SIPRI Yearbook 2022
Armaments, Disarmament and International Security

www.sipriyearbook.org

STOCKHOLM INTERNATIONAL PEACE RESEARCH INSTITUTE

Signalistgatan 9
SE-169 72 Solna, Sweden
Telephone: + 46 8 655 9700
Email: sipri@sipri.org
Internet: www.sipri.org

SIPRI Yearbook 2022

Armaments, Disarmament and International Security

**STOCKHOLM INTERNATIONAL
PEACE RESEARCH INSTITUTE**

OXFORD UNIVERSITY PRESS
2022

Great Clarendon Street, Oxford OX2 6DP,
United Kingdom

Oxford University Press is a department of the University of Oxford.
It furthers the University's objective of excellence in research, scholarship,
and education by publishing worldwide. Oxford is a registered trade mark of
Oxford University Press in the UK and in certain other countries

Published in the United States of America by Oxford University Press
198 Madison Avenue, New York, NY 10016, United States of America

British Library Cataloguing in Publication Data
Data available

Library of Congress Cataloging in Publication Data
Data available
ISBN 978–0–19–288303–2

Typeset and originated by SIPRI
Printed in the UK by
Bell & Bain Ltd., Glasgow

Credit: Figures 6.1 and 7.1 by Hugo Ahlenius, Nordipil, <https://nordpil.se/>

SIPRI Yearbook 2022 is also published online at
<http://www.sipriyearbook.org>

Contents

Preface   xix
Abbreviations and conventions   xxi
SIPRI Yearbook online   xxiv

Introduction

1. Introduction: International stability and human security in 2021   3
    DAN SMITH

  I. *Ukraine and the immediate consequences of the war*   5
  II. *The broader security horizon in 2021*   12

Part I. Armed conflict and conflict management, 2021

2. Global developments in armed conflict, peace processes and   27
   peace operations
    Overview
    IAN DAVIS AND CLAUDIA PFEIFER CRUZ

  I. *Tracking armed conflicts and peace processes*   29
    IAN DAVIS

    Defining armed conflict—Significant features of armed conflicts
    in 2021—Consequences of armed conflicts in 2021—Peace
    processes in 2021—Impact of Covid-19 on armed conflict

    Box 2.1. Definitions and types of armed conflict   32
    Figure 2.1. Armed conflict, by number of conflict-related deaths, 30
    2021
    Table 2.1. Estimated conflict-related fatalities by region, 2018–21   36
    Table 2.2. Categories of conflict-related violence, 2020–21   37
    Table 2.3. Number of peace agreements, 2012–21   40
    Table 2.4. Peace agreements in January to June 2021   42

  II. *Global and regional trends and developments in multilateral*   45
    peace operations
    CLAUDIA PFEIFER CRUZ, JAÏR VAN DER LIJN AND TIMO SMIT

    Multilateral peace operations in 2021—Personnel deployments—
    Organizations conducting multilateral peace operations—The
    main troop- and police-contributing countries—Other
    multilateral operations—Multilateral peace operations after
    Afghanistan—Conclusions

    Figure 2.2. Number of multilateral peace operations, by type of   46
    conducting organization, 2012–21
    Figure 2.3. Number of multilateral peace operations, by region,   47
    2012–21

Figure 2.4. Number of personnel in multilateral peace operations, 52
by type of conducting organization, 2012–21

Figure 2.5. Number of personnel in multilateral peace operations, 53
by region, 2012–21

Figure 2.6. Largest multilateral peace operations as of 31 Dec. 2021 54

Figure 2.7. Fatalities among international personnel in United 56
Nations peace operations, 2012–21

Figure 2.8. Fatality rates for uniformed personnel in United 57
Nations peace operations, 2012–21

Figure 2.9. Main contributors of military and police personnel 60
as of 31 Dec. 2021

Table 2.5. Number of multilateral peace operations and personnel 48
deployed by region and type of organization, 2021

III. *Table of multilateral peace operations, 2021* 71
CLAUDIA PFEIFER CRUZ

Table 2.6. Multilateral peace operations, 2021 72

3. Armed conflict and peace processes in the Americas 75

Overview
MARINA CAPARINI

I. *Key general developments in the region* 77
MARINA CAPARINI AND IAN DAVIS

Gang violence and other political violence as armed conflict—
Rising authoritarianism in Latin America and political instability
in the United States—The impact of Covid-19, food insecurity and
natural disasters

Table 3.1. Estimated conflict-related fatalities in Americas, 2018–21 78

II. *Armed conflict in North America and the Caribbean* 82
MARINA CAPARINI

Violence and organized crime in Mexico—Haiti

Table 3.2. Estimated conflict-related fatalities in Mexico, 2018–21 83

III. *Armed conflict in Central America* 88
MARINA CAPARINI AND IAN DAVIS

El Salvador—Guatemala—Honduras

IV. *Armed conflict in South America* 92
MARINA CAPARINI AND IAN DAVIS

Colombia—Brazil—Venezuela

Box 3.1. The blurred nature of armed conflict in Brazil 100
Table 3.3. Estimated conflict-related fatalities in Colombia, 2018–21 94
Table 3.4. Estimated conflict-related fatalities in Brazil, 2018–21 98

4. Armed conflict and peace processes in Asia and Oceania   103

    Overview
    IAN DAVIS

    I. *Key general developments in the region*   105
       IAN DAVIS

       Interstate armed conflict in Central Asia—The impact of Covid-19

       Table 4.1. Estimated conflict-related fatalities in Asia and   106
       Oceania, 2017–21

    II. *Flashpoints in the conflict dynamics in East Asia*   109
       FEI SU

       Korean Peninsula—East and South China Sea—Taiwan Strait

    III. *Armed conflict and peace processes in South Asia*   113
       IAN DAVIS AND JINGDONG YUAN

       Armed conflict in Afghanistan—Territorial disputes in Kashmir
       between China, India and Pakistan—India's internal armed
       conflicts and intercommunal tensions—Pakistan's internal armed
       conflicts

       Box 4.1. Timeline of key Afghanistan-related events, 1979–2021   116
       Table 4.2. Estimated conflict-related fatalities in Afghanistan,   114
       2017–21
       Table 4.3. Estimated conflict-related fatalities in India,   124
       2016–21
       Table 4.4. Estimated conflict-related fatalities in Pakistan,   126
       2016–2021

    IV. *Armed conflict and peace processes in South East Asia*   127
       IAN DAVIS

       Armed conflict in Myanmar—Armed conflict in Indonesia—
       Armed conflict in the Philippines—Armed conflict in Thailand

       Table 4.5. Estimated conflict-related fatalities in Myanmar,   128
       2016–21
       Table 4.6. Estimated conflict-related fatalities in the Philippines,   134
       2016–21

5. Armed conflict and peace processes in Europe   137

    Overview
    IAN DAVIS

    I. *Key general developments in the region*   139
       IAN DAVIS

       The interstate armed conflict between Armenia and Azerbaijan—
       Tensions between Russia and the West—Unresolved conflicts

II. *Armed conflict in Ukraine and the risk of spillover to a major*   149
interstate war
IAN DAVIS

The humanitarian impact of the armed conflict and the role of
the OSCE—Russia's March–April 2021 military mobilization—
Ukraine's proposed revisions to the peace process—Russia's
November–December military mobilization—Outlook

6. Armed conflict and peace processes in the Middle East and   155
North Africa

Overview
IAN DAVIS

I. *Key general developments in the region*   157
IAN DAVIS

Shifting alliances, rivalries and regional diplomacy—Other
regional cross-cutting issues—Armed conflict and prospective
state collapse in Lebanon

Table 6.1. Estimated conflict-related fatalities in the Middle East   158
and North Africa, 2017–21

II. *Armed conflict and peace processes in Iraq, Syria and Turkey*   164
SHIVAN FAZIL

Armed conflict in Iraq—Armed conflict in Syria—Armed conflict
between Turkey and Kurdish insurgent groups

Table 6.2. Estimated conflict-related fatalities in Iraq, 2016–21   166
Table 6.3. Estimated conflict-related fatalities in Syria, 2017–21   172
Table 6.4. Estimated conflict-related fatalities in Turkey, 2016–21   174

III. *The Israeli–Palestinian conflict and peace process*   175
IAN DAVIS

An escalation in Gaza and rioting within Israel—Outlook

IV. *Armed conflict and peace processes in North Africa*   179
IAN DAVIS

Armed conflict in Egypt—Armed conflict and the peace process
in Libya—Protests in Tunisia—Escalating tensions in Western
Sahara

Table 6.5. Estimated conflict-related fatalities in Libya, 2012–21   182

V. *Armed conflict and peace processes in Yemen*   185
IAN DAVIS

Key developments in the three conflict zones in 2021—The peace
process—The humanitarian crisis, conflict fatalities and alleged
war crimes—Outlook

Figure 6.1. Areas of control and conflict in Yemen, May 2021   186

Table 6.6. Estimated conflict-related fatalities in Yemen, 2015–21   190

7. Armed conflict and peace processes in sub-Saharan Africa   193

Overview
IAN DAVIS

I. *Key general developments in the region*   195
IAN DAVIS

The role of armed groups and criminal networks—External
actors—Election-related violence—Water insecurity and climate
change

Table 7.1. Estimated conflict-related fatalities in sub-Saharan   196
Africa, 2017–21

II. *Armed conflict and peace processes in West Africa*   202
ANNELIES HICKENDORFF AND ISSAKA K. SOUARÉ

Key general developments in the region—Multinational peace
and security operations—Internal armed conflicts (including the
role of armed self-defence groups)

Table 7.2. Active external national and multilateral peace and   208
counterterrorism operations in the Sahel and Lake Chad regions,
2021

Table 7.3. Estimated conflict-related fatalities in the   210
Liptako-Gourma region, 2017–21

Table 7.4. Estimated conflict-related fatalities in Mali, 2013–21   212

Table 7.5. Estimated conflict-related fatalities in Nigeria,   213
by region, 2017–21

III. *Armed conflict and peace processes in Central Africa*   215
IAN DAVIS

Cameroon—The Central African Republic—Chad—The
Democratic Republic of the Congo

Table 7.6. Estimated conflict-related fatalities in Cameroon,   216
2013–21

Table 7.7. Estimated conflict-related fatalities in the Central   218
African Republic, 2013–21

Table 7.8. Estimated conflict-related fatalities in the Democratic   222
Republic of the Congo, 2013–21

IV. *Armed conflict and peace processes in East Africa*   224
IAN DAVIS

Ethiopia—Mozambique—Somalia—South Sudan—Sudan

Figure 7.1. East Africa, including the Horn of Africa   225

Table 7.9. Estimated conflict-related fatalities in Ethiopia, 2013–21   226

Table 7.10. Estimated conflict-related fatalities in Mozambique, 2013–21   228

Table 7.11. Estimated conflict-related fatalities in Somalia, 2013–21   230

Table 7.12. Estimated conflict-related fatalities in South Sudan, 2013–21   234

Table 7.13. Estimated conflict-related fatalities in Sudan, 2013–21   238

Part II. Military spending and armaments, 2021

8. Military expenditure and developments in arms production   243

Overview
NAN TIAN

I. *Global developments in military expenditure, 2021*   245
NAN TIAN, XIAO LIANG, DIEGO LOPES DA SILVA AND
ALEXANDRA MARKSTEINER

Military burden, government priorities and reductions in
military expenditure—Trends in military expenditure, 2012–21—
The largest military spenders in 2021

Box 8.1. Variations in economic data and associated consequences   248
for military expenditure data

Box 8.2. Definition, sources and methods for SIPRI military   260
expenditure

Figure 8.1. Military expenditure, by region, 2012–21   249

Figure 8.2. Changes in military spending and gross domestic   250
product, by country, 2020

Figure 8.3. Changes in military spending and gross domestic   251
product, by country, 2021

Figure 8.4. Military burden, regional averages, 2012–21   257

Table 8.1. Military expenditure and military burden, by region,   246
2012–21

Table 8.2. Key military expenditure statistics, by region and   256
subregion, 2021

Table 8.3. The 15 countries with the highest military expenditure   258
in 2021

II. *Regional developments in military expenditure, 2021*   262
NAN TIAN, LUCIE BÉRAUD-SUDREAU, XIAO LIANG,
DIEGO LOPES DA SILVA AND ALEXANDRA MARKSTEINER

Africa—The Americas—Asia and Oceania—Europe—The Middle
East

Figure 8.5. Changes in military expenditure by subregion, 2012–21   263
and 2020–21

Table 8.4. Components of US military expenditure, fiscal years   266
2017–21

Table 8.5. Components of China's military expenditure, 2017–21   272

III. *Arms-producing and military services companies, 2020*   287
ALEXANDRA MARKSTEINER, LUCIE BÉRAUD-SUDREAU, NAN TIAN,
DIEGO LOPES DA SILVA AND ALEXANDRA KUIMOVA

The effects of the Covid-19 pandemic on arms production—
Regional and national developments in the Top 100

Figure 8.6. Total arms sales of companies in the SIPRI Top 100,   288
2002–20

Table 8.6. Trends in arms sales of companies in the SIPRI Top 100,   289
2011–20

Table 8.7. Regional and national shares of arms sales for   290
companies in the SIPRI Top 100, 2019–20

9. International arms transfers   297

Overview
SIEMON T. WEZEMAN

I. *Developments in arms transfers, 2017–21*   299
SIEMON T. WEZEMAN, ALEXANDRA KUIMOVA AND PIETER D. WEZEMAN

Key developments in 2021 related to arms transfers—Conflicts
and tensions as drivers of arms transfers

Box 9.1. Definitions and methodology for SIPRI data on   302
international arms transfers

Figure 9.1. The trend in international transfers of major arms,   300
1952–2021

II. *Developments among the suppliers of major arms, 2017–21*   304
SIEMON T. WEZEMAN, ALEXANDRA KUIMOVA AND PIETER D. WEZEMAN

The United States—Russia—France—Other major suppliers

Table 9.1. The 40 largest suppliers of major arms and their main   306
recipients, 2017–21

Table 9.2. Selected major arms on order or chosen for future orders   308
from the five largest arms suppliers for delivery after 2021

Table 9.3. Deliveries by arms category by the 10 largest suppliers   309
of major arms, 2017–21

Table 9.4. The 10 largest suppliers of major arms and their   310
recipients, by region, 2017–21

III. *Developments among the recipients of major arms, 2017–21*   317
SIEMON T. WEZEMAN, ALEXANDRA KUIMOVA AND PIETER D. WEZEMAN

Africa—The Americas—Asia and Oceania—Europe—The Middle
East

Table 9.5. The 50 largest recipients of major arms and their main   320
suppliers, 2017–21

Table 9.6. Imports of major arms, by region and subregion, 2012–16   322
and 2017–21

IV. *The financial value of states' arms exports*   334
PIETER D. WEZEMAN, ALEXANDRA KUIMOVA AND SIEMON T. WEZEMAN

Table 9.7. The financial value of states' arms exports according to   336
national government and industry sources, 2011–20

10. World nuclear forces   341
Overview
HANS M. KRISTENSEN AND MATT KORDA
Table 10.1. World nuclear forces, January 2022   342

I. *United States nuclear forces*   343
HANS M. KRISTENSEN AND MATT KORDA

The role of nuclear weapons in US military doctrine—Strategic
nuclear forces—Non-strategic nuclear forces

Table 10.2. United States nuclear forces, January 2022   344

II. *Russian nuclear forces*   355
HANS M. KRISTENSEN AND MATT KORDA

The role of nuclear weapons in Russian military doctrine—
Strategic nuclear forces—Non-strategic nuclear forces

Table 10.3. Russian nuclear forces, January 2022   356

III. *British nuclear forces*   369
HANS M. KRISTENSEN AND MATT KORDA

The role of nuclear weapons in British military doctrine—
Revisions to British nuclear policy—Nuclear weapon
modernization—Sea-based missiles

Table 10.4. British nuclear forces, January 2022   370

IV. *French nuclear forces*   375
HANS M. KRISTENSEN AND MATT KORDA

The role of nuclear weapons in French military doctrine—
Nuclear weapon modernization—Aircraft and air-delivered
weapons—Sea-based missiles

Table 10.5. French nuclear forces, January 2022   376

V. *Chinese nuclear forces*   380
HANS M. KRISTENSEN AND MATT KORDA

The role of nuclear weapons in Chinese military doctrine—
Aircraft and air-delivered weapons—Land-based missiles—Sea-
based missiles

Table 10.6. Chinese nuclear forces, January 2022   382

VI. *Indian nuclear forces* 391
HANS M. KRISTENSEN AND MATT KORDA

The role of nuclear weapons in Indian military doctrine—Aircraft and air-delivered weapons—Land-based missiles—Sea-based missiles—Cruise missiles

Table 10.7. Indian nuclear forces, January 2022 392

VII. *Pakistani nuclear forces* 398
HANS M. KRISTENSEN AND MATT KORDA

The role of nuclear weapons in Pakistani military doctrine—Aircraft and air-delivered weapons—Land-based missiles—Sea-based missiles

Table 10.8. Pakistani nuclear forces, January 2022 400

VIII. *Israeli nuclear forces* 404
HANS M. KRISTENSEN AND MATT KORDA

The role of nuclear weapons in Israeli military doctrine—Military fissile material production—Aircraft and air-delivered weapons—Land-based missiles—Sea-based missiles

Table 10.9. Israeli nuclear forces, January 2022 406

IX. *North Korean nuclear forces* 410
HANS M. KRISTENSEN AND MATT KORDA

The role of nuclear weapons in North Korean military doctrine—Fissile material and warhead production—Land-based missiles—Sea-based missiles

Table 10.10. North Korean forces with potential nuclear capability, January 2022 412

X. *Global stocks and production of fissile materials, 2021* 424
MORITZ KÜTT, ZIA MIAN AND PAVEL PODVIG
INTERNATIONAL PANEL ON FISSILE MATERIALS

Table 10.11. Global stocks of highly enriched uranium, 2021 426
Table 10.12. Global stocks of separated plutonium, 2021 428
Table 10.13. Significant uranium enrichment facilities and capacity worldwide, 2021 430
Table 10.14. Significant reprocessing facilities worldwide, 2021 432

Part III. Non-proliferation, arms control and disarmament, 2021

11. Nuclear disarmament, arms control and non-proliferation 435
Overview
TYTTI ERÄSTÖ, VITALY FEDCHENKO AND LORA SAALMAN

I.   *Bilateral and multilateral nuclear arms control involving China,*   437
     Russia and the United States
     LORA SAALMAN

     Russia–USA New START—Russia–USA strategic stability
     dialogue—Prospects for a China–USA strategic stability
     dialogue—Prospects for multilateral strategic stability
     dialogues—Conclusions

     Table 11.1. Russian and United States aggregate numbers of   438
     strategic offensive arms under New START, as of 5 February 2011
     and 1 September 2021

II. *The Joint Comprehensive Plan of Action on Iran's nuclear programme* 449
     TYTTI ERÄSTÖ

     Key developments in Iran's nuclear programme relevant to
     the JCPOA—Outstanding issues under Iran's Comprehensive
     Safeguards Agreement—Diplomatic efforts to restore the
     JCPOA—Prospects for the JCPOA

III. *Multilateral nuclear arms control, disarmament and*   460
     non-proliferation treaties and initiatives
     TYTTI ERÄSTÖ AND VITALY FEDCHENKO

     The postponed review conference of the Non-Proliferation
     Treaty—The Treaty on the Prohibition of Nuclear Weapons—The
     Conference on the Establishment of a Middle East Zone Free
     of Weapons of Mass Destruction—Twenty-five years of the
     Comprehensive Nuclear-Test-Ban Treaty

12. Chemical, biological and health security threats   471
     Overview
     FILIPPA LENTZOS AND UNA JAKOB

I.   *The unfolding Covid-19 pandemic*   473
     FILIPPA LENTZOS

     Milestones of the pandemic in 2021—Studies into the origins of
     SARS-CoV-2—A pandemic treaty—Conclusions

II. *Biological weapon disarmament and non-proliferation*   483
     FILIPPA LENTZOS

     The 2020 meetings of experts—The First Committee of the UN
     General Assembly—The 2020 meeting of states parties and the
     2021 Preparatory Committee—The evolving China–Russia–
     United States relationship—Conclusions

III. *Allegations of chemical weapons use in Syria* 496
UNA JAKOB

Ongoing work of the FFM and DAT, and other activities—Second
report of the Investigation and Identification Team—The decision
to invoke the compliance procedure under CWC Article XII

Table 12.1. Overview of ad hoc mechanisms of the Organisation 498
for the Prohibition of Chemical Weapons to address the issue of
chemical weapons in Syria

IV. *Chemical arms control and disarmament* 504
UNA JAKOB

Use of novichok agents—Other developments in the
OPCW—Outlook

13. Conventional arms control and regulation of new weapon 513
technologies

Overview
IAN DAVIS

I. *Multilateral regulation of inhumane weapons and other* 515
conventional weapons of humanitarian concern
IAN DAVIS AND GIOVANNA MALETTA

Incendiary weapons—Explosive weapons in populated
areas—Cluster munitions—Landmines, improvised explosive
devices and explosive remnants of war—Armed uncrewed aerial
vehicles—The United Nations Programme of Action on Small
Arms and Light Weapons

Table 13.1. Meetings of the Certain Conventional Weapons 516
Convention in 2021

II. *Intergovernmental efforts to address the challenges posed by* 532
autonomous weapon systems
LAURA BRUUN

Approaching the sixth review conference of the CCW
Convention—The legal, ethical and military challenges posed
by AWS—Options for addressing the challenges posed by
AWS—Outlook

III. *The withdrawal of Russia from the Treaty on Open Skies* 545
ALEXANDER GRAEF

The impact of the US withdrawal on the treaty and Russian
reactions—The position of the new US administration—Russian
withdrawal procedures and international reactions—Addressing
the consequences of the Russian withdrawal—Outlook

IV. *International transparency in arms procurement and military*   551
expenditure as confidence-building measures
PIETER D. WEZEMAN AND SIEMON T. WEZEMAN

The United Nations Register of Conventional Arms—The
United Nations Report on Military Expenditures—Regional
transparency mechanisms—Conclusions

V. *Cyberspace and the malicious use of information and*   558
communications technology
ALLISON PYTLAK

Cyber governance structures within the United Nations—
Regional cyber governance initiatives—National cyber
initiatives and policy—Non-governmental and collaborative
initiatives—Conclusions

VI. *Developments in space security*   572
NIVEDITA RAJU

Reports of weapon tests by China and Russia—Growing interest
in lunar activities—Looking ahead: Discussions on responsible
behaviour in space

14. Dual-use and arms trade controls   581
Overview
MARK BROMLEY

I. *The Arms Trade Treaty*   583
GIOVANNA MALETTA AND ANDREA EDOARDO VARISCO

Treaty implementation—Transparency and reporting—Treaty
universalization and international assistance—The financial
situation of the ATT—Conclusions

Figure 14.1. Number of Arms Trade Treaty states parties   588
submitting annual reports, 2015–20
Table 14.1. Arms Trade Treaty numbers of ratifications, accessions   590
and signatories, by region

II. *Multilateral arms embargoes*   595
MARK BROMLEY AND PIETER D. WEZEMAN

United Nations arms embargoes: Developments and
contraventions—European Union arms embargoes:
Developments and implementation challenges—Conclusions

Table 14.2. Multilateral arms embargoes in force during 2021   596

III. *The multilateral export control regimes*   610
KOLJA BROCKMANN

The Australia Group—The Missile Technology Control
Regime—The Nuclear Suppliers Group—The Wassenaar
Arrangement—Conclusions

Table 14.3. The four multilateral export control regimes   612

IV. *Developments in the European Union's dual-use and arms trade*   620
controls
MARK BROMLEY, KOLJA BROCKMANN AND GIOVANNA MALETTA

The EU dual-use regulation—The EU foreign direct investment
screening regulation—European and United States cooperation
on export controls—The EU common position on arms
exports—Conclusions

Table 14.4. Submissions of information to the European Union   628
annual report on arms exports, 2011–20

Annexes

Annex A. Arms control and disarmament agreements   635

    I. *Universal treaties*   636
    II. *Regional treaties*   659
    III. *Bilateral treaties*   669

Annex B. International security cooperation bodies   674

    I. *Bodies with a global focus or membership*   674
    II. *Bodies with a regional focus or membership*   683
    III. *Strategic trade control regimes*   697

Annex C. Chronology 2021   701

About the authors   711
Errata   715
Index   717

Preface

This edition of the SIPRI Yearbook was produced against the background of Russia's invasion of Ukraine and the international crisis arising out of it. As one of the largest armed conflicts in Europe since World War II, the war in Ukraine has led to the displacement of 13 million Ukrainians. Given the enormity of the war and its reverberations, the Yearbook's introduction (chapter 1) breaks from usual practice—which is to focus on the events of the year before publication, in this case 2021—to reflect on the much-changed security environment that is unfolding at the time of writing. The remainder of the Yearbook, however, retains its usual time-bound focus on events in 2021.

Like the previous year, 2021 was heavily defined by the Covid-19 pandemic. By the end of 2021, the world was starting to lift Covid restrictions, reopen international borders and resuscitate trade and normal economic functioning. Nevertheless, the emergence of Covid-19 variants meant that the global distribution of vaccines, which began in December 2020, continued to be an essential part of protecting people everywhere from the disease and of decreasing the risk of yet further variants emerging. But the promise of Covid-19 vaccines in ending the pandemic can only be realized if all countries resolve to pull together to optimize the strategic use of the limited but growing vaccine supply.

If international cooperation is achieved on this global health issue, it may also point the way forward for more collaborative approaches in other areas, such as in addressing climate change, resolving the crisis in nuclear arms control, and managing and peacefully settling local and regional conflicts. Although the international context in 2021 was shaped by deep geopolitical divisions among the great powers, there remain opportunities for other coalitions of international actors to step up to the plate with ideas for re-energizing the ailing international body politic (chapter 1).

Part I of the Yearbook covers armed conflicts and conflict management in 2021. It catches key moments and trends in both conflict escalation and peacebuilding. Chapter 2 focuses on armed conflicts and peace processes, looking at the multifaceted root causes of both and summarizing their latest developments. Multilateral peace operations feature prominently. Active armed conflicts occurred in at least 46 states in 2021: 8 in the Americas, 9 in Asia and Oceania, 3 in Europe, 8 in the Middle East and North Africa, and 18 in sub-Saharan Africa (chapters 3–7). The increase in the severity of several armed conflicts in 2021 led to an increase in conflict fatalities, ending the welcome downward trend of recent years.

Parts II and III focus on issues related to armament and disarmament. Much of the Institute's work in these areas is based on original, rigorous data collection that forms the foundation of SIPRI's databases. Part II is devoted to military spending and armaments, including comprehensive assessments of recent trends in military expenditure and arms production (chapter 8), international arms transfers (chapter 9), and world nuclear forces, including the nuclear modernization programmes current in all the nuclear-armed states (chapter 10). Global military spending rose again in 2021, passing the $2 trillion milestone, but the volume of global arms transfers saw a slight drop.

Part III covers non-proliferation, arms control and disarmament. Chapter 11 explains that it was another difficult year for nuclear arms control. On the positive side of the ledger, Russia and the United States agreed an extension to New START and the Treaty on the Prohibition of Nuclear Weapons entered into force. On the negative side, the remaining parties to the Joint Comprehensive Plan of Action to limit Iran's nuclear programme failed to reach agreement on a way forward and Russia followed the USA in withdrawing from the Open Skies Treaty. Chapter 12 discusses the latest developments in the Covid-19 pandemic, including the highly politicized nature of the international effort to identify the source of the disease. The chapter also explores allegations of chemical weapons use and other developments in chemical and biological security threats. Chapter 13 includes a round-up of the multilateral regulation of inhumane weapons and other conventional weapons of humanitarian concern in 2021, while chapter 14 reports on efforts to strengthen controls on the trade in conventional arms and dual-use items.

This year's 53rd edition of the SIPRI Yearbook features contributions from 37 authors. Its content has been refereed extensively and a dedicated editorial team ensures that it conforms to the highest publishing standards. The communications, library, operations and IT staff at SIPRI all contribute in different ways to the Yearbook's production and distribution. I would like to take this opportunity to express my gratitude to everybody involved, within SIPRI and beyond—especially our external reviewers, whose insights and suggestions always lead to material improvements in the content.

Disinformation continues to be a significant threat to liberal democracies, and the war in Ukraine and the Covid-19 crisis have resulted in the further spread of misinformation and conspiracy theories. The Yearbook's focus on the facts is vital in countering such misinformation and 'fake news', and SIPRI's commitment to authenticating the facts means that the volume remains an indispensable global public good. This will continue to be the case as the Institute helps to chart a course for emerging from the war in Ukraine and other armed conflicts with more equitable, resilient and sustainable societies.

Dan Smith
Director, SIPRI
Stockholm, May 2022

Abbreviations and conventions

ABM	Anti-ballistic missile
ACLED	Armed Conflict Location & Event Data Project
AG	Australia Group
ALCM	Air-launched cruise missile
APC	Armoured personnel carrier
APM	Anti-personnel mine
ASAT	Anti-satellite
ASEAN	Association of Southeast Asian Nations
ATT	Arms Trade Treaty
AU	African Union
BCC	Bilateral Consultative Commission (of the Russian–US New START treaty)
BWC	Biological and Toxin Weapons Convention
CAR	Central African Republic
CBM	Confidence-building measure
CBW	Chemical and biological weapon/warfare
CCM	Convention on Cluster Munitions
CCW	Certain Conventional Weapons (Convention)
CD	Conference on Disarmament
CFSP	Common Foreign and Security Policy (of the EU)
CSBM	Confidence- and security-building measure
CSDP	Common Security and Defence Policy (of the EU)
CSTO	Collective Security Treaty Organization
CTBT	Comprehensive Nuclear-Test-Ban Treaty
CTBTO	Comprehensive Nuclear-Test-Ban Treaty Organization
CW	Chemical weapon/warfare
CWC	Chemical Weapons Convention
DDR	Disarmament, demobilization and reintegration
DPRK	Democratic People's Republic of Korea (North Korea)
DRC	Democratic Republic of the Congo
ECOWAS	Economic Community of West African States
ERW	Explosive remnants of war
EU	European Union
EWIPA	Explosive weapons in populated areas
FFM	Fact-finding mission
FMCT	Fissile material cut-off treaty
FY	Financial year
G7	Group of Seven (industrialized states)
GDP	Gross domestic product
GGE	Group of government experts
GLCM	Ground-launched cruise missile
HCOC	Hague Code of Conduct
HEU	Highly enriched uranium
IAEA	International Atomic Energy Agency
ICBM	Intercontinental ballistic missile
ICC	International Criminal Court
ICJ	International Court of Justice
IED	Improvised explosive device
IGAD	Intergovernmental Authority on Development
IHL	International humanitarian law
INF	Intermediate-range Nuclear Forces (Treaty)
ISAF	International Security Assistance Force

ISU	Implementation Support Unit	P5	Five permanent members of the UN Security Council
JCPOA	Joint Comprehensive Plan of Action	PAROS	Prevention of an arms race in outer space
LAWS	Lethal autonomous weapon systems	POA	Programme of Action to Prevent, Combat and Eradicate the Illicit Trade in Small Arms and Light Weapons in All its Aspects (UN)
LEU	Low-enriched uranium		
MENA	Middle East and North Africa		
MIRV	Multiple independently targetable re-entry vehicle	R&D	Research and development
MRBM	Medium-range ballistic missile	SADC	Southern African Development Community
MTCR	Missile Technology Control Regime	SALW	Small arms and light weapons
NAM	Non-Aligned Movement	SAM	Surface-to-air missile
NATO	North Atlantic Treaty Organization	SLBM	Submarine-launched ballistic missile
NGO	Non-governmental organization	SLCM	Sea-launched cruise missile
		SORT	Strategic Offensive Reductions Treaty
NNWS	Non-nuclear weapon state		
NPT	Non-Proliferation Treaty	SRBM	Short-range ballistic missile
NSG	Nuclear Suppliers Group	START	Strategic Arms Reduction Treaty
NWS	Nuclear weapon state		
OAS	Organization of American States	TPNW	Treaty on the Prohibition of Nuclear Weapons
OECD	Organisation for Economic Co-operation and Development	UAE	United Arab Emirates
		UAV	Unmanned aerial vehicle
		UN	United Nations
OEWG	Open-ended working group	UNHCR	UN High Commissioner for Refugees
OHCHR	Office of the UN High Commissioner for Human Rights	UNODA	UN Office for Disarmament Affairs
OPCW	Organisation for the Prohibition of Chemical Weapons	UNROCA	UN Register of Conventional Arms
		UNSC	UN Security Council
OSCC	Open Skies Consultative Commission	WA	Wassenaar Arrangement
		WHO	World Health Organization
OSCE	Organization for Security and Co-operation in Europe	WMD	Weapon(s) of mass destruction

Conventions

..	Data not available or not applicable
–	Nil or a negligible figure
( )	Uncertain data
b.	Billion (thousand million)
kg	Kilogram
km	Kilometre (1000 metres)
m.	Million
th.	Thousand
tr.	Trillion (million million)
$	US dollars
€	Euros

Geographical regions and subregions

Africa	Consisting of North Africa (Algeria, Libya, Morocco and Tunisia, but excluding Egypt) and sub-Saharan Africa
Americas	Consisting of North America (Canada and the USA), Central America and the Caribbean (including Mexico), and South America
Asia and Oceania	Consisting of Central Asia, East Asia, Oceania, South Asia (including Afghanistan) and South East Asia
Europe	Consisting of Eastern Europe (Armenia, Azerbaijan, Belarus, Georgia, Moldova, Russia and Ukraine) and Western and Central Europe (with South Eastern Europe)
Middle East	Consisting of Egypt, Iran, Iraq, Israel, Jordan, Kuwait, Lebanon, Syria, Turkey and the states of the Arabian peninsula

Note: The boundaries, names and designations used in the maps in this volume do not imply any endorsement or acceptance by SIPRI of claims or stances in disputes over specific territories.

SIPRI Yearbook online

www.sipriyearbook.org

The full content of the SIPRI Yearbook is also available online. With the SIPRI Yearbook online you can

- access the complete SIPRI Yearbook on your desktop or handheld device for research on the go
- navigate easily through content using advanced search and browse functionality
- find content easily: search through the whole SIPRI Yearbook and within your results
- save valuable time: use your personal profile to return to saved searches and content again and again
- share content with colleagues and students easily via email and social networking tools
- enhance your research by following clearly linked references and web resources

How to access the SIPRI Yearbook online

Institutional access

The SIPRI Yearbook online is available to institutions worldwide for a one-time fee or by annual subscription. Librarians and central resource coordinators can contact Oxford University Press to receive a price quotation using the details below or register for a free trial at <http://www.oxford online.com/freetrials/>.

Individuals can recommend this resource to their librarians at <http://www.oup.com/library-recommend/>.

Individual subscriptions

The SIPRI Yearbook online is available to individuals worldwide on a 12-month subscription basis. Purchase details can be found at <http://www.oup.com/>.

Contact information

Customers within the Americas

Email: oxfordonline@oup.com
Telephone: +1 (800) 624 0153
Fax: +1 (919) 677 8877

Customers outside the Americas

Email: institutionalsales@oup.com
Telephone: +44 (0) 1865 353705
Fax: +44 (0) 1865 353308

Introduction

**Chapter 1. Introduction: International stability
and human security in 2021**

1. Introduction: International stability and human security in 2021

DAN SMITH

The international security horizon at the end of 2021 was dominated by two intensifying confrontations involving nuclear-armed great powers. One was between Russia and Ukraine, with the United States and its allies vocally opposing the Russian military build-up on Ukraine's borders; the other was between China and the USA, as the former intensified its pressure on Taiwan.[1] Although neither confrontation had exploded into open warfare by the end of 2021, Russia invaded Ukraine on 24 February 2022 and full-scale war ensued. In the case of China and Taiwan, the outcome at the time of writing (mid April 2022) remains uncertain, although air incursions continued in 2022.[2]

In recent years, the SIPRI Yearbook, of which this is the 53rd edition, has tracked and analysed deterioration in international peace and security. It now appears the process has reached, if not a culmination—since who knows what may yet ensue?—then at least an important milestone. This justifies and perhaps necessitates a change in focus for this edition's introductory chapter. In general, the Yearbook is largely timebound to the year preceding the year of publication. While this remains the case for all other chapters in this edition, this introduction needs to reflect not only on 2021 but on a much-changed environment that is unfolding at the time of writing—that is, it needs to take into account the war in Ukraine, as well as its impact on the broader security horizon. That is the topic of the first section of this chapter; thereafter, it scans the broader security horizon, looking at the continuing impact of climate change and the Covid-19 pandemic, nuclear arms control, geopolitical tensions, the West's withdrawal of forces from Afghanistan and the problem of conflict management.

To focus on Ukraine in the first section below is not intended to downplay the significance of events that rightly received considerable attention in 2021, such as the storming of the US Capitol on 6 January, the military coup d'état in Myanmar that began on the morning of 1 February, the war in Ethiopia, or the withdrawal of the USA and North Atlantic Treaty Organization (NATO) allies from Afghanistan in July and August. Part I of this Yearbook explores these events and issues (chapters 3–7). The war in Ukraine, however, has

---

[1] 'Record number of China planes enter Taiwan air defence zone', BBC News, 5 Oct. 2021.
[2] 'Taiwan reports new large-scale Chinese air force incursion', Al Jazeera, 23 Jan. 2022.

administered a shock to the international system that far outreaches the reverberations of the crises of 2021.

The strength of this effect cannot be explained by the misunderstanding that war has returned to Europe after many years of peace. The truth is that war is no stranger to Europe, even in recent times. There was war in 2020 between Armenia and Azerbaijan; since 2014 in Ukraine itself; in 2008 in Georgia; in the 1990s and around the turn of the century within Russia, in Chechnya; and in the 1990s in former Yugoslavia and all three countries of the South Caucasus.

The disruptive effect of the war in Ukraine is rooted in an act of aggression that constitutes a breach of the United Nations Charter by one of the five permanent members (P5) of the UN Security Council. There have previously been actions of, at best, dubious legality, where international laws and agreements have been bent, skirted and broken by others among the P5. However, many observers—especially but not only in the West—regard Russia's invasion of Ukraine as unprecedented in the era since the UN's foundation, attacking the fundamentals of contemporary international relations. This perception is underlined by the repeated warnings given by Russian spokespeople that the use of nuclear weapons has not been ruled out.[3] At the same time, Russia has alleged that there are Western laboratories researching chemical and biological weapons (CBW) in Ukraine.[4] These allegations have been interpreted in the West as a means for Russia to prepare the ground for its own CBW use.[5] Against this background, relations between Russia and the USA reached a new nadir. Taken together, these developments in the first months of 2022 mark a watershed moment in international politics.

All this suggests to many in Europe that existing security arrangements in the region must be fundamentally rethought. Although, as explored below, not all governments worldwide have responded in the same way to the war, decisions about European security do have wider ramifications. These arrangements are part of the framework of relations between two great powers and form a core part of global politics. Changes in the basic terms of European security will likely affect the security set-up in other regions too, not least in North East Asia in the context of poor relations between China

[3] Karmanau, Y. et al., 'Putin puts nuclear forces on high alert, escalating tensions', AP News, 28 Feb. 2022; Sevastopulo, D. and Qinio, A., 'Putin puts world on alert with high-stakes nuclear posturing', *Financial Times*, 7 Mar. 2022; and Faulconbridge, G., 'Putin ally warns of nuclear dystopia due to United States', Reuters, 23 Mar. 2022.

[4] Teslova, E., 'Russia says documents suggests "components of bioweapons were being developed in Ukraine"', Anadolu Agency, 9 Mar. 2022; Finnegan, C., 'Russia escalates false chemical weapons claims about US, Ukraine by bringing them to UN', ABC News, 11 Mar. 2022; and Pilkington, E. and Oladipo, G., 'What are Russia's biological weapons claims and what's actually happening?', *The Guardian*, 22 Mar. 2022.

[5] US Department of State, 'The Kremlin's allegations of chemical and biological weapons laboratories in Ukraine', Press statement, 9 Mar. 2022; and Spinelli, D., 'One more thing to worry about: Putin may be paving the way to use chemical weapons in Ukraine', Mother Jones, 8 Mar. 2022.

and the USA. While the full consequences of the war in Ukraine are not yet known, it is safe to assume that they will be far-reaching.

I. Ukraine and the immediate consequences of the war

The extended consequences of the war will be shaped not only by Russia's action but by the responses of the USA and its allies in Europe and beyond. As well as pure strategic and security considerations, these responses are being shaped by public and political perception and sentiment. It is evident that public and political opinion, especially but not only in Europe, have been shaken by the war. The risk of escalation—whether in terms of conflict spreading more widely across the continent or levels of violence further increasing (or both), with Russia's nuclear forces placed on a higher state of alert—has likewise had an unsettling effect.[6]

The human and social impact of the war is visible in over 5 million people becoming refugees from Ukraine within two months of the invasion, along with harrowing evidence collected by the UN of apparent war crimes.[7] The destruction of Ukrainian cities by Russian forces attacking civilian areas with artillery bombardments has not only left a major physical and economic reconstruction task, but also has potentially devastating health impacts arising from the destruction of hospitals, sewage systems, clean water supplies and other public health infrastructure.[8] In addition, the destruction of buildings releases large volumes of dust, containing cement, metals and industrial compounds—this dust is easily ingested and bears serious health risks.[9] The provinces of Donetsk and Lohansk in eastern Ukraine have already, since 2014, suffered severe disruption and damage to health infrastructure, which further warfare will only compound.[10] Moreover, since both Russia and Ukraine are major food producers, there is a high risk that the war will have severe human consequences further afield. The loss of the planting season in parts of Ukraine and the interruption in normal trading with Russia due to sanctions mean the prospects are bleak for the millions of people worldwide

---

[6] Karmanau et al. (note 3).

[7] United Nations High Commissioner for Refugees (UNHCR), 'Operational data portal', accessed 24 Apr. 2022; and UN News, 'UN's Bachelet condemns "horrors" faced by Ukraine's civilians', 22 Apr. 2022.

[8] Roberts, L., 'Surge of HIV, tuberculosis and Covid feared amid war in Ukraine', *Nature*, 15 Mar. 2022.

[9] Garrity, A., 'Conflict rubble: A ubiquitous and under-studied toxic remnant of war', Conflict and Environment Observatory, 10 July 2014.

[10] Buckley, C. J., Clem, R. S. and Herron, E. S., 'An assessment of attributing public healthcare infrastructure damage in the Donbas five years after Euromaidan: Implications for Ukrainian state legitimacy', *Eurasian Geography and Economics*, vol. 60, no. 1 (2019).

whose diets depend on wheat and other staples from the two countries.[11] This will compound the problem that, worldwide, food insecurity has been increasing since 2015.[12] The same factors will make it harder to meet global humanitarian needs—in recent years, Ukraine has been the source of half the wheat used by the World Food Programme, the world's largest humanitarian agency.[13]

The US and European responses

The response of the USA, the European Union (EU) and other governments opposing the invasion followed three main strands. First, they sought to isolate Russia politically, succeeding with a UN General Assembly resolution opposing the war (although without naming it as a war), which was supported by 141 member states and opposed by only 5, while 35 abstained.[14] Second, they imposed much harsher sanctions than had generally been foreseen, characterized as the most comprehensive set of multilateral economic sanctions ever applied to a major global economy.[15] And, third, within three weeks, 33 states decided to send lethal or non-lethal military aid to Ukraine.[16]

There has been considerable emphasis in the West on not only sending military aid to Ukraine but applying economic sanctions against Russia. Economic sanctions do not have a strong track record of achieving policy goals,

[11] World Food Programme (WFP), 'Ukraine war: More countries will "feel the burn" as food and energy price rises fuel hunger, warns WFP', 11 Mar. 2022; Delgado, C., 'War in the breadbasket: The ripple effects on food insecurity and conflict risk beyond Ukraine', SIPRI WritePeace blog, 1 Apr. 2022; Tschunkert, K. and Bourhrous, A., 'War in the breadbasket: The impacts of the war in Ukraine on food security and stability in Lebanon', SIPRI WritePeace blog, 4 Apr. 2022; and Riquier, M., 'War in the breadbasket: Hunger and the humanitarian fallout from the war in Ukraine', SIPRI WritePeace blog, 6 Apr. 2022.

[12] Delgado, C. and Smith, D., *Global Hunger Index 2021: Hunger and Food Systems in Conflict Settings* (Welthungerhilfe/Concern Worldwide: Bonn/Dublin, 2021).

[13] Beasley, D., 'The Ukraine war could leave hundreds of millions hungry around the world', *Washington Post*, 7 Mar. 2022.

[14] 'General Assembly resolution demands end to Russian offensive in Ukraine', UN News, 2 Mar. 2022.

[15] Anderson, S. R. et al., 'What sanctions has the world put on Russia?', Lawfare, 4 Mar. 2022.

[16] Duthois, T. and AFP, 'Ukraine war: Which countries are sending weapons and aid to forces fighting the Russian invasion?', Euronews, 3 Mar. 2022; Weaver, M., 'What weapons have other countries supplied to Ukraine?', *The Guardian*, 17 Mar. 2022; Al Jazeera, 'Which countries are sending military aid to Ukraine?', 28 Feb. 2022; Roblin, S., 'Putin has a problem: Ukraine is getting an arsenal of weapons from the West', 1945, 4 Mar. 2022; Qalliu, B., 'Albania sent military equipment to Ukraine', Exit News, 18 Mar. 2022; Reuters, 'Australia will fund lethal weapons for Ukraine says PM Morrison', 7 Mar. 2022; *Japan News*, 'Japan to send defense equipment to Ukraine', 4 Mar. 2022; Reuters, 'Spain to send grenade launchers and machine guns to Ukraine, minister says', 2 Mar. 2022; and Collins, K. et al., 'Biden announces hundreds of millions in new security aid for Ukraine following Zelensky's speech', CNN, 17 Mar. 2022.

although they are an effective means of moral signalling.[17] However, the economic instruments mobilized by the states opposing Russia may exact a price from Russia for its actions, even though they also look likely to impose a heavy economic burden on the West, and on the global economy as a whole.[18]

The immediate responses of European states may have significant long-term consequences. The EU quickly decided to finance weaponry for Ukraine, belying its well-earned reputation for being slow and indecisive on security issues.[19] Meanwhile, Germany, which has previously been reluctant to increase military spending, rapidly expanded its military budget for 2022–25.[20] Significantly, Finland openly acted against clearly expressed Russian interests and preferences for the first time in 80 years, and, like Sweden, started a domestic political discussion about joining NATO, despite strongly voiced Russian objections and warnings about potential countermeasures.[21]

Taken together, as they unfolded within the first few weeks of the invasion, these measures began to look like a potential step change in Europe's security concepts and architecture. For several years, Russia has systematically sidelined the Organization for Security and Co-operation in Europe (OSCE) when it comes to handling key issues such as Russia's seizure of Crimea and occupation of two eastern Ukrainian provinces in 2014, or the reignition of war between Armenia and Azerbaijan in 2020. Now, following the invasion, many observers—including those instinctively sympathetic to the OSCE as expressing a post-cold war aspiration for a comprehensive, cooperative framework for security policies in Europe—are likely to question the organization's practical role. A need will likely remain for a forum where European states, regardless of adversarial relations between them, can benefit from addressing shared problems of strategic instability in a security landscape

[17] Staibano, C. and Wallensteen, P. (eds), *International Sanctions: Between Wars and Words* (Routledge: London, 2005); Alavifar, S. A. and Zaernyuk, V. M., 'Analyzing the success rate of strategic and tactical economic sanctions: A strategy for Russian economic planning', Proceedings of the International Conference on Industrial Engineering and Operations Management, Kuala Lumpur, Malaysia, 8–10 Mar. 2016.

[18] Roth, A., '"We're going back to a USSR": Long queues return for Russian shoppers as sanctions bite', *The Guardian*, 23 Mar. 2022; and International Monetary Fund (IMF), *World Economic Outlook: War Sets Back the Global Recovery* (IMF: Washington, DC, Apr. 2022).

[19] European Commission, 'Statement by President von der Leyen on further measures to respond to the Russian invasion of Ukraine', 27 Feb. 2022.

[20] Sheahan, M. and Marsh, S., 'Germany to increase defence spending in response to "Putin's war"—Scholz', Reuters, 27 Feb. 2022; and Marksteiner, A., 'Explainer: The proposed hike in German military spending', SIPRI WritePeace blog, 25 Mar. 2022.

[21] 'Ukraine War: Russia warns Sweden and Finland against NATO membership', BBC News, 11 Apr. 2022; Faulconbridge, G., 'Russia warns of nuclear, hypersonic deployment if Sweden and Finland join NATO', Reuters, 14 Apr. 2022; Erlandger, S. and Lemola, J., 'Despite Russian warnings, Finland and Sweden draw closer to NATO', *New York Times*, 13 Apr. 2022; Yle, 'Yle poll: Support for NATO membership hits record high', 14 Mar. 2022; and Al Jazeera, 'Majority of Swedes in favour of joining NATO', 21 Apr. 2022.

beset by fast unfolding technological change.[22] The OSCE's future role may lie in a return to its origins in the cold war as the *Conference on* Security and Cooperation in Europe, from which the OSCE emerged in the November 1990–December 1994 period.[23]

The OSCE's distinctive characteristic has been its standing as the only pan-European security institution. Its capacity to act has been weakened over recent years, and a further weakening or possible redirection to a purely forum role—important though that could be—will inevitably strengthen some states' reliance on arrangements covering a smaller geographic area, in particular NATO and the EU. Uncertainties are to be found here too, however. Given the forcible reassertion of core hard security threats and challenges, NATO's renewed prominence and sense of purpose come as no surprise. Yet there are abundant uncertainties about NATO's future if the US presidential election in 2024 returns either Donald J. Trump or a candidate with similar views about the alliance to the White House. Trump expressed repeated scepticism about NATO both before and during his administration, even giving serious consideration to announcing the USA's withdrawal from NATO in 2018.[24] Likewise, it will take more than a month dominated by a single crisis of paramount importance to dispel uncertainty about the EU's capacity to be an international actor. It is not pre-ordained that the EU will retain both its increased focus on security and its greater cohesion once the immediate impetus of the war in Ukraine has dissipated.[25] By the end of the second month of war, some analysts were already noting that the EU's unity was fraying.[26]

Against this background of uncertainty about the big institutions for security and cooperation, developments are unfolding among cooperative security arrangements of less scope and ambition than NATO. Notable here are the EU's Permanent Structured Cooperation (PESCO), established in December 2017 with 25 members, including 4 non-members of NATO (Austria, Finland, Ireland and Sweden); the 13-state European Intervention Initiative, established in 2018 following a proposal by French President Emmanuel Macron; and the German-initiated Framework Nations Concept, launched

---

[22] Favaro, M., 'Strengthening the OSCE's role in strategic stability', Atlantic Council Strategic Insights memo, 12 Jan. 2022.

[23] Organization for Security and Co-operation in Europe (OSCE), 'History', accessed 1 Apr. 2022.

[24] Haines, T., 'Trump: NATO is obsolete and expensive: "Doesn't have the right countries in it for terrorism"', Real Clear Politics, 27 Mar. 2016; Pothier, F. and Vershbow, A., *NATO and Trump* (Atlantic Council: Washington, DC, June 2017), pp. 1–2; Barnes, J. E. and Cooper, H., 'Trump discussed pulling US from NATO, aides say amid new concerns over Russia', New York Times, 14 Jan. 2019; Crowley, M., 'Allies and former US officials fear Trump could seek NATO exit in a second term', New York Times, 3 Sep. 2020; and Alfaro, M., 'Bolton says Trump might have pulled the US out of NATO if he had been reelected', Washington Post, 4 Mar. 2022.

[25] Lehne, S., 'Making EU foreign policy for a geopolitical world', Carnegie Europe, 14 Apr. 2022.

[26] Dempsey, J., 'Europe's fading unity over Ukraine', Carnegie Europe, 21 Apr. 2022.

in 2013, aimed at broad intra-European defence cooperation.[27] The United Kingdom-led Joint Expeditionary Force was established in 2014, consisting of two states outside NATO (Finland and Sweden) and three outside the EU (Iceland, Norway and the UK), along with five that are members of both (Denmark, Estonia, Latvia, Lithuania and Netherlands).[28] There are also agreements of more limited scope, including the Franco-German Brigade and other arrangements within the Eurocorps framework, a 2018 trilateral Finland–Sweden–USA agreement, a France–Greece agreement concluded in October 2021, and a Poland–UK–Ukraine agreement made in February 2022, just before the war began.[29]

These diverse agreements and arrangements may be understood as compensating for the uncertainty surrounding the future roles of NATO and the EU. However, the fact that there are so many of them suggests that none has managed to carve out an indispensable security role. Indeed, whatever attractions these initiatives may hold for individual governments, their profusion threatens both to absorb resources and contribute to overall uncertainty.[30]

Both the sense of crisis itself and its effects, in terms of hardening positions, clarifying sentiment and overriding divisions, may dissipate relatively quickly once the most intense phase is over. However, the full effects of decisions taken in the immediate period will take years to unfold, and years or even decades to undo if—once the moment of crisis has passed—second thoughts arise. Whatever the outcome, war in Ukraine has raised serious questions both within Europe and beyond about political alignments and strategic preferences.

The broader responses and issues

As the UN General Assembly resolution in March 2022 showed, opposition to Russian actions in Ukraine was widespread. However, it was not all couched in the same terms, nor did it all lead to action such as sanctions.

Some close US allies, such as Japan and South Korea, adopted positions similar to that of the USA in the first months of the war, including providing

---

[27] Permanent Structured Cooperation (PESCO) website, <https://pesco.europa.eu>; Zandee, D. and Kruyver, K., *The European Intervention Initiative: Developing a Shared Strategic Culture for European Defence* (Clingendael: The Hague, Sep. 2019); and Major, C. and Möller, C., 'The Framework Nations Concept: Germany's contribution to a capable European defence', SWP Comments no. 52, Stiftung Wissenscahaft und Politik, Dec. 2014.

[28] Wharton, J., 'What is the Joint Expeditionary Force?', Forces Net, 16 Mar. 2022; and *The Economist*, 'Boris Johnson tells The Economist about his anti-Russia coalition', 19 Mar. 2022.

[29] Eurocorps, 'History', [n.d.]; 'Greek Parliament approves defence pact with France', Reuters, 7 Oct. 2022; and British Foreign, Commonwealth & Development Office, 'United Kingdom, Poland and Ukraine foreign ministers' joint statement, February 2022', Press release, 17 Feb. 2022.

[30] Frisell, E. H. and Sjökvist, E., *Military Cooperation Around Framework Nations: A European Solution to the Problem of Limited Defence Capabilities* (FOI: Stockholm, Feb. 2019).

aid and imposing sanctions.[31] In the Middle East, however, Saudi Arabia and the United Arab Emirates (UAE)—both long-standing regional allies of the USA—rebuffed US diplomacy and refused to increase their oil output as a means of restraining the rise in oil prices and helping stabilize the world economy against the disruptive effects of war and sanctions.[32] This may reflect other issues, including the two Gulf states' disagreements with the US administration of Joe Biden about the potential revival of the Iran nuclear deal (see below), discomfort with previous US policy under the administration of Barack Obama, and resentment at a perceived lack of support for their pursuit of war in Yemen since 2015. Against this background, some commentators are discussing a major realignment of policies by Saudi Arabia and the UAE, with a much clearer connection to China creating a new balance in their relationship with the USA.[33]

Other states criticized Russia's actions but avoided aligning with the West, opposing the breaching of sovereignty and forceful changing of borders, while insisting that disputes be settled by peaceful means. Such, for example, was India's position.[34]

China's position was similar. In February 2022, China and Russia avowed that their friendship has no limits, with no areas where cooperation is off the table.[35] This built on the 2021 extension of their 2001 treaty of friendship, which was renewed for a further 20 years.[36] Nonetheless, China was one of 35 states abstaining from the UN General Assembly vote condemning the invasion of Ukraine. Its position both respected Ukraine's sovereignty and criticized NATO enlargement, a key reason presented by Russian President Vladimir Putin for the war.[37] China has also stated its support for settling the conflict peacefully. A few weeks into the war, it remained unclear whether China would maintain this carefully nuanced position or opt for a more partisan stance in line with its long-standing relationship with Russia.[38]

---

[31] Smith, S. A., 'Tokyo condemns Putin's war, aids Ukraine', Council on Foreign Relations, 8 Mar. 2022; and Shin, H. and Kim, C., 'South Korea bans exports of strategic items to Russia, joins SWIFT sanctions', Reuters, 28 Feb. 2022.

[32] Di Paola, A. and Tobben, S., 'Saudi Arabia hikes oil prices as crude surges on Ukraine War', Bloomberg, 4 Mar. 2022; and Gambrell, J., 'Analysis: Oil prices, Ukraine war create Saudi pivot point', AP News, 1 Apr. 2022.

[33] Chulov, M., 'Biden rebuffed as US relations with Saudi Arabia and UAE hit new low', The Guardian, 3 Apr. 2022.

[34] Roy, A., 'Japan's Kishida and India's Modi discuss response to Ukraine crisis', Reuters, 19 Mar. 2022.

[35] Joint Statement of the Russian Federation and the People's Republic of China on the international relations entering a new era and the global sustainable development, 4 Feb. 2022.

[36] Isachenkov, V., 'Russia, China declare friendship treaty extension, hail ties', AP News, 28 June 2021; and Treaty of Good-Neighborliness and Friendly Cooperation Between the People's Republic of China and the Russian Federation, 16 July 2001, PA-X Agreements Database.

[37] Reuters, 'China says it respects Ukraine's sovereignty and Russia's security concerns', 25 Feb. 2022.

[38] Jiangtao, S., 'China has a choice to make on Ukraine, and the world is watching', South China Morning Post, 15 Mar. 2022; and Blanchette, J., 'The worse things go for Putin in Ukraine, the more China will back him', Washington Post, 24 Mar. 2022.

Around half of African states voted for the UN General Assembly resolution condemning Russia's invasion, with the others either abstaining or absent, apart from Eritrea, which voted against.[39] Responding to Russia's recognition of Donetsk and Lohansk in eastern Ukraine as independent states, Kenya's permanent representative to the UN made a particularly eloquent and widely quoted statement condemning Russian actions during a UN Security Council debate prior to the invasion.[40] The clarity and firmness of the condemnation of Russia was accompanied by equally straightforward criticism of 'the trend in the last few decades of powerful states, including members of this Security Council, breaching international law with little regard'.[41] This is a valuable challenge to the West's assumption of the moral high ground in the Ukraine crisis. While the West may be on the side of international law in this crisis, in the eyes of many it has not always been on such firm ground, leading to criticism of it for double standards and a selective moral approach.[42] The 2020 edition of this Yearbook found reason to decry the tendency in international politics towards not taking the rule of law and the norms accompanying it sufficiently seriously.[43] It is important that the Ukraine crisis becomes a moment when the necessity of rebuilding respect for international law is recognized, and equally important to acknowledge that Western powers have also breached it.

Ukraine is one of the few states to have relinquished ownership of nuclear weapons. Like Belarus and Kazakhstan, it did so in the aftermath of the break-up of the Soviet Union and, like them, did not at the time have the capacity for operational control over the thousands of weapons the Soviet Union's dissolution left in its hands. When it decided not to keep them, it received security assurances in the form of the Budapest Memorandum, a 1994 agreement with Russia, the UK and the USA.[44] The signatories bound themselves to 'respect the independence and sovereignty and the existing borders of Ukraine' (Article 1); 'refrain from the threat or use of force against the territorial integrity or political independence of Ukraine' (Article 2); and 'seek immediate United Nations Security Council assistance to Ukraine . . . if Ukraine should become a victim of an act of aggression' (Article 4). Thus, Russia's invasion of Ukraine not only violated the UN Charter but also broke its 1994 undertaking of non-aggression against Ukraine. Its occupation of

---

[39] United Nations, 'General Assembly resolution demands end to Russian offensive in Ukraine', UN News, 2 Mar. 2022.

[40] 'Russia recognizes independence of Ukraine separatist regions', Deutsche Welle, 21 Feb. 2022.

[41] Statement by Ambassador Martin Kimani during the Security Council Urgent Meeting on the Situation in Ukraine, 21 Feb. 2022.

[42] Obadare, E., 'Analyzing the Russia–Ukraine conflict from an African standpoint', Council on Foreign Relations, 3 Mar. 2022.

[43] *SIPRI Yearbook 2020*, pp. 19–23.

[44] Memorandum on security assurances in connection with Ukraine's accession to the Treaty on the Non-Proliferation of Nuclear Weapons, 5 Dec. 1994.

Crimea and of the eastern Ukrainian provinces of Donetsk and Luhansk in 2014 had already challenged the viability of the Budapest Memorandum, although not its validity.

Whether Ukraine would have faced Russian military action if it had kept nuclear weapons is necessarily speculative. In 1994 it would have been extremely unsafe for Ukraine to retain nuclear weapons, because it could not exert proper command and control over them and the risks of nuclear theft and subsequent terrorism were high; there can be no doubt it was the right decision.[45] Further, nuclear weapon ownership is not a panacea for security against attack: there have been armed clashes between nuclear-armed adversaries—China and the Soviet Union in 1969, and India and Pakistan persistently since 1999. Nonetheless, this speculation may be pertinent for some other governments pondering their choices in the face of nuclear-armed states in their region. Some argue that North Korea may regard the war as justifying its decision to develop nuclear weapons.[46] The crisis may also increase support in South Korea for either the USA redeploying nuclear weapons to the Korean Peninsula, or for developing nuclear weapons autonomously, while Japan has seen discussion of the nuclear option resurface.[47] The vast majority of the world's states have rejected nuclear weapons and embraced the goal of nuclear non-proliferation, because that is a safer and more secure path to take than heading towards a world with many nuclear weapons. War in Ukraine should not alter that underlying judgement.

II. The broader security horizon in 2021

Global trends

By the end of 2021, although Russia was threatening Ukraine, war had not yet begun. Meanwhile, China continued to put pressure on Taiwan.[48] In both cases the USA, supported to varying degrees by its allies, was involved in pushing back against the other two great powers. These confrontations capped a year in which, to the extent that the security situation can be weighed and measured, the overall balance was unchanged. After several years of significant deterioration in international security, the overall situ-

---

[45] Kelly, J., 'Despite the threat it faces, Ukraine was right to give up its nuclear weapons', German Marshall Fund of the United States, 22 Feb. 2022; and Knopf, J. W., 'Why the Ukraine war does not mean more countries should seek nuclear weapons', *Bulletin of the Atomic Scientists*, 12 Apr. 2022.

[46] Hong, A., 'Why Ukraine matters for the Korean Peninsula', KEI, 18 Feb. 2022.

[47] Larsen, M. S., 'Talk of a nuclear deterrent in South Korea', *Foreign Policy*, 9 Sep. 2021; Shin, M., 'Nearly three-quarters of South Koreans support nuclear weapons development', *The Diplomat*, 22 Feb. 2022; *The Economist*, 'An uncomfortable debate about nuclear weapons resurfaces in East Asia', 19 Mar. 2022; and Wingfield-Hayes, R., 'Will Ukraine invasion push Japan to go nuclear?', BBC News, 26 Mar. 2022.

[48] *The Economist*, 'China is ratcheting up military pressure on Taiwan', 9 Oct. 2021.

ation neither deteriorated further nor improved in 2020 and 2021.[49] This is the trajectory of risk in international security that the Bulletin of the Atomic Scientists also traces.[50] Such assessments necessarily contain an element of subjective judgement but, if conducted transparently, consistently and on the basis of solid evidence, they are worthwhile.

The evidence of persistent insecurity was all around in 2021. The number of armed conflicts was little changed compared to 2020 and, by the end of 2021, no significant new peace process had been launched, nor had there been any breakthrough in the ones that were already underway. In Asia, conflict fatalities—which had fallen by nearly 50 per cent in 2020 compared to the previous year—rose by 59 per cent in 2021, largely due to conflict in Afghanistan and Myanmar.[51] Asia became the region with the most conflict-related fatalities in 2021; however, sub-Saharan Africa was the region with the most armed conflicts (occurring in 18 of 49 states) and estimated conflict fatalities increased by 19 per cent compared to 2020.[52]

Global military spending continued to rise, as it has done every year since 2015, reflecting perceptions among many governments that their security context has deteriorated in a way that requires them to build up their military strength. Whatever the validity of an individual government's decision to increase military spending, an overall increase in global military spending is a sure sign of an increasingly insecure world. The increase in 2021 was 0.7 per cent, considerably less than the 3.1 per cent increase registered in 2020. Despite this relative deceleration, which may be due to the economic impact of the Covid-19 pandemic, the global total passed the $2 trillion milestone to stand at $2113 billion.[53] Reflecting the same reading of continuing global and regional insecurity, the nine states that possess nuclear weapons were all engaged in upgrading their nuclear arsenals.[54]

Climate change and Covid-19

The long-term pressure of climate change and the global Covid-19 pandemic both continued in 2021. Both have implications for peace and security.

In August 2021 the Intergovernmental Panel on Climate Change (IPCC) produced the first report in its sixth assessment cycle on the physical science basis for understanding global warming and climate change.[55] The science, like the climate crisis itself, has now developed to the point where it can be

---

[49] *SIPRI Yearbook 2021*, pp. 3–4.
[50] Bulletin of the Atomic Scientists, Science and Security Board, 'At doom's doorstep: It is 100 seconds to midnight. 2022 Doomsday Clock Statement', 20 Jan. 2022.
[51] See chapter 4, sections III and IV, in this volume.
[52] See chapter 7 in this volume.
[53] See chapter 8 in this volume.
[54] See chapter 10 in this volume.
[55] Allen, R. P. et al., *AR6 Climate Change 2021: The Physical Science Basis* (IPCC: Geneva, 7 Aug. 2021).

stated unequivocally that human influence has warmed the atmosphere, ocean and land, and that widespread and rapid changes—many of them unprecedented over centuries or even millennia—have occurred in the atmosphere, ocean, cryosphere and biosphere, affecting climate and weather in every region.

Looking ahead, the IPCC foresees that global surface temperature will continue increasing until at least the middle of the century, exceeding the ceiling set for global warming by the 2015 Paris Agreement on climate change unless there are deep reductions in greenhouse gas (GHG) emissions. Of the main GHGs, the level of carbon dioxide in the atmosphere is higher than at any time for at least 2 million years, while the levels of methane and nitrous oxide are higher than for at least 800 000 years. It is of particular concern that many changes caused by past and future GHG emissions will be irreversible for centuries to millennia, especially changes in the ocean, ice sheets and global sea level.

Impacts arising from extreme weather events and sea-level rises feed insecurity and conflict risk via clearly defined pathways.[56] Moreover, the relationship between climate change and insecurity is two-way: not only does the former interact with the socio-economic and political landscape to generate insecurity, but the latter can make it harder to respond to the challenge of climate change. To the degree that international cooperation is required to address the task of mitigating global warming and thus slowing climate change, a hostile international environment characterized by confrontation and distrust does not represent a conducive setting for finding solutions.

The 26th UN Climate Change Conference of the Parties (COP26) was held in Glasgow in November 2021. While the conference's concluding statement was regarded by many as a step forward compared to previous statements of intent and policy, it fell considerably short of what was needed.[57] Positives included accelerating the process of making national commitments more ambitious.[58] Overall, however, global warming will continue. If all promises are fulfilled, the rise in global average temperature will nonetheless be greater than the 1.5°C limit set by the 2015 Paris Agreement as the desirable goal; policies now in place will push the temperature increase over 2°C.[59]

---

[56] Mobjörk, M., Krampe, F. and Tarif, K., 'Pathways of climate insecurity: Guidance for policymakers', SIPRI Policy Brief, Nov. 2020.

[57] Åberg, A. et al., *COP26: What Happened, What Does This Mean, and What Happens Next?* (Chatham House: London, 15 Nov. 2021), p. 1; and *New York Times*, '6 takeaways from the UN climate conference', 13 Nov. 2021.

[58] Hoicka, C. et al., 'COP26: Experts react to the UN climate summit and Glasgow Pact', The Conversation, 13 Nov. 2021.

[59] Climate Action Tracker, 'Warming projections global update', Nov. 2021; and Hausfather, Z. and Forster, P., 'Analysis: Do COP26 promises keep global warming below 2C?', Carbon Brief, 10 Nov. 2021. See also Intergovernmental Panel on Climate Change (IPCC), *Mitigation of Climate Change: Summary for Policymakers* (IPCC: Geneva, 2022).

Strikingly, the president of COP26 tearfully apologized at the end of the conference for last-minute changes that watered down the conference statement's green commitments, with an undertaking to 'phase out' coal replaced by an intent to 'phase down'.[60]

At the same time, both the immediate and indirect consequences of the Covid-19 pandemic continued to unfold in 2021. Reported deaths from the disease totalled 4.1 million for the year, reaching a cumulative total of 5.94 million.[61] This data, however, is generally regarded as unreliable for several reasons, including methodological shortcomings and deficiencies in many national reporting systems. To correct for these, estimates of the death toll often take into account excess mortality—how many more people died than normal in a given period. Including excess mortality, the World Health Organization (WHO) estimates the Covid-19 death toll to be 60 per cent greater than reported deaths.[62] Other estimates give figures over three times higher than reported deaths: one estimate based on excess mortality suggests 17.1–19.6 million deaths by the end of 2021, while another that also includes prevalence of the disease in its modelling offers a 'best estimate' of 20 million.[63]

Although international scientific efforts to produce vaccines against Covid-19 were remarkably efficient, there was much to question regarding the use and distribution of the vaccines. Inevitably, the richer countries stood first in line, the poorest ones last. The WHO warned of the severe health risks of 'vaccine nationalism'—a me-first approach to immunization.[64] UN Secretary-General Antonio Guterres identified these risks in the following terms: '. . . more deaths. More shattered health systems. More economic misery. And a perfect environment for variants to take hold and spread.'[65] The economic consequences of vaccine nationalism are also potentially dire, including for countries stocking up with more vaccine doses than they need.[66]

---

[60] Reuters, '"Deeply sorry": UK's Sharma offers apology for last-minute changes to climate deal', 13 Nov. 2021.

[61] World Health Organization (WHO), 'The true death toll of Covid-19: Estimating global excess mortality', accessed 29 Mar. 2022; and Wang, H. et al., 'Estimating excess mortality due to the Covid-19 pandemic: A systematic analysis of Covid-19-related mortality, 2020–21', *The Lancet*, 10 Mar. 2022.

[62] WHO (note 61).

[63] Wang et al. (note 61); and *The Economist*, 'The pandemic's true death toll', accessed 23 Mar. 2022.

[64] Eaton, L., 'Covid-19: WHO warns against "vaccine nationalism" or face further virus mutations', *BMJ*, vol. 372, no. 292 (1 Feb. 2021).

[65] United Nations, Secretary-General, 'Vaccine nationalism, hoarding putting us all at risk, Secretary-General tells World Health Summit, warning Covid-19 will not be last global pandemic', Press Release SG/SM/20986, 24 Oct. 2021.

[66] Kretchmer, H., 'Vaccine nationalism—and how it could affect us all', World Economic Forum, 1 June 2021.

Studies of the economic costs of vaccine nationalism suggest figures ranging from $1.2 trillion to $9 trillion a year.[67]

The 2021 edition of this Yearbook traced how the pandemic's wider social, economic and political impacts have raised security concerns because of deepening inequalities and weakening democracy, both of which have been tied to increased risk of conflict.[68] Evidence in 2021 confirmed that the trend of deepening inequalities was continuing—including along economic, gender, racial and ethnic lines, as well as inequalities between countries—with the impact of the pandemic a contributory factor.[69] Likewise, several centres monitoring democracy confirmed a continued deterioration in its quality in 2021.[70] While this trend can partly be attributed to restrictions imposed on political rights for public health reasons, such as limiting public gatherings, a larger part of the problem is opportunistic exploitation of the pandemic to justify anti-democratic measures.

Arms control and nuclear non-proliferation

The year 2021 began with three pressing, unanswered questions about arms control. The first was whether the Russian–US Treaty on Measures for the Further Reduction and Limitation of Strategic Offensive Arms (New START) would be renewed for a further five years by the 5 February deadline. The second question was whether the twice-deferred review conference (RevCon) of the Nuclear Non-Proliferation Treaty (NPT), originally scheduled for April 2020, would proceed as planned in April 2021. And the third question was whether the USA under the new Biden administration would rejoin the Joint Comprehensive Plan of Action (JCPOA), commonly known as the Iran nuclear deal.

In the event, the new US administration made clear it wanted to extend New START and Russia stood by its long-held commitment to doing so. The Trump administration had delayed action, seeking at one point to make it conditional on Chinese participation, which the Chinese government con-

---

[67] Hafner, M. et al., *Covid-19 and the Cost of Vaccine Nationalism* (RAND Corporation: Santa Monica, CA, 2020); and United Nations, *Our Common Agenda: Report of the Secretary-General* (UN: New York, 2021), p. 53.

[68] *SIPRI Yearbook 2021*, pp. 17–19.

[69] Ahmed, N. et al., *Inequality Kills: The Unparalleled Action Needed to Combat Unprecedented Inequality in the Wake of Covid-19* (Oxfam: Oxford, Jan. 2022).

[70] International Institute for Democracy and Electoral Assistance, *The Global State of Democracy 2021: Building Resilience in a Pandemic Era* (International IDEA: Stockholm, Nov. 2021); *The Economist*, 'A new low for global democracy: More pandemic restrictions damaged freedoms in 2021', 9 Feb. 2022; Freedom House, *Freedom in the World 2022: The Global Expansion of Authoritarian Rule* (Freedom House: Washington, DC, 2022); and Boese, V. A., *Democracy Report 2022: Autocratization Changing Nature?* (V-Dem Institute: Gothenburg, Mar. 2022).

sistently ruled out, and then proposing an extension limited to just one year.[71] The full five-year extension was swiftly agreed two days before the deadline.[72] Preserving the one remaining bilateral nuclear arms control treaty between Russia and the USA kept open the opportunity to breathe new life into bilateral arms control. At the same time, it placed the spotlight on unresolved questions, such as whether (and how) to include China in the framework of negotiations—something that has been argued for by some US critics of New START.[73] This logically raises the question of whether to include the other six states that own nuclear weapons—the UK, France, Israel, India, Pakistan and North Korea—in arms control talks.[74] Given the parlous state of relations between the three great powers, however, this would seem out of the question, meaning that these states' nuclear weapons remain outside any agreed framework of limitation.

The NPT RevCon was deferred again until January 2022 due to the Covid-19 pandemic, before, late in 2021, being further postponed to August 2022.[75] The context in which it will convene in 2022 is characterized not only by nuclear concerns surrounding the crisis in Ukraine, but also by problems that go further back. In contrast to the plethora of arms control, reduction and disarmament treaties and agreements achieved in the 1990s, the 2010s were characterized by a crumbling arms control architecture, the arrival of North Korea among the small group of states that own nuclear weapons (probably in 2017 according to leaked US intelligence assessments) and the eight other nuclear-armed states all taking steps to enhance their arsenals.[76] The crisis in nuclear arms control and continued nuclear weapon possession by the nine states named above has long since led to frustration with the NPT by a number of states seeking quicker progress towards full nuclear disarmament, and formed part of the backdrop against which the Treaty on the Prohibition of Nuclear Weapons (TPNW) was opened for signature in 2017.[77]

[71] Reif, K. and Bugos, S., 'US, Russia extend new START for five years', *Arms Control Today*, Mar. 2021.

[72] 'New Start: US and Russia extend nuclear treaty', BBC News, 3 Feb. 2021. See also chapter 11, section I, in this volume.

[73] Reif, K., 'Bolton renews new START criticism', *Arms Control Today*, Sep. 2019.

[74] *SIPRI Yearbook 2021*, pp. 6–9. See also chapter 11, section I, in this volume.

[75] Zlauvinen, G., Letter from President-designate regarding the Tenth Review Conference of the Parties on the Non-proliferation of Nuclear Weapons, 21 July 2021; and Zlauvinen, G., Letter from President-designate regarding the Tenth Review Conference of the Parties on the Non-proliferation of Nuclear Weapons, 30 Dec. 2021.

[76] *SIPRI Yearbook 2019*, pp. 10–16; and Pollack, J. D., 'What do intelligence leaks about North Korea tell us?', Brookings, 9 Aug. 2017. See also chapter 11, section III, in this volume. Note that the phrase 'states that own nuclear weapons' is used instead of the shorter and more obvious term 'nuclear weapon states', as the latter is also used to designate those states permitted under the NPT to own nuclear weapons (i.e. the five permanent members of the UN Security Council).

[77] *SIPRI Yearbook 2019*, pp. 13–15; and Thakur, R. (ed.), *The Nuclear Ban Treaty* (Routledge: London, 2022).

Having been ratified by 50 states, the TPNW entered into force in January 2021.[78]

Iran's development of nuclear technology has long been controversial in the West and the Middle East. The country does not possess nuclear weapons and is a party to the NPT, meaning it has forsworn developing, producing or owning them. It has never acknowledged having a programme to develop nuclear weapons, nor has it ever been proven that the country has one, although there are indications of a possible programme before 2003 and further programme-relevant activities continuing until 2009.[79] Suspicions of Iran's intentions were widespread, however, and between 2006 and 2010 the UN Security Council passed six resolutions demanding an end to its uranium enrichment programme, five of which had sanctions attached.[80] The JCPOA blocked the country's path to developing nuclear weapons until at least 2030.[81] Under the Trump administration, however, the USA announced in 2018 that it would withdraw from its obligations under the deal, which it proceeded to do the following year despite the International Atomic Energy Agency's confirmation that Iran was fully implementing its own obligations.[82] Like other critics of the agreement, the administration's case for pulling out was based on Iran's actions in regional conflicts and its missile programme, as well as the 15-year time limit on the JCPOA. After the US withdrawal, Iran started breaching the JCPOA limits. Negotiations on restoring the deal began in 2021 but had not been completed by the end of the year.[83]

During 2021 the P5 of the UN Security Council—China, France, Russia, the UK and the USA—worked together in an informal group, with the rotating chair held by France, on a joint statement about nuclear war. Harking back to an epochal statement by the Soviet and US leaders Mikhail Gorbachev and Ronald Reagan following a 1985 meeting in Geneva, the P5 statement, issued on 3 January 2022, affirms that 'nuclear war cannot be won and must never be

---

[78] Treaty on the Prohibition of Nuclear Weapons, opened for signature 20 Sep. 2017, entered into force 22 Jan. 2021, UN Office for Disarmament Affairs.

[79] Quevenco, R., 'IAEA board adopts landmark resolution on Iran PMD case', International Atomic Energy Agency (IAEA), 15 Dec. 2015; and Kerr, P. K., *Iran's Nuclear Program: Status*, Congressional Research Service (CRS) Report for Congress RL34544 (US Congress, CRS: Washington, DC, 20 Dec. 2019).

[80] Arms Control Association, 'UN Security Council Resolutions on Iran', Jan. 2022.

[81] *SIPRI Yearbook 2016*, pp. 673–88; and *SIPRI Yearbook 2017*, pp. 505–510.

[82] IAEA, 'Verification and monitoring in the Islamic Republic of Iran in light of United Nations Security Council Resolution 2231 (2015)', Report by the Director General, GOV/2018/24, 24 May 2018.

[83] Abadi, C., 'The Iran nuclear deal's long year of negotiations and uncertainty', *Foreign Policy*, 24 Dec. 2021; Lynch, C., 'A last-ditch effort to save the Iran deal', *Foreign Policy*, 28 Dec. 2022; Al Jazeera, 'Iran says nuclear agreement can be reached if US sanctions lifted', 6 Jan. 2022; and Fassihi, F. and Jakes, L., 'Trading threats, the US and Iran inch closer to a nuclear pact', *New York Times*, 12 Jan. 2022. See also chapter 11, section II, in this volume.

fought'.[84] While the Gorbachev–Reagan declaration was followed by historic talks on nuclear disarmament, the new statement is unlikely to have such an impact. Nonetheless, it is valuable not only due to its recognition of the risks posed by the existence of nuclear weapons, but because, taken at face value, it offers a logic for constraint in the behaviour of great powers and other states owning nuclear weapons. There is a clear disjuncture between for-swearing nuclear war and being willing to start one—yet only China among the P5 has a nuclear 'no-first-use' policy. Equally, it raises questions about continuing down the nuclear modernization path on which all members of the P5 are set.[85] Indeed, the statement recognizes this by stating the wish to avoid a nuclear arms race among signatories. Moreover, the desire to prevent a nuclear war logically implies avoiding any conflictual and confrontational behaviour that might lead to nuclear weapon use by design or accident.

The P5 statement was aimed at the NPT RevCon that had been planned for January 2022. The further postponement of the RevCon until August 2022 ostensibly offered breathing space during which the P5 could work towards outlining the practical measures they could take to act on the logic of their joint statement. The mounting crisis over Russia–Ukraine relations and the eventual war mean that possibility is unlikely to be fulfilled.

Geopolitics

The departure of the Trump administration in the USA and its replacement by the Biden administration was widely expected to lead to a less turbulent and more peaceful period in international relations. The 2021 edition of SIPRI Yearbook warned that such expectations were likely misplaced. On the one hand, the USA is no longer the sole hegemon on the global stage as it was in the 1990s and, on the other hand, there remained many areas of poten-tial friction with both China and Russia.[86]

The Biden administration has been more critical and abrasive of Russia than the Trump administration was. In March 2021 the US president infuri-ated Russian media and diplomats by agreeing when an interviewer asked if he regarded the Russian president as a killer.[87] From the start, the Biden

---

[84] Ronald Reagan Presidential Library & Museum, 'Joint Soviet–United States statement on the summit meeting in Geneva', 21 Nov. 1985; and French Ministry for Europe and Foreign Affairs, 'Joint statement of the leaders of the five nuclear-weapon states on preventing nuclear war and avoiding arms races', 3 Jan. 2022.

[85] Gibbons, R. D., 'Five nuclear weapon states vow to prevent nuclear war while modernizing arsenals', *Bulletin of the Atomic Scientists*, 17 Jan. 2022.

[86] *SIPRI Yearbook 2021*, p. 22.

[87] CNN, 'Biden: I think Putin is a killer', 17 Mar. 2021; Gessen, M., 'How Biden rattled Putin', *New Yorker*, 19 Mar. 2021; Chernova, A., Ullah, Z. and Picheta, R., 'Russia reacts angrily after Biden calls Putin a "killer"', CNN, 18 Mar. 2021; and Troianovski, A., 'Russia erupts in fury over Biden's calling Putin a killer', *New York Times*, 18 Mar. 2021.

administration's approach has included trying to strengthen US alliances and undoing divisions sown by the Trump administration's policies and rhetoric.[88] Despite visible tension among allies over the lack of consultation by the US administration in handling the withdrawal from Afghanistan, there were signs that the public view of the USA among allies improved over the course of 2021.[89] It was always likely that this would be unwelcome to Russia, given the possibility that its government would see such efforts as a process of building unity against it. The summit meeting between presidents Biden and Putin in June 2021 was described by both parties as polite but marked by clearly stated disagreements.[90] Agreement was limited to the setting up of working groups of officials to tackle several key issues, including cyber-security, and initiating a dialogue on strategic stability.[91] Overall, some commentators formed the impression that, aside from nuclear arms control, the Biden administration viewed Russia as having little role to play in key issues, suggesting that, while the USA is central to how Russia understands the world, for US policymakers, Russia is a distraction.[92] With the war in Ukraine, however, Russia has returned to the centre of US attention.

Relations between China and the USA are also in a long-term process of deterioration, characterized by political competition, strategic confrontation and economic rivalry. China's annual economic growth over the past four decades has averaged close to 10 per cent for most of that time.[93] Although growth was much slower during 2020, the first year of the Covid-19 pandemic, China's was the only major economy that grew *at all* that year.[94] Some analysts argue that China's economy is already larger than the USA's by one measure and will likely outstrip it by all measures during the 2020s, although a contrary analysis suggests that will happen much later, if ever.[95] As the rising power of the current period, China chafes at the US assumption of superiority, at the global military reach the USA continues to display, and at an international system that it sees as unfairly shaped to US advantage.

---

[88] Blinken, A. J., 'Reaffirming and reimagining America's alliances', Speech at NATO headquarters, Brussels, by US Secretary of State, 24 Mar. 2021.

[89] Karnitschnig, M., 'Disbelief and betrayal: Europe reacts to Biden's Afghanistan "miscalculation"', Politico, 17 Aug. 2021; Walt, S. M., 'The real reason US allies are upset about Afghanistan', *Foreign Policy*, 27 Aug. 2021; Wike, R. et al,. 'America's image abroad rebounds with transition from Trump to Biden', Pew Research Center, 10 June 2021; and Griffiths, B. D., 'Global approval of the US shot up 15 points during Biden's first year after crashing under Trump, new polling finds', Insider, 12 Apr. 2022.

[90] Sanger, D. E., Shear, M. D. and Troianovski, A., 'Biden and Putin express desire for better relations at summit shaped by disputes', *New York Times*, 16 June 2021 (updated 31 Oct. 2021).

[91] White House, 'US–Russia presidential joint statement on strategic stability', 16 June 2021.

[92] Greene, S., 'How to speak with Moscow when there's nothing to talk about', *Moscow Times*; and Hill, F., 'The Kremlin's strange victory', *Foreign Affairs*, vol. 100, no. 6 (Nov./Dec. 2021), p. 44.

[93] Hirst, T., 'A brief history of China's economic growth', World Economic Forum, 30 July 2015.

[94] Jones, L., Palumbo, D. and Brown, D., 'Coronavirus: How the pandemic has changed the world economy', BBC News, 24 Jan. 2021.

[95] Farley, R., 'Can China's economy overtake the United States?', *The Diplomat*, 23 July 2021; and Zhu, E. and Orlik, T., 'When will China rule the world? Maybe never', Bloomberg, 5 July 2021.

In the USA, the bipartisan consensus on opposition to China's rise is reminiscent of the consensus that existed regarding the Soviet threat. One aspect of the US response is the 'trade war' initiated in 2018, which has been fought out by each side imposing high trade tariffs on the other.[96] By the first quarter of 2021, the higher tariffs had become the new normal, although commerce between the two countries continued to flourish despite this.[97] Even so, the atmosphere between China and the USA remains sour. The trilateral security pact launched in September 2021 between Australia, the UK and the USA—known as AUKUS—sent a clear political message of alliance against China.[98] Whether this should be regarded as a rerun of the US–Soviet cold war, with a change in the cast of characters, is hotly debated. One line of thinking in the USA treats confrontation between two great powers as inevitable, while another points to the economic and commercial links that tie China and the USA together in a way that was never true of the cold war rivals.[99]

Against this difficult background, the joint Chinese and US statement on enhancing climate action issued at COP26 in November 2021 was a welcome sign that, despite division on other challenges, cooperation is possible on this global issue.[100] Although the two countries offered strong statements of intent rather than binding commitments, their coming together over climate change augured well. Pragmatic cooperation may well be possible even in such a seemingly unfavourable international context.

The Western withdrawal from Afghanistan

In August 2021 the 20-year Western intervention in Afghanistan ended in failure, with many Afghans who had supported or participated in the Western presence in their country left stranded as forces pulled out. Under the Trump administration, the USA made an agreement with the Taliban in February 2020 to withdraw all US and allied forces from Afghanistan within 14 months—before 1 May 2021.[101] President Biden's decision to largely respect and implement this agreement confirmed that Western intervention in

---

[96] Wong, D. and Koty, A. C., 'The US–China trade war: A timeline', China Briefing, 25 Aug. 2020.

[97] Bown, C. P., 'US–China trade war tariffs: An up-to-date chart', Peterson Institute for International Economics (PIIE), 16 Mar. 2021; and Gordon, N., 'For all the "decoupling" rhetoric, US–China trade is booming', Fortune, 23 July 2021.

[98] Wintour, P., 'What is the Aukus alliance and what are its implications?', The Guardian, 16 Sep. 2021.

[99] Mearsheimer, J. J., 'The inevitable rivalry: America, China, and the tragedy of great-power politics', Foreign Affairs, vol. 100, no. 6 (Nov./Dec. 2021); and Brands, H. and Gaddis, J. L., 'The new Cold War: America, China, and the echoes of history', Foreign Affairs, vol. 100, no. 6 (Nov./Dec. 2021).

[100] US Department of State, 'US–China Joint Glasgow Declaration on Enhancing Climate Action in the 2020s', Media note, 10 Nov. 2021.

[101] Agreement for Bringing Peace to Afghanistan between the Islamic Emirate of Afghanistan which is not recognized by the United States as a state and is known as the Taliban and the United States of America, 29 Feb. 2020.

Afghanistan would end. In April 2021 the administration decided to delay the withdrawal until September.[102] The withdrawal then went ahead, descending into chaos as it became clear that the Taliban's victory would be swift and comprehensive. Amid the cacophony of recrimination that followed in the USA, the plain facts were that its war was over and the Taliban returned to power.[103]

In addition to the consequences suffered by the people of Afghanistan, there seemed likely to be several levels of geopolitical impact. US and Western influence would clearly be much diminished in the region, leaving space for both China and Russia to assert their interests. Some critics argued that the failure in Afghanistan drew a line under the 'global war on terrorism' launched by President George W. Bush after the al-Qaeda terrorist attacks on the USA of 11 September 2001—a war, they argued, which had likewise failed.[104] This, however, was strongly contested, despite acknowledgement of the costs of the campaign against terrorism.[105] A clearer if—for the USA and its allies—even more uncomfortable consequence of the withdrawal and its immediate aftermath is the impact of defeat on US prestige. This holds the possibility of simultaneously encouraging adversaries, demoralizing allies, weakening alliances, and discouraging states sitting on the fence from coming down on the US side.

Conflict management and risk

Beyond the calculation of advantage and disadvantage arising from intensified rivalry between the great powers, one problem highlighted in the previous two editions of this Yearbook is that contentiousness in global geopolitics diminishes the capacity for managing and helping resolve local and regional conflicts. This issue was again conspicuous in 2021.

Warfare in Ethiopia continued with no effective international conflict management stepping up to curtail the violence. No joint international action took place over the conflict between Armenia and Azerbaijan, which had erupted into open warfare in 2020. Similarly, there was an apparent incapacity to address what UN Secretary-General Guterres referred to

---

[102] Holland, S., Ali, I. and Stewart, P., 'Biden set to withdraw US troops from Afghanistan by Sept. 11', Reuters, 13 Apr. 2021.

[103] Axios, 'Pence says Biden solely responsible for Afghanistan crisis', 18 Aug. 2021; and *The Guardian*, 'Top US general says Afghan collapse can be traced to Trump–Taliban deal', 29 Sep. 2021. See also chapter 4, section III, in this volume.

[104] O'Donnell, L., 'The failed War on Terror', Friedrich Neumann Foundation for Freedom, 7 Oct. 2021; and France 24, '"Total Failure": The war on terror 20 years on', 26 Aug. 2021.

[105] Brands, H. and O'Hanlon, M., 'The War on Terror has not yet failed: A net assessment after 20 years', *Survival*, vol. 63, no. 4 (2021); and Ackerman, E., 'Winning ugly', *Foreign Affairs*, vol. 100, no. 5 (Sep./Oct. 2021).

as an 'epidemic of coup d'etats' in 2021.[106] This was not only evident in the UN Security Council, which generally does not take action aimed at reversing coups, but seemingly among regional organizations and other potential actors.[107]

The course of 2021 saw armed conflicts, terrorism and violence in many countries and regions, covered in part I of this Yearbook. In many of the affected countries, the conflict is protracted and violence endemic; in some cases, what can be seen is a re-emergence of conflicts that were thought to be over. The risk in these countries and regions is that war in Ukraine and a need to address other crises detracts from the energy and focus that international actors—not least the UN—need to draw on to address these conflicts. Accepting these levels of conflict and violence as a new normal would potentially consign many of the countries whose conflicts are described in part I to years of strife, immiseration and suffering.

A way forward?

The scale of human need in the face of the security, health and environmental challenges outlined above is daunting. The international system is not managing to cope and the great powers are not focused on responding.[108] In recent years, the same challenge has been identified in successive editions of the Yearbook: can energy and a sense of direction in the UN compensate for the lack of global leadership from the great powers? How might it be possible to achieve a balance in world affairs when the great powers are focused on their rivalries with each other? Now, as the international system reels under the impact of the war in Ukraine, is there space for anything else on the international agenda?

To the degree that it is possible to identify a way forward, the answer may lie in politics rather than in policies. The UN secretary-general's 2021 report, 'Our Common Agenda', maps out the approach and policies required to navigate the maze of current dilemmas and crises and so reach a prosperous, secure and sustainable future.[109] It has been estimated that some 400 reports a year are issued in the secretary-general's name—this one stands out from the rest not only because of the scope of the topic and its level of ambition, but because it was based on a mandate from the UN General Assembly's declaration to mark the UN's 75th anniversary.[110] There are also, it should be

---

[106] Nichols, M., '"An epidemic" of coups, UN chief laments, urging Security Council to act', Reuters, 26 Oct. 2021.

[107] Gowan, R. and Pradhan, A., 'Why the UN Security Council stumbles in responding to coups', International Crisis Group, 24 Jan. 2022.

[108] Tisdall, S., 'The world is ablaze: Xi, Putin and Biden must join the firefighters', The Guardian, 19 Dec. 2021.

[109] United Nations (note 67).

[110] UN Association–UK, 'UN briefing: Our common agenda', 10 Sep. 2021.

added, many other important reports—both recently produced and currently being composed—that set out crucial components of a way forward on the interrelated challenges faced by humanity.

If the vision set out in the UN secretary-general's report for a more effective, inclusive and networked multilateralism is to get policy traction, it cannot rely solely on the clarity of its ideas. This is the problem faced by all such reports. Impact is defined not merely by quality but by timing and the readiness of (at least some of) the audience to band together as a constituency to drive policies forward. Thus, to be implemented, 'Our Common Agenda' needs political support from a large, diverse and sufficiently effective coalition of states. If the supposition that the great powers are currently too distracted, lack the bandwidth or have other priorities is correct, then such a coalition must have three components. First, it must include middle and lesser powers to provide financing, energy, focus, foresight and political muscle. Second, it must include the UN system and regional multilateral organizations for the purposes of conflict resolution and violence prevention. And, third, it must include civil society organizations to mobilize public energy and engagement.

Part I. Armed conflict and conflict management, 2021

Chapter 2. Global developments in armed conflict, peace processes and peace operations

Chapter 3. Armed conflict and peace processes in the Americas

Chapter 4. Armed conflict and peace processes in Asia and Oceania

Chapter 5. Armed conflict and peace processes in Europe

Chapter 6. Armed conflict and peace processes in the Middle East and North Africa

Chapter 7. Armed conflict and peace processes in sub-Saharan Africa

2. Global developments in armed conflict, peace processes and peace operations

Overview

This chapter describes general developments in 2021 in armed conflicts and peace processes (for detailed regional coverage see chapters 3–7), as well as global and regional trends and developments in multilateral peace operations.

Section I explores definitions of 'armed conflicts' and outlines some of the main features and consequences of the active armed conflicts that occurred in at least 46 states in 2021 (one less than in 2020): 8 in the Americas, 9 in Asia and Oceania, 3 in Europe, 8 in the Middle East and North Africa (MENA) and 18 in sub-Saharan Africa. As in preceding years, most took place within a single country (intrastate), between government forces and one or more armed non-state group(s). Three were major armed conflicts (with more than 10 000 conflict-related deaths in the year)—in Afghanistan (approximately 42 000 reported fatalities), Yemen (18 500) and Myanmar (11 100)—and 19 were high-intensity armed conflicts (with 1000–9999 conflict-related deaths): in Nigeria (9900), Ethiopia (8880), Mexico (8300), Syria (5900), the Democratic Republic of the Congo (5700), Brazil (5500), Somalia (3300), Iraq (2700), Burkina Faso (2400), South Sudan (2100), Mali (1900), Sudan (1700), Central African Republic (1700), Niger (1500), Cameroon (1400), Pakistan (1400), Colombia (1300), Mozambique (1200) and the Philippines (1100). Only three armed conflicts were fought between states: the low-level border clashes between India and Pakistan, Armenia and Azerbaijan, and Kyrgyzstan and Tajikistan. Two other armed conflicts were fought between state forces and armed groups aspiring to statehood (between Israel and the Palestinians and between Turkey and the Kurds). Most of the armed conflicts were internationalized.

The total estimated number of conflict-related fatalities increased to about 150 000 in 2021, a 13 per cent increase since 2020. The increase was driven by significant increases in Asia and Oceania (59 per cent increase)—mostly due to increases in Afghanistan, Myanmar and Pakistan—and sub-Saharan Africa (19 per cent increase). Estimated conflict-related fatalities fell for the third consecutive year in MENA.

While conflict-related fatalities have generally shown a downward trend in recent years, other impacts of armed conflict (sometimes in combination with additional factors) appear to have increased, including population displacement, food insecurity, humanitarian needs and violations of international humanitarian law. Most peace processes either stalled or suffered serious setbacks during 2021. Nonetheless, some of the greatest decreases in armed violence in 2021 took place in contexts where ceasefires and power-sharing agreements had been reached in 2020: in Libya, Nagorno-Karabakh and Syria. The Covid-19 pandemic had minimal impact on armed conflicts in 2021—in most cases armed conflict levels persisted or even increased.

Section II describes the trends in multilateral peace operations. There were 63 active operations in 2021—an increase of one compared to the previous year. Three ended in 2021: the North Atlantic Treaty Organization-led Resolute Support Mission (RSM) in Afghanistan; the African Union Human Rights Observers and Military Experts Mission in Burundi; and the Organization for Security and Co-operation in Europe Observer Mission at the Russian Check-points Gukovo and Donetsk—and four started: the United Nations Integrated Transition Assistance Mission in Sudan; the Russian–Turkish Joint Monitoring Centre in Azerbaijan; the Southern Africa Development Community Mission in Mozambique; and the European Union Military Training Mission in Mozambique.

Despite an increase in the number of multilateral peace operations, the number of personnel deployed in them decreased by 12 per cent during 2021, from 127 124 on 31 December 2020 to 111 858 on 31 December 2021. This reduction was mainly driven by the closing of two multilateral peace operations, namely the RSM and the UN–AU Hybrid Operation in Darfur, which completed its mandate on 31 December 2020. The UN remained the leading organization in the field, with responsibility for about a third of all multilateral peace operations and more than two-thirds of all personnel deployed in them. Multilateral peace operations in sub-Saharan Africa continued to account for most personnel deployed in multilateral peace operations globally.

The AU Mission in Somalia remained the largest multilateral peace operation in 2021. Ethiopia remained the top troop contributor, followed by Uganda and Bangladesh. In 2021 the fatality rate for deaths due to all causes was lower than in the previous year. However, the annual fatality rate for hostile deaths of international personnel in UN peace operations increased again after having fallen in 2020, which was likely a result of reduced activities due to Covid-19 measures. The UN Multidimensional Integrated Stabilization Mission in Mali continued to be the deadliest peace operation in terms of both hostile deaths and overall fatalities.

The trend of increasing multilateral operations activity in the grey areas outside the scope of SIPRI's definition of a multilateral peace operation also continued in 2021, with the deployment of the joint international 'peacekeeping mission' to the Solomon Islands. Another trend in 2021 was the intensification of geopolitical rivalries between Western countries and Russia and China, affecting mission mandates, closures and restructuring.

Table 2.6 in section III provides further details on the different multilateral peace operations and the organizations deploying them.

IAN DAVIS AND CLAUDIA PFEIFER CRUZ

I. Tracking armed conflicts and peace processes

IAN DAVIS

In 2021 active armed conflicts occurred in at least 46 states (1 less than in 2020): 8 in the Americas; 9 in Asia and Oceania (2 more than in 2020); 3 in Europe; 8 in the Middle East and North Africa (MENA); and 18 in sub-Saharan Africa (3 less than in 2020)—see chapters 3–7 respectively.[1] As in preceding years, most took place within a single country (intrastate) between government forces and one or more non-state armed groups (NSAGs) or between such groups. Only three were fought between states (the low-level border clashes between India and Pakistan, Armenia and Azerbaijan, and Kyrgyzstan and Tajikistan), while two were fought between state forces and armed groups aspiring to statehood, with fighting sometimes spilling beyond recognized state borders (the conflicts between Israel and the Palestinians, and between Turkey and the Kurds).

Of the intrastate conflicts, 3 were major armed conflicts (10 000 or more conflict-related deaths in the year)—in Afghanistan (approximately 42 000 reported fatalities), Yemen (18 500) and Myanmar (11 100)—and 19 were high-intensity armed conflicts (1000–9999 conflict-related deaths in the year): in Nigeria (9900), Ethiopia (8880), Mexico (8300), Syria (5900), the Democratic Republic of the Congo (DRC, 5700), Brazil (5500), Somalia (3300), Iraq (2700), Burkina Faso (2400), South Sudan (2100), Mali (1900), Sudan (1700), the Central African Republic (CAR, 1700), Niger (1500), Cameroon (1400), Pakistan (1400), Colombia (1300), Mozambique (1200) and the Philippines (1100) (see figure 2.1). However, these categorizations should be considered tentative, as fatality information is unreliable.[2] Two of the three major armed conflicts (Afghanistan and Yemen) and most of the high-intensity armed conflicts were internationalized, involving foreign elements that may have led to the conflict being prolonged or exacerbated.

This section discusses the definitions of 'armed conflict' and related terms used in chapters 2–7, before highlighting the salient (and largely continuing) features of the armed conflicts and their main consequences in 2021, as well as key developments in peace processes.

---

[1] For the definitions of 'armed conflict' and related terms used in chapters 2–7 see the 'defining armed conflict' subsection and box 2.1 below.

[2] Armed Conflict Location & Event Data Project (ACLED), 'FAQs: ACLED fatality methodology', 27 Jan. 2020. On casualty counting see also *SIPRI Yearbook 2016*, pp. 247–61; and Delgado, C., 'Why it is important to register violent deaths', SIPRI WritePeace blog, 30 Mar. 2020.

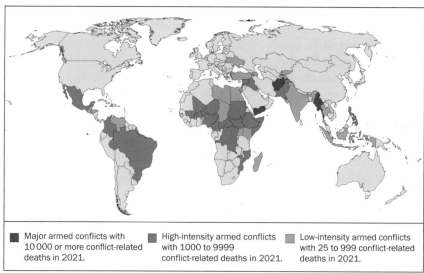

Major armed conflicts with 10 000 or more conflict-related deaths in 2021.

High-intensity armed conflicts with 1000 to 9999 conflict-related deaths in 2021.

Low-intensity armed conflicts with 25 to 999 conflict-related deaths in 2021.

Figure 2.1. Armed conflict, by number of conflict-related deaths, 2021

Defining armed conflict

Armed conflicts are often complex and multifaceted, featuring multiple actors with diverse and changeable objectives. This complexity can pose a major challenge for both the legal and conceptual categorization of armed conflict, as well as for thinking on peacebuilding and conflict prevention.[3]

Legal definitions

Determining the existence of an 'armed conflict' within the framework of international law differs according to whether the conflict occurs between states (interstate or international armed conflict), or between a state and one or more non-state groups, or among two or more non-state groups (intra-state armed conflict, or 'non-international armed conflict' (NIAC) under international humanitarian law).[4] Assessing a situation as an 'armed conflict' and further defining the nature of the armed conflict—international or non-international—is also crucial for determining the level of protection

---

[3] The complexity is captured in United Nations and World Bank, *Pathways for Peace: Inclusive Approaches to Preventing Violent Conflict* (World Bank: Washington, DC, 2018).

[4] For primary sources on the definition of armed conflicts see the 1949 Geneva Conventions common Article 2 and 1977 Additional Protocol I, Article 1 (international), and 1949 Geneva Conventions common Article 3 and Additional Protocol II, Article 1 (non-international)—International Committee of the Red Cross (ICRC), 'Treaties, states parties and commentaries'. See also e.g. ICRC, 'How is the term "armed conflict" defined in international humanitarian law?', Opinion Paper, Mar. 2008; and ICRC, *International Humanitarian Law and the Challenges of Contemporary Armed Conflicts* (ICRC: Geneva, Oct. 2019), pp. 50–52, 58–59, 75–76.

granted to non-combatants, defining the status of a combatant, and determining the level of obligations towards captured adversaries.

While there can be complications in classifying an international armed conflict—for example, foreign or multinational forces intervening in an armed conflict that does not otherwise have an international character, or extraterritorial uses of force by a state—it is usually more complicated to classify non-international ones. There is often no clear dividing line between intrastate armed conflicts and smaller-scale incidents of internal violence, such as riots or organized crime gangs. The threshold for an intrastate armed conflict must be evaluated on a case-by-case basis by weighing up a range of indicative data. The two key thresholds relevant to the classification of a NIAC are (*a*) protracted armed violence and (*b*) the actors involved demonstrating a certain degree of organization. The evaluation of (*a*) might include: duration of the conflict; frequency and intensity of the acts of violence and military operations, as well as the degree of continuity between them; the nature of the weapons used; displacement of civilians; territorial control by opposition forces; and the number of victims (including the dead, wounded and displaced people). Under (*b*), while states automatically meet the threshold, armed groups are assessed on a case-by-case basis, with possible considerations including whether explicit political goals have been stated; the presence of a command structure; a basic system of disciplinary rules and mechanisms; and the group's logistical and operational capability.[5]

Conceptual definitions used in this Yearbook

For the purpose of data gathering and analysing the number of and trends in armed conflicts, there is a need for simpler and more stringent definitions, both of an 'armed conflict' and its different types. However, the complexity in defining an armed conflict is reflected in the differences between the main datasets on violence and conflict, each of which has its own definitions and methodology.[6] This part of the Yearbook (chapters 2–7)—which is based predominantly on data from the Armed Conflict Location & Event Data Project (ACLED)—offers a primarily descriptive (rather than quantitative) synopsis of trends and events in 2021 affecting key armed conflicts.[7] It defines an 'armed conflict' as involving the use of armed force between two or more states or NSAGs (i.e. it covers both state-based and non-state armed conflict), and distinguishes armed conflicts according to three major categories: (*a*) interstate, (*b*) intrastate and (*c*) extrastate (see box 2.1).

---

[5] Vité, S., 'Typology of armed conflicts in international humanitarian law: Legal concepts and actual situations', *International Review of the Red Cross*, vol. 91, no. 873 (Mar. 2009), pp. 69–94.

[6] For an overview of the major advances in the collection and availability of armed conflict data see *SIPRI Yearbook 2016*, pp. 191–200.

[7] For more on events in 2021 related to armaments, disarmament and international security see annex C in this volume.

Box 2.1. Definitions and types of armed conflict

Armed conflict involves the use of armed force between two or more states or non-state armed groups (NSAGs). For the purposes of part I of this Yearbook, there is a threshold of battle-related violence causing 25 or more deaths in a given year. With the caveat that data on conflict deaths is often imprecise and tentative, the chapters categorize such conflicts as *major* (10 000 or more conflict-related deaths in the current year), *high intensity* (1000–9999 deaths) or *low intensity* (25–999 deaths).

Armed conflict can be further categorized as follows:

Interstate (international) armed conflict—the use of armed force by one or more state(s) against another state or states—is now rare and mostly occurs at lower intensities or shorter durations. While territorial, border and other disputes persist among states, they seldom escalate to armed conflict.

Intrastate (non-international) armed conflict is the most common form of armed conflict today and usually involves sustained violence between a state and one or more NSAGs fighting with explicitly political goals (e.g. taking control of the state or part of its territory). However, it can also include armed conflict between NSAGs, sometimes with less clear goals. Intrastate armed conflict can also be classified as follows:

- *Subnational armed conflict* is typically confined to particular areas within a sovereign state, with economic and social activities in the rest of the country proceeding relatively untroubled. This kind of conflict often takes place in stable, middle-income countries with relatively strong state institutions and capable security forces. Sometimes it takes place in a troubled border region within a large country that expanded geographically in the past or that has arbitrarily drawn borders.

- *Civil war* involves most of the country and results in at least 1000 conflict-related deaths in a given year.

Either type of intrastate conflict is considered internationalized if there is significant involvement by a foreign entity (excluding United Nations peace operations) that is clearly prolonging or exacerbating the conflict—such as armed intervention in support of, or provision of significant levels of weapons or military training to, one or more of the conflict parties by a foreign government or non-state actor, including private military companies.

Extrastate armed conflict occurs between a state and a political entity that is not widely recognized as a state but has long-standing aspirations of statehood (e.g. the Israeli–Palestinian conflict). Such conflicts, which are rare, may take place both inside and outside the state boundaries recognized by the international community.

Note: These definitions are used indicatively and are not based on legal conclusions. Thus, the conflict situations discussed in chapters 2–7 of this Yearbook may be characterized differently under international humanitarian law.

In defining a series of violent events as an armed conflict, a threshold of 25 reported battle-related deaths in a year is used. Fatality figures are collated from four event types: battles; explosions/remote violence; protests, riots and strategic developments; and violence against civilians.[8] Once the threshold of 25 battle-related deaths has been crossed, the fatalities from the other three event types are added to give a total number of 'conflict-related fatalities'.

---

[8] ACLED, 'ACLED definitions of political violence and protest', 11 Apr. 2019.

Thus, not every situation of armed violence amounts to an armed conflict. For example, although criminal violence can threaten the authority and capability of a state as much as an armed conflict, law enforcement activities unconnected to an armed conflict fall outside the scope of this definition (even if a state's military is involved). However, if the criminal violence involves state forces and/or organized NSAGs, and battle-related fatalities exceed the threshold, it is treated here as an armed conflict.

The difficulties in distinguishing between high levels of criminal violence and armed conflict is illustrated by the situation in the Americas (see chapter 3). The assessment that there were eight armed conflicts in the Americas in 2021 is based on ACLED's battle-related fatality figures, principally involving armed violence between state security forces and criminal gangs, or inter-gang violence. However, in only two of those countries—Colombia and Mexico—did the conflicts meet the complex legal definition of a NIAC. This was despite the other six countries experiencing levels of lethality, territorial control by non-state actors, and forced displacement and migration that are in keeping with traditional conceptions of armed conflict. Given these impacts and the lethality of gang–state violence, there is growing debate about whether international humanitarian law definitions of armed conflict require adjustment.[9]

Significant features of armed conflicts in 2021

Most armed conflicts since the cold war have been fought by a combination of regular armies, militias and armed civilians. Fighting is often intermittent, with a wide range of intensities and brief ceasefires, and rarely occurs on well-defined battlefields. While the nature of most armed conflicts is context specific, this subsection highlights some of the most significant features of several armed conflicts in 2021.

The International Committee of the Red Cross estimates that around 600 armed groups were active around the world in 2021, with at least 100 of them considered to be parties to a NIAC.[10] An estimated 60–70 million people reside in areas under the control of NSAGs.[11] Armed groups in many countries (e.g. CAR, Iraq, Libya, Nigeria, South Sudan, Syria, Ukraine and Yemen)

---

[9] See e.g. Applebaum, A. and Mawby, B., 'Gang violence as armed conflict: A new perspective on El Salvador', Policy Brief, Georgetown Institute for Women, Peace and Security, Nov. 2018; Ryan, K. O., '"Urban killing fields": International humanitarian law, gang violence, and armed conflict on the streets of El Salvador', *International and Comparative Law Review*, vol. 20, no. 1 (2020), pp. 97–126; and Chaparro, L. and Deslandes, A., 'Where's the aid for Mexicans displaced by gang violence?', New Humanitarian, 1 July 2021.

[10] Demeyere, B., 'Editorial: Non-state armed groups', *International Review of the Red Cross*, vol. 102, no. 915 (2021).

[11] Fidelis-Tzourou, M. and Sjöberg, A., 'Forgotten freedoms: The right to free expression in areas controlled by non-state armed groups', Armed Groups and International Law, 23 Oct. 2020.

were, in addition to being involved in military operations against state forces or other armed groups, providing services and governance normally associated with the state (from health care to security and justice). Despite the growing numbers of NSAGs, state forces remained the most powerful and violent actors in 2021, participating in 46 per cent of all political violence (down from 52 per cent in 2020).[12]

Most armed conflicts in 2021 were fought with conventional arms. Armed uncrewed aerial vehicles (UAVs), or drones, were increasingly used to conduct attacks in many situations of armed conflict, including in Ethiopia, Nagorno-Karabakh, Syria, Ukraine and Yemen.[13] UAV technology has proliferated greatly in recent years, with over 100 states currently operating military drones, and several armed non-state groups using commercial drones equipped with explosives.[14]

Forced recruitment of child soldiers and the use of sexual violence are widely perpetrated in armed conflict. In 2020 (the most recent year for which data is available) 8521 children were recruited and used as soldiers (as compared to 7747 in 2019), with Somalia remaining the country with the highest case number of cases (1716 in 2020).[15] Research suggests that the risk of children being recruited for use in armed conflict has increased steadily over the past 30 years.[16] In an annual report on conflict-related sexual violence, the UN secretary-general listed 18 countries of concern and 52 parties to conflict that were credibly suspected of having committed or instigated sexual violence in 2020 (the year covered by the report).[17] Such violence continued over the course of 2021 in many of these countries of concern. In Ethiopia, for example, sexual violence was widely reported, with an estimated 22 500 survivors seeking clinical care (up from 5611 in 2020).[18]

During many of the armed conflicts, especially the major and high-intensity conflicts, other international humanitarian law violations were also committed, including the use of starvation to achieve military ends;

---

[12] Lay, T., *ACLED 2021: The Year in Review* (ACLED: Mar. 2022), pp. 15–19.

[13] Gatopoulos, A., 'How armed drones may have helped turn the tide in Ethiopia's war', Al Jazeera, 10 Dec. 2021; and Khurshudyan, I. and Stern, D., 'Why Ukraine's Turkish-made drone became a flashpoint in tensions with Russia', *Washington Post*, 15 Jan. 2022.

[14] Gettinger, D., 'Drone databook update: March 2020', Mar. 2020, Center for the Study of the Drone; and Manson, K., 'Low-cost warfare: US military battles with "Costco drones"', *Financial Times*, 5 Jan. 2022. On calls to regulate armed UAVs see chapter 13, section I, in this volume.

[15] United Nations, General Assembly and Security Council, 'Children and armed conflict', Report of the Secretary-General, A/75/873–S/2021/437, 6 May 2021, pp. 2, 19.

[16] Haer, R. et al., 'Children at risk of being recruited for armed conflict, 1990–2020', Conflict Trends no. 6, Peace Research Institute Oslo, 2021.

[17] United Nations, Security Council, 'Conflict-related sexual violence', Report of the Secretary-General, S/2021/312, 30 Mar. 2021.

[18] Marks, S. and Walsh, D., '"They told us not to resist": Sexual violence pervades Ethiopia's war', *New York Times*, 1 Apr. 2021; and UN Population Fund Ethiopia, 'Preparedness and response plan for the Tigray crisis', April 2021, p. 2. On the armed conflict in Ethiopia see chapter 7, section IV, in this volume.

the denial of humanitarian aid; forced displacement; and attacks on aid and health workers, hospitals and schools. The rules meant to protect civilians in war are being broken regularly and systematically, with the consequence that such violations appear to be on the increase.[19]

Consequences of armed conflicts in 2021

Armed conflicts result in loss of life and life-changing injuries, displacement of civilian populations, and destruction of infrastructure and institutions. They also have long-term economic, developmental, political, environ-mental, health and social consequences.

Conflict-related fatalities

In 2021 the total estimated number of conflict-related fatalities increased by 13 per cent compared to 2020 (see table 2.1), despite a third consecutive year of reduced fatalities in MENA.[20] The increase in 2021 was driven by significant increases in Asia and Oceania (59 per cent increase)—mostly due to increases in Afghanistan, Myanmar and Pakistan—and sub-Saharan Africa (19 per cent increase). Conflict-related fatalities increased in all four event types in 2021 (see table 2.2). Battle-related fatalities increased by 11 per cent compared to 2020, despite the number of such events having declined by 13 per cent, accounting for 58 per cent of total estimated conflict-related fatalities in 2021.

Civilians were also increasingly targeted in 2021. ACLED recorded a 12 per cent increase in political violence targeting of civilians, with 33 331 events reported in 2020 compared to 37 185 in 2021 (of which 46 per cent were attributable to anonymous armed groups and 16 per cent to state forces); and an 8 per cent increase in civilian fatalities, with 35 889 reported fatalities in 2020 compared to 38 658 in 2021. The countries with the most civilian targeting in 2021 were Mexico (6298 events), Brazil (3262 events), Myanmar (2564 events), Syria (2517 events) and Nigeria (1580). In Mexico and Brazil the attacks were mainly perpetrated by anonymous or unidentified gangs (often making it difficult to determine whether the victim was a 'civilian' or a

---

[19] See e.g. United Nations, Security Council, 'Protection of civilians in armed conflict', Report of the Secretary-General, S/2021/423, 3 May 2021; and Metcalfe-Hough, V., 'Advocating for humanity? Securing better protection of civilians affected by armed conflict', Briefing Note, Humanitarian Policy Group, Nov. 2020.

[20] This assessment is based on ACLED data. For comparison see the Uppsala Conflict Data Program (UCDP), which reported total deaths from organized violence reaching a 15-year high in 2014, with about 103 000 deaths, and generally declining since then. UCDP's most recent data for 2019 showed almost 75 600 deaths, a decrease for the fifth successive year. Pettersson, T. and Öberg, M., 'Organized violence, 1989–2019', *Journal of Peace Research*, vol. 57, no. 4 (2020), pp. 597–613.

Table 2.1. Estimated conflict-related fatalities by region, 2018–21

Region	2018	2019	2020	2021
Americas	21 557	20 200	17 633	18 397
Asia and Oceania	49 888	48 755	36 325	57 877
Europe	1 084	482	7 312	278
Middle East and North Africa	76 512	53 430	34 117	28 506
Sub-Saharan Africa	26 504	26 620	37 683	44 848
Total	**175 545**	**149 487**	**133 070**	**149 906**

Note: Fatality figures are collated from four event types: battles; explosions/remote violence; protests, riots and strategic developments; and violence against civilians—see Armed Conflict Location & Event Data Project (ACLED), 'ACLED definitions of political violence and protest', 11 Apr. 2019.
Source: ACLED, 'Dashboard', accessed 29 Mar. 2022.

member of a criminal group), while in Myanmar it was primarily state forces, in Syria rebel groups and in Nigeria identity militias.[21]

Separate data on global trends and patterns in terrorism show a downward trend in deaths and in the impact of terrorism.[22] The Global Terrorism Index 2022 reports that the number of terrorism-related deaths worldwide fell by 1.2 per cent between 2020 and 2021, with the 7142 deaths recorded in 2021 a third of what they were at their peak in 2015. These reductions in fatalities occurred despite a 17 per cent increase in the number of attacks globally, to 5226. The data also shows a shift in the dynamics of terrorism. First, terrorism has become increasingly concentrated in regions and countries with political instability and conflict, such as the Sahel, Afghanistan and Myanmar—48 per cent of terrorism deaths globally in 2021 occurred in sub-Saharan Africa. Second, primarily politically motivated terrorism has overtaken religiously motivated terrorism, with five times more of the former than the latter in the period 2017–21.[23]

Forced displacement

While conflict-related fatalities have generally shown a downward trend in recent years, other impacts of armed conflict (sometimes in combination with

---

[21] Lay (note 12), pp. 18–22. ACLED categorizes 'political violence' as all events coded with event types 'battles', 'explosions/remote violence', and 'violence against civilians', as well as all events coded with sub-event type 'mob violence' under the 'riots' event type.

[22] There is no single internationally accepted definition of what constitutes terrorism. In the absence of an agreed definition, it is recognized that states sometimes identify 'terrorist' suspects in light of their own national interests, while others may consider the same actors to be insurgents or fighting for self-determination. Beyond al-Qaeda, the Islamic State and the Taliban, non-state armed groups as diverse as the Liberation Tigers of Tamil Eelam in Sri Lanka, the Revolutionary Armed Forces of Colombia (FARC), the Communist Party of Nepal, the Kurdistan Workers' Party in Turkey, the Communist Party of the Philippines, Hamas in Palestine and the Irish Republican Army (IRA) have been listed as terrorists.

[23] Institute for Economics & Peace (IEP), *Global Terrorism Index 2022: Measuring the Impact of Terrorism* (IEP: Sydney, Mar. 2022), p. 2.

Table 2.2. Categories of conflict-related violence, 2020–21

Event type	No. of events 2020	2021	Percentage change (2020–21)	Fatalities 2020	2021	Percentage change (2020–21)
Battles	37 755	32 660	*–13*	78 455	87 134	*11*
Explosions/ remote violence	25 499	25 382	*–0.5*	21 465	25 626	*19*
Protests, riots and strategic developments	164 698	184 796	*12*	3 358	3 911	*16*
Violence against civilians	24 892	27 964	*12*	29 792	33 251	*12*
Total	**252 844**	**270 802**		**133 070**	**149 922**	

Note: For definitions of event types, see Armed Conflict Location & Event Data Project (ACLED), 'ACLED definitions of political violence and protest', 11 Apr. 2019.
Source: ACLED, 'Dashboard', accessed 30 Mar. 2022.

other factors) appear to have increased, including population displacement, food insecurity, humanitarian needs, and violations of international humanitarian law. Armed conflict is a major driver of displacement, which reached record levels in 2021. At the beginning of 2021, 82.4 million people (approximately 1 per cent of humanity and more than double the number 10 years ago) were forcibly displaced, including 48 million internally displaced persons and 26.4 million refugees.[24]

These record numbers continued into the first six months of 2021, with conflict and violence triggering further large internal displacements, mainly in sub-Saharan Africa (e.g. 1.7 million people in Ethiopia, 0.73 million in the DRC and 0.29 million in Nigeria) and Asia (e.g. 0.34 million in Afghanistan and 0.24 million in Myanmar).[25] As of mid 2021, more than two-thirds of all refugees were from just five countries: Syria (6.8 million), Venezuela (4.1 million), Afghanistan (2.6 million), South Sudan (2.2 million) and Myanmar (1.1 million).[26] Protracted displacement crises continued in many other places, including Burkina Faso, Burundi, Cameroon, CAR, Colombia, El Salvador, Guatemala, Haiti, Honduras, Iraq, Libya, Mali, Mozambique, Somalia, Sudan and Yemen.[27]

Food insecurity

Armed conflict also continued to be one of the main drivers of food insecurity in 2021. In its September 2021 update the Global Report on Food Crises estimates that 161 million people in 42 countries faced acute food insecurity in the

---

[24] UN High Commissioner for Refugees (UNHCR), *Global Trends: Forced Displacement in 2020* (UNHCR: Copenhagen, 18 June 2021).

[25] Internal Displacement Monitoring Centre, 'Internal displacement at mid-year: 10 situations in review, 2021 mid-year update', 11 Apr. 2022.

[26] UNHCR, 'Refugee data finder', updated 10 Nov. 2021.

[27] UN Office for the Coordination of Humanitarian Affairs (OCHA), *Global Humanitarian Overview 2022* (UN OCHA: Geneva, Dec. 2021).

first eight months of 2021 due to the triple impact of conflict, climate shocks and the socio-economic consequences of the Covid-19 pandemic.[28] However, given this estimate did not cover all the countries at risk, and the situation worsened in some countries at the end of the year, a record high of up to 283 million people across 80 countries were likely to have been food insecure or at high risk in 2021 (up from 270 million across 79 countries in 2020).[29] This worsening situation reflects increases in acute food insecurity in some of the most conflict-affected countries, most notably Afghanistan, CAR, the DRC, Ethiopia, Haiti, Myanmar, Nigeria, Somalia, South Sudan, Sudan, Syria and Yemen.[30] Afghanistan became one of the world's largest hunger crises in 2021, with acute food insecurity affecting 22.8 million people (more than half the population), including 8.7 million people facing emergency levels of food insecurity.[31]

Conflict continued to be the primary driver of acute food insecurity in sub-Saharan Africa, where 12 of the 15 countries facing the greatest food insecurity in 2021 were also experiencing conflict.[32] The DRC, for example, was experiencing one of the worst humanitarian crises in the world, with an estimated 26.2 million people (about 27 per cent of the population) facing acute food insecurity—the largest of any single African country.[33] This was primarily due to ongoing armed violence and intercommunal conflicts in the eastern and north-eastern regions of the country. Similarly, in Ethiopia about 7 million people across three conflict-afflicted regions—Afar, Amhara and Tigray—were in need of food assistance by the end of September 2021.[34]

---

[28] Food Security Information Network, '2021 global report on food crises: September 2021 update', Sep. 2021, p. 3.

[29] UN OCHA (note 27), p. 26.

[30] UN OCHA (note 27), pp. 25–30. On food insecurity and conflict see also von Grebmer, K. et al., *Global Hunger Index 2021: Hunger and Food Systems in Conflict Settings* (Deutsche Welthungerhilfe e. V./Concern Worldwide: Bonn/Dublin, Oct. 2021); Food and Agriculture Organization of the UN (FAO), International Fund for Agricultural Development (IFAD), UN Children's Fund (UNICEF), World Food Programme (WFP) and World Health Organization (WHO), *The State of Food Security and Nutrition in the World 2021: Transforming Food Systems for Food Security, Improved Nutrition and Affordable Healthy Diets for All* (FAO: Rome, 2021); and Delgado, C., Murugani, V. and Tschunkert, K., *Food Systems in Conflict and Peacebuilding Settings: Pathways and Interconnections* (SIPRI: Stockholm, June 2021).

[31] Integrated Food Security Phase Classification, 'Afghanistan: Integrated Food Security Phase Classification snapshot: September 2021–March 2022', 25 Oct. 2021.

[32] The 15 countries with the highest acute food insecurity were: Burkina Faso, Cameroon, CAR, Chad, the DRC, Ethiopia, Kenya, Mozambique, Niger, Nigeria, Sierra Leone, Somalia, South Sudan, Sudan and Zimbabwe. Only Kenya, Sierra Leone and Zimbabwe were without armed conflict in 2021.

[33] Integrated Food Security Phase Classification, 'Democratic Republic of Congo: Integrated Food Security Phase Classification snapshot: March 2021', 30 March 2021; and Integrated Food Security Phase Classification, 'Democratic Republic of the Congo (DRC): Acute malnutrition situation September 2021–March 2022 and Projection for April–August 2022', 4 Oct. 2021.

[34] United Nations, 'Tigray: Food aid reaches Afar and Amhara, but situation still "dire"', UN News, 5 Oct. 2021.

Children and armed conflict

Large numbers of children suffer the consequences of armed conflicts: in 2020 (the latest year for which figures are available), 452 million children— more than one-sixth of children worldwide—were living in areas affected by armed conflict (a rise of 6 per cent compared to 2019).[35] In addition to fatalities through direct injury, children suffer the indirect effects of conflict, including malnutrition, disease and human rights violations. The UN secretary-general's annual report on children and armed conflict documented more than 26 000 incidents of 'grave violations' against children in conflicts around the world in 2020 (a 4 per cent increase compared to 2019), includ- ing the recruitment and use of children by armed groups, killing, maiming, harassment, rape and sexual violence, and abductions and attacks on schools and hospitals. The highest numbers of grave violations were verified in Afghanistan, the DRC, Somalia, Syria and Yemen.[36]

Economic costs

Armed conflict also imposes substantial economic costs on society. Though calculating the economic costs of violence is extremely difficult, one study estimated the global cost to be $15 trillion in 2020, or 11.6 per cent of global gross domestic product (GDP). This was a slight increase on the 2019 calcu- lation, mainly due to higher levels of military expenditure. However, the economic impact of armed conflict in 2020 was estimated to have decreased by 7.6 per cent to $448 billion, with this decline attributable to fewer deaths from terrorism and lower GDP losses from conflict. The economic impact of violence in the 10 most affected countries in 2020 averaged 35.7 per cent of GDP, while in the 10 most peaceful countries the average was just 4.2 per cent of GDP. The single largest component of the model in 2020 was global military expenditure (42.9 per cent of the total), followed by internal security spending (31.3 per cent) and private security expenditure (7.9 per cent).[37]

Environmental costs

Finally, armed conflict contributes to the deteriorating condition of the global environment, with consequences for sustainable development, human security and ecosystems—vulnerabilities that are being amplified by

---

[35] Østby, G. et al., 'Children affected by armed conflict, 1990–2020', Conflict Trends no. 4, Peace Research Institute Oslo, 2021.

[36] United Nations, General Assembly and Security Council, 'Children and armed conflict', Report of the Secretary-General, A/75/873–S/2021/437, 6 May 2021, p. 2.

[37] IEP, *Global Peace Index 2021: Measuring Peace in a Complex World* (IEP: Sydney, June 2021), pp. 37–48. On global military expenditure in 2021 see chapter 8 in this volume.

Table 2.3. Number of peace agreements, 2012–21

2012	2013	2014	2015	2016	2017	2018	2019	2020	2021[a]
63	43	81	70	79	74	81	48	21	7

[a] Covers Jan.–June 2021 only.

Source: PA-X Peace Agreements Database, Political Settlements Research Programme, University of Edinburgh, accessed 1 Apr. 2022.

increasingly unpredictable climate patterns.[38] Climate change poses multidimensional challenges to peace. In 2021 climate-related shocks continued to amplify drivers of violence in several countries and regions. Four interrelated pathways from climate change to violent conflict have been identified: (*a*) livelihoods; (*b*) migration and mobility; (*c*) armed group tactics; and (*d*) elite exploitation.[39] In Africa greater food and water insecurity, loss of livelihoods, additional pressure on natural resources, growing water scarcity, and more climate-linked human displacements contributed to increased violence in 2021. In South Sudan, for example, several years of catastrophic flooding displaced hundreds of thousands, including herders who moved south to the Equatoria region. This climate-induced forced migration aggravated pre-existing grievances and intercommunal tensions over land and power in the region.[40] Similarly, in the Sahel the erosion of traditional land-use arrangements due to climate change inflamed farmer–herder disputes, uprooting hundreds of thousands of people and contributing to the rise of jihadist and self-defence groups.[41]

The African Union and its member states have already recognized the risks that changing weather patterns pose to the continent. In November 2021, for example, the AU's Peace and Security Council emphasized the importance of climate-sensitive planning within peacekeeping and post-conflict reconstruction missions, as well as broader development agendas, to avoid armed conflict relapse in fragile communities.[42] Cooperation over water

---

[38] See e.g. Scartozzi, C. M., 'Reframing climate induced socioenvironmental conflicts: A systematic review', *International Studies Review*, vol. 23, no. 3 (16 Aug. 2021); and von Uexkull, N. and Buhaug, H., 'Security implications of climate change: A decade of scientific progress', *Journal of Peace Research*, vol. 58, no. 1 (Jan. 2021). On the linkages between climate change and arms transfers see Grand-Clément, S., Kruczkiewicz, A. and Miralles, M. M., 'A darker shade of "Code Red": Arms and climate change', Conflict and Environment Observatory, 2 Dec. 2021.

[39] Mobjörk, M., Krampe, F. and Tarif, K., 'Pathways of climate insecurity: Guidance for policymakers', SIPRI Policy Brief, Nov. 2020.

[40] See chapter 7, section IV, in this volume.

[41] Hegazi, F., Krampe, F. and Smith, E. S., *Climate-related Security Risks and Peacebuilding in Mali*, SIPRI Policy Paper no. 60 (SIPRI: Stockholm, Apr. 2021); Tarif, K., 'Climate change and violent conflict in West Africa: Assessing the evidence', SIPRI Insights on Peace and Security no. 2022/3, Feb. 2022; and chapter 7, section II, in this volume.

[42] 'Communiqué of the 1051st meeting of the AU PSC on "Climate Change and Peace and Security: The need for an Informed Climate-Security-Development nexus for Africa"', PSC/PR/COMM.1051 (2021), 26 Nov. 2021. Also see 'Communiqué of the 984th meeting of the AU PSC at the level of Heads of State and Government on "Sustainable Peace in Africa: Climate Change and its Effects on Peace and Security in the Continent"', AU PSC/AHG/COMM.1 (CMLXXXIV), 9 Mar. 2021.

resources, for example, can help prevent the escalation of tensions and build resilience to the impacts of climate change.[43] At the global level, however, cooperation has been harder to achieve due to increased geopolitical tensions. For example, a modest draft resolution focused on improving the UN Security Council's analysis of links between climate change and instability in countries and regions was vetoed by Russia in December 2021. India also opposed the draft, while China abstained.[44]

Peace processes in 2021

Like the conflicts they attempt to address, peace processes are also increasingly complex, multidimensional and internationalized, involving a wide range of actors, activities and outcomes.[45] In addition, there is a growing number of peace agreement databases and collections.[46] The evidence suggests that, despite increasing numbers of armed conflicts, there have been fewer peace agreements in recent years, with a particularly strong decrease likely in 2021 compared to the previous nine years (see table 2.3). The Covid-19 pandemic and a divided—and hence less influential—UN Security Council may be partly responsible for the lower number of peace agreements in 2020–21.[47] There were seven new peace agreements in the first half of 2021 (see table 2.4).

Peacebuilding efforts typically include: ceasefire negotiations; signing of peace agreements; multilateral peace operations; disarmament, demobilization and reintegration of former combatants (often supported as part of UN peace operations); power-sharing arrangements; and state-building measures. These are all designed to bring about sustainable peace among parties to a conflict.[48] Despite increased efforts in recent years to make peace

[43] For lessons learned from existing cooperative initiatives see Kim, K. et al., *Water Cooperation in the Horn of Africa: Addressing Drivers of Conflict and Strengthening Resilience* (SIPRI: Stockholm, Dec. 2021).

[44] AP News, 'Russia vetoes UN Security Council resolution linking climate crisis to international peace', *The Guardian*, 13 Dec. 2021; and International Crisis Group, 'How UN member states divided over climate security', 22 Dec. 2021. See also discussion on climate change in the Introduction, section II, of this volume.

[45] Wolff, S., 'The making of peace: Processes and agreements', Armed Conflict Survey, vol. 4, no. 1 (2018), pp. 65–80.

[46] Examples include: UN Peacemaker, Peace Agreements Database; UN Peacemaker and University of Cambridge, Language of Peace Database; University of Edinburgh, Political Settlements Research Programme, PA-X Peace Agreements Database; University of Notre Dame, Kroc Institute for International Peace Studies, Peace Accords Matrix; and UCDP, UCDP Peace Agreement Dataset.

[47] On the lack of cooperation in the international system and Western tensions with China and Russia see chapter 1, chapter 4, section II, and chapter 5, section I, in this volume.

[48] On multilateral peace operations see section II in this chapter, and in relation to disarmament, demobilization and reintegration see UN Peacekeeping, 'Disarmament, demobilization and reintegration', accessed 11 Apr. 2022. On various interpretations of the term 'peace', as well as other tools for realizing peace, see *SIPRI Yearbook 2017*, pp. 211–52; and Caplan, R., *Measuring Peace: Principles, Practices, and Politics* (Oxford: Oxford University Press, 2019).

Table 2.4. Peace agreements in January to June 2021

Country	Date of agreement	Agreement	Conflict level	Stage
India/ Pakistan	25 Feb. 2021	Joint statement	Interstate	Renewal
Mali	24 Jan. 2021	Peace agreement between the Dogon and Peulh communities[a]	Intrastate/ local	Framework–partial
Mali	22 Jan. 2021	Peace agreement between the Dogon and Peulh communities[b]	Intrastate/ local	Framework–partial
Mali	12 Jan. 2021	Peace agreement between the Dogon and Peulh communities[c]	Intrastate/ local	Framework–partial
Senegal/ Casamance	9 Apr. 2021	Joint statement	Intrastate	Pre-negotiation
South Sudan	25 Mar.2021	Lou Nuer–Dinka Bor–Murle Action for Peace, Jonglei State	Intrastate/ local	Framework–partial
Sudan	28 Mar. 2021	Declaration of Principles between the Transitional Government of Sudan and the Sudan People's Liberation Movement-North	Intrastate	Framework–partial

Renewal = a short agreement to renew previous commitments; Framework–partial = agreements that concern parties engaged in discussion and agreeing to substantive issues to resolve a conflict, but which only deal with some of the issues; Pre-negotiation = an agreement that aims to get parties to the point of negotiating over the incompatibilities at the heart of a conflict.

[a] Dogon and Peulh communities of Madougou and Barapirely.

[b] Dogon and Peulh communities of Dougoutènè I, Dougoutènè II, KoporoKendié Na, Koporo Pen, Pel Maoudé and Youdiou.

[c] Dogon and Peulh communities of Bondo, Dioungani and Koro.

Source: PA-X Peace Agreements Database, Political Settlements Research Programme, University of Edinburgh, accessed 1 Apr. 2022.

processes more inclusive, women, community and grassroots organizations continue to be under-represented in the political–military hierarchies at the centre of most peace negotiations.[49] In the period 1990–2020 the percentage of peace agreements with provisions referencing women, girls and gender averaged only 22 per cent per year. After a generally positive trend that saw the figure rise to 49 per cent in 2013, it dropped back down to 8 per cent in 2017 before rising to 29 per cent in 2020 (i.e. 6 out of 21 peace agreements that year referenced women, girls and gender).[50]

Not all peace processes lead to sustainable peace. Inconclusive political settlements, a failure to address the root causes of a conflict, and ongoing insecurity and tensions have often led to non-compliance, violations and

[49] Caparini, M. and Alvarado Cóbar, J. F., 'Overcoming barriers to grassroots inclusion in peace processes', SIPRI WritePeace blog, 18 Feb. 2021; and Schneiker, A., 'The UN and women's marginalization in peace negotiations', *International Affairs*, vol. 97, no. 4 (July 2021), pp. 1165–82.

[50] Wise, L., 'Peace agreements with a gender perspective are still an exception, not the rule', LSE blog, 18 June 2021.

a recurrence of armed conflict. Since the mid 1990s most armed conflicts have been renewed outbreaks of old conflicts rather than conflicts over new issues, indicating that the root causes of conflicts are not being sufficiently addressed. Moreover, this blurred boundary between war and peace also makes it difficult to identify and conceptualize the end of an armed conflict.[51]

While many of the armed conflicts in 2021 were being addressed by ongoing or new peace processes, most—with a few notable exceptions, including a new ceasefire between India and Pakistan in their conflict over Kashmir—were either stalled or suffered serious setbacks. In Myanmar, for example, it was hoped that the November 2020 ceasefire between the Arakan Army and Myanmar's military might open up new opportunities for dialogue, but the military coup in February 2021 led to escalating violence across the country and an 18-fold increase in estimated conflict-related fatalities in 2021 compared to 2020. Similarly, in Sudan, the only sub-Saharan African country to make substantive progress in a peace process in 2020, a military coup occurred in October 2021 and conflict-related fatalities nearly doubled during the year.

Nonetheless, some of the greatest decreases in armed violence in 2021 took place in contexts where ceasefires and power-sharing agreements had been reached in 2020. In Libya, for example, where a nationwide ceasefire and a power-sharing agreement by rival governments was agreed in October 2020, estimated conflict fatalities decreased by 93 per cent in 2021 compared to the previous year. Elsewhere, as a result of the November 2020 ceasefire agreed in relation to the Nagorno-Karabakh conflict between Azerbaijan and Armenia, the number of fatalities was reduced from over 7000 in 2020 to just 57 in 2021. Similarly, in Syria, where a ceasefire was agreed in Idlib province in March 2020, the reduction was 29 per cent in 2021. In Yemen, however, despite the formation of a power-sharing cabinet between the Southern Transitional Council and the Hadi government in the southern governorates in late 2020, as well as international engagement in peace negotiations on the Houthi conflict, the decrease in estimated conflict-related fatalities was only 6 per cent (with over 28 000 estimated fatalities as fighting continued throughout 2021). Moreover, even where declines in violence occurred, the context remained deeply fragile and susceptible to further outbreaks of violence.

[51] De Franco, C., Engberg-Pedersen, A. and Mennecke, M., 'How do wars end? A multidisciplinary enquiry', *Journal of Strategic Studies*, vol. 42, no. 7 (2019), pp. 889–900. See also Krause, J., 'How do wars end? A strategic perspective', *Journal of Strategic Studies*, vol. 42, no. 7 (2019), pp. 920–45. On the peace agreement provisions consistently associated with successful war-to-peace transitions see Fontana, G., Siewert, M. B. and Yakinthou, C., 'Managing war-to-peace transitions after intra-state conflicts: Configurations of successful peace processes', *Journal of Intervention and Statebuilding*, vol. 15, no. 1 (2020), pp. 25–47.

Impact of Covid-19 on armed conflict

The UN secretary-general's call in 2020 for a Covid-19-related global cease-fire was largely ignored by the majority of conflict parties, who at best displayed a chiefly tokenistic commitment. Most of the ceasefires that took place were unilateral declarations, and many were temporary or conditional—overall, therefore, they represented only preliminary steps, with minimal material impact on levels of violence.[52] By the start of 2021 most conflict parties appeared to have adapted to the pandemic, which now simply formed part of the wider political context of armed conflicts and peace processes. Rather than being game-changing, the impact of Covid-19 on armed conflicts in 2020–21 was essentially minimal. In most cases armed conflict levels persisted, even increasing in a few instances due to conflict parties exploiting either state weakness or reduced international attention arising from the pandemic.[53] ACLED recorded a rise in demonstrations around the world in 2021 as social unrest continued to build during the second year of the pandemic, but only in Europe did most of these seem directly or indirectly attributable to Covid-19-related restrictions.[54] Some projections based on economic and development data estimate the pandemic may lead to increases in armed violence—driven by rising prices and falling incomes—in fragile states.[55]

[52] Guterres, A., 'The fury of the virus illustrates the folly of war', United Nations Covid-19 response, 23 Mar. 2020. See the discussion in *SIPRI Yearbook 2021*, pp. 43–46. On the Covid-19 pandemic see chapter 12, section I, in this volume.

[53] Ide, T., 'Covid-19 and armed conflict', *World Development*, vol. 140 (Apr. 2021); and Kishi, R., *A Year of Covid-19: The Pandemic's Impact on Global Conflict and Demonstration Trends* (ACLED: Apr. 2021).

[54] Lay (note 12), p. 3.

[55] Moyer, J. D. and Kaplan, O., 'Will the coronavirus fuel conflict?', *Foreign Policy*, 6 July 2020.

II. Global and regional trends and developments in multilateral peace operations

CLAUDIA PFEIFER CRUZ, JAÏR VAN DER LIJN AND TIMO SMIT

A key trend in 2021 was the continued decrease in the number of personnel deployed in multilateral peace operations globally. To a large extent this reflects the termination of the North Atlantic Treaty Organization (NATO)-led Resolute Support Mission (RSM) in Afghanistan and the establishment (or continuation) of smaller peace operations that have had relatively stable deployments. The discussions on exit strategies for some of the largest multilateral peace operations, such as the United Nations Organization Stabilization Mission in the Democratic Republic of the Congo (MONUSCO) and the African Union Mission to Somalia (AMISOM), are also indications of this trend. Moreover, peace operations continue to be concentrated in sub-Saharan Africa, with two out of the three new operations launched in the region. These two peace operations, both in Mozambique, also illustrate the increasing involvement of regional organizations—in this case, the European Union and the Southern Africa Development Community (SADC). In addition, complex constellations of peace operations, concentrated in a handful of host countries, continue to face coordination challenges. The involvement of private military companies in conflict-management efforts in crowded fields, such as the Central African Republic (CAR) and Mali, has also increased the complexity of these environments. Finally, disagreements between organizations, personnel contributors and funders of multilateral peace operations have continued across many operations, and combined with increasing geopolitical rivalries—particularly between Western countries and Russia and China—this often leads to discussions about mission mandates, closures and restructuring.

Multilateral peace operations in 2021

In 2021 the UN, regional organizations and alliances, and ad hoc coalitions of states carried out 63 multilateral peace operations in 38 countries/territories across the world (see figure 2.2)[1]—one more operation than in 2020. In fact, the

---

[1] See also table 2.6, this chapter, section III. The quantitative analysis draws on data collected by SIPRI to examine trends in peace operations. According to SIPRI's definition, a multilateral peace operation must have the stated intention of: (a) serving as an instrument to facilitate the implementation of peace agreements already in place; (b) supporting a peace process; or (c) assisting conflict prevention or peacebuilding efforts. Good offices, fact-finding or electoral assistance missions, and missions comprising non-resident individuals or teams of negotiators are not included. Since all SIPRI data is reviewed on a continual basis and adjusted when more accurate information becomes available, the statistics in this chapter may not fully correspond with data found in previous editions of the SIPRI Yearbook or other SIPRI publications.

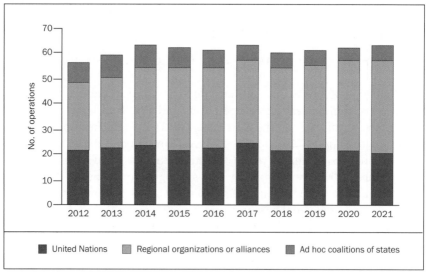

Figure 2.2. Number of multilateral peace operations, by type of conducting organization, 2012–21

number of active multilateral peace operations has remained relatively stable since 2013, when CAR and Mali became hotspots (see figure 2.3). In 2021 CAR hosted five operations, deploying a combined average of 15 000 personnel, while Mali hosted four operations, deploying approximately 16 000 personnel. Along with Somalia and South Sudan, these were the countries/territories with the largest number of deployments in 2021. In accordance with the general trend, the largest number of operations—22—took place in sub-Saharan Africa, with 19 taking place in Europe, 14 in the Middle East and North Africa, 5 in Asia and 3 in the Americas (see table 2.5).

New multilateral peace operations

Four multilateral peace operations started in 2021: the UN Integrated Transition Assistance Mission in Sudan (UNITAMS); the Russian–Turkish Joint Monitoring Centre in Azerbaijan (RTJMC); the SADC Mission in Mozambique (SAMIM); and the EU Military Training Mission in Mozambique (EUTM Mozambique).

UNITAMS was established on 3 June 2020 by UN Security Council Resolution 2524 with the objective of supporting the Sudanese democratic transition. Despite UNITAMS' deployment beginning in October 2020, the mission only started delivering its mandated objectives in January 2021. Though the mission's mandate—to support the transition process in Sudan—was extended for another year on 3 June 2021,[2] it was later called

---

[2] UN Security Council Resolution 2579, 3 June 2021.

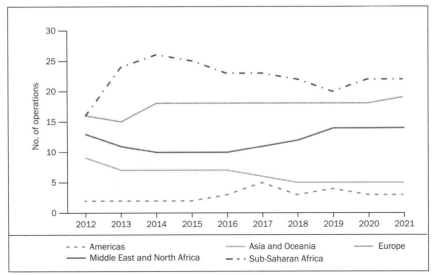

Figure 2.3. Number of multilateral peace operations, by region, 2012–21

into question by the October military coup in Sudan and the stalling of the democratic transition.[3]

The RTJMC in Aghdam district in Azerbaijan became operational on 30 January 2021. Established by a memorandum of understanding between Russia and Turkey, it monitors implementation of the ceasefire agreement between the Armenian and Azerbaijani forces signed on 10 November 2020 in the Nagorno-Karabakh war. As of 31 December 2021 the RTJMC was estimated at 60 personnel members from Russia and 60 from Turkey. Monitoring of the ceasefire has been carried out using uncrewed aerial vehicles (UAVs) and the evaluation of other sources—although the centre did not specify which sources.[4] It is the first time UAVs have been used as the primary platform to monitor a ceasefire.

On 23 June 2021 the Extraordinary SADC Summit of Heads of State and Government held in Maputo established SAMIM in response to escalating violent extremism in the northern Mozambiquan province of Cabo Delgado.[5] Less than a month later, on 15 July 2021, the mission was deployed in the region. SAMIM's mandate includes supporting Mozambique to combat terrorism and acts of violent extremism in Cabo Delgado; strengthening and maintaining peace and security, as well as restoring law and order, in affected

---

[3] United Nations, Security Council, 'Security Council briefing on the Integrated Transition Assistance Mission in Sudan (UNITAMS)', 11 Dec. 2021.

[4] 'Russia and Turkey Open Monitoring Centre for Nagorno-Karabakh', Reuters, 30 Jan. 2021. On the armed conflict in Nagorno-Karabakh see chapter 5, section I, in this volume.

[5] Southern Africa Development Community (SADC), Communiqué of the Extraordinary Summit of the SADC Heads of State and Government, 23 June 2021. On the armed conflict in Mozambique see chapter 7, section IV, in this volume.

Table 2.5. Number of multilateral peace operations and personnel deployed by region and type of organization, 2021

Conducting organization	Americas	Asia and Oceania	Europe	Middle East and North Africa	Sub-Saharan Africa	**World**
Operations	3	5	19	14	22	63
United Nations	2	2	2	7	7	20
Regional organization or alliance	1	1	14	6	15	37
Ad hoc coalition	–	2	3	1	–	6
Personnel	301	337	8 108	14 289	88 823	111 858
United Nations	277	301	1 015	12 459	65 291	79 343
Regional organization or alliance	24	–	5 942	676	23 532	30 174
Ad hoc coalition	–	36	1 151	1 154	–	2 341

– = not applicable.

Note: Numbers of active operations cover the year 2021, including operations closed during the year; personnel figures are as of 31 Dec. 2021.

Source: SIPRI Multilateral Peace Operations Database, accessed 1 Apr. 2022.

areas of Cabo Delgado; and supporting Mozambique, in collaboration with humanitarian agencies, to continue providing humanitarian relief to populations affected by terrorist activities. Although the mission's duration was foreseen as lasting for three months, continued instability in the area led to it being extended for an additional three months on 5 October 2021. Both SADC and Mozambican President Filipe Nyusi did not reject the possibility of a further extension of the mission.

As of the end of 2021 SAMIM comprised military personnel from eight SADC member states: Angola, Botswana, the Democratic Republic of the Congo (DRC), Lesotho, Malawi, South Africa, Tanzania and Zimbabwe. Though the mission's authorized level of personnel is 2916, as of 31 December 2021 it is estimated to consist of 1077 personnel, of which the largest contingent is South African.[6] SAMIM has worked in collaboration with the Mozambique Armed Defence Forces (Forças Armadas de Defesa de Moçambique, FADM) and other troops deployed to Cabo Delgado, such as the 1000-personnel strong Joint Force of the Rwanda Defence Force (RDF) and the Rwanda National Police (RNP). This Joint Force is not a multilateral peace operation, but a single-country contingent deployed at the request of

---

[6] International Crisis Group, 'Winning peace in Mozambique's embattled north', Africa Briefing no. 178, 10 Feb. 2022.

the Mozambique government, and has worked closely with the FADM and SAMIM.[7]

EUTM Mozambique was established by the Council of the EU on 12 July 2021 and launched on 15 October 2021.[8] The mission is mandated to build the capacity of FADM units that will eventually become part of a military quick reaction force, the rationale being that this will provide the Mozambique government with a more sustainable and effective military capability to combat armed groups in Cabo Delgado province. EUTM Mozambique will provide these units with training and non-lethal equipment, which is a novelty for EU military training missions. This equipment (which includes vehicles and a field hospital) is financed under the European Peace Facility, a new EU funding instrument that became operational in 2021.[9]

EUTM Mozambique's mandate will end two years after the mission has achieved full operational capability, which is expected in the spring of 2022. As of 31 December 2021 the missions consisted of 70 military personnel (out of an authorized strength of 118), with most troops from Portugal, the former colonial power in Mozambique. Unlike SAMIM and the Rwandese forces in Mozambique, the EU mission will conduct its training activities at locations in the south of the country, close to the capital Maputo, rather than operating in Cabo Delgado itself.[10]

These newly established missions follow the overall trend of smaller operations with small deployments. Although relatively speaking SAMIM is larger, it cannot be considered a large-scale operation along the lines of AMISOM or multidimensional UN operations such as the UN Multidimensional Integrated Stabilization Mission in the Central African Republic (MINUSCA) and the UN Multidimensional Integrated Stabilization Mission in Mali (MINUSMA).

Closed multilateral peace operations

Three multilateral peace operations ended in 2021: the NATO-led RSM in Afghanistan; the AU Human Rights Observers (HROs) and Military Experts (MEs) Mission in Burundi; and the Organization for Security

---

[7] Rwandan Ministry of Defence, 'Rwanda deploys joint force to Mozambique', 10 July 2021.

[8] Council Decision (CFSP) 2021/1143 of 12 July 2021 on a European Union Military Training Mission in Mozambique (EUTM Mozambique), *Official Journal of the European Union*, L247, 13 July 2021; and Council Decision (CFSP) 2021/1818 of 15 Oct. 2021 launching the European Union Military Training Mission in Mozambique (EUTM Mozambique), *Official Journal of the European Union*, L368, 18 Oct. 2021.

[9] Council Decision (CFSP) 2021/2032 of 19 Nov. 2021 on an assistance measure under the European Peace Facility to support military units trained by the EU Training Mission in Mozambique, *Official Journal of the European Union*, L415, 22 Nov. 2021.

[10] European Parliament, Subcommittee on Security Defence, An update on the state of play with EU Training Mission in Mozambique with Vice-Admiral Hervé Bléjean, Director General of the EU Military Staff (EUMS), 26 Jan. 2022.

and Co-operation in Europe (OSCE) Observer Mission at the Russian Checkpoints Gukovo and Donetsk.

The RSM was launched at the beginning of 2015 by NATO at the invitation of the Afghan government and in accordance with UN Security Council Resolution 2189.[11] The mission was established as a non-combat successor operation to the International Security Assistance Force (ISAF), its objective being to train, advise and assist Afghan security forces and institutions to develop their capacities.

Though the mission was terminated in early September 2021, its drawdown had already started the previous year following an agreement signed in February 2020 between the United States and the Taliban. In accordance with the agreement, the USA was to withdraw all its forces from Afghanistan by May 2021. One of the main arguments for the US withdrawal was that given increasing geopolitical rivalries it needed to undertake a strategic turn towards the Asia Pacific region, and towards China in particular.[12] Given that the withdrawal was progressive and relatively fast, it is difficult to estimate the number of personnel deployed immediately before the RSM's date of termination. Nevertheless, in February 2021 9592 troops from 36 contributing countries were deployed by the RSM.

The AU HROs and MEs Mission in Burundi was established on 13 June 2015 and deployed the following month in response to rising political violence surrounding President Pierre Nkurunziza's pursuance of a third term and a failed coup attempt.[13] The mission was designed to monitor, document and report on the country's human rights and security situation, and to strengthen protection and access to justice for victims of human rights violations. Although the original plan was to deploy 100 HROs and 100 MEs by March 2017, the maximum strength reached by the mission was only 45 HROs and 26 MEs, in July 2016. This was due to lack of funds, a perception that the situation in the country had undergone relative improvement, and resistance from the host government towards maintaining the mission.

On 20 May 2020, despite the recent death of Pierre Nkurunziza, Burundi held relatively peaceful elections. Although the country has been politically stable since the elections, human rights violations, particularly arrests and forced disappearances of political opposition, remain a concern. The AU Peace and Security Council decided to end the HROs and MEs Mission in Burundi on 31 May 2021 given the progress and positive developments

---

[11] UN Security Council Resolution 2189, 12 Dec. 2014.

[12] White House, 'Remarks by President Biden on the way forward in Afghanistan', 14 Apr. 2021.

[13] African Union, Communiqué of the 515th Meeting of the Peace and Security Council of the African Union at the Level of Heads of State and Government on Burundi, 13 June 2015.

witnessed in the country.[14] At the time the mission was terminated, it was composed of eight HROs and two MEs.[15]

The OSCE Observer Mission became operational on 24 July 2014 to monitor cross-border movements between Russia and Ukraine at the checkpoints of Gukovo and Donetsk. The mission was established at the request of Russia given the conflict in the Donbas region of Ukraine, and was based on the 2014 Minsk Protocol, in which Russia and Ukraine committed to an immediate ceasefire in the region. The protocol envisaged permanent OSCE monitoring and verification of the Russia–Ukraine border. The mission was discontinued on 30 September 2021 following Russia's objection to a further mandate extension, despite other OSCE countries—such as the United Kingdom and the USA—having advocated for expansion of the mission's scope.[16] Ukraine criticized the decision, considering it an attestation of Russia's plans to provide material support to separatists in Ukraine's Donetsk and Luhansk regions.[17] At the time of its discontinuation, the mission was operating with 21 permanent international personnel.

Personnel deployments

Over the past decade there has been a general trend towards a declining number of personnel deployed globally in multilateral peace operations.[18] In fact, December 2021 saw the lowest number of personnel deployed in multilateral peace operations during the period 2012–21 (see figure 2.4). Over 2021 the number of personnel deployed decreased from 127 124 to 111 858—a decline of approximately 12 per cent. Combined with the slight increase in the number of operations deployed in 2021, the trend continues towards more but smaller operations. Since MINUSCA's establishment in 2014, no large-scale mission has been launched.[19]

[14] AU, Communiqué of the 993rd Meeting of the Peace and Security Council of the African Union at the Level of Heads of State and Government on the AU Human Rights Observers and Military Experts Mission in Burundi, 27 Apr. 2021.

[15] Amani Africa, 'Discussion on the AU human rights observers and military experts to the Republic of Burundi', 27 Apr. 2021.

[16] US Embassy & Consulates in Russia, 'Planned closure of the OSCE Border Observer Mission', Sep. 20, 2021; and British Foreign, Commonwealth & Development Office, 'Russia decision to close OSCE Observer Mission at 2 Russian border checkpoints: UK statement', 16 Sep. 2021. On the armed conflict in Ukraine see chapter 5, section II, in this volume.

[17] Ukrainian Ministry of Foreign Affairs, 'Statement by the Ministry of Foreign Affairs of Ukraine on Russia's intention not to extend the mandate of the OSCE Observer Mission at the Russian Checkpoints Gukovo and Donetsk', 2 Sep. 2021.

[18] The number of personnel deployed in multilateral peace operations, unless otherwise specified, refers exclusively to international personnel and does not include national personnel employed in these operations.

[19] Though the RSM, a large-scale mission, was established in 2015, it was a follow-up mission to ISAF and so began with large contingents already on the ground.

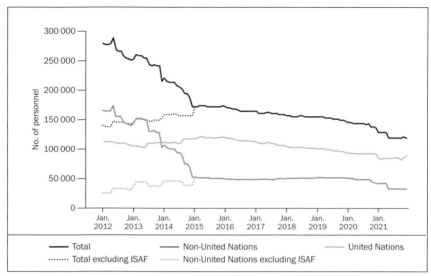

Figure 2.4. Number of personnel in multilateral peace operations, by type of conducting organization, 2012–21

ISAF = International Security Assistance Force.

Note: Monthly data, last observation is Dec. 2021.

The significant decrease in the number of personnel deployed from 2020 to 2021 can be explained by the closing of two of the largest multilateral peace operations active in 2020, namely the RSM in Afghanistan and the UN–AU Hybrid Operation in Darfur (UNAMID). At the time they were terminated, these operations together accounted for approximately 16 000 personnel deployed. In fact, much of the downward trend in personnel numbers over recent years is explained by the drawdown of troops from Afghanistan, which for a significant period was host to the largest multilateral peace operation, with more than 130 000 troops on the ground between 2010 and 2011 (when the RSM's predecessor, ISAF, was deployed).

Though both the RSM and UNAMID closed in 2021, their discontinuation had already been decided in previous years, with discussions in the Security Council on UNAMID's closure having begun in 2018.[20] In the case of the RSM, the agreement between the USA and the Taliban that envisaged the withdrawal of US troops from Afghanistan by May 2021 had been signed back in February 2020.[21] Therefore, the steep decline in the number of personnel deployed in peace operations globally in 2021 was already expected towards the end of 2020.

---

[20] UN Security Council Resolution 2559, 22 Dec. 2020.

[21] US Department of State, 'Agreement for bringing peace to Afghanistan between the Islamic Emirate of Afghanistan which is not recognized by the United States as a state and is known as the Taliban and the United States of America', 29 Feb. 2020.

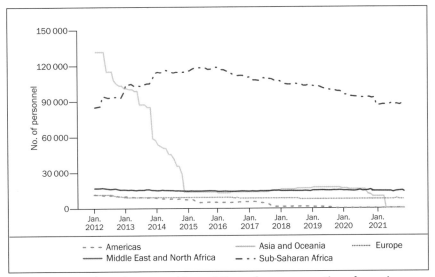

Figure 2.5. Number of personnel in multilateral peace operations, by region, 2012–21

Note: Monthly data, last observation is Dec. 2021.

Sub-Saharan Africa continues to host the highest number of multilateral peace operations (22 of the 63 peace operations active in 2021), including 7 of the 10 largest operations active on 31 December 2021. Moreover, 79 per cent of all international peace operations personnel deployed at the end of 2021 were assigned to this region (see figure 2.5). Even so, the number of personnel deployed in sub-Saharan Africa has decreased since 2015, the year following MINUSCA's establishment, and over the course of 2021 it declined further from 94 201 to 88 823. However, this decline of 6 per cent was lower than the global downward trend.

Organizations conducting multilateral peace operations

United Nations

The UN remains the main organization deploying multilateral peace operations, accounting for about one third of all operations and 71 per cent of all personnel deployed on 31 December 2021. In 2021 the UN deployed 20 multilateral peace operations—one fewer than in 2020. Over the course of 2021 the number of personnel deployed in UN peace operations decreased by 8.5 per cent from 86 712 to 79 343. This represents the continuation of a trend since 2015, with larger operations drawing down or closing in subsequent years.

The decrease in 2021 is largely due to the closing of UNAMID in Sudan, which still had 6623 deployed personnel at the time of its termination on 31 December 2020. UNITAMS, the UN peace operation established in the

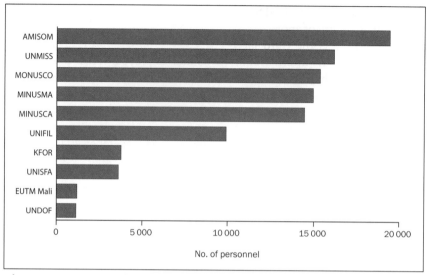

Figure 2.6. Largest multilateral peace operations as of 31 Dec. 2021

AMISOM = African Union Mission in Somalia; EUTM Mali = EU Training Mission Mali; KFOR = Kosovo Force; MINUSCA = United Nations Multidimensional Integrated Stabilization Mission in the Central African Republic; MINUSMA = UN Multidimensional Integrated Stabilization Mission in Mali; MONUSCO = UN Organization Stabilization Mission in the Democratic Republic of the Congo; UNDOF = UN Disengagement Observer Force; UNIFIL = UN Interim Force in Lebanon; UNISFA = UN Interim Security Force for Abyei; UNMISS = UN Mission in South Sudan.

country ahead of UNAMID's closure, is a much smaller special political mission, with 98 personnel deployed as of the end of December 2021. Although some of the largest UN peace operations, such as MINUSCA and MONUSCO, increased in size during 2021, this has not been sufficient to counterbalance the effect of UNAMID's closure. Even so, 7 of the 10 largest multilateral peace operations in December 2021 were UN peacekeeping operations.

Since 2019 the UN Mission in South Sudan (UNMISS) has been the largest UN peace operation, although its size has decreased since then (see figure 2.6). As of 31 December 2021 it deployed 16 140 international personnel, representing a decrease of 7.1 per cent over the course of the year.

MONUSCO was the second largest UN peace operation on 31 December 2021, with 15 313 personnel deployed. For the first time since 2016, MONUSCO personnel increased, by 3.8 per cent over the course of the year. Although the mission continues to prepare its transition plan,[22] on 20 December 2021, having considered the political instability and recurring violence in the DRC, the

---

[22] United Nations, Security Council, 'Senior official in Democratic Republic of Congo spotlights violence in eastern provinces, outlines mission transition plans, briefing Security Council', SC/14655, 5 Oct. 2021.

Security Council maintained the mission's strategic priorities and authorized personnel strength of approximately 16 000.[23]

MINUSMA was the third largest UN peace operation on 31 December 2021, with 14 917 international personnel deployed. This represents a decrease of less than 1 per cent compared to the end of the previous year. By contrast, MINUSCA's personnel number increased by 2.2 per cent over the same period to 14 423 on 31 December 2021. Lastly, the UN Interim Force in Lebanon (UNIFIL) continues to be the only major UN operation outside sub-Saharan Africa, deploying 9871 personnel as of 31 December 2021. Over the past 10 years, this number has remained relatively stable under pressure from the parties to the conflict that wish UNIFIL to keep this level of commitment.

Fatalities in United Nations peace operations

Over the course of 2021, 92 international personnel and 32 local staff died while serving in UN peace operations (see figure 2.7).[24] This was two less fatalities than in 2020, which had been considerably more deadly than preceding years due to illnesses, particularly Covid-19. Of the 92 international personnel who died, 64 were military personnel, 26 were international civilian personnel, and 2 were police. The fatality rate for uniformed personnel in 2021 was 0.85 per 1000 uniformed personnel (see figure 2.8).

In 2021 peacekeepers died from three main causes: illness (48, of which 10 were due to Covid-19), accidents (9) and malicious acts (24). In addition, for 11 peacekeepers the cause of death was yet undetermined or unknown. Despite hostile deaths tending to receive the most attention, such fatalities comprised only 26 per cent of all deaths during 2021. This is, however, an 11 per cent increase compared to 2020, when Covid-19 measures likely reduced activities.

MINUSMA continues to register the highest number of deaths among deployed personnel, with 35 fatalities. With a total of 19 hostile deaths in 2021, compared to 6 in 2020, MINUSMA has returned to the higher levels of hostile deaths it saw prior to the Covid-19 pandemic.[25] These 19 fatalities in MINUSMA account for 79 per cent of the 24 hostile deaths experienced by UN peace operations in 2021. Excluding MINUSMA, fatality rates of uniformed personnel due to malicious acts within UN peace operations remain at near all-time-low levels—it was only in 2019 that fewer hostile deaths were recorded per 1000 uniformed personnel deployed.

---

[23] UN Security Council Resolution 2612, 20 Dec. 2021.

[24] The figures for fatalities in this section do not include the UN's personnel category described as 'other', and refer to international personnel unless otherwise specified.

[25] During 2021 restrictions related to the Covid-19 pandemic, such as a reduction in patrols, reduced personnel's exposure to the risk of attack.

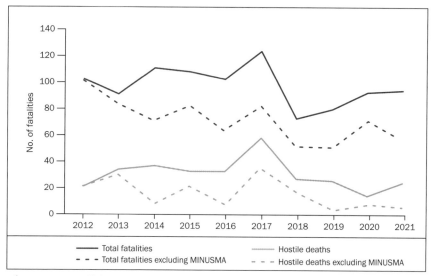

Figure 2.7. Fatalities among international personnel in United Nations peace operations, 2012–21

MINUSMA = UN Multidimensional Integrated Stabilization Mission in Mali.

Regional organizations and alliances

Regional organizations and alliances led 37 multilateral peace operations in 2021—one more than in 2020. There were two new operations in this category, both in Mozambique: SAMIM and EUTM Mozambique. As of 31 December 2021 multilateral peace operations established by regional organizations or alliances deployed a total of 30 174 personnel, a decrease of 21 per cent compared to the 38 140 personnel deployed the previous year. Once again, this decline is largely explained by the closure of the NATO-led RSM.

Four African regional organizations—the AU, the Economic Community of West African States (ECOWAS), the Intergovernmental Authority on Development (IGAD), and SADC—conducted a total of nine multilateral peace operations. While the number of operations deployed by African regional organizations remained the same over the course of 2021, the total number of personnel deployed by these organizations increased by 5 per cent from 20 496 to 21 562.

The AU conducted most of the African operations and was also the organization deploying most personnel. In fact, since 2015 AMISOM has been the largest multilateral peace operation, with 19 384 personnel in the field as of 31 December 2021. The AU also conducted the AU Mission in Libya and the AU Observer Mission to the Central African Republic (MOUACA). In addition, despite the closure of the AU HROs and MEs Mission in Burundi, the organization continued to maintain two small political missions in CAR and Mali.

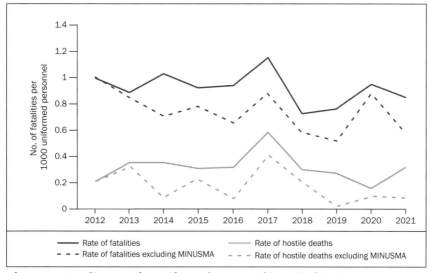

Figure 2.8. Fatality rates for uniformed personnel in United Nations peace operations, 2012–21

MINUSMA = UN Multidimensional Integrated Stabilization Mission in Mali.

Following a decrease in the number of deployed troops in 2020, AMISOM maintained its number of personnel throughout 2021. Though the mission aims to transition its efforts to the Somali government and its mandate was set to run out on 31 December 2021, troop-contributing countries and the AU expect to maintain a significant presence into the near future. The main stakeholders involved have expressed concerns about the potential expansion of al-Shabab in the wake of any eventual discontinuation of AMISOM—echoing the Taliban's rapid takeover of Afghanistan following the withdrawal of US and other international forces, including the RSM.

There was general agreement on the need to restructure the mission. During 2021 there were discussions between Somalia and the AU regarding the future of AMISOM and the establishment of an interim operation to facilitate the transfer of security responsibilities to Somali security agencies.[26] The report issued by an independent assessment team in May 2021 recommended that AMISOM be replaced by a hybrid AU–UN multidimensional stabilization mission starting in January 2022, financed under the peacekeeping budget.[27]

---

[26] AU, Communiqué of the 978th Meeting of the Peace and Security Council of the African Union on the consideration of the Report of the Chairperson of the Commission on the situation in Somalia and the implementation of the African Union Mission in Somalia (AMISOM) mandate, 9 Feb. 2021. On the armed conflict in Somalia see chapter 7, section IV, in this volume.

[27] AU, 'Report of the Independent Assessment Team on the African Union's engagement in and with Somalia post 2021', 30 May 2021.

In October 2021, however, the Somali government rejected the proposal.[28] AMISOM's mandate was subsequently renewed until the end of March 2022 in order to allow the AU, the Somali government, troop contributors and donors to agree on the mission's future.[29]

The ECOWAS Mission in Gambia (ECOMIG), in place since January 2017 to address the constitutional crisis that followed the 2016 national elections, was the only multilateral peace operation led by ECOWAS in 2021. As of 31 December 2021 it deployed approximately 1000 personnel, primarily military. IGAD also led a single multilateral peace operation, the Ceasefire and Transitional Security Arrangements Monitoring and Verification Mechanism (CTSAMVM), which since 2018 has been monitoring compliance with the South Sudan peace agreement. Prior to that, the mission—under different names—successively monitored other ceasefire agreements. Finally, SADC established SAMIM in June 2021, with the objective of addressing extremist violence across northern Mozambique (see above).

Regional organizations and alliances from the northern hemisphere—the EU, NATO and the OSCE—conducted 27 multilateral peace operations during 2021, one more than in 2020. Nevertheless, by December 2021 two of these operations had closed, namely the NATO-led RSM and the OSCE Observer Mission at the Russian Checkpoints Gukovo and Donetsk. The closure of RSM explains the steep 51 per cent decrease in the combined number of personnel deployed by these organizations, from 17 614 on 31 December 2020 to 8 588 on 31 December 2021. Whereas the OSCE only deploys peace operations in member states, the EU and NATO only conduct peace operations in non-member states.

The EU conducted 15 peace operations in 2021, comprising 5 military and 10 civilian missions—one more than in 2020. The deployment of EUTM Mozambique brought the total number of EU military training missions to four, with other EUTMs active in CAR, Mali and Somalia. Though some EU member states proposed establishing a similar mission in Ukraine, this was not supported by the Council of the EU.[30] Meanwhile, EUTM RCA suspended its training activities due to the growing influence of the Russian private military company Wagner Group in CAR, following reports that it had effectively taken command of a Central African Armed Forces (Forces Armées Centrafricaines, FACA) battalion that had previously been trained by the EU mission. In December, the arrival of Wagner Group operatives in Mali also raised the possibility of the EU pausing or discontinuing EUTM

---

[28] AU, Communiqué of the 1042nd Meeting of the Peace and Security Council of the African Union at the Level of Heads of State and Government on the update on the situation in Somalia, 28 Oct. 2021.

[29] UN Security Council Resolution 2614, 21 Dec. 2021.

[30] Dutch House of Representatives, 'Verslag informele Raad Buitenlandse Zaken Defensie d.d. 1 en 2 september 2021' [Report of the informal meeting of defence ministers of the Foreign Affairs Council of the Council of the EU, 1–2 September 2021], 16 Sep. 2021.

Mali's activities, which were already challenged by the absence of civilian control over the Malian armed forces following the most recent military coup in 2021.[31] The number of personnel deployed in EU multilateral peace operations increased 9.9 per cent, from 2992 on 31 December 2020 to 3289 on 31 December 2021.

NATO conducted three multilateral peace operations in 2021, the same number as in 2020. This, however, includes the RSM, which was terminated in 2021. NATO had been active in Afghanistan since 2003, when it assumed command of ISAF. The number of personnel in NATO peace operations decreased 68 per cent in 2021, to 4270 on 31 December 2021. Prior to the decision to end the RSM, NATO had decided in February 2021 to proceed with a gradual expansion of the NATO Mission in Iraq (NMI), which advises the Iraq armed forces. One important reason for this expansion was that the US-led Operation Inherent Resolve, which NMI has been relying on for protection as well as logistical and medical support, is drawing down. However, by the end of 2021 the expansion of NMI, which consists of approximately 500 military and civilian personnel, had yet to begin.

The OSCE conducted nine multilateral peace operations in 2021, although only eight were active by the end of the year. As of 31 December 2021 the organization had 1029 personnel deployed in these eight operations, mostly in the OSCE Special Monitoring Mission (SMM) to Ukraine, which consisted of 827 international personnel, in addition to local personnel from the host country. This makes the SMM the largest civilian mission globally. Despite the deteriorated situation on the ground, the mission's mandate was almost not renewed in March 2021 after Armenia blocked consensus on the decision for several weeks—allegedly to express its discontent with the OSCE's handling of the Nagorno-Karabakh conflict.[32] Hours before the mandate was set to expire, however, consensus was reached on extending it for a further year. Most of the other OSCE operations have been active since the 1990s and maintained fewer than 30 international personnel in 2021.

Ad hoc coalitions

Ad hoc coalitions of states conducted six multilateral peace operations in 2021, one more than in 2020. These were the International Monitoring Team in Mindanao, the Philippines; the Office of the High Representative (OHR) in Bosnia and Herzegovina; the Joint Control Commission (JCC) Joint Peacekeeping Forces in the disputed Trans-Dniester region of Moldova; the Multinational Force and Observers (MFO) in the Sinai Peninsula; the Neutral Nations Supervisory Commission on the Korean peninsula; and the RTJMC

---

[31] 'EU suspends military training in Central Africa over Russian mercenaries', Reuters, 15 Dec. 2021.
[32] Liechenstein, S., 'OSCE Ukraine Mission extended in last-minute breakthrough', Security and Human Rights Monitor, 31 Mar. 2021.

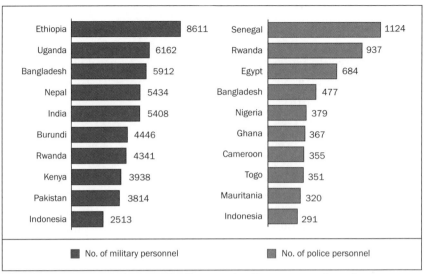

Figure 2.9. Main contributors of military and police personnel as of 31 Dec. 2021

in Azerbaijan. The number of personnel deployed in multilateral peace operations in this category increased by 3 per cent in 2021, from 2272 on 31 December 2020 to 2341 on 31 December 2021. This increase is mainly due to the establishment of the RTJMC in 2021, with the other missions' deployments remaining relatively constant.

In July 2021 Russia submitted a resolution, co-sponsored by China, to the UN Security Council to close the OHR on the basis that the Bosnian parties had achieved progress.[33] Russia and China were the only members of the Security Council to vote in favour of the resolution. This episode came just a few weeks after Russia had refused the appointment of German politician Christian Schmidt to the OHR post.[34] The OHR has caused disagreements between Russia and Western governments for years given the former's support to the Serbia and its desire to close the office. These tensions increasingly overlap with geopolitical rivalries affecting decisions on peace operations. Out of discontent with the OHR appointment, in November 2021 Russia also threatened to veto the renewal of EUFOR Althea's mandate, the EU force deployed to oversee the implementation of the Dayton Peace Agreement in Bosnia–Herzegovina.[35]

[33] United Nations, Security Council, 'Security Council turns down resolution that would end powers of Bosnia and Herzegovina High Representative', SC/14585, 22 July 2021.

[34] 'UN rejects Russian bid to scrap Bosnia peace envoy post', Deutsche Welle, 23 July 2021.

[35] Ruge, M., 'Peace of the action: The Kremlin's plans in Bosnia and Ukraine', European Council on Foreign Relations, 11 February 2022.

The main troop- and police-contributing countries

As of 31 December 2021 the 10 largest contributors of military personnel accounted for 52 per cent of all military personnel deployed globally in multilateral peace operations. While Ethiopia has remained the largest military personnel contributor (see figure 2.9) since 2014, its contribution has decreased for the fourth year in a row, down from 10 124 on 31 December 2020 to 8611 on 31 December 2021. This 15 per cent decline can be explained by the closing of UNAMID, to which the country was the third main contributor. Aside from this, Ethiopia has been providing personnel to the major multilateral peace operations in the Horn of Africa, namely AMISOM, UNMISS and the UN Interim Security Force for Abyei (UNISFA). In August 2021 the Sudanese government requested that the UN withdraw the Ethiopian peacekeepers from UNISFA due to deteriorating Sudan–Ethiopia relations arising from disputes over the the Fashaga border area, where Ethiopian farmers cultivate land claimed by Sudan. Nonetheless, as of the end of 2021 Ethiopia remained by far the largest contributor to the mission, with no indication that its contributions were being significantly affected by conflict in the country's Tigray region.

Four other sub-Saharan African countries feature among the 10 largest contributors of military personnel in 2021: Burundi, Kenya, Rwanda and Uganda. Burundi, Kenya and Uganda rank highly mainly due to their contributions to AMISOM. Rwanda, meanwhile, is the largest troop contributor to MINUSCA and UNMISS, two of the UN's largest peace operations.

South Asia is the other region well represented in multilateral peace operations, with Bangladesh, India, Nepal and Pakistan among the main contributors of military personnel due to their participation in UN peace operations. Bangladesh is the largest troop contributor to MINUSMA and Pakistan is the largest troop contributor to MONUSCO. Due to the closure of UNAMID, Pakistan's troop contribution fell by 752 over the course of 2021, to 3813 as of 31 December 2021.

The novelty in the 2021 list of top contributors is that the USA dropped out of the top 10, while Indonesia entered the list in 10th position. US contributions to multilateral peace operations were already declining due to the drawdown of forces in Afghanistan. With the closure of the RSM, US troop contributions decreased by some 68 per cent over the course of 2021, from 3640 at the end of 2020 to 1145 as of 31 December 2021. As such, it went from being the 10th largest contributor to peace operations in December 2020 to the eighteenth largest contributor in December 2021. The USA has remained the largest contributor of military personnel to the Kosovo Force (KFOR) and the MFO. Indonesia has been a key contributor of troops to UNIFIL and MONUSCO, and its contributions remained virtually the same over 2021.

The top 10 contributing countries of police personnel to multilateral peace operations together provided 64 per cent of all police personnel in 2021. Senegal has continued to be the main contributor of police personnel to peace operations, although its personnel contribution declined by 208 over the course of 2021, standing at 1124 as of 31 December 2021. Despite this 16 per cent decrease, Senegal provided 14 per cent of all police personnel deployed to multilateral peace operations. As in 2020, it is followed by Rwanda, Egypt and Bangladesh. Nepal, Burkina Faso and Jordan dropped out of the 2021 top 10 contributors of police personnel, to be replaced by Cameroon, Indonesia and Mauritania. It is noteworthy that in 2021 the top 10 contributors for both military and police personnel were exclusively African and Asian countries.

Other multilateral operations

In recent years there has been an ongoing trend of establishing multilateral operations that fall outside the scope of SIPRI's definition of a multilateral peace operation. The Joint Force of Group of Five for the Sahel (JF-G5S) and the Multinational Joint Task Force (MNJTF) in the Lake Chad Basin belong to this category. Both operations consist of uniformed personnel (mainly military) operating primarily within their own territory, meaning they cannot be considered a multilateral peace operation. A November 2021 Report of the UN Secretary-General to the Security Council proposed creating a UN support office to the JF-G5S,[36] while NATO has also been exploring options for enhanced support to the mission.[37] Nevertheless, these discussions had not developed further by the end of 2021. Meanwhile, in March 2020 a number of EU member states established the European multinational Special Operations Forces Task Force Takuba, comprising European special forces under French command in support of the Malian Armed Forces in coordination with the JF-G5S. Confined to the objective of countering terrorism in the Liptako-Gourma region and with no UN Security Council mandate, this operation does not meet the SIPRI definition of a multilateral peace operation.[38]

The EU has continued two military naval operations in the context of its Common Security and Defence Policy (CSDP). The EU Naval Force (NAVFOR) Atalanta, in the Gulf of Aden, functions in support of the Somali

[36] United Nations, Security Council, 'Joint Force of the Group of Five for the Sahel', Report of the Secretary-General, S/2021/940, 11 Nov. 2021.

[37] United Nations, Security Council, Letter dated 4 October 2021 from the Secretary-General addressed to the President of the Security Council, S/2021/850, 8 Oct. 2021.

[38] On 27 March 2020 the governments of Belgium, Czech Republic, Denmark, Estonia, France, Germany, Mali, Niger, the Netherlands, Norway, Portugal, Sweden and the UK issued a political statement expressing support for the creation of the task force. French Ministry of the Armed Forces, 'Task Force Takuba: political statement by the governments of Belgium, Czech Republic, Denmark, Estonia, France, Germany, Mali, Niger, the Netherlands, Norway, Portugal, Sweden and the United Kingdom', 27 Mar. 2020.

government to prevent, deter and repress acts of piracy and armed robbery off the coast of the country. Elsewhere, the main task of the EU NAVFOR Irini is implementing the UN arms embargo on Libya in the Mediterranean Sea.[39]

Since the ceasefire between Armenia and Azerbaijan established on 10 November 2020, Russia has maintained a 'peacekeeping contingent' of 1960 personnel along the disputed area and the Lachin corridor—a road connecting Nagorno-Karabakh with Armenia. Under the trilateral agreement, the deployment is for five years with an automatic five-year extension unless one of the parties objects.[40] Despite the trilateral agreement, it is not considered a peace operation as it consists of a unilateral force. It has established 27 checkpoints, and in August 2021 began conducting daily patrols in different regions, only deploying to the frontline upon receiving alerts from the local population or parties.[41]

The joint international 'peacekeeping mission' to the Solomon Islands was established at the end of November 2021 at the request of the national government following violent anti-government protests. It comprised forces from Australia, New Zealand, Fiji Islands and Papua New Guinea. At the end of December Australia and New Zealand announced a plan to drawdown their troops within the peacekeeping force, although some Australian military personnel was to remain to provide 'command, communications, logistics and air movement' support to the joint peacekeeping effort with police.[42] In contrast to the 2003 Regional Assistance Mission to Solomon Islands (RAMSI), the 2021 'peacekeeping mission' is not considered a multilateral peace operation for two main reasons. First, it is not based on the Biketawa Declaration, a framework agreed by the leaders of the Pacific Islands Forum for coordinating responses to regional crises; nor is it mandated by the UN Security Council. Second, rather than being established following a peace agreement or ceasefire, it was a response to civil unrest.

Multilateral peace operations after Afghanistan

During the 20 years between the start of the US-led intervention that toppled the Taliban government in 2001 and the withdrawal of US and allied troops in 2021, Afghanistan has hosted four multilateral peace operations: the NATO-led International Security Assistance Force (ISAF) and its successor Resolute Support Mission (RSM); the EU Police Mission in Afghanistan (EUPOL

---

[39] Council Decision (CFSP) 2020/472 of 31 Mar. 2020 on a European Union military operation in the Mediterranean (EUNAVFOR MED IRINI), *Official Journal of the European Union*, L101/4, 1 Apr. 2020.

[40] Russia Presidency, [Statement by the President of the Republic of Azerbaijan, the Prime Minister of the Republic of Armenia and the President of the Russian Federation], 10 Nov. 2021 (in Russian).

[41] Vartanyan, O., 'A risky role for Russian peacekeepers in Nagorno-Karabakh', Italian Institute for International Political Studies, 10 Nov. 2021.

[42] 'Australia's peacekeeping mission in Solomon Islands to be wound down', SBS News, 22 Dec. 2021.

Afghanistan); and the UN Assistance Mission in Afghanistan (UNAMA). One of them—ISAF—was the largest multilateral peace operation ever deployed, as well as being the first peace operation mounted by NATO outside Europe. The closure of the RSM and the subsequent Taliban victory heralds the end of an era.

The prominent role of these efforts in the broader multilateral peace operations landscape, the enormous investments made in Afghanistan, and the limited results these have arguably produced, explain why the Taliban victory features prominently in debates on the future of UN and non-UN multilateral peace operations. This raises the question of what its impact will be.

Consolidating a trend away from nation and state-building

The day after Kabul fell to the Taliban, President Biden argued that the US mission in Afghanistan was never supposed to have been nation building, counterinsurgency or bringing democracy, but instead should have been narrowly focused on counterterrorism.[43]

The façade of a state that his predecessors had created in Afghanistan collapsed the moment international support was withdrawn. Commentators were quick to reflect that nation building had been 'a fool's errand' and 'over-ambitious if not downright naïve'.[44] It spelled a 'tragedy' that had been '20 years in the making', relying on a theory that was 'only half right, at best; and in Afghanistan, it was dead wrong'.[45] Indeed, policymakers had presumed that nation and state-building in Afghanistan could be imposed on society from above by foreign forces. However, most frequently states have been built and power centralized under state institutions based on compromise and cooperation, drawing on the consent and support of populations.[46]

Before becoming president of Afghanistan, Ashraf Ghani, as a scholar, emphasized the importance of the state gaining legitimacy through performing economic, social and political functions. He argued that the international community should not micromanage each project based on 'microaccountabilities', but 'connect to an overall goal of global stability and prosperity'.[47] Once Ghani attained high office, however, the continued corruption of his government became one of the main reasons its popular

---

[43] White House, 'Remarks by President Biden on Afghanistan', 16, Aug. 2021.

[44] Price, G., 'Why Afghan nation-building was always destined to fail', Chatham House, 10 Sep. 2021.

[45] Acemoglu, D., 'Why nation-building failed in Afghanistan', Project Syndicate, 20 Aug. 2021.

[46] Acemoglu (note 45).

[47] Ghani, A. and Lockhart, C., *Fixing Failed States: A Framework for Rebuilding a Fractured World* (Oxford University Press: Oxford, 2008).

support collapsed, ultimately leading to Ghani being forced to hand over power to the Taliban.[48]

Despite these critical reflections, during the first two decades of the 2000s the common ground between the permanent members of an increasingly polarized Security Council was that democratization, human rights and protection of civilians could be balanced with the 'restoration' or 'extension of state authority'. This form of state-building made the liberal peace agenda more acceptable to China and Russia, to whom state sovereignty, or even regime security, is important. Consequently, large multidimensional UN peacekeeping operations in places such as CAR, the DRC and Mali were mandated to extend state authority.[49] However, during the second half of the 2010s, based on the already apparent failures in Afghanistan and Iraq, as well as the slow progress made in many such peacekeeping operations, the Security Council lost its appetite for new multidimensional peacekeeping operations.[50]

As a result, MINUSMA in 2013 and MINUSCA in 2014 remain the last two large-scale multidimensional peacekeeping operations established. By contrast, the UN's efforts in Libya, Syria and Yemen have been much more limited. With the Taliban's return to power in Afghanistan constituting the end of an era, there are increasing calls for further reflection on the approach applied in the country. Germany, for example, is to review its international military deployments.[51] French president Emmanuel Macron claims that even before the return of the Taliban in Afghanistan he had already drawn the lesson that the West cannot build a state in Mali and the Sahel.[52]

As such, the Taliban takeover in Afghanistan has reinvigorated an already existing discussion, consolidating the trend away from large-scale multidimensional nation and state-building interventions in countries experiencing armed conflict.

---

[48] Special Inspector General for Afghanistan Reconstruction (SIGAR), *What We Need to Learn: Lessons From Twenty Years of Afghanistan Reconstruction* (SIGAR: Arlington, VA, Aug. 2021); and Kopplin, Z., 'Afghanistan collapsed because corruption had hollowed out the state', *The Guardian*, 30 Aug. 2021.

[49] Osland, K. and Peter, M., 'UN peace operations in a multipolar order: Building peace through the rule of law and bottom-up approaches', *Contemporary Security Policy*, vol. 42, no. 2 (2021), pp. 197–210; and Lukunka, B., Rendtorff–Smith, S. and Donati, M., *Presence, Capacity and Legitimacy: Implementing Extension of State Authority Mandates in Peacekeeping* (UN Departments of Peacekeeping Operations and Field Support Policy, Evaluation and Training Division Policy and Best Practices Service, 2017).

[50] United Nations, Security Council, 8877th meeting, New York, 12 Oct. 2021, S/PV.8877.

[51] Glucroft, W., 'After Afghanistan: Germany rethinks its military missions', Deutsche Welle, 19 Aug. 2021.

[52] Clemenceau, F., 'Exclusif. Afghanistan, réfugiés, Irak, terrorisme … Emmanuel Macron s'explique dans le JDD' [Exclusive: Afghanistan, refugees, Iraq, terrorism … Emmanuel Macron explains himself in the JDD], *Le Journal du Dimanche*, 28 Aug. 2021.

Undetermined impact on the credibility of international support

It is not only in Afghanistan that donor frustration and fatigue has been on the rise. In Somalia, for example, the EU and USA have been frustrated with the limited progress made on key transitional milestones and in the electoral process. The EU has withheld budgetary support to the Somali government over the delayed elections and is reducing its support for AMISOM.[53] In Mali, meanwhile, it has led to tensions between the junta and France, culminating in the planned departure of France's Barkhane operation from Mali and its redeployment to neighbouring countries in the region.[54] The US decision to pull out from Afghanistan and stop investing in 'endless international state-building projects' that lack significant progress may also provide impetus to host country elites, potentially signalling that if international support is to be secured, progress must be made in terms of democratization, transitions and fighting corruption.[55]

On the other hand, the fall of Afghanistan may also lead to a diminishment in the credibility of international assistance and military efforts, due to a perception that they cannot be strategically sustained. In particular, the solidity of US security guarantees are being questioned by several Asian and East European allies.[56] Moreover, host governments may feel they need to decrease their dependence on international troops,[57] or alternatively seek diversification of international security assistance, such as in Mali with regard to the Wagner Group.[58]

There is, however, one major difference between, on the one hand, the USA and NATO in Afghanistan and, on the other, the French in the Sahel, and, in particular, the EU in the Western Balkans and African neighbouring states in the Sahel and Somalia—in the latter cases, the main intervening parties have a much clearer stake in regional stability and are therefore more committed to their investments. Nonetheless, there remains a risk that violent extremists may underestimate the extent of these commitments and so be encouraged to step up their activities.

Providing inspiration for armed groups, instilling fears in host governments

The Taliban's victory in Afghanistan has inspired and emboldened armed groups, particularly al-Qaida affiliates, in other places, demonstrating that

---

[53] Mahmood, O. and Ainte, A., 'Could Somalia be the next Afghanistan?', *Foreign Policy*, 22 Sep. 2021.

[54] 'France, European allies announce military withdrawal from Mali', Al Jazeera, 17 Feb. 2022.

[55] Mahmood and Ainte (note 53).

[56] Kelly, L. and Samuels, B., 'US credibility with military allies at risk over Afghanistan pullout', *The Hill*, 22 Aug. 2021; and O'Hanlon, M., 'After Afghanistan, where next? Biden must show resoluteness', Brookings Institution Order from Chaos blog, 20 Aug. 2021.

[57] Kahiye, M., 'Security experts warn al-Shabab may try to emulate Taliban in Somalia', VOA, 16 Aug. 2021.

[58] 'Reports of Russian mercenary deal in Mali trigger French alarm', France 24, 14 Sep 2021.

their struggles can bear fruit. This is evidenced by the celebratory pronouncements made by such jihadist movements.[59] In Somalia, for example, Islamist
group Harakat al-Shabab al-Mujahideen (Mujahedin Youth Movement, or
al-Shabab) responded with 'God is great', while in Mali, Iyad Ag Ghaly—
leader of Jama'at Nusrat al-Islam wal-Muslimin (the Group for the Support
of Islam and Muslims, or JNIM)—compared the withdrawal of foreign
forces in Afghanistan to the French drawdown in the Sahel by stating 'We are
winning',[60] and praised his 'brothers" strategy of 'two decades of patience'.[61]

At the same time, fears have increased among embattled governments and
elites of a similar situation occurring in their own countries. Somalia's armed
forces would arguably be even less prepared than their counterparts in
Afghanistan for a similar situation, as they have received much less support
and Somalia has been unable to purchase weapons due to an arms embargo.[62]
The Malian press has also drawn comparisons with Afghanistan.[63] Against
this backdrop, Macron's decision to drawdown from Mali is perceived by
some violent extremists as the first step towards making Mali France's
'Afghanistan'.[64] Even so, it remains unclear how the Taliban's victory will
ultimately affect violent extremist groups' funding and recruitment.[65] Thus,
the long-term operational impacts on multilateral peace operations remain
to be seen.

*Consolidating existing trends in regional focus, personnel contributions and
deploying organizations*

With the end of the Western presence in Afghanistan, the era in which Central
Asia represented a primary focus area for multilateral peace operations
has come to an end. From 2010 to 2012, Central Asia—due to the efforts in
Afghanistan—hosted the largest proportion of personnel deployed in peace
operations. By the time of ISAF's closure at the end of 2014 this title had
already been passed to Africa, in part due to increased personnel numbers
in the continent. In reflecting on the Taliban victory, Nigerian President
Muhammadu Buhari observed that the 'War on Terror' is not winding down,
but shifting to a new frontline in Africa. Moreover, he complained that
Western partners, 'bruised by their Middle East and Afghan experiences',

---

[59] Drevon, J. et al., 'How Islamist militants elsewhere view the Taliban's victory in Afghanistan',
International Crisis Group, 27 Oct. 2021; and 'America's flight from Afghanistan will embolden jihadists
around the world', *The Economist*, 28 Aug. 2021.

[60] Byaruhanga, C., 'Africa's jihadists: What Taliban takeover of Afghanistan means', BBC News,
21 Aug. 2021.

[61] Paquette, D. and Noack, R., 'France's drawdown in West Africa fuels local extremists' hope for a
Taliban-style victory', *Washington Post*, 27 Aug. 2021.

[62] Byaruhanga (note 60).

[63] Byaruhanga (note 60).

[64] Chutel, L., 'Will the War on Terror move to Africa?', *Foreign Policy*, 25 Aug. 2021.

[65] Drevon et al. (note 59); and 'America's flight from Afghanistan will embolden jihadists around the
world' (note 59).

do not prioritize Africa and that the fight against terrorism was never in fact global.[66]

Indeed, the closure of the RSM signifies an end to the period in which European and North American countries have played a prominent role in multilateral peace operations. For example, 2021 is the first time since 2006 that the USA is not among the top 10 contributors. Intervention fatigue has led NATO members to stay away from new 'forever wars' like those in Iraq and Afghanistan, and as a result they chose not to play the role of the 'world's policeman' in Syria.[67] Additionally, amid increasing geopolitical rivalries, the USA withdrew from Afghanistan in part to focus its attention on balancing China and Russia. It is therefore unlikely that the USA will continue to play a prominent role in multilateral peace operations.[68] The same likely holds true for European countries, with the transition from ISAF to the RSM in 2014 having already sparked a debate on what to do next with their armed forces. Given that UN peacekeeping operations in Africa were in need of high-tech niche forces, contributing to such operations was considered.[69] Indeed, to some extent there was a 'return' to UN peacekeeping, though it was limited and focused mainly on MINUSMA.[70] Now, with the continued rise of China and Russia's resurgence, 'grey zone operations' and 'hybrid warfare' have replaced 'counterinsurgency' and 'counterterrorism' as the dominant phrases in Europe's military vocabulary.[71] Moreover, even when European countries do consider activities that extend beyond territorial defence, this is now mainly confined to increasing their involvement in multilateral operations that fall within the context of counterterrorism, rather than multilateral peace operations—and even within this realm, France has already decided to decrease its presence in Mali.[72]

Consequently, NATO's role in multilateral peace operations is also likely to decrease, with the drawdown of ISAF having already brought to a close the 2010–13 period when NATO was the organization deploying the largest number of personnel in multilateral peace operations. Since then, NATO has shifted its focus from out-of-area operations to its core tasks of deterrence and territorial defence. The end of the RSM and the US presence in Afghanistan

---

[66] Buhari, M., 'Africa needs more than US military aid to defeat terror', *Financial Times*, 15 Aug. 2021.

[67] Aydıntaşbaş, A. et al., 'The fall of the Afghan government and what it means for Europe', European Council on Foreign Relations, 25 Aug. 2021.

[68] White House (note 43).

[69] Nadin, P., 'After Afghanistan: A return to UN peacekeeping?', UN University, 5 Mar. 2014.

[70] Koops, J. and Tercovich, G. (eds), 'A European return to UN peacekeeping?', *International Peacekeeping*, vol. 23, no. 5 (2016); Karlsrud, J. and Novosseloff, A., *Doing Less With More? The Difficult 'Return' of Western Troop Contributing Countries to United Nations Peacekeeping* (Global Governance Institute: Brussels, Feb. 2020); and Boutellis, A. and Beary, M., *Sharing the Burden: Lessons from the European Return to Multidimensional Peacekeeping* (International Peace Institute: New York, Jan. 2020).

[71] Heisler, J., 'Is UN peacekeeping losing its appeal?', VOA, 22 July 2021.

[72] 'France, European allies announce military withdrawal from Mali' (note 54).

has, however, forced European countries to face up to the fact that they are heavily dependent on US capabilities, having not been in a position to even evacuate their own personnel and local staff from Afghanistan without US support. In response, the EU is likely to seek strategic autonomy. At the same time, it cannot ignore trouble spots in its neighbourhoods. Therefore, while the EU is likely to resist stabilization interventions, it may opt for clearly defined military activities with achievable goals for which it has the necessary means to deliver.[73] With this in mind, calls have been made to strengthen EU CSDP capabilities for the deployment of civilian and military CSDP missions.[74]

Conclusions

The year 2021 saw two major developments that could impact the future of multilateral peace operations: first, peace operations in the field being affected by the exacerbation of geopolitical rivalries between the West on the one hand and China and, particularly, Russia on the other; and, second, the Taliban's victory in Afghanistan.

The US drawdown in Afghanistan was based on a strategic decision to rebalance its forces towards China. Meanwhile, Russia's refusal to renew the mandate and subsequent closure of the OSCE Observer Mission at the Gukovo and Donetsk checkpoints, as well as its attempts to reject the appointment of a new OHR in Bosnia-Herzegovina and later calls for the position to be discontinued altogether, indicate how increasing geopolitical tensions between Western countries and Russia are impacting multilateral peace operations. The closure of the OSCE operation in particularly widened the divide between Russia and the West over Ukraine, raising concerns over potential escalation of the conflict. Additionally, the presence of the Wagner Group in the conflict in CAR, in support of the FACA, has led organizations conducting peace operations in the country (namely, the UN and the EU) to urge the government to cut ties with the group—unsuccessfully thus far. EUTM RCA suspended its training activities, with questions raised about the future deployment of EUTMs in places where the Wagner Group is active. Mali could be the next country to have its EUTM suspended.

The Taliban victory in Afghanistan is likely to consolidate ongoing trends in peace operations—especially given that the international presence in the country had already been reduced since 2014, and that the interventions in Afghanistan and Iraq were already increasingly considered failures. Sub-Saharan Africa will likely remain the focus of interventions both within

---

[73] Aydıntaşbaş et al. (note 67).
[74] Pietz, T., 'After Afghanistan, EU crisis intervention should go big, not go home', World Politics Review, 1 Sep. 2021.

and outside the scope of multilateral peace operations, as not only are other regions too contentious due to great power interests, but African countries continue to have an interest in having peace operations on their soil. Additionally, given intensifying tensions between the West and Russia, NATO is likely to place greater focus on territorial defence of the alliance. This means that North American and European countries will be even less likely to make significant personnel contributions to peace operations. However, the EU may not be able to ignore instability at its borders, with increasing tensions in Ukraine potentially providing new impetus to civilian and military CSDP missions and operations. At the same time, the demand for multilateral action may increase due to violent extremist groups taking inspiration from the Taliban's victory, with host country governments, fearing abandonment, considering diversifying their sources of support.

The rapid takeover of Afghanistan by the Taliban following the RSM drawdown has raised concerns about a similar turn of events in Somalia—that is, a potential al-Shabab victory following the eventual termination of AMISOM. Discussions about exit strategies for other large operations, such as MONUSCO, also indicate that the trend towards smaller missions is likely to continue. Nevertheless, developments in Afghanistan have intensified concerns about transitional phases and exit strategies.[75]

Counterintuitively, the impact of the Taliban's victory may be that international responses will become even more militarized, even where there is no military solution to a conflict. The general perception is that nation and state-building has failed, and that large-scale multidimensional peace operations are not effective. If countries and organizations do feel a need to intervene they will likely prefer focused counterterrorism conflict-management activities (e.g. airstrikes/drones, and training and supporting local partners), as these are seen as more attainable. The intervention in Afghanistan failed largely because the state and security apparatus that was established was insufficiently inclusive, and failed to deliver economic opportunities to the country's populations. As a consequence, it did not gain enough support. A perverse effect of the Taliban's victory may therefore be a stronger emphasis on supporting security institutions. However, in the absence of broader state-building, including around governance and inclusivity, such measures are unlikely to lead to conflict resolution and may even aggravate conflict.

---

[75] UN Security Council Resolution 2594, 9 Sep. 2021.

III. Table of multilateral peace operations, 2021

CLAUDIA PFEIFER CRUZ

Table 2.6 provides data on the 63 multilateral peace operations conducted in 2021, including operations that were either launched or terminated during the year.

The table lists operations conducted under the authority of the United Nations, operations conducted by regional organizations and alliances, and operations conducted by ad hoc coalitions of states. UN operations are divided into two subgroups: (*a*) observer and multidimensional peacekeeping operations run by the Department of Peace Operations; and (*b*) special political and peacebuilding missions.

The table draws on the SIPRI Multilateral Peace Operations Database, which provides information on all UN and non-UN peace operations conducted since 2000, including location, dates of deployment and operation, mandate, participating countries, number of personnel, budget and fatalities.

Table 2.6. Multilateral peace operations, 2021

Unless otherwise stated, all figures are as of 31 Dec. 2021. Operations that closed in 2021 are shown in italic type—their personnel numbers represent the last month in which these operations were active and they are not included in the aggregate figures.

Operation	Start	Location	Mil.	Pol.	Civ.
UN peacekeeping operations			**66 220**	**7 302**	**3 498**
UNTSO	1948	Middle East	150	–	70
UNMOGIP	1951	India/Pakistan	42	–	20
UNFICYP	1964	Cyprus	803	61	40
UNDOF	1974	Syria (Golan)	1 122	–	48
UNIFIL	1978	Lebanon	9 629	–	242
MINURSO	1991	Western Sahara	204	2	73
MONUSCO	1999	DRC	13 078	1 643	592
UNMIK	1999	Kosovo	9	10	92
UNISFA	2011	Abyei	3 415	49	146
UNMISS	2011	South Sudan	13 896	1 416	828
MINUSMA	2013	Mali	12 419	1 744	754
MINUSCA	2014	CAR	11 453	2 377	593
UN special political missions			**1 168**	**98**	**1 057**
UNAMA	2002	Afghanistan	1	–	238
UNAMI	2003	Iraq	245	–	248
UNITAMS	2021	Sudan	–	21	77
UNSMIL	2011	Libya	236	–	153
UNSOM	2013	Somalia	629	12	149
UNVMC	2017	Colombia	53	52	111
UNMHA	2019	Yemen	4	–	33
BINUH	2019	Haiti	–	13	48
AU			**18 600**	**732**	**66**
AMISOM	2007	Somalia	18 586	732	66
MISAHEL	2013	Mali	–	–	..
MISAC	2014	CAR	–	–	..
AU Observer Mission in Burundi	*2015*	*Burundi*	*2*	*–*	*8*
AU Mission in Libya	2020	Libya	..	..	..
MOUACA	2020	CAR	14	–	–
ECOWAS			**875**	**125**	**1**
ECOMIG	2017	Gambia	875	125	1
EU[a]			**2 046**	**–**	**1 243**
EUFOR ALTHEA	2004	Bosnia and Herzegovina	526	–	14
EUBAM Rafah	2005	Palestinian territories	–	–	9
EUPOL COPPS	2005	Palestinian territories	–	–	48
EULEX Kosovo	2008	Kosovo	–	–	222
EUMM Georgia	2008	Georgia	–	–	216
EUTM Somalia	2010	Somalia	165	–	12

Operation	Start	Location	Mil.	Pol.	Civ.
EUCAP Sahel Niger	2012	Niger	–	–	124
EUTM Mali	2013	Mali	1 109	–	103
EUBAM Libya	2013[b]	Libya	–	–	53
EUAM Ukraine	2014	Ukraine	–	–	165
EUCAP Sahel Mali	2015	Mali	–	–	152
EUTM Mozambique	2021	Mozambique	70	–	3
EUTM RCA	2016	CAR	176	–	2
EUAM Iraq	2017	Iraq	–	–	66
EUAM RCA	2020	CAR	–	–	54
NATO			**4 270**	–	–
KFOR	1999	Kosovo	3 770	–	–
RSM	*2015*	*Afghanistan*	*9 592*	–	–
NMI	2018	Iraq	500	–	–
IGAD			–	–	86
CTSAMVM	2015	South Sudan	–	–	86
OAS			–	–	24
MAPP/OEA	2004	Colombia	–	–	24
OSCE			–	–	**1 029**
OSCE Mission to Skopje	1992	North Macedonia	–	–	31
OSCE Mission to Moldova	1993	Moldova	–	–	13
OSCE PRCIO	1995	Azerbaijan (Nagorno-Karabakh)	–	–	6
OSCE Mission to Bosnia and Herzegovina	1995	Bosnia and Herzegovina	–	–	35
OSCE Presence in Albania	1997	Albania	–	–	18
OMIK	1999	Kosovo	–	–	81
OSCE Mission to Serbia	2001	Serbia	–	–	18
OSCE SMM	2014	Ukraine	–	–	827
OSCE Observer Mission at the Russian Checkpoints Gukovo and Donetsk	*2014*	*Russia*	–	–	*21*
SADC			**1 077**		
SAMIM	2021	Mozambique	1 077	–	–
Ad hoc coalition of states			**2 318**	**3**	**20**
NNSC	1953	South Korea	10	–	–
MFO	1982	Egypt (Sinai)	1 154	–	..
JCC	1992	Moldova (Trans-Dniester)	1 015	–	–
OHR	1995	Bosnia and Herzegovina	–	–	16
IMT	2004	Philippines (Mindanao)	19	3	4
Russian–Turkish Joint Monitoring Centre (RTJMC)	2021	Azerbaijan (Nagorno-Karabakh)	120	–	–

– = not applicable; . . = information not available; AMISOM = African Union Mission in Somalia; AU = African Union; BINUH = United Nations Integrated Office in Haiti; CAR = Central African

Republic; Civ. = international civilian personnel; CTSAMVM = Ceasefire and Transitional Security Arrangements Monitoring and Verification Mechanism; DRC = Democratic Republic of the Congo; ECOMIG = ECOWAS Mission in the Gambia; ECOWAS = Economic Community of West African States; EU = European Union; EUAM Iraq = EU Advisory Mission in Support of Security Sector Reform in Iraq; EUAM RCA = EU Advisory Mission in the CAR; EUAM Ukraine = EU Advisory Mission for Civilian Security Sector Reform Ukraine; EUBAM Libya = EU Integrated Border Management Assistance Mission in Libya; EUBAM Rafah = EU Border Assistance Mission for the Rafah Crossing Point; EUCAP Sahel Mali = EU Common Security and Defence Policy (CSDP) Mission in Mali; EUCAP Sahel Niger = EU CSDP Mission in Niger; EUFOR ALTHEA= EU Military Operation in Bosnia and Herzegovina; EULEX Kosovo = EU Rule of Law Mission in Kosovo; EUMM Georgia = EU Monitoring Mission in Georgia; EUPOL COPPS = EU Police Mission for the Palestinian Territories; EUTM Mali = EU Training Mission Mali; EUTM Mozambique = EU Training Mission Mozambique; EUTM RCA = EU Training Mission in the CAR; EUTM Somalia = EU Training Mission Somalia; IGAD = Intergovernmental Authority on Development; IMT = International Monitoring Team; JCC = Joint Control Commission Peacekeeping Force; KFOR = Kosovo Force; MAPP/OEA = Organization of American States Mission to Support the Peace Process in Colombia; MFO = Multinational Force and Observers; Mil. = military personnel (troops and military observers); MINURSO = UN Mission for the Referendum in Western Sahara; MINUSCA = UN Multidimensional Integrated Stabilization Mission in the CAR; MINUSMA = UN Multidimensional Integrated Stabilization Mission in Mali; MISAC = AU Mission for the CAR and Central Africa; MISAHEL = AU Mission for Mali and the Sahel; MONUSCO = UN Organization Stabilization Mission in the DRC; MOUACA = AU Military Observers Mission in the CAR; NATO = North Atlantic Treaty Organization; NMI = NATO Mission Iraq; NNSC = Neutral Nations Supervisory Commission; OAS = Organization of American States; OHR = Office of the High Representative; OMIK = OSCE Mission in Kosovo; OSCE = Organization for Security and Co-operation in Europe; OSCE SMM = OSCE Special Monitoring Mission in Ukraine; Pol. = police; PRCIO = Personal Representative of the Chairman-in-Office on the Conflict Dealt with by the OSCE Minsk Conference; RSM = Resolute Support Mission; RTJMC = Russian–Turkish Joint Monitoring Centre; SADC = Southern Africa Development Community; SAMIM = SADC Mission in Mozambique; UN = United Nations; UNAMA = UN Assistance Mission in Afghanistan; UNAMI = UN Assistance Mission in Iraq; UNDOF = UN Disengagement Observer Force; UNFICYP = UN Peacekeeping Force in Cyprus; UNIFIL = UN Interim Force in Lebanon; UNISFA = UN Interim Security Force for Abyei; UNITAMS = UN Integrated Transition Assistance Mission in Sudan; UNMHA = UN Mission to Support the Hodeidah Agreement; UNMIK = UN Interim Administration Mission in Kosovo; UNMISS = UN Mission in South Sudan; UNMOGIP = UN Military Observer Group in India and Pakistan; UNSMIL = UN Support Mission in Libya; UNSOM = UN Assistance Mission in Somalia; UNTSO = UN Truce Supervision Organization; UNVMC = UN Verification Mission in Colombia.

[a] Figures on international civilian staff may include uniformed police.

[b] EUBAM Libya was established in 2013 but did not qualify as a multilateral peace operation prior to 1 Jan. 2019.

Source: SIPRI, Multilateral Peace Operations Database, accessed 1 Apr. 2022. Data on multilateral peace operations is obtained from the following categories of open source: (*a*) official information provided by the secretariat of the organization concerned; (*b*) information provided by the operations themselves, either in official publications or in written responses to annual SIPRI questionnaires; and (*c*) information from national governments contributing to the operation under consideration. In some instances, SIPRI researchers may gather additional information on an operation from the conducting organizations or governments of participating states by means of telephone interviews and email correspondence. These primary sources are supplemented by a wide selection of publicly available secondary sources, including specialist journals, research reports, news agencies, and international, regional and local newspapers.

3. Armed conflict and peace processes in the Americas

Overview

Several armed conflicts meeting the non-international armed conflict (NIAC) threshold, as defined under international law, were active in Colombia and Mexico in 2021. In Colombia at least three parallel and overlapping conflicts continued: one between the government and the Ejército de Liberación Nacional (ELN) and another between the government and dissident armed groups of the Fuerzas Armadas Revolucionarias de Colombia-Ejército del Pueblo (FARC-EP)'s former Eastern Bloc; and one between rival cartels the ELN and the Autodefensas Gaitanistas de Colombia (AGC). In Mexico three NIACs exist: one between the government and the Sinaloa Cartel and another between the government and the Cártel Jalisco Nueva Generación (CJNG); and one between the two rival cartels. In addition to these NIACs, there were various other situations of violence within the territories of Mexico and Colombia involving cartels, gangs and armed groups.

Six additional countries in the Americas—Brazil, El Salvador, Guatemala, Haiti, Honduras and Venezuela—experienced high levels of violence in 2021, which did not however meet the threshold required to be considered NIACs. Despite this, they are referred to in this yearbook as 'armed conflicts' on the basis of the number of battle-related fatalities involved.

Brazil saw a rise in estimated battle and other conflict-related deaths in 2021, and violence against civilians caused as many deaths as battles. The nature of armed conflict in Brazil is complex and difficult to define, as illustrated by the fact that approximately 57 per cent of the 2620 battle-related deaths were attributable to violence between state forces and unidentified armed groups or violence between police and political militias, while 42 per cent involved inter-political militia violence. In Venezuela government forces committed acts of violence as the state challenged its loss of control over swathes of territory to gangs and armed groups. Skirmishes between the Venezuelan military and dissident FARC group 10th Front occurred near the border between Venezuela and Colombia, while the 10th Front and Second Marquetalia clashed over control of drug trafficking routes and territory.

Guatemala and El Salvador saw growing violence, authoritarianism and corruption in 2021. In Guatemala the government shut down an anti-corruption body and arrested prosecutors who had begun investigating President Alejandro Giammettei for alleged bribery. In El Salvador President Nayib Bukele consolidated power by dismantling institutional checks and balances.

SIPRI Yearbook 2022: Armaments, Disarmament and International Security
www.sipriyearbook.org

Despite political violence and killings, 2021 closed on a more hopeful note in Honduras. Xiomara Castro, the region's only woman leader, was elected to president, replacing President Hernández. Even so, the country remains beset by high levels of poverty, violent crime and corruption.

In Haiti the assassination of the president deepened political instability. Mass displacement surged, driven by the compounding effects of extreme poverty, corruption, pervasive gang violence and natural disaster impacts.

There were three multilateral peace operations active in the Americas in 2021: two in Colombia and one in Haiti.

MARINA CAPARINI

I. Key general developments in the region

MARINA CAPARINI AND IAN DAVIS

Eight countries in the Americas experienced active armed conflicts in 2021 (the same as in 2020): one in North America—Mexico (high-intensity subnational armed conflict, including three armed conflicts meeting the thresholds of non-international armed conflicts (NIACs) as defined under international law), and one in the Caribbean—Haiti (low-intensity subnational armed conflict), as discussed in section II; three in Central America—El Salvador, Guatemala and Honduras (all low-intensity subnational armed conflicts), as discussed in section III; and three in South America—Brazil (high-intensity subnational armed conflict), Colombia (three NIACs as well as other high-intensity subnational armed conflicts) and Venezuela (low-intensity subnational armed conflict), as discussed in section IV. Across the region as a whole, conflict-related fatalities have remained relatively constant over the past four years, though with a slight overall decline compared to 2018 (see table 3.1).

The region was host to three multilateral peace operations in 2021, the same as in 2020: two in Colombia (see section IV) and one in Haiti (see section II). The number of personnel in multilateral peace operations in the Americas remained very low compared to the numbers of personnel deployed in other regions, decreasing from 303 on 31 December 2020 to 301 on 31 December 2021.[1]

This section briefly covers the three main cross-cutting armed conflict-related trends and political developments in the region in 2021: (*a*) the instability caused by armed gang violence and other armed violence; (*b*) rising levels of authoritarianism; and (*c*) the impact of Covid-19, food insecurity and natural disasters.

Gang violence and other political violence as armed conflict

The assessment that there are eight armed conflicts in the Americas is based on battle-related fatality figures provided by new Armed Conflict Location & Event Data Project (ACLED) data on the region (backdated to 2018). In previous years the Americas section in this yearbook adhered to the definition of armed conflict in international humanitarian law (IHL). However, to ensure consistency with the approach adopted in other regions covered by the yearbook (as defined in chapter 2), the definition of armed conflict in the Americas has been broadened beyond this strict legal definition

---

[1] SIPRI, Multilateral Peace Operations Database, accessed 1 Apr. 2022. See also chapter 2, sections II and III, in this volume.

Table 3.1. Estimated conflict-related fatalities in Americas, 2018–21

Country	2018	2019	2020	2021
Brazil	6 471	4 905	5 020	5 489
Colombia	861	726	847	1 238
El Salvador	935	848	297	363
Guatemala	787	1 098	558	653
Haiti	229	373	520	579
Honduras	672	928	656	594
Mexico	9 801	9 361	8 407	8 280
Venezuela	741	1 106	453	229
Total	**20 497**	**19 345**	**16 758**	**17 425**

Notes: Fatality figures are collated from four event types: battles; explosions/remote violence; protests, riots and strategic developments; and violence against civilians—see Armed Conflict Location & Event Data Project (ACLED), 'ACLED definitions of political violence and protest', 11 Apr. 2019. A country is treated as being in an armed conflict if there were 25 or more battle-related deaths in a given year—see chapter 2, section I, in this volume. The first available year for data on conflicts in the region in the ACLED database is 2018.

Source: ACLED, 'Dashboard', accessed 15 Feb. 2022.

and now includes other situations of violence, principally battle-related violence between state security forces and criminal gangs, and inter-gang violence.[2] While this violence is usually characterized as criminal rather than as conflict, and may not necessarily meet the stringent thresholds for armed conflict under IHL, it is often as lethal as traditional armed conflict. Moreover, it involves other major impacts normally associated with armed conflict, such as significant levels of territorial control by non-state actors, forced displacement and migration flows, and movement restrictions. Given these impacts and the lethality of gang–state violence—a prominent feature of all the countries listed in table 3.1—there is growing debate about whether IHL definitions of armed conflict require adjustment.[3]

Organized crime and gang violence vary widely across the region, and discussion of their political, sociological and legal dimensions is beyond the scope of this chapter. Nonetheless, insecurity and confrontations between state forces and armed gangs, or between the gangs themselves, are briefly highlighted in relation to the ACLED conflict data. The boundaries between localized acts of violence, violence linked to cartels and other organized crime actors, and an internal armed conflict in the region are likely to remain blurred (see especially the discussion on Brazil in section IV). According to InSight Crime, a non-governmental investigative organization, most of the region's countries experienced a marked increase in homicides over the

---

[2] For conflict definitions and typologies see chapter 2, section I, in this volume.

[3] See e.g. Applebaum, A. and Mawby, B., 'Gang violence as armed conflict: A new perspective on El Salvador', Georgetown Institute for Women, Peace and Security, Nov. 2018; Ryan, K. O., '"Urban killing fields": International humanitarian law, gang violence, and armed conflict on the streets of El Salvador', *International and Comparative Law Review*, vol. 20, no. 1 (2020), pp. 97–126; and Chaparro, L. and Deslandes, A., 'Where's the aid for Mexicans displaced by gang violence?', New Humanitarian, 1 July 2021.

course of 2021 as pandemic lockdown measures were lifted, law enforcement was strained due to illness, and a sharp deterioration in economic conditions made youth more susceptible to recruitment by criminal gangs.[4]

The region also stands out in terms of other forms of political violence. In 2021 Mexico remained one of the most dangerous places for journalists in the western hemisphere, while elsewhere across the Americas a number of journalists survived shooting attacks.[5] Over the past decade, nearly 80 per cent (140) of murders of journalists in the Americas have taken place in Brazil, Colombia, Mexico and Honduras.[6] Moreover, Latin America has also been the site of the greatest number of lethal attacks on land and environmental defenders, including a disproportionate number of attacks against indigenous people. In 2020 (the latest regional figures available) three out of four killings of environmental defenders took place in Latin America, with the region containing 7 of the 10 countries with the highest number of such deaths.[7] Colombia had the highest number of attacks, with 65 defenders killed, followed by Mexico (30) and Brazil (20), while Nicaragua saw the highest per capita number of killings with 12 deaths.[8]

Rising authoritarianism in Latin America and political instability in the United States

Alongside these armed conflicts, authoritarian rule persisted in Cuba, Haiti, Nicaragua and Venezuela, which were categorized as 'not free' in the 2021 Freedom House ratings of people's access to political rights and civil liberties, while eight other countries in the region were categorized as 'partly free': Bolivia, Colombia, Dominican Republic, El Salvador, Guatemala, Honduras, Mexico and Paraguay.[9] In El Salvador and Guatemala authorities cracked down on the political opposition and weakened or dismantled institutional checks and balances, including the independent judiciary, media and civil society. In Argentina, Bolivia, Brazil, Colombia, El Salvador, Guatemala, Haiti and Peru popular dissatisfaction was expressed in public demonstrations over issues relating to autocratic rule, poor governance, corruption, Covid-19 responses, economic hardship, violence against women, police brutality and

---

[4] InSight Crime, 'InSight Crime's 2021 homicide round-up', 1 Feb. 2022.

[5] Southwick, N. and de la Serna, C. M., 'A press freedom crisis unfolds in Latin America', Committee to Protect Journalists, 8 Dec. 2021.

[6] Reporters Without Borders, '2011–2020: A study of journalist murders in Latin America confirms the importance of strengthening protection policies', 13 May 2021.

[7] Global Witness, *Last Line of Defence: The Industries Causing the Climate Crisis and Attacks Against Land and Environmental Defenders* (Global Witness, Sep. 2021), p. 12.

[8] Global Witness (note 7), p. 11.

[9] Freedom House, 'Countries and territories: Global freedom scores', accessed 21 Mar. 2022.

other human rights abuses, and environmental and indigenous land concerns.[10]

The year opened with an attack on the United States Capitol by supporters
of President Donald Trump seeking to overturn the election of Joe Biden.
This directly resulted in five deaths, while four police personnel guarding the
Capitol on the day of the riot subsequently committed suicide (of which one
has been officially acknowledged as a direct line-of-duty death).[11] Impeachment charges against Trump ended in his being acquitted of 'incitement of
insurrection' by the Republican-controlled Senate in February 2021.[12]

A comprehensive review of the domestic terrorism threat ordered by
President Biden identified two main threat sources: violent racially or
ethnically motivated white supremacists; and anti-government or anti-
authority violent extremists, including those belonging to militias.[13] In June
2021, Biden launched the country's first-ever strategy to counter domestic
terrorism, declaring it the most urgent terrorism threat to the country.[14] The
strategy aims to enhance information-sharing across government; prevent
recruitment and mobilization; disrupt and deter domestic terrorism; and
address long-term contributing factors.[15]

The impact of Covid-19, food insecurity and natural disasters

The Covid-19 pandemic contributed to deepening poverty and food insecurity, in some cases exacerbating instability, displacement and violence across
the Americas. Although some countries responded effectively, the region was
disproportionately affected due to leaders—Brazilian President Jair Bolsonaro and outgoing US President Trump in particular—denying the seriousness
of Covid-19 and implementing weak pandemic response, which in turn inter-
acted with deep societal inequalities and governance challenges.[16] Despite
constituting less than 8.4 per cent of the world's population, Latin America
accounted for over 30 per cent of all global deaths due to Covid by October

---

[10] Carnegie Endowment for International Peace, 'Global Protest Tracker', accessed 22 Mar. 2022.

[11] Inskeep, S., 'Timeline: What Trump told supporters for months before they attacked', NPR, 8 Feb.
2021; Healy, J., 'These are the 5 people who died in the Capitol riot', *New York Times*, 11 Jan. 2021
(updated 22 Feb. 2021); and Reilly, R. J. and Caldwell, L. A., 'DC police officer's suicide after Jan. 6 riot
declared line-of-duty death', NBC News, 10 Mar. 2022.

[12] Fandos, N. and Shear, M. D., 'Trump impeached for abuse of power and obstruction of Congress',
New York Times, 18 Dec. 2019 (updated 10 Feb. 2021); and Levine, S. and Gambino, L., 'Donald Trump
acquitted in second impeachment trial', *The Guardian*, 14 Feb. 2021.

[13] White House, 'Fact sheet: National strategy for countering domestic terrorism', 15 June 2021.

[14] National Security Council, *National Strategy for Countering Domestic Terrorism* (White House:
Washington, DC, June 2021). See also Byman, D. L., 'Assessing the right-wing terror threat in the
United States a year after the January 6 insurrection', Brookings Institute, 5 Jan. 2022.

[15] White House (note 13).

[16] Lewis, T., 'How the US pandemic response went wrong—and what went right—during a year of
COVID', *Scientific American*, 11 Mar. 2021.

2021.[17] Similarly, by the end of 2021 the Covid-19 death rate in the USA reached almost 825 000 and exceeded that of all other large, high-income countries.[18]

Despite the estimated 6.2 per cent GDP growth in 2021 evidencing economic recovery in the Latin America and Caribbean subregion, the pandemic resulted in a prolonged health and social crisis linked to underlying problems of inequality, poverty and vulnerability, particularly affecting the lower income strata.[19] This situation was exacerbated by unequal access to or acceptance of vaccines in the subregion.[20]

During 2020 food insecurity in Latin America and the Caribbean had increased to its highest point since 2000, with a 30 per cent jump from 2019 to 2020 alone (Haiti and Venezuela experienced the most pronounced rise).[21] With 40.9 per cent of the population experiencing moderate or severe food insecurity in 2020, up from 31.9 per cent in 2019, this represented the most pronounced increase in food insecurity of all regions in the world.[22] Further, the continued impact of hurricanes and a higher number of natural disasters in 2020 caused El Salvador, Guatemala and Honduras to experience a 60 per cent growth in populations requiring humanitarian assistance in 2021.[23] According to the United Nations Office for the Coordination of Humanitarian Affairs (UN OCHA), internal displacement flows in 2021 reached unprecedented levels, with Brazil, Cuba, Guatemala and Honduras listed among the top 25 countries in the world in terms of new displacements due to disaster or conflict.[24] By November 2021 more than 1.6 million migrants had arrived at the US–Mexico border during the 2021 fiscal year, more than four times the figure for the previous fiscal year, and the highest number on record.[25]

---

[17] United Nations, 'COVID-19 cases and deaths in the Americas triple in 2021', UN News, 15 Dec. 2021.

[18] Mueller, B. and Lutz, E., 'US has far higher Covid death rate than other wealthy countries', *New York Times*, 1 Feb. 2022; and Centers for Disease Control and Prevention, 'Trends in number of COVID-19 cases and deaths in the US reported to CDC, by state/territory', accessed 30 Mar. 2022.

[19] UN Office for the Coordination of Humanitarian Affairs (UN OCHA), 'Global humanitarian overview 2022: Latin America and the Caribbean'.

[20] Pan American Health Organization (PAHO), 'The region of the Americas surpasses 100 million COIVD-19 cases', 22 Dec. 2021.

[21] Food and Agriculture Organization of the UN (FAO), International Fund for Agricultural Development (IFAD), Pan American Health Organization (PAHO), UN Children's Fund (UNICEF) and World Food Programme (WFP), *Latin America and the Caribbean: Regional Overview of Food Security and Nutrition 2021: Statistics and Trends* (FAO: Santiago, 2021), pp. 5, 8.

[22] FAO, IFAD, PAHO, UNICEF and WFP (note 21), p. 8.

[23] UN OCHA (note 19).

[24] UN OCHA (note 19).

[25] Gramlich, J. and Scheller, A., 'What's happening at the US–Mexico border in 7 charts', Pew Research Center, 9 Nov. 2021.

II. Armed conflict in North America and the Caribbean

MARINA CAPARINI

Two countries in North America and the Caribbean were the locations of armed conflict in 2021: Mexico and Haiti. Three non-international armed conflicts exist in Mexico: one between the government and the Sinaloa Cartel and another between the government and the Jalisco Cartel New Generation (Cártel Jalisco Nueva Generación, CJNG); and one between the two rival cartels. In addition, there are estimated to be hundreds of smaller gangs and factions involved in crime and violence, as well as continued state forces involvement in human rights violations, disappearances and violence. In Haiti the armed conflict is related to gang violence.

Violence and organized crime in Mexico

Mexico has numerous criminal gangs and groups. In 2019 the Mexican government identified 37 cartels or criminal groups operating in the country,[1] though this is viewed as a significant underestimate, with some sources conservatively estimating the existence of 463 groups between 2009 and 2019.[2] Many of these are factions of larger groups and, despite being small local actors, account for much of the violence affecting Mexico.[3] Estimated conflict-related fatalities in the four-year period (2018–21) averaged just under 9000 per year (see table 3.2).

The homicide rate—another indicator of armed violence—continued to reach a high level in 2021: over 30 000 murders were registered, equating to a rate of 26 per 100 000 people. Nevertheless, this represented a 3 per cent decline from 2020, after hitting a record high in 2018.[4] Despite the overall decline, femicides (the murder of women arising from gender-based violence) increased 2.7 per cent in 2021 to 1004.[5]

The main cartels

The Sinaloa Cartel, the most powerful drug trafficking organization in the western hemisphere, is headed by Ismael Zambada García (El Mayo) and the three sons of former leader Joaquin 'El Chapo' Guzmán, who in 2019 was imprisoned for life in the United States. In September 2021 the USA tripled

---

[1] Monroy, J., 'Reconoce gobierno la operación de 37 cárteles del narco, en el país' [Government acknowledges 37 drug cartels are operating in the country], *El Economista*, 19 May 2019.

[2] Esberg, J., 'More than cartels: Counting Mexico's crime rings', International Crisis Group, 8 May 2020.

[3] Esberg (note 2).

[4] InSight Crime, 'InSight Crime's 2021 homicide round-up', 1 Feb. 2022.

[5] 'Murders in Mexico fall 3.6% in 2021, but femicides rise', Reuters, 21 Jan. 2022.

Table 3.2. Estimated conflict-related fatalities in Mexico, 2018–21

Event type	2018	2019	2020	2021
Battles	2 129	1 892	1 525	1 492
Explosions/remote violence	2	1	1	2
Protests, riots and strategic developments	112	83	63	50
Violence against civilians	7 558	7 385	6 818	6 736
Total	**9 801**	**9 361**	**8 407**	**8 280**

Note: The first available year for data on Mexico in the Armed Conflict Location & Event Data Project (ACLED) database is 2018. For definitions of event types, see ACLED, 'ACLED definitions of political violence and protest', 11 Apr. 2019.
Source: ACLED, 'Dashboard', accessed 15 Feb. 2022.

the reward offered for information leading to the arrest or conviction of the 75-year old Zambada to \$15 million.[6] An internal power struggle between cells affiliated with Zambada and those affiliated with Guzmán's sons resulted in violent purges and struggles over turf.[7]

The rival CJNG, led by Nemesio Oseguera Cervantes, 'El Mencho', has aggressively expanded across the country. By 2021 Mexico's Financial Intelligence Unit identified CJNG as the cartel with the widest presence in the country, with operations in 27 out of 32 states.[8] CJNG also has a growing presence outside of Mexico, having become a major source of drugs smuggled into the USA and expanded rapidly into Central and South America.[9] Oseguera has evaded capture despite a \$10 million bounty offered by the US government in 2018. However, in November the Mexican military arrested Oseguera's wife, Rosalinda González Valencia, who is suspected of coordinating the CJNG's finances.[10]

Continuing high levels of violence and homicides occurred throughout 2021 due to the struggle between CJNG and the Sinaloa Cartel for control of certain territories, with CJNG seeking to expand its reach throughout the country and become the dominant cartel.[11] CJNG used commercially bought drones armed with explosives and shrapnel to attack targets such as state officials and rival gangs, a practice that is being copied by other criminal gangs. In response, the defence ministry announced plans to deploy an anti-drone system capable of monitoring and disabling them.[12]

---

[6] US Department of State, 'Department of State offers reward for information to bring Mexican drug trafficking cartel leader to justice', press statement, 22 Sep. 2021.

[7] 'Sinaloa Cartel's internal dispute extends into Sonora, Baja California', *Mexico News Daily*, 1 Dec. 2021.

[8] Gándara, S. R. and InSight Crime, 'Mexico ablaze as Jalisco Cartel seeks criminal hegemony', InSight Crime, 5 Jan. 2022.

[9] US Drug Enforcement Administration, *2020 National Drug Threat Assessment* (US Department of Justice: Washington, DC, Mar. 2021); and Chaparro, L., 'Mexico's powerful Jalisco cartel is flexing its muscles at opposite ends of Latin America', Insider, 19 Oct. 2021.

[10] Spocchia, G., 'Wife of Mexican drug lord El Mencho arrested', *The Independent*, 16 Nov. 2021.

[11] Gándara and InSight Crime (note 8).

[12] Saito, H., 'Weaponized drones in Mexico: Game-changer or gimmick?', InSight Crime, 6 May 2021.

Mexico continued to suffer widespread disappearances, with a total of 18 533 people reported missing over the course of 2021, of whom 9573 were not subsequently located.[13] This represents a decline from the previous year's figure of 21 226, and from the 2019 peak of 23 110.[14] According to the Office of the United Nations High Commissioner for Human Rights (OHCHR), the number of disappeared children, adolescents and women underwent a 'notable increase' following the onset of the Covid-19 pandemic.[15] In November the UN Committee on Enforced Disappearances drew attention to systemic impunity and impediments to access to justice in Mexico, calling on the state to provide the resources and political will to search for disappeared persons and investigate the circumstances of their disappearance.[16]

The run-up to the June mid-term elections saw clashes between rival cartels, criminal groups and security forces, as well as the assassination of several political candidates, signalling the persistent attention paid by criminal groups to gaining political influence. During the period September 2020–April 2021, 69 politicians, including 22 candidates, were assassinated.[17] In addition to the cartels/criminal groups' efforts to influence the political sphere, the co-option and corruption of state institutions, particularly at a local level, remained rampant.[18]

Reporting on crime, corruption and violence has proven deadly in Mexico. In 2021, for the third consecutive year, Reporters Without Borders declared Mexico to be the world's most dangerous country for journalists, with at least 47 killed over the past five years and at least seven journalists killed in 2021.[19]

The role of the military in law enforcement

In 2020 President Andrés Manuel López Obrador issued a Presidential Agreement, assigning an array of public security functions to the armed forces until 2024.[20] The role of the military in law enforcement and in other

---

[13] Government of Mexico, National Search Commission, 'Estadistica del RNPDNO por filtros' [RNPDNO statistics by filters], accessed 30 Mar. 2022. Total figure includes all non-located and located people who disappeared.

[14] Government of Mexico (note 13).

[15] Office of the United Nations High Commissioner for Human Rights (OHCHR), 'Press conference following the visit of the committee on Enforced Disappearances to Mexico', 26 Nov. 2021.

[16] OHCHR (note 15).

[17] Ernst, F., 'Violence erupts as Mexico's deadly gangs aim to cement power in largest ever elections', *The Guardian*, 29 Apr. 2021.

[18] Ernst (note 17).

[19] Reporters Without Borders, 'Mexique: RSF se mobilise pour la protection des journalistes et contre l'impunité à l'occasion d'une mission pour la liberté de la presse' [Mexico: RSF mobilizes for the protection of journalists and against impunity during a mission for press freedom], 24 Dec. 2021.

[20] Mexican Secretariat for Home Affairs, 'ACUERDO por el que se dispone de la Fuerza Armada permanente para llevar a cabo tareas de seguridad pública de manera extraordinaria, regulada, fiscalizada, subordinada y complementaria' [AGREEMENT whereby the permanent Armed Forces are available to carry out public security tasks in an extraordinary, regulated, supervised, subordinate and complementary manner], *Diario Oficial de la Federación*, 11 May 2020.

government services continued to expand under López Obrador in 2021. By February 2021 three-quarters of the over 100 000 members of the National Guard, which replaced the Federal Police when it was dissolved in 2018, were active members of the armed forces, commanded by a retired general.[21] Moreover, over 90 per cent of the organization's personnel remained uncertified at the expiration of the two-year deadline set out in the May 2019 law establishing the National Guard.[22]

In June 2021 López Obrador announced that jurisdiction of the National Guard (which is defined in the Constitution as a civilian police institution) would be moved from the civilian Ministry of Security and Citizen Protection to the Ministry of National Defence (Secretaría de la Defensa Nacional, SEDENA), the government department responsible for managing Mexico's army and the air force.[23] The announcement was viewed as formalizing SEDENA's de facto control over the National Guard's land, facilities, recruitment and state-level presence. In addition, the only remaining civilian element within the National Guard—consisting in late 2020 of around 26 000 former personnel from the Federal Police, decreasing to just over 23 000 by early 2022—were, according to a leaked official memo, to be replaced in a process beginning in September 2021 by military police, who would take over their duties supervising highways, ports and airports.[24]

Military involvement in law enforcement has been strongly criticized due to the heavy-handed tactics that have been deployed in the fight against the drug trade and organized crime. These have resulted in widespread human rights violations, including continuing allegations of torture being used to obtain confessions and extract information. The involvement of the security forces in enforced disappearances since 2006 is also considered widespread.[25]

Outlook

Despite reductions in the rates of homicides and disappearances in 2021, the outlook for public security in Mexico remains poor. Cartels continue to operate throughout the country and clash with their rivals to control territory, as seen most notably in the intense rivalry between the Sinaloa Cartel and the CJNG. The cartels and other criminal groups commit violent crime and extortion with impunity, and—as seen in the mid-term elections—are increasingly seeking to protect and expand their interests by

[21] 'Mexico's president is giving the armed forces new powers', *The Economist*, 29 Apr. 2021.

[22] Ford, A., 'Why Mexico's National Guard remains vastly unqualified', InSight Crime, 9 June 2021.

[23] 'AMLO va por reformas para que Guardia Nacional pase al Ejército y eliminar pluris' [AMLO pursues reforms to transfer the National Guard to the Army and eliminate duplication], Animal Politico, 15 June 2021.

[24] Angel, A., 'Aun sin reforma, Sedena ya controla bases, dirección y reclutamiento de la Guardia Nacional' [Even without reform, Sedena already controls the bases, direction and recruitment of the National Guard], Animal Politico, 1 Sep. 2021.

[25] Human Rights Watch, 'Mexico: Events of 2020', World Report 2021.

interfering in who gains political office. Contrary to his election platform of demilitarizing public security, López Obrador has progressively inserted the army into key policing and public security roles, as well as other sectors of public administration. However, if systemic corruption and state capture by the cartels remains unaddressed, especially at the local and regional level, then substituting the military for other state officials is unlikely to improve the safety or security of Mexicans.

Haiti

Haiti experienced a precipitous deterioration throughout 2021, with the state rocked by the assassination of the president, a continuing constitutional crisis, a major natural disaster, rampant corruption, mismanagement of the economy, fuel shortages, chronic gang violence, and an epidemic of kidnapping for ransom that targeted rich and poor alike. Armed gangs have controlled parts of Haiti—especially the poorest districts of the capital Port-au-Prince—for many years, capitalizing on the chronic insecurity to build local support.[26] The main form of armed violence in Haiti involves conflicts between the gangs and state security forces. The Armed Conflict Location & Event Data Project (ACLED) recorded 579 conflict-related deaths in Haiti in 2021 (the third consecutive year of increase), up from 517 in 2020, of which 315 were battle-related deaths.[27]

In February 2021 mass protests took place demanding the resignation of President Jovenel Moïse, amid accusations he was holding onto power illegitimately after having dissolved parliament and continued to rule by presidential decree. While the judiciary sided with the opposition, Moïse enjoyed the support of both the USA and—allegedly—the gangs that have come to dominate the country.[28] In July the situation deteriorated further when Moïse was assassinated at his home in mysterious circumstances by a group of mercenaries.[29]

A constitutional crisis ensued. Although Ariel Henry was appointed acting prime minister on 21 July, he faced resistance from criminal groups and political leaders.[30] Other figures called for the USA or the UN to help stabilize

---

[26] Insecurity Insight, 'Haiti: Situation report—Gangs and the Haitian State', 12 Nov. 2021.

[27] Armed Conflict Location & Event Data Project (ACLED), 'Dashboard', accessed 25 Mar. 2022.

[28] '"Down with the dictatorship": Protests continue in Haiti', Al Jazeera, 15 Feb. 2021; and Isaac, H., Paultre, A. and Abi-Habib, M., 'Haiti braces for unrest as a defiant president refuses to step down', *New York Times*, 7 Feb. 2021 (updated 7 July 2021).

[29] Tharoor, I., 'The spiraling chaos of Haiti's crisis', *Washington Post*, 12 July 2021; and 'Haiti president's assassination: What we know so far', BBC News, 20 Jan. 2022.

[30] 'Haiti appoints Ariel Henry as new prime minister after president's assassination', France 24, 21 July 2021.

the country, although many civil society actors opposed foreign intervention given Haiti's long history of destructive foreign interference.[31]

In August a 7.2 magnitude earthquake devastated the south of the country, with humanitarian relief efforts impeded by gang violence.[32] Gang activity, including kidnappings and inter-gang rivalry, remained rampant, enabled by police corruption, a weak judicial system and the highest rate of poverty in the Americas.[33]

In early November the 'G9 an famni' criminal alliance blocked access to the Varreux oil terminal outside Port-au-Prince in order to destabilize the government, demanding Ariel Henry's resignation and the withdrawal of state security forces from the area. While a negotiated agreement on unknown terms resulted in the lifting of the blockade several weeks later, the crisis demonstrated the extent to which Haiti's gangs wield power.[34] Unrest and upheaval continued to spur migration, mostly towards the USA. However, since taking office the Biden administration has used Trump-era public health measures to authorize the expulsion of thousands of asylum-seekers, either directly to Haiti or back across the border to Mexico, which has largely failed to register asylum-seekers.[35]

The UN Integrated Office in Haiti continued to advise the Haitian government on promoting political stability and good governance, advancing a peaceful and stable environment, and protecting and promoting human rights. It also provided guidance on dialogue and reforms, elections, police professionalism, community violence reduction and gang violence, justice reform, and human rights protection and accountability.[36] In view of the series of shocks experienced by Haiti in 2021, in October the UN Security Council requested a review of the mission's mandate, with the aim of enabling it to more effectively promote the rule of law, human rights, and engagement between the authorities and civil society.[37]

[31] '"We have the moral high ground": A civil society-led vision for Haiti's future', World Politics Review, 27 Aug. 2021.

[32] Perlmutter, L., 'A gang war is messing up earthquake relief in Haiti', Vice, 16 Aug. 2021.

[33] Porter, C. and Kitroeff, N., '"It's terror": In Haiti, gangs gain power as security vacuum grows', New York Times, 21 Oct. 2021 (updated 27 Oct. 2021).

[34] Wilson, M., 'A Faustian bargain: The cost of restoring Haiti's fuel supply', InSight Crime, 18 Nov. 2021.

[35] Borger, J., 'Senior state department official calls Biden's deportation of Haitians illegal', The Guardian, 4 Oct. 2021.

[36] UN Security Council Resolution 2476, 25 June 2019.

[37] UN Security Council Resolution 2600, 15 Oct. 2021.

III. Armed conflict in Central America

MARINA CAPARINI AND IAN DAVIS

This section briefly reviews the low-intensity (less than 1000 conflict-related fatalities) subnational armed conflicts in El Salvador, Guatemala and Honduras in 2021, all of which are related to gang violence (see section I). Two of the most infamous street gangs in the Americas—rivals Mara Salvatrucha (MS13) and the 18th Street Gang (Barrio 18)—have an especially strong influence in all three countries.

There were also political tensions in several other states in the region. Since the 2018 unrest in Nicaragua over changes to the state social security system, for example, at least 355 individuals have died and more than 108 000 have fled the country.[1] In 2021 the government of President Daniel Ortega cracked down on political dissent, creating an extremely polarized environment in the run-up to November's presidential and legislative elections.[2] The Sandinista Liberation Front formally won 75 per cent of the vote, returning Daniel Ortega to a fourth consecutive term in office.[3] On 13 November the Organization of American States issued a statement claiming the elections were 'not free, fair or transparent and lack democratic legitimacy', prompting Nicaragua's decision to begin the process of with-drawing from the regional bloc.[4]

El Salvador

In El Salvador gangs are increasingly pitted against state forces and each other in a political struggle to gain control over territory and populations. The two rival gangs behind much of the violence are MS13 and Barrio 18, with the latter split into two factions (Revolucionarios and Sureños).[5] The Armed Conflict Location & Event Data Project (ACLED) recorded 363 conflict-related deaths in El Salvador in 2021 (up from 297 in 2020 but

---

[1] Organization of American States (OAS), 'IACHR updates death toll records of human rights crisis', 15 Nov. 2021; and United Nations Refugee Agency (UNHCR), 'UNHCR calls for more support for Nicaraguans forced to flee', 16 Apr. 2021.

[2] AP News, 'Nicaragua arrests 7th presidential contender ahead of November vote', VOA, 24 July 2021; CIVICUS, 'Nicaragua added to human rights watchlist as government clamps down on civil society ahead of presidential election', Press release, 23 Sep. 2021; and Miller, L., 'The secret-poll watchers of Nicaragua: How they monitored a questionable presidential election', *Los Angeles Times*, 10 Nov. 2021.

[3] Murray, C. and Stott, M., 'Ortega crushes opponents to win "pantomime" Nicaragua election', *Financial Times*, 7 Nov. 2021.

[4] Feyche, M., 'OAS assembly condemns Nicaragua's election', Jurist, 14 Nov. 2021; and 'Under fire for "sham" vote, Nicaragua begins withdrawal from OAS', Al Jazeera, 19 Nov. 2021.

[5] Farber, J., 'War in peace: Exploring the roots of El Salvador's gang violence', Council on Hemispheric Affairs, 18 July 2016; and Wheeler, W., *State of War: MS-13 and El Salvador's World of Violence* (Columbia Global Reports: New York, Jan. 2020).

a third lower compared to 2018), of which 151 were battle-related deaths commonly involving armed gangs.[6] President Nayib Bukele came to power in 2019 on a wave of populism, having promised to confront the gangs. This has involved sending soldiers and police to gang strongholds as part of his so-called 'territorial control plan'. While murder rates have dropped significantly in recent years, political repression has increased.[7] Nonetheless, President Bukele remained one of the most popular leaders in the region, with an approval rating of 85.1 per cent according to a December 2021 poll.[8] In particular, despite having implemented stringent lockdown measures in 2020, his response to the Covid-19 pandemic enjoyed high support from the public.[9] Bukele's New Ideas party won a landslide victory in the legislative and municipal elections of 28 February 2021, giving it a two-thirds supermajority in the legislative assembly. Nonetheless, disregard for institutional checks and balances continued through 2021, with parliament endorsing the sacking of the attorney-general and five judges.[10]

Guatemala

ACLED recorded 653 conflict-related deaths in Guatemala in 2021 (a slight increase from 558 in 2020), of which 378 were attributed to 'battles' involving armed gangs.[11] The homicide rate for 2021 was 16.6 per 100 000, with 2843 registered for the year—266 more than in 2020.[12] Gang violence has in recent years been estimated to account for around 40 per cent of homicides in urban areas where gangs are prevalent.[13] These killings overlap with other causes of homicide, including those related to drug trafficking and organized crime, and social and economic conflict.[14] Guatemala has many criminal groups, ranging from the sizeable and influential (MS13 and Barrio 18) to smaller local gangs. They include former and active members of the security forces and police, as well as long-time criminals and some Mexican and Colombian drug trafficking organizations.[15]

---

[6] Armed Conflict Location & Event Data Project (ACLED), 'Dashboard', accessed 15 Feb. 2022.

[7] Robbins, S., 'El Salvador's gangs send message in blood', Insight Crime, 16 Dec. 2021.

[8] Renteria, N., 'Majority of Salvadorans approve of Bukele's leadership, poll shows', Reuters, 15. Dec. 2021.

[9] 'Why Salvadoreans love their populist president, Nayib Bukele', *The Economist*, 2 Mar. 2021; and World Health Organization, 'COVID-19 country case studies: El Salvador', Mar. 2021, p. 4.

[10] 'El Salvador's parliament sacks the country's top judges', *The Economist*, 8 May 2021; and Avelar, B. and Lopez, O., 'Raids on independent groups in El Salvador raise fears of repression', *New York Times*, 23 Nov. 2021.

[11] ACLED (note 6), accessed 15 Feb. 2022.

[12] InSight Crime, 'InSight Crime's 2021 homicide round-up', 1 Feb. 2022.

[13] Dudley, S., 'Homicides in Guatemala: Conclusions and recommendations', InSight Crime, 20 Apr. 2017.

[14] Dudley (note 13).

[15] InSight Crime, 'Guatemala profile', 28 Feb. 2021.

Guatemala experienced months of public unrest after Congress passed an emergency budget in November 2020 that terminated pandemic assistance programmes, reduced hunger relief, and cut education and health budgets. In the face of sustained public protests, which included setting fire to the Congress building, the government retracted the budget. Public protests also focused on the failure of the government to address Guatemala's endemic problem of corruption and impunity.[16]

Honduras

ACLED recorded 594 conflict-related deaths in Honduras in 2021 (a slight decrease from 656 in 2020), of which 521 were attributed to 'violence against civilians' and 60 to 'battles' involving armed gangs.[17] According to InSight Crime's rankings for 2021, Honduras remained Central America's most—and Latin America's third most—deadly country. The number of homicides rose to 3651 in 2021, up from 3599 in 2020, equating to a homicide rate of 38.6 per 100 000.[18] 'Massacres'—defined as the killing of three or more people, often gang-related—occurred on a weekly basis throughout the year.[19] The primary gangs present in Honduras are MS13 and Barrio 18, which operate mainly in urban areas such as Tegucigalpa or San Pedro Sula or in rural areas close to the border with El Salvador. Their main operations are extortion and drug trafficking.[20]

The country also experienced pronounced political violence, with the UN Human Rights Office in Honduras recording 63 cases of political violence, including 29 killings, between the September 2020 announcement of upcoming primary elections and the local, general and presidential elections on 28 November 2021.[21] The election saw leftist opposition candidate Xiomara Castro win the presidency with 53 per cent of the vote, ousting the scandal-ridden and highly unpopular National Party that had held power for the previous 12 years.[22] Castro was voted in after a campaign dominated by debates about state corruption, drug money and increasing authoritarianism

---

[16] 'Guatemala's top tribunal comes under pressure', *The Economist*, 22 Apr. 2021; and Reuters, 'Thousands protest in Guatemala demanding president's resignation', US News and World Report, 29 July 2021.

[17] ACLED (note 6), accessed 15 Feb. 2022.

[18] InSight Crime (note 12).

[19] Ordóñez, E., 'Unas 168 personas murieron en 53 masacres que se registraron en Honduras en 2021' [Some 168 people died in 53 massacres in Honduras in 2021], *El Heraldo*, 13 Dec. 2021.

[20] InSight Crime, 'Honduras profile', 15 Feb. 2021.

[21] Office of the United Nations High Commissioner for Human Rights (OHCHR), 'Honduras: Ensure people can vote without fear or coercion—Bachelet', Press release, 23 Nov. 2021

[22] AP News, 'Honduras to get first female president after ruling party concedes defeat', *The Guardian*, 1 Dec. 2021.

under President Hernández.[23] In March 2021 Hernández's brother had been convicted in a US court for 'state-sponsored drug trafficking', indicating the degree of complicity some Honduran elites—including the president himself—have in the gang-related violence.[24] Despite fears of a repeat of the violently contested 2017 presidential election, which saw 23 people die in protests opposing the election results declaring Hernández the winner despite findings of serious irregularities, the strengthening of electoral safeguards appeared to prevent similar irregularities in the November elections.[25]

Castro—the wife of Manuel Zelaya, who was deposed as president in a 2009 coup—became Honduras' first woman president and Latin America's only female leader. Heading a coalition of opposition parties, Castro faces significant challenges. Honduras has the second highest poverty rate in Latin America (after Haiti), with nearly two-thirds—5.5 million people—of its population living in poverty.[26] Migration from Honduras towards the USA surged due to the aftermath of the 2020 hurricanes, poverty and pervasive street gang violence.[27]

[23] 'A court case rocks the president of Honduras', *The Economist*, 18 Mar. 2021; and Palmer, E. and Semple, K., 'A damning portrait of presidential corruption, but Hondurans sound resigned', *New York Times*, 23 Mar. 2021.

[24] 'US court sentences Honduran president's brother to life imprisonment', *The Guardian*, 30 Mar. 2021.

[25] Moncada, M. A., 'Elections in Honduras: The end of a 12-year regime', Blavatnik School of Government, University of Oxford, blog, 1 Feb. 2022; and AP News (note 22).

[26] Contreras, F., 'Extreme poverty in Honduras forces many to migrate', CGTN, 19 May 2021.

[27] Kitroeff, N., '"We are doomed": Devastation from storms fuels migration in Honduras', *New York Times*, 6 Apr. 2021 (updated 28 Nov. 2021).

IV. Armed conflict in South America

MARINA CAPARINI AND IAN DAVIS

This section discusses the armed conflicts in Colombia, Brazil and Venezuela. The main focus is on Colombia, where at least three parallel and overlapping conflicts continued in 2021: one between the government and the National Liberation Army (Ejército de Liberación Nacional, ELN) and another between the government and dissident armed groups of the Revolutionary Armed Forces of Colombia-People's Army (Fuerzas Armadas Revolucionarias de Colombia-Ejército del Pueblo, FARC-EP)'s former Eastern Bloc; and one between rival cartels the ELN and the Gaitanista Self-Defence Forces of Colombia (Autodefensas Gaitanistas de Colombia, AGC). In Brazil the armed conflict involved a complicated picture of state–gang violence, while in Venezuela the armed violence centred on rebel groups operating along the border with Colombia, as well as armed criminal activity.

Colombia

Armed conflict worsened in Colombia in 2021, with a 70 per cent increase in organized political violence compared to the previous year and civilians targeted in over half of documented attacks.[1] Moreover, there was an increase in violent events from 778 in 2020 to 1766 in 2021, as well as a 46 per cent increase in the resulting reported fatalities, from 847 in 2020 to 1238 in 2021 (see table 3.3).[2]

Colombia continued to experience three parallel non-international armed conflicts (NIACs): one between the Colombian government and the ELN; the second between the Colombian government and fighters of the former Eastern Bloc (Bloque Oriental); and the third between the ELN and the AGC.[3] In addition, the International Committee of the Red Cross (ICRC) reports that two additional NIACs exist in the country: one between the Colombian government and the People's Liberation Army (Ejército Popular de Liberación, EPL), and one between the ELN and the EPL in Catatumbo region.[4] No peace agreement has yet been negotiated between the Colombian government and the ELN. Colombia is also experiencing forms of violence that are not considered NIACs by international humanitarian law experts, but which are governed by domestic law and international human rights law.

---

[1] Castro, B., '10 conflicts to worry about in 2022: Colombia', Armed Conflict Location & Event Data Project (ACLED), accessed 25 Mar. 2022.

[2] ACLED, 'Dashboard', accessed 22 Jan. 2022.

[3] Rule of Law in Armed Conflicts (RULAC), 'Colombia', 19 Mar. 2021.

[4] International Committee of the Red Cross, 'Colombia: Five armed conflicts—what's happening?', 30 Jan. 2019.

November 2021 saw the fifth anniversary of the 2016 peace agreement that brought an end to the 52-year conflict between the Colombian government and the FARC-EP, the country's largest armed group. The accord resulted in the formal dissolution of the FARC-EP and the demobilization of its members—according to the United Nations, by the end of 2021 a total 13 613 former FARC-EP members were accredited as demobilized.[5] Though most FARC-EP fighters demobilized, a small minority rejected the peace agreement and formed their own FARC-EP dissident groups, and some who had demobilized subsequently joined the FARC-EP dissidents in response to attacks by other armed groups. These groups have filled the power vacuum created by the FARC-EP's demobilization, with conflict involving the dissidents and other armed groups continuing to increase in many rural areas in 2021.

While disarmament of the FARC-EP has been a major success of the 2016 peace agreement, demobilized ex-combatants have yet to be fully reintegrated into civic life and several political, economic and rural reforms have stalled.[6] By September 2021 some 29 per cent of the accords had been fully implemented, a mere 2 per cent increase from 2020, reflecting the complexity of the aspects to be addressed.[7]

Multilateral peace operations

The UN Verification Mission (UNVM) in Colombia verifies the reintegration of former FARC-EP members into political, economic and social life; the security guarantees for former FARC-EP members, their families and communities; and the comprehensive security and protection programmes for communities in the territories most affected by the conflict.[8] On 31 December 2021 the UNVM counted 216 international personnel, of whom 53 were military, 52 police and 111 civilians.[9] In 2021 the UNVM was further mandated with verifying compliance with and implementation of the sentences issued by the Special Jurisdiction for Peace (Jurisdicción Especial para la Paz, JEP).[10] The jurisdiction of the JEP encompasses all crimes that took place during the armed conflict over the course of its 50-plus years—as well as being responsible for prosecuting the most serious 'international crimes',

---

[5] United Nations Verification Mission in Colombia, Report of the Secretary-General, Infographics, 25 Sep. 2021 to 27 Dec. 2021, S/2021/1090.

[6] International Crisis Group, *A Fight by Other Means: Keeping the Peace with Colombia's FARC*, Latin America Report no. 92 (International Crisis Group: Brussels, 30 Nov. 2021), pp. 32–33.

[7] Long, G., 'Colombia: Why peace remains elusive five years after Farc deal', *Financial Times*, 19 Sep. 2021.

[8] UN Security Council Resolution 2366, 10 July 2017; and UN Security Council Resolution 2377, 14 Sep. 2017.

[9] SIPRI, Multilateral Peace Operations Database, accessed 1 Apr. 2022.

[10] UN Security Council Resolution 2574, 11 May 2021.

Table 3.3. Estimated conflict-related fatalities in Colombia, 2018–21

Event type	2018	2019	2020	2021
Battles	233	188	148	325
Explosions/remote violence	87	83	18	51
Protests, riots and strategic developments	21	21	63	117
Violence against civilians	520	434	618	745
Total	**861**	**726**	**847**	**1 238**

Note: The first available year for data on Colombia in the Armed Conflict Location & Event Data Project (ACLED) database is 2018. For definitions of event types, see ACLED, 'ACLED definitions of political violence and protest', 11 Apr. 2019.
Source: ACLED, 'Dashboard', accessed 15 Feb. 2022.

such as crimes against humanity, it can also grant amnesties and pardons for regular crimes linked to the conflict.[11]

The Organization of American States Mission to Support the Peace Process in Colombia (Misión de Apoyo al Proceso de Paz en Colombia) is a political and technical mission tasked with assisting peace efforts in the areas most affected by internal armed conflict, crime and inequality.[12] In 2021 it had 24 civilian international personnel.[13] The mission—whose mandate was renewed for a further three years on 12 October 2021—is currently involved in verifying ceasefire and disarmament, demobilization and reintegration activities.[14]

The armed groups

The ELN is Colombia's largest remaining leftist guerrilla group following the 2016 peace agreement. It has an estimated 4000–5000 members, and has strengthened its position and presence in recent years.[15] Although the ELN entered negotiations with the government in 2017, no peace deal was agreed and talks were suspended in 2019 after the group bombed a police academy, killing 21 people.[16] Duque's government has since increased counter-insurgency operations against the ELN, killing one of its top commanders in October 2021.[17] The Colombian government demands that if peace talks

[11] Morales, A., 'The rocky road to peace: Current challenges at the Special Jurisdiction for Peace in Colombia', EJIL: Talk! Blog of the European Journal of International Law, 3 May 2021.

[12] 'Convenio entre el Gobierno de la Republica de Colombia y la Secretaria General de la Organización de los Estados Americanos para el Acompañamiento al proceso de proceso de paz en Colombia' [Agreement between the government of the Republic of Colombia and the Secretary General of the Organization of American States for accompaniment to the peace process in Colombia], 4 Feb. 2004.

[13] SIPRI (note 9).

[14] 'OEA amplía mandato de mission de apoyo a la paz en Colombia' [OAS extends mandate of peace support mission in Colombia], AP News, 12 Oct. 2021.

[15] 'ELN: Ejército de Liberación Nacional/National Liberation Army' [ELN: National Liberation Army/National Liberation Army], *Americas Quarterly*, 26 Jan. 2021.

[16] Villalba, J. and Risquez, R., 'ELN car bomb in Bogotá takes fight to Colombia's cities', InSight Crime, 24 Jan. 2019.

[17] Charles, M., 'Internal divisions hamper peace overtures from Colombia's ELN', World Politics Review, 20 Oct. 2021.

are to resume then the ELN must cease kidnapping, the forced recruitment of children, the use of antipersonnel mines, and drug trafficking. The ELN, meanwhile, maintains that its activities should be addressed through negotiations.[18] The ELN's complex decentralized structure contributes to the group's apparently contradictory approach whereby leaders express a commitment to resume peace negotiations while continuing to launch attacks on transportation and other infrastructure.[19]

The ELN has to an extent filled the vacuum created by the demobilization of the FARC-EP and derives an estimated 60 per cent of its income from illegal mining in Venezuela and Colombia.[20] Clashes between the ELN and state forces continued in Chocó, Valle del Cauca, Arauca, Catatumbo and Magdalena Media departments in 2021, causing forced displacement and confinement, and driving humanitarian need.[21] The ELN also continued to carry out attacks on energy infrastructure and oil companies.[22]

Fighters from the Eastern Bloc of the former FARC-EP—mainly the 1st, 7th and 40th 'fronts' that have not accepted the 2016 peace agreement—are also considered by Rule of Law in Armed Conflicts (RULAC) and the ICRC to be involved in a NIAC with the Colombian government.[23] Contrary to this view, however, the Office of the UN High Commissioner for Human Rights (OHCHR) does not regard any of the FARC-EP dissident groups as parties to a NIAC.[24] Numerous FARC-EP dissident groups of varying sizes have emerged since the peace agreement, often taking the names of the former FARC-EP fronts that held the area in question. These dissident factions contribute to the complex security situation, and are often involved in coercing local communities and criminal rackets.[25] Several dissident commanders have also sought to regain land and property handed over by the FARC-EP under the peace agreement to compensate victims, which was a major cause of violence in the departments of Meta and Caquetá in 2021.[26]

On 30 November 2021 the US State Department removed the original FARC-EP (it refers to this as the FARC), which signed the peace agreement, from its list of terrorist organizations. This de-listing enables the implemen-

---

[18] UN Verification Mission in Colombia, Report of the Secretary-General, S/2021/1090, 27 Dec. 2021, para. 95.

[19] Charles (note 17).

[20] 'ELN: Ejército de Liberación Nacional/National Liberation Army' (note 15).

[21] UN Verification Mission in Colombia (note 18), para. 96.

[22] Griffin, O., 'Colombia ELN guerillas claim responsibility for attacks on oil infrastructure', Reuters, 15 Oct. 2021; and International Crisis Group, *A Broken Canopy: Preventing Deforestation and Conflict in Colombia*, Latin America Report no. 91 (International Crisis Group: Brussels, 4 Nov. 2021), p. 11.

[23] Pappier, J. and Johnson, K., 'Does the FARC still exist? Challenges in assessing Colombia's "post conflict" under international humanitarian law', Human Rights Watch, 22 Oct. 2020.

[24] United Nations, General Assembly, 'Situation of human rights in Colombia', Report of the United Nations High Commissioner for Human Rights, A/HRC/43/3/Add.3, 26 Feb. 2020, para. 9.

[25] International Crisis Group (note 6), p. 28.

[26] Florez, A. and Acosta, L., 'FARC dissidents want old land back in Colombia's Caquetá and Meta', InSight Crime, 23 July 2021.

tation of certain peace accord provisions, including through reintegration programmes for demobilized combatants. However, the de-listing did not apply to dissident FARC units that have refused to demobilize, with two such units added to the US list of foreign terrorist organizations: the Fuerzas Armadas Revolucionarias de Colombia-Ejército Popular (FARC-EP), an armed group under the leadership of Néstor Gregorio Vera Fernández (alias Iván Mordisco) that adopted the name of the now-demobilized FARC; and Segunda Marquetalia, a group founded in 2019 and led by former FARC-EP second-in-command Luciano Marin Arango (alias Iván Márquez), which operates independently of the former Eastern Bloc units.[27]

Rivalry between the Segunda Marquetalia and the dissident FARC group 10th Front increased in 2021 with clashes in Apure, Venezuela.[28] Moreover, the 10th Front also increasingly engaged in conflict with the ELN in the Arauca region of Colombia, resulting in civilian deaths, kidnappings, and forced displacement and confinement. The former allies were allegedly competing over territorial control and linked economic interests, specifically extortion rackets.[29]

Elsewhere, the AGC, a right-wing paramilitary/criminal offshoot of the United Self-Defence Forces of Colombia (Autodefensas Unidas de Colombia, AUC), consolidated its control over the north of Chocó department. In August the ELN broke its non-aggression pact with the AGC and sought to expand towards the centre and south of the department, resulting in increased forced displacement and confinement, as well as homicides and violence against civilians, with indigenous and Afro-Colombian communities particularly impacted.[30] The AGC relies on the same illicit markets as the ELN.[31]

Insecurity in rural regions increased in 2021 due to attacks by ELN guerrillas, FARC dissidents, and paramilitary successor groups. Indigenous and Afro-Colombian leaders, human rights defenders, journalists and community activists were targeted.[32] According to the OHCHR, FARC dissidents, the ELN and paramilitary groups between them committed 82 'massacres' (defined as the killing of three or more civilians in the same incident by the same perpetrator) between January and September 2021, exceeding the 76 documented in 2020.[33] Between January and November

---

[27] Hansler, J., 'US removes Colombia's FARC from terrorism blacklist', CNN, 30 Nov. 2021; and Pappier and Johnson (note 23).

[28] InSight Crime, 'Second Marquetalia', 27 Jan. 2022.

[29] Collins, J., 'Colombia's "peace dividend" isn't paying off', World Politics Review, 7 Jan. 2022.

[30] Intersectoral Emergency Response Mechanism (MIRE) and ACAPS, 'Colombia: Regional needs analysis: Chocó', 22 Dec. 2021.

[31] Ebus, B., 'Five years after the "peace", the Colombian communities living in forced confinement', New Humanitarian, 25 Nov. 2021.

[32] Human Rights Watch, 'Colombia: Events of 2021', World Report 2022.

[33] Human Rights Watch (note 32).

2021 at least 72 300 people were displaced by armed conflict, an increase of almost 196 per cent compared to the same period in 2020.[34]

According to a survey held in November 2021, perceptions of insecurity were most pronounced in urban areas, where 45 per cent reported feeling unsafe. Such feelings of insecurity were most pronounced in the capital Bogotá, where fully 84 per cent of respondents felt unsafe and 52.7 per cent stated they had been the victim of a crime in the preceding 12 months.[35]

Protests

In 2020 Colombia's GDP suffered its biggest decrease in 50 years, dropping by 6.8 per cent—a result of Covid-19-related curbs that triggered mass unemployment and bankruptcies.[36] In 2021, however, the Colombian economy rebounded, with GDP expanding by a record 10.6 per cent, although poverty and unemployment rates remained above pre-pandemic levels.[37] In April, May and June massive but mostly peaceful protests and a general strike against the government were triggered by a proposal for regressive tax reforms—which would have hit working-class Colombians by increasing the cost of staples—a controversial health bill, and the proposal to pay $4.5 billion for 24 F-16 fighter aircraft at a time when 42 per cent of Colombians are living in poverty.[38] The protests focused on continuing high levels of inequality, killings of social movement leaders, police violence, corruption and lack of government transparency. The violent response of the police and armed paramilitary groups under the protection of the police resulted in thousands of documented human rights abuses. For the period 28 April–31 July 2021 covering the national strike and widespread demonstrations, the OHCHR verified 46 deaths (44 civilians and 2 police officers); recorded numerous instances of unnecessary or disproportionate use of force, as well as sexual violence, by police; and highlighted a failure by police to respond to attacks by armed individuals on demonstrators.[39] Given this, the OHCHR stressed that law enforcement officers must abide by principles such as legality, precaution and necessity when policing demonstrations, and that force only be used as a last resort. It called on the Colombian government to make good its pledge to reform the Colombian National Police—which falls under the jurisdiction

---

[34] UN Office for the Coordination of Humanitarian Affairs (UN OCHA), 'Colombia: Impacto y tendencias humanitarias entre enero y noviembre de 2021' [Colombia: Humanitarian Impact and Trends between January and November 2021], 30 Dec. 2021.

[35] 'Qué tan inseguros se sienten los colombianos, estos son los datos según la encuesta de Invamer' [How insecure Colombians feel, these are the data according to Invamer's survey], Infobae, 6 Dec. 2021.

[36] World Bank, 'GDP growth (annual %)—Colombia', accessed 30 Mar. 2022; and Medina. O., 'Record expansion: Colombia's economy grows the most in 115 years', Al Jazeera, 15 Feb. 2022.

[37] Medina (note 36).

[38] 'Colombian government seems determined to buy the new fighter jets for $4.5 billion', Infobae, 28 Mar. 2021.

[39] United Nations, 'UN rights office urges Colombia to reform policing of protests', UN News, 15 Dec. 2021.

Table 3.4. Estimated conflict-related fatalities in Brazil, 2018–21

Event type	2018	2019	2020	2021
Battles	3 055	2 616	2 391	2 620
Explosions/remote violence	1	0	0	3
Protests, riots and strategic developments	65	15	46	36
Violence against civilians	3 350	2 274	2 583	2 830
Total	**6 471**	**4 905**	**5 020**	**5 489**

Note: The first available year for data on Brazil in the Armed Conflict Location & Event Data Project (ACLED) database is 2018. For definitions of event types, see ACLED, 'ACLED definitions of political violence and protest', 11 Apr. 2019.
Source: ACLED, 'Dashboard', accessed 15 Feb. 2022.

of the Ministry of Defence—and introduce civilian control, as well as improve oversight and accountability mechanisms.[40]

Colombia continues to be one of the most dangerous countries in the world for land and environmental activists, with at least 145 activists killed in 2021 compared to 182 murdered over the course of 2020.[41] According to Colombia's ombudsman's office overseeing the protection of human and civil rights, at least 145 community leaders, trade unionists and representatives of rural communities were killed in 2021, most by illegal armed groups. Even so, this represented a fall from the 182 activists reportedly killed in 2020.[42]

Outlook

Although the peace agreement between the Colombian government and the FARC-EP has held and the majority of FARC fighters have been demobilized, Colombia saw increasing rates of armed conflict involving other non-state armed groups and FARC-EP dissident groups throughout 2021. Disproportionate police violence during the protests and general strike have weakened trust in the police, its overseers in the Ministry of Defence, and the administration of President Duque more generally. This will be an important factor should social unrest continue, which is a likely scenario given that the issues driving the general strike and protests remain largely unresolved. Increased urban perceptions of insecurity and the high rate of killings of environmental activists and indigenous and social leaders indicate public security challenges will, along with the parallel armed conflicts, continue to pose challenges for both national and local government into 2022.

---

[40] 'Colombia's Duque announces police reforms as protest leaders call off talks', France 24, 7 June 2021; and United Nations (note 39).

[41] 'Nearly 150 activists killed in Colombia in 2021: Rights ombudsman', Al Jazeera, 18 Jan. 2022.

[42] 'Colombia saw 145 activists killed in 2021, ombudsman says', BBC News, 18 Jan. 2022.

Brazil

In the four-year period of 2018–21 estimated conflict-related deaths in Brazil averaged around 5470 per year, largely divided between two categories: 'battles' and 'violence against civilians' (see table 3.4). Approximately 57 per cent of the 2620 battle-related deaths in 2021 were attributable to violence between state forces and unidentified armed groups or violence between police and political militias (sometimes associated with a particular politician or party), while 42 per cent involved inter-political militia violence. ACLED reported Brazil as having 3262 events with direct civilian targeting in 2021, the second highest in the world after Mexico. Anonymous or unidentified gangs were the primary perpetrators of this civilian targeting, which was particularly noticeable in the northern Amazonas state.[43]

Many poor urban communities in Brazil, especially in the city of Rio de Janeiro, have been subject to severe levels of armed violence for decades, involving armed gangs, paramilitary militias formed in opposition to the gangs, and the police and security forces. Two of the most powerful criminal groups—First Capital Command (Primeiro Comando da Capital, PCC) and Red Command (Comando Vermelho)—began as prison gangs but have since transformed into transnational crime organizations.[44] The proliferation of firearms—new gun registrations in Brazil doubled in 2020 compared to 2019—has added to the complex landscape of armed violence (see box 3.1).[45] Police violence remains an important factor: in 2020 the number of people killed by Brazilian police rose to 6416 (an average of over 17 per day), the seventh year in a row this figure has increased.[46]

President Jair Bolsonaro's popularity waned in 2021 as internal and external criticism intensified. Rising unemployment, high inflation and an end to the preceding year's federal emergency aid meant a population already severely affected by the Covid-19 pandemic experienced further economic strains.[47] In 2021 the country registered almost 40 000 homicides—though in absolute terms this figure far exceeds those of Mexico, Colombia and Venezuela, Brazil's homicide rate of 18.5 per 100 000 fell well below those countries and represented a slight decline from the 2020 rate.[48] Brazil has one of the world's highest mortality rates from the Covid-19 pandemic,

---

[43] Lay, T., 'ACLED 2021: The year in review', ACLED, Mar. 2022, pp. 20–21.

[44] InSight Crime, 'Brazil profile', 8 Sep. 2020; and Hinz, C., 'Brazil's policing is a war of men: Civilians are caught in the crossfire', openDemocracy, 13 Feb. 2022.

[45] Watson, K., 'Jair Bolsonaro and guns: A US culture war waging in Brazil', BBC News, 15 Nov. 2021.

[46] Barbon, J., 'Mortes pela polícia crescem de novo e triplicam em 7 anos no Brasil' [Police killings increase again and triple in 7 years in Brazil], Folha de Sao Paulo, 15 July 2021.

[47] 'Brazilians are increasingly going hungry', The Economist, 15 May 2021; and Rosati, A., 'Brazil's inflation ends 2021 above 10%, testing central bank', Bloomberg, 11 Jan. 2022.

[48] InSight Crime, 'InSight Crime's 2021 homicide round-up', 1 Feb. 2022.

Box 3.1. The blurred nature of armed conflict in Brazil

The complex nature of Brazil's conflict landscape presents difficult methodological challenges. Classifying Brazil as having multiple armed conflicts (as a result of battle-deaths being above 25 or more per year) may be seen as controversial, due to the nature of the organized armed groups in Brazil. Unlike the situation in Mexico, which has a handful of highly organized and long-standing criminal groups, in Brazil the degree of organization, structure, power and capacity of these groups is much more diffuse. There are two main types of non-state armed groups that operate in Brazil: drug trafficking groups and local armed groups. The latter are often referred to as political or police militias (and largely consist of current and former police officers and soldiers). However, these armed groups are also continuously evolving and forming alliances incorporating both state and criminal actors. This merging of crime and politics has been described as 'criminal insurgency'. Thus, the armed groups control large urban areas and carry out protection, welfare assistance, and other services that should be provided by state institutions. Moreover, the level and nature of gang violence affects and challenges the existing political order, and, as shown by table 3.4, the level of battle and other conflict-related fatalities is in keeping with a high-intensity armed conflict.

Sources: ACLED, 'ACLED methodology and coding decisions around political violence and demonstrations in Brazil', Feb. 2020; ACLED, 'Gang violence: Concepts, benchmarks and coding rules', Feb. 2020; InSight Crime, 'Brazil profile', 9 Sep. 2020; AFP, 'Brazil militias control more than half of Rio: Study', TRT World, 20 Oct. 2020; Baker, N. D. and Leão, G., 'Parties of crime? Brazil's *facções criminosas*: Good governance and bad government', *Small Wars Journal*, 19 July 2021; Hernandez, A., 'Against the current: Brazil's dangerous militias', Deutsche Welle, 4 Sep. 2019; and Ramos da Cruz, C. and Ucko, D. H., 'Beyond the *Unidades de Polícia Pacificadora*: Countering Comando Vermelho's criminal insurgency', *Small Wars & Insurgencies*, vol. 29, no. 1 (2018), pp. 38–67.

---

with over 619 000 confirmed deaths by the end of 2021.[49] By October 2021 mass protests were taking place demanding the impeachment of President Bolsonaro over his mishandling of the response.[50]

Venezuela

Armed conflict in Venezuela in 2021 involved clashes between state security forces and Colombian armed groups in the border state of Apurea, as well as recurring (but seemingly declining) levels of urban gang warfare and killings by security forces of citizens 'resisting authority'.[51] The Armed Conflict Location & Event Data Project (ACLED) recorded 229 conflict-related

---

[49] Statista, 'Number of confirmed cases and deaths of coronavirus (COVID-19) in Brazil from Feb. 26, 2020 to Mar. 27, 2022', accessed 30 Mar. 2022.

[50] Phillips, T., 'Mass protests in Brazil call for Jair Bolsonaro's impeachment', *The Guardian*, 2 Oct. 2021. See also Brito, R., 'Brazil Senate committee approves report calling for Bolsonaro to be indicted', Reuters, 26 Oct. 2021.

[51] InSight Crime, 'Venezuela profile', 10 Nov. 2020; Reuters, 'Venezuela: Intense gun battles rage in Caracas between gangs and police', *The Guardian*, 8 July 2021; Poulet, M., 'Venezuela–Colombia border: A look back at several months of conflict in Apure State', France 24, 4 June 2021; and Observatorio Venezolano de Violencia, 'Informe annual de violencia 2021' [Annual Report on Violence 2021], 28 Dec. 2021.

deaths in Venezuela in 2021 (the second consecutive year of decline and a significant decrease from the 1106 estimated conflict-related deaths in 2019), 90 of which were attributed to 'battles' between the different armed gangs and groups, including their clashes with Venezuelan state security forces.[52]

Following sporadic military clashes that began in September 2020 and resumed in the first two months of the 2021, the Venezuelan military launched 'Operation Bolivarian Shield 2021' in March in Apure, near the Colombian border, against the 10th Front, a dissident FARC armed group. For decades the FARC was seen as an ally of the Venezuelan state after President Hugo Chávez invited the rebel group to take sanctuary on its territory in support of his 'Bolivarian revolution'. After the 2016 peace agreement and the FARC's demobilization, the dissident 10th Front faction had taken over territorial operations in the cross-border criminal economy, allegedly in league with the local Venezuelan military.[53] The falling out between the 10th Front and the Venezuelan state has been attributed to the emergence of factional rivalries and competition among the 10th Front, Second Marquetalia and the ELN over criminal markets, with the state's presence having declined across the country.[54] In particular, the 10th Front has become involved in a struggle for control of territory, trafficking and other illegal operations with the Second Marquetalia—another Colombian armed group formerly linked to the FARC-EP, which is alleged to have political connections in Caracas.[55]

Significant numbers of state security forces, albeit poorly trained and equipped, were deployed to Apure. However, the estimated 300 members of the 10th Front benefited from close familiarity with the area and long-established relations with local communities, as well as contacts within the local military, which leaked information about upcoming operations. This enabled the group to successfully wage guerrilla warfare, which in turn led to rapidly increasing rates of desertion from the state security forces following an ambush on 23 April 2021 in which 12 soldiers were killed and 8 captured.[56] The military subsequently withdrew in late May.[57]

The perception that the Venezuelan military was deployed at least in part to aid the Second Marquetalia in its inter-factional struggle with the 10th Front over control of territory for illegal operations, together with the apparent failure of the operation, allegedly undermined the confidence in President Nicolás Maduro and the high command felt by those within the security forces' ranks.[58] It also underscored that, having provided a safe

[52] ACLED (note 2), accessed 15 Feb. 2022.

[53] InSight Crime, 'Apure's proxy war', 13 Oct. 2021.

[54] Martinez-Gugerli, K., 'FAQ on recent borderland violence in Apure', Venezuelan Politics and Human Rights blog, 3 June 2021; and InSight Crime (note 53).

[55] InSight Crime (note 53).

[56] 'Colombian armed group captured 8 Venezuelan soldiers—NGO', Reuters, 10 May 2021.

[57] InSight Crime, 'The Venezuelan military: Outfought and outmatched', 13 Oct. 2021.

[58] InSight Crime (note 57).

haven for Colombian armed groups, Venezuela no longer controls parts of its own territory.

Venezuela had the second highest homicide rate in Latin America in 2021 at 40.9 per 100 000—although if one excludes disappearances, this falls to 33 per 100 000.[59] Homicides were highest in the capital Caracas, where in January 2021 the state security forces launched raids on the gang led by Carlos Luis Revete (alias 'El Koki'), which had taken over the La Vega neighbourhood, leaving at least 23 people dead, and in June in Cota 905 neighbourhood, leaving 27 dead.[60] El Koki had ruled Cota 905 with seeming impunity since 2017, when the state designated the area a Peace Zone, rendering it off-limits to local police.[61] In a context of state erosion through corruption and the effects of sanctions, the gang has provided a variety of services to the population, including food, financial assistance for medicine and funerals, and the sponsoring of sports teams and cultural events.[62] Similarly, other organized crime gangs allegedly exercise territorial control over several of the capital's neighbourhoods.[63] Renewed state efforts in 2021 eventually pushed El Koki out of La Vega and Cota 905, with El Koki still at large by year end.[64]

Economic and political developments

A long-running and increasingly severe economic crisis in Venezuela resulted in three out of every four (76.6 per cent) Venezuelans living in extreme poverty in 2021, a rise from 67.7 per cent in 2020.[65] By mid 2021, 2.3 million people were severely food insecure and a further 7 million people moderately food insecure. The resulting humanitarian crisis has led to over 5.6 million people leaving the country.[66]

Despite the collapse of the oil industry, which is the main source of government revenue, President Maduro maintained his grip politically with the military's support.[67]

---

[59] InSight Crime (note 48).

[60] Glorimar Fernández, 'Monitor de Víctimas contabilizó 27 personas asesinadas en operativos contra banda del "Koki"' [Victims' Monitor counts 27 people killed in operations against the "Koki" gang], El Pitazo, 29 July 2021; and InSight Crime, 'El Koki's victory—An urban invasion in Caracas', 25 June 2021.

[61] InSight Crime (note 60).

[62] Herrera, I. and Kurmanaev, A., 'Bouncy castles and grenades: Gangs erode maduros' grip on Caracas', New York Times, 30 May 2021.

[63] Herrera and Kurmanaev (note 62).

[64] InSight Crime, 'Why did Venezuela's peace zones backfire so badly?', 25 Jan. 2022.

[65] 'Venezuela crisis: Three in four in extreme poverty, study says', BBC News, 30 Sep. 2021.

[66] 'Venezuela crisis' (note 65).

[67] Otis, J., 'The US predicted his downfall but Maduro strengthens his grip on power in Venezuela', NPR, 8 Dec. 2021.

4. Armed conflict and peace processes in Asia and Oceania

Overview

Nine countries in Asia and Oceania experienced active armed conflicts in 2021 (two more than in 2020). These consisted of three in South Asia (section III), namely Afghanistan (major internationalized civil war), India (low-intensity combined interstate border and subnational armed conflicts) and Pakistan (high-intensity combined interstate border and subnational armed conflicts); four in South East Asia (section IV), namely a major armed conflict in Myanmar and low-intensity subnational armed conflicts in Indonesia, the Philippines and Thailand; and a new low-intensity interstate conflict in Central Asia between Kyrgyzstan and Tajikistan, where an outbreak of border clashes resulted in more than 25 battle-related deaths, taking it above the armed conflict threshold. Total conflict-related fatalities in Asia and Oceania increased by 59 per cent in 2021 (having fallen by nearly 50 per cent in 2020), mostly due to conflict-related fatalities increasing in Afghanistan, Myanmar and Pakistan.

Three trends remained a cause for concern in 2021: (a) the growing Chinese–United States rivalry, combined with an increasingly assertive Chinese foreign policy (see section II); (b) a range of complex threats and conflicts falling within the broad terrorism/counterterrorism rubric, involving both states and non-state actors; and (c) the growing impact of weather and climate hazards—especially floods, storms and droughts—in many of the region's countries. The Covid-19 pandemic appeared to have minimal impact on the region's armed conflicts in 2021, despite profound impacts on human security more generally.

Only a few of the armed conflicts were being addressed by ongoing or new peace processes in 2021. South and North Korea, China and the US agreed 'in principle' to declare a formal end to the Korean War (see section II). In Afghanistan the war effectively came to an end after the Taliban took control of the country following the final withdrawal of US and North Atlantic Treaty Organization forces. There was a new ceasefire between India and Pakistan regarding their ongoing interstate armed conflict over Kashmir, as well as a slight thawing in China–India relations. There were five multilateral peace operations active in Asia and Oceania in 2021—the same number as in 2020.

The war in Afghanistan was set to end in time for the 20th anniversary of the terrorist attacks on the United States of 11 September 2001 with the agreed withdrawal of US troops. However, the withdrawal precipitated the rapid collapse of the Afghan government and the Taliban's triumphant return to power in Kabul. This left several lingering questions concerning the group's ability to govern and unify the country, the future of human rights and the role of women, and the likely response by regional powers and the rest of the international community. In particular, the Taliban faced a growing economic and humanitarian crisis driven by displacement, drought, the Covid-19 pandemic and an extreme dependency on external funds, much of which was suspended following their takeover.

The territorial conflict between India and Pakistan over Kashmir has generally involved relatively low levels of armed violence, largely consisting of regular artillery fire exchanges and other clashes between Indian and Pakistani forces along the Line of Control (LOC), and militant attacks and Indian counter-insurgency operations inside Jammu and Kashmir. However, following a United Arab Emirates-brokered ceasefire in February (the first such agreement since 2003), there was a significant drop in the number of ceasefire violations along the LOC. The ceasefire also enabled further bilateral dialogue between the parties, although this appears unlikely to overcome their divisions on Kashmir and other issues. After the deadly Chinese–Indian clashes in the Galwan Valley in 2020, there was a return to relative stability in territorial disputes along the Line of Actual Control (LAC) in 2021, although both countries increased troop deployments and improved infrastructure on their respective sides of the LAC.

In Pakistan increased violence involving Taliban-affiliated groups in the north-western province of Khyber Pakhtunkhwa and Baloch separatist fighters in the south-western province of Balochistan led to an uptick in conflict-related deaths in 2021.

In Myanmar a military coup at the beginning of February 2021 ended the recent short period of civilian rule and led to escalating protests and violence throughout the country. The armed conflict was transformed from a low-intensity to a major armed conflict, with over 11 000 conflict-related deaths in 2021. At the end of the year government forces and resistance forces—a loose coalition of ethnic armed groups and civilian militias—were locked in a violent stalemate, which Association of Southeast Asian Nations-led diplomacy seemed unlikely to break. In addition to armed violence and regime oppression, Myanmar faced a growing humanitarian crisis characterized by deepening economic recession, internal displacement, collapsing healthcare, and surging poverty and food insecurity.

Two long-running insurgencies in the Philippines continued in 2021 at relatively low levels of violence: one in the Muslim-majority areas of the southern Philippines' Mindanao region and another involving the New People's Army of the Communist Party of the Philippines. However, as in recent years, it was the 'war on drugs' that appeared to produce the most fatalities in the Philippines during 2021.

IAN DAVIS

I. Key general developments in the region

IAN DAVIS

Nine countries in Asia and Oceania experienced active armed conflicts in 2021 (two more than in 2020). These consisted of three in South Asia, namely Afghanistan (major internationalized civil war), India (low-intensity interstate border and subnational armed conflicts) and Pakistan (interstate border and subnational armed conflicts that when combined amount to high-intensity violence), as discussed in section III; four in South East Asia, namely a major armed conflict in Myanmar and low-intensity subnational armed conflicts in Indonesia, the Philippines and Thailand, as discussed in section IV; and a new low-intensity interstate armed conflict in Central Asia between Kyrgyzstan and Tajikistan, as discussed below.[1] After a significant decline in total conflict-related fatalities in the region in 2020 (compared to 2019), the situation was reversed in 2021 with a 59 per cent increase (compared to 2020). This was largely due to a rise in fatalities in Afghanistan prior to the war ending, a large increase in fatalities in Myanmar following the military coup in February 2021 and a spike in violence in Pakistan (see table 4.1).

Alongside these armed conflicts, parts of Asia and Oceania continued to be affected by instability arising from a variety of causes, often with important subregional differences. Moreover, while the region—especially East Asia—has experienced a dramatic reduction in armed conflict over the past 40 years, a reversal of this positive trend appears to be underway.[2] Three trends remained a cause for concern in 2021. First, the Chinese–United States rivalry continued to fester and expand in 2021, drawing in other countries and provoking increased tensions in East Asia, especially in relation to Taiwan and the South China Sea (see section II). Second, a range of complex threats and conflicts falling within the broad terrorism/counterterrorism rubric, involving both states and non-state actors, continued to have far-reaching consequences across many parts of Asia. Under the umbrella of this second trend, at least three key strands could be discerned: (*a*) violence related to identity politics, based on ethnic and/or religious polarization (some of which has long-term roots), such as the Hindu-nationalist paramilitary group, the Rashtriya Swayamsevak Sangh, in India, and Buddhist extremist groups operating in Myanmar, Sri Lanka and Thailand;[3] (*b*) violence involving

---

[1] For conflict definitions and typologies see chapter 2, section I, in this volume.

[2] World Bank Group and United Nations, *Pathways for Peace: Inclusive Approaches for Preventing Violent Conflict* (International Bank for Reconstruction and Development/World Bank: Washington, DC, 2018), pp. 11–12, 19; and Bellamy, A. J., *East Asia's Other Miracle: Explaining the Decline of Mass Atrocities* (Oxford University Press: 2017).

[3] Ramachandran, S., 'India: Fanning the flames of extremism and terror at home', *Terrorism Monitor*, vol. 18, no. 1 (14 Jan. 2020), pp. 7–9; and Gunasingham, A., 'Buddhist extremism in Sri Lanka and Myanmar: An examination', *Counter Terrorist Trends and Analyses*, vol. 11, no. 3 (Mar. 2019), pp. 1–6.

Table 4.1. Estimated conflict-related fatalities in Asia and Oceania, 2017–21

Country	2017	2018	2019	2020	2021
Afghanistan	36 618	43 295	41 279	31 327	42 031
India	1 403	2 149	1 533	1 289	989
Indonesia	49	167	212	124	124
Kyrgyzstan	–	4[a]	8[a]	2[a]	32[b]
Myanmar	1 407	264	1 495	659	11 061
Pakistan	1 725	1 226	1 157	825	1 378
Philippines	4 367	2 106	1 703	1 486	1 139
Tajikistan	–	64[a]	66[a]	22[a]	20[b]
Thailand	94	231	172	102	66
Total	**45 663**	**49 506**	**47 625**	**35 816**	**56 840**

– = not applicable.

[a] Battle-related deaths were below 25.

[b] Combined battle-related deaths exceeded 25.

Note: Fatality figures are collated from four event types: battles; explosions/remote violence; protests, riots and strategic developments; and violence against civilians—see Armed Conflict Location & Event Data Project (ACLED), 'ACLED definitions of political violence and protest', 11 Apr. 2019. A country is treated as being in an armed conflict if there were 25 or more battle-related deaths in a given year—see chapter 2, section I, in this volume.

Source: ACLED, 'Dashboard', accessed 26–27 Jan. 2022.

transnational violent jihadist groups, including the presence of actors linked to the Islamic State in Afghanistan, Bangladesh, India, Indonesia, Malaysia, New Zealand, Pakistan, the Philippines and Sri Lanka;[4] and (c) the use (and abuse) by several states of the terrorism narrative, counterterrorism laws and anti-Covid measures in order to stifle genuine dissent, civil society groups and minorities.[5]

The third trend is the growing impact of weather and climate hazards—especially floods, storms and droughts—in many of the region's countries.[6] For example, of the 11 climate-exposed 'highly vulnerable countries of concern' (i.e. those least likely to be able to adapt to climate change) identified in the latest US National Intelligence Assessment on climate change, 5 are in South and East Asia: Afghanistan, India, Myanmar, Pakistan and North Korea.[7]

---

[4] Menon, P., 'Police in New Zealand kill "extremist" who stabbed six in supermarket', Reuters, 3 Sep. 2021; Chew, A., 'Isis supporters in Indonesia, Malaysia call for more violence after attack during holy period for Muslims and Christians', *South China Morning Post*, 30 Mar. 2021; and United Nations, Security Council, 'Twelfth report of the Secretary-General on the threat posed by ISIL (Da'esh) to international peace and security and the range of United Nations efforts in support of Member States in countering the threat', S/2021/98, 29 Jan. 2021, p. 7.

[5] Omelicheva, M. Y. et al., 'Asia and the "Global War on Terror"', *The Diplomat*, 1 Sep. 2021.

[6] See e.g. World Meteorological Organization (WMO), *State of the Climate in Asia 2020*, WMO-no. 1273 (WMO: Geneva, Oct. 2021); and 'China floods: Nearly 2 million displaced in Shanxi province', BBC News, 11 Oct. 2021.

[7] National Intelligence Council, 'National intelligence estimate: Climate change and international responses increasing challenges to US national security through 2040', Oct. 2021, pp. 11–15. On Afghanistan's vulnerability to the effects of climate change see Norwegian Institute of International Affairs (NUPI) and SIPRI, 'Afghanistan', Climate, peace and security fact sheet, Feb. 2022.

Only a few of the armed conflicts discussed in this chapter were being addressed by ongoing or new peace processes in 2021. South and North Korea, China and the USA agreed 'in principle' to declare a formal end to the Korean War (1950–53), almost 70 years after the conflict ended in an armistice on 27 July 1953 (see section II). In Afghanistan the war effectively ended after the Taliban took control of the country following the final withdrawal of US and North Atlantic Treaty Organization (NATO) forces (see section III), and in February 2021 a United Arab Emirates-brokered ceasefire was agreed between India and Pakistan regarding their ongoing interstate armed conflict over Kashmir. The status quo between India and China in Kashmir broke down in 2020 and tensions over their border dispute continued in 2021, albeit with a slight thaw in their relations (see section III). In South East Asia Myanmar was excluded from the Association of Southeast Asian Nations (ASEAN) summit in October 2021 for failing to adhere to a regional peace process agreed in April, following a military coup in February (see section IV).

There were five multilateral peace operations in Asia and Oceania in 2021—the same number as in 2020. The NATO-led Resolute Support Mission (RSM) officially closed in September 2021; there were no new operations in Asia or Oceania in 2021. The number of personnel in multilateral peace operations in Asia and Oceania decreased by 97 per cent in 2021, from 9941 on 31 December 2020 to 337 on 31 December 2021. By and large, this was due to NATO's withdrawal from Afghanistan and the closing of the RSM (see section III).[8]

Interstate armed conflict in Central Asia

Since the collapse of the Soviet Union at the end of 1991, Central Asia has seen a broad spectrum of violence, including several armed conflicts. One of the main sources of tension has been the complex range of territorial, border and water disputes that have persisted in the region.[9] In 2021 the picture was mixed: while a territorial agreement was reached between Kyrgyzstan and Uzbekistan, a new outbreak of border clashes flared between Kyrgyzstan and Tajikistan. The latter resulted in more than 25 battle-related deaths, taking it above the armed conflict threshold.

The most complicated border negotiations involved the Ferghana Valley, where a myriad of enclaves exist and all three countries sharing it—Kyrgyzstan, Tajikistan and Uzbekistan—have both historical claims

---

[8] For a full list of multilateral peace operations see chapter 2, section III, table 2.6.

[9] International Crisis Group, *Central Asia: Border Disputes and Conflict Potential*, Asia Report no. 33 (International Crisis Group: Brussels, 4 Apr. 2002); Murzakulova, A., 'The Soviet water legacy in Central Asia', *The Diplomat*, 1 Sep. 2021; and Helf, G., 'Looking for trouble: Sources of violent conflict in Central Asia', United States Institute of Peace, Special Report no. 489, Nov. 2020.

and economic interests. In March 2021 Kyrgyzstan and Uzbekistan finally reached agreement on their long-standing border disputes, including those in the Ferghana Valley.[10] However, the border conflict between Kyrgyzstan and Tajikistan, which is particularly tense due to over a third of the 1000 kilometre border being disputed, flared up again in late April 2021. The four days of armed clashes over a water dispute killed at least 55 people and displaced about 10 000 before a ceasefire was agreed on 1 May.[11] To further ease tension both sides withdrew troops from the border area and agreed to joint security controls.[12]

Another clash occurred on the Kyrgyzstan–Tajikistan border in July, with tensions remaining high throughout the remainder of 2021.[13] By the end of the year the Armed Conflict Location & Event Data Project (ACLED) had recorded 32 fatalities in Kyrgyzstan and 20 in Tajikistan.[14]

The impact of Covid-19

As was the case in 2020 the Covid-19 pandemic appears to have had minimal impact on the region's armed conflicts in 2021. More generally, the pandemic is likely to unravel decades of economic and social progress in some of the more fragile parts of Asia. For example, India's economy contracted by 6.6 per cent in the fiscal year 2020–21, its worst performance in over four decades and among the worst performances globally.[15] One study suggested that the pandemic led to a staggering rise in inequality across Asia in 2020, destroying 147 million jobs and pushing 148 million people into poverty, while the region's billionaires grew their wealth by $1.46 trillion.[16]

[10] 'Kyrgyzstan, Uzbekistan sign deal to end border disputes', Eurasianet, 26 Mar. 2021.

[11] 'Deadly fighting on Kyrgyzstan–Tajikistan border kills at least 31', BBC News, 30 Apr. 2021; Abdülkerimov, B., 'Death toll rises to 55 from Kyrgyz–Tajik border clashes', Anadolu Agency, 5 May 2021; and 'Kyrgyzstan, Tajikistan agree new ceasefire after border clashes', Al Jazeera, 1 May 2021.

[12] 'Kyrgyzstan, Tajikistan agree to joint security controls along disputed border', RFE/RL, 18 May 2021.

[13] AFP, 'Kyrgyz border guard killed in shootout with Tajik forces', *Times of India*, 9 July 2021; and Imanaliyeva, A., 'Kyrgyzstan fortifies border as negotiations with Tajikistan drag on', Eurasianet, 26 Oct. 2021.

[14] Armed Conflict Location & Event Data Project (ACLED), 'Dashboard', accessed 25 Jan. 2022.

[15] National Statistical Office, Ministry of Statistics & Programme Implementation, Government of India, 'Press note on first revised estimates of national income, consumption expenditure, saving and capital formation for 2020–21', 31 Jan. 2022.

[16] Seery, E., *Rising to the Challenge: The Case for Permanent Progressive Policies to Tackle Asia's Coronavirus and Inequality Crisis* (Oxfam: Oxford, Jan. 2022).

II. Flashpoints in the conflict dynamics in East Asia

FEI SU

Great power competition continued to affect regional security in East Asia in 2021, with intensified rivalry between China and the United States. These trends solidified as a result of evolving US partnerships designed to counter China's influence in the region—including the exploration of partnerships with likeminded countries in Europe and Asia through the Quadrilateral Security Dialogue (Quad); the creation of a trilateral security pact between Australia, the United Kingdom and the United States (AUKUS); and closer coordination with allies Japan and South Korea. There were also growing concerns over China's assertive foreign policy and military actions in the Taiwan Strait and South China Sea (SCS). Moreover, China and Russia's deteriorating relations with the West and their rivalry with the US helped bring the two sides closer together.[1]

Chinese–US relations have shifted from a cooperative and competitive relationship towards one of competition and confrontation.[2] This rising geo-political tension has the potential to lead to escalation in several unsolved disputes and dormant security risks. This section briefly explores key developments in three areas—the Korean Peninsula, the East and South China seas, and the Taiwan Strait—that have the potential to seriously impact regional security dynamics.

Korean Peninsula

Despite several missile launches early in the year and again in September, the North Korean nuclear issue was less of an urgent priority for the relevant parties in 2021.[3] One notable development for the peace process on the Korean Peninsula, though, was an end-of-war declaration promoted by South Korean President Moon Jae-in aimed at formally ending the Korean War and incentivizing North Korea back to the negotiating table.[4] However, despite an active campaign and widespread discussion in South Korea, as well as a generally supportive stance from China, the USA and North Korea were seemingly less enthusiastic.[5] Opposing US voices argued that 'rewarding' North Korea in this way without any commitment to denuclearization would

---

[1] Russian International Affairs Council 2021, 'Russia–China dialogue: The 2021 model'. On Russia's relations with the West see chapter 5, section I, in this volume.

[2] Medeiros E. S., *Major Power Rivalry in East Asia* (Council on Foreign Relations: New York, Apr. 2021).

[3] On North Korea's nuclear weapons programme see chapter 10, section IX, in this volume.

[4] Choi, J. K., 'Reflections on the ROK–US Alliance and the Republic of Korea's place in the world', *Global Asia*, Dec. 2021.

[5] Hwang, J., 'An end-of-war declaration is not an impossible dream', *The Hankyoreh*, 7 Nov. 2021.

undermine stability and security on the Peninsula.[6] Meanwhile, North Korea, in responding to Moon's speech at the United Nations on the declaration, rejected the proposal and emphasized that the USA needed to withdraw its 'hostile policy' as a prerequisite to any discussions on the declaration.[7] Although South Korea and the USA had by the end of 2021 finally agreed to work on drafting the declaration, North Korea's stance remained uncertain.[8]

East and South China Sea

Tensions between China and Japan over their long-standing territorial dispute in the East China Sea continued in 2021. In November a Chinese naval vessel entered Japanese territorial waters, the first such incursion since 2017.[9] To help prevent escalation of the conflict, the defence ministers from the two sides agreed to set up a military hotline by the end of 2022.[10]

Meanwhile, no substantial progress was made in 2021 in negotiations between China and ASEAN countries over an SCS Code of Conduct (COC). This was partly due to the focus on Covid-19 and partly due to the divergent views maintained by the two sides. Amid the continued delay in finalizing the COC, there were increased concerns over China's use of maritime militias in the region. In March 2021 there were around 220 Chinese fishing boats at Whitsun Reef, prompting a diplomatic protest from the Philippines.[11] Later in September another protest was filed from the Philippines following the presence of Chinese fishing vessels in the vicinity of Iroquois Reef.[12] In addition, more than 26 military exercises were conducted by the Chinese People's Liberation Army (PLA) in the SCS over a three-month period between May and August.[13]

China also passed a new law expanding the duties and practices of the China Coast Guard (CCG), including granting it the power and capability to stop or prevent threats from foreign vessels, and dismantle structures built by other claimant countries in its jurisdictional waters. Application of the CCG law over disputed waters may further complicate the security situation in the

---

[6] Kim, Y. et al., Korean end of war declaration letter to National Security Advisor Jake Sullivan, 7 Dec. 2021.

[7] 'N. Korea proposes talks if South Korea lifts "hostility"', *Asahi Shimbun*, 24 Sep. 2021.

[8] 'Moon plans to end Korean War before leaving office', *Korea Joongang Daily*, 23 Dec. 2021.

[9] 'Chinese naval ship sailed in Japanese waters this week', *Japan Times*, 20 Nov. 2021; and 'Chinese naval ship sailed in Japan waters this week: Defense Ministry', Kyodo News, 20 Nov. 2021.

[10] Lendon, B., 'Japan and China agree to set up defense hotline amid territorial tensions', CNN, 28 Dec. 2021.

[11] Lendon, B., 'China's little blue men are taking over the SCS', ASEAN Post, 13 Apr. 2021.

[12] Centre for Strategic & International Studies (CSIS), 'There and back again: Chinese militia at Iroquois Reef and Union Banks', 22 Oct. 2021.

[13] Xuanzun, L., 'PLA holds 100+ drills in all Chinese sea areas in 3 months, "sets up strategic defense perimeter"', *Global Times*, 24 Aug. 2021.

area, as jurisdictional waters are not well defined in the law.[14] Moreover, the permission given to the CCG to use force in performing its duties, alongside the continuing modernization of its capacity with military-grade equipment and converted warships, is another concerning factor that may increase the risk of conflict in the region.[15]

Chinese actions aside, the SCS was also crowded with players from outside the region.[16] In February 2021 a French nuclear submarine patrolled in the SCS; later in the year a British aircraft carrier strike group held a joint military exercise; and in December 2021 a German warship entered the SCS for the first time in nearly 20 years. In addition, the newly formed AUKUS received a mixed reaction among ASEAN countries. The Philippines responded positively, expressing interest in enhancing its collaboration with AUKUS by inviting the UK to participate as an observer—alongside Australia and Japan—in its annual military exercise with the USA in 2022.[17] However, Indonesia and Malaysia expressed somewhat reserved views.[18]

Taiwan Strait

The question of whether China might use force to achieve unification with Taiwan returned to prominence in 2021. In recent years China has increased its incursions into the Taiwan Strait, which it says are training exercises, to near daily frequency. In response Taiwan proposed a record $16.8 billion military budget in September 2021.[19] A month later, over a period of three days, 93 Chinese aircraft (the largest number ever to do so) flew into Taiwan's Air Defense Identification Zone, coinciding with the celebration of China's National Day.[20]

---

[14] Permal S., 'Beijing bolsters the role of the China Coast Guard', CSIS, 1 Mar. 2021; and National People's Congress of People's Republic of China, '中华人民共和国海警法' [Law of China Coast Guard], 22 Jan. 2021.

[15] Office of the Secretary of Defense, *Military and Security Developments Involving the People's Republic of China 2021* (US Department of Defense: Washington, DC, Nov. 2021); Erickson, A. S., Hickey, J. and Holst, H., 'Surging second sea force: China's maritime law enforcement forces, capabilities, and future in the gray zone and beyond', *Naval War College Review*, vol. 72, no. 2 (2019), Article 4; and Huang, K., 'How does converting a Chinese navy ship into a coastguard vessel aid Beijing's maritime mission?', *South China Morning Post*, 20 Feb. 2022.

[16] 'French nuclear submarine patrolled in South China Sea—Navy', Reuters, 9 Feb. 2021; Lendon, B., 'UK's HMS Queen Elizabeth aircraft carrier pictured in South China Sea', CNN, 30 July 2021; and 'First German warship in almost two decades enters South China Sea', Reuters, 15 Dec. 2021.

[17] 'UK military might observe renewed full-scale Balikatan drills in Philippines', Radio Free Asia, 14 Oct. 2021.

[18] Curran, B., 'AUKUS, China Sea tensions put Indonesia in tight spot, analysts say', VOA, 23 Oct. 2021; and Darmawan, A. R., 'AUKUS adds fuel to the South China Sea dispute', East Asia Forum, 1 Nov. 20212.

[19] Chung, L., 'Taiwan's biggest defence budget includes US$1.4 billion for new warplanes', *South China Morning Post*, 26 Aug. 2021; and Grevatt, J., 'Taiwan proposes defence budget increase for 2022', Janes, 27 Aug. 2021.

[20] 'Record Chinese aircraft sorties near Taiwan prompt US warning', *Wall Street Journal*, 3 Oct. 2021.

The Biden administration has embraced strategic ambiguity in its Taiwan policy, which theoretically allows the USA to work with both China and Taiwan. Without a formal commitment to Taiwan, however, there is a risk of uncertainty. This has led to debates over whether the USA should adopt greater strategic clarity and commit to defending Taiwan in the event of a Chinese attack.[21] On a practical level the US has demonstrated a clearer stance through selling arms to Taiwan, military training, and transiting through the Taiwan Strait during its Freedom of Navigation Operations in the SCS.[22]

The potential conflict over the Taiwan Strait has also received attention from Japan. In the Joint Statement of the US–Japan Security Consultative Committee in March 2021 the Taiwan issue was referenced for the first time since 1969.[23] This raised speculation as to whether Japan would align with the USA to defend Taiwan in the event of an attack by China. However, in April 2021 Japanese Prime Minister Yoshihide Suga clarified that Japan 'does not presuppose military involvement at all'.[24] Instead, Japan committed to expanded economic cooperation and political support for Taiwan.[25]

---

[21] Haass R. and Sacks D., 'The growing danger of US ambiguity on Taiwan', *Foreign Affairs*, 13 Dec. 2021.

[22] Ng, T., 'US warship transits South China Sea to challenge "unlawful maritime claims"', *South China Morning Post*, 20 May 2021; and Borger, J. and Davidson, H., 'Secret group of US military trainers has been in Taiwan for at least a year', *The Guardian*, 7 Oct. 2021.

[23] Ministry of Foreign Affairs of Japan, 'Japan–US Security Consultative Committee (Japan–US "2+2")', 16 Mar. 2021; and Shigeta, S. and Miki, R., 'Taiwan in US–Japan statement: show of resolve or diplomatic calculus?', Nikkei Asia, 18 Apr. 2021.

[24] Lo, K. and Huang, K., 'Japan expected to take position of "ambiguity" on Taiwan issue', *South China Morning Post*, 21 Apr. 2021.

[25] Liff A. P. and Hass R., 'Japan–Taiwan relations: A look back on 2021 and look ahead to 2022', Brookings, 20 Jan. 2021.

III. Armed conflict and peace processes in South Asia

IAN DAVIS AND JINGDONG YUAN

Security challenges in South Asia—Afghanistan, Bangladesh, Bhutan, India, Maldives, Nepal, Pakistan and Sri Lanka—include interstate rivalry, border disputes, nuclear weapon risks, terrorism, and internal threats arising from a combination of ethnic, religious and political tensions, often exacerbated by oppressive state security forces. Environmental and climate-related challenges include high levels of water stress, floods and droughts, and moderate to severe food insecurity.[1]

This section focuses on Afghanistan, and the armed conflicts between and within India and Pakistan. The long-running and devastating war in Afghanistan, and the territorial disputes involving India and Pakistan (as well as China) over the Kashmir region are crucial barometers for peace and stability in South Asia. The war in Afghanistan was set to end in time for the 20th anniversary of the terrorist attacks on the United States of 11 September 2001 with the agreed withdrawal of US troops. However, the withdrawal precipitated the rapid collapse of the Afghan government and the Taliban's triumphant return to power in Kabul. In terms of Kashmir, an uneasy stalemate largely prevailed in 2021. South Asia remains one of the regions most affected by armed conflicts involving non-state groups and/or state security forces.

Armed conflict in Afghanistan

The current phase of the war in Afghanistan (2001–21) effectively ended in August 2021 with the departure of foreign troops and the return to power of the Taliban.[2] However, some limited violence continued and the scale of fighting earlier in the year meant that it remained the deadliest armed conflict in the world in 2021 (in terms of conflict-related fatalities), and the humanitarian outlook continued to be stark. There were over 42 000 estimated fatalities over the course of the year, a 34 per cent increase from 2020 (see table 4.2). Most of these were combat related and involved Afghan government forces and the Taliban. Meanwhile, the United Nations Assistance Mission in Afghanistan (UNAMA) continued to document high levels of violence against civilians. It recorded 5183 civilian casualties (1659 fatalities and 3524 injuries) in the first half of 2021, a 47 per cent increase compared to

---

[1] Institute for Economics & Peace (IEP), *Ecological Threat Register 2020: Understanding Ecological Threats, Resilience and Peace* (IEP: Sydney, Sep. 2020).

[2] The Taliban, or 'students' in the Pashto language, is an ultraconservative political and religious faction that emerged in the early 1990s in Afghanistan (and northern Pakistan) following the withdrawal of Soviet troops from Afghanistan. For more on the Taliban see chapter 4, section III.

Table 4.2. Estimated conflict-related fatalities in Afghanistan, 2017–21

Event type	2017	2018	2019	2020	2021
Battles	26 325	31 744	26 251	22 566	31 769
Explosions/remote violence	9 596	10 894	14 445	7 545	9 027
Protests, riots and strategic developments	259	287	198	409	309
Violence against civilians	438	370	385	807	926
Total	36 618	43 295	41 279	31 327	42 031

Notes: The first available year for data on Afghanistan in the Armed Conflict Location & Event Data Project (ACLED) database is 2017. For definitions of event types, see ACLED, 'ACLED definitions of political violence and protest', 11 Apr. 2019.
Source: ACLED, 'Dashboard', accessed 25 Jan. 2022.

the first six months of 2020. This reversed the trend seen over the past four years of decreasing civilian casualties in the first six months of the year.[3]

The US withdrawal and the Taliban's return to power

Only days after the US and North Atlantic Treaty Organization (NATO) military forces withdrew from Afghanistan, the Taliban took control of major cities and installed themselves in the presidential palace in Kabul. In a televised speech on the 14 April 2021 President Biden announced that a US troop withdrawal from what he called the 'forever war' in Afghanistan would begin on 1 May and be completed by 11 September 2021—the 20th anniversary of the terrorist attacks on the United States in 2001 (see timeline in box 4.1).[4] Following an agreement between the USA and the Taliban in February 2020, both the United States and NATO had been gradually reducing their troop presence.[5] Under that process a deadline of 1 May 2021 had initially been agreed for a full troop withdrawal. However, with various further rounds of peace discussions and proposals in February–April 2021 failing to yield results, and violence escalating, Biden extended it to the 11 September 2021 (later adjusted to 31 August 2021).[6] Given that the mission was unsustainable

[3] United Nations Assistance Mission in Afghanistan (UNAMA), 'Afghanistan: Protection of civilians in armed conflict midyear update: 1 January to 30 June 2021', July 2021.

[4] White House, 'Remarks by President Biden on the way forward in Afghanistan', 14 Apr. 2021.

[5] 'Agreement for bringing peace to Afghanistan between the Islamic Emirate of Afghanistan which is not recognized by the United States as a state and is known as the Taliban and the United States of America', 29 Feb. 2020. For more information on the various international peace processes in Afghanistan see *SIPRI Yearbook 2019*, chapter 2, section III, pp. 62–65. For the main developments in Afghanistan in 2019–20 see *SIPRI Yearbook 2020*, pp. 92–94; and *SIPRI Yearbook 2021*, pp. 95–101.

[6] See e.g. Isachenkov, V., 'Russia hosts Afghan peace conference, hoping to boost talks', AP News, 18 Mar. 2021; Shalizi, H., 'Afghan leader proposes peace road map in three phases—document', Reuters, 4 Apr. 2021; and Gannon, K., 'US-backed Afghan peace meeting postponed as Taliban balk', ABC News, 21 Apr. 2021. On the US internal debate about extending the deadline see Afghanistan Study Group, *Afghanistan Study Group Final Report: A Pathway for Peace in Afghanistan* (United States Institute of Peace: Washington, DC, Feb. 2021); and Cooper, H., Schmitt, E. and Sanger, E., 'Debating exit from Afghanistan, Biden rejected generals' views', *New York Times*, 17 Apr. 2021.

without US forces, NATO and other troop-contributing countries agreed to follow suit.[7]

As the 1 May deadline passed, the Taliban launched a major offensive against Afghan security forces, prompting a rural collapse and a series of negotiated surrenders by Afghan government forces.[8] In June 2021, as the Taliban gained control of several more districts across the country, a US intelligence assessment suggested that the Afghan government could fall to the Taliban earlier than had previously been anticipated—as soon as six months after US troops withdrew.[9] Similarly, General Austin Miller, the US military commander in Afghanistan, warned that the country could descend into civil war after the withdrawal of US troops.[10] On 2 July 2021 US troops handed over Bagram Air Base, the hub of the US war effort inside Afghanistan, to the Afghan government, and on 8 July President Biden specified a new completion date of 31 August for the US withdrawal.[11] Talks between the Afghan government and the Taliban in Doha continued to be deadlocked, with an ascendant Taliban now having little incentive to negotiate a settlement.[12]

By early August 2021, amidst allegations of Taliban war crimes and further assassinations of government officials and military personnel, journalists and civil society activists, the Taliban reportedly controlled over half of Afghanistan, including many of the country's 34 provincial capitals.[13] With new intelligence assessments that the Afghan government could fall within 30 days, the Biden administration and other Western governments began preparing for a potential evacuation of their embassy staff and nationals.[14] The Taliban's rapid takeover of the country continued: by 13 August Kandahar

[7] Aburakia, M. N., 'Germany and UK to follow US out of Afghanistan', Deutsche Welle, 14 Apr. 2021; and North Atlantic Treaty Organization (NATO), 'North Atlantic Council Ministerial Statement on Afghanistan', Press release, 14 Apr. 2021.

[8] Zucchio, D. and Rahim, N., 'A wave of Afghan surrenders to the Taliban picks up speed', New York Times, 27 May 2021.

[9] Schnell, M., 'Intel analysis: Afghan government could collapse six months after troops withdraw', The Hill, 23 June 2021.

[10] Mitchell, C., 'Troop withdrawal from Afghanistan could lead to "civil war", says top US commander', The Times, 30 June 2021.

[11] 'Afghanistan: US troops depart Bagram Airfield after nearly 20 years', Deutsche Welle, 2 July 2021; and Miller, Z. and Madhani, A., '"Overdue": Biden sets Aug.31 for US exit from Afghanistan', AP News, 8 July 2021.

[12] 'Afghan rivals agree to meet again after inconclusive Doha talks', Al Jazeera, 18 July 2021; and Gannon, K., 'To reach a peace deal, Taliban says Afghan president must go', AP News, 24 July 2021.

[13] Varshalomidze, T. and Siddiqui, U., 'US, UK accuse Taliban of "war crimes" in south Afghan town', Al Jazeera, 2 Aug. 2021; Sediqi, A. Q., 'Gunmen kill two female Supreme Court judges in Afghanistan: Police', Reuters, 17 Jan. 2021; Stewart, P., Ali, I. and Shalizi, H., 'Afghan pilots assassinated by Taliban as US withdraws', Reuters, 9 July 2021; and Gannon, K. and Akhgar, T., 'Taliban kill Afghan media chief in Kabul, take southern city', AP News, 6 Aug. 2021.

[14] Gibbons-Neff, T. et al., 'US is sending 3,000 troops back to Afghanistan to begin evacuations', New York Times, 12 Aug. 2021.

Box 4.1. Timeline of key Afghanistan-related events, 1979–2021

1979–89	Occupying Soviet forces battle loosely allied US-backed insurgents, many of whom seek competing outcomes for Afghanistan when the Soviet withdrawal occurs, giving way to civil war.
1989–96	Civil war among Afghan warlords destroys the capital, Kabul, with the Taliban emerging as the most powerful faction.
1996	The ultraconservative Taliban seize power in Afghanistan.
11 Sep. 2001	Osama bin Laden and his al-Qaida network attack targets in the USA using commercial aircraft, killing 2997 people.
7 Oct. 2001	US President George W. Bush announces the US-led military intervention in Afghanistan (Operation Enduring Freedom), which leads to the eventual toppling of the Taliban.
Dec. 2001	The Bonn Agreement provides a foundation for US and NATO-backed state-building efforts, including the establishment of the International Security Assistance Force (ISAF), as authorized by the UN Security Council, and the installation of Hamid Karzai as Afghan president.
Mar. 2003	US-led coalition invades Iraq, beginning another lengthy military engagement (Iraq War 2003–11) parallel to the Afghanistan conflict.
11 Aug. 2003	Amid increasing violence, NATO takes over lead of ISAF, which is mandated by the UN. The effort is NATO's first-ever commitment outside of Europe.
2006	NATO expands its peacekeeping operation to the southern portion of the country.
2009	US President Barack Obama announces a temporary 'troop surge' to Afghanistan.
2011	Responsibility for security is gradually transitioned from ISAF to Afghan forces. On 2 May Barack Obama announces the death of Osama bin Laden in Pakistan following a raid by US Special Forces.
Summer 2013	Afghan forces take the lead for security operations across the country.
2014–15	The security transition process is completed and Afghan forces assume full security responsibility at the end of 2014 (and the end of the ISAF mission). NATO launches a new, smaller non-combat mission ('Resolute Support') on 1 January 2015 to provide further training, advice and assistance to Afghan security forces and institutions.
2017	President Obama abandons plans to withdraw US forces by the end of his presidency and maintains 5500 troops in Afghanistan when he leaves office.
July 2018	The USA enters official negotiations with the Taliban without involving the elected Afghan government or NATO partners.
Feb. 2020	The USA and the Taliban sign the Doha Agreement, in which the former promises to fully withdraw its troops by May 2021 and the latter commits to conditions, including stopping attacks on US and coalition forces (but not Afghan government forces). The agreement receives unanimous backing from the UN Security Council and is welcomed by NATO.
Sep. 2020	Intra-Afghan peace talks begin in the Qatari capital, Doha, but soon stall.

| 14 Apr. 2021 | President Joe Biden says the USA's longest war will end and troops will be withdrawn by 11 September, the 20th anniversary of the terrorist attacks on the United States in 2001. |
| June–Aug. 2021 | The Taliban make rapid battlefield gains across the country and the takeover is completed on 15 August with the capture of Kabul. The US troop withdrawal is completed on 30 August, marking the end of the 2001–21 war in Afghanistan. |

and Herat, two of Afghanistan's largest cities, had fallen, and by 14 August only Kabul and Jalalabad remained under Afghan government control.[15]

On 15 August the Taliban captured Kabul and claimed victory after President Ashraf Ghani fled the country.[16] President Biden defended the Afghanistan withdrawal and blamed the rapid Taliban takeover on the Afghan army's unwillingness to fight.[17] Subsequent reporting suggested that the Afghan government's collapse was accelerated by an undercover network of Taliban operatives that had infiltrated government ministries and other state-backed organizations.[18] In the days and weeks that followed, the USA and its NATO allies and partners sought to evacuate thousands of their personnel and partners from Kabul International Airport, which was overrun with thousands of Afghans attempting to flee. Around 6000 US soldiers were deployed to the airport to provide security and restore order. In chaotic scenes reminiscent of the US withdrawal from Saigon at the end of the Vietnam War in 1975, Afghans were seen clinging to a US Air Force plane as it attempted to take off.[19] President Biden rejected requests by European allies to extend the withdrawal deadline for US troops beyond 31 August.[20]

With this final deadline looming, two final tragic incidents occurred to bookend the war: first, attacks on Kabul airport on 26 August by the Islamic State's Afghan affiliate, Islamic State Khorasan Province (ISKP), killed as many as 200 Afghans seeking to flee the country, as well as 13 US soldiers; and second, three days later, the USA carried out a drone strike that killed

---

[15] 'Kandahar falls, Taliban on way to Kabul's gates' *Hindustan Times*, 14 Aug. 2021; and Graham-Harrison, E. and Savage, M., 'Last major Afghan city in the north falls to the Taliban', *The Guardian*, 14 Aug. 2021.

[16] 'Afghanistan conflict: Kabul falls to Taliban as president flees', BBC News, 16 Aug. 2021; and 'Afghan president says he left country to avoid bloodshed', Reuters, 15 Aug. 2021.

[17] White House, 'Remarks by President Biden on Afghanistan', 16 Aug. 2021. On the rapid disintegration of the Afghan Airforce see Stewart, P., 'Special report: Pilots detail chaotic collapse of the Afghan Air Force', Reuters, 29 Dec. 2021.

[18] Trofimov, Y. and Stancati, M., 'Taliban covert operatives seized Kabul, other Afghan cities from within', *Wall Street Journal*, 28 Nov. 2021.

[19] Harding, L. and Doherty, B., 'Kabul airport: Footage appears to show Afghans falling from plane after takeoff', *The Guardian*, 16 Aug. 2021. On analogies between Afghanistan and Vietnam see Gawthorpe, A., 'Afghanistan and the real Vietnam analogy', *The Diplomat*, 18 Aug. 2021.

[20] Landler, M. and Shear, M. D., 'Biden sticks to Afghan deadline, resisting pleas to extend evacuation', *New York Times*, 24 Aug. 2021.

10 civilians—not Islamic State militants as US officials initially claimed[21] (the Pentagon later acknowledged a 'breakdown in process' in the errant strike but nothing that called for 'personal accountability').[22] The last US plane departed from Kabul on 31 August and President Biden declared the war 'over', while repeating his earlier vow to continue to 'hunt down' the Islamic State. He also framed the evacuation effort as an historic accomplishment that resulted in more than 120 000 people being evacuated from Afghanistan.[23] Nonetheless, hundreds of US and allied citizens, as well as tens of thousands of vulnerable Afghans who worked with the international community, remained in the country and faced an uncertain fate.[24]

The Taliban announced their interim government on 7 September—an all-male, mostly Pashtun assortment of veterans from the 1990s Taliban govern-ance and leaders in the 20-year war—and also seized Panjshir province, the last armed opposition in Afghanistan.[25] By the end of 2021 no government had formally recognized the Taliban, although several states were expected to do so in the near future.[26] Moreover, several official inquiries were underway within the USA and NATO to assess the lessons learnt from the intervention, and there was a growing literature on the causes of the Western nation-building failures in Afghanistan.[27] An inquiry by the International Criminal Court into alleged crimes committed by the Taliban and the Islamic State was also pending.[28] One area of uncertainty was the potential impact of the Taliban's success on other Islamist insurgents around the world and the wider 'global war on terrorism'.[29]

---

[21] Sprunt, B., 'Biden pledges to strike back after attack kills 13 US service members in Kabul', NPR, 26 Aug. 2021; Smith, D., 'US admits Kabul strike killed 10 civilians and not Islamic State militants', The Guardian, 17 Sep. 2021; and Borger, J., '"Honest mistake": US strike that killed 10 Afghan civilians was legal—Pentagon', The Guardian, 4 Nov. 2021.

[22] Schmitt, E., 'No US troops will be punished for deadly Kabul strike, Pentagon chief decides', New York Times, 13 Dec. 2021.

[23] White House, 'Remarks by President Biden on the end of the war in Afghanistan', 31 Aug. 2021.

[24] Pikulicka-Wilczewska, A., 'Under Taliban rule: Calm chaos prevails in Kabul', The Diplomat, 18 Sep. 2021.

[25] 'In power, the Taliban's divisions are coming to the fore', The Economist, 2 Oct. 2021; Bahiss, I., 'Afghanistan's Taliban extend their interim government', International Crisis Group, 28 Sep. 2021; and 'Hardliners get key posts in a new Taliban government', BBC News, 7 Sep. 2021.

[26] Anderson, S. R., 'History and the recognition of the Taliban', Lawfare, 26 Aug. 2021; and 'Afghan embassies don't recognise the Taliban', The Economist, 2 Oct. 2021.

[27] See e.g. Lamb, C., 'Chronicle of a defeat foretold: Why America failed in Afghanistan', Foreign Affairs, July/Aug. 2021; Miller, L., 'Biden's Afghanistan withdrawal: A verdict on the limits of American power', Survival, vol. 63 no. 3 (2021), pp. 37–44; Mehra, T. and Coleman, J., 'The fall of Afghanistan: A blow to counter-terrorism and rule of law efforts', International Centre for Counter-Terrorism (ICCT), 23 Aug. 2021; and Coll, S. and Entous, A., 'The secret history of the US diplomatic failure in Afghanistan', New Yorker, 10 Dec. 2021.

[28] Wintour, P., 'ICC asked to relaunch inquiry into Taliban and IS "war crimes"', The Guardian, 27 Sep. 2021.

[29] See e.g. International Crisis Group, 'How Islamist militants elsewhere view the Taliban's victory in Afghanistan', ICG Commentary, 27 Oct. 2021; and 'America's flight from Afghanistan will embolden jihadists around the world', The Economist, 28 Aug. 2021. On the implications for the future of international peace operations see chapter 2, section II, in this volume.

Consequences of the 20-year war and the outlook

Four multilateral peace operations were deployed to Afghanistan between 2001 and 2021, with the failure to deliver the planned political transformation proving immensely costly to the Afghan population.[30] During the 20-year conflict there were an estimated 176 000 direct war deaths (including 69 000 Afghan security forces, 53 000 opposition fighters, 46 000 Afghan civilians, 3500 coalition forces, 4000 US contractors, and 500 journalists and humanitarian workers). While an accurate accounting of the monetary cost of the war is difficult to determine, reliable estimates suggest around $2 trillion.[31]

The fallout from the Taliban takeover in Afghanistan left several lingering questions at the end of 2021 about the group's ability to govern and unify the country, the future of human rights and the role of women, and the likely response of regional powers and the rest of the international community. First, the Taliban faced a growing economic and humanitarian crisis driven by displacement, drought, the Covid-19 pandemic and an extreme dependency on external funds, much of which was suspended following their takeover. The beginning of 2022 saw 24.4 million people in Afghanistan requiring humanitarian need—more than half the population and four times greater than the number in 2019.[32] Moreover, more than 8 million people were on the cusp of famine.[33]

Second, the Taliban faced a rising threat from ISKP. In October and November 2021 ISKP carried out a series of attacks against Taliban security forces and civilian targets, and there remained a real possibility of these attacks mutating into a more widespread and powerful ISKP insurgency that could both challenge Taliban rule and threaten the USA.[34]

[30] See Pfeifer, C. and van der Lijn, J., 'Multilateral peace operations in Afghanistan between 2001 and 2021', SIPRI Topical Backgrounder, 16 Sep. 2021.

[31] Watson Institute for International and Public Affairs, Brown University, 'US costs to date for the war in Afghanistan', Aug 2021; and 'Afghanistan: What has the conflict cost the US and its allies?', BBC News, 3 Sep. 2021.

[32] UN Office for the Coordination of Humanitarian Affairs (UN OCHA), *Humanitarian Response Plan: Afghanistan 2022* (UN OCHA: Jan. 2022); Jamal, U., 'A humanitarian crisis looms over Afghanistan', *The Diplomat*, Issue 85, Dec. 2021; and International Crisis Group, *Beyond Emergency Relief: Averting Afghanistan's Humanitarian Catastrophe*, Asia Report no. 317 (International Crisis Group: Brussels, 6 Dec. 2021). On the impact of the pandemic in Afghanistan see Mercy Corps, *A Clash of Contagions: The Impact of COVID-19 on Conflict in Nigeria, Colombia and Afghanistan* (Mercy Corps: Portland, OR, June 2021).

[33] Carpenter, C., 'Western sanctions are condemning Afghanistan to famine', World Politics Review, 10 Dec. 2021; and Integrated Food Security Phase Classification (IPC), 'IPC Acute Food Insecurity Analysis, Sept. 2021–Mar. 2022', Oct. 2021.

[34] Gibbons-Neff, T., Sahak, S. and Shah, T., 'Dozens killed in ISIS attack on military hospital in Afghanistan's capital', *New York Times*, 2 Nov. 2021; Reuters, 'Islamic State in Afghanistan could have capacity to strike US next year', *The Guardian*, 26 Oct. 2021; and Giustozzi, A., 'The Taliban's homemade counterinsurgency', Royal United Services Institute (RUSI) Commentary, 4 Jan. 2022.

Third, the Taliban faced an ongoing challenge in terms of gaining international recognition. Although the group tried to project a more restrained image of its new government compared to its first time in power (1996–2001), promising rights for women and girls and some freedom of expression, reports suggested that such rights were in fact under attack and receding.[35] In turn, the international community was divided on how to deal with the Taliban. Western governments, for example, faced the dilemma of how to deliver humanitarian aid to the country without being seen to endorse the Taliban government, especially since economic support from some other regional powers—such as Russia and China—was likely to be less conditional.[36] The US government threatened to undertake 'over the horizon' attacks on ISKP in Afghanistan, while not ruling out cooperation with the Taliban in addressing the ISKP threat.[37] Hence, a spectrum of responses can be expected from the international community: from aid engagement and dialogue with the Taliban at one end to isolation, sanctions and even assistance to certain (non-ISKP) opponents at the other. During the Group of Twenty (G20) virtual summit in October 2021, for example, President Biden stressed that aid should be provided via independent international organizations and not directly to the Taliban, while the European Union stated any aid would be conditional on the Taliban's behaviour.[38]

Overall, therefore, many of the underlying causes and drivers of conflict in Afghanistan are likely to continue, with the prospects for peace in the country remaining low.

Territorial disputes in Kashmir between China, India and Pakistan

China–India border disputes

After the deadliest clashes in decades between China and India in Galwan Valley in June 2020, 2021 marked a year of relative stability in territorial disputes along the Line of Actual Control (LAC). Bilateral trade registered a historic high of $125 billion despite unresolved border disputes, the Covid-19

---

[35] See e.g. Nader, Z. and Ferris-Rotman, A., 'They stayed to fight the Taliban. Now the protesters are being hunted down', *The Guardian*, 4 Nov. 2021; and AFP, 'West condemns Taliban over "summary killings" of ex-soldiers and police', *The Guardian*, 5 Dec. 2021.

[36] On the agendas of regional powers, especially Russian and Chinese, vis-à-vis Afghanistan see International Crisis Group, 'With the Taliban back in Kabul, regional powers watch and wait', ICG Commentary, 26 Aug. 2021; Girard, B., 'The myth of China's "value-free" diplomacy: Afghanistan and beyond', *The Diplomat*, Issue 83, Oct. 2021; and Graham-Harrison, E., 'Russia holds high-profile Afghanistan talks with Taliban', *The Guardian*, 20 Oct. 2021.

[37] Burke, J., 'Biden's "over the horizon" counter-terrorism strategy comes with new risks', *The Guardian*, 18 Aug. 2021.

[38] 'Afghanistan crisis: G20 leaders pledge to avert economic catastrophe', BBC News, 12 Oct. 2021; and Council of the European Union, 'Council conclusions on Afghanistan', 15 Sep. 2021.

pandemic, Indian bans on Chinese apps and calls to boycott Chinese goods.[39] At the sidelines of the Shanghai Cooperation Organization (SCO) meeting in the Tajik capital of Dushanbe in September, the Chinese and Indian foreign ministers agreed on the importance of maintaining stability in the border region.[40] While periodic small-scale skirmishes occurred over the course of the year, no major border clashes took place. The 13th round of India–China Corps Commander level meeting was held on 10 October 2021—though little progress was made, both sides agreed to maintain communication and stability on the ground.[41] There were some indications that the Chinese People's Liberation Army (PLA) began a partial pull back from the Pangong Lake area in January–February, with satellite images showing forward positions being dismantled. However, a complete drawdown of forces has yet to be achieved.[42] The standoff at the Depsand Plains—where the PLA is also building infrastructure—continued, with each side seeking to block the other's access to key patrol points.[43]

Meanwhile, both China and India increased deployment of troops along the western (Ladakh) and eastern (Arunachal Pradesh) sectors of the disputed border. India tripled its troop numbers in the contentious eastern area of Ladakh to 50 000, including re-deploying an entire strike corps from its border with Pakistan. For its part, China maintained over 60 000 troops opposite Ladakh and continued to build up infrastructure allowing faster movement of its forces to the LAC.[44]

Perhaps the most significant development was the infrastructural construction on both sides of the LAC. China has maintained the lead in building roads, bridges, outposts and villages. A new bridge was built over the Pangong Lake linking the northern and southern banks, cutting the time for troop movements from about 12 to 3–4 hours.[45] Across from Arunachal Pradesh on the Chinese side of the LAC, enclaves of buildings have been constructed near the Doklam area, which in 2017 witnessed over 70 days of standoff between Chinese and Indian troops in the Bhutan–China–India

---

[39] Krishnan, A., 'India's trade with China crosses $125 billion, imports near $100 billion', *The Hindu*, 15 Jan. 2022; Bhalla, K., 'One year of Chinese apps ban—Indian alternatives take over TikTok', Business Insider India, 29 June 2021; and Nair, R., 'India's imports from China rise despite boycott calls, pandemic. But this may not last', The Print, 9 Aug. 2021.

[40] 'Chinese, Indian FMs agree to safeguard border peace, tranquility', Xinhuanet, 17 Sep. 2021.

[41] Government of India, Ministry of External Affairs, '13th round of India–China Corps Commander Level Meeting', 11 Oct. 2021.

[42] Pollock, J., 'Eyeball to eyeball at Pangong Tso: Why Sino–Indian tensions will continue', South Asian Voices, 6 May 2021.

[43] Peri, D., 'Patrol blocking in Depsang by both sides will take time to resolve', *The Hindu*, 27 July 2021.

[44] Mashal, M. and Kumar, H., 'For India's military, a juggling act on two hostile fronts', *New York Times*, 24 Sep. 2021; and ANI, 'China maintaining around 60,000 troops opposite Ladakh, Indian preparedness also at high level', *Times of India*, 3 Jan. 2022.

[45] Bhalla, A., 'Chinese construction of bridge on Pangong Lake on for two months, extremely close to LAC', *India Today*, 3 Jan. 2022.

trijunction area.[46] India, on the other hand, has also been constructing a network of tunnels, bridges and roads in Ladakh to enable rapid troop movements to the contested border areas.[47] The Modi government planned to develop sparsely populated areas through the roll-out of the Vibrant Villages Programme to counter similar efforts on the Chinese side, as well as to strengthen India's claims to disputed territories. According to Indian reports, under Phase 2 of the India–China Border Roads (ICBR) project, 32 roads will be built. The Indian defence minister recently inaugurated 63 bridges along the Sino–Indian border regions.[48]

In late December 2021 Beijing announced its decision to 'standardize' names of 15 places in Arunachal, which China calls 'Zangnan' (Southern Tibet), to reinforce its legitimate claims to an area currently under Indian administration.[49] Spanning over 90 000 square kilometres, the eastern sector is the largest disputed territory between the two countries and is increasingly assuming greater geopolitical significance for China.[50] In recent years China has sped up infrastructure construction in the border regions, including building over 600 'model Xiaokang villages' (moderately prosperous villages) since 2017 and providing $1 billion in subsidies to residents living in the border region, as well as for regional development.[51] In response India stepped up its infrastructure development in Arunachal, with $150 million allocated in 2021.[52] Clearly, both Beijing and New Delhi have sought to keep open conflicts under control, while at the same time continuing—even intensifying—efforts to improve infrastructure in the border regions and strengthen military deployments. This has become the new normal in how the two countries manage their territorial disputes.

India–Pakistan disputes over Kashmir

India and Pakistan began 2021 with a United Arab Emirates (UAE)-brokered ceasefire announced in late February. For the first time the two countries'

---

[46] 'Satellite images show Chinese infrastructure in Arunachal Predash and near Doklam: Reports', Scroll.in, 18 Nov. 2021.

[47] 'India hastens to build strategic Ladakh tunnel amid China conflict', Deutsche Welle, 15 Nov. 2021.

[48] Singh, J., 'India to accelerate construction of roads along Chinese border: Sources', *India Today*, 17 June 2020; Bhaumik, A., 'India to have "viberant" border villages to counter China's territorial claims', *Deccan Herald*, 1 Feb. 2022; and Rajagopalan, R. P., 'Unabating tension with China spurs India's border infrastructure efforts', *The Diplomat*, 1 Jul 2021.

[49] Liu, C., 'China standardizes names of 15 more places in Zangnan "based on sovereignty, history"', *Global Times*, 30 Dec. 2021.

[50] Panda, J., 'Arunachal Predash in Beijing's security calculus: Watching the Eastern Sector of the Sino–Indian border', South Asian Voices, 27 Jan. 2022.

[51] Press Trust of India, 'China increases subsidies for residents living close to Indian border in Tibet', *Hindustan Times*, 10 Sep. 2017.

[52] Singh, V., 'Centre clears over ₹ 1,100 crore for more roads in Arunachal', *The Hindu*, 18 Feb. 2021.

militaries issued a joint statement after talks,[53] agreeing to the 'strict observance of the truce along the Line of Control' and to use the hotline to communicate and 'resolve potential misunderstandings'.[54] Subsequent reports suggested that senior intelligence officers from the two countries held secret talks in Dubai in January 2021,[55] with this back-channel diplomacy facilitating dialogue on a roadmap towards normalization after two years of intense conflict and confrontation.[56] The UAE's mediation role between the two nuclear-armed South Asian states was further confirmed when the Gulf country invited the Indian and Pakistani foreign ministers for separate talks in April.[57]

The February ceasefire was the first such agreement since 2003, although analysts doubted its sustainability given the many failures over the past seven decades of conflict. One promising sign was the significant drop in the number of ceasefire violations along the Line of Control (LOC), from more than 4645 in 2020 to around 592 in 2021.[58] The thaw also resulted in India and Pakistan issuing assignment visas to each other's diplomats after a gap of 28 months.[59] There were also reports that, having undergone a diplomatic downgrading in 2019, their respective high commissioners could be reinstated to the other's capital.[60] The Permanent Indus Commission held its first meeting in three years on water-related issues, as mandated by the 1960 Indus Water Treaty, and for the first time in history there was discussion of Indian armed forces participating in the SCO-sponsored joint military exercises in Pakistan.[61]

The ceasefire also appeared to open further dialogue opportunities. Both Pakistani Prime Minister Imran Khan and Pakistani Chief of Army Staff General Bajwa called for peace and trade with India, emphasizing that the two countries needed to bury the past and move forward. However,

---

[53] Sen, S. R., 'UAE brokering secret India–Pakistan peace roadmap: Officials', Bloomberg, 22 Mar. 2021; and 'For first time in 18 years, India, Pakistan agree to "strictly" observe LoC ceasefire', The Wire, 25 Feb. 2021.

[54] Masood, S., Mashal, M. and Humar, H., 'Pakistan and India renew pledge cease-fire at troubled border', New York Times, 7 Oct. 2021.

[55] Reuters, 'Indian and Pakistani intelligence officials held secret talks in Dubai to break Kashmir stand-off', South China Morning Post, 15 Apr. 2021.

[56] Reuters, 'India and Pakistan held secret talks to try to break Kashmir impasse', CNBC, 14 Apr. 2021.

[57] Basu, N., 'Jaishankar, Qureshi in Abu Dhabi as UAE seeks "functional" ties between India, Pakistan', The Print, 17 Apr. 2021.

[58] Shah, K., 'Will the ceasefire on India Pakistan border sustain?', Observer Research Foundation, 29 Sep. 2021; and Pande, A., 'The new "thaw" between Pakistan and India in context', The Hill, 22 Mar. 2021.

[59] ANI, 'India, Pakistan issue diplomatic visas to each other after 28 months', Economic Times, 24 Aug. 2021.

[60] Basu, N., 'India, Pakistan could upgrade diplomatic ties, Delhi may let SAARC meet happen in Islambad', The Print, 25 Feb. 2021.

[61] Chakravarty, P., 'Signs of thaw between India, Pakistan as border ceasefire holds', RFI, 13 Apr. 2021; and Rej, A., 'India–Pakistan ceasefire details emerge—along with possibility of joint military exercises', The Diplomat, 23 Mar. 2021.

Table 4.3. Estimated conflict-related fatalities in India, 2016–21

Event type	2016	2017	2018	2019	2020	2021
Battles	1 008	811	1 216	576	660	468
Explosions/remote violence	69	64	157	114	15	37
Protests, riots and strategic developments	282	209	240	309	320	193
Violence against civilians	303	319	536	534	294	291
Total	**1 662**	**1 403**	**2 149**	**1 533**	**1 289**	**989**

Notes: The first available year for data on India in the Armed Conflict Location & Event Data Project (ACLED) database is 2016. For definitions of event types, see ACLED, 'ACLED definitions of political violence and protest', 11 Apr. 2019.
Source: ACLED, 'Dashboard', accessed 26 Jan. 2022.

Bajwa put the onus on India to 'take the first step' and 'create a conducive environment, particularly in occupied Kashmir'.[62] While the reaction of Indian analysts to Pakistan's calls for reconciliation were lukewarm, there were strong economic and political reasons for this approach.[63] Pakistan's chronic economic malaise and the financial difficulties it faces after the USA cut its financial support by $440 million in 2019, alongside growing domestic unrest, have led to Pakistan's political and military leadership reassessing the importance of economic security. This may explain the growing interest in pursuing peace and trade with India, even without resolution of their territorial disputes, a model adopted by India and China in the late 1980s.[64]

Even so, deep-seated mistrust between India and Pakistan, and the two countries' diametrically opposed views of the Kashmir issue continue to be major obstacles to the improvement of bilateral relations.

India's internal armed conflicts and intercommunal tensions

In addition to the armed conflict zone in Kashmir, 2021 saw an ongoing non-international armed conflict in India between the Indian government and the Naxalites (Maoist rebels in rural areas of central and eastern India). The Maoist insurgency started in 1967 and entered its current phase in 2004.[65] While Maoist violence usually remains low intensity, a large-scale attack in central Chhattisgarh state in April 2021 killed 22 and injured over 30 security

---

[62] 'Read: Full text of Gen Bajwa's speech at the Islamabad Security Dialogue', *Dawn*, 18 Mar. 2021; and 'Time to bury the past and move forward: COAS Bajwa on Indo–Pak Ties', *Dawn*, 18 Mar. 2021.

[63] Asthana, S. B., 'Pakistan seeking peace with India: Is it for real?', WION, 2 Apr. 2021.

[64] Raghavan, P., 'Explained: Why is Pakistan lifting its ban on Indian imports?', *Indian Express*, 3 Apr. 2021.

[65] On the history of the conflict see Sahoo, N., *Half a Century of India's Maoist insurgency: An Appraisal of State Response*, ORF Occasional Paper 198 (Observer Research Foundation: New Dehli, June 2019).

forces personnel in the deadliest Naxalite attack on Indian security forces since 2017.[66]

While there were several low-level insurgencies in the north-east of India in 2021, attacks by insurgent groups were rare. In Nagaland, peace talks were initiated in 1997 between the Indian government and the National Socialist Council of Nagaland-Isak-Muivah (NSCN-IM)—the main separatist group in Nagaland—and the Naga National Political Groups. A framework agreement was reached in 2015, but talks stalled in 2020 and the deadlock remained unbroken in 2021.[67] The killing of 14 civilians by the Indian army in Nagaland on 4 December 2021 increased tensions and led to calls for the repeal of the 1958 Armed Forces (Special Powers) Act.[68]

Intercommunal (mainly Hindu–Muslim) tensions remained a key security issue in India in 2021, with discrimination against Muslims reportedly having increased significantly in recent years.[69] In addition, a wave of farmers' protests over reforms to the agricultural sector led to periodic violence during the year (and the subsequent repeal of the farm laws).[70] Overall, conflict-related fatalities in India in 2021 fell for the third year in a row (see table 4.3), with almost 50 per cent of battle-deaths occurring in Jammu and Kashmir (see above).

Pakistan's internal armed conflicts

The Pakistan government is involved in low-level non-international armed conflicts with various armed groups acting within its territory, particularly Taliban-affiliated groups in the north-western Khyber Pakhtunkhwa province and Baloch separatist fighters in the south-western province of Balochistan. In both these provinces violence increased in 2021, indicating a resurgence of both the Tehreek-i-Taliban Pakistan (TTP) and the Baloch separatist movement. Battle-related fatalities and deaths in Pakistan have declined considerably since the 2013–15 period (when total annual conflict-

---

[66] 'Indian security personnel killed after ambush by Maoists', Al Jazeera, 4 Apr. 2021.

[67] Tiwary, D. and Roy, E., 'Explained: Why has peace process for Naga Accord been stuck, what is the way forward?', Indian Express, 13 Oct. 2021.

[68] The 1958 Armed Forces (Special Powers) Act is in force in Jammu and Kashmir, Nagaland and parts of Manipur, Assam and Arunachal Pradesh. It gives extra-judicial powers to the Indian security forces in designated disturbed areas. Kalita, P., 'After killing of civilians, chorus against "draconian" armed forces law gets louder', Times of India, 6 Dec. 2021.

[69] See e.g. Maskara, S., 'Cow protection legislation and vigilante violence in India', Armed Conflict Location & Event Data Project (ACLED), 3 May 2021; and Alam, A., '"Shown their place": Muslim livelihoods under attack in India', Al Jazeera, 27 Sep. 2021.

[70] Bozhinova, K., Satre, J. and Rajagopal, S., 'An unlikely success: Demonstrations against farm laws in India', ACLED, 17 Dec. 2021; and Aswani, T., 'India's farmers signal lack of trust in Modi government', The Diplomat, 22 Nov. 2021.

Table 4.4. Estimated conflict-related fatalities in Pakistan, 2016–2021

Event type	2016	2017	2018	2019	2020	2021
Battles	1 173	891	479	630	522	784
Explosions/remote violence	815	668	410	185	151	262
Protests, riots and strategic developments	40	16	44	14	50	83
Violence against civilians	188	150	293	328	102	249
Total	**2 216**	**1 725**	**1 226**	**1 157**	**825**	**1 378**

Note: For definitions of event types, see Armed Conflict Location & Event Data Project (ACLED), 'ACLED definitions of political violence and protest', 11 Apr. 2019.
Source: ACLED, 'Data export tool', accessed 24 Jan. 2022.

related deaths were estimated to have averaged 4800) but witnessed an uptick in 2021 (see table 4.4).[71]

The current phase of the Baloch insurgency started in 2003, but has been at a relatively low level since 2012. Baloch separatist groups have increasingly targeted the China–Pakistan economic corridor, prompting Prime Minister Imran Khan to pledge to start talks with the groups.[72] By the end of the year, however, there was little sign of such talks having commenced.[73]

There were concerns that the Taliban takeover of Afghanistan would embolden Islamic militant groups in Pakistan, such as the TTP, which had already stepped up attacks against the Pakistani security forces, as well as other targets.[74] An attack on a bus in July that killed 10 Chinese workers and 3 Pakistanis was attributed to the TTP.[75] However, the Pakistan government also sought to use the influence of the Afghan Taliban over the TTP to start a reconciliation process, and in November 2021 a one-month ceasefire was agreed.[76] However, the ceasefire ended on 8 December, with domestic opposition to the reconciliation process meaning its future remained uncertain as of the end of 2021.[77]

---

[71] See also Pak Institute for Peace Studies (PIPS), 'Pakistan security report 2021', *Conflict & Peace Studies*, vol. 14, no. 1 (Jan.–June 2022).

[72] Sheikh, S. R., 'Pakistan seeks peace with anti-China Baloch rebels', *Asia Times*, 17 July 2021; and Haq, R., 'Baloch leaders sceptical of govt's plan for dialogue with insurgents', *Dawn*, 9 July 2021.

[73] PIPS (note 71), pp. 35–36.

[74] Ellis-Petersen, H. and Baloch, S. M., 'Pakistan divided over success of Taliban in Afghanistan', *The Guardian*, 17 Aug. 2021; Giustozzi, A., 'The resurgence of the Tehrik-i-Taliban Pakistan', RUSI Commentary, 12 Aug. 2021; and Ni, V., 'China condemns bombing of hotel hosting ambassador', *The Guardian*, 22 Apr. 2021.

[75] Masood, S. and Myers, S. L., 'Blast that killed Chinese workers in Pakistan was a terrorist attack, officials say', *New York Times*, 16 July 2021.

[76] Jamal, U., 'Imran Khan seals deal with the Tehreek-i-Taliban in Pakistan', *The Diplomat*, 16 Nov. 2021; and Shehzad, R., 'Govt, TTP agree to cease fire', *Express Tribune*, 8 Nov. 2021.

[77] Khan, I., 'TTP declares end to ceasefire', *Dawn*, 10 Dec. 2021; and PIPS (note 71), pp. 34–35.

IV. Armed conflict and peace processes in South East Asia

IAN DAVIS

This section focuses on the armed conflict in Myanmar, which was transformed from a low-intensity armed conflict (less than 1000 conflict-related fatalities) in 2020 to a major armed conflict (more than 10 000 conflict-related fatalities) in 2021. It also reviews the low-intensity subnational armed conflicts in Indonesia, the Philippines and Thailand. In the Philippines, when fatalities from the 'war on drugs' are added to those from the subnational armed conflict, the number of conflict-related deaths rises to over 1100. Some of Asia's most organized Islamist extremist groups are active in South East Asia, most notably in Indonesia and the Philippines.[1]

Armed conflict in Myanmar

Insurgencies have persisted for much of the past seven decades in Myanmar's Chin, Kachin, Kayah, Kayin, Mon, Rakhine and Shan states. Various armed insurgent groups have fought the country's armed forces, known as the Tatmadaw, over political control of territory, ethnic minority rights, and access to and control over natural resources. These long-running armed conflicts are now structured along complex ethnic and/or religious lines, and include about 20 ethnic armed groups and hundreds of armed militias mainly located in the country's border regions.[2] A military coup at the beginning of February 2021 ended the recent short period of partial civilian rule—the Myanmar military has ruled the country for most of the past 60 years—and led to escalating protests and violence throughout the country. According to the Armed Conflict Location & Event Data Project (ACLED), conflict-related deaths in Myanmar increased to over 11 000 in 2021, taking it into the category of a major armed conflict (see table 4.5).[3]

The military coup, civil disobedience and armed resistance

Having achieved a landslide victory in the November 2020 general election, Aung San Suu Kyi's National League for Democracy (NLD) was set to return to power for another five-year term. However, voting was cancelled in several areas dominated by ethnic minorities (most of Rakhine State and

---

[1] United Nations, Security Council, 'Twenty-eighth report of the Analytical Support and Sanctions Monitoring Team submitted pursuant to resolution 2368 (2017) concerning ISIL (Da'esh), Al-Qaida and associated individuals and entities', S/2021/655, 21 July 2021, pp. 16–17.

[2] International Crisis Group, *Identity Crisis: Ethnicity and Conflict in Myanmar*, Asia Report no. 312 (International Crisis Group: Brussels, 28 Aug. 2020).

[3] On the methodological challenges for the recording of political violence amidst the complexity of the disorder in Myanmar see Armed Conflict Location & Event Data Project (ACLED), 'ACLED methodology and coding decisions around political violence in Myanmar', Nov. 2019.

Table 4.5. Estimated conflict-related fatalities in Myanmar, 2016–21

Event type	2016	2017	2018	2019	2020	2021
Battles	277	297	150	1 248	381	6 203
Explosions/remote violence	69	42	36	85	127	2 554
Protests, riots and strategic developments	10	13	9	30	8	647
Violence against civilians	257	1 055	69	132	143	1 657
Total	**613**	**1 407**	**264**	**1 495**	**659**	**11 061**

Note: For definitions of event types, see Armed Conflict Location & Event Data Project (ACLED), 'ACLED definitions of political violence and protest', 11 Apr. 2019.

Source: ACLED, 'Dashboard', accessed 26 Jan. 2022.

parts of Shan, Karen and Kachin states), ostensibly due to security concerns. This disenfranchised an estimated 1.5 million people (out of approximately 38 million eligible to vote), in addition to about 1.1 million Rohingya who had long been denied citizenship and voting rights.[4] Moreover, the military-backed Union Solidarity and Development Party claimed widespread electoral fraud (without evidence) and called for a rerun of the elections with military involvement.[5] The NLD rejected such claims and international observers described the election as credible.[6] Nonetheless, civil–military relations remained strained at the beginning of 2021.

On 1 February 2021 Myanmar's military seized control of the country, detaining several leaders of the NLD—including President Win Myint and State Counsellor Aung San Suu Kyi—and declaring a state of emergency. Against a backdrop of widespread international condemnation (see below), the coup triggered nationwide mass protests and general strikes led by public sector workers and labour unions, which the military responded to using a range of repressive measures, including an internet blackout, online censorship and digital surveillance.[7] From 20 February 2021 onwards the military's response to the waves of protests and civil disobedience grew more violent, incorporating killings, torture and arbitrary detentions. Widespread human rights violations potentially amounting to crimes against humanity

[4] International Crisis Group, 'Majority rules in Myanmar's second democratic election', Asia Briefing no. 163, 22 Oct. 2020; Ratcliffe, R., 'Aung San Suu Kyi's party returns to power in Myanmar', *The Guardian*, 13 Nov. 2020; and Ratcliffe, R., 'Myanmar minorities, including Rohingya, excluded from voting in election', *The Guardian*, 6 Nov. 2020.

[5] Strangio, S., 'What's next for Myanmar's military proxy party?', *The Diplomat*, 26 Nov. 2020.

[6] See e.g. Carter Center, 'Election Observation Mission, Myanmar, General Election, November 8, 2020, preliminary statement', 10 Nov. 2020.

[7] 'Myanmar junta cracks down on crowds defying protest ban', AP News, 10 Feb. 2021; 'Myanmar coup: Protesters face up to 20 years in prison under new law', BBC News, 15 Feb. 2021; 'A boycott by bureaucrats is undermining the coup in Myanmar', *The Economist*, 18 Feb. 2021; and Beech, H., 'Myanmar's military deploys digital arsenal of repression in crackdown', *New York Times*, 1 Mar. 2021.

were documented.[8] According to Thailand-based human rights group Assistance Association for Political Prisoners, state security forces had killed 1384 people and detained over 11 200 protesters by the end of 2021.[9]

In April 2021 elected lawmakers ousted in the coup formed a National Unity Government (NUG)—a parallel administration in exile.[10] The vast majority of anti-coup demonstration events held in the first half of 2021 were peaceful on the part of the protesters, despite the excessive force used by the military.[11] However, the protests began to fragment, with some protesters turning to armed resistance in local anti-regime militias, known as 'people's defence forces' (PDFs). The NUG had called for the establishment of the PDFs on 5 May 2021 and while a significant proportion of them appeared to be politically aligned to the NUG, many also seemed to be operating autonomously.[12] Most of the subsequent fighting between the Tatmadaw and the lightly-armed PDFs took place in rural areas of Chin State and Sagaing Region, as well as Kayah State. The Tatmadaw responded with indiscriminate attacks on populated areas using artillery, airstrikes and helicopter gunships.[13]

On 7 September the NUG declared a 'people's defensive war' against the military junta, and later the same month claimed to have killed at least 1700 regime troops over the previous three months.[14] The remainder of the year saw the NUG and the Tatmadaw locked in an increasingly violent conflict, which included the indiscriminate use of weapons by the latter.[15] The formation of militias loyal to the Tadmadaw in the aftermath of the coup further complicated an already super-fragmented conflict landscape.[16]

---

[8] See e.g. Human Rights Watch, 'Myanmar: Coup leads to crimes against humanity', 31 July 2021; United Nations, Human Rights Council, 'Report of the Independent Investigative Mechanism for Myanmar', A/HRC/48/18, 5 July 2021; and United Nations, Human Rights Council, 'Written updates of the Office of the United Nations High Commissioner for Human Rights on the situation of human rights in Myanmar', A/HRC/48/67, 16 Sep. 2021.

[9] Since the military coup the Assistance Association for Political Prisoners has catalogued those killed and detained by the security forces. See their website: <https://aappb.org/>. See also multiple media reports, e.g. Mandhana, N., 'Myanmar protesters return after security forces kill at least 90 people', *Wall Street Journal*, 28 Mar. 2021; Solomon, F., 'Chinese factories burn in Myanmar's deadliest weekend of protests since coup', *Wall Street Journal*, 15 Mar. 2021; and 'Myanmar crackdown on protests, widely filmed, sparks outrage', AP News, 4 Mar. 2021.

[10] 'Opponents of Myanmar coup announce unity government', Al Jazeera, 16 Apr. 2021.

[11] Bynum, E., 'Myanmar's Spring Revolution', ACLED, 22 July 2021.

[12] 'Myanmar's shadow government forms People's Defense Force', The Irrawaddy, 5 May 2021.

[13] International Crisis Group, 'Taking aim at the Tatmadaw: The new armed resistance to Myanmar's coup', Asia Briefing no. 168, 28 June 2021.

[14] The NUG posted its declaration on its Facebook page on 7 Sep. 2021. See also 'Declaration of war necessary as international pressure fails: Myanmar shadow govt', The Irrawaddy, 9 Sep. 2021; and 'Over 1,700 Myanmar junta soldiers killed in past three months, civilian govt says', The Irrawaddy, 14 Sep. 2021.

[15] International Crisis Group, 'The deadly stalemate in post-coup Myanmar', Asia Briefing no. 170, 20 Oct. 2021; and AFP, 'Myanmar massacre: Two Save the Children staff among the dead', *The Guardian*, 28 Dec. 2021.

[16] Selth, A., 'Myanmar's military numbers', The Interpreter, 17 Feb. 2022.

A military-installed 'caretaker government' was announced on 1 August 2021, with Min Aung Hlaing given the position of prime minister and elections promised by August 2023.[17] In December 2021 Aung San Suu Kyi was sentenced by a military court to four years of detention for alleged incitement and breaching Covid-19 restrictions, although the sentence was swiftly reduced to two years by Min Aung Hlaing. Further charges were expected to be made in January 2022 in relation to illegal possession of walkie-talkies.[18]

Impact of the coup on the existing armed conflicts

Armed conflict also resumed or escalated between the Myanmar military and ethnic armed groups in several of the country's border regions.[19] In March–June 2021, for example, thousands fled to Thailand as a result of airstrikes on civilian settlements in Karen State and subsequent fighting between the Myanmar military and the Karen National Union (KNU), one of the main signatories to the 2015 Nationwide Ceasefire Agreement (NCA).[20] Some of the clashes were linked to anti-coup protests—the KNU, for example, supported the protests—while others appeared to be mainly related to territorial control of strategic areas, such as the fighting between the Kachin Independence Organisation, a non-signatory to the NCA, over control of the jade mines in Kachin State.[21] In addition, inter-ethnic unity between armed groups resisting the military has been undermined by territorial disputes and military clashes between such groups, particularly in Shan State.[22]

Until a temporary ceasefire was agreed in November 2020, the armed conflict between government forces and the ethnic Rakhine Arakan Army in western Myanmar had seen some of the most serious fighting in recent years.[23] Within days of the military coup the junta reaffirmed its commitment to the ceasefire, thereby enabling it to focus on the emerging PDFs. In November 2021, however, the ceasefire broke down, adding another battleground for the Myanmar military and a further serious challenge to the return of Rohingya refugees forcibly displaced in 2017.[24]

---

[17] International Crisis Group (note 15), pp. 9–10.

[18] AP News, 'Aung San Suu Kyi testifies in Myanmar court as lawyers barred from speaking about her case', *The Guardian*, 27 Oct. 2021; and 'Aung San Suu Kyi: Myanmar court sentences ousted leader in widely criticised trial', BBC News, 6 Dec. 2021.

[19] On the peace process in Myanmar see *SIPRI Yearbook 2021*, pp. 114–15.

[20] 'Thousands flee to Thailand after Myanmar's army's air strikes on villages: activist group, media', Reuters, 28 Mar. 2021; and 'Myanmar rebel group says has captured military base near Thai border', France 24, 27 Apr. 2021. On the NCA see *SIPRI Yearbook 2021*, p. 114.

[21] Global Witness, 'Jade and conflict: Myanmar's vicious circle', 29 June 2021.

[22] Bynum (note 11).

[23] United League of Arakan/Arakan Army, 'Statement no. 41/2020', 12 Nov. 2020; Office of the Commander-in-Chief of the Defence Services, 'Statement on ceasefire and eternal peace', 12 Nov. 2020; and International Crisis Group, 'From elections to ceasefire in Myanmar's Rakhine state', Asia Briefing no. 164, 23 Dec. 2020.

[24] AFP, 'UN's "deep concern" at Myanmar fighting between Rakhine rebels and military', *The Guardian*, 11 Nov. 2021.

The NUG has sought to build political and military alliances with the ethnic armed groups, including by promising a federal system for Myanmar, and a significant amount of political and military cooperation against the military regime was underway by the end of 2021.[25]

The international response

The coup was widely condemned by parts of the international community and the United Nations Security Council called for all those detained to be released.[26] In February the United States and several other states announced sanctions on the military leaders who directed the coup.[27] Additional US and European Union sanctions were imposed in late March, with the former also suspending all trade agreements and investment with Myanmar.[28]

The international diplomatic response was led by the Association of Southeast Asian Nations (ASEAN).[29] At a special summit organized by ASEAN in April 2021, which coup leader Min Aung Hlaing attended, a five-point plan to exit the crisis was agreed. This included an immediate cessation of violence, the delivery of humanitarian aid and the appointment of an ASEAN envoy to facilitate dialogue among the parties.[30] However, it took a further three months to appoint the envoy, who was then blocked from visiting Myanmar.[31] As a consequence of this lack of cooperation and failure to implement the plan, Min Aung Hlaing was excluded from the ASEAN summit on 26 October.[32] Overall, though, the effectiveness of the ASEAN-led diplomatic effort has been severely limited by its consensus-based non-interference approach, internal divisions and the refusal of the Myanmar military junta to cooperate.[33]

The question of who represents Myanmar at the UN—the military junta or the NUG—remained unresolved at the end of 2021.[34] China and Russia

---

[25] International Crisis Group, *Myanmar's Coup Shakes up its Ethnic Conflicts*, Asia Report no. 319 (International Crisis Group: Brussels), 12 Jan. 2022.

[26] United Nations, Security Council, 'Security Council press statement on situation in Myanmar', SC/14430, 4 Feb. 2021; and United Nations, Security Council, 'Statement by the President of the Security Council', S/PRST/2021/5, 10 Mar. 2021.

[27] 'Myanmar ruler calls for end to protests as US imposes sanctions', Reuters, 11 Feb. 2021; and 'UK and Canada impose sanctions on Myanmar generals after coup', Reuters, 18 Feb. 2021.

[28] 'US suspends all trade engagement with Myanmar until elected government returns', Reuters, 29 Mar. 2021; and 'EU and US sanctions step up pressure on Myanmar military over coup', Reuters, 22 Mar. 2021.

[29] For a brief description and list of members of ASEAN see annex B, section II, in this volume.

[30] 'ASEAN chairman's statement on the leaders meeting', Nikkei Asia, 24 Apr. 2021; and 'ASEAN "consensus" urges Myanmar junta to end violence', Nikkei Asia, 24 Apr. 2021.

[31] 'ASEAN appoints Brunei diplomat as envoy to Myanmar', Reuters, 4 Aug. 2021.

[32] Ministry of Foreign Affairs of Brunei, 'Statement of the Chair of the ASEAN Foreign Ministers' Meeting', 16 Oct. 2021; and Reuters, 'Asean summit starts with Myanmar junta excluded for ignoring peace deal', *The Guardian*, 26 Oct. 2021.

[33] Samet, O., 'There is no ASEAN consensus on Myanmar', *The Diplomat*, 22 June 2021.

[34] Nichols, M., 'UN committee agrees Taliban, Myanmar junta not allowed in UN for now', Reuters, 1 Dec. 2021.

remained Myanmar's two main foreign partners, while Japan and Thailand remained influential with regard to trade and investment.[35]

The humanitarian crisis

In addition to armed violence and regime oppression, Myanmar faced a growing country-wide humanitarian crisis characterized by deepening economic recession, collapsing healthcare, and surging poverty and food insecurity.[36] In November 2021 UN Emergency Relief Coordinator Martin Griffiths warned that the country's humanitarian situation was deteriorating, with more than 3 million people in need of life-saving aid.[37] At the end of 2021 over 320 000 people remained internally displaced due to violence since the military coup. This was in addition to the 340 000 people already living in protracted displacement in Rakhine, Chin, Shan and Kachin states.[38]

State-backed systematic persecution in 2017 forcibly displaced more than 700 000 Rohingya people—members of a predominantly Sunni Muslim ethnic group—from Rakhine State.[39] Continuing persecution and armed conflict led to further displacement, and as of the end of 2021 about 850 000 Rohingya remained in refugee camps in southern Bangladesh—the largest and densest refugee settlement in the world.[40] Insecurity for these refugees was also growing, with little prospect of repatriation and the Bangladesh government preparing to relocate thousands of them to a seasonally inundated island.[41]

Armed conflict in Indonesia

Sporadic attacks by groups associated with the Islamic State and al-Qaeda continued in Indonesia in 2021.[42] However, it was the long-running insurgency in Papua that was the focus of most of the combat-related armed violence in the country, including the death of Indonesia's top intelligence

---

[35] 'Japan's much-touted go-between has little sway over Myanamar junta', The Irrawaddy, 9 Sep. 2021; and Zhabina, A., 'China in post-coup Myanmar—closer to recognition, further from "Pauk-phaw"', PRIF Blog, 21 Dec. 2021.

[36] International Crisis Group (note 15), pp. 8–9.

[37] United Nations, 'Myanmar: 3 million in need of humanitarian aid, "world is watching" UN relief chief warns generals', UN News, 8 Nov. 2021.

[38] UN Office for the Coordination of Humanitarian Affairs (OCHA), 'Myanmar: Humanitarian update no. 14', 17 Jan. 2022.

[39] On the Rohingya crisis in 2017 see SIPRI Yearbook 2018, pp. 49–52. Also see Ahmed, I., 'Special issue on the Rohingya crisis: From the guest editor's desk', Asian Journal of Comparative Politics, vol. 5, no. 2 (2020), pp. 85–88; and Nishikawa, Y., 'The reality of protecting the Rohingya: An inherent limitation of the responsibility to protect', Asian Security, vol. 16, no. 1 (2020), pp. 90–106.

[40] Ahmed, K., 'UN quizzed over role in prison-like island camp for Rohingya refugees', The Guardian, 15 Oct. 2021.

[41] Hasnat, S. and Yasir, S., 'They were promised a new home. Then they tried to escape it', New York Times, 10 Oct. 2021.

[42] United Nations (note 1). On the domestic roots of Islamic State-inspired groups in Indonesia see Sumpter, C. and Franco, J., 'Islamist militancy in Indonesia and the Philippines: Domestic lineage and sporadic foreign influence', International Centre for Counter-Terrorism, 15 Sep. 2021.

official in the province in April 2021 and a subsequent troop surge by the Indonesia armed forces.[43] According to ACLED, there were 124 conflict-related deaths in Indonesia in 2021 (the same as in 2020), with 74 of these related to armed conflict (battles or explosions/remote violence).[44]

Armed conflict in the Philippines

Two intrastate armed conflicts emerged in the Philippines in the late 1960s: one in the Muslim-majority areas of the Mindanao region of the southern Philippines and another involving the New People's Army (NPA) of the Communist Party of the Philippines, concentrated mainly in rural areas across the country.[45] However, as in recent years, it was the war on drugs that appeared to result in the most fatalities during 2021.

The establishment in March 2019 of Bangsamoro Autonomous Region in the southern Philippines was a major step towards ending the almost 50-year Moro separatist conflict, although many challenges remained.[46] An 80-member Bangsamoro Transition Authority was appointed to govern the region until 2022, when elections for a Bangsamoro parliament and government were due to take place, and in October 2021 this political transition period was extended until 2025.[47] A small number of armed groups operating outside the peace process, some with links to the Islamic State, appeared to be in decline.[48]

Equally elusive, despite sporadic peace talks, has been the goal of ending the 50-year-old insurgency by the NPA—the armed wing of the Communist Party of the Philippines and its political umbrella organization, the National Democratic Front. Despite government forces claiming battlefield successes during the year, as of the end of 2021 there appeared to be no prospect of ending the insurgency.[49]

---

[43] Paddock, R. C. and Suhartono, M., 'Indonesian general is killed in rebel ambush, sparking fears of retaliation', *New York Times*, 27 Apr. 2021; Strangio, S., 'Indonesia deploys forces to troubled Papua region', *The Diplomat*, 5 May 2021; and James, R., '"We are living in a war zone": Violence flares in West Papua as villagers forced to flee', *The Guardian*, 11 May 2021.

[44] ACLED, 'Dashboard', accessed 26 Jan. 2022.

[45] For background on these two conflicts see Åkebo, M., 'Ceasefire rationales: A comparative study of ceasefires in the Moro and Communist conflicts in the Philippines', *International Peacekeeping*, vol. 28, no. 3 (2021), pp. 366–92.

[46] On key developments in the Philippines in 2019–20 see *SIPRI Yearbook 2020*, pp. 105–107; and *SIPRI Yearbook 2021*, pp. 115–17.

[47] Engelbrecht, G., 'The Philippines: Three more years for the Bangsamoro transition', International Crisis Group, 29 Oct. 2021.

[48] Yeo, K., 'Hungry and tired: The decline of militancy in Mindanao', The Strategist, 11 June 2021; and Yeo, K., 'How will the Taliban affect violent extremism in Mindanao?', *The Diplomat*, Issue 83, Oct. 2021. See also Sumpter and Franco (note 42).

[49] Broome, J., 'An end in sight for the Philippines' Maoist insurgency?', *The Diplomat*, 19 Feb. 2021; 'Philippines military says 16 communist rebels killed in raid', Reuters, 16 Aug. 2021; and Gomez, J., 'Key leader of decades-old insurgency in the Philippines is killed', *Los Angeles Times*, 21 Nov. 2021.

Table 4.6. Estimated conflict-related fatalities in the Philippines, 2016–21

Event type	2016	2017	2018	2019	2020	2021
Battles	898	2013	608	531	539	442
Explosions/remote violence	73	56	41	48	34	18
Protests/riots and strategic developments	9	4	4	4	20	7
Violence against civilians	3 546	2 294	1 453	1 120	893	672
Total	**4 526**	**4 367**	**2 106**	**1 703**	**1 486**	**1 139**

Notes: The first available year for data on the Philippines in the Armed Conflict Location & Data Project (ACLED) database is 2016. For definitions of event types, see ACLED, 'ACLED definitions of political violence and protest', 11 Apr. 2019.
Source: ACLED, 'Data export tool', accessed 27 Jan. 2022.

The war on drugs and contested casualty statistics

While the number of civilians killed in the Philippines in 2021 is uncertain and disputed, indications are that the government's war on drugs, initiated when President Duterte took office in 2016, continued to result in more deaths than the insurgencies (see table 4.6)—although, overall, conflict-related fatalities in the Philippines fell for the fifth year in a row. Concerns about the war on drugs are part of wider concerns about repression of human rights and the targeting of political opponents, activists and journalists.[50] According to the government the estimated death toll in the anti-drugs campaign between 1 July 2016 and 30 September 2021 was 6201, although ACLED estimated the figure to be at least 7742 (as of 12 November 2021) and domestic human rights groups suggest drug war killings could be up to four times higher than the government number.[51] In September 2021 the International Criminal Court (ICC) announced an investigation into alleged state crimes committed during the period between 2011 and March 2019, when the Philippines left the court. The ICC said that while relevant crimes appeared to have continued after that date, it was limited to investigating those suspected to have occurred while the Philippines was a member.[52]

---

[50] 'Philippines downgraded as civic freedoms deteriorate', CIVICUS Monitor, 8 Dec. 2020. On the linkages between the Covid-19 pandemic and state repression see Agojo, K. N. M., 'Policing a pandemic: Understanding the state and political instrumentalization of the coercive apparatus in Duterte's Philippines', *Journal of Developing Societies*, vol. 37, no. 3 (2021), pp. 363–86.
[51] The government's official numbers are periodically published under its #RealNumbersPH campaign on Facebook—see Philippine Drug Enforcement Agency, '#RealNumbers from July 01, 2016 to September 30, 2021'; and Kishi, R. and Buenaventura, T., 'The drug war rages on in the Philippines: New data on the civilian toll, state responsibility, and shifting geographies of violence', ACLED, 18 Nov. 2021.
[52] International Criminal Court, 'Situation in the Philippines: ICC Pre-Trial Chamber I authorises the opening of an investigation', Press release, 15 Sep. 2021; Engelbrecht, G., 'Philippines: The International Criminal Court goes after Duterte's drug war', International Crisis Group, 17 Sep. 2021; and Aspinwall, N., 'The ICC will probe Duterte. Will he get off scot-free?', *The Diplomat*, Issue 83, Oct. 2021.

Armed conflict in Thailand

The decades-old non-international armed conflict in the south of Thailand between the military government and various secessionist groups continued in 2021, but at lower levels of violence. ACLED recorded 66 conflict-related deaths in Thailand in 2021 (down from 102 in 2020 and the third consecutive year of decline), with 40 of these related to armed conflict (battles or explosions/remote violence).[53] More than 7000 people have been killed in the conflict since 2004.

Malaysian-brokered peace talks started in 2015 between the government and Mara Patani, an umbrella organization of Thai Malay secessionists groups. The most significant insurgent group—the National Revolutionary Front (Barisan Revolusi Nasional, BRN)—had been boycotting the talks, but in January 2020 the group met with government officials for the first time in a formal peace dialogue.[54] However, the talks stalled and by the end of 2020 state–insurgent violence had resumed. There was no resumption of face-to-face peace talks in 2021, although some technical-level discussions between the parties took place online (due to the Covid-19 pandemic). However, reports suggested that talks would resume in January 2022.[55]

Pro-democracy demonstrations and other protests continued in Thailand in 2021, although these were more sporadic than the 2020 protests due to increased repression. The demands for constitutional and monarchical reform also expanded to criticism of the government's handling of the Covid-19 pandemic and the impact on the economy.[56] The continuation of emergency rules and police crackdowns on activists failed to halt the protests.

[53] ACLED, 'Dashboard', accessed 27 Jan. 2022.

[54] International Crisis Group, *Southern Thailand's Peace Dialogue: Giving Substance to Form*, Asia Report no. 304 (International Crisis Group: Brussels, 21 Jan. 2020). On the role of religion as a motivating frame within the BRN see Chalermsripinyorat, R., 'Islam and the BRN's armed separatist movement in Southern Thailand', *Small Wars & Insurgencies*, vol. 32, no. 6 (2021), pp. 945–76.

[55] Pathan, D., 'Thailand: Could one of Asia's deadliest conflicts be coming to an end?', United States Institute of Peace, 7 Sep. 2021; and Azmi, H. and Ahmad, M., 'Sources: Thailand, BRN rebels to resume in-person peace talks next month', Benar News, 23 Dec. 2021.

[56] Kuhakan, J. and Setboonsang, C., 'Thai anti-govt protesters clash with police in Bangkok', Reuters, 7 Aug. 2021; and Ratcliffe, R., '"Everything has exploded now": On the streets with Thailand's protesters', *The Guardian*, 24 Sep. 2021.

5. Armed conflict and peace processes in Europe

Overview

Two armed conflicts were active in Europe in 2021: the interstate border conflict between Armenia and Azerbaijan for control of Nagorno-Karabakh, and the ongoing, low-intensity, internationalized, subnational armed conflict in Ukraine. In late 2021, a second large-scale Russian military build-up near Ukraine's borders raised fears of the conflict in Ukraine escalating into a major interstate armed conflict (see section II).

After being on a low simmer for months, the armed conflict in Donbas escalated again in March and April 2021 as Russian-backed rebels and Ukrainian government forces clashed in violation of the July 2020 ceasefire agreement. Tensions further increased as Russia deployed tens of thousands of additional troops along the border with Ukraine in late March–early April 2021. In November, with peace talks stalled, Russia once again deployed thousands of troops near its borders with Ukraine, having only partially pulled back its forces from the April build-up. Though Russia's motives and objectives appeared deliberately ambiguous, President Vladimir Putin seemed to be using the threat of invasion to secure both a more acquiescent Ukraine and extensive changes in the European security order, as well as project strength at home.

The Ukraine conflict was the focal point for persistent tensions between Russia and the rest of Europe over several issues, including cyberattacks, the treatment of Russian opposition leader Alexei Navalny, the political crisis in Belarus, and strengthening bilateral security cooperation between China and Russia. In December 2021, these tensions culminated with Russia tabling security demands in two draft treaties due to be discussed over a series of early January 2022 meetings with the United States and the North Atlantic Treaty Organization (NATO) (see section I). Russia stressed that failure to endorse the documents would lead to an unspecified but serious military response, though there was very little in the texts that was likely to be accepted by either the USA or NATO.

Elsewhere in Europe, tensions persisted in largely quiescent but unresolved conflicts in the post-Soviet space, the Western Balkans and Cyprus. The November 2020 ceasefire between Armenia and Azerbaijan largely held in areas where Russian peacekeepers were deployed, but in other areas sporadic clashes and ceasefire violations kept it above the armed conflict threshold. There were also serious and complex security challenges in Europe's southern neighbourhood and beyond, especially in the eastern Mediterranean. There were 19 multilateral peace operations active in Europe in 2021, one more than in the previous year.

IAN DAVIS

I. Key general developments in the region

IAN DAVIS

There were three countries with active armed conflicts on their territory in Europe in 2021: the low-intensity interstate border conflict between Armenia and Azerbaijan for control of Nagorno-Karabakh (see below), and the low-intensity, internationalized, subnational, armed conflict in Ukraine.[1] In Ukraine, the collapse of peace talks and a second large-scale Russian military build-up near Ukraine's borders in late 2021 raised fears of the simmering conflict boiling over into a major interstate armed conflict (see section II).

Although most of Europe has been relatively peaceful for at least the past two decades, two main areas of tension remain (as explained in more detail below): persistent tensions between Russia and most of the rest of Europe; and several long-standing unresolved conflicts, especially, but not limited to, the post-Soviet space and the eastern Mediterranean.

As was the case in 2020 the impact of Covid-19 on the two armed conflicts in Europe appeared minimal, although the pandemic's direct and indirect impacts on conflict dynamics and European security more broadly may take years to unfold. In addition to large numbers of deaths, the pandemic continued to require restrictions on freedom of movement, although both mortality rates and policy responses to Covid-19 varied widely between European countries.[2]

There were 19 multilateral peace operations in Europe in 2021, one more than in the previous year. The Russian–Turkish Joint Monitoring Centre (RTJMC) opened in Azerbaijan and the OSCE Observer Mission at the Russian Checkpoints Gukovo and Donetsk was discontinued. The number of personnel deployed increased by 0.6 per cent, from 8063 on 31 December 2020 to 8108 on 31 December 2021.[3]

The interstate armed conflict between Armenia and Azerbaijan

Having flared up again in 2020, the interstate Armenia–Azerbaijan armed conflict over the disputed territory of Nagorno-Karabakh was nominally ended by a Russian-brokered truce in November 2020.[4] The six weeks

---

[1] For conflict definitions and typologies see chapter 2, section I, in this volume.

[2] See e.g. Emric, E. and Niksic, S., 'As deaths rise, vaccine opponents find a foothold in Bosnia', AP News, 30 Sep. 2021; and Higgins, A., 'In Romania, hard-hit by Covid, doctors fight vaccine refusal', *New York Times*, 8 Nov. 2021.

[3] On the European Union's civilian crisis management in Europe and beyond see Smit, T., 'Strengthening EU civilian crisis management: The civilian CSDP Compact and beyond', SIPRI Insights on Peace and Security no. 2021/5, Nov. 2021. For a full list of multilateral peace operations see chapter 2, section III, table 2.6.

[4] On the history of the conflict see *SIPRI Yearbook 2021*, pp. 127–29; and Broers, L., *Armenia and Azerbaijan: Anatomy of a Rivalry* (Edinburgh University Press: Edinburgh, 2019).

of fighting had resulted in Azerbaijan regaining control of about a third of Nagorno-Karabakh, as well as most of the adjacent territories.[5] However, while the truce largely held in 2021, the situation remained unstable, with battle-related deaths from sporadic clashes and ceasefire violations keeping it above the threshold for an armed conflict. According to the Armed Conflict Location & Event Data Project (ACLED), there were 57 conflict-related deaths in 2021 (24 in Armenia and 33 in Azerbaijan), compared to over 7000 in 2020.[6]

Renewed clashes in 2021

Under the November 2020 ceasefire agreement, Armenia and Azerbaijan agreed to the deployment of 1960 Russian peacekeepers. In January 2021 Russia and Turkey opened a joint ceasefire-monitoring centre in Azerbaijan, using drones to track violations.[7] The ceasefire was largely preserved in areas where military personnel were stationed. Between January and June 2021, for example, only 33 cross-border clashes took place, compared to 2600 during the same period in 2020.[8] These clashes mainly occurred where there were no Russian forces, including along parts of the Azerbaijani–Armenian border. With opposing Armenian and Azerbaijan military positions only 30–100 metres apart—before the 2020 war, they were hundreds of metres apart—the front line's new topography is more unstable.[9] Border clashes and ceasefire violations escalated significantly in July 2021 and again in November.[10]

In January 2021, Russian President Vladimir Putin hosted the first post-war meeting between the leaders of Armenia and Azerbaijan, with an agreement reached to create new transportation infrastructure aimed at 'unblocking' the region's many closed borders.[11] While representatives from Russia, Armenia and Azerbaijan met again in August to discuss progress on transport and communications issues, little other diplomatic progress was made during the year. In particular, the Organization for Security and Co-operation in Europe (OSCE) Minsk process remained in limbo after Azerbaijani President Ilham

---

[5] On the armed conflict in 2020 see *SIPRI Yearbook 2021*, pp. 129–32. On the role of arms transfers in the conflict see Wezeman, P. D., Kuimova, A. and Smith, J., 'Arms transfers to conflict zones: The case of Nagorno-Karabakh', SIPRI Topical Backgrounder, 30 Apr. 2021.

[6] Armed Conflict Location & Event Data Project (ACLED), 'Dashboard', accessed 21 Jan. 2022.

[7] 'Russia and Turkey open monitoring centre for Nagorno-Karabakh', Reuters, 30 Jan. 2021.

[8] Holcomb, F., 'Armenia and Azerbaijan: Ceasefire largely holds, but tensions remain', in ACLED, *Mid-Year Update: 10 Conflicts to Worry About in 2021*, Aug. 2021, pp. 20–22.

[9] International Crisis Group, *Post-war Prospects for Nagorno-Karabakh*, Europe Report no. 264 (International Crisis Group: Brussels, 9 June 2021), p. 7.

[10] 'Armenia, Azerbaijan report casualties after renewed fighting on border', RFE/RL, 17 Nov. 2021.

[11] Balmforth, T. and Soldatkin, V., 'Putin hosts first post-war talks between leaders of Azerbaijan, Armenia', Reuters, 11 Jan. 2021; and Kucera, J., 'Leaders of Armenia and Azerbaijan hold first post-war meeting', Eurasianet, 11 Jan. 2021.

Aliyev declared the Nagorno-Karabakh conflict 'resolved'.[12] During the United Nations General Assembly on 24 September 2021, the OSCE Minsk Group co-chairs (France, Russia and the United States) convened the first meeting between the Armenian and Azerbaijani foreign ministers since the war.

Outlook

Fundamental questions remain regarding Nagorno-Karabakh's status, who will provide security and services for its residents, how to manage humanitarian aid, and whether the ceasefire will hold. Talks have yet to begin on addressing post-war issues, including demarcation of the new borders between Armenia and the regions reclaimed by Azerbaijan in the 2020 war, and other measures aimed at stabilizing the situation on the ground. As such, Nagorno-Karabakh is likely to remain an area of low-intensity conflict and tension at least for the medium term.

Tensions between Russia and the West

Tensions persisted throughout 2021 between Russia and most of the rest of Europe and the USA over issues as diverse as cyberattacks, Ukraine (see section II), the treatment of Russian opposition leader Alexei Navalny, the political crisis in Belarus, and strengthening bilateral security cooperation between China and Russia.[13] There are competing explanations for this political–military climate of mistrust.[14]

In February, the European Union (EU) imposed travel bans and asset freezes on associates of Vladimir Putin in response to the jailing of Navalny

---

[12] International Crisis Group (note 9), p. 4. For a brief description and list of members of the OSCE Minsk Group see annex B, section II, in this volume. On the history of the Minsk Group process see Remler, P. et al., 'OSCE Minsk Group: Lessons from the past and tasks for the future', ed. Institute for Peace Research and Security Policy at the University of Hamburg, *OSCR Insight 2020: Corona, War, Leadership Crisis* (Nomos: Baden-Baden, 2020); and Guliyev, F. and Gawrich, A., 'OSCE mediation strategies in Eastern Ukraine and Nagorno-Karabakh: A comparative analysis', *European Security*, vol. 30, no. 4 (2021), pp. 569–88.

[13] See e.g. Sanger, D. E., Perlroth, N. and Barnes, J. E., 'As understanding of Russian hacking grows, so does alarm', *New York Times*, 2 Jan. 2021; and Chan, M., 'Afghan crisis draws China and Russia closer on Central Asian stability as both step up army drills', *South China Morning Post*, 27 Aug. 2021. On these geopolitical divisions within arms control for biological and chemical weapons, see chapter 12, sections II and IV, in this volume.

[14] On the deteriorating relationship between Russia and the USA/Europe see *SIPRI Yearbook 2018*, pp. 11–12; *SIPRI Yearbook 2019*, pp. 18–19; and *SIPRI Yearbook 2020*, pp. 114–15. See also Stent, A., *Putin's World: Russia Against the West and With the Rest* (Twelve: New York, 2019); Orenstein, M. A., *The Lands in Between: Russia vs. the West and the New Politics of Hybrid War* (Oxford University Press: New York, 2019); Hill, F., 'The Kremlin's strange victory: How Putin exploits American dysfunction and fuels American decline', *Foreign Affairs*, Nov./Dec. 2021; and Sarotte, M. E., 'Containment beyond the Cold War: How Washington lost the post-Soviet peace', *Foreign Affairs*, Nov./Dec. 2021. On increases in military expenditure in Europe see chapter 8, sections I and II, in this volume.

for alleged parole violations.[15] In March the USA applied sanctions on seven senior Russian government officials and 14 entities associated with Russian biological and chemical agent production in response to allegations of Russian cyber espionage and the poisoning of Navalny.[16] In April the US government announced extensive new sanctions on 32 Russian entities and individuals, and formally attributed the 2019–20 SolarWinds hacking attack to the SVR (Sluzhba Vneshney Razvedki), Russia's foreign intelligence agency. Additionally, 10 Russian diplomats were expelled from the Russian embassy in Washington, DC.[17] In response, Russia expelled 10 US diplomats and blacklisted eight US officials.[18] Further tit-for-tat expulsions took place later in April between Russia and Czechia over an espionage row.[19]

Belarus

The internal governance crisis in Belarus that began in August 2020 continued in 2021, as did the deepening of ties with Russia.[20] One of year's most serious incidents occurred in May, when Belarus forced a plane flying through Belarusian airspace while carrying prominent opposition journalist Roman Protasevich—along with approximately 170 other passengers—to land in the capital, Minsk. After the plane landed, Protasevich was arrested by Belarusian authorities. The EU responded by closing European airports to Belarus's state airline and advising the carriers of member states to avoid Belarusian airspace.[21] The continuing crackdown of dissidents in Belarus sparked further EU and US sanctions.[22] In retaliation, the Belarus government provoked a migrant crisis by transporting refugees to the Lithuanian and Polish borders.[23]

---

[15] Emmott, R. and Siebold, S., 'EU to impose sanctions on Russians over Navalny by March summit, diplomats say', Reuters, 18 Feb. 2021.

[16] Holland, S. and Mohammed, A., 'US imposes sanctions on Russia over poisoning of Navalny', Reuters, 2 Mar. 2021.

[17] Sanger, D. E. and Kramer, A. E., 'US imposes stiff sanctions on Russia, blaming it for major hacking operation', *New York Times*, 15 Apr. 2021; and White House, 'Fact sheet: Imposing costs for harmful foreign activities by the Russian government', 15 Apr. 2021.

[18] Roth, A., 'Russia expels 10 US diplomats as part of retaliation for sanctions', *The Guardian*, 16 Apr. 2021; and Russian Ministry of Foreign Affairs, 'Foreign Ministry statement on measures in response to hostile US actions', 16 Apr. 2021.

[19] Cameron, R., 'Spy row revs up Czech–Russian tensions', BBC News, 8 May 2021.

[20] On the political crisis in Belarus in 2020 see *SIPRI Yearbook 2021*, pp. 122–24; and 'The protest movement in Belarus: Resistance and repression', *Strategic Comments*, vol. 27 no. 2 (2021), pp. i–iii.

[21] Troianovski, A., 'Belarus is isolated as other countries move to ban flights', *New York Times*, 24 May 2021; and 'Having hijacked a Ryanair plane, Belarus draws closer to Russia', *The Economist*, 26 May 2021 (Updated 27 May 2021).

[22] On the expanded EU arms embargo on Belarus see chapter 14, section II, in this volume.

[23] Pempel, K., 'Poland to build fence, double troop numbers on Belarus border', Reuters, 23 Aug. 2021; Nielsen, N., 'EU ready to impose more sanctions against Belarus', EU Observer, 6 Oct. 2021; and Talmazan, Y., 'Suffering of migrants intensifies amid standoff on Poland–Belarus border', NBC News, 10 Nov. 2021. On the role of military technologies used to track and control refugees on the EU's borders see Ahmed, K. and Tondo, L., 'Fortress Europe: The millions spent on military-grade tech to deter refugees', *The Guardian*, 6 Dec. 2021.

Russia's support for Belarus was a key factor in sustaining President Alexander Lukashenko's government. At a summit between President Putin and President Lukashenko in September 2021, for example, it was reported that progress had been made towards integrating the two countries' economies.[24] The meeting was followed by the quadrennial Zapad-2021 military exercises (focused on Russia's Western Military District and Belarus), which were much more of a joint Russian–Belarusian effort than previous iterations, leaving Western analysts concerned that the exercise might lead to a more permanent Russian military presence inside Belarus.[25]

Militarization and diplomacy

The actions of Russia described above, along with other long-standing political tensions, have led to several highly militarized and contested security contexts both within Europe and further afield, including confrontations in Africa, the Arctic, and the Middle East and North Africa (MENA).[26] In the communique for the North Atlantic Treaty Organization (NATO) summit in Brussels on 14 June 2021, for example, 'Russia's aggressive actions' were highlighted as a key threat to transatlantic security. The leaders of NATO countries committed to updating the alliance's strategic concept with the aim of considering new threats and clarifying that Article 5 of NATO's founding treaty—which establishes the principle of collective defence for the alliance—applies to threats in space and cyberattacks.[27] EU member states were also working on a new defence policy, the so-called 'strategic compass', which is due to be adopted in 2022.[28]

A further deterioration of relations between NATO and Russia occurred in October, when the latter announced it would end its diplomatic engagement with NATO in response to the alliance's expulsion of eight Russian diplomats alleged to be undeclared intelligence officers.[29] Post-cold war efforts in building trust between Russia and NATO had centred on the 2002 NATO–Russia Council (NRC) and the 1997 NATO–Russia Founding Act.[30] However, after Russia annexed Ukraine's Crimean peninsula in 2014, NATO suspended all

---

[24] Roth, A., 'Putin and Lukashenko move to integrate economies of Russia and Belarus', *The Guardian*, 9 Sep. 2021.

[25] Whitmore, B., 'Concerns mount over Russia–Belarus military exercises', Atlantic Council, 28 July 2021; Kofman, M., 'Zapad 2021: What we learned from Russia's massive military drills', *Moscow Times*, 23 Sep. 2021; and Johnson, R., 'NATO's big concern from Russia's Zapad exercise: Putin's forces lingering in Belarus', Breaking Defense, 4 Oct. 2021.

[26] Lee, M., 'US, Russia at odds over military activity in the Arctic', AP News, 20 May 2021.

[27] Brussels Summit Communiqué, Issued by the heads of state and government participating in the meeting of the North Atlantic Council in Brussels 14 June 2021, Press Release (2021) 086, 14 June 2021.

[28] EU External Action Service, 'A Strategic Compass for the EU', Factsheet, 15 Nov. 2021.

[29] Kramer, A. E., 'Russia breaks diplomatic ties with NATO', *New York Times*, 18 Oct. 2021.

[30] Founding Act on Mutual Relations, Cooperation and Security Between NATO and the Russian Federation Signed in Paris, France, 27 May 1997. For a summary of the NATO–Russia Council see annex B, section II, in this volume.

practical civilian and military cooperation with Russia. While some channels were left open for dialogue on Ukraine and other matters, the general view within NATO was that Russia no longer accepted the principles enshrined in the Founding Act, such as national sovereignty and the inviolability of borders.[31] With the suspension of Russia's diplomatic mission to NATO, the avenues for NATO–Russia dialogue narrowed even further.

The decay of confidence-building measures in Europe is also symbolized by the crisis in European arms control, which includes the termination of the 1987 Treaty on the Elimination of Intermediate-Range and Shorter-Range Missiles (INF Treaty), the withering of the Open Skies regime, and the lack of progress on the 2011 Vienna Document on Confidence- and Security-Building Measures.[32] This has meant that incidents of military brinkmanship—such as occurred between Russian forces and a British warship near Crimea in June 2021—are at greater risk of military escalation.[33]

Nonetheless, there has been room for diplomacy on certain issues. Most significantly, the USA and Russia were able to extend the New START nuclear agreement in February 2021 by five years following talks between President Joe Biden and President Putin.[34] Similarly, senior US and Russian diplomats met in May, and despite serious differences struck an optimistic tone about potential future cooperation on combating the Covid-19 pandemic, climate change, the nuclear programmes in North Korea and Iran, and the Afghanistan war.[35] In June Biden and Putin met in Geneva for their first face-to-face summit since the former took office, in an attempt to arrest deteriorating relations. The admittedly low bar set for the meeting seemed to be met, with both sides agreeing to keep talking about arms control and strategic stability.[36]

EU leaders have also struggled to define a common agenda on managing their disagreements with Russia.[37] A French–German proposal for a separate EU–Russia summit to open space for dialogue on issues such as climate change, energy, health, and the fight against terrorism and organized crime

---

[31] See e.g. Polish Ministry of Foreign Affairs, 'Polish foreign policy strategy 2017–2021', p. 2; and British Foreign, Commonwealth & Development Office, 'Seventh anniversary of Russia's illegal annexation of Crimea: UK statement', 4 Mar. 2021.

[32] For a summary of the INF Treaty see annex A, section III, in this volume. On the Open Skies Treaty see chapter 13, section III, and annex A, section II, in this volume. For a summary and other details of the 2011 Vienna Document see annex A, section II, in this volume.

[33] Sabbagh, D. and Roth, A., 'Britain acknowledges surprise at speed of Russian reaction to warship', *The Guardian*, 24 June 2021.

[34] See chapter 11, section I, in this volume.

[35] Pamuk, H., 'Blinken, Lavrov agree to work together despite differences', Reuters, 19 May 2021.

[36] Troianovski, A., Matsnev, O. and Nechepurenko, I., 'Biden and Putin say the talks went well, but divisions remain on issues like cyberattacks and human rights', *New York Times*, 16 June 2021; and Braw, E., 'The Biden–Putin meeting: Every little helps', European Leadership Network Commentary, 2 Sep. 2021.

[37] See e.g. Borrell, J., 'My visit to Moscow and the future of EU–Russia relations', EU External Action Service, 7 Feb. 2021.

was dropped following criticism from other EU member states, particularly Poland and the Baltic states.[38] Instead, a new review of EU policy towards Russia (in the context of the developing EU strategic compass and closer cooperation with NATO) suggests a dual-track of push back/containment and engagement.[39]

Russia sets out security demands

In December 2021 relations between the West and Russia worsened again, with further tit-for-tat expulsions of US and Russian diplomats, and US intelligence assessments that Russia was preparing to invade Ukraine (see section II)—which Russia denied.[40] A further round of joint Russia–Belarus military exercises announced in late December 2021 (and due to take place in Belarus in February 2022) raised additional concerns that Russia might also attack Ukraine's northern flank from Belarusian territory.[41]

Many Western analysts considered Russia's triggering of a new crisis with Ukraine as being due, at least in part, to a desire to force a wider security shift with the West.[42] Seemingly to this end, on 17 December 2021 Russia released two draft security agreements—one with NATO and the other with the USA—which set out a number of proposals, including: (*a*) an end to NATO military activity in member states in central and eastern Europe that joined the alliance after 1997; (*b*) no further expansion of NATO membership, particularly to Ukraine; (*c*) no intermediate or shorter-range missiles deployed close enough to hit the territory of the other side; (*d*) no military exercises of more than one military brigade in an agreed border zone; (*e*) an agreement that parties refrain from considering each other as adversaries and attempt to resolve disputes peacefully; and (*f*) a prohibition on the deployment of nuclear weapons outside of national territories.[43] While most of the proposals were both not new and seriously at odds with the views of most Western countries,

---

[38] Siebold, S., Emmott, R. and Baczynska, G., 'France and Germany drop Russia summit plan after EU's east objects', Reuters, 25 June 2021.

[39] European Commission, High Representative of the Union for Foreign Affairs and Security Policy, 'Joint communication to the European Parliament, the European Council and the Council, On EU–Russia relations—push back, constrain and engage', JOIN(2021) 20 final, 16 June 2021.

[40] Simmons, A. M. and Mauldin, W., 'Russia expels some US diplomats in latest tit-for-tat action', *Wall Street Journal*, 2 Dec. 2021.

[41] 'Russia, Belarus announce plans for more joint military drills', RFE/RL, 30 Dec. 2021.

[42] See e.g. Melvin, N., 'The West surrendered its strategic ambiguity in the Black Sea', RUSI Commentary, 21 Dec. 2021; and 'Russia's menacing of Ukraine is unlikely to induce NATO to retreat', *The Economist*, 8 Jan. 2022. For an explanation of Russian motives see Trenin, D., 'What Putin really wants in Ukraine', *Foreign Affairs*, 28 Dec. 2021; and Gromyko, A., 'What is driving Russia's security concerns?', European Leadership Network Commentary, 20 Jan. 2022.

[43] Russian Ministry of Foreign Affairs, 'Treaty between the United States of America and the Russian Federation on security guarantees', draft, unofficial translation, 17 Dec. 2021; and Russian Ministry of Foreign Affairs, 'Agreement on measures to ensure the security of the Russian Federation and member states of the North Atlantic Treaty Organization', draft, unofficial translation, 17 Dec. 2021.

their detailed elaboration in this format underlined Russia's intention to seek change the European security framework.[44]

Senior Russian officials stressed that failure to endorse the documents would lead to an unspecified but serious 'military-technical' response. Despite this, there was very little in the texts that was likely to be accepted by either the USA or NATO.[45] On 21 December NATO Secretary General Jens Stoltenberg announced, 'Any dialogue with Russia needs to be based on the core principles of European security and to address NATO's concerns about Russia's actions. And it needs to take place in consultation with NATO's European partners, including with Ukraine'.[46] Similarly, a senior US official said, 'There are some things that we're prepared to work on and that we do believe that there's merit in having a discussion . . . There are other things in those documents that the Russians know will be unacceptable'.[47] Nonetheless, agreement was reached to discuss the proposals with Russia in three separate meetings in January 2022: a USA–Russia bilateral meeting on 10 January; a meeting of the NRC on 12 January; and in the broader format of the OSCE on 13 January.

Unresolved conflicts

There are several long-standing simmering or frozen conflicts in Europe, especially in the post-Soviet space where five de facto statelets claiming independence from Soviet Union successor states—Abkhazia, Nagorno-Karabakh, South Ossetia, Trans-Dniester, and the portions of Ukraine's Donbas now controlled by Russian-backed separatists—remain unrecognized by most states around the world.[48] Similar conditions apply in Cyprus, Northern Ireland and the Western Balkans.[49] In these conditions of neither war nor peace, seemingly minor disputes can quickly escalate. In the Western Balkans in September 2021, for example, NATO peacekeepers stepped up patrols along the Kosovo–Serbia border amid heightened tensions between

---

[44] Baklitskiy, A. A., 'Putin's demand for security guarantees: Not new and not to be taken literally, but not to be ignored', Bulletin of the Atomic Scientists, 14 Jan. 2022.

[45] 'Putin warns of "military–technical" response to Western "aggression"', Moscow Times, 21 Dec. 2022; and Podvig, P., 'Russia threatened a "military–technical" response for unmet demands. What could that mean?', Bulletin of the Atomic Scientists, 18 Jan. 2022.

[46] Joint press conference by NATO Secretary General Jens Stoltenberg with the Prime Minister of Romania Nicolae Ciucă, 21 Dec. 2021.

[47] US Department of State, 'Telephonic press briefing with Dr Karen Donfried, Assistant Secretary of State, Bureau of European and Eurasian Affairs', 21 Dec. 2021.

[48] On frozen conflicts see Klosek, K. C. et al., 'Frozen conflicts in world politics: A new dataset', Journal of Peace Research, vol. 58, no. 4 (2021), pp. 849–58.

[49] On Northern Ireland see Edwards, A. and McGrattan, C., 'Ireland, 2021: A century of insurgency, terrorism and security challenges', Small Wars & Insurgencies, vol. 32, no. 4–5 (2021), pp. 587–97; Dixon, P., 'Bringing politics back in: Interpretations of the peace process and the security challenge in Northern Ireland', Small Wars & Insurgencies, vol. 32, no. 4–5 (2021), pp. 812–36; and 'Northern Ireland's unhappy centenary', The Economist, 17 Apr. 2021.

the two countries over a minor motoring regulation dispute.[50] Similarly, in Bosnia and Herzegovina in late 2021, Serbian leadership took steps to undermine federal institutions, sparking the worst political crisis in 20 years.[51]

Security challenges in the eastern Mediterranean

There are also serious and complex security challenges in Europe's southern neighbourhood and beyond.[52] One of the most significant areas of tension in 2021 continued to be in the eastern Mediterranean, where Turkey was pitted against Cyprus and Greece, and the disagreements continued to draw in the EU, Egypt, Libya, and other states with geopolitical and economic interests in the region. Turkish–Western relations have deteriorated over multiple issues, including oil and gas exploration, maritime delimitation, the wars in Iraq, Libya and Syria, migration, Turkey's democratic backsliding, stalled EU membership negotiations, and the long-standing Cyprus conflict.[53]

Bilateral Greek–Turkish talks aimed at addressing some of these underlying issues started in 2002 but broke down in 2016 after 60 rounds of meetings. At least three separate strands of exploratory talks resumed in the first half of 2021. First, on 25 January 2021, Greece and Turkey resumed exploratory talks on maritime issues.[54] Second, talks within the NATO-led 'deconfliction' process initiated in 2020 continued.[55] Third, talks resumed on attempting to resolve the Cyprus conflict. The foreign ministers of Greece, Turkey and the United Kingdom (Cyprus's three guarantor powers) joined Greek Cypriot and Turkish Cypriot representatives for UN-led talks in Geneva.[56] None of these talks registered a significant breakthrough, however, and the UN Security Council, in renewing the UN Peacekeeping Force in Cyprus mandate in July, called on leaders of the two Cypriot communities to 'free' the technical committees 'from obstructions in their work' and 'to empower them to . . . enhance intercommunal contacts'.[57]

---

[50] Butcher, J. and Boffey, D., 'Tensions rise at Kosovo border as number plate row escalates', *The Guardian*, 2 Oct. 2021.

[51] 'International envoy warns of Bosnia breakup amid tensions', Euronews, 2 Nov. 2021; and MacDowall, A., 'A neglected crisis in Bosnia threatens to boil over', World Politics Review, 23 Nov. 2021.

[52] On armed conflicts in Afghanistan, MENA and sub-Saharan Africa see, respectively, chapter 4, section III, and chapters 6 and 7, in this volume.

[53] For an overview of the multifaceted dispute see International Crisis Group, *Turkey–Greece: From Maritime Brinkmanship to Dialogue*, Europe Report no. 263 (International Crisis Group: Brussels, 31 May 2021). For developments in 2020 see *SIPRI Yearbook 2021*, pp. 125–26.

[54] Ozerkan, F. and Akkoc, R., 'Greece, Turkey hold first crisis talks since 2016', Digital Journal, 25 Jan. 2021.

[55] 'Turkey, Greece complete 9th round of NATO technical talks', *Daily Sabah*, 7 Feb. 2021.

[56] Smith, H., 'Greek and Turkish Cypriot leaders to hold talks on resuming peace process', *The Guardian*, 26 Apr. 2021.

[57] UN Security Council Resolution 2587, 29 July 2021.

Relations between Greece and Turkey were further strained by new developments in their bilateral arms race.[58] Over the course of 2021, Greece entered into significant new military cooperation arrangements with France, Israel and the USA, while Turkey deepened military cooperation with Spain.[59] Turkey's intricate foreign policy positions also posed complexities within the eastern Mediterranean and beyond. For example, Turkey has worked both with and against Russia in northern Syria, has different interests from Russia in the South Caucasus, and has been involved in multiple disagreements with NATO allies, especially over the procurement of an advanced missile defence system from Russia.[60]

---

[58] Karagiannis, E., 'The coming naval arms race in the Eastern Mediterranean', Royal United Services Institute Commentary, 22 July 2021; and *SIPRI Yearbook 2021*, pp. 317–18.

[59] 'France and Greece hedge their bets with a new defence pact', *The Economist*, 2 Oct. 2021; Carassava, A., 'Greece, Israel seal $1.6 Billion defense deal', VOA, 8 Jan. 2021; Pamuk, H., 'Blinken says renewed US–Greece defense deal to advance stability in Eastern Mediterranean', Reuters, 15 Oct. 2021; and Michalopoulos, S., 'Greece fumes over new Spain–Turkey armament deal', Euractiv, 19 Nov. 2021.

[60] See e.g. 'Turkey says Greek–French defense pact harms NATO alliance', AP News, 1 Oct. 2021; 'Turkey and Russia: Are they rivals or cooperating competitors?', *Times of India*, 11 Oct. 2021; and Miller, Z. and Boak, J., 'Biden tells Erdogan US and Turkey must avoid crises', AP News, 31 Oct. 2021.

II. Armed conflict in Ukraine and the risk of spillover to a major interstate war

IAN DAVIS

Ukraine has been the focus of Europe's main territorial conflict since the annexation of Crimea by Russia in March 2014 and the outbreak of armed conflict in eastern Ukraine shortly thereafter. The initial causes of this conflict and the extent to which it represents a non-international armed conflict with primarily domestic origins or a foreign intervention by Russia remain intensely contested.[1] The conflict centres on clashes between Russian-backed non-state armed groups and the Ukrainian government in two regions, Donetsk and Luhansk, which are part of an area known as Donbas. While Russia has consistently denied the presence of its military forces in Donbas, Western and Ukrainian officials assert that Russia supports the separatists with military forces, equipment and funding. In May 2021 Ukraine estimated that almost 3000 Russian military personnel, mostly in command and control positions, were present in eastern Ukraine, with the total number of Russia-led fighters estimated at more than 35 000.[2]

In this chapter, the armed conflict in 2021 is defined as a low-intensity, internationalized, subnational armed conflict.[3] A new ceasefire agreement in July 2020 led to much lower levels of violence and military and civilian casualties for the next six months.[4] However, fundamental disagreements at the root of the conflict persisted throughout 2021, with more intense outbreaks of fighting taking place from late March 2021 onwards along the 450 kilometre line of contact that divides Donbas.

The conflict is also driven by and helps drive the wider geopolitical confrontation between Russia and Western powers. The internationalized nature of the conflict took on a new dimension in 2021 as Russia amassed troops on its border with Ukraine, first in March–April and again in November, in moves widely interpreted within Western circles as a potential prelude to a new invasion of Ukraine—although Russia denied this. At the

---

[1] For a discussion on the initial causes of the conflict in Ukraine see *SIPRI Yearbook 2016*, pp. 143–57; and Clem, R. S., 'Clearing the fog of war: Public versus official sources and geopolitical storylines in the Russia–Ukraine conflict', *Eurasian Geography and Economics*, vol. 58, no. 6 (2017), pp. 592–612. On the various armed groups fighting in conflict see Galeotti, M., *Armies of Russia's War in Ukraine* (Osprey Publishing: Oxford, 2019).

[2] Permanent Mission of Ukraine to the International Organizations in Vienna, 'Statement on Russia's on-going aggression against Ukraine and illegal occupation of Crimea', 27 May 2021. On Russia's hybrid warfare operations in Ukraine see McCrory, D., 'Russian electronic warfare, cyber and information operations in Ukraine', *RUSI Journal*, vol. 165, no. 7 (2021), pp. 34–44.

[3] For conflict definitions and typologies see chapter 2, section I, in this volume. For details of the internationalized nature of the armed conflict see *SIPRI Yearbook 2020*, pp. 123–25.

[4] On casualty trends in the conflict see International Crisis Group, 'Visualising the dynamics of combat and negotiations in Donbas', International Crisis Group Commentary, 3 Aug. 2021.

end of December 2021, despite emerging diplomatic efforts (see section I), there had been no withdrawal of Russian troops, and further troops had been deployed on exercises in neighbouring Belarus. As such, the situation remained tense.

The Ukrainian government receives arms and military assistance from the United States and other North Atlantic Treaty Organization (NATO) member states, with the USA having allocated more than $2.7 billion in security assistance to Ukraine since 2014.[5] In September 2021, the USA announced plans to provide 'a new $60 million package for additional Javelin anti-armour systems and other defensive lethal and non-lethal capabilities'.[6]

Many Russians believe parts of Ukraine to be a historical province of Russia, and in July 2021 President Putin published an essay arguing that Russians and Ukrainians were 'one people'.[7] However, an opinion poll conducted just after Putin's article was published showed that 70 per cent of Ukrainians disagreed with this view.[8]

The humanitarian impact of the armed conflict and the role of the OSCE

The armed conflict between Ukrainian government forces and Russian-backed separatists has led to over 13 000 deaths since April 2014, including at least 3390 civilian deaths.[9] However, battle-related deaths and civilian casualties in Donbas have been much lower since 2018 compared to previous years: there were an estimated 145 conflict-related deaths in 2021 (a slight increase from 113 in 2020).[10] At least 2.9 million people needed humanitarian assistance during 2021 and at least 1.4 million people remained internally displaced.[11] In addition, eastern Ukraine has some of the world's

---

[5] On Western support for Ukraine see Fasola, N. and Wood, A. J., 'Reforming Ukraine's Security Sector', *Survival*, vol. 63 no. 2 (2021), pp. 41–54; White House, 'Joint Statement on the US–Ukraine Strategic Partnership', 1 Sep. 2021; and US Department of State, 'US Security Cooperation with Ukraine', 20 Jan. 2022.

[6] US Department of Defense, 'Readout of Secretary of Defense Lloyd J. Austin III's meeting with Ukrainian President Volodymyr Zelenskyy and Minister of Defense Andrii Taran', 31 Aug. 2021. On arms imports by Ukraine in 2021 see chapter 9, section III, in this volume.

[7] President of Russia, 'Article by Vladimir Putin "On the historical unity of Russians and Ukrainians"', 12 July 2021. For a critique of these claims see Wilson, A., 'Russia and Ukraine: "One People" as Putin claims?', RUSI Commentary, 23 Dec. 2021.

[8] [Citizens' assessment of the main theses of Putin's article, 'On the historical unity of Russians and Ukrainians' (July–Aug. 2021)], Razumkov Center, 11 Aug. 2021 (in Ukrainian).

[9] Office of the UN High Commissioner for Human Rights (OHCHR), *Report on the Human Rights Situation in Ukraine: 1 February to 31 July 2021* (OHCHR: 2021), pp. 8–9; and OHCHR, *Report on the Human Rights Situation in Ukraine: 16 November 2019 to 15 February 2020* (OHCHR: 2020), p. 8.

[10] Armed Conflict Location & Event Data Project (ACLED), 'Dashboard', accessed 21 Jan. 2021.

[11] 'Ukraine, situation report', UN Office for the Coordination of Humanitarian Affairs (UN OCHA), 22 Oct. 2021; and Welt, C., *Ukraine: Background, Conflict with Russia, and US Policy*, Congressional Research Service (CRS) Report for Congress R45008 (US Congress, CRS: Washington, DC, 5 Oct. 2021), p. 15.

worst landmine contamination, with deaths and injuries from mines and unexploded ordnance increasing markedly in recent years.[12]

The Organization for Security and Co-operation in Europe (OSCE) operates a Special Monitoring Mission (SMM) in Ukraine, consisting of around 827 international unarmed civilian personnel. Although the SMM is deployed throughout Ukraine, it focuses on monitoring ceasefire violations and the presence of heavy weaponry within defined security zones in eastern Ukraine. The SMM issues daily and spot monitoring reports on the security situation and facilitates the delivery of humanitarian aid.[13] A separate OSCE observer mission at the Russian checkpoints Gukovo and Donetsk (both within Russia) to monitor border crossings to and from eastern Ukraine ended on 30 September 2021 after Russia refused to support a renewal of its mandate.[14]

Russia's March–April 2021 military mobilization

After being on a low simmer for months, the armed conflict in Donbas escalated again in March and April 2021 as Russian-backed rebels and Ukrainian government forces clashed, in violation of the July 2020 ceasefire agreement.[15] Tensions further increased in late March–early April as Russia deployed tens of thousands of additional troops along the border with Ukraine. The US European Command raised its watch level to 'potential imminent crisis' in response to the movement of Russian forces, while Ukrainian President Volodymyr Zelensky called on NATO to create an accelerated path for Ukrainian membership.[16] Russia said the troops on Ukraine's border were engaged in military exercises and although the rationale for their presence was unclear, it was likely about geopolitical posturing

---

[12] Organization for Security and Co-operation in Europe (OSCE), *Thematic Report, The Impact of Mines, Unexploded Ordnance and Other Explosive Objects on Civilians in the Conflict-Affected Regions of Eastern Ukraine, November 2019–March 2021* (OSCE: May 2021); and Flint, J., 'As the threat of war looms in Eastern Ukraine, AOAV examines the country's landmine problem', AOAV, 7 Dec. 2021. On the impact of landmines see also chapter 13, section I, in this volume.

[13] For OSCE SMM daily and ad hoc reports on the crisis in Ukraine see <https://www.osce.org/ukrainecrisis>. For analysis of the SMM see Härtel, A., Pisarenko, A. and Umland, A., 'The OSCE's special monitoring mission to Ukraine', *Security and Human Rights*, vol. 31, no. 1–4 (2021), pp. 121–54.

[14] OSCE, 'Chairperson-in-Office expressed regret that no consensus could be reached on extension of mandate of Observer Mission', 16 Sep. 2021. For further details on the SMM in Ukraine see chapter 2, section II, in this volume.

[15] 'Kremlin urges France and Germany to stop Ukraine conflict crossing "dangerous line"', Reuters, 4 Mar. 2021.

[16] Kramer, A. E., 'Fighting escalates in Eastern Ukraine, signaling the end to another cease-fire', *New York Times*, 30 Mar. 2021; Polityuk, P. and Soldatkin, V., 'Ukraine calls for path into NATO after Russia masses troops', Reuters, 6 Apr. 2021; and 'A Russian military build-up on Ukraine's border prompts alarm', *The Economist*, 14 Apr. 2021.

rather than a potential prelude to invasion.[17] Although tensions were temporarily assuaged when Russia started to pull back its forces in late April, the situation in Donbas remained fraught.

Ukraine's proposed revisions to the peace process

The 2015 Minsk II agreement ended the major fighting and set out steps for the conflict parties (Ukrainian government, separatist statelets and Russia) to take in order to bring about peace in Donbas.[18] These steps were meant to lead to the breakaway areas of Donetsk and Luhansk being reintegrated into Ukraine while offering them a measure of autonomy. In contrast to its policy toward Crimea, Russia officially recognized the areas controlled by separatists in eastern Ukraine as Ukrainian territory. Russian motives appeared to be for a Russian-friendly autonomous Donbas to remain in Ukraine, thereby securing continuing leverage over Ukraine's foreign and domestic policy. The local separatist leaders were already financially and politically obligated to Russia, and Russia had granted citizenship to more than 525 000 residents in separatist-controlled parts of eastern Ukraine.[19]

The peace process had stalled due to fundamental disagreements among the conflict parties about the nature of the conflict and their involvement in it, as well as the implementation of the Minsk agreements.[20] The core of the stalemate lay within the sequencing of some of Minsk II's key measures, which remained ambiguous. While Ukraine emphasized the need for a permanent ceasefire and withdrawal of Russian forces, both on principle and as a prerequisite for creating a secure environment to hold free and fair local elections in the separatist-controlled Donbas, Russia continued to deny a military presence and reject responsibility for ceasefire violations and the failure to withdraw heavy weapons. Russia also called on Ukraine, irrespective of the security environment, to fulfil certain political measures,

---

[17] International Crisis Group, 'Responding to the new crisis on Ukraine's borders', International Crisis Group Statement, 20 Apr. 2021; Isachenkov, V., 'Kremlin says it fears full-scale fighting in Ukraine's east', AP News, 9 Apr. 2021; and 'Ukraine rules out offensive against Russia-backed separatists', Al Jazeera, 9 Apr. 2021.

[18] 'Package of measures for the implementation of the Minsk agreements' (Minsk II Agreement), 12 Feb. 2015. See also 'Protocol on the results of consultations of the Trilateral Contact Group with respect to the joint steps aimed at the implementation of the peace plan of the president of Ukraine, P. Poroshenko, and the initiatives of the president of Russia, V. Putin' (Minsk Protocol, or Minsk I Agreement), 5 Sep. 2014.

[19] International Crisis Group, *Rebels Without a Cause: Russia's Proxies in Eastern Ukraine*, Europe Report no. 254 (International Crisis Group: Brussels, 16 July 2019); and 'Nearly 530,000 Donbass citizens receive Russian citizenship in simplified procedure', Tass, 2 May 2021.

[20] For developments in the peace process in 2019–20 see *SIPRI Yearbook 2020*, pp. 126–28; and *SIPRI Yearbook 2021*, pp. 134–36. For analysis on the Russian and Ukrainian positions on the Minsk agreements see International Crisis Group, 'Responding to Russia's new military buildup near Ukraine', Europe Briefing no. 92, 8 Dec. 2021, pp. 3–6.

including granting permanent special status to the separatist-controlled areas and related constitutional reforms.

In April 2021 President Zelensky called for the Minsk II agreement to be revised through new negotiations within an expanded Normandy Format (an informal forum established by France, Germany, Russia and Ukraine in 2014) that would include Canada, the United Kingdom and the USA. He also reiterated that Ukraine was not bound to offer permanent (as opposed to temporary) autonomy to Donbas. Russia refused to open talks on this basis.[21]

On 23 August 2021, the eve of the 30th anniversary of Ukraine's independence, an inaugural Crimea Platform summit was organized by President Zelensky in Kyiv. Designed as an international coordination mechanism aimed at reinforcing the message that the 2014 annexation of Crimea would never be accepted, the summit was attended by representatives from 46 countries and international organizations.[22]

Russia's November–December military mobilization

In November Russia once again deployed thousands of troops near its borders with Ukraine, having only partially pulled back its forces from the April build-up. According to Ukrainian and Western officials about 100 000 Russian troops, along with military equipment, were deployed in proximity to the Ukrainian border.[23] The troop build-up was characterized by one US official as 'much larger and on a much more lethal scale' than that preceding the annexation of Crimea in 2014, while a US intelligence assessment suggested that Russia could begin an offensive involving up to 175 000 troops staged at different points along the border with Ukraine in early 2022.[24] NATO, the USA and other member states expressed grave concern, warning Moscow against a military operation against Ukraine.[25] Russian officials continued to deny that its troops posed any threat to Ukraine, and instead accused Ukraine

---

[21] Hall, B., 'Ukrainian leader calls for revamp of peace process to end Donbas war', *Financial Times*, 26 Apr. 2021; and Hall, B. and Olearchyk, R., 'Zelensky forced to "face reality" over peace talks with Russia', *Financial Times*, 3 May 2021. On the Normandy Format see Wintour, P., 'Ukraine tensions: What is the Normandy format and has it achieved anything?', *The Guardian*, 26 Jan. 2022.

[22] Socor, V., 'Crimea platform: Ukraine's initiative to raise the costs of Russia's occupation', *Eurasia Daily Monitor*, vol. 18, no. 25 (15 Feb. 2021); and Yavuz, T., 'Crimean platform summit reaffirms support for Ukraine', Anadolu Agency, 24 Aug. 2021.

[23] Schwirtz, M. and Reinhard, S., 'How Russia's military is positioned to threaten Ukraine', *New York Times*, 7 Jan. 2022; and Roth, A., Blood, D. and de Hoog, N., 'Russia–Ukraine crisis: Where are Putin's troops and what are his options?', *The Guardian*, 17 Dec. 2021.

[24] Gaouette, N., Hansler, J. and Atwood, K., 'Russian military capacity on Ukraine's border is on a "more lethal scale" than 2014 Crimea invasion, US official says', CNN, 8 Dec. 2021; and Harris, S. and Sonne, P., 'Russia planning massive military offensive against Ukraine involving 175,000 troops, US intelligence warns', *Washington Post*, 3 Dec. 2021.

[25] NATO, 'Statement by the North Atlantic Council on the situation in and around Ukraine', Press Release 189 (2021), 16 Dec. 2021; and Maynes, C., 'US and Russian officials have agreed to discuss Ukraine tensions and role of NATO', NPR, 25 Dec. 2021.

and Western states of 'provocations'.[26] The situation was clouded by a lack of Russian transparency and conflicting assessments of the crisis.[27]

During a video call on 7 December 2021, President Biden warned President Putin that the USA and its allies would meet a military invasion of Ukraine with strong economic penalties, moves to bolster Ukrainian defences, and the fortifying of support for NATO member states in Eastern Europe.[28] A similar warning to Russia was issued by the G7 group on 12 December, calling on the country to 'de-escalate, pursue diplomatic channels, and abide by its international commitments on transparency of military activities'.[29] In another telephone conversation on 30 December 2021, Biden and Putin restated their positions. Despite failing to reach agreement on defusing tensions, the exchange set the scene for further diplomatic talks between the USA and Russia in January 2022 (see section I).[30]

Outlook

At the end of 2021 concerns about the fresh build-up of Russian forces on Ukraine's border prompted grave concerns about the potential for escalation, even to the point of full-blown interstate war. Russia's motives and objectives were not entirely clear, and in all probability intentionally ambiguous. However, Russia appeared to be using the threat of invasion to achieve a more acquiescent Ukraine and extensive changes in the European security order (as discussed in section I), as well as to project strength to a domestic audience.[31] While negotiations due to take place in January 2022 seemed unlikely to reach any initial agreement, it was hoped that the talks might lead to more substantive and sustained diplomacy. In the event of a Russian invasion of Ukraine, Western leaders were discussing economic sanctions on Russia and greater defensive support for Ukraine rather than a direct military response. Nonetheless, the risk of a wider escalation remained a real possibility. On 24 February 2022, Russia invaded Ukraine.[32]

---

[26] 'Attempts to solve Ukrainian crisis by force will trigger serious consequences—Kremlin', Tass, 21 Nov. 2021; and 'Russia says Ukraine has deployed half its army to Donbass conflict zone', Reuters, 1 Dec. 2021.

[27] 'Kyiv seeks to align its forces in information warfare', Intelligence Online, 10 Jan. 2022; and 'The information warfare between Kyiv and Moscow reaches fever pitch', Intelligence Online, 29 Nov. 2021.

[28] White House, 'Readout of President Biden's video call with President Vladimir Putin of Russia', 7 Dec. 2021; and Roth, A., 'Biden promises eastern Europeans support in event of Russian attack on Ukraine', The Guardian, 9 Dec. 2021.

[29] US Department of State, 'G7 Foreign Ministers' Statement on Russia and Ukraine', 12 Dec. 2021.

[30] White House, 'Statement by Press Secretary Jen Psaki on President Biden's phone call with President Vladimir Putin of Russia', 30 Dec. 2021; and Renshaw, J. and Soldatkin, V., '"Serious" talk between Biden and Putin sets the stage for diplomacy', Reuters, 31 Dec. 2021.

[31] Roth, A., 'Vladimir Putin passes law that may keep him in office until 2036', The Guardian, 5 Apr. 2021.

[32] On the Russian invasion of Ukraine see chapter 1, section I, in this volume.

6. Armed conflict and peace processes in the Middle East and North Africa

Overview

There were eight states with active armed conflicts in the Middle East and North Africa (MENA) in 2021 (the same as in 2020): Egypt, Iraq, Israel (Palestine), Lebanon, Libya, Syria, Turkey and Yemen. Compared with 2020, conflict-related fatalities in 2021 fell in all conflicts apart from Israel–Palestine and Lebanon. Total conflict-related fatalities in the region fell for the fourth consecutive year, down about 75 per cent since 2017. Yemen was the region's only major armed conflict (annual fatalities greater than 10 000 people), and aside from Iraq and Syria (high-intensity armed conflicts), the remaining armed conflicts were all low intensity (25–999 deaths). Many of the conflicts were interconnected, involving regional and international powers, as well as numerous non-state actors. The rapid fall in conflict-related fatalities in the region reflected a small shift towards greater regional stability, with the caveat that many of the underlying economic and political drivers of conflict remained unaddressed.

The most destabilizing and high-risk interstate rivalries in 2021 continued to be between Iran (and its allies in Iraq, Lebanon, Syria and Yemen) and an ad hoc group of four states: Israel, Saudi Arabia, the United Arab Emirates and the United States. However, increased diplomacy mitigated some of these regional rivalries in 2021. Four other cross-cutting issues shaped security dilemmas in the region: the impact of the Covid-19 pandemic; the continuing wave of large, sustained protest movements across many states; ongoing threats from violent jihadist groups; and increased competition over water, alongside growing climate change impacts (section I). There were 14 multilateral peace operations in the MENA region in 2021, the same as in 2020.

There were complex and interlinked armed conflicts in Iraq, Syria and Turkey (section II). The situation in Syria remained volatile, with particularly intensive clashes during the third quarter of the year. Turkey and its aligned Syrian militias intensified their attacks in the Kurdish-controlled territory within north-east Syria. The Idlib ceasefire brokered by Russia and Turkey in 2020 that cemented their roles as power brokers in Syria remained in force. Iraq continued to be a fragile state, with weak institutions and a growing rift between the government and some militias. Iran-backed Shia parties with links to these militias suffered a setback in early Iraqi parliamentary elections. Turkey continued its military operations in northern Iraq, while the protracted conflict in the south-east of Turkey also persisted.

SIPRI Yearbook 2022: Armaments, Disarmament and International Security
www.sipriyearbook.org

The underlying dynamics of the Israeli–Palestinian conflict continued into 2021, with a new US presidency and a new Israeli coalition government adding additional layers of uncertainty (section III). In May 2021 the conflict in Gaza escalated again, with Israel and Hamas fighting an 11-day war, their fourth in 14 years. The conflict in Gaza also sparked unrest in the West Bank, as well as an unprecedented general strike among Palestinians across Israel, Gaza and the West Bank, and large-scale street protests and mob violence between Palestinians and Jews within Israel's mixed cities and towns. The economic and humanitarian costs of the Israeli occupation to the Palestinian people continued to be severe, with 2.1 million Palestinians projected to need humanitarian assistance in 2022

North Africa (section IV) is undergoing a convergence of crises, with negative spillover impacting the stability of neighbouring states in the eastern Mediterranean and sub-Saharan Africa. Egypt's low-level Sinai insurgency continued in 2021, with no end or decisive outcome in sight. The 40-year territorial dispute over Western Sahara between Morocco and the Popular Front for the Liberation of Saguia el Hamra and Río de Oro (Polisario Front) heated up again. While not at the level of an armed conflict in 2021, it nonetheless contributed to a rise in Algeria–Morocco tensions. In Libya an internationally backed ceasefire agreed in October 2020 largely held during 2021. Despite the establishment of a new interim unity government for the first time since 2014, postponement of the elections due to take place on 24 December 2021 provoked heightened levels of uncertainty in the peacebuilding roadmap. Moreover, it left the political reconciliation process in the balance, opening up the risk that rival armed forces in Libya may once again mobilize.

The civil war in Yemen continued throughout the year, further exacerbating one of the world's worst humanitarian crises (section V). The political, security, military, economic and humanitarian situation in Yemen further deteriorated during 2021, with over half a million people on the brink of famine. Despite the new US administration committing to a more diplomatic approach, in practice it remained a staunch Saudi ally, with its 'new' approach appearing to have little impact on the ground. The Houthis made significant territorial gains during 2021, and despite Saudi Arabia increasingly looking for a means to exit the war, the prospects of a political settlement remained remote. At the end of 2021, following seven years of territorial fragmentation and proliferating armed groups and sub-conflicts, the United Nations Special Envoy reported that the conflict was escalating. If it continues through 2030, the total conflict-attributable death toll could reach 1.3 million people.

IAN DAVIS

I. Key general developments in the region

IAN DAVIS

There were eight states in the Middle East and North Africa (MENA) with active armed conflicts in 2021 (the same as in 2020): Egypt (low-intensity, subnational armed conflict); Iraq (high-intensity, subnational armed conflict); Israel (low-intensity, extrastate armed conflict); Lebanon (low-intensity, subnational armed conflict); Libya (internationalized low-intensity, subnational armed conflict); Syria (internationalized civil war); Turkey (low-intensity, extrastate and subnational armed conflict); and Yemen (major internationalized civil war).[1] Many of these conflicts were interconnected, involving regional and international powers, as well as numerous non-state actors.

Developments in Lebanon are discussed below, while the other armed conflicts and related peace processes are covered in subsequent sections: Iraq, Syria and Turkey (section II); the Israeli–Palestinian conflict (section III); Egypt, Libya and Morocco, which was on the cusp of an armed conflict as the situation escalated in Western Sahara (section IV); and Yemen (section V).

Compared with 2020, conflict-related fatalities in 2021 fell in all conflicts apart from Israel–Palestine and Lebanon (see table 6.1). Total conflict-related fatalities in the region fell for the fourth consecutive year (a situation reflected in the cases of Egypt, Iraq, Syria and Turkey), down about 75 per cent since 2017. The decrease is linked to ceasefires in Libya and Syria in 2020. As was the case in 2020, there was limited evidence in 2021 of any clear correlation between the Covid-19 pandemic and a change in the nature or intensity of armed conflicts in the region. However, the pandemic may yet increase the underlying drivers and structural factors conducive to communal tensions, and it clearly added another layer of complexity to the region's existing humanitarian challenges.[2]

While the war in Yemen was the region's only remaining major armed conflict in 2021, a number of tensions and post-conflict situations continued to cause unrest. Nonetheless, the conflict fatalities data not only reflected lower rates of armed violence but also a small shift towards greater regional stability. This was emphasized by increased diplomacy mitigating some regional rivalries (see below). However, with many of the underlying economic and political causes of the 2011 Arab Spring remaining unaddressed, and other

---

[1] For conflict definitions and typologies see chapter 2, section I, in this volume.
[2] Counter-Terrorism Committee Executive Directorate, 'The impact of the COVID-19 pandemic on terrorism, counter-terrorism and countering violent extremism', Update, Dec. 2021. On regional responses to the pandemic see Altunışık, M., 'Pandemic regionalism or not? The MENA region in the shadow of Covid-19', *International Spectator*, vol. 56, no. 2 (2021), pp. 38–55.

Table 6.1. Estimated conflict-related fatalities in the Middle East and North Africa, 2017–21

Country	2017	2018	2019	2020	2021
Egypt	1 544	1 112	1 003	626	264
Iraq	32 027	5 621	3 717	2 805	2 750
Israel–Palestine	136	344	178	47	397
Lebanon	389	36[a]	25[a]	48	73
Libya	1 708	1 228	2 294	1 560	115
Syria	54 391	30 134	15 638	8 211	5 861
Turkey	2 925	1 927	957	552	297
Yemen	17 589	34 269	28 056	19 766	18 454
Total	**110 709**	**74 671**	**51 868**	**33 615**	**28 211**

[a] Battle-related deaths were below 25.

Notes: Fatality figures are collated from four event types: battles; explosions/remote violence; protests, riots and strategic developments; and violence against civilians—see Armed Conflict Location & Event Data Project (ACLED), 'ACLED definitions of political violence and protest', 11 Apr. 2019. A country is treated as being in an armed conflict if there were 25 or more battle-related deaths in a given year—see chapter 2, section I, in this volume.

Source: ACLED, 'Dashboard', accessed 8–17 Feb. 2022.

cross-cutting concerns continuing (as discussed below), this period of relative stability may be short-lived.

There were 14 operations in 2021, the same number as in 2020. None of the operations that were active started or ended during the year. The number of personnel in the MENA region decreased by 2.2 per cent, from 14 615 on 31 December 2020 to 14 289 on 31 December 2021.[3]

Shifting alliances, rivalries and regional diplomacy

In MENA, interstate and intrastate fault lines intersect in complex ways, with shifting alliances and rivalries. The most destabilizing and high-risk interstate rivalries in 2021 continued to be between Iran (and its allies in Iraq, Lebanon, Syria and Yemen) and an ad hoc group of four states: Israel, Saudi Arabia, the United Arab Emirates (UAE) and the United States. Saudi Arabia and the UAE (and to a lesser extent some of the other states in the Gulf) have actively been opposing Iran in Iraq, Lebanon, Syria and Yemen, while Israeli opposition to Iran has been focused on Lebanon and Syria, as well as Iran's nuclear programme. As was the case in 2018–20, Israel attacked Iranian and Iranian-aligned targets in Syria on several occasions in 2021, and was suspected of further sabotage attacks against Iran's nuclear programme.[4]

---

[3] For global and regional trends in multilateral peace operations see chapter 2, sections II and III, in this volume.

[4] See e.g. AFP, 'Deadliest Israeli airstrikes on Syria in years kill 57, say observers', *The Guardian*, 13 Jan. 2021; D'Agostino, S., 'Alleged sabotage at Iran's Natanz nuclear facility comes amid talks on reviving the Iran nuclear deal', Bulletin of the Atomic Scientists, 12 Apr. 2021; and AFP, 'Israeli airstrike sets port of Latakia ablaze, says Syrian media', *The Guardian*, 28 Dec. 2021.

Israel also escalated its military operations against Hezbollah in Lebanon in August 2021, supplementing artillery exchanges with airstrikes for the first time since 2014.[5] Russia and Turkey continued to be influential external actors—sometimes rivals—in the region, while China adopted a more prominent economic and diplomatic role.[6]

Several new or existing channels of high-level diplomacy helped calm regional tensions during 2021. First, Syria continued to push to normalize relations with several states that had previously supported opposition forces during Syria's civil war. Jordan, for example, reopened its border crossing with Syria in late September 2021.[7] Second, a three-and-a-half-year dispute between Qatar and other Gulf states—which had led to Bahrain, Egypt, Saudi Arabia and the UAE imposing a blockade against Qatar—was formally ended by a reconciliation deal agreed in January 2021. Though the diplomatic breakthrough at the Gulf Cooperation Council summit led to restored relations and the blockade being lifted, foreign policy differences are likely to persist, especially in relation to the Horn of Africa.[8]

Third, two of the region's most interventionist states, Turkey and the UAE, sought to reduce their bilateral political tensions through increased economic collaboration.[9] In the wake of a peace deal in Libya (see section IV), Turkey also began diplomatic overtures towards Egypt, having broken off relations in 2013.[10] Fourth, and most significantly, direct talks between Iran and Saudi Arabia began in April 2021, mediated by Iraq. Several further rounds of direct talks followed, centred primarily on issues related to Yemen.[11] Although the prospects of significant diplomatic progress between the two countries are likely to remain modest, an incremental process of

---

[5] 'Hezbollah launches rocket fire in response to Israeli air raids', Al Jazeera, 6 Aug. 2021.

[6] Borshchevskaya, A., 'Russia's strategic success in Syria and the future of Moscow's Middle East policy', Lawfare, 23 Jan. 2022; Ghiselli, A. and Giuffrida, M. G. E., 'China as an offshore balancer in the Middle East and North Africa', RUSI Journal, vol. 165, no. 7 (2020), pp. 10–20; and Simon, S., 'China and the Persian Gulf in the aftermath of a US withdrawal', Quincy Institute for Responsible Statecraft, Quincy Brief no. 17, Sep. 2021.

[7] Cambanis, T., 'Syria's Middle East neighbors are thawing ties with Damascus', World Politics Review, 4 Oct. 2021; and 'Syria's Assad calls Jordan's king amid thaw in relations', AP News, 3 Oct. 2021.

[8] 'Qatar crisis: Saudi Arabia and allies restore diplomatic ties with Emirate', BBC News, 5 Jan. 2021; and 'Gulf rivalries are spilling into Africa's Horn', The Economist, 11 Feb. 2021. For an overview and membership of the Gulf Cooperation Council see Annex B, section II, in this volume. On conflict in the Horn of Africa see chapter 7, section IV, in this volume.

[9] Bakir, A., 'Turkey and the UAE: Making amends and talking business in post-Trump era', Middle East Eye, 2 Sep. 2021; and 'Building economic ties top swift Turkey–UAE talks', Daily Sabah, 7 Sep. 2021. For a review of all the region's military interventions in the period 2010–20 see Petti, M. and Parsi, T., No Clean Hands: The Interventions of Middle Eastern Powers, 2010–2020, Quincy Paper no. 8 (Quincy Institute for Responsible Statecraft, 19 July 2021).

[10] Elerian, M., 'Turkey and Egypt open the door to a diplomatic thaw', World Politics Review, 25 Mar. 2021.

[11] 'Saudi and Iran held talks aimed at easing tensions, say sources', Reuters, 18 Apr. 2021; and Mabon. S., 'Yemen: Talks between Saudi Arabia and Iran offer hopes for an end to bitter seven-year civil war', Political Anthropologist, 10 Oct. 2021.

Saudi–Iranian détente would help lower political and strategic tensions in the region. To this end, Iraq and France co-organized a regional summit in Baghdad in August 2021, while an earlier summit in June 2021 brought together the leaders of Egypt, Iraq and Jordan.[12]

Finally, there were signs during 2021 that one of the most difficult regional rivalries—the Iranian–US conflict, which had threatened to escalate into a region-wide interstate military conflict in 2019–20—might enter a new period of détente. Iranian–US relations have been largely adversarial since the 1979 Islamic Revolution, deteriorating further in recent years due to the USA's withdrawal from the 2015 multilateral nuclear agreement with Iran (Joint Comprehensive Plan of Action, JCPOA) and the USA's coercive policy of applying 'maximum pressure' colliding with Iran's policy of 'maximum resistance'.[13] In 2019–20 this led to a series of serious military confrontations, raising the risk of a regional conflagration.[14] In 2021, however, despite continuing tensions, occasional naval encounters and US airstrikes against Iran-backed militias in the Iraq–Syria border region, Iranian and US diplomats met and discussed reviving the JCPOA.[15] Although gaps between the two sides narrowed during the early rounds of indirect talks, the election in June 2021 of a new Iranian president, Ebrahim Raisi, further complicated negotiations.[16] By the end of the year a renewed nuclear deal had still not been agreed, risking a return to confrontation.[17]

In December 2021 Israel's prime minister and the UAE's de facto leader met for the first time in history, amid fears that the Iran nuclear talks might collapse and concerns about the shrinking role of the USA in the Middle East.[18] A few days earlier the USA had announced it was ending its combat

---

[12] Republic of Iraq, Ministry of Foreign Affairs, 'Final communique of the Baghdad Conference for Cooperation and Partnership', 28 Aug. 2021; Mamouri, A., 'Baghdad conference to establish cooperation, partnership in region', Al-Monitor, 30 Aug. 2021; and Harvey, K. and Riedel, B., 'Egypt, Iraq and Jordan: A new partnership 30 years in the making?', Brookings, 2 July 2021.

[13] US Department of State, Office of the Spokesperson, 'Advancing the US maximum pressure campaign on Iran', Fact sheet, 22 Apr. 2019. On the US withdrawal from the JCPOA see *SIPRI Yearbook 2019*, pp. 381–86. On Iran's defence posture and key foreign policy objectives see Katzman, K., 'Iran's foreign and defense policies', Congressional Research Service Report R44017, 11 Jan. 2021; and Eisenstadt, M., 'Iran's gray zone strategy: Cornerstone of its asymmetric way of war', *PRISM*, vol. 9, no. 2 (Mar. 2021).

[14] On developments in 2019–20 see *SIPRI Yearbook 2020*, pp. 5–8, 132–34; and *SIPRI Yearbook 2021*, pp. 11–12, 141–43.

[15] See e.g. Burns, R., 'US ship fires warning shots in encounter with Iranian boats', AP News, 10 May 2021; and Schmitt, E., 'US carries out airstrikes in Iraq and Syria', *New York Times*, 27 June 2021. On developments in the JCPOA see chapter 11, section II, in this volume.

[16] Gladstone, R., 'Khamenei adds to doubts on Iran nuclear deal talks', *New York Times*, 28 July 2021; and International Crisis Group, *Iran: The Riddle of Raisi*, Middle East Report no. 224 (International Crisis Group: Brussels, 5 Aug. 2021).

[17] Wintour, P., 'US and Israel exploring "plan B" for if Iran does not resume nuclear talks', *The Guardian*, 13 Oct. 2021.

[18] Grove, T., Kalin, S. and Said, S., 'Fear of Iran, shrinking US role in Middle East push rivals together', *Wall Street Journal*, 13 Dec. 2021.

mission in Iraq, instead shifting its armed forces in the country (numbering roughly 2500) to a training and advisory role (see section II).

Other regional cross-cutting issues

Three other cross-cutting issues shaped security dilemmas in the region in 2021: (a) the continuing wave of large, sustained protest movements across many states; (b) ongoing threats from violent jihadist groups; and (c) increased competition over water, alongside growing climate change impacts.[19]

Anti-government protests have occurred in many states in the region since 2018 (as part of a second wave of protests following the 2011–12 uprisings).[20] Key reasons driving the protests include extreme levels of inequality, economic austerity and corruption, as well as calls for broader political and democratic rights.[21] With the exception of Tunisia, such rights remain largely unfulfilled (and even Tunisia took a backward step in July 2021 when the president invoked emergency powers and suspended parliament—see section IV).[22] The wide-ranging socio-economic consequences of the Covid-19 pandemic and the declining status of oil-based economies have exacerbated some of these grievances.[23] Government responses have combined repression with compromise in order to maintain the status quo and avoid social and political reforms. External actors, with their focus on mitigating threats to regional and international security, have also contributed to preservation of the status quo.[24]

Although the Salafi-jihadist threat in MENA and globally has become fractured and localized, the Islamic State (IS) in particular continued to drive or influence a number of disparate groups in Iraq and Syria.[25] Western coalition forces continued to attack the groups with sporadic airstrikes, while

---

[19] For earlier developments in these issues see *SIPRI Yearbook 2019*, pp. 81–87; *SIPRI Yearbook 2020*, pp. 132–36; and *SIPRI Yearbook 2021*, pp. 139–46.

[20] O'Driscoll, D. et al., *Protest and State–Society Relations in the Middle East and North Africa*, SIPRI Policy Paper no. 56 (SIPRI: Stockholm, Oct. 2020); and 'Identity crisis: The Arab world', Special Report, *The Economist*, 28 Aug. 2021.

[21] See e.g. Gambrell, J., 'Protests spread across once-quiet Oman as economy flounders', AP News, 25 May 2021; Chehayeb, K., 'Lebanon's PM-designate Saad Hariri resigns as crisis escalates', Al Jazeera, 15 July 2021; and 'Iraq Kurdish police fire warning shots as students protest', France 24, 23 Nov. 2021.

[22] Fabiani, R., 'Tunisia's leap into the unknown', International Crisis Group, 28 July 2021.

[23] Bourhrous, A., 'Trust and coercion in times of emergency: COVID-19 and structures of authority in North Africa', SIPRI Essay, 13 Aug. 2020; and Mann, Y., 'Oil—A factor promoting or undermining stability in the countries of the Middle East?', *Comparative Strategy*, vol. 40, no. 5 (2021), pp. 455–67.

[24] O'Driscoll et al. (note 20), pp. 50–59.

[25] United Nations, Security Council, 'Thirteenth report of the Secretary-General on the threat posed by ISIL (Da'esh) to international peace and security and the range of United Nations efforts in support of Member States in countering the threat', S/2021/682, 27 July 2021; and Clarke, C. P., 'Twenty years after 9/11: What is the future of the global jihadi movement?', *CTC Sentinel*, vol. 14, no. 7 (Sep. 2021), pp. 91–105.

thousands of individuals suspected of belonging to IS remained in detention camps.[26] In Syria, new locally oriented jihad movement Hayat Tahrir al-Sham gained supremacy, achieving control over parts of north-west Syria.[27] In Yemen, al-Qaeda in the Arabian Peninsula remained a threat despite having been weakened by fragmentation into local factions.[28]

Linkages in MENA between water scarcity, climate change and insecurity issues are 'complex, diverse and multi-directional'.[29] Most states in the region are facing medium to high exposure to ecological threats, such as food insecurity and water stress, which is exacerbating forced displacement and rural to urban migration.[30] Climate change and water stress have played a role—whether direct or indirect—in the region's recent and ongoing conflicts and protests.[31]

Armed conflict and prospective state collapse in Lebanon

Since Lebanon's 15-year civil war ended in 1990, stability within the country has remained elusive due to rival militias, sectarian tensions, corruption and deep-rooted socio-economic inequalities. Hezbollah, which is by far the strongest faction in Lebanon, is better equipped even than the national army.[32] The economic, political and humanitarian crises in the country worsened in 2021, leading to further low-level armed clashes.[33]

Lebanon had been operating under a caretaker government since August 2020, when Prime Minister Hassan Diab resigned along with his ministers following the catastrophic explosion at Beirut's port that killed more than 200 people. In September 2021 a new government led by Prime Minister Najib Mikati was formed. However, the investigation into the port explosion widened divisions in government, sparking violence in October 2021 be-

---

[26] Sabbagh, D., 'RAF engaged in 10-day attack on ISIS in Iraq this spring', *The Guardian*, 8 Apr. 2021; and Altier, M. B., 'Lessons for reintegrating Islamic State detainees', Lawfare, 7 Mar. 2021.

[27] Thomson, M., 'IS brutality returning to Syrian towns', BBC News, 7 Feb. 2021; and Lister, C., 'Twenty years after 9/11: The fight for supremacy in Northwest Syria and the implications for global jihad', *CTC Sentinel*, vol. 14, no. 7 (Sep. 2021), pp. 44–62.

[28] Kendall, E., 'Twenty years after 9/11: The jihadi threat in the Arabian Peninsula', *CTC Sentinel*, vol. 14, no. 7 (Sep. 2021), pp. 63–75.

[29] Schaar, J., 'A confluence of crises: On water, climate and security in the Middle East and North Africa', SIPRI Insights on Peace and Security no. 2019/4, July 2019.

[30] Institute for Economics & Peace (IEP), *Ecological Threat Register 2020: Understanding Ecological Threats, Resilience and Peace* (IEP: Sydney, Sep. 2020).

[31] See e.g. Ide, T. et al., 'Pathways to water conflict during drought in the MENA region', *Journal of Peace Research*, vol. 58, no. 3 (2021), pp. 568–82; and Motamedi, M., 'Violence escalates in water-shortage protests in Iran's Khuzestan', Al Jazeera, 21 July 2021.

[32] Saab, B. Y., 'Hezbollah amid Lebanese collapse', Lawfare, 21 Feb. 2021.

[33] International Crisis Group, *Managing Lebanon's Compounding Crises*, Middle East Report no. 228 (International Crisis Group: Brussels, 28 Oct. 2021); and 'A year after the Beirut blast: Still no bottom to Lebanon's crisis', *The Economist*, 5 Aug. 2021. On the work of the World Food Programme in Lebanon see Tschunkert, K., *The World Food Programme's Contribution to Improving the Prospects for Peace in Lebanon* (SIPRI: Stockholm, Sep. 2021).

tween, reportedly, supporters of Hezbollah and the Lebanese Forces party.[34] The situation remained unstable, with estimated battle-related deaths from sporadic clashes keeping it above SIPRI's threshold for an armed conflict. According to the Armed Conflict Location & Event Data Project (ACLED) there were 73 conflict-related deaths in 2021 (29 battle-related), compared to 48 in 2020 (40 battle-related).[35] At the end of 2021 Lebanon was on the verge of state collapse.[36]

---

[34] 'How an investigation led to a gun battle in Lebanon', *The Economist*, 23 Oct. 2021; and 'Lebanon: Hezbollah, Lebanese Forces trade blame over deadly protests', Deutsche Welle, 14 Oct. 2021.

[35] Armed Conflict Location & Event Data Project (ACLED), 'Dashboard', accessed 8 Feb. 2022.

[36] Bourhrous, A. et al., *Reform Within the System: Governance in Iraq and Lebanon*, SIPRI Policy Paper no. 61 (SIPRI: Stockholm, Dec. 2021); Bourhrous, A., 'Fixing the economy and public service provision in Lebanon', SIPRI Policy Brief, Dec. 2021; and Wimmen, H., 'Lebanon: A journey to the end of the state', International Crisis Group, 24 Nov. 2021.

II. Armed conflict and peace processes in Iraq, Syria and Turkey

SHIVAN FAZIL

This section outlines how the complex and interconnected armed conflicts in Iraq, Syria and Turkey unfolded during 2021. The situation in Syria remained volatile, with clashes particularly intensive during the third quarter of the year. Iraq remained a fragile state, afflicted by weak institutions and a growing rift between the government and some militias. Iran-backed Shia parties with links to these militias suffered a setback in early parliamentary elections. Turkey's military operations in northern Iraq continued unabated, as did the protracted conflict in south-east Turkey. In Syria, Turkey and its aligned Syrian militias intensified their attacks in the Kurdish-controlled territory in the north-east. The Idlib ceasefire brokered in 2020 by Russia and Turkey—which cemented their roles as power brokers in Syria—remained in force, while the Kurdish forces in control of the territory in the north-east remained fearful of waning United States influence and the country's pivot away from the region following the Afghanistan withdrawal.

Armed conflict in Iraq

Post-conflict Iraq remains scarred by interrelated political, economic and security challenges, weak institutions and low levels of accountability, which have penetrated the economy and hindered the performance of the state.[1] In 2021 the country remained caught in the middle of tensions between the USA and Iran. Unable to rein in the Iranian-backed militias targeting US assets in Iraq or stop the USA from retaliating, Iraq continued to face threats to its stability four years after the territorial defeat of Islamic State (IS). Although the number of IS attacks were lower in 2021 compared to the previous year, the group persisted with its insurgency. Several sophisticated attacks in the third quarter of 2021 indicated a higher level of operational effectiveness and ambition, with IS continuing to seek the spark for renewed sectarian conflict.[2] In addition, despite the improved security situation, IS carried out deadly suicide explosions in crowded Baghdad markets in January and July.[3]

---

[1] Fazil, S., 'Fixing the economy and public service provision in Iraq', SIPRI Policy Brief, Dec. 2021; and Bourhrous, A. et al., *Reform Within the System: Governance in Iraq and Lebanon*, SIPRI Policy Paper no. 61 (SIPRI: Stockholm, Dec. 2021).

[2] Arraf, J. 'Iraq is caught in the middle as US and Iran spar on its soil', *New York Times*, 28 June 2021; 'Islamic State down but not out in Syria and Iraq: Pentagon report', Al-Monitor, 26 Nov. 2021; and Offices of Inspector General, *Operation Inherent Resolve: Lead Inspector General Report to the United States Congress*, 1 Oct.–31 Dec. 2021, 2022.

[3] 'Dozens killed in Baghdad suicide bombings', Al-Monitor, Jan. 2021; and 'Explosion at Baghdad's Sadr City injures at least 15', Al-Monitor, 1 July 2021.

Iraq's economy is still recovering from the twin shocks in 2020 of the oil price plunge and the Covid-19 pandemic. While the prospects for Iraq's economy improved with the recovery in global oil prices in 2021, key stumbling blocks remain in the form of the spread of new Covid-19 variants, the growing impacts of climate change, setbacks in the security situation and the derailing of economic reform implementation.[4] In August Iraq resumed talks with the International Monetary Fund for loans of up to $4 billion.[5] The dire economic situation saw thousands of Iraqis, mostly from the Kurdistan Region of Iraq (KRI), flee the country, with many ending up stranded at the Belarus–Poland border. The Iraqi government repatriated thousands of its nationals after they had failed in their attempts to enter the European Union (EU).[6]

The rift continued to grow between the government and some factions among the Popular Mobilization Forces (PMF)—an Iraqi state-sponsored umbrella organization composed of several predominantly Shia militias (some supported by Iran)—and smaller militias groups comprised by ethno-religious minorities in the country's north. Tensions reached a crescendo in November when Prime Minister Mustafa al-Kadhimi survived a drone attack on his residence.[7] Although no group claimed responsibility for the attack, suspicions fell on the Iran-aligned militias that had suffered a setback in the general elections (see below).[8] The attack also spotlighted divisions between the government and the Iran-backed militias, with questions raised about Iran's influence over these groups when it joined other countries in condemning the attack.[9] Despite the Iraqi government's attempts to integrate the PMF into the Iraqi Security Forces, progress remained slow.

In August Iraq hosted a high-level summit aimed at de-escalating regional tensions, with several heads of states, as well as Saudi and Iranian officials, in attendance. The meeting, co-organized with France, was seen as showcasing both Iraq's efforts to become a neutral meditator in the region's crises and re-engage with the world, and its attempts to rebalance relations with its neighbours after decades of conflict.[10] Iraq also hosted direct talks between Saudi Arabia and Iran, signalling a possible de-escalation in tensions and rapprochement following years of rivalry, which had often spilled over into neighbouring countries.[11] In July Iraq and the USA held another round of strategic dialogue, agreeing to end the presence of US combat troops in Iraq

---

[4] World Bank, 'Iraq's Economic Update, October 2021', 7 Oct. 2021.
[5] 'Iraq says its gone back to IMF for loan of up to $4 billion', Bloomberg, 5 Aug. 2021.
[6] 'Belarus: Iraq to fly migrants back to Baghdad in first repatriation flight', Euronews, 15 Nov. 2021.
[7] 'Iraqi PM al-Kadhimi survives drone attack on his home', BBC News, 7 Nov. 2021.
[8] 'Iraq PM says his would-be assassins have been identified', BBC News, 8 Nov. 2021.
[9] Yuan, S., 'Is Iran losing some of its grip on Shia militias in Iraq?', Al Jazeera, 12 Nov. 2021.
[10] 'Iraq hosts summit aimed at easing regional tensions', Al Jazeera, 28. Aug. 2021.
[11] AFP, 'Rivals Iran and Saudi Arabia hold talks in Baghdad', France 24, 19 Apr. 2021.

Table 6.2. Estimated conflict-related fatalities in Iraq, 2016–21

Event type	2016	2017	2018	2019	2020	2021
Battles	24 605	15 220	2 736	1 736	1 470	1 522
Explosions/remote violence	25 654	13 926	2 517	1 272	897	859
Protests, riots and strategic developments	319	58	57	469	114	37
Violence against civilians	5 755	2 823	311	240	324	332
Total	**56 333**	**32 027**	**5 621**	**3 717**	**2 805**	**2 750**

Notes: The first available year for data on Iraq in the Armed Conflict Location & Event Data Project (ACLED) database is 2016. For definitions of event types, see ACLED, 'ACLED definitions of political violence and protest', 11 Apr. 2019.
Source: ACLED, 'Dashboard', accessed 8 Feb. 2022.

by the end of 2021, at which point the US security relationship transitioned to an advisory role.[12]

Turkey's airstrikes and military ground operations against the Kurdistan Workers' Party (Partiya Karkerên Kurdistan, PKK) in northern Iraq continued into 2021. The operations wreaked havoc, aggravating tensions between various Kurdish factions on the one hand and between Turkey and Iraq on the other. Shelling and bombing, including the targeting of a refugee camp, resulted in the destruction of homes and livelihoods, triggering the displacement of villagers.[13] In the KRI, there were renewed clashes between PKK fighters and Peshmerga of the Kurdistan Democratic Party (KDP) in June.[14] The PKK accused the KDP of assisting Turkey's operations, while the latter insisted the PKK's presence in the KRI invites Turkey's attacks.[15] Turkey was also accused of deforestation activities in northern Iraq.[16] Drought and heat stress became more acute across the country in 2021 due to climate change and upstream damming by Turkey and Iran.[17]

In addition, Iran launched airstrikes against members of the Kurdistan Democratic Party of Iran, an exiled Kurdish separatist group in the KRI. Although no casualties were reported, these were the first such attacks since an Iranian missile strike in 2018. The Kurdish separatist groups from Iran

---

[12] Governments of the United States of America and the Republic of Iraq, 'Joint Statement on the US–Iraq Strategic Dialogue', US Department of State, 26 July 2021.

[13] 'Turkish drone attack kills three civilians in northern Iraq Kurdish refugee camp', France 24, 5 June 2021; and AFP, 'Iraqi Kurds in border zone flee Turkey's hunt for PKK', France 24, 9 June 2021.

[14] Glynn, S., 'Turkey's invasion of northern Iraq could lead to Kurdish civil war', openDemocracy, 2 July, 2021.

[15] Zaman, A., 'Turkey's anti-PKK assault leaves Kurds more divided', Al-Monitor, 6 July 2021.

[16] Tastekin, F., 'Massive Turkey-led logging in Iraqi Kurdistan causes outcry', Al-Monitor, 11 June 2021; and 'KRG calls for an end to Turkey's deforestation of the Kurdistan Region', GOV.KRD, 31 May 2021.

[17] Pawson, M., '"All the trees have died": Iraqis face intensifying water crisis', Al Jazeera, 5 Nov. 2021; and 'Water crisis and drought threaten 12 million in Syria, Iraq', Al Jazeera, 23 Aug. 2021.

mostly reside inside the KRI territories, and Iran has on many occasions urged Iraq to expel these groups.[18]

Overall, conflict-related fatalities continued to decline in 2021, a trend that started with declared victory over IS in 2018 (see table 6.2).

In June the Iraqi government vowed to close the remaining internally displaced persons (IDP) camps despite criticism from humanitarian and rights groups that its resettlement plans for families displaced by IS fighting were inadequate.[19] Following a wave of camp closures that began in 2020, humanitarian agencies reported that returnees faced dire conditions, with their homes still destroyed and villages lacking basic services during winter and the Covid-19 pandemic. Unresolved tensions over affiliations to IS were reported to have triggered new waves of evictions after the IDPs were made to return to their villages.[20] The situation in Sinjar, the Yezidi hometown in north-western Iraq, remained volatile despite a 2020 agreement between the Iraqi government and the Kurdistan Regional Government to normalize the town's administrative and security situation. In 2021 the town remained entangled in a geopolitical competition between the two governments on the one hand, and between Turkey and Iran-backed militias on the other. In August and December, Turkey launched airstrikes against the local Yezidi armed groups it deemed to be PKK affiliates.[21] PMF factions refused to leave, instead bringing in more fighters to reinforce their control over the town in response to Turkey's threatened incursions.[22] Overall, the humanitarian situation in Iraq, including the KRI, remained challenging, with almost 1.2 million IDPs (including new displacements by a resurgent IS in Diyala) as of the third quarter of 2021.[23]

Early parliamentary elections

In October 2021 early parliamentary elections were held: the first vote in Iraq since mass protests hit the country in 2019, toppling the then government, and also the first to be held under a new electoral law demanded by the protestors. Both the EU and the United Nations sent monitors, with the

---

[18] 'Iran launches air strikes on Kurdish separatist group in northern Iraq', Middle East Eye, 9 Sep. 2021; and 'Iran asks Iraq to expel Iranian rebels from Kurdistan region', Reuters, 10 Aug. 2021.

[19] Qazi, S. and Botane, K., 'Iraq: IDPs say they are being threatened to leave camp', Al Jazeera, 1 Feb. 2021.

[20] Al Khateeb, F., 'Returning Iraqis face dire conditions following camp closures', UNHCR, 27 May 2021; and Human Rights Watch, 'Iraq: Apparent familial feud drives illegal evictions', 11 Aug. 2021.

[21] Kittleson, S., 'Turkey targets PKK-linked Yazidis inside Iraq', Al-Monitor, 13 Dec. 2021; and '"Deaths, injuries" as Turkish air raid hits clinic in Iraq's Sinjar', New Arab, 17 Aug. 2021.

[22] Porter, L., 'Despite government promises, lives in Sinjar remain on hold', New Humanitarian, 30 Mar. 2021.

[23] International Organization for Migration (IOM), Displacement Tracking Matrix, 'Iraq Master List Report 123 (August–September 2021)'; and IOM, Displacement Tracking Matrix, 'Attacks in Muqdaya, Diyala', DTM emergency tracking.

latter enacting one of its largest ever electoral assistance projects.[24] Special provisions were made to register IDPs, allowing them to vote in their districts of origin.[25] Despite the high stakes, low turnout overshadowed a largely 'well managed and competitive' vote, with disillusioned Iraqis fearing it would only serve to reinforce a political system that had failed them.[26] The movement headed by the Shia cleric and politician Muqtada al-Sadr emerged as the biggest winner, while the pro-Iran Shia parties linked to the PMF suffered a major setback. Iran-backed parties rejected the results, mobilizing their followers to organize sit-in protests that turned violent after clashing with security forces in Baghdad.[27] The UN Security Council condemned the attempts to discredit the election and deplored the use of violence to settle election-related grievances, including threats against the UN mission and electoral commission.[28] Groups and independent candidates connected to the 2019 mass protests won a handful of seats, despite facing a campaign of intimidation that deterred many from participating.[29] The formation of the new government, which is expected to be completed in 2022, is a process often subject to intense negotiations and fraught with backdoor deals over the distribution of ministries. This is especially so this time around, as fractures within ethno-sectarian blocs have started to emerge, preventing the formation of large parliamentary blocs.[30]

Armed conflict in Syria

In 2021 the Syrian civil war—initially triggered by the 2011 uprising against the regime of Bashar al-Assad—remained an ongoing multisided armed conflict involving regional and international powers and their proxies. Since 2018 there has been a clear de-escalation in war due to the Syrian government's consolidation of territorial control and the territorial defeat of IS in 2019. Despite a further decrease in large-scale hostilities due to the Idlib ceasefire, the situation remained volatile, with intense clashes during the third quarter of 2021.[31]

---

[24] Fazil. S. and O'Driscoll, D., 'Iraqis go to the polls on October 10. What happens next?', Euronews, 4 Oct. 2021.

[25] United Nations Assistance Mission for Iraq (UNAMI), 'Elections for Iraq's Council of Representatives: Participation of internally displaced persons', Oct. 2021, Fact Sheet no. 9, 3 Oct. 2021.

[26] Chulov, M., 'Turnout at Iraqi national election sluggish as many boycott polls', *The Guardian*, 11 Oct. 2021; and European Union Election Observation Mission Iraq, 'Preliminary statement', 12 Oct. 2021.

[27] 'Pro-Iranian groups reject early Iraq election results as "scam"', Al Jazeera, 12 Oct. 2021; and 'Protests against Iraq election results turn violent', Al Jazeera, 5 Nov. 2021.

[28] Lederer, E., 'UN condemns attempts to discredit Iraq's recent election', ABC News, 15 Nov. 2021.

[29] AFP, 'Iraqis head to polls for early election shunned by activists', France 24, 10 Oct. 2021.

[30] Fazil (note 1); and Fazil, S., 'Government formation in gridlock while Iraq faces an array of challenges', LSE Blog, 17 Feb. 2022.

[31] Muaz, A., 'The state of Syria: Q2 2021–Q3 2021', ACLED.

The government of Bashar al-Assad remained in control of around two-thirds of the country, with armed opposition focused on two areas: Idlib province in the north-west, and the north-east, which is partially ruled by the Kurds. The armed conflict has attracted a complex and changing cast of fighters, including regional and global powers: Russia and Turkey in the north-west; and Russia, Turkey and the USA in the north-east. The UN-mediated peace process remained deadlocked in 2021 (see below), with key differences apparent within the Astana Group (Turkey, Russia and Iran) process: Russia and Iran support the Syrian government and the Syrian military's eventual retaking of Idlib, where Turkey-backed rebels and other armed opposition groups remain in control.[32] Iran continued its entrenchment in the south-west and in the east through further military build-up, while Israel continued its air strikes against Iran-aligned targets in order to maintain the buffer between itself and the Iranian-backed Syrian government.[33] The USA also carried out air strikes in eastern Syria's Deir ez-Zor province, along the border with Iraq, against Iran-backed militias.[34] In addition, IS remained a threat.[35]

The north-west: Turkey's quagmire despite the ceasefire in Idlib

There were no major military operations or changes in territorial control demarcation lines in the north-west of Syria in 2021. While implementation of the 5 March 2020 ceasefire agreement between Russia and Turkey remained in force, joint Russian–Turkish patrols to monitor the agreement were suspended. Nevertheless, small-scale attacks continued in Idlib, with Syrian/Russian attacks targeting civilians described as war crimes by rights groups.[36] The situation remained tense despite a decrease in hostilities attributable to the redeployment of Syrian government forces to the south following renewed clashes with opposition rebels in Daraa, the birthplace of the Syrian uprising (see below). In September, prior to a Russian–Turkish presidential summit, Russia increased its airstrikes against Turkey-backed rebels and opposition-held areas in Aleppo and Idlib.[37] Escalating violence, concerns

[32] 'Erdogan makes urgent appeal to West on grim 10-year mark of Syria's war', Al-Monitor, 19 Mar. 2021.

[33] Dukhan, H. and Alhamad, A., 'Iran's growing network of influence among eastern Syrian tribes', Fikra Forum, Washington Institute for Near East Policy, 6 Apr. 2021; and Caspit, B., 'Israel loses patience with Iranian entrenchment in Syria', Al-Monitor, 12 Nov. 2021.

[34] 'Biden takes first military action with Syria strike on Iran-backed militias', BBC News, 26 Feb. 2021; and 'Luce, D. and Gains, M., 'US airstrike in Syria on Iranian-backed militia killed one fighter, wounded two, Pentagon says', NBC News, 1 Mar. 2021.

[35] 'Oil workers killed in Islamic State attack in Syria', Al-Monitor, 3 Dec. 2021.

[36] 'Syria/Russia: 12 civilians dead in Idlib artillery attacks', Human Rights Watch, 8 Dec. 2021; and McLoughlin, P., 'Syrian regime, Russia guilty of 'war crimes' in Idlib over Ariha bombing: White Helmets', New Arab, 21 Oct. 2021.

[37] al-Kanj, S., 'Russia bombs Turkey's allies in Syria ahead of Putin-Erdogan summit', Al-Monitor, 28 Sep. 2021.

over a possible new military offensive, and attacks against refugee camps in Aleppo and Idlib provinces led to a new wave of civilian displacement.[38]

Turkey's involvement in the Syrian crisis has turned into a quagmire without any easy exit.[39] The Turkish armed forces and Turkey-backed Syrian rebels continued to battle against the Syrian Democratic Forces (SDF), with clashes primarily in Manbij (Aleppo), Tell Abiad (Raqqa) and Dardara (al-Hassakah). In September Turkish forces were reported to have used drone strikes against the SDF in locations further from the frontline after three Turkish soldiers were killed in Idlib, the last stronghold of Turkish-backed rebels in the north-west. Turkey also launched attacks against US-backed Kurdish forces in the north-east (see below).[40]

In addition, there were splits and infighting among the Turkey-backed rebels referred to as the Syrian National Army (SNA). In September several factions affiliated with the SNA merged under a new alliance known as the Syrian Liberation Front in a bid to end the infighting and power struggle between Turkey's allied factions in the north.[41] The merger could also be seen as part of Turkey's efforts to enhance the image of rebel forces accused of al-Qaeda affiliation, which Turkey supports against both Syrian government forces and the US-backed SDF.[42]

The north-east: Turkey steps up its attacks

In 2019 a protracted but ultimately partial withdrawal of US forces from the north-eastern area of Syria led to a new Turkish military offensive, which was halted only by a Russian–Turkish agreement on 22 October 2019.[43] Turkish forces retained seized territory while Russian and Syrian forces were expected to control the remainder of a 'safe zone' on the Syria–Turkey border. As such, a challenging but fragile stalemate continued in north-eastern Syria throughout 2021. The SDF, led primarily by the People's Protection Units (Yekîneyên Parastina Gel, YPG), protected the autonomous administration it continued to govern in most of the north-east not held by Turkey or its Syrian allies.

In the third quarter of 2021 Turkey stepped up its attacks, deploying drone strikes against the YPG across multiple fronts, including in Qamishli, Aleppo

---

[38] al-Khateb, K., 'Massive displacement wave amid fears of renewed battles in Idlib', Al-Monitor, 17 Sep. 2021.

[39] 'Turkey faces gathering storm in Syria', Al-Monitor, 17 Sep. 2021.

[40] al-Khateb, K., 'Turkish-backed Syrian forces intensify attacks on US-aligned Syrian Kurdish group', Al-Monitor, 14 Sep. 2021; and Tastekin, F., 'Turkey's blind eye to jihadis worsens its predicaments in Syria', Al-Monitor, 16 Sep. 2021.

[41] al-Kanj, S., 'Turkey-backed Syrian opposition groups merge under new banner', Al-Monitor, 16 Sep. 2021.

[42] al-Kanj, S., 'Syrian jihadist group ramps up efforts to oust rivals from Idlib', Al-Monitor, 2 July 2021.

[43] 'Full text of Turkey, Russia agreement on northeast Syria', Al Jazeera, 22 Oct. 2019.

and al-Hassakah. The SDF general command, which had unilaterally ceased offensive military activities in order to facilitate responses to the Covid-19 pandemic, vowed to retaliate against the attacks. Turkey also hinted at yet another military ground operation into the Kurdish-controlled territory in north-eastern Syria.[44] Aside from shelling and drone attacks, Turkey weaponized water supplies in its war against the Kurds in Syria.[45] In addition to Turkey's limited release of water from its dams into the Euphrates river, Turkish-backed armed groups blocked north-east Syria's water lifeline by cutting off the vital Khabur river, the most important tributary of the Euphrates. This exacerbated already existing climate-related risks, with severe consequences for communities dependent on irrigation.[46] Turkey's escalations and threats of new military ground operations raised concerns among Kurdish forces, who feel abandoned by the USA. The Afghanistan withdrawal added to their fears of a complete US withdrawal from the region.[47]

The humanitarian crisis, conflict casualties and war crimes

The year 2021 marked the 10th anniversary of the uprising and war—a long decade of trauma that, according to various estimates, has cost over half a million lives. On top of this, more than half the country's pre-war population of 22 million have become either refugees or internally displaced. In 2021 Syria remained the world's largest refugee crisis, with 6.7 million IDPs and 6.6 million external refugees hosted mainly by the neighbouring countries of Jordan, Turkey and Lebanon.[48] Syria and its economy are still in ruins, with 12 million on the brink of starvation.[49] The deepening of the economic crisis triggered the return of street protests in the south of the country's besieged town of Daraa, known as the cradle of the 2011 Syrian uprising.[50] Although there are no reliable casualty statistics, a leading United Kingdom-based monitoring group estimate a death toll of over 606 000 since the start of the uprising.[51] In 2016 the UN envoy estimated over 400 000 Syrians had died in the war. Since then, ACLED has estimated there have been over

---

[44] al-Kanj, S., 'Syrian Kurdish parties feel abandoned by US in wake of Turkish-backed attack', Al-Monitor, 8 Sep. 2021; and Omer, Z. and Kajjo, S., '3 killed in suspected Turkish drone attack in NE Syria', VOA, 9 Nov. 2021.

[45] Zaman, A., 'Turkey's war of attrition against Syria's Kurds', Al-Monitor, 17 Nov. 2021.

[46] Zwijnenburg, W., 'Killing the Khabur: How Turkish-backed armed groups blocked northeast Syria's water lifeline', PAX for Peace, 3 Nov. 2021; and 'Water crisis and drought threaten 12 million in Syria, Iraq', Al Jazeera, 23 Aug. 2021.

[47] Mohammed, Z. and Majeed, R., 'Afghanistan fall renews Kurdish fears of US withdrawal in Iraq, Syria', VOA, 20 Aug. 2021.

[48] UNHCR, 'Syria refugee crisis explained', 5 Feb. 2021.

[49] World Food Programme, 'Twelve million Syrians now in the grip of hunger, worn down by conflict and soaring food prices', 17 Feb. 2021.

[50] Dadouch, S., 'In the cradle of the Syrian revolution, renewed violence shows reconciliation is still elusive', Washington Post, 19 Sep. 2021.

[51] 'Syria war: UN calculates new death toll', BBC News, 24 Sep. 2021.

Table 6.3. Estimated conflict-related fatalities in Syria, 2017–21

Event type	2017	2018	2019	2020	2021
Battles	26 575	16 007	8 416	4 357	2 467
Explosions/remote violence	25 236	11 848	5 925	2 810	2 472
Protests, riots and strategic developments	222	18	63	21	17
Violence against civilians	2 358	2 261	1234	1 023	905
Total	**54 391**	**30 134**	**15 638**	**8 211**	**5 861**

Notes: The first available year for data on Syria in the Armed Conflict Location & Event Data Project (ACLED) database is 2016. For definitions of event types, see ACLED, 'ACLED definitions of political violence and protest', 11 Apr. 2019.

Source: ACLED, 'Dashboard', accessed 9 Feb. 2022.

100 000 additional fatalities, including approximately 5900 in 2021 (which is lower than 2020, see table 6.3).

The peace processes and Syria's potential return to the Arab fold

The main peace efforts in Syria have included long-standing UN-mediated talks, regular discussions by the more military-focused Astana Group (Iran, Russia and Turkey), an October 2018 Quartet Meeting (France, Germany, Russia and Turkey), and a fragile patchwork of localized de-escalation agreements and ceasefires. In October 2019 150 delegates (50 each from the government, opposition and civil society) met in Geneva to begin drafting a new Syrian constitution—the first step in a political process expected to lead to UN-supervised elections. However, little progress was made at the three subsequent rounds of negotiations in 2019–20. Although two further rounds of negotiations were held in 2021 (25–29 January and 18–21 October), these again failed to reach any breakthrough.[52] The UN Special Envoy for Syria described the October session as a 'big disappointment', despite an earlier announcement of a breakthrough in constitutional talks between the opposition and regime negotiating teams.[53] With the Syrian constitutional process gridlocked, the prospects of an end to the civil war seem remote. In December Russia and Turkey urged the Kurds to engage with Damascus and underlined their support for Syria's territorial integrity.[54] In May Bashar al-Assad was reelected for another seven-year term in a presidential election widely rejected by Western states as 'illegitimate' and 'neither free nor fair',

[52] United Nations, '"We can't continue like this": UN envoy's grim assessment of Syria peace process', UN News, 29 Jan. 2021; and 'Syria: Latest round of talks on constitution begins in Geneva', Al Jazeera, 25 Jan. 2021.

[53] United Nations, '"Big disappointment" over lack of Syria constitution agreement', UN News, 22 Oct. 2021; and McLoughlin, P., 'Constitutional crisis: The Syria peace talks that are going nowhere', New Arab, 6 Dec. 2021.

[54] 'Russia, Turkey press Syrian Kurds to engage with Damascus', Reuters, 22 Dec. 2021.

given that it was held outside the framework set out in UN Security Council Resolution 2254.[55]

Nonetheless, external actors continued to adjust their positions vis-à-vis Syria in 2021, with the desire for regional stability seemingly stronger than that of ousting al-Assad.[56] Having survived a decade of war, al-Assad seemed poised to return to the world stage, despite opposition from the West. Many of the Arab states that cut him off after the outbreak of the civil war or opposed his rule by supporting opposition rebels have begun rebuilding ties, with the country making further inroads to end its isolation in 2021. In September Jordan reopened its border with Syria. Egypt and the United Arab Emirates (UAE) made concerted efforts to restore relations between Syria and the Arab world, as well as the country's membership in the Arab League.[57] Oman, Kuwait, Jordan, Bahrain and the UAE all reopened their embassies, with the latter exploring avenues for future cooperation and investment.[58] Also noteworthy was an agreement allowing the delivery of Egyptian gas and Jordanian electricity to Lebanon via Syria, which had not yet taken place by the end of 2021 due to Jordan and Egypt seeking reassurances from the USA regarding whether this would constitute a violation of Syria sanctions.[59] However, despite many overtures there is lack of consensus among the Arab states regarding a complete rapprochement. With the peace process gridlocked, a sustained ceasefire that freezes the conflict may have a broad consensus.

Armed conflict between Turkey and Kurdish insurgent groups

Turkey's military operations in northern Syria and Iraq are driven by decades-long armed conflict in the south-east of Turkey between Turkish armed forces and the PKK. However, since the outbreak of the Syrian conflict, Turkey's efforts have focused on preventing the Syrian Kurds from achieving a degree of political autonomy inside Syria following their US-supported military and political gains. As noted above, Turkey also continued its military incursions into northern Iraq in 2021, and in October threatened to launch a

---

[55] 'Assad wins Syrian election dismissed as farce by critics', BBC News, 27 May 2021; and 'Syria elections: Polls open as Western countries slam "illegitimate" vote', Deutsche Welle, 26 May 2021.

[56] 'Joint op-ed by 18 foreign ministers on the fight against impunity for crimes committed in Syria', Government Offices of Sweden, 31 Mar. 2021.

[57] Saied, M., 'Egypt steps up efforts to "restore Syria's position in the Arab world"', Al-Monitor, 30 Sep. 2021.

[58] Sherlock, R., 'Arab nations that opposed Assad's regime have begun rebuilding ties with Syria', NPR, 14 July 2021; and 'UAE foreign minister meets Syria's Assad, US slams visit to "dictator"', France 24, 10 Nov. 2021.

[59] 'Egypt, Jordan, Syria agree to export gas to crisis-stricken Lebanon', Al-Monitor, 8 Sep. 2021; and Harris, B. and Joyce, K., 'Arab states get cold feet over Egypt-to-Lebanon gas deal', The National, 22 Feb. 2022.

Table 6.4. Estimated conflict-related fatalities in Turkey, 2016–21

Event type	2016	2017	2018	2019	2020	2021
Battles	3 650	2 303	1 638	765	413	214
Explosions/remote violence	1 370	521	253	174	118	64
Protests, riots and strategic developments	14	4	8	4	1	1
Violence against civilians	166	97	28	14	20	18
Total	**5 200**	**2 925**	**1 927**	**957**	**552**	**297**

Notes: The first available year for data on Turkey in the Armed Conflict Location & Event Data Project (ACLED) database is 2016. For definitions of event types, see ACLED, 'ACLED definitions of political violence and protest', 11 Apr. 2019.

Source: ACLED, 'Dashboard', accessed 9 Feb. 2022.

new military offensive in the Kurdish-controlled autonomous administration in northern Syria.

The armed conflict between Turkish armed forces and the PKK inside Turkey continued in 2021, with two independent sources estimating fatalities in the range of 300–350. According to International Crisis Group 344 people were killed in 2021 (25 civilians, 268 PKK rebels and 51 state security forces), compared to 341 in 2020, taking the total number of deaths to 5731 since the resumption of hostilities in July 2015.[60] ACLED, meanwhile, estimated there were 297 conflict-related fatalities in 2021, indicating a continuous decline in fatalities since 2016 (see table 6.4).

Resolution of this protracted conflict is predicated on the Turkish peace process with the Kurds (also known as the resolution process, which collapsed in July 2015) resuming, as well as the establishment of peaceful relations between Turkey and the YPG in Syria, which Turkey views as an extension of the PKK. However, the prospect of either seems remote given Turkey's continuing crackdown on the pro-Kurdish Peoples' Democratic Party, which is battling for its political survival in the Turkish courts. Moreover, its former co-leader remains in prison despite calls for his release, including from the European Court of Human Rights.[61]

[60] International Crisis Group, 'Turkey's PKK conflict: A visual explainer'.

[61] Cupolo, D., 'Top Turkish court accepts revised indictment to ban pro-Kurdish party', Al-Monitor, 21 June 2021; and Kucukgocmen, A., 'European Court of Human Rights says Turkey must free Demirtas', Reuters, 22 Dec. 2020.

III. The Israeli–Palestinian conflict and peace process

IAN DAVIS

The history of Israel's occupation of the Gaza Strip, Golan Heights and West Bank—territories it captured in the 1967 Arab–Israeli War—is well known and much commented upon.[1] Israeli settlement expansion in the occupied territories has added to recent instability, especially in the West Bank. Developments in 2020—the new US 'peace plan', the threatened annexation of parts of the West Bank, and Israeli normalization agreements (the Abraham accords) with Bahrain, Morocco, Sudan and the United Arab Emirates—had suggested a potentially significant shift in the regional Arab–Israeli conflict.[2] However, despite further marginalization of the Palestinians, the underlying reality in the local Israeli–Palestinian conflict remained largely unchanged. There appeared little prospect of resolving the principal Israeli–Palestinian territorial dispute, including Israel's occupation in its various forms, or of ending Palestinian political divisions. These underlying conflict dynamics continued in 2021, with a new US presidency and a new Israeli coalition government adding additional layers of uncertainty. In May 2021 the conflict escalated again, with Israel and Hamas fighting an 11-day war, their fourth in 14 years. The economic and humanitarian costs of the Israeli occupation to the Palestinian people also continued to be severe, with 2.1 million Palestinians projected to need humanitarian assistance in the occupied territories in 2022.[3]

An escalation in Gaza and rioting within Israel

In recent years frequent military exchanges between Hamas and/or the Islamic Jihad Movement in Palestine (rockets fired into Israel) and Israel (air strikes in Gaza) have been punctuated by often short-lived ceasefire arrangements. On 10 May 2021 the conflict escalated again after weeks of protests in East Jerusalem, triggered by plans to evict Palestinian families

---

[1] See e.g. Shlaim, A., *The Iron Wall: Israel and the Arab World* (W. W. Norton: New York, 2014); Thrall, N., *The Only Language They Understand: Forcing Compromise in Israel and Palestine* (Metropolitan Books: New York, 2017); and Anziska, S., *Preventing Palestine: A Political History from Camp David to Oslo* (Princeton University Press: Princeton, NJ, 2018).

[2] For developments in 2020 see *SIPRI Yearbook 2021*, pp. 160–65. On the impact of the Abraham accords see 'The Palestinian cause no longer binds the Arab world', *The Economist*, 24 Aug. 2021; Fulton, J. and Yellinek, R., 'UAE–Israel diplomatic normalization: A response to a turbulent Middle East region', *Comparative Strategy*, vol. 40, no. 5 (2021), pp. 499–515; and Falah, G.-W., 'How should one read Trump's map of the "deal of the century"?', *Third World Quarterly*, vol. 42, no. 12 (2021), pp. 3030–50.

[3] United Nations Office for the Coordination of Humanitarian Affairs (UN OCHA), *Global Humanitarian Overview 2022* (UN OCHA: 2021), pp. 107–10; and 'Palestinians condemn Israel's move to send vaccines overseas', Al Jazeera, 25 Feb. 2021.

displaced in 1948 and now living in the Sheikh Jerrah area. This prompted Palestinian armed factions in Gaza to fire rockets into Israel and the Israeli military to retaliate with heavy bombardments of Gaza.[4]

Following growing international pressure, a ceasefire brokered by Egypt was agreed on 20 May (coming into effect a day later), ending 11 days of fighting that killed at least 242 Palestinians in Gaza and 12 people in Israel. The Israeli military said that it carried out over 1500 air, land and sea strikes on sites in Gaza—including a tunnel network allegedly used by Hamas to move weapons and combatants. In addition, the military strikes destroyed houses, medical facilities and roads throughout Gaza, as well as a 12-story building in Gaza City that housed several media outlets. Palestinian armed groups launched more than 4000 rockets at Israel, most of which were shot down by Israeli defences, landed in unpopulated places or fell short within Gaza.[5]

The conflict in Gaza also sparked unrest in the West Bank—where 34 Palestinians were killed in May 2021—an unprecedented general strike by Palestinian citizens across Israel and the occupied territories, and large-scale street protests and mob violence between Palestinians and Jews within Israel's mixed cities and towns, prompting warnings that the disorder could lead to civil war.[6]

On 27 May 2021 the United Nations Human Rights Council agreed to establish a panel to investigate potential 'violations of international humanitarian law' by both Israel and Hamas during the May 2021 clashes.[7] A more wide-ranging investigation had already been announced in March 2021 by the International Criminal Court (ICC) in relation to alleged war crimes by both sides, focusing on events beginning in 2014. Israel and the United

---

[4] Federman, J. and Akram, F., 'Israel, Hamas escalate heavy fighting with no end in sight', AP News, 12 May 2021. On the evolution and conduct of the conflict see International Crisis Group and US/Middle East Project, *Beyond Business as Usual in Israel–Palestine*, Middle East Report no. 225 (International Crisis Group: Brussels, 10 Aug. 2021); and Zonzsein. M., 'Why Jerusalem cannot be "taken off the table"', International Crisis Group, 16 Dec. 2021.

[5] International Crisis Group and US/Middle East Project (note 4); UN OCHA, 'Escalation in the Gaza Strip, the West Bank and Israel', Flash Update no. 12, 23 May 2021; Kingsley, P., Yee, V. and Bengali, S., 'Israel's attack on a press building in Gaza draws condemnations', *New York Times*, 16 May 2021; and Airwars, *'Why Did They Bomb Us?' Urban Civilian Harm in Gaza, Syria and Israel From Explosive Weapons Use* (Airways: London, Dec. 2021).

[6] 'Israel bombards Gaza as it confronts mob violence at home', *The Economist*, 14 May 2021; Walsh, D. and Nagourney, E., 'Warnings of "civil war" as Arabs and Jews face off violently in Israel's streets', *New York Times*, 13 May 2021; and 'Israeli forces open fire on Palestinians; hundreds wounded', Al Jazeera, 9 July 2021.

[7] UN Human Rights Council, 'Human Rights Council establishes International Commission of Inquiry to investigate violations in the Occupied Palestinian Territory, including East Jerusalem, and in Israel', 27 May 2021.

States are opposed to the ICC investigation.[8] Moreover, in April 2021 the non-governmental organization Human Rights Watch accused Israel of committing the crimes against humanity of apartheid and persecution, following a similar analysis from the Israeli organization B'Tselem in January 2021.[9] In October Israel designated six Palestinian human rights groups as terrorist organizations.[10] In the West Bank, tensions increased in the last four months of 2021 as Israel moved forward with plans to build some 3000 homes for Israeli settlers, despite criticism from the Biden administration and several European countries.[11] Attacks by Israeli settlers against Palestinians spiked in this period.[12]

Despite some limited Israeli airstrikes on Gaza in mid June, after Palestinian groups sent incendiary balloons into southern Israel, and further strikes in August, the fragile ceasefire in Gaza remained in place during 2021.[13] Total annual casualties in the Israel–Palestine conflict were at their highest since 2018 (when 299 Palestinians were killed and more than 29 000 were injured by Israeli forces, mostly in protests along the Gaza–Israel border). In 2021 Israeli forces killed 339 Palestinians (257 in the Gaza Strip and 82 in the West Bank), with 18 796 injured; while Palestinians killed 11 Israelis (compared to 3 in 2020) and injured at least 157 others.[14] Overall, the Israel–Palestine conflict has claimed over 14 000 lives since 1987, with its asymmetric nature highlighted by the fact that Palestinians account for 87 per cent of the deaths.[15]

---

[8] 'Kamala Harris tells Netanyahu that US opposes ICC probe of Israel', Al Jazeera, 5 Mar. 2021; Office of the Prosecutor, 'Statement of ICC Prosecutor, Fatou Bensouda, respecting an investigation of the situation in Palestine', International Criminal Court (ICC), 3 Mar. 2021; and Williams, D., 'Israel to tell ICC it does not recognise court's authority', Reuters, 8 Apr. 2021.

[9] Human Rights Watch, 'Gaza: Apparent war crimes during May fighting', 27 July 2021; Human Rights Watch, 'Palestinian rockets in May killed civilians in Israel, Gaza', 12 Aug. 2021; B'Tselem, 'A regime of Jewish supremacy from the Jordan river to the Mediterranean sea', 12 Jan. 2021; and Human Rights Watch, 'A threshold crossed: Israeli authorities and the crimes of apartheid and persecution', 27 Apr. 2021. On the application of the laws of war to the conflict see also Carpenter, C., 'Three myths about the laws of war and the Israel–Hamas conflict', World Politics Review, 21 May 2021.

[10] Kingsley, P., 'Israel accuses 6 Palestinian rights groups of terrorism', New York Times, 22 Oct. 2021.

[11] AP News, 'Five Palestinians shot dead in gun battles with Israeli troops in West Bank', The Guardian, 27 Sep. 2021; and Carey, A. and Gold, H., 'Israeli settlement plans in the West Bank draw condemnation from US, UK, Europe', CNN, 28 Oct. 2021.

[12] Hendrix, S., '"Hate crime" attacks by Israeli settlers on Palestinians spike in the West Bank', Washington Post, 29 Nov. 2021.

[13] 'Israel launches air raids on Gaza, first since truce with Hamas', Al Jazeera, 15 June 2021; Kingsley, P., 'Israel strikes Gaza again, after militants set fires in Israel', New York Times, 17 June 2021; and Reuters, 'Israeli aircraft strike Hamas sites in Gaza as hostilities escalate', The Guardian, 21 Aug. 2021.

[14] UN OCHA, 'Occupied Palestinian territory: Data on casualties', accessed 9 Feb. 2022.

[15] 'The Israel–Palestine conflict has claimed 14,000 lives since 1987', The Economist, 18 May 2021.

Outlook

There were no significant efforts in 2021 to re-energize the long-moribund two-state peace process—i.e. addressing the core issues of Palestinian statehood, demarcating borders and granting rights to Palestinian refugees— and the recent one-sided US peace initiative effectively ended with the change in the US presidency. With the prospects of a negotiated solution increasingly remote, the enduring conflict between Israel and Palestine looks set to continue for the medium term, with further outbreaks of armed violence, like the 11-day war in Gaza in May, seemingly likely.

IV. Armed conflict and peace processes in North Africa

IAN DAVIS

A decade on from the 2011 Arab Spring, North Africa—here comprising Algeria, Egypt, Libya, Morocco and Tunisia—is undergoing a convergence of crises, with negative spillover impacting the stability of neighbouring states in sub-Saharan Africa (see chapter 7) and the eastern Mediterranean (see chapter 5).[1] This section briefly discusses Egypt, Libya, Tunisia and the growing conflict in Western Sahara.

Armed conflict in Egypt

In 2021 the Egyptian government remained involved in a non-international armed conflict against the non-state armed group Wilayat Sinai (also known as Islamic State–Sinai Province) in the Sinai Peninsula. The Sinai insurgency (2011–present) deteriorated in 2014 when Islamist militants in Sinai embraced Islamic State and carried out large-scale attacks on civilian targets.[2] A state of emergency has existed in northern Sinai since October 2014, as well as in the country as a whole between April 2017 and October 2021.[3] The government is accused of human rights abuses in its military campaign and of using counterterrorism measures to silence dissent more widely.[4] The low-level armed conflict continued in 2021 with no end or decisive outcome in sight.[5] Estimated total conflict-related fatalities in Egypt in 2021 (264 fatalities) fell for the fifth successive year and are at their lowest level since 2012.[6]

Armed conflict and the peace process in Libya

There has been armed conflict in Libya since an armed rebellion, supported by Western military intervention, deposed Muammar Gaddafi in 2011. Although the armed conflict began as a civil war between Libya's rival east-

---

[1] There is no single accepted definition of North Africa. Some definitions include Sudan in North Africa. The conflict in Sudan is discussed in chapter 7, section IV, in this volume.

[2] On the historical developments and socio-political causes leading to the rise of Sinai province and its military build-up see Ashour, O., 'Sinai's insurgency: Implications of enhanced guerrilla warfare', *Studies in Conflict & Terrorism*, vol. 42, no. 6 (2019), pp. 541–58.

[3] Reuters, 'Egypt's President Sisi ends state of emergency for the first time in years', *Global Times*, 26 Oct. 2021. On developments in Egypt in 2018–20 see *SIPRI Yearbook 2019*, pp. 87–88; *SIPRI Yearbook 2020*, pp. 157–58; and *SIPRI Yearbook 2021*, pp. 166–67.

[4] Wintour, P., '"Not just Giulio Regeni": Hundreds have died in Egyptian custody, says report', *The Guardian*, 11 Dec. 2020; Human Rights Watch, 'Egypt: Massive Sinai demolitions likely war crimes', 17 Mar. 2021; and Human Rights Watch, '"Security forces dealt with them": Suspicious killings and extrajudicial executions by Egyptian security forces', 7 Sep. 2021.

[5] 'Egypt: Eight soldiers killed in Sinai "anti-terrorism" operations', Al Jazeera, 1 Aug. 2021; and 'Egyptian military consolidates grip on northern Sinai', Reuters, 20 Oct. 2021.

[6] Armed Conflict Location & Event Data Project (ACLED), 'Dashboard', accessed 10 Feb. 2022.

and west-based political authorities, it quickly became a regional proxy war. There is a strong economic dimension to the conflict, with competition among internal and external actors for control of key economic levers such as the central bank and oil revenues.[7] A United Nations-led peace process in 2020 offered new grounds for optimism that were largely borne out by further progress in 2021.[8] However, the postponement of the elections due to take place on 24 December 2021 created new levels of uncertainty in the peacebuilding roadmap.

The Libyan peace process

The Libyan peace process has three tracks: economic, military and political. During 2020 there had been progress mainly along the latter two of these tracks: the political track evolved into the Libyan Political Dialogue Forum (LPDF), while the military track led to a 23 October 2020 agreement on a permanent ceasefire covering all areas of Libya.[9] The new agreement required armed groups and military units to return to their respective bases (with some earmarked for demobilization), foreign mercenaries to depart within three months, and the creation of a joint military force and a way to monitor violations.[10] At the end of 2020 the UN was proposing to bring in monitors to oversee the ceasefire.[11]

The first round of talks within the LPDF took place in Tunisia in November 2020, where it was agreed to hold elections on 24 December 2021—the 70th anniversary of Libya's independence.[12] However, the November 2020 statement was vague on the exact terms of follow-up actions, and six rounds

---

[7] Carpenter, S., 'Waging economic war, Libyan strongman wants access to Central Bank cash', Forbes, 31 Jan. 2020.

[8] On the Libyan conflict and peace processes in 2016–20 see SIPRI Yearbook 2017, pp. 83–84; SIPRI Yearbook 2018, pp. 74–75; SIPRI Yearbook 2019, pp. 94–98; SIPRI Yearbook 2020, pp. 158–62 and SIPRI Yearbook 2021, pp. 167–73. On the complex interaction between localized and national conflicts in Libya since 2011 see Thornton, C., 'The Libyan carousel: The interaction of local and national conflict dynamics in Libya', ed. British Academy, Local Peace Processes (British Academy: London, Sep. 2021), pp. 22–29.

[9] 'Agreement for a complete and permanent ceasefire in Libya' (unofficial translation), 23 Oct. 2020; United Nations Support Mission in Libya (UNSMIL), 'UNSMIL statement on the resumption of intra-Libyan political and military talks', 10 Oct. 2020; and Zaptia, S., 'Immediate and permanent ceasefire agreement throughout Libya signed in Geneva', Libya Herald, 23 Oct. 2020.

[10] International Crisis Group, 'Fleshing out the Libya ceasefire agreement', MENA Briefing no. 80, 4 Nov. 2020.

[11] Wintour, P., 'UN to bring in monitors to observe Libya's widely flouted ceasefire', The Guardian, 1 Jan. 2021.

[12] British Foreign, Commonwealth & Development Office, 'Libyan Political Dialogue Forum and the Berlin Conference: Joint statement', Press release, 23 Nov. 2020.

of online follow-up meetings in 2020 failed to reach consensus on a legal framework for moving the electoral process forward.[13]

A breakthrough occurred in March 2021 with the establishment of a unified government for the first time since 2014. In a peaceful handover of power, the Government of National Unity—headed by Prime Minister Abdelhamid Dabaiba and a three-person Presidency Council—was accepted by both the internationally recognized Government of National Accord based in Tripoli and the rival Tobruk-based House of Representatives in the east of the country. This represented an important milestone towards unifying Libyan political institutions.[14] However, the new government faced several key challenges, including reunifying parallel financial institutions and the fragmented military, removing foreign military advisers and mercenaries (mainly Turkish forces in western Libya and Russian-linked private military contractors in central and southern Libya), and delivering a credible electoral roadmap.

On 23 June 2021 representatives of Libya's new interim national unity government joined foreign stakeholders at an international conference co-sponsored by the UN and Germany in Berlin aimed at renewing foreign commitment to supporting Libya's peace process.[15] However, conflicting visions for the country both among foreign governments and within the Libyan delegations continued to hinder progress in the implementation of the political, military and financial tracks.[16] In addition, tensions increased in June 2021 between rival armed coalitions in western Libya, while in the south IS launched its first attack since May 2020.[17]

In the second half of 2021 tensions increased around the electoral process. A legal framework for the election was adopted unilaterally by the House of Representatives but was rejected by other groups. Presidential candidates were disqualified and then readmitted.[18] Ján Kubiš, the UN Special Envoy

---

[13] International Crisis Group, 'Negotiations run aground, threatening political and economic stalemate', Crisis Group Libya Update no. 1, 11 Dec. 2020; and International Crisis Group, 'Foreign actors drive military build-up amid deadlocked political talks', Crisis Group Libya Update no. 1, 24 Dec. 2020.

[14] United Nations, Security Council, United Nations Support Mission in Libya, Report of the Secretary-General, S/2021/451, 11 May 2021; United Nations, Security Council, 'Statement by the President of the Security Council', S/PRST/2021/6, 12 Mar. 2021; and 'The prospects for Libya's interim government', Strategic Comments, vol. 27, no. 2 (2021), pp. iv–vi.

[15] United Nations, Security Council, Annex to the letter dated 23 June 2021 from the Permanent Representative of Germany to the United Nations addressed to the President of the Security Council Second Berlin Conference on Libya, S/2021/595, 24 June 2021.

[16] United Nations, Security Council, Letter dated 6 Aug. 2021 from the Secretary-General addressed to the President of the Security Council, S/2021/716, 9 Aug. 2021; and 'Doubts on elections multiply', Africa Confidential, vol. 62, no. 17 (26 Aug. 2021).

[17] United Nations, Security Council, United Nations Support Mission in Libya, Report of the Secretary-General, S/2021/752, 25 Aug. 2021, pp. 5–6.

[18] See e.g. 'Libya election panel rejects Gaddafi's son as presidential candidate', Reuters, 24 Nov. 2021; and 'Libya court reinstates Gaddafi presidential bid amid election chaos', Reuters, 2 Dec. 2021.

Table 6.5. Estimated conflict-related fatalities in Libya, 2012–21

Event type	2012	2013	2014	2015	2016	2017	2018	2019	2020	2021
Battles	458	197	2 381	2 000	2 201	972	742	1 234	802	53
Explosions/remote violence	27	87	483	715	864	509	363	948	643	44
Protests, riots and strategic developments	21	83	11	30	18	0	0	0	5	0
Violence against civilians	46	76	475	336	250	227	123	112	110	18
Total	**552**	**443**	**3 350**	**3 081**	**3 333**	**1 708**	**1 228**	**2 294**	**1 560**	**115**

Notes: For definitions of event types, see Armed Conflict Location & Event Data Project (ACLED), 'ACLED definitions of political violence and protest', 11 Apr. 2019.
Source: ACLED, 'Dashboard', accessed 10 Feb. 2022.

for Libya who was supposed to help oversee the process, resigned in November.[19] As the date of the election approached there were fears that violence would ensue. On 15 December militias briefly surrounded government offices in Tripoli.[20]

With the election at risk of being marred by disputes that might potentially lead to boycotts, disputed results and even armed violence, it became impossible to hold presidential elections on 24 December as planned. As such, on 22 December the Libyan electoral commission officially postponed the poll. Although a new date was expected within 30 days, as of the end of 2021 it remained unclear when the election would go ahead.[21]

An improving humanitarian situation and lower conflict-related fatalities

As a result of the improving security situation in 2021, the overall humanitarian situation saw some improvements across Libya, including a nearly 25 per cent decrease in the number of internally displaced persons to 213 000 people (compared to some 278 000 at the start of 2021).[22] With nearly 598 000 migrants, Libya serves as a major transit checkpoint for those hoping to reach Europe. As such, the smuggling of migrants and people trafficking in the Mediterranean Sea off Libya's coast remained key humanitarian concerns in 2021.[23] As of the end of 2021 an estimated 800 000 people still needed some form of humanitarian assistance—while this represented

[19] AFP, 'Libya: UN special envoy quits a month before presidential elections', *The Guardian*, 23 Nov. 2021.
[20] 'Armed militias deploy around key sites in Tripoli amid mounting doubts over ballot', *Arab Weekly*, 16 Dec. 2021.
[21] United Nations, 'Libyan elections postponed, new date expected within 30 days', UN News, 23 Dec. 2021.
[22] UN Office for the Coordination of Humanitarian Affairs (UN OCHA), *Global Humanitarian Overview 2022* (UN OCHA: 2021), pp. 104–106.
[23] United Nations, Security Council, Implementation of resolution 2546 (2020), Report of the Secretary-General, S/2021/767, 2 Sep. 2021; and 'UN demands Libya inquiry into shooting of escaping migrants', Reuters, 12 Oct. 2021.

a 36 per cent decrease compared to the beginning of the year, protests were growing about deteriorating living conditions.[24]

In an October 2021 report the UN Independent Fact-Finding Mission on Libya found reasonable grounds to believe that war crimes had been committed in the country, and that violence perpetrated in prisons and against migrants might amount to crimes against humanity.[25] Libya remained relatively peaceful throughout 2021 as the ceasefire largely held. Although there were some limited clashes among armed groups, the total annual number of estimated conflict-related deaths fell to its lowest level since the start of the conflict in 2011 (see table 6.5).

Outlook

The political reconciliation process remains in the balance due to the postponement of the presidential elections, with the risk that rival forces in Libya could once again mobilize. Achieving consensus on the electoral framework and resolving disputes over the eligibility of some of the presidential candidates continues to be key to keeping the peace process on track.

Protests in Tunisia

Despite Tunisia's revolution in 2011 often being portrayed as the sole success of the Arab Spring, it has not led to economic or political stability, with a 2021 surge in the Covid-19 pandemic further fuelling long-standing anti-government protests.[26] In July 2021 Tunisian President Kais Saïed sacked the country's prime minister and senior ministers, and suspended parliament for 30 days—a move political opponents called 'unconstitutional' or a coup.[27] The political crisis deepened in August as President Saïed indefinitely extended the suspension of parliament, then proceeded to announce in December that it would remain suspended until December 2022. A referendum on constitutional amendments is promised in July 2022, followed by a general election in December 2022.[28]

---

[24] UN OCHA (note 22); and Report of the Secretary-General, S/2021/767 (note 23).

[25] UN Human Rights Council, Report of the Independent Fact-Finding Mission on Libya, A/HRC/48/83 (advance and unedited version), 1 Oct. 2021.

[26] On the protests in Tunisia see O' Driscoll, D. et al., *Protest and State–Society Relations in the Middle East and North Africa*, SIPRI Policy Paper no. 56 (SIPRI: Stockholm, Oct. 2020), pp. 29–31.

[27] 'Tunisia's PM sacked after violent Covid protests', BBC News, 26 July 2021; and Foroudi, L., 'Ennahda calls for dialogue to resolve Tunisia's political crisis', Al Jazeera, 27 July 2021. Also see Rivera-Escartin, A., 'Tunisia's democratisation process: When "consensus democracy" undermines democratic consolidation', *Third World Quarterly* (2021).

[28] 'Tunisia's president extends suspension of parliament until further notice', Africanews, 24 Aug. 2021; and Reuters, 'Tunisia's president calls constitutional referendum followed by elections in 2022', *The Guardian*, 14 Dec. 2021.

Escalating tensions in Western Sahara

In November 2020 the 40-year territorial dispute over Western Sahara between Morocco and the Popular Front for the Liberation of Saguia el Hamra and Río de Oro (Polisario Front) erupted once more when the Polisario Front ended a 1991 ceasefire and launched attacks on Moroccan forces. The attacks followed a military operation by Moroccan forces in the buffer zone monitored by the UN Mission for the Referendum in Western Sahara.[29] Morocco controls about 80 per cent of Western Sahara, with the Polisario Front controlling the remainder of the territory.[30] At the start of 2021, with the peace process stalled, the risk of military escalation was growing.

In May–July 2021 Morocco was involved in separate diplomatic disputes with Spain, Germany and Algeria, although all were linked in some way to Western Sahara.[31] In August 2021 Algeria (which supports the Polisario Front) cut diplomatic ties with Morocco, then a month later closed its airspace to all Moroccan aircraft.[32] It was hoped that Staffan de Mistura's appointment as the UN Secretary-General's new personal envoy for the region, after a two-year search to fill the position, could re-energize the peace process.[33] However, ahead of a UN Security Council meeting on Western Sahara on 28 October, Polisario Front leader Brahim Ghali vowed to continue hostilities against Morocco unless it agreed to organize a referendum on self-determination.[34]

Although low-level clashes between the Polisario Front and Moroccan security forces continued in 2021, battle-related fatalities (12 in total) remained below SIPRI's threshold for an armed conflict. However, there were also 33 fatalities from 'explosions and remote violence', indicating that an armed conflict may already have resumed, although Morocco denied this was the case.[35]

[29] Dahir, A. L., 'Western Sahara independence group ends truce with Morocco', *New York Times*, 14 Nov. 2020.

[30] 'Things are heating up in Western Sahara', *The Economist*, 6 Nov. 2021.

[31] 'New diplomatic tension between Algeria and Morocco', Africanews, 19 July 2021; Green, A., 'Morocco is weaponizing migration to punish Spain on Western Sahara', World Politics Review, 21 May 2021; and Holleis, J. and Driouich, H., 'Tensions rise between Morocco and Germany', Deutsche Welle, 8 May 2021.

[32] 'Algeria cuts diplomatic ties with Morocco over "hostile actions"', Al Jazeera, 24 Aug. 2021; and 'Algeria closes airspace to Moroccan aviation as dispute deepens', Reuters, 23 Sep. 2021. On military spending rivalry between Algeria and Morocco see chapter 8, section II, in this volume.

[33] United Nations, 'Secretary-General appoints Staffan de Mistura of Italy personal envoy for Western Sahara', Press release, 6 Oct. 2021; and International Crisis Group, *Relaunching Negotiations Over Western Sahara*, MENA Report no. 227 (International Crisis Group: Brussels, 14 Oct. 2021).

[34] 'Western Sahara: Polisario Front leader vows attacks on Morocco will continue', Africanews, 17 Oct. 2021.

[35] ACLED, 'Dashboard', accessed 17 Feb. 2022; and *The Economist* (note 30).

V. Armed conflict and peace processes in Yemen

IAN DAVIS

The roots of the current multiparty war and humanitarian crisis in Yemen are complex and contested.[1] The Houthi insurgency began in 2004 when Hussein Badreddin al-Houthi, a leader of the Zaidi Shia, launched an uprising against the Yemeni government. Al-Houthi was killed in that uprising, with the insurgents going on to become known as the Houthis (the official name is Ansar Allah). In 2014, after several years of growing violence, the country descended into a new phase of civil war between the internationally recognized government of President Abdrabbuh Mansur Hadi and an uneasy alliance of Iran-backed Houthis and forces loyal to former president Ali Abdallah Saleh that controlled the capital, Sanaa, and large parts of the country.[2]

Since March 2015 a coalition led by Saudi Arabia has been intervening militarily on the side of President Hadi, although the coalition itself is divided by conflicts and rivalries. In addition to the United Arab Emirates (UAE), the coalition includes Bahrain, Egypt, Jordan, Kuwait, Morocco, Qatar (until 2017), Senegal and Sudan, either supplying ground troops or carrying out air strikes. The coalition has also received substantial international support (including arms transfers) from Canada, France, the United Kingdom and the United States.[3] A United Nations arms embargo on Yemen, which prohibits transfers to non-state actors in the country, has been continuously violated since it was imposed in 2015. In 2021, for example, the UN Panel of Experts on Yemen revealed that the Houthis had been able to produce uncrewed aerial vehicles (UAVs) and rockets using components sourced from the commercial market in Europe, the Middle East and Asia.[4]

Despite UN-mediated attempts to end the civil war—including the 2018 Stockholm Agreement, the 2019 Riyadh Agreement, and fresh attempts to broker a nationwide ceasefire in 2021—the armed conflict continued

---

[1] See *SIPRI Yearbook 2018*, pp. 80–82. See also e.g. Orkaby, A., 'Yemen's humanitarian nightmare: The real roots of the conflict', *Foreign Affairs*, Nov./Dec. 2017; and al-Hamdani, R. and Lackner, H., 'Talking to the Houthis: How Europeans can promote peace in Yemen', European Council on Foreign Relations, Policy Brief, Oct. 2020.

[2] On the national dialogue process in 2014 that failed to avert war see Elayah, M., van Kempen, L. and Schulpen, L., 'Adding to the controversy? Civil society's evaluation of the national conference dialogue in Yemen', *Journal of Intervention and Statebuilding*, vol. 14, no. 3 (2020), pp. 431–58.

[3] On arms transfers to Saudi Arabia and the UAE see chapter 9, sections II and III, in this volume. For a list of the main conflict actors and armed groups see United Nations, Human Rights Council, 'Situation of human rights in Yemen, including violations and abuses since September 2014', Report of the group of eminent international and regional experts on Yemen, A/HRC/48/20, Advanced edition, 10 Sep. 2021, Annex IV.

[4] United Nations, Security Council, 'Final report of the Panel of Experts on Yemen established pursuant to Security Council resolution 2140 (2114)', S/2022/50, 26 Jan. 2022, pp. 23–25. On the UN arms embargo on Yemen see chapter 14, section II, in this volume.

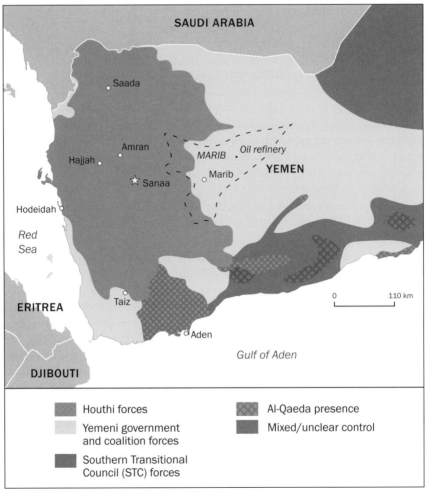

Figure 6.1. Areas of control and conflict in Yemen, May 2021

UAE = United Arab Emirates

Source: 'Houthi rebels look to take Marib, prolonging Yemen's war', *The Economist*, 8 May 2021.

throughout 2021, further exacerbating one of the world's worst humanitarian crisis.[5]

In recent years there have been at least three main conflict zones to this major internationalized civil war in Yemen (see figure 6.1): (*a*) in the north, between the coalition-backed Yemeni government and Houthi forces, including a Saudi Arabia–Yemen border conflict; (*b*) on the Red Sea coast, between Houthi and UAE-backed Joint Forces (that are only loosely affiliated with the

---

[5] On the Stockholm and Riyadh agreements and other developments in Yemen in 2018–20 see *SIPRI Yearbook 2019*, pp. 108–14; *SIPRI Yearbook 2020*, pp. 163–70; and *SIPRI Yearbook 2021*, pp. 175–82.

Yemeni government); and (*c*) in the south between the Yemeni government and the Southern Movement, a fragile coalition of separatist groups operating in Aden, Hadramaut and Shabwa, and represented politically by the UAE-backed Southern Transitional Council (STC). Another dimension to the armed conflict is the US-led counterterrorism campaign against radical armed groups—mainly al-Qaeda in the Arabian Peninsula (AQAP) and the local affiliate of the rival Islamic State—that operate mainly in the south. The USA has been carrying out regular air strikes against AQAP, or its antecedents, in Yemen since at least 2009. The frequency of US air strikes against AQAP has been steadily decreasing, with none officially reported in 2021 (although five were suspected by an independent monitor).[6]

Key developments in the three conflict zones in 2021

Military activity in Yemen continued to ebb and flow during 2021, with oil- and gas-rich Marib and Shabwa governorates the strategic focus of intermittent fighting. In February 2021 the Houthis began their attack on Marib governorate, and within weeks there were escalations on other frontlines. Heavy fighting continued for much of the year across frontlines in Marib governorate and by mid 2021 came within kilometres of Marib city.[7] The Houthi offensive led to large waves of displacement within the governorate. The Houthis also carried out multiple cross-border attacks on Saudi Arabia (including on oil facilities) using a combination of UAVs, short-range artillery, and cruise and ballistic missiles, with Saudi Arabia conducting retaliatory airstrikes on Houthi-controlled areas in Yemen.[8]

In the southern governorate in 2020 there were indications that the Riyadh Agreement—signed in November 2019 by the Yemeni government (backed by Saudi Arabia) and the STC (backed by the UAE)—was beginning to unravel. The situation seemingly improved when the STC agreed in December 2020 to join a newly constituted Hadi government in exchange for allowing the government to move back to Aden. However, on 30 December 2020 an attack was launched on Aden airport, moments after a plane carrying members of the new government landed.[9] The fractured relationship between the STC and the Yemeni government was reaffirmed on 16 March 2021 when

---

[6] Airwars, 'Declared and alleged US actions in Yemen'.

[7] United Nations, S/2022/50 (note 4), pp. 2, 8–9, 61–65; 'Houthi rebels look to take Marib, prolonging Yemen's war', *The Economist*, 8 May 2021; and 'Dozens killed in northern Yemen as battle for strategic city of Marib flares', France 24, 19 June 2021.

[8] United Nations, S/2022/50 (note 4), pp. 2, 20–23; Reuters, 'Saudi-led coalition launches air strikes on Yemeni capital', France 24, 7 Mar. 2021; Reuters, 'US "alarmed" by frequency of attacks on Saudi after Houthis target oil heartland', 8 Mar. 2021; and 'Saudi forces intercept ballistic missiles and drones fired from Yemen', *The Guardian*, 5 Sep. 2021.

[9] McKernan, B., 'Aden airport blasts kill 26 in attack "directed at Yemen government"', *The Guardian*, 30 Dec. 2020.

supporters of the STC stormed the Maasheq Presidential Palace in Aden. As of the end of 2021 the STC and its affiliated forces continued to control the governorate and the Yemeni government had no effective security presence in Aden.[10]

On the Red Sea coast, UN Security Council Resolution 2586 (2021) extended the mandate of the UN Mission to Support the Hodeidah Agreement (UNMHA), which was created in January 2019 to lead and support the Redeployment Coordination Committee (RCC)—a Houthi–Hadi working group formed to oversee the Hodeidah ceasefire—until 15 July 2022.[11] In the first half of 2021, while ceasefire violations and spikes in hostilities persisted, there was a continued reduction in reported violence and no major territorial shifts between the parties.[12] In November, however, the Joint Forces evacuated their positions from large parts of the governorate to reinforce the Marib and Shabwa fronts, with Houthi forces taking control of most of the vacated areas.[13]

Throughout the year there was a continued risk of a major oil spill from the *Safer* oil tanker, moored off the west coast of Yemen, 60 kilometres north of Hodeidah. With almost no maintenance since 2015, the *Safer*—carrying 1.1 million barrels of oil (four times the amount involved in the Exxon Valdez spill in 1989)—risked causing a major oil spill, with catastrophic environmental and humanitarian consequences. While the UN has sought to undertake assessment and salvage operations, the Houthis have not yet provided the necessary written security guarantees.[14]

The peace process

UN-brokered negotiations between the Yemeni government and the Houthis started in March 2020. The negotiations sought to reach agreement on a joint declaration that would include a nationwide ceasefire, economic and humanitarian measures, and resumption of the political process aimed at comprehensively resolving the conflict. In short, the UN was trying to sequence three distinct tracks—the Stockholm Agreement, the Riyadh Agreement and the Saudi Arabia–Houthi border de-escalation talks—into a single UN-led process to end the war. However, the process was criticized for excluding women and civil society groups.[15]

[10] United Nations, S/2022/50 (note 4), pp. 14–15.

[11] UN Security Council Resolution 2586, 14 July 2021.

[12] United Nations, Security Council, Letter dated 3 June 2021 from the Secretary-General addressed to the President of the Security Council, S/2021/528, 4 June 2021.

[13] United Nations, S/2022/50 (note 4), pp. 9–12.

[14] Wintour, P., 'Rotting Red Sea oil tanker could leave 8m people without water', *The Guardian*, 11 Oct. 2021.

[15] International Crisis Group, *The Case for More Inclusive—and Effective—Peacemaking in Yemen*, Middle East Report no. 221 (International Crisis Group: Brussels, 18 Mar. 2021).

Impact of the new US presidency and a new Saudi initiative

In February 2021 the new US administration announced changes in its policy towards Yemen, including ending the designation of the Houthis as a foreign terrorist organization and terminating support for what it called the Saudi-led coalition's 'offensive operations' in the conflict. President Biden also appointed a new US envoy to Yemen, Tim Lenderking.[16] However, the 'new' US approach appeared to have little impact on the conflict in 2021. Despite the commitment to a more diplomatic approach, the USA in practice remained a staunch Saudi ally—for example, supporting proposed weapons sales of air-to-air missiles and related equipment to Saudi Arabia worth a reported $650 million. A US Senate resolution that would have banned the sales was defeated in December 2021.[17]

On 22 March 2021 Saudi Arabia proposed a nationwide ceasefire in Yemen, with the plan including the reopening of some air and sea links, as well as the start of political negotiations. The Houthis, though, claimed that the initiative fell short of their demands.[18] At the regional level, Saudi–Iranian direct talks began in April 2021 in Iraq (see section I), while from June 2021 Oman led a mediation effort in the Yemen conflict backed by both the USA and Saudi Arabia.[19] However, the US criticized the Houthis for continuing to refuse to engage meaningfully on a ceasefire and political talks in Oman.[20] In September 2021 the new UN Special Envoy to Yemen, Hans Grundberg, declared that the country was 'stuck in an indefinite state of war' and that resuming negotiations to end the conflict would not be easy.[21] As of the end of 2021, movement towards a sustainable political solution to end the conflict remained stalled.[22]

---

[16] White House, 'Remarks by President Biden on America's place in the world', 4 Feb. 2021. On the impact of the US terrorist designation system on the conflict see van der Kroft, L., 'Yemen's Houthis and the terrorist designation system', International Centre for Counter-Terrorism, Policy Brief, June 2021.

[17] Desiderio, A., 'Senate backs Biden admin weapons sale to Saudi Arabia', Politico, 7 Dec. 2021.

[18] 'Yemen conflict: Saudi Arabia puts forward peace plan', BBC News, 22 Mar. 20201; and El Yaakoubi, A., 'Saudi Arabia proposes ceasefire in Yemen, Houthis sceptical', Reuters, 22 Mar. 2021.

[19] Al-Kharusi, M. and Borck, T., 'Omani mediation: A chance for Yemen?', RUSI Commentary, 7 Sep. 2021; and 'Riyadh and Washington back Oman as mediator in Yemen conflict', Intelligence Online, 15 Oct. 2021.

[20] 'US envoy says Yemen Houthi militia not trying to reach cease-fire', *Arab News*, 5 June 2021.

[21] The meeting record of the first briefing by the Special Envoy for Yemen, Hans Grundberg, in United Nations, Security Council, 'The situation in the Middle East', S/PV.8854, 10 Sep. 2021, pp. 2–3. On the UN envoy appointment see Salisbury, P., 'A new UN envoy is an opportunity for a new approach in Yemen', International Crisis Group Commentary, 18 June 2021.

[22] United Nations, Security Council, 'Warring parties in Yemen must talk even if they "are not ready" to put down arms, Special Envoy tells Security Council, describing escalating violence', SC/14735, 14 Dec. 2021.

Table 6.6. Estimated conflict-related fatalities in Yemen, 2015–21

Event type	2015	2016	2017	2018	2019	2020	2021
Battles	9 167	8 508	10 884	21 801	16 646	14 777	12 407
Explosions/remote violence	8 048	6 895	6 519	12 010	10 897	4 299	5 697
Protests, riots and strategic developments	77	14	17	40	174	77	74
Violence against civilians	228	242	169	418	339	613	276
Total	**17 520**	**15 659**	**17 589**	**34 269**	**28 056**	**19 766**	**18 454**

Notes: The first available year for data on Yemen in the Armed Conflict Location & Event Data Project (ACLED) database is 2015. For definitions of event types, see ACLED, 'ACLED definitions of political violence and protest', 11 Apr. 2019.

Source: ACLED, 'Dashboard', accessed 17 Feb. 2022.

The humanitarian crisis, conflict fatalities and alleged war crimes

The UN has described the humanitarian crisis in Yemen as the worst in the world since 2018, and in February 2021 the UN's Emergency Relief Coordinator warned of the 'worst famine the world has seen in decades'.[23] According to the UN Office for the Coordination of Humanitarian Affairs, around 20.7 million people in Yemen currently require some form of humanitarian or protection assistance, as a result of protracted conflict, disease outbreaks, the Covid-19 pandemic, flooding, import restrictions, and an economic and fuel crisis. More than 16.2 million of them (over half the population) faced significant food insecurity in 2021.[24] Additionally, international funding fell far short of the levels required to address the humanitarian crisis. In March 2021 the UN Secretary-General said the $1.7 billion that had been pledged was less than half the $3.85 billion it was seeking for 2021.[25]

The UN Development Programme estimates that 377 000 people have died in the Yemeni war since 2015 (including 154 000 due to direct attacks and 223 000 indirectly caused by disease, malnutrition or other consequences of the conflict), with over 18 400 people killed in direct attacks in 2021 alone (see table 6.6).[26]

---

[23] United Nations, 'Five million Yemenis "one step away from famine"—UN relief coordinator tells Security Council', UN News, 18 Feb. 2021.

[24] UN Office for the Coordination of Humanitarian Affairs (UN OCHA), *Global Humanitarian Overview 2022* (UN OCHA: 2021), pp. 115–18; Schulman, S., 'Yemenis' daily struggles between conflict and climate change', *RUSI Journal*, vol. 166, no. 1 (2021), pp. 82–92; and Cole, J. et al., 'Conflict, collapse and Covid-19', *RUSI Journal*, vol. 166, no. 3 (2021), pp. 10–19. On food insecurity in Yemen see also Murugani, V. et al., *Food Systems in Conflict and Peacebuilding Settings: Case Studies of Yemen and Venezuela* (SIPRI: Stockholm, Dec. 2021). On the economic conflict in Yemen see International Crisis Group, *Brokering a Ceasefire in Yemen's Economic Conflict*, Middle East Report no. 231 (International Crisis Group: Brussels, 20 Jan. 2022).

[25] Nichols, M., 'UN says disappointing $1.7 billion pledged for Yemen, impossible to avert famine', Reuters, 1 Mar. 2021.

[26] Hanna, T., Bohl, D. K. and Moyer, J. D., *Assessing the Impact of War in Yemen: Pathways for Recovery* (UN Development Programme: Sana'a, Nov. 2021), p. 32.

All parties to the conflict have faced allegations of crimes under international law over the past six years, including from a UN-established group of experts. Repeated calls by the expert group for prompt investigations into alleged violations and prosecutions of those responsible were ignored.[27] In October 2021 the UN Human Rights Council narrowly voted against a resolution to extend the work of the group. This marked the first time in the Council's 15-year history that a resolution had been defeated, reflecting international divisions on the issue. Human rights groups accused Saudi Arabia of heavy lobbying against the resolution.[28] The Houthis continued to recruit child soldiers and between 1 January 2020 and 31 May 2021 nearly 2000 child recruits died on the battlefield.[29]

Outlook

The political, security, military, economic and humanitarian situation in Yemen deteriorated further during 2021. The Houthis made significant territorial gains, and despite Saudi Arabia increasingly looking for a means to exit the war, the prospects of a political settlement in Yemen remain remote. After seven years of territorial fragmentation and the proliferation of armed groups and sub-conflicts, the UN Special Envoy reported at the end of 2021 that the conflict was escalating and could open a new chapter in the multi-party war in Yemen.[30] If the armed conflict continues through 2030, the total conflict-attributable death toll could reach 1.3 million people.[31]

[27] United Nations, A/HRC/48/20 (note 3). See also United Nations, S/2022/50 (note 4), pp. 39–45.
[28] Reuters, '"We have failed Yemen": UN human rights council ends war crime probe', *The Guardian*, 7 Oct. 2021; and Kirchgaessner, S., 'Saudis used "incentives and threats" to shut down UN investigation in Yemen', *The Guardian*, 1 Dec. 2021.
[29] United Nations, S/2022/50 (note 4), pp. 44, 134–48.
[30] United Nations, Security Council, 8929th meeting, 'The situation in the Middle East', S/PV.8929, 14 Dec. 2021.
[31] Estimated by the UN Development Programme see Hanna, Bohl and Moyer (note 26).

7. Armed conflict and peace processes in sub-Saharan Africa

Overview

At least 18 states in sub-Saharan Africa (out of a total of 49) experienced active armed conflict in 2021. High-intensity armed conflicts occurred in 12 states— Nigeria (9913 estimated conflict-related deaths); Ethiopia (8958); the Democratic Republic of the Congo (DRC) (5683); Somalia (3261); Burkina Faso (2373); South Sudan (2156); Mali (1910); the Central African Republic (CAR) (1707); Sudan (1652); Niger (1460); Cameroon (1395); and Mozambique (1158)—and low-intensity, subnational armed conflicts in a further 6 (Benin, Burundi, Chad, Kenya, Madagascar and Uganda). Eleven of these 18 countries suffered higher estimated conflict-related fatalities in 2021 than in 2020, with the total increase for the region standing at about 19 per cent.

Almost all the armed conflicts were internationalized. Conflict dynamics and ethnic and religious tensions were often rooted in a combination of state weakness, corruption, ineffective delivery of basic services, competition over natural resources, inequality and a sense of marginalization. Four other cross-cutting issues (section I) shaped security dilemmas in sub-Saharan Africa in 2021: (a) the presence of armed groups and criminal networks; (b) the security activities of external actors; (c) election-related violence; and (d) water insecurity and the growing impact of climate change. There were four successful military coups (in Chad, Mali, Guinea and Sudan) and three failed coups (in CAR, Niger and Sudan) in the region in 2021, compared to just one coup in 2020 (in Mali). There was no substantive progress in any of the region's peace processes in 2021, although sub-Saharan African states continued to host more multilateral peace operations—22—than any other region of the world.

Burkina Faso, Mali, Niger and Nigeria were West Africa's hotspots of insecurity in 2021, mainly due to the attacks of armed groups, some operating beyond their respective national borders (section II). Security forces countering these armed groups included national, regional and international forces, as well as local self-defence groups. In June 2021 France announced a drawdown of the 5000 Barkhane troops in Mali, to be replaced by the European multinational Task Force Takuba, which was established in 2020.

The security situation in Nigeria worsened in 2021, with a 27 per cent increase in conflict-related fatalities compared to 2020, due largely to the high number of conflicts between farmers and herders in the Middle Belt, a sharp rise in banditry in the north-west, and intensifying uprisings by separatists in the south-east.

There was some cautious optimism regarding the course of the conflict with Boko Haram in 2021, following the surrender of thousands of its fighters.

Central Africa (section III) contains some of the world's severest and most protracted crises. Large-scale violence continued in the eastern DRC as external and Congolese armed groups engaged in multiple armed conflicts with the government, alongside a resurgence of intercommunal violence. In Cameroon the anglophone separatist insurgency in the Southwest and Northwest regions, as well as the insurgency in the Far North region (part of the wider Lake Chad crisis), continued, while in CAR the security situation became even more volatile as government forces, backed by Russian private military companies (PMCs) and Rwandan troops, fought to recapture territory from armed groups. Due to the growing influence of the Russian PMCs, France suspended aid to and military cooperation with the CAR government in June 2021, and the European Union mission suspended its training activities in December.

In East Africa (section IV) 9 of the 22 states or territories were involved in active armed conflict in 2021, with 5 in particular—Ethiopia, Mozambique, Somalia, South Sudan and Sudan—experiencing sharp escalations or continuing large-scale armed violence that have helped give rise to more than 9.6 million people being internally displaced and more than 4.7 million people becoming refugees across East Africa. Grave violations against civilians continued to be committed in the region, while at least 33.8 million people were severely food insecure. Disputes over resource allocation and access have also been significant in the region.

The armed conflict in the Tigray region of northern Ethiopia between federal government forces and the Tigray People's Liberation Front worsened during 2021, with the expansion of the conflict to the neighbouring regions of Amhara and Afar causing a deepening humanitarian crisis. The war fluctuated wildly over the course of 2021, reaching a stalemate at the end of the year. While the government's planned national dialogue offered some grounds for optimism, finding solutions to Ethiopia's deeply rooted conflicts is likely to be a lengthy process.

The insurgency in Cabo Delgado province in the north of Mozambique continued in 2021, leading to a regional military intervention in July 2021. However, the conflict's root causes, including a more equitable distribution of the province's mineral and hydrocarbon resources, remained unaddressed. In Somalia, al-Shabab remained a major threat despite the continued presence of an African Union-led peace operation.

In South Sudan, despite some progress towards implementation of the 2018 peace agreement, intercommunal violence continued to impact communities across multiple parts of the country. In Sudan, despite the optimism arising from the October 2020 Juba Peace Agreement with various opposition armed groups, the situation deteriorated in 2021: there was a military coup in October and a near doubling of estimated conflict-related fatalities during the year.

IAN DAVIS

I. Key general developments in the region

IAN DAVIS

At least 18 states in sub-Saharan Africa experienced active, subnational armed conflict in 2021, compared to 21 (Angola, Côte d'Ivoire and Guinea being the three additional countries) in 2020. Low-intensity armed conflicts (fewer than 1000 conflict-related deaths) occurred in 6 states, and high-intensity armed conflicts (1000–9999 deaths) occurred in 12—two more than in 2020. The Central African Republic (CAR) and Sudan moved from being low-intensity armed conflicts in 2020 to high-intensity armed conflicts in 2021.[1]

Eleven of the 18 armed conflict countries (Benin, Burkina Faso, Niger, Nigeria, CAR, Chad, Ethiopia, Kenya, Somalia, Sudan and Uganda) had higher estimated conflict-related fatalities in 2021 than in 2020, translating into an increase of about 19 per cent across the region as a whole (see table 7.1). A doubling of estimated fatalities in Ethiopia, a 27 per cent increase in Nigeria, and persistently high levels in the Democratic Republic of the Congo (DRC) were the most significant contributing factors.

Most of the armed conflicts were internationalized, with many of them overlapping across states and regions due to the involvement of external state actors—whether directly or through proxies—and/or the transnational activities of armed groups and criminal networks. Conflict dynamics and ethnic and religious tensions were often rooted in a combination of state weakness, corruption, ineffective delivery of basic services, competition over natural resources, inequality and a sense of marginalization. Among the world's economies for which poverty can be measured, 18 of the 20 poorest countries in 2021 were in sub-Saharan Africa, as were 33 of the 46 least developed countries (LDCs).[2] Aside from Cameroon, Kenya and Nigeria, all the countries in the region with armed conflicts in 2021 were LDCs.[3]

Developments in each of the armed conflicts and any related peace processes are discussed in more detail in subsequent sections of this chapter: West Africa (section II), Central Africa (section III) and East Africa (section IV). While many of the armed conflicts were the subject of ongoing

---

[1] For conflict definitions and typologies see chapter 2, section I, in this volume. For armed conflicts in North Africa see chapter 6, section IV, in this volume.

[2] World Bank, *Poverty and Shared Prosperity 2020: Reversals of Fortune* (International Bank for Reconstruction/World Bank: Washington, DC, Oct. 2020), p. 13; and United Nations Conference on Trade and Development (UNCTAD), *The Least Developed Countries Report 2021* (UN: Geneva, 2021), p. ix.

[3] Of course, this means that the other 18 LDCs in sub-Saharan Africa were not involved in an armed conflict in 2021. Thus, while poverty and armed conflict are thought to be closely interconnected, the poverty–conflict nexus is not straightforward. See e.g. Mueller, H. and Techasunthornwat, C., *Conflict and Poverty*, Policy Research Working Paper no. 9455 (World Bank Group, 2020); and Braithwaite, A., Dasandi, N. and Hudson, D., 'Does poverty cause conflict? Isolating the causal origins of the conflict trap', *Conflict Management and Peace Science*, vol. 33 no. 1 (2016), pp. 45–66.

Table 7.1. Estimated conflict-related fatalities in sub-Saharan Africa, 2017–21

Country	2017	2018	2019	2020	2021
West Africa					
Benin	15[a]	31[a]	37[a]	64	93
Burkina Faso	117	303	2 216	2 303	2 373
Côte D'Ivoire	43[a]	16[a]	45[a]	132	38[a]
Guinea	47[a]	39[a]	41[a]	145	28[a]
Mali	946	1747	1 875	2 854	1 910
Niger	240	506	729	1 126	1 460
Nigeria	4 948	6 220	5 416	7 781	9 913
Subtotal	**6 356**	**8 862**	**10 359**	**14 405**	**15 815**
Central Africa					
Angola	67	41[a]	23[a]	74	150[a]
Cameroon	741	1 663	1 303	1 764	1 395
Central African Republic	1 829	1 171	596	446	1 707
Chad	296	259	567	738	831
Congo, Democratic Republic of the	3 211	3 192	3 806	6 056	5 683
Subtotal	**6 144**	**6 326**	**6 295**	**9 078**	**9 766**
East Africa					
Burundi	285[a]	327	305	331	303
Ethiopia	1 355	1 565	667	4 057	8 958
Kenya	745	407	269	311	391
Madagascar	210	142	350	354	304
Mozambique	129	224	664	1 785	1 158
Somalia	6 143	5 420	4 513	3 249	3 261
South Sudan	4 841	1 700	1 811	2 380	2 156
Sudan	1 291	1 054	776	957	1 652
Uganda	66	146[a]	163	282	499
Subtotal	**15 065**	**10 985**	**9 518**	**13 706**	**18 682**
Total	**27 565**	**26 173**	**26 172**	**37 189**	**44 263**

Notes: Fatality figures are collated from four event types: battles; explosions/remote violence; protests, riots and strategic developments; and violence against civilians—see Armed Conflict Location & Event Data Project (ACLED), 'ACLED definitions of political violence and protest', 11 Apr. 2019. A country is treated as being in an armed conflict if there were 25 or more battle-related deaths in a given year (see chapter 2, section I, in this volume).

[a] Battle-related deaths were below 25.

Source: ACLED, 'Dashboard', accessed 16 Mar.–11 Apr. 2021.

peace processes in 2021, all were either stalled or suffered serious setbacks, with no substantive progress seen in any of them. Even in Sudan, where a series of peace agreements were signed in 2020 with various opposition armed groups, culminating in the October 2020 Juba Peace Agreement, a military coup occurred in October 2021 and conflict-related fatalities nearly doubled during the year (see section IV).

There were 22 multilateral peace operations active in sub-Saharan Africa in 2021[4]—more than in any other region of the world. The European

---

[4] The peace operations were deployed across 10 countries—see chapter 2, section II, in this volume.

Union (EU) and the Southern Africa Development Community (SADC) each deployed a new peace operation to Mozambique in 2021: the SADC Mission in Mozambique (SAMIM) and the EU Military Training Mission in Mozambique (EUTM Mozambique).[5] Meanwhile, the number of personnel in multilateral peace operations in sub-Saharan Africa decreased for the sixth consecutive year, from 94 201 on 31 December 2020 to 88 823 on 31 December 2021—a fall of 5.7 per cent. Nonetheless, the missions deployed in sub-Saharan Africa accounted for over three-quarters of the personnel deployed in multilateral peace operations globally.[6]

As in 2020 the Covid-19 pandemic appeared to have minimal direct impact on most of the region's armed conflicts in 2021, although there were reports of some Covid-19 responses being 'weaponized' to clamp down on human rights.[7] In the longer term, however, the pandemic may affect some of the key political, social and economic drivers of peace and conflict in the region. In 2020 sub-Saharan Africa's economy registered a record contraction of 1.9 per cent, and the Covid-19 crisis was exacerbated by a shortage of vaccines. Although the region's economy was projected to grow by 3.7 per cent in 2021, this represented the lowest recovery rate among the world's regions (as measured by the International Monetary Fund), thereby widening the income gap between sub-Saharan Africa and the rest of the world.[8] Four other cross-cutting issues shaped security challenges in sub-Saharan Africa in 2021: (*a*) the presence of armed groups and criminal networks; (*b*) the security activities of external actors; (*c*) election-related violence; and (*d*) water insecurity and the growing impact of climate change.[9]

The role of armed groups and criminal networks

Not only were non-state armed groups of varying capacity, size and objectives involved in all the armed conflicts in sub-Saharan Africa in 2021, they threatened security and civic participation in multiple other countries in the region. A broad typology would include jihadist groups, ethnic separatists (such as the Sudan Liberation Movement/Army and the Ambazonia Restoration Forces), communal or self-defence militias (often state-linked) and criminal networks, but there are few clear demarcation lines and groups

---

[5] For further details see chapter 2, section II, in this volume. For developments in Mozambique see section IV in this chapter.

[6] For further details see chapter 2, sections II and III, in this volume.

[7] See e.g. Amnesty International, 'Sub-Saharan Africa: The devastating impact of conflicts compounded by COVID-19', 7 Apr. 2021.

[8] International Monetary Fund (IMF), *Regional Economic Outlook, Sub-Saharan Africa: One Planet, Two Worlds, Three Stories* (IMF: Washington, DC, Oct. 2021).

[9] On developments in some of these issues in 2018–20 see *SIPRI Yearbook 2019*, pp. 115–21; *SIPRI Yearbook 2020*, pp. 176–79; and *SIPRI Yearbook 2021*, pp. 187–94.

often share overlapping characteristics. The violence is not just between governments and armed groups, but includes inter-group violence.

Armed groups have increasingly developed strong Salafi jihadist ideologies and forged ties with jihadist movements predominantly active in the Middle East and North Africa (MENA), namely al-Qaeda and the Islamic State. The epicentre of jihadist violence has now shifted from MENA to sub-Saharan Africa, and is particularly pronounced in central Sahel, Lake Chad, the Great Lakes and the Horn of Africa, and more recently northern Mozambique.[10] In addition to the influence and inflow of violent extremists from MENA, this rise in jihadist activity has been attributed to a number of factors, including ideology, poverty, corruption, local grievances, separatist movements, pre-existing intercommunal violence between herders and farmers over land rights (aggravated by the effects of climate change), weak state presence, and lack of economic opportunities for young people.[11] The dominant military counterterrorism approach adopted by states and external actors (see below) has often failed to address the influence of foreign jihadist movements or these deeper community grievances, or to strengthen the state's civic presence. Abuses by security force and a perceived lack of access to justice and protection drives recruitment into extremist organizations and other armed groups.[12]

Community-based or village-based self-defence groups (sometimes referred to as communal defence militias or identity militias) in sub-Saharan Africa tend to emerge where state security forces lack influence, resources or trust. Often formed along socio-economic, ethnic or political lines, these groups depend on popular support and frequently cooperate with state security forces or other armed groups. Meanwhile, porous borders, corruption, and weak justice and law enforcement systems have enabled transnational criminal activities by armed and organized crime groups to proliferate.[13]

---

[10] United Nations, Security Council, 'Fourteenth report of the Secretary-General on the threat posed by ISIL (Da'esh) to international peace and security and the range of United Nations efforts in support of member states in countering the threat', S/2022/63, 28 Jan. 2022, pp. 4–6.

[11] Stanicek, B. and Betant-Rasmussen, M., 'Jihadist networks in sub-Saharan Africa: Origins, patterns and responses', European Parliament Briefing, European Parliamentary Research Service, Sep. 2021.

[12] Stanicek and Betant-Rasmussen (note 11); Coleman, J. et al., *Dynamics of Support and Engagement: Understanding Malian Youths' Attitudes Towards Violent Extremism* (UN Interregional Crime and Justice Research Institute and the International Centre for Counter-Terrorism: Feb. 2021); Faleg, G. and Mustasilta, K., 'Salafi-Jihadism in Africa: A winning strategy', European Union Institute for Security Studies, Brief no. 12, June 2021; and International Crisis Group, *A Course Correction for the Sahel Stabilisation Strategy*, Africa Report no. 299 (International Crisis Group: Brussels, 1 Feb. 2021).

[13] For a comparative analysis of organized crime in Africa see ENACT, *Africa Organised Crime Index 2021: Evolution of Crime in a Covid World* (ENACT: Nov. 2021).

External actors

Sub-Saharan Africa is increasingly treated as an arena for geopolitical and commercial competition. In the Horn of Africa, for example, there are actors from Asia, Europe, MENA and North America.[14] Most Western forces deployed in the region are there to train and build capacity in local, national or subregional forces, largely with the aim of countering transnational jihadist groups.[15] France has a long tradition of maintaining a significant military footprint in sub-Saharan Africa, but more recently has made efforts to reduce it through multilateral arrangements with African and European states. This reorientation accelerated in 2021 with the announcement of Operation Barkhane's drawdown (with an expected reduction of French troops in the region from 5100 to roughly 3000) and its gradual replacement by the European Takuba Task Force under French command (see section II).[16] The French presence has been increasingly complicated by Russia's expanding influence, especially in Mali and CAR, and the intervention's lack of visible success.[17] Russia's military relationships in sub-Saharan Africa appear to be growing, with two new military cooperation agreements signed in 2021: with Ethiopia and Nigeria (the latter also has similar cooperation agreements with China and the United States).[18] Also more visible has been Russia's use of private military companies, especially the Wagner Group, reportedly present in at least 10 African countries, including CAR, Mali and Sudan.[19]

While the USA claims to maintain a 'light and relatively low-cost footprint' in Africa as a whole, independent estimates suggest at least 6000 military personnel are deployed across 13 countries in the sub-Saharan Africa region.[20] China's military presence in sub-Saharan Africa is linked to its growing

[14] Melvin, N. J., 'The foreign military presence in the Horn of Africa region', SIPRI Background Paper, Apr. 2019; and Lanfranchi, G., 'Geopolitics meets local politics in the Horn of Africa', *Clingendael Spectator*, 1 Dec. 2021. Also see section IV in this chapter.

[15] Garamone, J., 'US engagement needed to build security, prosperity on African continent', US Department of Defense, 12 Apr. 2021; and Hickendorff, A. and Acko, I., 'The European Union Training Mission in the Central African Republic: An assessment', SIPRI Background Paper, Feb. 2021.

[16] Salaün, T. and Irish, J., 'France ends West African Barkhane military operation', Reuters, 10 June 2021; and French Presidency, 'Propos liminaires du Président de la République à l'occasion de la conférence de presse conjointe à l'issue du Sommet du G5 Sahel' [Opening remarks by the President of the Republic at the joint press conference following the G5 Sahel Summit], 9 July 2021.

[17] Kante, M. I., 'France has started withdrawing its troops from Mali: What is it leaving behind?', The Conversation, 25 Oct. 2021.

[18] Morsy, A., 'Russia rejects attempts to link its military cooperation with Ethiopia with GERD dispute', Ahram Online, 24 July 2021; and Bedarride, D., 'Nigeria signs major military cooperation agreement with Russia to expand influence in Africa', Ecom News Afrique, 1 Sep. 2021.

[19] Dalaa, M. and Aksoy, H. A., 'Russia's Wagner Group reportedly deployed in Africa', Anadolu Agency, 5 Mar. 2021; and Jones, S. G. et al., *Russia's Corporate Soldiers: The Global Expansion of Russia's Private Military Companies* (Center for Strategic and International Studies: Washington, DC: July 2021).

[20] Turse, N., 'Pentagon's own map of US bases in Africa contradicts is own claim of "light" footprint', The Intercept, 27 Feb. 2020; and Husted, T. F. et al., *Sub-Saharan Africa: Key Issues and US Engagement*, Congressional Research Service (CRS) Report for Congress R45428 (US Congress, CRS: Washington, DC, 17 Feb. 2021), pp. 16–19.

economic presence, as well as its role as a leading supplier (compared to other permanent members of the UN Security Council) of UN peacekeepers in the region.[21] Finally, the region has also become a theatre for Middle East and North African power struggles, with Turkey and the Gulf states particularly active in the Horn of Africa (section IV).[22]

Election-related violence

Election transition processes can be a major source of instability in sub-Saharan Africa. The causes of electoral instability and violence in the region are multidimensional but broadly fall into two categories: the underlying power structures in new and emerging democracies, and flaws in the electoral process itself.[23] Several important national and local elections taking place in the region in 2021 faced the risk of pre- or post-election violence.[24] However, while some elections were marred by serious irregularities and security clampdowns, most took place without incident. Of the electoral violence that did flare up, the most serious occurrences were seen in CAR, Ethiopia, Niger, Uganda and Zambia.[25] Somalia's protracted indirect election process was repeatedly delayed during 2021 amidst political instability and violence (see section IV).[26]

A further indication of the fragility of democracy in sub-Saharan Africa was the occurrence of four successful military coups (in Chad, Mali, Guinea and Sudan) and three failed coups (in CAR, Niger and Sudan) in 2021, compared to just one coup in 2020 (in Mali). The number of coup attempts in Africa averaged around four a year between 1960 and 2000, before dropping to around two a year until 2019.[27] In September 2021 UN Secretary-General

[21] 'America worries about China's military ambitions in Africa', *The Economist*, 11 Dec. 2021.

[22] 'Gulf rivalries are spilling into Africa's Horn', *The Economist*, 11 Feb. 2022.

[23] Kovacs, M. S. and Bjarnesen, J. (eds), *Violence in African Elections: Between Democracy and Big Man Politics* (Nordic Africa Institute/Zed Books: Uppsala/London, 2018). See also the discussion in *SIPRI Yearbook 2019*, pp. 117–20. On the linkages between violence and democracy in Africa see Obiagu, U. C., 'A third wave? Creeping autocracy in Africa', *African Studies Quarterly*, vol. 20, no. 1 (Jan. 2021), pp. 114–24.

[24] Electoral Institute for Sustainable Democracy in Africa, '2021 African election calendar', Dec. 2021.

[25] 'CAR post-election violence displaces more than 200,000 people: UN', Al Jazeera, 29 Jan. 2021; 'Ethiopia votes in test for PM Abiy amid reports of abuses', AP News, 21 June 2021; 'Niger: 2 killed in protests against election results', Deutsche Welle, 25 Feb. 2021; Human Rights Watch, 'Uganda: Elections marred by violence', 21 Jan. 2021; and 'Zambia deploys army to curb violence ahead of elections', Al Jazeera, 1 Aug. 2021.

[26] United Nations, 'Completion of Somalia elections more important than ever: UN envoy', UN News, 17 Nov. 2021.

[27] Durmaz, M., '2021, the year military coups returned to the stage in Africa', Al Jazeera, 28 Dec. 2021; and Mwai, P., 'Are military takeovers on the rise in Africa?', BBC News, 2 Feb. 2022. On reasons for the rise in coups see Goldberg, M. L., 'Why have there been so many coups in Africa recently?', UN Dispatch, 14 Feb. 2022.

António Guterres voiced concern that 'military coups are back', blaming a lack of international unity in response to military interventions.[28]

Water insecurity and climate change

Climate-related security risks include 'forced migration and displacement, livelihood insecurity, food and water insecurity, rising levels of intercommunal conflict between pastoralists and farmers, protracted cross-border resource conflicts and unsustainable resource exploitation'.[29] Insecurity and armed conflict in sub-Saharan Africa affects local and national capacities to mitigate and adapt to climate vulnerability. In Mali and Somalia, for example, climate change has amplified existing challenges, including those faced by peace operations, and strengthened radical groups.[30]

Most countries in sub-Saharan Africa are dependent on rain-fed agriculture, making the region particularly vulnerable to changes in climatic conditions, such as seasonal floods and prolonged droughts. Somalia in 2021, for instance, experienced its third consecutive season of below-average rainfall, with the country's central and southern areas enduring moderate-to-severe drought conditions and water shortages.[31] These climatic conditions were a major driver of conflict in Somalia in 2021 (see section IV). Similarly, conflict over access to water in Cameroon displaced over 21 000 people in August 2021 (see section III). Accessing safe drinking water represents a challenge for more than 300 million people in rural areas of sub-Saharan Africa.[32] Arguably the highest profile water resource dispute in the region is between Egypt, Ethiopia and Sudan over the River Nile. These tensions have been exacerbated by Ethiopia's construction of the Grand Ethiopian Renaissance Dam, as well as a shifting regional power struggle.

[28] United Nations, Secretary-General, 'Secretary-General's address to the 76th Session of the UN General Assembly', 21 Sep. 2021.

[29] Aminga, V. and Krampe, F., 'Climate-related security risks and the African Union', SIPRI Policy Brief, May 2020.

[30] Eklöw, K. and Krampe, F., *Climate-related Security Risks and Peacebuilding in Somalia*, SIPRI Policy Paper no. 53 (SIPRI: Stockholm, Oct. 2019); and Hegazi, F., Krampe, F. and Smith E. S., *Climate-related Security Risks and Peacebuilding in Mali*, SIPRI Policy Paper no. 60 (SIPRI: Stockholm, Apr. 2021).

[31] Oxfam, 'Parts of Somalia hit by severe, climate-fueled drought', 14 Dec. 2021.

[32] Food and Agriculture Organization of the UN (FAO), *The State of Food and Agriculture: Overcoming Water Challenges in Agriculture* (FAO: Rome, 2020), p. 21.

II. Armed conflict and peace processes in West Africa

ANNELIES HICKENDORFF AND ISSAKA K. SOUARÉ

Five of the 15 states in West Africa experienced internal armed conflict in 2021: Benin, Burkina Faso, Mali, Niger and Nigeria.[1] The focus of this section is, however, on high-intensity armed conflicts (1000–9999 conflict-related deaths in the year), thereby excluding Benin (which had less than 100 estimated conflict-related deaths in 2021). Conflict-related fatalities decreased in Mali compared to 2020, but increased in Burkina Faso, Niger and Nigeria. This section is divided into three main themes: (*a*) key developments in the region; (*b*) multilateral peace and counterterrorism operations; and (*c*) internal armed conflicts, including the role of self-defence armed groups and current circumstances in Burkina Faso, Mali, Niger and Nigeria.

Key general developments in the region

Many states in West Africa face severe governance and security challenges. These are linked mainly to state weakness, political and economic mismanagement, economic fragility, and climate change. Several armed groups continue to be active, while state armed forces (military and police) are, in most countries, weak, dysfunctional and under-equipped.

Despite the Covid-19 pandemic, four presidential elections were held in the region in 2021: in Niger (2nd round, February); in Benin (April); in Cabo Verde (October); and in Gambia (December). In Senegal, anticipated regional and local elections (originally scheduled for June 2019) were postponed for a third time, to January 2022. The opposition asserted that the delay of the polls—widely seen as a test of President Macky Sall's popularity—was deliberate.[2] Two military coups occurred—in Mali (May) and Guinea (September)—as well as a failed coup in Niger, which added to regional governance and humanitarian challenges.

The impact of Covid-19 in West Africa appeared to remain relatively limited in 2021 compared to other regions of the world. Vaccination rates, however, were low.[3] As of the end of October 2021 only 3 per cent of Burkina Faso's, 4 per cent of Mali's, 5 per cent of Niger's, and 6 per cent Nigeria's

---

[1] For conflict definitions and typologies see chapter 2, section I, in this volume.

[2] Soumaré, M., 'Macky Sall a-t-il voulu le report des élections locales?' [Did Macky Sall want to postpone the local elections?], *Jeune Afrique*, 1 Apr. 2021.

[3] United Nations Office for the Coordination of Humanitarian Affairs (OCHA), *Global Humanitarian Overview 2022* (UN OCHA: Geneva, Dec. 2021), p. 37; and United Nations, Security Council, 'Report of the Secretary-General on the activities of the United Nations Office for West Africa and the Sahel', S/2021/1091, 15 Dec. 2021.

population had been fully vaccinated, though Cabo Verde registered a 36 per cent vaccination rate.[4]

In addition, with more than 80 per cent of the region's population reliant on agriculture and pastoral activities, the impact of climate change has led to high levels of food insecurity. An international index measuring both climate vulnerability and readiness to respond to climate change effects ranked Burkina Faso, Mali, Niger and Nigeria among the countries most exposed to the physical effects of climate change.[5]

Transnational armed groups

Burkina Faso, Mali, Niger and Nigeria were hotspots of armed conflict in West Africa in 2021. All four countries experienced attacks by armed groups, some operating beyond their respective national borders. In Nigeria the main armed groups were Boko Haram (also known as Jamā'at Ahl as-Sunnah lid-Da'wah wa'l-Jihād, or JAS) and the Islamic State West Africa Province (ISWAP). Both groups launched attacks in the north-east of the country as well as in neighbouring Niger and Cameroon, with Boko Haram claiming some attacks in Chad.[6]

In the Liptako-Gourma region—comprising the tri-border areas of Mali, Niger and Burkina Faso—the main transnational armed groups active in 2021 were Ansarul Islam, Katiba Serma, the Islamic State in the Greater Sahara (ISGS), and Jama'a Nusrat ul-Islam wa al-Muslimin (JNIM), an umbrella coalition of al-Qaeda-aligned groups composed of al-Qaeda in the Islamic Maghreb, Ansar Eddine, al-Mourabitoune and Katiba Macina.[7] These groups attacked both state armed forces and civilians.

In Senegal authorities reportedly dismantled a cell affiliated with JNIM in the eastern town of Kidira, prompting President Macky Sall to attend, for the first time, the ordinary session of the summit of the Authority of Heads of State of the Group of Five for the Sahel (G5 Sahel), held in N'Djamena, Chad, on 15 February 2021.[8]

Security forces countering these armed groups included national, regional and international forces, as well as local self-defence groups. These non-state

---

[4] UN OCHA (note 3), p. 37.

[5] Notre Dame Global Adaptation Initiative (ND GAIN), 'Country index', July 2021, accessed 19 Jan. 2022.

[6] Kindzeka, M. E., 'Cameroon says Boko Haram has intensified attacks for supplies', VOA, 30 Mar. 2021; and 'Chad army says at least 26 soldiers killed in Lake Chad attack', Reuters, 5 Aug. 2021.

[7] International Crisis Group, *Mali: Enabling Dialogue with the Jihadist Coalition JNIM*, Africa Report no. 306 (International Crisis Group: Brussels, 10 Dec. 2021).

[8] Presidency of Senegal, 'Le Président Macky Sall quitte Dakar pour prendre part à la séance élargie du Sommet du G5 Sahel à N'djaména' [President Macky Sall leaves Dakar to take part in the enlarged session of the G5 Sahel Summit in N'djaména], Press release, 15 Feb. 2021; and 'Senegal uncovers Jihadist cell in east of country', Defense Post, 9 Feb. 2021.

armed groups displayed varying degrees of legal recognition by and formal collaboration with state authorities.

Several leaders among the armed groups were killed in 2021, including Abubakar Shekau, the long-time leader of Boko Haram, with conflicting reports about the circumstances of his death; Adnan Abu Walid al-Sahrawi, the leader of ISGS, reportedly killed by forces of the French military-led Operation Barkhane; and Abu Musab al-Barnawi, head of ISWAP, and, subsequently, his immediate successor, Malam Bako, who were both reportedly killed in military operations by Nigerian forces.[9]

Election-related violence

Of the four presidential elections that took place in the region in 2021, only the Cabo Verde election was free of violence. In Niger long-time minister Mohamed Bazoum won the presidency in the second round (first round, 27 December 2020) to succeed Mahamadou Issoufou, who had served the maximum two terms in office allowed by the constitution. Both Bazoum and Issoufou are from the Nigerien Party for Democracy and Socialism (PNDS-Tarayya), which brought Issoufou to power in 2011. Bazoum defeated former president Mahamane Ousmane (1993–96), becoming the country's first president to take office in a peaceful transfer of power. However, Ousmane rejected the result, claiming irregularities and fraud. This contestation led to violent protests across the country and a government crackdown on protestors. Among hundreds arrested was opposition leader and former prime minister Hama Amadou, who was allied with Ousmane. An attempted military coup took place two days before Bazoum's inauguration on 2 April 2021—the attackers had reportedly come from a nearby airbase but were defeated by the presidential guard.[10]

In Benin incumbent president Patrice Talon was declared winner of the April presidential election in the first round, with some 86 per cent of votes. Several opposition leaders had boycotted the election, while others were barred from standing or were arrested. In the weeks around the elections, constitutionalist-turned-opposition leader, Frédéric Joel Aïvo, as well as another prominent opposition leader, Reckya Madougou were arrested and imprisoned, and in December 2021 these two leaders were sentenced to,

---

[9] 'ISWAP militant group says Nigeria's Boko Haram leader is dead', Reuters, 7 June 2021; 'Macron says French forces killed Islamic State leader in Sahara', Reuters, 16 Sep. 2021; 'Nigerian military confirms death of ISWAP leader Abu Musab al-Barnawi', *The Guardian* (Nigeria), 14 Oct. 2021; and 'Nigerian army says Islamic State West Africa's new leader killed in military operation', Reuters, 29 Oct. 2021.

[10] Abdou, N. H., 'Despite post-election violence, Niger achieves democratic breakthrough', United States Institute of Peace, 12 Mar. 2021; Akinpelu, Y., 'Attempted coup foiled in Niger days to historic handover', *Premium Times*, 31 Mar. 2021; and 'Niger "coup" thwarted days before inauguration', BBC News, 31 Mar. 2021.

respectively, 10 and 20 years in jail.[11] Violence was registered in parts of the country before and during the election.[12]

In Gambia incumbent Adama Barrow was re-elected for a second term in office, gaining around 53 per cent of the vote in the first round of the 4 December poll, thereby defeating his former ally-cum-rival, Ousainou Darboe, who garnered 28 per cent. Two other candidates shared the remaining votes. Though most observers attested to the credibility and transparency of the electoral process,[13] contestation by Darboe and the other losing candidates raised tensions, leading the police to disperse their supporters with tear gas. Sporadic violence was registered but largely circumscribed.[14]

Military coups and transitional regimes

An attempted military coup was thwarted by security forces in Niger in March 2021 and successful coups registered in Mali in May and Guinea in September.

In Mali it was a 'coup within a coup', in that Colonel Assimi Goïta had staged a first coup against elected president, Ibrahim Boubacar Keita, on 18 August 2020.[15] Following regional pressure, particularly from the Economic Community of West African States (ECOWAS), the military junta had appointed a civilian president, Bah Ndaw, and civilian prime minister, Mouctar Ouane, with Goïta retaining the post of vice-president. However, dissatisfied with the transitional government's ministerial choices in a government reshuffle, Colonel Goïta staged a second coup on 24 May 2021, arresting both the Ndaw and Ouane. Goïta then proclaimed himself head of state and assumed the transitional presidency.[16]

In Guinea Colonel Mamadi Doumbouya, head of the army's special forces, staged a military coup on 5 September 2021 that overthrew President Alpha Condé. In March 2020 the latter had forced through a constitutional change allowing him to stand for a third term in the October 2020 presidential

---

[11] Thantan, M., 'Bénin: L'opposant Joël Aïvo condamné à dix ans de prison' [Benin: Opposition leader Joël Aïvo sentenced to ten years in prison], *Jeune Afrique*, 7 Dec. 2021; and AFP, 'Benin opposition leader sentenced to 20 years in jail', France 24, 11 Dec. 2021.

[12] West Africa Network for Peacebuilding (WANEP), 'Élection Présidentielle de 2021: La violence électorale passera-t-elle encore par le Bénin?' [2021 Presidential Election: Will electoral violence again pass through Benin?], WARN Policy Brief, Apr. 2021; and CIVICUS, 'Benin: Protests and violence precede controversial presidential elections without main opposition', 5 May 2021.

[13] Price, N., 'Presidential election in the Gambia', press statement, US Department of State, 7 Dec. 2021; Busari, K. and Olawoyin, O., '#GambiaDecides2021: Adama Barrow wins Gambia presidential election', *Premium Times*, 5 Dec. 2021; and Crowe, P., 'Gambian opposition parties reject election results', *The Guardian*, 6 Dec. 2021.

[14] Saine, P., 'Gambia police disperse protesters contesting president's re-election', Reuters, 7 Dec. 2021.

[15] See *SIPRI Yearbook 2021*, pp. 195–202.

[16] Wing, S. D., 'Another coup in Mali? Here's what you need to know', *Washington Post*, 28 May 2021.

elections.[17] Doumbouya was sworn in as transitional president on 1 October 2021 and, six days later, appointed Mohamed Beavogui—an international civil servant recently retired from the United Nations system—as prime minister.[18]

As per their agreed policy against military coups, both ECOWAS and the African Union suspended Mali and Guinea from their decision-making organs.[19] ECOWAS held two extraordinary summits on both countries and imposed sanctions on the juntas running them, which in turn pledged a swift return to civilian rule.

In Mali it was agreed that the transition would last for a maximum of 18 months from the first coup, culminating in presidential elections in February 2022. However, in December 2021 the military junta organized a general gathering for 'state reformation', at the end of which it asked for the transition to be prolonged for up to five years, which as of the end of 2021 it seemed likely ECOWAS would reject.[20] In Guinea the transitional authorities had, as of the end of 2021, not yet fixed a timeline for the transition.

Human security

The human security situation in West Africa, and particularly in the Sahel, in 2021 was marked by general insecurity, political violence, forced displacement, malnutrition, the spread of diseases among displaced populations—both internally displaced persons (IDPs) and refugees—droughts, food insecurity, school closures, and the abduction and abuse of young girls and women. In 2021 the UN designated several parts of the Sahel as having become humanitarian high-risk zones since 2020, with deterioration observed in Burkina Faso, Mali, Niger and Nigeria.[21] More than 2 million people in the Central Sahel became or remained internally displaced in 2021, while about half a million resided as refugees in other countries in the region.[22]

In its September 2021 update the *Global Report on Food Crises* reported a global rise in the number of people facing catastrophe—that is, households extremely food deprived and experiencing a collapse in livelihoods. Along

---

[17] Foucher, V. and Depagne, R., 'Condé's removal clears the way for army to regain control of Guinea', International Crisis Group, 8 Sep. 2021.

[18] 'Guinea junta names development veteran Mohamed Beavogui prime minister', Africanews, 7 Oct. 2021.

[19] Souaré, I. K., 'The African Union as a norm entrepreneur on military coups d'état in Africa (1952–2012): An empirical assessment', *Journal of Modern African Studies*, vol. 52, no. 1 (Mar. 2014), pp. 69–94.

[20] Africanews, 'Assises nationales au Mali : une transition jusqu'à 5 ans?,' [National Conferences in Mali: A transition up to 5 years?], Africanews, 31 Dec. 2021.

[21] UN OCHA, 'Sahel INFORM/Indice de risque 2017–2021' [Sahel INFORM/Risk Index 2017–2021], accessed 15 Feb. 2022.

[22] UN High Commissioner for Refugees (UNHCR), 'Decade of Sahel conflict leaves 2.5 million people displaced', 14 Jan. 2022.

with Yemen and South Sudan, Burkina Faso falls in the highest phase classification of this index.[23]

Schools, colleges and universities in northern Nigeria were the target of a wave of kidnappings for ransom in 2021.[24] Between January and September there were some 20 attacks on schools, with 1436 children abducted, 16 murdered and over 200 missing. Mass kidnappings included the seizure of 279 students from a female secondary school in Zamfara State on 26 February, the abduction of 200 children in Niger State in June and the snatching of 140 pupils in Kaduna State in July.[25] The insecurity forced hundreds of schools to close, deepening the humanitarian and educational crisis. As of 29 November 2021, 934 schools in northern Nigeria were closed, depriving over a million children of education.[26]

Multinational peace and security operations

Several multinational peace and security operations have been deployed to address insecurities in West Africa, mainly in the Sahel region. The largest of these is the UN Multidimensional Integrated Stabilization Mission in Mali (MINUSMA), which was established in 2013. MINUSMA focuses on peacekeeping and stabilization of the country through ssupporting implementation of the Algiers agreement (2015), the political transition, the restoration of state authority, and the protection of civilians.[27] A number of other missions were conducting security-related, often counterterrorism, operations, rather than traditional peace operations.[28] The French military Operation Barkhane deployed in Burkina Faso, Chad, Mali, Mauritania and Niger since 2014, with its headquarters in the Chadian capital, is a key example of a security-related force focused on regional counterterrorism.[29]

---

[23] Global Network Against Food Crisis, '2021 Global Report on Food Crisis, September 2021 update', Sept. 2021

[24] Obasi, N., 'Halting repeated school kidnappings in Nigeria', International Crisis Group, 5 Mar. 2021.

[25] Obiezu, T. '279 Kidnapped Nigerian schoolgirls released by their captors', VOA, 2 Mar. 2021; 'Nigeria rules out paying ransom for hundreds of kidnapped school children', France 24, 2 June 2021; and Maishanu, A. A., 'Police confirm abduction in Kaduna school, say 26 students rescued', *Premium Times*, 5 July 2021.

[26] UNICEF Nigeria, 'First day of school "indefinitely postponed" for at least 1 million Nigerian students', Press release, 15 Sep. 2021; and UN OCHA, 'Lake Chad Basin: Humanitarian snapshot', 2 Dec. 2021.

[27] UN Security Council Resolution 2584, 29 June 2021.

[28] For a discussion on the differences between 'multilateral peace operations' and 'multilateral other operations' see chapter 2, section II, in this volume.

[29] France describes Operation Barkhane as having a counterterrorism role. See France Ministry of the Armed Forces, 'Operation Barkhane', accessed 1 Apr. 2021. Given there is no single internationally accepted definition of what constitutes terrorism, however, counterterrorism measures can generate controversy. Counterterrorism instruments vary from heavily securitized responses (including killing armed fighters on the battlefield) to holistic national and international strategies aimed at preventing and countering violent extremism.

Table 7.2. Active external national and multilateral peace and counterterrorism operations in the Sahel and Lake Chad regions, 2021

Launched or established	Name	Contributing countries/ organizations	Force level (No. of personnel deployed)	Country of deployment
2012	EU Capacity Building Mission Sahel Niger	EU member states	124	Niger
2013	Multidimensional Integrated Stabilization Mission in Mali	UN (mainly African countries, Bangladesh, China, Egypt and Germany)	14 917	Mali
2013	EU Training Mission in Mali	EU member states	1212	Mali
2014[a]	Multinational Joint Task Force	Benin (no troops), Cameroon, Chad, Niger and Nigeria	10 620	Cameroon, Chad, Niger and Nigeria
2014[b]	Operation Barkhane	France	4 800	Burkina Faso, Chad, Mali and Niger
2015	EU Capacity Building Mission Sahel Mali	EU member states	152	Mali
2017	Joint Force of the Group of Five for the Sahel	Burkina Faso, Chad, Mali, Mauritania and Niger	5 300	Burkina Faso, Chad, Mali, Mauritania and Niger
2020	Task Force Takuba	Belgium, Czech Republic, Denmark, Estonia, France, Italy, Hungary, Netherlands, Portugal and Sweden	800	Liptako-Gourma region

[a] Initiated as a solely Nigerian force in 1994; expanded to include Chad and Niger in 1998.
[b] Succeeded Operation Serval, which was launched in Jan. 2013 and ended in July 2014.
Source: SIPRI, Multilateral Peace Operations Database, accessed 1 Apr. 2022.

Operation Barkhane collaborates closely with the G5 Sahel Joint Force, one of the two regional counterterrorism task forces in the region. The second regional operation is the Multinational Joint Task Force (MNJTF), created by the AU and the Lake Chad Basin Commission to fight Boko Haram in the Lake Chad region. The force has so far consisted of troops from Cameroon, Chad, Niger and Nigeria.[30]

Since March 2020 the mandate of the European Union Training Mission (EUTM) in Mali has been broadened to include not only capacity building of the Malian army, but providing assistance to the national armed forces of the other G5 Sahel countries, with priority placed on Burkina Faso and Niger.[31]

[30] See *SIPRI Yearbook 2021*, pp. 197–202.
[31] European Union External Action, 'General Maio visits Niger to discuss the new mandate of EUTM Mali', 21 May 2021.

On the civilian side, the EU Capacity Building Mission (EUCAP) Sahel Mali and EUCAP Sahel Niger are building the capacity of, respectively, the Malian and Nigerien internal security forces, while a EUCAP Sahel Mali's Regional Advisory and Coordination Cell (RACC) in Mauritania supports regional and cross border cooperation in the Sahel (see table 7.2).[32]

Coordination between these complex constellations of multilateral peace (and other) operations has been a challenge and their effectiveness mixed, whether at the military level or in terms of restoring state authority. In particular, more needs to be done to differentiate between civilians and combatants in the areas they operate.[33] Furthermore, national and regional security forces regularly face accusations of human rights abuses, including conducting extrajudicial killings during counterterrorism operations.[34]

On 10 June 2021, amid rapidly escalating tensions between Mali and France,[35] President Emmanuel Macron announced a drawdown of the 5000 Barkhane troops in Mali.[36] French soldiers were to be replaced by the European multinational Task Force Takuba, which had been set up for this purpose in 2020 under Operation Barkhane's command. Composed of special forces and logistical and tactical support from some 12 European countries, Takuba is tasked with advising, assisting and accompanying Malian Armed Forces and regional troops.[37] French forces closed their bases in Kidal and Tessalit in northern Mali in November, and in Timbuktu on 15 December.[38]

Against a background of increasingly widespread anti-French resentment in the region, Mali's transitional government engaged in closer security cooperation with Russia. On 23 December 2021 France and 15 other Western nations issued a statement condemning the alleged deployment of Russian

[32] EU Capacity Building Mission (EUCAP) Sahel Mali, 'EUCAP Sahel Mali', accessed 19 Jan. 2022; and EUCAP Sahel Niger, 'EUCAP Sahel Niger', accessed 19 Jan. 2022.

[33] International Crisis Group, *What Role for the Multinational Joint Task Force in Fighting Boko Haram*, Africa Report no. 291 (International Crisis Group: Brussels, 7 July 2020).

[34] Human Rights Watch, *World Report 2022: Events of 2021* (Human Rights Watch: New York, 2022); and Zandonni, G., Staius T. and Aksar, M., '"No room for dialogue": How abuses by Niger's foreign-funded army derail its anti-jihadist fight', New Humanitarian, 30 Nov. 2021.

[35] Bensimon, C. and Vincent, E., 'Au Sahel, un convoi de l'armée française face à la colère populaire' [In the Sahel, a French Army convoy faces popular anger], *Le Monde*, 30 Nov. 2021; and Melly, P., 'Why France faces so much anger in West Africa', BBC News, 5 Dec. 2021.

[36] 'Emmanuel Macron annonce "La fin de l'opération Barkhane en tant qu'opération extérieure"' [Emmanuel Macron announces 'the end of Operation Barkhane as an external operation'], RFI, 10 June 2021; and Irish, J., 'Mali junta wiping its feet on blood of French soldiers, says angry France', Reuters, 29 Sep. 2021.

[37] 'Task Force Takuba: Political statement by the governments of Belgium, Czech Republic, Denmark, Estonia, France, Germany, Mali, Niger, the Netherlands, Norway, Portugal, Sweden and the United Kingdom', 23 Mar. 2020; and 'Europe deploys Takuba task force in Mali as France draws down troops', RFI, 16 Dec. 2021.

[38] United Nations, Security Council, 'Situation in Mali', Report of the Secretary-General, S/2021/1117, 4 Jan. 2022.

Table 7.3. Estimated conflict-related fatalities in the Liptako-Gourma region, 2017–21

Provinces (state)	2017	2018	2019	2020 (%)	2021 (%)
Boucle du Mouhoun, Centre-Nord, Est, Nord and Sahel (Burkina Faso's part of Liptako-Gourma)	77	266	2 123	2 261 (*98*)	2 219 (*94*)
Total Burkina Faso				2 303	2 372
Gao, Ménaka and Mopti (Malian part of Liptako-Gourma)	568	1 409	1 658	2 230 (*78*)	1 375 (*72*)
Total Mali				2 852	1 910
Tillabéri (Nigerien part of Liptako-Gourma in Niger)	62	170	263	680 (*60*)	905 (*62*)
Total Niger				1 126	1 460
Total Liptako-Gourma	707	1 845	4 044	5 171	4 482

Note: Percentages are of total national conflict-related fatalities.
Source: Armed Conflict Location & Event Data Project (ACLED), 'Data export tool', accessed 16 Mar. 2022. Data per region is available from 11 Jan. 2017.

private military company the Wagner Group.[39] The situation at the end of 2021 not only raises questions about potential impacts on the Western military presence in the Sahel—particularly France and Task Force Takuba— but the consequences for MINUSMA and the G5 Sahel Joint Force, which rely on French strategic and logistical support.[40]

Internal armed conflicts (including the role of armed self-defence groups)

In 2021 armed violence in West Africa mainly manifested itself through attacks by armed groups, intercommunity and intracommunity tensions, violent disputes between farmers and herders, and banditry and organized crime, with a particular hotspot of insecurity being the tri-border Liptako-Gourma region. While the number of conflict-related fatalities in this tri-border region decreased, mainly because of a decrease in fatalities in Mali, it remained higher than the 2019 level (see table 7.3).

Burkina Faso

The security situation in Burkina Faso continued to deteriorate in 2021, with armed groups continuing their attacks against government forces and public infrastructure, as well as against unarmed civilian populations. The total

---

[39] Belgium, Canada, Czech Republic, Denmark, Estonia, France, Germany, Italy, Lithuania, Netherlands, Norway, Portugal, Romania, Spain, Sweden, United Kingdom, 'Statement on the Deployment of the Wagner Group in Mali', 23 Dec. 2021.
[40] Lebovich, A., 'After Barkhane: What France's military drawdown means for the Sahel', European Council on Foreign Relations, 2 July 2021.

number of IDPs in Burkina Faso rose to more than 1.5 million by the end of 2021, meaning that six in ten of the Sahel's IDPs are now Burkinabe.[41] On 5 June the village of Solhan in the north-eastern Sahel region was attacked by gunmen, who reportedly executed some 138 civilians.[42] In August about 80 people were killed in an attack on a civilian convoy that was being escorted by gendarmes near the town of Arbinda in the north of the country. The death toll included about 20 gendarmes and pro-government militia.[43] Similar attacks killed about 53 gendarmes and civilians in Inata in the Sahel region bordering Mali in November; and an estimated 41 members of the pro-government Homeland Defence Volunteers (Volontaires pour la défense de la patrie, VDP) in the northern Loroum province in December.[44] The legalization and use of the VDP was one of the various strategies—which included changing the defence minister and the army chief of staff—deployed by the Burkina Faso government in its attempts to find solutions to these attacks.[45] Explanations given for the persistence of the attacks include the alleged dysfunctionality of the defence and security forces; a lack of equipment and adequate resources; and the weakness of the state presence in the most affected localities.

Mali

Mali registered less conflict-related fatalities in 2021 compared to 2020, although the security situation remained poor. More than 400 000 people were displaced inside the country—a 30 per cent increase from the previous year.[46] There was little progress in implementing the 2015 Agreement on Peace and Reconciliation, particularly regarding some of the fundamental pending issues, such as the disarmament, demobilization and reintegration (DDR) process, the finalization of institutional and political reforms, and the effective implementation of development projects. Even so, the signatory parties appeared to maintain good working relations, with improved dialogue observed between them.[47]

---

[41] UN High Commissioner for Refugees (UNHCR), 'Decade of Sahel conflict leaves 2.5 million people displaced', 14 Jan. 2022.

[42] Amnesty International, 'Burkina Faso: In the wake of the Solhan massacre, the priority must be to protect the people', 7 June 2021.

[43] Ndiaga, T., 'Death toll from Burkina Faso attack rises to 80', Reuters, 20 Aug. 2021.

[44] 'Burkina Faso President criticizes army "dysfunctions" after deadly attack', Africanews, 18 Nov. 2021; and 'Burkina Faso begins two-day mourning period after dozens killed in ambush', France 24, 26 Dec. 2021.

[45] Tisseron, A., *Pandora's Box: Burkina Faso, Self-Defense Militias and VDP Law in Fighting Jihadism* (Friedrich-Ebert-Stiftung: Dakar, 2021).

[46] UNHCR (note 41).

[47] Carter Center, *Report of the Independent Observer: Observations on the Implementation of the Agreement on Peace and Reconciliation in Mali, Resulting from the Algiers Process* (Carter Center: Bamako/Atlanta, Aug. 2021).

Table 7.4. Estimated conflict-related fatalities in Mali, 2013–21

Event type	2013	2014	2015	2016	2017	2018	2019	2020	2021
Battles	547	301	316	210	563	759	831	1657	1159
Explosions/remote violence	191	39	27	32	144	177	234	262	285
Protests, riots and strategic developments	7	1	5	7	3	28	4	27	10
Violence against civilians	138	41	80	71	238	783	806	903	456
Total	**883**	**382**	**428**	**320**	**948**	**1 747**	**1 875**	**2 849**	**1 910**

Note: For definitions of event types, see Armed Conflict Location & Event Data Project (ACLED), 'ACLED definitions of political violence and protest', 11 Apr. 2019.
Source: ACLED, 'Data export tool', accessed 17 Mar. 2022.

Throughout the year civilians and security forces were subject to deadly attacks by armed groups, particularly in the centre of the country where extremist groups are interwoven with local self-defence militias and armed groups, exacerbating local and community tensions. With 20 hostile deaths in 2021, compared to 6 in 2020, there was a clear uptick in MINUSMA fatalities due to malicious acts, which returned to the levels seen prior to the Covid-19 pandemic (see chapter 2). On 8 August 2021 suspected members of ISGS reportedly raided several villages in the Gao region (north), killing at least 51 civilians. On 3 December suspected Katiba Macina elements ambushed a public bus near Songho village, in the Mopti region (centre), reportedly killing 32 civilians. A few days later Katiba Macina militants clashed with elements of the self-defence militia called Dana Ambassagou, leaving some 10 militia members dead near Baima village.[48] In addition, landmines and improvised explosive devices killed 285 people (see table 7.4).

Niger

There was a rise in conflict-related fatalities in Niger from 1126 in 2020 to 1460 in 2021, which can partly be explained by increasing violence in the Liptako-Gourma region (accounting for 62 per cent of total national fatalities). For example, on 15 March 2021 gunmen killed at least 58 civilians as they were returning from a weekly market in the Tillabéri region, while a week later unidentified gunmen attacked the villages of Intazayene, Bakorate and Wistane in Tahoua region, killing at least 137 people.[49] In early December an attack on the Fianto base of the G5 Sahel's Joint Force in the Tillabéri region killed about 29 soldiers.[50] The number of IDPs in Tillabéri and Tahoua regions increased by 53 per cent over the course of 2021.[51]

[48] International Crisis Group, 'Tracking conflict worldwide, Africa—Mali', CrisisWatch, Dec. 2021.
[49] United Nations, 'UN chief reaffirms solidarity with Niger, as second deadly attack rocks country', UN News, 24 Mar. 2021.
[50] 'West Africa: Explosions, attacks in Mali, Niger kill over 100', Deutsche Welle, 5 Dec. 2021.
[51] UNHCR (note 41).

Table 7.5. Estimated conflict-related fatalities in Nigeria, by region, 2017–21

States	2017	2018	2019	2020	2021
Adamawa, Borno and Yobe (north-east)	3 022	2 591	2 221	3465	3 212
Kaduna, Katsina, Kebbi, Sokoto and Zamfara (north-west)	146	1 095	1 920	2793	3 523
Benue, Plateau, Nasarawa, Niger (Middle Belt)	424	1 441	347	617	1 750
Ebonyi, Enugu, Anambra, Imo, Abia (south-east)	325	160	114	110	649
Delta (south)	97	60	55	121	84
Total	**4 869**	**4947**	**6 243**	**7781**	**9 913**

Source: Armed Conflict Location & Event Data Project (ACLED), 'Dashboard', accessed 13 Jan. 2022.

Nigeria

The security situation in Nigeria worsened in 2021, with a 27 per cent increase in conflict-related fatalities compared to 2020 (see table 7.5). This can be explained by the high number of conflicts between farmers and herders in the Middle Belt, a sharp rise in banditry in the north-west, and intensifying uprisings by separatists in the south-east.[52] In 2021 conflict-related fatalities in the north-west were on the same level as in the north-east of the country (Adamawa State, Borno State and Yobe State). These states, and particularly Borno State, remained the epicentre of the Boko Haram-related armed conflict in the Lake Chad region, comprising parts of Cameroon, Chad, Niger and Nigeria. As of 22 December 2021 the Lake Chad region hosted an estimated 5.5 million displaced people, of whom 76 per cent were in Nigeria.[53] Forced displacement and grave human rights violations, including killings, sexual violence, abduction and the recruitment of child soldiers, remained widespread.

There was some cautious optimism in 2021 regarding the conflict with Boko Haram following the surrender of thousands of its fighters. The surrender was attributed to a combination of infighting between armed groups, pressure from security forces, and a controversial amnesty programme aimed at senior jihadist commanders introduced following the death of Boko Haram's leader Abubakar Shekau in May.[54]

[52] Beaumont, P., 'Failed state? Why Nigeria's fragile democracy is facing an uncertain future', *The Guardian*, 25 Oct. 2021; Tanko, A., 'Nigeria's security crises—five different threats', BBC News, 19 July 2021; and International Crisis Group, *Ending Nigeria's Herder–Farmer Crisis: The Livestock Reform Plan*, Africa Report no. 302 (International Crisis Group: Brussels, 4 May 2021).

[53] International Organization for Migration (IOM), 'Regional Displacement Tracking Matrix (DTM): Lake Chad Basin crisis', IOM Monthly Dashboard no. 39, 22 Dec. 2021.

[54] Anyadike, O., 'Nigeria's secret programme to lure top Boko Haram defectors', New Humanitarian, 19 Aug. 2021; and Kurtzer, J., 'Boko Haram's leader is dead: What are the humanitarian and security implications?', Center for Strategic and International Studies, 15 June 2021.

In the south-east, clashes between separatist group the Indigenous People of Biafra (IPOB) and state authorities intensified, with an almost sixfold increase of conflict-related fatalities in 2021—to 649—compared to 2020. Violent protests broke out following the arrest of IPOB's leader, Nnamdi Kanu, in June.[55] IPOB has been accused of attacks on police stations, government offices, prisons, and the homes of politicians and community leaders. An alleged IPOB attack on Owerri prison, Imo state, in early April 2021 resulted in one of the country's largest ever jailbreaks, with 1844 prisoners escaping.[56]

---

[55] Orjinmo, N., 'Nnamdi Kanu's arrest leaves Nigeria's Ipob separatists in disarray', BBC News, 4 July 2021.

[56] Akinwotu, E., 'Nearly 2,000 prisoners escape jail in south-east Nigeria', *The Guardian*, 5 Apr. 2021.

III. Armed conflict and peace processes in Central Africa

IAN DAVIS

Four of the nine Central African states were involved in armed conflicts in 2021: Cameroon, the Central African Republic (CAR), Chad and the Democratic Republic of the Congo (DRC). Central Africa contains some of the world's severest and most protracted crises. Despite most of the region's countries being resource rich, these natural resources have often been a driver for competition and corruption (and hence weak governance), leading to high levels of poverty and food insecurity. The impact of climate change also drives life-threatening levels of vulnerability.[1] Conflict in the region's hotspots in 2021 persisted (in Cameroon and the DRC) or worsened (in CAR and Chad).

Cameroon

The two main but unrelated armed conflicts in Cameroon continued in 2021: the anglophone separatist insurgency in the Southwest and Northwest regions; and the Boko Haram insurgency in the Far North region (part of the wider Lake Chad crisis). Both persisted in 2021, and although total estimated conflict-related fatalities in Cameroon fell by 21 per cent compared to 2020, only three of the last nine years had higher fatality levels (see table 7.6). The two conflicts have displaced nearly 1 million Cameroonians internally, while the country also hosts over 340 000 refugees fleeing insecurity in neighbouring CAR, and 120 000 Nigerians displaced by the Boko Haram and Islamic State in West Africa Province (ISWAP) insurgencies.[2] The number of people requiring humanitarian support in Cameroon fell slightly from 4.4 million in 2020 to 4 million in 2021 (out of a total population of 27.2 million).[3]

The conflict in the Lake Chad region

Conflict over natural resources in the Lake Chad basin intensified in 2021, with the number of people displaced continuing to increase. In August intercommunal clashes between herders and fishermen/farmers in Logone-Birni over access to water displaced over 23 000 people, including almost 9000 who sought refuge in Chad. The Far North region also experienced drought in 2021 (after exceptional flooding in 2020), severely reducing crop

---

[1] United Nations Office for the Coordination of Humanitarian Affairs (OCHA), *Global Humanitarian Overview 2022* (UN OCHA: Dec. 2021), pp. 182–85.

[2] UN High Commissioner for Refugees (UNHCR), 'Cameroon MCO', Fact Sheet, Jan. 2022.

[3] UN OCHA (note 1), p. 190.

Table 7.6. Estimated conflict-related fatalities in Cameroon, 2013–21

Event type	2013	2014	2015	2016	2017	2018	2019	2020	2021
Battles	17	1 223	959	340	280	1 081	678	937	862
Explosions/remote violence	0	33	202	175	223	31	22	62	62
Protests, riots and strategic developments	1	0	0	11	48	7	2	41	36
Violence against civilians	14	110	278	195	190	544	601	724	435
Total	**32**	**1 366**	**1 439**	**721**	**741**	**1 663**	**1 303**	**1 764**	**1 395**

Notes: For definitions of event types, see Armed Conflict Location & Event Data Project (ACLED), 'ACLED definitions of political violence and protest', 11 Apr. 2019.
Source: ACLED, 'Dashboard', accessed 11 Apr. 2022.

yields and triggering acute food insecurity.[4] Further violent clashes occurred between Arab Shoa cattle herders and Massa farmers and Mousgoum fishermen in December.[5] In addition, Boko Haram and ISWAP continued to carry out attacks and commit serious human rights abuses, mostly targeting farmers and fishermen in remote areas. One study recorded 37 attacks by Boko Haram in Cameroon in 2021, resulting in 58 deaths.[6]

The conflict in anglophone Cameroon

The origins of the anglophone crisis lie in colonial-era divisions of territory between Britain and France. Today, 5 million people in the Northwest and Southwest regions—about one-fifth of the country's population—speak mainly English and have their own legal and educational systems. The anglophone demand for an autonomous republic called Ambazonia, which dates back to at least 1985, turned violent in October 2017.[7] Protests by anglophone teachers and lawyers against the use of French in anglophone schools and courts were harshly repressed, leading to an armed insurgency by separatist militias.

In 2021 education and health facilities continued to be targeted by armed separatist groups. In September, for example, two out of every three schools in Cameroon's anglophone regions were closed, leaving more than 700 000 students without education.[8] At least 29 attacks on health care facilities were

---

[4] Bourgois, X., 'Dwindling rains in northern Cameroon spark conflict and displacement', UNHCR, 10 Nov. 2021; and Hoinathy, R. and Delanga, C., 'Cameroon's community violence adds to Lake Chad Basin security woes', ISS Today, 4 Oct. 2021.

[5] Kouagheu, J. and Ramadane, M., 'North Cameroon violence between farmers, herders kills 22; residents flee', Reuters, 9 Dec. 2021.

[6] Institute for Economics & Peace (IEP), *Global Terrorism Index 2022: Measuring the Impact of Terrorism* (IEP: Sydney, Mar. 2022), p. 25.

[7] International Crisis Group, *Cameroon's Anglophone Crisis at the Crossroads*, Africa Report no. 250 (International Crisis Group: Brussels, 2 Aug. 2017). On developments in 2018 see *SIPRI Yearbook 2019*, pp. 124–25.

[8] United Nations, 'Violence in Cameroon, impacting over 700,000 children shut out of school', UN News, 2 Dec. 2021; and Human Rights Watch, '"They are destroying our future": Armed separatist attacks on students, teachers, and schools in Cameroon's Anglophone region', 16 Dec. 2021.

reported between January and June, while the use of improvised explosive devices by separatists also increased.[9]

Attempts at finding a solution to the conflict have been limited and ineffectual. After a national dialogue in October 2019 (that excluded all separatists), the government announced in January 2020 a new 'special status' for the two anglophone regions.[10] However, questions remained over the government's commitment to engage in dialogue and grant political concessions to separatist groups. Swiss mediation efforts also failed to break the deadlock.[11] In February 2021 the Vatican's secretary of state, Cardinal Pietro Parolin, visited Cameroon and announced the readiness of the Catholic Church to facilitate a dialogue between the government and separatist groups.[12] Cameroon's prime minister, Joseph Dion Ngute, visited the anglophone regions in October to call for peace, but added that those who refused to disarm would be killed.[13]

The Central African Republic

Since 2013, despite the presence of multinational peace operations—currently the UN Multidimensional Integrated Stabilization Mission in the Central African Republic (MINUSCA)—almost the entire territory of CAR has been affected by conflict and violence provoked by shifting alliances of armed groups. A 2019 peace agreement and ceasefire between the government and 14 armed groups (the Political Agreement for Peace and Reconciliation in the Central African Republic, hereafter Political Agreement) initially curbed some of the violence.[14] Nonetheless, regular attacks against civilian populations, including conflict-related sexual violence, as well as killings and other crimes and violations at the hands of the ex-Seleka and anti-Balaka armed groups, have continued.[15]

---

[9] Health Cluster, World Health Organization, 'Cameroon: Attacks on health care in the North-West and South-West regions (1 Jan–30 Jun 2021)', 7 July 2021; Kindzeka, M. E., 'Cameroon military says rebels turning to IEDs as numbers fall', VOA, 11 May 2021; and Centre for Human Rights and Democracy in Africa, 'Cameroon: The indiscriminate and disproportionate use of an improvised explosive device at the Buea Trade Fair event is unacceptable', 13 Dec. 2021.

[10] Bone, R. M. and Nkwain, A. K., 'Cameroon grants "special status" its restive regions. They don't feel special', African Arguments, 13 Jan. 2020.

[11] Jeune Afrique, 'Cameroon's Anglophone crisis: Rivalries hamper peace talks', Africa Report, 11 Aug. 2020.

[12] Finnan, D., 'Cameroon: Can Vatican visit to Cameroon break the Anglophone crisis stalemate?', AllAfrica, 5 Feb. 2021.

[13] Kindzeka, M. E., 'Cameroon Prime Minister visits English-speaking western regions to ask for peace', VOA, 8 Oct. 2021.

[14] The agreement is annexed to United Nations, Security Council, 'Letter dated 14 February 2019 from the Secretary-General addressed to the President of the Security Council', S/2019/145, 15 Feb. 2019. On developments in CAR in 2019 see *SIPRI Yearbook 2020*, pp. 196–99.

[15] The Seleka, meaning an 'alliance movement' in Sango, was created in 2012, while the anti-Balaka, a collection of 'self-defence' armed groups, emerged in 2013. Since 2015 there has been a proliferation of armed groups in CAR as a result of divisions within the ex-Seleka and the anti-Balaka, mainly along ethnic lines and regional origins, or based on economic interests. See Vircoulon, T., *Écosystème des groupes armés en Centrafrique* [Ecosystem of Armed Groups in Central Africa] (IFRI: Paris, Apr. 2020).

Table 7.7. Estimated conflict-related fatalities in the Central African Republic, 2013–21

Event type	2013	2014	2015	2016	2017	2018	2019	2020	2021
Battles	1 223	1 144	191	443	1 250	624	350	331	724
Explosions/remote violence	4	105	12	1	10	2	7	0	75
Protests, riots and strategic developments	122	105	56	8	14	25	4	5	4
Violence against civilians	1 210	2 264	266	287	555	520	235	110	904
Total	**2 559**	**3 618**	**525**	**739**	**1 829**	**1 171**	**596**	**446**	**1 707**

Notes: For definitions of event types, see Armed Conflict Location & Event Data Project (ACLED), 'ACLED definitions of political violence and protest', 11 Apr. 2019.
Source: ACLED, 'Dashboard', accessed 11 Apr. 2022.

The security situation became even more volatile during 2021 as government forces, backed by Russian private military companies (PMCs) and Rwandan troops, fought to recapture territory from armed groups.[16] Estimated conflict-related fatalities increased to over 1700 in 2021, after three consecutive years of decline (see table 7.7). The political situation also remained fragile in the aftermath of the presidential and legislative elections of December 2020.[17] Over half (3.1 million people) the population required humanitarian assistance and protection at the end of 2021, and one in four of the country's population was displaced, either within or outside CAR.[18]

The internationalized armed conflict

On 19 December 2020 six rebel groups controlling two-thirds of the country's territory formed the Coalition of Patriots for Change (CPC). This occurred after CAR's Constitutional Court rejected the candidacy of former president François Bozizé, who remains influential among anti-Balaka militia groups and the Gbaya community (the country's largest ethnic group). The newly formed CPC escalated attempts to obstruct the 27 December election and attempted a military coup in January 2021.[19] At the request of the CAR government, Russia and Rwanda deployed additional forces to support MINUSCA and government forces.[20] The temporary deployment of 300 Russian military instructors complemented existing Russian private military contractors, who had been present in CAR since at least 2018,

---

[16] Several Russian PMCs have reportedly been conducting activities in CAR, including the Wagner Group, Sewa Security Services and Patriot. See Arnold T. D., 'The geoeconomic dimensions of Russian private military and security companies', *Military Review*, Nov.–Dec. 2019; and Office of the UN High Commissioner for Human Rights (OHCHR), 'CAR: Experts alarmed by government's use of "Russian trainers", close contacts with UN peacekeepers', Press release, 31 Mar. 2021.

[17] On developments in 2020 see *SIPRI Yearbook 2021*, pp. 211–14.

[18] UN OCHA (note 1), p. 194.

[19] United Nations, Security Council, 'Central African Republic', Report of the Secretary-General, S/2021/146, 16 Feb. 2021, pp. 1–2; and 'Central African Republic: One year later, Central Africans still remember the failed coup of January 13, 2021', Radio Ndeke Luka, 14 Jan. 2022.

[20] 'Rwanda bolsters force in CAR as rebels "held back"', BBC News, 21 Dec. 2020.

mostly associated with the Wagner Group (and thought to number 1200–2000 personnel).[21]

The security situation remained fragile throughout 2021, particularly in the west, north-west and centre of the country, with continued clashes between mainly CPC-affiliated armed groups and national military forces assisted by Russian PMCs and Rwandan troops. These clashes resulted in significant fatalities, displacement and reported human rights abuses by all parties.[22] The CAR and allied forces were able to recapture several towns from armed groups during the first half of 2021, diminishing the operational capabilities of the CPC and confining it to the far north-west of the country.[23]

In April 2021 Unity for Peace in Central Africa (UPC), then the biggest of the CPC-affiliated armed groups, withdrew from the coalition and sought talks with the government.[24] By the end of July much of the frontline fighting against the CPC was being carried out by the Russian PMCs, with government troops occupying the captured positions after they had been secured by the contractors.[25] Russia's increasing influence at the expense of France in the latter's former colony had led to a disinformation campaign between the two countries in December 2020, and in June 2021 France suspended aid and military cooperation with the CAR government.[26] In December 2021 the European Union Military Training Mission in Central African Republic (EUTM RCA) also suspended its training activities due to the growing influence of the Russian PMCs.[27]

The political context and implementation of the Political Agreement

Although only 35 per cent of the 1.85 million registered voters took part in the December 2020 presidential and legislative elections—due to insecurity,

---

[21] Schreck, C., 'What are Russian military contractors doing in the Central African Republic?', RadioFreeEurope/RadioLiberty, 1 Aug. 2018; 'Russia sends 300 military instructors to Central African Republic', BBC News, 22 Dec. 2020; and Bax, P., 'Russia's influence in the Central African Republic', International Crisis Group, 3 Dec. 2021. On the role of the Wagner Group in Africa see Olivier, M., 'Russia/Africa: Wagner, an investigation into Putin's mercenaries', Africa Report, 28 July 2021.

[22] UNHCR, 'Central African Republic: UN report calls for urgent end to mounting human rights abuses and violations', Press release, 4 Aug. 2021; and Surprenant, A., 'Central African troops and Russian mercenaries accused of abuses in anti-rebel offensive', New Humanitarian, 29 Apr. 2021.

[23] United Nations, Security Council, 'Central African Republic', Report of the Secretary-General, S/2021/571, 16 June 2021, pp. 5–6; United Nations, Security Council, 'Central African Republic', Report of the Secretary-General, S/2021/867, 12 Oct. 2021, pp. 4–5; and Munshi, N., 'Central African Republic troops beat back rebels with Russian help', *Irish Times*, 26 Jan. 2021.

[24] 'Powerful armed group in Central African Republic vows to leave rebel coalition', France 24, 6 Apr. 2022.

[25] Olivier, M., 'Russia/Africa: Wagner, an investigation into Putin's mercenaries', Africa Report, 28 July 2021.

[26] 'French and Russian Facebook trolls fight it out in CAR elections', Al Jazeera, 15 Dec. 2020; and 'France suspends aid, military support for Central African Republic', Reuters, 9 June 2021.

[27] 'EU suspends military training in Central Africa over Russian mercenaries', Reuters, 15 Dec. 2021; and Bax (note 21). On the impact of Russian PMCs on multilateral peace operations in CAR and elsewhere in Africa see chapter 2, section II, in this volume.

voting did not take place in roughly 40 per cent of the 140 National Assembly seats—President Faustin-Archange Touadéra secured the win with over 53 per cent of the vote.[28] He was inaugurated on 30 March 2021 and in April–June conducted national consultations with a variety of stakeholders, excluding armed groups affiliated with the CPC. On 10 June President Touadéra announced the imminent launch of a 'republican dialogue' and requested the international community's support.[29] An organizing committee for the republican dialogue was established on 30 June and inaugurated on 1 September.[30]

Efforts to reinvigorate implementation of the Political Agreement continued in 2021, but only limited progress was made in disarmament and demobilization, and in the training and operationalization of the mixed security units.[31] The government, with the support of MINUSCA, did have some success with local-level dialogue and reconciliation efforts.[32] At a mini-summit of the International Conference on the Great Lakes Region on 16 September a joint roadmap to revitalize the peace process was adopted, notably calling for the declaration of a ceasefire by the CAR government.[33] On 15 October Touadéra declared a unilateral ceasefire to allow civilians access to aid, but even so military operations continued.[34] In November 2021 MINUSCA's mandate was extended for a further 12 months until 15 November 2022.[35]

Having been founded in 2015, the CAR Special Criminal Court (SCC)—composed of national and international staff and applying a blend of national and international law—became operational in 2021.[36] Despite obstructions from government officials, the SCC has a mandate to investigate, prosecute and judge serious human rights violations and grave breaches of international criminal and humanitarian law committed in CAR since 1 January 2003. In November 2021 the SCC arrested former leader of the UPC turned minister Hassan Bouba, charging him with war crimes and crimes against humanity.[37]

---

[28] United Nations, 'Central African Republic: Respect final results of the election, UN and partners urge', UN News, 5 Jan. 2021.

[29] United Nations, S/2021/571 (note 23), p. 2.

[30] United Nations, S/2021/867 (note 23), pp. 1–2.

[31] United Nations, S/2021/867 (note 23), pp. 2–3.

[32] United Nations, S/2021/867 (note 23), p. 4.

[33] Final communiqué of the Mini-Summit of ICGLR on the political and security situation in the Central African Republic, 16 Sep. 2021.

[34] Yongo, J., 'Central African Republic declares unilateral ceasefire in fight with rebels', Reuters, 16 Oct. 2021.

[35] UN Security Council Resolution 2605, 12 Nov. 2021.

[36] UN Multidimensional Integrated Stabilization Mission in the Central African Republic (MINUSCA), 'CAR Special Criminal Court (SCC) now fully operational', 9 June 2021.

[37] Human Rights Watch, 'Central African Republic: Minister faces atrocity charges', 24 Nov. 2021.

Chad

Chad has been one of the most important regional states in the fight against armed groups in the Central Sahel and Lake Chad regions (see section II). In 2021 the country was affected by growing insecurity both within its borders and in neighbouring countries. In addition to the political and military turmoil following the killing of President Idriss Déby in April 2021, attacks by Boko Haram and Chadian armed groups, as well as intercommunal violence, continued.[38] These conflicts flowed partly from farmer–herder competition, but also from deeper identity-based rivalries over land and power-sharing. There were an estimated 831 conflict-related fatalities in 2021, the third consecutive annual increase and the largest total seen in the past decade.[39] The combined effects of armed conflict, health emergencies and climate change resulted in 5.5 million people—one-third of the population—needing humanitarian assistance in 2021. Chad was host to over 528 000 refugees and asylum seekers in 2021—a figure that rises to over 1 million if internally displaced persons (IDPs) and Chadian returnees are included—making it one of the largest refugee host countries in Africa. Meanwhile, severe food insecurity affected more than 1.8 million people.[40]

In April 2021 President Idriss Déby was killed in clashes with the armed group, Front for Change and Concord in Chad (FACT), which had invaded from Libya.[41] Unwilling to adhere to the constitution's succession plan, the military organized a coup and installed Déby's son, Mahamat, as leader of a 15-member Transitional Military Council (TMC). The TMC announced that it would rule Chad for an 18-month period, renewable once, during which time it would organize an inclusive national dialogue prior to elections.[42] By early May the army had pushed the FACT insurgents back into Libya. However, the security context continued to be tense for the remainder of the year.

The Democratic Republic of the Congo

The DRC—the second-largest country in Africa, with a population of about 80 million—is suffering from one of the longest and most complex crises in the world. Armed conflict, epidemics and natural disasters have combined with high levels of poverty and weak public infrastructure and services, with

---

[38] 'At least two dozen Chadian soldiers killed in suspected jihadist attack', France 24, 5 Aug. 2021; and UN OCHA, 'Chad: Overview of intercommunal conflicts', 6 Aug. 2021.

[39] Armed Conflict Location & Event Data Project (ACLED), 'Dashboard', accessed 11 Apr. 2022.

[40] UN OCHA (note 1), p. 197.

[41] 'Rebels threaten to march on capital as Chad reels from president's battlefield death', Reuters, 21 Apr. 2021.

[42] Eizenga, D., 'Chad's "political transition" is a smokescreen for military rule', World Politics Review, 12 Oct. 2021.

Table 7.8. Estimated conflict-related fatalities in the Democratic Republic of the Congo, 2013–21

Event type	2013	2014	2015	2016	2017	2018	2019	2020	2021
Battles	1 093	603	748	898	1 364	1 790	1 966	3 349	3 002
Explosions/remote violence	77	10	13	4	108	9	15	1	101
Protests, riots and strategic developments	16	38	65	145	79	63	129	204	299
Violence against civilians	787	579	936	693	1 660	1 330	1 696	2 502	2 281
Total	**1 973**	**1 230**	**1 762**	**1 740**	**3 211**	**3 192**	**3 806**	**6 056**	**5 683**

Notes: For definitions of event types, see Armed Conflict Location & Event Data Project (ACLED), 'ACLED definitions of political violence and protest', 11 Apr. 2019.

Source: ACLED, 'Dashboard', accessed 11 Apr. 2022.

competition over land and mineral resources a primary driver of conflict.[43] Since the end of the 1998–2003 Second Congo War, conflict has persisted in the eastern DRC, where dozens of armed groups remain and a major UN peacekeeping force—the UN Organization Stabilization Mission in the DRC (MONUSCO)—has been deployed since 2010.[44] The armed groups vary in capacity, size and objectives.[45] MONUSCO personnel increased by 3.8 per cent over the course of 2021—the first increase since 2016—and on 20 December 2021 the UN Security Council extended the mission's mandate to 20 December 2022, with an authorized personnel strength of approximately 16 000. A transition plan for the mission's drawdown and eventual exit continues to be discussed.[46]

While most of the DRC's 26 provinces were stable in 2021, several of the eastern provinces (particularly Ituri and North Kivu) faced continued instability from external and Congolese armed groups engaged in multiple armed conflicts with the government, as well as a resurgence of intercommunal violence. The high levels of violence in the eastern DRC recorded in 2020 continued into 2021, reflected in the estimated conflict-related fatalities for these two years being the highest recorded in the 2013–21 period (see table 7.8). Serious and widespread human rights and international humanitarian law violations continued to take place in the eastern DRC, including conflict-related sexual violence and grave violations

---

[43] For detailed analysis of the armed conflict see United Nations, Security Council, Final report of the Group of Experts on the Democratic Republic of the Congo, S/2020/482, 2 June 2020.

[44] The UN Organization Mission in the DRC (MONUC) was deployed in 1999 and succeeded by MONUSCO in 2010.

[45] For details of the armed groups see United Nations, S/2020/482 (note 43), pp. 5–12; and Vogel C. et al., *The Landscape of Armed Groups in Eastern Congo: Missed Opportunities, Protracted Insecurity and Self-fulfilling Prophecies* (Kivu Security Tracker: Feb. 2021).

[46] UN Security Council Resolution 2612, 20 Dec. 2021; and United Nations, 'Senior official in Democratic Republic of Congo spotlights violence in eastern provinces, outlines mission transition plans, briefing Security Council', SC/14655, 5 Oct. 2021. On developments in MONUSCO see also chapter 2, section II, in this volume.

against children.[47] As part of this ongoing, complex and multi-layered humanitarian crisis, 26.2 million people faced acute food insecurity in 2021 (the highest absolute number ever recorded globally), while an estimated 5.5 million people remained internally displaced—the largest IDP population in Africa—including 1.5 million people displacements in 2021.[48]

The armed conflicts in eastern DRC

A temporary 'state of siege' in North Kivu and Ituri provinces was declared by President Felix Tshisekedi on 3 May 2021. These special measures included the replacement of all civil authorities—including elected governors—with military authorities granted the power to arrest and prosecute civilians.[49] The state of siege was extended multiple times during the year and was still extant at the end of December 2021. Even so, the security situation in the two provinces continued to deteriorate as a result of ongoing armed group activity, causing further population displacement.[50]

Some of the most violent clashes in North Kivu were between government forces and the Allied Democratic Forces, an Islamist armed group that originated in Uganda. In Ituri, the Cooperative for the Development of Congo, a loose association of ethnic Lendu militias, carried out attacks against civilians. Attacks on civilians and government forces by armed groups in other provinces included, in South Kivu, local Mai-Mai armed groups and external armed groups such as the Burundian Resistance for Law in Burundi (RED-Tabara); and in Katanga, attacks by the secessionist group Bakata-Katanga and other militias.[51] A new Demobilization, Disarmament, Community Recovery and Stabilization programme introduced by the government during the second half of 2021 has the potential to meet armed group grievances if implemented successfully.[52]

---

[47] United Nations, Security Council, 'United Nations Organization Stabilization Mission in the Democratic Republic of the Congo', Report of the Secretary-General, S/2021/987, 1 Dec. 2021, pp. 5–6; Amnesty International (AI), *Amnesty International Report 2021/22: The State of the World's Human Rights* (AI: London, 2022), pp. 145–49; and United Nations, General Assembly and Security Council, 'Children and armed conflict', Report of the Secretary-General, A/75/873-S/2021/437, 6 May 2021, pp. 8–10.

[48] Integrated Food Security Phase Classification, 'Democratic Republic of Congo: Integrated Food Security Phase Classification snapshot: March 2021', 30 Mar. 2021; and UN OCHA (note 1), p. 201.

[49] United Nations, Security Council, 'United Nations Organization Stabilization Mission in the Democratic Republic of the Congo', Report of the Secretary-General, S/2021/587, 21 June 2021, p. 2.

[50] Human Rights Watch, 'DR Congo: Massacres persist despite martial law', 15 Sep. 2021; and United Nations, 'Human rights abuses intensifying in eastern DR Congo—UNHCR', UN News, 10 Sep. 2021.

[51] United Nations, Security Council, 'United Nations Organization Stabilization Mission in the Democratic Republic of the Congo', Report of the Secretary-General, S/2021/807, 17 Sep. 2021, pp. 3–4; and United Nations, S/2021/987 (note 47), pp. 3–4.

[52] Kivu Security Tracker, 'Does the new disarmament and demobilization program stand a chance of success?', 10 Sep. 2021.

IV. Armed conflict and peace processes in East Africa

IAN DAVIS

East Africa comprises 22 states or territories, 9 of which were involved in active armed conflicts in 2021 (see figure 7.1). This section focuses on five of these armed conflicts: in Ethiopia, Mozambique, Somalia, South Sudan and Sudan (which all saw sharp escalations or continuing large-scale armed violence in 2021). There were more than 9.6 million internally displaced persons (IDPs) and more than 4.7 million refugees across East Africa, primarily due to conflict and violence in these five countries. Grave violations against civilians, including conflict-related sexual violence, continued to be committed in the region, while at least 33.8 million people were severely food insecure.[1]

Most East African conflicts are in the Horn of Africa.[2] States in this subregion are particularly fragile due to a complex mix of reasons, including restricted access to natural resources, inter-group tensions, poverty and inequality, and weak state institutions.[3] Over the past decade, a growing number of external actors have prioritized counterterrorism and anti-piracy efforts in the Horn of Africa. This has created a crowded playing field— including China, India, the United States and other Western powers (France, Germany, Italy, Japan, Spain and the United Kingdom) and several Middle Eastern countries (Egypt, Iran, Qatar, Saudi Arabia, Turkey and the United Arab Emirates)—leading to growing geopolitical tensions, rivalries and risks of destabilizing proxy conflicts.[4]

Disputes over resource allocation and access have also been significant in the region. For example, the dispute involving Egypt, Ethiopia and Sudan over sharing of the eastern Nile waters remained deadlocked in 2021.[5] Many of the region's social, political and economic challenges are compounded by the impacts of climate change, including droughts and floods.[6] Three consecutive failed rainy seasons, coupled with increased temperatures,

---

[1] United Nations Office for the Coordination of Humanitarian Affairs (OCHA), *Global Humanitarian Overview 2022* (UN OCHA: Dec. 2021), p. 146.

[2] Geographically, the Horn of Africa is normally understood to comprise Djibouti, Eritrea, Ethiopia and Somalia. There are also broader definitions (as used here) that comprise these four core countries plus all or parts of Kenya, the Seychelles, South Sudan, Sudan and Uganda.

[3] Adeto, Y. A., 'State fragility and conflict nexus: Contemporary security issues in the Horn of Africa', ACCORD, 22 July 2019.

[4] Melvin, N., 'The foreign military presence in the Horn of Africa region', SIPRI Background Paper, Apr. 2019; and 'Gulf rivalries are spilling into Africa's Horn', *The Economist*, 11 Feb. 2021. On geopolitical tensions in the Middle East and North Africa see chapter 6, section I, in this volume.

[5] Asala, K., 'Tension over Nile waters between Ethiopia, Sudan and Egypt explained', Africanews, 8 Apr. 2021; and United Nations, Security Council, 8816th meeting, 'Peace and security in Africa', S/PV.8816, 8 July 2021.

[6] For a regional analysis of environment, peace and security linkages in the region with specific focus on water security and governance see Krampe, F. et al., *Water Security and Governance in the Horn of Africa*, SIPRI Policy Paper no. 54 (SIPRI: Stockholm, Mar. 2020).

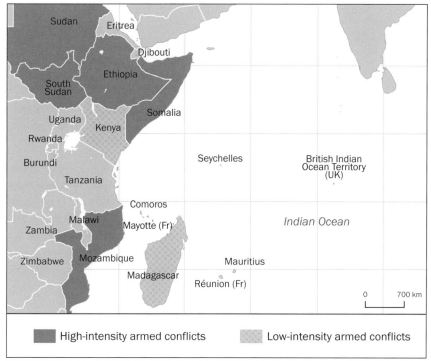

Figure 7.1. East Africa, including the Horn of Africa

particularly in Somalia and Kenya, caused the region's most severe drought in decades.[7]

Ethiopia

The armed conflict that broke out in the Tigray region of northern Ethiopia in November 2020 between the former administration of the northern Tigray region—the Tigray People's Liberation Front (TPLF)—and federal government forces worsened during 2021, with the conflict's expansion to the neighbouring regions of Amhara and Afar causing a deepening humanitarian crisis. By the end of September 2021 the number of people in the three regions in need of food assistance had increased from 5.2 million to about 7 million, and the number of IDPs stood at more than 2.4 million.[8] In addition to the crisis in northern Ethiopia, long-standing intercommunal tensions in other parts of the country and regional border disputes drove humanitarian

[7] Famine Early Warning Systems Network, 'The Eastern Horn of Africa faces an exceptional prolonged and persistent agro-pastoral drought sequence', 1 Dec. 2021.

[8] United Nations, 'Tigray: Food aid reaches Afar and Amhara, but situation still "dire"', UN News, 5 Oct. 2021.

Table 7.9. Estimated conflict-related fatalities in Ethiopia, 2013–21

Event type	2013	2014	2015	2016	2017	2018	2019	2020	2021
Battles	418	237	566	999	877	730	193	1 663	5 351
Explosions/remote violence	48	2	16	15	2	22	17	235	510
Protests, riots and strategic developments	33	53	177	749	131	241	170	225	38
Violence against civilians	85	43	52	752	345	572	287	1 934	3 059
Total	**584**	**335**	**811**	**2 515**	**1 355**	**1 565**	**667**	**4 057**	**8 958**

Notes: For definitions of event types, see Armed Conflict Location & Event Data Project (ACLED), 'ACLED definitions of political violence and protest', 11 Apr. 2019.

Source: ACLED, 'Dashboard', accessed 6 Apr. 2022.

need in 2021. Across the country, 25.9 million people needed humanitarian assistance (up from 11.7 million in 2020) due to a combination of high levels of armed conflict and insecurity from climate shocks, disease outbreaks and a declining economy. The displacement trend in Ethiopia saw a rise in the number of IDPs from 3.2 million in 2018 to 4.2 million at the end of 2021.[9] Estimated conflict-related fatalities in Ethiopia doubled in 2021 compared with 2020 (see table 7.9).

The armed conflict in Tigray and neighbouring regions

The political roots of the war in the Tigray region—located in the north of Ethiopia, bordering Eritrea and Sudan, with a population of about 6 million people (out of a total Ethiopian population of about 115 million)—reflect a power struggle between Tigrayan elites (who once dominated Ethiopia's military and ruling coalition) and the Ethiopian government led by Prime Minister Abiy Ahmed.[10] The war pitted TPLF forces against Ethiopian government forces (consisting of armed forces, federal police, regional police and regional militias), with the latter supported by Amhara regional forces and Eritrean forces.[11] The Ethiopian government, having captured the Tigrayan capital, Mekelle, on 28 November 2020 and declared victory over the TPLF, was in the ascendancy at the start of 2021.[12] During the year, however, the course of the war fluctuated wildly.

In the first half of 2021 the Ethiopian government's occupation of Tigray resulted in the deaths of thousands of civilians and the destruction of civil infrastructure in the region. Eritrean troops were accused of committing

[9] UN OCHA (note 1), pp. 155–57.

[10] Gardner, T., 'How Abiy's effort to redefine Ethiopia led to war in Tigray', World Politics Review, 8 Dec. 2020; and Burke, J., 'Rise and fall of Ethiopia's TPLF—from rebels to rulers and back', *The Guardian*, 25 Nov. 2020.

[11] Beaumont, P., 'Diplomats back claims Eritrean troops have joined Ethiopia conflict', *The Guardian*, 8 Dec. 2020.

[12] Anna, C., 'UN: Ethiopia's victory claim doesn't mean war is finished', AP News, 29 Nov. 2020. On developments in 2020 see *SIPRI Yearbook 2021*, pp. 218–21.

massacres and looting.[13] By the end of June 2021, however, the TPLF insurgency had wrested back control of the region, before pushing south and east through the Amhara and Afar regions.[14] A joint UN–Ethiopian investigation into the conflict, covering the period November 2020–June 2021, concluded that all parties to the conflict committed human rights violations, and that war crimes and crimes against humanity may have been committed.[15]

By November 2021 the TPLF, acting in coordination with the Oromo Liberation Army (OLA)—insurgents from Ethiopia's most populous region, Oromia—were threatening the federal government in Addis Ababa.[16] The conflict in both Amhara and Afar regions led to further large-scale displacement, civilian casualties and sexual violence.[17] With the risk of a widening civil war, the government declared a nationwide state of emergency.[18] At the end of November the TPLF were within 130 kilometres of Addis Ababa, before being stopped by federal forces and their allies. By the end of 2021 most of the TPLF gains from earlier in the year had been reversed. A 'popular mobilization' of additional forces and the Ethiopian government forces' advantage in heavy weapons and total air control were key to their battlefield success. Armed drones supplied by Turkey and others (unconfirmed reports suggest China, Iran and/or the United Arab Emirates) also played a role.[19]

The TPLF claimed that their withdrawal from Afar and Amhara regions was strategic and a 'decisive opening for peace'.[20] Similarly, the Ethiopian

[13] Ethiopian Human Rights Commission (EHRC), 'Investigation into grave human rights violations in Aksum—preliminary findings', 24 Mar. 2021; and Human Rights Watch, 'Ethiopia: Eritrean forces massacre Tigray civilians', 5 Mar. 2021.

[14] Akinwotu, E., 'Interim government of Tigray flees as rebels seize capital', *The Guardian*, 28 June 2021.

[15] EHRC and Office of the UN High Commissioner for Human Rights (OHCHR), 'Report of the Ethiopian Human Rights Commission (EHRC)/Office of the United Nations High Commissioner for Human Rights (OHCHR) joint investigation into alleged violations of international human rights, humanitarian and refugee law committed by all parties', 3 Nov. 2021.

[16] 'Ethiopia's Tigray forces seek new military alliance', Reuters, 11 Aug. 2021; and Hamza, M. M., 'TPLF–OLA alliance is a prelude to Tigray's secession', Ethiopia Insight, 2 Sep. 2021.

[17] Amnesty International, *Ethiopia: 'I Don't Know If They Realized I Was a Person': Rape and Sexual Violence in the Conflict in Tigray, Ethiopia* (Amnesty International: 11 Aug. 2021).

[18] Wintour, P., 'Ethiopia declares state of emergency as Tigrayan rebels gain ground', *The Guardian*, 2 Nov. 2021.

[19] Mitzer, S. and Oliemans, J., 'Wing Loong is over Ethiopia: Chinese UCAVs join the battle for Tigray', Oryx, 11 Oct. 2021, Zwijnenburg, W., 'Is Ethiopia flying Iranian-made armed drones?', Bellingcat, 17 Aug. 2021; 'UAE air bridge provides military support to Ethiopia gov't', Al Jazeera, 25 Nov. 2021; Spicer, J. Paravinci, G. and Coskun, O., 'US concerned over Turkey's drone sales to conflict-hit Ethiopia', Reuters, 22 Dec. 2021; Anna, C., 'Ethiopia says PM, a Nobel Peace laureate, is at battlefront', AP News, 24 Nov. 2021; and Gatopoulos, A., 'How armed drones may have helped turn the tide in Ethiopia's war', Al Jazeera, 10 Dec. 2021. On arms transfers to Ethiopia see also chapter 9, section III, in this volume.

[20] 'Tigrayan fighters announce they are withdrawing from rest of Ethiopia', Deutsche Welle, 20 Dec. 2021.

Table 7.10. Estimated conflict-related fatalities in Mozambique, 2013–21

Event type	2013	2014	2015	2016	2017	2018	2019	2020	2021
Battles	116	43	41	45	40	39	269	880	717
Explosions/remote violence	3	0	0	0	0	0	8	73	105
Protests, riots and strategic developments	3	3	3	2	71	6	20	19	23
Violence against civilians	22	11	4	58	18	179	367	813	313
Total	**144**	**57**	**48**	**105**	**129**	**224**	**664**	**1 785**	**1 158**

Notes: For definitions of event types, see Armed Conflict Location & Event Data Project (ACLED), 'ACLED definitions of political violence and protest', 11 Apr. 2019.

Source: ACLED, 'Dashboard', accessed 6 Apr. 2022.

government announced a temporary halt to its advance into the Tigray region, paving the way for a planned national dialogue in 2022.[21]

Other key developments in 2021

Ethiopian security forces were also fighting several other anti-government insurgencies during 2021, with those in Oromia and Benshangul-Gumuz regions particularly virulent.[22] Intercommunal tensions over unequal access to land and resources also continued to fuel violence. A coalition of eight anti-government factions, including the OLA, was formed in November 2021.[23]

In the mid-year general election, which had been postponed twice due to the Covid-19 pandemic, the ruling Prosperity party won 410 of 436 seats in the federal parliament, assuring a second term for Prime Minister Abiy. Opposition parties cited harassment and intimidation, and voting was delayed or cancelled in 111 constituencies (of 547 constituencies nationally) owing to insecurity and logistical problems.[24]

Border tensions between Ethiopia and Sudan, which had escalated in late December 2020 in the fertile al-Fashaga borderland, continued in 2021, resulting in inter-state clashes between Sudanese and Ethiopian troops.[25] Relations between the two countries were already strained due to the dispute over the Grand Ethiopian Renaissance Dam on the River Nile. In December 2021 Sudanese forces announced full control over the disputed region. The recurrent clashes raised fears of an escalation that could draw in regional allies.[26]

---

[21] 'Ethiopia government says military won't cross into Tigray for now', Reuters, 24 Dec. 2022.

[22] Ochieng, Z., 'Ethiopia grapples with Oromo attacks', News Africa, 1 July 2021; and Sew, M., 'EIEP: Marginalization and persecution in Ethiopia's Benishangul-Gumuz', Ethiopia Insight, 10 Aug. 2021.

[23] Pamuk, H. and Fick, M., 'New alliance wants to oust Ethiopia's PM by talks or force', Reuters, 5 Nov. 2021.

[24] 'Ethiopia election: Abiy Ahmed wins with huge majority', BBC News, 11 July 2021.

[25] 'Six Sudanese soldiers killed in Ethiopian attack—Sudan military sources', Reuters, 28 Nov. 2021.

[26] International Crisis Group, 'Containing the volatile Sudan–Ethiopia border dispute', Africa Briefing no. 173, 24 June 2021; and 'Sudanese army deployed along the disputed border with Ethiopia', Africanews, 15 Dec. 2021.

Outlook

While the government's planned national dialogue offered some grounds for optimism, finding solutions to Ethiopia's numerous deeply rooted and complex conflicts is likely to be a lengthy process. Intercommunal grievances across Ethiopia and the ethno-federalist system of governance, which is used to compete for contested territory and governance rights, will make politically negotiated settlements difficult to agree and implement.

Mozambique

The insurgency in Cabo Delgado province in the north of Mozambique, which began in 2017, continued to escalate in the first half of 2021. The conflict also became more internationalized, with both Rwanda and the Southern African Development Community (SADC) authorizing military deployments in July 2021 in support of Mozambican government forces. These forces managed to drive the insurgents out of their main strongholds, but smaller-scale attacks continued. Throughout 2021 the crisis in Cabo Delgado deepened the needs of displaced people, with an estimated 745 000 IDPs in northern Mozambique by September 2021, while more than 900 000 people were severely food insecure. At the end of 2021 at least 1.5 million people needed humanitarian assistance and protection in northern Mozambique.[27] Overall, estimated conflict-related fatalities in Mozambique decreased by about 35 per cent in 2021 (compared to 2020) but remained almost twice as high compared to 2019 (see table 7.10).

International intervention in Cabo Delgado

The main insurgent group in Cabo Delgado is Ansar al-Sunna, although locals call it 'al-Shabab' (there is no connection to the al-Shabab group in Somalia). Motivations for joining the group are diverse: though some are committed jihadists, many are likely driven by economic and political exclusion.[28] During 2019 the group reportedly pledged allegiance to the Islamic State and analysts now refer to it as being part of the Islamic State Central Africa Province.[29] Despite the extent of the group's fragmentation and links to the Islamic State being difficult to discern, the US government designated the insurgents

---

[27] UN OCHA (note 1), pp. 163–65.

[28] On the roots of the insurgency see International Crisis Group, *Stemming the Insurrection in Mozambique's Cabo Delgado*, Africa Report no. 303 (International Crisis Group: Brussels, 11 June 2021), pp. 3–24; and Jentzsch, C., 'Ignorance, denial and insurgency in Mozambique', Africa is a Country, 17 Dec. 2021.

[29] On the origins of Islamist groups in northern Mozambique see Habibe, S., Forquilha, S. and Pereira, J., *Islamic Radicalization in Northern Mozambique: The Case of Mocímboa da Praia*, Cadernos IESE no. 17/2019 (Institute for Social and Economic Studies: Maputo, Sep. 2019).

Table 7.11. Estimated conflict-related fatalities in Somalia, 2013–21

Event type	2013	2014	2015	2016	2017	2018	2019	2020	2021
Battles	1 985	2 893	2 785	3 729	2 686	3 034	2 154	1 891	1 989
Explosions/remote violence	543	955	784	1 518	2 493	1 765	1 696	869	804
Protests, riots and strategic developments	15	19	8	27	74	48	23	24	81
Violence against civilians	629	602	562	676	890	573	640	465	387
Total	**3 172**	**4 469**	**4 139**	**5 950**	**6 143**	**5 420**	**4 513**	**3 249**	**3 261**

Notes: For definitions of event types, see Armed Conflict Location & Event Data Project (ACLED), 'ACLED definitions of political violence and protest', 11 Apr. 2019.

Source: ACLED, 'Dashboard', accessed 6 Apr. 2022.

an international terrorist organization in March 2021.[30] With Mozambique state forces stretched by the conflict, local communities formed self-defence militias. The government also increasingly relied on military assistance from private security contractors from South Africa.[31]

In March 2021 Ansar al-Sunna attacked the coastal town of Palma, close to a major liquefied natural gas project run by French company Total, and in late April Total suspended its operations.[32] By the end of May 2021 pressure was building for Mozambique to accept international military assistance to contain the insurrection.[33] In June 2021 the SADC Summit established the SADC Mission in Mozambique (SAMIM) and on 15 July it was deployed to the region. Although the mission has an authorized ceiling of just under 3000 personnel, by the end of 2021 only about a third of this number had been deployed.[34] Although initially mandated for three months, the mission was extended for an additional three months on 5 October 2021. SAMIM operates in cooperation with Mozambique government forces and a Rwanda Joint Force contingent, initially numbering 1000 personnel, that had also arrived in July.[35]

Government and allied foreign forces began to recapture territory in the second half of 2021. In August 2021, for example, the port town of Mocímboa

[30] US Department of State, 'State Department terrorist designations of ISIS affiliates and leaders in the Democratic Republic of the Congo and Mozambique', 10 Mar. 2021; and Hamming, T. R., 'The Islamic State in Mozambique', Lawfare, 24 Jan. 2021.

[31] 'Paramount and Lionel Dyck massively boost Nyusi's firepower', Africa Intelligence, 10 Dec. 2020; and Cenola, T. and Kleinfeld, P., 'Mozambique's Cabo Delgado: Militants advance as aid access shrinks', New Humanitarian, 21 Dec. 2020.

[32] Burke, J. and Beaumont, P., 'Isis claims deadly attack in northern Mozambique', *The Guardian*, 29 Mar. 2021; and Ahmed, K., 'Mozambique insurgency: 20,000 still trapped near gas plant six weeks after attack', *The Guardian*, 7 May 2021.

[33] See e.g. International Crisis Group, *Stemming the Insurrection in Mozambique's Cabo Delgado*, Africa Report no. 303 (International Crisis Group: Brussels, 11 June 2021).

[34] Southern Africa Development Community (SADC), Communiqué of the Extraordinary Summit of the SADC Heads of State and Government, 23 June 2021. For further details on SAMIM's mandate and personnel deployed see chapter 2, section II, in this volume.

[35] Ministry of Defence, Republic of Rwanda, 'Rwanda deploys joint force to Mozambique', 10 July 2021. For further details about the Rwanda Joint Force see chapter 2, section II, in this volume.

daPraia, which had been the centre of the insurgency and captured by Ansar al-Sunna a year earlier, was reclaimed in an operation led by the Rwanda Joint Force.[36] By the end of 2021 the Rwanda Joint Force contingent had increased to 2500 troops.[37]

Outlook

While the international military intervention dealt a significant blow to the insurgency, small groups of insurgents continued to destabilize pockets of territory in Cabo Delgado and spread into neighbouring Niassa province and Tanzania.[38] Resolving the crisis will require measures aimed at addressing root causes, including a more equitable distribution of the proceeds from the province's mineral and hydrocarbon resources.[39]

Somalia

Since 2012 the main armed conflict in Somalia has been between the Somali government, backed by the African Union Mission in Somalia (AMISOM) and US forces, and al-Shabab insurgents, which still dominate most rural parts of south-central Somalia. Government forces have struggled to mount a cohesive response, partly due to ongoing political factionalism in Somalia. In addition, Somalia's rural populations continued to suffer from clan-based violence, with weak state security forces unable to prevent clashes over water and pasture resources.[40] Overall, estimated conflict-related fatalities in 2021 were similar to 2020, and although these two years were the lowest in the past eight years, annual fatalities remained above 3200 (see table 7.11).

This armed violence has contributed to a prolonged humanitarian crisis in Somalia, which is also characterized by climate shocks (such as floods), drought, disease outbreaks (including the Covid-19 pandemic in 2020–21) and weak social protection. A third consecutive season of below-average rainfall caused water shortages in 2021, adding to food insecurity. The number of people in need of humanitarian assistance increased from 4.2 million in 2019 to 7.7 million in 2021, while the number of IDPs rose from 770 000 in 2019 to 2.9 million in 2021.[41]

---

[36] 'Why Mozambique invited foreign troops to fight its jihadists', *The Economist*, 14 Aug. 2021.

[37] International Crisis Group, 'Winning peace in Mozambique's embattled north', Africa Briefing no. 178, 10 Feb. 2022, p. 4.

[38] International Crisis Group (note 37), pp. 7–9; and Miguel, R. and Baptista, A., 'Officials say insurgency in northern Mozambique is spreading', VOA, 17 Dec. 2021.

[39] Hanlon, J., 'Mozambique's jihadists and the "curse" of gas and rubies', BBC News, 18 Sep. 2020.

[40] Hujale, M. and Davies, L., '"Nothing to eat": Somalia hit by triple threat of climate crisis, Covid and conflict', *The Guardian*, 23 Aug. 2021.

[41] UN OCHA (note 1), pp. 168–71. On the impact of climate-related change in livelihood options and migration, as well as peacebuilding in Somalia, see also Eklöw, K. and Krampe, F., *Climate-related Security Risks and Peacebuilding in Somalia*, SIPRI Policy Paper no. 53 (SIPRI: Stockholm, Oct. 2019).

The future of AMISOM and US forces

In 2018 the AU Peace and Security Council adopted a security transition plan for AMISOM for the gradual transfer of security responsibilities to Somali forces, with final withdrawal of the mission to take place by the end of 2021.[42] An independent assessment in May 2021 recommended that it be replaced by a hybrid AU–UN multidimensional stabilization mission.[43] In October 2021, however, the Somali government rejected the proposal and AMISOM's mandate was subsequently renewed until the end of March 2022 in order to allow the AU, the Somali government, troop contributors and donors to agree on the mission's future.[44]

The USA continued its engagement in Somalia, conducting 12 air strikes in 2021 (compared to 54 in 2020), with an independent assessment recording 19 incidents in 2021 (and 72 in 2020).[45] The USA has been carrying out air strikes against al-Shabab in Somalia since 2007 and from a US airbase in Niger since 2019. The number of air strikes in 2021 was the lowest since 2015. In December 2020 President Donald J. Trump announced the withdrawal of all US troops from Somalia (thought to number about 700), and on 17 January 2021 the US military confirmed that the drawdown had been completed.[46] However, reports suggested that many of these troops had been repositioned to neighbouring countries in East Africa and were 'commuting' to deployments in Somalia. US training of allied forces and special operations activity also continued.[47]

Political fragmentation and Somalia's federalism

Political relations between the federal government and some of the federal member states remained tense in 2021. Electoral processes and the decision by Somalia's parliament in April 2021 to extend the incumbent president's mandate by two years were the primary sources of tension.[48] Power-sharing

---

[42] Oluoch, F., 'AMISOM ready to withdraw', East African, 10 Nov. 2018. On developments within AMISOM in 2018 see SIPRI Yearbook 2019, pp. 169–71. On the force strength of AMISOM and other mission developments in 2021 see chapter 2, sections II and III, in this volume.

[43] African Union, 'Report of the Independent Assessment Team on the African Union's engagement in and with Somalia post 2021', 30 May 2021.

[44] AU, Communiqué of the 1042nd Meeting of the Peace and Security Council of the African Union at the Level of Heads of State and Government on the update on the situation in Somalia, 28 Oct. 2021; UN Security Council Resolution 2614, 21 Dec. 2021; and International Crisis Group, 'Reforming the AU Mission in Somalia', Africa Briefing no. 176, 15 Nov. 2021.

[45] Airwars, 'Declared and alleged US actions in Somalia', accessed 6 Apr. 2022.

[46] Cooper, H., 'Trump orders all American troops out of Somalia', New York Times, 4 Dec. 2020; and Anna, C., 'US military says its troop removal from Somalia is complete', AP News, 17 Jan. 2021.

[47] Myers, M., 'US troops now "commuting to work" to help Somalia fight al-Shabab', Military Times, 27 Apr. 2021; and Turse, N., 'Washington is not telling the truth about US troops in Somalia', Responsible Statecraft, 3 Nov. 2021.

[48] Walsh, D., 'Somalia's president extends term by two years, drawing condemnation', New York Times, 14 Apr. 2021; and Sperber, A., 'Back from the brink? Somalia's political crisis explained', New Humanitarian, 20 May 2021.

arrangements along clan lines are common at all levels of Somali governance. In September 2020 it was decided to maintain the country's indirect voting system, whereby state legislatures and clan delegates select lawmakers for the national parliament, who in turn choose the president. However, for most of 2021 the electoral process remained contested and subject to delays amid disagreement between Somalia's political leaders.[49] By the end of 2021 the election of the 54-member Senate chamber had been completed, and over half of the 275 lawmakers in the House of the People had also been elected. Once the latter election process is completed the long-awaited presidential elections will take place in 2022.[50]

South Sudan

On 9 July 2021 South Sudan marked its 10th anniversary as an independent state. The year also marked the 10th anniversary of the establishment of the UN Mission in South Sudan (UNMISS).[51] Although a post-independence civil war (2013–15) was curtailed by a 2015 peace agreement, the legacy of violence continued in the form of an armed conflict waged primarily between two groups: the Sudan People's Liberation Movement (SPLM) led by President Salva Kiir, and the Sudan People's Liberation Army-in-Opposition (SPLM/A-IO) and the Nuer White Army, led by Vice President Riek Machar. Although the main division in the subsequent conflict has been between the Dinka and Nuer ethnic groups, underlying conflict dynamics are primarily political and vary considerably across the country. Opposition groups have become more fractured and localized.

Kiir and Machar signed a new peace deal in September 2018—the Revitalized Agreement on the Resolution of the Conflict in the Republic of South Sudan—but since then implementation has been contested, partial and slow.[52] In February 2020 one of the key deadlocks was broken by the formation of a long-awaited unity government, alongside changes to the number and boundaries of regional states (with the number of such states reduced from 32 to 10). Though some progress was made in 2021 in implementing the 2018 peace agreement, armed conflict continued to impact communities in multiple parts of the country, and further fragmentation of SPLM/A-IO occurred.[53]

---

[49] Kahiye, M., 'Somali elections delayed again; no new date set', VOA, 26 July 2021.

[50] 'Somali president, PM trade accusations over delays to ongoing elections', Reuters, 27 Dec. 2021.

[51] On personnel numbers and other developments within UNMISS in 2021 see chapter 2, sections II and III, in this volume.

[52] Intergovernmental Authority on Development (IGAD), Revitalised Agreement on the Resolution of the Conflict in the Republic of South Sudan, 12 Sep. 2018.

[53] United Nations, Security Council, Final report of the Panel of Experts on South Sudan submitted pursuant to resolution 2521 (2020), S/2021/365, 15 Apr. 2021. On developments in South Sudan in 2017–21 see SIPRI Yearbook 2018, pp. 99–100; SIPRI Yearbook 2019, pp. 140–43; SIPRI Yearbook 2020, pp. 208–11; and SIPRI Yearbook 2021, pp. 225–28.

Table 7.12. Estimated conflict-related fatalities in South Sudan, 2013–21

Event type	2013	2014	2015	2016	2017	2018	2019	2020	2021
Battles	1 340	4 456	2 309	2 541	3 395	1 133	825	1 701	1 203
Explosions/remote violence	18	61	61	46	18	30	10	12	5
Protests, riots and strategic developments	0	11	24	1	4	5	4	7	11
Violence against civilians	2 999	1 886	1 208	958	1 424	532	972	660	937
Total	**4 357**	**6 414**	**3 602**	**3 546**	**4 841**	**1 700**	**1 811**	**2 380**	**2 156**

Notes: For definitions of event types, see Armed Conflict Location & Event Data Project (ACLED), 'ACLED definitions of political violence and protest', 11 Apr. 2019.

Source: ACLED, 'Dashboard', accessed 6 Apr. 2022.

The humanitarian situation

Humanitarian needs in South Sudan remained exceptionally high in 2021 due to years of persistent armed conflict, enduring economic and climate-related vulnerabilities, and weak basic services. Over two-thirds (8.4 million people) of the population needed humanitarian assistance, and the country faced its highest levels of food insecurity and malnutrition since declaring independence: an estimated 7.2 million people were acutely food insecure from April to July 2021, and over half a million people were brought back from the brink of famine during the year.[54] A third consecutive year of flooding affected 809 000 people, while humanitarian operations were disrupted by increased levels of violence against humanitarian workers. Some 4 million people in South Sudan were displaced during 2021 due to conflict, insecurity and weather shocks (1.7 million people internally displaced and an additional 2.3 million refugees in neighbouring countries).[55]

More broadly, a climate of repression and political intolerance, arbitrary arrests, disappearances and extrajudicial killings continued in 2021. The armed conflicts were characterized by gross human rights violations and abuses, with South Sudanese women and girls facing extreme levels of conflict-related sexual violence: over 65 per cent of South Sudanese women have experienced sexual or physical violence—double the global average.[56] Economic crimes were described by the UN Human Rights Council as 'constituting a grand-scale theft of the nation's oil and non-oil fiscal revenues'.[57]

---

[54] UN OCHA (note 1), p. 4.

[55] UN OCHA (note 1), pp. 172–77.

[56] UN OCHA (note 1), p. 146; and United Nations, Human Rights Council, 'Conflict-related sexual violence against women and girls in South Sudan', A/HRC/49/CRP.4, 21 Mar. 2022.

[57] United Nations, Human Rights Council, Report of the Commission on Human Rights in South Sudan, A/HRC/49/78, 15 Feb. 2022, p. 18. See also United Nations, Human Rights Council, 'Human rights violations and related economic crimes in the republic of South Sudan', A/HRC/48/CRP.3, 23 Sep. 2021; and International Crisis Group, *Oil or Nothing: Dealing With South Sudan's Bleeding Finances*, Africa Report no. 305 (International Crisis Group: Brussels, 6 Oct. 2021).

Implementation of the 2018 peace agreement and ongoing conflict

Implementation of the 2018 peace agreement continued, albeit with further delays and missed deadlines. Key benchmarks for the transition achieved in 2021 included: completion of the appointment of governors for all 10 regional states (January); appointment of 550 legislators for the reconstituted national parliament (11 May) and its subsequent inauguration (30 August); establishment of a taskforce to oversee and coordinate transitional justice and other judicial reforms (10 May); and the launch of a constitution-making process (25 May).[58] Electoral preparations are due to be conducted in parallel with the constitution-making process, with elections potentially slated for early 2023 (although there is no consensus on the exact timeline).[59] A major challenge, however, was the lack of progress in transitional security arrangements. These are pivotal to almost every aspect of the agreement, but the formation, graduation and deployment of unified forces continued to be delayed.[60]

While violence directly attributable to the conflict parties to the civil war has reduced significantly since 2018, the scale and intensity of intercommunal violence has increased in virtually every region of the country.[61] In June 2021 UNMISS reported that more than 80 per cent of civilian casualties suffered that year were attributable to intercommunal violence and community-based militias.[62] There was a particularly fierce upsurge in fighting in June–October 2021 in Western Equatoria.[63]

This widespread violence is reflected in the continuing high level of estimated conflict-related fatalities in 2021 (see table 7.12), although violence against civilians documented by UNMISS saw a 42 per cent reduction in 2021 compared to 2020. At least 3414 civilians were subject to killing, injury, abduction or conflict-related sexual violence in South Sudan in 2021 according to UNMISS, compared to 5850 in 2020. These incidents resulted in

---

[58] United Nations, Security Council, 8801st meeting, 'Reports of the Secretary-General on the Sudan and South Sudan', S/PV.8801, 21 June 2021.

[59] United Nations, Security Council, 8859th meeting, 'Reports of the Secretary-General on the Sudan and South Sudan', S/PV.8859, 15 Sep. 2021.

[60] United Nations, Security Council, 8931st meeting, 'Reports of the Secretary-General on the Sudan and South Sudan', S/PV.8931, 15 Dec. 2021.

[61] For details see United Nations, Security Council, 'Situation in South Sudan', Report of the Secretary-General, S/2021/566, 14 June 2021, pp. 4–5; United Nations, Security Council, 'Situation in South Sudan', Report of the Secretary-General, S/2021/784, 9 Sep. 2021, pp. 4–6; and United Nations, Security Council, 'Situation in South Sudan', Report of the Secretary-General, S/2021/1015, 7 Dec. 2021, pp. 3–5. For analysis of the forces and structures that regulate, permit, or intensify intercommunal conflicts see Watson, D., 'Surface tension: "Communal" violence and elite ambitions in South Sudan', Armed Conflict Location & Event Data Project (ACLED), 19 Aug. 2021.

[62] United Nations, S/PV.8801 (note 58), p. 3.

[63] International Crisis Group, 'South Sudan's other war: Resolving the insurgency in Equatoria', Africa Briefing no. 169, 25 Feb. 2021; and Amnesty International, 'South Sudan: Survivors describe killings, mass displacement and terror amid fighting in Western Equatoria', 9 Dec. 2021.

1907 civilian deaths (compared to 2425 civilian deaths from armed violence in 2020).[64]

Sudan

A major transition of power occurred in Sudan in 2019 following the removal of President Omar al-Bashir by the Sudanese army. Under a subsequent power-sharing agreement reached between the Sudanese Transitional Military Council and a coalition of opposition and protest groups, Sudan was scheduled to hold elections following a 39-month period of shared rule between the military and civilian groups.[65] The new transitional administration inherited a deepening economic and humanitarian crisis, as well as a legacy of armed conflict in Darfur (involving a fragmented mosaic of non-state armed groups) and in the southern border states of Blue Nile and South Kordofan (where the Sudan People Liberation Movement-North (SPLM-N) controls significant chunks of territory).[66] Some of the armed groups from Darfur were also present in Libya and South Sudan. In 2020 further significant but complex peace agreements were reached with the main armed groups.[67] A military coup in October 2021, however, produced a new crisis in Sudan's political transition process.

From peace process to military coup

On 3 October 2020 the Sudanese government and representatives of several armed groups signed the Juba Agreement for Peace in Sudan (JPA), a highly complex agreement that brought together and expanded the individual agreements signed earlier in the year.[68] It consisted of 10 different chapters—including 6 chapters of bilateral agreements with the different armed groups—and set out in considerable detail the future federal system. Moreover, it established a complicated web of transnational justice mechanisms and extensive transitional security arrangements, as well as implementation deadlines for many of these issues.[69] While there was

---

[64] Human Rights Division, UN Mission in South Sudan, 'Annual brief on violence affecting civilians, January–December 2021', Feb. 2022.

[65] Burke, J. and Salih, Z. M., 'Sudanese military and protesters sign power-sharing accord', *The Guardian*, 17 July 2019.

[66] For details of the armed groups in Darfur see United Nations, Security Council, Final report of the Panel of Experts on the Sudan, S/2022/48, 24 Jan. 2022, pp. 17–23. On the key armed opposition groups in Sudan as a whole see *SIPRI Yearbook 2021*, table 7.15, p. 230.

[67] On developments in Sudan in 2019–20 see *SIPRI Yearbook 2020*, pp. 211–14; and *SIPRI Yearbook 2021*, pp. 228–32.

[68] Juba Agreement for Peace in Sudan between the Transitional Government of Sudan and the Parties to the Peace Process, Official English version, 3 Oct. 2020.

[69] Al-Ali, Z., 'The Juba Agreement for Peace in Sudan: Summary and analysis', Version 5, International IDEA, 23 Oct. 2020.

positive support for the JPA in many parts of Sudan, eastern Sudan became the epicentre of demonstrations against it.[70]

Though the Sudanese government and the signatory armed groups continued to support the JPA in 2021, progress on implementation—aside from power-sharing arrangements—was either slow (on security arrangements) or negligible (in respect of provisions relating to IDPs, refugees, nomads and herders, land, justice and accountability).[71] The expected funding from international donors to implement the JPA's provisions did not materialize, jeopardizing its overall implementation and the peace process.[72] Furthermore, by mid 2021, tensions between the civilian and military sides of the transitional government were growing.[73]

After several rumoured coup attempts and one failed coup attempt on 21 September 2021, a military coup occurred on 25 October 2021. Prime Minister Hamdok, senior officials and political activists were arrested, triggering widespread protests and condemnation.[74] At least 44 people were killed, and hundreds were injured as a result of the excessive use of force by security forces.[75] Implementation of the JPA also became more problematic, especially as bilateral development cooperation measures to support the transition were suspended following the military coup, as was Sudan's membership of the AU.[76] After weeks of domestic and international efforts to find a way out of the crisis, a political agreement was reached on 21 November that included the reinstatement of Prime Minister Hamdok. However, there was significant opposition to this new agreement from large segments of Sudanese society, and it did little to assuage the concerns of foreign partners and donors—especially given Hamdok resigned just 42 days after his reinstatement.[77]

Conflict and humanitarian needs

In 2021 parts of Sudan—including Darfur, Blue Nile and South Kordofan—witnessed increased insecurity and localized violence. Clashes occurred among armed groups and with the security forces. There were also attacks on

---

[70] United Nations, Security Council, Final report of the Panel of Experts on the Sudan, S/2021/40, 13 Jan. 2021, pp. 7, 11–12.

[71] United Nations, S/2022/48 (note 66), pp. 6–9, 14–17.

[72] Takpiny, B., 'South Sudan's peace deal under serious threat, warns UN', Anadolu Agency, 8 Dec. 2021.

[73] Zaidan, Y., 'Sudan's democratic transition needs a jumpstart', World Politics Review, 13 July 2021.

[74] 'Condemnation, civil disobedience actions against Sudan military coup continue', Dabanga, 28 Oct. 2021; and 'Marches of the Millions: Sudan doctors count 98 injured from tear gas and stun grenades', Dabanga, 2 Dec. 2021.

[75] United Nations, Security Council, 8925th meeting, 'Reports of the Secretary-General on the Sudan and the South Sudan', S/PV.8925, 10 Dec. 2021, p. 2. See also Human Rights Watch, 'US Congressional briefing statement: Human rights situation in Sudan', 13 Dec. 2021.

[76] 'African Union, World Bank suspend Sudan over military coup', Africanews, 27 Oct. 2021.

[77] 'Sudan's Hamdok resigns as prime minister amid political deadlock', Al Jazeera, 2 Jan. 2022.

Table 7.13. Estimated conflict-related fatalities in Sudan, 2013–21

Event type	2013	2014	2015	2016	2017	2018	2019	2020	2021
Battles	5 595	3 049	2 440	2 939	851	700	321	565	1 037
Explosions/remote violence	479	263	263	294	33	28	17	13	13
Protests, riots and strategic developments	342	15	9	27	34	37	213	34	83
Violence against civilians	380	831	756	639	373	289	225	345	519
Total	**6 796**	**4 158**	**3 468**	**3 899**	**1 291**	**1 054**	**776**	**957**	**1 652**

Notes: For definitions of event types, see Armed Conflict Location & Event Data Project (ACLED), 'ACLED definitions of political violence and protest', 11 Apr. 2019.

Source: ACLED, 'Dashboard', accessed 6 Apr. 2022.

villages and communities hosting IDPs and outbreaks of violence involving nomads, pastoralist communities and farmers, mostly due to disputes over land ownership, access to resources and criminality.[78] Finally, clashes between Sudanese and Ethiopian forces occurred in the fertile al-Fashaga borderland.[79] Overall, estimated conflict-related fatalities increased by over 70 per cent in 2021 (and battle-related fatalities almost doubled) compared to 2020, reaching the highest level since 2016 (see table 7.13). Sexual and gender-based violence remained endemic in Darfur.[80]

Sudan has had a UN inter-agency humanitarian appeal for at least 20 consecutive years, with humanitarian needs in Sudan continuing to rise in 2021 due to localized conflict, climatic events, disease outbreaks and economic crisis: 14.3 million people needed humanitarian assistance by the end of the year, up from 7.5 million at the end of 2020. Over 365 000 people were displaced during 2021, many of whom had already been displaced as a result of earlier crises and conflict. The country also hosts about 1.2 million refugees and asylum seekers (two-thirds from South Sudan), making Sudan one of the top 10 refugee-hosting countries in the world. Heavy rains and floods affected about 314 000 people during the year, and during the first nine months of 2021 about 1.6 million cases of malaria were reported across Sudan.[81]

Having been deployed in Darfur since 2007, the joint UN–AU Hybrid Operation in Darfur (UNAMID)—a major joint peace operations mission that at its height in 2007 was authorized to have about 26 000 personnel—closed on 31 December 2020 and by 30 June 2021 had completed the withdrawal of its remaining 6600 personnel. It was replaced on 1 January 2021 with the much smaller special political mission (just under 100 personnel), UN Integrated

---

[78] See e.g. 'At least 138 have died in ongoing West Darfur attacks while Jebel Moon leaders sign non-aggression pledge', Dabanga, 10 Dec. 2021; and United Nations, S/2022/48 (note 66), pp. 25–28.

[79] International Crisis Group (note 26); and '20 Sudan troops killed in Ethiopia border clash', Dabanga, 29 Nov. 2021.

[80] United Nations, S/2022/48 (note 66), pp. 29–31.

[81] UN OCHA (note 1), pp. 21, 178–81.

Transition Assistance Mission in Sudan (UNITAMS).[82] The transfer of arms and other military materiel into Darfur continued, in violation of the UN arms embargo.[83]

Outlook

The future of the Sudanese transition remains uncertain, with the military coup of 25 October a major setback for a civilian-led democratic future. Slow implementation of the JPA and rising intercommunal tensions in Darfur and other areas of the country remain sources of concern.

---

[82] United Nations, 'Withdrawal of Hybrid Peacekeeping Operation in Darfur completed by 30 June deadline, under-secretary-general tells Security Council, outlining plans to liquidate assets', SC/14587, 27 July 2021. On the closure of UNAMID and comparisons of mission size with UNITAMS see chapter 2, sections II and III, in this volume.

[83] The UN embargo on Sudan prohibits transfers to non-state actors in the region of Darfur. For further details see chapter 14, section II, in this volume.

Part II. Military spending and armaments, 2021

Chapter 8. Military expenditure and developments in arms production

Chapter 9. International arms transfers

Chapter 10. World nuclear forces

8. Military expenditure and developments in arms production

Overview

Global military expenditure rose for the seventh consecutive year in 2021 to reach US$2113 billion. This was the highest level since SIPRI started estimating total world military expenditure and the first time that it has exceed $2 trillion (see section I). Military spending accounted for 2.2 per cent of global gross domestic product (GDP), equivalent to $268 per person. World spending was 0.7 per cent higher than in 2020 and 12 per cent higher than in 2012.

A striking observation from two years of the Covid-19 pandemic is that the upward trajectory of military spending remained unchanged despite pandemic-induced economic fluctuations. However, while the world allocated more to the military in absolute terms, overall government budgets grew faster than military budgets. In 2021 countries appropriated an average of 6.0 per cent of their total government spending for their militaries. This was down from 6.1 per cent in 2020 and from 6.6 per cent in 2012. Thus, it seems that governments have not been prioritizing the military over other public policy initiatives. Instead, they appear to be investing more funds in the military while simultaneously allocating even more to non-military expenditure.

The urgency of meeting the Sustainable Development Goals (SDGs) of Agenda 2030 and the targets of the 2015 Paris Agreement on climate change highlights the lost opportunity that military spending represents. Diverting a small fraction of the $2 trillion to these goals could do much to improve security in the broader sense and contribute towards achieving the SDGs. During 2021 the United Nations reaffirmed various initiatives to reverse the upward trend of military expenditure within its disarmament efforts. These included a call by the UN secretary-general in his report on the Women and Peace and Security Agenda for the urgent reduction of excessive military spending and greater investment in social infrastructure and human security.

Spending rose in 2021 in three of the five geographical regions: by 3.5 per cent in Asia and Oceania, 3.0 per cent in Europe and 1.2 per cent in Africa (see section II). The increase in Africa was the third consecutive year of growth. Nigeria had a particularly high rate of growth: the 56 per cent increase to $4.5 billion was its highest annual increase since 1975. Interstate tensions, intrastate conflicts and the fight against violent Islamist extremism remain key security considerations in the region. The increase in military spending in Asia and Oceania continued an uninterrupted upward trend dating back to at least 1989. China allocated an estimated $293 billion to its military in 2021, a

4.7 per cent increased since 2020. The 2021 Chinese budget forms the first year of the 14th five-year plan, which includes goals for military modernization and reform. Spending also rose in other major spenders in Asia and Oceania: by 0.9 per cent in India, 7.3 per cent in Japan and 4.7 per cent in South Korea. In Europe, heightened geopolitical tensions were a significant factor in the increase in military spending by Central and West European states. They prioritized the recapitalization of their armed forces' equipment. In Eastern Europe, Russia's military spending grew for the third consecutive year in 2021—up by 2.9 per cent to reach $65.9 billion. Russian military spending was revised upwards several times over the course of the year. The top-up allocations were probably spent on operational activities as Russia built up its forces on the borders of Ukraine.

Military spending fell in the Middle East by 3.3 per cent and in the Americas by 1.2 per cent. Military spending trends in the Americas are driven primarily by changes in spending by the United States, which spent $801 billion in 2021. This represented a nominal increase of 2.9 per cent but a real-terms decrease of 1.4 per cent. This discrepancy is attributable to the highest rate of inflation since 1982. In 2021 the USA ended its nearly two-decade long military presence in Afghanistan. Between 2001 and 2021, the US government spent more than $2.3 trillion on the war there, including investing $85 billion to bolster the Afghan security forces. The decrease in spending in the Middle East was mainly due to the 17 per cent fall in the spending of Saudi Arabia, which accounted for 30 per cent of the regional total. Part of the decrease was offset by a 11 per cent increase in Iranian military expenditure. This made Iran the 14th biggest military spender in 2021, the first time since 1992 that it had ranked among the top 15.

A further indication of the health of the military sector amid the pandemic can be found in the arms sales of the world's largest arms-producing and military services companies (section III). The arms sales of the 100 largest of these companies (the SIPRI Top 100) totalled $531 billion in 2020. Arms production around the world was largely resilient to the shock of the Covid-19 pandemic and the resulting economic downturn: while the global economy contracted by 3.1 per cent in 2020, the aggregated arms sales of the Top 100 increased. The USA hosted the highest number of companies ranked in the Top 100 of any country worldwide, with 41 arms companies. Together, their arms sales amounted to $285 billion. This was followed by the combined arms sales of $66.8 billion of the five Chinese companies ranked in the Top 100.

NAN TIAN

I. Global developments in military expenditure, 2021

NAN TIAN, XIAO LIANG, DIEGO LOPES DA SILVA AND
ALEXANDRA MARKSTEINER

Global military expenditure is estimated to have reached US$2113 billion in 2021.[1] This was the first time that global spending on military activities had surpassed $2 trillion, and in real terms it was higher than at any time since the end of the cold war.[2] The 2021 total was 0.7 per cent higher in real terms than in 2020 and 12 per cent higher than in 2012. The increase in 2021 represented the seventh consecutive year of increases in military spending.

Global military expenditure as measured in current 2021 US dollars was substantially higher than the total measured in 2020 constant US dollars (see table 8.1). This large discrepancy is related to the depreciation of the US dollar against major global currencies in 2021 (see box 8.1). The loss in value of the US dollar against the majority of currencies meant that the 2021 financial value of military expenditure once converted from local currency to US dollars using 2021 exchange rates was much higher than when using 2020 exchange rates (on SIPRI's definition, sources and methods for calculating military expenditure see box 8.2 at the end of this section).

The global military burden—that is, world military expenditure as a share of world gross domestic product (GDP)—is estimated to have been 2.2 per cent in 2021. After a global recession caused by the Covid-19 pandemic in 2020, when world GDP fell by 3.1 per cent, a sharp economic rebound was estimated for 2021, with global GDP projected to rise by 5.9 per cent.[3] As a result, the global military burden fell by 0.1 percentage point. Military spending per capita rose for the fifth consecutive year in 2021, up to $268 from $256 in 2020, as the growth in nominal military spending continued to surpass projected world population growth (1.0 per cent). In 2021, countries appropriated an average of 5.9 per cent of their government budgets to the military, the same as in 2020, but well below the level of 6.4 per cent in 2012.

Military expenditure rose in 2021 in three of the five geographical regions (see figure 8.1 and section II). The rate of increase was highest in Asia and Oceania, at 3.5 per cent, taking the estimated regional total to $586 billion in 2021. This was followed by Europe, with an overall increase of 3.0 per cent to $418 billion, and Africa, with growth of 1.2 per cent to $39.7 billion.

---

[1] All figures for spending in 2021 are quoted in current 2021 United States dollars. Except where otherwise stated, figures for increases or decreases in military spending are expressed in constant 2020 US dollars, often described as changes in 'real terms' or adjusted for inflation.

[2] Of the 168 countries for which SIPRI attempted to estimate military expenditure in 2021, relevant data was found for 152. See the notes in table 8.1 for more details on estimates in world and regional totals.

[3] International Monetary Fund (IMF), *World Economic Outlook: Recovery during a Pandemic—Health Concerns, Supply Disruptions, and Price Pressures* (IMF: Washington, DC, Oct. 2021), p. 5.

Table 8.1. Military expenditure and military burden, by region, 2012–21

Figures for 2012–21 are in US$ b. at constant (2020) prices and exchange rates, unless otherwise stated. Figures for 2021 in the right-most column, marked *, are in current US$ b. Figures may not add up to the given totals because of the conventions of rounding.

	2012	2013	2014	2015	2016	2017	2018	2019	2020	2021	2021*
World total	**1 791**	**1 757**	**1 751**	**1 779**	**1 787**	**1 810**	**1 859**	**1 932**	**1 992**	**2 007**	**2 113**
Geographical regions											
Africa	(36.0)	38.4	40.0	(38.4)	37.1	36.5	34.7	35.8	36.4	(36.9)	(39.7)
North Africa	(14.0)	15.9	17.0	(17.3)	(17.4)	(16.9)	(16.4)	(17.4)	(18.3)	(18.0)	(19.6)
Sub-Saharan Africa	(21.9)	22.5	23.0	(21.1)	19.8	19.7	18.4	18.4	18.1	18.8	20.1
Americas	883	821	776	761	758	757	779	819	856	846	883
Central America and the Caribbean	6.3	6.7	7.0	6.8	7.4	7.0	7.6	8.4	10.2	10.0	11.0
North America	835	771	724	711	709	706	726	766	802	792	827
South America	42.1	43.9	44.4	43.9	41.9	44.2	45.2	44.5	44.3	44.1	45.3
Asia and Oceania	374	391	411	435	456	477	495	519	534	553	586
Central Asia	1.5	1.7	1.7	1.7	1.6	1.5	1.6	2.0	1.8	1.7	1.8
East Asia	249	262	277	294	306	320	337	354	368	386	411
Oceania	22.0	21.9	23.6	25.8	28.2	28.3	28.0	29.1	30.5	31.6	35.3
South Asia	67.0	66.8	70.6	71.7	78.0	83.4	87.8	92.7	90.1	90.8	95.1
South East Asia	34.7	38.2	37.9	41.6	42.2	43.9	40.7	41.9	44.3	43.2	43.1
Europe	329	324	327	336	348	339	346	364	381	393	418
Central and Western Europe	266	257	255	258	266	272	280	294	310	319	342
Eastern Europe	63.8	66.7	71.9	77.7	81.6	66.9	65.7	69.2	71.5	73.2	76.3
Middle East	169	183	196	(208)	(188)	(201)	(205)	(195)	(184)	(178)	(186)
World military spending per capita (current US$)	245	242	239	229	226	233	240	247	256	268	
Average military spending as a share of total government expenditure (%) [a]	6.4	6.5	6.4	6.4	6.4	6.4	6.2	6.3	5.9	5.9	

Military burden [b]									
World	2.3	2.3	2.2	2.3	2.2	2.2	2.1	2.2	2.3	2.2
Africa	1.8	1.9	2.2	1.8	1.9	1.7	1.6	1.7	1.7	1.6
Americas	1.5	1.5	1.4	1.4	1.4	1.5	1.4	1.4	1.5	1.4
Asia and Oceania	1.6	1.6	1.7	1.8	1.8	1.7	1.7	1.7	1.8	1.7
Europe	1.5	1.5	1.5	1.5	1.5	1.5	1.5	1.7	1.8	1.8
Middle East	4.6	4.7	4.8	5.4	5.3	5.0	4.7	4.6	4.7	4.3

( ) = total based on country data accounting for less than 90% of the regional total.

Notes: The totals for the world and regions are estimates, based on data from the SIPRI Military Expenditure Database. When military expenditure data for a country is missing for a few years, estimates are made, most often on the assumption that the rate of change in that country's military expenditure is the same as that for the region in which it is located. When no estimates can be made, countries are excluded from all totals here are excluded from the totals. The countries excluded from all totals here are Cuba (Americas); Djibouti, Eritrea and Somalia (Africa); North Korea, Turkmenistan and Uzbekistan (Asia and Oceania); and Syria and Yemen (Middle East). Totals for regions cover the same groups of countries for all years. The SIPRI military expenditure figures are presented on a calendar-year basis, calculated on the assumption of an even rate of expenditure throughout the financial year. Further detail on sources and methods can be found in box 8.2 and 'Sources and methods' for the SIPRI Military Expenditure Database on the SIPRI website.

[a] These figures represent the average budget shares that countries (for which data was available) allocated to their militaries.

[b] The military burden of a country is its military spending as a share of its gross domestic product (GDP), both measured in current US dollars. The military spending of a region is the average military burden of the countries in the region for which data is available. The world military burden is world military spending as a share of world GDP.

Sources: SIPRI Military Expenditure Database, Apr. 2022; International Monetary Fund, World Economic Outlook Database, Oct. 2021, <https://www.imf.org/external/pubs/ft/weo/2021/02/weodata/index.aspx>; International Monetary Fund, International Financial Statistics Database, Sep. 2021, <http://data.imf.org/IFS>; and United Nations, Department of Economic and Social Affairs, Population Division, 'World population prospects 2019', Aug. 2019, <https://population.un.org/wpp/Download/Standard/Population/>.

Box 8.1. Variations in economic data and associated consequences for military expenditure data

Depreciation in the US dollar

For comparability purposes, SIPRI provides global military expenditure estimates in US dollars. In 2021 a combination of lower interest rates and high inflation (as measured by the consumer price index, CPI) in the United States resulted in substantial depreciation of the US dollar against all major currencies. This, in combination with higher than usual CPI inflation in many countries, led to significant numerical differences in global, regional and country-level military expenditure when comparing 2021 spending using constant 2020 US dollars versus current 2021 US dollars. For example, measured in current 2021 US dollars, China's military spending amounted to $293 billion in 2021, while it was only $270 billion when measured in constant 2020 US dollars (see section II).

Data reliability: Gross domestic product

A significant development in 2021 was the decrease in the quality and availability of comparable data on gross domestic product (GDP). International Finance Statistics (IFS) from the International Monetary Fund (IMF) is the most reliable source of GDP data. In the IMF's most recent data release, actual GDP data for 2020 was only available for 68 countries. The majority of GDP data for 2020 and all of the GDP data for 2021 is based on estimates provided by the IMF World Economic Outlook (WEO). This substantially affects analysis of military burden as a result, since most GDP data used in calculating military burden is based on estimates.

For the Middle East, estimated military spending in 2021 fell by 3.3 per cent to $186 billion, and in the Americas spending was down by 1.2 per cent to $883 billion.

This section continues by providing an updated assessment of the impact of the Covid-19 pandemic on military expenditure, covering such topics as the affordability of military spending, government priorities and the renewed discussions taken up by the United Nations on military spending reductions. It then describes the global trends in military expenditure over the period 2012–21 and identifies the 15 countries with the highest military spending in 2021. Regional and subregional trends and the spending of individual countries are discussed in section II.

Military burden, government priorities and reductions in military expenditure

One of the striking observations in the aftermath of the first year of the Covid-19 pandemic was the opposite directions taken by global GDP on the one hand and global military expenditure on the other.[4] In 2020, as the world contended with the worst economic fallout since the great depression of 1929, military spending rose by 3.1 per cent, to almost $2 trillion. As the world's economy fell while military spending rose, the result was the biggest annual

---

[4] See Tian, N. et al., 'Global developments in military expenditure 2020', *SIPRI Yearbook 2021*.

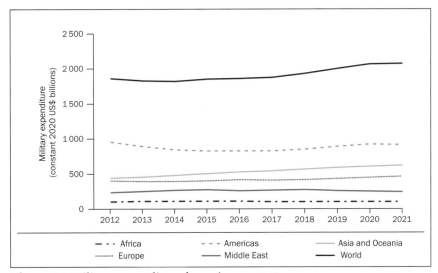

Figure 8.1. Military expenditure, by region, 2012–21

Source: SIPRI Military Expenditure Database, Apr. 2022.

increase in global military burden since the global financial and economic crisis in 2009. In other words, there was a sharp and substantial rise in the burden of military activities on the economy.

One year on, 2021 marked a significant turnaround and a resumption of the declining trend in military burden of 2015–18. While most countries continued to allocate more resources to military expenditure, the International Monetary Fund (IMF) estimates that there was a substantial recovery in the global economy, surpassing the growth of military spending.[5] As a result, the military burden fell in most countries, which contributed to a fall in the global military burden, from 2.3 per cent in 2020 to 2.2 per cent in 2021.

The relationship between the growth of military expenditure and the growth of GDP can be visualized graphically: plotting changes in military spending growth on the vertical axis and growth in GDP on the horizontal axis shows how changes in GDP interact with changes in military spending (see figures 8.2 and 8.3). Considering the four quadrants of each graph, the countries situated in the upper-left quadrant have rising military spending coupled with decreasing GDP, while countries in the lower-left quadrant have decreasing GDP coupled with decreasing military spending. The lower-right quadrant represents increases in GDP and decreases in military spending, while the upper-right quadrant shows countries with increases in both GDP and military spending.

Comparing 2020 with 2021, the scatter plot for 2021 (figure 8.3) is almost a mirror reflection (at the vertical axis) of the graph for 2020 (figure 8.2).

[5] International Monetary Fund (note 3), p. 5.

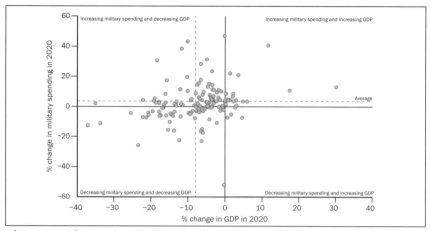

Figure 8.2. Changes in military spending and gross domestic product, by country, 2020

Source: SIPRI Military Expenditure Database, Apr. 2022.

Whereas most countries in 2020 coupled increasing military spending with decreases in GDP (the upper-left quadrant in figure 8.2), most countries in 2021 coupled increasing military spending with increases in GDP (the upper-right quadrant in figure 8.3). This means that the trajectory of military spending remained unchanged despite economic fluctuations induced by the Covid-19 pandemic.

Government spending priorities

Whereas military expenditure as a share of GDP quantifies the economic burden of the armed forces, military spending as a share of total government expenditure can help shed light on how governments allocate their limited financial resources. This indicator thus provides a more direct measure of government priorities than the military burden indicator. The trade-off between military and healthcare spending has been a particularly salient discussion during the Covid-19 pandemic, as governments have faced critical decisions on the prioritization of different types of spending—from healthcare expenditure via economic stimulus packages to military procurement.[6]

In 2021 countries allocated an average of 5.9 per cent of their government budgets to their militaries.[7] This was the same as in 2020 but down from 6.4 per cent in 2012. Within the general decreasing trend in the share of

---

[6] Becker, S., Mölling, C. and Schütz, T., 'Deterrence and defense in times of Covid-19: Europe's political choices', German Council on Foreign Relations (DGAP) Policy Brief no. 9, Apr. 2020; and Garcia, D., 'Redirect military budgets to tackle climate change and pandemics', *Nature*, 20 Aug. 2020.

[7] This figure does not refer to the share of total expenditure by the governments of the world that was dedicated to the military. Instead, it represents the average budget shares that countries (for which data was available) allocated to their militaries.

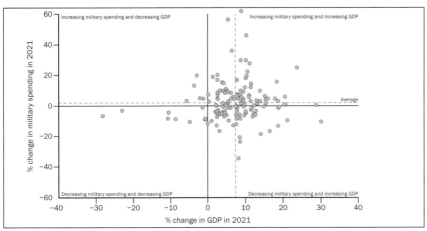

Figure 8.3. Changes in military spending and gross domestic product, by country, 2021

Source: SIPRI Military Expenditure Database, Apr. 2022.

government expenditure spent on military activities, there were significant regional differences. On average, countries in the Americas and Europe allocated the smallest portion of their government budgets to their armed forces, with respective proportions of 4.0 per cent and 4.7 per cent. Among European countries, the average share in 2021 was 0.1 percentage point higher than in 2020, whereas the average American share remained unchanged. Countries in Africa appropriated an average of 6.1 per cent of their government budgets for their armed forces (0.3 percentage points lower than in 2020), whereas governments in Asia and Oceania spent an average of 6.7 per cent (0.2 percentage points higher). With an average share of 12 per cent, Middle Eastern countries allocated by far the largest proportion of their government budgets to military activities in 2021. Compared to 2020, however, this was a decline of 0.3 percentage points.

These figures suggest that, while global military expenditure has been on the rise, government budgets have grown at an even faster pace. This trend was particularly pronounced during the first year of the Covid-19 pandemic. As public outlays increased and stimulus packages were adopted to stabilize economies in freefall and to fund social welfare programmes, government budgets ballooned. For example, the United States government's financial response to the economic fallout of the pandemic was equivalent to 27 per cent of the USA's GDP.[8] The share of government spending allocated to military activities thus dropped. This meant that the proportion of US

---

[8] Taylor, A., 'How the $1.9 trillion US stimulus package compares with other countries' coronavirus spending', *Washington Post*, 5 Apr. 2021.

government expenditure spent on the military decreased by 0.3 percentage points between 2019 and 2020.

That said, the downward trend in military spending as a share of total government expenditure has been underway for some time. Over the decade 2012–21, the average share shrank by 0.5 percentage points. Many countries appear to be simultaneously investing more funds in their armed forces and in other government programmes, instead of prioritizing military spending over other public policy initiatives.

Opportunity costs of military spending and initiatives to reduce military expenditure

The opportunity costs of military spending represents the missed opportunity for spending on other expenditure items such as human development (e.g. healthcare, education or foreign aid) embodied by the choice to spend money on the military. Concerns regarding the opportunity costs of excessive military expenditure have long been emphasized by global disarmament efforts. Diversion of money spent on the military towards social and economic development was suggested by international organizations and civil society as early as the founding of the United Nations, in 1945, and the first special session of the UN General Assembly on disarmament, in 1978.[9] Following the end of the cold war, declining military spending gave rise to renewed calls to redirect the funds for social expenditure and development aid, before global spending started to increase again in 1999.[10]

Countries with different levels of military spending and economic development face similar choices between competing priorities in allocating finite public resources. For the biggest spenders, reducing military expenditure can release resources for development aid. Total official development assistance (ODA) from members of the Development Assistance Committee (DAC) of the Organisation for Economic Co-operation and Development (OECD) was $161 billion in 2020, equivalent to 13 per cent of the military expenditure of DAC countries in 2020, which totalled $1.23 trillion.[11] Yet the opportunity costs of military spending are critical for low-income countries, many of which have a higher share of military expenditure to government spending than the rest of the world. High military expenditure and inadequate social

---

[9] Charter of the United Nations, opened for signature 26 June 1945, entered into force 24 Oct. 2015, Article 26; and United Nations, General Assembly, Final document of the 10th special session, A/RES/S-10/2, 30 June 1978, para. 35.

[10] UN Development Programme (UNDP), *Human Development Report 1994* (Oxford University Press: Oxford, 1994); and Hewitt, D. P., *Military Expenditure: International Comparison of Trends*, International Monetary Fund (IMF) Working Paper no. WP/91/54 (IMF: Washington, DC, May 1991).

[11] Organisation for Economic Co-operation and Development (OECD), 'COVID-19 spending helped to lift foreign aid to an all-time high in 2020', 13 Apr. 2021.

spending in these states contribute to further insecurity and perpetuate military, social and economic vulnerability.[12]

With global military expenditure surpassing $2 trillion for the first time in 2021, the world entered 2022 at the halfway mark between the adoption in 2015 of the Agenda for Sustainable Development and the Paris Agreement on climate change and their target date of 2030.[13] Before the Covid-19 pandemic, it was estimated that the annual financing gap for developing countries to achieve the Sustainable Development Goals (SDGs) of the 2030 Agenda was $2.5 trillion. This gap was predicted to increase by $1.7 trillion because of the pandemic.[14] Meanwhile, the World Health Organization (WHO) has estimated that $16 billion funding is needed urgently from governments to ensure equitable global access to Covid-19 tests, treatments and vaccines.[15] Under the Paris Agreement, developed countries also promised to provide $100 billion a year to developing countries to combat climate change (SDG Target 13.A).

The effort to close these funding gaps has reinvigorated the agenda of rebalancing military expenditure and human security.[16] For example, the $16 billion need identified by WHO is equivalent to only 0.8 per cent of world military spending in 2021. At the 26th UN Climate Change Conference (COP26) in Glasgow, United Kingdom, in 2021, developed countries reaffirmed the $100 billion commitment, which would amount to 8.1 per cent of developed countries' military spending in 2021.[17] Furthermore, the UN Educational, Scientific and Cultural Organization (UNESCO) estimates that the annual financing gap for reaching universal primary and secondary education (SDG Target 4.1) in low- and lower middle-income countries is $39 billion, equivalent to 1.8 per cent of global military spending in 2021.[18]

---

[12] Calvo Rufanges, J. and Royo Aspa, J. M., *Democratic Republic of Congo: A Review of 20 Years of War* (Centre Delàs d'Estudis per la Pau: Barcelona, Apr. 2016); and Saba, C. S. and Ngepah, N., 'A cross-regional analysis of military expenditure, state fragility and economic growth in Africa', *Quality & Quantity*, vol. 53, no. 6 (Nov. 2019).

[13] UN General Assembly Resolution 70/1, 'Transforming our world: The 2030 Agenda for Sustainable Development', 25 Sep. 2015; and Paris Agreement, adopted 2 Dec. 2015, opened for signature 2 Apr. 2016, entered into force 4 Nov. 2016.

[14] Organisation for Economic Co-operation and Development (OECD), *Global Outlook on Financing for Sustainable Development 2021: A New Way to Invest for People and Planet* (OECD: Paris, 2020), p. 16.

[15] World Health Organization (WHO), 'ACT-Accelerator calls for fair share-based financing of US$ 23 billion to end pandemic as global emergency in 2022', News release, 9 Feb. 2022.

[16] Brzoska, M., Omitoogoon, W. and Sköns, E., *The Human Security Case for Rebalancing Military Expenditure* (SIPRI: Stockholm, May 2022); Sabbagh, D., '"Colossal waste": Nobel laureates call for 2% cut to military spending worldwide', *The Guardian*, 14 Dec. 2021; and Garcia (note 6).

[17] Organisation for Economic Co-operation and Development (OECD), *Forward-looking Scenarios of Climate Finance Provided and Mobilised by Developed Countries in 2021–2025*, Technical note (OECD: Paris, 2021); and British Government, 'COP26 presidency compilation of 2021–2025 climate finance commitments', Press release, Oct. 2021.

[18] UN Educational, Scientific and Cultural Organization (UNESCO), 'Pricing the right to education: The cost of reaching new targets by 2030', Policy Paper no. 18, ED/EFA/MRT/2015/PP/18, July 2015.

Under these circumstances, the UN has reaffirmed various initiatives to reverse the upward trend in military expenditure within its disarmament efforts in addition to several pronouncements over the years. One prime example is the report of the UN secretary-general on the Women and Peace and Security (WPS) Agenda. In his 2020 report on WPS, the secretary-general identifies reversing the upward trajectory in global military spending as one of the goals for the next decade.[19] In 2021 he furthered the initiative by issuing another urgent call for the reduction of excessive military spending and greater investment in social infrastructure and human security.[20]

Trends in military expenditure, 2012–21

The 0.7 per cent increase in global military expenditure in 2021 was the seventh consecutive annual increase in spending since 2015. Over the decade 2012–21, world spending rose by 12 per cent, split into two different trends. Between 2012 and 2014, military spending was on a downward trajectory, falling 2.3 per cent over the three-year period. Thereafter, annual military expenditure rose consistently, averaging 2.0 per cent per year or a total increase of 15 per cent between 2014 and 2021.

Trends in world military spending are mostly driven by the world's largest spenders. The United States and China, the two largest spenders, together allocated $1.1 trillion to military activities in 2021, accounting for 52 per cent of world spending. A change in military spending by either the USA or China therefore has a substantial effect on the global trend. Changes by other major spenders—such as India, the United Kingdom, the Russian Federation, France or Saudi Arabia—mainly affect regional or subregional spending trends. At times these changes have come together to affect world military spending, albeit to a much lesser extent.

The 2.3 per cent or $40.9 billion (in 2020 constant US dollars) fall in global military spending over the period 2012–14 was primarily due to cuts in US military expenditure. Over this period, US spending fell by 13 per cent or $109 billion (in 2020 constant US dollars) following the first major withdrawal of US troops from Afghanistan and Iraq.[21] However, the total fall in world spending between 2012 and 2014 was only 38 per cent of the drop in US spending: world spending would have fallen by a far greater amount if the US decrease had not been offset by increases by emerging economies such as China, India, Russia and Saudi Arabia. Spending by these four countries rose

---

[19] United Nations, Security Council, 'Women and peace and security', Report of the Secretary-General, S/2020/946, 25 Sep. 2020, para. 113.

[20] United Nations, Security Council, 'Women and peace and security', Report of the Secretary-General, S/2021/827, 27 Sep. 2021.

[21] On the increases and decreases in US military spending in the early 2010s see Tian, N. et al., 'Global developments in military expenditure', *SIPRI Yearbook 2019*.

by $58 billion (in 2020 constant US dollars), offsetting over half of the US decrease. The trend reversal—from decrease to increase—in world military spending since 2015 can be explained by the slowdown in the rate of decrease in US spending and the spending increases by other major spenders such as China, India, France, Germany and (until 2017) Russia. While US military spending fell 7.7 per cent in 2013 and 6.2 per cent in 2014, in 2015 it fell by only 2.3 per cent. From 2018, the USA returned to increases in military spending, and the rate of increase in world military spending also rose. World spending rose by 3.9 per cent in 2019, which coincided with a 5.7 per cent increase in US spending. The global rise in price levels in 2021 played a major role in dampening the real-terms increase in military expenditure.

Between 2012 and 2021, spending increased in all regions other than the Americas (–4.2 per cent; see table 8.2); the highest increase was in Asia and Oceania (48 per cent), followed by Europe (19 per cent), the Middle East (5.6 per cent) and Africa (2.5 per cent). Among the 13 subregions, spending fell over the decade in only two: sub-Saharan Africa (–14 per cent) and North America (–5.1 per cent). The five largest subregional increases were in Central America and the Caribbean (58 per cent), East Asia (55 per cent), Oceania (43 per cent), South Asia (36 per cent) and North Africa (29 per cent).

The decline in military spending in sub-Saharan Africa since 2012 was the result of spending decreases by four of the five countries with the largest military expenditure in the subregion at the time: Angola, South Africa, South Sudan and Sudan. In North America, the decrease was solely the result of cuts in the USA's military budget.

Spending increased in all 17 Central European countries between 2012 and 2021. This was due to the growing threat perceptions of Russia, which was manifested in a political will to reach the military expenditure target of 2 per cent of GDP for member states of the North Atlantic Treaty Organization (NATO). The increased spending was in the form of expensive weapon-modernization programmes.[22]

All but one of the countries in Central America and the Caribbean, East Asia, Oceania, and South Asia increased military spending over the period 2012–21 (the exception being Papua New Guinea in Oceania).

The global military burden of 2.2 per cent in 2021 was 0.1 percentage point lower than in both 2020 and 2012. Between 2012 and 2018 the trend in world military burden was on a decline, down 0.2 percentage points, despite a 3.8 per cent increase in military spending (figure 8.4). This decrease was largely the result of recovering levels of GDP following the 2009 global financial and economic crisis. Thus, while the world spent more and more on the military in absolute terms over 2012–18, it dedicated a smaller proportion of

[22] Tian, N., Lopes da Silva, D. and Wezeman, P. D., 'Spending on military equipment by European members of the North Atlantic Treaty Organization', *SIPRI Yearbook 2020*.

Table 8.2. Key military expenditure statistics, by region and subregion, 2021

Expenditure figures are in US$, at current prices and exchange rates. Changes are in real terms, based on constant (2020) US dollars.

Region/subregion	Military expenditure, 2021 (US$ b.)	Change (%) 2020–21	Change (%) 2012–21	Major changes, 2020–21 (%)[a] Increases		Decreases	
World	**2 113**	0.7	12				
Africa[b]	(39.7)	1.2	2.5				
North Africa	(19.6)	–1.7	29	Nigeria	56	Togo	–35
Sub-Saharan Africa[b]	20.1	4.1	–14	Senegal	30	Mozambique	–24
				Benin	28	Niger	–20
				Zambia	20	DRC	–23
Americas[c]	883	–1.2	–4.2				
Central America and the Caribbean[c]	11.0	–2.5	58	Bolivia	20	Argentina	–15
North America	827	–1.2	–5.1	Trinidad and Tobago	19	Jamaica	–12
South America	45.3	–0.6	4.7	Honduras	17	Dominican Rep.	–7.0
				Uruguay	10	Peru	–4.9
Asia and Oceania[d]	586	3.5	48				
Central Asia[e]	1.8	–0.8	14	Malaysia	9.1	Indonesia	–15
East Asia[f]	411	4.9	55	Japan	7.3	Mongolia	–9.7
Oceania	35.3	3.5	43	Singapore	7.1	Kyrgyzstan	–8.8
South Asia	95.1	0.8	36	South Korea	4.7	Thailand	–8.5
South East Asia	43.2	–2.3	25				
Europe	418	3.0	19				
Central and Western Europe	342	3.1	20	Croatia	62	Switzerland	–13
Eastern Europe	76.3	2.3	15	Greece	46	Ukraine	–8.5
				Finland	36	Slovakia	–8.4
				N. Macedonia	30	Hungary	–5.9
Middle East[g]	186	–3.3	5.6				
				Kuwait	25	Saudi Arabia	–17
				Iran	11	Oman	–9.6
				Egypt	8.2	Iraq	–5.1

( ) = uncertain estimate; DRC = Democratic Republic of the Congo; N. = North; Rep. = Republic.

[a] These lists shows the countries with the largest increases or decreases for each region as a whole, rather than by subregion. Countries with a military expenditure in 2021 of less than $100 million, or $50 million in Africa, are excluded.

[b] These figures exclude Djibouti, Eritrea and Somalia.

[c] These figures exclude Cuba.

[d] These figures exclude North Korea, Turkmenistan and Uzbekistan.

[e] These figures exclude Turkmenistan and Uzbekistan.

[f] These figures exclude North Korea.

[g] These figures exclude Syria and Yemen.

Source: SIPRI Military Expenditure Database, Apr. 2022.

total resources to the military. The declining trend in world military burden stopped in 2019 and 2020. This was mainly due to military spending rising faster than GDP in 2019 and the Covid-19-related economic recession in 2020, when GDP fell by 3.1 per cent while military spending rose by 3.1 per

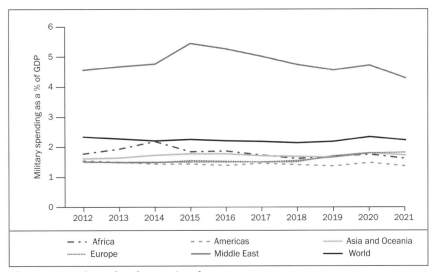

Figure 8.4. Military burden, regional averages, 2012–21

Note: The military burden is military expenditure as a share of gross domestic product. The military burden of a region is the average military burden of the countries in the region for which data is available.

Source: SIPRI Military Expenditure Database, Apr. 2022.

cent. The military burden fell once again in 2021, mainly due to the economic rebound following the global recession in 2020 (see above).

On average, states in the Middle East had the highest military burden in 2021, at 4.3 per cent of GDP. This was followed by states in Europe, with a substantially lower average of 1.8 per cent, in Asia and Oceania with 1.7 per cent, in Africa with 1.6 per cent, and in the Americas with 1.4 per cent. Between 2012 and 2021, the average military burden increased for states in Europe (0.3 percentage points) and Asia and Oceania (0.1 percentage point), while it fell in the Middle East (–0.3 percentage points), the Americas (–0.2 percentage points) and Africa (–0.1 percentage point).

The largest military spenders in 2021

Military spending by the 15 largest military spenders reached $1717 billion in 2021, accounting for 81 per cent of global military expenditure (see table 8.3). The United States (accounting for 38 per cent of world military spending in 2021) and China (14 per cent) remained by far the two largest spenders. There were, however, some notable changes in ranking among the top 15 between 2020 and 2021. The United Kingdom and France each moved up two ranks, becoming the fourth and sixth largest spenders in 2021, respectively. After a 17 per cent drop in its military spending, Saudi Arabia fell from fourth largest spender in 2020 to eighth largest in 2021. Iran increased its military spending

Table 8.3. The 15 countries with the highest military expenditure in 2021

Expenditure and GDP figures are in US$, at current prices and exchange rates. Changes are in real terms, based on constant (2020) US dollars.

Rank[a]		Country	Military expenditure, 2021 ($ b.)	Change (%)		Military expenditure as a share of GDP (%)[b]		Share of world military expenditure, 2021 (%)
2021	2020			2020–21	2012–21	2021	2012	
1	1	USA	801	–1.4	–6.1	3.5	4.5	38
2	2	China	[293]	4.7	72	[1.7]	[1.7]	[14]
3	3	India	76.6	0.9	33	2.7	2.6	3.6
4	6	UK	68.4	3.0	3.7	2.2	2.4	3.2
5	5	Russia	65.9	2.9	11	4.1	3.7	3.1
Subtotal top 5			1 305	..	..	..	..	62
6	8	France	56.6	1.5	13	1.9	1.9	2.7
7	7	Germany	56.0	–1.4	24	1.3	1.2	2.7
8	4	Saudi Arabia	[55.6]	–17	–15	[6.6]	[7.7]	[2.6]
9	9	Japan	54.1	7.3	18	1.1	1.0	2.6
10	10	South Korea	50.2	4.7	43	2.8	2.5	2.4
Subtotal top 10			1 578	..	..	..	..	75
11	11	Italy	32.0	4.6	9.8	1.5	1.4	1.5
12	12	Australia	31.8	4.0	42	2.0	1.7	1.5
13	13	Canada	26.4	3.1	40	1.3	1.1	1.3
14	18	Iran	24.6	11	–17	2.3	2.8	1.2
15	14	Israel	24.3	3.1	35	5.2	5.6	1.2
Subtotal top 15			1 717	..	..	..	..	81
World			**2 113**	**0.7**	**12**	**2.2**	**2.3**	**100**

.. = not applicable; [ ] = estimated figure; GDP = gross domestic product.

[a] Rankings for 2020 are based on updated military expenditure figures for 2020 in the current edition of the SIPRI Military Expenditure Database. They may therefore differ from the rankings for 2020 given in *SIPRI Yearbook 2021* and in other SIPRI publications in 2021.

[b] These figures are based on GDP estimates from International Monetary Fund, World Economic Outlook Database, Oct. 2021, <https://www.imf.org/external/pubs/ft/weo/2021/02/weodata/index.aspx>; and International Monetary Fund, International Financial Statistics Database, Sep. 2021.

Source: SIPRI Military Expenditure Database, Apr. 2022.

by 11 per cent, making it the 14th largest military spender in 2021. This is the first time in 20 years that Iran has ranked among the top 15 military spenders.

All but three countries in the top 15 had higher military expenditure in 2021 than in 2012. The exceptions were the USA (–6.1 per cent), Iran (–17 per cent) and Saudi Arabia (–15 per cent). Of the 12 countries that increased their military spending over the period 2012–21, the lowest increase was the 3.7 per cent rise by the UK, far below the five largest increases made by China (72 per cent), the Republic of Korea (South Korea, 43 per cent), Australia (42 per cent), Canada (40 per cent) and Israel (35 per cent). The reasons behind these increases range from long-term expensive military modernization programmes (i.e. China) to regional security concerns and threat perceptions (i.e. Australia, Israel and South Korea).

Despite continued increases in military spending in the majority of the top 15 spenders, their military burdens decreased as the world economy rebounded from the 2020 Covid-19-related recession. The most notable change in military burden in 2021 was the fall of 2.6 percentage points observed in Saudi Arabia. This sharp fall was the result of contrasting trends in GDP and military spending: a 17 per cent decrease in military expenditure was coupled with a predicted 16 per cent real-terms rise in GDP. Other notable decreases in military burdens in 2021 were from India (–0.2 percentage points), Israel (–0.2 percentage points), Russia (–0.2 percentage points) and the USA (–0.2 percentage points).

Notwithstanding the sharp fall, Saudi Arabia still had the highest military burden (6.6 per cent) among the 15 biggest military spenders in 2021. Seven other countries in the top 15—Israel (5.2 per cent), Russia (4.1 per cent), the USA (3.5 per cent), South Korea (2.8 per cent), India (2.7 per cent), Iran (2.3 per cent) and the UK (2.2 per cent)—also had a military burden higher than or equal to the global military burden of 2.2 per cent. Japan continued to have the lowest military burden among the 15, devoting 1.1 per cent of its GDP to military expenditure, albeit the highest level since 1960.

Box 8.2. Definition, sources and methods for SIPRI military expenditure[a]

Definition

The main purpose of the data on military expenditure is to provide an identifiable measure of the scale of financial resources absorbed by the military.

Although the lack of sufficiently detailed data makes it difficult to apply a common definition of military expenditure on a worldwide basis, SIPRI has adopted a definition as a guideline. Where possible, SIPRI military expenditure data includes all current and capital (including for procurement) expenditure on (a) the armed forces, including peacekeeping forces; (b) defence ministries and other government agencies engaged in defence projects; (c) paramilitary forces, when judged to be trained and equipped for military operations; and (d) military space activities. This should include expenditure on personnel, including salaries of military and civil personnel, retirement pensions of military personnel, and social services for personnel; operations and maintenance; procurement; military research and development; infrastructure spending; and military aid (in the military expenditure of the donor country). Civil defence, current expenditure on previous military activities (e.g. veterans' benefits, demobilization, conversion and weapon destruction) and military involvement in non-military activities (e.g. policing) are not included.

In practice, it is not possible to apply this definition for all countries, and in many cases SIPRI is confined to using the national data provided. Priority is then given to the choice of a uniform definition for each country in order to achieve consistency over time, rather than adjusting the figures for single years according to a common definition. In the light of these difficulties, military expenditure data is most appropriately used for comparisons over time and may be less suitable for close comparison between individual countries.

Sources of information

The SIPRI military expenditure figures are presented on a calendar-year basis. The only exception is the United States, for which data is reported on a financial-year basis.

SIPRI data reflects the official data reported by national governments. Such data is obtained directly from official publications such as budget documents, public finance statistics, reports of national audit agencies and government responses to questionnaires sent out by SIPRI. This official data is also available indirectly in reports published by the United Nations, the International Monetary Fund (IMF) and the North Atlantic Treaty Organization (NATO). In a few cases, the original government documents are not available to SIPRI, for example because they are not published, but the content of these documents may be reported in newspapers.

As a general rule, SIPRI takes national data to be accurate until there is convincing information to the contrary. Estimates are made primarily when the coverage of official data does not correspond to the SIPRI definition or when no consistent time series is available that covers the entire period covered by the data.

Military spending and military capability

Military spending measures the current level of resources devoted to renewing, replacing, expanding and maintaining military capability. Extreme caution should be exercised in drawing a link between a country's level of military expenditure and its degree of military capability, as many factors contribute to military capability. Further, other intervening factors may affect the degree to which military expenditure succeeds in buying military capability.

Thus, military spending does not reflect the stock of capabilities represented by factors such as weapons, training or knowledge. However, SIPRI military expenditure data can be directly used for comparisons of the national allocation of financial resources, for instance comparing it with spending on health services or education and as an indicator of military burden.

Military spending measured using market exchange rates

SIPRI uses market exchange rates (MERs) or, where applicable, fixed official exchange rates, to convert local currency military expenditure data into US dollars (whether current or constant prices). However, the prices of many goods and services on domestic markets are determined in partial or complete isolation from the rest of the world. Therefore, MERs do not always accurately reflect differences in price levels between countries.

An alternative is to use purchasing power parity (PPP) conversion factors (or PPP exchange rates). The PPP dollar rate of a country's currency is defined by the World Bank as 'the number of units of a country's currency required to buy the same amount of goods and services in the domestic market as a US dollar would buy in the United States'.[b] PPP rates are designed to control for differences in price levels and thus provide a measure of the real purchasing power of the gross domestic product (GDP) of each country.

However, since PPP rates are statistical estimates, the reliability GDP-based PPP rates is lower than for MERs, which are calculated on the basis of collected price data for a basket of goods and services for benchmark years. Between benchmark years, the PPP rates are extrapolated forward using ratios of prices indexes, either GDP deflators or consumer price indexes. Like all statistical estimates, they are subject to a margin of error.

Furthermore, GDP-based PPP rates are of limited relevance for the conversion of military expenditure data into US dollars.[c] Such PPP rates are designed to reflect the purchasing power for goods and services that are representative of spending patterns in each country, that is, primarily for civilian goods and services. Military expenditure is used to purchase a number of goods and services that are not typical of national consumption patterns. The extent to which this data reflects the amount of military goods and services that the military budget can buy is not known. Due to these uncertainties, SIPRI uses market exchange rates to convert military expenditure data into US dollars, despite their limitations.

[a] For more information see SIPRI Military Expenditure Database, 'Frequently asked questions', [n.d.].

[b] World Bank DataBank, 'Metadata glossary', [n.d.].

[c] See e.g. Ward, M., 'International comparisons of military expenditures: Issues and challenges of using purchasing power parities', *SIPRI Yearbook 2006*.

II. Regional developments in military expenditure, 2021

NAN TIAN, LUCIE BÉRAUD-SUDREAU, XIAO LIANG,
DIEGO LOPES DA SILVA AND ALEXANDRA MARKSTEINER

Total world military expenditure reached US$2113 billion in 2021.[1] States in the Americas accounted for the largest share of the total, 42 per cent. It was followed by Asia and Oceania, with a 28 per cent share, Europe, with 20 per cent, and the Middle East, with an estimated 8.8 per cent share. Africa accounted for the smallest share, only 1.9 per cent of world military expenditure.

This section reviews the main trends in military expenditure in 2021 and over the period 2012–21 from a regional perspective. It describes how specific developments have affected national decision-making on military spending as well as subregional and regional trends. For analysis of global trends see section I.

Africa

Military expenditure in Africa increased by 1.2 per cent in real terms in 2021 to $39.7 billion.[2] The spending pattern over the decade 2012–21 can be divided in three distinct periods: spending rose for three successive years in 2012–14, followed by four years of decline in 2015–18 and then three consecutive years of increases. The 4 countries included in North Africa accounted for 49 per cent of Africa's military spending, while the 46 countries covered in sub-Saharan Africa accounted for the remaining 51 per cent.

North Africa

Military expenditure by countries in North Africa reached $19.6 billion in 2021, down 1.7 per cent compared to 2020 but still 29 per cent higher than in 2012 (see figure 8.5). Algeria and Morocco drive trends in North African spending. Together, the two countries account for about three-quarters of the subregion's spending. Unresolved military and economic rivalries between the two and continued territorial disagreements over contested Western Sahara underpin the long-term tension and the increase in military expenditure in the subregion.[3]

---

[1] All figures for spending in 2021 are quoted in current 2021 US dollars. Except where otherwise stated, figures for increases or decreases in military spending are expressed in constant 2020 US dollars, often described as changes in 'real terms' or adjusted for inflation.

[2] This total excludes Djibouti, Eritrea and Somalia, for which it was impossible to make a reliable series of estimates for inclusion in the regional total.

[3] On the conflict in Western Sahara see chapter 6, section IV, in this volume.

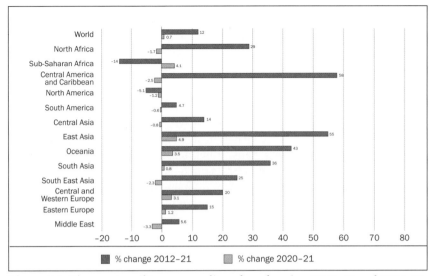

Figure 8.5. Changes in military expenditure by subregion, 2012–21 and 2020–21

Source: SIPRI Military Expenditure Database, Apr. 2022.

At $9.1 billion, Algeria was the largest spender in the subregion and the region. Despite a fall of 6.1 per cent in 2021, its spending was still 16 per cent higher than in 2012. In contrast, at $5.4 billion, Morocco's military expenditure was up by 3.4 per cent since 2020 and 48 per cent higher than in 2012. Morocco has steadily sought to bolster its military capability through arms procurement deals with the United States, France and China.[4]

Sub-Saharan Africa

Military expenditure in sub-Saharan Africa in 2021 was $20.1 billion, up 4.1 per cent from 2020 but still 14 per cent lower than in 2012.[5] The increase in 2021 was the first in the subregion since 2014.

The rise in sub-Saharan African military spending in 2021 was primarily due to increases in Nigeria's military expenditure. Its military spending rose by 56 per cent to $4.5 billion in 2021 in response to a plethora of security challenges, ranging from violent extremism via farmer–herder conflict, banditry and kidnapping, to separatist insurgencies and attacks on state oil production.[6] An initial 9.4 per cent increase (91 billion naira or $228 million) in the Nigerian military budget was supplemented in July 2021 with an additional

---

[4] Boukhars, A., 'Reassessing the power of regional security providers: The case of Algeria and Morocco', *Middle Eastern Studies*, vol. 55, no. 2 (2018). On the arms transfers to Morocco see also chapter 9, section III, in this volume.

[5] The total for sub-Saharan Africa excludes the Comoros and Sao Tome and Principe, which are not in the SIPRI Military Expenditure Database and are assumed to have low expenditure, and Djibouti, Eritrea and Somalia.

[6] On the armed conflict and security challenges in Nigeria see chapter 7, section II, in this volume.

716 billion naira ($1.8 billion).[7] This supplementary budget was equal to three-quarters of the initial military budget. Disaggregated information in the supplementary budget shows that this additional funding was for capital expenditure for the Nigerian armed forces.[8] Part of the additional military budget could thus have been used to pay for weapon systems delivered to the Nigerian military in 2021. These included combat aircraft from Brazil and China and off-shore patrol vessels from the Netherlands and France.[9]

The downward trend in sub-Saharan Africa's spending between 2014 and 2020 can be explained by persistent reductions in military spending by four of the subregion's five biggest spenders, as ranked in 2014: Angola, South Africa, Sudan and South Sudan. Principal of those was the sharp fall in spending in South Sudan, down 94 per cent between 2014 and 2020. This was followed by decreases of 73 per cent by Angola, 68 per cent by Sudan and 4.3 per cent by South Africa. The worsening economic conditions and continued low oil prices, slumps in oil production, and slow economic recovery were central to lower military spending in Angola, Sudan and South Sudan.[10] In South Africa, which has a more robust and diverse economy, almost a decade of stagnant economic performance led to a fall in military budgets.[11]

With the continued decline in the military expenditure of Angola, Sudan and South Sudan in 2021, the subregion's top 5 spenders were Nigeria, South Africa, Kenya, Uganda and Angola. In the cases of Kenya and Uganda, both have faced similar counterinsurgency challenges in recent years: Kenya's fight against al-Shabab and Uganda's armed conflict against the Allied Democratic Forces (ADF).[12] Over the 2014–21 period, military expenditure rose by 241 per cent in Uganda but remained relatively stable in Kenya, up by only 6.4 per cent.

In 2021 four sub-Saharan African countries experienced military coups— Chad in April, Mali in May, Guinea in September and Sudan in October—while there was also a failed coup in Niger in March.[13] A core justification by military leaders for the coups has been dissatisfaction with the government's ability to combat Islamist extremism, either through effective military strategy or

---

[7] 'Buhari signs N982 billion supplementary budget for 2021', *Premium Times* (Abuja), 26 July 2021.

[8] Nigerian Budget Office of the Federation, 'Supplementary appropriation bill 2021', p. 4.

[9] On arms transfers to Nigeria see also chapter 9, section III, in this volume.

[10] Tian, N. and Lopes da Silva, D., 'Debt, oil and military expenditure', *SIPRI Yearbook 2018*.

[11] International Monetary Fund (IMF), *South Africa: Staff Report for the 2021 Article IV Consultation*, IMF Country Report no. 22/37 (IMF: Washington, DC, 21 Jan. 2022); DefenceWeb, 'Budget cuts mean South Africa is losing its sovereign capability, defence industry', 31 May 2020; and Leone, D., 'South African Air Force Gripen fighter jets are grounded since September and they won't fly again until late January 2022 at the earliest. Here's why', Aviation Geek Club, 25 Dec. 2021.

[12] On armed conflict in the Horn of Africa see chapter 7, section IV, in this volume.

[13] Zeigler, S. M., 'Are military coups back in style in Africa?', Rand Corporation, 1 Dec. 2021. See also the discussion in chapter 7 of this volume.

by providing the military with equipment to combat the worsening security situation.[14]

In the five-year period 2017–21, military spending rose in three of the five countries that suffered either a coup or a coup attempt in 2021: Chad (31 per cent), Guinea (1.3 per cent) and Mali (12 per cent). It fell in Niger (–11 per cent) and Sudan (–73 per cent).

Military expenditure increases in some of these coup-affected countries are often explicitly meant to fund the fight against Islamist extremism. In Mali, for example, additional resources were allocated to the military in accordance with the Law on Military Policy and Programming for 2015–19 and the Law on Interior Security Policy and Programming for 2017–21 to improve operational capacity and military capability.[15] In contrast, despite a deteriorating security situation, worsening economic conditions resulted in budgetary cuts across military and non-military sectors in Chad and Sudan.[16]

The economic burden of the military in these coup-affected countries is higher than in non-coup-affected countries in sub-Saharan Africa. Between 2017 and 2021 the average military burden—that is, military spending as a share of gross domestic product (GDP)—of countries in sub-Saharan Africa was 1.5 per cent. In comparison, the average military burden between 2017 and 2021 of these five counties ranged from 1.6 per cent in Guinea to 2.9 per cent in Mali, all higher than the subregional average.

The Americas

Military expenditure in the Americas reached $883 billion in 2021. Spending in the region fell for the first time since 2017, down 1.2 per cent in real terms compared to 2020 and 4.2 per cent lower than in 2012. While spending fell in all three subregions—Central America and the Caribbean, North America, and South America—the regional decrease was mainly due to the fall in spending by the United States. North American countries (i.e. the USA and Canada) accounted for 94 per cent of total regional spending in 2021, with 5.1 per cent in South America, and 1.2 per cent in Central America and the Caribbean.

---

[14] Maclean, R., 'Five African countries. Six coups. Why now?', *New York Times*, 31 Jan. 2022; and Mishra, A., 'Coups are making a comeback in Africa, but what's driving them?', Observer Research Foundation, 1 Nov. 2021.

[15] International Security Sector Advisory Team (ISSAT), 'Mali SSR background note', Geneva Centre for Security Sector Governance (DCAF), 11 Feb. 2019; Loi de Finances 2018 [Finance Act 2018], Malian Law no. 2017-073 of 26 Dec. 2017, pp. 22–23; and La Sirène, 'Loi d'orientation et de programmation de la sécurité intérieure : 446 milliards F CFA pour ne rien faire . . . Salif mérite-t-il encore la confiance d'IBK ?' [Law on Interior Security Policy and Programming: 446 billion CFA francs for doing nothing . . . Does Salif still deserve the confidence of IBK?', Mali Jet, 3 May 2018.

[16] 'Sudan to cut government spending, increase social spending', Reuters, 27 June 2021; and Amnesty International (AI), *Strangled Budgets, Silenced Dissent: The Human Cost of Austerity Measures in Chad* (AI: London, 2018), pp. 7–13.

Table 8.4. Components of US military expenditure, fiscal years 2017–21

Figures are current US$ b. unless otherwise stated. Figures may not add up to the given totals because of the conventions of rounding.

	2017	2018	2019	2020	2021*a*
Department of Defense	569	601	654	690	712
Military personnel	145	146	156	161	175
Operation and maintenance	245	257	272	279	287
Procurement	104	113	125	139	137
Research, development, testing and evaluation	68	77	89	100	103
Other (construction, housing etc.)	6.8	8.6	12	11	11
Department of Energy, atomic energy defence activities	20	21	23	25	27
Other defence-related activities	9.3	9.5	9.3	9.7	9.4
National Intelligence Program, military-related activities	[41]	[45]	[45]	[47]	[46]
Department of State, international security assistance	7.1	6.8	6.8	6.7	6.7
Transfers to fund southern border wall construction	..	..	−3.6	..	..
Total	**647**	**686**	**734**	**778**	**801**
Military expenditure as share of GDP (%)	*3.3*	*3.3*	*3.4*	*3.7*	*3.5*

.. = not applicable; [ ] = estimated figure; FY = fiscal year; GDP = gross domestic product.

a Figures for FY 2021 are estimates.

Sources: SIPRI Military Expenditure Database, Apr. 2021; US Office of Budget and Management, 'Table 3.2—Outlays by function and sub-function: 1962–2026', 28 May 2021; Federation of American Scientists (FAS), Intelligence Resource Program, 'Intelligence budget data', [n.d.]; and US Department of State, *Congressional Budget Justification: Department of State, Foreign Operations and Related Programs—Fiscal Year 2022* (Department of State: Washington, DC, 2021).

North America

North American military spending amounted to $827 billion in 2021. This represented a decrease of 1.2 per cent compared to 2020 and a fall of 5.1 per cent since 2012. Given the size of the US military budget, which makes up 38 per cent of the world total, North American military expenditure is driven primarily by decisions made in Washington (see below). Canadian military spending totalled $26.4 billion in 2021, up by 3.1 per cent since 2020. Canada allocated 1.3 per cent of its GDP to its military, whereas the USA allocated 3.5 per cent. As the Canadian and US economies recovered in the aftermath of the pandemic-induced crash in 2020, the military burden of both countries decreased in 2021.

United States military spending. The USA spent $801 billion on military activities during the 2021 fiscal year (see table 8.4).[17] Following SIPRI

[17] The US fiscal year runs from 1 Oct. until 30 Sep. The 2021 fiscal year thus started in Oct. 2020.

methodology, this total includes funding for the National Intelligence Program and international security assistance. Compared to 2020, there was a nominal increase of 2.9 per cent but a real-terms decrease of 1.4 per cent. This discrepancy is attributable to a rising US inflation rate.[18]

The US military budget for the 2021 fiscal year was prepared, negotiated and passed during the final year of the administration of US President Donald J. Trump. When the national budget request was first published in February 2020, it allocated a total of $754 billion to national defence. This figure included funding for the Department of Defense (DOD), military-related nuclear activities and other defence-related activities.[19] Adjusted for inflation, the DOD's budget request was 2.7 per cent less than the amount enacted for the 2020 fiscal year.[20]

The budget process was delayed by congressional disputes over the scope of economic relief measures amid the Covid-19 pandemic. It was not until December 2020, two and a half months into the new fiscal year, that the US Congress approved the National Defense Authorization Act (NDAA) for 2021, an omnibus spending bill that specifies the level of funding for the DOD.[21]

When broken down into different funding categories, the US military budget for 2021 sheds light on shifting strategic priorities and military planning assumptions. The budget line with the largest increase between 2020 and 2021 was that for military personnel. In 2021 active-duty members of the armed services received an average pay rise of 2.7 per cent, as well as a higher basic housing allowance.[22] This explains why the budget category for military personnel grew by a nominal 8.7 per cent despite projections of personnel strength being unchanged.

To finance the planned overhaul of the US nuclear arsenal and expand nuclear capabilities as laid out in the 2018 Nuclear Posture Review, funding for military-related nuclear activities increased by 8.0 per cent in nominal terms in 2021.[23] In May 2021 the Congressional Budget Office projected the 10-year cost of maintaining and modernizing the US nuclear arsenal to be $634 billion until 2030.[24]

---

[18] US Department of Labor, Bureau of Labor Statistics, 'Consumer price index—January 2022', USDL-22-0191, 10 Feb. 2022.

[19] US Office of Management and Budget, *A Budget for America's Future: Fiscal Year 2021 Budget of the US Government* (US Government Publishing Office: Washington, DC, 2020), pp. 116, 129.

[20] Harrison, T. and Daniels, S. P., *Analysis of the FY 2021 Defense Budget* (Rowman & Littlefield: Lanham, MD, Aug. 2020), pp. 2, 5.

[21] O'Brien, C., 'Senate passes defense bill, setting up veto showdown with Trump', Politico, 11 Dec. 2020.

[22] Losey, S., 'Troops would see 2.7% pay raise under proposed DOD budget', Military.com, 28 May 2021.

[23] Reif, K., 'US nuclear budget skyrockets', *Arms Control Today*, vol. 50, no. 2 (Mar. 2020); and US Department of Defense (DOD), *Nuclear Posture Review* (DOD: Arlington, VA, Feb. 2018). On US nuclear weapon modernization see chapter 10, section I, in this volume.

[24] Bennet, M., 'Projected costs of US nuclear forces, 2021 to 2030', US Congressional Budget Office (CBO), May 2021.

Investment in the research, development, testing and evaluation (RDT&E) of new weapon systems has become a staple of recent budget requests. In 2021 a total of $103 billion was appropriated for this category, a nominal increase of 3.0 per cent compared to the previous year. Incoming US President Joe Biden has vowed to continue on this course; his defence budget request for the 2022 fiscal year forecasted a 6.5 per cent nominal increase in RDT&E funding.[25]

In contrast, appropriations for the procurement of weapon systems shrank by 1.4 per cent in nominal terms between 2020 and 2021. The largest cuts were for shipbuilding, aircraft and ground systems.[26] The decrease in procurement funding alongside a renewed focus on RDT&E may indicate that the DOD is rebalancing its portfolio to favour new technologies over legacy systems.

One of the defining moments of 2021 was the end of the nearly two-decade-long international military presence in Afghanistan, as the USA and its partners in the North Atlantic Treaty Organization (NATO) withdrew their remaining troops.[27] Estimates of the total cost of the US war in Afghanistan exceed $2.3 trillion over 20 years.[28] While most of this money was spent on military operations, the USA also devoted substantial financial resources to reconstruction activities and military aid to Afghanistan. For instance, between 2001 and 2021 the US government invested around $85 billion in an effort to bolster the Afghan security forces.[29] Following the collapse of the Afghan government and the Taliban takeover in August 2021, the US departments of Defense and State reallocated funds that had previously been made available for reconstruction in Afghanistan to other departmental activities.[30]

A few months before the US operation in Afghanistan drew to a close, President Biden published his first budget request, which allocated $768 billion to national defence in the 2022 fiscal year.[31] When the request was handed over to the US Congress, however, the DOD's funding had been boosted by an additional $25 billion. Members of the Congress voting in favour of this increase pointed out the need to hedge against rising inflation and to bolster US capabilities amid long-term strategic competition with China and Russia.[32]

---

[25] Harrison, T. and Daniels, S. P., *Analysis of the FY 2022 Defense Budget: Funding Trends and Issues for the Next National Defense Strategy* (Rowman & Littlefield: Lanham, MD, Dec. 2021).

[26] Harrison and Daniels (note 20), p. 12.

[27] Council on Foreign Relations (CFR), 'Timeline: The US war in Afghanistan 1999–2021', Sep. 2021. On the war in Afghanistan see chapter 4, section III, in this volume.

[28] Costs of War Project, 'US costs to date for the war in Afghanistan', Brown University, Watson Institute for International and Public Affairs, Aug. 2021.

[29] US Special Inspector General for Afghanistan Reconstruction (SIGAR), Quarterly report to the United States Congress, 30 Jan. 2022, pp. 41–42.

[30] US Special Inspector General for Afghanistan Reconstruction (note 29).

[31] Harrison and Daniels (note 25), pp. 3–4.

[32] Eversden, A., 'NDAA passes Senate at $740 billion; heads to Biden's desk', Breaking Defense, 15 Dec. 2021.

The budget request for the 2022 fiscal year was also the first since 2001 not to appropriate funds for Overseas Contingency Operations (OCO). This supplemental fund was created to finance the wars in Afghanistan and Iraq but soon became a means of circumventing spending caps and covering activities unrelated to overseas operations.[33] Following a debt ceiling crisis, the 2011 Budget Control Act (BCA) was passed to reduce the ballooning US budget deficit by imposing limits on defence and non-defence spending over the coming decade.[34] Even though these caps were routinely raised, most recently in 2019, it was not enough to cover all US military spending.[35] To finance the deficit, resources were thus appropriated under OCO, which is not subject to the BCA. In 2021, the most recent year during which defence planners made use of the OCO fund, $69 billion was appropriated under this category.[36]

Central America and the Caribbean

Military spending in Central America and the Caribbean was $11.0 billion in 2021. This was a 2.5 per cent drop compared to 2020 but a 58 per cent rise compared to 2012. The use of military forces to combat criminal activity remains the main driver of military spending in the subregion.[37]

Mexico's military spending dropped by 3.4 per cent in 2021 to $8.7 billion. The decline was mainly due to an economic contraction. Because military spending fell to the same extent as GDP, Mexico's military burden remained unchanged at 0.7 per cent. Mexico is by far the largest spender in Central America and the Caribbean—it accounted for nearly 80 per cent of the subregion's total military spending in 2021. The composition of Mexico's military spending has mirrored the growing use of the military in police operations.[38] Despite the cut in overall military expenditure in 2021, spending on the National Guard increased by 35 per cent. As a result, spending on the National Guard as a share of Mexico's total military expenditure rose from 11 per cent in 2020 to 16 per cent in 2021.

[33] McGarry, B. W. and Morgenstern, E. M., *Overseas Contingency Operations Funding: Background and Status*, US Congressional Research Service (CRS) Report to Congress R44519 (US Congress, CRS: Washington, DC, 6 Sep. 2019).

[34] Budget Control Act of 2011, US Public Law 112–5, signed into law 2 Aug. 2011. See also Sköns, E. and Perlo-Freeman, S., 'The United States' military spending and the 2011 budget crisis', *SIPRI Yearbook 2012*.

[35] McGarry, B. W., *The Defense Budget and the Budget Control Act: Frequently Asked Questions*, US Congressional Research Service (CRS) Report to Congress R44039 (US Congress, CRS: Washington, DC, 30 Sep. 2019).

[36] Harrison and Daniels (note 20), p. 2.

[37] On the armed conflict between state forces and armed gangs in Central America see chapter 3, section III, in this volume.

[38] On the armed conflict in Mexico between state security forces and drug cartels see chapter 3, section II, in this volume.

The use of military forces in combatting organized crime is also a driver of military spending in El Salvador. At $383 million, El Salvador's military spending increased by 6.8 per cent in 2021. The growth was largely related to the use of the armed forces in public security missions. In 2021, over 10 000 troops—nearly half of armed forces personnel—were deployed under the Territorial Control Plan, a public security policy aimed at combatting El Salvador's criminal gangs.[39] Salvadoran President Nayib Bukele plans to double the size of the armed forces by 2026, from 20 000 to 40 000 troops.[40] In pursuit of this goal, the approved budget for 2022 projects the highest military spending since the end of the 1979–92 civil war.[41]

South America

South America's military spending was relatively unchanged in 2021, at $45.3 billion—a mere 0.6 per cent drop compared to 2020. Military spending growth was relatively limited over the decade 2012–21, at 4.7 per cent. Brazil accounted for 42 per cent of the subregion's total military expenditure in 2021, followed by Colombia (23 per cent) and Chile (14 per cent).

Brazil's military spending in 2021 was $19.2 billion, a 4.3 per cent decrease compared to 2020. This was the third consecutive year of decline. Budget execution increased from 88 per cent in 2020 to 90 per cent in 2021, which was more in line with budget execution rates prior to the pandemic. Despite the budget cut, Brazil was still able to pursue some of its strategic armament programmes.[42] For instance, the FX-2 programme—the goal of which is to replace Brazil's ageing fleet of combat aircraft—continued to receive funds. At $266 million, actual expenditure on the FX-2 programme in 2021 was 9.4 per cent higher than initially budgeted. The FX-2 programme includes acquisition of 36 Gripen combat aircraft from the Swedish company Saab.[43] Other notable ongoing programmes were the construction of a nuclear-powered submarine (the PROSUB programme) and the development of the Astros 2020 artillery system.[44]

Colombia's military spending rose 4.7 per cent in 2021, to $10.2 billion. This was 30 per cent higher than in 2012. Since the 2016 peace agreement that ended the conflict between the government and the Revolutionary Armed

[39] SWI swissinfo.ch, 'Más de 10.000 militares son parte de un plan contra pandillas en El Salvador' [More than 10 000 soldiers are part of an anti-gang plan in El Salvador], 20 July 2021. See also the discussion in chapter 3, section III, in this volume.

[40] López, A., 'El Salvador duplicará sus efectivos militares de 20.000 a 40.000 en cinco años' [El Salvador to double its military personnel from 20,000 to 40,000 in five years], Infodefensa, 22 July 2021.

[41] Bernal, D., Jordán, L. and Urbina, J., 'El Ejército, el que más crece en presupuesto' [The army, the budget that grows the most], *Prensa Gráfica* (San Salvador), 2 Oct. 2021.

[42] Caiafa, R., 'Brasil planeja investir 20 bilhões de dólares em Defesa durante 2021' [Brazil plans to invest 20 billion dollars in Defense during 2021], Infodefensa, 13 Oct. 2020.

[43] On this and other Brazilian arms imports see chapter 9, section III, in this volume.

[44] On armed violence in Brazil see chapter 3, section IV, in this volume.

Forces of Colombia–People's Army (Fuerzas Armadas Revolucionarias de Colombia–Ejército del Pueblo, FARC-EP), Colombia's military spending has grown every year except for 2018. The rising trend can be attributed to the ongoing conflicts between the government and other armed groups, such as the National Liberation Army (Ejército de Liberación Nacional, ELN), as well as against former members of FARC-EP who have rejected the peace accord and formed splinter groups of their own.[45]

Asia and Oceania

Military spending in Asia and Oceania totalled $586 billion in 2021. This was 3.5 per cent higher than in 2020 and up 48 per cent since 2012, continuing an uninterrupted upward trend dating back to at least 1989.[46] Over the decade 2012–21, military spending rose in all five subregions of Asia and Oceania. The regional increase was due primarily to the rise in Chinese and Indian military spending, which in 2021 accounted for 63 per cent of total spending in the region, up from 51 per cent in 2012.

Central Asia

The combined total military expenditure in 2021 for the countries in Central Asia for which data is available was $1.8 billion, accounting for 0.3 per cent of total spending in Asia and Oceania. The total for Central Asia, which is comprised of spending figures for Kazakhstan, Kyrgyzstan and Tajikistan, was down 0.8 per cent in 2021 but was 14 per cent higher than in 2012. Military spending information has not been publicly available for Turkmenistan since 1999 and for Uzbekistan since 2003.

Kazakhstan was the largest spender in the subregion. At $1.6 billion, it accounted for 89 per cent of the subregional total.

East Asia

Military expenditure in East Asia totalled $411 billion in 2021, an increase of 4.9 per cent since 2020 and of 55 per cent since 2012. The increase in 2021 marked the 27th consecutive year of rising spending in East Asia.[47] The three biggest spenders in the subregion were China (71 per cent of the total), Japan (13 per cent) and the Republic of Korea (South Korea, 12 per cent). Together, these three countries accounted for 97 per cent of total East Asian spending,

---

[45] On the armed conflict in Colombia see chapter 3, section IV, in this volume.

[46] No data is available for North Korea, Turkmenistan or Uzbekistan for 2012–21 and they are not included in the totals for Asia and Oceania. Data for Viet Nam is not available for the years 2019–21. For Myanmar official data on the military budget is available for most years but is not used as there is significant spending outside the official budget. Incomplete data for Tajikistan, which indicates an increase, is included in the total.

[47] On geopolitical tensions in East Asia see chapter 4, section II, in this volume.

Table 8.5. Components of China's military expenditure, 2017–21

Figures are in b. yuan at current prices unless otherwise stated.

	2017	2018	2019	2020	2021
Official Chinese figures					
National defence (central and local)	1 044	1 128	1 213	1 292	1 381
Additional items included in SIPRI's estimate of China's total military expenditure					
People's Armed Police (central and local)	113	123	124	130	139
China Coast Guard	[8.1]	[9.2]	[11.1]	[11.8]	[12.7]
Payments to demobilized and retired soldiers	118	124	140	189	202
Additional military RDT&E spending*a*	[139]	[153]	[173]	[158]	[158]
Additional military construction spending*a*	0.2	0.1	0.1	0.1	0.1
Arms imports*b*	[1.3]	[0.9]	[0.5]	–	–
Total (yuan b.)	**1 424**	**1 538**	**1 660**	**1 781**	**1 893**
Total (US$ b. at current prices)	**210**	**233**	**240**	**258**	**293**
Military expenditure as a share of GDP (%)	*1.7*	*1.7*	*1.7*	*1.8*	*1.7*

[ ] = estimated figure; GDP = gross domestic product; RDT&E = research, development, testing and evaluation.

a Some spending on military RDT&E and military construction is also included in the main national defence budget.

b By 2020 all arms imports are estimated to be paid for by the equipment expenditure reported in the official defence budget.

Sources: Chinese Ministry of Finance, Budget Department, [2021 central budget expenditure table], 23 Mar. 2021 (in Chinese); and Chinese Ministry of Finance, Budget Department, Various national budget expenditure tables for years 2017–20 (in Chinese).

dwarfing the spending of the two other countries in the subregion, Mongolia and Taiwan.[48]

Chinese military spending. China, the world's second largest spender, allocated an estimated $293 billion to its military in 2021, an increase of 4.7 per cent since 2020 and of 72 per cent compared to 2012 (see table 8.5). China's military spending has grown for 27 consecutive years—the longest streak by any country in the SIPRI Military Expenditure Database. The 4.7 per cent rate of increase in 2021 was the same as in 2020 and equalled the slowest annual growth in Chinese spending since 1995. Despite the ongoing property market slump, the pursuit of a 'zero Covid' policy and a regulatory crackdown on technology companies, China's GDP is estimated to have increased by 8.4 per cent in 2021.[49] Its military burden thus fell by 0.1 percentage points, to 1.7 per cent of GDP.

[48] Figures may not add up to the given totals because of the conventions of rounding.

[49] 'China's economy slowed at end of 2021 amid COVID outbreaks', Deutsche Welle, 17 Jan. 2022; and Huang, E., 'China's tech crackdown could last decades, but won't stop long-term investors, says wealth manager', CNBC, 23 Nov. 2021.

The 2021 Chinese military budget forms part of the first year of the country's 14th five-year plan, which covers a wide range of social, economic development and national security initiatives in 2021–25.[50] An element of the new five-year plan is the application of Xi Jinping Thought on Socialism with Chinese Characteristics for a New Era—the policies and ideology of Chinese President Xi Jinping—to strengthening the military and the continued modernization of the People's Liberation Army (PLA).[51] While complete 'mechanization' (i.e. modernization of military equipment) was supposed to be achieved by 2020, the 2021–25 plan still mentions 'mechanization' as part of the military strengthening process.[52]

China's continued increases in military spending are further proof of the Communist Party of China's support for strengthening the military as a governing priority under President Xi.[53] Both Xi Jinping Thought and the 14th five-year plan note two significant dates for the Chinese military: modernization by 2035 and transforming into a 'world class' military by 2049.[54] The 14th five-year plan sets an additional goal: to strengthen the military via training, reform, science and technology, and information and intelligence by 2027.[55] While the goal is vague and may just be a propaganda slogan, it reinforces the narrative of progress in China's long-term military modernization plan.[56]

SIPRI's military expenditure figures for China differ from the official national defence budget. The SIPRI figure for 2021 is 37 per cent or 512 billion yuan ($79 billion) higher than the figure published in the official state budget. The annually published national defence budget does not include important elements of what SIPRI defines as military expenditure, some of which are listed in other parts of the official state budget.

---

[50] Tiezzi, S., 'China's fifth plenum: What you need to know', The Diplomat, 29 Oct. 2020.

[51] Xinhua, [Two sessions authorized for release, draft outline of the plan: Accelerate the modernization of national defence and the military to achieve unity of a prosperous country and a strong military], 3 May 2021 (in Chinese). On Xi Xinping Thought see Buckley, C., 'Xi Jinping thought explained: A new ideology for a new era', New York Times, 26 Feb. 2018.

[52] Fravel, M. T., 'China's "world-class military" ambitions: Origins and implications', Washington Quarterly, vol 43, no. 1 (2020), p. 87; and Chinese State Council, China's National Defense in the New Era, Defence White Paper (Chinese State Council Information Office: Beijing, July 2019), chapter II.

[53] Buckley, C. and Myers S. L., 'Xi Jinping presses military overhaul, and two generals disappear', New York Times, 11 Oct. 2017.

[54] Campbell, C., China's Military: The People's Liberation Army (PLA), US Congressional Research Service (CRS) Report for Congress R46808 (US Congress, CRS: Washington, DC, 4 June 2021); Nouwens, M., 'Is China speeding up military modernisation? It may, but not yet', The Interpreter, Lowy Institute, 4 Nov. 2020; Buckley (note 51); and Noon, N. and Bassler, C., 'Schrodinger's military? Challenges for China's military modernization ambitions', War on the Rocks, 14 Oct. 2021.

[55] Xinhua, [Proposal of the Central Committee of the Communist Party of China on formulating the 14th Five-year Plan for National Economic and Social Development and Long-term Goals for 2035], 3 Nov. 2020 (in Chinese).

[56] Hart, B., Glaser, B. S. and Funaiole, M. P., 'China's 2027 goal marks the PLA's centennial, not an expedited military modernization', China Brief, Jamestown Foundation, 26 Mar. 2021.

SIPRI's estimate of Chinese military expenditure is comprised of seven components.[57] Official information is available for four: national defence, the People's Armed Police, payments to demobilized and retired soldiers, and additional military construction spending. Together, these four categories accounted for 91 per cent of total spending in 2021. Estimates are made for two of the remaining three components, the China Coast Guard and additional funding for military RDT&E. The combined share of these two components was 9.0 per cent of the total in 2021. Since 2020, the cost of arms imports paid for outside the national defence budget is assumed to be zero and fully accounted for within the official defence budget.[58]

Japanese military spending. Military spending by Japan was $54.1 billion in 2021.[59] Following the initial approval of the 2021/22 budget in December 2020, the Japanese government passed a supplementary budget for total government spending in November 2021 that added an additional 774 billion yen ($7.0 billion) to the military budget for 2021/22.[60] The result was a 7.3 per cent increase in military spending in 2021 compared to 2020, the highest annual growth rate since 1972. Moreover, at 1.1 per cent of GDP, Japan's military burden in 2021 according to SIPRI data surpassed the threshold of 1 per cent of GDP for the first time since 1960.[61] Over the decade 2012–21 Japanese spending rose by 18 per cent. The main drivers of Japan's increased spending have been the growing perceived security threats from China, the Democratic People's Republic of Korea's (DPRK, or North Korea) and Russia.[62]

Around 55 per cent of the supplementary military budget was for advance payments to Japanese military companies for procurement of new equipment. This was stated to be a way to ease the financial situation faced by Japanese arms-producing companies in the wake of the Covid-19 pandemic.[63]

South Korean military spending. South Korean military expenditure reached $50.2 billion in 2021. The implementation of the 2021 military budget followed a similar trajectory to that of 2020. After the initial proposed budgetary increase of 5.4 per cent, the South Korean government revised its military budget, cutting 563 billion won ($492 million) or 1.1 per cent

---

[57] Tian, N. and Su, F., *A New Estimate of China's Military Expenditure* (SIPRI: Stockholm, Jan. 2021).

[58] Tian and Su (note 57), pp. 4–6.

[59] The SIPRI figures for Japan's military expenditure do not include spending by the Ministry of Defense on the emergency measures for disaster prevention and mitigation and building national resilience, which is considered non-military activity.

[60] Japanese Ministry of Finance, 'Overview of the supplementary budget for FY2021', Nov. 2021; and Grevatt, J. and MacDonald, A., 'Japan adds USD6.8 billion to 2021 defence budget', Janes, 29 Nov. 2021.

[61] Takahashi, K., 'Japan approves record extra defense budget', The Diplomat, 26 Nov. 2021.

[62] Japanese Ministry of Defense, 'National defense program guidelines for FY 2019 and beyond', 18 Dec. 2018.

[63] Takahashi (note 61).

from the initial budget.[64] The savings from the military expenditure cut were redirected into a 35 trillion won ($30.6 billion) economic relief and pandemic-recovery package.[65]

As a result, South Korea's military expenditure increased by 4.7 per cent in 2021. This was the 22nd consecutive year in which South Korean military expenditure has risen: over the period 1999 to 2021, allocations to the military increased by 142 per cent. The increase in South Korean spending came amid continued development of nuclear weapons and testing of ballistic missiles by North Korea, in violation of United Nations Security Council resolutions.[66]

Oceania

At $35.3 billion in 2021, military spending in Oceania rose by 3.5 per cent between 2020 and 2021 and by 43 per cent over the decade from 2012. Australia accounted for 90 per cent of the subregion's total in 2021.

Australia's military expenditure in 2021 was US$31.8 billion. This was 4.0 per cent higher than in 2020 and 42 per cent higher than in 2012. The economic burden of Australia's military activities amounted to 2.0 per cent of its GDP in 2021, unchanged since 2020 but 0.3 percentage points higher than in 2012.

On 16 September 2021, Australia, the United Kingdom and the United States announced the signing of a trilateral security pact.[67] Termed AUKUS, the agreement includes the procurement by Australia of eight nuclear-powered submarines and closer cooperation on cyber, artificial intelligence (AI) and quantum technologies.[68] While China was not mentioned in the official AUKUS agreement, Australia has publicly stated in documents such as the 2020 Defence Strategic Update that China's increased assertiveness and pursuit of greater influence in the Indo-Pacific region directly affects Australia's security environment.[69]

---

[64] South Korean Ministry of Economy and Finance, '2021 budget proposal: 2021 budget drawn up to speed up turnaround and prepare for the future', Press release, 1 Sep. 2020; Grevatt, J. and MacDonald, A., 'South Korea cuts 2021 defence budget', Janes, 3 Aug. 2021; and Yonhap, 'Govt. cut W560b won of defense budget, including for F-35A plan, for COVID-19 extra budget', *Korea Herald*, 2 Aug. 2021.

[65] Grevatt and MacDonald (note 64); and South Korean Ministry of Economy and Finance (MOEF), Budget Office, *Recovery for All: Korea's Fiscal Response to COVID-19* (MOEF: Seoul, 29 Oct. 2021), p. 3.

[66] Grevatt, J. and MacDonald, A., 'South Korea finalise USD46.32 billion defence budget for 2022', Janes, 3 Dec. 2021. On North Korea's nuclear weapon and ballistic missile programmes see chapter 10, section IX, in this volume.

[67] Morrison, S., Australian Prime Minister, Johnson, B., British Prime Minister, and Biden, J. R., US President, Joint leaders statement on AUKUS, Australian Department of the Prime Minister and Cabinet, 16 Sep. 2021. See also Borger, J. and Sabbagh, D., 'US, UK and Australia forge military alliance to counter China', *The Guardian*, 16 Sep. 2021.

[68] Clarke, M., 'The AUKUS nuclear submarine deal: Unanswered questions for Australia', The Diplomat, 22 Sep. 2021.

[69] Australian Department of Defence (DOD), *2020 Defence Strategic Update* (DOD: Canberra, 2020), pp. 11, 15. See also Wintour, P., 'As China threat rises, can AUKUS alliance recover from rancorous birth?', *The Guardian*, 23 Nov. 2021; and Clarke (note 68).

The immediate implication of the AUKUS agreement was the cancellation of a 2016 deal with Naval Group, a French company, for the supply of 12 diesel-powered submarines to Australia. Reported to be worth 90 billion Australian dollars (US$67 billion), the French deal had been denounced in the Australian public debate as too costly.[70] Although Australia is yet to choose between British and US submarines under the AUKUS agreement, the new submarine deal is estimated to cost as much as 171 billion Australian dollars (US$128 billion).[71] The Australian Parliamentary Budget Office estimates that military spending could rise from the current 43.6 billion Australian dollars in 2021 to 75.7 billion Australian dollars by 2031.[72] Part of this increase is probably due to a need to absorb the costs of the AUKUS agreement, including the nuclear submarine programme.

South Asia

Military spending in South Asia increased again to $95.1 billion in 2021 after a real-terms decrease in 2020 of 2.7 per cent. Spending in 2021 was 0.8 per cent higher than in 2020 and 36 per cent higher than in 2012.

India is the largest military spender in South Asia, making up 81 per cent of the subregion's total in 2021. Its budget of $76.6 billion also ranked as the second highest in Asia and Oceania and the third highest in the world. This was up by 0.9 per cent from 2020 and by 33 per cent from 2012. India's economy recovered from a sharp contraction in 2020 to grow by 9.5 per cent in 2021 after undergoing a devastating wave of Covid-19 in the first half of 2021. The military burden consequently dropped to 2.7 per cent of GDP after reaching 2.9 per cent in 2020, the highest value in the decade 2012–21.

In 2021, 60 per cent of India's total military budget was allocated to personnel expenses such as salaries and military pensions. Around one-quarter is generally spent on capital outlays, which continued to grow after a big surge in 2020. About 12 per cent of the spending in 2021 went to paramilitary forces, including the Indo-Tibetan Border Police, the budget of which rose by 9.1 per cent in the context of the Ladakh border confrontation with China.[73]

Amid ongoing, albeit de-escalated, stalemates on two fronts—with China and Pakistan—the Indian government has placed self-reliance and

---

[70] Shepherd, T., 'Australia's Aukus nuclear submarines could cost as much as $171bn, report finds', *The Guardian*, 13 Dec. 2021; and Galloway, A., 'Defence knew submarines would cost almost $80b five years ago', *Sydney Morning Herald*, 13 Oct. 2020.

[71] Nicholls, A., Dowie, J. and Hellyer, M., *Implementing Australia's Nuclear Submarine Programme* (Australian Strategic Policy Institute: Canberra, Dec. 2021), p. 72.

[72] Cheung, A. et al., *Beyond the Budget 2021–22: Fiscal Outlook and Scenarios*, Report no. 02/2021 (Parliamentary Budget Office: Canberra, 2021); and Wright, S., 'Subs get to sail past $100 billion as defence call on budget grows', *Sydney Morning Herald*, 20 Sep. 2021.

[73] On the armed conflict in the border areas of China, India and Pakistan see chapter 4, section III, in this volume.

modernization of its armed forces as its top military priorities.[74] In a push to strengthen the indigenous arms industry and local research and development (R&D) capabilities, 64 per cent of capital outlays in 2021 were earmarked for domestic equipment acquisitions.[75]

Pakistan's military spending fell for the third consecutive year in 2021, to $11.3 billion, a decrease of 0.7 per cent since 2020. This came against the backdrop of rising inflation during the Covid-19 pandemic as well as the ceasefire agreement reached with India over Kashmir in February 2021.[76] At 3.8 per cent of GDP in 2021, Pakistan's military burden was the highest in Asia and Oceania. Pakistan also spent the highest share of total government expenditure on the military (18 per cent) in Asia and Oceania.

Afghanistan's military budget for 2021, adopted by the government of President Ashraf Ghani, increased by 1.8 per cent to $278 million. Following the Taliban's seizure of power in August 2021, in early 2022 the new government released its first quarterly budget, which followed the same format with regards to military expenditure as the budgets of the previous government.[77]

South East Asia

Military spending in South East Asia decreased by 2.3 per cent between 2020 and 2021 to $43.2 billion. This was the third time since 2012 that the subregion's total military spending fell. The other two instances were a small decrease of 0.7 per cent in 2014 and a decrease of 7.3 per cent in 2018, when Indonesia and Malaysia each reduced military expenditure in a context of economic downturn and electoral campaigns. These variations, supported by fluctuations in the military burden, show that military spending in South East Asia is sensitive to economic downturns and political events.[78]

The Covid-19 pandemic had an impact on military expenditure in South East Asia. For instance, Singapore's military expenditure was revised downward during 2020 explicitly because of the pandemic.[79] It rose again in 2021, reaching $11.1 billion (a growth of 7.1 per cent) but did not grow as fast as the country's health expenditure. Health spending rose from a 13 per cent share

[74] 'Sitharaman allocates Rs 4.78 lakh crore to defence budget for 2021–22, "highest in 15 years"', Asian News International, 1 Feb. 2021.

[75] On the Indian arms industry see Fleurant, A., 'Arms production and military services', *SIPRI Yearbook 2015*; and Jackson, S. T. and Grinbaum, M., 'The Indian arms-production and military services industry', *SIPRI Yearbook 2012*.

[76] On the ceasefire see chapter 4, section II, in this volume.

[77] Afghan Ministry of Finance (MOF), [Quarterly national budget 1400] (MOF: Kabul, 21 Dey 1400 [11 Jan. 2022]) (in Pashto).

[78] Ball, D. et al., *Asia's New Geopolitics: Military Power and Regional Order*, Adelphi Series vol. 59, nos 478–480 (Routledge: Abingdon, 2021), pp. 71–124.

[79] Heijmans, P., 'Singapore faces defense budget cutbacks amid virus impact', Bloomberg, 29 June 2020; and Parameswaran, P., 'What does Singapore's new defense budget say about the country's security thinking', The Diplomat, 24 Feb. 2020.

of total government spending in 2020 to 18 per cent in 2021, higher than the military expenditure share (11 per cent in 2020 and 15 per cent in 2021).[80]

The downward trend in the subregion's military spending was driven overall by its second and third largest spenders, Indonesia and Thailand, which both reduced their military expenditure in 2021: Indonesia by 15 per cent to $8.3 billion and Thailand by 8.5 per cent to $6.6 billion.[81] The decrease in Indonesia casts doubts over its budgetary capacity to absorb the costs of the projected purchases of 42 Rafale combat aircraft (estimated at $8.1 billion) and 36 F-15 combat aircraft (announced as $13.9 billion).[82] In the past, Indonesia has resorted to foreign loans to procure its military equipment, but has already encountered difficulties in paying for its current joint combat aircraft development programme with South Korea.[83]

Europe

Total military spending in Europe in 2021 amounted to $418 billion. This was 3.0 per cent higher than in 2020 and 19 per cent higher than in 2012.

Central and Western Europe

The military expenditure of the states in Central and Western Europe totalled $342 billion in 2021, 3.1 per cent higher than in 2020. This represented the seventh consecutive year of growth. While military expenditure growth was slower in 2021 than in 2019 (5.1 per cent) and 2020 (5.2 per cent), it was still higher than in 2017 (2.3 per cent) and 2018 (2.9 per cent). Over the decade 2012–21, the subregion's military expenditure grew by more than 20 per cent.

The economies of countries in Central and Western Europe rebounded quickly after the Covid-19-induced recession of 2020. GDP in the eurozone—the 19 members of the European Union (EU) that have adopted the euro as a common currency—contracted by 6.3 per cent in 2020 but was projected to grow by 5.0 per cent in 2021. The trend was even more pronounced in the United Kingdom, where economic output declined by 9.8 per cent in 2020

---

[80] Singaporean Ministry of Finance (MOF), *The Revenue and Expenditure Estimates for the Financial Year 2012/2022*, Cmd 5 of 2021 (MOF: Singapore, 2021), p. 12. The figure for military spending as a proportion of total government spending may differ from figures in government documents as SIPRI uses IMF government spending figures.

[81] Gregatt, J. and MacDonald, A., 'Covid-19: Thailand proposes 2021 defence budget reduction', *Jane's Defence Weekly*, 2 July 2020; and Grevatt, J., 'Indonesia sets 2022 defence budget at USD9.3 billion', *Jane's Defence Weekly*, 25 Aug. 2021.

[82] Hummel, T. and Widianto, S., 'France seals $8.1 billion deal with Indonesia to sell 42 Rafale jets', Reuters, 10 Feb. 2022; and US Defense Security Cooperation Agency, 'Indonesia—F-15ID aircraft', New Release no. 22-13, 10 Feb. 2022.

[83] Rahmat, R., 'Amid funding challenges, Indonesia eyes A400M for aerial tanker requirements', *Jane's Defence Weekly*, 11 Oct. 2021; and Yonhap, 'S. Korea cuts Indonesia's payment for joint fighter development', *Korea Herald*, 15 Nov. 2021.

but increased by 6.8 per cent in 2021.[84] At the same time, financial policies remained expansive, as the circulation of the virus led to further mobility and economic restrictions and governments continued to support companies and jobs.[85] As a result, government budget deficits worsened in 2021 compared to 2020.[86]

Of the 36 countries in Central and Western Europe for which SIPRI provides military spending data, 21 increased military spending as a share of total government spending in 2021. This reflects the continued priority that Central and West European governments assigned to allocating public expenditure to their armed forces, despite the Covid-19 pandemic. In 2021 the strategic situation and threat perceptions thus weighed more heavily in the decision-making of Central and West European governments than fiscal and economic conditions.[87]

In 2021 the European Commission's European Defence Fund (EDF) came into force, building on two previous military research funding mechanisms: the Preparatory Action on Defence Research (2017–19) and the European Defence Industrial Development Programme (2019–20). Over the period 2021–27 a total of €8.0 billion ($9.5 billion) is earmarked for the EDF in the EU's 2021–27 Multiannual Financial Framework (MFF) and €5.0 billion ($5.9 billion) is to be financed outside the EU budget for the European Peace Facility (EPF).[88] In addition, the MFF also includes €1.7 billion ($2.0 billion) for 'military mobility' over the seven-year period. This expenditure is earmarked to overhaul dual-use transport infrastructure, which will facilitate the circulation of military personnel and equipment across Europe.[89] All this expenditure is in addition to national military spending by EU countries; it is currently not included in the SIPRI estimate of world military spending.

The $9.7 billion increase in Central and West European military spending in 2021 was mostly driven by procurement and R&D.[90] According to NATO, 18 of its European members increased the share of their military expenditure spent on equipment in 2021, some quite starkly, such as Croatia

---

[84] International Monetary Fund (IMF), *World Economic Outlook, October 2021: Recovery during a Pandemic—Health Concerns, Supply Disruptions, and Price Pressures* (Washington DC: Oct. 2021), p. 5.

[85] European Central Bank (ECB), *Economic Bulletin*, no. 8/2021, p. 47.

[86] International Monetary Fund (IMF), World Economic Outlook Database, Oct. 2021, <https://www.imf.org/en/Publications/WEO/weo-database/2021/October>

[87] On the growing geopolitical tensions in Europe see chapter 5, section I, in this volume.

[88] European Commission, 'The European Defence Fund', 30 June 2021; European Commission, 'Multiannual Financial Framework 2021–2027 (in commitments)—Current prices', Jan. 2021; and European External Action Service (EEAS), 'Questions and answers: The European Peace Facility', 22 Mar. 2021.

[89] European Commission, 'Defence Union: Further progress made towards military mobility in the EU', 27 Sep. 2021.

[90] Tian, N., Lopes da Silva, D. and Wezeman, P. D., 'Spending on military equipment by European members of the North Atlantic Treaty Organization', *SIPRI Yearbook 2020*.

(+33 percentage points) and Greece (+26 percentage points).[91] Both countries planned purchases of Rafale combat aircraft from France.[92]

There were similar surges in spending on equipment by non-NATO countries in Central and Western Europe. For instance, Finland's acquisition of military equipment jumped from €789 million ($899 million) in 2020 to €2.3 billion ($2.7 billion) in 2021, the same year it signed a procurement deal for 64 F-35 combat aircraft at an approximate cost of $9.4 billion.[93] Sweden's procurement spending plans increased from 14.8 billion kronor ($1.6 billion) to 17.8 billion kronor ($2.1 billion) between 2020 and 2021.[94] Hence, in a context of heightened geopolitical tensions, Central and West European states appeared to prioritize the procurement of their armed forces' equipment in their military spending.

The United Kingdom's military expenditure amounted to $68.4 billion in 2021, up by 3.0 per cent from 2020. The UK's military burden was 2.2 per cent of GDP in 2021, above the NATO target of 2 per cent. Over the period 2012–21, the UK's military expenditure grew by only 3.7 per cent, the slowest of all countries in Central and Western Europe. In 2021 the British government published its Integrated Review of Security, Defence, Development and Foreign Policy. This included the announcement of a £24.0 billion ($33.0 billion) increase in the Ministry of Defence's budget (the largest component of SIPRI's estimate of British military spending) over four years.[95] This incorporates £6.6 billion ($9.1 billion) for military R&D. The additional spending is also expected to fund a new Space Command, sustain the nuclear weapon programme, and support the modernization of the British Royal Air Force and the British Royal Navy with the introduction of new types of weapon system.[96] The Defence Command Paper gave more indications of the priorities for the British armed forces. New emphasis is put on emerging military capabilities in the AI or cyber domains, while the number of personnel in the British Army will be reduced from 76 000 to 72 500 by 2025, and legacy platforms will be retired (e.g. the Type 23 frigates).[97]

---

[91] NATO, 'Defence expenditure of NATO countries (2014–2021)', Press Release no. PR/CP(2021)094, 11 June 2021.

[92] 'France confirms deal with Greece for six more Rafale fighter jets', France 24, 12 Sep. 2021; and 'Croatia signs deal to buy 12 French fighter jets during visit by Macro', France 24, 25 Nov. 2021.

[93] Finnish Ministry of Finance, 'Statsbudgeten 2022, Huvudtitel 27: Försvarsministeriets förvaltningsområde' [State budget 2022, Main title 27: Administrative area of the Ministry of Defence], 2021, pp. 3–4; and Lehto, E. and Stone, M., 'Finland orders 64 Lockheed F-35 fighter jets for $9.4 bln', Reuters, 10 Dec. 2021.

[94] Swedish government, 'Utgiftsområde 6—Försvar och samhällets krisberedskap' [Expenditure area 6—Defence and civil protection], Proposition 2020/21:1, 2020, p. 8.

[95] See Béraud-Sudreau, L. and Tian, N., 'Reassessing SIPRI's military expenditure estimate for the United Kingdom', SIPRI Topical Backgrounder, 9 Feb. 2021.

[96] British Government, *Global Britain in a Competitive Age: The Integrated Review of Security, Defence, Development and Foreign Policy*, CP 403 (Her Majesty's Stationery Office: London, Mar. 2021).

[97] British Ministry of Defence, *Defence in a Competitive Age*, CP 411 (Her Majesty's Stationery Office: London, Mar. 2021); and Brooke-Holland, L., 'Defence Command Paper 2021: Summary', Briefing Paper no. 9181, British House of Commons Library, 19 Mar. 2021.

French military expenditure reached $56.6 billion in 2021, a 1.5 per cent increase over 2020. Over the decade 2012–21, French military spending grew by 13 per cent. The military burden was 1.9 per cent of GDP in 2021. France's military spending in 2021 was in line with the Law on Military Planning (Loi de Programmation Militaire, LPM) for 2019–25. The government had originally tabled an increase in the funding outlined in the LPM for 2021. However, this was postponed due to the financial uncertainty during the Covid-19 pandemic.[98] According to the Ministry of Armed Forces, one of the reasons that prompted the government not to proceed with the increase was that the military burden had risen automatically, due to the economic crisis, to reach 2 per cent, which could have prematurely indicated that the French armed forces had completed their modernization process.[99] The government thus wanted to wait for the economic situation to settle before reassessing spending plans for the final three years of the LPM.[100]

Germany, the third largest military spender in Central and Western Europe, spent $56.0 billion in 2021, a fall of 1.4 per cent. Its military burden in 2021 was 1.3 per cent of GDP. A new coalition government came to power in September 2021, composed of the Social Democratic, Green and Free Democratic parties. The coalition agreement includes a goal to invest 3 per cent of Germany's GDP jointly in diplomacy, development and commitments to NATO.[101] This phrasing moves away from the NATO target of 2 per cent of GDP to be spent on 'defence expenditure' and tends to include military spending as part of a wider approach to security, including other aspects of human security and international commitments (see section I).[102]

Eastern Europe

Military spending in Eastern Europe increased by 2.3 per cent between 2020 and 2021 to $76.3 billion, and by 15 per cent between 2012 and 2021. Russia, which accounted for 86 per cent of the total, drove this trend.

The Russian Federation's military spending reached $65.9 billion in 2021. This represented a real-terms growth of 2.9 per cent compared to 2020, confirming Russia's upward trajectory since 2018. This came after a period of decline in 2017 and 2018 due to economic difficulties in the wake of Western

[98] Castex, J., French Prime Minister, Statement on the updating of the Law on Military Programming, French Senate, 23 June 2021 (in French).

[99] Mackenzie, C., 'Despite pressure from lawmakers and pandemic, French defense budget to remain unchanged'. *Defense News*, 5 Oct. 2020.

[100] French Senate, Legislative update on the Law on Military Programming, Response to Written Question no. 22 683, 9 Sep. 2021 (in French).

[101] German Social Democratic Party (SPD), Bündnis 90/The Greens and Free Democratic Party (FDP), *Mehr Fortschritt wagen: Bündnis für Freiheit, Gerechtigkeit und Nachhaltigkeit* [Daring more progress: Alliance for freedom, justice and sustainability], Coalition agreement (SDP/The Greens/FDP: Berlin, 26 Nov. 2021), p. 144.

[102] On this wider approach see also Brzoska, M., Omitogoon, W. and Sköns, E., *The Human Security Case for Rebalancing Military Expenditure* (SIPRI: Stockholm, May 2022).

sanctions and a period of lower commodity prices. Russia's military burden remained relatively high in 2021, at 4.1 per cent, among the highest 15 in the world.

Russian military spending growth in 2021 can be attributed to the government's budget surplus due to high commodity prices. Average oil prices were $70 per barrel in 2021, while Russia's breakeven oil price—that is, when income from oil sales covers the cost of extraction—was estimated to be around $40 per barrel.[103] The higher commodity prices generated additional revenue for the Russian government, which relies on commodity exports for a large proportion of its income.[104] In September 2021, Russia's current account surplus from higher oil export revenue rose to $82 billion—a level that had not been reached for 14 years.[105] Russia did not reallocate the windfall revenue solely to foreign exchange savings, but also for additional public spending, including on its armed forces. [106]

The 2021 'national defence' budget, which accounts for three-quarters of total Russian military spending, was revised several times.[107] In the Budget Law of 8 December 2020, 'national defence' for 2021 was set at 3118 billion roubles ($42.3 billion).[108] When the subsequent draft budget was submitted in September 2021, 'national defence' for 2021 was revised to 3381 billion roubles ($45.9 billion).[109] Eventually, information from the State Treasury regarding actual spending for the year 2021 showed that 3573 billion roubles ($48.4 billion) had been spent under this budget line.[110] The top-up allocations are likely to have been spent on operational activities, given that additional funds could not be easily allocated to weapon production and procurement. In late 2021, Russia amassed troops alongside the Ukrainian

---

[103] World Bank, 'World Bank commodities price data', 2 Feb. 2022, p. 1; and International Monetary Fund (IMF), *Russian Federation: Staff Report for the 2020 Article IV Consultation*, IMF Country Report no. 21/36 (IMF: Washington, DC, 19 Jan. 2021), p. 38.

[104] World Bank, 'Amidst strong economic rebound in Russia, risks stemming from COVID-19 and inflation build, says World Bank report', Press Release no. 2022/ECA/38, 1 Dec. 2021.

[105] World Bank, *Amidst Strong Economic Recovery, Risks Stemming from COVID-19 and Inflation Build—Special Focus on Russia's Green Transition: Pathways, Risks and Robust Policies*, Russia Economic Report no. 46 (World Bank: Washington, DC, Dec. 2021), p. xii.

[106] On the relationship between oil revenue and military expenditure see Tian and Lopes da Silva (note 10).

[107] Wezeman, S. T., 'Russia's military spending: Frequently asked questions', SIPRI Topical Backgrounder, 27 Apr. 2020; and Cooper, J., *Russian Military Expenditure: Data, Analysis and Issues* (Swedish Defence Research Agency: Stockholm, Sep. 2013). On the other quarter of Russian military spending—comprised of social support, pensions, paramilitary forces, support for the nuclear weapons complex, and other expenditure by the Ministry of Defence such as health, education and housing—see Tian, N. et al., 'Regional developments in military expenditure, 2019', *SIPRI Yearbook 2020*.

[108] Russian Ministry of Finance, [On the federal budget for 2021 and for the planning period 2022 and 2023], Dec. 2020, p. 47 (in Russian).

[109] Russian State Duma, Defence Committee, [On the federal budget for 2022 and for the planning period of 2023 and 2024], 14 Oct. 2021, p. 5 (in Russian).

[110] Russian Federal Treasury, Budget Execution, Monthly report for January 2022, 8 Feb. 2022.

border and demanded a guarantee that Ukraine will not join NATO and that the alliance will refrain from expanding eastwards.[111]

Despite a certain degree of disaggregation in the official military budget, 48 per cent of total Russian military expenditure in 2021 is labelled as 'classified' within three broad categories: the Ministry of Defence, applied R&D, and other spending. This includes part of the spending on the nuclear weapons complex, which, according to budgetary documents, will increase in the coming years.[112] This is partly due to the production of a new generation of intercontinental ballistic missiles (ICBMs).[113]

Several countries in Eastern Europe are or have been involved in armed conflict or are facing regional tensions. Ukraine's military spending rose steeply after Russia's annexation of Crimea and its support of separatists in the Donbas region in 2014.[114] Overall, its military spending rose by 72 per cent in 2014–21 and by 142 per cent over the decade 2012–21. The upward trend was interrupted in 2021 by an 8.5 per cent drop in military spending, to $5.9 billion. This accounted for 3.2 per cent of the country's GDP in 2021. The USA has been increasing military aid to Ukraine since 2014. Between 2015 and 2021, US military aid to Ukraine totalled $717 million (which is included in the military spending of the USA, not Ukraine—see box 8.2 in section I).

Territorial disputes and skirmishes between Armenia and Azerbaijan have continued since the 2020 conflict over Nagorno-Karabakh.[115] Armenia and Azerbaijan both had high military burdens in 2021: 4.4 per cent and 5.3 per cent, respectively. While Azerbaijan's military spending grew by 16 per cent between 2020 and 2021, reaching $2.7 billion, Armenia's decreased by 5.2 per cent to $619 million.

The Middle East

Military expenditure in the Middle East is estimated to have totalled $186 billion in 2021, down 3.3 per cent since 2020 but 5.6 per cent higher than in 2012.[116] For over a decade, until 2021, SIPRI had been unable to estimate military spending by Qatar (now the fifth largest spender in the region and the 22nd in the world) or provide an estimate for the region since 2014. Newly

---

[111] Bertrand, N., Sciutto, J. and Lillis K. B., 'Russia continues to amass new troops near Ukraine's border despite Biden urging Putin to de-escalate tensions', CNN, 17 Dec. 2021; and Roth, A., 'Russia issues list of demands it says must be met to lower tensions in Europe', *The Guardian*, 17 Dec. 2021. See also chapter 5 in this volume.

[112] Russian Ministry of Finance, [On the federal budget for 2022 and for the planning period 2023 and 2024], Dec. 2021, p. 71 (in Russian).

[113] Gady, F.-S., 'Russia's RS-28 Sarmat ICBM to enter serial production in 2021', The Diplomat, 31 Oct. 2018; and Bratersky, A., 'Russian nuclear weapons stand out in defense budget request', *Defense News*, 1 Nov. 2021. On Russian nuclear forces see chapter 10, section II, in this volume.

[114] On the armed conflict in Ukraine see chapter 5, section II, in this volume.

[115] Forestier-Walker, R., 'Armenia and Azerbaijan's new-old border war', Al Jazeera, 19 Nov. 2021.

[116] This total excludes Syria and Yemen but includes an estimate for the UAE.

available data for Qatar allows a regional estimate to be made once more, although data for the United Arab Emirates (UAE) remains unavailable.

Six of the 10 countries with the highest military burden are in the Middle East: Oman, which spent 7.3 per cent of its GDP on the military (the highest level in the world), Kuwait at 6.7 per cent, Saudi Arabia at 6.6 per cent, Israel at 5.2 per cent, Jordan at 5.0 per cent and Qatar at 4.8. per cent. In contrast to 2020, the military burden fell in most countries of the Middle East in 2021. This was mostly due to a rapid economic recovery from pandemic-related disruptions. The largest fall in military burden was in Saudi Arabia, where it dropped 2.6 percentage points.

Saudi Arabia's estimated military expenditure in 2021 was $55.6 billion, which is a fall of 17 per cent compared with 2020. The decrease came amid reports that Saudi Arabia had begun to withdraw its military forces from Yemen, but the Saudi Arabian government rejected the claims and stated that the troops were simply being redeployed.[117] Saudi Arabia's military spending has followed a downward trend since 2015, largely due to a sharp fall in oil prices that put its economy under strain.[118] Saudi Arabia's economy showed signs of recovery as oil prices began to rise in 2020–21, but this has not yet led to a corresponding increase in military spending.[119]

The cut in Saudi Arabian spending in 2021 was the largest since 2016, when military spending fell by 28 per cent. Public expenditure as a whole has been decreasing, yet military spending as a share of public expenditure has also declined: it fell from 23 per cent in 2019 to 21 per cent in 2021. Budget lines such as education, health and social development have been relatively stable as a share of public expenditure. Despite shrinking, military spending is still the largest proportion of Saudi Arabia's public expenditure.

Iran's planned military spending rose for the first time in four years in 2021, to $24.6 billion. The annual increase of 11 per cent was approved despite Iran's continuing economic problems due to the effects of many years of sanctions: US sanctions on Iran's oil exports have severely affected government revenue, resulting in a soaring budget deficit.[120] The rise in military spending coincided with continued strained relations with the United States, the Arab states of the Gulf and Israel, and its proxy war in Syria.[121] The increase also took

---

[117] El Yaakoubi, A. and Mukhshaf, R., 'Saudi-led coalition says troops redeploying in Yemen, not withdrawing', Reuters, 11 Nov. 2021. On the armed conflict in Yemen see chapter 6, section V, in this volume.

[118] On the relationship between oil revenue and military expenditure see Tian and Lopes da Silva (note 10).

[119] Nereim, V., 'Saudi Arabia's economic growth stays near decade-high as oil powers rebound', Bloomberg, 10 Feb. 2022.

[120] Rome, H., 'Iran in 2021: The economy', Iran Primer, US Institute of Peace, 15 Dec. 2021.

[121] Al-Monitor, 'Gulf states cooperate on defense, Iran and economic integration at summit', 15 Dec. 2021; and Akbarzadeh, S., Gourlay, W. and Ehteshami, A., 'Iranian proxies in the Syrian conflict: Tehran's "forward-defence" in action', *Journal of Strategic Studies*, 4 Jan. 2020, pp. 12–14. On developments in Iranian–US relations see also chapter 6, section I, in this volume.

place as Iran adopted a more assertive diplomatic stance in the negotiations concerning the Joint Comprehensive Plan of Action (JCPOA) on its nuclear programme.[122]

The budget of the Islamic Revolutionary Guard Corps (IRGC) continued to grow in 2021. The increase of 14 per cent took spending on the IRGC to 38 per cent of Iran's total military spending. This followed a 15 per cent increase in 2020 compared to 2019, when the IRGC budget was 34 per cent of Iran's total military budget. The rising trend will probably continue: the proposed budget for 2022 foresees a 141 per cent nominal increase for the IRGC budget (in the context of a high inflation rate).

In 2021 Israel's military spending rose 3.1 per cent to $24.3 billion. In addition, Israel receives military aid from the USA, which in 2021 totalled $3.8 billion, including $500 million for missile defence.[123] This continued a streak of growth since 2010, amounting to a 39 per cent rise. The most recent increase continues the 3–4 per cent annual growth projections of the 2030 Security Concept, a multi-year military modernization programme presented in 2018.[124] It also allows Israel to pursue the 2019 Momentum Plan, a military programme aiming to strengthen the capabilities of the armed forces, the Israel Defense Forces (IDF).

Israel spent two years without a properly approved state budget because of a political stand-off in the Knesset, the parliament. As a result, military spending in 2021 and 2020 was based on the 2019 budget with top-up allocations. In 2021 the Knesset finally agreed to a budget that projects a significant rise in military spending for 2022.[125] This suggests that the change in government following elections in 2021 will not affect Israel's commitment to ongoing military modernization programmes nor does it represent a shift in threat perception.[126] The Israeli government continued to express severe concerns about Iran's nuclear capabilities in 2021.[127] A senior official of the Mossad, Israel's national intelligence agency, affirmed that the country would do 'whatever it takes' to prevent Iran from building a nuclear weapon.[128]

In 2021 Qatar's military spending was $11.6 billion, equivalent to 4.8 per cent of Qatari GDP. Qatar's military spending accounted for 22 per cent of the state budget, the largest share among all sectors. Health, for example, took

---

[122] On developments in the JCPOA see chapter 11, section II, in this volume.

[123] US military aid is accounted for in US military spending, not Israel's (see box 8.2 in section I). Sharp, J. M., *US Foreign Aid to Israel*, US Congressional Research Service (CRS) Report for Congress RL33222 (US Congress, CRS: Washington, DC, 18 Feb. 2022), p. 2.

[124] Tian et al. (note 107), pp. 251–52; and Israeli Prime Minister's Office, 'PM Netanyahu presents "2030 Security Concept" to the Cabinet', 15 Aug. 2018.

[125] Ahronheim, A., 'Israel finally has a budget, and so does the IDF—analysis', *Jerusalem Post*, 4 Nov. 2021.

[126] Al Jazeera, 'Israel swears in new government, ending Netanyahu's 12-year rule', 13 June 2021.

[127] Knell, Y., 'Iran nuclear programme: Threat of Israeli strike grows', BBC News, 23 Nov. 2021.

[128] Kube, C. and De Luce, D., 'Tensions rising between US and Iran; New Year's seen as potential flashpoint', NBC News, 20 Dec. 2021.

8.5 per cent. SIPRI does not have military expenditure data for Qatar for the period 2011–20 but estimates that Qatari spending increased by 434 per cent between 2010 and 2021. This is by far the steepest rise among members of the Gulf Cooperation Council (GCC) for the period.[129] During those years, Qatar sent troops to assist the Libyan rebels who overthrew the regime of Muammar Gaddafi; backed the Syrian opposition; and expanded its armed forces and modernized its military equipment with several arms-import programmes.[130]

Turkey's military spending fell for the second consecutive year in 2021, by 4.4 per cent to $15.5 billion. The decline took place amid a severe currency and debt crisis that has hit the country since 2018.[131] Despite the recent cuts, Turkish military spending grew by 63 per cent in the decade 2012–21. The surge coincided with Turkey's expanding foreign policy engagement in the Middle East and North Africa.[132] Another driver of Turkish military spending has been the pursuit of military procurement autarky by 2023.[133] The Defence Industry Support Fund received a little over a fifth of Turkey's total military spending in 2021, slightly higher than in 2020. This fund was created in 1985 to help develop Turkey's arms industry through direct support to a wide range of indigenous firms and enterprises in the defence sector.[134] However, it remains unclear how the recent cuts in military spending will affect Turkey's aim of reducing its reliance on arms imports.

[129] Data for the UAE is available only until 2014.

[130] Wezeman, P. D. and Kuimova, A., 'Military spending and arms imports by Iran, Saudi Arabia, Qatar and the UAE', SIPRI Fact Sheet, May 2019.

[131] Kubilay, M. M., 'Turkey's self-made currency crisis', Middle East Institute, 3 Dec. 2021.

[132] On Turkey's involvement in the armed conflicts in the Middle East and North Africa see chapter 6, sections II and IV, in this volume.

[133] Kurç, Ç., 'Between defence autarky and dependency: The dynamics of Turkish defence industrialization', *Defence Studies*, vol. 17, no. 3 (2017).

[134] Özlü, H., 'The foundation and development of Turkey's defense industry in the context of national security strategy', *Perceptions*, vol. 26, no. 2 (autumn–winter 2021), p. 229; and *Daily Sabah*, 'Turkey creates defense industry investment fund', 13 June 2021.

III. Arms-producing and military services companies, 2020

ALEXANDRA MARKSTEINER, LUCIE BÉRAUD-SUDREAU, NAN TIAN,
DIEGO LOPES DA SILVA AND ALEXANDRA KUIMOVA

The combined arms sales of the world's 100 largest arms-producing and military services companies (the SIPRI Top 100) were $531 billion in 2020.[1] This represents an increase of 1.3 per cent on their arms sales in 2019.[2] This increase continued an uninterrupted upward trend since 2015 (see figure 8.6 and table 8.6), roughly correlating with rising global military expenditure levels. The arms sales of the Top 100 were 17 per cent higher in 2020 than in 2015 (the first year for which SIPRI included Chinese firms in its ranking).

This section reviews developments in the arms production and military services industry in 2020 (the most recent year for which consistent data on arms sales of the Top 100 is available). It first assesses the effects of the Covid-19 pandemic on arms production before reviewing developments in the major arms-producing countries and regions. 'Arms sales' are defined here as sales of military goods and services to military customers domestically and abroad.[3]

The effects of the Covid-19 pandemic on arms production

Arms production around the world was largely resilient against the shock of the Covid-19 pandemic and the resulting economic downturn. While the global economy contracted by 3.1 per cent in 2020, the total arms sales of the Top 100 and military spending both increased.

This resilience can be attributed to at least three key factors. First, the arms industry, like many other economic sectors, benefited from expansionary financial policies in 2020, the first year of the pandemic. Military manufacturers were largely shielded by sustained government demand for military goods and services. Second, some states rolled out specific measures to mitigate the effects of government-mandated lockdowns on their arms-producing companies, such as accelerated payments or order schedules. Third, because arms-procurement contracts usually span several years, many

---

[1] Unless otherwise stated, all financial figures—including arms sales figures—in this section are presented in nominal (current) 2020 US dollars, while percentage changes and shares are in constant 2020 US dollars (i.e. in real terms). For further detail on the SIPRI Top 100 see the SIPRI Arms Industry Database, Dec. 2021.

[2] This change of 1.3% refers to the arms sales in 2019 and 2020 of the 100 companies in the Top 100 for 2020. Table 8.6 shows the change of 0.8% in the sales of the Top 100 for 2020 compared to the slightly different set of companies in the Top 100 for 2019. The latter figure is lower since, by definition, the companies that left the Top 100 between 2019 and 2020 would have had a lower rate of change in arms sales than those that joined.

[3] For further details see SIPRI Arms Industry Database, 'Sources and methods', [n.d.].

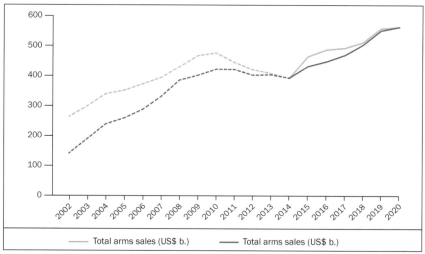

Figure 8.6. Total arms sales of companies in the SIPRI Top 100, 2002–20

Note: There was a series break between 2014 and 2015, when Chinese companies were first included in the data set. The arms sales of the Top 100 for 2015 (including Chinese companies) were 14 per cent higher than those of the Top 100 for 2014 (which exclude Chinese companies) primarily due to this change. However, even if Chinese arms companies are excluded, total Top 100 arms sales would still have increased by 0.8 per cent between those years.

Source: SIPRI Arms Industry Database, Dec. 2021.

arms-producing companies were able to capitalize on a backlog of orders placed before the outbreak of the health crisis.

However, despite these and other factors, global arms production was not fully immune to the impact of the pandemic. In many cases, measures taken to slow the spread of the virus disrupted supply chains and delayed deliveries. The pandemic also affected restructuring, as exemplified by the cancelled merger of Hexcel and Woodward. These two United States-based companies, which both produce components for military aircraft, had agreed to merge in January 2020. They abandoned the effort in April, citing the disruptions and uncertainties caused by the pandemic.[4] Had the merger taken place as planned, the resulting company would probably have entered the Top 100 in 2020.

During the first year of the Covid-19 pandemic, many companies involved in both the civilian and military sectors increased their arms sales as a proportion of their total sales. This could have meant that their military sales grew faster or declined at a slower rate than their civilian sales, or that military sales remained stable while civilian sales fell. This illustrates the relative resilience of the demand for military goods and services, which—even

[4] Hexcel, 'Woodward and Hexcel announce mutual termination of merger agreement', Press release, 6 Apr. 2020.

Table 8.6. Trends in arms sales of companies in the SIPRI Top 100, 2011–20

	2011	2012	2013	2014	2015	2016	2017	2018	2019	2020
Arms sales in current prices and exchange rates										
Total ($b.)	420	405	406	398	428	441	458	484	521	531
Change (%)		–3.6	0.2	–2.0	..	3.0	3.9	5.7	7.6	1.9
Arms sales in constant (2020) prices and exchange rates										
Total ($b.)	439	419	410	397	454	471	476	491	527	531
Change (%)		–4.6	–2.1	–3.2	..	3.7	1.1	3.2	7.3	0.8

|| = series break.

Note: Figures for each year refer to the companies in the SIPRI Top 100 in that year, so the data covers a different set of companies each year. On the series break between 2014 and 2015 see the notes to figure 8.6.

Source: SIPRI Arms Industry Database, Dec. 2021.

before the pandemic—was somewhat insulated from the business cycles experienced in the commercial sector.

Regional and national developments in the Top 100

The United States

With 41 arms companies, the United States hosted the highest number of companies ranked in the Top 100 for 2020 of any country worldwide (see table 8.7). Together, their arms sales amounted to $285 billion, an increase of 1.9 per cent compared with 2019. US companies accounted for 54 per cent of the combined arms sales of the Top 100.

Since 2018, the top five arms companies in the ranking have all been based in the USA. Lockheed Martin, by far the largest arms company in the world, has occupied the top rank every year since 2009. In 2020 its revenue from arms sales totalled $58.2 billion, or 11 per cent of the Top 100's total arms sales. Of the companies included in the 2020 ranking, Lockheed Martin recorded the largest absolute year-on-year growth in arms sales, of $4.2 billion (or 7.7 per cent in real terms). Raytheon Technologies is the world's second largest arms company, with arms sales of $36.8 billion in 2020. It was formed by the merger of Raytheon and United Technologies Corporation (UTC) in 2020. The 2020 arms sales of the merged company were 5.7 per cent lower than the combined (pro forma) arms sales of these two firms in 2019. Boeing, one of the world's largest military aerospace manufacturers, ranked third. Due to the Covid-19 pandemic and the impact of government-mandated lockdowns and travel restrictions on commercial aviation, Boeing's total sales fell by $19.6 billion in 2020. Its arms sales also decreased, by 5.9 per cent from $34.1 billion in 2019 to $32.1 billion in 2020. Northrop Grumman ranked fourth, with arms sales of $30.4 billion or 5.7 per cent of the Top 100 total.

Table 8.7. Regional and national shares of arms sales for companies in the SIPRI Top 100, 2019–20

Arms sales figures are in constant (2020) US$. Figures for 2019 refer to the companies in the Top 100 for 2020, not the slightly different set of companies in the Top 100 for 2019. Changes between 2019 and 2020 are in real terms, based on constant (2020) US$. Figures may not add up to the given totals because of the conventions of rounding.

No. of companies	Region/ Country[a]	Arms sales ($m.)		Change in arms sales, 2019–20 (%)	Share of Top 100 sales, 2020 (%)
		2020	2019		
41	United States	285 040	279 708	1.9	54
26	Europe	109 280	108 227	1.0	21
7	United Kingdom	37 490	35 289	6.2	7.1
6	France	24 740	26 807	–7.7	4.7
2	Trans-European[b]	16 040	15 463	3.7	3.0
2	Italy	13 820	13 497	2.4	2.6
4	Germany	8 910	8 799	1.3	1.7
1	Sweden	3 390	3 302	2.6	0.6
1	Poland	1 490	1 687	–12	0.3
1	Ukraine	1 320	1 295	2.0	0.2
1	Norway	900	776	16	0.2
1	Spain	1 180	1 310	–10	0.2
5	China	66 750	65 761	1.5	13
9	Russia	26 360	28 180	–6.5	5.0
19	Other arms producers	43 070	41 643	3.4	8.1
3	Israel	10 440	10 108	3.3	2.0
5	Japan	9 880	9 624	2.7	1.9
4	South Korea	6 500	6 216	4.6	1.2
3	India	6 500	6 390	1.7	1.2
1	United Arab Emirates	4 750	4 679	1.5	0.9
1	Turkey	2 200	1 966	12	0.4
1	Singapore	1 890	1 665	14	0.4
1	Canada	910	996	–8.6	0.2
100	**Total**	**530 500**	**523 518**	**1.3**	**100**

[a] Figures for a country or region refer to the arms sales of the Top 100 companies headquartered in that country or region, including those by subsidiaries in another country or region. They do not reflect the sales of arms actually produced in that country or region.

[b] The 2 companies classified as 'trans-European' are Airbus and MBDA.

Source: SIPRI Arms Industry Database, Dec. 2021.

General Dynamics was in fifth position, with arms sales of $25.8 billion, equivalent to 4.9 per cent of the total.

To reinforce its military advantage and hedge against perceived threats emanating from what it considers to be its strategic competitors (i.e. China and Russia), the USA has been investing more heavily in research and development and the procurement of next-generation weapon systems.[5] This has prompted a wave of mergers and acquisitions in the US arms industry in recent years, with some companies seeking to broaden their product portfolios to gain a competitive edge when bidding for contracts.

The all-stock merger-of-equals between Raytheon and UTC, which was finalized in April 2020, was one of the largest mergers in the history of the arms industry. The multibillion-dollar merger of L3 Technologies and Harris was completed a year earlier, in June 2019. The resulting company, L3Harris Technologies, ranked 10th in 2020. The trend continued in 2021 with the merger of Peraton and Perspecta as well as the acquisition of FLIR Systems by Teledyne Technologies (ranked 89th in 2020) for $8.2 billion.

The trend of mergers and acquisitions is particularly pronounced in the space sector. For example, in 2018 Northrop Grumman acquired Orbital ATK, a space systems contractor (ranked 47th in 2017), for approximately $9.2 billion. The acquisition by KBR (ranked 43rd in 2020) of Centauri, a provider of space and directed energy capabilities, was finalized in October 2020.

However, the US Department of Defense has become concerned about mergers and acquisitions in the arms industry, signalling that the US government may put an end to this trend.[6] For instance, although Lockheed Martin announced plans in 2020 to buy competitor Aerojet Rocketdyne (ranked 75th) for $4.4 billion, the acquisition was later blocked by a US government regulatory agency.[7]

China

The combined arms sales of the five Chinese companies included in the Top 100 ranking amounted to an estimated $66.8 billion in 2020—1.5 per cent more than the same five companies in 2019. With a 13 per cent share of total Top 100 arms sales, Chinese arms companies in the Top 100 had the second highest total arms sales in 2020, behind US firms. The rise of China as a major arms producer has been driven by its aim to become more self-reliant in weapon production and by the implementation of ambitious modernization

---

[5] Tian, N., Lopes da Silva, D. and Marksteiner, A., 'Global developments in military expenditure, 2020', *SIPRI Yearbook 2021*. On a similar trend in 2021 see section II.

[6] Lopez, C. T., 'DOD report: Consolidation of defense industrial base poses risks to national security', US Department of Defense, 16 Feb. 2022; and US Office of the Under Secretary of Defense for Acquisition and Sustainment, *State of Competition within the Defense Industrial Base* (Department of Defense: Arlington, VA, Feb. 2022). See also Béraud-Sudreau, L., 'COVID-19: A new wave of European arms industry consolidation?', SIPRI Essay, 7 Sep. 2020.

[7] Lockheed Martin, 'Lockheed Martin terminates agreement to acquire Aerojet Rocketdyne', Press release, 13 Feb. 2022.

programmes.[8] All five Chinese arms companies ranked among the top 20, with three in the top 10.

With estimated arms sales of $17.9 billion in 2020, China North Industries Group Corporation (NORINCO, ranked 7th) is China's largest arms-producing company. The arms sales of NORINCO, a land systems specialist, rose by 12 per cent in 2020, in part because the company deepened its involvement in emerging technologies and contributed to the development of the BeiDou military–civil satellite navigation system. Estimated arms sales of the Aviation Industry Corporation of China (AVIC, ranked 8th), China's main military aircraft producer, declined by 1.4 per cent in 2020 to $17.0 billion. However, the decrease is probably due to exchange rate fluctuations, as its arms sales increased in nominal terms. The third Chinese company with arms sales high enough to rank in the top 10 was China Electronics Technology Group Corporation (CETC, ranked 9th), the country's leading producer of military electronics. At $14.6 billion, CETC's arms sales fell by 6.0 per cent in 2020. China Aerospace Science and Industry Corporation (CASIC, ranked 12th), one of China's leading producers of missile and space systems, also recorded a drop in arms sales. CASIC's arms sales of $11.9 billion in 2020 were 2.8 per cent lower than in 2019. The fifth Chinese company in the Top 100 was China South Industries Group Corporation (CSGC, ranked 20th), which manufactures military vehicles. CSGC's arms sales rose by 13 per cent in 2020 to $5.4 billion.

All the Chinese companies in the Top 100 are state-owned enterprises that produce both military and civilian products. Most of the revenue generated by these five companies is derived from civilian sales. Arms sales as a share of total sales range from 16 per cent for CSGC to 43 per cent for CETC.

Europe

There were 26 European companies ranked in the Top 100 in 2020. Together, they accounted for 21 per cent of total Top 100 arms sales or $109 billion, up by 1.0 per cent compared with 2019. Of these firms, seven are headquartered in the United Kingdom, six in France, four in Germany, two in Italy and one each in Norway, Poland, Spain, Sweden and Ukraine. A further two, Airbus and MBDA, are categorized as 'trans-European' since their ownership and control structures are spread across more than one European country.

The arms sales of the seven companies based in the UK amounted to $37.5 billion in 2020, equivalent to 7.1 per cent of the Top 100 total. Their arms sales were 6.2 per cent higher in 2020 than in 2019. BAE Systems (ranked

---

[8] Chinese State Council, *China's National Defense in the New Era* (State Council Information Office: Beijing, July 2019); and Cheung, T., 'Keeping up with the *Jundui*: Reforming the Chinese defense acquisition, technology, and industrial system', eds P. C. Saunders et al., *Chairman Xi Remakes the PLA: Assessing Chinese Military Reforms* (National Defense University Press: Washington, DC, 2019).

6th) was the only European arms company to rank in the top 10. Its arms sales increased by 6.6 per cent to $24.0 billion in 2020. Almost half of this, or $11.9 billion, was from sales made by BAE System's US subsidiary. Two of the British companies in the Top 100 recorded decreases in arms sales in 2020: the arms sales of Babcock International (ranked 39th) decreased by 4.6 per cent, while those of Meggitt (ranked 95th) fell by 7.9 per cent. The largest relative increase in arms sales among British companies was recorded by Melrose Industries (ranked 69th), a producer of aerospace components. Its arms sales grew by 41 per cent in 2020 to $1.5 billion, which the company attributed to high demand for its military aerospace engines.[9]

With combined arms sales of $24.7 billion, the six arms companies based in France accounted for 4.7 per cent of total Top 100 arms sales. This represents a decrease of 7.7 per cent between 2019 and 2020. The arms sales of four of these six companies decreased. The arms sales of Thales (ranked 14th), the largest French arms company, fell by 5.8 per cent in 2020 to $9.1 billion. Naval Group (ranked 31st) recorded a drop in arms sales of 11 per cent to $3.8 billion. Both Thales and Naval Group ascribed their losses to operational interruptions caused by the Covid-19 pandemic.[10] The largest percentage decrease in arms sales of any company in the Top 100 was reported by Dassault Aviation Group (ranked 32nd). Its arms sales declined by 37 per cent, mainly due to a sharp drop in export deliveries of its Rafale combat aircraft in 2020 compared with 2019, when deliveries peaked. Safran (ranked 25th) recorded the largest percentage increase in arms sales among French companies in the Top 100. Its arms sales grew by 24 per cent to reach $4.5 billion in 2020, which the company attributed to increased sales of sighting and navigation systems.[11]

The combined arms sales of the two trans-European firms ranked in the Top 100 were $16.0 billion in 2020 or 3.0 per cent of the Top 100 total. Airbus (ranked 11th) reported arms sales of $12.0 billion in 2020, up by 5.7 per cent on 2019. The arms sales of MBDA (ranked 30th), a joint venture specializing in missiles, decreased by 1.7 per cent in 2020 to $4.1 billion.

With $13.8 billion in total arms sales, the two ranked companies based in Italy accounted for 2.6 per cent of the Top 100 total. Arms sales by Leonardo (ranked 13th) were $11.2 billion in 2020—a decrease of 1.5 per cent on 2019. Fincantieri (ranked 47th), a shipbuilder, recorded a 23 per cent increase in arms sales in 2020. Significant fluctuations in annual arms sales are common among shipbuilding companies because of long production timelines.

---

[9] Melrose Industries, *Annual Report 2020* (Melrose: Birmingham, Mar. 2021), p. 15.
[10] Thales, 'Investor meeting', Nov. 2021, p. 36; and Naval Group, *Rapport financier 2020* [Financial report 2020] (Naval Group: Paris, Mar. 2021), p. 6.
[11] Safran, 'Full year 2020 earnings', 15 Feb. 2021, p. 9.

The arms sales of the four ranked companies headquartered in Germany reached $8.9 billion in 2020, equivalent to 1.7 per cent of the total for the Top 100. This was a slight increase of 1.3 per cent compared with 2019. Rhein-metall, the largest German arms company, ranked 27th with arms sales of $4.2 billion. This represented a year-on-year growth of 5.2 per cent, explained in part by higher sales of armoured fighting and transportation vehicles. The arms sales of Hensoldt (ranked 78th), a military electronics specialist, also grew in 2020, by 7.9 per cent. The arms sales of the other two German companies declined in 2020: those of shipbuilder ThyssenKrupp (ranked 55th) by 3.7 per cent and those of Krauss-Maffei Wegmann (ranked 70th), a land systems manufacturer, by 7.5 per cent.

The five other European companies listed in the Top 100 for 2020 were Saab of Sweden (ranked 36th), PGZ of Poland (ranked 68th), UkrOboronProm of Ukraine (ranked 77th), Navantia of Spain (ranked 84th) and Kongsberg Gruppen of Norway (ranked 100th).

The Russian Federation

The nine Russian companies in the ranking accounted for 5.0 per cent of total Top 100 arms sales in 2020.[12] Their combined arms sales fell by 6.5 per cent to $26.4 billion in 2020. This marked a continuation of the downward trend observed since 2017, when the total arms sales of these same nine firms peaked at $31.5 billion. Russian arms sales fell in 2020 even though the Russian government stated that it had provided assistance to the arms industry in order to dampen the negative effects of the Covid-19 pandemic.

Russian firms recorded some of the sharpest declines in arms sales among the Top 100. Arms sales of Almaz-Antey (ranked 17th) decreased by 31 per cent, of Russian Helicopters (ranked 81st) by 13 per cent and of United Ship-building Corporation (ranked 33rd) by 11 per cent. This downturn can be attributed to several factors. The foremost factor was the ending of the State Armament Programme (Gosudarstvennuyu Programmu Vooruzheniya, GPV) for 2011–20, a major modernization plan for the Russian armed forces.[13] The funding allocated to arms procurement in the follow-up GPV, for the period up to 2027, is lower in real terms.[14] Furthermore, some arms export deliveries were delayed due to the pandemic, which may have contributed to the overall decline in Russian arms exports in 2020, thus driving down arms company revenues.

[12] Ten Russian companies ranked in the Top 100 for 2018. The 10th company, High Precision Systems (which ranked 46th in 2018), cannot be ranked in the Top 100 for 2019–20 due to a lack of reliable data.

[13] Cooper, J., *Russia's State Armament Programme to 2020: A Quantitative Assessment of Implementation 2011–2015*, Swedish Defence Research Agency (FOI) Report no. FOI-R--4239--SE (FOI: Stockholm, Mar. 2016).

[14] Conolly, R. and Boulègue, M., *Russia's New State Armament Programme Implications for the Russian Armed Forces and Military Capabilities to 2027* (Chatham House: London, May 2018).

Despite these factors, some Russian companies increased their arms sales significantly in 2020. For example, United Aircraft Corporation (ranked 21st) increased its arms sales by 16 per cent, while those of KRET (ranked 58th) grew by 22 per cent and those of Russian Electronics (ranked 71st) by 39 per cent.

Other arms-producing countries and their companies

Collectively, the arms sales of the 19 companies in the Top 100 based outside the USA, China, Russia and the rest of Europe totalled $43.1 billion in 2020— an increase of 3.4 per cent on 2019. This represented 8.1 per cent of the total arms sales of the Top 100. Five of these companies are based in Japan, four in the Republic of Korea (South Korea), three each in Israel and India, and one each in Canada, Singapore, Turkey and the United Arab Emirates (UAE).

Together, the three companies based in Israel had arms sales of $10.4 billion or 2.0 per cent of the Top 100 total. Their arms sales increased by 3.3 per cent compared with 2019. The arms sales of Elbit Systems (ranked 28th) were $4.2 billion in 2020, up by 1.4 per cent on 2019. This growth was mainly due to increased sales of military aircraft equipment and the acquisition of the Harris Night Vision business from L3Harris Technologies.[15] The arms sales of Israel Aerospace Industries (ranked 35th) grew by 11 per cent in 2020 to reach $3.5 billion. Rafael's arms sales fell by 2.2 per cent to $2.7 billion in 2020.

The total arms sales of the five companies headquartered in Japan was $9.9 billion, equivalent to 1.9 per cent of the total for the Top 100.[16] Their combined arms sales rose by 2.7 per cent in 2020 despite decreases by three companies: Kawasaki Heavy Industries (ranked 53rd), IHI Corporation (ranked 90th) and Mitsubishi Electric (ranked 97th). These reductions were outweighed by substantial increases in the arms sales of Mitsubishi Heavy Industries (ranked 26th) and Fujitsu (ranked 76th). The arms sales of Mitsubishi Heavy Industries grew by 11 per cent in 2020 to reach $4.4 billion, while Fujitsu's were up by 23 per cent to $1.3 billion.

With combined arms sales of $6.5 billion in 2020, the four companies based in South Korea accounted for 1.2 per cent of the Top 100 total.[17] Their arms sales were 4.6 per cent higher in 2020 than in 2019. The arms sales of three of these companies increased in 2020. The arms sales of the largest South Korean arms company, Hanwha Aerospace (ranked 50th), rose marginally (by 0.3 per cent). The arms sales of LIG Nex1 (ranked 73rd) increased by 9.6 per cent to reach $1.4 billion. This company only sells military products and does not appear to have been affected by the pandemic. Hanwha Corporation (ranked

---

[15] Elbit Systems, Annual report for 2020, Form 20-F, US Securities and Exchange Commission (SEC), 24 Mar. 2021, p. F-18.

[16] Data on Japanese companies were provided by the Mitsubishi Research Institute.

[17] Data on South Korean companies were provided by the Korea Institute for Industrial Economics and Trade (KIET).

85th) also recorded a significant growth in arms sales (19 per cent), driven by its guided weapons business.

Three companies based in India were included in the 2020 ranking. Their total arms sales of $6.5 billion were 1.7 per cent higher in 2020 than in 2019 and accounted for 1.2 per cent of the Top 100 total. The arms sales of Hindustan Aeronautics (ranked 42nd) rose by 1.5 per cent and those of Bharat Electronics (ranked 66th) rose by 4.0 per cent. Indian Ordnance Factories (ranked 60th) increased its arms sales marginally (by 0.2 per cent). Domestic procurement helped to shield Indian companies from the negative economic consequences of the pandemic. In 2020 the Indian government announced a phased ban on imports of more than 100 different types of military equipment to support domestic companies and enhance self-reliance in arms production.[18]

Edge (ranked 23rd) is a UAE-based conglomerate created in 2019 through the consolidation of 25 smaller entities. Its estimated arms sales reached $4.8 billion in 2020. Turkey-based Aselsan (ranked 51st) had arms sales of $2.2 billion in 2020, an increase of 12 per cent on 2019. The arms sales of Singapore-based ST Engineering (ranked 61st) amounted to $1.9 billion in 2020. They were up by 14 per cent compared with 2019. CAE (ranked 98th), a flight-simulator company headquartered in Canada, had arms sales of $910 million in 2020, a decrease of 8.6 per cent on 2019.

[18] Indian Ministry of Defence, 'MOD's big push to Amanirbhar Bharat initiative; Import embargo on 101 items beyond given timelines to boost indigenisation of defence production', Press release, 9 Aug. 2020.

9. International arms transfers

Overview

The volume of international transfers of major arms in 2017–21 was 4.6 per cent lower than in 2012–16 and 3.9 per cent higher than in 2007–11. The volume of transfers in 2017–21 was among the highest since the end of the cold war, but was still around 35 per cent lower than the totals for 1977–81 and 1982–86, when arms transfers peaked. States' arms acquisitions, often from foreign suppliers, are largely driven by armed conflict and political tensions (see section I). There are strong indications that tensions are increasing in most regions and it is thus likely that there will be more demand for major arms in the coming years, much of which will be fulfilled by international transfers.

SIPRI has identified 60 states as exporters of major arms in 2017–21, but most are minor exporters. The 25 largest suppliers accounted for 99 per cent of the total volume of exports, and the five largest suppliers in the period—the United States, Russia, France, China and Germany—accounted for 77 per cent of the total volume of exports (see section II). Since 1950, the USA and Russia (or the Soviet Union before 1992) have consistently been by far the largest suppliers. However, the USA's arms exports were 108 per cent higher than Russia's in 2017–21, compared with 34 per cent higher in 2012–16, and the gap is likely to increase. In 2017–21 the USA's arms exports accounted for 39 per cent of the global total and were 14 per cent higher than in 2012–16. In contrast, Russia's arms exports decreased by 26 per cent and its share of the global total dropped from 24 per cent in 2012–16 to 19 per cent in 2017–21. Exports by France, the third largest supplier, grew by 59 per cent between 2012–16 and 2017–21, while China's and Germany's exports decreased by 31 per cent and 19 per cent respectively.

SIPRI has identified 163 states as importers of major arms in 2017–21. The five largest arms importers were India, Saudi Arabia, Egypt, Australia and China, which together accounted for 38 per cent of total arms imports (see section III). The region that received the largest volume of major arms supplies in 2017–21 was Asia and Oceania, accounting for 43 per cent of the total, followed by the Middle East, which received 32 per cent, Europe (13 per cent), Africa (5.8 per cent) and the Americas (5.5 per cent). Between 2012–16 and 2017–21, the flow of arms to Europe (19 per cent) and the Middle East (2.8 per cent) increased, while flows to Africa (–34 per cent), the Americas (–36 per cent) and Asia and Oceania (–4.7 per cent) decreased.

Most of the 163 importers are directly involved in armed conflict or in tensions with other states in which the imported major arms play an important role.

Many of the exporters are direct stakeholders or participants in at least some of the conflicts and tensions, which partly explains why they are willing to supply arms, even when the supply may seem to contradict their stated arms export policies.

While SIPRI data on arms transfers does not represent their financial value, many arms-exporting states do publish figures on the financial value of their arms exports (see section IV). This data is not consistent but gives a rough indication of the financial aspect of arms exports. Based on this data, SIPRI estimates that the total value of the global arms trade was at least US$112 billion in 2020 (the most recent year for which financial data is available), compared with $87 billion (in constant 2020 US dollars) in 2011. The total value of the arms trade in 2020 was about 0.5 per cent of the total value of global international trade in 2020.

SIEMON T. WEZEMAN

I. Developments in arms transfers, 2017–21

SIEMON T. WEZEMAN, ALEXANDRA KUIMOVA AND PIETER D. WEZEMAN

The volume of international transfers of major arms in 2017–21 was 4.6 per cent lower than in 2012–16, but was 3.9 per cent higher than in 2007–11 and 30 per cent higher than in 2002–2006 when arms transfers were at their lowest volume for any five-year period since 1952–56 (see figure 9.1).[1] However, the total volume in 2017–21 was still around 35 per cent lower than the peak reached in the periods 1977–81 and 1982–86, at the height of the cold war.

Despite a 4.7 per cent drop in imports of major arms by states in Asia and Oceania between 2012–16 and 2017–21, Asia and Oceania remained the region with the highest volume of arms imports and accounted for 43 per cent of the global total. Arms imports to Africa (–34 per cent) and the Americas (–36 per cent) also fell over the same period and these regions' shares of total global arms transfers decreased. In contrast, the flow of arms to states in the Middle East increased by 2.8 per cent between 2012–16 and 2017–21, and the region's share of the global total rose from 30 per cent to 32 per cent. This is a higher share than in any of the seven other consecutive five-year periods since 1982–86. There was also a marked increase (of 19 per cent) in arms transfers to states in Europe, raising the region's share of the global total from 10 per cent in 2012–16 to 13 per cent in 2017–21.

The five largest arms exporters in 2017–21 were the United States, Russia, France, China and Germany (see section II). The five states that imported the most arms in the period were India, Saudi Arabia, Egypt, Australia and China (see section III).

While many states have recently placed orders for advanced major arms or plan to make such orders in the near future, the information available remains limited in most cases. This makes it extremely difficult to provide even very rough predictions of global trends in arms transfers, no matter whether these are near- or long-term forecasts. Nonetheless, the indications—especially the perception among many states that security threats are increasing (which acts as a driver of arms transfers) and the continued growth in military spending (which acts as an enabler)—suggest that there will be more, rather than less, demand for major arms in the coming years. Much of this demand will be met

---

[1] Except where indicated, the information on the arms deliveries and orders referred to in this section is taken from the SIPRI Arms Transfers Database. For a definition of 'major arms' and a description of how the volume of transfers is measured see box 9.1 in this section. Since year-on-year deliveries can fluctuate, SIPRI compares consecutive multi-year periods—normally five-year periods. This provides a more stable measure of trends in transfers of major arms. The figures here may differ from those in previous editions of the SIPRI Yearbook because the Arms Transfers Database is updated annually.

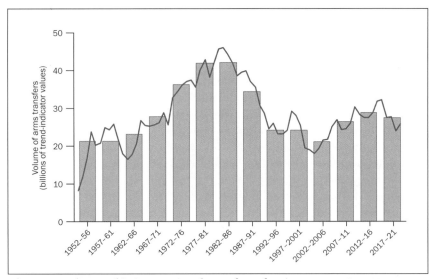

Figure 9.1. The trend in international transfers of major arms, 1952–2021

Note: The bar graph shows the average annual volume of arms transfers for five-year periods and the line graph shows the annual totals. See box 9.1 in this section for an explanation of the SIPRI trend-indicator value.

Source: SIPRI Arms Transfers Database, Mar. 2022.

by arms imports as many states are still unable to produce domestically all the major arms they believe they need.

Key developments in 2021 related to arms transfers

As was also the case in 2020, the Covid-19 pandemic had some direct and indirect effects on arms transfers in 2021.[2] For example, several exporters, importers and producers reported delays in some arms programmes as supply chains were disrupted or deliveries were rescheduled due to travel restrictions.[3] However, these problems seem to have had only a marginal impact on arms production and arms transfers in 2020 and 2021. One important reason for this is that most major arms delivered or planned for delivery in 2020–21 were ordered years earlier and in most cases production was well under way before the pandemic hit.

The indirect impact of the pandemic on arms transfers is less easy to determine. The pandemic led to a global economic downturn in 2020–21, but

---

[2] See also Wezeman, S., Kuimova, A. and Wezeman, P., 'International arms transfers and developments in arms production', *SIPRI Yearbook 2021*.

[3] See e.g. Capaccio, A., 'Lockheed reduces planned F-35s for 2022, citing Covid's impact', Bloomberg, 27 Sep. 2021; Nanuam, W., 'Navy chief will drop his submarine fund request', *Bangkok Post*, 7 Jan. 2022; and Manaranche, M., 'Australia delivers Austal-built Guardian-class patrol boat to Kiribati', Naval News, 18 June 2021.

this seems to have had only a limited effect on arms acquisitions.[4] Notably, despite the fact that the USA reportedly lowered its annual production targets for the next few years for the F-35 combat aircraft due to both the direct and indirect effects of the pandemic, the targets remained at a higher level than in previous years.[5] Thailand's postponement of an order for two submarines from China, valued at around US$700 million, was one of the few clear cases of a significant pandemic-related change to a planned acquisition.[6] Many states, by contrast, made major decisions about new arms import contracts in 2020 and 2021 (see section III).

Agreements or even orders for major arms do not, however, always lead to actual deliveries. This phenomenon was highlighted by several cases in 2021 where agreements for large orders of major arms were cancelled. These included an agreement between the United Arab Emirates (UAE) and the USA for F-35 combat aircraft, an Australian order for submarines from France, and Egyptian and Indonesian orders for Su-35 combat aircraft from Russia. In all these cases, the importer opted instead for similar types of arms from another supplier (see section III for more detail on all four cases).

The Australian case is notable for several reasons. The decision to cancel the order for French submarines and start negotiations with the USA and the United Kingdom for the acquisition of nuclear-powered submarines was at least partly aimed at strengthening Australia's alliance with those two states. It also raised issues related to the risk of nuclear proliferation since the submarines will probably use highly enriched uranium (HEU) as fuel. HEU can be used in nuclear weapon programmes. Australia does not plan to produce the nuclear fuel or process it after use; the reactors will instead have fuel installed to last for the lifetime of the submarines. Australia plans to keep the fuel under international safeguards to prevent diversion. However, other non-nuclear states may now perceive that the path is clear to follow the Australian example and acquire their own nuclear-powered submarines but with an indigenous and potentially unsafeguarded HEU fuel capability.[7]

---

[4] For further detail on military expenditure, including arms procurement spending, in 2021 see chapter 8 in this volume.

[5] Tirpak, J. A., 'New F-35 Lot 15-17 deal hung up on inflation, Covid-19 mitigation costs', *Air Force Magazine*, 26 Jan. 2022; and Lockheed Martin, 'Pentagon and Lockheed Martin agree to F-35 production baseline', News release, 27 Sep. 2021.

[6] Nanuam (note 3).

[7] Carlson, J., 'AUKUS nuclear-powered submarine deal: Non-proliferation aspects', Asia–Pacific Leadership Network, Commentary, 17 Sep. 2021; Tilemann, J., 'Nuclear submarines: Mitigating the proliferation impacts', Asia–Pacific Leadership Network, 22 Sep. 2021; Acton, J. M., 'Why the AUKUS submarine deal is bad for nonproliferation: And what to do about it', Carnegie Endowment for International Peace, Commentary, 21 Sep. 2021; and Center for Arms Control and Non-proliferation, 'Low-enriched uranium for naval reactors', Fact sheet, 8 Nov. 2021. For further detail on global stocks of HEU see chapter 10, section X, in this volume.

Box 9.1. Definitions and methodology for SIPRI data on international arms transfers

The SIPRI Arms Transfers Database contains information on deliveries of major arms to states, international organizations and non-state armed (i.e. rebel) groups from 1950 to 2021. A new set of data is published annually, replacing the data in earlier editions of the SIPRI Yearbook or other SIPRI publications.

Definitions

SIPRI's definition of 'transfer' includes sales, manufacturing licences, aid, gifts, and most loans or leases. The item must have a military purpose: the recipient must be the armed forces or paramilitary forces or intelligence agency of another country, a non-state armed group, or an international organization.

The SIPRI Arms Transfers Database only includes 'major arms', which are defined as (*a*) most aircraft, including unmanned aerial vehicles; (*b*) air defence missile systems and larger air defence guns; (*c*) air refuelling systems; (*d*) most armoured vehicles; (*e*) artillery over 100 millimetres in calibre; (*f*) engines for combat-capable aircraft and other larger aircraft, for combat ships and larger support ships, and for most armoured vehicles; (*g*) guided missiles, torpedoes, and most guided bombs and shells; (*h*) larger sensors (radars, sonars and many passive electronic sensors); (*i*) most ships; (*j*) larger ship-borne weapons (naval guns, missile launch systems and anti-submarine weapons); (*k*) reconnaissance satellites; and (*l*) most gun or missile-armed turrets for armoured vehicles.

In cases where an air refuelling system, engine, sensor, naval gun or other ship-borne system, or turret (items c, f, h, j and l) is fitted on a platform (vehicle, aircraft or ship), the transfer only appears as a separate entry in the database if the item comes from a different supplier from that of the platform.

The SIPRI trend-indicator value

SIPRI has developed a unique system for measuring the volume of transfers of major arms using a common unit, the trend-indicator value (TIV). The TIV is intended to represent the transfer of military resources. Each weapon has its own specific TIV. Second-hand and second-hand but significantly modernized arms are given a reduced TIV. SIPRI calculates the volume of transfers by multiplying the weapon-specific TIV with the number of arms delivered in a given year. SIPRI TIV figures do not represent the financial values of arms transfers.

Conflicts and tensions as drivers of arms transfers

Active armed conflicts and increasing tensions between states are arguably the main drivers of arms acquisitions by states. At least 5 of the top 10 importers of major arms in 2017–21 (India, Saudi Arabia, Egypt, Pakistan and the UAE) were engaged in armed conflicts in 2021. In some cases the conflicts were internal against rebel groups (e.g. Egypt and India), while others were either external in support of other states against rebel groups (e.g. Saudi Arabia and the UAE) or external against other states (e.g. India and Pakistan). All these conflicts involved the use of major arms, most of which were imported. Three other members of the top 10 (China, Japan and South Korea) were embroiled in intrastate tensions in 2021 where major arms were used as a show of force to indicate resolve (e.g. China in the South China Sea, and Japan and China in the East China Sea).

The link between arms acquisition on the one hand and conflict and tensions on the other is visible not just for the largest importers; most of the 163 states identified by SIPRI as recipients of major arms in 2017–21 were directly involved in an armed conflict or in tensions where imported major arms played a role. From the list of importers, it is also clear that the level of imports of major arms does not necessarily correspond to the level of conflict or tensions. For example, sub-Saharan states are generally among the smallest importers globally, often importing less advanced arms in very limited numbers; however, many of those states are involved in armed conflict in which the imported major arms play an important role. This is highlighted in section III in this chapter on arms importers. The only region relatively free from armed conflict and major intrastate tensions is South America, and SIPRI data shows a significant decrease in arms imports by states in that region in recent years.

Arms-exporting states are often direct or indirect participants in the conflicts or tensions affecting the states to which they supply major arms. This partly explains why some arms exporters are willing to supply arms (sometimes as aid) even when the supply may seem to contradict the exporter's stated arms export policies. Section II in this chapter on arms exporters provides several examples.

II. Developments among the suppliers of major arms, 2017–21

SIEMON T. WEZEMAN, ALEXANDRA KUIMOVA AND PIETER D. WEZEMAN

SIPRI has identified 60 states as exporters of major arms in 2017–21.[1] The five largest suppliers of arms during that period—the United States, Russia, France, China and Germany—accounted for 77 per cent of all arms exports (see table 9.1). This is slightly higher than in 2012–16 and 2007–11, when the top five—the same five states—accounted for 74 per cent in both periods. US and French arms exports rose between 2012–16 and 2017–21, while Russian, Chinese and German arms exports fell.

The top 25 arms exporters supplied 99 per cent of the world's arms exports in 2017–21 (see table 9.1). Of these 25 states, 15 are in the Euro–Atlantic space (i.e. North America and Europe, including Russia), 4 are in Asia and Oceania, 4 are in the Middle East (including Turkey), 1 is in Africa and 1 is in South America.[2] States in North America (i.e. Canada and the USA) and Europe together accounted for 87 per cent of all arms exports in 2017–21. The top five West European arms exporters—France, Germany, Italy, the United Kingdom and Spain—supplied 24 per cent of total global arms exports in 2017–21, compared with 21 per cent in 2012–16. Three states outside Europe and North America were among the top 10 arms exporters in 2017–21: China, South Korea and Israel.

The concentration of suppliers in the Euro–Atlantic space has been a feature of the entire period covered by the SIPRI Arms Transfers Database (1950–2021). Many of the states listed in the top 25 for 2017–21 have also appeared in this list in previous periods: 23 were among the top 25 in 2012–16, 21 in 2007–11 and 20 in 2002–2006.

The two largest arms exporters, the USA and Russia, have long dominated the international supply of arms. However, the gap between the two states in terms of their shares of global arms exports continues to widen: the USA's arms exports were 108 per cent higher than Russia's in 2017–21, compared with 34 per cent higher in 2012–16 and 22 per cent higher in 2007–11. Known pending deliveries from the USA and Russia, and indications from plans for major arms acquisitions by many of the larger importers, strongly suggest that the gap will increase further in the coming years. For example, combat aircraft have in recent years made up the majority of US and Russian arms

---

[1] Except where indicated, the information on the arms deliveries and orders referred to in this section is taken from the SIPRI Arms Transfers Database. For a definition of 'major arms' and a description of how the volume of transfers is measured see box 9.1 in section I of this chapter. The figures here may differ from those in previous editions of the SIPRI Yearbook because the Arms Transfers Database is updated annually.

[2] On SIPRI's regional coverage see the list of conventions in this volume and the SIPRI website.

exports, but by the end of 2021 the USA had pending deliveries for a total of 905 combat aircraft, while Russia had export orders for just 60 (see table 9.2). In addition, by the end of 2021, several states were very close to placing large orders for combat aircraft from the USA. Canada, for example, plans to order 88 combat aircraft and has expressed a preference for F-35s from the USA.[3] Having reportedly cancelled their orders for Russian Su-35 aircraft, Egypt and Indonesia are both likely to order equivalent combat aircraft from the USA (see below). For most other types of major arms, pending exports from the USA far outnumber those of Russia. Notably, France has a significantly higher number of combat aircraft awaiting delivery (188) than Russia and its pending exports of several other types of major arms are also far higher than those of Russia, raising the real possibility of France overtaking Russia to become the world's second largest exporter of major arms within a few years.

The rest of this section reviews the arms exports and arms export policies of the top three suppliers in 2017–21 and then provides an overview of arms exports by some of the other major suppliers in the period.

The United States

The USA's arms exports grew by 14 per cent between 2012–16 and 2017–21, increasing its global share from 32 per cent to 39 per cent. The USA delivered major arms to 103 states in 2017–21, far more than any other supplier. Aircraft were the USA's main arms export in 2017–21, making up 62 per cent of its total arms exports (see table 9.3), followed by missiles (17 per cent) and armoured vehicles (10 per cent). By the end of 2021, there was a long list of large contracts for US arms exports, with deliveries planned from 2022 to the end of the decade. Of these, the planned deliveries of a total of 905 combat aircraft, including 600 F-35s, to 23 countries are among the most significant.

The Middle East accounted for 43 per cent of total US arms exports in 2017–21 (see table 9.4), a slight drop on the 47 per cent share in 2012–16. A total of 33 per cent of US arms exports went to states in Asia and Oceania in 2017–21, compared with 34 per cent in 2012–16. US arms exports to Europe increased by 105 per cent, with European states receiving 18 per cent of total US arms exports in 2017–21.

The growth in US arms exports between 2012–16 and 2017–21 was largely due to increases in arms exports to Saudi Arabia, Australia, South Korea and Japan—the four main recipients of US arms exports in 2017–21. US arms exports to Saudi Arabia rose by 106 per cent and it alone accounted for 23 per cent of total US arms exports in the period. US arms exports to

---

[3] Canadian Government, Public Services and Procurement Canada, 'Canada moves closer to delivering 88 advanced fighter jets for the Royal Canadian Air Force as it begins negotiations with the top-ranked bidder, the US Government and Lockheed Martin, for the F-35', News release, 28 Mar. 2022.

Table 9.1. The 40 largest suppliers of major arms and their main recipients, 2017–21

Rank 2017–21	Rank 2012–16[a]	Exporter	Share of total global exports (%) 2012–16	Share of total global exports (%) 2017–21	Change in volume (%) from 2012–16 to 2017–21	Main recipients (share of exporter's total exports, %), 2017–21 1st	2nd	3rd
1	1	United States	32	39	14	Saudi Arabia (23)	Australia (9.4)	South Korea (6.8)
2	2	Russia	24	19	-26	India (28)	China (21)	Egypt (13)
3	3	France	6.4	11	59	India (29)	Qatar (16)	Egypt (11)
4	4	China	6.4	4.6	-31	Pakistan (47)	Bangladesh (16)	Thailand (5.0)
5	5	Germany	5.4	4.5	-19	South Korea (25)	Egypt (14)	United States (6.1)
6	7	Italy	2.5	3.1	16	Egypt (28)	Turkey (15)	Qatar (9.0)
7	6	United Kingdom	4.7	2.9	-41	Oman (19)	Saudi Arabia (19)	United States (19)
8	14	South Korea	1.0	2.8	177	Philippines (16)	Indonesia (14)	United Kingdom (14)
9	10	Spain	2.2	2.5	10	Australia (51)	Turkey (13)	Belgium (8.6)
10	9	Israel	2.5	2.4	-5.6	India (37)	Azerbaijan (13)	Viet Nam (11)
11	11	Netherlands	2.0	1.9	-12	Indonesia (18)	United States (16)	Mexico (10)
12	16	Turkey	0.7	0.9	31	Turkmenistan (16)	Oman (16)	Qatar (14)
13	12	Sweden	1.2	0.8	-35	Pakistan (24)	United States (24)	Brazil (15)
14	8	Ukraine	2.5	0.7	-72	China (39)	Thailand (15)	Russia[c] (13)
15	13	Switzerland	1.0	0.7	-35	Australia (25)	Denmark (12)	France (8.7)
16	21	Australia	0.3	0.6	98	Canada (33)	Chile (29)	United States (18)
17	15	Canada	0.8	0.5	-41	Saudi Arabia (47)	UAE (22)	Australia (6.8)
18	19	UAE	0.3	0.4	17	Egypt (31)	Jordan (24)	Algeria (15)
19	20	South Africa	0.3	0.3	-5.8	UAE (26)	United States (21)	India (12)
20	18	Belarus	0.5	0.3	-42	Serbia (34)	Vietnam (25)	Uganda (14)
21	24	Brazil	0.2	0.3	48	France (23)	Nigeria (13)	Chile (11)
22	17	Norway	0.6	0.3	-57	Oman (27)	United States (21)	Lithuania (14)
23	31	India	0.1	0.2	119	Myanmar (50)	Sri Lanka (25)	Armenia (11)
24	22	Czechia	0.3	0.2	-36	United States (28)	Ukraine (26)	Uganda (13)
25	26	Jordan	0.1	0.2	5.0	United States (40)	Egypt (36)	Armenia (10)

26	33	Belgium	0.1	59	<0.05	Saudi Arabia	(61)	Indonesia	(24)	Argentina	(5.9)
27	38	Indonesia	0.1	58	0.1	Philippines	(69)	Senegal	(19)	Nepal	(6.6)
28	23	Finland	0.2	-62	0.1	Poland	(56)	United Kingdom	(22)	Portugal	(6.2)
29	28	Portugal	0.1	-40	0.1	Romania	(95)	Cabo Verde	(2.5)	Colombia	(2.5)
30	37	Serbia	0.1	2.1	0.1	Cyprus	(40)	Bangladesh	(28)	Turkmenistan	(7.1)
31	32	Denmark	0.1	-28	0.1	Portugal	(29)	Argentina	(23)	Malaysia	(22)
32	..	Lithuania	..	..	<0.05	Angola	(97)	Ukraine	(3.2)	..	..
33	30	Bulgaria	0.1	-66	<0.05	Côte d'Ivoire	(39)	Saudi Arabia	(25)	Angola	(20)
34	57	Pakistan	<0.05	5 800	<0.05	Nigeria	(92)	Azerbaijan	(3.4)	Qatar	(3.4)
35	36	Austria	0.1	-41	<0.05	Latvia	(42)	Australia	(23)	Czechia	(11)
36	27	Poland	0.1	-76	<0.05	Ukraine	(30)	Germany/Nepal[b]	(13)	Lithuania	(6.4)
37	..	Qatar	..	..	<0.05	Pakistan	(64)	Somalia	(19)	Burkina Faso	(7.1)
38	42	Slovakia	<0.05	15	<0.05	Azerbaijan	(62)	Senegal	(26)	Saudi Arabia	(7.7)
39	..	Greece	..	..	<0.05	Canada	(100)	..	..	..	..
40	64	Colombia	<0.05	..	<0.05	Guatemala/Honduras[b]	(42)	Peru	(17)	..	..

.. = not available or not applicable; – = no deliveries; <0.05 = between 0 and 0.05; UAE = United Arab Emirates.

Notes: Percentages below 10 are rounded to 1 decimal place; percentages over 10 are rounded to whole numbers.

[a] The rank order for suppliers in 2012–16 differs from that published in *SIPRI Yearbook 2017* because of subsequent revision of figures for these years.

[b] The two importers received the same volume of arms transfers from the exporter.

[c] This involved transport aircraft produced in Russia until 2018 under licences granted before Ukraine banned arms sales to Russia in 2014.

Source: SIPRI Arms Transfers Database, Mar. 2022.

Table 9.2. Selected major arms on order or chosen for future orders from the five largest arms suppliers for delivery after 2021

Figures are units of major arms.

	Supplier				
	USA	Russia	France	China	Germany
Combat aircraft	905	60	188	85	–
Helicopters	788	235	310	–	68
Transport aircraft	37	–	6	1	–
Major surface ships	4	4	14	3	14
Submarines	–	1	7	9	17
Tanks	654	500	–	174	44
Other armoured vehicles	2 633	238	540	–	1 390
Surface-to-air missile systems	32	16	3	–	21

– = no orders.

Note: Orders are as of 31 Dec. 2021.

Source: SIPRI Arms Transfers Database, Mar. 2022.

Australia increased by 78 per cent, while those to South Korea and Japan rose by 66 per cent and 173 per cent respectively.

These large increases were partly offset by decreases in exports to several states that have been among the largest recipients of US arms in previous periods. The United Arab Emirates (UAE), for example, was the 2nd largest recipient of US arms in 2012–16, but was only the 8th largest in 2017–21. Similarly, Turkey dropped from 3rd to 21st largest and Taiwan from 4th to 15th largest. In the case of Turkey, the decline was directly linked to a severe political rift with the USA and there were few pending US arms deliveries to Turkey by the end of 2021.[4] In contrast, based on known pending deliveries, US arms exports to the UAE are expected to remain high and arms exports to Taiwan are expected to increase significantly over the coming five years.

Developments in US arms export policy in 2021

Soon after the administration of President Joe Biden took office in January 2021, it started a review of US arms export policies and decisions.[5] In February 2021 President Biden announced that the USA was ending all support for offensive operations by the coalition led by Saudi Arabia involved in the war in Yemen, including relevant arms sales to Saudi Arabia.[6] The most important outcome of the ensuing review of US arms exports to Saudi Arabia appears to have been the suspension of the sale of an unknown quantity of guided

[4] Zanotti, J. and Thomas, C., *Turkey: Background and US Relations In Brief*, Congressional Research Service (CRS), Report for Congress R44000 (US Congress, CRS: Washington, DC, 30 Dec. 2021), p. 1.

[5] Blinken, A. J., US Secretary of State, US Department of State, Remarks to the press, Washington, DC, 27 Jan. 2021.

[6] White House, 'Remarks by President Biden on America's place in the world', 4 Feb. 2021. On the armed conflict in Yemen see chapter 6, section V, in this volume.

Table 9.3. Deliveries by arms category by the 10 largest suppliers of major arms, 2017–21

Figures are the percentage share of each category of major arms in the exports of the 10 largest suppliers in 2017–21.

Arms category	Supplier										
	USA	Russia	France	China	Germany	Italy	UK	South Korea	Spain	Israel	World[a]
Aircraft	62	48	56	28	12	43	39	12	44	6.8	47
Air defence systems	2.9	6.4	1.9	6.6	1.7	–	0.7	–	–	16	3.6
Armoured vehicles	10	11	2.5	21	15	6.1	0.8	0.9	0.9	0.5	10
Artillery	0.2	0.2	0.8	1.8	0.8	1.7	5.3	19	0.6	1.2	1.3
Engines	2.6	16	5.5	–	13	<0.05	13	–	–	–	6.2
Missiles	17	12	12	16	11	3.7	14	0.4		41	13
Naval weapons	0.9	0.6	0.3	0.2	–	2.6	–	–	–	0.5	0.6
Satellites	–	0.2	1.0	–	–	–	–	–	–	1.5	0.2
Sensors	2.8	1.1	4.3	2.9	8.6	5.2	2.8	–	2.7	17	3.8
Ships	1.3	4.5	15	23	38	37	7.1	68	52	9.9	13
Other	–	0.3	0.1	–	–	0.8	17	–	<0.05	5.7	0.9

– = no deliveries; <0.05 = between 0 and 0.05.

Notes: On SIPRI's categories of major arms see box 9.1 in section I of this chapter. Percentages below 10 are rounded to 1 decimal place; percentages over 10 are rounded to whole numbers.

    [a] 'World' is the share of each category for all suppliers globally.

Source: SIPRI Arms Transfers Database, Mar. 2022.

bombs, which had been agreed in 2020 by the administration of President Donald J. Trump.[7] The Biden administration also reviewed a letter of agreement for the sale of 50 F-35 combat aircraft to the UAE signed by the Trump administration in January 2021. In April 2021 it decided to proceed with the sale, but negotiations were eventually suspended by the UAE in December (see below).[8] In addition, the Biden administration worked on a new US Conventional Arms Transfer policy in 2021, which is expected to put more emphasis during the arms export decision-making process on the human rights conditions in potential recipient states.[9] This policy had not been finalized as at the end of 2021.

Based on the existing contracts at the end of 2021, it appeared that the Biden administration had not, by that point, altered US arms export policies

    [7] Blanchard, C. M., *Saudi Arabia: Background and US Relations*, Congressional Research Service (CRS), Report for Congress RL33533 (US Congress, CRS: Washington, DC, 5 Oct. 2021), pp. 2, 28.

    [8] Katzman, K., *The United Arab Emirates (UAE): Issues for US Policy*, Congressional Research Service (CRS), Report for Congress RS21852 (US Congress, CRS: Washington, DC, 28 Oct. 2021), p. 16.

    [9] Kirshner, J., 'Will Biden's Conventional Arms Transfer policy be an evolution or a revolution?', Breaking Defense, 14 Jan. 2022; and Cohen, J., 'Biden's Conventional Arms Transfer policy review could be a turning point', CATO Institute, Commentary, 29 Nov. 2021.

Table 9.4. The 10 largest suppliers of major arms and their recipients, by region, 2017–21

Figures are the percentage shares of the supplier's total volume of exports of major arms delivered to each recipient region in 2017–21.

Recipient region	Supplier									
	USA	Russia	France	China	Germany	Italy	UK	South Korea	Spain	Israel
Africa	2.6	14	3.4	13	3.8	6.7	0.2	0.2	0.8	1.2
Americas	2.2	<0.05	5.0	<0.05	10	7.0	25	7.8	12	15
Asia and Oceania	33	61	47	79	40	16	21	63	56	57
Europe	18	5.5	4.9	0.4	18	7.4	10	24	13	26
Middle East	43	20	37	7.2	29	63	44	5.2	18	–

– = no deliveries; <0.05 = between 0 and 0.05.

Notes: Percentages below 10 are rounded to 1 decimal place; percentages over 10 are rounded to whole numbers. Figures may not always add up to 100% because of the conventions of rounding and because some suppliers exported small volumes of major arms to unidentified recipients or to international organizations that cannot be linked to a particular region.

Source: SIPRI Arms Transfers Database, Mar. 2022.

in a way that was likely to have a major effect on the total volume of arms exported by the USA in the short term. For example, by the end of 2021, pending deliveries to Saudi Arabia included 51 F-15SA combat aircraft—a type that has been used by Saudi Arabia to attack targets in Yemen—ordered in 2011.[10] In 2021 the USA also continued to sign major arms deals with states in all regions of the world. As was the case under previous administrations, the Biden administration generally presented its arms deals as being a key element of US foreign and security policy.

The USA has established policies and legislation aimed at limiting the global influence of China and Russia. These policies and laws continued to have an important effect on US arms trade relations in 2021, both in terms of the potential volume of arms involved and in terms of the USA's strategic interests.

One key piece of legislation in this area is the 2017 Countering America's Adversaries Through Sanctions Act (CAATSA), which, among other things, gives the US government the authority to restrict US arms exports to countries that buy arms from Russia.[11] In 2017–21 the act had a notable impact on US arms exports to Turkey—a long-term ally of the USA and member of the North Atlantic Treaty Organization (NATO). Invoking CAATSA, the USA halted deliveries of the first batch of up to 100 F-35 combat aircraft to Turkey

[10] See e.g. 'Yemen war: Democrats introduce bill to stop US support for Saudi air force', Middle East Eye, 2 Feb. 2022; and Naar, I., 'Saudi-led coalition begins air raids on Houthis in Yemen capital Sanaa', The National, 18 Jan. 2022.

[11] Countering America's Adversaries Through Sanctions Act, US Public Law 115-44, signed into law 2 Aug. 2017.

in 2019 after Turkey imported S-400 surface-to-air missile (SAM) systems from Russia. The USA imposed further related sanctions against Turkey under CAATSA in 2020.[12] The two states did not find a solution to the disagreement in 2021 and US arms exports to Turkey remained very low.

In 2018 India also ordered S-400 systems from Russia and the first batch was delivered in 2021. In contrast to its reaction to Turkey's acquisition of S-400s, the USA did not impose any specific restrictions on arms deliveries to India during 2021.[13] In 2017–21 India was the ninth largest recipient of US arms exports. The arms transfers made during the period are generally seen as an important part of efforts to strengthen strategic ties between the USA and India, especially considering that both states perceive China to be a major military threat. This possibly explains why the USA has so far declined to invoke CAATSA against India.

In December 2021 the UAE suspended negotiations on a contract for 50 F-35s that both the Trump and Biden administrations had already agreed to in principle. The decision was at least partly in reaction to US pressure on the UAE aimed at halting the UAE's planned acquisition of 5G telecommunication technology from China.[14]

Russia

Russia's arms exports fell by 26 per cent between 2012–16 and 2017–21, and its share of global arms exports decreased from 24 per cent to 19 per cent. Russia delivered major arms to 45 states in 2017–21. In contrast to the USA, Russia's deliveries in 2017–21 were more concentrated as four states—India, China, Egypt and Algeria—together received 73 per cent of total Russian arms exports. Asia and Oceania remained the largest recipient region of Russian arms, accounting for 61 per cent of total Russian arms exports, followed by the Middle East (20 per cent) and Africa (14 per cent). Aircraft were Russia's main arms export in 2017–21. They accounted for 48 per cent of its total arms exports, followed by engines, mainly for aircraft (16 per cent), and missiles (12 per cent).

The overall drop in Russian arms exports between 2012–16 and 2017–21 was almost entirely due to decreases in arms exports to Algeria, India and Viet Nam. While India remained the chief recipient of Russian arms in 2017–21, Russian arms exports to India fell by 47 per cent between 2012–16 and 2017–21. Arms exports to Viet Nam and Algeria, which were the second and third largest recipients of Russian arms in 2012–16, decreased by

[12] Zanotti and Thomas (note 4), pp. 7–9.

[13] Basu, N. and Philip, S. A., 'US unlikely to impose CAATSA sanctions on India for S-400, but other Russian deals won't be easy', The Print, 3 Dec. 2021.

[14] England, A. and Kerr, S., 'UAE suspends talks with US over purchase of F35 fighter jets', *Financial Times*, 14 Dec. 2021.

71 per cent and 17 per cent, respectively, between the two periods. The decline in Russia's arms supplies to these states appears to be largely attributable to demand-side factors. These include national procurement cycles, whereby high levels of deliveries of major arms are followed by lower levels as the new arms are integrated in the armed forces, and efforts by these states to diversify their respective arms supplier bases to fulfil their arms procurement plans (see section III).[15] Although a number of arms export contracts signed over the past 10 years had been completed by the end of 2021—including deliveries of 42 Su-30MKI combat aircraft to India and 42 Mi-28NE combat helicopters to Algeria—several large Russian arms deliveries are still pending. These include 8 S-400 SAM systems, 4 Talwar frigates and 1 Project-971I nuclear-powered submarine to India and a total of 28 combat aircraft to Algeria (22) and Viet Nam (6).

Substantial increases in Russia's arms exports to China (60 per cent) and Egypt (723 per cent)—which in 2017–21 became the second and third largest recipients of Russian arms, respectively—did not offset the other decreases in its arms exports. In 2017–21 both China and Egypt received SAM systems and combat aircraft from Russia.

Notably, the delivery status of several major Russian arms deals remained uncertain as at the end of 2021. Among these deals was the implementation of a contract, signed in 2019, for 24 Su-35 combat aircraft for Egypt. The reasons for the delay in implementing the Su-35 deal are unclear but may be attributed to a combination of factors, including disruption to Russia's planned production and delivery schedules arising from the Covid-19 pandemic, and pressure reportedly applied on Egypt by the USA that the deal risked triggering US sanctions under CAATSA.[16] In early 2022 multiple media outlets reported that the deal might have been cancelled.[17]

In 2017–21 Russia continued to be the main arms supplier to many states of the former Soviet Union. Russian deliveries of major arms in the period included eight Su-30MK combat aircraft to Kazakhstan and four Tor-M2 air defence systems to Belarus. Russia's military cooperation with Kazakhstan and Belarus, including through arms transfers, is aimed at maintaining the military potential of those states 'to prevent a military threat and repel

---

[15] Ybarra, M., 'The politics of selling weapons to Algeria', *National Interest*, 7 Mar. 2019; and Gady, F., 'India's Army approves "Emergency Purchase" of 240 Israeli anti-tank guided missiles', The Diplomat, 17 Apr. 2019.

[16] [Source: Russia started production of Su-35 for Egypt], TASS, 16 May 2020 (in Russian); and Cornwell., A., 'Egypt risks US sanctions over Russian fighter jet deal: US official', Reuters, 18 Nov. 2019.

[17] See e.g. Martin, T., 'Suspected collapse of Su-35 deal sees US agree Egyptian F-15 order', Shephard Media, 18 Mar. 2022; and Malyasov, D., 'Egypt, Algeria, Indonesia reject Su-35 fighter jet deals with Russia', Defence Blog, 4 Jan. 2022.

aggression in the common defense space'.[18] After a 26 per cent increase in Russian arms exports to Kazakhstan between 2012–16 and 2017–21, Kazakhstan became the sixth largest recipient of Russian major arms and the top importer of Russian arms among the states of the former Soviet Union. It accounted for 4.0 per cent of all Russian arms supplies in 2017–21. Russian arms exports to Belarus increased by 66 per cent between 2012–16 and 2017–21. Belarus received 2.7 per cent of total Russian arms exports in 2017–21.

Russia was also among the main arms suppliers to both Armenia and Azerbaijan in 2017–21. It supplied nearly all of Armenia's major arms and accounted for 22 per cent of Azerbaijan's arms imports. The arms deliveries to Armenia and Azerbaijan took place while the states were in conflict with each other, and played a major role in the full-blown war between the two states in 2020.[19] The war ended in November 2020 with a ceasefire brokered by Russia, which was supported by a Russian peacekeeping force.[20] Only one order for Russian major arms has been identified for either state since the ceasefire agreement: a pending delivery of four Mi-8 armed helicopters for Armenia.

France

In 2017–21 French arms exports accounted for 11 per cent of the global total after increasing by 59 per cent between 2012–16 and 2017–21. At the regional level, 47 per cent of French arms exports went to Asia and Oceania in 2017–21 and 37 per cent went to the Middle East. Aircraft were France's main arms export in 2017–21, making up 56 per cent of its total arms exports, followed by ships, accounting for 15 per cent.

France delivered major arms to 65 states in 2017–21, but the three largest recipients—India, Qatar and Egypt—together accounted for 56 per cent of French arms exports in that period (see table 9.1). With a 29 per cent share of French arms exports, India was by far the largest recipient. France has delivered major arms to India every year since 1961, but the volume of deliveries in 2017–21 was at its highest level for any five-year period since 1950 and was almost 11 times higher than in 2012–16. French arms export relations with Qatar and Egypt have not been as consistent as those with India. The volume of French arms deliveries to Qatar was more than 25 times higher in 2017–21 than its relatively low level in 2012–16. After a break of 11 years, French arms exports to Egypt resumed in 2012–16 and remained at a similar

[18] Belarussian Embassy in Russia, [Military cooperation with the Russian Federation], [n.d.] (in Russian); and Khrolenko, A., [What weapons does Russia supply to Kazakhstan], Sputnik Kazakhstan, 18 Mar. 2019 (in Russian).

[19] Smith, J., Wezeman, P. D. and Kuimova, A., 'Arms transfers to conflict zones: The case of Nagorno-Karabakh', SIPRI Topical Backgrounder, 30 Apr. 2021.

[20] On the interstate conflict between Armenia and Azerbaijan see chapter 5, section I, in this volume.

level in 2017–21. India (54), Qatar (30) and Egypt (18) together received a total of 102 Rafale and Mirage-2000-5 combat aircraft and associated equipment from France in 2017–21. These deliveries accounted for more than 70 per cent of the arms exports from France to each of these three recipients.

In 2021 France concluded export agreements for a total of 188 Rafale combat aircraft with Croatia (12), Egypt (30), Greece (24), Indonesia (42) and the UAE (80). Delivery of all 188 will probably take until at least the end of the 2020s. The fact that the Rafale does not include US components or technology and is thus not covered by US export rules—which for example led to restrictions on sales to Egypt after the 2013 coup—is probably one of the reasons why some states have ordered it instead of other types of combat aircraft.[21] France's willingness to provide credit arrangements for the costly acquisitions is another key reason. The Croatian, Egyptian and Indonesian orders were all largely paid for with loans from French banks guaranteed by the French state.[22]

Other major suppliers

China

In 2017–21 China accounted for 4.6 per cent of total global arms exports. Chinese arms exports decreased by 31 per cent between 2012–16 and 2017–21. A total of 79 per cent of Chinese arms exports went to Asia and Oceania in 2017–21. China delivered major arms to 48 states in 2017–21, but 47 per cent of its arms exports went to just one state, Pakistan, which is one of China's closest allies. Most of China's pending deliveries (see table 9.2) are also destined for Pakistan. Pakistan has become increasingly reliant on China for its arms supplies, partly because of the deterioration in its political relations with other exporters, most notably the USA. China has become one of the largest producers of major arms (including the relevant components), many of which are entirely of indigenous design. It now offers advanced systems, including submarines with air-independent propulsion and the J-10C combat aircraft, which has advanced sensors and missiles as well as a Chinese engine rather than the Russian engine used in the earlier J-10. Despite this, many of the world's largest arms importers remain very reluctant to order Chinese major arms, at least partly for political reasons.

Germany

German arms exports made up 4.5 per cent of the global total in 2017–21. They were 19 per cent lower than in 2012–16 and 49 per cent lower than in 2007–11.

---

[21] Seibt, S., 'With billions in new deals, France's Rafale fighter makes a comeback', France 24, 5 Dec. 2021.

[22] Oliver, D., 'Rafale success hits headwind over India', *Armada International*, 11 Jan. 2022.

Germany delivered major arms to 53 states in 2017–21. A total of 40 per cent of German arms exports went to states in Asia and Oceania, 29 per cent went to states in the Middle East and 18 per cent went to states in Europe. South Korea was by far the largest recipient of German arms exports in 2017–21, with Egypt becoming the second largest. The delivery of 4 Type-214 submarines and 239 Taurus KEPD-350 long-range (up to 400 kilometres) air-to-surface missiles from Germany contributed significantly to the military capabilities South Korea is accumulating as a response to the threat it perceives from North Korea. The delivery of 3 Type-209/1400 submarines accounted for the bulk of German arms exports to Egypt in 2017–21.

Ships were Germany's main arms export in 2017–21, accounting for 38 per cent of its total arms exports. This will most likely continue to be the case for at least the next few years as it has pending deliveries for 14 frigates and 17 submarines, most of which are scheduled for delivery by 2030.

Italy

Italy's arms exports in 2017–21 were 16 per cent higher than in 2012–16 and 33 per cent higher than in 2007–11. Italian arms exports amounted to 3.1 per cent of the global total in 2017–21. The Middle East accounted for 63 per cent of Italian arms exports in the period. The delivery of two frigates to Egypt accounted for 23 per cent of total Italian arms exports in 2017–21. The frigates were originally produced for the Italian navy and were already undergoing sea trials by the time they were sold to Egypt in 2020, meaning that they could be adapted to Egyptian requirements and delivered by early 2021.[23] Other major deliveries included 51 T-129B combat helicopters to Turkey and a Fincantieri-3000 frigate to Qatar. Based on known arms agreements with pending deliveries, Italy will remain a major exporter in the coming years. Deliveries planned for 2023–24, for example, include 28 Typhoon combat aircraft to Kuwait, 3 frigates to Qatar and the first of 6 FREMM frigates ordered by Indonesia.

The United Kingdom

The UK was the world's seventh largest arms exporter in 2017–21 and sup-plied 2.9 per cent of total global arms exports. Deliveries related to a deal with Saudi Arabia for a total of 72 Typhoon combat aircraft ended in 2017, leading to a 41 per cent fall in British arms exports between 2012–16 and 2017–21. The main orders with pending deliveries are for 24 Typhoons to Oman, which are likely to be delivered by 2025, and a total of 26 frigates to Australia (9), Canada (15) and Indonesia (2). The frigates were ordered in 2019–21 and are the first newly produced major warships ordered from the UK since 2007.

---

[23] Groizeleau, V., 'L'Italie livre en catimini une première FREMM à la marine égyptienne' [Italy secretly delivers a first FREMM to the Egyptian Navy], Mer et Marine, 5 Jan. 2021.

Deliveries will be spread over many years, with the final batch of ships scheduled for delivery in the 2040s.

South Korea

South Korea was the eighth largest arms exporter in 2017–21 with a 2.8 per cent share of the global total. Its arms exports were 177 per cent higher than in 2012–16. Asia and Oceania accounted for 63 per cent of South Korean arms exports in 2017–21, followed by Europe with 24 per cent. South Korea also further developed its arms export relations in other regions, especially the Middle East. In 2021, for example, Egypt selected artillery and the UAE selected SAM systems from South Korea for major military procurement projects.

III. Developments among the recipients of major arms, 2017–21

SIEMON T. WEZEMAN, ALEXANDRA KUIMOVA AND PIETER D. WEZEMAN

SIPRI has identified 163 states as importers of major arms in 2017–21.[1] The top five arms importers—India, Saudi Arabia, Egypt, Australia and China—together received 38 per cent of total arms imports in 2017–21 (see table 9.5). India, Saudi Arabia and China were also among the top five importers in 2012–16, and India and China were among the top five importers in 2007–11. At the regional level, Asia and Oceania accounted for 43 per cent of arms imports in 2017–21 (see table 9.6), followed by the Middle East (32 per cent), Europe (13 per cent), Africa (5.8 per cent) and the Americas (5.5 per cent).

In addition to the 163 importing states, two international organizations—the North Atlantic Treaty Organization (NATO) and the African Union—and non-state rebel forces in Libya, Sudan (Darfur), Syria and Yemen received major arms in 2017–21. Of these, only NATO received a significant volume (0.5 per cent of the global total).

This section reviews significant developments among the main recipients of arms in each region in turn.

Africa

Between 2012–16 and 2017–21, imports of major arms by African states decreased by 34 per cent. Russia was the largest supplier to Africa, accounting for 44 per cent of arms exports to the region, followed by the USA (17 per cent), China (10 per cent) and France (6.1 per cent).

The overall drop in African arms imports was mainly driven by decreases in imports by Algeria and Morocco—the two largest arms importers in the region.

Algeria and Morocco

In 2017–21 Algeria accounted for 44 per cent of total African arms imports. This amounted to 2.6 per cent of global arms transfers, making it the 11th largest arms importer in the world. Its regional rival Morocco received 17 per cent of African arms imports, equivalent to 1.0 per cent of the global total. It was the 25th largest arms importer in 2017–21. Despite the ongoing tensions between the two states, particularly with regard to the conflict in

---

[1] Except where indicated, the information on the arms deliveries and orders referred to in this section is taken from the SIPRI Arms Transfers Database. For a definition of 'major arms' and a description of how the volume of transfers is measured see box 9.1 in section I of this chapter. The figures here may differ from those in previous editions of the SIPRI Yearbook because the Arms Transfers Database is updated annually.

Western Sahara, their arms imports decreased significantly between 2012–16 and 2017–21.[2]

Algeria's arms imports fell by 37 per cent between 2012–16 and 2017–21. In recent years it has attempted to diversify its arms supplier base but continued to rely heavily on imports of Russian arms in 2017–21. Although the volume of Algeria's arms imports from Russia decreased by 17 per cent between 2012–16 and 2017–21, Russia remained the largest arms supplier to Algeria and accounted for 81 per cent of all Algerian arms imports in 2017–21. Germany, the second largest arms exporter to Algeria, accounted for 6.4 per cent of Algerian arms imports over the same period.

Morocco's arms imports dropped by 27 per cent between 2012–16 and 2017–21. It received major arms from several arms exporters in 2017–21, but its arms supplier base became more concentrated compared with the previous five-year period. The USA remained Morocco's main supplier of major arms and its share of Moroccan arms imports increased from 42 per cent in 2012–16 to 76 per cent in 2017–21. China (14 per cent) had the second largest share, followed by France (8.4 per cent).

The arms transfer relations between the USA and Morocco, which is a key ally of the USA in Africa, are likely to continue to grow in importance in the coming years as both states signed an agreement in 2020 intended to further enhance defence cooperation between them through 2030.[3] This new level of cooperation can already be illustrated by the fact that Morocco has several large pending deliveries of major arms from the USA—including for 24 F-16 Block-72 combat aircraft and 24 AH-64E combat helicopters—that are expected to be implemented in the coming five years.

Sub-Saharan Africa

States in sub-Saharan Africa accounted for 2.0 per cent of total global arms imports in 2017–21. Taken together, their arms imports were 35 per cent lower in 2017–21 than in 2012–16. In 2017–21 the five largest arms importers in the subregion were Angola, Nigeria, Ethiopia, Mali and Botswana. In 2017–21 Angola, Nigeria, Ethiopia and Mali all had a diversified supplier base, receiving major arms from West European states as well as China, Russia and the USA, while Botswana received arms only from West European states and the USA. Angola received 62 per cent of its major arms imports in 2017–21 from Russia, but none of the other four states received more than 49 per cent of their major arms from a single supplier.

In 2017–21 Angola's arms imports were 2.6 times higher than in the previous five-year period and accounted for 0.4 per cent of the global total. Deliveries

---

[2] On tensions in Western Sahara see chapter 6, section IV, in this volume.

[3] Garamone, J., 'US, Morocco chart defense cooperation through 2030', US Department of Defense, News release, 2 Oct. 2020.

included 12 Su-30MK combat aircraft from Russia and 12 K-8W light combat/ trainer aircraft from China as well as a total of 134 second-hand pieces of artillery from Belarus and Bulgaria—which was more than four times the volume of artillery imports of all other sub-Saharan states combined.

Amid ongoing external and domestic security challenges, including attacks by armed Islamist groups such as Boko Haram, Nigeria received major arms from 13 suppliers in 2017–21. Deliveries included 272 tanks and other armoured vehicles from China, 7 Mi-35M combat helicopters from Russia, 3 JF-17 combat aircraft from Pakistan, 12 Super Tucano light combat aircraft from Brazil (via the USA) and 9 patrol craft from France. Some of these recently delivered arms were put to use almost immediately in counter-insurgency operations.[4]

Ethiopia received air-defence equipment from Russia and Ukraine during the first three years of the period 2017–21. While no transfers of major arms from these states have been identified for 2020–21, several transfers by other suppliers are known to have taken place in that period, including deliveries of multiple rocket launchers from China and unmanned aerial vehicles (UAVs) from Turkey. A number of media outlets reported that Ethiopia may have also received some other UAVs, possibly produced by Iran and by China.[5] However, information on the actual supplier states, the delivery dates and the number of units transferred to Ethiopia remained uncertain as at the end of 2021.[6]

Ongoing armed conflict in the Sahel region coincided with increased arms imports by Mali—which is a member of the Joint Force of the Group of Five for the Sahel—between 2012–16 and 2017–21. In 2017–21 Mali received 130 armoured vehicles from the United Arab Emirates (UAE) and 4 light combat aircraft from Brazil. South Africa also supplied 102 armoured vehicles, of which at least 70 were paid for by Germany as military aid. The largest arms supplier to Mali in 2017–21 was Russia, which delivered 4 armed transport helicopters and 4 combat helicopters.

Botswana, the fifth largest arms importer in the subregion, accounted for 0.1 per cent of the global total in 2017–21. Although it was not involved in any open conflict during this period, its arms imports increased more than fivefold from 2012–16. In 2017–21 deliveries to Botswana included 45 infantry fighting vehicles from Switzerland and surface-to-air missile (SAM) systems from France.

---

[4] Lake, J., 'Now there's Thunder in the Nigerian sky', Times Aerospace, 12 Jan. 2022; and Malyasov, D., 'Nigerian anti-terrorism operation marks combat debut of Chinese VT4 tank', Defence Blog, 12 Jan. 2021. On the armed conflict in Nigeria see chapter 7, section II, in this volume.

[5] Zwijnenburg, W., 'Is Ethiopia flying Iranian-made armed drones?', Bellingcat, 17 Aug. 2021; and Zwijnenburg, W., 'Are Emirati armed drones supporting Ethiopia from an Eritrean air base?', Bellingcat, 19 Nov. 2020.

[6] Mwai, P., 'Tigray conflict: What do we know about drone strikes in Ethiopia?', BBC News, 31 Jan. 2022. On the armed conflict in Ethiopia see chapter 7, section IV, in this volume.

Table 9.5. The 50 largest recipients of major arms and their main suppliers, 2017–21

Rank 2017–21	Rank 2012–16[a]	Importer	Share of total global imports (%) 2012–16	Share of total global imports (%) 2017–21	Change in volume (%) from 2012–16 to 2017–21	Main suppliers (share of importer's total imports, %), 2017–21 1st	2nd	3rd
1	1	India	14	11	−21	Russia (46)	France (27)	United States (12)
2	2	Saudi Arabia	8.2	11	27	United States (82)	France (5.1)	United Kingdom (5.0)
3	9	Egypt	3.2	5.7	73	Russia (41)	France (21)	Italy (15)
4	10	Australia	3.2	5.4	62	United States (67)	Spain (24)	Switzerland (3.3)
5	4	China	4.4	4.8	4.1	Russia (81)	France (9.1)	Ukraine (5.9)
6	22	Qatar	1.3	4.6	227	United States (46)	France (36)	Italy (6.1)
7	13	South Korea	2.3	4.1	71	United States (63)	Germany (27)	France (7.8)
8	8	Pakistan	3.2	3.0	−11	China (72)	Germany (6.4)	Russia (5.6)
9	3	UAE	4.5	2.8	−41	United States (61)	Sweden (6.2)	Russia (5.3)
10	26	Japan	1.0	2.6	152	United States (98)	United Kingdom (1.7)	Sweden (0.7)
11	5	Algeria	3.9	2.6	−37	Russia (81)	Germany (6.4)	France (3.7)
12	21	United Kingdom	1.4	2.5	74	United States (77)	South Korea (16)	Germany (3.2)
13	12	United States	2.5	2.4	−9.6	United Kingdom (23)	Netherlands (13)	France (12)
14	17	Israel	1.5	1.9	19	United States (92)	Germany (6.9)	Italy (1.0)
15	14	Indonesia	2.1	1.7	−24	South Korea (23)	United States (23)	Netherlands (19)
16	49	Norway	0.3	1.6	343	United States (83)	South Korea (10)	Italy (4.0)
17	7	Turkey	3.2	1.5	−56	Italy (30)	United States (22)	Spain (21)
18	16	Singapore	1.6	1.4	−20	France (54)	United States (22)	Germany (7.9)
19	40	Netherlands	0.6	1.3	116	United States (94)	Germany (5.0)	Australia (0.3)
20	11	Viet Nam	2.9	1.3	−56	Russia (56)	Israel (19)	South Korea (6.6)
21	6	Iraq	3.4	1.2	−66	Russia (44)	United States (35)	Italy (10)
22	25	Italy	1.0	1.2	15	United States (72)	Germany (17)	Israel (5.8)
23	31	Thailand	0.9	1.1	20	South Korea (28)	China (20)	Ukraine (9.9)
24	18	Bangladesh	1.5	1.0	−35	China (71)	Russia (9.2)	United Kingdom (5.2)
25	24	Morocco	1.3	1.0	−27	United States (76)	China (14)	France (8.4)
26	28	Afghanistan	0.9	0.9	−4.1	United States (97)	Brazil (2.0)	Belarus (1.1)

27	23	Oman	1.3	0.9	-34	United Kingdom (63)	Turkey (16)	Norway (8.1)
28	29	Kuwait	0.9	0.9	-6.3	United States (56)	France (26)	Italy (9.4)
29	52	Philippines	0.3	0.9	142	South Korea (53)	United States (16)	Israel (8.7)
30	27	Canada	1.0	0.9	-14	United States (43)	Australia (23)	Israel (12)
31	37	Kazakhstan	0.7	0.8	8.1	Russia (91)	Spain (2.2)	China (2.1)
32	38	Jordan	0.6	0.7	11	United States (37)	Netherlands (17)	UAE (14)
33	33	Brazil	0.8	0.7	-17	United Kingdom (19)	Sweden (18)	France (17)
34	15	Taiwan	1.9	0.7	-68	United States (99)	Germany (0.4)	Italy (0.3)
35	32	Myanmar	0.9	0.6	-32	China (36)	Russia (27)	India (17)
36	41	Poland	0.6	0.6	3.4	United States (35)	Italy (12)	South Korea (12)
37	20	Azerbaijan	1.4	0.5	-63	Israel (61)	Russia (22)	Belarus (6.6)
38	115	NATO^b	0.0	0.5	1 991	France (69)	United States (26)	Spain (3.7)
39	56	Belarus	0.3	0.5	62	Russia (100)	China (0.1)	..
40	58	France	0.2	0.5	97	United States (42)	United Kingdom (16)	Brazil (15)
41	65	Angola	0.2	0.4	161	Russia (62)	Lithuania (10)	China (9.5)
42	53	Denmark	0.3	0.4	21	United States (57)	Switzerland (21)	Germany (15)
43	55	Chile	0.3	0.4	15	Australia (48)	Germany (17)	United States (13)
44	46	Malaysia	0.4	0.4	-13	Turkey (23)	China (16)	South Korea (15)
45	35	Mexico	0.7	0.4	-53	Netherlands (52)	United States (34)	France (9.8)
46	48	Nigeria	0.4	0.4	-7.2	China (29)	Russia (22)	Pakistan (11)
47	133	Serbia	<0.05	0.3	3 207	Russia (61)	Belarus (32)	Germany (4.3)
48	39	Turkmenistan	0.6	0.3	-47	Turkey (45)	Italy (31)	France (6.8)
49	63	Romania	0.2	0.3	86	United States (49)	Portugal (25)	Israel (13)
50	30	Greece	0.9	0.3	-66	United Kingdom (37)	United States (12)	Israel (3.5)

.. = not available or not applicable; <0.05 = between 0 and 0.05; NATO = North Atlantic Treaty Organization; UAE = United Arab Emirates.

Notes: Percentages below 10 are rounded to 1 decimal place; percentages over 10 are rounded to whole numbers.

^a The rank order for recipients in 2012–16 differs from that published in *SIPRI Yearbook 2017* because of subsequent revision of figures for these years.

^b The data is for imports by the organization itself, not the total imports by NATO member states.

Source: SIPRI Arms Transfers Database, Mar. 2022.

Table 9.6. Imports of major arms, by region and subregion, 2012–16 and 2017–21

Figures for volume of imports are SIPRI trend-indicator values (TIV).

Recipient region	Volume of imports (TIV)		Change in volume from 2012–16 to 2017–21 (%)	Share of total imports (%)	
	2012–16	2017–21		2012–16	2017–21
Africa	11 995	7 949	−34	8.4	5.8
North Africa	7 794	5 211	−33	5.5	3.8
Sub-Saharan Africa	4 196	2 735	−35	2.9	2.0
Americas	11 773	7 537	−36	8.3	5.5
Central America and the Caribbean	1 449	666	−54	1.0	0.5
North America	4 928	4 394	−11	3.5	3.2
South America	5 371	2 419	−55	3.8	1.8
Asia and Oceania	61 662	58 734	−4.7	43	43
Central Asia	2 066	1 898	−8.1	1.4	1.4
East Asia	13 960	16 705	20	9.8	12
Oceania	4 746	7 531	59	3.3	5.5
South Asia	27 401	22 335	−18	19	16
South East Asia	13 489	10 265	−24	9.5	7.5
Europe	14 850	17 654	19	10	13
Central Europe	1 503	2 737	82	1.1	2.0
Eastern Europe	3 331	2 078	−38	2.3	1.5
Western Europe	10 016	12 840	28	7.0	9.4
Middle East	42 108	43 305	2.8	30	32
Other [a]	104	131	26	0.1	0.1

Notes: The SIPRI TIV is an indicator of the volume of arms transfers and not their financial value. The method for calculating the TIV is described in box 9.1 in section I of this chapter. Percentages below 10 are rounded to 1 decimal place; percentages over 10 are rounded to whole numbers.

[a] 'Other' refers to unidentified recipients or to international organizations that cannot be linked to a particular region.

Source: SIPRI Arms Transfers Database, Mar. 2022.

The Americas

Arms imports by states in the Americas decreased by 36 per cent between 2012–16 and 2017–21. This followed a decrease of 21 per cent between 2007–11 and 2012–16. The USA and Canada were the largest importers of major arms in the Americas in 2017–21, accounting respectively for 43 per cent and 15 per cent of the regional total.

The fall in arms imports to the Americas was largely due to a 55 per cent reduction in arms imports by South American states between 2012–16 and 2017–21. In 2017–21 arms imports by South American states were lower than in any five-year period in the past half century. The sharp drop in Venezuelan arms imports between 2012–16 and 2017–21 was one of the key reasons for the overall subregional decrease. Venezuela was the largest arms importer in South America in 2012–16 and accounted for 39 per cent of total arms transfers to the subregion. Venezuela has been badly affected by a severe economic crisis since 2013, which has had an impact on its arms procurement. Venezuela's arms imports in 2017–21 were 96 per cent lower than in 2012–16 and its share of the subregional total fell to 3.8 per cent. Arms transfers to several other large importers in South America also decreased: Brazil's fell by 17 per cent, Colombia's by 67 per cent and Peru's by 54 per cent. In contrast, Chile's arms imports increased by 15 per cent, mainly due to the delivery of two second-hand frigates from Australia.

Brazil and Chile were the largest arms importers in South America in 2017–21, accounting respectively for 37 per cent and for 21 per cent of arms deliveries to the subregion. Brazil is the only state in South America with substantial pending deliveries of arms. These include over 1100 armoured vehicles mainly from Italy, 5 submarines (including one with nuclear propulsion) from France, 4 frigates from Germany and 31 combat aircraft from Sweden. These pending deliveries dwarf those of all other South American states and, while several of these states have plans to acquire new combat aircraft, submarines or frigates, none had placed, or even appeared close to placing, such an order by the end of 2021.

Asia and Oceania

Arms imports by states in Asia and Oceania decreased by 4.7 per cent between 2012–16 and 2017–21. This followed a 25 per cent increase between 2002–2006 and 2007–11, and a further 9.3 per cent increase between 2007–11 and 2012–16. Asia and Oceania remained the largest recipient region, accounting for 43 per cent of global arms imports. Of the 10 largest importers in 2017–21, 6 are in Asia and Oceania: India, Australia, China, South Korea, Pakistan and Japan. The USA accounted for 30 per cent of arms imports by states in the region, followed by Russia with 26 per cent and France with 12 per cent.

For many states in Asia and Oceania, a growing perception of China as a threat is the main driver of arms imports.[7] This at least partly explains why Asia and Oceania has been by far the largest recipient region over the past 30 years as well as the particularly high levels of arms imports by India and many states in East Asia, South East Asia, and Oceania. Current known orders indicate that arms imports by states in Asia and Oceania will remain at a high overall level for at least the coming five years. There is one state in the region, however, that is likely to see a sharp reduction in its arms imports. Afghanistan was the 26th largest arms importer in the world in 2017–21, accounting for 0.9 per cent of the global total, with most of its supplies coming from the

---

[7] On geopolitical tensions in East Asia see chapter 4, section II, in this volume.

USA in the form of military aid. Since the return to power of the Taliban in August 2021, the USA and other Western suppliers have stopped deliveries of major arms to Afghanistan. It is doubtful that the new government would be able to fund significant acquisitions of major arms within the next few years, but even if it could, it seems unlikely that any of the world's main suppliers would be willing to deliver such arms to the Taliban.[8]

India and Pakistan

Arms imports by India decreased by 21 per cent between 2012–16 and 2017–21. Despite this, India was the world's largest importer of major arms in 2017–21 and accounted for 11 per cent of total global arms imports in the period.

Russia was the largest supplier of major arms to India in both 2012–16 and 2017–21, but India's imports of Russian arms dropped by 47 per cent between the two periods as several large programmes for Russian arms wound down. This, combined with India's increased efforts to diversify its arms supplier base, meant that Russia's share of total Indian arms imports fell from 69 per cent to 46 per cent. In contrast, India's arms imports from France increased more than tenfold, making it India's second largest arms supplier in 2017–21.

Because of perceived growing threats from Pakistan and China and because of significant delays in the production of its own major arms, India has large-scale plans for future arms imports. The drop in India's arms imports is, therefore, probably a temporary result of its slow and complex procurement process as well as its shift in suppliers.

Arms imports by Pakistan decreased by 11 per cent between 2012–16 and 2017–21, but it remained the eighth largest importer globally in 2017–21. Pakistan's political rift with the USA, which dates back to around 2007, has resulted in a significant reduction in US arms supplies to Pakistan, either as aid or in sales, over the past decade.[9] US arms deliveries in 2012–16 were 65 per cent lower than in 2007–11 and dropped by another 92 per cent between 2012–16 and 2017–21. This brought the share of US deliveries to only 1.4 per cent of total arms imports by Pakistan in 2017–21. The USA's unwillingness to supply arms has caused Pakistan to rely even more heavily on imports from China. China accounted for 67 per cent of Pakistan's arm imports in 2012–16 and for 72 per cent in 2017–21. In 2021 the USA refused to allow the export of engines of US design intended for combat helicopters Pakistan had ordered from Turkey, whereupon Pakistan cancelled the order and opened

---

[8] See also Kuimova, A. and Wezeman, S. T., 'Transfers of major arms to Afghanistan between 2001 and 2020', SIPRI Topical Backgrounder, 3 Sep. 2021. On the armed conflict in Afghanistan see chapter 4, section III, in this volume.

[9] Kronstadt, K. A., 'Pakistan–US relations', In Focus, Congressional Research Service, 8 July 2021.

negotiations with China for an alternative combat helicopter.[10] While the USA restricted almost all arms exports to Pakistan in 2017–21, several West European states continued to deliver major arms. These included Sweden and Italy, which accounted for 6.4 per cent and 5.3 per cent of Pakistan's arms imports, respectively.

India and Pakistan are embroiled in a long-standing conflict with each other over territorial claims to Kashmir, and their acquisitions of major arms often follow an action–reaction pattern.[11] For example, in 2017 India acquired 36 Rafale combat aircraft from France. One reason why India chose the Rafale was because it was supplied with the Meteor air-to-air missile, which has better capability than the US and Chinese missiles Pakistan used on its combat aircraft at that time. Pakistan had acquired the US and Chinese missiles some years before as they had better capability than the Russian missiles deployed on Indian combat aircraft at that time.[12] In 2021 Pakistan ordered 25 J-10C combat aircraft from China in response to India's acquisition of Rafales.[13] Notably, the J-10C can use the PL-15 air-to-air missile, which reportedly has the same range as, or possibly an even longer range than, the Meteor.[14]

Australia

Arms imports by Australia rose by 62 per cent between 2012–16 and 2017–21, making it the fourth largest arms importer globally in 2017–21. The USA accounted for 67 per cent of Australia's imports of major arms, followed by Spain with 24 per cent. The most significant imports included a total of 50 F-35A and EA-18G combat aircraft as well as 11 P-8A anti-submarine aircraft from the USA, and 3 Hobart destroyers from Spain.

Australia also has several large orders with pending deliveries, mostly from the United Kingdom and the USA. Notably, in 2021 Australia cancelled an order of up to 12 conventionally powered (i.e. not nuclear-powered) submarines from France. The decision came as Australia expanded its security cooperation with the UK and the USA under a trilateral agreement (AUKUS

---

[10] Bekdil, B. E., Ansari, U. and Gould, J., 'Pakistan extends delayed T129 helo deal with Turkey—again', *Defense News*, 15 Mar. 2021; and Herschelman, K., 'Pakistan cancels attack helicopter project with Turkey, opting for China', Janes, 6 Jan. 2022.

[11] On the armed conflict in the Kashmir region, including tensions between India and China, see chapter 4, section III, in this volume.

[12] 'Why IAF is counting on 1 missile on the Rafale fighter to counter China', *The Week*, 30 June 2020; and 'Rafale "game changer" SCALP and Meteor missiles give India a formidable edge', *Economic Times*, 18 Dec. 2020.

[13] 'Pakistan acquires J-10C fighter jets from China to counter India's rafale', *Daily Times*, 30 Dec. 2021.

[14] 'Pakistan officially inducts Chinese-built J-10C fighter jets', Airforce Technology, 14 Mar. 2022; Bronk, J., *Russian and Chinese Combat Air Trends: Current Capabilities and Future Threat Outlook*, Whitehall Report 3-20 (Royal United Services Institute, RUSI: London, Oct. 2020), p. 36; and Chuanren, C., 'New Chinese weapons seen on J-10C fighter', AIN Online, 20 July 2017.

agreement), directed mainly against China. As part of the AUKUS agreement, Australia ordered or selected several types of long-range (400–900 kilometres) land-attack missile from the USA. In addition, the UK and the USA offered to supply at least eight nuclear-powered submarines to Australia.[15] The details of the proposed submarine deal had not been defined as at the end of 2021.

The changes to Australia's submarine programme are an example of how arms acquisition plans can sometimes change rapidly as well as the long time frame between selection and final delivery of major arms. Australia originally planned to replace 6 existing submarines with 10 to 12 boats for delivery from 2026 at a cost of around US$20 billion. In 2014 Australia appeared to favour a submarine of Japanese design. However, in 2016 it signed an agreement with France for 12 submarines at a cost of US$38 billion, with delivery planned for the early 2030s. By early 2021, the cost had increased to around US$70 billion and the start of delivery had been delayed until 2033 or 2034. The new nuclear submarine programme under the proposed deal with the UK and the USA is for much larger boats with more armaments, but at a higher cost—one estimate for the eight submarines was around US$120 billion. If the proposed deal is agreed, delivery would most likely start only in the 2030s or even the 2040s.[16]

East Asia

East Asia accounted for 12 per cent of global imports of major arms in 2017–21. Arms imports by East Asian states rose by 20 per cent between 2012–16 and 2017–21, reflecting the increasing tensions in the subregion. Of the 6 states in East Asia, 3 (China, South Korea and Japan) were among the 10 largest arms importers in 2017–21, despite all 3 having arms industries that can produce indigenous designs covering much or even most of their demands for major arms.

Chinese arms imports remained stable between 2012–16 and 2017–21 and mainly came from Russia in both periods. However, China's arms imports are likely to decrease in the next few years as its industry is now capable of producing all types of major arms and their components. Engines from Russia for Chinese J-10, J-15, J-20 and H-6K combat aircraft and Y-20 transport aircraft make up a significant proportion of China's arms imports. These engines accounted for 39 per cent of total Chinese arms imports in 2017–21. The imports were needed because China's development of indigenous

---

[15] Australian Department of Defence, 'Australia to pursue nuclear-powered submarines through new trilateral enhanced security partnership', Joint media statement, 16 Sep. 2021; and LaGrone, S., 'CNO Gilday: Developing, building Australian nuclear submarine could take decades', USNI News, 23 Sep. 2021.

[16] LaGrone (note 15); and Nicholls, A., Dowie, J. and Hellyer, M., *Implementing Australia's Nuclear Submarine Programme* (Australian Strategic Policy Institute: Canberra, Dec. 2021).

alternatives was beset with technical problems during most of this period. However, by 2021 it appeared that China had mastered series production of indigenous engine designs and Chinese production of combat and transport aircraft progressed to versions with Chinese engines.[17]

Arms imports by South Korea grew by 71 per cent and those by Japan rose by 152 per cent. The USA was the main supplier to both states in 2017–21. While both South Korea and Japan have large arms industries that are capable of developing many of the most advanced major arms and from which the bulk of their respective acquisitions is sourced, they continue to be partly reliant on foreign suppliers, especially for advanced ('fifth generation') combat aircraft, long-range air defence systems and helicopters. South Korea received, among other major arms, 36 F-35A combat aircraft, 8 Patriot SAM systems and 18 AH-64E combat helicopters from the USA, and 4 Type-214 submarines from Germany. Japan's imports included 27 F-35As and 38 helicopters from the USA. Many of the imports by South Korea and Japan involve production under licence or local production of some components. Both states have active programmes to develop their own advanced combat aircraft, air defence systems and helicopters, and South Korea commissioned its first indigenous submarine in 2021.[18]

Taiwan's arms imports were 68 per cent lower in 2017–21 than in 2012–16. However, its arms imports will increase in the coming five years based on recent orders signed with the USA for 66 F-16V combat aircraft, 108 M-1A2 tanks, and coastal defence systems with Harpoon anti-ship missiles. The US arms sales to Taiwan came as China continued to ramp up pressure on Taiwan, including through increased military activity around and directed towards Taiwan.[19] China not only protested against the sales, as it has done after similar USA–Taiwan deals, but also started to target US companies involved in the sales. In 2020 several major US arms companies were named by China as being sanctioned over sales to Taiwan.[20]

Myanmar

Compared with some other arms-importing states in Asia and Oceania, Myanmar received a relatively low volume of arms deliveries during the

---

[17] Farley, R. and Lovell, J. T., 'Why China struggles to produce an indigenous jet engine', *National Interest*, 2 Sep. 2021; and Lendon, B., 'China has upgraded its best stealth fighter jet with domestic-made engines', CNN, 29 Sep. 2021.

[18] Manaranche, M., 'ROK Navy commissions her first KSS III submarine', Naval News, 13 Aug. 2021. All submarines acquired by Japan since the mid 1950s have been of indigenous design. See e.g. *Jane's Fighting Ships*, various issues.

[19] Brown, D., 'China and Taiwan: A really simple guide to a growing conflict', BBC News, 12 Jan. 2022.

[20] McDonald, J., AP News, 'China to sanction Boeing, Lockheed and Raytheon over Taiwan arms sales', *Defense News*, 26 Oct. 2020; and AP News, 'China sanctions Raytheon, Lockheed over Taiwan deal', *Defense News*, 22 Feb. 2022.

past decade. Its arms imports decreased by 32 per cent between 2012–16 and 2017–21. Nevertheless, Myanmar accounted for 0.6 per cent of total global arms imports in 2017–21, despite the widespread criticism of its violent military campaign against the Rohingya minority since 2016 and the repression of citizens by the military after the coup in February 2021. Imported major arms were employed by the military in both cases and continue to be used for such purposes.[21] China, Russia and India were Myanmar's main arms suppliers in 2017–21. Deliveries included 30 combat-capable aircraft, with 20 Yak-130s coming from Russia and a total of 10 JF-17s and K-8s coming from China. India delivered 1 submarine and its armaments.

Europe

In 2017–21 arms imports by European states were 19 per cent higher than in 2012–16. The USA accounted for 54 per cent of the region's arms imports in 2017–21, followed by Russia (7.9 per cent) and Germany (6.2 per cent). The increase in European arms imports coincided with rising tensions between most European states and Russia, particularly with regard to Ukraine since 2014.

The three largest importers of major arms in Europe in 2017–21 were the UK, Norway and the Netherlands. All three increased their arms imports significantly between 2012–16 and 2017–21, ranging from 74 per cent for the UK to 116 per cent for the Netherlands and 343 per cent for Norway. They imported a total of 71 F-35 combat aircraft from the USA, which accounted for the bulk of their respective arms imports in 2017–21.

Other European states are also expected to increase their arms imports significantly over the coming decade, based on recent orders for major arms. Poland, for example, made several notable arms procurement decisions in 2017–21. Although its national arms industry will supply part of Poland's armament requirements, most of the new procurement programmes will involve arms imports, in particular from the USA. By the end of 2021, Polish arms procurement agreements with the USA included deals for 32 F-35s, 70 JASSM-ER long-range (1000 km) air-to-ground missiles, 250 M-1A2 tanks, 20 HIMARS multiple rocket launchers with 30 ATACMS ballistic missiles, and 4 Patriot SAM systems.

While the overall volumes of arms imported remained relatively small compared with much larger European states, the three Baltic states (Estonia, Latvia and Lithuania) increased their arms imports significantly between

---

[21] See e.g. United Nations, Human Rights Council, Enabling Atrocities: UN Member States' Arms Transfers to the Myanmar Military, Conference room paper of the Special Rapporteur on the situation of human rights in Myanmar, A/HRC/49/CRP.1, 22 Feb. 2022. On the armed conflict in Myanmar see chapter 4, section IV, in this volume.

2012–16 and 2017–21. These increases ranged from 113 per cent for Latvia to 119 per cent for Estonia and 152 per cent for Lithuania.

As at the end of 2021, several states in Western Europe had large orders of major arms with pending deliveries. The most significant of these are for aircraft and naval vessels. Examples of pending deliveries of aircraft include a total of 331 F-35s, which will be supplied by the USA to the UK (112), Finland (64), Italy (45), Switzerland (36), Belgium (34), the Netherlands (22) and Norway (18). The USA will also deliver 4 P-8A anti-submarine aircraft to Norway, 5 to Germany and the last aircraft from an order of 9 to the UK. In the naval domain, pending transfers mainly involve contracts between European states. Examples include planned deliveries from Germany of four Type-212 submarines to Norway and two to Italy, and a planned delivery from France of four Gowind-2500 frigates to Romania.

Four states in Europe imported major arms from Russia in 2017–21. Belarus, Russia's closest ally, received almost all of its major arms from Russia, while Armenia received 82 per cent of its major arms from Russia. The other two states—Azerbaijan (which received 22 per cent of its major arms from Russia) and Serbia (61 per cent)—were less reliant on Russia for their arms imports.

Ukraine

Despite the armed conflict in the east of the country with rebel forces supported by Russia that continued throughout 2017–21 and its inventory of generally older types of major arms that are in many cases coming to the end of their useful lives, Ukraine's imports of major arms were very limited in 2017–21 and accounted for only 0.1 per cent of total global arms imports in the period.[22] Most of the deliveries of major arms to Ukraine in 2017–21 had more of a political than military significance and were mainly intended to show support for Ukraine as tensions with Russia intensified. The transfer to Ukraine with potentially the largest military impact on its conflict with the rebel forces on its eastern flank was Turkey's delivery of 12 Bayraktar TB-2 armed UAVs in 2019–21. These were a new capability for Ukraine and were reportedly first used against rebel forces in 2021. Additional deliveries of UAVs from Turkey were pending as at the end of 2021.[23] As the tensions between Russia and Ukraine worsened in late 2021, raising the spectre of a Russian invasion, the USA sent additional military aid—such as deliveries of Javelin light, but advanced, anti-tank missiles—and agreed to make further supplies in 2022, including another 300 Javelin missiles. In addition, Estonia

---

[22] For further detail on Ukraine's inventory of major arms see e.g. International Institute for Strategic Studies, *The Military Balance 2022* (Routledge: Abingdon, Feb. 2022), pp. 211–15. On the armed conflict in Ukraine see chapter 5, section II, in this volume.

[23] 'More Bayraktar TB2 UCAS for Ukraine', Scramble, 17 Jan. 2022; and Jennings, G., 'Ukraine conflict: Turkey airlifts additional TB2 UCAVs to Ukraine', Janes, 2 Mar. 2022.

agreed in December 2021 to supply around 50 Javelin missiles to Ukraine as aid.[24]

Czechia was the main supplier of major arms to Ukraine in 2017–21, accounting for 41 per cent of total Ukrainian arms imports and delivering 87 BMP-1 infantry fighting vehicles and 56 self-propelled guns—all second-hand equipment of Soviet origin. The USA was the second largest supplier, accounting for 31 per cent. US deliveries, mainly as aid, included 540 Javelin missiles. France, Lithuania, Poland and Turkey were Ukraine's only other suppliers of major arms in 2017–21.

The low level of arms transfers to Ukraine in 2017–21 is partly explained by its limited financial resources.[25] It also has a local arms industry capable of producing some major arms and a large, albeit ageing, inventory of military equipment. In addition, up until the Russian invasion in February 2022, several European Union (EU) member states, including Germany, had been reluctant to provide Ukraine with military equipment due to concerns that transfers of major arms could contribute to conflict escalation or hinder a dialogue with Russia on a peaceful solution.[26]

The Middle East

Arms imports by states in the Middle East were 2.8 per cent higher in 2017–21 than in 2012–16. This followed an 86 per cent increase between 2007–11 and 2012–16. Four of the top 10 arms-importing states in 2017–21 are in the Middle East: Saudi Arabia, Egypt, Qatar and the UAE. The USA accounted for 53 per cent of arms imports by states in the region, followed by France (12 per cent) and Russia (11 per cent).

The Gulf region

As the conflict in Yemen continued and tensions between several states and Iran remained high, arms imports played an important role in security developments in the Gulf region in 2017–21.[27] Saudi Arabia, for example, increased its arms imports by 27 per cent between 2012–16 and 2017–21.

---

[24] 'State planning artillery, missile system supply to Ukrainian armed forces', ERR.ee, 31 Dec. 2021. Many NATO and EU member states decided to supply weapons, including major arms, to Ukraine in early 2022—just before or after the start of the Russian invasion of Ukraine on 24 Feb. 2022. This included states that had previously been reluctant to supply weapons. The data presented here covers decisions and deliveries until 31 Dec. 2021. The decisions and deliveries made in 2022 are thus not included.

[25] For further detail on Ukraine's military expenditure see chapter 8, section II, in this volume.

[26] Minzarari, D. and Stewart, S., 'The logic of defence assistance to Ukraine: A strategic assessment', SWP Comment no. 42, German Institute for International and Security Affairs (SWP), 9 July 2021; Neukirch, R., 'Germany's position on weapons for Ukraine makes no sense: Balderdash from Berlin', *Der Spiegel*, 28 Jan. 2022; and Kurmayer, N. J., 'Germany rejects military aid to Ukraine, prefers political solution', Euractiv, 2 June 2021.

[27] On the armed conflict in Yemen see chapter 6, section V, in this volume.

It received 11 per cent of total global arms imports, making it the second largest arms importer in the world, just behind India. The USA accounted for 82 per cent of Saudi Arabian arms imports in 2017–21. US arms supplies included 97 F-15SA combat aircraft, a type used by Saudi Arabia in the war in Yemen, and 8 Patriot air defence systems, a type used against missiles fired by Houthi rebels in Yemen. The USA also supplied thousands of guided bombs, although further deliveries of such bombs were reportedly suspended in 2021 by the administration of President Joe Biden. Several other states have restricted arms exports to Saudi Arabia partly because of its military operations in Yemen. For example, Germany maintained in 2021 significant restrictions on arms exports to Saudi Arabia, which were first imposed in 2018.[28] Nevertheless, such restrictions had only a limited effect on the overall capacity of Saudi Arabia to import major arms and, by the end of 2021, several deliveries from other states were pending. These included 51 F-15SA combat aircraft from the USA, 5 Avante-2200 frigates from Spain and hundreds of LAV-700 armoured vehicles from Canada.

During 2017–21, the UAE was active in the war in Yemen as well as in the war in Libya. Despite this, its arms imports dropped by 41 per cent between 2012–16 and 2017–21, taking it from the third largest to the ninth largest arms importer globally. Based on pending deliveries under current contracts, however, the volume of arms imports by the UAE is likely to remain at a high level in the coming five years. The largest of these deals, for 80 Rafale combat aircraft from France, was agreed in 2021 and deliveries are expected to start in 2027.

Some major arms-supplying states have restricted arms exports to the UAE because of its role in the war in Yemen but, as with Saudi Arabia, these restrictions appear to have had only a limited impact on the UAE's ability to acquire arms. For example, in 2019 Italy restricted exports of arms to the UAE (and Saudi Arabia) that might be used in Yemen. However, in July 2021, after the UAE threatened to limit its military and trade relations with Italy, the restrictions were significantly loosened.[29]

Qatar's arms imports grew by 227 per cent between 2012–16 and 2017–21, propelling it from being the 22nd largest arms importer to the 6th largest. For the large-scale expansion of its armed forces that began in around 2010, Qatar has turned to several of the world's major arms suppliers. In 2017–21 Qatar received 46 per cent of its arms imports from the USA and 36 per cent from France. By the end of 2021, Qatar had large deliveries of major arms pending from the USA, France, Italy and the UK.

---

[28] 'Saudi-Arabien kritisiert deutschen Rüstungsexportstopp' [Saudi Arabia criticizes German arms export ban], *Der Spiegel*, 23 Feb. 2022.

[29] Amante, A., 'Italy eases curbs on arms sales to Saudi Arabia and UAE', Reuters, 6 July 2021.

Kuwait was outside the top 25 arms importers in 2017–21. However, it will probably be among this group in future years as it has pending deliveries scheduled for 2021–23 for 28 F/A-18E combat aircraft and 109 tanks from the USA and 26 Typhoon combat aircraft from Italy.

Iran's arms imports remained at a very low level in 2017–21 (at less than 0.05 per cent of global arms imports, compared with 0.3 per cent in 2012–16). Although the United Nations lifted its decade-long arms embargo on Iran in 2020, there was no publicly available evidence, as at the end of 2021, that Iran had since ordered or received notable volumes of major arms from abroad.[30]

Egypt

Egypt was the third largest arms importer in the world in 2017–21. Its arms imports accounted for 5.7 per cent of the global total and were 73 per cent higher than in 2012–16. The USA, which has been giving military aid to Egypt since 1978, was the largest arms supplier to Egypt in every five-year period between 1977 and 2016. However, arms imports from the USA fell by 70 per cent between 2012–16 and 2017–21. The USA accounted for only 6.5 per cent of Egyptian arms imports in 2017–21, making it the fifth largest supplier of major arms to Egypt.

Partly because of frictions with the USA since Egypt's military coup in 2013, Egypt has intensified its efforts to diversify its arms supplier base. Following the USA's decision in 2013 to suspend temporarily its military aid and arms deliveries to Egypt, Russia and France were among the first arms exporters to reaffirm their willingness to supply major arms to Egypt.[31] In 2017–21 Russia emerged as Egypt's largest supplier and accounted for 41 per cent of Egyptian arms imports, followed by France (21 per cent), Italy (15 per cent) and Germany (11 per cent).

Given that Egypt remains one of the USA's most important strategic partners in the Middle East, it seems likely that US arms exports to Egypt will start to grow again in the near future—even despite the concerns raised repeatedly by various civil society organizations and US politicians over Egypt's record of human rights violations.[32] The restrengthening of arms trade relations between the two states can be illustrated by the ongoing negotiations between Egypt and the USA for the purchase of F-15EX combat aircraft.[33] The F-15EX is very similar in capabilities to the Su-35 produced

---

[30] On multilateral arms embargoes see chapter 14, section II, in this volume.

[31] '3.2 billion euros of Egypt–French arms deal financed by loan from Paris: Sisi', Reuters, 1 Mar. 2015; and 'Russia, Egypt seal preliminary arms deal worth $3.5 billion: Agency', Reuters, 17 Sep. 2014.

[32] O'Brien, C., 'Senate rejects bid to block $2B sale of military planes to Egypt', Politico, 10 Mar. 2022; and US Department of State, 'US relations with Egypt', Bilateral Relations Fact Sheet, 5 Jan. 2021. On the armed conflict in Egypt see chapter 6, section IV, in this volume.

[33] Jennings, G., 'US to supply F-15s to Egypt', Janes, 16 Mar. 2022.

by Russia and this development suggests that Egypt's order for Su-35s from Russia may have been suspended or cancelled (see section II).

Israel

Israeli arms imports increased by 19 per cent between 2012–16 and 2017–21. The USA accounted for 92 per cent of Israeli arms imports in 2017–21, which included 31 F-35 combat aircraft and thousands of guided bombs supplied as military aid. The F-35, Israel's most advanced combat aircraft, has since 2018 been used in air strikes on targets in Gaza, Lebanon and Syria.[34] It is also widely considered to be a key component of Israel's capacity to potentially attack targets in Iran.[35] Pending arms imports by Israel include 17 F-35s and 2 tanker aircraft from the USA, and 4 MEKO frigates, 1 Dolphin submarine and 3 Dakar submarines from Germany.

[34] Pfeffer, A., 'Hamas in Gaza, Iranians in Syria: Israel's F-35 strikes carried message to both enemies and allies', *Haaretz*, 24 May 2018.

[35] Lewis, O., 'Netanyahu says Israel "mightier" as first F-35 fighter jets arrive', Reuters, 12 Dec. 2016; and Gross, J. A., 'In first, Israeli F-35s train in Italy with Iran in their sights', *Times of Israel*, 6 June 2021.

IV. The financial value of states' arms exports

PIETER D. WEZEMAN, ALEXANDRA KUIMOVA AND SIEMON T. WEZEMAN

Official data on the financial value of states' arms exports in the years 2011–20 is presented in table 9.7. The data is taken from reports by—or direct quotes from—national governments. The stated data coverage reflects the language used by the original source. National practices in this area vary, but the term 'arms exports' generally refers to the financial value of the arms actually delivered; 'arms export licences' generally refers to the financial value of the licences for arms exports issued by the national export licensing authority; and 'arms export agreements' or 'arms export orders' refers to the financial value of contracts or other agreements signed for arms exports.

The arms export data for the states in table 9.7 is based on national definitions and methodologies and is thus not necessarily comparable across countries. There is no internationally agreed definition of what constitutes 'arms' and governments use different lists when collecting and reporting data on the financial value of their arms exports. In addition, there is no standardized methodology concerning the collection and reporting of such data, with some states reporting on export licences issued or used and other states using data collected from customs agencies.

According to SIPRI's statistics on arms transfers, states that produce official data on the financial value of their arms exports accounted for over 90 per cent of the total volume of deliveries of major arms. By adding together the data in table 9.7 it is therefore possible to attain a rough estimate of the financial value of the total global arms trade. However, there are significant limitations in using this data to make such an estimate. First, as noted above, the data sets used are based on different definitions and methodologies and are not directly comparable. Second, several states (e.g. the United States and the United Kingdom) do not release data on arms exports but only on arms export agreements and licences, while other states (e.g. China) do not release any data on arms exports, licences, agreements or orders. Nonetheless, by adding together the data that states have made available on the financial value of their arms exports as well as estimates for those that only provide data on arms export licences, agreements or orders it is possible to roughly estimate the total value of the global arms trade. The estimate of the financial value of the global international arms trade for 2020—the latest year for which relevant data is available—was at least US$112 billion.[1] However, the true figure is likely to be higher.

It is difficult to assess the trend in the value of the global arms trade over time because countries do not always report consistently on their arms

---

[1] For a full description of the methodology used to calculate this figure see the SIPRI website.

export figures each year. This means that comparisons of the value of the global arms trade in different years provide only a very rough indication of trends over time. Nevertheless, the available data suggests a significant real-terms increase over time in the value of the global arms trade from at least $87 billion in 2011 (in constant 2020 US dollars) to at least $112 billion in 2020. Despite this increase, the estimated value of the global arms trade for 2020 is about 0.5 per cent of the value of the total global trade of all products and services in 2020.[2]

[2] The value of the total global trade in all products and services in 2020 was US$22 trillion. World Trade Organization (WTO), *World Trade Statistical Review 2021* (WTO: Geneva, 2021), p. 11.

Table 9.7. The financial value of states' arms exports according to national government and industry sources, 2011–20

Figures are in constant (2020) US$ m. Conversion to constant US dollars is made using the market exchange rates of the reporting year and the US consumer price index (CPI). Years are calendar years unless otherwise stated.

State	2011	2012	2013	2014	2015	2016	2017	2018	2019	2020	Explanation of data
Australia[a]	..	..	1 200	1 606	3 451	897	1 287	3 778	3 734	1 852	Arms export licences
Austria	688	659	776	778	407	762	452	363	385	485	Arms exports
	2 610	2 251	3 502	1 310	1 313	4 748	2 388	1 843	1 958	1 582	Arms export licences
Belgium	1 336	1 403	904	6 546	1 350	1 489	882	1 416	3 247	3 389	Arms export licences
Bosnia and Herzegovina	66	59	58	97	127	124	124	144	..	..	Arms exports
	91	67	165	187	279	364	352	283	..	..	Arms export licences
Bulgaria	369	317	347	585	1 698	1 210	1 451	931	696	745	Arms exports
	357	505	724	1 201	774	1 501	1 653	1 275	971	1 239	Arms export licences
Canada[b]	737	1 176	735	788	577	584	838	1 645	2 866	1 466	Arms exports
Croatia	56	74	127	103	47	88	81	119	49	81	Arms exports
	245	345	1 050	699	463	452	539	465	607	551	Arms export licences
Czechia	293	397	425	620	682	822	682	664	702	767	Arms exports
	553	384	484	726	899	410	606	474	627	339	Arms export licences
Denmark	..	..	34	65	93	134	108	100	187	219	Arms exports
	379	322	1 154	213	162	242	244	324	177	166	Arms export licences
Estonia	560	4	4	6	17	11	76	45	12	80	Arms exports
Finland	155	84	329	323	119	157	125	156	128	91	Arms exports
	294	171	507	329	438	117	233	214	119	349	Arms export licences
France	6 051	5 472	4 984	5 867	7 511	8 492	8 012	8 474	11 250	4 911	Arms exports
	5 833	4 843	5 724	5 579	7 339	8 326	7 907	8 371	11 720	4 838	Arms exports
Germany	10 424	6 977	10 140	11 920	20 492	16 628	8 262	11 092	9 432	5 543	Arms export licences
	2 055	1 370	1 376	2 644	1 883	2 984	3 157	938	934	1 570	Arms exports[c]
	8 659	6 813	8 622	5 764	9 517	8 167	7 430	5 869	9 084	6 641	Arms export licences
	8 607	6 043	3 680	3 691	6 007	70	387	18	576	458	Arms export licences[d]

Country	Category										
Hungary	Arms exports	29	39	47	48	56	23	52	45	60	55
	Arms export licences	250	391	757	627	1 554	702	695	482	646	584
India [e]	Arms exports	..	97	130	178	351	244	758	1 254	1 311	114
Ireland	Arms exports	43	68	91	125	52	75	30	40	48	55
	Arms export licences	..	..	..	..	..	..	..	..	..	..
Israel	Arms export agreements	6 696	..	7 266	6 188	6 224	7 009	9 714	7 730	7 289	8 300
	Arms exports	1 636	4 360	4 089	4 829	3 892	3 405	3 428	2 989	2 707	3 075
Italy	Arms exports	..	..	..	..	..	..	..	..	..	..
	Arms export licences	8 418	6 025	3 170	3 845	9 546	17 456	11 324	5 814	4 631	4 479
Korea, South	Arms exports	2 741	2 652	3 795	3 949	3 867	2 758	3 294	..	..	..
Latvia	Arms exports	<1	<1	<1	4	1	<1	106	13	15	3
Lithuania	Arms exports	77	28	24	27	33	49	85	116	59	76
	Arms export licences	82	29	32	22	71	110	71	55	56	55
Montenegro	Arms exports	..	4	4	13	5	1	7	10	..	..
	Arms export licences	6	7	9	16	13	10	11	22	..	55
Netherlands	Arms exports	1 235	1 191	373	363	717	675	792	696	505	761
	Arms export licences	665	1 363	1 421	2 996	1 057	1 689	958	782	1 046	800
Norway [f]	Arms exports	734	751	624	511	442	460	684	611	525	658
Pakistan [g]	Arms exports	12	15	14	19	66	33	61	..	..	..
	Arms export agreements	28	32	24	61	103	73	25	..	..	..
Poland	Arms exports	..	..	496	574	510	457	562	592	443	446
	Arms export licences	1 358	917	1 266	1 334	1 537	1 463	1 287	1 894	2 179	1 613
Portugal	Arms exports	40	45	260	227	231	712	193	255	444	203
	Arms export licences	50	75	215	369	82	291	70	209	197	120
Romania	Arms exports	210	120	261	231	195	216	230	237	163	132
	Arms export licences	294	259	437	361	266	287	314	248	175	200
Russia	Arms exports	15 763	17 134	17 442	17 055	15 833	16 175	>15 000	16 491	>15 000	>15 000
Serbia	Arms exports	200	211	193	342	423	485	292	505	..	..
	Arms export licences	456	505	903	876	885	997	865	803	..	..
Slovakia	Arms exports	16	36	46	53	69	72	82	113	77	105
	Arms export licences	48	106	180	389	343	248	273	230	213	303

State	2011	2012	2013	2014	2015	2016	2017	2018	2019	2020	Explanation of data
Slovenia	14	6	4	7	13	18	29	14	17	21	Arms exports
	19	13	13	4	38	51	61	79	57	325	Arms export licences
South Africa	1 455	1 456	363	300	234	305	272	368	285	189	Arms export licences
Spain	3 888	2 829	5 765	4 646	4 505	4 832	5 174	4 527	4 581	4 131	Arms exports
	4 592	11 145	6 374	5 317	12 930	6 619	25 096	13 873	11 436	30 276	Arms export licences
Sweden	2 465	1 624	2 037	1 268	966	1 383	1 387	1 348	1 742	1 773	Arms exports
	1 931	1 320	1 676	714	641	7 790	1 003	1 004	1 446	1 623	Arms export licences
Switzerland	1 131	842	553	673	507	451	479	538	741	960	Arms exports
Turkey	940	1 353	1 544	1 801	1 807	1 809	1 836	2 097	2 775	2 279	Arms exports
UK	9 955	15 661	17 021	15 301	12 846	8 584	12 186	19 249	14 204	10 128	Arms export orders [h]
	11 201	3 858	7 718	3 750	9 711	4 712	8 985	3 845	6 592	4 487	Arms export licences
Ukraine	1 155	1 154	1 111	..	622	830	..	790	919	981	Arms exports
USA [i]	22 484	19 781	22 584	21 235	23 126	22 765	32 270	..	..	..	Arms exports [j]
	29 730	70 696	26 088	34 306	49 008	53 745	54 459	65 378	55 741	59 577	Arms export licences [k]
	29 730	70 696	26 088	34 306	49 008	29 672	52 129	..	..	..	Arms export agreements [l]
	..	..	..	..	..	36 264	44 265	57 366	56 069	50 782	Arms export agreements [m]

.. = data not available.

Notes: The countries included in this table are those that provide official data on the financial value of either 'arms exports', 'contracts signed for arms exports', 'arms export orders placed' or 'licences for arms exports' for at least 6 of the 10 years covered and where the annual average of the values given in at least one of the data sets for each state exceeds $10 million. The arms export data for the different states in this table is not necessarily comparable and may be based on significantly different definitions and methodologies.

[a] Figures for Australia cover the period 1 July–30 June (e.g. the 2020 figure covers the period 1 July 2020–30 June 2021).
[b] Figures for Canada exclude exports to the USA.
[c] These figures only include exports of 'war weapons' as defined under German legislation.
[d] These figures include arms export licences for international collaborative projects.
[e] Figures for India cover the period 1 Apr.–31 Mar. (e.g. the figure for 2020 covers the period 1 Apr. 2020–31 Mar. 2021).
[f] Figures for Norway exclude dual-use goods and defence-related services.
[g] Figures for Pakistan for 2009–17 cover the period 1 Apr.–31 Mar. (e.g. the figure for 2017 covers the period 1 Apr. 2017–31 Mar. 2018).

h Figures cover defence equipment and additional aerospace equipment and services.

i Figures for the USA are for the period 1 Oct.–30 Sep. (e.g. the figure for 2020 covers the period 1 Oct. 2019–30 Sep. 2020.

j Figures include items sold under the government-to-government Foreign Military Sales programme as well as direct commercial sales by US companies to foreign governments.

k Figures only include items sold as direct commercial sales; they do not include sales under the government-to-government Foreign Military Sales programme.

l Figures were calculated by the reporting authority using an old methodology. Arms export agreements are counted as such if the US government and recipient government signed a Letter of Agreement. Figures only include items sold under the government-to-government Foreign Military Sales programme; they do not include direct commercial sales by US companies to foreign governments.

m Figures were calculated using a new methodology that the reporting authority adopted starting in 2020. Arms export agreements are counted as such if the US government and recipient government signed a Letter of Agreement and an initial payment was made. Figures only include items sold under the government-to-government Foreign Military Sales programme; they do not include direct commercial sales by US companies to foreign governments.

Sources: Reports by—or direct quotes from—national governments. For a full list of sources and all available financial data on arms exports see the 'Financial value of the global arms trade' page of the SIPRI website.

10. World nuclear forces

Overview

At the start of 2022, nine states—the United States, Russia, the United Kingdom, France, China, India, Pakistan, Israel and the Democratic People's Republic of Korea (DPRK, or North Korea)—possessed approximately 12 705 nuclear weapons, of which 9440 were estimated to be in military stockpiles for potential use. About 3732 of these warheads were estimated to be deployed with operational forces (see table 10.1), and around 2000 of these were kept in a state of high operational alert.

Overall, the number of nuclear warheads in the world continues to decline. However, this is primarily due to the USA and Russia dismantling retired warheads. Global reductions of operational warheads appear to have stalled, and their numbers may be rising again. At the same time, both the USA and Russia have extensive and expensive programmes under way to replace and modernize their nuclear warheads, missile and aircraft delivery systems, and nuclear weapon production facilities (see sections I and II).

The nuclear arsenals of the other nuclear-armed states are considerably smaller (see sections III–IX), but all are either developing or deploying new weapon systems or have announced their intention to do so. China is in the middle of a significant modernization and expansion of its nuclear arsenal, and India and Pakistan also appear to be increasing the size of their nuclear weapon inventories. In 2021 the UK announced its intention to increase the cap for its nuclear stockpile. North Korea's military nuclear programme remains central to its national security strategy and it may have assembled up to 20 warheads.

The availability of reliable information on the status of the nuclear arsenals and capabilities of the nuclear-armed states varies considerably. The USA, the UK and France have declared some information. Russia refuses to publicly disclose the detailed breakdown of its strategic nuclear forces, even though it shares the information with the USA. China releases little information about force numbers or future development plans. The governments of India and Pakistan make statements about some of their missile tests but provide no information about the status or size of their arsenals. North Korea has acknowledged conducting nuclear weapon and missile tests but provides no information about the size of its nuclear arsenal. Israel has a long-standing policy of not commenting on its nuclear arsenal.

The raw material for nuclear weapons is fissile material, either highly enriched uranium or separated plutonium (see section X).

HANS M. KRISTENSEN AND MATT KORDA

SIPRI Yearbook 2022: Armaments, Disarmament and International Security
www.sipriyearbook.org

Table 10.1. World nuclear forces, January 2022

All figures are approximate and are estimates based on assessments by the authors. The estimates presented here are based on publicly available information and contain some uncertainties, as reflected in the notes to tables 10.1–10.10.

State	Year of first nuclear test	Deployed warheads[a]	Stored warheads[b]	Total stockpile[c]	Retired warheads	Total inventory
United States	1945	1 744[d]	1 964[e]	3 708	1 720[f]	5 428
Russia	1949	1 588[g]	2 889[h]	4 477	1 500[f]	5 977
United Kingdom	1952	120	60	180	45[i]	225[j]
France	1960	280	10[k]	290	..	290
China	1964	–	350	350	–	350
India	1974	–	160	160	..	160
Pakistan	1998	–	165	165	..	165
Israel	..	–	90	90	..	90
North Korea	2006	–	20	20	..	20[l]
Total		**3 732**	**5 708**	**9 440**	**3 265**	**12 705**

.. = not applicable or not available; – = nil or a negligible value.

Note: SIPRI revises its world nuclear forces data each year based on new information and updates to earlier assessments. The data for Jan. 2022 replaces all previously published SIPRI data on world nuclear forces.

[a] These are warheads placed on missiles or located on bases with operational forces.

[b] These are warheads in central storage that would require some preparation (e.g. transport and loading on to launchers) before they could be deployed.

[c] Some states, such as the USA, use the official term 'stockpile' to refer to this subset of warheads, while others, such as the UK, often use 'stockpile' to describe the entire nuclear inventory. SIPRI uses the term 'stockpile' to refer to all deployed warheads as well as warheads in central storage that could potentially be deployed after some preparation.

[d] This figure includes c. 1344 warheads deployed on ballistic missiles and c. 300 stored at bomber bases in the USA, as well as c. 100 non-strategic (tactical) nuclear bombs deployed outside the USA at North Atlantic Treaty Organization partner bases.

[e] This figure includes c. 100 non-strategic nuclear bombs stored in the USA.

[f] This figure is for retired warheads awaiting dismantlement.

[g] This figure includes c. 1388 strategic warheads deployed on ballistic missiles and c. 200 deployed at heavy bomber bases.

[h] This figure includes c. 977 strategic and c. 1912 non-strategic warheads in central storage.

[i] This figure refers to retired warheads that have not yet been dismantled. It seems likely that they will be reconstituted to become part of the UK's total stockpile over the coming years (see note j).

[j] The British government declared in 2010 that its nuclear weapon inventory would not exceed 225 warheads. It is estimated here that the inventory remained at that number in Jan. 2022. A planned reduction to an inventory of 180 warheads by the mid 2020s was ended by a government review published in 2021. The review introduced a new ceiling of 260 warheads.

[k] The 10 warheads assigned to France's carrier-based aircraft are thought to be kept in central storage and are not normally deployed.

[l] In previous editions of the SIPRI Yearbook, this figure referred to the number of nuclear warheads that North Korea could potentially build with the amount of fissile material it has produced. However, SIPRI's estimate for Jan. 2022 is that North Korea has assembled up to 20 warheads. This is the first time that figures for North Korea have been included in the global totals.

I. United States nuclear forces

HANS M. KRISTENSEN AND MATT KORDA

As of January 2022, the United States maintained a military stockpile of approximately 3708 nuclear warheads, around 100 fewer than the estimate for January 2021. Approximately 1744 of these—consisting of about 1644 strategic and roughly 100 non-strategic (tactical) warheads—were deployed on ballistic missiles and bomber bases. In addition, about 1964 warheads were held in reserve and around 1720 retired warheads were awaiting dismantlement (30 fewer than the previous year's estimate), giving a total inventory of approximately 5428 nuclear warheads (see table 10.2).

These estimates are based on publicly available information regarding the US nuclear arsenal and SIPRI estimates.[1] In 2010 the USA for the first time declassified the entire history of its nuclear weapon stockpile size.[2] Both the annual US stockpile size and the annual number of dismantled warheads were declassified every subsequent year. However, the administration of President Donald J. Trump halted this transparency process in 2019, refusing to disclose any numbers for 2018–19.[3] In 2021 the administration of President Joe Biden restored nuclear transparency by declassifying both numbers for the entire history of the US nuclear arsenal until September 2020.[4] This effort revealed that the US nuclear stockpile consisted of 3750 warheads in September 2020, 3805 warheads in 2019 and 3785 warheads in 2018.[5] The US stockpile is expected to continue to decline gradually over the next decade as nuclear modernization programmes consolidate some nuclear weapon types.

In 2021 the USA remained in compliance with the final warhead limits prescribed by the 2010 Russian–US Treaty on Measures for the Further Reduction and Limitation of Strategic Offensive Arms (New START), which places a cap on the numbers of US and Russian deployed strategic nuclear forces.[6] The most recent data exchange, on 1 September 2021, listed the USA deploying 1389 warheads attributed to 665 ballistic missiles and heavy

---

[1] Kristensen, H. M. and Korda, M., 'Estimating world nuclear forces: An overview and assessment of sources', SIPRI Topical Backgrounder, 14 June 2021.

[2] See e.g. US Department of Defense, 'Increasing transparency in the US nuclear weapons stockpile', Fact sheet, 3 May 2010.

[3] Kristensen, H. M., 'Trump administration again refuses to disclose nuclear stockpile size', FAS Strategic Security Blog, Federation of American Scientists, 3 Dec. 2020.

[4] US Department of State, 'Transparency in the US nuclear weapons stockpile', Fact sheet, 5 Oct. 2021.

[5] US Department of State (note 4).

[6] For a summary and other details of New START see annex A, section III, in this volume. On the negotiation of the renewal of New START see chapter 11, section I, in this volume.

Table 10.2. United States nuclear forces, January 2022

All figures are approximate and some are based on assessments by the authors.

Type	Designation	No. of launchers	Year first deployed	Range (km)[a]	Warheads x yield	No. of warheads[b]
Strategic nuclear forces		**746**				**3 508**[c]
Aircraft (bombers)		*107/66*[d]				*788*[e]
B-52H	Stratofortress	87/46	1961	16 000	20 x AGM-86B ALCMs 5–150 kt[f]	500[g]
B-2A	Spirit	20/20	1994	11 000	16 x B61-7, -11, B83-1 bombs[h]	288
Land-based missiles (ICBMs)		*400*				*800*[i]
LGM-30G Minuteman III						
	Mk12A	200	1979	13 000	1–3 x W78 335 kt	600[j]
	Mk21 SERV	200	2006	13 000	1 x W87 300 kt	200[k]
Sea-based missiles (SLBMs)		*14/280*[l]				*1 920*[m]
UGM-133A Trident II D5(LE)						
	Mk4	..	1992	>12 000	1–8 x W76-0 100 kt	–[n]
	Mk4A	..	2008	>12 000	1–8 x W76-1 90 kt	1 511
	Mk4A	..	2019	>12 000	1 x W76-2[o] 8 kt	25
	Mk5	..	1990	>12 000	1–8 x W88 455 kt	384
Non-strategic nuclear forces						**200**[p]
F-15E	Strike Eagle	..	1988	3 840	5 x B61-3, -4	80
F-16C/D	Falcon	..	1987	3 200[q]	2 x B61-3, -4	60
F-16MLU	Falcon (NATO)	..	1985	3 200	2 x B61-3, -4	30
PA-200	Tornado (NATO)	..	1983	2 400	2 x B61-3, -4	30
Total stockpile						**3 708**[r]
Deployed warheads						1 744
Reserve warheads						1 964
Retired warheads awaiting dismantlement						**1 720**[s]
Total inventory						**5 428**[t]

.. = not available or not applicable; – = nil or a negligible value; ALCM = air-launched cruise missile; ICBM = intercontinental ballistic missile; kt = kiloton; NATO = North Atlantic Treaty Organization; SERV = security-enhanced re-entry vehicle; SLBM = submarine-launched ballistic missile.

[a] For aircraft, the listed range is for illustrative purposes only; actual mission range will vary according to flight profile, weapon payload and in-flight refuelling.

[b] These figures show the total number of warheads estimated to be assigned to nuclear-capable delivery systems. Only some of these warheads have been deployed on missiles and at air bases.

[c] Approximately 1644 of these strategic warheads were deployed on land- and sea-based ballistic missiles and at bomber bases. The remaining warheads were in central storage. This number is different from the number of deployed strategic warheads counted by the 2010 Russian–US Treaty on Measures for the Further Reduction and Limitation of Strategic Offensive Arms (New START) because the treaty attributes one weapon to each deployed bomber, even though bombers do not carry weapons under normal circumstances Additionally, the treaty does not count weapons stored at bomber bases and, at any given time, some nuclear-powered ballistic missile submarines (SSBNs) are not fully loaded with warheads and are thus not counted under the treaty.

[d] The first figure is the total number of bombers in the inventory; the second is the number of bombers that are counted as nuclear-capable under New START. The USA has declared that it

will deploy no more than 60 nuclear bombers at any given time but normally only about 50 are deployed (45 were counted as deployed under New START as of Sep. 2021), with the remaining aircraft in overhaul.

[e] The estimate of c. 788 warheads assigned to strategic bombers is a decrease from the estimate of c. 848 warheads in *SIPRI Yearbook 2021*. The decrease is not the result of a recent retirement of weapons but of a reassessment of the number of warheads that are assigned to the bombers. Of the c. 788 bomber weapons, c. 300 (200 ALCMs and 100 bombs) were deployed at the bomber bases; all the rest were in central storage. Many of the gravity bombs are no longer fully active and are slated for retirement after deployment of the B61-12 in the early 2020s.

[f] The B-52H is no longer configured to carry nuclear gravity bombs.

[g] In 2006 the US Department of Defense decided to reduce the number of ALCMs to 528 missiles. Burg, R., Director of Strategic Security in the Air, Space and Information Operations, 'ICBMs, helicopters, cruise missiles, bombers and warheads', Statement before the Subcommittee on Strategic Forces, US Senate Armed Services Committee, 28. Mar. 2007, p. 7. Since then, the number has probably decreased gradually to around 500 as some missiles and warheads have probably been taken out of service and not been replaced.

[h] Strategic gravity bombs are assigned to B-2A bombers only. The maximum yields of strategic bombs are 360 kt for the B61-7, 400 kt for the B61-11 and 1200 kt for the B83-1. However, all these bombs, except the B-11, have lower-yield options. Most B83-1s have been moved to the inactive stockpile and B-2As rarely exercise with the bomb.

[i] Of the 800 ICBM warheads, only 400 were deployed on the missiles. The remaining warheads were in central storage.

[j] Only 200 of these W78 warheads were deployed, as each ICBM has had its warhead load reduced to carry a single warhead; all of the remaining warheads were in central storage.

[k] SIPRI estimates that another 340 W87 warheads might be in long-term storage outside the stockpile for use in the W78 replacement warhead (W87-1) programme.

[l] The first figure is the total number of nuclear-powered ballistic missile submarines (SSBNs) in the US fleet; the second is the maximum number of missiles that they can carry. However, although the 14 SSBNs can carry up to 280 missiles, 2 vessels are normally undergoing refuelling overhaul at any given time and are not assigned missiles. The remaining 12 SSBNs can carry up to 240 missiles, but 1 or 2 of these vessels are usually undergoing maintenance at any given time and may not be carrying missiles.

[m] Of the 1920 SLBM warheads, c. 944 were deployed on submarines as of Sep. 2021; all the rest were in central storage. Although each D5 missile was counted under the 1991 Strategic Arms Reduction Treaty as carrying 8 warheads and the missile was initially flight tested with 14, the US Navy has reduced the warhead load of each missile to an average of 4–5 warheads. D5 missiles equipped with the new low-yield W76-2 are estimated to carry only 1 warhead each.

[n] It is assumed here that all W76-0 warheads have been replaced by the W76-1.

[o] According to US military officials, the new low-yield W76-2 warhead will normally be deployed on at least two of the SSBNs on patrol in the Atlantic and Pacific oceans.

[p] Approximately 100 of the 200 tactical bombs are thought to be deployed across six NATO air bases outside the USA. The remaining bombs were in central storage in the USA. Older B61 versions will be dismantled once the B61-12 is deployed. The maximum yields of tactical bombs are 170 kt for the B61-3 and 50 kt for the B61-4. All have selective lower yields. The B61-10 was retired in 2016.

[q] Most sources list an unrefuelled ferry range of 2400 kilometres, but Lockheed Martin, which produces the F-16, lists 3200 km.

[r] Of these 3708 weapons, c. 1744 were deployed on ballistic missiles, at bomber bases in the USA and at six NATO air bases outside the USA; all the rest were in central storage.

[s] Up until 2018, the US government published the number of warheads dismantled each year, but the administration of President Donald J. Trump ended this practice. The administration of President Joe Biden restored transparency in 2021, but publication of the 2018, 2019 and 2020 data showed that far fewer warheads had been dismantled than assumed (e.g. only 184 in 2020).

Nonetheless, dismantlement of the warheads has continued, leaving an estimated 1720 warheads in the dismantlement queue.

^{t} In addition to these intact warheads, more than 20 000 plutonium pits were stored at the Pantex Plant, Texas, and perhaps 4000 uranium secondaries were stored at the Y-12 facility at Oak Ridge, Tennessee.

Sources: US Department of Defense, various budget reports and plans, press releases and documents obtained under the Freedom of Information Act; US Department of Energy, various budget reports and plans; US Air Force, US Navy and US Department of Energy, personal communications with officials; *Bulletin of the Atomic Scientists*, 'Nuclear notebook', various issues; and the authors' estimates.

bombers.[7] The numbers of deployed warheads presented here differ from the numbers reported under New START because the treaty attributes one weapon to each deployed bomber, even though bombers do not carry weapons under normal circumstances. Additionally, the treaty does not count weapons stored at bomber bases and, at any given time, some nuclear-powered ballistic missile submarines (SSBNs) are not fully loaded with warheads and are thus not counted under the treaty.

The role of nuclear weapons in US military doctrine

According to the 2018 Nuclear Posture Review (NPR), 'The United States would only consider the employment of nuclear weapons in extreme circumstances to defend the vital interests of the United States, its allies, and partners.'[8] The NPR further clarifies that the USA reserves the right to first use of nuclear weapons in a conflict, and could use nuclear weapons in response to 'significant non-nuclear strategic attacks' on 'the US, allied, or partner civilian population or infrastructure, and attacks on US or allied nuclear forces, their command and control, or warning and attack assessment capabilities'.[9]

The USA under the Biden administration continued to implement the 2018 NPR throughout 2021, including several large-scale nuclear weapon programmes initiated under the administration of President Barack Obama and accelerated and expanded by the Trump administration, which cover modernization programmes for all three legs of the nuclear triad (see 'Strategic nuclear forces' below).

The 2018 NPR's justification for the development of two nuclear 'supplements'—the W76-2 low-yield warhead and a nuclear sea-launched cruise missile (SLCM-N)—reflected important doctrinal changes in US nuclear

---

[7] US Department of State, 'Notification containing data for each category of data contained in part two of the protocol', 1 Sep. 2021, retrieved by request from the US Department of State, Bureau of Arms Control, Verification and Compliance, 26 Jan. 2022.

[8] US Department of Defense (DOD), *Nuclear Posture Review 2018* (DOD: Arlington, VA, Feb. 2018), p. 21.

[9] US Department of Defense (note 8), p. 21.

planning. According to the NPR, the W76-2 is intended to provide the USA with a prompt low-yield capability aimed at deterring Russia from what the NPR suggested was a greater willingness to use nuclear weapons first—an alleged doctrinal shift that independent experts have questioned.[10] Both the W76-2 and SLCM-N appear intended to restrengthen US non-strategic nuclear weapon capabilities, which had reduced in importance for the US military since the end of the cold war. This included, according to the NPR, the option of responding to non-nuclear strategic attacks, which would constitute first use of nuclear weapons—the very act that the NPR criticizes Russia for including in its alleged doctrine.[11]

Strategic nuclear forces

US offensive strategic nuclear forces include heavy bomber aircraft, land-based intercontinental ballistic missiles (ICBMs) and SSBNs. These forces, together known as the triad, changed little during 2021.[12] SIPRI estimates that a total of 3508 nuclear warheads were assigned to the triad, of which an estimated 1644 warheads were deployed on ballistic missiles and at heavy bomber bases.

Aircraft and air-delivered weapons

As of January 2022, the US Air Force (USAF) operated a fleet of 152 heavy bombers: 45 B-1Bs, 20 B-2As and 87 B-52Hs.[13] Of these, 66 (20 B-2As and 46 B-52Hs) were nuclear-capable and 45 (11 B-2As and 34 B-52Hs) were counted as deployed under New START as of 1 September 2021.[14] The B-2A can deliver gravity bombs (B61-7, B61-11 and B83-1) and the B-52H can deliver the AGM-86B/W80-1 nuclear air-launched cruise missile (ALCM). SIPRI estimates that approximately 788 warheads were assigned to strategic bombers, of which about 300 are deployed at bomber bases and ready for

---

[10] US Department of Defense (note 8), pp. 8, 53–55. See also e.g. Ven Bruusgaard, K., 'Here's why US tactical nukes are a bad idea', *National Interest*, 10 Dec. 2018; Oliker, O. and Baklitskiy, A., 'The Nuclear Posture Review and Russian "de-escalation": A dangerous solution to a nonexistent problem', War on the Rocks, 20 Feb. 2018; and Oliker, O., 'Russia's nuclear doctrine: What we know, what we don't, and what that means', Center for Strategic and International Studies (CSIS), 5 May 2016.

[11] US Office of the Under Secretary of Defense for Policy, 'Strengthening deterrence and reducing nuclear risks, part ii: The sea-launched cruise missile-nuclear (SLCM-N)', *Arms Control and International Security Papers*, vol. 1, no. 11 (23 July 2020), p. 3; and US Department of Defense (note 8), p. xiii. For further detail on the Nuclear Posture Review see Kristensen, H. M., 'US nuclear forces', *SIPRI Yearbook 2019*.

[12] The reduction in bomber weapons compared with *SIPRI Yearbook 2021* is not the result of new cuts but of new stockpile numbers causing a reassessment of the estimate.

[13] In Sep. 2021 the US Air Force retired 17 B-1B heavy bombers; the remaining 45 B-1Bs will be decommissioned once the B-21 enters service in the mid 2020s.

[14] US Department of State (note 7).

delivery on relatively short notice.[15] Both the B-2As and B-52Hs are currently undergoing modernization intended to improve their ability to receive and transmit secure nuclear mission data.[16]

The development of the next-generation long-range strike bomber, known as the B-21 Raider, was well under way by the end of 2021 and the first two test aircraft were being constructed.[17] In July 2021 the USAF released its visual rendering of the B-21, indicating a flying-wing design similar to that of the B-2, along with a fact sheet noting that the B-21 would eventually be able to conduct uncrewed operations.[18] The B-21 will be capable of delivering two types of nuclear weapon: the B61-12 guided nuclear gravity bomb, which is scheduled to begin full-scale production in May 2022 and is also designed to be deliverable from shorter-range non-strategic aircraft (see below); and the long-range standoff weapon (LRSO) ALCM, which is in development. In June 2021 the acting administrator of the National Nuclear Security Administration (NNSA) noted in US Senate testimony that the W80-4 warhead—being developed for the LRSO—would probably be delayed due to the ongoing Covid-19 pandemic, and the first production unit was not expected until US financial year 2025.[19]

The B-21 is scheduled to enter service in the mid 2020s. At the end of 2021, six were in production, with roll-out and first flight expected in mid 2022.[20] The new bomber will replace the B-1B bombers—which are not nuclear-capable—at Dyess Air Force Base (AFB) in Texas and Ellsworth AFB in South Dakota. This, along with the reinstatement of nuclear-weapon storage capability at Barksdale AFB in Louisiana, will result in the number of US bomber bases with such capability increasing from two in 2021 to five by the early 2030s.[21] In June 2021 the USAF announced that Ellsworth AFB would

---

[15] The estimate of *c.* 788 warheads assigned to strategic bombers is a decrease from the estimate of *c.* 848 warheads in *SIPRI Yearbook 2021*. The decrease is not the result of a recent retirement of weapons but of a reassessment of the number of warheads that are assigned to the bombers.

[16] US Department of Defense (DOD), *Fiscal Year (FY) 2021 Budget Estimates: Air Force: Justification Book*, vol. 3a, Research, Development, Test & Evaluation, Air Force, vol. III, part 1 (DOD: Arlington, VA, Feb. 2020), pp. 109–82, 203–21.

[17] Tirpak, J., 'Second B-21 under construction as bomber moves toward first flight', *Air Force Magazine*, 15 Jan. 2021.

[18] US Air Force, US Secretary of the Air Force Public Affairs, 'Air Force releases new B-21 Raider artist rendering', Press release, 6 July 2021; and US Air Force, 'B-21 Raider', Fact sheet, 6 July 2021.

[19] Verdon, C., Statement, US Senate Armed Services Committee hearing on Department of Energy and National Nuclear Security Administration on Atomic Energy Defense Activities in Review of the Defense Authorization Request for Fiscal Year 2022 and the Future Years Defense Program, 24 June 2021; and 'NNSA assessing Covid-related delays to warhead refurbs; results in spring', Exchange Monitor, 8 Feb. 2022.

[20] Hadley, G., 'Six B-21s in production, fuel control software already tested', *Air Force Magazine*, 9 Feb. 2022.

[21] Dawkins, J. C., Commander, 8th Air Force and Joint-Global Strike Operations Center, Barksdale AFB, 'B21 General Dawkins intro', YouTube, 19 Mar. 2020, 01:35; and Kristensen, H. M., 'USAF plans to expand nuclear bomber bases', FAS Strategic Security Blog, Federation of American Scientists, 17 Nov. 2020.

be the first base to receive the B-21.[22] The USAF plans to acquire at least 100 (but possibly as many as 145) B-21 bombers by the mid 2030s.[23] However, funding decisions made by the US Congress will determine the final number.

Land-based missiles

As of January 2022, the USA deployed 400 Minuteman III ICBMs in 450 silos across three missile wings, with the 50 empty silos kept in a state of readiness for reloading with stored missiles if necessary.[24] Each Minuteman III ICBM was armed with either a 335-kiloton W78 or a 300-kt W87 warhead. Missiles carrying the W78 can be uploaded with up to two more warheads for a maximum of three multiple independently targetable re-entry vehicles (MIRVs). ICBMs with the W87 can only be loaded with one warhead. SIPRI estimates that there are 800 warheads assigned to the ICBM force, of which 400 are deployed on the missiles.[25]

The USAF has scheduled its next-generation ICBM, the Ground Based Strategic Deterrent (GBSD) weapon system, to begin replacing the Minuteman III in 2028, with full replacement by 2036.[26] Each GBSD will be able to carry up to two W87 or W87-1 MIRVs (see below)—for a maximum of 800 warheads across all GBSDs—but will probably carry only one warhead under normal circumstances. The USAF is expected to conduct its first flight test of the system in 2023.[27] The projected cost of the programme has continued to increase and the absence of competition in the bidding process for the contract may have eliminated any potential to make savings up front.[28] In May 2021 the US Congressional Budget Office (CBO) estimated that the cost of acquiring and maintaining the ICBMs would total approximately $82 billion over the 10-year period 2021–30, approximately $20 billion more than the CBO had previously estimated for the period 2019–28.[29] The cost is

---

[22] Cisneros, M., 'AFCEC leads bed-down efforts for B-21 Raider stealth bomber', Ellsworth Air Force Base, Press release, 22 Nov. 2021.

[23] Tirpak, J. A., 'A new bomber vision', *Air Force Magazine*, 1 June 2020.

[24] Willett, E., 'AF meets New START requirements', US Air Force Global Strike Command, Press release, 28 June 2017.

[25] For further detail on the warheads and yields see Kristensen, H. M. and Korda, M., 'US nuclear forces', *SIPRI Yearbook 2021*, p. 341.

[26] Richard, C. A., Commander, US Strategic Command, Statement before the US Senate Armed Services Committee, 13 Feb. 2020, p. 9. For further detail on the GBSD see Kristensen and Korda (note 25), p. 341.

[27] Tirpak, J., 'New GBSD will fly in 2023; no margin left for Minuteman', *Air Force Magazine*, 14 June 2021. The requirements for reaching initial operating capability are deploying 20 GBSD missiles loaded with legacy W87-0/Mk21 warheads and re-entry vehicles, upgrading 20 Minuteman III launch facilities to GBSD standards, and operationally certifying 3 GBSD launch control centres and 1 integrated command centre.

[28] Reif, K., 'New ICBM replacement cost revealed', *Arms Control Today*, vol. 47, no. 2 (Mar. 2017); and Burns, R., 'Pentagon estimates cost of new nuclear missiles at $95.8B', AP News, 20 Oct. 2020.

[29] US Congressional Budget Office, 'Projected costs of US nuclear forces, 2021 to 2030', May 2021, p. 10; and US Congressional Budget Office, 'Projected costs of US nuclear forces, 2019 to 2028', Jan. 2019, p. 9.

likely to increase further, which perhaps calls into question the decision not to extend the life of the existing Minuteman III.

The USAF is also modernizing the nuclear warheads that will be used to arm the GBSD.[30] The projected cost of the programme for the replacement warhead, known as the W87-1, is between \$11.8 billion and \$15 billion, but this estimate does not include costs associated with production of plutonium pits for the warhead (see below).[31] In March 2021 the NNSA completed its review of requirements for the W87-1, a key milestone that allows the programme to progress to the next stage of its development.[32]

Sea-based missiles

The US Navy operates a fleet of 14 Ohio-class SSBNs, of which 12 are normally considered to be operational and 2 are typically undergoing refuelling and overhaul at any given time. Eight of the SSBNs are based at Naval Base Kitsap in Washington state and six at Naval Submarine Base Kings Bay in Georgia.

Each Ohio-class SSBN can carry up to 20 Trident II D5 submarine-launched ballistic missiles (SLBMs). To meet the New START limit on deployed launchers, 4 of the 24 initial missile tubes on each submarine were deactivated so that the 12 deployable SSBNs can carry no more than 240 missiles.[33] Around 8 to 10 SSBNs are normally at sea, of which 4 or 5 are on alert in their designated patrol areas and ready to fire their missiles within 15 minutes of receiving the launch order. The US SSBN fleet conducts about 30 deterrent patrols per year.[34]

The Trident II D5 SLBMs carry two basic warhead types: the 455-kt W88 and the W76, which exists in two versions, the 90-kt W76-1 and the low-yield W76-2.[35] The NNSA has begun modernizing the ageing W88 warhead, and the first production unit for the W88 Alt 370 was completed on 1 July 2021.[36] Each SLBM can carry up to eight warheads but normally carries an average of four or five. SIPRI estimates that around 1920 warheads were assigned to the SSBN fleet, of which about 944 were deployed on missiles.[37]

---

[30] For further detail on the GBSD see Kristensen and Korda (note 25), pp. 341–42.

[31] US Department of Energy, National Nuclear Security Administration (NNSA), *Fiscal Year 2021 Stockpile Stewardship and Management Plan: Biennial Plan Summary*, Report to Congress (NNSA: Washington, DC, Dec. 2020), pp. 5-32, 5-33.

[32] Sirota, S., 'NNSA completes requirements review of GBSD's W87-1 warhead', Inside Defense, 22 Apr. 2021.

[33] US Navy Office of Information, 'Fleet ballistic missile submarines—SSBN', Fact sheet, updated 25 May 2021.

[34] See e.g. Kristensen, H., 'US SSBN patrols steady, but mysterious reduction in Pacific in 2017', FAS Strategic Security Blog, Federation of American Scientists, 24 May 2018.

[35] The older W76-0 version has been, or remains in the process of being, retired. For further detail on these warheads see Kristensen and Korda (note 25), pp. 342–43.

[36] US Department of Energy, National Nuclear Security Administration (NNSA), 'NNSA completes first production unit of W88 Alteration 370', 13 July 2021.

[37] US Department of State, Bureau of Arms Control, Verification and Compliance, 'New START Treaty aggregate numbers of strategic offensive arms', Fact sheet, 1 Dec. 2020.

The newest warhead, the low-yield W76-2, was first deployed in late 2019 on USS *Tennessee* (SSBN-734), which patrols the Atlantic Ocean, and has now been deployed on SSBNs in both the Atlantic and the Pacific.[38] It is a modification of the W76-1 and is estimated to have an explosive yield of about 8 kt.[39]

Since 2017, the US Navy has been replacing its Trident II D5 SLBMs with an enhanced version, known as the D5LE (LE for 'life extension'), with the upgrade scheduled for completion in 2024.[40] In 2021 the US Navy conducted several flight tests of the D5LE SLBM, which is equipped with the new Mk6 guidance system.[41] The D5LE will arm Ohio-class SSBNs for the remainder of their service lives (up to 2042) and will be deployed on the United Kingdom's Trident submarines (see section III). A new class of SSBN, the Columbia class, will initially also be armed with the D5LE, but from 2039 these will eventually be replaced with an upgraded SLBM, the D5LE2.[42] The first Columbia-class SSBN—USS *Columbia* (SSBN-826)—is scheduled to start patrols in 2031.[43]

To arm the D5LE2, the NNSA has begun early design development of a new nuclear warhead, known as the W93, to complement the W76 and W88 warheads. This would be the first brand-new warhead developed by the USA since the end of the cold war. The W93 warhead will be housed in a new Mk7 re-entry body (aeroshell) that will also be delivered to the British Royal Navy (see section III). Production of the W93 is scheduled to begin in the mid 2030s.[44]

Warhead production

From the end of the cold war, the USA relied on refurbishment of existing warhead types for its nuclear forces, but since around 2018 it has shifted to an expanded production capacity intended to produce new warheads. This plan depends heavily on the USA's ability to produce new plutonium pits. Whereas production capacity in 2021 was limited (to around 10 plutonium pits per year), the NNSA plans to produce up to 30 pits in 2026 and

[38] Arkin, W. M. and Kristensen, H. M., 'US deploys new low-yield nuclear submarine warhead', FAS Strategic Security Blog, Federation of American Scientists, 29 Jan. 2020; and US Department of Defense, 'Statement on the fielding of the W76-2 low-yield submarine launched ballistic missile warhead', Press release, 4 Feb. 2020.

[39] US military officials, Private communications with the authors, 2019–20.

[40] Wolfe, J., Director of US Strategic Systems Programs, Statement before the Subcommittee on Strategic Forces, US Senate Armed Services Committee, 1 May 2019, p. 4.

[41] US Navy, 'USS Wyoming successfully tests Trident II D5LE missiles', Press release, 18 Sep. 2021.

[42] Wolfe, J., Director of US Strategic Systems Programs, 'FY2021 budget request for nuclear forces and atomic energy defense activities', Statement before the Subcommittee on Strategic Forces, US House of Representatives Armed Services Committee, 3 Mar. 2020, p. 5.

[43] Wolfe (note 42), p. 3.

[44] US Department of Defense, 'W93/Mk7 Navy warhead: Developing modern capabilities to address current and future threats', White paper, May 2020, p. 2. Part of this document is available online. For further detail on this warhead programme see Kristensen and Korda (note 25), p. 343.

at least 80 pits per year by 2030 to meet the demands of the US nuclear modernization programmes.[45] In order to fulfil these objectives, the NNSA is modernizing its plutonium facility (PF-4) at Los Alamos National Laboratory in New Mexico and creating a new plutonium processing facility at Savannah River in South Carolina.[46]

In June 2021 the acting administrator of the NNSA announced to the US Congress what outside experts had long predicted—that the NNSA's goal of producing up to 80 pits per year by 2030 would not be possible.[47] This indicates that some of the aforementioned nuclear weapon programmes will probably face delays or that new delivery systems could be initially deployed with legacy warheads.[48]

Non-strategic nuclear forces

US non-strategic (tactical) nuclear forces include nuclear bombs delivered by several types of short-range fighter-bomber aircraft, as well as potentially a future nuclear-armed SLCM.

Air force weapons

The USA, as of January 2022, had one basic type of air-delivered non-strategic weapon in its stockpile—the B61 gravity bomb, which exists in two versions: the B61-3 and the B61-4.[49] An estimated 200 tactical B61 bombs remained in the stockpile.

SIPRI estimates that the USAF has deployed approximately 100 of the B61 bombs for potential use by fighter-bomber aircraft at six air bases in five other member states of the North Atlantic Treaty Organization (NATO): Kleine Brogel in Belgium; Büchel in Germany; Aviano and Ghedi in Italy; Volkel in the Netherlands; and İncirlik in Turkey.[50] The remaining (c. 100) B61 bombs

[45] US Department of Energy, National Nuclear Security Administration (NNSA), 'Plutonium pit production', Fact sheet, Apr. 2019; and US Government Accountability Office (GAO), *Nuclear Weapons: NNSA Should Further Develop Cost, Schedule, and Risk Information for the W87-1 Warhead Program*, Report no. GAO-20-73 (GAO: Washington, DC, Sep. 2020), pp. 14–15.

[46] US Department of Energy (note 45).

[47] Demarest, C., 'Plutonium pit production in SC might happen in 2035. The target was 2030', *Aiken Standard*, 12 June 2021. See also e.g. US Government Accountability Office (note 45), p. 5; and Hunter, D. E. et al., 'Independent assessment of the two-site pit production decision: Executive summary', Institute for Defense Analyses document no. NS D-10711, May 2019, p. 4.

[48] US Air Force (USAF), *Report on Development of Ground-Based Strategic Deterrent Weapon*, Report to eight congressional committees (USAF: [Arlington, VA,] May 2020), p. 4. The USAF is already anticipating that the W87-1 will not be completed on time and is therefore planning for the GBSD to reach initial operational capability with legacy warheads.

[49] A third version, the B61-10, was retired in Sep. 2016. US Department of Energy, National Nuclear Security Administration (NNSA), *Fiscal Year 2018 Stockpile Stewardship and Management Plan*, Report to Congress (NNSA: Washington, DC, Nov. 2017), figures 1.1–1.7, pp. 1–13.

[50] For a detailed overview of the dual-capable aircraft programmes of the USA and its NATO allies see Kristensen (note 11), pp. 299–300; and Andreasen, S. et al., *Building a Safe, Secure, and Credible NATO Nuclear Posture* (Nuclear Threat Initiative: Washington, DC, Jan. 2018).

are thought to be stored at Kirtland AFB in New Mexico for potential use by US aircraft in support of allies outside Europe, including in East Asia.[51] USA-based fighter wings for this mission include the 366th Fighter Wing at Mountain Home AFB in Idaho.[52]

The USA has completed development of the new B61-12 guided nuclear bomb, which will replace all existing versions of the B61 (both strategic and non-strategic). Delivery was scheduled to start in 2020 but production problems in 2019 caused delays; the first production unit was completed in November 2021, and full-scale production is scheduled for May 2022.[53] Certification training by the air forces of the countries where the bombs will be based is likely to begin in 2023. The new version is equipped with a guided tail-kit that enables it to hit targets more accurately, meaning that it can use lower yields against targets and thus generate less radioactive fallout.[54]

Operations to integrate the incoming B61-12 on existing USAF and NATO aircraft continued in 2021. The USAF plans to integrate the B61-12 on seven types of aircraft operated by the USA or its NATO allies: the B-2A, the new B-21, the F-15E, the F-16C/D, the F-16MLU, the F-35A and the PA-200 (Tornado).[55] The Tornado's age prevents it from using the B61-12's new guided tail-kit function, and the aircraft will instead deliver the B61-12 as a 'dumb' bomb akin to the older B61-3s and B61-4s.

Germany plans to retire its Tornado aircraft by 2030, and would require a new dual-capable aircraft if it intended to remain part of NATO's nuclear-sharing mission. In November 2021 the incoming coalition government confirmed that its intention was for Germany to remain part of the mission.[56]

Navy weapons

As noted above, the 2018 NPR established a requirement for a new nuclear-armed SLCM—the SLCM-N.[57] In 2019 the US Navy began an 'analysis of alternatives' study for the new weapon, which was reportedly completed in 2021.[58]

[51] US Department of Defense (note 8), p. 48.

[52] Heflin, L., '53rd Wing WSEP incorporates NucWSEP, enhances readiness for real world operations', Air Combat Command, Press release, 9 Sep. 2021.

[53] Mehta, A., 'How a $5 part used to modernize nuclear warheads could cost $850 million to fix', *Defense News*, 25 Sep. 2019; and US Department of Energy, National Nuclear Security Administration (NNSA), 'NNSA completes first production unit of B61-12 life extension program', 2 Dec. 2021.

[54] Kristensen, H. M. and McKinzie, M., 'Video shows earth-penetrating capability of B61-12 nuclear bomb', FAS Strategic Security Blog, Federation of American Scientists, 14 Jan. 2016.

[55] US Air Force (USAF), *Acquisition Annual Report Fiscal Year 2018: Cost-effective Modernization* (USAF: Arlington, VA, [n.d.]), p. 24.

[56] Siebold, S. and Wacket, M., 'Germany to remain part of NATO's nuclear sharing under new government', Reuters, 24 Nov. 2021.

[57] US Department of Defense (note 8), pp. 54–55.

[58] Wolfe (note 42).

The USA eliminated all non-strategic naval nuclear weapons after the end of the cold war. Completion of the SLCM-N would therefore mark a significant change in US Navy strategy.[59] In a leaked memorandum from June 2021, the acting Secretary of the Navy recommended that the SLCM-N be defunded, noting that 'the Navy cannot afford to simultaneously develop the next generation of air, surface, and subsurface platforms and must prioritize these programs balancing the cost of developing next generation capabilities against maintaining current capabilities'.[60] If the Biden administration decides to continue with the programme and the US Congress agrees to fund it, then the new missile could be deployed on attack submarines by the end of the 2020s. This could potentially result in the first significant increase in the size of the US nuclear weapon stockpile since 1996.

[59] Kristensen, H. M., 'Declassified: US nuclear weapons at sea', FAS Strategic Security Blog, Federation of American Scientists, 3 Feb. 2016.

[60] Shelbourne, M. and LaGrone, S., 'SECNAV memo: New destroyer, fighter or sub: You can only pick one; cut nuclear cruise missile', USNI News, 8 June 2021.

II. Russian nuclear forces

HANS M. KRISTENSEN AND MATT KORDA

As of January 2022, Russia maintained a military stockpile of approximately 4477 nuclear warheads, around 20 fewer than the estimate for January 2021. About 2565 of these were offensive strategic warheads, of which roughly 1588 were deployed on land- and sea-based ballistic missiles and at bomber bases. Russia also possessed approximately 1912 non-strategic (tactical) nuclear warheads. All of the non-strategic warheads are thought to be at central storage sites.[1] An estimated additional 1500 retired warheads were awaiting dismantlement (260 fewer than the estimate for 2021), giving a total inventory of approximately 5977 warheads (see table 10.3).

These estimates are based on publicly available information about the Russian nuclear arsenal and the authors' estimates. Because of a lack of transparency, estimates and analysis of Russia's nuclear weapon developments come with considerable uncertainty, particularly with regard to Russia's sizable stockpile of non-strategic nuclear weapons. However, it is possible to formulate a reasonable assessment of the progress of Russia's nuclear modernization by reviewing satellite imagery and other forms of open-source intelligence, official statements, industry publications and interviews with military officials.[2]

In September 2021 Russia declared 1458 deployed warheads attributed to 527 strategic launchers, thus remaining in compliance with the final warhead limits prescribed by the 2010 Russian–United States Treaty on Measures for the Further Reduction and Limitation of Strategic Offensive Arms (New START).[3] This treaty places a cap on the numbers of Russian and US deployed strategic nuclear forces. The numbers of deployed warheads presented here differ from the numbers reported under New START because the treaty attributes one weapon to each deployed bomber, even though bombers do not carry weapons under normal circumstances. Additionally, the treaty does not count weapons in storage and, at any given time, some nuclear-powered ballistic missile submarines (SSBNs) are not fully loaded with warheads and are thus not counted under the treaty.

---

[1] For an overview of Russia's nuclear weapon storage facilities see Podvig, P. and Serrat, J., *Lock Them Up: Zero-deployed Non-strategic Nuclear Weapons in Europe* (United Nations Institute for Disarmament Research: Geneva, 2017).

[2] Kristensen, H. M. and Korda, M., 'Estimating world nuclear forces: An overview and assessment of sources', SIPRI Topical Backgrounder, 14 June 2021.

[3] US Department of State, Bureau of Arms Control, Verification and Compliance, 'New START Treaty aggregate numbers of strategic offensive arms', Fact sheet, 1 Sep. 2021. For a summary and other details of New START see annex A, section III. On the negotiation of the renewal of New START see chapter 11, section I, in this volume.

Table 10.3. Russian nuclear forces, January 2022

All figures are approximate and some are based on assessments by the authors.

Type/ Russian designation (NATO designation)	No. of launchers	Year first deployed	Range (km)[a]	Warheads x yield	No. of warheads[b]
Strategic nuclear forces	**516**				**2 565**[c]
Aircraft (bombers)	68[d]				580[e]
Tu-95MS6/16/M (Bear-H)[f]	55	1984/ 2015	6 500– 10 500	6–16 x 200 kt AS-15A or AS-23B ALCMs	448
Tu-160/M/M2 (Blackjack)	13	1987/ 2021	10 500– 13 200	12 x 200 kt AS-15A or AS-23B ALCMs, bombs	132
Land-based missiles (ICBMs)	306				1 185[g]
RS-20V Voevoda (SS-18 Satan)	40	1988	11 000– 15 000	10 x 500–800 kt	400[h]
RS-18 (SS-19 Stiletto)	0	1980	10 000	6 x 400 kt	0[i]
Avangard (SS-19 Mod 4)[j]	6	2019	10 000	1 x HGV	6
RS-12M Topol (SS-25 Sickle)	9[k]	1988	10 500	1 x 800 kt	9
RS-12M1 Topol-M (SS-27 Mod 1/mobile)	18	2006	10 500	1 x [800 kt]	18
RS-12M2 Topol-M (SS-27 Mod 1/silo)	60	1997	10 500	1 x [800 kt]	60
RS-24 Yars (SS-27 Mod 2/mobile)	153	2010	10 500	[4 x 250 kt]	612[l]
RS-24 Yars (SS-27 Mod 2/silo)	20	2014	10 500	4 x [250 kt]	80
RS-28 Sarmat (SS-X-29)	..	[2022]	>10 000	[10 x 500 kt]	–
Sea-based missiles (SLBMs)	10/160[m]				800[n]
RSM-50 Volna (SS-N-18 M1 Stingray)	0/0	1978	6 500	3 x 50 kt	0[o]
RSM-54 Sineva/Layner (SS-N-23 M2/3)	5/80	2007/ 2014	9 000	4 x 100 kt[p]	320[q]
RSM-56 Bulava (SS-N-32)	5/80	2012	>8 050	[6 x 100 kt]	480[r]
Non-strategic nuclear forces					**1 912**[s]
Navy weapons	..				935
Submarines/surface ships/naval aircraft	..			Land-attack cruise missiles, sea-launched cruise missiles, anti-submarine weapons, surface-to-air missiles, depth bombs, torpedoes[t]	935
Air force weapons	260				500
Tu-22M3 (Backfire-C)	60	1974	..	3 x ASMs, bombs	300
Su-24M/M2 (Fencer-D)	70	1974	..	2 x bombs	70[u]
Su-34 (Fullback)	120	2006	..	2 x bombs	120[u]
Su-57 (Felon)	–	[2024]	..	[bombs, ASMs]	..
MiG-31K (Foxhound)	10	2018	..	1 x ALBM	10

Type/ Russian designation (NATO designation)	No. of launchers	Year first deployed	Range (km)[a]	Warheads x yield	No. of warheads[b]
Air, coastal and missile defence	*886*				*387*
53T6 (SH-08, Gazelle)	68	1986	30	1 x 10 kt	68
S-300/400 (SA-20/21)	750[v]	1992/ 2007	..	1 x low kt	290
3M55/P-800 Oniks (SS-N-26 Strobile), 3K55/K300-P Bastion (SSC-5 Stooge)	60	2015	>400	1 x [10–100 kt]	25
SPU-35V Redut (SSC-1B Sepal)	8[w]	1973	500	1 x 350 kt	4
Army weapons	*164*				*90*
9K720 Iskander-M (SS-26 Stone), 9M728 Iskander-K (SSC-7 Southpaw)	144	2005	350	1 x [10–100 kt]	70[x]
9M729 (SSC-8)	20	2016	2 350	1 x [10–100 kt]	20[y]
Total stockpile					**4 477**
Deployed warheads					1 588
Reserve warheads					2 889
Retired warheads awaiting dismantlement					**1 500**
Total inventory					**5 977**

.. = data not available or not applicable; – = nil or a negligible value; [ ] = uncertain SIPRI estimate; ALBM = air-launched ballistic missile; ALCM = air-launched cruise missile; ASM = air-to-surface missile; HGV = hypersonic glide vehicle; kt = kiloton; ICBM = intercontinental ballistic missile; NATO = North Atlantic Treaty Organization; SLBM = submarine-launched ballistic missile.

[a] For aircraft, the listed range is for illustrative purposes only; actual mission range will vary according to flight profile, weapon payload and in-flight refuelling.

[b] These figures show the total number of warheads estimated to be assigned to nuclear-capable delivery systems. Only some of these warheads have been deployed on missiles and at air bases.

[c] Approximately 1588 of these strategic warheads were deployed on land- and sea-based ballistic missiles and at bomber bases. The remaining warheads were in central storage. This number is different from the number of deployed strategic warheads counted by the 2010 Russian–United States Treaty on Measures for the Further Reduction and Limitation of Strategic Offensive Arms (New START) because the treaty attributes one weapon to each deployed bomber, even though bombers do not carry weapons under normal circumstances. Additionally, the treaty does not count weapons stored at bomber bases and, at any given time, some nuclear-powered ballistic missile submarines (SSBNs) are not fully loaded with warheads and are thus not counted under the treaty.

[d] All of Russia's long-range strategic bombers are nuclear-capable. Of these, only about 50 are thought to be counted as deployed under New START. Because of ongoing bomber modernization, there is considerable uncertainty about how many bombers are operational.

[e] The maximum possible payload on the bombers is more than 800 nuclear weapons but, given that only some of the bombers are fully operational, SIPRI estimates that only about 580 weapons have been assigned to the long-range bomber force, of which approximately 200 might be deployed and stored at the two strategic bomber bases. The remaining weapons are thought to be in central storage facilities.

[f] There are two types of Tu-95MS aircraft: the Tu-95MS6, which can carry 6 AS-15A missiles internally; and the Tu-95MS16, which can carry an additional 10 AS-15A missiles externally, for a total of 16 missiles. Both types were being modernized in 2021. The modernized aircraft (Tu-95MSM) can carry 8 AS-23B missiles externally and possibly 6 internally, for a total of 14 missiles.

[g] These ICBMs can carry a total of 1185 warheads, but SIPRI estimates that they have had their warhead load reduced to approximately 812 warheads, with the remaining warheads in storage.

[h] It is possible that, as of Jan. 2022, the RS-20Vs carried only five warheads each to meet the New START limit for deployed strategic warheads. It is also possible that one of the four RS-20V regiments started an upgrade in late 2021 to convert to the Avangard.

[i] It is possible that the remaining RS-18s have been retired, although activities continued at some regiments.

[j] The missile uses a modified RS-18 ICBM booster with an HGV payload.

[k] It is possible that one regiment at Barnaul, Altai krai, has not yet completed upgrade to RS-24. In 2021 one additional regiment at Yurya, Kirov oblast, had nine RS-12M launchers and was expected to upgrade to the RS-24 in 2022; however, the regiment served a back-up launch transmission function and was not nuclear-armed. Therefore, it is not included in this table.

[l] Two more road-mobile regiments were being upgraded from RS-12M to RS-24. It is possible that, as of Jan. 2022, the RS-24s carried only three warheads each to meet the New START limit on deployed strategic warheads.

[m] The first figure is the total number of nuclear-powered ballistic missile submarines (SSBNs) in the Russian fleet; the second is the maximum number of missiles that they can carry. Of Russia's 10 operational SSBNs in 2021, 1 or 2 were in overhaul at any given time and did not carry their assigned nuclear missiles and warheads (see note n).

[n] The warhead load on SLBMs is thought to have been reduced for Russia to stay below the New START warhead limit. Additionally, at any given time, one or two SSBNs were in overhaul and did not carry nuclear weapons. Therefore, it is estimated here that only around 576 of the 800 SLBM warheads have been deployed.

[o] The last remaining Delta III-class SSBN was converted to an attack submarine in mid 2021. Therefore, it no longer carries the RSM-50.

[p] The current version of the RSM-54 SLBM might be the Layner (SS-N-23 M3), a modification of the previous version—the Sineva (SS-N-23 M2). However, the US Air Force's National Air and Space Intelligence Center (NASIC) did not include the Layner in its 2020 report on ballistic and cruise missile threats, and there is some uncertainty regarding its status and capability. In 2006 US intelligence estimated that the missile could carry up to 10 warheads, but it lowered the estimate to 4 in 2009. The average number of warheads carried on each missile has probably been limited to 4 multiple independently targetable re-entry vehicles (MIRVs) to meet the New START limits.

[q] SIPRI estimates that, at any given time, only 256 of these warheads have been deployed on four operational Delta IV submarines, with the fifth boat in overhaul. The actual number may even be lower as two boats often undergo maintenance at the same time.

[r] It is possible that, as of Jan. 2022, Bulava SLBMs carried only four warheads each for Russia to meet the New START limit on deployed strategic warheads.

[s] According to the Russian government, non-strategic nuclear warheads are not deployed with their delivery systems but are kept in storage facilities. Some storage facilities are near operational bases. It is possible that there are more unreported nuclear-capable non-strategic systems.

[t] Only submarines are assumed to be assigned nuclear torpedoes.

[u] These estimates assume that half of the aircraft have a nuclear role.

[v] As of Jan. 2022, there were at least 80 S-300/400 sites across Russia, each with an average of 12 launchers, each with 2–4 interceptors. Each launcher has several reloads.

[w] It is assumed that all SPU-35V Redut units, except for a single silo-based version in Crimea, had been replaced by the K-300P Bastion by Jan. 2022.

ˣ This estimate assumes that around half of the dual-capable launchers have a secondary nuclear role. In its 2020 report, NASIC listed the 9M728 as 'Conventional, Nuclear Possible'.

ʸ This figure assumes that there are five 9M729 battalions, each with four launchers, for a total of 80 missiles. Each launcher is assumed to have at least one reload, for a total of at least 160 missiles. Most missiles are thought to be conventional, with 4–5 nuclear warheads per battalion, for a total of about 20.

Sources: Russian Ministry of Defence, various press releases; US Department of State, START Treaty Memoranda of Understanding, 1990–July 2009; New START aggregate data releases, various years; US Air Force, National Air and Space Intelligence Center (NASIC), *Ballistic and Cruise Missile Threat 2020* (NASIC: Wright-Patterson Air Force Base, OH, July 2020); US Department of Defense (DOD), *Nuclear Posture Review 2018* (DOD: Arlington, VA, Feb. 2018); DOD, *2019 Missile Defense Review* (DOD: Arlington, VA, 2019); US Office of the Deputy Assistant Secretary of Defense for Nuclear Matters, *Nuclear Matters Handbook 2020* (DOD: Arlington, VA, Mar. 2020); DOD, various Congressional testimonies; BBC Monitoring; Russian news media; Russian Strategic Nuclear Forces website; International Institute for Strategic Studies, *The Military Balance*, various years; Cochran, T. B. et al., *Nuclear Weapons Databook*, vol. 4, *Soviet Nuclear Weapons* (Harper & Row: New York, 1989); *IHS Jane's Strategic Weapon Systems*, various issues; US Naval Institute, *Proceedings*, various issues; *Bulletin of the Atomic Scientists*, 'Nuclear notebook', various issues; and authors' estimates.

The role of nuclear weapons in Russian military doctrine

Russia's deterrence policy (last updated in 2020) lays out explicit conditions under which it could launch nuclear weapons: to retaliate against an ongoing attack 'against critical governmental or military sites' by ballistic missiles, nuclear weapons or other weapons of mass destruction (WMD), and to retaliate against 'the use of conventional weapons when the very existence of the state is in jeopardy'.[4] This formulation is largely consistent with previous public iterations of Russian nuclear policy, despite US allegations of a shift towards greater reliance on potential first use of nuclear weapons (see section I).[5]

Strategic nuclear forces

As of January 2022, Russia had an estimated 2565 warheads assigned for potential use by strategic launchers: long-range bombers, land-based intercontinental ballistic missiles (ICBMs) and submarine-launched ballistic missiles (SLBMs). This is a decrease of approximately 20 warheads compared with January 2021, due to fluctuations in the arsenal caused by the gradual replacement of some heavy ICBMs with newer ICBMs that carry fewer warheads, as well as the dismantlement of two SSBNs.

---

[4] Russian Ministry of Foreign Affairs, 'Basic principles of state policy of the Russian Federation on nuclear deterrence', Approved by Russian Presidential Executive Order no. 355, 2 June 2020.

[5] US Department of Defense (DOD), *Nuclear Posture Review 2018* (DOD: Arlington, VA, Feb. 2018), p. 30.

Aircraft and air-delivered weapons

As of January 2022, Russia's Long-Range Aviation command operated a fleet of approximately 68 operational heavy bombers, comprising 13 Tu-160 (Blackjack) and 55 Tu-95MS (Bear) bombers.[6] Not all of these counted as deployed under New START and some were undergoing various upgrades. The maximum possible payload on the bombers is more than 800 nuclear weapons but, since only some of the bombers were fully operational, it is estimated here that the number of assigned weapons was lower—around 580. SIPRI estimates that approximately 200 of these weapons were probably stored at the two strategic bomber bases: Engels in Saratov oblast and Ukrainka in Amur oblast.[7]

Modernization of the bombers—which includes upgrades to their avionics suites, engines and long-range nuclear and conventional cruise missiles—continued but remained subject to delays.[8] The upgraded Tu-95MS is known as the Tu-95MSM and the upgraded Tu-160 is known as the Tu-160M. The upgraded bombers are capable of carrying the new Kh-102 (AS-23B) nuclear air-launched cruise missile. In his end-of-year defence report, President Vladimir Putin indicated that four Tu-95MS aircraft were upgraded in 2021 and delivery of two Tu-160Ms was scheduled for 2022.[9] It seems likely that all of the Tu-160s and most of the Tu-95s will eventually be upgraded to maintain a bomber force of perhaps 50–60 operational aircraft. Russia has also resumed production of the Tu-160M airframes to produce at least 10 brand-new Tu-160M2 bombers with new engines and advanced communications suites.[10] The maiden flight of the first Tu-160M2 was initially expected in late 2021, but was delayed until January 2022.[11]

The modernized Tu-95MSM, Tu-160M and Tu-160M2 bombers are intended to be only a temporary bridge to Russia's next-generation bomber: the PAK-DA. This is a subsonic aircraft whose flying-wing design may look similar to that of the USA's B-2 bomber. Construction of the first PAK-DA's cockpit reportedly began in May 2020, with final assembly of the first aircraft postponed from 2021 to 2023, and serial production expected to begin in

---

[6] For the missiles, aircraft and submarines discussed in this section, a designation in parentheses (e.g. Blackjack) following the Russian designation (e.g. Tu-160) is that assigned by the North Atlantic Treaty Organization (NATO). The Tu-95MS exists in two versions: the Tu-95MS16 (Bear-H16) and the Tu-95MS6 (Bear-H6).

[7] Podvig, P., 'Strategic aviation', Russian Strategic Nuclear Forces, 7 Aug. 2021.

[8] President of Russia, 'Meeting with workers of Gorbunov Kazan aviation factory and Tu-160M pilots', 25 Jan. 2018.

[9] President of Russia, 'Expanded meeting of the Defence Ministry Board', 21 Dec. 2021.

[10] 'Tu-160M2, Tu-22M3M bombers to get communications suite from latest Su-57 fighter', TASS, 12 Aug. 2020.

[11] 'First newly-built Tu-160M to make maiden flight in 4th quarter of 2021', TASS, 30 Dec. 2020; and United Aircraft Corporation (@UAC_Russia_eng), 'Today, the first newly manufactured strategic missile carrier Tu-160M performed its maiden flight from the airfield of the Kazan Aviation Plant. The flight took place at an altitude of 600 meters and lasted about 30 minutes', Twitter, 12 Jan. 2022.

2028 or 2029.[12] The PAK-DA will eventually replace all Tu-95s and Tu-160s as well as the Tu-22s deployed with non-strategic forces (see below).[13]

Land-based missiles

As of January 2022, Russia's Strategic Rocket Forces (SRF)—the branch of the armed forces that controls land-based ICBMs—consisted of 12 missile divisions grouped into 3 armies, deploying an estimated 306 ICBMs of different types and variations (see table 10.3).[14] These ICBMs can carry a maximum of about 1185 warheads, but SIPRI estimates that they have had their warhead load reduced to around 812 warheads, to keep Russia below the New START limit for deployed strategic warheads. These ICBMs carry approximately half of Russia's estimated 1588 deployed strategic warheads.

At the end of 2021, Russia's ICBM force was most of the way through a significant modernization programme to replace all Soviet-era missiles with new types. The missiles will not be replaced on a one-for-one basis, meaning that Russia will probably have fewer missiles after the modernization is completed. The programme also involves substantial reconstruction of silos, launch control centres, garrisons and support facilities.[15] The modernization programme, which began in the late 1990s, appears to be progressing more slowly than previously envisioned. In December 2021 Colonel General Sergey Karakaev, commander of the SRF, stated that around 83 per cent of the ICBM force had been modernized, which is significantly lower than the goal announced in 2014 of 97 per cent of modernization completed by the end of 2020.[16] In November 2020 the chief designer of the RS-24 Yars (SS-27 Mod 2) missile suggested that the last Soviet-era ICBM would be phased out by 2024.[17] However, this seems unlikely based on SIPRI's assessment of the probable time frame for replacing the RS-20V (SS-18) (see below).

The bulk of the modernization programme has focused on the RS-24 Yars, a version of the RS-12M1/2 Topol-M (SS-27 Mod 1) deployed with multiple independently targetable re-entry vehicles (MIRVs). In December 2020

[12] 'PAK DA demonstrational model to be ready by 2023: Source', TASS, 2 Aug. 2021; 'Russia begins construction of the first PAK DA strategic bomber: Sources', TASS, 26 May 2020; and Lavrov, A., Kretsul, R. and Ramm, A., [PAKage agreement: The latest bomber assigned a deadline for production], *Izvestia*, 14 Jan. 2020 (in Russian).

[13] 'Russia to test next-generation stealth strategic bomber', TASS, 2 Aug. 2019.

[14] One of these ICBM divisions, the 40th missile regiment at Yurya, Kirov oblast, was being modernized alongside the rest of the ICBM force; however, the regiment's ICBMs are believed to serve as back-up launch code transmitters and therefore have not been armed with nuclear weapons.

[15] See e.g. Kristensen, H. M., 'Russian ICBM upgrade at Kozelsk', FAS Strategic Security Blog, Federation of American Scientists, 5 Sep. 2018.

[16] [Russia's indisputable argument], Interview with Karakaev, S. V. (Col. Gen.), *Krasnaya Zvezda*, 17 Dec. 2021 (in Russian); and 'Russian TV show announces new ICBM to enter service soon', TRK Petersburg Channel 5, 21 Apr. 2014, Translation from Russian, BBC Monitoring.

[17] 'Russia to complete rearming Strategic Missile Force with advanced Yars ICBMs by 2024', TASS, 2 Nov. 2020.

the Russian Ministry of Defence's television channel declared that approximately 150 mobile and silo-based RS-24 ICBMs had been deployed.[18] SIPRI estimates that, as of January 2022, this number had grown to approximately 173 mobile- and silo-based RS-24 missiles, including four completed mobile divisions (Irkutsk, Nizhniy Tagil, Novosibirsk and Yoshkar-Ola), with two more in progress (Barnaul and Vypolzovo—sometimes referred to as Bologovsky).[19] The upgrade to the Barnaul division was scheduled for completion by April 2022, and SIPRI estimates that this division has already been fully disarmed of its older RS-12M Topol (SS-25) ICBMs in preparation for receiving the new RS-24.[20] In addition, one completed mobile division at Teykovo, Ivanovo oblast, was equipped with both the single-warhead RS-12M1 Topol-M (SS-27 Mod 1) and MIRV-equipped RS-24 ICBMs. The first silo-based RS-24s have been installed at Kozelsk, Kaluga oblast; one regiment of 10 silos was completed in 2018, and the second regiment was completed in 2020.[21] In December 2021 Colonel General Karakaev announced that the third regiment at Kozelsk had begun combat duty with new RS-24 ICBMs; however, commercial satellite imagery indicated that the necessary infrastructure upgrades had only been completed at a couple of the regiment's silos.[22] Given how long it took to upgrade the previous two regiments, it is unlikely that the third regiment will be completed by the 2024 target date. It is likely that the 60 RS-12M2 Topol-M (SS-27 Mod 1) silos at Tatishchevo, Saratov oblast, will eventually also be upgraded to the RS-24.

In December 2021 Russia completed the rearmament of its first regiment of six RS-18 (SS-19 Mod 4) missiles equipped with the Avangard hypersonic glide vehicle (HGV) system.[23] The missiles were installed in former RS-20V silos at Dombarovsky, Orenburg oblast. Russia has been installing Avangard-equipped missiles at a rate of two per year in upgraded complexes with new facilities, fences and Dym-2 perimeter defence systems.[24] Russia plans to install the first two missiles in the second Avangard regiment at Dombarovsky in 2022 or 2023 (construction was already well under way in

[18] Levin, E., [Strategic Rocket Forces commander names the number of Yars complexes entering combat duty], *Krasnaya Zvezda*, 8 Dec. 2020 (in Russian).

[19] Tikhonov, A., [You won't catch them by surprise], *Krasnaya Zvezda*, 28 May 2018 (in Russian); and [The commander of the Strategic Missile Forces announced the completion of the rearmament of the Tagil division], RIA Novosti, 29 Mar. 2018 (in Russian).

[20] [The Barnaul division of the Strategic Rocket Forces will be completely re-equipped with the Yars complex in 2022], TASS, 20 Jan. 2022 (in Russian); and authors' estimates.

[21] [Two regiments of the Strategic Rocket Forces will be re-equipped with 'Yars' missile systems in 2021], TASS, 21 Dec. 2020 (in Russian); and authors' assessment based on observation of satellite imagery.

[22] [Russia's indisputable argument] (note 16); and authors' assessment based on observation of satellite imagery.

[23] President of Russia (note 9).

[24] Russia Insight, 'BREAKING! Russia's new top secret "toy" revealed: "Dym" small arms system protects RS-24 Yars ICBMs', YouTube, 21 Dec. 2018.

2021), with the entire regiment's rearmament scheduled for completion by the end of 2027.[25]

Russia has also been developing a new 'heavy' liquid-fuelled, silo-based ICBM, known as the RS-28 Sarmat (SS-X-29), as a replacement for the RS-20V. Like its predecessor, the RS-28 is expected to carry a large number of MIRVs (possibly as many as 10), but some might be equipped with one or more Avangard HGVs. After manufacturing-related delays, full-scale flight testing of the RS-28 was scheduled to begin in early 2022 at the new proving ground at Severo-Yeniseysky, Krasnoyarsk krai, with serial production expected to begin in mid 2022—although this would depend on a successful flight-test programme.[26] In December 2021 Colonel General Karakaev announced that the first RS-28 ICBMs would assume combat duty at the ICBM complex at Uzhur, Krasnoyarsk krai, sometime in 2022.[27] Satellite imagery indicates that, as of January 2022, the regiment's older RS-20Vs had already been removed to prepare for the incoming RS-28 ICBMs.[28]

In December 2021 Karakaev also declared the development of 'a new mobile ground-based missile system'. This could be a reference to the development programme for the future Osina-RV ICBM, which is reportedly derived from the RS-24.[29] It is also possible that Karakaev was referring to Russia's 'Kedr' project, which reportedly includes research and development on next-generation missile systems.[30] The Kedr ICBM will probably be fielded sometime around 2030.

Russia conducted several small- and larger-scale exercises with road-mobile and silo-based ICBMs during 2021. These included combat patrols for road-mobile regiments, simulated launch exercises for silo-based regiments, and participation in command staff exercises.[31]

Sea-based missiles

As of January 2022, the Russian Navy had a fleet of 10 operational nuclear-armed SSBNs. The fleet included five Soviet-era Delfin-class or Project 667BDRM (Delta IV) SSBNs and five (of a planned total of 10) Borei-class or Project 955 (Dolgorukiy) SSBNs. The number of SSBNs is lower

---

[25] [Russia's indisputable argument] (note 16); and 'Russia's 1st regiment of Avangard hypersonic missiles to go on combat alert by yearend', TASS, 10 Aug. 2021.

[26] President of Russia (note 9); Safronov, I. and Nikolsky, A., [Tests of the latest Russian nuclear missile start at the beginning of the year], *Vedomosti*, 29 Oct. 2019 (in Russian); and Военно-болтовой (@warbolts), [This is not the first time in the course of litigation details are revealed about the progress of the ROC on the creation of advanced weapons...], Telegram, 4 Jan. 2022 (in Russian).

[27] [Russia's indisputable argument] (note 16).

[28] Authors' assessment based on observation of satellite imagery.

[29] [Russia's indisputable argument] (note 16); and Военно-болтовой (@warbolts), [The missile system with the index '15P182' is being created by JSC 'Corporation' MIT], Telegram, 15 June 2021 (in Russian).

[30] 'Russia develops new-generation Kedr strategic missiles system', TASS, 1 Mar. 2021.

[31] See e.g. 'Yars ICBM launchers embark on combat patrols in Siberia drills', TASS, 26 July 2021.

than the previous year's estimate because in 2021 Russia's last Kalmar-class or Project 667BDR (Delta III) SSBN was reclassified as a multi-purpose submarine, and one Delfin-class SSBN was withdrawn from the navy to prepare for its disposal in 2022.[32]

The two newest Borei submarines are of an improved design, known as Borei-A or Project 955A. After delays due to technical issues during sea trials, the first Borei-A was accepted into the navy in June 2020.[33] The second Borei-A was delivered to the navy in December 2021, following a test launch of a Bulava SLBM from the vessel in October.[34] The third Borei-A was launched in December 2021, meaning that it is not expected to be delivered to the navy before December 2022.[35] The next four Borei-A SSBNs are scheduled for delivery in the mid to late 2020s; the first two keels were laid in 2015 and 2016, while the last two keels were laid in August 2021.[36] Eventually, five Borei SSBNs will be assigned to the Northern Fleet (in the Arctic Ocean) and five will be assigned to the Pacific Fleet, replacing all remaining Delfin-class SSBNs.[37]

Each of the 10 operational SSBNs can be equipped with 16 ballistic missiles and the Russian SSBN fleet can carry a total of 800 warheads.[38] However, one or two SSBNs are normally undergoing repairs and maintenance at any given time and are not armed. It is also possible that the warhead load on some missiles has been reduced to meet the total warhead limit under New START. As a result, SIPRI estimates that only about 576 of the 800 warheads have been deployed.

In 2021 the Russian Navy continued to develop the Poseidon or Status-6 (Kanyon), a long-range, strategic nuclear-powered torpedo intended for future deployment on two new types of special-purpose submarine: (*a*) the K-329 Belgorod or Project 09852—a converted Antei-class or Project 949A (Oscar-II) guided-missile submarine (SSGN)—and (*b*) the Khabarovsk-class

---

[32] [Guarantor of stability in the Asia-Pacific region], Interview with Dmitriev, V. (Vice Admiral), *Krasnaya Zvezda*, 19 Mar. 2021 (in Russian); and 'Russian Navy to decommission Delta IV-class strategic nuclear-powered submarine in 2022', TASS, 28 Apr. 2021.

[33] Russian Ministry of Defence, [On Russia Day, the newest Borei-A class strategic missile submarine 'Prince Vladimir' was inaugurated into the Navy], 12 June 2020 (in Russian).

[34] Sevmash, [The ceremony of handing over to the Navy of two nuclear submarines 'Prince Oleg' and 'Novosibirsk' took place at Sevmash], 21 Dec. 2021 (in Russian); and Lindemann, I., [Missile submarine 'Prince Oleg' launched 'Bulava' from the White Sea], TV Zvezda, 21 Oct. 2021 (in Russian).

[35] Sevmash, [The ceremony of pulling out of the boathouse of the nuclear submarine 'Generalissimo Suvorov' took place at Sevmash], 25 Dec. 2021 (in Russian).

[36] Sevmash, [Nuclear-powered submarine cruisers 'Dmitry Donskoy' and 'Prince Potemkin' laid down at Sevmash], 23 Aug. 2021 (in Russian).

[37] [Source: Two more 'Borei-A' strategic submarines will be built at 'Sevmash' by 2028], TASS, 30 Nov. 2020 (in Russian).

[38] The Delfin-class or Project 667BDRM (Delta IV) SSBNs carry RSM-54 Sineva/Layner (SS-N-23 M2/3) SLBMs, while the Borei(-A)-class or Project 955(A) SSBNs carry RSM-56 Bulava (SS-N-32) SLBMs. Each RSM-54 can carry up to four warheads, while each RSM-56 can carry up to six warheads. It is assumed that each RSM-56 has had its warhead load reduced to four warheads, to meet New START limits.

or Project 09851 submarine, based on the Borei-class SSBN hull.[39] The Belgorod was originally scheduled for delivery to the navy by the end of 2020 but returned to dry dock in October 2021 following delayed sea trials.[40] The official transfer of the Belgorod to the Pacific Fleet was expected to take place in July 2022.[41] The Belgorod and the Khabarovsk submarines will each be capable of carrying up to six Poseidon torpedoes.[42]

The Russian Navy conducted military exercises with its ballistic missile submarines throughout 2021. Notably, in March 2021 three SSBNs—two Delfin-class vessels and possibly a Borei-class vessel—simultaneously surfaced alongside each other near the North Pole during Russia's Umka-2021 major Arctic exercise.[43]

Non-strategic nuclear forces

There is no universally accepted definition of 'tactical', 'non-strategic' or 'theatre' nuclear weapons. Generally speaking, these terms refer to shorter-range weapons that are not covered by arms control agreements regulating long-range strategic forces.

Different agencies within the US intelligence community have offered varying estimates of Russian non-strategic nuclear weapons. The 2018 US Nuclear Posture Review stated that Russia had 'up to 2000' non-strategic nuclear weapons, while the US Defense Intelligence Agency in 2021 suggested a lower range of '1000 to 2000'.[44] These examples reflect both the degree of uncertainty associated with estimating Russian non-strategic nuclear forces, and the variations in estimates between different US governmental agencies.

SIPRI estimates that, as of January 2022, Russia had approximately 1912 warheads assigned for potential use by non-strategic forces—an unchanged estimate from the previous year. Russia's non-strategic nuclear weapons—most of which are dual-capable, meaning that they can also be

---

[39] Sutton, H. I., 'Khabarovsk-class-submarine', Covert Shores, 20 Nov. 2020; and Sutton, H. I., 'Poseidon torpedo', Covert Shores, 22 Feb. 2019.

[40] ['Poseidon' drone carrier submarine 'Belgorod' to be handed over to the fleet in 2021], TASS, 24 Dec. 2020 (in Russian); and Sutton, H. I., 'The submarine which came in from the cold: Belgorod under cover', Covert Shores, 6 Oct. 2021.

[41] 'Russian Navy to receive special-purpose sub with nuclear-armed drones in summer: Sources', TASS, 26 Jan. 2022.

[42] [Second 'Poseidon' carrier submarine planned to be launched in spring–summer 2021], TASS, 6 Nov. 2020 (in Russian).

[43] Russian Ministry of Defence, [Integrated arctic expedition of the Russian Navy and the Russian Geographical Society 'Umka-21'], YouTube, 26 Mar. 2021 (in Russian).

[44] US Department of Defense (note 5), p. 53; and Berrier, S., Director, US Defense Intelligence Agency, 'Worldwide threat assessment', Statement for the record, US Senate Armed Services Committee, 26 Apr. 2021.

armed with conventional warheads—are intended for use by ships and submarines, aircraft, air- and missile-defence systems, and army missiles.

Russia's non-strategic nuclear weapons chiefly serve to compensate for perceived weaknesses in its conventional forces, to provide regional attack options, and to maintain overall parity with the total US nuclear force level. There has been considerable debate about the role that non-strategic nuclear weapons have in Russian nuclear strategy, including potential first use.[45]

Navy weapons

The Russian military service that is thought to be assigned the highest number of non-strategic nuclear weapons is the navy, with an estimated 935 warheads for use by land-attack cruise missiles, anti-ship cruise missiles, anti-submarine rockets, depth bombs, and torpedoes delivered by ships, submarines and naval aviation.

The nuclear version of the long-range, land-attack Kalibr submarine-launched cruise missile (SLCM), also known as the 3M-14 (SS-N-30A), is a significant new addition to the navy's stock of weapons.[46] It has been integrated on numerous types of surface ship and attack submarine, including the new Yasen/-M or Project 885/M (Severodvinsk) SSGN.[47] The second boat of this class completed its sea trials in late 2020, hitting a target over 1000 kilometres away with a Kalibr cruise missile, and became operational with the Northern Fleet in 2021.[48] The next Yasen-M SSGN was delivered to the Pacific Fleet in December 2021, indicating that it will probably become operational in 2022.[49]

Other notable navy weapons include the 3M-55 (SS-N-26) SLCM and the future 3M-22 Tsirkon (SS-NX-33) hypersonic anti-ship missile (although

[45] On this debate see e.g. US Department of Defense (note 5), p. 30; Kofman, M. and Fink, A. L., 'Escalation management and nuclear employment in Russian military strategy', War on the Rocks, 23 June 2020; Oliker, O., 'Moscow's nuclear enigma: What is Russia's arsenal really for?', *Foreign Affairs*, vol. 97, no. 6 (Nov./Dec. 2018); Stowe-Thurston, A., Korda, M. and Kristensen, H. M., 'Putin deepens confusion about Russian nuclear policy', Russia Matters, 25 Oct. 2018; Tertrais, B., 'Russia's nuclear policy: Worrying for the wrong reasons', *Survival*, vol. 60, no. 2 (Apr. 2018); and Ven Bruusgaard, K., 'The myth of Russia's lowered nuclear threshold', War on the Rocks, 22 Sep. 2017.

[46] There is considerable confusion about the designation of what is commonly referred to as the Kalibr missile. The Kalibr designation actually refers not to a specific missile but to a launcher for a family of weapons that, in addition to the 3M-14 (SS-N-30/A) land-attack versions, includes the 3M-54 (SS-N-27) anti-ship cruise missile and the 91R anti-submarine missile. For further detail see US Navy, Office of Naval Intelligence (ONI), *The Russian Navy: A Historic Transition* (ONI: Washington, DC, Dec. 2015), pp. 34–35.

[47] It is important to caution that although a growing number of vessels are capable of launching the dual-capable 3M-14, it is uncertain how many of them have been assigned a nuclear role.

[48] 'Newest Russian submarine hits target 1000 km away with Kalibr cruise missile', TASS, 23 Nov. 2020; and 'Defense ministry announces Kazan missile-carrying submarine joins Russian Navy', TASS, 7 May 2021.

[49] Manaranche, M., 'Yasen-M class SSGN "Novosibirsk" begins its sea trials', Naval News, 2 July 2021; and Sevmash (note 34).

it is unclear whether the Tsirkon is dual-capable), which will begin serial production and delivery to the navy in 2022.[50]

Air force weapons

The second largest stock of non-strategic nuclear weapons is assigned to the Russian Air Force, which is estimated to have approximately 500 nuclear warheads for use by Tu-22M3 (Backfire-C) intermediate-range bombers, Su-24M (Fencer-D) fighter-bombers, Su-34 (Fullback) fighter-bombers and MiG-31K (Foxhound) attack aircraft.[51] The new Su-57 (Felon) combat aircraft, also known as PAK-FA, is dual-capable, and the first serial production units were delivered in 2020 and 2021.[52]

The MiG-31K is equipped with the new 9A-7760 Kinzhal air-launched ballistic missile, which in 2021 was operational with the Southern Military District and Northern Fleet, and will eventually be integrated into the Western and Central Military Districts by 2024.[53] Russia has also begun introducing the nuclear-capable Kh-32 air-to-surface missile, an upgrade of the Kh-22N (AS-4) used on the Tu-22M3.[54]

Air-, coastal- and missile-defence weapons

The third largest stock of non-strategic nuclear weapons is assigned to Russian air-, coastal- and missile-defence forces, which are estimated to have around 387 nuclear warheads. Most have been assigned for use by dual-capable S-300 and S-400 air-defence forces and the Moscow A-135 missile-defence system. Russian coastal-defence units are believed to have been assigned a small number of nuclear weapons. Russia has also been developing the S-500 air-defence system, which might potentially be dual-capable, but there is no publicly available authoritative information confirming a nuclear role.[55] It is likely that the stock of warheads associated with Russia's air-, coastal- and missile-defence forces will eventually decrease due to the improving capabilities of conventional air-defence interceptors—including

[50] 'Russia's Tsirkon sea-launched hypersonic missile enters final stage of trials: Top brass', TASS, 20 Jan. 2022.

[51] US Department of Defense, 'US nuclear deterrence policy', Fact sheet, 1 Apr. 2019, p. 3; International Institute for Strategic Studies, *The Military Balance 2021* (Routledge: London, 2021); and authors' estimate. It is possible that the Su-30SM is also capable of delivering nuclear weapons.

[52] D'Urso, S., 'First serial production Su-57 Felon delivered to the Russian Aerospace Forces', *The Aviationist*, 30 Dec. 2020; and Rob Lee (@RALee85), 'Two new "serial" Su-57 fighters (bort red 02 and 52, including RF-81775) photographed in Novosibirsk', Twitter, 3 Feb. 2022.

[53] President of Russia (note 9); 'Russia's upgraded MiG-31 fighters to provide security for Northern Sea Route', TASS, 26 Nov. 2021; and [Add hypersonic: Another military district will be armed with 'Daggers'], *Izvestia*, 7 June 2021 (in Russian).

[54] US Department of Defense (note 5), p. 8.

[55] Podvig, P., 'Missile defense in Russia', Working paper, Federation of American Scientists (FAS), Project on Nuclear Dynamics in a Multipolar Strategic BMD World, May 2017.

the Nudol and Aerostat systems under development in 2021—and the retirement of legacy warheads.

Army weapons

The Russian Army has the smallest stock of non-strategic nuclear weapons, an estimated 90 warheads to arm 9K720 Iskander-M (SS-26) short-range ballistic missiles (SRBMs) and 9M729 (SSC-8) ground-launched cruise missiles (GLCMs). As of January 2022, the dual-capable Iskander-M had completely replaced the Tochka (SS-21) SRBM in 12 missile brigades.[56] The 9M728 Iskander-K (SSC-7) GLCM might also be dual-capable.

The dual-capable 9M729 GLCM was cited by the USA as its main reason for withdrawing from the 1987 Treaty on the Elimination of Intermediate-Range and Shorter-Range Missiles (INF Treaty) in 2019.[57] SIPRI estimates that four or five 9M729 battalions have so far been co-deployed with four or five of the Iskander-M brigades. Following President Putin's October 2020 declaration of willingness to impose a moratorium on future 9M729 deployments in European territory, subject to conditions, the Russian foreign ministry in December 2021 published a draft security agreement that included a ban on deployment of Russian and US missiles with ranges previously covered by the now defunct INF Treaty in areas where they could reach the other side's territory.[58]

There have been suggestions that the Russian Army may also have stocks of nuclear artillery shells and landmines, but the publicly available evidence is conflicting.[59]

[56] Authors' assessment based on observation of satellite imagery.

[57] US Department of State, Bureau of Arms Control, Verification and Compliance, 'INF Treaty at a glance', Fact sheet, 8 Dec. 2017. For a summary and other details of the INF Treaty see annex A, section III, in this volume. See also Topychkanov, P. and Davis, I., 'Russian–US nuclear arms control and disarmament', *SIPRI Yearbook 2020*; and Kile, S. N., 'Russian–US nuclear arms control and disarmament', *SIPRI Yearbook 2018*.

[58] President of Russia, 'Statement by Vladimir Putin on additional steps to de-escalate the situation in Europe after the termination of the Intermediate-Range Nuclear Forces Treaty (INF Treaty)', 26 Oct. 2020; and Russian Ministry of Foreign Affairs, Agreement on Measures to Ensure the Security of the Russian Federation and Member States of the North Atlantic Treaty Organization, Unofficial translation, 17 Dec. 2021. See also Kristensen, H. M. and Korda, M., 'Russian nuclear forces', *SIPRI Yearbook 2020*, p. 356.

[59] E.g. the 2018 US Nuclear Posture Review did not list nuclear artillery shells or landmines, but a statement by former US Department of Defense official Ellen M. Lord before a US Senate subcommittee in May 2019 did mention them. US Department of Defense (note 5); and Lord, E. M., Under Secretary for Acquisition and Sustainment, Statement before the Subcommittee on Strategic Forces, US Senate Armed Services Committee, 1 May 2019, p. 3.

III. British nuclear forces

HANS M. KRISTENSEN AND MATT KORDA

As of January 2022, the United Kingdom's nuclear weapon inventory consisted of approximately 225 warheads (see table 10.4)—an unchanged estimate from the previous year. This estimate is based on publicly available information on the British nuclear arsenal and conversations with British officials. The authors consider the British government to have generally been more transparent about its nuclear activities than many other nuclear-armed states—for example, by having declared the size of its nuclear weapon inventory in 2010 and the number of warheads it intends to keep in the future. However, the UK has never declassified the history of its inventory or the actual number of warheads it possesses, and in 2021 declared that it will no longer publicly disclose figures for the country's operational stockpile, deployed warheads or deployed missile numbers.[1]

The role of nuclear weapons in British military doctrine

The British government has stated that it remains 'deliberately ambiguous about precisely when, how, and at what scale [it] would contemplate the use of nuclear weapons'.[2] However, British policy also states that the UK 'would consider using ... nuclear weapons only in extreme circumstances of self-defence, including the defence of ... NATO [North Atlantic Treaty Organization] Allies'.[3]

The UK is the only nuclear-armed state that operates a single type of nuclear weapon: the country's nuclear deterrent is entirely sea-based. The UK possesses four Vanguard-class nuclear-powered ballistic missile submarines (SSBNs) that carry Trident II D5 submarine-launched ballistic missiles (SLBMs).[4] In a posture known as continuous at-sea deterrence (CASD), which began in 1969, one British SSBN carrying approximately 40 warheads is on patrol at all times.[5] While the second and third SSBNs

---

[1] British Government, *Global Britain in a Competitive Age: Integrated Review of Security, Defence, Development and Foreign Policy*, CP 403 (HM Stationery Office: London, Mar. 2021), pp. 76–77. On the challenges of collecting information on world nuclear forces more generally see Kristensen, H. M. and Korda, M., 'Estimating world nuclear forces: An overview and assessment of sources', SIPRI Topical Backgrounder, 14 June 2021.

[2] British Government, *National Report of the United Kingdom of Great Britain and Northern Ireland, pursuant to Actions 5, 20 and 21 of the Treaty on the Non-Proliferation of Nuclear Weapons (NPT) Review Conference 2010 for the 10th NPT Review Conference* (British Ministry of Defence: London, Nov. 2021), p. 9.

[3] British Government (note 1), p. 76.

[4] Mills, C., *Replacing the UK's Strategic Nuclear Deterrent: Progress of the Dreadnought Class*, Briefing Paper no. CBP-8010 (House of Commons Library: London, 2 Mar. 2021), p. 7.

[5] British Ministry of Defence, 'UK's nuclear deterrent (CASD)', 17 Mar. 2021.

Table 10.4. British nuclear forces, January 2022

All figures are approximate and some are based on assessments by the authors.

Type/designation	No. of launchers	Year first deployed	Range (km)	Warheads x yield	No. of warheads
Sea-based missiles (SLBMs)	4/64[a]				*120*
Trident II D5	48[b]	1994	>10 000[c]	1–8 x 100 kt[d]	120
Total operationally available warheads					**120**[e]
Other stored warheads					105[f]
Total inventory					**225**[g]

kt = kiloton; SLBM = submarine-launched ballistic missile.

[a] The first figure is the total number of nuclear-powered ballistic missile submarines (SSBNs) in the British fleet; the second is the maximum number of missiles that they can carry. However, the total number of missiles carried is lower (see note b). Of the four SSBNs, one is in overhaul at any given time.

[b] The three operational SSBNs can carry a total of 48 Trident SLBMs. The United Kingdom has purchased the right to 58 missiles from a pool shared with the United States Navy.

[c] The Trident II D5 missiles on British SSBNs are identical to the Trident II D5 missiles on US Navy SSBNs, which have demonstrated a range of more than 10 000 km in test flights.

[d] The British warhead is called the Holbrook, a modified version of the USA's W76 warhead, with a potential lower-yield option.

[e] Of the 120 operationally available warheads, approximately 40 are deployed on the single SSBN that is at sea at any given time.

[f] This figure includes *c.* 45 retired warheads that have not yet been dismantled. It seems likely that they will be reconstituted to become part of the UK's total stockpile over the coming years (see note g). Many of the stored warheads that have not been retired are thought to be undergoing upgrade from the Mk4 to the Mk4A.

[g] The British government declared in 2010 that its inventory would not exceed 225 warheads, and that the UK would reduce the number of warheads in its overall nuclear stockpile to no more than 180. Despite these stated intentions, the UK's nuclear inventory appears to have remained at approximately 225 warheads throughout the decade 2010–20. The integrated review of security, defence, development and foreign policy undertaken in 2020 and published in early 2021 introduced a new ceiling of 260 warheads.

Sources: British Ministry of Defence, white papers, press releases and website; British House of Commons, *Hansard*, various issues; *Bulletin of the Atomic Scientists*, 'Nuclear notebook', various issues; and authors' estimates.

remain in port and could be put to sea in a crisis, the fourth would probably be unable to deploy because it would be in the midst of extensive overhaul and maintenance.

The UK operates its submarines at a 'reduced alert' level with detargeted missiles, meaning that it could take days—rather than minutes—to fire nuclear missiles in a crisis.[6] This distinguishes British nuclear policy from that of countries such as Russia or the United States, which are postured to launch nuclear missiles at a moment's notice and could be prompted to launch without first receiving a wholly accurate confirmation of an adversarial

[6] British Ministry of Defence, 'The UK's nuclear deterrent: What you need to know', 17 Feb. 2022.

first strike. In order to command its submarines in the event of a degraded command and control environment, the British government uses a system of pre-written 'letters of last resort' to issue possible retaliatory orders: on a prime minister's first day in office, after being briefed on the precise damage that a Trident missile could cause, the prime minister is expected to offer preplanned instructions regarding the UK's response in the event of a nuclear crisis.[7]

Revisions to British nuclear policy

For approximately 15 years, the British government had been in the process of reducing the number of operationally available warheads and the size of its overall nuclear stockpile, until a sudden policy shift occurred in 2021.

In 2006 the British Ministry of Defence (MOD) announced that the country would be 'reducing the number of operationally available warheads from fewer than 200 to fewer than 160'.[8] By May 2010, the MOD had also reduced the country's overall nuclear stockpile from approximately 240 to 245 warheads in 2006 to no more than 225 warheads.[9]

In October 2010 the British government's strategic defence and security review (SDSR) announced additional plans for reductions: the number of warheads carried by each submarine would be reduced from 48 to 40 and the number of operational missiles on each submarine would also be reduced; the number of operationally available nuclear warheads would be reduced from fewer than 160 to no more than 120; and the overall nuclear stockpile would be reduced from no more than 225 warheads to no more than 180.[10] The 2015 SDSR reaffirmed these planned reductions and announced that the number of operationally available nuclear warheads had already been reduced from fewer than 160 to no more than 120, and that all Vanguard-class SSBNs 'now carr[ied] 40 nuclear warheads and no more than eight operational missiles' (see below).[11]

Despite these reductions and the government's stated intentions about gradually further reducing the overall nuclear stockpile, from 2010 until 2021 the size of the UK's stockpile remained constant at approximately

---

[7] Norton-Taylor, R., 'Theresa May's first job: Decide on UK's nuclear response', *The Guardian*, 12 July 2016.

[8] British Ministry of Defence, *The Future of the United Kingdom's Nuclear Deterrent*, White Paper, CM 6994 (HM Stationery Office: London, Dec. 2006), p. 8.

[9] British Ministry of Defence, 'Response to Freedom of Information Act request made by Rob Edwards: Ref. 25-03-2013-173601-014', 25 July 2013.

[10] British Government, *Securing Britain in an Age of Uncertainty: The Strategic Defence and Security Review*, Cm 7948 (HM Stationery Office: London, 2010), p. 38.

[11] Fallon, M., British secretary of state for defence, 'Statement on nuclear deterrent', *Hansard*, 20 Jan. 2015, column 4WS; and British Government, *National Security Strategy and Strategic Defence and Security Review 2015: A Secure and Prosperous United Kingdom*, Cm 9161, (HM Stationery Office: London, 2015), p. 34.

225 warheads. While warheads removed from operationally available service throughout this period were placed into storage, they were not dismantled, contrary to what many analysts believed at the time.[12]

In its integrated review of security, defence, development and foreign policy, published in March 2021, the British government revealed a marked shift in policy by announcing a significant increase to the upper limit of its nuclear stockpile, to up to no more than 260 warheads.[13] British officials clarified that the target of 180 warheads stated in the 2010 and 2015 SDSRs 'was indeed a goal, but it was never reached, and it has never been our cap'.[14] In addition, in its 2021 national report in advance of the planned 2022 10th review conference of the parties to the 1968 Treaty on the Non-Proliferation of Nuclear Weapons, the British government stated that the 260 number 'is a ceiling, not a target, and it is not our current stockpile number'.[15]

It is unclear what exactly has prompted the UK to reverse decades of gradual disarmament policy. British government officials have offered differing and somewhat vague explanations for the increase in the UK's overall nuclear stockpile, but following the integrated review's publication, Ben Wallace, the British secretary of state for defence, explicitly pointed to improvements in Russia's ballistic missile defence capabilities as one driving factor.[16] It is also possible that raising the limit on its nuclear stockpile could enable the UK to deploy its SSBNs with a full load of Trident missiles and warheads. If the UK intends to increase the size of its nuclear stockpile, this would position the UK with China and Russia as the three members out of the five permanent members of the United Nations Security Council that are increasing the sizes of their nuclear stockpiles.

Nuclear weapon modernization

The UK's lead SSBN, HMS *Vanguard*, entered service in December 1994, while the last submarine in the class, HMS *Vengeance*, entered service in February 2001 with an expected service life of 25 years.[17] The 2015 SDSR stated the government's intention to replace the Vanguard-class submarines with four new SSBNs, known as the Dreadnought class.[18]

---

[12] British officials, Interviews with the authors, May 2021.

[13] British Government (note 1) p. 76.

[14] Aidan Liddle (@AidanLiddle), the UK's permanent representative to the Conference on Disarmament, 'That cap was maintained in 2015. 180 was indeed a goal, but it was never reached, and it has never been our cap. And by the way, we're talking about ceilings, not targets, or indeed our actual numbers', Twitter, 16 Mar. 2021. This information was also later confirmed by other officials. British officials, Interviews with the authors, May 2021.

[15] British Government (note 2), p. 11.

[16] BBC Politics (@BBCPolitics) '#Marr: Do we need 80 new nuclear weapons? Defence Secretary Ben Wallace: "We need a credible nuclear deterrent"', Twitter, 21 Mar. 2021.

[17] Mills (note 4).

[18] British Government (note 11), para. 4.73.

The new Dreadnought-class submarines were originally expected to begin entering into service by 2028, but this has been delayed until the early 2030s. The service life of the Vanguard-class SSBNs has been commensurately extended to an overall lifespan of approximately 37 to 38 years.[19] The UK is participating in the US Navy's programme to extend the service life of the Trident II D5 missile. The first and second life-extended versions are known as D5LE and D5LE2, respectively; the D5LE will function until the early 2060s and the D5LE2 until the mid 2080s.[20]

The warhead carried on the Trident II D5 is called the Holbrook, which is currently being upgraded to accommodate the USA-produced Mk4A re-entry body, in a collaboration between the British MOD's Atomic Weapons Establishment and US nuclear laboratories. British defence officials have suggested that 'the Mk4A programme will not increase the destructive power of the warhead'.[21] However, the Mk4A is equipped with a new fuze system incorporating new technology that significantly increases the system's ability to conduct nuclear strike missions against hardened targets.[22] British defence officials have acknowledged the enhanced capability.[23] According to Nukewatch, a UK-based disarmament group that tracks warhead convoys across the country, it is possible that sufficient Mk4A-upgraded warheads had been produced by the end of 2021 to arm the UK's Vanguard-class SSBNs.[24]

The British government in 2020 announced its intention to replace the Holbrook with a new warhead, which will use the Mk7 aeroshell to be developed for the new US W93 warhead.[25] Although the administration of US President Joe Biden is expected to continue the W93 programme started under the previous administration, British defence officials stated in 2021 that the UK's warhead replacement programme would move forward regardless of the status of the USA's W93 programme.[26]

---

[19] Mills (note 4).

[20] Mills (note 4).

[21] British Ministry of Defence, 'Defence in the media: 8 June 2016', Defence in the Media blog, 8 June 2016.

[22] Kristensen, H. M., McKinzie, M. and Postol, T., 'How US nuclear force modernization is undermining strategic stability: The burst-height compensating super-fuze', Bulletin of the Atomic Scientists, 1 Mar. 2017.

[23] Norton-Taylor, R., 'Trident more effective with US arming device, tests suggest', The Guardian, 6 Apr. 2011.

[24] Nukewatch, 'Warhead convoy movements summary 2021', 2021.

[25] Wallace, B., British secretary of state for defence, 'Nuclear deterrent', Written Statement HCWS125, British Parliament, 25 Feb. 2020; and Wolfe, J., Director of US Strategic Systems Programs, 'FY2022 budget request for nuclear forces and atomic energy defense activities', Statement before the Subcommittee on Strategic Forces, US Senate Armed Forces Committee, 12 May 2021, pp. 6–7. For further detail see Kristensen, H. M. and Korda, M., 'British nuclear forces', SIPRI Yearbook 2021.

[26] Mehta, A., 'UK official: American warhead decision won't impact British nuclear plans', Defense News, 13 Apr. 2021.

The new Dreadnought-class submarines will have 12 launch tubes—a reduction from the 16 carried by the Vanguard-class (see below). Delivery of the first batch of missile tubes, which are produced in the USA, was initially delayed, but, as of January 2022, all 12 of the tubes required for the first SSBN in the class (HMS *Dreadnought*) had been delivered and were in the process of being integrated into the SSBN's pressure hull.[27] The Dreadnought-class is expected to be significantly stealthier than its predecessor, as a result of its hull design and electric-drive propulsion.[28]

The cost of the Dreadnought programme has been a source of concern and controversy since its inception.[29] In its annual update to the parliament in December 2021, the MOD reported that a total of £10.4 billion ($14.3 billion) had been spent on the programme's concept, assessment and delivery phases as of 31 March 2021—of which £1.9 billion ($2.6 billion) was spent in financial year 2020/21.[30]

Sea-based missiles

The current Vanguard-class SSBNs can each be armed with up to 16 Trident II D5 SLBMs. The UK does not own the missiles, but has purchased the right to 58 Trident SLBMs from a pool shared with the US Navy at the US Strategic Weapons Facility in Kings Bay, Georgia.[31] Previously, under limits set out in the 2010 SDSR and reaffirmed by the 2015 SDSR, when on patrol, the submarines would be armed with no more than 8 operational missiles with a total of 40 nuclear warheads.[32] However, after the 2021 integrated review's policy changes, it is possible that these limits are no longer applicable and that the number of deployed missiles and warheads on each submarine could therefore increase.

[27] British Ministry of Defence, 'The United Kingdom's future nuclear deterrent: The 2021 update to Parliament', 16 Dec. 2021.

[28] Sutton, H. I., 'First submarine to use new stealth technology', Naval News, 3 Nov. 2021; O'Rourke, R., *Navy Columbia (SSBN-826) Class Ballistic Missile Submarine Program: Background and Issues for Congress*, Congressional Research Service (CRS) Report R41129 (US Congress, CRS: Washington, DC, 19 Oct. 2021), p. 41; and O'Rourke, R., *Electric-drive Propulsion for US Navy Ships: Background and Issues for Congress*, Congressional Research Service (CRS) Report RL30622 (US Congress, CRS: Washington, DC, 31 July 2000), pp. 11–12.

[29] Mills (note 4). See also Kristensen and Korda (note 25), p. 361.

[30] British Ministry of Defence (note 27).

[31] Allison, G., 'No, America doesn't control Britain's nuclear weapons', UK Defence Journal, 20 July 2019.

[32] Fallon (note 11); and British Government (note 11), p. 34.

IV. French nuclear forces

HANS M. KRISTENSEN AND MATT KORDA

As of January 2022, France's nuclear weapon stockpile consisted of about 290 warheads, the same number as in January 2021. The warheads are allocated for delivery by 48 submarine-launched ballistic missiles (SLBMs) and approximately 50 air-launched cruise missiles (ALCMs) produced for land- and carrier-based aircraft (see table 10.5). However, the 10 warheads assigned to France's carrier-based aircraft are thought to be kept in central storage and are not normally deployed. The estimate of France's nuclear weapon stockpile is based on publicly available information.[1] France is relatively transparent about many of its nuclear weapon activities and has in the past publicly disclosed the size of its stockpile and details of its nuclear-related operations.[2]

The role of nuclear weapons in French military doctrine

France considers all of its nuclear weapons to be strategic and reserved for the defence of France's 'vital interests'.[3] While this concept has appeared in various governmental white papers and presidential speeches for several decades, what constitutes France's 'vital interests' remains unclear, and President Emmanuel Macron has implied that these 'vital interests' could increasingly take on a European dimension.[4] No changes to French military doctrine were announced in 2021.

Nuclear weapon modernization

President Macron has reaffirmed the French government's commitment to the long-term modernization of France's air- and sea-based nuclear deterrent forces.[5] Current plans include the modernization of France's nuclear-powered ballistic missile submarines (SSBNs, or *sous-marins nucléaires lanceurs d'engins*, SNLEs), SLBMs, aircraft and ALCMs (see below). The 2018 Law on Military Planning (Loi de Programmation Militaire, LPM) for

---

[1] For additional information see Kristensen, H. M. and Korda, M., 'Estimating world nuclear forces: An overview and assessment of sources', SIPRI Topical Backgrounder, 14 June 2021.

[2] Macron, E., French President, Speech on defence and deterrence strategy (in French, with English translation), École de Guerre, Paris, 7 Feb. 2020.

[3] Tertrais, B., *French Nuclear Deterrence Policy, Forces and Future: A Handbook*, Recherches & Documents no. 04/2020 (Fondation pour la Recherche Stratégique: Paris, Feb. 2020), pp. 25–29, 62–63.

[4] Macron (note 2). See also Kristensen, H. M. and Korda, M., 'French nuclear forces', *SIPRI Yearbook 2021*.

[5] Macron, E., French President, Speech on the challenges and priorities of defence policy (in French), Toulon, 19 Jan. 2018.

Table 10.5. French nuclear forces, January 2022

All figures are approximate and some are based on assessments by the authors.

Type/designation	No. of launchers	Year first deployed	Range (km)[a]	Warheads x yield	No. of warheads
Land-based aircraft					
Rafale BF3[b]	40	2010–11	2 000	1 x <300 kt TNA[c]	40
Carrier-based aircraft					
Rafale MF3[b]	10	2010–11	2 000	1 x <300 kt TNA[c]	10[d]
Sea-based missiles (SLBMs)	4/64[e]				240
M51.2[f]	48[g]	2017	>9 000[h]	4–6 x 100 kt TNO	240
M51.3[i]	–	[2025]	>[9 000]	[up to 6] x [100 kt] TNO	–
Total stockpile					**290**[j]

[] = uncertain SIPRI estimate; – = nil or a negligible value; kt = kiloton; SLBM = submarine-launched ballistic missile; TNA = *tête nucléaire aéroportée* (air-launched nuclear warhead); TNO = *tête nucléaire océanique* (sea-based nuclear warhead).

[a] For aircraft, the listed range is for illustrative purposes only; actual mission range will vary according to flight profile, weapon payload and in-flight refuelling.

[b] The BF3 and MF3 aircraft both carry the ASMP-A (*air–sol moyenne portée–améliorée*) air-launched cruise missile (ALCM). Most sources report that the ASMP-A has a range of 500–600 kilometres, although some suggest that it might be over 600 km.

[c] The TN81 warhead for the original ASMP had an estimated yield of 300 kt, but the new TNA warhead has a so-called medium energy yield.

[d] The 10 warheads assigned to France's carrier-based aircraft are thought to be kept in central storage and are not normally deployed.

[e] The first figure is the total number of nuclear-powered ballistic missile submarines (SSBNs) in the French fleet; the second is the maximum number of missiles that they can carry. However, the total number of missiles carried is lower (see note g). Of the four SSBNs, one is in overhaul at any given time.

[f] The last M51.1 missiles were offloaded from *Le Terrible* in late 2020 in preparation for a one-year refuelling overhaul and upgrade to the more advanced M51.2 missile.

[g] France has 48 SLBMs in service—enough to equip the three operational SSBNs.

[h] The M51.2 has a 'much greater range' than the M51.1 according to the French Ministry of the Armed Forces.

[i] The M51.3 is under development and has not yet been deployed.

[j] In Feb. 2020 President Emmanuel Macron reaffirmed that the arsenal 'is currently under 300 nuclear weapons'. A few of the warheads are thought to be undergoing maintenance and inspection at any given time.

Sources: Speeches (in French) of French presidents and defence ministers: Macron, E., Speech on defence and deterrence strategy, École de Guerre, Paris, 7 Feb. 2020; Parly, F., Speech, ArianeGroup, Les Mureaux, 14 Dec. 2017; Hollande, F., Speech on nuclear deterrence, Istres Air Base, 19 Feb. 2015; Sarkozy, N., Speech on the new defence policy, Porte de Versailles, 17 June 2008; Sarkozy, N., Speech on the white paper on national defence and security, nuclear deterrence and the non-proliferation of nuclear weapons, Cherbourg, 21 Mar. 2008; Chirac, J., Speech on France's defence policy, Île Longue, Brest, 19 Jan. 2006. Other sources: French Ministry of Defence/Ministry of the Armed Forces, various publications; French National Assembly, various defence bills; *Air Actualités*, various issues; *Aviation Week & Space Technology*, various issues; *Bulletin of the Atomic Scientists*, 'Nuclear notebook', various issues; Tertrais, B., *French Nuclear Deterrence Policy, Forces and Future: A Handbook*, Recherches & Documents no. 04/2020 (Fondation pour la Recherche Stratégique: Paris, Feb. 2020); and authors' estimates.

2019–25 allocated €37 billion ($43.7 billion) for maintenance and modernization of France's nuclear forces and infrastructure.[6] This is a significant nominal increase on the €23 billion ($30.5 billion) allocated to nuclear forces and associated infrastructure by the LPM for 2014–19.[7]

The 2022 budget of the Ministry of the Armed Forces (France's defence ministry) allocated €5.3 billion ($6.3 billion) to nuclear weapon-related activity, which is €0.3 billion more than in the 2021 budget.[8] France intends to spend a total of €25 billion ($29.5 billion) on nuclear modernization between 2019 and 2023.[9]

Aircraft and air-delivered weapons

The airborne component of the French nuclear forces consists of land- and carrier-based aircraft. The French Air and Space Force has 40 deployed nuclear-capable Rafale BF3 aircraft based at Saint-Dizier Air Base in northeast France. The French Naval Nuclear Air Force (Force aéronavale nucléaire, FANu) consists of a squadron of 10 Rafale MF3 aircraft for deployment on the aircraft carrier *Charles de Gaulle*. The FANu and its nuclear-armed missiles are not permanently deployed but can be rapidly deployed by the French president in support of nuclear operations.[10]

The Rafale aircraft are equipped with medium-range air-to-surface cruise missiles (*air–sol moyenne portée–améliorée*, ASMPA), which are currently being refurbished, with delivery expected in 2022 or 2023.[11] The ASMPA missiles are equipped with a new warhead, the *tête nucléaire aéroportée*

---

[6] Agence-France Presse, 'Macron promulgue la loi de programmation militaire 2019-2025' [Macron signs the Law on Military Planning for 2019–2025], *Le Figaro*, 13 July 2018; Loi relative à la programmation militaire pour les années 2019 à 2025 [Law on Military Planning for the Years 2019 to 2025], French Law no. 2018-607 of 13 July 2018, *Journal Officiel de la République Française*, 14 July 2018; and Agence-France Presse, 'France to spend 37 bn euros on upgrading nuclear arsenal', France 24, 8 Feb. 2018. The total defence budget approved for the seven-year period was €295 billion ($348 billion). On France's military expenditure see chapter 8, sections I and II, in this volume.

[7] Loi relative à la programmation militaire pour les années 2014 à 2019 [Law on Military Planning for the Years 2014 to 2019], French Law no. 2013-1168 of 18 Dec. 2013, *Journal Officiel de la République Française*, 19 Dec. 2013.

[8] French Ministry of the Armed Forces (MAF), *Projet de loi de finances: Année 2022* [Finance bill: Year 2022] (MAF: Paris, Sep. 2021), p. 43; and Rose, M., 'Amid arms race, Macron offers Europe French nuclear wargames insight', Reuters, 7 Feb. 2020.

[9] Groizeleau, V., 'Dissuasion: 25 milliards en cinq ans pour le renouvellement des deux composantes' [Deterrence: 25 billion in five years for the renewal of the two components], Mer et Marine, 2 Oct. 2019.

[10] Pintat, X. et al., 'Rapport d'information fait au nom de la commission des affaires étrangères, de la défense et des forces armées par le groupe de travail "La modernisation de la dissuasion nucléaire"' [Information report made on behalf of the Committee on Foreign Affairs, Defense and the Armed Forces by the working group 'Modernization of nuclear deterrence'], Report of the French Senate no. 560, 23 May 2017.

[11] For further detail see Kristensen and Korda (note 4), p. 366.

(TNA), which the missile's producer (MBDA) says has a 'medium energy' yield.[12]

The Ministry of the Armed Forces has begun developing a successor: a fourth-generation air-to-surface nuclear missile (*air–sol nucléaire de 4e génération*, ASN4G) with enhanced stealth and manoeuvrability to counter potential technological improvements in air defences.[13] The ASN4G is scheduled to reach initial operational capability in 2035.[14] France's Rafale aircraft are also being modernized, and flight trials for the latest F4 configuration with new radars and targeting capabilities began in May 2021.[15]

Sea-based missiles

The main component of France's nuclear forces is the Strategic Oceanic Force (Force océanique stratégique, FOST). It consists of four *Le Triomphant*-class SSBNs based on the Île Longue peninsula near Brest, north-west France. Each is capable of carrying 16 SLBMs. However, at any given time one SSBN is out of service for overhaul and maintenance work, and is not armed. France has 48 SLBMs in service—enough to equip the three operational SSBNs.

The French Navy (Marine nationale) maintains a continuous at-sea deterrence posture with one SSBN on patrol at all times. It has conducted more than 500 such patrols since 1972.[16]

France's SLBM, the M51, is being upgraded. The first version, the M51.1, was capable of carrying up to six TN-75 warheads in multiple independently targetable re-entry vehicles (MIRVs), each with an explosive yield of 100 kilotons. Over the past several years, the M51.1 has been gradually replaced by the M51.2, an upgraded version with greater range and improved accuracy. With the deployment of the M51.2 on *Le Téméraire* in mid 2020, the only SSBN left to receive this upgrade, *Le Terrible*, began its major refit in late 2020.[17] Thus, the M51.1 had been officially removed from service by early 2021.

---

[12] MBDA, 'ASMPA: Air-to-ground missile, medium range, enhanced', Fact sheet, [n.d.].

[13] French Ministry of the Armed Forces, 'La dissuasion nucléaire' [Nuclear deterrence], *Actu Défense*, 14 June 2018, p. 1; and Tran, P., 'France studies nuclear missile replacement', *Defense News*, 29 Nov. 2014.

[14] Medeiros, J., '"Faire FAS": 55 ans de dissuasion nucléaire aéroportée' ['Go FAS': 55 years of airborne nuclear deterrence], *Air Actualités*, Oct. 2019, p. 36.

[15] Jennings, G., 'France begins Rafale F4 flight trials', Janes, 21 May 2021.

[16] French Ministry of the Armed Forces, '500e patrouille d'un sous-marin nucléaire lanceur d'engins' [500th patrol of a nuclear-powered ballistic missile submarine], 12 Oct. 2018.

[17] French Ministry of the Armed Forces and Naval Group, 'Le SNLE *Le Terrible* transféré de l'Île Longue à la base navale de Brest pour son grand carénage' [The SSBN *Le Terrible* transferred from Île Longue to the Brest naval base for its major refit], Press release, 8 Jan. 2021.

The M51.2 is designed to carry a new, stealthier nuclear warhead, the *tête nucléaire océanique* (TNO), which has a reported yield of up to 100 kt.[18] To allow for targeting flexibility, some of the missiles have fewer warheads than others.[19] France has also commenced design work on another upgrade, the M51.3, which will have improved accuracy. The first M51.3 missiles are scheduled to replace their M51.2 predecessors and become operational in 2025.[20]

In April 2021 France conducted a successful test launch of the M51 from the missile testing site near Biscarosse in south-west France; however, the impact area referenced in the notice to mariners was significantly offset from a regular ballistic trajectory.[21] This could potentially indicate that the launch included a test of a manoeuvrable re-entry vehicle or a post-boost capability. This was the 10th test of the M51.

In the LPM for 2019–25, the French government announced that it would produce a third-generation SSBN, designated the SNLE 3G.[22] The programme was officially launched in early 2021.[23] The SNLE 3G will eventually be equipped with a further modification of the M51 SLBM, the M51.4.[24] The construction of the first of four submarines in the class is scheduled to begin in 2023 and is expected to be completed by 2035. The other three submarines will be delivered on a schedule of one boat every five years.[25] In 2021 France dismantled its second of five retired SSBNs and plans to complete the deconstruction programme by 2026.[26]

---

[18] Groizeleau (note 9); and Groizeleau, V., 'Dissuasion: F. Hollande détaille sa vision et l'arsenal français' [Deterrence: F. Hollande outlines his vision and the French arsenal], Mer et Marine, 20 Feb. 2015.

[19] Tertrais (note 3), p. 57.

[20] French Ministry of the Armed Forces, 'Missiles balistiques stratégiques (MSBS)' [Strategic ballistic missiles], 28 Jan. 2020; and Parly, F., French minister of the armed forces, Speech (in French), ArianeGroup, Les Mureaux, 14 Dec. 2017.

[21] French Ministry of the Armed Forces, 'Succès d'un tir d'essai de missile M51 sans charge militaire', 28 Apr. 2021; and Dr Marco Langbroek (@Marco_Langbroek), 'Navigational Warnings suggest that France will be test-firing an #ICBM from DGA Essais de Missiles near Biscarosse towards Bermuda between Apr 28–May 21. Target area does not fit a simple ballistic trajectory', Twitter, 25 Apr. 2021.

[22] French Ministry of the Armed Forces, 'Projet de loi de programmation militaire, 2019–2025' [Military Planning Bill, 2019–2025], Press kit, Feb. 2018, p. 38.

[23] French Ministry of the Armed Forces, 'Florence Parly, ministre des armées, annonce le lancement en réalisation des sous-marins nucléaires lanceurs d'engins de 3e génération (SNLE 3G)' [Florence Parly, minister of the armed forces, announces the launch of the 3rd-generation nuclear-powered ballistic missile submarines (SNLE 3G)], 19 Feb. 2021; and Mackenzie, C., 'France to begin building new ballistic missile subs', *Defense News*, 22 Feb. 2021.

[24] Tertrais (note 3), pp. 56, 60, 65.

[25] French Ministry of the Armed Forces (note 23); Groizeleau (note 9); and Mackenzie (note 23).

[26] Naval Group, 'Naval Group starts the deconstruction of a third French nuclear-powered ballistic missile submarine in Cherbourg', News release, 15 Sep. 2021.

V. Chinese nuclear forces

HANS M. KRISTENSEN AND MATT KORDA

As of January 2022, China maintained an estimated total stockpile of about 350 nuclear warheads. This estimate is higher than the 'low-200' warheads reported in the United States Department of Defense (US DOD) 2020 report to the US Congress; however, the DOD's estimate only referred to 'operational' nuclear warheads and therefore presumably excluded warheads assigned to the newer launchers that were in the process of being fielded.[1] As a result, even though SIPRI's estimate of China's total inventory is the same as for January 2021, the ratio of stockpiled and other stored warheads has changed because additional and new launchers became operational during 2021. These warheads have been assigned to China's operational land- and sea-based ballistic missiles and to nuclear-configured aircraft (see table 10.6). Although it is expected to increase significantly in the next decade, China's nuclear stockpile as at January 2022 remained much smaller than that of either Russia or the USA.

SIPRI's estimate of 350 warheads relies on publicly available information on the Chinese nuclear arsenal.[2] China itself has never declared the size of its nuclear arsenal. Occasionally, Chinese officials reference open-source estimates as a means of discussing China's nuclear weapon programme publicly or in diplomatic negotiations.[3] As a result, many of the assessments here rely on data from the US DOD and must therefore be treated with a degree of caution. For example, in 2021 the US DOD estimated that China 'likely intends to have at least 1000 warheads by 2030'; however, this claim relies on several assumptions about China's future force posture and plutonium production that have not yet been fully realized.[4]

The role of nuclear weapons in Chinese military doctrine

The Chinese government's declared aim is to maintain its nuclear capabilities at the minimum level required for safeguarding national security. The goal is 'deterring other countries from using or threatening to use nuclear

---

[1] US Department of Defense, *Military and Security Developments Involving the People's Republic of China 2020*, Annual Report to Congress (Office of the Secretary of Defense: Arlington, VA, 1 Sep. 2020), p. 85.

[2] Kristensen, H. M. and Korda, M., 'Estimating world nuclear forces: An overview and assessment of sources', SIPRI Topical Backgrounder, 14 June 2021.

[3] See e.g. Chinese Ministry of National Defense, 'China reiterates it will not join so-called China–US–Russia arms control negotiations', 9 July 2020.

[4] US Department of Defense, *Military and Security Developments Involving the People's Republic of China 2021*, Annual Report to Congress (Office of the Secretary of Defense: Arlington, VA, 3 Nov. 2021), p. 90; and Sokolski, H. D. (ed.), *China's Civil Nuclear Sector: Plowshares to Swords?*, Nonproliferation Policy Education Center (NPEC), Occasional Paper no. 2102 (NPEC: Arlington, VA, Mar. 2021).

weapons against China'.[5] For decades, China did so with an arsenal of mainly liquid-fuelled land-based ballistic missiles and a few sea-based ballistic missiles, with a small stockpile of gravity bombs available for bombers as a semi-dormant back-up capacity. Since around 2017, China has started to put in place a triad of nuclear forces—solid-fuelled mobile and siloed land-based missiles, nuclear-powered ballistic missile submarines (SSBNs), and bombers with a full, re-established nuclear mission—in order to strengthen its nuclear deterrence and counterstrike capabilities in response to what it sees as a growing threat from other countries.[6]

Despite the continuing growth in the sophistication and size of its nuclear arsenal, there is no official public evidence that the Chinese government has deviated from its long-standing core nuclear policies, including its no-first-use (NFU) policy.[7] Although US officials have publicly and increasingly questioned China's NFU policy in recent years, the US DOD's 2021 report to the US Congress on China's military power acknowledged that 'there has also been no indication that national leaders are willing to publicly attach such additions, nuances, or caveats [to the NFU policy]'.[8]

In April 2021 the commander of US Strategic Command stated before the US Congress that 'increasing evidence suggests China has moved a portion of its nuclear force to a Launch on Warning (LOW) posture and . . . [is] adopting a limited "high alert duty" strategy'.[9] Additionally, in July 2021 an official from the US Department of State noted that 'Since 2017 PLA [the People's Liberation Army] has also conducted exercises involving launch-on-warning, and now has deployed at least one satellite into orbit for its [LOW] posture'.[10]

The Chinese posture has always involved procedures for loading warheads onto launchers in a crisis, but with warheads kept in central storage, separate from their delivery vehicles, during peacetime.[11] The US DOD's 2021 report

---

[5] Chinese State Council, *China's National Defense in the New Era* (Information Office of the State Council: Beijing, July 2019), chapter 2.

[6] Fabey, M., 'China on faster pace to develop nuclear triad, according to Pentagon, analysts', Jane's, 3 May 2019; and 'Chinese military paper urges increase in nuclear deterrence capabilities', Reuters, 30 Jan. 2018.

[7] Santoro, D. and Gromoll, R., 'On the value of nuclear dialogue with China', Pacific Forum, *Issues & Insights* (special report), vol. 20, no. 1 (Nov. 2020); and Kulacki, G., 'Would China use nuclear weapons first in a war with the United States?', The Diplomat, 27 Apr. 2020.

[8] Zhou, L., 'China should "fine-tune" nuclear weapons policy amid US pressure, ex-diplomat says', *South China Morning Post*, 22 Sep. 2021; and US Department of Defense (note 4), pp. 90–91.

[9] Richard, C. A., Commander, United States Strategic Command, Statement before the US Senate Armed Services Committee, 20 Apr. 2021.

[10] Shashank Joshi (@shashj), '. . . PRC is building nuclear reactors and [ENR] facilities, while seeking to portray them as having only civilian purposes. Since 2017 PLA has also conducted exercises involving launch-on-warning, and now has deployed at least one satellite into orbit for its [LoW] posture', Twitter, 29 July 2021.

[11] Stokes, M. A., *China's Nuclear Warhead Storage and Handling System* (Project 2049 Institute: Arlington, VA, 12 Mar. 2010), p. 8; Li, B., 'China's potential to contribute to multilateral nuclear disarmament', *Arms Control Today*, vol. 41, no. 2 (Mar. 2011); and US Department of Defense (note 4), p. 91.

Table 10.6. Chinese nuclear forces, January 2022

All figures are approximate and some are based on assessments by the authors.

Type/Chinese designation (US designation)	No. of launchers	Year first deployed	Range (km)[a]	Warheads x yield[b]	No. of warheads[c]
Aircraft	20[d]				20
H-6K (B-6)	20	2009	3 100	1 x bomb	20
H-6N (B-6N)	–	2021	..	1 x ALBM	–
H-20 (B-20)	–	[2025]	..	..	–
Land-based missiles[e]	398				258
DF-4 (CSS-3)	6[f]	1980	5 500	1 x 3 300 kt	6
DF-5A (CSS-4 Mod 2)	10	1981	12 000	1 x 4 000–5 000 kt	10
DF-5B (CSS-4 Mod 3)	10	2015	13 000	5 x 200–300 kt	50
DF-5C (CSS-4 Mod 4)	..	[2020s]	13 000	[MIRV]	..
DF-15 (CSS-6)	..	1990	600	1 x .. [g]	..
DF-17 (CSS-22)	36[h]	2020	>1 800	1 x HGV[i]	..
DF-21A/E (CSS-5 Mod 2/6)	40[j]	2000/2016	>2 100[k]	1 x 200–300 kt	40[l]
DF-26 (CSS-18)	200	2016	4 000	1 x 200–300 kt	20[m]
DF-31 (CSS-10 Mod 1)	6	2006	7 200	1 x 200–300 kt	6
DF-31A/AG (CSS-10 Mod 2)[n]	72	2007/2018	11 200	1 x 200–300 kt	72
DF-41 (mobile version) (CSS-20)	18[o]	2020	12 000	3 x 200–300 kt	54
Sea-based missiles (SLBMs)	6/72[p]				72
JL-2 (CSS-N-14)	72	2016	>7 000	1 x 200–300 kt	72
JL-3 (CSS-N-X-..)	..	[2020s][q]	>10 000	[MIRV]	..
Total stockpile	**490**				**350**[r]

.. = not available or not applicable; – = nil or a negligible value; [ ] = uncertain SIPRI estimate; ALBM = air-launched ballistic missile; HGV = hypersonic glide vehicle; kt = kiloton; MIRV = multiple independently targetable re-entry vehicle; SLBM = submarine-launched ballistic missile.

[a] For aircraft, the listed range is for illustrative purposes only; actual mission range will vary according to flight profile, weapon payload and in-flight refuelling.

[b] Warhead yields are listed for illustrative purposes. Actual yields are not known, except that older and less accurate missiles were equipped with megaton-yield warheads. Newer long-range missile warheads probably have yields of a few hundred kilotons, and it is possible that some warheads have even lower yield options.

[c] Figures are based on estimates of one warhead per nuclear-capable launcher, except for the MIRV-capable DF-5B, which can carry up to five warheads, and the MIRV-capable DF-41, which is estimated to carry three warheads. China's warheads are not thought to be deployed on launchers under normal circumstances but kept in storage facilities. All estimates are approximate.

[d] The number of bombers only counts those estimated to be assigned a nuclear role. H-6 bombers were used to deliver nuclear weapons during China's nuclear weapon testing programme (one test used a fighter-bomber) and models of nuclear bombs are exhibited in military museums. It is thought (but not certain) that a small number of H-6 bombers previously had a secondary contingency mission with nuclear bombs. The United States Department of Defense (US DOD) reported in 2018 that the People's Liberation Army Air Force was reassigned a nuclear mission.

[e] China defines missile ranges as short-range, <1000 kilometres; medium-range, 1000–3000 km; long-range, 3000–8000 km; and intercontinental range, >8000 km.

f The US DOD's 2021 report to the US Congress still listed the old liquid-fuelled DF-4 as an element of China's fixed intercontinental ballistic missile (ICBM) force, but the DF-4 is generally believed to be in the process of being retired.

g The US Central Intelligence Agency concluded in 1993 that China 'almost certainly' had developed a warhead for the DF-15, but it is unclear whether the capability was fielded.

h This number is based on the assumption that two DF-17 brigades were operational and up to two more were under preparation as of Jan. 2022.

i The DF-17 carries an HGV with an unknown payload. The US DOD's 2021 report to the US Congress noted that the DF-17 is 'primarily a conventional platform' but that it could 'be equipped with nuclear warheads'.

j In 2017 the US Air Force's (USAF) National Air and Space Intelligence Center reported that China had 'fewer than 50' Mod 2 launchers. The Mod 6 is thought to be a replacement for the Mod 2.

k The range of the nuclear-armed DF-21 variants (CSS-5 Mod 2 and Mod 6) is thought to be greater than the 1750 km reported for the original (CSS-5 Mod 1), which has been retired. The USAF has reported the range as 2150 km.

l It is assumed that nuclear launchers do not have any reloads, unlike conventional versions (DF-21C and DF-21D) that are assumed to have one reload.

m The DF-26 is a dual-capable launcher. It is thought that its mission is primarily conventional and that only a few launchers are assigned nuclear warheads. Only one nuclear warhead is assumed for each of the DF-26's missiles that have been assigned a nuclear mission, with any reloads assumed to be conventional.

n The DF-31AG is thought to carry the same missile as the DF-31A.

o This number assumes two brigades were operational as of Jan. 2022. It is possible that the number of launchers is closer to 24.

p The first figure is the total number of operational nuclear-powered ballistic missile submarines (SSBNs) in the Chinese fleet; the second is the maximum number of missiles that they can carry. Two additional Jin-class (Type 094) SSBNs joined the fleet in 2021 to give a total of six SSBNs.

q US officials have suggested that the JL-3 might have already become operational; however, it is thought that the system is intended to arm the future Type 096 SSBN, which will not be ready for several years.

r The US DOD's 2021 report to the US Congress stated that the 'operational' stockpile was in the low 200s and increasing. Since then, the DF-41 and two additional submarines have become operational (see notes o and p). Consequently, SIPRI estimates that the total stockpile is larger and includes approximately 350 warheads.

Sources: US Air Force (USAF), National Air and Space Intelligence Center, *Ballistic and Cruise Missile Threat*, various years; USAF Global Strike Command, various documents; US Central Intelligence Agency, various documents; US Defense Intelligence Agency, various documents; US Department of Defense, *Military and Security Developments Involving the People's Republic of China*, Annual Report to Congress, various years; Kristensen, H. M., Norris, R. S. and McKinzie, M. G., *Chinese Nuclear Forces and US Nuclear War Planning* (Federation of American Scientists/Natural Resources Defense Council: Washington, DC, Nov. 2006); *Bulletin of the Atomic Scientists*, 'Nuclear notebook', various issues; Google Earth satellite imagery; and authors' estimates.

reaffirmed that China 'almost certainly keeps the majority of its nuclear force on a peacetime status—with separated launchers, missiles, and warheads'.[12] A transition to a LOW posture, where space-based sensors could detect an incoming attack before impact, does not necessarily require China to keep

[12] US Department of Defense (note 4), pp. 90–91.

warheads on delivery vehicles under normal circumstances, and doing so would constitute a significant change to the country's long-held nuclear custodial practices. But missile brigades need training to be ready to load the warheads. The US DOD's 2021 report stated that the PLA Rocket Force (PLARF) brigades conduct 'combat readiness duty' and 'high alert duty' drills, which 'apparently includes assigning a missile battalion to be ready to launch and rotating to standby positions as much as monthly for unspecified periods of time'.[13]

Aircraft and air-delivered weapons

Chinese medium-range bombers have long had a capability of delivering nuclear weapons and were used to conduct more than 12 atmospheric nuclear tests in the 1960s and 1970s. Until 2018, the capability was not fully operational and was probably a back-up contingency mission. As a result, until 2018, SIPRI continued to assess that China maintained a small inventory of gravity bombs for secondary contingency use by Hong-6, or H-6 (B-6) bombers.[14]

In 2018, however, the US DOD reported that the PLA Air Force (PLAAF) was 'newly re-assigned a nuclear mission'.[15] In its 2021 report, the US DOD concluded that China in 2019 had 'signaled the return of the airborne leg of its nuclear triad after the PLAAF publicly revealed the H-6N (B-6N) as its first nuclear-capable air-to-air refuelable bomber', and noted that as of 2020, the H-6N had been operationally fielded.[16] Legacy H-6 bombers did not include an air-to-air refuelling probe, which significantly limited their long-range targeting capability.

Since at least 2015, China has been developing two new air-launched ballistic missiles (ALBMs), one of which is assessed by the USA to be potentially nuclear-capable.[17] This missile, which can be carried by the H-6N bomber and is designated as CH-AS-X-13 by the USA, may be a variant of the Dong Feng-21, or DF-21 (CSS-5), medium-range ballistic missile (MRBM), or

[13] US Department of Defense (note 4), pp. 90–91.

[14] For the aircraft, missiles and submarines discussed here, a designation in parentheses (in this case B-6) following the Chinese designation (in this case H-6) is that assigned by the USA.

[15] US Department of Defense, *Military and Security Developments Involving the People's Republic of China 2018*, Annual Report to Congress (Office of the Secretary of Defense: Arlington, VA, 16 May 2018), p. 75.

[16] US Department of Defense (note 4), pp. 55–56.

[17] US Department of Defense (note 4), pp. 55–56; Ashley, R., Director, US Defense Intelligence Agency, 'Worldwide threat assessment', Statement for the record, US Senate Armed Services Committee, 6 Mar. 2018, p. 8; US Air Force, National Air and Space Intelligence Center (NASIC), *Ballistic and Cruise Missile Threat 2020* (NASIC: Wright-Patterson Air Force Base, OH, July 2020), p. 37; and Stewart, V. R., Director, US Defense Intelligence Agency, 'Worldwide threat assessment', Statement for the record, US Senate Armed Services Committee, 9 Feb. 2016.

possibly the DF-15.[18] The first base to be equipped with this capability might be Neixiang, Henan province, where an H-6N bomber was observed flying with the possible new ALBM in October 2020.[19] In its 2021 report, the US DOD stated that 'The PRC has possibly already established a nascent "nuclear triad" with the development of a nuclear-capable air-launched ballistic missile . . . and improvement of its ground and sea-based nuclear capabilities', potentially indicating that it assessed the ALBM to be operational.[20] Even so, the 'viability' of the triad would depend on the survivability and capability of each leg.

In addition to the intermediate-range H-6 bomber, the PLAAF has been developing its first long-range strategic bomber, known as the H-20 (B-20), with an anticipated range of at least 8500 kilometres and a stealthy design.[21] The aircraft might be in production within 10 years, according to the US DOD.[22] The US DOD has also suggested that the H-20 will be dual-capable— that is, able to deliver both conventional and nuclear weapons.[23]

Land-based missiles

China's nuclear-capable land-based ballistic missile arsenal has been under-going significant modernization as China replaces its ageing silo-based, liquid-fuelled missiles with large numbers of new mobile and silo-based, solid-fuelled models.

Intercontinental ballistic missiles

In 2021 commercial satellite imagery revealed that China had started con-struction of what appeared to be more than 300 new missile silos across at least three distinct fields in northern China.[24] On several separate occasions, different elements of the US government appeared to validate the open-

[18] Wright, T., 'Chinese PLAAF H-6N pictured carrying large missile', International Institute for Strategic Studies, 23 Oct. 2020; and Panda, A., 'Revealed: China's nuclear-capable air-launched ballistic missile', The Diplomat, 10 Apr. 2018.

[19] Lee, R., 'China's Air Force might be back in the nuclear business', The Diplomat, 9 Sep. 2020; and Rod Lee (@roderick_s_lee), 'The video footage of an H-6N with a possible air-launched ballistic missile appears to be taken at this location just outside Neixiang Afld. This corroborates my theory that the 106th bde operates H-6N's and, per the CMPR suggesting nuclear-capable ALBMs, is a nuclear unit', Twitter, 17 Oct. 2020.

[20] US Department of Defense (note 4), p. 90.

[21] US Department of Defense (note 4), p. 85.

[22] US Office of the Deputy Assistant Secretary of Defense for Nuclear Matters, Nuclear Matters Handbook 2020 (US Department of Defense: Arlington, VA, Mar. 2020), figure 1.1, p. 3.

[23] US Department of Defense (note 4), p. 85.

[24] Lewis, J. and Eveleth, D., 'Chinese ICBM silos', Arms Control Wonk, 2 July 2021; Korda, M. and Kristensen, H. M., 'China is building a second nuclear missile silo field', FAS Strategic Security Blog, Federation of American Scientists, 26 July 2021; and Lee, R., 'PLA likely begins construction of an intercontinental ballistic missile silo site near Hanggin Banner', China Aerospace Studies Institute, 12 Aug. 2021.

source assessment that the construction sites were associated with China's missile programme.[25] If China eventually fills each suspected silo site with a single-warhead missile, the number of warheads attributed to China's intercontinental ballistic missile (ICBM) force, estimated at January 2022 as around 190 warheads, could more than double to approximately 450 warheads. If each suspected silo were filled with a missile equipped with three multiple independently targetable re-entry vehicles (MIRVs), this number could rise to approximately 1000 warheads. However, as of January 2022 it was unclear how China plans to operate the new silos, whether they will all be filled, how many warheads each missile would carry, and whether a portion of them could potentially have conventional strike roles.[26]

Notably, China's new silo fields are located deeper inside China than any other known ICBM base and are beyond the reach of US conventional cruise missiles. This, combined with the large number of silos, could suggest that one of the main drivers of the construction effort is to reduce the vulnerability of China's nuclear arsenal from long-range conventional strikes.

In its 2021 report to the US Congress, the US DOD estimated that China's operational arsenal included 100 ICBMs, and that the number of warheads on Chinese ICBMs capable of reaching the USA was expected to grow to 200 by 2025.[27] Additionally, the report noted that China appeared to be doubling the number of launchers in some ICBM brigades, although this could be the result of redistributing existing launchers.[28]

The silo-based, liquid-fuelled, two-stage DF-5 (CSS-4) family of missiles—which first entered into service in the early 1980s—were believed to be China's longest-range ICBMs as at the end of 2021. Along with the road-mobile, solid-fuelled, three-stage DF-31A/AG (CSS-10 Mod 2) ICBM and the new solid-fuelled, three-stage DF-41 (CSS-20) ICBM, DF-5s are capable of targeting all of continental USA and Europe.

China is believed to have deployed at least two mobile DF-41 brigades—totalling around 18 launchers—and appeared to be preparing for the

---

[25] US Strategic Command (@US_Stratcom), 'This is the second time in two months the public has discovered what we have been saying all along about the growing threat the world faces and the veil of secrecy that surrounds it', Twitter, 27 July 2021; Shashank Joshi (@shashj), 'State Dept. told me: "This build-up is deeply concerning, raises questions about the PRC's intent, and reinforces the importance of pursuing practical measures to reduce nuclear risks"', Twitter, 29 July 2021; and US Department of Defense (note 4), pp. 60–62.

[26] Roderick Lee of the United States Air Force's China Aerospace Studies Institute—who disclosed the third Chinese silo complex at Hanggin Banner in Aug. 2021—suggests that circumstantial evidence could indicate that China might consider using some of its new ICBM silos in a conventional strike role. Lee, R., 'A case for China's pursuit of conventionally armed ICBMs', The Diplomat, 17 Nov. 2021.

[27] US Department of Defense (note 4), pp. 60–62.

[28] US Department of Defense (note 4), p. 61; and Decker Eveleth (@dex_eve), 'Ok, this is a bit of an overstatement: TEL garages have doubled at 644, the DF-41 OT&E brigade, possibly indicating ~24 launchers. At other new ICBM units, number of garages has actually gone down, from 12 to 8. Possible the PLARF is redistributing existing DF-31AG launchers', Twitter, 3 Nov. 2021.

integration of additional DF-41 brigades.[29] The US DOD assessed in 2020 and 2021 that China might ultimately plan to deploy the DF-41 in both mobile and silo-based modes, in some or all of China's new missile silo fields, and potentially in a rail-based mode as well.[30] However, the new silo fields were still only in the early stages of construction in late 2021.[31]

The US DOD's 2021 report states that China has also begun developing a new missile called the DF-27, which could have a range of 5000–8000 km.[32] However, public information about this new missile is scarce and rife with unsubstantiated rumours.

After many years of research and development, China has modified a small number of ICBMs to deliver nuclear MIRVs, apparently to improve the penetration capabilities of its warheads in response to advances in US and, to a lesser extent, Russian and future Indian missile defences. The DF-5B (CSS-4 Mod 3) is a MIRV-capable variant of the DF-5 that can carry up to five warheads, two more than previously assumed.[33] A second variant under development, the DF-5C (CSS-4 Mod 4), can reportedly also deliver multiple warheads. Some US media reports have suggested that it might be capable of carrying up to 10 warheads, but it seems more likely that it will carry a number similar to that of the DF-5B version.[34] There has been speculation that the DF-41 is able to carry 6–10 warheads, but there is significant uncertainty about the actual capability, and it is likely to carry fewer than its maximum capacity in order to maximize range. SIPRI cautiously estimates that the DF-41 carried 3 warheads as at January 2022.

China reportedly conducted two tests of what appeared to be a hypersonic boost-glide system in July and August 2021.[35] According to the US Office of the Director of National Intelligence, at least one test 'flew completely around the world', indicating that the test might have been of an orbital bombardment system.[36] Additionally, the US DOD noted that at least one test fired a missile mid-flight over the South China Sea.[37] Other credible details

---

[29] US Department of Defense (note 4), p. 62; and Rod Lee (@roderick_s_lee), 'More evidence that 651 Bde has DF-41s: An officer assigned to 651 Bde inspecting a probable 41 TEL in garrison. Known 651 Bde personalities state that in the past few years, the brigade has been swapping out for a new missile that was featured in the 2019 parade', Twitter, 28 Dec. 2021.

[30] US Department of Defense (note 4), p. 62; and US Department of Defense (note 1), p. 56.

[31] Gertz, B., 'Exclusive: China building third missile field for hundreds of new ICBMs', *Washington Times*, 12 Aug. 2021.

[32] US Department of Defense (note 4), p. 62.

[33] US Department of Defense (note 4), p. 61; and Lewis, J. G., 'China's belated embrace of MIRVs', eds M. Krepon, T. Wheeler and S. Mason, *The Lure and Pitfalls of MIRVs: From the First to the Second Nuclear Age* (Stimson Center: Washington, DC, May 2016), pp. 95–99.

[34] Gertz, B., 'China tests missile with 10 warheads', Washington Free Beacon, 31 Jan. 2017.

[35] Sevastopulo, D., 'China conducted two hypersonic weapons tests this summer', *Financial Times*, 20 Oct. 2021. See also chapter 13, section VI, in this volume.

[36] US Office of the Director of National Intelligence (ODNI), *Annual Threat Assessment of the US Intelligence Community* (ODNI: McLean, VA, 7 Feb. 2022), p. 7.

[37] Sevastopulo (note 35).

about this new system are scarce; however, if the initial reporting is accurate, then the system may be intended to counter advances in US missile defences.

Intermediate- and medium-range ballistic missiles

In 2016 the PLARF began the deployment of the dual-capable DF-26 (CSS-18) intermediate-range ballistic missile (IRBM). This missile has an estimated maximum range exceeding 4000 km and can therefore reach targets in India, the South China Sea, and the western Pacific Ocean, including the US strategic base on Guam.[38] The missile is equipped with a manoeuvrable re-entry vehicle (MaRV) that can be swapped with another warhead at a rapid pace, thus theoretically allowing the PLARF to switch the missile's mission between precision conventional strikes and nuclear strikes against ground targets—and even conventional strikes against naval targets—at the last minute.[39] The majority of the DF-26s are thought to serve a conventional mission with a smaller number assigned a nuclear role. In its 2021 report, the US DOD noted that: 'The DF-26 is the PRC's first nuclear-capable missile system that can conduct precision strikes, and therefore, is the most likely weapon system to field a lower-yield warhead in the near-term.'[40] It remains unclear, however, whether low-yield options have been produced for China's nuclear forces.

China appears to be producing the DF-26 in significant numbers, and in 2021 the US DOD estimated that China might have up to 200 launchers and 300 missiles in its inventory, although SIPRI estimates that only a small number of those have a nuclear role.[41] The launcher number might also be on the higher end of an estimated range and could also include launchers in production as of January 2022. There were sightings of the missile at several PLARF brigade bases during 2021, and PLARF brigades conducted several exercises that featured multiple waves of missile strikes, reloads and relocations.[42]

The US DOD's 2021 report indicated a sizable increase in China's MRBM force, from 150 launchers and 150-plus missiles in 2020 to 250 launchers and 600 missiles in 2021.[43] Most of these are conventional versions, and the numbers are probably on the higher end of an estimated range and could also include launchers and missiles in production. SIPRI estimates that, as of January 2022, around 40 of the PLARF's MRBMs were nuclear

---

[38] US Department of Defense (note 4), p. 61.

[39] Pollack, J. H. and LaFoy, S., 'China's DF-26: A hot-swappable missile?', Arms Control Wonk, 17 May 2020; Deng, X., 'China deploys Dongfeng-26 ballistic missile with PLA Rocket Force', *Global Times*, 26 Apr. 2018; and US Department of Defense (note 4), p. 61.

[40] US Department of Defense (note 4), p. 93.

[41] US Department of Defense (note 4), p. 163.

[42] Liu, X., 'PLA Rocket Force practices night DF-26 missile launch', *South China Morning Post*, 9 June 2021.

[43] US Department of Defense (note 4), p. 163; and US Department of Defense (note 1), p. 166.

DF-21s (CSS-5). The DF-21 is a two-stage, solid-fuelled mobile missile. The original DF-21 (CSS-5 Mod 1), which was first deployed in 1991, has been retired. An upgraded variant, the DF-21A (CSS-5 Mod 2), was first deployed in 1996 and an enhanced version, possibly known as the DF-21E (CSS-5 Mod 6), was fielded in 2017.[44] Two other versions of the DF-21 (DF-21C and DF-21D) are armed with conventional warheads.

The PLARF has also begun fielding the new DF-17 (CSS-22) MRBM equipped with a hypersonic glide vehicle (HGV).[45] The US DOD's 2021 report noted that the DF-17 is 'primarily a conventional platform', but that it could 'be equipped with nuclear warheads'.[46] As of January 2022, the DF-17 was operational in at least two brigades, with integration under way in several additional brigades.[47]

Sea-based missiles

In 2021 China continued to pursue its long-standing strategic goal from the early 1980s of developing and deploying a sea-based nuclear deterrent. According to the US DOD's 2021 report, the PLA Navy (PLAN) has constructed six Type 094 SSBNs.[48] The two newest boats—Type 094A, believed to be variants of the original design—were handed over to the PLAN in April 2020 and one of them formally entered service in April 2021.[49] The US DOD's 2021 report assessed that these six operational Type 094 SSBNs constitute China's 'first credible, sea-based nuclear deterrent'.[50]

China's four original Type 094 submarines can each carry up to 12 three-stage, solid-fuelled Julang-2, or JL-2 (CSS-N-14), submarine-launched ballistic missiles (SLBMs). The JL-2 is a sea-based variant of the DF-31 ICBM. It has an estimated maximum range in excess of 7000 km and is believed to carry a single nuclear warhead.[51]

There has been considerable speculation about whether the missiles on China's SSBNs are mated with warheads under normal circumstances; there appear to be no credible public reports that China has commenced

[44] O'Halloran, J. C. (ed.), *IHS Jane's Weapons: Strategic, 2015–16* (IHS Jane's: Coulsdon, 2015), pp. 21–22; and US Department of Defense (note 4), p. 93.

[45] US Department of Defense (note 4), p. 61.

[46] US Department of Defense (note 4), p. 61.

[47] Rod Lee (@roderick_s_lee), 'The PLA appears to be fielding the (likely hypersonic) DF-17 at an operational unit, suggesting the DF-17 has achieved at least initial operational capability. PRC television footage from 29 December shows a probable DF-17 TEL at the PLARF's 627 Brigade in Jieyang', Twitter, 30 Dec. 2020; Chan, M., 'Chinese military beefs up coastal forces as it prepares for possible invasion of Taiwan', *South China Morning Post*, 18 Oct. 2020; and authors' estimates.

[48] US Department of Defense (note 4), p. 49.

[49] Chan, M., 'China's new nuclear submarine missiles expand range in US: Analysts', *South China Morning Post*, 2 May 2021.

[50] US Department of Defense (note 4), p. 49.

[51] US Air Force (note 17), p. 33.

nuclear-armed patrols. The routine deployment of nuclear weapons on China's SSBNs would constitute a significant change to the country's long-held practice of keeping nuclear warheads in central storage in peacetime and would pose operational challenges for its nuclear command-and-control arrangements. During a war, geographic choke points and advanced US anti-submarine warfare capabilities could force China to deploy its nuclear submarines in a protective bastion within the South China Sea, rather than sail them past Japan and out into the Pacific Ocean. These constraints significantly limit Chinese SSBNs from targeting continental USA.

The US DOD's 2021 report indicates that the PLAN has begun construction of its next-generation SSBN, Type 096, and a potential hull section was visible in commercial satellite imagery from February 2021.[52] Reports vary widely on the design parameters, but the new submarine is expected to be larger and quieter than the Type 094 and could possibly be equipped with more missile launch tubes. Given the expected lifespans of the current Type 094 and the next-generation Type 096 SSBNs, the PLAN is expected to operate both types concurrently. In 2021 the US DOD assessed that China could have up to eight SSBNs by 2030.[53]

The Type 096 SSBN will be armed with a successor to the JL-2: the JL-3 SLBM, which is thought to use technologies from the land-based DF-41 ICBM and have a longer range than the JL-2. The US Air Force's National Air and Space Intelligence Center has assessed that the JL-3 will be capable of carrying multiple warheads and have a range of more than 10 000 km.[54] According to the US DOD, the JL-3's longer range could enable the PLAN to deploy its SSBNs in bastions in the South China Sea and the Bohai Gulf, to enhance their survivability.[55]

[52] US Department of Defense (note 4), p. 49; and Sutton, H. I., 'First image of China's new nuclear submarine under construction', Naval News, 1 Feb. 2021.
[53] US Department of Defense (note 4), p. 49.
[54] US Air Force (note 17), p. 37.
[55] US Department of Defense (note 4), p. 91.

VI. Indian nuclear forces

HANS M. KRISTENSEN AND MATT KORDA

As of January 2022, India was estimated to have a growing stockpile of about 160 nuclear weapons—a small increase from the previous year (see table 10.7). These weapons were assigned to a maturing nuclear triad of aircraft, land-based missiles and ballistic missile submarines. The warhead estimate is based on calculations of India's inventory of weapon-grade plutonium, the estimated number of operational nuclear-capable delivery systems, India's nuclear doctrine, publicly available information on the Indian nuclear arsenal, and private conversations with defence officials.[1] The Indian government itself has not provided much public information about the size of its nuclear forces, other than conducting occasional parade displays and making announcements about missile flight tests. India has continued to expand the size and capability of its nuclear weapon inventory as well as its infrastructure for producing nuclear warheads.

The role of nuclear weapons in Indian military doctrine

Until the early 2010s, the limited ranges of India's initial nuclear systems meant that their only credible role was to deter Pakistan. However, with the development over the subsequent decade of longer-range missiles capable of targeting all of China, it appears that India has placed increased emphasis on China in recent years. It remains to be seen how this development, as well as recent border clashes with China and Pakistan, will affect India's nuclear arsenal and strategy.[2] While India has adhered to a nuclear no-first-use policy since 1999, this pledge was qualified by a 2003 caveat that India could use nuclear forces to retaliate against attacks by non-nuclear weapons of mass destruction (WMD).[3] This 2003 statement was reaffirmed as recently as 2018, and could still be in place as official policy.[4] Doubts about India's commitment to the no-first-use policy have increased, and although India is believed to store its warheads separate from its delivery systems, there has been increasing evidence of some parts of India's nuclear arsenal

---

[1] Kristensen, H. M. and Korda, M., 'Estimating world nuclear forces: An overview and assessment of sources', SIPRI Topical Backgrounder, 14 June 2021.

[2] On the border tensions in 2021 between China and India and between India and Pakistan see chapter 4, section III, in this volume.

[3] Indian Ministry of External Affairs, 'The Cabinet Committee on Security reviews [o]perational-ization of India's nuclear doctrine', Press release, 4 Jan. 2003; and Indian Embassy in Washington, DC, 'Draft report of National Security Advisory Board on Indian nuclear doctrine', 17 Aug. 1999.

[4] Indian Prime Minister's Office, 'Prime Minister felicitates crew of INS Arihant on completion of nuclear triad', Press release, 5 Nov. 2018.

Table 10.7. Indian nuclear forces, January 2022

All figures are approximate and some are based on assessments by the authors.

Type/designation	No. of launchers	Year first deployed	Range (km)[a]	Warheads x yield[b]	No. of warheads[c]
Aircraft[d]	48				48
Mirage 2000H	32	1985	1 850	1 x 12 kt bomb	32
Jaguar IS	16	1981	1 600	1 x 12 kt bomb	16
Rafale	–	[2022]	2 000	–	–
Land-based missiles	64				64
Prithvi-II	24	2003	250[e]	1 x 12 kt	24
Agni-I	16	2007	>700	1 x 10–40 kt	16
Agni-II	16	2011	>2 000	1 x 10–40 kt	16
Agni-III	8	2018	>3 200	1 x 10–40 kt	8
Agni-IV	–	[2022]	>3 500	1 x 10–40 kt	–
Agni-V	–	[2022]	>5 000	1 x 10–40 kt	–
Agni-VI	–	[2025]	>6 000	1 x 10–40 kt	–
Agni-P	–	[2025]	1 000–2 000	[2 x 10–40 kt MIRV]	–
Sea-based missiles	3/14[f]				16
Dhanush	2	2013	400	1 x 12 kt	4[g]
K-15 (B-05)[h]	12[i]	2018	700	1 x 12 kt	12
K-4	–[j]	[2025]	3 500	1 x 10–40 kt	–
Other stored warheads[k]					32
Total stockpile	126				**160**[k]

– = nil or a negligible value; [ ] = uncertain SIPRI estimate; kt = kiloton; MIRV = multiple independently targetable re-entry vehicle.

[a] For aircraft, the listed range is for illustrative purposes only; actual mission range will vary according to flight profile, weapon payload and in-flight refuelling.

[b] The yields of India's nuclear warheads are not known. The 1998 nuclear tests demonstrated yields of up to 12 kt. Since then, it is possible that boosted warheads have been introduced with a higher yield, perhaps up to 40 kt. There is no open-source evidence that India has developed two-stage thermonuclear warheads.

[c] Aircraft and several missile types are dual-capable—that is, they can be armed with either conventional or nuclear warheads. This estimate counts an average of one nuclear warhead per launcher. All estimates are approximate.

[d] Other aircraft that could potentially have a secondary nuclear role include the Su-30MKI.

[e] The Prithvi-II's range is often reported as 350 kilometres. However, the United States Air Force's National Air and Space Intelligence Center sets the range at 250 km.

[f] The first figure is the number of operational vessels—two ships and one nuclear-powered ballistic missile submarine (SSBN); the second is the maximum number of missiles that they can carry. India has launched two SSBNs, but only one—INS *Arihant*—was believed to be operational as of Jan. 2022, and was believed to have only a limited operational capability. The other SSBN—INS *Arighat*—was being fitted out and might become operational during or after 2022.

[g] Each Sukanya-class patrol ship equipped with Dhanush missiles was thought to have possibly one reload.

[h] Some sources have referred to the K-15 missile as 'Sagarika', which was the name of the missile development project rather than the missile itself.

[i] Each SSBN has 4 missile tubes, each of which can carry 3 K-15 submarine-launched ballistic missiles (SLBMs), for a total of 12 missiles per SSBN. SIPRI estimates that around 12 additional K-15 missiles and warheads have been produced for deployment on INS *Arighat* and might become operational during or after 2022 (see notes f and k).

j Each missile tube will be able to carry one K-4 SLBM once it becomes operational.

k In addition to the approximately 128 warheads estimated to be assigned to operational forces, SIPRI estimates that around 32 warheads might have been produced to arm Agni-IV and Agni-V missiles (*c.* 20 warheads) and K-15 missiles (*c.* 12 warheads for INS *Arighat*), for a total estimated stockpile of around 160 warheads. India's stockpile is expected to continue to increase.

Sources: Indian Ministry of Defence, annual reports and press releases; International Institute for Strategic Studies, *The Military Balance*, various years; US Air Force, National Air and Space Intelligence Center (NASIC), *Ballistic and Cruise Missile Threat*, various years; Indian news media reports; *Bulletin of the Atomic Scientists*, 'Nuclear notebook', various issues; and authors' estimates.

being kept at a much higher state of readiness.[5] This growing emphasis on increased readiness and quicker ability to launch has prompted some analysts to consider the possibility that India could be transitioning towards a counterforce nuclear posture with the goal of targeting an adversary's nuclear weapons early in a crisis, before they could be used.[6] However, other analysts have challenged those claims, citing a lack of evidence and pointing to other ways in which declaratory policy has remained consistent.[7]

Aircraft and air-delivered weapons

Aircraft are the most mature component of India's nuclear strike capabilities. India has several types of combat aircraft with performance characteristics that make them suitable as nuclear delivery platforms, including the Mirage 2000H, Jaguar IS and Rafale. However, with the exception of the Mirage 2000H, for which there is at least one detailed source that describes how the aircraft was converted for a nuclear strike role in the 1990s, there are no official sources that confirm their nuclear-capable roles. Given this significant uncertainty, SIPRI estimates that approximately 48 nuclear bombs have been assigned to Indian aircraft.

The Indian Air Force (IAF) has reportedly certified its Mirage 2000H combat aircraft for delivery of nuclear gravity bombs.[8] The IAF has begun upgrading 51 of these aircraft with new mission computers, radar, navigation, avionics, and communications systems, as well as a life-extension programme intended to keep the aircraft in service until the 2040s.[9] It has also been

---

[5] For further detail see Kristensen, H. M. and Korda, M., 'Indian nuclear forces', *SIPRI Yearbook 2021*.

[6] Clary, C. and Narang, V., 'India's counterforce temptations: Strategic dilemmas, doctrine, and capabilities', *International Security*, vol. 43, no. 3 (2019); and Kaushal, S. et al., 'India's nuclear doctrine: The Agni-P and the stability–instability paradox', Royal United Services Institute (RUSI), 8 July 2021.

[7] Rajagopalan, R., *India and Counterforce: A Question of Evidence*, ORF Occasional Paper no. 247 (Observer Research Foundation: New Delhi, May 2020).

[8] Kampani, G., 'New Delhi's long nuclear journey: How secrecy and institutional roadblocks delayed India's weaponization', *International Security*, vol. 38, no. 4 (spring 2014), pp. 94, 97–98.

[9] Philip, S. A., 'Why India is set to miss 2021 deadline to upgrade Mirage 2000 fighters', The Print, 7 Oct. 2021.

widely reported in Indian media sources that the IAF's Jaguar IS combat aircraft might also be certified to deliver nuclear gravity bombs.[10]

In addition to the Mirage 2000H, India has acquired 36 Rafale combat aircraft from France, scheduled for full delivery by early 2022.[11] According to the Indian Ministry of Defence (MOD), the 'Rafale will provide IAF the strategic deterrence and requisite capability cum technological edge'.[12] It is unclear whether this language indicates a future nuclear role for the Rafales, and there have been other instances where the Indian MOD used similar language to describe non-nuclear systems.[13] However, at the time of the sale, Indian defence officials reportedly told the media that the decision to purchase the Rafales was based on its ability to be converted for a nuclear strike role.[14]

Land-based missiles

The Indian Army's Strategic Forces Command operates four types of mobile nuclear-capable ballistic missile: the short-range Prithvi-II (250 kilometres) and Agni-I (700 km); the medium-range Agni-II (>2000 km); and the intermediate-range Agni-III (>3200 km).[15] As of January 2022, three new land-based ballistic missiles were in development: the Agni-P (1000–2000 km), the Agni-IV (>3500 km) and the Agni-V (>5000 km); while a variant with an even longer range, the Agni-VI (6000 km), was in the design stage of development.[16]

The Agni-P and Agni-V missiles achieved significant milestones in 2021, with test launches, respectively, in June and December, and in October.[17] The

---

[10] See e.g. Cohen, S. and Dasgupta, S., *Arming Without Aiming: India's Military Modernization* (Brookings Institution Press: Washington, DC, 2010), pp. 77–78; and Shukla, A., 'Jaguar fighter gets 20-year lease of life with DARIN-III avionics', *Business Standard*, 24 Nov. 2016.

[11] Gupta, S., '36th Rafale to have all India specific enhancements, arrives Jan 2022', *Hindustan Times*, 10 Sep. 2021; and NDTV, '3 of 4 remaining Rafale jets will arrive on time in February: Air Force chief', 18 Dec. 2021.

[12] Indian Ministry of Defence (MOD), *Annual Report 2018–19* (MOD: New Delhi, 2019), p. 43.

[13] See e.g. Tiwary, A. K., 'IAF: The strategic force of choice', *Indian Defence Review*, vol. 22, no. 3 (July–Sep. 2007); and Major, F. H., 'Indian Air Force in the 21st century: Challenges and opportunities', *Journal of Defence Studies*, vol. 2, no. 1 (summer 2008).

[14] Singh, S., 'Behind Rafale deal: Their "strategic" role in delivery of nuclear weapons', *Indian Express*, 18 Sep. 2016; and Malhotra, J., 'India favoured Rafale also because of its "nuclear advantage"', *The Print*, 15 Feb. 2019.

[15] The Prithvi-II's range is often reported as 350 km. However, the range is set at 250 km in information provided by the United States. See e.g. US Air Force, National Air and Space Intelligence Center (NASIC), *Ballistic and Cruise Missile Threat 2020* (NASIC: Wright-Patterson Air Force Base, OH, July 2020), p. 17.

[16] Vikas, S. V., 'Why India may not test Agni 6 even if DRDO is ready with technology', OneIndia, 10 July 2019.

[17] Indian Ministry of Defence (MOD), 'DRDO successfully flight tests new generation Agni P ballistic missile', Press release, 28 June 2021; Indian MOD, 'Surface to surface ballistic missile, Agni-5, successfully launched from APJ Abdul Kalam Island', Press release, 27 Oct. 2021; and Indian MOD, 'New generation ballistic missile "Agni P" successfully test-fired by DRDO', Press release, 18 Dec. 2021.

medium-range Agni-P (described by the Indian MOD as a next-generation nuclear-capable ballistic missile) reportedly incorporates technology developed specifically for the Agni-V programme, including advanced navigation and new mobile canisterized launch systems, which will reduce the time required to place the missiles on alert in a crisis.[18] The solid-fuelled Agni-P can reportedly manoeuver upon re-entry, which could allow the missile to evade regional missile defences.[19] It is expected that the Agni-P will eventually replace India's first-generation Agni-I missile, and possibly the Prithvi-II and Agni-II missiles, once the system becomes operational. The three-stage, solid-fuelled Agni-V was test launched for the eighth time in October 2021.[20] Notably, this was the first user trial for the system, meaning that its integration into the Indian armed forces is likely to take place in 2022 or 2023.[21]

India has also begun developing a land-based, short-range version (750 km) of the K-15 submarine-launched ballistic missile (SLBM), known as the Shaurya. Because the K-15 is nuclear-capable, media reports have also widely attributed nuclear capability to the Shaurya.[22] No official government statement has confirmed this, however, and with only three or four flight tests, reports about imminent deployment seem premature.[23] The United States Air Force's National Air and Space Intelligence Center (NASIC) did not mention the Shaurya in its ballistic and cruise missile reports of 2020 and 2017.[24] Because of the high level of uncertainty about the status of the Shaurya, it is not included in SIPRI's estimate for January 2022.

India seems to have been pursuing a technology development programme for multiple independently targetable re-entry vehicles (MIRVs). Notably, the June 2021 Agni-P test appeared to use two decoys to simulate a MIRV-equipped payload, with defence sources suggesting that a functional MIRV capability would take another two years to develop and flight test; however, given the inherent technological barriers to developing an operational MIRV

---

[18] 'DRDO successfully flight tests new generation Agni P ballistic missile' (note 17); and Rout, H. K., 'India test fires new generation nuclear capable Agni-Prime missile off Odisha coast', *New Indian Express*, 28 June 2021.

[19] Philip, S. A., 'Agni Prime is the new missile in India's nuclear arsenal. This is why it's special', The Print, 30 June 2021; and Zhen, L., 'India's latest Agni-P missile no great threat to China: Experts', *South China Morning Post*, 1 July 2021.

[20] 'Surface to surface ballistic missile, Agni-5, successfully launched from APJ Abdul Kalam Island' (note 17).

[21] Gupta, S., 'Strategic Forces Command conducts Agni V trial, hits target 5,000 km away', *Hindustan Times*, 28 Oct. 2021.

[22] See e.g. Press Trust of India, 'India successfully test-fires nuclear capable hypersonic missile Shaurya', *Hindustan Times*, 3 Oct. 2020; and Gupta, S., 'Govt okays induction of nuke-capable Shaurya missile amid Ladakh standoff', *Hindustan Times*, 6 Oct. 2020.

[23] Subramanian, T. S. and Mallikarjun, Y., 'India successfully test-fires Shourya missile', *The Hindu*, 24 Sep. 2011; and Press Trust of India, '"Shaurya" successfully test fired', *The Hindu*, 3 Oct. 2020.

[24] United States Air Force (note 15), p. 17; and US Air Force, NASIC, *Ballistic and Cruise Missile Threat 2017* (NASIC: Wright-Patterson Air Force Base, OH, June 2017).

capability, it could take much longer.[25] It is also possible that the Agni-V, and eventually the intercontinental Agni-VI, could be equipped with MIRVs.[26]

Sea-based missiles

With the aim of creating an assured second-strike capability, India has continued to develop the naval component of its nascent nuclear triad and build a fleet of four to six nuclear-powered ballistic missile submarines (SSBNs).[27] The first SSBN, INS *Arihant*, was launched in 2009, formally commissioned in 2016 and completed its first 'deterrence patrol' in 2018, although it is doubtful that the submarine's missiles carried nuclear warheads during the patrol; it is unlikely that India's submarines will carry a nuclear payload during peacetime.[28] SIPRI estimates that 12 nuclear warheads were delivered for potential deployment by INS *Arihant* and another 12 produced for a second SSBN, INS *Arighat*. INS *Arihant* appears to have only a limited operational capability relative to its successors, given its less powerful reactor and fewer missile tubes.

INS *Arighat* was launched in November 2017 and was undergoing advanced sea trials in 2021 ahead of its expected commissioning into the Indian Navy in 2022.[29] A third submarine, known as S4, was reportedly launched in November 2021, and a fourth was expected to be launched in 2023.[30]

Photographs indicate that INS *Arihant* and INS *Arighat* have each been equipped with a four-tube vertical-launch system and could carry up to 12 two-stage, 700-km-range K-15 (which may have been renamed to the B-05) SLBMs.[31] India's third and fourth submarines are expected to be larger than its first two. They will reportedly have eight launch tubes to hold up to 24 K-15 missiles or 8 K-4 missiles, which are in development.[32]

---

[25] Pandit, R., 'Key trial of 5,000-km ICBM Agni-V in October', *Times of India*, 24 Sep. 2021.

[26] Rout, H. K., 'India to conduct first user trial of Agni-V missile', *New Indian Express*, 13 Sep. 2021.

[27] Davenport, K., 'Indian submarine completes first patrol', *Arms Control Today*, vol. 48, no. 10 (Dec. 2018).

[28] Dinakar, P., 'Now, India has a nuclear triad', *The Hindu*, 18 Oct. 2016; Indian Prime Minister's Office (note 4); Davenport (note 27); and Joshi, Y., 'Angels and dangles: Arihant and the dilemma of India's undersea nuclear weapons', War on the Rocks, 14 Jan. 2019.

[29] Bhattacharjee, S., 'Third Arihant class submarine quietly launched in November', *The Hindu*, 4 Jan. 2022. Until its launch, the submarine was assumed to be named INS *Aridhaman*.

[30] Chris Biggers (@CSBiggers), 'India quietly launched S4 in November 2021 at SBC . . .', Twitter, 28 Dec. 2021; and Unnithan, S., 'A peek into India's top secret and costliest defence project, nuclear submarines', *India Today*, 10 Dec. 2017.

[31] Indian Defence Research and Development Organisation (DRDO), 'MSS—achievements', 6 Sep. 2019.

[32] Bhattacharjee (note 29); and Hans Kristensen (@nukestrat), 'New submarine cover (17°42'23"N, 83°16'23"E) constructed at Vizag is 40m longer than first one. India's third SSBN will be longer with more missile tubes than the 4 on first two boats. Current missile compartment is ~15m with tubes in row instead of pairs as other navies have', Twitter, 12 Mar. 2021.

The K-4 is a two-stage, 3500-km-range SLBM being developed by the Indian Defence Research and Development Organisation (DRDO). The K-4 will eventually replace the K-15, although with only four or eight missiles per submarine, depending on the number of launch tubes.[33] The DRDO has also started to develop extended-range versions: the K-5, which will reportedly have a range in excess of 5000 km, and the K-6, which will have an even longer range.[34] With only two successful launches, which took place in January 2020 after two previous attempts failed, and none from a submarine, as of January 2022, the K-4 still seemed to be several years from operational capability.[35]

India's first naval nuclear weapon, the Dhanush missile, is a version of the dual-capable Prithvi-II that can be launched from two Sukanya-class offshore patrol vessels often seen at the Mumbai and Karwar naval bases on India's west coast.[36] Although NASIC has listed the Dhanush system as deployed, its usefulness in combat is highly questionable, given the slow speed and high degree of vulnerability of the Sukanya-class vessels.[37] Therefore, the system will probably be retired when the SSBN programme with longer-range missiles matures.

Cruise missiles

There have been numerous claims in news articles and on private websites that some Indian cruise missiles are nuclear-capable. These claims concern the ground- and air-launched Nirbhay subsonic cruise missile and the supersonic air-, ground-, ship- and submarine-launched BrahMos cruise missile.[38] However, no official or authoritative source has attributed nuclear capability to India's cruise missiles. Therefore, they are not included in SIPRI's estimate for January 2022.

[33] Jha, S., 'India's undersea deterrent', The Diplomat, 30 Mar. 2016; and United States Air Force (note 15), p. 30.

[34] Unnithan (note 30).

[35] Peri, D., 'India successfully test-fires 3,500-km range submarine-launched ballistic missile K-4', The Hindu, 19 Jan. 2020; and Pandit, R., 'DRDO: Arihant's N-capable missile "ready to roll"', Times of India, 25 Jan. 2020.

[36] 'Nuke-capable Dhanush and Prithvi-II launched', New Indian Express, 12 Mar. 2011; and Indian Ministry of Defence (note 12), p. 100.

[37] US Air Force (note 24).

[38] See e.g. Pandit, R., 'India successfully tests its first nuclear-capable cruise missile', Times of India, 8 Nov. 2017; Gady, F.-S., 'India successfully test fires indigenous nuclear-capable cruise missile', The Diplomat, 8 Nov. 2017; and Mitra, J., 'Nuclear BrahMos: on the anvil?', South Asian Voices, 10 July 2018.

VII. Pakistani nuclear forces

HANS M. KRISTENSEN AND MATT KORDA

According to SIPRI estimates, Pakistan possessed approximately 165 nuclear warheads as of January 2022, around the same number as the previous year (see table 10.8). The Pakistani government has never publicly disclosed the size of its nuclear arsenal. Limited official public data and widespread exaggerated news stories about Pakistan's nuclear weapons mean that analysing the number and types of Pakistani warheads and delivery vehicles is fraught with uncertainty.[1] The estimates in this section are based on the authors' analysis of Pakistan's nuclear posture, fissile material production, public statements by Western officials, and private conversations with Pakistani officials. The development of several new delivery systems and growing accumulation of fissile materials suggests that Pakistan's nuclear weapon arsenal and fissile material stockpile are likely to continue to expand over the next decade, although projections vary considerably.[2]

The role of nuclear weapons in Pakistani military doctrine

Pakistan has been pursuing the development and deployment of new nuclear weapons and delivery systems as part of its 'full spectrum deterrence posture' in relation to India.[3] According to Pakistan, its full spectrum nuclear weapon posture includes long-range missiles and aircraft as well as several short-range, lower-yield nuclear-capable weapon systems.[4] Pakistan's emphasis on non-strategic (tactical) nuclear weapons is specifically intended to be a reaction to India's 'Cold Start' doctrine, which revolves around maintaining the capability to launch large-scale conventional strikes or incursions against Pakistani territory at a level below the threshold at which Pakistan would

---

[1] Kristensen, H. M. and Korda, M., 'Estimating world nuclear forces: An overview and assessment of sources', SIPRI Topical Backgrounder, 14 June 2021.

[2] See e.g. Sundaresan, L. and Ashok, K., 'Uranium constraints in Pakistan: How many nuclear weapons does Pakistan have?', *Current Science*, vol. 115, no. 6 (25 Sep. 2018); Salik, N., 'Pakistan's nuclear force structure in 2025', Regional Insight, Carnegie Endowment for International Peace, 30 June 2016; and Jones, G. S., 'Pakistan's nuclear material production for nuclear weapons', Proliferation Matters, 16 Feb. 2021. See also Berrier, S., Director, US Defense Intelligence Agency, 'Worldwide threat assessment', Statement for the record, US Senate Armed Services Committee, 26 Apr. 2021. On Pakistan's fissile material stockpile see Kile, S. N. and Kristensen, H. M., 'Pakistani nuclear forces', *SIPRI Yearbook 2019*; International Panel on Fissile Materials, 'Pakistan', 31 Aug. 2021; and section X of this chapter.

[3] Kidwai, K., Keynote address and discussion session, South Asian Strategic Stability: Deterrence, Nuclear Weapons and Arms Control (Workshop), International Institute for Strategic Studies (IISS) and Centre for International Strategic Studies (CISS), 6 Feb. 2020. For a detailed assessment of Pakistan's nuclear posture see Tasleem, S. and Dalton, T., 'Nuclear emulation: Pakistan's nuclear trajectory', *Washington Quarterly*, vol. 41, no. 4 (winter 2019).

[4] Pakistani Inter Services Public Relations (ISPR), Press release no. PR-94/2011-ISPR, 19 Apr. 2011.

retaliate with nuclear weapons.[5] In 2015 a retired member of Pakistan's National Command Authority suggested that 'by introducing the variety of tactical nuclear weapons in Pakistan's inventory', Pakistan has 'blocked the avenues for serious military operations by the other side'.[6] In June 2021 Pakistani Prime Minister Imran Khan stated in an interview, 'I'm not sure whether we're growing [the nuclear arsenal] or not because as far as I know … the only one purpose [of Pakistan's nuclear weapons]—it's not an offensive thing', further noting that 'Pakistan's nuclear arsenal is simply as a deterrent, to protect ourselves'.[7]

Aircraft and air-delivered weapons

At the end of December 2021, Pakistan had a small stockpile of gravity bombs. Two versions of the Ra'ad (Hatf-8) air-launched cruise missile (ALCM) were being developed to supplement this stockpile by providing the Pakistan Air Force (PAF) with a nuclear-capable standoff capability at ranges of 350–600 kilometres.[8] There is no publicly available evidence to suggest that either version of the Ra'ad ALCM had been operationally deployed as of January 2022.

Pakistan has several types of combat aircraft with performance characteristics that make them suitable as nuclear delivery platforms, including the Mirage III, the Mirage V, the F-16 and the JF-17. However, no official sources have confirmed their nuclear-capable roles. Given this significant uncertainty, SIPRI assesses that the Mirage III and possibly the Mirage V are the most likely to have a nuclear-delivery role. The Mirage III has been used for developmental test flights of the nuclear-capable Ra'ad ALCM, while the Mirage V is believed to have been given a strike role with Pakistan's small arsenal of nuclear gravity bombs.[9] The nuclear capability of Pakistan's F-16 fighter-bombers is uncertain. Many analysts continue to assign a potential nuclear role to these aircraft based on reports in the late 1980s that

---

[5] Kidwai (note 3); and Saalman, L. and Topychkanov, P., *South Asia's Nuclear Challenges*, SIPRI Report (SIPRI: Stockholm, Apr. 2021). For a US diplomatic assessment of India's 'Cold Start' strategy see Roemer, T., US Ambassador to India, 'Cold Start: A mixture of myth and reality', Cable New Delhi 000295, 16 Feb. 2010. Although Indian officials had previously denied the existence of the Cold Start doctrine, India's chief of the army staff acknowledged its existence in an interview with *India Today* in 2017. Unnithan, S., '"We will cross again"', *India Today*, 4 Jan. 2017.

[6] Kidwai, K., Conversation transcript, Carnegie Endowment for International Peace, 23 Mar. 2015, p. 5.

[7] Laskar, R. H., 'Pakistan PM Imran Khan again seeks US intervention on Kashmir', *Hindustan Times*, 21 June 2021.

[8] For further detail on the Ra'ad ALCM see Kristensen, H. M. and Korda, M., 'Pakistani nuclear forces', *SIPRI Yearbook 2021*, p. 387.

[9] International Institute for Strategic Studies (IISS), *The Military Balance 2022* (Routledge: London, 2022), p. 297; and Dominguez, G., 'Pakistan test-launches longer-range variant of Ra'ad II ALCM', Janes, 19 Feb. 2020.

Table 10.8. Pakistani nuclear forces, January 2022

All figures are approximate and some are based on assessments by the authors.

Type/designation	No. of launchers	Year first deployed	Range (km)[a]	Warheads x yield[b]	No. of warheads[c]
Aircraft[d]	36				36
Mirage III/V	36[e]	1998	2 100	1 x 5–12 kt bomb or Ra'ad ALCM (in development)[f]	36
Land-based missiles	118[g]				118
Abdali (Hatf-2)	10	2015	200	1 x 5–12 kt	10
Ghaznavi (Hatf-3)	16	2004	300	1 x 5–12 kt	16
Shaheen-I (Hatf-4)	16	2003	750	1 x 5–12 kt	16
Shaheen-IA[h]	–	..	900	1 x 5–12 kt	–
Shaheen-II (Hatf-6)	16	2014	2 000	1 x 10–40 kt	16
Shaheen-III[i]	–	[2023]	2 750	1 x 10–40 kt	–
Ghauri (Hatf-5)	24	2003	1 250	1 x 10–40 kt	24
Nasr (Hatf-9)	24	2013	70	1 x 5–12 kt	24
Ababeel	–	..	2 200	MRV or MIRV[j]	–
Babur/-1A GLCM (Hatf-7)[k]	12	2014/[early 2020s]	350/450	1 x 5–12 kt	12
Babur-2 GLCM[l]	–	..	900	1 x 5–12 kt	–
Sea-based missiles					
Babur-3 SLCM	–	[2025]	450	1 x 5–12 kt	–
Other stored warheads[m]					11
Total stockpile	**154**				**165**[m]

. . = not available or not applicable; – = nil or a negligible value; [ ] = uncertain SIPRI estimate; ALCM = air-launched cruise missile; GLCM = ground-launched cruise missile; kt = kiloton; MIRV = multiple independently targetable re-entry vehicle; MRV = multiple re-entry vehicle; SLCM = sea-launched cruise missile.

[a] For aircraft, the listed range is for illustrative purposes only; actual mission range will vary according to flight profile, weapon payload and in-flight refuelling.

[b] The yields of Pakistan's nuclear warheads are not known. The 1998 nuclear tests demonstrated a yield of up to 12 kt. Since then, it is possible that boosted warheads have been introduced with higher yields. There is no open-source evidence that Pakistan has developed two-stage thermonuclear warheads.

[c] Aircraft and several missile types are dual-capable—that is, they can be armed with either conventional or nuclear warheads. Cruise missile launchers (aircraft and land- and sea-based missiles) can carry more than one missile. This estimate counts an average of one nuclear warhead per launcher. Pakistan does not deploy its warheads on launchers but keeps them in separate storage facilities.

[d] There are unconfirmed reports that Pakistan modified for a nuclear weapon delivery role some of the 40 F-16 aircraft procured from the United States in the 1980s. However, it is assumed here that the nuclear weapons assigned to aircraft are for use by Mirage aircraft. When the Mirage IIIs and Vs are eventually phased out, it is possible that the JF-17 will take over their nuclear role in the Pakistan Air Force.

[e] Pakistan possesses many more than 36 Mirage aircraft, but this table only includes those that are assumed to have a nuclear weapon delivery role.

[f] The Ra'ad (Hatf-8) ALCM has a claimed range of 350 km and an estimated yield of 5–12 kt. However, there is no available evidence to suggest that the Ra'ad has been deployed and therefore it is not included in the operational warhead count. In 2017 the Pakistani military displayed a

Ra'ad-II variant with a reported range of 600 km. It was test flown for the first time in 2020 and several additional flights will be needed before it becomes operational.

g Some launchers might have one or more missile reloads.

h It is unclear whether the Shaheen-IA has the same designation as the Shaheen-I.

i The designation for the Shaheen-III is unknown.

j The Pakistani military in 2017 claimed that the Ababeel can deliver multiple warheads using MIRV technology, but does not appear to have provided any further information since then.

k Pakistan has been upgrading its original Babur GLCMs to Babur-1As by improving their avionics and target engagement systems to enable engagement against both land and sea targets. The original Babur's range is listed as 350 km by the US Air Force's National Air and Space Intelligence Center, while Pakistan claims that the improved Babur-1A's range is 450 km.

l The Babur-2 GLCM is sometimes referred to as the Babur-1B.

m In addition to the approximately 154 warheads estimated to be assigned to operational forces, SIPRI estimates that around 11 warheads have been produced to arm future Shaheen-III and cruise missiles, for a total estimated stockpile of about 165 warheads. Pakistan's warhead stockpile is expected to continue to increase.

Sources: Pakistani Ministry of Defence, various documents; US Air Force, National Air and Space Intelligence Center, *Ballistic and Cruise Missile Threat*, various years; International Institute for Strategic Studies, *The Military Balance*, various years; *Bulletin of the Atomic Scientists*, 'Nuclear notebook', various issues; and authors' estimates.

Pakistan was modifying them to deliver nuclear weapons.[10] At the end of 2021, Pakistan was also operating more than 100 JF-17 aircraft, and intended to acquire around another 188 JF-17s to replace the ageing Mirage III and Mirage V aircraft.[11] When the Mirage aircraft are eventually phased out, it is possible that the JF-17 will take over their nuclear role in the PAF and that the Ra'ad ALCM will be integrated onto the JF-17.[12] However, in the light of these considerable uncertainties, it is not possible for SIPRI to make an assessment as to whether Pakistan's F-16s and JF-17s have a dedicated nuclear weapon-delivery role and therefore they are omitted from table 10.8.

Land-based missiles

As of January 2022, Pakistan's nuclear-capable ballistic missile arsenal comprised short- and medium-range systems.

Pakistan has deployed four types of solid-fuelled, road-mobile short-range ballistic missiles: Abdali (also designated Hatf-2), Ghaznavi (Hatf-3), Shaheen-I (Hatf-4) and Nasr (Hatf-9). The dual-capable Ghaznavi was test

---

[10] For further detail on the role of the F-16s see Kristensen, H. M. and Kile, S. N., 'Pakistani nuclear forces', *SIPRI Yearbook 2020*, p. 370.

[11] International Institute for Strategic Studies (IISS), *The Military Balance 2019* (Routledge: London, 2019), pp. 298–99; Warnes, A., 'PAC Kamra rolls out final 14 JF-17B fighters for Pakistan Air Force', Janes, 31 Dec. 2020; Khan, B., 'Why is the Pakistan Air Force procuring 26 JF-17B fighters?', Quwa, 19 Jan. 2020; and 'Pakistan aeronautical complex delivers new JF-17B batch', Quwa, 2 Jan. 2021.

[12] Fisher, R., 'JF-17 Block II advances with new refuelling probe', *Jane's Defence Weekly*, 27 Jan. 2016; 'Ra'ad ALCM: The custodian of Pakistan's airborne nuclear deterrence', PakDefense, 6 Dec. 2020; and 'Update on Pakistan: "JF-17 Thunder's integration with RA'AD II ALCM"', Pakistan Strategic Forum, 8 July 2020.

launched twice in 2021, after which the PAF listed its range as 290 km.[13] The Shaheen-IA, an extended-range version of the Shaheen-I that was still in development, was test launched twice in 2021—once to a range of 900 km.[14] With the exception of the Abdali, Pakistan displayed all its nuclear-capable short-range missiles at the Pakistan Day Parade in March 2021.[15]

The arsenal also included two types of medium-range ballistic missile: the liquid-fuelled, road-mobile Ghauri (Hatf-5), with a range of 1250 km; and the two-stage, solid-fuelled, road-mobile Shaheen-II (Hatf-6), with a range of 2000 km.[16] The Shaheen-II has been test launched seven times since 2004, with the most recent launch taking place in 2019.[17] A longer-range variant in development, the Shaheen-III, has been test launched only twice—in 2015 and early 2021—and had not yet been deployed as of January 2022.[18] This missile has a claimed range of 2750 km, making it the longest-range system that Pakistan has tested to date. Notably, the Shaheen-III, but not the Shaheen-II, was displayed at the Pakistan Day Parade in March 2021.[19] The Pakistani government claimed in 2017 that the Ababeel (a variant of the Shaheen-III under development) could deliver multiple warheads, using multiple independently targetable re-entry vehicle (MIRV) technology, but has not conducted any subsequent test launches of the missile.[20]

In addition to expanding its arsenal of land-based ballistic missiles, Pakistan continued in 2021 to develop the nuclear-capable Babur (Hatf-7) ground-launched cruise missile. The United States Air Force's National Air and Space Intelligence Center has claimed that the Babur has a range of

[13] Pakistani Inter Services Public Relations (ISPR), 'Pakistan conducted a training launch of surface to surface ballistic missile Ghaznavi', Press release no. PR-141/2021-ISPR, 12 Aug. 2021; and ISPR, 'Pakistan today conducted a successful training launch of surface to surface ballistic missile Ghaznavi, capable of delivering nuclear and conventional warheads up to a range of 290 kilometers', Press release no. PR-19/2021-ISPR, 3 Feb. 2021.

[14] Pakistani Inter Services Public Relations (ISPR), 'Pakistan conducted successful flight test of Shaheen-1A surface to surface ballistic missile', Press release no. PR-199/2021-ISPR, 25 Nov. 2021; and ISPR, 'Pakistan conducted successful flight test of Shaheen-1A surface to surface ballistic missile, having a range of 900 kilometers', Press release no. PR-59/2021-ISPR, 26 Mar. 2021.

[15] Pakistani Inter Services Public Relations (ISPR), DG ISPR (@OfficialDGISPR), 'Pakistan Day Parade: March 2021', Twitter, 24 Mar. 2021.

[16] United States Air Force, National Air and Space Intelligence Center (NASIC), *Ballistic and Cruise Missile Threat 2020* (NASIC: Wright-Patterson Air Force Base, OH, July 2020), p. 25.

[17] Pakistani Inter Services Public Relations (ISPR), 'Pakistan conducted successful training launch of surface to surface ballistic missile Shaheen-II', Press release no. PR-104/2019-ISPR, 23 May 2019.

[18] Pakistani Inter Services Public Relations (ISPR), 'Shaheen 3 missile test', Press release no. PR-61/2015-ISPR, 9 Mar. 2015; and Jamal, S., 'Pakistan tests nuclear-capable Shaheen-III ballistic missile', *Gulf News*, 20 Jan. 2021.

[19] Pakistani Inter Services Public Relations (note 15).

[20] Pakistani Inter Services Public Relations (ISPR), Press release no. PR-34/2017-ISPR, 24 Jan. 2017. The US Air Force's National Air and Space Intelligence Center (NASIC) also describes the 2017 test as involving 'the MIRV version of the Ababeel'. US Air Force (note 16), p. 25. On the Ababeel see also Kile and Kristensen (note 2), p. 335.

350 km.[21] Pakistan has test launched the Babur approximately a dozen times since 2005 and has used it in army field training since 2011, which indicates that the system is probably operational. Pakistan has been upgrading the Babur's avionics and navigation systems to enable target engagement both on land and at sea; the upgraded version is known as the Babur-1A. Following the system's most recent test in February 2021, the Pakistani military stated that the Babur-1A's range was 450 km.[22] An extended-range version known as the Babur-2 (sometimes referred to as the Babur-1B) has a claimed range of 900 km—double that of the Babur-1A. Pakistan test launched the Babur-2 in 2016, 2018, 2020 (which resulted in a failure) and most recently in December 2021.[23]

Sea-based missiles

As part of its efforts to achieve a secure second-strike capability, Pakistan has sought to create a nuclear triad by developing a sea-based nuclear force. The Babur-3 submarine-launched cruise missile (SLCM) is intended to establish a nuclear capability for the Pakistan Navy's three Agosta-90B diesel–electric submarines.[24] Pakistan test launched the Babur-3 first in 2017 and again in 2018.[25]

China was still expected to deliver the first of eight air-independent propulsion-powered Hangor-class submarines to Pakistan in 2022, possibly for a nuclear role with the Babur-3 SLCM.[26] If Pakistan does intend to deploy both nuclear and conventional missiles on its attack submarines, this could ultimately create issues around entanglement of nuclear and non-nuclear capabilities, with the potential risk of unintended escalation.[27]

---

[21] US Air Force, National Air and Space Intelligence Center (NASIC), *Ballistic and Cruise Missile Threat 2017* (NASIC: Wright-Patterson Air Force Base, OH, June 2017), p. 37.

[22] Pakistani Inter Services Public Relations (ISPR), ISPR Official, 'Press release no. PR24/2021, Pak conducted successful launch of Babur cruise missile -11 Feb 2021(ISPR)', YouTube, 11 Feb. 2021.

[23] Pakistani Inter Services Public Relations (ISPR), 'Pakistan conducted a successful test of an enhanced range version of the indigenously developed Babur cruise missile', Press release no. PR-142/2018-ISPR, 14 Apr. 2018; Gupta, S., 'Pakistan's effort to launch 750km range missile crashes', *Hindustan Times*, 23 Mar. 2020; and ISPR, 'Pakistan conducted a successful test of an enhanced range version of the indigenously developed Babur cruise missile 1B', Press release no. PR-222/2021-ISPR, 21 Dec. 2021.

[24] Pakistani Inter Services Public Relations (ISPR), Press release no. PR-10/2017-ISPR, 9 Jan. 2017; and Panda, A. and Narang, V., 'Pakistan tests new sub-launched nuclear-capable cruise missile. What now?', The Diplomat, 10 Jan. 2017.

[25] Pakistani Inter Services Public Relations (ISPR), 'Pakistan conducted another successful test fire of indigenously developed submarine launched cruise missile Babur having a range of 450 kms', Press release no. PR-125/2018-ISPR, 29 Mar. 2018. Reports of a ship-launched cruise missile test in 2019 might have been for a different missile. Gady, F.-S., 'Pakistan's Navy test fires indigenous anti-ship/ land-attack cruise missile', The Diplomat, 24 Apr. 2019.

[26] Khan, B., 'Profile: Pakistan's new Hangor submarine', Quwa, 11 Nov. 2019.

[27] For further discussion on entanglement in the South Asian context see Saalman and Topychkanov (note 5).

VIII. Israeli nuclear forces

HANS M. KRISTENSEN AND MATT KORDA

As of January 2022, Israel was estimated to have a stockpile of around 90 nuclear warheads (see table 10.9), the same number as in January 2021. This estimate is on the lower end of a possible range that other analysts have estimated could reach as high as 300 nuclear weapons; however, SIPRI assesses that these larger estimates are probably too high.[1] Israel continues to maintain its long-standing policy of nuclear ambiguity: it neither officially confirms nor denies that it possesses nuclear weapons.[2] This lack of transparency means there is significant uncertainty about the size of Israel's nuclear arsenal and the yields and characteristics attributed to its weapons.[3] The estimate here is largely based on calculations of Israel's inventory of weapon-grade plutonium and the number of operational nuclear-capable delivery systems. The locations of the storage sites for the warheads, which are thought to be stored partially unassembled, are unknown.

The role of nuclear weapons in Israeli military doctrine

Since the late 1960s, the Israeli government has repeated that Israel 'won't be the first to introduce nuclear weapons into the Middle East'.[4] However, to accommodate the apparent fact that Israel possesses a significant nuclear arsenal, Israeli policymakers have previously interpreted 'introducing nuclear weapons' as testing, publicly declaring or actually using nuclear capability, which, according to available open-access sources, Israel has not yet done.[5] Another caveat may be that the warheads are not fully assembled under normal circumstances (i.e. the nuclear cores would be stored and managed separately from their delivery systems). It is unclear what

---

[1] Luscombe, B., '10 questions: Jimmy Carter', *Time*, 30 Jan. 2012; and Clifton, E., 'Powell acknowledges Israeli nukes', *Lobe Log*, 14 Sep. 2016.

[2] For further detail on Israel's 'strategic ambiguity' policy see Cohen, A., 'Israel', eds H. Born, B. Gill and H. Hänggi, *Governing the Bomb: Civilian Control and Democratic Accountability of Nuclear Weapons* (SIPRI and Oxford University Press: Oxford, 2010), pp. 152–68.

[3] Kristensen, H. M. and Korda, M., 'Estimating world nuclear forces: An overview and assessment of sources', SIPRI Topical Backgrounder, 14 June 2021.

[4] This formulation was first expressed during Israel's negotiations with the United States over the purchase of 50 F-4 Phantom aircraft in the late 1960s. During these negotiations, it was made explicitly clear that both sides had very different opinions about what 'introducing nuclear weapons' meant; however, these competing interpretations allowed the two sides to look the other way, thus satisfying both their security interests and alliance relationships while 'agreeing to disagree' over their interpretations of what 'introducing nuclear weapons' actually meant. The most recent public iteration of this policy by an Israeli head of state was made by Benjamin Netanyahu in 2011. Prime Minister's Office, 'PM Netanyahu's interview with Piers Morgan of CNN', 17 Mar. 2011.

[5] Cohen, A. and Burr, W., 'Israel crosses the threshold', Electronic Briefing Book no. 189, National Security Archive, 28 Apr. 2006; and Cohen, A. and Burr, W., 'The US discovery of Israel's secret nuclear project', Electronic Briefing Book no. 510, National Security Archive, 15 Apr. 2015.

circumstances would prompt Israel to 'introduce' nuclear weapons into the region under its own narrow definition. It is believed that one such scenario would involve a crisis that poses an existential threat to the State of Israel, such as a full-scale conventional attack.

In 2021 Israeli Prime Minister Naftali Bennett and United States President Joe Biden met to reaffirm that the USA would not pressure Israel to disarm or join the 1968 Treaty on the Non-Proliferation of Nuclear Weapons (Non-Proliferation Treaty, NPT), and that any arms control agreement would not negatively impact Israel's nuclear arsenal.[6] This has reportedly been a ritual performed with every US president since the administration of President Bill Clinton.

Military fissile material production

Declassified US government documents indicate that Israel may have assembled its first nuclear weapons in the late 1960s, using plutonium produced by the Israel Research Reactor 2 (IRR-2) at the Negev Nuclear Research Center near Dimona, in southern Israel.[7] This heavy water reactor, which was commissioned in 1963, is not under International Atomic Energy Agency (IAEA) safeguards. There is little publicly available information about its operating history and power capacity (see section X).[8]

The International Panel on Fissile Materials (IPFM) estimates that, as of the beginning of 2020, Israel may have a stockpile of 850–1120 kilograms of plutonium.[9] Another analyst estimates a lower amount, approximately 530 kg, depending on assumptions about the reactor efficiency.[10] Assuming that its warhead arsenal is likely to consist of single-stage, boosted fission weapons, Israel could potentially use the larger number estimated by the IPFM to build anywhere between 170 and 278 nuclear weapons. However, as with other nuclear-armed states, Israel is unlikely to have converted all of its plutonium into warheads and has probably assigned nuclear weapons to only a limited number of launchers. Moreover, the available tritium required to boost the warheads would represent an additional constraint on the

[6] Ravid, B., 'Biden and Israeli PM renewed agreement on covert nuclear program', Axios, 1 Sep. 2021; and Entous, A., 'How Trump and three other US presidents protected Israel's worst-kept secret: Its nuclear arsenal', New Yorker, 18 June 2018.

[7] For a history of Israel's nuclear weapon programme see Cohen, A., The Worst-kept Secret: Israel's Bargain with the Bomb (Columbia University Press: New York, 2010); Burr, W. and Cohen, A., 'Duplicity and self-deception: Israel, the United States, and the Dimona inspections, 1964–65', Briefing Book no. 733, National Security Archive, 10 Nov. 2020; and Cohen, A. and Burr, W., 'How Israel built a nuclear program right under the Americans' nose', Haaretz, 17 Jan. 2021.

[8] Glaser, A. and Miller, M., 'Estimating plutonium production at Israel's Dimona reactor', 52nd annual meeting of the Institute of Nuclear Materials Management (INMM), 17–21 July 2011.

[9] International Panel on Fissile Materials, 'Countries: Israel', 31 Aug. 2021.

[10] Jones, G. S., 'Estimating Israel's stocks of plutonium, tritium and heu', Proliferation Matters, 18 Sep. 2018, p. 6.

Table 10.9. Israeli nuclear forces, January 2022

All figures are approximate and some are based on assessments by the authors.

Type/designation	No. of launchers	Year first deployed	Range (km)[a]	No. of warheads
Aircraft	*125/50[b]*			*30*
F-16I	100/25	1980	1 600	30
F-15	25/25	1998	4 450	. .[c]
Land-based missiles	*50*			*50[d]*
Jericho II	25	1990	>1 500	25
Jericho III	25	[2011]	[>4 000]	25[e]
Sea-based missiles	*5/20[f]*			*10*
'Popeye' variant SLCM	20	[2002]	[<1 500]	10
Total stockpile	**120**			**90[g]**

. . = not available or not applicable; [ ] = uncertain SIPRI estimate; SLCM = sea-launched cruise missile.

[a] Aircraft range is for illustrative purposes only; actual range will vary according to flight profile, weapon payload and in-flight refuelling.

[b] The first figure is the total number of aircraft in the inventory; the second is the number of aircraft that might be adapted for a nuclear strike mission.

[c] The United States Air Force's F-15E Strike Eagle has been given a nuclear role. It is not known whether the Israeli Air Force has added nuclear capability to this aircraft, but when Israel sent half a dozen F-15s from Tel Nof Air Base to the United Kingdom in Sep. 2019, a US official privately commented that Israel had sent its nuclear squadron.

[d] Commercial satellite images show what appear to be 23 caves or bunkers for mobile Jericho launchers at Sdot Micha Air Base. High-resolution satellite imagery that became available in 2021 indicates that each cave appears to have two entrances, which suggests that each cave could hold up to 2 launchers. If all 23 caves are full, this would amount to 46 launchers.

[e] The Jericho III is gradually replacing the older Jericho II, if this has not happened already. A longer-range version of the Jericho ballistic missile with a new solid rocket motor may be under development.

[f] The first figure is the total number of Dolphin-class submarines in the Israeli fleet; the second is the estimated maximum number of missiles that they can carry. In addition to six standard 533 millimetre torpedo tubes, Israel's submarines are reportedly equipped with four additional, specially designed 650 mm tubes that could potentially be used to launch nuclear-armed SLCMs.

[g] Given the unique lack of publicly available information about Israel's nuclear arsenal, this estimate comes with a considerable degree of uncertainty.

Sources: Cohen, A., *The Worst-kept Secret: Israel's Bargain with the Bomb* (Columbia University Press: New York, 2010); Cohen, A. and Burr, W., 'Israel crosses the threshold', *Bulletin of the Atomic Scientists*, vol. 62, no. 3 (May/June 2006); Cohen, A., *Israel and the Bomb* (Columbia University Press: New York, 1998); US National Security Archive, various document collections related to Israel's nuclear weapon programme and declassified US government documents relating to Israel's nuclear weapon capability; Albright, D., Berkhout, F. and Walker, W., SIPRI, *Plutonium and Highly Enriched Uranium 1996: World Inventories, Capabilities and Policies* (Oxford University Press: Oxford, 1997); International Institute for Strategic Studies, *The Military Balance*, various years; *IHS Jane's Strategic Weapon Systems*, various issues; Fetter, S., 'Israeli ballistic missile capabilities', *Physics and Society*, vol. 19, no. 3 (July 1990); *Bulletin of the Atomic Scientists*, 'Nuclear notebook', various issues; and authors' estimates.

number of weapons Israel could build. As a result, SIPRI estimates that Israel has approximately 90 warheads, rather than several hundred.

Having produced enough plutonium for Israel to produce some weapons, IRR-2 may now be operated primarily to produce the tritium needed to boost those weapons.[11] Shutdown of the ageing reactor was scheduled for 2003 but has been postponed until at least 2023. The Israel Atomic Energy Commission is reportedly examining ways to extend its service life until the 2040s.[12] Satellite imagery indicates that significant construction started at the Negev Nuclear Research Center in late 2018 or early 2019 and continued throughout 2021, with a large dig several storeys deep located near the reactor.[13] It is unclear whether the construction is related to life-extension operations at Dimona.

Aircraft and air-delivered weapons

Approximately 30 of Israel's nuclear weapons are estimated to be gravity bombs for delivery by F-16I aircraft. It is possible that some F-15 aircraft could also play a nuclear role.[14] When Israel sent half a dozen F-15s from Tel Nof Air Base to the United Kingdom for an exercise in September 2019, a US official privately commented that Israel had sent its nuclear squadron.[15]

Nuclear gravity bombs without nuclear cores would probably be stored at protected facilities near one or two air force bases. It is possible that Tel Nof Air Base in central Israel and Hatzerim Air Base in the Negev desert might have nuclear missions. Israel is also acquiring 50 F-35s from the USA, which are particularly suitable for deep strike operations, although it is unclear whether Israel would use them for that role.[16]

Land-based missiles

Up to 50 warheads are thought to be assigned for delivery by land-based Jericho ballistic missiles, although the Israeli government has never publicly confirmed that it possesses the missiles.[17] The missiles are believed to be located, along with their mobile transporter-erector-launchers (TELs), in

---

[11] Kelley, R. and Dewey, K., 'Assessing replacement options for Israel's ageing Dimona reactor', *Jane's Intelligence Review*, 20 Nov. 2018; and International Panel on Fissile Materials (note 9).

[12] Bob, Y. J., 'Experts agree Dimona nuke reactor can exceed original life expectancy', *Jerusalem Post*, 12 July 2019.

[13] Gambrell, J., 'Secretive Israeli nuclear facility undergoes major project', AP News, 25 Feb. 2021.

[14] Israeli Air Force, 'The F-15I as the IAF's Strategic Aircraft', 19 Jan. 2016; and Israeli Air Force, '19 years of "Ra'am"', 19 Jan. 2017.

[15] US military official, Interview with the author (Kristensen, H. M.), Oct. 2019.

[16] Lockheed Martin, 'Israel's 5th generation fighter', [n.d.].

[17] For further detail see Kristensen, H. M. and Korda, M., 'Israeli nuclear forces', *SIPRI Yearbook 2021*.

caves or bunkers at Sdot Micha Air Base near Zekharia, about 25 kilometres west of Jerusalem. High-resolution satellite imagery that became available in 2021 showed that an upgrade of the bunkers is ongoing, and indicated that each suspected Jericho missile bunker might be capable of storing two launchers. Given that there are 23 caves or bunkers visible in satellite imagery, this lends support to the estimate of approximately 50 mobile missile launchers. Each cluster of bunkers also appears to be coupled with a covered high-bay drive-through facility, potentially for missile handling and warhead loading. A nearby complex with its own internal perimeter has four tunnels to underground facilities that could be used for warhead storage.

Israel is upgrading its arsenal of missiles from the solid-fuelled, two-stage Jericho II medium-range ballistic missile to the Jericho III intermediate-range ballistic missile. The newer and more capable Jericho III is a three-stage missile with a longer range, exceeding 4000 km. It first became operational in 2011 and might now have replaced the Jericho II.[18] In recent years—including 2015, 2017, 2019, 2020 and possibly 2021—Israel has conducted several test launches of what it calls 'rocket propulsion systems', although it is possible that some of these tests could be related to the development of Israeli space-launch vehicles, which use solid rocket motors.[19] In April 2021 video footage captured a blast at Sdot Micha Air Base that external analysts suggested was likely to be another rocket engine test; however—unlike its previous rocket propulsion tests—the Israeli Ministry of Defence did not confirm it as such.[20]

Sea-based missiles

Israel operates five German-built Dolphin-class (Dolphin-I and Dolphin-II) diesel–electric submarines, and plans to take delivery of at least four more submarines.[21] It is possible that the newer enlarged Dolphin-II submarines could be equipped with a vertical launch system that could carry new types of missile.[22] In early 2022 Israel signed a deal with Germany to procure three submarines, which will be known as the Dakar class, to replace the three

---

[18] O'Halloran, J. C. (ed.), 'Jericho missiles', *IHS Jane's Weapons: Strategic, 2015–16* (IHS Jane's: Coulsdon, 2015), p. 53.

[19] Agence France-Presse, 'Israel tests rocket propulsion system', *Defense News*, 5 May 2015; Israeli Ministry of Defense (@Israel_MOD), 'A few moments ago, Israel conducted a test launch of a rocket propulsion system around central Israel', Twitter, 29 May 2017; Kubovich, Y., 'Israel carries out test launch for rocket propulsion system', *Haaretz*, 6 Dec. 2017; and Israeli Ministry of Defense (@Israel_MOD), 'The Israel Ministry of Defense has completed a test of a rocket propulsion system from a military base in central Israel. The test launch was scheduled in advance and carried out as planned', Twitter, 31 Jan. 2020.

[20] Lewis, J., 'Israeli rocket motor test', Arms Control Wonk, 23 Apr. 2021.

[21] SIPRI Arms Transfers Database, Mar. 2022.

[22] Sutton, H. I., 'Israel's submarine secret: New dolphin-IIs could have VLS', Naval News, 19 Jan. 2022.

oldest Dolphin-class boats.[23] In addition to six standard 533 millimetre torpedo tubes, Israel's submarines are equipped with four additional, specially designed 650 mm tubes.[24] Both the German and Israeli governments have stated that these tubes are 'for the transfer of special forces and the pressure-free stowage of their equipment'; however, the unusual diameter has led many to speculate that Israel has modified some or all of the submarines to carry indigenously produced nuclear-armed sea-launched cruise missiles (SLCMs), giving it a sea-based nuclear strike capability.[25] Additionally, a 2012 media report—which remains one of the most significant exposés on the topic—quoted several former German defence ministry officials stating that they had always assumed that Israel would use the submarines for nuclear weapons.[26] If this is true, the naval arsenal might include about 10 cruise missile warheads for the submarines. Israel's submarines have their home port at Haifa on the Mediterranean coast. In recent years—including in 2021—they have occasionally sailed through the Suez Canal, as a possible deterrence signal to Iran.[27]

[23] 'Israel signs $3.4 bln submarines deal with Germany's Thyssenkrupp', Reuters, 20 Jan. 2022.

[24] Sutton, H. I., 'History of Israeli subs', Covert Shores, 20 May 2017; and Bergman, R. et al., 'Israel's deployment of nuclear missiles on subs from Germany', Der Spiegel, 4 June 2012.

[25] Bergman et al. (note 24).

[26] Bergman et al. (note 24). See also Frantz, D., 'Israel's arsenal is point of contention', Los Angeles Times, 12 Oct. 2003; and Sutton (note 24).

[27] See e.g. 'Iranian state media claims Israeli submarine passed through Suez into Red Sea', Times of Israel, 10 Aug. 2021.

IX. North Korean nuclear forces

HANS M. KRISTENSEN AND MATT KORDA

The Democratic People's Republic of Korea (DPRK, or North Korea) maintains an active but highly opaque nuclear weapon programme. SIPRI estimates that, as of January 2022, North Korea possessed approximately 20 nuclear weapons, but that it probably possessed sufficient fissile material for approximately 45–55 nuclear devices (see table 10.10). These estimates are based on calculations of the amount of fissile material—plutonium and highly enriched uranium (HEU)—that North Korea is believed to have produced for use in nuclear weapons (see section X), North Korea's nuclear weapon testing history and its observable missile forces. Analysing the numbers and types of North Korean warheads and delivery vehicles is fraught with uncertainty due to limited official public data and the fact that North Korean state media sources can be subject to manipulation, misinterpretation or exaggeration. Most of the data presented here is derived from sources outside North Korea, including satellite imagery, United States government reports and statements, and expert analyses.[1]

In 2021 North Korea did not conduct any nuclear explosive tests or flight tests of long-range ballistic missiles, despite the government's announcement in January 2020 that it would no longer observe its self-imposed moratorium from 2018 on conducting either type of test.[2] However, North Korea did conduct several tests of short-range ballistic missiles (SRBMs)—including tests from new types of launcher—as well as new land-attack cruise missiles, hypersonic glide vehicles (HGVs), and submarine-launched ballistic missiles (SLBMs).

Additionally, in January 2021 North Korean leader Kim Jong Un announced at the eighth congress of the ruling Workers' Party of Korea (WPK) that, since the previous congress in 2016, North Korea had 'already accumulated nuclear technology developed to such a high degree as to miniaturize, lighten and standardize nuclear weapons and to make them tactical ones and to complete the development of a super-large hydrogen bomb'. Kim also emphasized the need to 'develop the nuclear technology to a higher level and make nuclear weapons smaller and lighter for more tactical uses'.[3] The 'super-large hydrogen bomb' might refer to a weaponized design of the large-yield device with a suspected thermonuclear yield that was tested in 2017,

---

[1] Kristensen, H. M. and Korda, M., 'Estimating world nuclear forces: An overview and assessment of sources', SIPRI Topical Backgrounder, 14 June 2021.

[2] Nebehay, S., 'North Korea abandons nuclear freeze pledge, blames "brutal" US sanctions', Reuters, 21 Jan. 2020.

[3] Korean Central News Agency, 'On report made by Supreme Leader Kim Jong Un at eighth party congress of WPK', National Committee on North Korea, 9 Jan. 2021.

while the smaller and lighter weapons might be intended for deployment on one or several of the new shorter-range missiles test launched in 2021.[4]

The role of nuclear weapons in North Korean military doctrine

The 2013 law on nuclearization—one of the most recent official documents pertaining to North Korean nuclear doctrine—states that North Korea's nuclear arsenal would only be used 'to repel invasion or attack from a hostile nuclear weapons state and make retaliatory strikes', and that nuclear weapons would not be used against non-nuclear states 'unless they join a hostile nuclear weapons state in its invasion and attack on the DPRK'.[5] In a speech marking the 75th anniversary of the ruling WPK in October 2020, Kim Jong Un reiterated North Korea's pledge not to use nuclear weapons 'preemptively'.[6] This does not constitute a no-first-use policy, however, since Kim made it clear that he could turn to nuclear weapons if 'any forces infringe upon the security of our state'.[7]

As with other nuclear-armed states, it seems unlikely that North Korea would use its nuclear weapons outside of extreme circumstances where the continued existence of the state and its leadership was in question. However, in the event of such a scenario, it is possible that North Korea would use its nuclear weapons in an attempt to forestall adversarial action. Occasionally, North Korea has signalled or explicitly mentioned which targets it intends to prioritize in the event of imminent invasion. North Korea has specifically indicated that it would first target the Blue House, the executive office and official residence of the head of state of the Republic of Korea (South Korea), most likely as a response to the public acknowledgement by South Korea of its preparations to conduct 'decapitation' strikes aimed at eliminating North Korea's political and military leadership early in a conflict.[8] North Korea has stated that to forestall a conventional invasion, its second wave of targets would be US military bases in the Asia–Pacific region and continental USA.[9] Some nuclear weapons would probably be held in reserve to threaten targets

[4] For detail on North Korea's nuclear test in late 2017 see Fedchencko, V., 'Nuclear explosions, 1945–2017', *SIPRI Yearbook 2018*.

[5] Law on Consolidating the Position of Nuclear Weapons State for Self-Defence, adopted 1 Apr. 2013, Articles 4 and 5. For a translation see Korean Central News Agency, 'Law on consolidating position of nuclear weapons state adopted', Korea News Service, 1 Apr. 2013, available via GlobalSecurity.org.

[6] 'Kim Jong Un's October speech: More than missiles', 38 North, 13 Oct. 2020.

[7] 'Kim Jong Un's October speech' (note 6).

[8] Korean Central News Agency, 'Crucial statement of KPA Supreme Command', Korea News Service, 23 Feb. 2016, available via GlobalSecurity.org; and Choe, S. H., 'South Korea plans "decapitation unit" to try to scare North's leaders', *New York Times*, 12 Sep. 2017.

[9] Ko, Y. H., 'North Korean missile proliferation', Statement before the Subcommittee on International Security, Proliferation and Federation Services, US Senate Hearing no. 105-241, 21 Oct. 1997; Korean Central News Agency (note 8); and Allard, L., Duchâtel, M. and Godement, F., 'Pre-empting defeat: In search of North Korea's nuclear doctrine', European Council on Foreign Relations, 22 Nov. 2017.

Table 10.10. North Korean forces with potential nuclear capability, January 2022

All figures are approximate and some are based on assessments by the authors. The inclusion of a missile in this table does not necessarily indicate it is known to have a nuclear role. Some systems have been excluded because it is unlikely that they have a nuclear or operational role.

Type/ North Korean designation (US designation)[a]	Year first displayed	Range (km)	Description and status
Land-based missiles			
Hwasong-5/-6 (Scud-B/-C)	1984/1990	300/500	Single-stage, liquid-fuelled SRBMs launched from 4-axle wheeled TEL. NASIC estimates fewer than 100 Hwasong-5 and -6 launchers. Operational.
(KN18/KN21)	2017	250/450	Hwasong-5 and -6 variants with separating manoeuvrable warhead. Flight tested in May and Aug. 2017 from wheeled and tracked TELs. Status unknown; may have been superseded by newer solid-fuelled SRBMs.
(KN23/KN24[b]/KN25)	2018/2019	380–800	New generation of solid-fuelled SRBMs. Resemble Russia's Iskander-M, South Korea's Hyunmoo-2B, and the USA's ATACMS SRBMs. Successfully flight tested several times from wheeled, tracked and rail-based launchers since 2019. Status unknown; probably operational.
Hwasong-7 (Nodong/Rodong)	1993	>1 200	Single-stage, liquid-fuelled MRBM launched from 5-axle wheeled TEL. NASIC estimates fewer than 100 Hwasong-7 launchers. Operational.
Hwasong-9 (KN04/Scud-ER)	2016	1 000	Single-stage, liquid-fuelled Scud extended-range variant launched from 4-axle wheeled TEL. Flight tested in 2016. Probably operational.
Pukguksong-2 (KN15)	2017	>1 000	Two-stage, solid-fuelled MRBM launched from tracked TEL. Land-based version of Pukguksong-1 SLBM. Flight tested in 2017. Probably operational.
Land-attack cruise missile	2021	1 500	Flight tested multiple times in 2021 from wheeled TEL. Under development.
Hwasong-8/Unnamed 'Hypersonic Missile'	2021	>1 000	Two versions of HGV carried by a shortened Hwasong-12 booster. Hwasong-8 flight tested in Sep. 2021 with unknown result; unnamed missile successfully flight tested twice in Jan. 2022. Both systems displayed at exhibition in Oct. 2021. Under development.

Type/ North Korean designation (US designation)[a]	Year first displayed	Range (km)	Description and status
Hwasong-10 (BM-25/Musudan)	2010	>3 000	Single-stage, liquid-fuelled IRBM launched from 6-axle wheeled TEL. NASIC estimates fewer than 50 Hwasong-10 launchers. Several failed flight tests in 2016. Status unknown; may have been superseded.
Hwasong-12 (KN17)	2017	>4 500	Single-stage, liquid-fuelled MRBM launched from 8-axle wheeled TEL. Flight tested several times in 2017 with mixed success. Deployment status unknown.
Hwasong-14 (KN20)	2017	>10 000	Two-stage, liquid-fuelled ICBM launched from 8-axle wheeled TEL. First ICBM. Successfully flight tested twice in 2017. Deployment status unknown; may have been superseded.
Hwasong-15 (KN22)	2017	>12 000	Two-stage, liquid-fuelled ICBM launched from 9-axle wheeled TEL. Successfully flight tested in Nov. 2017. Displayed at parade in Oct. 2020 and at exhibition in Oct. 2021. Deployment status unknown.
Hwasong-17 (KN28)[c]	2020	14 000	Two-stage, liquid-fuelled ICBM launched from 11-axle wheeled TEL. Largest ICBM to date, possibly capable of carrying MIRVs and penetration aids. No known flight tests. Displayed at parade in Oct. 2020 and at exhibition in Oct. 2021. Under development.
Sea-based missiles			
Pukguksong-1 (KN11)	2014	>1 000	Two-stage, solid-fuelled SLBM. Flight tested several times in 2015 and 2016 with mixed success. Displayed at exhibition in Oct. 2021. Deployment status unknown; may have been superseded.
Pukguksong-3 (KN26)	2017	1 900– 2 500	Two-stage, solid-fuelled SLBM. Successfully flight tested in Oct. 2019. Deployment status unknown.
Pukguksong-4	2020	3 500– 5 400	Two-stage, solid-fuelled SLBM. Appears wider than Pukguksong-1 and shorter than Pukguksong-3. No known flight tests. Displayed at parade in Oct. 2020. Deployment status unknown.
Pukguksong-5	2021		Two-stage, solid-fuelled SLBM. Roughly same length as Pukguksong-3 with elongated shroud; possibly capable of carrying MIRVs and penetration aids. No known flight tests. Displayed at parade in Jan. 2021 and at exhibition in Oct. 2021. Deployment status unknown.

Type/ North Korean designation (US designation)[a]	Year first displayed	Range (km)	Description and status
Small 'New Type' SLBM	2021	400–600	Appears to deviate from traditional Pukguksong SLBM design, instead bearing similarities to KN23 SRBM. Displayed at exhibition in Oct. 2021 and successfully flight tested a week later. Deployment status unknown; probably under development.
Total warheads		**20**[d]	

HGV = hypersonic glide vehicle; ICBM = intercontinental ballistic missile; IRBM = intermediate-range ballistic missile; MIRV = multiple independently targetable re-entry vehicle; MRBM = medium-range ballistic missile; NASIC = United States National Air and Space Intelligence Center; SLBM = submarine-launched ballistic missile; SRBM = short-range ballistic missile; TEL = transporter-erector-launcher.

[a] Information about the status and capability of North Korea's missiles comes with significant uncertainty. This table includes missiles that could potentially have a nuclear capability, whether or not confirmed as being equipped with nuclear warheads or assigned nuclear missions. Several missiles may have been intended for development of technologies that will eventually become operational on newer missiles. There is no publicly available evidence that North Korea has produced an operational nuclear warhead for delivery by an ICBM.

[b] North Korea refers to the KN24 as the 'Hwasong-11Na', which could be considered akin to 'Hwasong-11B', as 'Na' (나) is the second letter in the Korean (Hangul) alphabet. This indicates that the KN24 is an improvement on or replacement for the original Hwasong-11 SRBM, which the US Department of Defense designates as the KN02 (Toksa).

[c] This missile was previously assumed to be designated the Hwasong-16; however, it was revealed at North Korea's Oct. 2021 Defence Development Exhibition that it is called the Hwasong-17.

[d] SIPRI estimates that North Korea might have produced enough fissile material to build between 45 and 55 nuclear warheads; however, it is likely that it has assembled fewer warheads, perhaps around 20, of which only a few would be thermonuclear warheads and nearly all would be lower-yield single-stage fission warheads.

Sources: US Department of Defense (DOD), *2019 Missile Defense Review* (DOD: Arlington, VA, 2019); US Air Force, National Air and Space Intelligence Center, *Ballistic and Cruise Missile Threat*, various years; *IHS Jane's Strategic Weapon Systems*, various editions; Hecker, S., Stanford University, Personal communication, 2020; *Bulletin of the Atomic Scientists*, 'Nuclear notebook', various issues; published expert analyses; and the authors' estimates. For the estimated number of warheads see also Hecker, S., 'What do we know about North Korea's nuclear program?', Presentation, Dialogue on DPRK Denuclearization Roadmaps and Verification, Kyung Hee University, Global America Business Institute (GABI) and Natural Resources Defense Council (NRDC), 20 Oct. 2020; 'Estimating North Korea's nuclear stockpiles: An interview with Siegfried Hecker', 38 North, 30 Apr. 2021; and Fedchenko, V. and Kelley, R., 'New methodology offers estimates for North Korean thermonuclear stockpile', *Janes Intelligence Review*, Sep. 2020, pp. 44–49.

within the US mainland, in an attempt to 'decouple' the USA from its Asia–Pacific allies.

The North Korean announcement in 2021 to 'make nuclear weapons smaller and lighter for more tactical uses' could potentially indicate plans to have the capability to respond on a more limited scale to threats that do not meet the threshold for a full-scale nuclear attack.

Fissile material and warhead production

Plutonium production and separation capabilities

North Korea's plutonium production and separation capabilities for manufacturing nuclear weapons are located at the Yongbyon Nuclear Scientific Research Centre in North Pyongan province.[10] Since its inspectors were required to leave the country in 2009, the International Atomic Energy Agency (IAEA) has monitored North Korea's nuclear programme using open-source information and commercial satellite imagery.[11] Between December 2018 and July 2021 the IAEA found no signs that North Korea's ageing 5-megawatt-electric (MW(e)) graphite-moderated research reactor had been operational; however, in August 2021 the IAEA reported that 'since early July 2021, there have been indications, including the discharge of cooling water, consistent with the operation of the reactor'.[12] Despite the intermittent discharge of cooling water throughout the latter half of 2021, there were no other indicators of reactor operations, such as steam emissions from the generator building.[13]

The Yongbyon complex's Thermal Plant—which supplies steam to the Radiochemical Laboratory used for plutonium reprocessing—operated between February 2021 and July 2021 after a multi-year hiatus.[14] The IAEA noted in August 2021 that 'this five-month timeframe is consistent with the time required to reprocess a complete core of irradiated fuel', which could indicate the possible completion of a new reprocessing campaign in 2021.[15]

---

[10] For an assessment of North Korea's nuclear weapon production facilities and infrastructure see Hecker, S. S., Carlin, R. L. and Serbin, E. A., 'A comprehensive history of North Korea's nuclear program: 2018 update', Stanford University, Center for International Security and Cooperation, 11 Feb. 2019.

[11] Dixit, A., 'IAEA ready to undertake verification and monitoring in North Korea', International Atomic Energy Agency (IAEA), 4 Mar. 2019.

[12] IAEA, Board of Governors and General Conference, 'Application of safeguards in the Democratic People's Republic of Korea', Report by the Director General, GOV/2021/40-GC(65)/22, 27 Aug. 2021, para. 12; and Pabian, F., Town, J. and Liu, J., 'North Korea's Yongbyon nuclear complex: More evidence the 5 MWe reactor appears to have restarted', 38 North, 30 Aug. 2021.

[13] Pabian, Town and Liu (note 12); and Heinonen, O., Liu, J. and Pitz, S. J., 'North Korea's Yongbyon nuclear complex: 5 MWe reactor may still be operating', 38 North, 8 Oct. 2021.

[14] Makowsky, P., Pabian, F. and Liu, J., 'North Korea's Yongbyon nuclear center: Signs of activity at the radiochemical laboratory facilities', 38 North, 3 Mar. 2021; Pabian, F. et al., 'North Korea's Yongbyon nuclear center: Reprocessing status remains unclear', 38 North, 7 Apr. 2021; and Bermudez Jr, J. S. et al., 'Thermal imagery indicates activity at Yongbyon nuclear reprocessing facilities', Beyond Parallel, 15 Apr. 2021.

[15] IAEA, Board of Governors and General Conference, 'Application of safeguards in the Democratic People's Republic of Korea', Report by the Director General, GOV/2021/40-GC(65)/22, 27 Aug. 2021, para. 12.

Throughout 2021, commercial satellite imagery indicated that North Korea continued construction of a new experimental light water reactor (ELWR), which will eventually be capable of producing plutonium for nuclear weapons. The 2021 IAEA report noted that North Korea may have conducted infrastructure tests at the ELWR in March and April, but that 'it is not possible to estimate when the reactor could become operational'.[16]

In April 2021 Siegfried Hecker—the former Los Alamos National Laboratory director who was given unprecedented access to North Korean nuclear facilities over several years—estimated that North Korea's plutonium stocks were likely to be between 25 and 48 kilograms and could increase by up to 6 kg per year at full operation.[17]

Uranium enrichment capabilities

There is considerable uncertainty about North Korea's uranium enrichment capabilities and its stock of HEU. North Korea produces yellowcake—the raw material for reactor fuel rods—at its Pyongsan Uranium Concentrate Plant (Nam-chon Chemical Complex) in North Hwanghae province.[18] It is widely believed that North Korea has focused on the production of HEU for use in nuclear warheads to overcome its limited capacity to produce weapon-grade plutonium. In September 2021 a report by the United Nations panel of experts assessed that North Korea continued to conduct activities at the gas centrifuge enrichment plant located at the Yongbyon complex, and noted the presence of what might have been a liquid nitrogen tank trailer at the site in April 2021—possibly indicating that the plant was operational.[19] Additionally, satellite imagery analysis indicates that North Korea is expanding this uranium enrichment plant, possibly by adding up to 1000 new centrifuges—thus potentially increasing the plant's enrichment capacity by up to 25 per cent.[20]

Using commercial satellite imagery, several non-governmental researchers have identified an additional suspected covert uranium enrichment plant located at Kangson (or Kangsong), to the south-west of Pyongyang.[21] The

[16] IAEA, GOV/2021/40-GC(65)/22 (note 15), para. 12.

[17] 'Estimating North Korea's nuclear stockpiles: An interview with Siegfried Hecker', 38 North, 30 Apr. 2021.

[18] Bermudez Jr, J. S., Cha, V. and Jun, J., 'Current status of the Pyongsan Uranium Concentrate Plant (Nam-chon Chemical Complex) and January Industrial Mine', Beyond Parallel, 8 Nov. 2021; and Bermudez Jr, J. S., Cha, V. and Kim, D., 'Recent activity at the Pyongsan Uranium Concentrate Plant (Nam-chon Chemical Complex) and January Industrial Mine', Beyond Parallel, 26 Mar. 2021.

[19] United Nations, Security Council, Midterm report of the Panel of Experts submitted pursuant to resolution 2569 (2021), S/2021/777, 8 Sep. 2021, pp. 6–7.

[20] Lewis, J., Pollack, J. and Schmerler, D., 'North Korea expanding uranium enrichment plant at Yongbyon', Arms Control Wonk, 14 Sep. 2021; and Cohen, Z., 'Satellite images reveal North Korea expanding facility used to produce weapons-grade uranium', CNN, 16 Sep. 2021.

[21] Panda, A., 'Exclusive: Revealing Kangson, North Korea's first covert uranium enrichment site', The Diplomat, 13 July 2018; and Albright, D. and Burkhard, S., 'Revisiting Kangsong: A suspect uranium enrichment plant', Institute for Science and International Security Imagery Brief, 2 Oct. 2018.

2021 IAEA report noted that 'the Kangson complex shares infrastructure characteristics with the reported centrifuge enrichment facility at Yongbyon', and that its construction matched the IAEA's understanding of the construction sequence of North Korea's uranium enrichment plant.[22] However, the 2021 UN panel of experts report cautioned that, without access to the plant, it was not possible to confirm the nature and purpose of the activities being conducted on-site.[23] A classified intelligence assessment by the USA in 2018 reportedly concluded that North Korea probably had more than one covert uranium enrichment plant and that the country was seeking to conceal the types and numbers of production facilities in its nuclear weapon programme, although a more recent open-source assessment concluded that the increased production capacity at Pyongsan indicates that North Korea does not require another uranium milling facility of comparable size.[24]

Nuclear warhead production

It is unclear how many nuclear weapons North Korea has produced with its fissile material, how many have been deployed on missiles, and what the military characteristics of the weapons are. North Korea has demonstrated a thermonuclear capability (or a capability with suspected thermonuclear yield) once, in 2017.[25] There is no open-source evidence or state intelligence confirming North Korea's capability to deliver an operational nuclear warhead on an intercontinental ballistic missile (ICBM). Moreover, most of North Korea's nuclear tests demonstrated yields in the range of 5–15 kilotons. As a result, SIPRI estimates that North Korea has used only a small portion of its HEU for thermonuclear weapons and has probably used the majority for a larger number of fission-only single-stage weapons deliverable by a medium-range ballistic missile (MRBM) or possibly by an intermediate-range ballistic missile (IRBM).[26] For this reason, SIPRI estimates that North Korea could potentially produce 45–55 nuclear weapons with its inventory of fissile material as at January 2022; however, it is likely that the number of operational warheads is smaller, perhaps closer to 20.[27] This falls within the range offered by a July 2020 US Army study that stated: 'Estimates for North Korean nuclear weapons range from 20–60 bombs, with the capability

[22] IAEA, GOV/2021/40-GC(65)/22 (note 15), para. 14.

[23] United Nations, S/2021/777 (note 19), p. 7.

[24] Kube, C., Dilanian, K. and Lee, C. E, 'North Korea has increased nuclear production at secret sites, say US officials', NBC News, 1 July 2018; Nakashima, E. and Warrick, J., 'North Korea working to conceal key aspects of its nuclear program, US officials say', *Washington Post*, 1 July 2018; and Park, S. et al., 'Assessing uranium ore processing activities using satellite imagery at Pyongsan in the Democratic People's Republic of Korea', *Science and Global Security*, vol. 29, no. 3 (2021), pp. 111–44.

[25] Fedchenko (note 4).

[26] Ballistic missiles are typically divided into four range categories: short-range (less than 1000 km), medium-range (1000–3000 km), intermediate-range (3000–5500 km) and intercontinental (>5500 km).

[27] For additional assessments see 'Estimating North Korea's nuclear stockpiles' (note 17).

to produce 6 new devices each year.'[28] Although North Korea demolished tunnels and facilities at its nuclear test site in 2018, satellite images in 2021 and early 2022 indicated that the site had not been abandoned but kept in caretaker status, potentially allowing nuclear testing to resume.[29]

Land-based missiles

North Korea is increasing both the size and capability of its ballistic missile force, which consists of indigenously produced missile systems with ranges from a few hundred kilometres to more than 12 000 km.[30] Since 2016, it has pursued development and production of several missile systems with progressively longer ranges and increasingly sophisticated delivery capabilities.[31] There is considerable uncertainty about the operational status of North Korea's IRBMs and ICBMs. According to independent analyses, North Korea may have deployed long-range missiles at several missile bases.[32]

It is unclear which of North Korea's missiles can carry nuclear weapons. The available evidence suggests that some MRBMs and IRBMs are the most likely to have an operational nuclear capability, while the ICBMs being developed to fulfil the nuclear role specified in North Korea's military doctrine have not yet demonstrated a reliable atmospheric re-entry vehicle or a capability for terminal-stage guidance and warhead activation.[33] As such, it remains unclear whether North Korea's missiles would be able to deliver reliably a nuclear warhead to an intercontinental-range target without further development.[34]

It must be emphasized that inclusion of a specific North Korean missile in the following overview and in table 10.10 does not necessarily indicate that it is confirmed as nuclear-capable or as having a nuclear role.

Short-range ballistic missiles

As of January 2022, North Korea had several types of SRBM, including older liquid-fuelled systems, possibly based on Soviet R-17 Scud missiles, and newer

---

[28] United States Army, 'North Korean tactics', Army Techniques Publication no. 7-100.2, 24 July 2020, pp. 1–11.

[29] Lee, C., 'North Korea's saber-rattling rekindles nuclear test site questions', VOA, 26 Jan. 2022.

[30] United States Air Force, National Air and Space Intelligence Center (NASIC), *Ballistic and Cruise Missile Threat 2020* (NASIC: Wright-Patterson Air Force Base, OH, July 2020).

[31] James Martin Center for Nonproliferation Studies (CNS), The CNS North Korea Missile Test Database, Nuclear Threat Initiative, as of 24 Mar. 2022.

[32] Bermudez Jr, J. S. and Cha, V., 'Undeclared North Korea: The Yusang-ni missile operating base', Beyond Parallel, 9 May 2019; Frank, M. 'Continued construction at Yusang-ni missile base', Open Nuclear Network, 26 July 2021; and United Nations, Security Council, Final report of the Panel of Experts submitted pursuant to resolution 2515 (2020), S/2021/211, 4 Mar. 2021, annexes 16–18.

[33] Ali, I., 'US general says North Korea not demonstrated all components of ICBM', Reuters, 30 Jan. 2018; and Cohen, Z., Starr, B. and Crawford, J., 'Top general warns US may not see a North Korean attack coming', CNN, 27 Mar. 2019.

[34] Elleman, M., 'Does size matter? North Korea's newest ICBM', 38 North, 21 Oct. 2020.

solid-fuelled missiles of indigenous design. These newer missiles, known as the KN23, KN24 and KN25, have been tested more than 35 times since the beginning of 2019.[35] North Korea has also been modernizing its older SRBMs by equipping them with manoeuverable re-entry vehicles designed to evade regional (e.g. South Korean) missile-defence systems.[36] Notably, in September 2021 North Korea launched two KN23 SRBMs using a rail-mobile launcher for the first time; following the successful test, North Korea announced its intention to expand the regiment into a brigade, which could eventually consist of nine launchers with 18 KN23s.[37] Rail-mobile launchers would enable North Korea to move missiles around the country rapidly and significantly increase the survivability of its second-strike force.

While the older, less accurate SRBMs might have been developed with dual capability, there is no publicly available, authoritative information confirming a nuclear delivery role for the newer, more accurate SRBMs—although as noted above, in a May 2021 speech, Kim Jong Un hinted that North Korea's shorter-range systems might have a 'tactical' (i.e. non-strategic) nuclear role.[38] Independent assessments have suggested that a nuclear device that North Korea displayed in 2017—if, indeed, it was a functional nuclear device—might be too large to fit into these newer SRBMs.[39] However, if North Korea has miniaturized its nuclear warheads as claimed, these types of missile could be used in a dual-capable role to target US military facilities south of Seoul.

Medium- and intermediate-range ballistic missiles

Assuming that North Korea is able to produce a sufficiently compact warhead, the country's three types of MRBM—all of which were probably operational as of January 2022—are considered to be its most likely nuclear delivery systems. These three types include the single-stage, liquid-fuelled Hwasong-7 (Nodong/Rodong); the single-stage, liquid-fuelled Hwasong-9 (KN04/Scud-ER); and the two-stage, solid-fuelled Pukguksong-2 (KN15), a land-based variant of the Pukguksong-1 (KN11) SLBM.[40] All three missiles

---

[35] James Martin Center for Nonproliferation Studies (note 31).

[36] Panda, A., 'Introducing the KN21, North Korea's new take on its oldest ballistic missile', The Diplomat, 14 Sep. 2017.

[37] Korean Central News Agency, 'Secretary Pak Jong Chon guides launching drill of Railway Mobile Missile Regiment for inspection', KCNA Watch, 16 Sep. 2021; Xu, T., Shin, J. and Furukawa, K., 'The first DPRK missile launch from a rail-mobile launcher', Open Nuclear Network, 17 Sep. 2021; and Bermudez Jr, J. S., 'What is the significance of North Korea's rail-mobile ballistic missile launcher?', Beyond Parallel, 30 Sep. 2021.

[38] North Korean Ministry of Foreign Affairs, 'Great programme for struggle leading Korean-style socialist construction to fresh victory on report made by Supreme Leader Kim Jong Un at Eighth Congress of WPK', *Rodong Sinmun*, 9 Jan. 2021, available via KCNA Watch.

[39] Elleman, M., 'Preliminary assessment of the KN-24 missile launches', 38 North, 25 Mar. 2020.

[40] For the missiles and submarines discussed in this section, a designation in parentheses (e.g. Nodong/Rodong) following the North Korean designation (e.g. Hwasong-7) is that assigned by the US Department of Defense.

have ranges between 1000 and 1200 km, meaning that they could reach targets anywhere in South Korea or Japan.[41]

North Korea's development of the solid-fuelled Pukguksong-2 might be part of an effort to improve the survivability of its nuclear-capable ballistic missile systems. Solid-fuelled missiles can be fired more quickly than liquid-fuelled systems and require fewer support vehicles that might give away their position to overhead surveillance. In addition, the Pukguksong-2 is coupled with a tracked transporter-erector-launcher (TEL), allowing North Korea to launch it from hidden, off-road sites. Most other systems use wheeled launchers and thus require paved or relatively smooth roads—a rarity in North Korea's mountainous terrain. According to a 2021 UN panel of experts report, North Korea has also developed tracked launchers for some of its newer SRBM systems, including the KN23, KN24 and KN25.[42]

The Hwasong-10 (BM-25/Musudan) is a single-stage, liquid-fuelled missile with an estimated range exceeding 3000 km. The missile has a poor test rate and no flight tests of the Hwasong-10 are known to have been conducted since 2016–17; as such, SIPRI assesses that the Hwasong-10 programme might have been superseded by North Korea's more sophisticated missile programmes—in particular, the Hwasong-12 (KN17), a single-stage IRBM that is believed to have a new liquid-propellant booster engine that is also used for North Korea's ICBM programme.[43] The Hwasong-12 was test launched in 2017 but it is unclear whether it has been operationally deployed.[44]

In September 2021 North Korea tested a new missile called the Hwasong-8, which appeared to include an HGV carried by a modified Hwasong-12 booster. Notably, state media reported that the Hwasong-8 is the first North Korean missile to use a 'fuel ampoule', which involves placing pre-fuelled liquid-fuelled missiles in temperature-controlled canisters to facilitate faster launches.[45]

Intercontinental-range ballistic missiles

As of January 2022, North Korea was widely believed to have prioritized building and deploying an ICBM that could potentially deliver a nuclear warhead to targets in continental USA. However, as mentioned above, considerable uncertainty remained in assessments of North Korea's long-range

---

[41] United States Air Force (note 30).

[42] United Nations, S/2021/211 (note 32), annex 12.

[43] James Martin Center for Nonproliferation Studies (note 31).

[44] Elleman, M., 'North Korea's Hwasong-12 launch: A disturbing development', 38 North, 30 Aug. 2017.

[45] Korean Central News Agency, 'Hypersonic missile newly developed by Academy of Defence Science test-fired', KCNA Watch, 30 Sep. 2021; and Xu, T., 'Brief on the Defence Development Exhibition of the Democratic People's Republic of Korea', Open Nuclear Network, 18 Oct. 2021.

missile capabilities, and the US Air Force's most recent report, from 2020, did not list any of North Korea's ICBMs as deployed.[46]

The Hwasong-13 (KN08) had not been flight tested as of January 2022 and SIPRI assesses that it is unlikely to become an operational military system. North Korea has twice tested the Hwasong-14 (KN20), a prototype ICBM that first appeared in 2015 at a military parade in Pyongyang, but it is unclear if it was operational in 2021.[47] However, the Hwasong-14 was absent from North Korea's most recent military parade featuring ICBMs, which took place in 2020. This suggests that it may have been superseded by more sophisticated ICBM programmes.[48]

North Korea has been developing a new two-stage ICBM, the Hwasong-15 (KN22), which has a significantly larger second stage and more powerful booster engines than the Hwasong-14, as well as a new liquid-fuelled type of ICBM, the Hwasong-17.[49] The Hwasong-17 (thought to have the US designation KN28) would hypothetically be large enough to accommodate multiple warheads; however, such capabilities have not yet been demonstrated.[50]

In 2019 the US Department of Defense (DOD) indicated that North Korea had deployed one ICBM, the Taepodong-2; however, other official US sources have listed the missile as a space-launch vehicle that would need reconfiguration to be used as an ICBM and therefore it is not included in SIPRI's assessment for January 2022 of North Korean forces with potential nuclear capability.[51]

Cruise missiles

In September 2021 North Korea conducted test launches of a new land-attack cruise missile (LACM) at a claimed speed of roughly 200 metres per second to a range of 1500 km. Although North Korea has other cruise missiles in its arsenal, this is the first system that has been explicitly described as a 'strategic weapon', thus potentially implying a connection to North Korea's nuclear weapon programme.[52] The test launches followed Kim Jong Un's

[46] United States Air Force (note 30).

[47] United States Air Force (note 30), p. 27; Wright, D., 'North Korean ICBM appears able to reach major US cities', Union of Concerned Scientists, 28 July 2017; and Elleman, M., 'North Korea's Hwasong-14 ICBM: New data indicates shorter range than many thought', 38 North, 29 Nov. 2018.

[48] NK News, 'North Korea military parade 2020: livestream & analysis', YouTube, 10 Oct. 2020.

[49] For further detail see Kristensen, H. M. and Korda, M., 'North Korean nuclear forces', *SIPRI Yearbook 2021*, p. 402.

[50] Ankit Panda (@nktpnd), 'Real good catch by @ColinZwirko: North Korea's very large road-mobile ICBM seen at the end of the October 2020 is the *Hwasong-17*, NOT Hwasong-16 (KN28 to USIC)', Twitter, 13 Oct. 2021.

[51] United States Department of Defense, *Missile Defense Review 2019* (Office of the Secretary of Defense: Arlington, VA, Jan. 2019); and United States Air Force (note 30), p. 29.

[52] Shin, H. and Smith, J., 'N.Korea tests first "strategic" cruise missile with possible nuclear capability', Reuters, 13 Sep. 2021.

January 2021 statement on pursuing 'tactical' missiles and nuclear weapons.[53] Imagery of the LACM released by North Korean state media indicates that it might include a terminal guidance system—which would improve the missile's accuracy—and that it could be launched from a TEL that carries five missiles.[54] Notably, South Korean news sources subsequently reported that neither South Korea nor the USA were aware of the LACM launch until after the announcement in North Korean state media.[55] Given that this system is designed to circumvent radars and missile-defence systems by flying at lower altitudes on manoeuvrable trajectories, it could offer North Korea a new and unique capability to attack regional targets. Kim Jong Un's statement in January 2021 that this system's 'conventional warheads are the most powerful in the world' indicates that the LACM could either be dual-capable or exclusively conventional.[56]

Sea-based missiles

North Korea has continued to develop its family of Pukguksong ('Polaris') solid-fuelled SLBMs as part of an effort to improve the survivability of its nuclear-capable ballistic missile systems.[57] During North Korea's October 2020 military parade, a new type of SLBM was unveiled—the Pukguksong-4, which the UN panel of experts estimates has a maximum range between 3500 and 5400 km for payloads of 1300 kg and 650 kg, respectively.[58] At a military parade in January 2021, North Korea unveiled its new Pukguksong-5. Both the Pukguksong-4 and Pukguksong-5 are two-stage, solid-fuelled missiles and are wider than North Korea's previous Pukguksong SLBMs.[59]

In October 2021 North Korea unveiled a 'new type' of smaller SLBM with an unknown designation at its Defence Development Exhibition.[60] The missile appears to bear similar characteristics to North Korea's newer SRBM designs.[61] The same SLBM, which North Korea described as having 'flank mobility and gliding skip mobility', was reportedly test launched one week

---

[53] Korean Central News Agency, 'Newly-developed long-range cruise missiles test-fired', KCNA Watch, 13 Sep. 2021; and Van Diepen, V. H., 'Initial analysis of North Korea's "new type long-range cruise missile"', 38 North, 15 Sep. 2021.

[54] Xu (note 45).

[55] See e.g. Lee, C. J., [(Exclusive) 'Both pre- and post-detection of North Korean missiles failed . . . Korea–US information disaster'], *JoongAng*, 13 Sep. 2021 (in Korean).

[56] North Korean Ministry of Foreign Affairs (note 38).

[57] For further detail on North Korea's earlier Pukguksong family of missiles see Kristensen and Korda (note 49), p. 403.

[58] NK News (note 48); and United Nations, S/2021/211 (note 32), annex 11.

[59] United Nations, S/2021/777 (note 19), annex 18-2. The larger diameter of the missiles could potentially indicate that they are designed to carry penetration aids or even multiple warheads; however, such capabilities have not yet been demonstrated.

[60] Xu (note 45).

[61] Xu, T., 'Brief on the 19 October 2021 submarine-launched ballistic missile test of the Democratic People's Republic of Korea', Open Nuclear Network, 21 Oct. 2021.

later from the port of Sinpo to an approximate range of 590 km, landing in the Sea of Japan.[62] The test's short apogee of 60 km indicates that this new SLBM is likely to have a shorter range than many of the Pukguksong SLBMs.[63] The missile was launched using North Korea's single Gorae-class (Sinpo) experimental submarine, *8.24 Yongung*.[64] This submarine can hold and launch only a single SLBM.

In November 2020 the South Korean National Intelligence Service announced that North Korea was building a new ballistic missile submarine.[65] The vessel, designated Sinpo-C by the US DOD, appears to be based on a modified Project-633 (Romeo) diesel–electric submarine and to be fitted with three missile launch canisters.[66] According to a 2019 report by North Korea's state-run Korean Central News Agency, the submarine's operational deployment was 'near at hand'.[67]

[62] Korean Central News Agency, 'Academy of Defence science succeeds in test-launch of new-type SLBM', KCNA Watch, 20 Oct. 2021.

[63] 'N. Korea fires what seems to be SLBM toward East Sea: S. Korea', Yonhap News Agency, 19 Oct. 2021.

[64] Korean Central News Agency (note 62); Makowsky, P. and Liu, J., 'Sinpho South shipyard: Evidence of the SINPO-Class SSBA participation in recent SLBM test', 38 North, 21 Oct. 2021; and Bermudez Jr, J. S. and Cha, V., 'Sinpo South shipyard update: SLBM test launch', Beyond Parallel, 21 Oct. 2021.

[65] Bermudez Jr, J. S. and Cha, V., 'Sinpo South shipyard: Construction of a new ballistic missile submarine?', Beyond Parallel, 28 Aug. 2019; Cha, S., 'North Korea building two submarines, one capable of firing ballistic missiles: Lawmaker', Reuters, 3 Nov. 2020; and Dempsey, J. and Schmerler, D., 'Two halls enter: One sub leaves', Arms Control Wonk, 17 June 2021.

[66] Hotham, O., 'New North Korean submarine capable of carrying three SLBMs: South Korean MND', NK News, 31 July 2019; and Cha (note 65).

[67] 'NK leader inspects new submarine to be deployed in East Sea: State media', Yonhap News Agency, 23 July 2019.

X. Global stocks and production of fissile materials, 2021

MORITZ KÜTT, ZIA MIAN AND PAVEL PODVIG

INTERNATIONAL PANEL ON FISSILE MATERIALS

Materials that can sustain an explosive fission chain reaction are essential for all types of nuclear explosive, from first-generation fission weapons to advanced thermonuclear weapons. The most common of these fissile materials are highly enriched uranium (HEU) and plutonium. This section gives details of military and civilian stocks, as of the beginning of 2021, of HEU (table 10.11) and separated plutonium (table 10.12), including in weapons, and details of the current capacity to produce these materials (tables 10.13 and 10.14, respectively). The timeliness of the information here is constrained by the most recent annual declarations on civilian plutonium and HEU stocks to the International Atomic Energy Agency (IAEA; INFCIRC/549), which give data for 31 December 2020. The information in the tables is based on estimates prepared for the International Panel on Fissile Materials (IPFM).[1]

The production of both HEU and plutonium starts with natural uranium. Natural uranium consists almost entirely of the non-chain-reacting isotope uranium-238 (U-238) and is only about 0.7 per cent uranium-235 (U-235). Following mining, which produces a large amount of hazardous mining waste, conversion facilities turn uranium into gaseous uranium-hexafluoride. Using the gas, the concentration of U-235 in the uranium can be increased through isotopic separation (enrichment)—now carried out typically by using gas centrifuges and previously by gaseous diffusion technology.

Uranium that has been enriched to less than 20 per cent U-235 (typically, 3–5 per cent), known as low-enriched uranium, is suitable for use in power reactors. Uranium that has been enriched to contain at least 20 per cent U-235, known as HEU, is generally taken to be the lowest concentration practicable for use in weapons. However, to minimize the mass of the nuclear explosive, weapon-grade uranium is usually enriched to over 90 per cent U-235.

Plutonium is produced in nuclear reactors when U-238 in the fuel is exposed to neutrons. The plutonium is subsequently chemically separated from spent fuel in a hazardous reprocessing operation that generates large amounts of long-lived radioactive waste and can expose workers to high radiation doses.

---

[1] For further information see International Panel on Fissile Materials, 'Fissile material stocks', 4 Sep. 2021. For further information on the history, production and use of fissile materials and options for addressing the risks these materials pose see Feiveson, H. A. et al., *Unmaking the Bomb: A Fissile Material Approach to Nuclear Disarmament and Nonproliferation* (MIT Press: Cambridge, MA, 2014).

Plutonium comes in a variety of isotopic mixtures, most of which are weapon-usable. Weapon designers prefer to work with a mixture that predominantly consists of plutonium-239 (Pu-239) because of its relatively low rate of spontaneous emission of neutrons and gamma rays and the low level of heat generation from alpha decay. Weapon-grade plutonium typically contains more than 90 per cent Pu-239. The plutonium in typical spent fuel from power reactors (reactor-grade plutonium) contains 50–60 per cent Pu-239 but is weapon-usable, even in a first-generation weapon design.

The categories for fissile materials used in this section reflect the availability of these materials for weapon purposes. Material described as 'not directly available for weapons' is either material produced outside of weapon programmes or weapon-related material that states pledged not to use in weapons. This material, however, is not placed under international safeguards (such as through the IAEA or Euratom) or under bilateral monitoring. Safeguarded or monitored material is listed in a separate category. Starting this year, the data accounts only for unirradiated fissile material, a category that corresponds to the IAEA definition of 'unirradiated direct use material'.

All states that have a civil nuclear industry (i.e. that operate a nuclear reactor or a uranium enrichment plant) have some capability to produce fissile materials that could be used for weapons.

Table 10.11. Global stocks of highly enriched uranium, 2021

State	Total stock (tonnes)[a]	In weapons/ available for weapons (tonnes)	Not directly available for weapons, unsafeguarded (tonnes)	Not available for weapons, monitored/ under safeguards (tonnes)	Production status
China	14	14 ± 3	–	–	Stopped 1987–89
France[b]	29	25 ± 6	–	3.8	Stopped 1996
India[c]	4.5	–	4.5 ± 1.9	–	Continuing
Iran[d]	0.02	–	0.02	–	Continuing
Israel[e]	0.3	0.3	–	–	Unknown
Korea, North[f]	Uncertain	–	–	–	Uncertain
Pakistan[g]	4	4 ± 1.2	–	–	Continuing
Russia[h]	678	672 ± 120	6[i]	–	Continuing[j]
UK[k]	23	22	0.6[l]	–	Stopped 1962
USA[m]	495	361	134	–	Stopped 1992
Other states[n]	~4	–	–	~4	..
Total[o]	**1 250**	**1 100**	**145**	**10**	

.. = not available or not applicable; – = nil or a negligible value.

[a] The numbers in the table are for unirradiated highly enriched uranium (HEU). Most of this material is 90–93% enriched uranium-235 (U-235), which is typically considered weapon-grade. The estimates are for the start of 2021. Important exceptions are noted.

[b] A 2014 analysis offers grounds for a significantly lower estimate of the stockpile of weapon-grade HEU (between 6 ± 2 tonnes and 10 ± 2 tonnes), based on evidence that the Pierrelatte enrichment plant may have had both a much shorter effective period of operation and a smaller weapon-grade HEU production capacity than previously assumed.

[c] It is believed that India is producing HEU (enriched to 30–45%) for use as naval reactor fuel. The estimate is for HEU enriched to 30%.

[d] The data for Iran is the International Atomic Energy Agency's (IAEA) estimate as of 5 Nov. 2021. Iran started enriching uranium up to 20% on 4 Jan. 2021 and started enriching HEU up to 60% enrichment level on 17 Apr. 2021.

[e] Israel may have acquired illicitly c. 300 kilograms of weapon-grade HEU from the USA in or before 1965. Some of this material may have been consumed in the process of producing tritium.

[f] North Korea (the Democratic People's Republic of Korea, DPRK) is known to have a uranium enrichment plant at Yongbyon and possibly others elsewhere. Independent estimates of uranium enrichment capability and possible HEU production extrapolated to the beginning of 2021 suggest a potential accumulated HEU stockpile in the range 230–1180 kg.

[g] This estimate for Pakistan assumes total HEU production of 4.1 tonnes, of which c. 100 kg was used in nuclear weapon tests.

[h] This estimate assumes that the Soviet Union stopped all HEU production in 1988. It may therefore understate the amount of HEU in Russia (see also note j).

[i] This material is believed to be in use in various civilian as well as military-related research facilities.

[j] The Soviet Union stopped production of HEU for weapons in 1988 but kept producing HEU for civilian and non-weapon military uses. Russia continues this practice.

[k] The estimate for the United Kingdom reflects a declaration of 21.9 tonnes of military HEU as of 31 Mar. 2002, the average enrichment of which was not given.

[l] This figure is from the UK's INFCIRC/549 declaration to the IAEA for the start of 2021. As the UK has left the European Union, the material is no longer under Euratom safeguards.

[m] The amount of HEU held by the United States is given in actual tonnes, not 93%-enriched equivalent. In 2016 the USA declared that, as of 30 Sep. 2013, its HEU inventory was 585.6 tonnes,

of which 499.4 tonnes was declared to be for 'national security or non-national security programs including nuclear weapons, naval propulsion, nuclear energy, and science'. This material was estimated to include about 360.9 tonnes of HEU in weapons and available for weapons, 121.1 tonnes of HEU reserved for naval fuel and 17.3 tonnes of HEU reserved for research reactors. The remaining 86.2 tonnes of the 2013 declaration was composed of 41.6 tonnes 'available for potential down-blend to low enriched uranium or, if not possible, disposal as low-level waste', and 44.6 tonnes in spent reactor fuel. As of the end of 2020, the amount available for use had been reduced to c. 472.1 tonnes, which is estimated to include 96 tonnes of HEU in naval reserve and 15.2 tonnes reserved for research reactors. Between the end of the US financial year (FY) 2013 (30 Sep. 2013) and the end of FY 2020 (30 Sep. 2020), the amount of material to be downblended was reduced from 41.6 tonnes to 23 tonnes.

[n] The IAEA's 2020 annual report lists 156 significant quantities of HEU under comprehensive safeguards in non-nuclear weapon states as of the end of 2020. Assuming a significant quantity to be 25 kg of HEU, the total mass is estimated to be 4 tonnes. In INFCIRC/912 (from 2017) more than 20 states committed to reducing civilian HEU stocks and providing regular reports. So far, only 2 states have reported under this scheme. At the end of 2018 (time of last declaration), Norway held less than 4 kg of HEU for civilian purposes. As of 30 June 2019, Australia held 2.7 kg of HEU for civilian purposes.

[o] Totals are rounded to the nearest 5 tonnes.

Sources: International Panel on Fissile Materials (IPFM), *Global Fissile Material Report 2015: Nuclear Weapon and Fissile Material Stockpiles and Production* (IPFM: Princeton, NJ, 2015). *China*: Zhang, H., *China's Fissile Material Production and Stockpile* (IPFM: Princeton, NJ, 2017). *France*: International Atomic Energy Agency (IAEA), 'Communication received from France concerning its policies regarding the management of plutonium', INFCIRC/549/Add.5/25, 21 Sep. 2021; and Philippe, S. and Glaser, A., 'Nuclear archaeology for gaseous diffusion enrichment plants', *Science & Global Security*, vol. 22, no. 1 (2014), pp. 27–49. *Iran*: IAEA, Board of Governors, 'Verification and monitoring in the Islamic Republic of Iran in light of United Nations Security Council Resolution 2231 (2015)', Report by the Director General, GOV/2021/51, 17 Nov. 2021. *Israel*: Myers, H., 'The real source of Israel's first fissile material', *Arms Control Today*, vol. 37, no. 8 (Oct. 2007), p. 56; and Gilinsky, V. and Mattson, R. J., 'Revisiting the NUMEC affair', *Bulletin of the Atomic Scientists*, vol. 66, no. 2 (Mar./Apr. 2010). *North Korea*: Hecker, S. S., Braun, C. and Lawrence, C., 'North Korea's stockpiles of fissile material', *Korea Observer*, vol. 47, no. 4 (winter 2016), pp. 721–49. *Russia*: Podvig, P. (ed.), *The Use of Highly-Enriched Uranium as Fuel in Russia* (IPFM: Washington, DC, 2017). *UK*: British Ministry of Defence, 'Historical accounting for UK defence highly enriched uranium', Mar. 2006; and IAEA, 'Communications received from the United Kingdom of Great Britain and Northern Ireland concerning its policies regarding the management of plutonium', INFCIRC/549/Add.8/25, 13 Oct. 2021. *USA*: US Department of Energy (DOE), National Nuclear Security Administration, *Highly Enriched Uranium, Striking a Balance: A Historical Report on the United States Highly Enriched Uranium Production, Acquisition, and Utilization Activities from 1945 through September 30, 1996* (DOE: Washington, DC, Jan. 2001); White House, 'Transparency in the US highly enriched uranium inventory', Fact sheet, 31 Mar. 2016; US DOE, *FY 2021 Congressional Budget Request*, vol. 1, *National Nuclear Security Administration* (DOE: Washington, DC, Feb. 2020), p. 593; and US DOE, *Tritium and Enriched Uranium Management Plan through 2060*, Report to Congress (DOE: Washington, DC, Oct. 2015). *Non-nuclear weapon states*: IAEA, *IAEA Annual Report 2020* (IAEA: Vienna, 2020), Annex, Table A4, p. 139; IAEA, 'Communication dated 19 July 2019 received from the Permanent Mission of Norway concerning a joint statement on minimising and eliminating the use of highly enriched uranium in civilian applications', INFCIRC/912/Add.3, 15 Aug. 2019; and IAEA, 'Communication dated 23 January 2020 received from the Permanent Mission of Australia concerning the joint statement on minimising and eliminating the use of highly enriched uranium in civilian applications', INFCIRC/912/Add.4, 5 Mar. 2020.

Table 10.12. Global stocks of separated plutonium, 2021

State	Total stock (tonnes)[a]	In weapons/available for weapons (tonnes)	Not directly available for weapons, unsafeguarded (tonnes)	Not available for weapons, monitored/under safeguards (tonnes)	Military production status
China	2.9	2.9 ± 0.6	0.04[b]	–	Stopped in 1991
France	85.4	6 ± 1.0	–	79.4[c]	Stopped in 1992
India	9.2	0.71 ± 0.14	8.1 ± 4.3[d]	0.4	Continuing
Israel[e]	0.8	0.83 ± 0.1	–	–	Continuing
Japan	46.1	–	–	46.1[c]	–
Korea, North[f]	0.04	0.04	–	–	Continuing
Pakistan[g]	0.5	0.46 ± 0.16	–	–	Continuing
Russia	191	88 ± 8	88.3[h]	15[i]	Stopped in 2010
UK	119.3	3.2	116.1[c]	–	Stopped in 1995
USA[j]	87.8	38.4	46.4	3[k]	Stopped in 1988
Total[l]	**545**	**140**	**260**	**145**	

– = nil or a negligible value.

[a] Estimates are for the start of 2021. Important exceptions are noted.

[b] These numbers are based on China's INFCIRC/549 declaration to the International Atomic Energy Agency (IAEA) for the end of 2016. As of May 2022, this is the most recent declaration.

[c] The data for France, Japan and the United Kingdom is for the end of 2020, reflecting their most recent respective INFCIRC/549 declarations to the IAEA. Some states with civilian plutonium stocks do not submit an INFCIRC/549 declaration. Of these states, the Netherlands, Spain and Sweden store their plutonium abroad, but the total amounts are too small to be noted in the table.

[d] This material is the plutonium separated from spent power-reactor fuel. While such reactor-grade plutonium can, in principle, be used in weapons, it is labelled as 'not directly available for weapons' here since it is intended for breeder reactor fuel. It was not placed under safeguards in the 'India-specific' safeguards agreement signed by the Indian government and the IAEA on 2 Feb. 2009. India does not submit an INFCIRC/549 declaration to the IAEA.

[e] Israel is believed to be operating the Dimona plutonium production reactor. The estimate assumes partial use of the reactor for tritium production from 1997 onwards. The estimate is for the end of 2020. Without tritium production, the stockpile could be as high as 1070 kg.

[f] North Korea (the Democratic People's Republic of Korea, DPRK) reportedly declared a plutonium stock of 37 kg in June 2008. It is believed that it subsequently unloaded its 5 megawatt electric reactor three additional times, in 2009, 2016 and 2018. The stockpile estimate has been reduced to account for North Korea's six nuclear tests. North Korea's reprocessing facility operated again in 2021 for five months.

[g] As of the end of 2020, Pakistan was operating four plutonium production reactors at its Khushab site. This estimate assumes that Pakistan is separating plutonium from all four reactors.

[h] This material includes 63.3 tonnes of separated plutonium declared in Russia's 2021 INFCIRC/549 declaration as civilian. Russia does not make the plutonium it reports as civilian available to IAEA safeguards. This amount also includes 25 tonnes of weapon-origin plutonium stored at the Mayak Fissile Material Storage Facility, which Russia pledged not to use for military purposes.

[i] This material is weapon-grade plutonium produced between 1 Jan. 1995 and 15 Apr. 2010, when the last plutonium production reactor was shut down. It cannot be used for weapon purposes under the terms of a 1997 Russian–United States agreement on plutonium production reactors. The material is currently stored at Zheleznogorsk and is subject to monitoring by US inspectors.

[j] In 2012 the USA declared a government-owned plutonium inventory of 95.4 tonnes as of 30 Sep. 2009. In its 2021 INFCIRC/549 declaration, the most recent submitted, the USA declared 49.4 tonnes of unirradiated plutonium (both separated and in mixed oxide, MOX) as part of the stock identified as excess for military purposes (declaration for 31 Dec. 2020).

[k] The USA has placed about 3 tonnes of its excess plutonium, stored at the K-Area Material Storage Facility at the Savannah River Plant, under IAEA safeguards.

[l] Totals are rounded to the nearest 5 tonnes.

Sources: International Panel on Fissile Materials (IPFM), *Global Fissile Material Report 2015: Nuclear Weapon and Fissile Material Stockpiles and Production* (IPFM: Princeton, NJ, 2015). *Civilian stocks (except for India)*: declarations by countries to the International Atomic Energy Agency (IAEA) under INFCIRC/549. *China*: Zhang, H., *China's Fissile Material Production and Stockpile* (IPFM: Princeton, NJ, 2017). *Israel*: Glaser, A. and de Troullioud de Lanversin, J., 'Plutonium and tritium production in Israel's Dimona reactor, 1964–2020', *Science & Global Security*, vol. 29, no. 2 (2021). *North Korea*: Kessler, G., 'Message to US preceded nuclear declaration by North Korea', *Washington Post*, 2 July 2008; Hecker, S. S., Braun, C. and Lawrence, C., 'North Korea's stockpiles of fissile material', *Korea Observer*, vol 47, no. 4 (winter 2016), pp. 721–49; and IAEA, Board of Governors and General Conference, 'Application of safeguards in the Democratic People's Republic of Korea', Report by the acting director general, GOV/2019/33-GC(63)/20, 19 Aug. 2019. *Russia*: Russian–United States Agreement Concerning the Management and Disposition of Plutonium Designated as No Longer Required for Defense Purposes and Related Cooperation (Plutonium Management and Disposition Agreement), signed 29 Aug. and 1 Sep. 2000, amendment signed 5 Sep. 2006, entered into force 13 July 2011. *USA*: National Nuclear Security Administration (NNSA), *The United States Plutonium Balance, 1944–2009* (NNSA: Washington, DC, June 2012); and Gunter, A., 'K-Area overview/update', US Department of Energy, Savanah River Site, 28 July 2015.

Table 10.13. Significant uranium enrichment facilities and capacity worldwide, 2021

State	Facility name or location	Type	Status	Enrichment process[a]	Capacity (thousands SWU/yr)[b]
Argentina[c]	Pilcaniyeu	Civilian	Uncertain	GD	20
Brazil	Resende	Civilian	Expanding capacity	GC	45
China[d]	Lanzhou	Civilian	Operational	GC	2 600
	Hanzhong (Shaanxi)	Civilian	Operational	GC	2 000
	Emeishan	Civilian	Operational	GC	1 050
	Heping	Dual-use	Operational	GD	230
France	Georges Besse II	Civilian	Operational	GC	7 500
Germany	Urenco Gronau	Civilian	Operational	GC	3 800
India	Rattehalli	Military	Operational	GC	15–30
Iran[e]	Natanz	Civilian	Limited operation	GC	3.5–10
	Qom (Fordow)	Civilian	Limited operation	GC	0.7–2
Japan	Rokkasho[f]	Civilian	Resuming operation	GC	75
Korea, North	Yongbyon[g]	Uncertain	Operational	GC	8
Netherlands	Urenco Almelo	Civilian	Operational	GC	5 200
Pakistan	Gadwal	Military	Operational	GC	..
	Kahuta	Military	Operational	GC	15–45
Russia	Angarsk	Civilian	Operational	GC	4 000
	Novouralsk	Civilian	Operational	GC	13 300
	Seversk	Civilian	Operational	GC	3 800
	Zelenogorsk[h]	Civilian	Operational	GC	7 900
UK	Urenco Capenhurst	Civilian	Operational	GC	4 500
USA	Urenco Eunice	Civilian	Operational	GC	4 900

.. = not available or not applicable.

[a] The gas centrifuge (GC) is the main isotope-separation technology used to enrich uranium in uranium-235 (U-235), but a few facilities continue to use gaseous diffusion (GD).

[b] Separative work units per year (SWU/yr) is a measure of the effort required in an enrichment facility to separate uranium of a given content of U-235 into two components, one with a higher and one with a lower percentage of U-235. Where a range of capacities is shown, the capacity is uncertain or the facility is expanding its capacity.

[c] In Dec. 2015 Argentina announced the reopening of its Pilcaniyeu GD uranium enrichment plant, which was shut down in the 1990s. There is no evidence of actual production.

[d] Assessments of China's enrichment capacity in 2015 and 2017 identified new enrichment sites and suggested a much larger total capacity than had previously been estimated.

[e] In July 2015 Iran agreed the Joint Comprehensive Plan of Action (JCPOA), which ended uranium enrichment at Fordow but kept centrifuges operating and limited the enrichment capacity at Natanz to 5060 IR-1 centrifuges (equivalent to 3500–5000 SWU/yr) for 10 years. Since the withdrawal of the United States from the JCPOA in 2018, Iran has increased enrichment capacities at its facilities. As of 17 Nov. 2021, the International Atomic Energy Agency (IAEA) had verified 5229 IR-1 centrifuges (31 cascades), 1044 IR-2m centrifuges (6 cascades) and 348 IR-4 centrifuges (2 cascades) installed at the Natanz Fuel Enrichment Plant. Highly enriched uranium (HEU) production takes place at the Pilot Fuel Enrichment Plant at Natanz, with a capacity of up to 2000 SWU. At the Fordow Fuel Enrichment Plant, there were 1044 IR-1 and 189 IR-6 centrifuges as of Nov. 2021.

[f] The Rokkasho centrifuge plant has been in the process of being refitted with new centrifuge technology since 2011. Production since the start of retrofitting has been negligible.

[g] North Korea (the Democratic People's Republic of Korea, DPRK) revealed its Yongbyon enrichment facility in 2010. It appeared to be operational in 2021. It is believed that North Korea is operating at least one other enrichment facility.

[h] Zelenogorsk operates a centrifuge cascade for HEU production for fast reactor and research reactor fuel.

Sources: Indo-Asian News Service (IANS), 'Argentina president inaugurates enriched uranium plant', *Business Standard*, 1 Dec. 2015; 'Brazil's INB launches new centrifuge cascade', *Nuclear Engineering International*, 25 Nov. 2021; Zhang, H., 'China's uranium enrichment complex', *Science & Global Security*, vol. 23, no. 3 (2015), pp. 171–90; Zhang, H., *China's Fissile Material Production and Stockpile* (International Panel on Fissile Materials, IPFM: Princeton, NJ, 2017); Hecker, S. S., Carlin, R. L. and Serbin, E. A., 'A comprehensive history of North Korea's nuclear program', Stanford University, Center for International Security and Cooperation (CISAC), 2018 update; International Atomic Energy Agency (IAEA), Board of Governors, 'Verification and monitoring in the Islamic Republic of Iran in light of United Nations Security Council Resolution 2231 (2015)', Report by the Director General, GOV/2021/51, 17 Nov. 2021; and IAEA, Board of Governors, 'Verification and monitoring in the Islamic Republic of Iran in light of United Nations Security Council resolution 2231 (2015)', Report by the Director General, GOV/2022/4, 3 Mar. 2022. Enrichment capacity data is based on IAEA, Integrated Nuclear Fuel Cycle Information Systems (iNFCIS); Urenco, 'Global operations', [n.d.]; and IPFM, *Global Fissile Material Report 2015: Nuclear Weapon and Fissile Material Stockpiles and Production* (IPFM: Princeton, NJ, 2015).

Table 10.14. Significant reprocessing facilities worldwide, 2021

All facilities process light water reactor (LWR) fuel, except where indicated.

State	Facility name or location	Type	Status	Design capacity (tHM/yr)[a]
China[b]	Jiuquan pilot plant	Civilian	Operational	50
France	La Hague UP2	Civilian	Operational	1 000
	La Hague UP3	Civilian	Operational	1 000
India[c]	Kalpakkam (HWR fuel)	Dual-use	Operational	100
	Tarapur (HWR fuel)	Dual-use	Operational	100
	Tarapur-II (HWR fuel)	Dual-use	Operational	100
	Trombay (HWR fuel)	Military	Operational	50
Israel	Dimona (HWR fuel)	Military	Operational	40–100
Japan	JNC Tokai	Civilian	Reprocessing shut down[d]	(was 200)
	Rokkasho	Civilian	Start planned for 2022	800
Korea, North	Yongbyon (GCR fuel)	Military	Operational	100–150
Pakistan	Chashma (HWR fuel)	Military	Starting up	50–100
	Nilore (HWR fuel)	Military	Operational	20–40
Russia[e]	Mayak RT-1, Ozersk	Civilian	Operational	400
	EDC, Zheleznogorsk	Civilian	Starting up	250
UK	Sellafield B205 (Magnox fuel)	Civilian	To be shut down in 2022	1 500
	Sellafield Thorp	Civilian	Shut down in 2018	(was 1 200)
USA	H-canyon, Savannah River Site	Civilian	Operational	15

HWR = heavy water reactor; GCR = gas cooled reactor.

[a] Design capacity refers to the highest amount of spent fuel the plant is designed to process and is measured in tonnes of heavy metal per year (tHM/yr), tHM being a measure of the amount of heavy metal—uranium in these cases—that is in the spent fuel. Actual throughput is often a small fraction of the design capacity. LWR spent fuel contains c. 1% plutonium, and heavy water- and graphite-moderated reactor fuels contain c. 0.4% plutonium.

[b] China is building a pilot reprocessing facility near Jinta, Gansu province, with a capacity of 200 tHM/yr, to be commissioned in 2025. A second reprocessing plant of the same capacity is planned for the same site.

[c] As part of the 2005 Indian–United States Civil Nuclear Cooperation Initiative, India has decided that none of its reprocessing plants will be opened for International Atomic Energy Agency safeguards inspections.

[d] In 2014 the Japan Atomic Energy Agency announced the planned closure of the head-end of its Tokai reprocessing plant, effectively ending further plutonium separation activity. In 2018 the Japanese Nuclear Regulation Authority approved a plan to decommission the plant.

[e] Russia continues to construct a 250 tHM/yr pilot experimental centre at Zheleznogorsk. A pilot reprocessing line with a capacity of 5 tHM/yr was launched in June 2018.

Sources: Kyodo News, 'Japan approves 70-year plan to scrap nuclear reprocessing plant', 13 June 2018; and RIA Novosti, [Rosatom is ready to start 'green' processing of spent nuclear fuel], 29 May 2018 (in Russian). Data on design capacity is based on International Atomic Energy Agency, Integrated Nuclear Fuel Cycle Information Systems (iNFCIS); and International Panel on Fissile Materials (IPFM), *Global Fissile Material Report 2015: Nuclear Weapon and Fissile Material Stockpiles and Production* (IPFM: Princeton, NJ, 2015).

Part III. Non-proliferation, arms control and disarmament, 2021

Chapter 11. Nuclear disarmament, arms control and non-proliferation

Chapter 12. Chemical, biological and health security threats

Chapter 13. Conventional arms control and regulation of new weapon technologies

Chapter 14. Dual-use and arms trade controls

11. Nuclear disarmament, arms control and non-proliferation

Overview

On balance, 2021 was another difficult year for nuclear arms control and non-proliferation efforts. There was some positive news at the start of the year, when the Russian Federation and the United States agreed to an extension of the 2010 New Strategic Arms Reduction Treaty (New START) for another five years (see section I). However, questions remained as to whether the five-year extension of New START will yield a replacement agreement before 2026, as well as the extent to which both old and new weapon systems would be covered in a follow-on treaty.

Despite these concerns, a joint statement in June 2021 following a meeting between US President Joe Biden and Russian President Vladimir Putin proclaimed that 'a nuclear war cannot be won and must never be fought'. This repeated a 1985 declaration from then leaders Ronald Reagan and Mikhail Gorbachev and preceded a similar joint statement by China and Russia. Following this declaration, a bilateral Russian–US strategic stability dialogue held in July and September came to play a central role in maintaining communication channels between the two countries.

While Russia and the USA agreed to discuss future arms control options as part of the dialogue, the bipartisan view in the USA is that, for nuclear arms control to be effective, China must be engaged. Following a November 2021 meeting between Chinese President Xi Jinping and US President Biden, the US national security advisor stated that China is willing to carry forward discussions on strategic stability. However, China's official statements have been more muted, reflecting some of the challenges to China's participation in bilateral talks with the USA, much less trilateral talks with the USA and Russia.

The breakdown of the short-lived bilateral nuclear diplomacy between the Democratic People's Republic of Korea (DPRK, or North Korea) and the USA since 2019 continued into 2021. Despite having announced in January 2020 that it would no longer observe its unilateral moratoriums on nuclear test explosions and test flights of long-range ballistic missiles that it had declared in 2018, North Korea conducted no such tests during 2021. However, it continued development of its shorter-range ballistic missiles (see chapter 10).

The previously slow unravelling of the 2015 Joint Comprehensive Plan of Action (JCPOA) on Iran's nuclear programme sped up in 2021 (see section II). US sanctions remained in place and Iran stepped up its nuclear activities, notably by increasing the enrichment of uranium up to 60 per cent of the isotope uranium-235. Iran also began restricting for the first time the inspections by the International Atomic Energy Agency (IAEA) authorized under the JCPOA. Despite the stated intent by both the Biden administration and the new Iranian government of President Ebrahim Raisi to restore the JCPOA, the USA and the remaining JCPOA parties failed to reach an agreement in the seven rounds of negotiations that were held in two phases in 2021. Whether the JCPOA could still be revived remained an open question at the end of 2021.

In the case of multilateral nuclear arms control, disarmament and non-proliferation efforts, the most notable development was the entry into force of the 2017 Treaty on the Prohibition of Nuclear Weapons (TPNW) on 22 January 2021. The United Nations secretary-general described the entry into force as 'an important step towards a world free of nuclear weapons', while civil society portrayed it as a 'critical milestone'. The TPNW is the first treaty to establish a comprehensive ban on nuclear weapons, including their development, deployment, possession, use and threat of use. This prohibition has brought to the fore the tension between nuclear disarmament and nuclear deterrence: while civil society and many non-nuclear weapon states welcomed the entry into force of the treaty, the nuclear weapon states and their allies viewed it as undermining the existing nuclear order based on the 1968 Non-Proliferation Treaty (NPT) and have not joined the treaty.

The 10th review conference of the NPT was postponed due to the Covid-19 pandemic for a second year. Initially planned for April–May 2020, the review conference is now scheduled to take place in August 2022. It would have marked the 50th anniversary of the NPT's entry into force and a quarter of a century since the treaty was indefinitely extended. However, the annual UN Conference on the Establishment of a Middle East Zone Free of Nuclear Weapons and other Weapons of Mass Destruction held its second annual session in November–December 2021 despite the pandemic, albeit without the participation of Israel.

Another milestone in 2021 was the 25th anniversary of the 1996 Comprehensive Nuclear-Test-Ban Treaty (CTBT)—the international treaty that would ban all nuclear test explosions in all environments. While it has not yet entered into force, over the past quarter of a century the CTBT has established an international norm against nuclear testing and has had a significant impact by, for example, slowing down the development of nuclear weapon capabilities and curbing significant radioactive contamination. Its unique international global monitoring network of stations and laboratories for treaty verification has strengthened the nuclear non-proliferation and disarmament regime and become an unmatched source of data and technical expertise.

TYTTI ERÄSTÖ, VITALY FEDCHENKO AND LORA SAALMAN

I. Bilateral and multilateral nuclear arms control involving China, Russia and the United States

LORA SAALMAN

The process of nuclear arms control underwent both treaty extension and reconfigured engagement in 2021. At the start of the year, Russia and the United States agreed to an extension of the 2010 Treaty on Measures for the Further Reduction and Limitation of Strategic Offensive Arms (New START) for another five years, during which they would observe the limits and provisions set out in the treaty.[1] They also agreed to further engage through a bilateral strategic stability dialogue, rather than traditional arms control negotiations. The US government also issued statements indicating China's willingness to participate in bilateral strategic stability talks, albeit at a different level from those with Russia. This section covers these developments and analyses the prospects for multilateral strategic stability dialogues.

Russia–USA New START

Extension of the treaty

In January 2021, Russia and the USA agreed to extend their obligations under New START for another five years, until 5 February 2026.[2] This extension maintains the central provisions and limits of the treaty, which entered into force on 5 February 2011. It restricts Russia and the USA each to 700 deployed intercontinental ballistic missiles (ICBMs), deployed submarine-launched ballistic missiles (SLBMs) and deployed heavy bombers equipped for nuclear armaments; 1550 nuclear warheads on deployed ICBMs, deployed SLBMs and deployed heavy bombers equipped for nuclear armaments; and 800 deployed and non-deployed ICBM launchers, SLBM launchers and heavy bombers equipped for nuclear armaments.[3] The two sides met these limits by 5 February 2018.

Since the entry of New START into force, the two parties have conducted 328 on-site inspections, exchanged more than 23 100 notifications, held 19 meetings of the Bilateral Consultative Commission (BCC) and issued 42 biannual data exchanges on strategic offensive arms subject to the treaty.[4]

---

[1] For a summary and other details of New START see annex A, section III, in this volume.

[2] Blinken, A. J., 'On the extension of the New START treaty with the Russian Federation', US Department of State, 3 Feb. 2021; and State Duma, Federal Assembly of the Russian Federation, 'The State Duma adopted the President's bill on ratification of the agreement on extension of the New START treaty', 27 Jan. 2021.

[3] New START (note 1).

[4] US Department of State, 'New START treaty', Updated 3 Mar. 2022.

Table 11.1. Russian and United States aggregate numbers of strategic offensive arms under New START, as of 5 February 2011 and 1 September 2021

Category	Treaty limit[a]	Russia			United States		
		Feb. 2011	Sep. 2021	Change	Feb. 2011	Sep. 2021	Change
Deployed ICBMs, SLBMs and heavy bombers	700	521	527	+6	882	665	–217
Warheads on deployed ICBMs, SLBMs and heavy bombers[b]	1 550	1 537	1 458	–79	1 800	1 389	–411
Warheads on deployed ICBMs, SLBMs and heavy bombers[b]	800	865	742	–123	1 124	800	–324

ICBM = intercontinental ballistic missile; SLBM = submarine-launched ballistic missile.

[a] The treaty entered into force on 5 February 2011. The treaty limits had to be reached by 5 February 2018.

[b] Each heavy bomber, whether equipped with cruise missiles or gravity bombs, is counted as carrying only one warhead, even though the aircraft can carry larger weapon payloads.

Source: US Department of State, Bureau of Arms Control, Verification and Compliance, 'New START treaty aggregate numbers of strategic offensive arms', Fact sheets, 1 June 2011 and 28 Sep. 2021.

Table 11.1 provides a comparison of Russian and US aggregate numbers of strategic offensive arms under New START as of February 2011 and September 2021. While Russian reductions may be numerically less than those of the USA, this resulted from Russia having fewer strategic forces than the USA when the treaty entered into force in 2011.[5]

Compliance concerns and future challenges

Despite the extent to which New START has limited Russian and US nuclear arsenals, the compliance process has had its challenges. The Covid-19 pandemic has complicated the verification process, with an April 2021 report suggesting that no on-site inspections had been conducted for a year and a statement in December 2021 by Russia's deputy foreign minister, Sergey Ryabkov, noting that the 'practice of mutual inspection visits will resume as the sanitary situation improves'.[6] This has resulted in greater reliance on the BCC meetings and notification exchanges to enforce the treaty. Further, as emphasized by the US State Department, 'Each Party has the flexibility to determine for itself the structure of its forces subject to the central limits'.[7]

This is noteworthy in light of both countries' nuclear modernization programmes. While some newer systems may be covered under New START, including Russia's Avangard hypersonic glide vehicle and the Sarmat, a heavy ICBM equipped with multiple independently targetable re-entry vehicles

---

[5] Kristensen, H., 'First New START data after extension shows compliance', Federation of American Scientists, 6 Apr. 2021.

[6] Russian Ministry of Foreign Affairs, 'Deputy Foreign Minister Sergey Ryabkov's interview with Izvestia', 13 Dec. 2021.

[7] US Department of State (note 4).

(MIRVs), adjustments to the nuclear forces of both countries have raised some compliance concerns. For example, in May 2021 Russia's Ministry of Foreign Affairs (MFA) stated that the number of US launchers and bombers exceeded the limit outlined by New START, claiming it was unable to confirm that 56 launchers and 41 heavy bombers were no longer nuclear-capable, nor could it verify the removal of four underground missile silos.[8] Russia has also criticized the US procedures used to convert B-52H heavy bombers and Trident II SLBM launchers, which the USA maintains are compliant with treaty provisions.[9]

Moreover, questions remained as to whether the five-year extension of New START will yield a replacement agreement before 2026, as well as the extent to which both old and new weapon systems would be covered in a follow-on treaty. US officials have cited concerns over Russia's 'novel nuclear weapons of intercontinental range' and '1,000 to 2,000 "non-strategic" nuclear weapons' that are not limited under New START.[10] Russian officials have also expressed misgivings about the lack of inclusion of US long-range precision-guided conventional systems under the treaty.[11] In terms of newer systems, some experts suggest that Russia's Poseidon uncrewed underwater vehicle and Burevestnik nuclear-powered ground-launched cruise missile would be 'unlikely to upset the strategic balance in the foreseeable future'.[12] However, others have cited the development of these novel weapon platforms as challenges that must be addressed by future arms control agreements.[13]

Russia–USA strategic stability dialogue

Communication channels

Given the uncertainty about whether an arms control agreement will follow New START, the Russia–USA strategic stability dialogue has come to play a central role in maintaining communication channels between the two

---

[8] Loughrin, C., 'Russia raises concerns over US compliance with nuclear threat', Organization for World Peace, 18 June 2021.

[9] US Department of State, Bureau of Arms Control, Verification and Compliance, *Adherence to and Compliance with Arms Control, Nonproliferation and Disarmament Agreements And Commitments*, Report, 15 Apr. 2021; and US Department of State (note 4).

[10] Jenkins, B., 'Nuclear arms control: A new era?', Remarks of the US Under Secretary, NATO Conference on WMD Arms Control, Disarmament, and Nonproliferation, Copenhagen, 6 Sep. 2021.

[11] Antonov, A. I., 'Long-range precision-guided conventional weapons: Implications for arms control and strategic stability', Joint meeting of members of the Centre russe d'études politiques and the Trialogue Club International, PIR Center.

[12] Kristensen (note 5).

[13] Acton, J. M., MacDonald, T. and Vaddi, P., *Reimagining Nuclear Arms Control: A Comprehensive Approach* (Carnegie Endowment for International Peace: Washington, DC, 2021); and Wright, T., 'New START extension and next steps for arms control', International Institute for Strategic Studies, 19 Feb. 2021.

countries.[14] This format was created in 2017 under the administration of US President Donald J. Trump and carried forward following a June 2021 meeting between US President Joe Biden and Russian President Vladimir Putin from which they released a joint statement proclaiming that 'a nuclear war cannot be won and must never be fought', echoing a 1985 declaration from then leaders Ronald Reagan and Mikhail Gorbachev and preceding a similar joint statement by China and Russia.[15] Convened in July and September 2021, with a session scheduled for January 2022, the Russia–USA strategic stability dialogue featured the formation of two inter-agency expert working groups on 'principles and objectives for future arms control' and on 'capabilities and actions with strategic effects'.[16] Among the overall aims of this dialogue, led by Russian Deputy Foreign Minister Ryabkov and US Deputy Secretary of State Wendy Sherman, are maintaining engagement between Russia and the USA and laying the groundwork for a follow-on treaty to New START. The broader coverage of these strategic stability talks, in comparison with traditional arms control negotiations, reflects some of the longer-term aims of both countries.

US statements and aims

The US under secretary of state for arms control and international security, Bonnie Jenkins, has stated the USA is determined to use the extension period to 'pursue a new dialogue with Russia on what nuclear arms control measures should follow' New START, with discussions to include 'new kinds of intercontinental-range nuclear delivery systems' and 'all nuclear warheads, including those which have not been limited previously, like so-called non-strategic nuclear weapons'.[17] The US national security advisor, Jake Sullivan, has designated this five-year period as 'the beginning of the story on what is going to have to be serious, sustained negotiations around a whole set of nuclear challenges and threats that fall outside of the New

---

[14] A US Department of State report defines crisis stability as 'the absence of incentives for either side to believe it would benefit from initiating war in a crisis', and defines arms race stability as 'the absence of any reason to believe that building additional or different strategic forces by either side would alter this situation'. International Security Advisory Board, 'The nature of multilateral strategic stability', 27 Apr. 2016, pp. 1–2.

[15] White House, 'US–Russia presidential joint statement on strategic stability', Briefing Room statement, 16 June 2021; White House, 'Joint Soviet–United States statement on the summit meeting in Geneva', Ronald Reagan Presidential Library and Museum, 21 Nov. 1985; and Russian Embassy in the UK, 'Joint Statement of the Russian Federation and the People's Republic of China on the Twentieth Anniversary of the Treaty of Good Neighbourliness and Friendly Cooperation between the Russian Federation and the People's Republic of China, 28 June 2021', 29 June 2021.

[16] White House, 'US–Russia presidential joint statement on strategic stability' (note 15); and US Department of State, Office of the Spokesperson, 'Joint Statement on the outcomes of the US–Russia strategic stability dialogue in Geneva on September 30', Press release, 30 Sep. 2021.

[17] Jenkins (note 10).

START agreement, as well as other emerging security challenges'.[18] US Secretary of State Anthony Blinken has also stressed that the USA should use this extension to pursue with Russia, 'in consultation with Congress and US allies and partners, arms control that addresses all of its nuclear weapons'.[19]

Russian statements and aims

Russia's ambassador to the USA, Anatoly Antonov, stated that the September 2021 meeting featured discussion of 'not only specific types and classes of nuclear and non-nuclear weapons capable of performing strategic missions, but also the actions of the Sides that have a "strategic effect"', highlighting 'hypersonic and other high-precision non-nuclear weapons, including unmanned systems, with an emphasis on those that can be used for strategic missions', as well as 'quantitative and qualitative aspects of the balance of power between the two countries and their allies in terms of both nuclear and conventional weapons'.[20] Ambassador Antonov also noted Russia's interest in the 'nexus between strategic offensive and strategic defensive arms' and creation of the 'next agreement to replace the New START treaty'.[21] However, he emphasized that, while Russia aims for legally binding agreements on arms control, it does not rule out other formats. Further, Deputy Foreign Minister Ryabkov has stated that enlarging the dialogue framework to include more nuclear powers would be inevitable, with a particular focus on the United Kingdom and France given the former's 'recent decision to increase the maximum level of nuclear warheads by 40 percent—to 260 units'.[22]

Prospects for a China–USA strategic stability dialogue

US engagement of China

From the Trump administration's efforts to establish trilateral talks among China, Russia and the USA to the Biden administration's interest in incorporating China in bilateral and potentially future multilateral strategic stability talks, there is continuity, even if the approach differs. Moreover, much like former US administrations, US official statements and documents continue to link China and Russia by pairing their advances.[23] Thus, while the

---

[18] Reif, K. and Bugos, S., 'US, Russia extend New START for five years', Arms Control Association, Mar. 2021.

[19] Blinken (note 2).

[20] TASS, 'Russian–US dialogue on strategic stability develops in right direction—envoy', 25 Oct. 2021.

[21] TASS (note 20).

[22] Radio Free Europe, 'Russia wants Britain, France to join wider nuclear talks with US', 29 July 2021. On the changes in the British nuclear weapons posture see chapter 10, section III, in this volume.

[23] US Department of Defense (DOD), *Nuclear Posture Review Report* (DOD: Washington, DC, Apr. 2010), p. iv; and Saalman, L., *China and the US Nuclear Posture Review*, Carnegie Papers (Carnegie Endowment for International Peace: Washington, DC, Feb. 2011), p. 3.

Biden administration did not make US–Russian negotiations on New START extension contingent on Chinese participation, Under Secretary Jenkins has similarly referred to how the USA 'will apply and tailor the lessons we've learned in the Russia–US arms control process when possible to US–[China] discussions'.[24]

As part of this, the USA has taken a bilateral focus to establishing a US–China strategic stability dialogue, with National Security Advisor Sullivan stating that President Xi Jinping and President Joe Biden, during a meeting on 15 November, had agreed that they 'would look to begin to carry forward discussions on strategic stability' under a format 'guided by the leaders and led by senior empowered teams on both sides that cut across security, technology and diplomacy'.[25] While both Sullivan and a US National Security Council spokesperson have stressed that these talks would not be at the same level or formality as those between Russia and the USA, their statements suggest that there may be some traction for the USA to engage with China to ensure that their competition 'does not veer into conflict'.[26]

Secretary Blinken has made it clear that the USA will 'pursue arms control to reduce the dangers from China's modern and growing nuclear arsenal'.[27] Under Secretary Jenkins has also emphasized that China remains at the forefront of US formulation of a 'new era' of arms control, stating that 'both Russia and China are engaged in extensive, destabilizing nuclear buildup that poses new threats to collective security and endangers the international rules-based order'.[28] In arguing for engagement with China, she has stressed a 'hope that China will come to see that arms control is in its security interests' and 'not a trap designed to weaken China's defenses'.[29] This statement again reveals a relatively bipartisan view in the USA that, for future arms control to be effective, China must be part of this 'mechanism to reduce risk and the chance of unnecessary arms races'.[30]

China's response

In contrast with statements from US officials, China's response has been more muted. On the extension of New START, China's MFA spokesperson expressed support, stating that the 'two sides should follow the international

[24] Gordon, M. R., 'Trump administration weighs extending New START nuclear treaty', *Wall Street Journal*, 23 June 2020; and Jenkins (note 10).

[25] Brookings Institution, 'Readout from the Biden–Xi virtual meeting: Discussion with National Security Advisor Jake Sullivan', Webinar transcript, 16 Nov. 2021, p. 11; and Sevastopulo, D. and Mitchell, T., 'US and China agree to hold talks on nuclear arsenals', *Financial Times*, 16 Nov. 2021.

[26] Sevastopulo and Mitchell (note 25); and 'US says it is not engaged in formal arms control talks with China', Reuters, 17 Nov. 2021.

[27] Blinken (note 2).

[28] Jenkins (note 10).

[29] Jenkins (note 10).

[30] Jenkins (note 10); and Rose, F., 'Bringing China into the fold on arms control and strategic stability issues', Brookings Institution, 25 Sep. 2019.

consensus, fulfil their special and primary responsibilities on nuclear disarmament, and further drastically and substantively reduce their nuclear stockpile in a verifiable, irreversible and legally-binding manner, so as to create the conditions for realizing general and complete nuclear disarmament'.[31] However, this statement was more circumspect on the subject of China's participation in strategic stability talks, emphasizing that 'China will continue to participate in discussions on issues related to strategic stability within such framework[s] as the cooperation mechanism of the five nuclear-weapon states, the Conference on Disarmament and the [United Nations General Assembly] First Committee'.[32] Nevertheless, the spokesperson also noted China's willingness 'to maintain communication with all parties on issues relating to nuclear arms control through bilateral channels', not entirely closing the door on the potential for bilateral strategic stability talks between China and the USA.[33]

This being said, the precise format of China's involvement in dialogues remains unclear. Following the November 2021 meeting between President Biden and President Xi, official statements in Chinese were oblique as to the nature of future talks between China and the USA, stating that 'The two sides should enhance their understanding of each other's intentions through open and frank dialogue, and ensure that the competition between the two countries is fair and healthy and does not turn into a conflict' without directly referencing the term 'strategic stability'.[34] While a working paper released by the Chinese MFA in December 2021 referred to a desire 'to prevent a nuclear arms race and maintain strategic stability' and used the term 'constructive dialogue' multiple times, it noted that the nuclear disarmament process 'cannot be divorced from the realities of international security' and criticized US pursuit of 'overwhelming military superiority', 'global missile defence systems' and the potential deployment of 'intermediate missiles in the Asia-Pacific region and Europe'.[35] While these statements did not rule out China's participation in bilateral or multilateral strategic stability dialogues—instead reinforcing the need for such engagement—they still reflected some of China's ambivalence and the issues that would need to be addressed in such talks.

---

[31] Chinese State Council Information Office, 'China welcomes extension of New START nuclear treaty, responds to US accusation', Xinhua, Press release, 7 Feb. 2021.
[32] Chinese State Council Information Office (note 31).
[33] Chinese State Council Information Office (note 31).
[34] Chinese Embassy in the USA, [Xi Jinping and US President Biden hold a video meeting], 23 Nov. 2021 (in Chinese).
[35] Chinese Ministry of Foreign Affairs, [Working paper submitted by the Chinese delegation on nuclear disarmament], 28 Dec. 2021 (in Chinese).

Track-1 and track-1.5 precedents

In terms of format, there is a history of both track-1 and track-1.5 strategic dialogues and nuclear dialogues between China and the USA. At the track-1 level, the 'US–China Strategic and Economic Dialogue' was established in 2009 by US President Barack Obama and Chinese President Hu Jintao.[36] This dialogue expanded the coverage of previous high-level China–USA dialogues that focused on economic affairs to include strategic issues between both countries. US Secretary of State John Kerry and Chinese State Councillor Yang Jiechi co-chaired the strategic track, which dealt with such issues as international security, non-proliferation and counterterrorism, regional security and stability, climate change, energy and environment, military-to-military relations, among others.[37] However, while the inclusion of non-proliferation resulted in a pledge 'to work collaboratively to strengthen global non-proliferation and arms control regimes', as well as discussion of the review conference of the 1968 Treaty on the Non Proliferation of Nuclear Weapons (NPT), the Conference on Disarmament and the Global Nuclear Security Summit, there was no mention of bilateral nuclear forces and strategic stability.[38] Moreover, by 2017 the dialogue had been renamed as the 'US–China Comprehensive Economic Dialogue', reorienting its focus away from strategic relations and again towards economic affairs.[39]

At the track-1.5 level, the biannual 'China–US Strategic Nuclear Dynamics' dialogue was initiated in 2004 and assembled Chinese and US academics, think-tank experts, retired officials and military leaders, as well as government officials and active military personnel attending in their private capacity.[40] This dialogue featured such issues as strategic stability, mutual vulnerability, no first use, ballistic missile defence, extended deterrence, escalation and crisis management, arms control, transparency, non-proliferation and nuclear security. However, by 2019 US interlocutors had decided to suspend the dialogue for several reasons. First, there was a determination that Chinese interlocutors would not conduct a transition

---

[36] Shear, D. B., 'US–China relations: Maximizing the effectiveness of the strategic and economic dialogue', US Department of State, 10 Sep. 2009; and National Committee on American Foreign Policy, 'New report: US–China strategic and economic dialogues', 13 Sep. 2021.

[37] Shear (note 36).

[38] Shear (note 36).

[39] Shear (note 36).

[40] These talks were supported by the US Department of Defense and US Department of State, and funded almost entirely by the US Defense Threat Reduction Agency. The Center for Strategic and International Studies ran the talks during the first few years, followed by the Pacific Forum in collaboration with the Naval Postgraduate School and in partnership with the China Foundation for International and Strategic Studies and the China Arms Control and Disarmament Association, which are Chinese think tanks affiliated with, respectively, the People's Liberation Army and the Chinese Ministry of Foreign Affairs. Santoro, D. and Gromoll, R., 'On the value of nuclear dialogue with China: A review and assessment of the track 1.5 "China–US Strategic Nuclear Dynamics Dialogue"', *Issues and Insights*, vol. 20, no. 1 (Nov. 2020).

from track-1.5 to track-1 dialogue, despite repeated US requests.[41] Second, Chinese interlocutors were unable to hold the dialogue in China in 2018 and 2019, and Chinese delegates demonstrated a marked decrease in seniority at sessions held abroad.[42]

These experiences at both the track-1 and track-1.5 levels illustrate some of the challenges that are likely to arise as China and the USA discuss the potential of holding future bilateral strategic stability dialogues. The expectations of US interlocutors already appear to be tempered by the understanding that dialogues with China would be less formal than those with Russia, given that the latter talks with Russia 'are mature and have history'.[43] While echoing this sentiment, Under Secretary Jenkins has still emphasized that the lessons learned from the Russia–US arms control process will be factored into any dialogues with China.[44] Further, the work and meetings being conducted at the track-2 level—in the relative absence of talks at track-1 and track-1.5 levels—indicates that there is an extensive array of topics that could be addressed during a China–USA strategic stability dialogue, including but not limited to nuclear weapons, missile defence, weaponization of space, cybersecurity, artificial intelligence, dual-capable systems, precision-guided conventional strike advances and their impact on strategic stability.[45]

Prospects for multilateral strategic stability dialogues

Interest in multilateral engagement

Beyond bilateral talks, Chinese, Russian and US reports and statements indicate that there may be interest in the longer term in engagement on multilateral strategic stability. The International Security Advisory Board of the US Department of State issued a report in April 2017 that sought to extend 'strategic stability beyond the US–Russia Cold War construct to include nuclear weapons–possessing states', with the aim of reducing the deliberate or unintended escalation that can lead to nuclear war.[46] The report defined 'multi-national strategic stability [as] largely the sum of stability between

---

[41] Cossa, R., Glosserman, B. and Santoro, D., 'US–China strategic nuclear relations: Time to move to track-1 dialogue', *Issues and Insights*, vol. 15, no. 7 (9–10 Feb. 2015); and Santoro and Gromoll (note 40).

[42] Santoro and Gromoll (note 40).

[43] 'US says it is not engaged in formal arms control talks with China' (note 26).

[44] Jenkins (note 10).

[45] National Academies of Sciences, Engineering and Medicine, 'CISAC security dialogues', [n.d.]; Santoro, D., 'What should Washington expect from US–China strategic stability talks?', Pacific Forum PacNet no. 53, 17 Nov. 2021; Centre for Humanitarian Dialogue, 'Code of conduct on artificial intelligence in military systems', 18 Aug. 2021; Kim, P. (ed.), *Enhancing US–China Strategic Stability in an Era of Strategic Competition: US and Chinese Perspectives* (United States Institute of Peace: Washington, DC, 26 Apr. 2021); and Levite, A. E. et al., 'China–US cyber–nuclear C3 stability', Carnegie Endowment for International Peace and Shanghai Institutes for International Studies, Working paper, Apr. 2021.

[46] International Security Advisory Board (note 14), p. 1.

many pairs of nuclear weapons states', 'using the Cold War definition, with the understanding that in the modern world all nuclear weapons should be regarded as strategic'.[47] In doing so, it provided a draft list of characteristics and practices that can enhance multilateral strategic stability under the headings of policy and doctrine, force structure and posture, safety and security.

Two years later, Russia's Higher School of Economics University published a report—with the support of the Russian MFA and State Duma Committee on International Affairs—on strengthening multilateral strategic stability, mirroring the US official report in some content.[48] The report offered its own definition of multilateral strategic stability as 'a state of relations between nuclear powers which enables them to prevent any military clash between them, including intentional and unintentional ones, because any such clash may develop into a global nuclear war', while listing factors that strengthen strategic stability.[49] Much as in the US report, the Russian report focused on such topics as channels of military-to-military communication, Russia–USA and China–USA dialogues on nuclear doctrines and military strategies, nuclear multipolarity shaped by dyadic interactions, escalation caused by nuclear and non-nuclear weapons, and expansion of China's nuclear arsenal. Nevertheless, on the primary driver of strategic shifts, this Russian report also reflected views held in China on US threats to strategic stability, including the latter's development of ballistic missile defence and potential plans to deploy intermediate-range ballistic missile systems in the region.[50]

When these two reports are juxtaposed with a statement in June 2021 by China's state councillor and foreign minister, Wang Yi, entitled 'Uphold multilateralism to promote common security', it becomes evident that all three are in support of multilateral processes.[51] In the Chinese case, the emphasis is on multilateral 'comprehensive, cooperative and sustainable security' that advances 'international arms control, disarmament and nonproliferation processes'.[52] Given that the same sentence in Foreign Minister Wang's statement advocates for a multilateral strengthening of cooperative strategic risk reduction and deepening of strategic dialogue, this indicates China's potential openness to multilateral engagement on strategic stability on such topics as 'observing international arms control treaties,

[47] International Security Advisory Board (note 14), p. 2.

[48] Karaganov, S. and Suslov, D., 'The new understanding and ways to strengthen multilateral strategic stability', Higher School of Economics University, Sep. 2019; and International Security Advisory Board (note 14).

[49] Karaganov and Suslov (note 48), p. 34.

[50] Karaganov and Suslov (note 48), p. 7.

[51] Wang, Y., 'Uphold multilateralism to promote common security', Chinese Ministry of Foreign Affairs, 11 June 2021.

[52] Wang (note 51).

resolving non-proliferation issues through negotiations and improving global security governance'.[53]

Multilateral formats and discussions

Even if not under the label of strategic stability dialogues, multilateral engagement has already been underway. Reflecting the continuation of a process begun in 2007, the five permanent members of the United Nations Security Council (P5)—China, France, Russia, the UK and the USA—released a 'Joint Communique of the Non-Proliferation Treaty P5 Nations' in December 2021 on their joint obligations and aims under the NPT.[54] While the statement emphasized the importance of 'strategic stability', it was primarily as a by-product of their reaffirmations of (*a*) the importance of negotiations on nuclear disarmament; (*b*) the centrality of the NPT and the 1996 Comprehensive Nuclear-Test-Ban Treaty (CTBT); (*c*) updates on their respective nuclear doctrines and policies; (*d*) collaboration to reduce the risk of nuclear conflict; (*e*) review of the P5 glossary of key nuclear terms; (*f*) commitment to the objectives of nuclear weapon-free zones, (*g*) ongoing negotiation of the proposed fissile material cut-off treaty (FMCT) and (*h*) the benefits of the peaceful uses of nuclear energy.[55] Further, while efforts have been made to expand this grouping beyond NPT parties under the 'P5 Plus' format, there have been analyses that suggest this has exacerbated stalemates at such forums as the Conference on Disarmament on such initiatives as the FMCT.[56]

The intersection of these various formulations of multilateralism and strategic stability suggests that there is a foundation for future strategic stability talks that extend beyond Russia and the USA. However, the Russian and US reports still have a tendency to examine these dynamics as pairs or dyads, while US efforts to engage China in trilateral arms control negotiations have been met with resistance from the latter. This indicates that bilateral strategic stability dialogues will probably need to precede any multilateral strategic stability talks.[57] Moreover, the format and membership of any expanded grouping will have to be well thought out to minimize the chance of eliciting more stalemates or tensions, as encountered with the P5 Plus process.

---

[53] Wang (note 51).

[54] French Ministry of Europe and Foreign Affairs, 'P5 conference joint communiqué', 2–3 Dec. 2021.

[55] For a summary and other details of the CTBT and the NPT see annex A, section I, in this volume.

[56] European Leadership Network, 'The P-5 Plus talks and prospects for progress on a fissile material cut-off treaty', 9 Jan. 2013.

[57] Logan, D. C., 'Trilateral arms control: A realistic assessment of Chinese participation', 9 Aug. 2021, Stimson Center; Standish, R., 'The art of the trilateral deal? US nuke agreement with Russia, China proving difficult', Radio Free Europe, 28 June 2020; Fan, J., 'Trilateral negotiations on arms control? Not time yet', *China–US Focus*, 13 Sep. 2019; and Kroenig, M. and Massa, M. J., 'Toward trilateral arms control: Options for bringing China into the fold', Atlantic Council Issue Brief, 4 Feb. 2021.

Conclusions

While some scepticism remains as to whether the Russia–USA strategic stability dialogue will generate a follow-on agreement to New START by 2026, this five-year window provides an opportunity for the two countries to maintain official communication channels. The dialogue also offers a potential template for future engagement of China in bilateral official talks with the USA, even if at a different level. If a China–USA strategic stability dialogue occurs alongside that between Russia and the USA, these two sets of bilateral talks may further the chances of an eventual multilateral strategic stability dialogue. This future expansion of strategic stability dialogues could, much like the P5 Plus, also engage other countries that possess nuclear weapons, including France, India, Pakistan and the UK. However, for this to occur, bilateral strategic stability dialogues between Russia and the USA must endure and those between China and the USA must begin.

II. The Joint Comprehensive Plan of Action on Iran's nuclear programme

TYTTI ERÄSTÖ

The previously slow unravelling of the 2015 Joint Comprehensive Plan of Action (JCPOA) sped up in 2021, as Iran significantly increased its uranium-enrichment activities and curtailed the ability of the International Atomic Energy Agency (IAEA) to monitor its nuclear programme. In parallel, a new administration in the United States meant that a fresh start could be made on negotiations to revive the agreement.

The JCPOA had been concluded by Iran on one side and, on the other, the European Union (EU) and three European states—France, Germany and the United Kingdom (the E3)—and China, Russia and the USA.[1] The agreement appeared to end the crisis over Iran's nuclear programme that had begun in the early 2000s. The JCPOA—which was endorsed by United Nations Security Council Resolution 2231—was based on a compromise whereby Iran accepted limits on and strict monitoring of its proliferation-sensitive activities in return for the lifting of international sanctions on its nuclear programme. The IAEA was charged with monitoring and verifying the implementation of Iran's commitments under the JCPOA, alongside its normal verification activities under the Comprehensive Safeguards Agreement (CSA) with Iran.

The JCPOA was subsequently weakened by the decision of US President Donald J. Trump to withdraw the USA from the agreement in May 2018. In addition to reimposing the unilateral sanctions that had been lifted as part of the nuclear agreement, the USA added various new sanctions targeting the Iranian economy as well as civil nuclear cooperation under the JCPOA. Most of these US sanctions were secondary sanctions aimed at third parties. As such, they also undermined the ability of other JCPOA participants to fulfil their commitments under the agreement—notably because foreign banks avoid engaging with Iran out of fear of penalties from the US Department of the Treasury.[2]

---

[1] Joint Comprehensive Plan of Action (JCPOA), 14 July 2015, reproduced as annex A of UN Security Council Resolution 2231, 20 July 2015. On the agreement and its implementation see Rauf, T., 'Resolving concerns about Iran's nuclear programme', *SIPRI Yearbook 2016*; Rauf, T., 'Implementation of the Joint Comprehensive Plan of Action in Iran', *SIPRI Yearbook 2017*; Erästö, T., 'Implementation of the Joint Comprehensive Plan of Action in Iran', *SIPRI Yearbook 2018*; Erästö, T., 'Implementation of the Joint Comprehensive Plan of Action', *SIPRI Yearbook 2019*; Erästö, T., 'Implementation of the Joint Comprehensive Plan of Action', *SIPRI Yearbook 2020*; and Erästö, T., 'Implementation of the Joint Comprehensive Plan of Action on Iran's nuclear programme', *SIPRI Yearbook 2021*.

[2] See Erästö, *SIPRI Yearbook 2021* (note 1); and Batmanghelidj, E. et al., *Using 'Technical Guarantees' to Restore and Sustain the Iran Nuclear Deal*, Global Security Policy Brief (European Leadership Network/Bourse & Bazaar Foundation: London, Nov. 2021).

In May 2019 Iran responded by starting to gradually reduce adherence to its commitments under the agreement, and by 5 January 2020 it had ceased to observe all of its key operational limits.[3] Despite the stated intent by both the US administration of President Joe Biden and the new Iranian government of President Ebrahim Raisi to restore the JCPOA, the USA and the remaining JCPOA parties failed to reach an agreement in the seven rounds of negotiations that were held in two phases in 2021. At the same time, the US sanctions remained in place and Iran stepped up its nuclear activities, notably by increasing the enrichment of uranium up to 60 per cent of the isotope uranium-235. In addition, in 2021 Iran began restricting for the first time the IAEA inspections authorized under the JCPOA.

This section reviews developments related to the JCPOA. It focuses on Iran's nuclear-related commitments, while recognizing that the lifting of US sanctions forms an equally important part of the JCPOA. In addition, it describes unresolved issues related to Iran's past nuclear activities that the IAEA investigated under the terms of its CSA with Iran.

Key developments in Iran's nuclear programme relevant to the JCPOA

The JCPOA was designed to limit proliferation-sensitive nuclear activities whereby Iran could obtain weapon-grade fissile materials—highly enriched uranium (HEU) and plutonium. Excess stocks of enriched uranium and heavy water, as well as spent nuclear fuel, were to be shipped abroad under the agreement.[4] Iran ceased to observe these and other operational limits set out in the JCPOA in May 2019.[5] In 2021 Iran took two further significant steps in contravention to the agreement: it began to restrict the IAEA's additional verification activities under the JCPOA and increased the level of uranium enrichment, first up to 20 per cent in January, just below the threshold for classification as HEU, and then, in April, to 60 per cent—well over the threshold.[6] For nuclear explosive use, uranium would need to be enriched to 90 per cent.

---

[3] See Erästö, *SIPRI Yearbook 2020* (note 1).

[4] JCPOA (note 1). Heavy water is used in certain types of nuclear power plant to produce plutonium from natural uranium. Spent nuclear fuel is nuclear fuel that has been used and removed from a power reactor, and which still contains fissile materials that can be 'separated' from waste through reprocessing.

[5] Erästö, *SIPRI Yearbook 2020* (note 1); and Erästö, *SIPRI Yearbook 2021* (note 1).

[6] IAEA, Board of Governors, 'Verification and monitoring in the Islamic Republic of Iran in light of United Nations resolution 2231 (2015)', Report by the Director General, GOV/INF/2021/2, 4 Jan 2021; and IAEA, Board of Governors, 'Verification and monitoring in the Islamic Republic of Iran in light of United Nations resolution 2231 (2015)', Report by the Director General, GOV/INF/2021/26, 17 Apr. 2021.

'Continuity of knowledge' without the Additional Protocol

As part of the JCPOA, Iran agreed to provisionally implement its Additional Protocol to its CSA, which allowed the IAEA to conduct inspections in Iran outside the declared nuclear sites.[7] The JCPOA also permitted the IAEA to request access to non-nuclear sites beyond the normal scope of the Additional Protocol.[8]

In mid February 2021 Iran informed the IAEA that, from 23 February, it would stop the implementation of voluntary transparency measures, including the Additional Protocol.[9] The decision was based on a law approved by the Iranian Parliament in December 2020 that obliged the government to deny inspections beyond those required by the CSA 'if the other signatories to the JCPOA . . . fail to fully deliver on their commitments toward Iran and banking relations are not normalized and obstacles to exports and Iran's sale of oil products are not fully removed and [foreign exchange] proceeds from sales are not immediately and fully returned to the country'.[10]

On 21 February Iran and the IAEA reached a technical understanding that allowed exceptional verification and monitoring activities to continue for three months.[11] Specifically, Iran allowed the IAEA monitoring equipment at Iranian nuclear facilities to continue collecting and storing information, as agreed under the JCPOA, but the agency would not be allowed access to the recordings until a diplomatic solution on the restoration of the nuclear agreement was found.[12]

In the absence of a diplomatic breakthrough, in May the technical understanding was extended to 24 June.[13] After this, the status of the agreement remained uncertain for over two months. As a result, the IAEA voiced concerns about 'continuity of knowledge'. Not only would this continuity be necessary for the future resumption of verification and monitoring under a restored JCPOA, but it also required that the agency be able to service the

---

[7] Davenport, K., 'IAEA safeguards agreements at a glance', Arms Control Association, June 2020.

[8] Davenport, K. and Masterson, J., 'Explainer: Problems for IAEA monitoring in Iran', Iran Primer, United States Institute of Peace, 29 Nov. 2021.

[9] IAEA, Board of Governors, 'Verification and monitoring in the Islamic Republic of Iran in light of United Nations resolution 2231 (2015)', Report by the Director General, GOV/INF/2021/13, 16 Feb. 2021.

[10] Strategic Action Law for the Lifting of Sanctions and Protection of the Interests of the Iranian People, Iranian law approved 2 Dec. 2020, English translation by National Iranian American Council, 3 Dec. 2020.

[11] IAEA, Board of Governors, 'Verification and monitoring in the Islamic Republic of Iran in light of United Nations resolution 2231 (2015)', Report by the Director General, GOV/2021/10, 23 Feb. 2021; and Joint statement by the Vice-President of the Islamic Republic of Iran and Head of the AEOI and the Director General of the IAEA, IAEA, 21 Feb. 2021.

[12] Davenport, K., 'Iran, IAEA reach monitoring agreement', *Arms Control Today*, vol. 51, no. 2 (Mar. 2021).

[13] IAEA, Board of Governors, 'Verification and monitoring in the Islamic Republic of Iran in light of United Nations resolution 2231 (2015)', Report by the Director General, GOV/INF/2021/32, 25 June 2021.

monitoring and surveillance equipment and replace the data storage media every three months.[14]

On 12 September 2021 Iran and the IAEA reached a new agreement permitting IAEA inspectors to service the monitoring and surveillance equipment and to replace the storage media.[15] The agreement was implemented on 20–22 September at all Iranian facilities, except for the TESA Karaj centrifuge component manufacturing workshop near Tehran. Iran had removed four IAEA cameras at the facility after a 23 June attack by an uncrewed aerial vehicle (UAV), which it argued was conducted by Israel with the help of the IAEA cameras—a claim that the IAEA denied.[16] On 15 December Iran and the IAEA finally agreed that new cameras could be installed at Karaj.[17]

Despite these temporary agreements, the IAEA concluded in November that its 'verification and monitoring activities have been seriously undermined' because of Iran's 23 February decision.[18] Moreover, while the technical understanding had 'facilitated the maintenance of continuity of knowledge', its repeated prolongation was 'becoming a significant challenge to the Agency's ability to restore this continuity of knowledge'.[19] Nevertheless, remote monitoring at all Iranian enrichment facilities, as well as normal inspections under Iran's CSA, continued uninterrupted throughout 2021, ensuring the non-diversion of fissile material from civilian to military use.[20]

Activities related to enrichment and fuel

The JCPOA imposed a limit of 3.67 per cent on uranium enrichment—a limit that Iran had already breached since 2019 by enriching up to 5 per cent. On 4 January it took a step further by beginning to enrich uranium up to 20 per cent at the Fordow Fuel Enrichment Plant (FFEP), Qom province.[21] In addition to being a political move prescribed by the law passed in December, enrichment up to 20 per cent was part of a pre-existing Iranian plan

---

[14] IAEA, Board of Governors, 'Verification and monitoring in the Islamic Republic of Iran in light of United Nations resolution 2231 (2015)', Report by the Director General, GOV/2021/39, 7 Sep. 2021.

[15] IAEA, GOV/INF/2021/32 (note 13); and IAEA, Board of Governors, 'Verification and monitoring in the Islamic Republic of Iran in light of United Nations resolution 2231 (2015)', Report by the Director General, GOV/INF/2021/42, 12 Sep. 2021.

[16] IAEA, GOV/2021/39 (note 14); IAEA, Board of Governors, 'Verification and monitoring in the Islamic Republic of Iran in light of United Nations resolution 2231 (2015)', Report by the Director General, GOV/INF/2021/43, 26 Sep. 2021; IAEA, Board of Governors, 'Verification and monitoring in the Islamic Republic of Iran in light of United Nations resolution 2231 (2015)', Report by the Director General, GOV/2021/51, 17 Nov. 2021; and Middle East Monitor, 'Iran: Attack on Karaj plant "enabled" by hacking of IAEA's cameras', 20 Dec. 2021.

[17] IAEA, 'IAEA and Iran reach agreement on replacing surveillance cameras at Karaj facility', Press Release no. 82/2021, 15 Dec. 2021.

[18] IAEA, GOV/2021/51 (note 16), para. 52.

[19] IAEA, GOV/2021/51 (note 16), para. 53.

[20] Al Jazeera, 'Rafael Grossi: Does the UN's nuclear watchdog trust Iran?', Talk to Al Jazeera, 11 Dec. 2021.

[21] IAEA, GOV/INF/2021/2 (note 6).

to produce advanced nuclear fuel for the Tehran Research Reactor (TRR), which Iran had informed the IAEA about in January 2019.[22] According to the details of the plan that Iran supplied to the IAEA in December 2020, it would produce uranium metal at the Fuel Plate Fabrication Plant (FPFP), Isfahan, as part of a research and development (R&D) process that used uranium hexa-fluoride (UF_6) to produce uranium silicide (U_3Si_2).[23] In November 2021 the IAEA verified that Iran had produced two fuel plates using uranium silicide containing 20 per cent enriched uranium.[24] As some observers argued, the conversion of uranium to silicide reactor fuel reduced the proliferation risks of UF_6 enriched to 20 per cent; in the form of silicide—and especially in the form of uranium silicide plates, which were used by Iran in the conversion process—the material could no longer be enriched further.[25] Others, however, warned that Iran could use the equipment and experience gained in such a conversion to produce HEU for use in nuclear explosives in the future.[26] Most of Iran's 20 per cent enriched uranium stockpile nevertheless remained in the form of UF_6.[27]

On 17 April Iran increased the enrichment level of uranium processed at the Pilot Fuel Enrichment Plant (PFEP) at Natanz, Isfahan province, to 60 per cent.[28] Unlike the uranium fuel-production R&D activities described above, the decision to enrich uranium to 60 per cent lacked a civilian ration-ale. Although Iran had previously indicated that it might produce HEU to be used in nuclear-powered submarines, the circumstances suggested that the move mainly served the purpose of political messaging.[29] More specifically, Iran described the decision to enrich to 60 per cent as a response to a cyber-attack on the Natanz facility on 11 April.[30] Like previous cyberattacks against

---

[22] Strategic Action Law for the Lifting of Sanctions and Protection of the Interests of the Iranian People (note 10); and IAEA, Board of Governors, 'Verification and monitoring in the Islamic Republic of Iran in light of United Nations resolution 2231 (2015)', Report by the Director General, GOV/INF/2021/3, 13 Jan. 2021.

[23] IAEA, GOV/INF/2021/3 (note 22). On 28 June 2021 Iran informed the IAEA about another 4-stage process to produce uranium silicide, which was slightly different from the previously described 3-stage process. IAEA, Board of Governors, 'Verification and monitoring in the Islamic Republic of Iran in light of United Nations resolution 2231 (2015)', Report by the Director General, GOV/INF/2021/36, 6 July 2021.

[24] IAEA, GOV/2021/51 (note 16).

[25] Kelley, R., 'Iran is actually reducing its weapons-usable uranium inventory', IranSource, Atlantic Council, 28 Jan. 2021.

[26] Albright D. and Burkhard, S., 'Iran's recent, irreversible nuclear advances', Institute for Science and International Security, 22 Sep. 2021.

[27] IAEA, GOV/2021/51 (note 16), paras 44, 46.

[28] IAEA, GOV/INF/2021/26 (note 6).

[29] Kelley, R. E., 'Why is Iran producing 60 per cent-enriched uranium?', SIPRI, 29 Apr. 2021; and Islamic Consultative Assembly New Agency, 'Leader: Iran to increase uranium enrichment to 60% if needed', 22 Feb. 2021.

[30] 'Iran says key Natanz nuclear facility hit by "sabotage"', BBC News, 12 Apr. 2021; and 'Iran says 60% enrichment meant to show nuclear prowess, is reversible', Reuters, 20 Apr. 2021.

Natanz, this one was reportedly conducted by Israel.[31] Although the outgoing Iranian president, Hassan Rouhani, said in July that Iran had the technical capacity to enrich even to 90 per cent, in December the head of the Atomic Energy Organization of Iran (AEOI) stressed that the country would not go beyond 60 per cent even if the nuclear talks were to fail.[32]

As in 2019 and 2020, throughout 2021 Iran also continued uranium enrichment up to 5 per cent and breached the JCPOA provisions that restricted it to using only IR-1 centrifuges to increase its stock of enriched uranium.[33] For example, Iran used both IR-4 and IR-6 centrifuges for HEU production.[34]

Centrifuge manufacturing, mechanical testing and component inventory

The JCPOA regulates the manufacturing of uranium enrichment centrifuges by Iran. It notes that in 2025 Iran will start phasing out the old IR-1 centrifuges and begin using more advanced centrifuges. To prepare for that shift, the JCPOA allows limited R&D on certain advanced centrifuge types within certain limits—notably on the condition that such activities would not lead to the accumulation of enriched uranium. Moreover, the agreement allows Iran to commence manufacturing the advanced IR-6 and IR-8 centrifuges in 2023. It was also agreed that Iran would replace any operating IR-1 centrifuges that failed or got damaged by retrieving IR-1 centrifuges from storage, rather than produce new ones. Iran could only produce more IR-1 centrifuges when the number of IR-1 centrifuges in storage decreased to 500.[35]

In February 2021 the IAEA reported that the centrifuge components declared by Iran had been used for activities that went 'beyond those specified in the JCPOA', such as R&D activities on advanced centrifuges that led to the accumulation of enriched uranium.[36] Iran was also manufacturing centrifuge rotor tubes 'using carbon fibre that was not subject to continuous Agency containment and surveillance measures'.[37] Carbon fibre is used for advanced centrifuge types that spin at higher speeds than the IR-1 model, the rotor tubes of which are made of aluminium.[38]

For the remainder of the year, the verification related to centrifuge manufacturing was hampered by Iran's decision to end voluntary transparency measures. The IAEA reported in May that since 23 February it had had no

---

[31] 'Israel's alleged Natanz strike "as complex as Stuxnet", a major blow to Iran', *Times of Israel*, 10 July 2020.

[32] 'Rouhani: Iran able to produce 90%-enriched uranium', Fars News Agency, 14 July 2021; and 'Iran not to enrich uranium above 60% purity level: Nuclear chief', Tasnim News, 25 Dec. 2021.

[33] JCPOA (note 1); Erästö, *SIPRI Yearbook 2020* (note 1); and Erästö, *SIPRI Yearbook 2021* (note 1).

[34] IAEA, GOV/INF/2021/26 (note 6).

[35] JCPOA (note 1).

[36] IAEA, GOV/2021/10 (note 11), para. 37.

[37] IAEA, GOV/2021/10 (note 11), para. 38.

[38] Voûte, F. and Lincy, V., *Beyond the IR-1: Iran's Advanced Centrifuges and Their Lasting Implications*, Iran Watch Report (Wisconsin Project on Nuclear Arms Control: Washington, DC, Nov. 2021).

access to the data and recordings of the surveillance equipment monitoring Iran's mechanical testing of centrifuges.[39] Since that date, Iran also 'no longer provided declarations to the Agency of its production and inventory of centrifuge rotor tubes and bellows, nor . . . permitted the Agency to verify the items in the inventory'.[40] As in other facilities, the IAEA surveillance equipment nevertheless remained in place to continuously monitor Iran's centrifuge manufacturing-related activities. The only exception, as noted above, was a centrifuge component-manufacturing workshop at Karaj that does not handle nuclear materials.[41]

Enriched uranium stockpile

After 23 February, the IAEA reported that it was no longer able to verify Iran's total stockpile of enriched uranium—which by that time had exceeded the JCPOA limit of 300 kilogrammes by almost 10 times.[42] Nonetheless, the IAEA could still measure the enriched uranium product from enrichment cascades, even if it was no longer able to monitor material in process in the cascades, as it had done under JCPOA.[43] Together with Iran's declarations, this enabled the agency to provide precise estimates of the stockpile.

Thus, the IAEA estimated that Iran's enriched uranium stockpile first increased to 3241 kg in May, but then decreased to 2441 kg in September and reached 2490 kg in November.[44] The decrease was due to the consumption of the stockpile of low-enriched uranium as feed material for 20 and 60 per cent enrichment.[45]

Activities related to heavy water and reprocessing

Under the JCPOA, Iran agreed to redesign the heavy water reactor at Arak, Markazi province, in order to minimize the amount of plutonium in the spent nuclear fuel produced there. Iran also agreed to keep its stock of heavy water below 130 tonnes (reduced to 90 tonnes after commissioning of the Arak reactor) and not to reprocess spent fuel from any of its reactors, with an exception for producing medical and industrial radioisotopes.[46]

As in previous years, in 2021 the IAEA reported that Iran had neither pursued the construction of the Arak reactor based on its original design nor carried out reprocessing-related activities.[47] As on some previous occasions,

---

[39] IAEA, Board of Governors, 'Verification and monitoring in the Islamic Republic of Iran in light of United Nations resolution 2231 (2015)', Report by the Director General, GOV/2021/28, 31 May 2021.

[40] IAEA, GOV/2021/28 (note 39), para. 34.

[41] IAEA, GOV/INF/2021/43 (note 16).

[42] IAEA, GOV/2021/10 (note 11).

[43] IAEA, GOV/2021/51 (note 16).

[44] IAEA, GOV/2021/28 (note 39); IAEA, GOV/2021/39 (note 14); and IAEA, GOV/2021/51 (note 16).

[45] IAEA, GOV/2021/39 (note 14).

[46] JCPOA (note 1), annex I.

[47] See e.g. IAEA, GOV/2021/51 (note 16).

a February IAEA report noted that Iran had slightly exceeded the heavy water stock limit, with an inventory of 131 tonnes.[48] However, following Iran's decision in February to limit transparency measures under the JCPOA, it no longer informed the IAEA about its heavy water inventory or production, nor did it allow the agency to monitor heavy water stocks or the amount of heavy water produced at the Heavy Water Production Plant (HWPP) at Arak. The IAEA's monitoring equipment nevertheless remained operational at the HWPP.[49]

Outstanding issues under Iran's Comprehensive Safeguards Agreement

In February 2019 the IAEA detected natural uranium particles at a site that Iran had not declared to the IAEA—named Location 1 in IAEA reports.[50] The agency subsequently requested clarification on four Iranian locations that it suspected of having hosted nuclear material and activities prior to 2003.[51] These suspicions are apparently based on evidence presented to the IAEA by Israel, seized in 2018 from what the Israeli prime minister called a 'secret atomic warehouse' in Tehran.[52] One of the other locations (Location 2) is the suspected place of origin of undeclared 'natural uranium in the form of a metal disc'; another (Location 3) 'may have been used for the processing and conversion of uranium ore including fluorination in 2003'; while the fourth (Location 4) may have been used for 'outdoor, conventional explosive testing ... in 2003, including in relation to testing of shielding in preparation for the use of neutron detectors'.[53] While the issue of so-called possible military dimensions of Iran's past nuclear activities was formally closed with the adoption of the JCPOA, the IAEA has investigated this evidence in the framework of Iran's CSA.[54]

After three meetings of technical experts from the IAEA and Iran in April and May 2021, the agency found Iranian answers to its questions related to these four locations to be insufficient.[55] According to a May report by the IAEA, Iran had provided no new information on Location 1, no information at all on locations 2 and 3, and no 'substantiating documentation' to back its

---

[48] IAEA, GOV/2021/10 (note 11).

[49] See e.g. IAEA, GOV/2021/39 (note 14).

[50] Erästö, *SIPRI Yearbook 2020* (note 1).

[51] IAEA, Board of Governors, 'NPT Safeguards Agreement with the Islamic Republic of Iran', Report by the Director General, GOV/2021/15, 23 Feb. 2021.

[52] Sanger, D. E. and Specia, M., 'Israeli leader claims Iran has "secret atomic warehouse"', *New York Times*, 27 Sep. 2018.

[53] IAEA, GOV/2021/15 (note 51), para. 9.

[54] Erästö, *SIPRI Yearbook 2020* (note 1), p. 422; and Davenport, K., 'IAEA investigations of Iran's nuclear activities', Arms Control Association, Oct. 2021.

[55] IAEA, Board of Governors, 'NPT Safeguards Agreement with the Islamic Republic of Iran', Report by the Director General, GOV/2021/29, 31 May 2021.

statement on Location 4.[56] In September the IAEA director general, Rafael Grossi, stated that he was 'increasingly concerned' that, after two years, these safeguards issues still remained unresolved.[57] The Iranian view, in contrast, was that its answers had been sufficient and that the agency should announce that the issue had been resolved.[58]

An additional safeguards issue that emerged in 2021 was Iran's decision to include modified Code 3.1 of the Subsidiary Arrangements to its CSA among other transparency measures that it decided to end on 23 February.[59] Modified Code 3.1 obligates countries to inform the IAEA of plans to construct new nuclear facilities at an early stage.[60] According to the IAEA, Iran was under a legal obligation to implement the modified Code 3.1, which it had agreed to do prior to the JCPOA.[61] However, Iran 'informed the Agency that it does not have a plan to construct a new nuclear facility in the near future'.[62]

Diplomatic efforts to restore the JCPOA

The inauguration in January 2021 of Joe Biden as US president led to the recommencement of nuclear talks with Iran, based on Biden's campaign pledge to bring the USA back to the JCPOA. There was perceived to be a window of opportunity to reach an agreement in the months before the Iranian presidential election in June. However, it took the Biden administration until March to clarify the US position on the issue, which contributed to a delayed start to the talks, further narrowing the window.[63] On 6 April the USA and the remaining parties to the JCPOA—Iran, China, Russia, the EU and the E3—began talks in Vienna to restore the agreement, leading to six rounds of negotiations that were held until 20 June.

Iran and the USA negotiated indirectly, with other parties conveying messages between the two sides. By late April, three working groups had been established to address key sticking points: determining which sanctions the USA would need to lift; which measures Iran would need to take with respect to its nuclear programme; and how these steps should be sequenced to enable the parties to return to compliance with the JCPOA.[64] Despite expressions of hope by the negotiators during this time, the diplomatic process ended in

---

[56] IAEA, GOV/2021/29 (note 55), para. 24.

[57] IAEA, GOV/INF/2021/42 (note 15), para. 3.

[58] IAEA, Board of Governors, 'NPT Safeguards Agreement with the Islamic Republic of Iran', Report by the Director General, GOV/2021/42, 7 Sep. 2021.

[59] IAEA, GOV/INF/2021/13 (note 9).

[60] Davenport (note 7).

[61] IAEA, GOV/2021/15 (note 51).

[62] IAEA, GOV/2021/28 (note 39), para. 42.

[63] Costello, R., 'Why talks with Iran have faltered and what Biden can do to revive them', Responsible Statecraft, 14 Sep. 2021.

[64] Murphy, F. and Irish, J., 'Iran deal parties seek nuclear talks momentum, US briefs Gulf states', Reuters, 27 Apr. 2021.

June without results, and was then followed by a five-month hiatus during which the new administration of Ebrahim Raisi, the conservative winner of the Iranian presidential election, took over.

Iran's presidential elections were a complicating factor for the nuclear talks, as the conservative leaders and groups in Iran may have wanted to prevent the outgoing moderate government from gaining a diplomatic victory prior to the elections.[65] However, there were also major disagreements in the talks on substantive issues, notably the lifting of sanctions. While Iran demanded the lifting of all sanctions imposed as part of the Trump administration's 'maximum pressure' campaign, the US position was that only non-proliferation sanctions could be lifted.[66] In practice, however, it was difficult to draw the line between non-proliferation and other sanctions; for example, some of the sanctions imposed by the Trump administration on grounds of terrorism support had the same effect on Iran's oil and banking sectors as the sanctions whose lifting had been a key part of the JCPOA. While US officials reportedly acknowledged this problem, domestic politics in the USA made it difficult to amend the relevant legislation, including sanctions against the Iranian Revolutionary Guards Corps.[67] Iran also demanded guarantees that the USA would not withdraw from the agreement in the future, whereas the USA wanted Iran to agree to follow-on talks on issues such as missiles and regional security, going beyond the restoration of the JCPOA.[68]

The election of Raisi as Iran's president led to speculation that the new Iranian negotiation team would take a harder line in Vienna.[69] In practice, its main impact seemed to be the five-month delay in resuming the nuclear talks—during which the new administration was reportedly reviewing the country's approach on the nuclear issue.[70] At the same time, the EU, the E3 and the USA stressed the urgent need for Iran to reverse its nuclear escalation, with the E3 arguing that Iran's uranium enrichment activities had 'permanently and irreversibly' upgraded its nuclear capabilities.[71] Although the new Iranian negotiation team's position was described as 'maximalist' when nuclear talks finally resumed on 29 November, at the end of the sev-

[65] Rozen, L., '"Unbearably slow": Scant progress at latest Iran Vienna talks', Diplomatic, by Laura Rozen, 5 May 2021.

[66] Psaledakis, D. and Mohammed, A., 'US tiptoes through sanctions minefield toward Iran nuclear deal', Reuters, 17 Dec. 2021.

[67] Psaledakis and Mohammed (note 66).

[68] Rozen, L., 'US: Still "serious differences" to resolve for Iran deal, talks won't go on indefinitely', Diplomatic, by Laura Rozen, 25 June 2021.

[69] E.g. Schwartz, M. S., 'What the election of a new hard-line president in Iran means for the nuclear deal', NPR, 21 June 2021.

[70] Amwaj.media, 'Iranians debate whether nuclear talks delay may cost or help', 27 Sep. 2021.

[71] E3 statement to the IAEA on the Joint Comprehensive Plan of Action, 24 Nov. 2021.

enth round of talks the parties characterized the situation as being similar to where it had been in June.[72]

As the eighth round of talks started on 27 December, negotiators expressed cautious optimism that a solution might finally be within reach.[73] However, the E3 and the USA warned that 'time [was] running out' for the nuclear talks, with 'only "weeks" left' to reach an agreement.[74] At the end of the year, reports also referred to discussions on an 'interim deal' whereby Iran would freeze certain nuclear activities in return for some sanctions relief, although these were not confirmed by the negotiation parties.[75]

Prospects for the JCPOA

Uncertainty over the fate of the JCPOA persisted throughout 2021, with changes in both US and Iranian administrations creating delays and raising questions about each side's commitment to their stated goal of restoring the JCPOA. Questions over Iran's past nuclear activities and sabotage operations against its nuclear facilities further complicated matters. While Iran's fuel cycle activities led to heightened concerns about proliferation, reversing these advances based on JCPOA limits appeared easier than the lifting of US sanctions, for which the nuclear agreement did not provide a clear formula.

The situation in late 2021 seemingly pointed to three alternative futures. First, a successful conclusion of the Vienna talks in 2022 could restore the agreement, alleviating both international proliferation concerns and Iran's economic hardship, ideally also including mechanisms to hedge against unilateral withdrawals by any party in the future. Second, a failure of diplomatic efforts could lead to a continuation of the slow-motion crisis whereby the JCPOA, while formally in place and constituting an area of consensus in principle, would be hollowed out further by its lack of implementation by Iran and the USA. Third, the JCPOA parties and the USA might ultimately abandon the JCPOA as a viable framework for addressing their respective concerns.[76]

[72] Motamedi, M., 'Iran nuclear talks to resume "soon" after modest gains in Vienna', Al Jazeera, 17 Dec. 2021; and US Department of State, 'Senior State Department official on the JCPOA talks in Vienna', Special briefing, 17 Dec. 2021.

[73] Motamedi, M., 'Delegates at new round of Iran nuclear talks strike hopeful note', Al Jazeera, 27 Dec. 2021.

[74] Tirone, J. and Motevalli, G., 'West warns time's running out for the fraught nuclear talks', Bloomberg, 14 Dec. 2021; and Esfandiari, G., 'Will 2022 bring a revived Iran nuclear deal—or a hard-line plan B?', Radio Free Europe/Radio Liberty, 31 Dec. 2021.

[75] Ravid, B., 'Scoop: US floats interim Iran nuclear deal', Axios, 17 Nov. 2021; Esfandiari (note 74); and Lee, C. E., Kube, C. and De Luce, D., 'Russia proposed interim nuclear deal to Iran, with US knowledge, sources say', NBC News, 22 Jan. 2022.

[76] Tirone and Motevalli (note 74).

III. Multilateral nuclear arms control, disarmament and non-proliferation treaties and initiatives

TYTTI ERÄSTÖ AND VITALY FEDCHENKO

Multilateral nuclear arms control, disarmament and non-proliferation efforts take place in a number of forums. These include formal negotiating forums such as the Conference on Disarmament (CD) in Geneva and meetings associated with treaties such as the 1968 Non-Proliferation Treaty (NPT), the 1996 Comprehensive Nuclear-Test-Ban Treaty (CTBT) and the 2017 Treaty on the Prohibition of Nuclear Weapons (TPNW). A more recent multilateral process is the annual United Nations conference on the establishment of a zone free of weapons of mass destruction (WMD) in the Middle East.

This section reviews developments in 2021 in relation to these treaties and initiatives, looking in turn at the NPT, the TPNW, the Middle East conference and the CTBT. Developments in the Vienna negotiations on restoring the Joint Comprehensive Plan of Action (JCPOA) on Iran's nuclear programme are covered in section II. While the entry into force of the TPNW in January marked a milestone in efforts to strengthen the global norm on nuclear disarmament, the lack—once again—of significant nuclear developments in the CD in 2021 reflected the lack of practical progress towards that goal.[1]

The postponed review conference of the Non-Proliferation Treaty

The 10th review conference of the parties to the NPT was initially planned for April–May 2020.[2] Due to the ongoing Covid-19 pandemic, the conference was first delayed until January 2021, then August 2021 and then further postponed until 4–28 January 2022.[3]

Various state groupings issued statements and working papers in antici-pation of the conference. In December 2021 the five NPT-recognized nuclear weapon states—China, France, the Russian Federation, the United King-dom and the United States, known as the P5—issued a joint communiqué that emphasized, among other things, 'strategic risk reduction' but did not specify concrete measures for achieving this beyond a discussion on nuclear doctrines and policies.[4] Risk reduction is viewed as being one of the few areas

---

[1] For a description and other details of the CD see annex B, section I, in this volume.

[2] For a summary and other details of the NPT see annex A, section I, in this volume. On earlier developments see Erästö, T., Kile, S. N. and Fedchenko, V., 'Multilateral arms control, disarmament and non-proliferation treaties and initiatives', *SIPRI Yearbook 2021*.

[3] Zlauvinen, G., President-designate of the 10th NPT Review Conference, Letter to NPT states parties, 25 Oct. 2021

[4] P5 Conference, Joint communiqué, Paris, 2–3 Dec. 2021.

of common ground at the review conference.[5] It was also highlighted by other groupings, such as the Stockholm Initiative for Nuclear Disarmament and the Non-Proliferation and Disarmament Initiative (NPDI), which both consist of non-nuclear weapon states and also include states that are included in USA's extended nuclear deterrence 'umbrella'.[6] However, as the Group of the Non-Aligned States stressed, risk reduction is no substitute for nuclear disarmament.[7]

The key challenge to the NPT remains the lack of progress towards the commitment under Article VI of the treaty for all the parties to 'pursue negotiations in good faith on effective measures relating to . . . nuclear disarmament, and on a treaty on general and complete disarmament'. In addition to the lack of implementation of the disarmament steps that had been agreed by consensus at the review conferences in 1995, 2000 and 2010, uncertainty prevailed as to whether the P5 still viewed themselves as bound by those previous decisions.

The general mood of the review conference discussions was somewhat improved by the extension in February 2021 of the 2010 Russian–US New Strategic Arms Reduction Treaty (New START; see section I). However, by the end of the year there was still no sign of follow-on negotiations on further nuclear cuts by Russia and the USA, while nuclear modernization programmes continued in these two countries as well as in other nuclear-armed states.[8] At the same time, new developments created additional challenges for the NPT: the JCPOA further deteriorated during the year, and in March the UK decided to increase the cap on the number of warheads in its nuclear stockpile and reduce nuclear transparency.[9] In addition, in September the UK and the USA agreed to sell nuclear-powered submarines to Australia (the so-called AUKUS agreement), thereby allowing it to remove nuclear material from the NPT-mandated safeguards system.[10]

The UN High Representative for Disarmament Affairs, Izumi Nakamitsu, nevertheless characterized the mood in the run-up to the review conference

---

[5] van der Meer, S., 'Nuclear risk reduction as an interim success for the NPT Review Conference?', European Leadership Network, 23 June 2020.

[6] 10th NPT Review Conference, 'A nuclear risk reduction package', Working paper submitted by the Stockholm Initiative, NPT/CONF.2020/WP.9, 14 May 2021; and 10th NPT Review Conference, 'Recommendations for consideration by the Tenth Review Conference of the parties to the Treaty on the Non-Proliferation of Nuclear Weapons', Joint working paper submitted by the members of the Non-Proliferation and Disarmament Initiative, NPT/CONF.2020/WP.10, 10 Sep. 2021.

[7] 10th NPT Review Conference, 'Nuclear disarmament', Working paper submitted by the members of the Group of Non-Aligned States Parties to the NPT, NPT/CONF.2020/WP.20, 22 Nov. 2021.

[8] On these nuclear modernization programmes see chapter 10, sections I–IX, in this volume.

[9] See section II in this chapter and chapter 10, section III, in this volume; and British Government, *Global Britain in a Competitive Age: The Integrated Review of Security, Defence, Development and Foreign Policy*, CP 403 (Stationery Office: London, Mar. 2021), p. 76.

[10] Acton, J. M., 'Why the AUKUS submarine deal is bad for non-proliferation—and what to do about it', Carnegie Endowment for International Peace, 21 Sep. 2021.

scheduled for January 2022 as 'cautiously optimistic'.[11] At the same time, she appealed for states parties to show flexibility and 'civility in discourse' to ensure a successful outcome. While differences over the TPNW had marked previous NPT meetings, it seemed that compromise language acknowledging the entry into force of the TPNW in 2021 could help to avoid such differences undermining consensus at the NPT review conference.[12] In turn, Ambassador Gustavo Zlauvinen of Argentina, the president-designate of the review conference, stressed that state parties 'need to be ready . . . to engage in real direct dialogue and negotiations' rather than 'recitation of national positions'.[13] He also noted that the two years of consultations about the review conference with states parties had clarified the need for progress in the implementation of Article VI as well as practical nuclear risk-reduction measures.

Less than a week before the review conference was due to start, the meeting was postponed again due to a surge in Covid-19 infections in New York. Zlauvinen tentatively suggested 1–26 August 2022 as the new dates, subject to formal confirmation by the states parties.[14]

The Treaty on the Prohibition of Nuclear Weapons

The 2017 Treaty on the Prohibition of Nuclear Weapons entered into force on 22 January 2021, 90 days after the 50th state had ratified or acceded to it.[15] By the end of the year, the TPNW had 59 states parties and had been signed but not yet ratified by a further 30 states. The entry into force of the treaty was viewed as a major turning point in multilateral efforts to advance nuclear disarmament; the UN secretary-general, António Guterres, described it as 'an important step towards a world free of nuclear weapons', and civil society representatives described it as a 'critical milestone'.[16]

The TPNW is the first multilateral treaty establishing a comprehensive ban on nuclear weapons, including their development, production, testing, acquisition, stockpiling, transfer and possession, as well as their use and

---

[11] Nakamitsu, I., High Representative for Disarmament Affairs, Remarks at the Third Track 1.5 Meeting for Substantive Advancement of Nuclear Disarmament, 9 Dec. 2021.

[12] Kimball, D. G., 'NPT states prepare for a critical conference', *Arms Control Today*, vol. 51, no. 10 (Dec. 2021).

[13] Zlauvinen, G., 'Prospects of the upcoming X NPT Review Conference', Public lecture, PIR Center, 1 Nov. 2021.

[14] Deen, T., 'Review Conference on Nuclear Non-Proliferation Treaty stalled due to rising COVID-19 infections', InDepthNews, 1 Jan. 2022.

[15] For a summary and other details of the TPNW, including lists of the parties and signatories, see annex A, section I, in this volume. On its entry into force see Erästö et al. (note 2), pp. 435–37.

[16] United Nations, 'Guterres hails entry into force of treaty banning nuclear weapons', 22 Jan. 2021; and International Campaign to Abolish Nuclear Weapons (ICAN), 'The Treaty on the Prohibition of Nuclear Weapons enters into force', 22 Jan. 2021.

threat of use.[17] The treaty builds in particular on international humanitarian law and was inspired by an international initiative that highlighted the catastrophic humanitarian consequences of any use of nuclear weapons. The TPNW negotiations took place within the UN, initiated by a General Assembly decision in December 2016, and the treaty was adopted by the General Assembly with a majority vote of 122 states to 1 on 7 July 2017.[18]

The entry into force of the treaty paved the way for the next milestone— the first meeting of states parties (MSP1), which the treaty requires to be held within one year.[19] Initially scheduled for January 2022, MSP1 was subsequently postponed until 22–24 March 2022, to avoid an overlap with the planned NPT review conference, and then again until July 2022.[20]

Ambassador Alexander Kmentt of Austria, the president-designate of MSP1, argued that the meeting provides an opportunity 'to put the implementation of the treaty on a strong and solid track'.[21] Among other subjects, the meeting will be able to initiate discussion to clarify certain TPNW articles that are open to interpretation, such as what exactly it means to 'assist, encourage or induce' activities prohibited by the treaty in Article 1.[22]

According to Kmentt, the TPNW states parties view the treaty as 'an essential normative supplement and further development of and complement to the [NPT]'.[23] The nuclear weapon states, in contrast, have portrayed the TPNW and its approach of outlawing nuclear weapons as being a threat to the NPT-based international order.[24] As in previous years, in 2021 the outcome of voting in the UN General Assembly testified to this controversy; a resolution that called upon 'all States that have not yet done so to sign, ratify, accept, approve or accede to the Treaty at the earliest possible date' was supported by 128 votes, all from non-nuclear weapon states, whereas the 42 negative votes included all nine nuclear-armed states and their allies.[25] Two member states of the North Atlantic Treaty Organization (NATO)—Germany and Norway—

---

[17] For background see Kile, S. N., 'Treaty on the Prohibition of Nuclear Weapons', *SIPRI Yearbook 2018*; and Erästö, T., 'Treaty on the Prohibition of Nuclear Weapons', *SIPRI Yearbook 2019*.

[18] Kile (note 17), p. 314.

[19] TPNW (note 15), Article 8.

[20] Kmentt, A., President-designate of TPNW 1MSP, Letter to the UN secretary-general, 10 Aug. 2021, annexed to A/75/990, 16 Aug. 2021; and United Nations Office of Disarmament Affairs, 'Note verbale from the Secretary-General of the United Nations, dated 4 April 2022, on the convening of the first Meeting of States Parties to the TPNW', 4 Apr. 2022.

[21] Kmentt, A., Statement at the 2021 World Conference against A and H Bombs, 6 Aug. 2021.

[22] International Committee of the Red Cross (ICRC), 'The prohibition to assist, encourage or induce prohibited activities under the Treaty on the Prohibition of Nuclear Weapons', ICRC Briefing Note, 24 Apr. 2019.

[23] Kmentt (note 21).

[24] See Kile (note 17); and Erästö (note 17).

[25] UN General Assembly Resolution 76/34, 6 Dec. 2021, para. 8; and United Nations, Digital Library, 'Treaty on the Prohibition of Nuclear Weapons: Resolution / adopted by the General Assembly', Voting data, 6 Dec. 2021.

nevertheless announced their intention to attend MSP1 as observers.[26] This was viewed as a significant departure from the prevailing NATO policy line of opposing the TPNW, which has created pressure among member states to refrain from any action that might signal support for the treaty.[27] Kmentt noted that all states had been invited to the conference and he called for 'those who are still sceptical and stuck in the belief of the necessity of nuclear deterrence' to join and 'to engage with the profound humanitarian arguments on which the TPNW rests'.[28]

The Conference on the Establishment of a Middle East Zone Free of Weapons of Mass Destruction

Initially planned for November 2020 but postponed due to the pandemic, the second session of the Conference on the Establishment of a Middle East Zone Free of Nuclear Weapons and Other Weapons of Mass Destruction took place between 29 November and 3 December 2021 at UN Headquarters in New York.[29] The conference was convened by the UN secretary-general and presided over by Ambassador Mansour Al-Otaibi of Kuwait. It was attended by 19 Middle Eastern states and observed by China, France, Russia and the UK as well as relevant international organizations.[30] As at the first session, in 2019, the USA and the region's only nuclear-armed state, Israel, did not attend the meeting despite being invited.

In 2018 the UN General Assembly decided to hold annual conferences on establishment of a Middle East WMD-free zone until that goal is achieved.[31] That decision had been preceded by calls in the UN General Assembly since 1974 to free the Middle East of nuclear weapons, and by unproductive efforts since 1995 to promote a WMD-free zone in the region as part of the NPT review process. While this current UN process is therefore independent of the NPT review process, it builds on the NPT and, in particular, the Middle East Resolution adopted at the 1995 NPT review conference whereby the

---

[26] International Campaign to Abolish Nuclear Weapons (ICAN), 'Germany expected to observe TPNW MSP', 25 Nov. 2021.

[27] Davis, I., 'NATO Secretary General attempts to hold the line on nuclear sharing: Germany and Norway caught in the crosshairs', NATO Watch, 23 Nov. 2021.

[28] Kmentt (note 21).

[29] United Nations, Conference on the Establishment of a Middle East Zone Free of Nuclear Weapons and Other Weapons of Mass Destruction, 'Second session', Decision, A/CONF.236/DEC.5, 21 Sep. 2020.

[30] United Nations, Conference on the Establishment of a Middle East Zone Free of Nuclear Weapons and Other Weapons of Mass Destruction, Report on the work of its second session, A/CONF.236/2021/4, 3 Dec. 2021, para. 2.

[31] United Nations, General Assembly, 'Convening of a conference on the establishment of a Middle East zone free of nuclear weapons and other weapons of mass destruction', Decision 73/546, 22 Dec. 2018. For background see Erästö, T. and Kile, S. N., 'Multilateral nuclear arms control, disarmament and non-proliferation treaties and initiatives', SIPRI Yearbook 2020.

establishment of the Middle East WMD-free zone was linked to the decision to indefinitely extend the NPT.[32]

Among other issues, the conference report reaffirms the importance of Israel's accession to the NPT.[33] While it contains no reference to the TPNW, the report notes that a future treaty on a Middle East WMD-free zone 'should recognize the catastrophic humanitarian and environmental consequences' resulting from any WMD use.[34] Regarding verification, the report notes that 'the [zone] treaty should avoid duplicating other existing international arrangements and could rely on existing instruments, including the comprehensive safeguards of [the International Atomic Energy Agency (IAEA)] and the verification regime of the Organisation for the Prohibition of Chemical Weapons'—although these could be supplemented by a 'regional verification mechanism'.[35] The report also stressed the responsibility of all nuclear-armed states to provide legally binding negative security assurances to treaty members.[36]

The next session of the conference was scheduled for 14–18 November 2022. A working committee was established to continue deliberations during the intersessional period, to convene at least two meetings.

While critics have downplayed the significance of the conference, advocates see in it an opportunity to 'turn the Middle East from a region of global concern, where chemical weapons have been widely employed and where a potential nuclear-arms race could be unleashed at any moment, into a region with a legally binding and humanitarian-based regional security system, capable of dissolving former rivalries'.[37]

Twenty-five years of the Comprehensive Nuclear-Test-Ban Treaty

The year 2021 marked the 25th anniversary of the Comprehensive Nuclear-Test-Ban Treaty: on 10 September 1996 the UN General Assembly voted 158 to 3, with 5 abstentions, to adopt the treaty as negotiated at the CD.[38] By the end of 1996, 138 states had signed the treaty.[39] Ratifications by the Comoros

---

[32] Erästö and Kile (note 31); United Nations, A/CONF.236/2021/4 (note 30), para. 17; and 1995 NPT Review and Extension Conference, Resolution on the Middle East, 11 May 1995, NPT/CONF.1995/21 (Part I).

[33] United Nations, A/CONF.236/2021/4 (note 30), para. 18.

[34] United Nations, A/CONF.236/2021/4 (note 30), para. 21.

[35] United Nations, A/CONF.236/2021/4 (note 30), paras 30–31.

[36] United Nations, A/CONF.236/2021/4 (note 30), para. 46.

[37] Bandarra, L. and Dolev, S., 'Pathways to a WMD-free zone in the Middle East', *Bulletin of the Atomic Scientists*, 2 Dec. 2021.

[38] For a summary and other details of the CTBT see annex A, section I, in this volume.

[39] Arnett, E., 'The Comprehensive Nuclear Test-Ban Treaty', *SIPRI Yearbook 1997*, p. 403.

and Cuba in 2021 brought the total number of ratifying states to 170, while a further 15 had signed but not yet ratified.[40]

Upon its entry into force, the CTBT will prohibit its states parties from conducting 'any nuclear weapon test explosion or any other nuclear explosion' anywhere in the world.[41] However, before the CTBT can enter into force, it must be ratified by 44 states named in the treaty's Annex 2, which all had nuclear power or research reactors when the treaty was negotiated. Eight of these states—China, Egypt, India, Iran, Israel, the Democratic People's Republic of Korea (DPRK, or North Korea), Pakistan and the USA—have yet to do so.

While the CTBT is still not in force, steady progress is being made on the operational aspects of the treaty by the Preparatory Commission for the Comprehensive Nuclear-Test-Ban Treaty Organization (CTBTO). The commission is a plenary body composed of all the treaty's states signatories. It is assisted by a Provisional Technical Secretariat (PTS), which is working to establish the CTBT verification regime. When completed, this regime will consist of an International Monitoring System (IMS) with 321 seismic, hydroacoustic, infrasound and radionuclide monitoring stations and 16 laboratories around the globe to detect evidence of any nuclear explosion; and an International Data Centre (IDC) to process and analyse the data registered at the monitoring stations and transmit it to member states. As of 31 December 2021, 303 of these 337 facilities were certified operational, with the 304th station, PS35 in Peleduy, Russia, expected to be certified in early 2022.[42]

Election of the executive secretary

In 2021 the CTBTO was finally able to resolve the drawn-out and contentious process of selecting its next executive secretary, who oversees the staff of the PTS and the annual budget of approximately US$130 million.[43] The nomination and voting process was complicated in 2020 by disagreements on whether countries with unpaid financial dues could vote in the election of the executive secretary, the effects of the Covid-19 pandemic, and the decision of the outgoing executive secretary, Lassina Zerbo, to break with general practice across the UN system and the CTBT requirement (when it enters into force) for leaders of international organizations to serve no more than two consecutive terms.[44] The commission resolved the first and the

---

[40] CTBTO, 'Cuba joins the Comprehensive Nuclear-Test-Ban Treaty', Press release, 4 Feb. 2021; and CTBTO, 'Comoros becomes 170th state to ratify the CTBT', Press release, 19 Feb. 2021.

[41] CTBT (note 38), Article I(1).

[42] CTBTO, 'Station profiles', [n.d.]; and CTBTO, 'Beating snowstorms, Russia's last primary seismic station is installed', 11 Nov. 2021.

[43] CTBTO, *Business Continuity: Annual Report 2020* (CTBTO: Vienna, 2021), p. 91.

[44] On these three issues see Erästö et al. (note 2), pp. 438–40.

most contentious of the three issues on 26 March 2021, when it decided by consensus that any state that had taken part in the voting in December 2020, any new signatory (i.e. Cuba) and any other state that paid its assessed dues would be eligible to cast a vote.[45]

On 20 May 2021 Robert Floyd of Australia won the support of 96 states (exactly two-thirds of the states voting).[46] He started his term on 1 August 2021 as the fourth executive secretary, following Zerbo of Burkina Faso (2013–21), Tibor Tóth of Hungary (2005–13) and Wolfgang Hoffmann of Germany (1997–2005).[47]

Marking the 25th anniversary

In 2021 the CTBT member states conducted several events marking the 25th anniversary of the opening for signature of the treaty. On 23 and 24 September, in accordance with Article XIV of the treaty, the states that had ratified the CTBT convened the biannual Conference on Facilitating the Entry into Force of the CTBT, with other signatory states attending as observers.[48] In an address to the conference, a senior US official emphasized the support of the administration of President Joe Biden for the treaty and its commitment 'to work to achieve its entry into force'.[49] This represented a clear change from the policy of the previous administration, of President Donald J. Trump, which in 2020 is reported to have discussed the possibility of resuming nuclear weapon tests.[50] The USA also reiterated that it 'continues to observe its zero-yield nuclear explosive testing moratorium, and calls on all states possessing nuclear weapons to declare or maintain such a moratorium'.

On 27 September the UN Security Council dedicated a meeting to the CTBT. The CTBTO executive secretary, the head of the UN Office for Disarmament Affairs, civil society representatives and envoys from Ireland (then president of the Security Council), Estonia, the USA, China, Russia and other states spoke in support of the treaty.[51]

---

[45] Kimball, D. G., 'States finally settle on next leader for CTBTO', *Arms Control Today*, vol. 51, no. 5 (June 2021).

[46] Kimball (note 45).

[47] CTBTO, 'Robert Floyd takes office as CTBTO executive secretary', Press release, 2 Aug. 2021.

[48] Conference on Facilitating the Entry into Force of the Comprehensive Nuclear-Test-Ban Treaty, Report of the conference, CTBT-Art.XIV/2021/6, 30 Sep. 2021.

[49] Jenkins, B., US Under Secretary for Arms Control and International Security, Remarks to the Conference on Facilitating the Entry into Force of the Comprehensive Nuclear-Test-Ban Treaty, 23 Sep. 2021.

[50] Erästö et al. (note 2), pp. 442–43.

[51] United Nations, Security Council, 'Comprehensive Test-Ban Treaty "essential element of nuclear disarmament", high representative tells Security Council', SC/14645, 27 Sep. 2021.

The Security Council had previously addressed the CTBT five years earlier, when it marked the 20th anniversary of the treaty on 22 September 2016.[52] On that occasion it noted a joint statement on the CTBT made by the P5, in particular the part pointing out that 'a nuclear-weapon test explosion or any other nuclear explosion would defeat the object and purpose of the CTBT'.[53] Unlike in 2016, the 2021 Security Council session did not result in a joint statement or resolution due to the opposition of France.[54]

The impact of 25 years of the Comprehensive Nuclear-Test-Ban Treaty

During the 51 years between the first nuclear test, on 16 July 1945, and the opening for signature of the CTBT, six states conducted a total of 2048 nuclear test explosions.[55] During the subsequent 25 years, only 10 additional nuclear tests were conducted, all by three states outside the treaty—India, Pakistan and North Korea. While the CTBT's goal of a complete prohibition on 'any nuclear weapon test explosion or any other nuclear explosion' anywhere in the world has not been reached, the treaty has had a significant impact in five important areas.

First, the CTBT helped to slow down the research and development of global nuclear weapon capabilities. Although the treaty only bans nuclear test explosions of any yield and does not proscribe other nuclear weapon-related work, the ability of nuclear weapon states to improve existing nuclear warheads and reliably develop new ones has been severely limited by the treaty.[56] 'Live' nuclear test explosions are important for development of advanced warheads. For example, France required 22 nuclear tests to develop its TN-75 warhead.[57]

Second, the CTBT helped to curb significant radioactive contamination—both of the atmosphere globally and of the nuclear test sites locally. Nuclear weapon tests made the main man-made contribution to the exposure of the world population to radiation since 1945.[58]

---

[52] Rauf, T., '"Unfinished business" on the anniversary of the Comprehensive Nuclear-Test-Ban Treaty', 26 Sep. 2016.

[53] UN Security Council Resolution 2310, 23 Sep. 2016, para. 4; and Joint statement on the Comprehensive Nuclear-Test-Ban Treaty by the Nuclear Non-Proliferation Treaty nuclear-weapon states, 15 Sep. 2016.

[54] Kimball, D. G., 'On CTBT anniversary, UN members call for action', Arms Control Today, vol. 51, no. 8 (Oct. 2021).

[55] Those 6 states were the USA, the Soviet Union/Russia, the UK, France, China and India. Ferm, R., 'Nuclear explosions, 1945–96', SIPRI Yearbook 1997.

[56] Garwin, R. L. and Simonenko, V. A., 'Nuclear weapon development without nuclear testing', Pugwash Workshop on Problems in Achieving a Nuclear-Weapon-Free World, 25–27 October 1996.

[57] Norris, R. S., 'French and Chinese nuclear weapon testing?', Security Dialogue, vol. 27, no. 1 (Mar. 1996), p. 46.

[58] UN Scientific Committee on the Effects of Atomic Radiation (UNSCEAR), Sources and Effects of Ionizing Radiation, UNSCEAR 2000 Report to the General Assembly (United Nations: New York, 2000), pp. 5–6.

Third, it has been argued that the CTBT, even though it is still not universal and not in force, has introduced an international norm against nuclear testing. As pointed out by credible and influential non-proliferation and disarmament researchers, even though India and Pakistan—two nuclear-armed states that did not join the treaty—conducted testing campaigns after the CTBT was opened for signature, they then ceased and stated that they would not test further.[59] One researcher has even argued that Israel and North Korea have also been influenced by this norm.[60]

Fourth, in preparation for the treaty's entering into force, the CTBTO has created a unique international global monitoring network of stations and laboratories for treaty verification. The IMS demonstrated its proficiency by detecting and analysing data from all six known nuclear tests conducted by North Korea between 2006 and 2017.[61] In 2016 the UN Security Council recognized that the IMS and the IDC 'contribute to regional stability as a significant confidence-building measure, and strengthen the nuclear non-proliferation and disarmament regime'.[62] Despite its provisional status, the IMS has become for many countries 'a provider of global data that national technical means could not match'.[63]

Finally, the IMS data and reports produced by the PTS are made available to all signatory states, which often choose to use that data to foster earth sciences research and capacity building. In addition, the CTBTO awards contracts to operate its monitoring stations and radionuclide laboratories to local institutions. This has made the CTBTO an important contributor of data to scientific communities and a significant contributor to building and sustaining scientific capacity beyond the fields of nuclear non-proliferation and disarmament verification.[64]

---

[59] Bunn, G., 'The status of norms against nuclear testing', *Nonproliferation Review*, vol. 6, no. 2 (winter 1999), p. 5; Tannenwald, N., 'The great unraveling: The future of the nuclear normative order', N. Tannenwald and J. M. Acton, *Emerging Risks and Declining Norms in the Age of Technological Innovation and Changing Nuclear Doctrines* (American Academy of Arts and Sciences: Cambridge, MA, 2018), pp. 22–23.

[60] Kimball, D. G., 'Preserving the nuclear testing taboo', *Arms Control Today*, vol. 51, no. 7 (Sep. 2021).

[61] Fedchenko, V., 'Nuclear explosions, 1945–2017', *SIPRI Yearbook 2018*.

[62] UN Security Council Resolution 2310 (note 53), para. 7.

[63] Giovannini, F., 'The CTBT at 25 and beyond', *Arms Control Today*, vol. 51, no. 7 (Sep. 2021).

[64] CTBTO, 'Science and Technology—the conference series', [n.d.].

12. Chemical, biological and health security threats

Overview

In 2021 the Covid-19 pandemic continued to wreak, in the words of the World Health Organization (WHO), 'unprecedented devastation on global population health'. By the end of 2021, the WHO had received reports of over 286 million cases of Covid-19 worldwide, and there had been over 5.4 million recorded deaths. The actual number of infections and recorded deaths were likely to be considerably higher from undiagnosed cases and generally poor Covid-19-related data. The pandemic's global socio-economic impacts included economic recession, millions of job losses, extreme inequity, political divisions, and educational losses (see section I). The origins of the pandemic continued to be a politically divisive subject. A report by a joint WHO–China team in March 2021 concluded that of four origin hypotheses the 'most likely' pathway was that the virus jumped from one animal species to another before infecting people. However, the report was heavily criticized and the WHO concluded that all theories remained open. United States intelligence assessments were also inconclusive about the virus's origin but agreed that it was not developed as a biological weapon and that the Chinese government did not know about it prior to the outbreak. Although the origin question remained unresolved at the end of 2021, the WHO had established a permanent international scientific advisory group for origins of novel pathogens (SAGO), which was expected to play a vital role in the next phase of studies into the virus's origin.

The Covid-19 pandemic, and its public and socio-economic impacts, has shown that the international community needs to be much better prepared in responding to possible future pandemics. In December 2021, the World Health Assembly agreed to start a global process on a new international treaty to strengthen pandemic prevention, preparedness and response.

The pandemic also continued to impact the functioning of key biological disarmament and non-proliferation activities in 2021, as discussed in section II. Nevertheless, intersessional meetings of experts and the meeting of states parties under the 1972 Biological and Toxin Weapons Convention (BWC) that had been postponed in 2020 were held in 2021. While these meetings revealed areas of broad agreement among states on how best to strengthen the BWC, they also demonstrated significant areas of disagreement, with broader geopolitical tensions among China, Russia and the USA affecting the discussions. In response to US allegations of BWC non-compliance, China and Russia more closely coordinated their BWC diplomacy and counter-allegations against the

USA. *Finding sufficient common ground to successfully negotiate substantive outcomes will be challenging at the ninth review conference in 2022 but—with each of the three states articulating plans that address issues of compliance, transparency and accountability—there is potential for a workable compromise solution.*

Disagreements within the BWC were largely mirrored within the 1993 Chemical Weapons Convention (CWC), including continued efforts by a handful of actors to stop, hinder, undermine and contest the authority and work of investigation teams within the Organization for the Prohibition of Chemical Weapons (OPCW) and the United Nations (see section III). Investigations into Syrian chemical weapons use continued in 2021; although no new instances were reported, chemicals weapons use was confirmed or likely in 20 out of 80 cases investigated to date. By the end of 2021, according to the OPCW, Syria's declarations continued to contain 'identified gaps, inconsistencies, and discrepancies'. Divisions over the investigation into chemical weapons use in Syria, and the 2020 decision to invoke the compliance procedure under CWC Article XII, were again at the forefront of discussions at the second session of the 25th conference of the states parties (CSP) to the CWC in April 2021, and at the 26th CSP in November. These disagreements point to investigations becoming more contentious and complex—and important.

Outside of Syria, there were further developments in 2021 related to toxic chemicals from the novichok group of nerve agents, as well as other developments in the OPCW, covered in section IV. The poisoning of Russian citizen Alexei Navalny with a novichok nerve agent in August 2020 had still not been officially investigated or resolved by the end of 2021, and it continued to cause political tensions between Russia and a number of Western countries. The pandemic again disrupted routine and other inspections by the OPCW Technical Secretariat throughout 2021. Political divisions were still evident at the two CSPs and in OPCW Executive Council meetings, especially over the re-appointment of the OPCW director-general and the budget for 2022–23, as well as efforts to address the threat from chemicals that act on the central nervous system. On a more positive note, construction of the new Centre for Chemistry and Technology started in June 2021. The United States is the only declared possessor state party with chemical weapons yet to be destroyed, but it is expected to complete its remaining destruction activities (less than 3 per cent of its declared stockpiles) within the current timelines.

FILIPPA LENTZOS AND UNA JAKOB

I. The unfolding Covid-19 pandemic

FILIPPA LENTZOS

Milestones of the pandemic in 2021

In January 2021, the director-general of the World Health Organization (WHO) called for a collective worldwide commitment to ensure vaccination for health workers and those at high-risk in all countries in the first 100 days of 2021.[1] He urged all vaccine manufacturers from around the world to swiftly provide the necessary data to enable the WHO to consider vaccine candidates for emergency use listing. The Pfizer/BioNTech vaccine became the first vaccine against Covid-19 to receive emergency use validation, on 31 December 2020.[2] The Moderna mRNA-1273 vaccine followed suit on 25 January 2021, the AstraZeneca/Oxford vaccine on 15 February 2021, the Johnson & Johnson vaccine on 12 March 2021, and the Sinopharm vaccine on 7 May 2021.[3] By the end of 2021, the WHO had listed nine Covid-19 vaccines for emergency use.[4]

In his opening remarks to the Executive Board on 18 January 2021, the WHO director-general warned that the world was 'on the brink of a catastrophic moral failure', with equitable access to vaccines at serious risk as 'some countries and companies continue to prioritize bilateral deals . . . driving up prices and attempting to jump to the front of the queue'.[5] The ambitious Covax initiative—jointly led by Gavi, the Vaccine Alliance, the Coalition for Epidemic Preparedness Innovations (CEPI) and the WHO, and aimed at ensuring vaccine access for all countries—began its global roll-out on 24 February 2021 with Ghana receiving the first vaccine doses.[6] Over 100 countries had received more than 38 million vaccine doses from Covax within 42 days.[7] Yet Covax's first few months were plagued with insufficient

---

[1] World Health Organization (WHO) Director-General, 'WHO Director-General's opening remarks at the media briefing on COVID-19—11 January 2021', 11 Jan. 2021.

[2] WHO, 'WHO issues its first emergency use validation for a COVID-19 vaccine and emphasizes need for equitable global access', News release, 31 Dec. 2020.

[3] WHO, 'Interim recommendations for use of the Moderna mRNA-1273 vaccine against COVID-19', Interim guidance, 25 Jan. 2021; WHO, 'WHO lists two additional COVID-19 vaccines for emergency use and COVAX roll-out', News release, 15 Feb.2021; WHO, 'WHO adds Janssen vaccine to list of safe and effective emergency tools against COVID-19', News release, 12 Mar. 2021; and WHO, 'WHO lists additional COVID-19 vaccine for emergency use and issues interim policy recommendations', News release, 7 May 2021.

[4] WHO, 'WHO lists 9th COVID-19 vaccine for emergency use with aim to increase access to vaccination in lower-income countries', News release, 17 Dec. 2021.

[5] WHO Director-General, 'WHO Director-General's opening remarks at 148th session of the Executive Board', 18 Jan. 2021.

[6] WHO, 'COVID-19 vaccine doses shipped by the COVAX Facility head to Ghana, marking beginning of global rollout', Joint news release, 24 Feb. 2021.

[7] WHO, 'COVAX reaches over 100 economies, 42 days after first international delivery', News release, 8 Apr. 2021.

funds, low vaccine supplies, a limited willingness from high-income countries to share vaccines, and logistics challenges. December 2021, however, saw a last-minute surge in deliveries, with about 300 million vaccine doses shipped to low- and middle-income countries, including Bangladesh, Indonesia, the Philippines and Pakistan.[8] By the end of 2021, Covax had delivered roughly 910 million doses worldwide, though this fell far short of the two billion doses the initiative originally aimed for.[9]

As of 31 December 2021, 4.56 billion people worldwide had been vaccinated against Covid-19.[10] China had vaccinated well over a billion inhabitants, India over 800 million, the United States over 240 million, and Brazil and Indonesia over 160 million each.[11]

However, 2021 still ended with great uncertainty, as a burgeoning wave of the Omicron variant of SARS-CoV-2 rapidly swept across countries. First identified in South Africa and designated a 'variant of concern' by the WHO on 26 November 2021, Omicron was rapidly replacing the Delta variant.[12] The Delta variant was first identified in India and was the dominant strain globally for much of 2021; it was thought partly responsible for India's deadly second wave that began in February 2021. *The Economist* labelled these recurring waves of infection 'the era of predictable unpredictability'.[13]

Health and mortality impacts

According to the WHO *World Health Statistics 2021* report, the Covid-19 pandemic wrought 'unprecedented devastation on global population health'.[14] By the end of 2021, the WHO had received reports of over 286 million cases of Covid-19 worldwide. The actual number of infections is likely to be considerably higher from undiagnosed cases and generally poor Covid-19-related data. As of 31 December 2021, the WHO reported over 103 million cases in the Americas, over 102 million in Europe, nearly 45 million in South East Asia, over 17 million in the Eastern Mediterranean, over 7 million in Africa, and over 11 million in the Western Pacific. The five countries with the highest cumulative number of reported cases by the end of 2021 were, in descending order, the USA, India, Brazil, France and the United Kingdom.[15]

---

[8] Taylor, A., 'Covax vaccine deliveries surge in final stretch of 2021, with a record 300 million doses sent out in December', *Washington Post*, 1 Jan. 2022.

[9] Taylor (note 8).

[10] Ritchie, H. et al., 'Coronavirus (COVID-19) vaccinations', *Coronavirus Pandemic (COVID-19)* (Our World in Data, 2020).

[11] Richie et al. (note 10).

[12] WHO, 'Classification of Omicron (B.1.1.529): SARS-CoV-2 variant of concern', Statement, 26 Nov. 2021.

[13] 'The new normal is already here. Get used to it', *The Economist*, 18 Dec. 2021.

[14] WHO, *World Health Statistics 2021: Monitoring Health for the SDGs, Sustainable Development Goals* (WHO: Geneva, 2021), p. 1.

[15] WHO, 'WHO coronavirus (COVID-19) dashboard', [n.d.].

As of 31 December 2021, Covid-19 had caused over 5.4 million recorded deaths, with several million likely to have gone unrecorded. Reasons for unrecorded Covid-19 deaths include lack of pre-death testing and reliable tracking systems in most counties. In addition, the pandemic disrupted essential health services through 'widespread shortages' of medicines, staff and diagnostics, as well as 'hesitancy to seek medical treatment' for fear of infection, which may have indirectly caused an increase in fatalities from diseases other than Covid-19.[16] *The Economist*'s 'excess death tracker' attempted to provide a more accurate death toll from the pandemic by taking the number of people who die from any cause in a given region and period, and comparing it with a historical baseline from recent years. It assessed the number of global deaths as closer to 19 million, three times higher than the WHO figure.[17] Deaths reported to the WHO in the Americas numbered over 1.6 million, in Europe over 2.4 million, in South East Asia over 720 000, in the Eastern Mediterranean over 315 000, in Africa over 155 000 and in the Western Pacific over 155 000.[18] *The Economist*'s excess death tracker assessed that numbers in North America and in Latin America and the Caribbean should be increased by 20 per cent and 50 per cent, respectively. The WHO figures for Europe should be increased by 80 per cent, Asia by 700 per cent and Africa by 900 per cent. For the Western Pacific, the excess death tracker assessed a 300 per cent decrease on official estimates 'because Covid-19 claimed relatively few victims, while lifestyle changes lowered the toll from other causes such as flu'.[19]

By mid December 2021, more than 800 000 Americans were reported to have died from Covid-19, the highest recorded national death toll from the pandemic. The figure exceeds the populations of cities like Boston and Washington DC, and means nearly twice as many Americans have died during the pandemic than in World War II.[20]

According to mortality reports received by the WHO, the five countries with the highest cumulative number of total deaths by the end of 2021 were, in descending order, the USA, Brazil, India, Russia and Mexico.[21] *The Economist*'s excess death tracker reassessed that order to be India, Russia, the USA, Brazil and Mexico.[22] When the figures are adjusted for population size, the highest death rates were estimated by the excess death tracker to be, in descending order, in Bulgaria, North Macedonia, Russia, Lithuania and Peru.

---

[16] WHO, *World Health Statistics 2021* (note 14), p. 1.
[17] 'The pandemic's true death toll', *The Economist*, [n.d.].
[18] WHO, 'WHO coronavirus (COVID-19) dashboard' (note 15).
[19] 'The pandemic's true death toll' (note 17).
[20] 'Covid-19: US surpasses 800,000 pandemic deaths', BBC News, 15 Dec. 2021.
[21] WHO, 'WHO coronavirus (COVID-19) dashboard' (note 15).
[22] 'The pandemic's true death toll' (note 17).

At the end of 2021, the WHO report declared that Covid-19 had 'sharply shortened life expectancy' in many countries 'to a degree that has not been seen in decades'.[23] Health systems continued to be overwhelmed. Millions of people missed out on essential life-saving health services for non-communicable diseases and mental health. Progress against HIV, tuberculosis, malaria and other diseases stalled or went backwards, and millions of children missed out on vaccinations for other life-threatening diseases.

Economic, social and political impacts

Covid-19 also continued to generate significant economic, social and political impacts worldwide, including economic recession, millions of job losses, extreme inequity, political divisions and lost educational opportunities.

Spending and borrowing to build field hospitals, buy vaccines and provide emergency aid to business and the unemployed caused unprecedented levels of global debt in 2021, particularly in emerging markets, and further widened the gap between richer and poorer nations.[24] A broadening gap was also seen between richer and poorer people.[25] According to Oxfam's annual report on global inequality, the world's 10 richest individuals more than doubled their collective fortunes from $700 billion to $1.5 trillion between March 2020 and November 2021, and a new billionaire has been created every 26 hours since the pandemic began.[26] Meanwhile, 99 per cent of the world's population were worse off because of lockdowns, lower levels of international trade and less international tourism, and 160 million more people were pushed into poverty than would have been without the impact of the pandemic.[27] Deepening inequalities have weakened the economic, financial and social fabric of almost every nation, regardless of development status, and the International Labour Organization assessed the damage would likely 'take years to repair . . . with long-term consequences for labour force participation, household incomes, and social—and possibly political—cohesion'.[28]

The pandemic continued to expose and exacerbate long-standing gender and racial divides. Gender equality went backwards—an estimated 13 million fewer women in work in 2021 than in 2019, and over 20 million girls at risk of never returning to school—but the pandemic hit ethnic minority groups the hardest. The Oxfam inequality report, for example, assessed that, during the

---

[23] WHO, *World Health Statistics 2021* (note 14), p. 1.

[24] Institute of International Finance, Global Debt Monitor, 'Reassessing the pandemic impact', 14 Sep. 2021.

[25] Chancel, L. et al., *World Inequality Report 2022* (World Inequality Lab: Paris, Dec. 2021).

[26] Ahmed, N. et al., *Inequality Kills: The Unparalleled Action Needed to Combat Unprecedented Inequality in the Wake of COVID-19* (Oxfam International, Jan. 2022), p. 7.

[27] 'Wealth of world's 10 richest men doubled in pandemic, Oxfam says', BBC News, 17 Jan. 2022.

[28] International Labour Organization (ILO), *World Employment and Social Outlook: Trends 2022*, ILO Flagship Report (ILO: Geneva, 17 Jan. 2022), p. 3.

second wave of the pandemic in England, people of Bangladeshi origin were five times more likely to die of Covid-19 compared with the White British population.[29]

School closures continued in 2021, with exceptionally long closures in Latin America and South Asia. Affecting more than 1.6 billion learners, the global disruption to education caused by the pandemic is 'without parallel' and 'its effects on learning have been severe', according to a global education report.[30]

Studies into the origins of SARS-CoV-2

The origins of the pandemic continued to be a politically divisive subject in 2021. Very late in its tenure, on 15 January 2021, the outgoing Trump administration issued a fact sheet on the pandemic's origins.[31] It said the novel coronavirus causing Covid-19, SARS-CoV-2, could have first entered the human population through human contact with infected animals. Alternatively, it could have spilled over into the human population as a result of a lab accident, where 'initial exposure included only a few individuals and was compounded by asymptomatic infection'. The fact sheet noted that 'scientists in China have researched animal-derived coronaviruses under conditions that increased the risk for accidental and potentially unwitting exposure', and listed three elements deserving 'greater scrutiny'. All associated with the Wuhan Institute of Virology (the premier laboratory in China working on coronaviruses), these three elements were genetic experiments with coronaviruses, Covid-19-like illnesses in the autumn of 2019 and secret military activity at the institute. The US fact sheet said that 'any credible investigation into the origin of Covid-19 demands complete, transparent access to the research labs in Wuhan, including their facilities, samples, personnel, and records'.

The joint WHO–China mission, mandated by the World Health Assembly in May 2020 and plagued by delays, finally began its field visit to China in January 2021. After four weeks of work, including two weeks of quarantine imposed on the international experts by the Chinese government, it reported its highly anticipated findings at a press conference on 9 February 2021 in Wuhan, where the outbreak was first identified.[32] The co-heads of the mission, Peter Ben Embarek and Liang Wannian, laid out four origin hypotheses

---

[29] Ahmed et al. (note 26), p. 7.

[30] World Bank, UNESCO and UNICEF, *The State of the Global Education Crisis: A Path to Recovery* (World Bank: Washington, DC, 2021), p. 5.

[31] US Department of State, Office of the spokesperson, 'Activity at the Wuhan Institute of Virology', Fact sheet, 15 Jan. 2021.

[32] WHO, 'WHO media briefing from Wuhan on COVID-19 mission—9 February 2021', Press briefing (video), 9 Feb. 2021.

that had formed the basis of the mission's investigation. First, the virus could have jumped directly from an animal species to humans. Alternatively, and second, the virus could have leapt from one animal species to an intermediary animal host in which the virus further adapted before jumping to people. A third, and surprising, hypothesis, which had not featured in prior origin discussions, was that the virus could have been introduced to Wuhan via the food chain, for example from imported frozen products. A final hypothesis was that the virus could have been accidentally released through a lab-related incident. The joint mission, made up of Chinese scientists selected by China and an equal number of international experts selected by the WHO, concluded that the second hypothesis, where the virus jumped from one species to another before infecting people, was the 'most likely' pathway. While the mission reported that the direct spillover and food-chain ideas needed more investigation, Ben Embarek said the team dismissed the lab-leak hypothesis as 'extremely unlikely' and that it would not inform future studies into the origin of the virus.[33]

Although the findings of the joint mission were widely reported in the press as representing the findings of the WHO itself, they did not represent the official position of the WHO. This was made clear two days after the press conference briefing, when WHO Director-General Tedros Adhanom Ghebreyesus undercut the remarks by Ben Embarek and the team, by specifically stating that 'all hypotheses remain open and require further study'.[34]

The mission report was eventually released on 30 March 2021, seven weeks after the mission ended.[35] It showed that the joint team saw its priority as seeking a zoonotic origin, not as fully examining all possible sources of the pandemic. The published data supporting the report mostly presented reviews of Chinese studies that had not been published outside China, nor shared with or reviewed by the international scientific community. The report also showed that, well over a year after the initial outbreak, critical records and biological samples that could have provided essential insights into the pandemic's origin had not been accessed by the team and remained inaccessible. The international members of the joint team, by their own admission, relied on verbal assurances given to them by their Chinese counterparts rather than conducting an independent investigation. This was particularly the case when it came to the possibility of a research-related incident. The final process used by the joint team for assessing the likelihood of a natural spillover or a research-related incident—amounting to a show of hands by the

---

[33] WHO, 'COVID-19 Virtual Press conference transcript—9 February 2021', Press briefing (transcript), 9 Feb. 2021, 01:13:18.

[34] WHO Director-General, Opening remarks at the member states briefing on Covid-19, 11 Feb. 2021.

[35] Joint WHO–China Study Team, 'WHO-convened Global Study of Origins of SARS-CoV-2: China Part', Report, 30 Mar. 2021.

team members based on a superficial review—failed to reach basic standards of credible analysis and assessment. The report also showed that it was, at best, unclear whether the Chinese team members had the leeway to express their fair evaluation of the origin theories in the presence of their Chinese government minders. Finally, the report made clear that the team had used different evidentiary standards for the origin theories it assessed.

On the day the report came out, the WHO director-general further distanced himself and the WHO from the team's findings. In his closing remarks at the briefing where the team presented their report, the director-general stated that all origin hypotheses must still be examined, including the possibility of a lab-related incident; that China must be more forthright in sharing essential data and biological samples; and that the WHO was prepared to send additional missions and experts to China to thoroughly examine all origin hypotheses.[36]

A joint statement released on the same day by 14 countries, led by the USA, was also critical of the report.[37] It underscored the need for a transparent and independent analysis, 'free from interference and undue influence', and it voiced the countries' shared concern that the joint study 'lacked access to complete, original data and samples'. The European Union released a similar statement.[38] Independent experts also voiced concern about the joint mission's independence, investigation process and conclusions.[39]

On 13 May 2021, 18 leading scientists published a letter in the prestigious journal *Science* calling for a full investigation into all pandemic origin hypotheses, including a lab incident.[40] On 26 May 2021, US President Joe Biden issued a statement saying he had asked the US intelligence community to investigate the origin question and to report back to the White House in 90 days.[41] Over the course of May and June of 2021, the lab-leak theory was also given greater prominence in the media.[42]

---

[36] WHO Director-General, Remarks at the member state briefing on the report of the international team studying the origins of SARS-CoV-2, 30 Mar. 2021.

[37] US Department of State, Office of the spokesperson, 'Joint statement on the WHO-convened COVID-19 origins study', Press release, 30 Mar. 2021. The 13 other countries were Australia, Canada, Czechia, Denmark, Estonia, Israel, Japan, the Republic of Korea, Latvia, Lithuania, Norway, Slovenia and the UK.

[38] European External Action Service, 'EU Statement on the WHO-led COVID-19 origins study', 30 Mar. 2021.

[39] Butler, C. D. et al., 'Call for a full and unrestricted international forensic investigation into the origins of Covid-19', Open letter, 4 Mar. 2021; and Butler, C. D. et al., 'Call for a full investigation into the origins of Covid-19', Open letter, 7 Apr. 2021.

[40] Bloom, J. D. et al., 'Investigate the origins of COVID-19', Letter, *Science*, vol. 372, no. 6543 (14 May 2021).

[41] Biden, J., Statement on the investigation into the origins of COVID-19, White House Briefing Room, 26 May 2021.

[42] See e.g. Wade, N., 'The origin of COVID: Did people or nature open Pandora's box at Wuhan?', *The Bulletin*, 5 May 2021; Jacobsen, R., 'Exclusive: How amateur sleuths broke the Wuhan lab story and embarrassed the media', *Newsweek Magazine*, 2 June 2021; and Eban, K., 'The lab-leak theory: Inside the fight to uncover COVID-19's origins', *Vanity Fair*, 3 June 2021.

A statement by leaders of the Group of Seven (G7) nations, issued on 13 June 2021 at a meeting in Cornwall, UK, stressed that the second phase of the WHO-convened origins study should take place in China and be 'timely, transparent, expert-led, and science-based'.[43] At a press briefing on 15 July 2021, the WHO director-general told reporters that for the second phase of the origins study, the WHO was 'asking China to be transparent, open and cooperate, especially on the information, raw data that we asked for at the early days of the pandemic'.[44] The director-general expressed the view that there had been a 'premature push' to rule out the lab incident theory, saying, 'I was a lab technician myself, an immunologist, and I have worked in the lab, and lab accidents happen. It's common.' In opening remarks to the WHO member state information session on pandemic origins on 16 July 2021, the director-general made clear that operational plans and terms of reference for the second phase were still in development. He highlighted that the origins study 'is a scientific exercise that must be kept free from politics' and declared, 'For that to happen, we expect China to support this next phase of the scientific process by sharing all relevant data in a spirit of transparency. Equally, we expect all Member States to support the scientific process by refraining from politicising it.'[45]

At the information session, the director-general also announced that the WHO was establishing a permanent international scientific advisory group for origins of novel pathogens (SAGO), which would 'play a vital role in the next phase of studies into the origins of SARS-CoV-2'.[46] Five weeks later, on 20 August 2021, the call for experts to join SAGO came out along with the group's terms of reference.[47] The group eventually selected comprised 27 individuals, including several scientists from the previous joint WHO–China study.[48] SAGO met for the first time on 24 November 2021.[49] These meetings are private, and no public reports about the studies the group might undertake had been produced by the end of 2021. However, it is expected that SAGO will focus on areas identified in earlier statements of the WHO, namely: further examination of the raw data from the earliest cases and potential cases in 2019; integrated studies of humans, wildlife, captive and farmed animals, and the environment; studies prioritizing geographic areas where

---

[43] White House, 'Carbis Bay G7 summit communiqué', Briefing Room statement, 13 June 2021.

[44] WHO, Covid-19 virtual press conference, Transcript, 15 July 2021, 00:19:15.

[45] WHO Director-General, Opening remarks at the member state information session on origins, 16 July 2021.

[46] WHO Director-General (note 45).

[47] WHO, 'Call for experts to join Scientific Advisory Group for the Origins of Novel Pathogens', News release, 20 Aug. 2021; and WHO, Scientific Advisory Group for the Origins of Novel Pathogens (SAGO), Terms of reference, 20 Aug. 2021.

[48] SAGO, 'About us', [n.d.].

[49] WHO, 'First meeting of Scientific Advisory Group for the Origins of Novel Pathogens (SAGO)', News release, 24 Nov. 2021.

the virus first started circulating and neighbouring areas where other SARS-related coronaviruses have been found in non-human reservoirs; studies of animal markets in and around Wuhan; studies related to 'animal trace-back activities'; and audits of relevant laboratories and research institutions in Wuhan.[50]

On 24 August 2021 the US intelligence community delivered its classified report on pandemic origins to President Biden, and released a short, two-page unclassified summary on 27 August 2021.[51] The several agencies making up the intelligence community were divided on the origin question. Four agencies and the National Intelligence Council assessed with low confidence that the pandemic was most likely caused by natural spillover. One agency assessed with moderate confidence that it was caused by a laboratory-associated incident. Three institutions were unable to make a judgement either way. These different assessments resulted from 'how agencies weigh intelligence reporting and scientific publications, and intelligence and scientific gaps'.[52] The report said that, to reach a conclusive assessment, China's cooperation would most likely be needed. There were two things the intelligence agencies could agree on: first, that the virus was not developed as a biological weapon; and second, that the Chinese government did not have foreknowledge of the virus before the outbreak began. Most agencies also assessed, with low confidence, that SARS-CoV-2 was probably not genetically engineered, though two agencies believed there was insufficient evidence to draw that conclusion. On release of the report, President Biden said that while the review had finished, US 'efforts to understand the origins of this pandemic will not rest'.[53] He stressed that 'critical information about the origins of this pandemic exists in the People's Republic of China, yet from the beginning, government officials in China have worked to prevent international investigators and members of the global public health community from accessing it'.[54] He said the USA would continue to press China to fully share information and to cooperate with the WHO's second phase of the origins study. He concluded, 'We must have a full and transparent accounting of this global tragedy. Nothing less is acceptable.'[55]

The origin question remained unresolved at the end of 2021, amidst continuing debate politically, in the media and within the scientific community. Among scientists, opinions generally fall into four groups: those favouring the natural spillover theory, those favouring the research-related accident

---

[50] WHO Director-General (note 45); and WHO, 'WHO statement on advancing the next series of studies to find the origins of SARS-CoV-2', Statement, 12 Aug. 2021.

[51] US Office of the Director of National Intelligence, 'Key takeaways', 27 Aug. 2021.

[52] US Office of the Director of National Intelligence (note 51), p. 1.

[53] Biden, J., Statement on the investigation into the origins of COVID-19, White House Briefing Room, 27 Aug. 2021.

[54] Biden (note 53).

[55] Biden (note 53).

theory, those who remain open to both, and the majority who do not know and prefer, for various reasons, not to participate in the debate.

A pandemic treaty

In March 2021, 25 heads of government and international agencies called on the international community to work together towards a new international treaty for pandemic preparedness and response. Drawing parallels to how political leaders came together following the devastation of two world wars to forge the multilateral treaty system, the joint statement expressed the hope of building 'a more robust global health architecture to protect future generations'.[56] Published in several newspapers around the world, the statement envisioned a treaty 'to foster an all-of-government and all-of-society approach, strengthening national, regional and global capacities and resilience to future pandemics'.[57]

Meeting in a special session on 1 December 2021, the second-ever since the WHO's founding in 1948, the World Health Assembly agreed to start a global process on a treaty to strengthen pandemic prevention, preparedness and response.[58] The Assembly established an intergovernmental negotiating body to draft the treaty. This body's first meeting (to be held by 1 March 2022) would agree on ways of working and timelines, and its second meeting (before 1 August 2022) would discuss progress on a working draft of the treaty. The body would also hold public hearings to inform its deliberations; deliver a progress report to the 76th World Health Assembly in 2023; and submit its outcome for consideration by the 77th World Health Assembly in 2024.

Conclusions

At the end of 2021, there was still no end in sight to the Covid-19 pandemic. The new Omicron variant was rapidly spreading, and it was unclear whether the vaccines that had been developed would be effective against it—and future variants—and whether the exponential rise in infections would translate into severe disease, hospitalizations and deaths as for previous variants. Geopolitical tensions remained high, with investigations into the origins of the pandemic a particular point of contention. More encouragingly, there was agreement on initiating development of a new international treaty on preparing for and responding to pandemics.

---

[56] WHO, 'Global leaders unite in urgent call for international pandemic treaty', News release, 30 Mar. 2021.

[57] WHO (note 56).

[58] WHO, 'World Health Assembly agrees to launch process to develop historic global accord on pandemic prevention, preparedness and response', News release, 1 Dec. 2021.

II. Biological weapon disarmament and non-proliferation

FILIPPA LENTZOS

The principal legal instrument against biological warfare is the 1972 Convention on the Prohibition of the Development, Production and Stockpiling of Bacteriological (Biological) and Toxin Weapons and on their Destruction (Biological and Toxin Weapons Convention, BWC).[1] The treaty has 184 states parties and 4 signatory states. Ten states have neither signed nor ratified the convention. No state joined the treaty in 2021.

While the Covid-19 pandemic continued to affect the 2021 calendar of disarmament events, some meetings were able to take place in person, including BWC meetings. The BWC meetings of experts (MXs), originally scheduled for 25 August to 3 September 2020, were eventually held from 30 August to 8 September 2021 in Geneva. The First Committee of the United Nations General Assembly met from 4 October to 4 November 2021 in New York. The BWC meeting of states parties (MSP), originally scheduled for 8 to 11 December 2020, was held from 22 to 25 November 2021 in Geneva, and the first meeting of the ninth Preparatory Committee (PrepCom) was held on 20 December 2021, also in Geneva.

Increasing geopolitical tensions in 2021 between China, Russia and the United States were also visible in the biological field and resulted in allegations of non-compliance with the BWC.

The 2020 meetings of experts

The third, and last, set of five MXs ahead of the ninth review conference considered topics assigned to them by the 2017 MSP.[2] MX1, chaired by Kimmo Laukkanen of Finland, considered cooperation and assistance, with a particular focus on strengthening cooperation and assistance on peaceful uses of the life sciences and associated technologies (BWC Article X). The chair's summary report of the two-day meeting characterized the discussions as 'in-depth and substantive', with a 'large number of proposals' indicating 'clear interest' in making progress on strengthening cooperation and assistance.[3] MX2, chaired by Kazuhiro Nakai of Japan, considered developments

---

[1] For a summary and other details of the Convention on the Prohibition of the Development, Production and Stockpiling of Bacteriological (Biological) and Toxin Weapons and on their Destruction see annex A, section I, in this volume.

[2] For meeting agendas, reports, working papers, technical briefing presentations, side event details, the joint statement of civil society organizations and other documentation see BWC, 'BWC-Meetings of Experts (2020)', United Nations Office for Disarmament Affairs (UNODA) Meetings Place.

[3] BWC, Meeting of States Parties (MSP), 'Report of the 2020 Meeting of Experts on cooperation and assistance, with a particular focus on strengthening cooperation and assistance under Article X', BWC/MSP/2020/MX.1/2, 1 Oct. 2021, annex I, para. 3.

in the fields of science and technology related to the BWC. Topics discussed over the two-day meeting included methodologies for establishing a science and technology review mechanism, and standards and guiding principles for biorisk management. Many states expressed their support for the 'Tianjin Biosecurity Guidelines for Codes of Conduct for Scientists', including their endorsement at the ninth review conference and agreement on a mandate from the review conference to promote and promulgate them.[4]

The one-day MX3, chaired by Arman Baissuanov of Kazakhstan, considered a variety of proposals on strengthening national implementation and efforts undertaken by states parties to enhance domestic implementation of the BWC.[5] The two-day MX4, chaired by Ambassador Elena Kuzmanovska Biondic of North Macedonia, considered assistance, response and preparedness. The chair observed 'broad recognition of the need to make progress towards the operationalization of Article VII and a clear interest among delegations in advancing related proposals'.[6]

The final meeting—the one-day MX5 chaired by Grisselle del Carmen Rodriguez Ramirez of Panama on institutional strengthening of the convention—generated the most intense discussion and divergence of views.[7] Many, mostly Non-Aligned Movement (NAM), states repeated decades-old calls for resuming negotiations on a legally binding protocol to the BWC. A clear lack of consensus on pursuing such an approach was evident. Several Western Group states pointed out that this lack of consensus should not hinder efforts to strengthen the convention and called for a pragmatic approach to explore both legal and voluntary measures in greater depth. The USA said it would oppose any new calls that fail to address the technical and political challenges that precluded agreement on a verification protocol in 2001, noting that many of those issues still exist today and many may have gotten worse.

Russia introduced a proposal to establish a group of governmental experts from 2022 to 2026 to develop investigation procedures under Article VI. The proposal 'received much attention and was discussed at great length, with opinions differing as to its necessity'.[8] Several, mainly Western Group, states opposed the initiative, noting that it would compete with, or undermine, the UN Secretary-General's Mechanism for Investigation of Alleged Use

---

[4] BWC, MSP, 'Report of the 2020 Meeting of Experts on review of developments in the field of science and technology related to the Convention', BWC.MSP/2020/MX.2/2/Rev.1, 8 Oct. 2021, paras 19–22.

[5] BWC, MSP, 'Report of the 2020 Meeting of Experts on strengthening national implementation', BWC/MSP/2020/MX.3/2, 1 Oct 2021.

[6] BWC, MSP, 'Report of the 2020 Meeting of Experts on assistance, response and preparedness', BWC/MSP/2020/MX.4/2, 14 Oct. 2021, annex I, para. 3.

[7] BWC, MSP, 'Report of the 2020 Meeting of Experts on institutional strengthening of the Convention', BWC/MSP/2020/MX.5/2, 14 Oct. 2021, annex I.

[8] BWC, BWC/MSP/2020/MX.5/2 (note 7), annex I, para. 7.

of Chemical and Biological Weapons (Secretary-General's Mechanism, UNSGM). Russia also proposed establishing an open-ended working group to develop proposals for strengthening the BWC that could eventually be included in a legally binding instrument. While some delegations were very supportive, others observed pragmatically that current circumstances do not seem conducive to establishing such a working group.

MX5 also discussed Kazakhstan's proposal to establish an International Agency for Biological Safety, which it had first introduced at the UN General Assembly in 2020. Kazakhstan reported receiving positive feedback on the concept note it had distributed to the Geneva and New York missions in May and June 2021, respectively, offering a vision of the mandate, objectives and functions of the proposed agency; and stated that, if conditions permit, it would convene an international conference in 2022 to discuss different approaches on how to create the agency. Based on those discussions, Kazakhstan hoped to present a collective vision of the proposed agency at the ninth review conference. Points of contention raised by states included 'the underlying meaning of the proposed organization's accountability' to the UN Security Council, its relationship with the BWC Implementation Support Unit (ISU) and 'potential overlaps with existing bodies'.[9]

A proposal from the United Kingdom to delegate decision-making authority from the review conference to the MSP met with a clear divergence of views.[10] A working paper from Panama with 12 concrete suggestions to enhance gender equality and women's empowerment under the BWC was well received, with several states expressing their support for further advancing the discussion on gender equality in the forum.[11]

While there were areas of broad agreement among states on how best to strengthen the BWC, the MXs also demonstrated significant areas of disagreement, with broader geopolitical tensions affecting the discussions.

The First Committee of the UN General Assembly

The UN General Assembly committee on disarmament and international security (First Committee) convened from 4 October to 4 November 2021. In the general debate and thematic debate, 9 groups of states and 73 individual states referred to biological weapons in their statements. Most of the remarks emphasized the importance of the BWC and expressed support for the

---

[9] BWC, BWC/MSP/2020/MX.5/2 (note 7), annex I, para. 10.

[10] BWC, BWC/MSP/2020/MX.5/2 (note 7), annex I, para. 6. See also United Kingdom, 'Review conferences, decision making and future institutional strengthening of the Convention', Working paper, BWC/MSP/2020/MX.5/WP.1, 13 Aug. 2021.

[11] BWC, BWC/MSP/2020/MX.5/2 (note 7), annex I, para. 5. See also Panama, 'Enhancing gender equality and women's empowerment as an integral part of the institutional strengthening of the Biological Weapons Convention (BWC)', Working paper, BWC/MSP/2020/MX.5/WP.6, 30 Aug. 2021.

treaty. Many highlighted the need to universalize and implement the BWC effectively, including by adequately resourcing it. 'About a dozen' states referred in the first week to the Covid-19 pandemic in the context of biological threats, noting 'the need to strengthen biosecurity, biorisk management, and disease surveillance'.[12]

The ninth review conference of the BWC also provided a focus for states. India spoke about the need for states to 'work together, build convergences and achieve tangible outcomes'.[13] China and Russia urged states to adopt 'a constructive approach'.[14] The UK called for 'action, ambition and cooperation', while the USA emphasized the need to 'bring the Convention into the 21st century'.[15] Germany stated more firmly that a key deliverable for the review conference 'should be the establishment of a Scientific and Technological Experts Advisory Forum'—which most states agreed with in principle but diverged on the specifics.[16]

The NAM, the Association of Southeast Asian Nations (ASEAN) group and several other states—including China, Cuba, India, Iran and Russia—reiterated long-standing calls for a legally binding protocol to the BWC to ensure effective verification. The USA, which formally put an end to protocol negotiations in 2001 and which continued to advocate against a protocol, announced it 'will propose that States Parties adopt measures to strengthen the BWC immediately and, simultaneously, take steps to intensively explore measures to strengthen implementation and promote compliance'.[17] The USA did not elaborate further on these measures. The UN high representative for disarmament affairs suggested 'an innovative middle way that is responsive to scientific advances and the needs of developing countries, while rooted in international cooperation'.[18]

Russia called on 'everyone concerned to refrain from the militarization of public healthcare', yet it labelled efforts from several states to use voluntary

---

[12] Lentzos, F., 'Biological weapons', *First Committee Monitor*, vol. 19, no. 2 (9 Oct. 2021), p. 12, and no. 3 (16 Oct. 2021), p. 12.

[13] Sharma, P., Permanent representative of India to the Conference on Disarmament, Statement at the General Debate of the First Committee of the 76th session of the UN General Assembly, New York, 4 Oct. 2021, p. 2.

[14] Geng S., Chinese ambassador, Remarks on the release of the joint statement by the foreign ministers of China and Russia to the First Committee of the 76th session of the UN General Assembly, New York, 7 Oct. 2021, p. 6.

[15] United Kingdom, Statement to the First Committee of the 76th session of the UN General Assembly, New York, 6 Oct. 2021, p. 1; and Jenkins, B., US Under-secretary for arms control and international security, Remarks to the First Committee of the 76th session of the UN General Assembly, New York, 6 Oct. 2021, p. 4.

[16] Göbel, T., Ambassador and permanent representative of Germany to the Conference on Disarmament, Statement at the general debate of the First Committee of the 76th session of the UN General Assembly, New York, 5 Oct. 2021, p. 3.

[17] United States, Statement at the thematic debate on clusters 1–4, First Committee of the 76th session of the UN General Assembly, New York, 13 Oct. 2021, p. 1.

[18] Nakamitsu, I., UN high representative for disarmament affairs, Opening statement to the First Committee of the 76th session of the UN General Assembly, New York, 4 Oct. 2021, p. 5.

peer review as a way to enhance transparency about dual-use facilities and research as 'dubious', claiming that they 'lack impartial criteria for assessment and selection of participants'.[19] Ukraine spoke of the 'ruinous consequences of Russian aggression' negatively impacting Ukrainian biosafety and biosecurity.[20] Iran described Israel's rejection of BWC membership as 'endangering regional security'.[21]

A revised resolution on the UN Secretary-General's Mechanism

Russia introduced a draft resolution, co-sponsored by Nicaragua and Zimbabwe, on the UNSGM.[22] It was a revised version of a resolution introduced in 2020, co-sponsored by China, Nicaragua, and Venezuela, which faced an unprecedented defeat.[23]

The new draft resolution cut four of the nine operative paragraphs from the 2020 version, and introduced a revised version of another of the operative paragraphs. Two preambular paragraphs from 2020 were gone, but the rest remained intact and a new one was added. While the revised resolution went through two rounds of heavily contested consultations, much of the feedback Russia received, notably that the resolution undermines the UNSGM rather than strengthens it, did not appear to lead to any revisions.

The First Committee overwhelmingly rejected the draft resolution for a second time on 3 November 2021. There were 31 votes in favour, 64 votes against and 77 abstentions—figures very similar to the vote in 2020. Two individual paragraphs were also voted on, both rejected by even greater margins (26–58–68 and 25–88–68).

Before the vote took place, Slovenia on behalf of the European Union (EU) and other states (Albania, Australia, Canada, Georgia, Liechtenstein, Montenegro, Norway, Republic of North Macedonia, Ukraine and the UK), the USA, Switzerland and the Philippines all provided explanations of vote that urged states to vote against the draft resolution.

The US explanation noted that the revised resolution 'might appear less contentious', but claimed 'it would still undermine the UNSGM's integrity, independence, and impartial character'. The USA stated its particular concern about elements 'that would launch a formal process' for UN member

---

[19] Russia, Statement at the thematic debate on nuclear weapons, First Committee of the 76th session of the UN General Assembly, New York, 13 Oct. 2021, p. 7.

[20] Zlenko, A., Ukrainian second secretary, Statement at the thematic debate on clusters 1–4, First Committee of the 76th session of the UN General Assembly, New York, 13 Oct. 2021, p. 2.

[21] Balouji, H. A., First counselor of the permanent mission of Iran, Statement at combined thematic debate on nuclear weapons, other WMDs, outer space and conventional weapons, First Committee of the 76th session of the UN General Assembly, New York, 13 Oct 2021, p. 3.

[22] United Nations, General Assembly, 'Secretary-General's Mechanism for Investigation of Alleged Use of Chemical and Biological Weapons', Draft resolution, A/C.1/76/L.54, 14 Oct. 2021.

[23] Lentzos, F. and Littlewood, J., 'How Russia worked to undermine UN bioweapons investigations', *Bulletin of the Atomic Scientists*, 11 Dec. 2020.

states to critique the mechanism's guidelines and procedures 'without a compelling reason and without regard for existing review provisions', and questioned Russia's aim in introducing the resolution: 'It is clear that Russia does not intend to stop with this first step of critiquing the UNSGM's technical procedures and guidelines. Russia will continue pressing to steadily strip away the UN Secretary-General's prerogative to lead any technical review and update process in an objective manner.'[24]

The statement on behalf of the EU and other states was equally critical of Russia's motives: 'The ulterior motive behind this supposed need to review the SGM guidelines and procedures is to subordinate the SGM, and more specifically the Secretary General's decisional power as to whether to launch an investigation into alleged use of biological weapons, to the UN Security Council.'[25] The statement also highlighted the resolution's proposed review of the UNSGM guidelines and procedures as its key concern, noting that the resolution 'fails to mention' their 2007 review and update, and that they had 'worked adequately in a real-world situation in 2013, when the SGM was launched to investigate allegations of chemical weapons use in Syria'.[26]

Switzerland similarly made the point that the mechanism is functional and proved its value in Syria in 2013. Placing the resolution in the larger context of 'the erosion of key arms control instruments in recent years', Switzerland emphasized that the foundational principle of the UNSGM, namely its independence, is undermined by the draft resolution, as is the authority of the UN secretary-general—both of which 'must be protected and not diminished'.[27]

Iran's explanation of vote, also delivered before the vote, urged states to vote for the resolution.[28] Argentina, India and Mexico provided explanations of their abstentions after the vote.[29]

---

[24] USA, Explanation of vote L.54 on the UNSGM, First Committee of the 76th session of the UN General Assembly, New York, 3 Nov. 2021, p. 1.

[25] Slovenia on behalf of European Union member states, Explanation of vote L.54 on the UNSGM, First Committee of the 76th session of the UN General Assembly, New York, 3 Nov. 2021, p. 2.

[26] Slovenia on behalf of European Union member states (note 25), p. 2.

[27] Switzerland, Explanation of vote L.54 on the UNSGM, First Committee of the 76th session of the UN General Assembly, New York, 3 Nov. 2021.

[28] Iran, Explanation of vote L.54 on the UNSGM, First Committee of the 76th session of the UN General Assembly, New York, 2 Nov. 2021.

[29] Argentina, Explanation of vote L.54 on the UNSGM, First Committee of the 76th session of the UN General Assembly, New York, 2 Nov. 2021; India, Explanation of vote L.54 on the UNSGM, First Committee of the 76th session of the UN General Assembly, New York, 2 Nov. 2021; Mexico, Explanation of vote L.54 on the UNSGM, First Committee of the 76th session of the UN General Assembly, New York, 2 Nov. 2021; and United Nations, 'First Committee, 19th meeting (16th plenary meeting)—General Assembly, 76th session', UN Web TV, 2 Nov. 2021.

Sticking points

Both the First Committee and the General Assembly adopted draft resolution A/C.1/76/L.35 on the BWC without a vote (Resolution 76/67).[30] The resolution only contained two minor technical updates on the 2021 version.

India used the opportunity to express grievances about the BWC working capital fund. India said the fund should operate on the basis of assessed contributions by states parties, not through voluntary contributions (highlighting the OPCW working capital fund as a model), and not by non-state entities, referring to a contribution to the fund from the Nuclear Threat Initiative.[31]

The Philippines used the opportunity to focus on aligning agendas on disarmament and sustainable development. Heeding the UN secretary-general's 2018 call for 'a re-imagining of our efforts in WMD disarmament in the context of development', the Philippines agreed 'there is space for taking further steps to unlock the synergies between the disarmament paradigm and the sustainable development agenda'. It said the upcoming review conference can 'establish a more developed BWC institutional machinery that meets the challenges of the 21st century' and that it hoped a successful conference outcome would provide a basis for substantively updating the BWC resolution at the 77th session of the First Committee. The Philippines also joined calls for the resumption of multilateral negotiations for a legally binding verification protocol and highlighted the importance of initiatives to enhance international cooperation and assistance, particularly with respect to Article X and Article VII.[32]

The clear signal coming from the First Committee was that these two aspects—verification, and cooperation and assistance—will form fundamental sticking points at the ninth review conference.

---

[30] UN General Assembly Resolution 76/67, 'Convention on the Prohibition of the Development, Production and Stockpiling of Bacteriological (Biological) and Toxin Weapons and on Their Destruction', A/RES/76/67, 6 Dec. 2021; and Reaching Critical Will, 'Draft resolutions, voting results, and explanations of vote from First Committee 2021', [n.d.].

[31] India, Explanation of vote L.35 on the BWC, First Committee of the 76th session of the UN General Assembly, New York, 6 Dec. 2021; United Nations, 'General Assembly: 45th plenary meeting, 76th session', UN Web TV, 6 Dec. 2021; and 'Voluntary contributions', BWC Newsletter, Nov. 2021 (see summary table of the current status of the BWC working capital fund).

[32] Philippines, Explanation of vote L.35 on the BWC, First Committee of the 76th session of the UN General Assembly, New York, 6 Dec. 2021; and United Nations (note 31).

The 2020 meeting of states parties and the 2021 Preparatory Committee

The 2020 meeting of states parties (MSP) was postponed several times due to the Covid-19 pandemic, but eventually convened in November 2021.[33] The chair of the 2020 MSP, Ambassador Cleopa K. Mailu of Kenya, produced a report in advance of the meeting providing information on the 14 states not party to the BWC and on activities to promote universalization of the convention.[34]

Upon request from the 2019 MSP, the chair also produced a report to the 2020 MSP on the financial situation of the BWC and the implementation of the financial measures adopted in 2018. The report noted a 91.9 per cent collection rate for 2020 by the end of that year, compared with a 94.8 per cent collection rate for 2019.[35] The state party with by far the largest outstanding amount was Brazil, with Venezuela, United Arab Emirates and Argentina with the next largest outstanding amounts.[36] The working capital fund, established by the 2018 MSP, had received $628 801 as of 31 August 2021—82.7 per cent of the target level set for the fund. The fund was set aside in 2019, 2020 and 2021 as guarantee for contract renewals for ISU staff, but did not have to be used for this purpose because additional contributions were received in time to cover payroll charges.[37]

The ISU's annual report on its activities up to September 2021 reported that 2020 saw the highest number of confidence-building measures submitted, with reports received from 85 states parties (46.4 per cent), and that the figure for 2021 was likely to eclipse that figure because by the end of September 2021 it had already received 87 submissions (47.5 per cent).[38] A reminder letter sent by the ISU in early January 2022 stated that the final number of reports submitted by 31 December was 92 (50.3 per cent).[39] The annual report also stated that 129 states parties had nominated a national

---

[33] Permanent Mission of the Republic of Kenya to the United Nations and other International Organisations, Letter to the UN Office in Geneva, Chairperson of the 2020 BWC Meeting of States Parties, KMG/BWC-MSP-2020/44, 28 July 2020; Permanent Mission of the Republic of Kenya to the United Nations and other International Organisations, Letter to the UN Office in Geneva, Chairperson of the 2020 BWC Meeting of States Parties, KMG/BWC-MSP-2020/145, 9 Feb. 2021; and BWC, 'Report of the 2020 Meeting of Experts on strengthening national implementation', BWC/MSP/2020/MX.3/CRP.1, 3 Sep. 2021, para. 4.

[34] BWC, MSP, 'Report on universalization activities', BWC/MSP/2020/3, 27 Sep. 2021.

[35] BWC, MSP, 'Report on the overall financial situation of the Biological Weapons Convention', BWC/MSP/2020/5, 27 Sep. 2021, paras 7 and 9.

[36] United Nations Office for Disarmament Affairs, 'Outstanding amounts / prepayments by year and convention as at 31 January 2022', 31 Jan. 2022, p. 1.

[37] BWC, BWC/MSP/2020/5 (note 35), para. 15.

[38] BWC, MSP, 'Annual report of the Implementation Support Unit', BWC/MSP/2020/4, 27 Sep. 2021, paras 21–22.

[39] See United Nations Office for Disarmament Affairs, 'ISU sends out reminder letter', About the Biological Weapons Convention, Latest information, 15 Jan. 2022.

contact point; 77 offers of assistance from 10 states parties and one group of states parties had been made; and 51 requests for assistance, from 17 states parties, had been received.[40]

States parties submitted 16 working papers to the MSP, considerably more than the 5 produced for the 2019 MSP and the 11 for the 2018 MSP.[41] In the general debate, 56 states parties made statements.[42] There were eight virtual side events, organized by states, the United Nations Office for Disarmament Affairs (UNODA) and non-governmental organizations.

In reviewing the MXs, the MSP noted 'the value of the work' and welcomed 'the substantive discussions' of the MXs, but consideration of how to reflect the deliberations was 'inconclusive' and no consensus could be reached.[43] This is the third MSP in a row where no substantive outcome document was produced.

The MSP decided that an initial PrepCom meeting would be held in Geneva on 20 December 2021 to consider organizational aspects of the review conference. A second, more substantial, PrepCom meeting was scheduled for 4–11 April 2022. The MSP agreed the ninth review conference would be held in Geneva from 8 to 26 August 2022. The NAM was invited to nominate the president of the ninth review conference and chair of the PrepCom. Azerbaijan, as coordinator of the NAM, nominated Pakistan. Unusually, India and the Philippines raised objections to the nomination, and the MSP decided to provide the NAM more time for consultation.[44]

The one-day December PrepCom meeting elected Florian Antohi of Romania and Tancredi Francese of Italy as vice-chairs and reached understanding on a provisional agenda and draft rules of procedure for the review conference, for final adoption at the April PrepCom. The meeting also requested the ISU prepare eight background information documents for the review conference.

Several rounds of NAM consultations on a nomination for the review conference presidency failed to reach agreement by the end of 2021. The disarray and presumably ill feeling among the NAM delegations will likely make it harder to achieve consensus on substantive outcomes at the ninth review conference.

[40] BWC, BWC/MSP/2020/4 (note 38), paras 13 and 28.

[41] BWC, MSP, 'Report of the 2020 Meeting of States Parties', BWC/MSP/2020/7, 25 Nov. 2021, annex II; BWC, MSP, 'Report of the 2019 Meeting of States Parties', BWC/MSP/2019/7, 11 Dec. 2019, annex II; and BWC, MSP, 'Report of the 2018 Meeting of States Parties', BWC/MSP/2018/6, 11 Dec. 2018, annex II.

[42] BWC, BWC/MSP/2020/7 (note 41), para. 15.

[43] BWC, BWC/MSP/2020/7 (note 41), paras 26–28.

[44] BWC, BWC/MSP/2020/7 (note 41), paras 31–32. See also United Nations, '10th meeting, Biological Weapons Convention—Meeting of States Parties', UN Web TV, 26 Nov. 2021; and Guthrie, R., 'The extra day of the Meeting of States Parties and some reflections', BioWeapons Prevention Project, MSP report 6, 3 Dec. 2021.

The evolving China–Russia–United States relationship

Geopolitical tensions among the USA, China and Russia continued to spill over into the biological field in 2021, with allegations of BWC non-compliance aired in public reports and statements.[45]

The US arms control compliance report

While the USA has been concerned about Russian compliance with the BWC for many years, as reflected in its annual arms control compliance reports from the US Department of State, the 2021 compliance report, published on 15 April 2021, assessed outright that Russia maintains an offensive biological warfare programme and that Russia is in violation of the BWC. No new evidence was provided in the report to explain why the USA changed its assessment from 'concerns about Russian activities' in 2020 to 'Russia maintains an offensive [biological weapons] program' in 2021.[46] However, in August 2020 the USA added three key military biological facilities—the 48th Central Scientific Research Institute in Kirov, Sergiev Posad and Yekaterinburg—to the list of entities the USA considers to pose a security or foreign policy risk to its interests, making them subject to export control restrictions. The 2021 compliance report asserted that 'the United States has reasonable cause to believe these institutes are Russian Ministry of Defense facilities associated with the Soviet and Russian biological weapons program'.[47] The report further stated:

Russia is providing an incomplete acknowledgment of the former Soviet program, a lack of evidence of the dismantlement or cessation of key activities, and continues its ongoing secrecy efforts (including both the military facilities noted above and legislation criminalizing any disclosure of information about the former Soviet program). As such, Russia has not fulfilled its obligations under Article II to 'destroy or divert to peaceful purposes' the [biological weapons] specified in Article I of the Convention that it inherited from the Soviet Union.[48]

The 2021 compliance report also continued to raise concerns about China's compliance with Article I of the BWC. It asserted that 'China continues to develop its biotechnology infrastructure and pursue scientific cooperation with countries of concern', and that it 'has never acknowledged publicly or in

---

[45] On the geopolitical tensions between the USA and Russia see chapter 5, section I, in this volume. On the geopolitical tensions between the USA and China see chapter 4, section II, in this volume.

[46] US Department of State, *Adherence to and Compliance with Arms Control, Non-Proliferation, and Disarmament Agreements and Commitments* (US Department of State: Washington, DC, June 2020), p. 60; and US Department of State, *Adherence to and Compliance with Arms Control, Non-Proliferation, and Disarmament Agreements and Commitments* (US Department of State: Washington, DC, 15 Apr. 2021), p. 50.

[47] US Department of State, *Adherence to and Compliance with Arms Control, Non-Proliferation, and Disarmament Agreements and Commitments* (2021) (note 46), p. 52.

[48] US Department of State, *Adherence to and Compliance with Arms Control, Non-Proliferation, and Disarmament Agreements and Commitments* (2021) (note 46), p. 51.

diplomatic channels its past offensive [biological warfare] programme'.[49] The report declared that over the last year China 'engaged in activities with dual-use applications', highlighting toxin research and development undertaken at Chinese military medical institutions.

The report also raised previous concerns in relation to two other countries: that 'Iran has engaged in dual-use activities with potential for BW applications'; and that North Korea has an offensive biowarfare programme.[50]

Closer coordination by China and Russia on the BWC

During the 76th session of the First Committee of the General Assembly, on 7 October 2021, China and Russia released a joint statement for the first time, on strengthening the BWC. According to the Chinese Ministry of Foreign Affairs, the statement demonstrated 'the high level of the China–Russia comprehensive strategic coordination in a new era as well as the two countries' strong determination and responsible attitude towards safeguarding global biosecurity and defending multilateralism'.[51] The joint statement called on BWC states parties to develop operating standards for a BWC mechanism to investigate allegations of biological weapons use, emphasizing that BWC functions 'should not be duplicated by other mechanisms'.[52] The statement also expressed 'serious concerns' about 'military biological activities' of the USA 'and its allies' both within and outside their national territory. China and Russia alleged that over 200 US biological laboratories are deployed outside US national territory; that these laboratories function in a non-transparent manner; and that such activities pose serious risks for their own national security and the security of relevant regions. No such concerns have been formally raised within the context of the BWC.

The joint statement from China and Russia appears to signal a closer coordination of their policies on the BWC, and potentially complicates efforts to deliver a substantial outcome to the ninth review conference. It may also signal a greater emphasis on biological weapons in disinformation campaigns.

A two-track approach from the United States

Initially announced in the First Committee, the USA's new approach to strengthening the BWC was given prominence in a statement by US national

---

[49] US Department of State, *Adherence to and Compliance with Arms Control, Non-Proliferation, and Disarmament Agreements and Commitments* (2021) (note 46), pp. 46 and 52.

[50] US Department of State, *Adherence to and Compliance with Arms Control, Non-Proliferation, and Disarmament Agreements and Commitments* (2021) (note 46), pp. 47–49.

[51] Zhao, L., Chinese Ministry of Foreign Affairs press conference, 8 Oct. 2021, Transcript.

[52] Chinese Ministry of Foreign Affairs, 'Joint Statement by the Foreign Ministers of the People's Republic of China and the Russia Federation on Strengthening the Convention on the Prohibition of the Development, Production and Stockpiling of Bacteriological (Biological) and Toxin Weapons and on their Destruction', 7 Oct. 2021.

security advisor Jake Sullivan in advance of the BWC MSP. Sullivan said the USA was 'concerned that some nations still possess biological weapons programs, while other nations as well as nonstate actors seek to acquire them', and he urged 'all countries to take seriously the threat of biological weapons'.[53] Sullivan repeated the US intention to propose 'immediate action at the Review Conference on a number of practical measures that will build capacity to counter biological threats and benefit BWC members'.

Ambassador Bonnie Jenkins, US under-secretary for arms control and international security, further elaborated these measures and the US approach in her opening remarks to the BWC MSP in November 2021. Without naming specific countries, she said that 'Some states continue to possess sophisticated, well-established biological weapons programs', that 'non-state actors have shown continuing interest in acquiring [biological weapons] capabilities', and that 'widespread availability of sophisticated scientific and technological tools and methods is gradually eroding barriers to the development of biological weapons'.[54]

To overcome the political impasse of the last 20 years, the USA outlined a two-track approach. Track one sees the upcoming review conference taking 'near-term, concrete action' on a set of proposals that have been discussed at BWC meetings over the past few years, including 'creating a mechanism to review scientific advances', 'establishing a voluntary fund for technical cooperation' and 'enabling more agile decision-making'.[55]

Track two, addressing 'the harder issues', proposed that the ninth review conference establish 'a new expert working group to examine possible measures to strengthen implementation of the Convention, increase transparency, and enhance assurance of compliance'.[56] The vision was not, Ambassador Jenkins made clear, a return to the 1990s negotiations on a verification protocol. But while she firmly noted that current efforts should not be defined by past approaches, she did not rule out building on them either. Ambassador Jenkins announced the US Department of State will 'dedicate a senior official to drive' its new approach, and to play an active and constructive role in ensuring the success of the ninth review conference.[57] There was no mention, however, of how the new expert working group would be funded.

Allegations and counter-allegations at the 2020 meeting of states parties

In opening remarks to the BWC MSP, Russia claimed that significant expansion of military biomedical activities by the USA and its NATO allies, 'espe-

---

[53] White House, 'Statement by National Security Advisor Jake Sullivan on the US approach to strengthening the Biological Weapons Convention', Briefing Room statement, 19 Nov. 2021.

[54] Jenkins, B., US under-secretary for arms control and international security, Statement to the BWC MSP, Geneva, 22 Nov. 2021, pp. 1–2.

[55] Jenkins (note 54), pp. 2–3.

[56] Jenkins (note 54), p. 2.

[57] Jenkins (note 54), p. 4.

cially in countries near to us, raises questions about their true nature and content'.[58] Echoing Russia's accusations, China said that 'The bio-military activities carried out by the United States both in and outside its territory has caused serious compliance concerns' and that the USA's 'serious lack of transparency' in these activities 'poses a grave threat to the security of relevant states and regions'.[59] Responding to the 'truly appalling distortions of fact', the USA maintained the allegations were 'pure disinformation, plain and simple'.[60] The hundreds of laboratories Russia and China accuse of suspicious activity are not American facilities, explained the deputy head of the US delegation to the meeting. While they have been supported by the US Department of Defense's Cooperative Threat Reduction Program, they are public and animal health facilities that are owned and operated by the countries they are located in. He pushed back on claims that US activities lack transparency, emphasizing the irony of being lectured on transparency by Russia and China.

Conclusions

By the close of 2021, allegations of offensive weapons programmes and nefarious activities had rebounded in meetings rooms of the UN and ricocheted around the world in both credible and disreputable media. Yet the BWC, the bulwark against the return of biological weapons into the arsenals and war plans of states, has languished and efforts to strengthen it have been in a holding pattern for over 20 years since the USA scuppered the negotiations on a verification protocol in July 2001. The ninth review conference provides an opportunity to redress this situation. The prospects for making progress are better than they have been for over a decade. China, Russia and the USA have each articulated plans that address issues of compliance, transparency and accountability. Their approaches differ, but there is common ground to craft a workable compromise solution if these three states and others are determined enough. The most significant reason for hope is a change in the US approach to making the convention more robust. Yet, reaching consensus on anything in the BWC remains extremely difficult, and multiple challenges must be overcome if the ninth review conference is to deliver a new approach to biological weapons controls. It will not take much to prevent success and the festering allegations of non-compliance will not help the situation.

[58] Russia, Statement in general debate at the BWC MSP, Geneva, 22 Nov. 2021, pp. 2–3.

[59] Li, S., Chinese ambassador, Statement in general debate at the BWC MSP, Geneva, 22 Nov. 2021, p. 7.

[60] US Department of Defense, Defense Threat Reduction Agency, 'The US government responds to false allegations targeted at DoD CTR Program', YouTube, 11 Jan.2022.

III. Allegations of chemical weapons use in Syria

UNA JAKOB

The Organisation for the Prohibition of Chemical Weapons (OPCW) continued to investigate allegations of the use of chemical weapons in Syria and to clarify the status of Syria's chemical weapons programme. All chemical weapons facilities and stockpiles which Syria had declared upon its accession to the 1993 Chemical Weapons Convention (CWC) in 2013 were destroyed under OPCW verification by 2016.[1] However, since OPCW inspections have yielded indications that the initial declarations by the Syrian Arab Republic were neither complete nor accurate, and since chemical weapons attacks in Syria continued even after the destruction of the declared chemical weapons programme was completed, the OPCW has undertaken a number of activities to address the chemical weapons issue in Syria.[2] These activities are carried out by the Fact-Finding Mission (FFM), the Declaration Assessment Team (DAT) and the Investigation and Identification Team (IIT), and through inspections at sites that previous OPCW and United Nations investigations have found to be involved in Syria's chemical weapons activities (see table 12.1).[3]

Ongoing work of the FFM and DAT, and other activities

No new instances of chemical weapons use were reported in 2021. The governments of Russia and Syria continued to warn that terrorist organizations, allegedly supported by Western governments, were planning to stage chemical attacks in Syria in order to discredit the Syrian government.[4] However, the OPCW Technical Secretariat reported in March 2021 that none of the allegations brought forward by Syria could be independently verified.[5] The FFM continued its activities with regard to past alleged chemical weapons use in Syria but did not publish a new report in

---

[1] For a summary and other details of the Chemical Weapons Convention see annex A, section I, in this volume.

[2] See e.g. Arms Control Association, 'Timeline of Syrian chemical weapons activity, 2012–2021', Fact sheets & briefs, last reviewed May 2021.

[3] Organisation for the Prohibition of Chemical Weapons (OPCW), Executive Council, 'Progress in the elimination of the Syrian chemical weapons programme', Report by the Director-General, EC-98/DG.1, 23 July 2021, para. 24.

[4] See e.g. the note verbale in OPCW, Executive Council, 'Request for circulation of a document at the Ninety-Seventh Session of the Executive Council', EC-97/NAT.7, 23 June 2021, annex; Dabin, B., Al Ashkar, S. and Eyon, M., 'Foreign ministry: Attempts of fabricating chemical scenarios in Idleb won't affect Syria's stance in combating terrorism', SANA, 22 June 2021; and Ibrahim, M. H. D. and Eyon, M., 'Russian Defense Ministry: Al-Nusra terrorists with help of "White Helmets" fabricate chemical attack in Idleb', SANA, 3 July 2021.

[5] OPCW, Technical Secretariat, 'Information provided by the Syrian Arab Republic for consideration by the Technical Secretariat: Overview of processing', S/1934/2021, 10 Mar. 2021.

2021. The FFM had to date investigated a total of 80 allegations of chemical weapons use and confirmed such use or likely use in 20 cases.[6] The pandemic situation complicated the planning for further on-site activities. Moreover, the OPCW command post in Syria could not be continually staffed because the Syrian government delayed issuing visas for incoming staff members.[7] In spite of these impediments, the FFM travelled to Syria between 29 March and 13 April to collect information on 'an incident that took place in Kafr Zita, Hama, on 1 October 2016'.[8] The pertinent FFM report confirming the use of an industrial chlorine cylinder as a weapon in this incident was published on 1 February 2022.[9] Between 28 November and 10 December the FFM again deployed to Syria to gather information on four incidents that allegedly took place in the Hama governorate in 2017: in Khirbat Masasinah on 7 July and 4 August, in Qalib Al-Thawr, Al-Salamiya on 9 August, and in Al-Balil, Suran on 8 November.[10]

The DAT likewise continued its work to clarify concerns about the completeness and accuracy of Syria's initial declaration of its chemical weapons programme. According to the director-general's report in December 2021, these concerns include 'undeclared research, production, and/or weaponisation of unknown quantities of chemical weapons, and significant quantities of chemical warfare agents or precursors and chemical munitions whose fate has not yet been fully verified by the Secretariat'.[11] Of the 24 outstanding issues identified by the DAT since 2014, 4 have been resolved, and Syria has amended its initial declarations several times. However, by the end of 2021, 20 issues still remained unresolved, and Syria's declarations continued to contain 'identified gaps, inconsistencies, and discrepancies'.[12]

The 24th round of consultations of the DAT with representatives of the Syrian government took place in February 2021 but failed to resolve any outstanding issues.[13] The 25th round was initially scheduled for May but was

[6] OPCW Director-General, Opening remarks at 'Ten years of chemical weapons use in Syria: A look back and a look ahead', CWC Coalition webinar, 22 Feb. 2022, 00:13:20. See also OPCW Director-General, Statement at the United Nations Security Council, 3 June 2021, The Hague, Netherlands.

[7] OPCW, Executive Council, 'Progress in the elimination of the Syrian chemical weapons programme', Report by the Director-General, EC-98/DG.24, 24 Sep. 2021, para. 27.

[8] OPCW, Executive Council, 'Progress in the elimination of the Syrian chemical weapons programme', Report by the Director-General, EC-97/DG.3, 23 Apr. 2021, para. 20.

[9] OPCW, Technical Secretariat, 'Report of the OPCW Fact-Finding Mission in Syria regarding the incident of the alleged use of chemicals as a weapon in Kafr Zeita, Syrian Arab Republic, 1 October 2016', Note by the Technical Secretariat, S/2020/2022, 31 Jan. 2022.

[10] OPCW, Executive Council, 'Progress in the elimination of the Syrian chemical weapons programme', Report by the Director-General, EC-99/DG.3, 23 Dec. 2021, para. 29.

[11] OPCW, EC-99/DG.3 (note 10), para. 15.

[12] OPCW, Executive Council, 'Progress in the elimination of the Syrian chemical weapons programme', Report by the Director-General, EC-96/DG.13, 24 Feb. 2021, para. 13; and OPCW, EC-99/DG.3 (note 10), para. 29.

[13] OPCW, Executive Council, 'Progress in the elimination of the Syrian chemical weapons programme', Report by the Director-General, EC-97/DG.2, 24 Mar. 2021, para. 11.

Table 12.1. Overview of ad hoc mechanisms of the Organisation for the Prohibition of Chemical Weapons to address the issue of chemical weapons in Syria

Mechanism	Duration	Mandate	Source
Declaration Assessment Team (DAT)	Since 2014	Resolve identified gaps and inconsistencies in Syria's declarations	Established by OPCW director-general
Fact-Finding Mission (FFM)	Since 2014	Establish facts surrounding alleged chemical weapons use in Syria	Established by OPCW director-general, endorsed by OPCW Executive Council and UN Security Council
OPCW–UN Joint Investigative Mechanism (JIM)	2015–2017	Identify perpetrators of chemical weapons attacks established by the FFM	UN Security Council Resolution 2235
Investigation and Identification Team (IIT)	Since 2018	Identify those involved in cases of chemical weapons use established by the FFM but not investigated by the JIM	Decision by OPCW conference of states parties

OPCW = Organisation for the Prohibition of Chemical Weapons; UN = United Nations.

Sources: OPCW, Executive Council, 'Reports of the OPCW Fact-Finding Mission in Syria', Decision, EC-M-48/DEC.1(2015), 4 Feb. 2015; UN Security Council Resolution 2235, 7 Aug. 2015; OPCW, Conference of the States Parties, 'Addressing the threat from chemicals weapons use', Decision, C-SS-4/DEC.3, 27 June 2018; UN Security Council Resolution 2209, 6 Mar. 2015; and OPCW, 'Syria and the OPCW', [n.d.].

postponed several times and ultimately did not take place in 2021, as Syria at first did not confirm the meeting dates and later denied the visa for one DAT member.[14] In response, the Secretariat 're-emphasised that the Syrian Arab Republic cannot intervene in the selection of experts by the OPCW and reiterated that, in the absence of fulfilment of these obligations by the Syrian Arab Republic, the Secretariat will not be in a position to deploy the DAT to Damascus and will duly report on this situation through existing mechanisms'.[15]

One of the outstanding issues concerns a site which Syria declared as never having been used for chemical weapons production but where the DAT found indications for the presence of a nerve agent.[16] By December 2021, Syria had not yet fulfilled the Technical Secretariat's request to explain and fully declare

---

[14] OPCW, Executive Council, 'Progress in the elimination of the Syrian chemical weapons programme', Report by the Director-General, EC-97/DG.7, 25 May 2021, para. 14; OPCW, Executive Council, 'Progress in the elimination of the Syrian chemical weapons programme', Report by the Director-General, EC-98/DG.6, 24 Aug. 2021, para. 13; OPCW, EC-98/DG.24 (note 7), paras 14–17; and OPCW, EC-99/DG.3 (note 10), para. 29.

[15] OPCW, EC-99/DG.3 (note 10), para. 18.

[16] E.g. OPCW, EC-96/DG.13 (note 12).

all chemical weapons activities at this site.[17] Another issue yet to be clarified relates to a military attack which Syria reported in July 2021 to have taken place on 8 June 2021. This was of concern to the OPCW since the targeted site had housed a declared former chemical weapons production facility and was related to an outstanding issue on the DAT list. Moreover, Syria informed the Secretariat of the destruction in that attack 'of two chlorine cylinders related to the chemical weapon incident that took place in Douma, Syrian Arab Republic, on 7 April 2018'.[18] The FFM confirmed the use of chlorine as a chemical weapon in this incident in its report of March 2019.[19] After the report's publication, an intense debate developed over these findings and the process by which they were reached.[20] OPCW experts had last inspected the cylinders at a different site in November 2020, and the Technical Secretariat had 'advised the Syrian Arab Republic that it was not to open, move, or alter the containers or their contents in any way without seeking the prior written consent of the Secretariat'. Syria had not obtained such consent, nor had it, as of December 2021, provided the explanations requested by the Secretariat.[21]

The director-general also informed the OPCW Executive Council of analysis results of several samples collected in the course of earlier inspections. Inspections carried out in November 2020 at two facilities of the Syrian Scientific Studies and Research Centre (SSRC) did not reveal any 'substances or activities inconsistent with' Syria's obligations under the CWC.[22] However, samples taken from large-volume storage containers during the 23rd round of DAT consultations in September and October 2020 contained a 'neat chemical warfare agent' which Syria had not previously declared, and the circumstances in which the samples were found 'may imply undeclared production activities'.[23] Since Syria did not provide sufficient explanation, the DAT took this up as a new outstanding issue to be pursued in the next round of consultations.[24] While Syria claimed it had

---

[17] E.g. OPCW, Executive Council, 'Statement by the Director-General following discussions under agenda item 6(c) on the elimination of the Syrian chemical weapons programme', EC-96/DG.17, 9 Mar. 2021, p. 3; and OPCW, EC-99/DG.3 (note 10), para. 17.

[18] OPCW, EC-98/DG.1 (note 3), paras 20–21. See also OPCW, EC-98/DG.6 (note 14), para. 19; and OPCW, EC-99/DG.3 (note 10), para. 24.

[19] OPCW, Technical Secretariat, 'Report of the Fact-Finding Mission regarding the incident of alleged use of toxic chemicals as a weapon in Douma, Syrian Arab Republic, on 7 April 2018', Note by the Technical Secretariat, S/1731/2019, 1 Mar. 2019.

[20] McLeish, C., 'Allegations of use of chemical weapons in Syria', *SIPRI Yearbook 2020*, pp. 442–45.

[21] OPCW, EC-98/DG.1 (note 3), paras 22–23; and OPCW, EC-99/DG.3 (note 10), para. 24.

[22] OPCW, EC-97/DG.7 (note 14), para. 17.

[23] OPCW, EC-97/DG.3 (note 8), para. 12. See also e.g. OPCW, Executive Council, 'Progress in the implementation of decision C-SS-4/DEC.3 on addressing the threat from chemical weapons use', Report by the Director-General, EC-97/DG.13, 22 June 2021, para. 3.

[24] OPCW, EC-97/DG.13 (note 23), para. 4.

been cooperating with the DAT and complained about unfair treatment,[25] the Secretariat stated that the Syrian Arab Republic's submitted declarations 'still cannot be considered accurate and complete' as required by the CWC, the Executive Council decision of 2013, and UN Security Council Resolution 2118.[26]

Second report of the Investigation and Identification Team

The IIT was established within the OPCW Technical Secretariat pursuant to a decision at a special session of the conference of the states parties (CSP) in June 2018.[27] This decision, while supported by a majority of those OPCW member states present at the CSP, was and remains highly contested.[28] On 12 April 2021 the IIT published its second report, which covered a chemical weapons attack with chlorine that occurred on 4 February 2018 in Saraqib, Syria. The report presented a detailed account of the incident, the methodology applied in the investigations, and the results of its investigations, and concluded that:

there are reasonable grounds to believe that at approximately 21:22 on 4 February 2018, during ongoing attacks against Saraqib, a military helicopter of the Syrian Arab Air Force under the control of the Tiger Forces hit eastern Saraqib by dropping a least one cylinder. The cylinder ruptured and released a toxic gas, chlorine, which dispersed over a large area affecting 12 named individuals.[29]

This was the fourth chemical incident for which the IIT identified the Syrian Arab Air Force as the responsible party.[30] For its report, the IIT also

---

[25] Syrian Arab Republic, 'Statement by Ms Rana Alrifaiy, Chargé d'Affaires of the Permanent Mission of the Syrian Arab Republic to the OPCW, at the Ninety-seventh Session of the Executive Council under agenda item 6(c)', EC-97/NAT.47, 6 July 2021.

[26] OPCW, EC-99/DG.3 (note 10), para. 19; OPCW, Executive Council, 'Destruction of Syrian chemical weapons', Decision, EC-M-33/DEC.1, 27 Sep. 2013; and UN Security Council Resolution 2118, 27 Sep. 2013.

[27] OPCW, Conference of the States Parties, 'Addressing the threat from chemical weapons', Decision, C-SS-4/DEC.3, 27 June 2018.

[28] McLeish, C., 'Chemical weapons: Arms control and disarmament', *SIPRI Yearbook 2019*, pp. 425–26; and McLeish, C., 'Chemical arms control and disarmament', *SIPRI Yearbook 2020*, pp. 452–55.

[29] OPCW, Technical Secretariat, 'Second report by the OPCW Investigation and Identification Team pursuant to paragraph 10 of Decision C-SS-4/DEC.3 "Addressing the threat from chemical weapons use", Saraqib (Syrian Arab Republic)—4 February 2018', Note by the Technical Secretariat, S/1943/2021, 12 Apr. 2021, Executive Summary, para. 3.

[30] For the first three incidents see OPCW, Technical Secretariat, 'First report by the OPCW Investigation and Identification Team (IIT) pursuant to paragraph 10 of Decision C-SS-4/DEC.3 "Addressing the Threat From Chemical Weapons Use", Ltamenah (Syrian Arab Republic) 24, 25, and 30 March 2017', Note by the Technical Secretariat, S/1867/2020, 8 Apr. 2020. The OPCW–UN Joint Investigative Mechanism (JIM) identified Syria as perpetrator in another four incidents and the Islamic State in two cases. See United Nations, Security Council, Seventh report of the OPCW–UN JIM, S/2017/904, 26 Oct. 2017; Fourth report of the UN–OPCW JIM, S/2016/888, 21 Oct. 2016; and Third report of the OPCW–UN JIM, S/2016/738, 24 Aug. 2016.

considered and investigated alternative scenarios such as Syria's suggestion that the incident in Saraqib had been staged by terrorist groups to discredit the Syrian government. However, the IIT did not find evidence in support of this or any other alternative scenario.[31]

Due to the pandemic situation and restrictions on travel and physical meetings in place at the time, the 25th conference of the states parties (CSP25) was split into two parts, the first part being held from 30 November to 1 December 2020, and the second part from 20–22 April 2021.[32] The issue of chemical weapons in Syria was addressed during the latter. A large number of states parties referred to the IIT's conclusions then and especially at the 97th session of the Executive Council in July 2021 (EC97). Many of them expressed their support for and confidence in the work of the Technical Secretariat.[33] Many states parties also linked their comments to Decision C-25/DEC.9 taken at CSP25 to invoke the compliance procedure under Article XII of the CWC in relation to Syria (see below).[34] Some states parties, including China and India, while unequivocally condemning chemical weapons use, noted the pertinent OPCW reports and called for a cooperative solution to the outstanding problems.[35] Some others, notably Iran, Russia and Syria, continued to reject the IIT as illegitimate and the FFM and IIT findings as arrived at through flawed methodologies; they also stated that Syria was cooperating with the OPCW but was not being treated fairly or impartially.[36] Russia presented its own analysis of the IIT report to the Executive Council in which it questioned the IIT's methodology, the credibility of witnesses, and the scientific accuracy of some findings.[37] Syria continued to deny that it still possessed or had ever used chemical weapons and condemned chemical

---

[31] OPCW, S/1943/2021 (note 29), 12 Apr. 2021, p. 12 and passim.

[32] OPCW, 25th Conference of the States Parties (CSP25), 'Report of the Twenty-fifth Session of the Conference of the States Parties', C-25/5, 22 Apr. 2021. See McLeish, C., 'Chemical weapons: Arms control and disarmament', *SIPRI Yearbook 2021*, p. 495.

[33] For CPS25 see e.g. the statements of Estonia (C-25/NAT.123), the EU (C-25/NAT.103), France (C-15/NAT.119), Lithuania (C-25/NAT.93), Romania (C-25/NAT.105), San Marino (C-25/NAT.122), the UK (C-25/NAT.111) and the USA (C-25/NAT.97). For EC97 see e.g. the joint statement of Australia, Canada and New Zealand (EC-97/NAT.36); and the statements of Austria (EC-97/NAT.35), Chile (EC-97/NAT.38), Ecuador (EC-97/NAT.41), the EU (EC-97/NAT.22), Finland (EC-97/NAT.14), France (EC-97/NAT.51), Guatemala (EC-97/NAT.49), Republic of Korea (EC-97/NAT.17), Peru (EC-97/NAT.44), Poland (EC-97/NAT.13), Romania (EC-97/NAT.11), Saudi Arabia (EC-97/NAT.58), Slovakia (EC-97/NAT.20), Sweden (EC-97/NAT.9), Switzerland (EC-97/NAT.54), the UK (EC-97/NAT.57) and the USA (EC-97/NAT).

[34] OPCW, CSP25, 'Addressing the possession and use of chemical weapons by the Syrian Arab Republic', Decision, C-25/DEC.9, 21 Apr. 2021.

[35] OPCW, CSP25, Statements of China (EC-97/NAT.29) and India (EC-97/NAT.30). China also considered the establishment of the IIT as beyond the CWC's mandate.

[36] OPCW, EC97, Statements of Iran (EC-97/NAT.21), Russia (EC-97/NAT.42, pp. 1–2), and Syria (EC-97/NAT.48). See also OPCW, CSP25, statements of, e.g., Iran (C-25/Nat.107), Russia, and Russia on behalf of the Member States of the Collective Security Treaty Organisation (C-25/NAT.124).

[37] Russia, 'Analysis of the report by the Investigation and Identification Team of the Organisation for the Prohibition of Chemical Weapons on the chemical incident in Saraqib, Syrian Arab Republic on 4 February 2018', EC-97/NAT.8, 5 July 2021.

weapons use under any circumstance; it also repeatedly claimed that terrorist groups, supported by Western governments, had staged chemical weapons attacks in order to blame them on Syria.[38] The members of the UN Security Council expressed a similar range of views in response to a briefing by the UN high representative for disarmament affairs, Izumi Nakamitsu.[39]

The decision to invoke the compliance procedure under CWC Article XII

In response to the first IIT report in 2020, a group of 40 states tabled a draft decision at the 94th session of the Executive Council in July 2020 that was adopted by majority vote as Decision EC-94/DEC.2. Among other things, the decision condemned the use of chemical weapons by Syria, as reported by the IIT, and laid out a set of requirements that Syria was expected to fulfil within 90 days, including: declaring the facilities related to the chemical weapons used in the attacks which the IIT had investigated, declaring all current chemical weapons stocks and facilities, and resolving all outstanding issues identified by the DAT.[40] The 90-day deadline expired with Syria not having met any of the requirements.[41]

As recommended by the Executive Council in July 2020, CSP25 took up the issue mainly at its second session in April 2021. A group of 46 states parties tabled a draft decision to invoke CWC Article XII paragraph 2 for the first time, formally state Syria's non-compliance with the CWC, and suspend the right of Syria '(a) to vote in the Conference and the Council; (b) to stand for election to the Council; and (c) to hold any office of the Conference, the Council, or any subsidiary organs'.[42] Syria's membership rights would be reinstated once the director-general reported that the country had fulfilled the requirements set by the Executive Council in Decision EC-94/DEC.2.

Since no consensus could be reached on the draft decision, a vote had to be taken at CSP25. Before and after the vote, several states parties elaborated on their positions. Whereas supporters of the decision emphasized that this reaction to Syria's activities was appropriate and necessary, others

[38] See e.g. Dabi, B. and Eyon, M., 'Syria: States that politicize chemical file should be held accountable', SANA, 30 Nov. 2021; and Eyon, M., 'Sabbagh: Some countries still politicize chemical file in Syria', SANA, 4 Oct. 2021.

[39] United Nations, Security Council, 'Letter dated 8 April 2021 from the President of the Security Council addressed to the Secretary-General and the Permanent Representatives of the members of the Security Council', S/2021/337, 9 Apr. 2021, annexes II–XVII.

[40] OPCW, Executive Council, 'Addressing the possession and use of chemical weapons by the Syrian Arab Republic', Decision, EC-94/DEC.2, 9 July 2020. See McLeish, C., 'Allegations of use of chemical weapons in Syria', *SIPRI Yearbook 2021*, pp. 483–86.

[41] See e.g. OPCW, Executive Council, 'Implementation of EC-94/DEC.2 on addressing the possession and use of chemical weapons by the Syrian Arab Republic', Report by the Director-General, EC-96/DG.1, 14 Oct. 2020, paras 4–6.

[42] OPCW, C-25/DEC.9 (note 34), para. 7.

emphasized the value of dialogue, cooperation and consensus in the work of the OPCW. Opponents criticized the decision because in their view it entailed a further politicization of the OPCW or because they rejected the IIT.[43] A majority of 87 states parties voted in favour of the decision, 15 voted against it and 34 abstained. CSP25 thus adopted the document as Decision C-25/DEC.9, 'Addressing the possession and use of chemical weapons by the Syrian Arab Republic'.[44]

The debate at the 26th conference of the states parties in November showed a similar pattern as previous debates. Most states parties still supported the decision taken by CSP25 in April and called on Syria to fully restore its compliance and cooperate with the OPCW to that end. China and Russia stated once more that they did not consider the IIT, on whose work the decision was based, as legitimate; Russia even called its establishment a violation of the CWC and of the UN Charter. Syria repeated its unconditional condemnation of chemical weapons use and declared its willingness to further cooperate with the DAT, on the condition that one DAT team member be replaced. The Syrian representative also stated that Syria would not accept or work with the IIT which it, too, considered illegitimate, and that Decision EC-94/DEC.2 was drafted in a manner that made it impossible for Syria to comply with all of its terms.[45]

[43] For statements and explanations of votes on this matter see OPCW, 'Twenty-fifth Session of the Conference of States Parties: Documents', [n.d.].

[44] OPCW, C-25/DEC.9 (note 34), 21 Apr. 2021; and OPCW, C-25/5 (note 32), para. 9.24.

[45] See discussion under agenda item 9(d) in OPCW, 'CSP-26—29 November 2021—afternoon', Webcast, 29 Nov. 2021; and Syria, 'Statement by HE Ambassador Bassam Sabbagh, Permanent Representative of the Syrian Arab Republic to the OPCW, at the 25th session of the CSP', C-25/NAT.39, 30 Nov. 2021, p. 3.

IV. Chemical arms control and disarmament

UNA JAKOB

The Chemical Weapons Convention (CWC) contains a comprehensive and unequivocal prohibition of chemical weapons and warfare. As of December 2021, it had 193 states parties. Of the four states not party to the CWC, Israel has signed but not ratified it, and Egypt, North Korea and South Sudan have neither signed nor ratified or acceded to the CWC.[1]

This section provides an update on the case of the Russian citizen Alexei Navalny's poisoning in August 2020 with a novichok nerve agent, as well as other developments in the Organisation for the Prohibition of Chemical Weapons (OPCW) during 2021.[2] As of December 2021, the Navalny case had not yet been officially investigated or resolved, and it continued to cause political tensions between Russia and a number of Western countries, in particular France, Germany, Sweden, the United Kingdom and the United States.

Use of novichok agents

Sanctions related to the use of novichoks

The political repercussions of the novichok attack against Navalny carried over into 2021. The sanctions enacted by the European Union (EU) in October 2020 remained in place and were extended for one year on 11 October 2021.[3] They target six Russian government officials whom the EU holds responsible for 'inducing', 'providing support to' or 'assisting' the perpetrators of the attack against Navalny, as well as a research institute in Moscow for failing to 'destroy the stockpiles of chemical weapons'.[4] The UK maintains sanctions against the same targets as part of its own chemical weapons sanctions regime.[5] The USA, in coordination with the EU and the UK, also enacted two sets of sanctions in March and in August 2021.[6] In August, the USA and the UK also added seven individuals to their sanctions lists; all seven are

---

[1] For a summary and other details of the Chemical Weapons Convention see annex A, section I, in this volume.

[2] For background see McLeish, C., 'Use of novichok agents', *SIPRI Yearbook 2021*, pp. 489–93.

[3] McLeish (note 2), p. 492; and Council of the EU, 'EU sanctions against chemical weapons renewed for one year', Press release, 11 Oct. 2021.

[4] Council Implementing Regulation (EU) 2020/1480 of 14 October 2020 implementing Regulation (EU) 2018/1542 concerning restrictive measures against the proliferation and use of chemical weapons, *Official Journal of the European Union*, L341, 15 Oct. 2020; and Council of the EU (note 3).

[5] The Chemical Weapons (Sanctions) (EU Exit) Regulations 2019 (UK).

[6] US Department of State, 'US sanctions and other measures imposed on Russia in response to Russia's use of chemical weapons', Fact sheet, 2 Mar. 2021; US Department of State, 'United States imposes additional costs on Russia for the poisoning of Aleksey Navalny', Fact sheet, 20 Aug. 2021; and Congressional Research Service (CRS), 'Russia: the Navalny poisoning, chemical weapons use, and US sanctions', CRS *In Focus* report no. IF11872, Updated 26 Aug. 2021.

members of the Russian intelligence service FSB and allegedly took part in the attack on Navalny.[7]

Debates within the OPCW policy-making organs

In the debates during the 2021 meetings of the OPCW Executive Council and the conference of states parties (CSP), many delegations submitted statements condemning the use of a novichok agent.[8] The statements affirmed that such an attack against an individual constituted chemical weapons use and as such was completely unacceptable and a violation of the CWC and international norms; declared that those responsible for chemical weapons use must be held accountable, and there must be no impunity; called on Russia to fully investigate the incident and disclose all related information; and expressed their regret or concern that no technical assistance visit (TAV) to Russia had taken place. While the delegations of the EU, France, Germany, Sweden, the UK and the USA were the most outspoken on this issue, a group of 46 and later 55 states parties presented joint statements expressing their support for the positions outlined above.[9] Moreover, the UK and, more explicitly, the USA accused Russia of violating the CWC, with both countries calling on Russia to declare and destroy any remaining chemical weapons, including novichok agents.[10]

Russia continued to deny any responsibility for the case.[11] It did not accept the findings that a novichok agent was used on Russian territory in the first place, instead viewing this narrative as fabricated and politically motivated. The Russian delegation also suggested that the OPCW Technical Secretariat had not been acting in an impartial manner, and that several Western countries had refused to cooperate with Russia, in particular following Russia's requests to Germany, France and Sweden for legal assistance and coopera-

---

[7] British government, 'The UK sanctions list', Brexit Guidance, 6 July 2020 (updated 22 Dec. 2021); British Foreign, Commonwealth & Development Office, 'UK sanctions Russian FSB operatives over poisoning of Alexey Navalny', Press release, 20 Aug. 2021; and US Department of State, 'United States imposes additional costs on Russia for the poisoning of Aleksey Navalny' (note 6).

[8] See e.g. the statements of the EU, France, Germany, Sweden, the UK and the USA, as well as joint statements, at the 97th Session of the Executive Council (EC97) and the 26th Conference of the States Parties (CSP26).

[9] See the joint statements delivered at the 96th Session of the Executive Council (EC96) by Lithuania on behalf of 45 states EC-96/NAT.21, 9 Mar. 2021; and at CSP26 by Bulgaria on behalf of 55 states, 29 Nov. 2021.

[10] UK delegation to the OPCW, Statement on the use of a novichok nerve agent delivered at EC97, 19 July 2021; Roper, J., Statement by the permanent representative of the UK to the 98th session of the Executive Council (EC98), 4 Oct. 2021; US delegation statements at the 25th Conference of the States Parties (CSP25), C-25/NAT.98, 20 Apr. 2021; at EC96, EC-96/NAT.24, 9 Mar. 2021; and at EC97, EC-97/NAT.16, 6 July 2021.

[11] Russian delegation to the OPCW, Statement delivered at CSP25, C-25/NAT.48, 19 Feb. 2021; see also statement by Russia at CSP26 under agenda item 9—status of implementation of the Chemical Weapons Convention in OPCW, 'CSP-26—29 November 2021—afternoon', Webcast, 29 Nov. 2021.

tion under the CWC and the European Convention on Mutual Assistance in Criminal Matters.[12]

Invoking the consultation and clarification procedure under CWC Article IX

On 5 October 2021 the UK on behalf of 45 states parties invoked the consultation and clarification procedure contained in Article IX, paragraph 2 of the CWC.[13] This paragraph 2 provides:

States Parties should, whenever possible, first make every effort to clarify and resolve, through exchange of information and consultations among themselves, any matter which may cause doubt about compliance with this Convention, or which gives rise to concerns about a related matter which may be considered ambiguous. A State Party which receives a request from another State Party for clarification … shall provide the requesting State Party as soon as possible, but in any case not later than 10 days after the request, with information sufficient to answer the doubt or concern raised along with an explanation of how the information provided resolves the matter.

The group asked for information regarding Russia's actions and any planned further steps to explain, address and clarify the Navalny incident. They moreover requested Russia to share the results of its investigation with OPCW members and to inform member states about the status of its cooperation with the OPCW, in particular with regard to the TAV.[14] In its response, Russia did not address these questions directly but rather, as mentioned above, requested information and clarification from Germany, the UK, France, Sweden and the OPCW Technical Secretariat, which it considered essential for the decision to open its own criminal investigation.[15] Both sides have so far considered the other side's responses insufficient,[16] and Russia and the UK have already submitted further requests for information as official documents for the 99th session of the Executive Council, scheduled for March 2022.[17] The clarification process will likely continue in 2022.

---

[12] European Convention on Mutual Assistance in Criminal Matters, signed 20 June 1959, entered into force 12 June 1962.

[13] The request for clarification by the UK permanent representative to the OPCW, on behalf of 45 member states, was first submitted to Russia via the Technical Secretariat in Note Verbale no. 093/2021 on 5 Oct. 2021 and repeated in Note Verbale no. 109/2021, EC-99/NAT.1, 5 Nov. 2021.

[14] UK permanent representative to the OPCW, EC-99/NAT.1 (note 13).

[15] These requests referred to the role of certain individuals that were present on Navalny's flight to Berlin, to a possible piece of evidence currently in German custody, to the formula of the chemical agent identified in Navalny's biomedical samples, and to video footage from the TAV to Germany. See Russian permanent representative to the OPCW, Note Verbale no. 54, EC-98/NAT.13, 2 Nov. 2021; Note Verbale no. 44, EC-98/NAT.8, 7 Oct. 2021; and Note Verbale no. 58, EC-99/NAT.2, 15 Nov. 2021. Copies of the requests for legal assistance submitted by Russia to Germany, France and Sweden, as well as other related documents, are contained in the annexes to EC-98/NAT.8.

[16] See the notes verbales submitted at EC98, by France, no. 2021-0496245, EC-98/NAT.10, 18 Oct. 2021; Germany, no. 41/2021, EC-98/NAT.9, 18 Oct. 2021; Russia, no. 54, EC-98/NAT.13, 2 Nov. 2021; Sweden, EC-98/NAT.12, 18 Oct. 2021; and the UK, no. 101/2021, EC-98/NAT.11, 18 Oct. 2021.

[17] UK permanent representative to the OPCW, EC-99/NAT.1 (note 13); and Russian permanent representative to the OPCW, Note Verbale no. 58, EC-99/NAT.2 (note 15).

Other developments in the OPCW

Impact of the Covid-19 pandemic on OPCW activities and meetings

The meeting of the 25th conference of the states parties (CSP25) was originally scheduled for 2020 but was split into two sessions due to the pandemic situation.[18] The second session of CSP25 in April 2021 and the 26th conference of the states parties (CSP26) in November 2021, as well as the meetings of the Executive Council, were held as in-person meetings, albeit similar to 2020 with limited attendance and a webcast due to the pandemic restrictions.[19] Subsidiary bodies such as the Scientific Advisory Board (SAB) and the Advisory Board on Education and Outreach (ABEO) held their meetings virtually.[20] Germany, supported by 12 co-sponsors, tabled a draft decision at the 98th session of the Executive Council (EC98) in October 2021 that would enable the council to meet in a virtual format in emergency situations.[21] However, council members deferred the decision on this proposal to the next session, scheduled for March 2022.[22]

The Covid-19 pandemic again affected the activities of the Technical Secretariat in 2021.[23] Due to travel and other restrictions, the Secretariat could not carry out all its planned and mandated inspection and verification activities, but had to prioritize its missions.[24] Other routine activities were carried out as far as possible under pandemic conditions.[25] Regarding international assistance activities, meetings were held virtually where possible, but the number of journeys and activities had to be reduced; the Fellowship Programme was temporarily suspended but was able to resume towards the end of 2021.[26]

---

[18] OPCW, 25th Conference of the States Parties (CSP25), 'Report of the Twenty-fifth Session of the Conference of the States Parties', C-25/5, 22 Apr. 2021.

[19] See e.g. OPCW, Technical Secretariat, 'Update on the impact of the Covid-19 outbreak on the OPCW programme in 2021', Note by the Technical Secretariat, S/1996/2021, 5 Oct. 2021; and McLeish, C., 'Chemical weapons: Arms control and disarmament', *SIPRI Yearbook 2021*, p. 495.

[20] OPCW, Executive Council, 'Report on the activities of the Advisory Board on Education and Outreach covering the period 1 September 2020 to 31 August 2021', Note by the Director-General, EC-98/DG.17, 16 Sep. 2021; OPCW, Scientific Advisory Board (SAB), 'Report of the Scientific Advisory Board at its Thirty-first Session', SAB-31/1, 4 Mar. 2021; OPCW, SAB, 'Report of the Scientific Advisory Board at its Thirty-Second Session', SAB-32/1, 17 June 2021; and OPCW, SAB, 'Report of the Scientific Advisory Board at its Thirty-Third Session', SAB-33/1, 18 Nov. 2021.

[21] German permanent representative to the OPCW, Note Verbale no. 33/2021, 28 Sep. 2021, pp. 2–4 (Draft Decision: 'Allowing the Convening of Executive Council Meetings or Sessions in Extraordinary Circumstances').

[22] OPCW, Executive Council, Report of the 98th Session of the Executive Council, EC-98/5, 7 Oct. 2021, p. 14, para. 17.6.

[23] OPCW, S/1996/2021 (note 19). See also McLeish, C., 'Allegations of use of chemical weapons in Syria', *SIPRI Yearbook 2020*, pp. 494–95.

[24] See OPCW, Technical Secretariat, 'Update on the impact of the outbreak of the coronavirus disease (Covid-19) on the Organisation for the Prohibition of Chemical Weapons programme in 2021', Note by the Technical Secretariat, S/1930/2021, 18 Feb. 2021; and OPCW, S/1996/2021 (note 19).

[25] OPCW, S/1996/2021 (note 19), pp. 3–4.

[26] OPCW, S/1996/2021 (note 19), p. 4.

Re-appointment of the OPCW director-general

CSP26 re-appointed Fernando Arias as director-general for a second four-year term of office commencing in July 2022.[27] The EU and 22 states parties took the floor to express their strong support for Director-General Arias and for the renewal of his appointment. Russia criticized some changes it perceived in the OPCW's approach since Arias took office, including what it saw as a politicization of the OPCW and a turn away from the strictly impartial and technical work of the Technical Secretariat. The Russian representative also took issue with the fact that no alternative candidate was put forward for the appointment. In its explanation of vote, Russia stated that it disassociated itself from the consensus decision to renew the director-general's appointment.[28]

The OPCW budget for 2022–23

In 2021, states parties for the first time decided on a biannual budget for the OPCW, moving away from the previous yearly cycle. Neither at EC98 nor at CSP26 was there consensus on the draft programme and budget. In the Executive Council, a majority of 31 states parties supported the draft. Three states parties—China, Iran and Russia—voted against its adoption, and seven countries abstained.[29] At CSP26, of the 132 states present and voting, 102 voted in favour of the draft, 12 states opposed it and 18 abstained.[30] Several states offered explanations of their vote.[31] To highlight but a few examples, both Russia and Iran explained they did not wish to support a budget that includes funding for the IIT, reiterating their well-known position that the IIT is illegal and not covered by the CWC. Supporters of the draft budget pointed out that the OPCW needs a solid and predictable financial basis to carry out its work. Explanations offered for abstentions included concerns about the departure from consensus decisions on the budget; the move away from a zero nominal growth policy, which some states could not support for domestic political or economic reasons; concerns that the planned budget included funding for non-consensual items (such as the IIT); and dissatis-

[27] OPCW, CSP26, 'Renewal of the appointment of the Director-General', Decision, C-26/DEC.9, 30 Nov. 2021.

[28] OPCW, CSP26, 'Report of the Twenty-sixth Session of the Conference of the States Parties', 2 Dec. 2021, C-26/5, p. 16; and OPCW, 'CSP26—30 November 2021—Afternoon', Webcast, 30 Nov. 2021, Agenda item 22 (Appointment of the Director-General), 00:26:56 (intervention of Russia).

[29] OPCW, Executive Council, 'Draft Programme and Budget of the OPCW for 2022–2023', Decision, EC-98/DEC.5, 6 Oct. 2021; and OPCW, Executive Council, 'Report of the Ninety-eighth Session of the Executive Council', EC-98/5, 7 Oct. 2021, para. 10.19.

[30] OPCW, CSP26, 'Programme and Budget of the OPCW for 2022–2023', Decision, C-26/DEC.11, 1 Dec. 2021; and OPCW, C-26/5 (note 28), para. 13.4.

[31] OPCW, 'CSP-26—1 December 2021—morning', Webcast, 1 Dec. 2021, Agenda item 13 (Biennial Programme and Budget of the OPCW for 2022 and 2023), 1:29:39.

faction with transfers of funds away from the International Cooperation and Assistance Programme.[32]

Use of central nervous system–acting chemicals for law enforcement purposes

The use of chemicals acting on the central nervous system (CNS) for law enforcement purposes continued to be an issue in 2021. At the recommendation of the 96th Session of the Executive Council (EC96), CSP26 adopted the decision 'that the aerosolised use of CNS-acting chemicals is understood to be inconsistent with law enforcement purposes as a "purpose not prohibited" under the Convention'.[33] The topic was first officially discussed at the second CWC review conference in 2008 at the initiative of Switzerland. That country, later supported by Australia and subsequently the USA, continued to advocate a clarification by states parties that such use was prohibited by the CWC. This initiative built on and was supported by even earlier efforts undertaken by the International Committee of the Red Cross (ICRC) and civil society groups, as well as the work of the OPCW Scientific Advisory Board (SAB) on this issue.[34] In a 2018 report, the SAB stated that CNS-acting chemicals differ from riot control agents, which are permitted under the CWC for law enforcement purposes, due to their different properties and effects, and that 'chemicals that selectively modify CNS functions . . . can have a very low safety margin when delivered as an aerosol'.[35]

Like the draft programme and budget, this draft decision did not command consensus at either forum. Of the 128 states parties voting on this draft decision at CSP26, 85 supported it, 10 opposed it and 33 abstained.[36] In explaining their vote, several countries referred to the SAB's assessment as one reason for their positive vote. Some emphasized that the decision did not entail any additional financial or other obligations and that it was based on the scientific state of the art as elaborated by the SAB. Some proponents also suggested that further dialogue was necessary and desirable within the OPCW to achieve wider support for this decision. This view was also shared

---

[32] OPCW, Webcast (note 31). Some explanations of votes are also available as official documents at <https://www.opcw.org/resources/documents/csp26>. On the transfer of funds see e.g. OPCW, Executive Council, 'Transfers of funds during 2020', Note by the Director-General, EC-97/DG.12 and C-26/DG.3, 22 June 2021.

[33] OPCW, CSP26, 'Understanding regarding the aerosolised use of central nervous system-acting chemicals for law enforcement purposes', Decision, C-26/DEC.10, 1 Dec. 2021.

[34] Switzerland, Statement by HE Heinz Walker-Nederkoorn, Permanent representative of Switzerland to the OPCW, to the 26th CSP, The Hague, 1 Dec. 2021; and International Committee of the Red Cross, Statement at the 26th CSP to the CWC, 26 Nov. 2021.

[35] OPCW, Fourth Session of the Review Conference, 'Report of the Scientific Advisory Board on developments in science and technology for the Fourth Special Session of the Conference of the States Parties to review the operation of the Chemical Weapons Convention', RC-4/DG.1, 30 Apr. 2018, para. 97.

[36] OPCW, C-26/5 (note 28), para. 26.7. For the vote in the Executive Council see OPCW, Executive Council, 'Report of the Ninety-sixth Session of the Executive Council', EC-96/2, 12 Mar. 2021, para. 14.14.

by some states that had abstained; some explained they were dissatisfied with the process rather than the substance of the decision, and some cited principled opposition to the tendency to move away from consensus-based decisions towards more frequent voting in the OPCW. States opposed mostly criticized the decision for having no basis in the CWC, but rather constituting a de facto amendment of the convention and illegally circumventing the pertinent procedure under CWC Article VX. Iran and Russia explicitly disassociated themselves from the decision.[37] The ICRC welcomed the recommendation of EC96 and the draft decision but added, 'At the ICRC, we are of the view that the decision should not be interpreted as meaning that non-CNS-acting, non-aerosol-delivered toxic chemicals are therefore acceptable as weapons in law enforcement'.[38]

OPCW activities concerning international cooperation and assistance

In 2021 the OPCW Technical Secretariat carried out a range of measures, under Article XI of the CWC, to address international cooperation and exchange of chemicals, equipment and know-how for purposes not prohibited under the CWC. These activities included, for example, capacity building in the area of chemical safety and security, and the enhancement of laboratory capabilities.[39] However, several states parties expressed their concern that funds had been transferred out of the International Cooperation and Assistance (ICA) programme several times; for instance, the group of African states parties to the OPCW (African Group) called 'upon the Secretariat and states Parties to work collectively to address this concern and to come up with sustainable solutions that would enable the retention of unspent funds for future ICA activities'.[40] The Technical Secretariat also continued to implement the Africa Programme, which includes activities in the areas of capacity building, technical assistance, training, and exchanges among scientists including through fellowships. The ongoing pandemic restrictions meant that most of the activities had to be conducted online.[41] In October 2021 Algeria issued a statement on behalf of the African Group that, while welcoming the activities under the Africa Programme, suggested the programme should be covered by the regular OPCW budget instead of being funded through voluntary contributions.[42]

---

[37] See OPCW (note 31), agenda item 26 (Any other business), 00:02:11.

[38] International Committee of the Red Cross, Statement to CSP26, 29 Nov. 2021, p. 2.

[39] OPCW, Executive Council, 'Progress made and review of the status of the implementation of Article XI of the Chemical Weapons Convention', Report by the Director-General, EC-98/DG.9, C-26/DG.7, 2 Sep. 2021.

[40] Algerian permanent representative to the OPCW, Statement on behalf of the African Group, EC-98/NAT.20, 5 Oct. 2021, p. 4.

[41] OPCW, Executive Council, 'The Programme to Strengthen Cooperation with Africa on the Chemical Weapons Convention', Note by the Director-General, EC-98/DG.14, C-26/DG.12, 9 Sep. 2021.

[42] Algerian permanent representative to the OPCW (note 40), p. 4.

Destruction of chemical weapons in the United States

The USA, the only chemical weapons possessor state that has not yet completed the destruction of its declared chemical weapons, continued the elimination of its stockpile under OPCW verification. As of October 2021, it had destroyed over 97 per cent of its declared stockpiles and was planning to complete the destruction process according to schedule by 30 September 2023.[43]

The new OPCW Centre for Chemistry and Technology

The project to upgrade the OPCW Laboratory and Equipment Store to a Centre for Chemistry and Technology (ChemTech Centre) entered a new phase in 2021. Construction activities on the building started in June, and the contracts for security-related installations and laboratory furnishings were awarded in July and October, respectively.[44] The construction process is currently scheduled to be completed by the end of 2022. Voluntary contributions pledged to the project, from 51 countries, the EU and other donors, total around 33.7 million euros, covering the ChemTech Centre's estimated costs of around 33.4 million euros.[45]

Scientific Advisory Board of the OPCW

According to its reports, the SAB focused on three areas of work: the preparations of its report for the fifth CWC review conference, scheduled for 2023; ideas and plans for workshops within the chemicals industry; and the new temporary working group (TWG) on the analysis of biotoxins, which took up its work in 2021.[46] In his response to the SAB report on its 33rd session, Director-General Arias expressed his support for their recommendations, namely a joint workshop with the International Union of Pure and Applied Sciences (IUPAC) in preparation for the fifth review conference, a workshop on the role of artificial intelligence (AI) in chemistry, and enhancing outreach and capacity building with regard to dissemination technologies.[47]

---

[43] US permanent representative to the OPCW, Statement at the 98th Session of the Executive Council, EC-98/NAT.15, 5 Oct. 2021, p. 2; and OPCW, Executive Council, 'Overall progress with respect to the destruction of the remaining chemical weapons stockpiles', Report by the Director-General, EC-97/DG.18, 30 June 2021.

[44] OPCW, Technical Secretariat, 'Progress in the project to upgrade the OPCW Laboratory and Equipment Store to a Centre for Chemistry and Technology', Note by the Technical Secretariat, S/1956/2021, 17 May 2021, p. 3, and S/2003/2021, 9 Nov. 2021, p. 4.

[45] OPCW, S/2003/2021 (note 44), pp. 4–5.

[46] OPCW, SAB-31/1, SAB-32/1 and SAB-33-1 (note 20); OPCW, SAB, 'Summary of the first meeting of the Scientific Advisory Board's temporary working group on the analysis of biotoxins', SAB-32/WP.1, 6 May 2021; and OPCW, SAB, 'Summary of the second meeting of the Scientific Advisory Board's temporary working group on the analysis of biotoxins', SAB-33/WP.1, 15 Oct. 2021.

[47] OPCW, Executive Council, 'Response to the Report of the Thirty-second Session of the Scientific Advisory Board, 15–17 June 2021', Note by the Director-General, EC-98/DG.21, 22 Sep. 2021.

These recommendations tie in with the broader efforts of the SAB to identify, in cooperation with industry representatives, scientific and technological developments that are potentially relevant to the CWC or that may pose challenges for industry verification. They also reflect the SAB's own work in 2021 regarding the use of AI and computing power in the chemical industry, for example in advanced synthesis planning and dissemination technologies, among other things.[48]

The TWG on the analysis of biotoxins, chaired by SAB member Dr Daan Nort, comprised eight SAB members and six external experts. The TWG's focus was on the 'identification of materials of biological origin relevant to the Convention, analysis techniques and procedures, and current and future collaboration with other organisations'.[49]

OPCW Advisory Board on Education and Outreach

At its 10th session in February 2021, the ABEO agreed its strategic plan, which included focusing on enhancing e-learning opportunities, fostering the impact of capacity building, and continuing to work on awareness-raising about chemical safety and security.[50] The TWG on e-learning, established in September 2020, continued its work in 2021 by reviewing the Secretariat's existing e-learning offers, which aim to provide training and information to national authorities and other stakeholders about the central provisions of and obligations under the CWC.[51] The TWG also formulated recommendations for a future e-learning strategy, among other things, and presented its report to EC98. [52]

Outlook

At the time of writing, it was difficult to predict to what extent the Covid-19 pandemic will continue to affect the work and meetings of the OPCW in 2022. At the very least, there will probably be repercussions concerning the Technical Secretariat's inspection and verification activities. The problem of chemical weapons use will continue to play an important role in the OPCW's work, and it is unlikely that the existing political differences will be overcome in the short term. The Executive Council is expected to establish an open-ended working group which, together with the Technical Secretariat, is to start preparations for the fifth review conference, scheduled for May 2023.[53]

[48] OPCW, SAB-32/1 (note 20).
[49] OPCW, SAB-31/1 (note 20), p. 9.
[50] OPCW, Executive Council, EC-98/DG.17 (note 20), p. 2.
[51] OPCW, Technical Secretariat, 'OPCW E-learning', [n.d.].
[52] OPCW, EC-98/DG.17 (note 20), p. 6 (see the annex for the TWG report on e-learning); and Weinig, J.-G., Chair of the OPCW Advisory Board on Education and Outreach, Statement to CSP26, 29 Nov. to 3 Dec. 2021.
[53] OPCW, C-26/5 (note 28), para. 25.1.

13. Conventional arms control and regulation of new weapon technologies

Overview

Many of the contemporary debates on conventional arms control are shaped by the concept of 'humanitarian disarmament'. This can relate to weapons deemed to be inhumane—such as incendiary weapons, explosive weapons in populated areas (EWIPA), cluster munitions, and landmines, improvised explosive devices and explosive remnants of war—and other categories of conventional weapon that raise humanitarian concerns—such as small arms and light weapons (SALW) and armed uncrewed aerial vehicles (UAVs).

The main multilateral treaty for regulating inhumane weapons is the 1981 Certain Conventional Weapons (CCW) Convention, alongside the 1997 Anti-Personnel Mine Convention and the 2008 Convention on Cluster Munitions. While progress in implementing the latter two treaties continued in 2021, a handful of states once again obstructed advances in most of the agenda at the sixth review conference of the CCW Convention, in December (see section I).

After many years of failing to make progress to address the humanitarian harm of EWIPA within the CCW framework, a separate process led by Ireland aims to develop a political declaration on their use. After Covid-19-related delays, the consultation process restarted in 2021 and a political declaration is expected to be adopted in 2022. Equivalent concerns about the humanitarian implications of armed UAVs have so far failed to generate sufficient state support for a similar multilateral regulatory process.

One of the most prominent efforts within the CCW regime has been to consider the regulation of autonomous weapon systems (AWS; see section II). Since 2017 a group of governmental experts (GGE) has been leading these efforts. A critical juncture was reached in 2021 with the end of the GGE's current mandate and dialogue at the CCW review conference. As in previous years, the GGE's discussions in 2021 followed two tracks: one on substantial questions around legal, ethical and military aspects of the development and use of AWS, and the other on options related to the governance of AWS. The GGE had aimed to submit substantive recommendations to the conference, on both the normative and the operational frameworks guiding the development and use of AWS, as well as recommendations for the mandate of a future GGE. However, fundamental disagreements prevented consensus being reached on both items. The review conference eventually adopted a new—less ambitious—mandate, allowing GGE discussions on AWS to continue within the CCW framework in

2022. However, the lack of substantive progress may lead some states to seek alternative paths to achieving a legally binding instrument.

Some of the humanitarian impacts of SALW are addressed by the 2001 United Nations Programme of Action to Prevent, Combat and Eradicate the Illicit Trade in SALW in All its Aspects (POA) and the 2005 International Tracing Instrument (ITI). Implementation of both these politically binding instruments is reviewed at a biennial meeting of states (BMS). At the seventh BMS, in July 2021, states remained divided on the most contentious issues related to the implementation of the POA, including controls on ammunition, addressing new developments in SALW manufacturing, and creating links between the POA and other international processes (see section I).

Beyond arms control, international security can also be improved by states acting to build mutual confidence through transparency about their armaments (see section IV). However, the existing instruments within the UN and the Organization for Security and Co-operation in Europe (OSCE) are in urgent need of revitalization as participation in 2021 was low and parts of the submissions were incomplete. A more complex confidence-building mechanism is the 1992 Treaty on Open Skies. In November 2020 the United States withdrew from the treaty, and in January 2021 Russia announced that it would do the same (see section III). After the Russian withdrawal came into effect on 18 December 2021, most of the remaining parties to the treaty seemed determined to continue implementing it. However, at the end of the year the longer-term future of the treaty remained uncertain.

Several categories of weapon are not covered by a specific treaty and in more complex cases—such as the regulation of cyberspace or activity in space—the most appropriate approach may also be the subject of intense debate. Dialogue around the governance of information and communications technology (ICT) and cyber norms has taken place through a patchwork of initiatives (see section V). The main state-driven efforts continued in 2021 within two parallel UN processes: a GGE and an open-ended working group (OEWG). The 2019–21 OEWG concluded its work and a new OEWG, for 2021–25, was established. Despite international efforts to control the malicious use of ICT continuing to be hindered by differing interests and normative preferences of states and ongoing geopolitical tensions, 2021 was generally a productive year for cyber governance.

Meanwhile, developments in space security in 2021 centred on three issues (see section VI). There was continued development of offensive counterspace capabilities. This was demonstrated by new reported tests by China and Russia. Rising interest in lunar activities was shown by the development of two distinct international partnerships, one led by the USA and the other by China and Russia. Finally, there was widespread support for new discussions on responsible behaviour in space in the UN General Assembly, including agreement to convene a consensus-based OEWG to move discussions forward.

IAN DAVIS

I. Multilateral regulation of inhumane weapons and other conventional weapons of humanitarian concern

IAN DAVIS AND GIOVANNA MALETTA

Many of the contemporary debates on conventional arms control are shaped by the concept of 'humanitarian disarmament', which prioritizes the protection, security and well-being of people as opposed to states. This approach strives to increase the protection of civilians by reducing the human and environmental impacts of arms.[1] One of the main multilateral treaties designed for regulating weapons that are considered to cause unnecessary or unjustifiable suffering to combatants or to affect civilians indiscriminately is the 1981 Certain Conventional Weapons Convention (CCW Convention) and its five protocols. Their scope extends to landmines, incendiary weapons and explosive remnants of war (ERW), among other weapon types.[2] Since the CCW Convention is an umbrella treaty, agreements on additional weapon types can be regulated through the adoption of new protocols. In recent decades, however, there have been increasing tensions between the prioritization of humanitarian demands and the perceived military needs of certain states. Because the CCW regime operates by consensus, a small number of states that have chosen to retain or develop weapons seen as inhumane by others have simply vetoed or stalled progress on strengthening the treaty.[3]

As of 31 December 2021, there were 125 states parties to the CCW Convention and at least two of its five protocols; no new state joined in 2021.[4] The parties meet regularly at annual meetings and quinquennial review conferences. These meetings also consider the work of the groups of governmental experts (GGEs) convened since 2001 in various formats. Amended Protocol II and Protocol V have their own parallel implementation processes. Unlike in 2020, when all but three CCW-related meetings were postponed due to Covid-19 restrictions, all nine meetings took place in 2021 (see table 13.1). However, a handful of states once again obstructed advances in most of the CCW agenda. For example, at the sixth review conference, which took place

---

[1] See the discussions on humanitarian disarmament in Anthony, I., 'International humanitarian law: ICRC guidance and its application in urban warfare', *SIPRI Yearbook 2017*; and Davis, I. and Verbruggen, M., 'The Convention on Certain Conventional Weapons', *SIPRI Yearbook 2018*, p. 381. See also International Committee of the Red Cross (ICRC), 'International humanitarian law and the challenges of contemporary armed conflicts: Recommitting to protection in armed conflict on the 70th anniversary of the Geneva Conventions', *International Review of the Red Cross*, vol. 101, no. 911 (Aug. 2019).

[2] For a summary and other details of the CCW Convention see annex A, section I, in this volume.

[3] See e.g. the discussion on the 2016 CCW Review Conference in Davis, I. et al., 'Humanitarian arms control regimes: Key developments in 2016', *SIPRI Yearbook 2017*, pp. 554–61; and on developments since then in the 2018–21 editions of the SIPRI Yearbook.

[4] For lists of the CCW Convention states parties that have ratified the original, amended and additional protocols see annex A, section I, in this volume.

Table 13.1. Meetings of the Certain Conventional Weapons Convention in 2021

Dates	Meeting
3–13 August	GGE on LAWS
18 August	Protocol V meeting of experts
16–17 August	Amended Protocol II group of experts
6–8 September	Preparatory meeting for 6th CCW review conference
24 September–1 October	GGE on LAWS
2–8 December	GGE on LAWS
9 December	15th annual conference of the parties to Protocol V
10 December	23rd annual conference of the parties to Amended Protocol II
13–17 December	6th CCW review conference

GGE = group of governmental experts; LAWS = lethal autonomous weapon systems.
Note: All meetings took place in Geneva.

on 13–17 December 2021, a few countries were able to prevent progress on the main agenda item—a possible new protocol on autonomous weapon systems (AWS)—as well as in other important areas, such as efforts to strengthen controls on incendiary weapons and mines other than anti-personnel mines (MOTAPM).[5]

One of the consequences of this is that regulatory progress in some of these weapon types may be sought outside the CCW process by groups of small and middle-power states supported by civil society networks—as was the case on landmines, with the 1997 Anti-Personnel Mine (APM) Convention, and cluster munitions, with the 2008 Cluster Munitions Convention (CCM). Ireland is already leading a separate process to address the use of explosive weapons in populated areas (EWIPA).

Other categories of conventional weapon that raise humanitarian concerns are dealt with by other legal and political processes. For example, armed uncrewed aerial vehicles (UAVs) have been addressed to some extent by the United Nations General Assembly, the Missile Technology Control Regime (MTCR) and the 2013 Arms Trade Treaty (ATT). However, there is no dedicated multilateral process on the regulation of armed UAVs. Similarly, small arms and light weapons (SALW) are regulated by a series of regional and subregional treaties and by two politically binding agreements: the 2001 UN Programme of Action on SALW (POA) and the 2005 International Tracing Instrument (ITI). In both cases, there have been calls for further and tighter regulation.[6]

This section reviews the key developments and treaty negotiations that took place in 2021 in relation to weapons deemed to be inhumane and other

---

[5] 6th CCW Review Conference, Final document, CCW/CONF.VI/11 (Advance version), 10 Jan. 2022, part II, Final declaration. On criticism of the conduct and outcome of the Review Conference see Gisel, L., 'The ICRC urges states to achieve tangible results next year towards adopting new legally binding rules on autonomous weapons', Final statement by the International Committee of the Red Cross (ICRC), 17 Dec. 2021; and Acheson, R., Reaching Critical Will, 'Editorial: "Our position has not changed"', *CCW Report*, vol. 9, no. 13, 17 Dec. 2021.

[6] On the regional and subregional treaties regulating SALW see annex A, section II, in this volume.

weapons that raise humanitarian concerns. It first looks at weapon types addressed principally within the CCW regime and parallel frameworks (the CCM and APM Convention): incendiary weapons, EWIPA, cluster munitions, and landmines, improvised explosive devices (IEDs) and ERW. The challenges posed by AWS and the prominent intergovernmental efforts within the CCW regime to address them are discussed in section II. Given the deadlock, a new regulatory process outside the CCW framework to consider AWS now seems increasingly likely.[7] This section then looks at developments related to armed UAVs and SALW.

Incendiary weapons

Incendiary weapons produce heat and fire through the chemical reaction of a flammable substance. They cause extremely painful burn injuries that are difficult to treat and start fires that can destroy civilian infrastructure. Protocol III to the CCW Convention regulates the use of incendiary weapons, but critics argue that it is being undermined by two loopholes.[8] First, it prohibits the use of air-dropped incendiary weapons in civilian areas but permits the use of ground-launched versions under certain circumstances. Second, it does not encompass white phosphorus or other munitions that are 'primarily designed' to create smokescreens or to signal troops, yet still produce the same incendiary effects.

Over 20 states, the European Union (EU), the International Committee of the Red Cross (ICRC) and many non-governmental organizations (NGOs) have raised concerns about incendiary weapons since the fifth CCW review conference, in 2016, and many of them have called for further discussion of the issue.[9] Some have been calling for Protocol III to be reviewed and strengthened by banning the use of all incendiary weapons in civilian areas and by broadening the definition in the protocol to cover white phosphorus.

Ahead of the sixth CCW review conference, Human Rights Watch organized an open letter from more than 50 healthcare professionals, med-ical-related organizations and burn survivor groups urging governments to strengthen international law on these weapons.[10] While the CCW review conference agreed to condemn the use of incendiary weapons against civil-ians, Russia and Cuba blocked a widely supported proposal by Ireland to hold

---

[7] Carpenter, C., 'A better path to a treaty banning "killer robots" has just been cleared', World Politics Review, 7 Jan. 2022.

[8] Human Rights Watch (HRW) and International Human Rights Clinic, 'They Burn Through Everything': The Human Cost of Incendiary Weapons and the Limits of International Law (HRW: New York, Nov. 2020), pp. 38–39.

[9] Human Rights Watch and International Human Rights Clinic, 'Incendiary weapons: Assessing the problem', Feb. 2021.

[10] Humanitarian Disarmament, 'Open letter on incendiary weapons from healthcare professionals and burn survivor organizations', Nov. 2021.

informal consultations on Protocol III in 2022.[11] It thus seems likely that there will be recurring pressure to adopt this topic at CCW meetings in the coming years.

Explosive weapons in populated areas

The use of EWIPA—and especially the use of explosive weapons with a large destructive radius, an inaccurate delivery system or the capacity to deliver multiple munitions over a wide area—has frequently led to situations in which over 90 per cent of casualties in populated areas are civilian rather than combatants.[12] One study recorded 357 370 casualties (155 118 people killed and 202 252 injured) from explosive weapons in the decade 2011–20, 73 per cent of whom were civilians.[13] Of the recorded incidents, 60 per cent took place in populated areas, and civilians accounted for 91 per cent of the casualties (238 892) in those areas. The use of EWIPA also has reverberating effects, with impacts on water, sanitation, ecosystems, healthcare, education and psychological well-being.[14]

Moves to regulate EWIPA

The International Network on Explosive Weapons (INEW), a coalition of NGOs, was first to articulate EWIPA as an issue that demanded attention in the early 2010s.[15] This led to calls from an increasing number of states, successive UN secretary-generals, international bodies and other NGOs for measures to provide better protection for civilians and to prevent harm

---

[11] 6th CCW Review Conference, CCW/CONF.VI/11 (note 5), paras 89–91. Austria, Chile, Colombia, Costa Rica, Ireland, Mexico, the Netherlands, New Zealand, Norway, Panama, Peru, Switzerland and several NGOs supported work being undertaken on Protocol III. See Acheson, R., 'Incendiary weapons', *Reaching Critical Will*, *CCW Report*, vol. 9, no. 11 (15 Dec. 2021); and Acheson, R., 'Incendiary weapons', *Reaching Critical Will*, *CCW Report*, vol. 9, no. 13 (17 Dec. 2021).

[12] Action on Armed Violence (AOAV), *Explosive Violence Monitor 2019* (AOAV: London, 2020), p. 3. See also International Committee of the Red Cross (ICRC), 'Explosive weapons in populated areas', [n.d.]; and International Network on Explosive Weapons (INEW), 'Protecting civilians from the use of explosive weapons in populated areas', May 2020.

[13] The study was based on the monitoring of 29 000 incidents in 123 countries recorded by English-language media. Action on Armed Violence (AOAV), *A Decade of Explosive Violence Harm* (AOAV: London, May 2021), p. 9.

[14] For detailed taxonomies of these effects see Wille, C. and Malaret Baldo, A., *Menu of Indicators to Measure the Reverberating Effects on Civilians from the Use of Explosive Weapons in Populated Areas* (UNIDIR: Geneva, Feb. 2021); and Malaret Baldo, A. and Batault, F., *Second Menu of Indicators to Measure the Reverberating Effects on Civilians from the Use of Explosive Weapons in Populated Areas* (UNIDIR: Geneva, Feb. 2022). See also Action on Armed Violence (AOAV), *Blast Injury: The Reverberating Health Consequences from the Use of Explosive Weapon Use* (AOAV: London, 2020); Action on Armed Violence (AOAV), *The Broken Land: The Environmental Consequences of Explosive Weapons* (AOAV: London, 2020); and UN Children's Fund (UNICEF), *Water Under Fire*, vol. 3, *Attacks on Water and Sanitation Services in Armed Conflict and the Impacts on Children* (UNICEF: New York, 2021).

[15] See e.g. International Network on Explosive Weapons (INEW), *Stop Bombing Civilians: An Advocacy Guide on Explosive Weapons in Populated Areas* (INEW: London, [Sep. 2012]).

from EWIPA.[16] After many years of failing to make progress within the CCW framework, and as a result of this increasing international political pressure, a separate process gathered momentum in late 2019 and early 2020.[17]

This process was led by Ireland, which convened a series of open consultations with the aim of developing a political declaration to address the humanitarian harm arising from the use of EWIPA. Such a declaration would aim to establish a new international norm against the use of explosive weapons in towns and cities, which could in turn drive changes in military practice at the policy and operational levels. The Covid-19 pandemic meant that consultations scheduled for March 2020 and the planned adoption of the declaration in May 2020 were postponed, although another round of consultations was held online in 2020.

Developments in 2021

The Irish-led process restarted in January 2021, with Ireland releasing a revised draft declaration and holding consultations online to discuss it on 3–5 March 2021.[18] The written submissions (from 22 states, the Arab Group and 19 NGOs) largely welcomed the revised draft with reservations.[19] Several states (notably Australia, Belgium, Canada, Colombia, France, Israel, Lithuania, the United Kingdom and the United States) argued for qualifying language throughout the text that would be likely to weaken the declaration, while other states and most NGOs called for the draft declaration to be strengthened.[20] The ICRC, for example, argued for the commitment to be upgraded from 'restricting' to 'avoiding' the use of EWIPA.[21] The consultations are expected to be concluded in 2022.

---

[16] See e.g. Austrian Federal Ministry for Europe, Integration and Foreign Affairs, 'Vienna Conference on Protecting Civilians in Urban Warfare: Summary of the conference', Vienna, 1–2 Oct. 2019; and United Nations, 'Joint appeal by the UN secretary-general and the president of the International Committee of the Red Cross on the use of explosive weapons in cities', Press Release SG/2251, 18 Sep. 2019. For a list of 112 states and territories and 9 state groupings that have publicly acknowledged the harm caused by EWIPA in statements see International Network on Explosive Weapons (INEW), 'Political response', [n.d.].

[17] Irish Department of Foreign Affairs, 'Protecting civilians in urban warfare', [n.d.]. For developments in 2019–20 see Davis, I., 'Global instruments for conventional arms control', *SIPRI Yearbook 2020*, pp. 496–99; and Davis, I., 'Global and regional instruments for conventional arms control', *SIPRI Yearbook 2021*, pp. 508–10.

[18] Irish Department of Foreign Affairs, 'Draft Political Declaration on Strengthening the Protection of Civilians from the Humanitarian Consequences that can arise from the use of Explosive Weapons with Wide Area Effects in Populated Areas', Rev 1, 29 Jan. 2021.

[19] The written submissions are available at Irish Department of Foreign Affairs, 'Written submissions—3–5 March 2021 informal consultations', 23 Feb. 2021.

[20] For a detailed analysis of participant statements at the consultations see Reaching Critical Will, 'Report on the March 2021 consultations on a political declaration on the use of explosive weapons in populated areas', 12 Mar. 2021.

[21] International Committee of the Red Cross (ICRC), 'Draft political declaration on strengthening the protection of civilians from the humanitarian consequences that can arise from the use of explosive weapons with wide area effects in populated areas: Comments by the International Committee of the Red Cross (ICRC)', Feb. 2021.

The use of EWIPA was discussed in several other international forums in 2021. First, at the UN Security Council's annual open debate on the protection of civilians (POC), most participants voiced concerns about ongoing harms to civilians in armed conflict, with the majority specifically condemning the use of EWIPA and attacks on medical facilities and personnel.[22] The UN secretary-general's annual report on POC continued to emphasize the threats faced by civilians from the use of EWIPA, with a particular focus on the impact on healthcare services.[23] Second, many states voiced support for the political declaration process during the 2021 meetings of the UN General Assembly's First Committee (on disarmament and international security). Austria, Azerbaijan, Costa Rica, Iceland, Ireland, New Zealand, San Marino and Switzerland all raised concerns about the use of EWIPA in their national statements, as did the UN high representative for disarmament affairs, INEW and a group of 16 NGOs.[24] Third, nine delegations addressed EWIPA during the general exchange of views over the first two days of the sixth CCW review conference.[25] The issue of the use of EWIPA also came up in the context of the draft final declaration, but a reference to 'explosive weapons' in the preamble was deleted at the insistence of Russia, with the support of Cuba and Romania.[26]

While it seems likely that a political declaration will be adopted by some states in 2022, other states that regularly use EWIPA are likely to continue as before. Hence, the political declaration should be seen as only the first step towards establishing an effective norm against EWIPA.

Cluster munitions

Cluster munitions are air-dropped or ground-launched weapons that release smaller submunitions intended to kill enemy personnel or destroy vehicles. There are three main criticisms of cluster munitions: they disperse large

[22] United Nations, Security Council, Letter dated 27 May 2021 from the president of the Security Council, S/2021/505, 28 May 2021. For an analysis of the meeting see Acheson, R., 'Protecting civilians by preventing conflict', Reaching Critical Will, 4 June 2021.

[23] United Nations, Security Council, 'Protection of civilians in armed conflict', Report of the Secretary-General, S/2021/423, 3 May 2021.

[24] Nakamitsu, I., UN High Representative for Disarmament Affairs, Opening statement to the First Committee of the UN General Assembly, 4 Oct. 2021; Jaramillo, C., International Network on Explosive Weapons (INEW), Statement at the First Committee of the UN General Assembly, 8 Oct. 2021; Cottrell, L., Conflict and Environment Observatory, 'Protection of the environment in relation to armed conflicts', Statement at the First Committee of the UN General Assembly, 9 Oct. 2021; and Young, K., 'Explosive weapons in populated areas', Reaching Critical Will, *First Committee Monitor*, vol. 19, no. 2 (9 Oct. 2021).

[25] Varella, L., 'Use of explosive weapons in populated areas', Reaching Critical Will, *CCW Report*, vol. 9, no. 10 (14 Dec. 2021).

[26] 6th CCW Review Conference, CCW/CONF.VI/11 (note 5), part II, Final declaration; and Varella, L. and Acheson, R., 'Use of explosive weapons in populated areas', Reaching Critical Will, *CCW Report*, vol. 9, no. 11 (15 Dec. 2021).

numbers of submunitions imprecisely over an extended area; they frequently fail to detonate and are difficult to detect; and unexploded submunitions can remain explosive hazards for many decades.[27]

The humanitarian consequences of cluster munitions and the unacceptable harm to civilians that they cause are addressed by the 2008 Convention on Cluster Munitions.[28] The CCM establishes an unconditional prohibition on cluster munitions. It also requires the destruction of stockpiles within 8 years of entry into force of the Convention (Article 3), the clearance of areas contaminated by cluster munition remnants within 10 years (Article 4) and the provision of assistance for victims of such weapons (Article 5). As of 31 December 2021, the CCM had 110 parties and 13 signatory states, among which are former major producers and users of cluster munitions as well as affected states. In the UN General Assembly in December 2021, 146 states voted to adopt its seventh resolution supporting the CCM, with one vote against (Russia).[29]

Use and production of cluster munitions in 2020/21

No CCM state party has used cluster munitions since the convention was adopted and most of the states still outside the convention abide de facto by the ban on the use and production of these weapons. However, the Cluster Munition Coalition reported the use of cluster munitions in Azerbaijan, including Nagorno-Karabakh, and Syria during the period August 2020–July 2021.[30]

There is convincing evidence that both Armenia and Azerbaijan (neither a party to the CCM) used cluster munitions in the armed conflict in Nagorno-Karabakh in September–October 2020, although both denied doing so and each blamed the other side for this use.[31] Syrian government forces have used cluster munitions since 2012, probably with the support of Russia, and at least 687 cluster munition attacks by government forces were reported between

---

[27] Feickert, A. and Kerr, P. K., *Cluster Munitions: Background and Issues for Congress*, Congressional Research Service (CRS) Report for Congress RS22907 (US Congress, CRS: Washington, DC, 22 Feb. 2019).

[28] For a summary and other details of the CCM see annex A, section I, in this volume.

[29] UN General Assembly Resolution 76/47, 'Implementation of the Convention on Cluster Munitions', 6 Dec. 2021.

[30] Cluster Munition Coalition (CMC), *Cluster Munition Monitor 2021* (International Campaign to Ban Landmines–CMC: Geneva, Sep. 2021), pp. 1, 13–15. *Cluster Munition Monitor 2021* focuses on the calendar year 2020 with information included to Aug. 2021 where possible.

[31] Cluster Munition Coalition (note 30), pp. 13–14; Amnesty International, 'Armenia/Azerbaijan: Civilians must be protected from use of banned cluster bombs', 5 Oct. 2020; Human Rights Watch, 'Azerbaijan: Cluster munitions used in Nagorno-Karabakh', 23 Oct. 2020; and Williamson, H., 'Unlawful attack on medical facilities and personnel in Nagorno-Karabakh', Human Rights Watch, 26 Feb. 2021. On the armed conflict in Nagorno-Karabakh see Davis, I., 'The interstate armed conflict between Armenia and Azerbaijan', *SIPRI Yearbook 2021*; and chapter 5, section I, in this volume.

July 2012 and July 2021, including at least one new attack in 2020/21.[32] There were also unsubstantiated allegations of cluster munitions use in the Tigray region of Ethiopia in 2020/21.[33]

The Cluster Munition Coalition lists 16 states as producers of cluster munitions—Brazil, China, Egypt, Greece, India, Iran, Israel, North Korea, South Korea, Pakistan, Poland, Romania, Russia, Singapore, Turkey and the USA—none of them party to the CCM.[34] A lack of transparency means that it is unclear whether any of them were actively producing such munitions in 2020/21.

Cluster munition clearance and stockpile destruction

Stockpile destruction is one of the CCM's major successes. As of August 2021, 36 of the 41 states parties that had declared possession of cluster munitions had completed the destruction of their stockpiles.[35] This destruction of 1.5 million stockpiled cluster munitions containing 179 million submunitions represents the destruction of 99 per cent of all the cluster munitions and sub-munitions declared as stockpiled under the CCM.

The quantity of cluster munitions currently stockpiled by non-signatories to the CCM is unknown. Similarly, it is not possible to provide an accurate estimate of the total size of the area contaminated by cluster munition remnants, but at least 26 UN member states and 3 other states or areas remain contaminated by cluster munitions.[36] These include 10 CCM states parties— Afghanistan, Bosnia and Herzegovina, Chad, Chile, Germany, Iraq, Laos, Lebanon, Mauritania, and Somalia—and two signatory states—Angola and the Democratic Republic of the Congo (DRC). In addition, there are remnants in 14 non-signatory UN member states—Armenia, Azerbaijan, Cambodia, Georgia, Iran, Libya, Serbia, South Sudan, Sudan, Syria, Tajikistan, Ukraine, Viet Nam and Yemen—and 3 other states or areas—Kosovo, Nagorno-Karabakh and Western Sahara.

Over the past decade, six CCM state parties—the Republic of the Congo, Croatia, Grenada, Montenegro, Mozambique and Norway—have completed clearance of areas contaminated by cluster munition remnants.[37]

The second CCM review conference

Due to Covid-19-related restrictions, it was agreed to split the second review conference of the CCM into two parts: a virtual meeting (held on

---

[32] Cluster Munition Coalition (note 30), pp. 14–15. On the armed conflict in Syria see chapter 6, section II, in this volume.

[33] Cluster Munition Coalition (note 30), p. 15. On the armed conflict in Ethiopia see chapter 7, section IV, in this volume.

[34] Cluster Munition Coalition (note 30), pp. 16–18.

[35] Cluster Munition Coalition (note 30), pp. 2, 19–24.

[36] Cluster Munition Coalition (note 30), pp. 39–45.

[37] Cluster Munition Coalition (note 30), pp. 39–40.

25–27 November 2020) and a meeting in hybrid format (originally scheduled for 4–5 February 2021 but subsequently held on 20–21 September 2021 in Geneva).[38] The first part of the conference reviewed progress on CCM implementation and focused on procedural matters, including discussion of extension requests for stockpile destruction and clearance, and other financial and administrative issues.[39]

The second part adopted the Lausanne Action Plan to support implementation of the CCM in 2021–26, replacing the 2015 Dubrovnik Action Plan.[40] The new plan includes 50 concrete actions to implement the CCM. These cover treaty universalization, stockpile destruction, clearance of contaminated land, risk education, victim assistance, international cooperation and assistance, transparency, national implementation, and compliance. The conference also adopted a declaration, the Lausanne Declaration, expressing 'grave concern' about new cluster munition use since the first review conference, in 2015.[41]

The conference granted extensions of deadlines to Bulgaria and Peru for the completion of destruction of cluster munitions stockpiles.[42] It also granted extensions to Afghanistan, Bosnia and Herzegovina, Chile, Lebanon, and Mauritania for completing the clearance and destruction of cluster munition remnants.[43]

Landmines, improvised explosive devices and explosive remnants of war

Anti-personnel mines are mines that detonate on human contact—that is, they are 'victim-activated'—and therefore encompass improvised explosive devices that act as APMs, also known as 'improvised mines'.[44] APMs are prohibited under the 1997 Convention on the Prohibition of the Use, Stockpiling, Production and Transfer of Anti-Personnel Mines and on their Destruction (APM Convention).[45] As of 31 December 2021 there were 164 states parties to the APM Convention; no new states joined in 2021. Amended Protocol II of the CCW Convention also regulates (but does not entirely ban) landmines (i.e. APMs and MOTAPM or anti-vehicle mines), booby-traps and IEDs.

---

[38] For videos, documents and decisions of the two parts of the conference see CCM Implementation Support Unit, 'First part of the second review conference', 25–27 Nov. 2020; and 'Second part of the second review conference', 20–21 Sep. 2021.

[39] On the first part see Davis, *SIPRI Yearbook 2021* (note 17), p. 517.

[40] Convention on Cluster Munitions (CCM), *Lausanne Action Plan* (CCM Implementation Support Unit: Geneva, Sep. 2021). On the earlier plan see Convention on Cluster Munitions (CCM), *Dubrovnik Action Plan* (CCM Implementation Support Unit: Geneva, Sep. 2015).

[41] 2nd CCM Review Conference, Final report, CCM/CONF/2021/6, 6 Oct. 2021, annex I.

[42] 2nd CCM Review Conference, CCM/CONF/2021/6 (note 41), paras 32–46.

[43] 2nd CCM Review Conference, CCM/CONF/2021/6 (note 41), paras 49–76.

[44] See Seddon, B. and Malaret Baldo, A., *Counter-IED: Capability Maturity Model & Self-assessment Tool* (UN Institute for Disarmament Research: Geneva, 2020).

[45] For a summary and other details of the APM Convention see annex A, section I, in this volume.

A dedicated group of experts under this protocol has been working on these devices since 2009. Protocol V regulates ERW, including landmines, unexploded ordnance and abandoned explosive ordnance. IEDs are also discussed in the First Committee of the UN General Assembly, including through the submission of resolutions.

Use and Production of APMs in 2020–21

New use of APMs by states is now extremely rare. According to the International Campaign to Ban Landmines (ICBL), Myanmar (which is not a party to the APM Convention) is the only state to have used APMs in the period mid-2020 to October 2021, and it had been deploying them for the previous 20 years. New use was also suspected during the conflict in Nagorno-Karabakh in late 2020 but could not be verified.[46] More than 50 states have produced APMs in the past, but the ICBL identifies only 12 as current producers, and only 5 as probable active producers: India, Iran, Myanmar, Pakistan and Russia.[47]

While there is a de facto moratorium on the production and use of the weapon among most states in the world, the use of APMs, including victim-activated IEDs, by non-state armed groups in conflicts is a growing problem.[48] APMs were used by such groups in at least six states between mid-2020 and October 2021: Afghanistan, Colombia, India, Myanmar, Nigeria and Pakistan. There were also unconfirmed allegations of use by non-state armed groups in Cameroon, Egypt, Niger, the Philippines, Thailand, Tunisia and Venezuela.[49]

In 2020, the most recent year for which comparative data is available, the number of victims rose by 20 per cent compared to 2019, due to 'increased conflict and contamination' of land with improvised mines.[50] In total, over 7000 people were killed or injured in 54 countries and areas—the sixth successive year of high casualties, and in the past 20 years only lower than in 2001–2002 and 2016–17. The two states with the most casualties in 2020 were Syria (2729) and Afghanistan (1474).[51]

---

[46] International Campaign to Ban Landmines (ICBL), *Landmine Monitor 2021* (ICBL–Cluster Munition Coalition: Geneva, Nov. 2021), pp. 1, 8–10, 16. *Landmine Monitor 2021* focuses on the calendar year 2020 with information included up to Oct. 2021 where possible.

[47] International Campaign to Ban Landmines (note 46), p. 19. The other 7 listed producers are China, Cuba, North Korea, Singapore, South Korea, the USA and Viet Nam.

[48] E.g. Luke, D., *Old Issues, New Threats: Mine Action and IEDs in Urban Environments* (LSE Ideas: London, Feb. 2020).

[49] International Campaign to Ban Landmines (note 46), pp. 1, 11–14.

[50] International Campaign to Ban Landmines (note 46), p. 2.

[51] International Campaign to Ban Landmines (note 46), pp. 41–43.

APM clearance and stockpile destruction

An estimated 146 square kilometres of land were cleared of APMs in 2020 (compared to 156 km² in 2019) and more than 135 000 APMs were destroyed (compared to 122 000 in 2019).[52] Clearance operations were temporarily suspended in Angola, Chad, Senegal, Serbia, South Sudan and Zimbabwe in 2020 due to Covid-19-related restrictions.[53] In January 2021 the River Jordan was declared mine-free by Israel (not a party to the APM Convention), allowing religious ceremonies to take place there for the first time in more than 50 years.[54] The 60 states and other areas that are known to have mine contamination include 33 states parties to the APM Convention. Among them are some of the most mine-affected states in the world: Afghanistan, Bosnia and Herzegovina, Cambodia, Croatia, Ethiopia, Iraq, Turkey, Ukraine and Yemen.[55]

Collectively, states parties of the APM Convention have destroyed more than 55 million stockpiled APMs. Sri Lanka completed the destruction of its landmine stockpile in 2021.[56] That left only two parties with remaining stockpile-destruction obligations: Greece and Ukraine. The total remaining global stockpile of APMs is estimated to be less than 50 million, down from about 160 million in 1999. With the exception of Ukraine, the largest stockpilers are non-signatories: Russia (26.5 million), Pakistan (6 million), India (4–5 million), China (5 million), Ukraine (3.3 million) and the USA (3 million).[57]

Treaty-related developments in 2021

The lack of progress at the sixth CCW review conference also applied to landmine-related topics.[58] Early drafts of the final declaration of the review conference included three paragraphs related to MOTAPM. Among these was a proposal by Ireland to convene a group of experts to meet for three days in 2022 to discuss the implementation of international humanitarian law in relation to MOTAPM. The proposal was blocked by Cuba and Russia, but two other, preambular references to MOTAPM remained.[59]

---

[52] International Campaign to Ban Landmines (note 46), p. 3.

[53] International Campaign to Ban Landmines (note 46), pp. 58–61.

[54] Reuters, 'Mine-free River Jordan shrine ends 50 year wait for Epiphany', 10 Jan. 2021.

[55] International Campaign to Ban Landmines (note 46), pp. 28–40. On the landmine problem in Ukraine see Flint, J., 'As the threat of war looms in eastern Ukraine, AOAV examines the country's landmine problem', Action on Armed Violence, 7 Dec. 2021.

[56] APM Convention Implementation Support Unit, 'Nearly 12 000 landmines destroyed by Sri Lanka under the Mine Ban Convention', Press release, 30 Sep. 2021.

[57] International Campaign to Ban Landmines (note 46), pp. 3, 20–21.

[58] For a summary of state positions during the general exchange of views on 13–14 Dec. 2021 see Acheson, R., 'Mines', Reaching Critical Will, *CCW Report*, vol. 9, no. 10 (14 Dec. 2021).

[59] 6th CCW Review Conference, CCW/CONF.VI/11 (note 5), part II, Final declaration; and Acheson, R., 'Mines and cluster munitions', Reaching Critical Will, *CCW Report*, vol. 9, no. 13 (17 Dec. 2021).

At its meeting in August 2021, the group of experts of Amended Protocol II continued its discussion of IEDs.[60] The focus remained on voluntary exchange of information on national and multilateral measures and on best practices regarding identification, humanitarian clearance and civilian protection from IEDs. The group also agreed to an updated political declaration on IEDs, which was adopted by the annual conference of parties to Amended Protocol II and was welcomed by the CCW review conference.[61]

The 19th meeting of states parties of the APM Convention took place virtually on 15–19 November 2021 due to Covid-19 restrictions.[62] Seven states were granted extensions to their mine-clearance obligations under Article 5: Cyprus (until 2025), the DRC (2025), Guinea-Bissau (2022), Mauritania (2026), Nigeria (2025), Somalia (2027) and Turkey (2025).[63] States parties 'expressed serious concern' that Eritrea remained in non-compliance by not requesting an extension to its 2020 mine-clearance deadline.[64] The USA attended the annual meeting as an observer, as it has done since 2009. In 2020 the US administration of President Donald J. Trump had abandoned the policy of his predecessor of acceding to the treaty at some future date. In 2021 the new US administration was reported to be reviewing the possibility of returning to the former policy.[65]

Armed uncrewed aerial vehicles

UAVs are aircraft without any human pilot, also known as a drones or uncrewed aerial vehicles. UAVs are operated remotely (by a ground- or aircraft-based controller) or are pre-programmed. There are numerous civilian and military applications for UAVs. Military forces are increasingly using them for surveillance, logistics or communication, and armed versions for combat, also referred to as uncrewed combat aerial vehicles (UCAVs). At least 19 states currently operate armed UAVs, with at least another 15 states close to doing so.[66] Since 2015, at least 11 states—Egypt, Israel, Iraq, Iran, Nigeria, Pakistan, Saudi Arabia, Turkey, the United Arab Emirates, the UK

---

[60] Amended Protocol II to the CCW Convention, 23rd Annual Conference, 'Report on improvised explosive devices', CCW/AP.II/CONF.23/2, 11 Nov. 2021.

[61] Amended Protocol II to the CCW Convention, 23rd Annual Conference, Final document, CCW/AP.II/CONF.23/6 (Advance version), 11 Nov. 2021, annex V; and 6th CCW Review Conference, CCW/CONF.VI/11 (note 5), para. 81.

[62] On the proceedings, documents and statements by states parties see APM Convention, 'Nineteenth Meeting of the States Parties (19MSP)', 15–19 Nov. 2021.

[63] For details of each of the requests, additional information submitted by the state party, analysis and decisions see APM Convention, 19th Meeting of the States Parties, Draft final report, APLC/MSP.19/2021/CRP.1, 18 Nov. 2021, sections A–G.

[64] APM Convention, APLC/MSP.19/2021/CRP.1 (note 63), para. 91.

[65] Abramson, J., 'Countries grapple with 2025 landmine goal', Arms Control Today, vol. 51, no. 10 (Dec. 2021).

[66] Drone Wars, 'Who has armed drones?', July 2021.

and the USA—are known to have or suspected of having operated armed UAVs for counterterrorism operations, including in some cases for targeted killings.[67] In recent years they have also been deployed in support of armed groups or allied states in proxy wars or over disputed territories, including their decisive use in the Nagorno-Karabakh conflict in 2020.[68] Finally, the widespread proliferation of UAV technology has enabled non-state armed groups to carry out attacks using smaller military UAVs or by adapting commercial off-the-shelf UAVs.[69]

Many of the existing regulatory regimes, such as the Missile Technology Control Regime and the Arms Trade Treaty, are limited in scope and exclude some of the main UAV-producing countries—such as China (not in the MTCR), Turkey (not in the ATT) and Israel (in neither).[70] Yet concerns about the humanitarian implications of armed UAVs have been growing and there have been calls from civil society groups and independent experts for a new multilateral process to develop robust standards for the design, export and use of armed UAVs or even to ban them.[71] For example, in 2020 the UN secretary-general and the UN special rapporteur on extrajudicial killings called for the development of robust standards of oversight, transparency and accountability in the use of armed UAVs, and for effective multilateral measures to control their proliferation.[72]

To date, however, there has been no multilateral discussion to these ends, beyond a US-led process initiated in 2016 towards international standards on the export and subsequent use of armed UAVs.[73] In parallel, somewhat contradictory US efforts within the MTCR helped to relax controls to make it easier for US companies to compete in the international military UAV

---

[67] United Nations, Human Rights Council, 'Use of armed drones for targeted killings', Report of the Special Rapporteur on extrajudicial, summary or arbitrary executions, A/HRC/44/38, 15 Aug. 2020, para. 7.

[68] Arraf, J. and Schmitt, E., 'Iran's proxies in Iraq threaten US with more sophisticated weapons', *New York Times*, 4 June 2021; and Dixon, R., 'Azerbaijan's drones owned the battlefield in Nagorno-Karabakh—and showed future of warfare', *Washington Post*, 11 Nov. 2020.

[69] Schmitt, E., 'Papers offer a peek at ISIS' drones, lethal and largely off the shelf', *New York Times*, 31 Jan. 2017; and Chávez, K. and Swed, O., 'The proliferation of drones to violent nonstate actors', *Defence Studies*, vol. 21, no. 1 (2021).

[70] On the MTCR see chapter 14, section III, and annex B, section III, in this volume. For a summary and other details of the ATT see annex A, section I, in this volume. On the scope of the ATT see Holtom, P., 'Taking stock of the Arms Trade Treaty: Scope', SIPRI, Aug. 2021.

[71] See e.g. Levenson, M., 'What to know about the civilian casualty files', *New York Times*, 18 Dec. 2021; Krähenmann, S. and Dvaladze, G., 'Humanitarian concerns raised by the use of armed drones', Geneva Call, 16 June 2020; Callamard, A. and Rogers, J., 'We need a new international accord to control drone proliferation', *Bulletin of the Atomic Scientists*, 1 Dec. 2020; and European Forum on Armed Drones, 'Call to action', 7 Apr. 2016.

[72] United Nations, Security Council, 'Protection of civilians in armed conflict', Report of the Secretary-General, S/2020/366, 6 May 2020, para. 36; and United Nations, A/HRC/44/38 (note 67).

[73] Joint Declaration for the Export and Subsequent Use of Armed or Strike-Enabled Unmanned Aerial Vehicles (UAVs), US Department of State, 28 Oct. 2016. See also Enemark, C., 'On the responsible use of armed drones: The prospective moral responsibilities of states', *International Journal of Human Rights*, vol. 24, no. 6 (2020).

market.[74] Indeed, these calls for regulation have little apparent support among states. At meetings of the UN General Assembly's First Committee in 2021, only Armenia, Costa Rica, Cuba, the Holy See and Yemen referred to armed UAVs in their statements during the general and thematic debates and, as in previous years, no resolution was proposed on this issue. Armenia and Yemen raised specific concerns about the use of armed UAVs in Nagorno-Karabakh and the Yemeni conflict, respectively.[75] Similarly, at the CCW review conference, only Panama and Venezuela raised concerns about these weapons and called for the development of new standards.[76] As states avoid external pressure to restrict use of armed UAVs, future autonomous and swarming UAV capabilities are likely to be even harder to regulate.[77]

The United Nations Programme of Action on Small Arms and Light Weapons

The 2001 UN Programme of Action to Prevent, Combat and Eradicate the Illicit Trade in Small Arms and Light Weapons in All its Aspects and the 2005 International Instrument to Enable States to Identify and Trace, in a Timely and Reliable Manner, Illicit Small Arms and Light Weapons are politically binding agreements that were negotiated on the basis of consensus under the auspices of the First Committee of the UN General Assembly.[78] These instruments outline steps that states should take at the international, regional and national levels to counter the illicit trade in and diversion of SALW. The UN Office for Disarmament Affairs (UNODA) administers the two instruments, and states voluntarily submit a report every two years that outlines how they implement both the POA and the ITI.[79] In addition, states meet at a biennial meeting of states (BMS) to 'consider' implementation of both instruments and at sexennial review conferences that allow for a more in-depth assessment of the progress made on implementation.

---

[74] Stone, M., 'US relaxes rules to export more aerial drones', Reuters, 24 July 2020; and Stone, M., 'Biden wants to keep Trump policy that boosted armed drone exports—sources', Reuters, 25 Mar. 2021. On the MTCR see chapter 14, section III, and annex B, section III, in this volume.

[75] Muñoz, A., 'Armed drones', Reaching Critical Will, *First Committee Monitor*, vol. 19, no. 4 (22 Oct. 2021).

[76] Acheson, R., 'Other weapon issues', Reaching Critical Will, *CCW Report*, vol. 9, no. 10 (14 Dec. 2021).

[77] Verbruggen, M., 'Drone swarms: Coming (sometime) to a war near you. Just not today', *Bulletin of the Atomic Scientists*, 3 Feb. 2021; and Kallenborn, Z., 'Meet the future weapon of mass destruction, the drone swarm', *Bulletin of the Atomic Scientists*, 5 Apr. 2021.

[78] United Nations, General Assembly, Programme of Action to Prevent, Combat and Eradicate the Illicit Trade in Small Arms and Light Weapons in All its Aspects (POA), pp. 7–17 of A/CONF.192/15, 20 July 2001; and United Nations, General Assembly, International Instrument to Enable States to Identify and Trace, in a Timely and Reliable Manner, Illicit Small Arms and Light Weapons (International Tracing Instrument, ITI), Decision 60/519, 8 Dec. 2005.

[79] UN Office for Disarmament Affairs (UNODA), 'Programme of action on small arms and light weapons: National reports', [n.d.].

The seventh BMS (BMS7) took place in a hybrid format on 26–30 July 2021 under the chairmanship of Ambassador Martin Kimani of Kenya. It was originally scheduled to take place on 15–19 June 2020 but was postponed because of the Covid-19 pandemic. Physical meetings took place at the UN Headquarters in New York—with one delegate per state allowed in the room to attend in person—while civil society participation was entirely virtual.[80] The discussions and process leading to the final outcome of BMS7 continued to highlight recurring divisions among states on the most contentious issues related to the implementation of both the POA and the ITI. These included controls on ammunition in the scope of the POA, addressing new developments in SALW manufacturing, and creating links between the POA and other international processes.[81]

The inclusion of controls on ammunition was widely supported across different regional groupings, including members of the Caribbean Community (CARICOM) and of Mercosur (Mercado Común del Sur, Southern Common Market).[82] However, it continued to be opposed by a narrow group of states, including the USA, Iran and Egypt among others.[83] Despite this resistance, the final outcome document of BMS7 still included two references to ammunition, although these were largely based on language already agreed at the third review conference, in 2018.[84] One took note of the ongoing work of the UN governmental expert process considering problems 'arising from the accumulation of conventional ammunition stockpiles in surplus'. [85] The second reference continued to acknowledge that some states explicitly apply the POA to ammunition, adding that these states 'can integrate applicable policies and practices into their [SALW] control efforts with a view to strengthening the implementation of the [POA]'.[86]

As a result of states' informal consultations on the matter ahead of BMS7, the original draft of the BMS7 outcome document proposed the establishment of an open-ended technical expert group to discuss developments in

---

[80] UN Office for Disarmament Affairs (UNODA), 'Aide memoire for non-governmental organizations', 7 July 2021; and International Action Network on Small Arms (IANSA), 'Daily update day 1', BMS7, 26 July 2021.

[81] See e.g. Bromley, M., 'Control measures on small arms and light weapons', *SIPRI Yearbook 2019*, pp. 471–75; and Davis et al. (note 3), pp. 566–69.

[82] Mercosur has 5 member states: Argentina; Brazil; Paraguay; Uruguay and Venezuela (suspended since Dec. 2016).

[83] International Action Network on Small Arms (note 80); International Action Network on Small Arms (IANSA), 'Daily update day 4', BMS7, 29 July 2021; Geyer, K., Rafferty, J. and Pytlak, A., 'Reporting on statements', *Small Arms Monitor*, vol. 11, no. 2 (4 Aug. 2021), pp. 15–16; Statement by the Caribbean Community (CARICOM) on agenda item 6, BMS7, 26–30 July 2021; and Statement on behalf of Bolivia, Cuba, Iran, Nicaragua, Syria and Venezuela, BMS7, 26–30 July 2021.

[84] 3rd POA Review Conference, Report, A/CONF.192/2018/RC/3, 6 July 2018, annex, section I, para. 16, and section II, para. 18.

[85] 7th POA Biennial Meeting of States, Report, A/CONF.192/BMS/2021/1, 11 Aug. 2021, annex, para. 24.

[86] 7th POA Biennial Meeting of States, Report, A/CONF.192/BMS/2021/1 (note 85), annex, para. 36.

SALW manufacturing and the development of a good practice document on marking practices for modular and polymer weapons.[87] These proposals have been contested by states on different grounds. For example, the USA argued that the ITI already offers a 'sound framework' to deal with such developments.[88] In addition, others expressed concerns over the potential financial and technical burden of the proposals.[89] The proposal to produce a good practice document was eventually accepted, while states could only agree to 'consider a proposal' to establish an open-ended technical expert group at BMS8, scheduled for 2022.[90] Even this latter and weaker initiative was contested by Iran after the chair presented the final outcome document on the final day of BMS7. In an attempt to erase any reference to the possibility to advance discussions on the matter at BMS8, Iran—breaking consensus—called a vote on this specific paragraph, which was eventually adopted.[91]

The inclusion in the outcome document of explicit references to the synergies between the POA and other relevant international, legally binding instruments, such as the ATT and the 2001 UN Firearms Protocol, continued to be resisted by states that are not parties to these instruments and no real progress was made on this matter.[92] In contrast, BMS7 agreed on several gender-related provisions which call for, among other things, gender-balanced participation in relevant decision-making processes and information sharing on practices to mainstream gender perspectives

---

[87] 7th POA Biennial Meeting of States, Informal Consultations on Opportunities and Challenges Presented by Recent Developments in Small Arms and Light Weapons Manufacturing, Technology and Design, Facilitator's summary, 25 June 2021; and 7th POA Biennial Meeting of States, Outcome document, Draft 3, A/CONF.192/BMS/2021/CRP.2, 19 July 2021, paras 90, 92, annexed to letter from Kimani, M., BMS7 Chair-designate, 19 July 2021.

[88] Costner, S. R., USA, 'Thematic discussion on implementation of the UN International Tracing Instrument at the seventh Biennial Meeting of States (agenda item 7)', 27 July 2021; and International Action Network on Small Arms (note 83).

[89] International Action Network on Small Arms (note 83). See also Statement by Algeria, BMS7, 26–30 July 2021; Statement by Cuba, BMS7, 27 July 2021 (in Spanish); and Statement on behalf of Bolivia, Cuba, Iran, Nicaragua, Syria and Venezuela on agenda item 8, BMS7, 26–30 July 2021.

[90] 7th POA Biennial Meeting of States, A/CONF.192/BMS/2021/1 (note 85), annex, paras 42, 45, 47, 92, 94; and Rafferty, J. and Pytlak, A., 'Overview and analysis of the BMS7 outcome document', *Small Arms Monitor*, vol. 11, no. 2 (4 Aug. 2021), pp. 6–7.

[91] Pytlak, A., 'Act today for a better tomorrow', *Small Arms Monitor*, vol. 11, no. 2 (4 Aug. 2021), p. 1; and International Action Network on Small Arms (IANSA), 'Daily update day 5', BMS7, 30 July 2021, p. 2.

[92] International Action Network on Small Arms (note 83); Arms Trade Treaty (note 70); and Protocol against the Illicit Manufacturing of and Trafficking in Firearms, their Parts and Components and Ammunition, Supplementing the United Nations Convention against Transnational Organized Crime (UN Firearms Protocol), opened for signature 2 July 2001, entered into force 3 July 2005. See also Statement on behalf of Bolivia, Cuba, Iran, Nicaragua, Syria and Venezuela on agenda item 9, BMS7, 29 July 2021; Statement by Egypt, BMS7, 29 July 2021 (in Arabic); and 7th POA Biennial Meeting of States, A/CONF.192/BMS/2021/1 (note 85), annex, para. 54.

into SALW control policies.[93] Notably, BMS7 also linked the POA with the implementation of the Women and Peace and Security Agenda and with 'all relevant Goals and targets' of the 2030 Agenda for Sustainable Development, which had been opposed during the third review conference.[94] The inclusion of gender-oriented provisions in the final document remained contested by a few delegations, including Russia, which openly distanced themselves from such language.[95]

BMS7 highlighted both long-standing and emerging limitations in the POA decision-making processes. Politicized discussions made it difficult to achieve consensus on the final outcome and, thus, the realization of more ambitious results.[96] Further, the exclusion of civil society representatives from in-person meetings in New York was a step backwards in terms of transparency and inclusivity in POA processes. In addition to technical problems that at times affected the functioning of the online streaming, much time at BMS7 was spent on confidential, and thus offline, consultations among states.[97] BMS8 is scheduled to take place in 2022. This confronts states with two procedural challenges: finding ways to involve civil society in relevant meetings and preparing for the meeting in a more limited amount of time than usual.

---

[93] 7th POA Biennial Meeting of States, A/CONF.192/BMS/2021/1 (note 85), annex, paras 10, 52, 73–79. See also Rafferty and Pytlak (note 90), pp. 6–7; and International Action Network on Small Arms (IANSA), *Quick Guide: Results of the Seventh Biennial Meeting of States to Consider the Implementation of the Programme of Action (PoA)* (IANSA: New York, 1 Oct. 2021), pp. 3–4.

[94] 7th POA Biennial Meeting of States, A/CONF.192/BMS/2021/1 (note 85), annex, paras 68, 73; and UN General Assembly Resolution 70/1, 'Transforming our world: The 2030 Agenda for Sustainable Development', 25 Sep. 2015. See also Bromley (note 81), pp. 471–75.

[95] International Action Network on Small Arms (note 91); and Pytlak (note 91), p. 3.

[96] Pytlak (note 91), pp. 1–2.

[97] Pytlak (note 91), p. 4; and International Action Network on Small Arms (note 93), p. 7.

II. Intergovernmental efforts to address the challenges posed by autonomous weapon systems

LAURA BRUUN

The legal, ethical and security challenges posed by autonomous weapon systems (AWS) have since 2014 been the subject of intergovernmental discussions within the framework of the 1981 Convention on Certain Conventional Weapons (CCW Convention) under the auspices of the United Nations.[1] Since 2017, the discussions have been led by an open-ended group of governmental experts (GGE). The GGE was initially mandated to 'explore and agree on possible recommendations on options related to emerging technologies in the area of LAWS [lethal autonomous weapon systems]'.[2] After an amendment to its mandate in 2019, the GGE was also tasked with considering, clarifying and possibly further developing aspects of the relevant normative and operational framework.[3] A central question that has divided the GGE from the start relates to the extent to which the existing normative and operational framework needs to be clarified and further developed. That is, whether the existing rules of international law provide a sufficiently clear regulatory framework or whether new (legally binding) rules, standards or best practices are required to address the challenges associated with the use of AWS.

Approaching the sixth review conference of the CCW Convention

After almost a decade of work, intergovernmental efforts to address the challenges posed by AWS reached a critical juncture in 2021. The year marked the end of the GGE's current mandate, and the sixth review

---

[1] For a summary and other details of the Convention on Prohibitions or Restrictions on the Use of Certain Conventional Weapons which may be Deemed to be Excessively Injurious or to have Indiscriminate Effects (CCW Convention or 'Inhumane Weapons' Convention) and its protocols see annex A, section I, in this volume. On earlier discussions on the regulation of lethal autonomous weapon systems (LAWS) see Anthony, I. and Holland, C., 'The governance of autonomous weapon systems', *SIPRI Yearbook 2014*, pp. 423–31; Davis, I. et al., 'Humanitarian arms control regimes: Key developments in 2016', *SIPRI Yearbook 2017*, pp. 559–61; Davis, I. and Verbruggen, M., 'The Convention on Certain Conventional Weapons', *SIPRI Yearbook 2018*, pp. 383–86; Boulanin, V., Davis, I. and Verbruggen, M., 'The Convention on Certain Conventional Weapons and lethal autonomous weapon systems', *SIPRI Yearbook 2019*, pp. 452–57; Peldán Carlsson, M. and Boulanin, V., 'The group of governmental experts on lethal autonomous weapon systems', *SIPRI Yearbook 2020*, pp. 502–12; and Bruun, L., 'The group of governmental experts on lethal autonomous weapon systems', *SIPRI Yearbook 2021*, pp. 518–24.

[2] Since 2017, the GGE's mandate has run for terms of two years. CCW Convention, Fifth Review Conference, Report of the 2016 Informal Meeting of Experts on Lethal Autonomous Weapons Systems (LAWS), CCW/CONF.V/2, 10 June 2016, annex, para. 3. The GGE is 'open-ended' in the sense that it is open to participants from all CCW Convention states parties.

[3] CCW Convention, GGE on Emerging Technologies in the Area of LAWS, Report of the 2019 session, CCW/GGE.1/2019/3, 25 Sep. 2019, para. 26(d).

conference (RevCon) of the CCW Convention was held in December (see section I). The RevCon, which takes place every five years, was seen as an important opportunity for the GGE to consolidate its work, potentially agree on political commitments and identify a direction for the way forward. Preparations for the RevCon, notably in terms of consolidating views in consensus recommendations, were therefore central to the GGE's work in 2021. After more than a year of Covid-19 pandemic-related disruptions, the GGE was able to resume physical meetings in 2021. It met in Geneva for a total of 20 days between August and December—the highest number of meeting days the GGE had ever had in one year. The group also met for an informal, virtual exchange in June and most delegations met at an informal working seminar in November organized by the French delegation. States and civil society groups also contributed to the discussion through written commentaries and oral statements.[4] Several states did so jointly, reflecting old as well as new alliances (notably the newly established cross-regional Group of 13).[5]

As in previous years, the GGE's discussions in 2021 followed two tracks: one on substantial questions around legal, ethical and military aspects of the development and use of AWS, and the other on options related to the governance of AWS. This section summarizes key aspects discussed under both tracks and also considers the way forward. To reflect the emerging consensus that 'lethality' is not an intrinsic characteristic of AWS, this section adopts the broader term of 'autonomous weapon systems (AWS)', while noting that the GGE's work, so far, refers to 'lethal autonomous weapon systems (LAWS)' in line with its current mandate.

The legal, ethical and military challenges posed by AWS

Identifying and addressing the legal, ethical and military challenges associated with the development and use of AWS have been key aspects of the GGE's work since the formation of the group. While there are fundamentally different perceptions among delegations of the GGE as to the challenges posed by AWS, the group has managed to agree on some basic elements. The outline of this initial agreement is notably reflected in the GGE's 11 guiding

---

[4] All commentaries and working papers can be found on the meeting website, UN Office for Disarmament Affairs, Meetings Place, <https://meetings.unoda.org/section/ccw-gge-2021_documents _14090/>.

[5] The Group of 13 started as the Group of 6 in 2021 through an initiative by Costa Rica, Panama, Peru, the Philippines, Sierra Leone and Uruguay. It was later expanded to the Group of 10, then Group of 11 and finally Group of 13 by the end of 2021, with Argentina, Ecuador, El Salvador, Guatemala, Kazakhstan, Nigeria and Palestine joining the 6 original members.

principles as well as in past meeting outcome documents.[6] The GGE's aim in 2021 was to turn the progress made into substantial recommendations to submit at the RevCon. To that end, the Chair of the GGE in 2021, Ambassador Marc Pecsteen de Buytswerve of Belgium, presented a paper for the GGE to consider during its meeting sessions.[7] The chair's paper consolidated proposals made across several areas, and gave the GGE the opportunity to elaborate on substantial questions and expand areas of convergence. The central issues discussed by the GGE in 2021 included, but were not limited to, questions around the characterization of AWS, the application of international law, human–machine interaction (HMI), human responsibility and accountability, weapon reviews, and ethical considerations. Key aspects of the discussions are summarized in the following subsections.

The characterization of AWS

Questions on how to characterize AWS remained subject to debate in 2021. Many, but not all, delegations expressed that reaching a common understanding of the characteristics of AWS was an important step for the GGE to make progress, particularly for regulatory purposes.[8] With this in mind, the GGE assessed two new characterizations in 2021. Inspired by a French–German proposal, the chair's paper suggested distinguishing between fully autonomous weapon systems (FAWS) and partially autonomous weapon systems (PAWS).[9] This would set the basis for a regulatory delineation between weapon systems that are inherently unlawful and should be prohibited (i.e. FAWS) from those that may be lawful but subject to regulation (i.e. PAWS). However, the suggestion was questioned by several

---

[6] The guiding principles establish, among other things, that international humanitarian law (IHL) applies to LAWS; that humans, not machines, remain responsible for the use of LAWS; and that various types and degrees of human–machine interaction are needed to ensure compliance with international law. CCW Convention, CCW/GGE.1/2019/3 (note 3), annex IV. Past meeting outcome documents include: CCW Convention, GGE on Emerging Technologies in the Area of LAWS, Report of the 2017 session, CCW/GGE.1/2017/3, 22 Dec. 2017; and CCW Convention, GGE on Emerging Technologies in the Area of LAWS, Report of the 2018 session, CCW/GGE.1/2018/3, 23 Oct. 2018.

[7] The chair's paper was first circulated in an offline format. It was subject to a number of revisions from when it was first circulated in August until it was finally reviewed in December. An online version of a revised version from September is available on the Reaching Critical Will website. CCW Convention, GGE on Emerging Technologies in the Area of LAWS, 'Draft elements on possible consensus recommendations in relation to the clarification, consideration and development of aspects of the normative and operational framework on emerging technologies in the area of lethal autonomous weapons systems: Revised chair's paper', 20 Sep. 2021.

[8] Some delegations, such as Chile, argued that discussions around characteristics could be shelved until the start of negotiations on a potential new treaty and that a lack of commonly agreed characteristics should not prevent the GGE from making progress. CCW Convention, GGE on Emerging Technologies in the Area of LAWS, Statement by Chile, 1st session of 2021, 2nd meeting, Audio recording, 3 Aug. 2021.

[9] CCW Convention, GGE on Emerging Technologies in the Area of LAWS, 'Outline for a normative and operational framework on emerging technologies in the area of LAWS', Commentary by France and Germany, 2021; and CCW Convention, Revised chair's paper (note 7).

delegations. They doubted the regulatory feasibility of distinguishing between AWS based on levels of autonomy (see section III). The GGE also continued to discuss whether 'lethality' was a defining characteristic of AWS, and thereby whether the GGE's mandate should extend to AWS as a whole or only to LAWS. A small group of states, including India, Israel and Russia, insisted that the 'lethal' qualifier was important and that 'LAWS' should remain the focus of the GGE.[10] In contrast, the majority argued that the GGE should expand its focus to 'AWS', pointing, for example, to the fact that non-lethal AWS could also violate international humanitarian law (IHL).[11] Although discussions on characterization reached a new level of granularity in 2021, the issue remained an area of future work.

The application of international law to AWS

The GGE has established that international law, and in particular IHL, applies to LAWS.[12] However, questions on how IHL applies to AWS and what limits it places on them continued to divide the GGE in 2021, which had implications for the GGE's ability to reach consensus recommendations on this issue. Several states and civil society groups—including Austria and Brazil as well as the International Committee of the Red Cross (ICRC)—argued that IHL compliance demands qualitative value judgements that cannot be delegated to machines and that this should be reflected in the consensus recommendations.[13] Meanwhile, other delegations—including France, Japan, Russia and the United States—asserted that human involvement is not an explicit requirement in IHL and that delegating some tasks to machines

---

[10] See e.g. CCW Convention, GGE on Emerging Technologies in the Area of LAWS, Statement by Israel, 1st session of 2021, 6th meeting, Audio recording, 5 Aug. 2021; CCW Convention, GGE on Emerging Technologies in the Area of LAWS, Statement by Russia, 2nd session of 2021, 5th meeting, Audio recording, 28 Sep. 2021; and CCW Convention, GGE on Emerging Technologies in the Area of LAWS, Statement by India, 2nd session of 2021, 6th meeting, Audio recording, 28 Sep. 2021.

[11] See e.g. CCW Convention, GGE on Emerging Technologies in the Area of LAWS, Statements by Austria, Bulgaria, the International Committee of the Red Cross (ICRC), Portugal and Switzerland, 1st session of 2021, 3rd meeting, Audio recording, 4 Aug. 2021; and CCW Convention, GGE on Emerging Technologies in the Area of LAWS, Statement by Palestine on behalf of the then Group of 10 (Argentina, Costa Rica, Ecuador, El Salvador, Palestine, Panama, Peru, the Philippines, Sierra Leone and Uruguay), 2nd session of 2021, 5th meeting, Audio recording, 28 Sep. 2021.

[12] Guiding Principle (a). CCW Convention, CCW/GGE.1/2019/3 (note 3), annex IV, para. (a).

[13] See e.g. CCW Convention, GGE on Emerging Technologies in the Area of LAWS, 'Joint submission on possible consensus recommendations in relation to the clarification, consideration and development of aspects of the normative and operational framework on emerging technologies in the area of lethal autonomous weapons systems', Commentary by Austria, Brazil, Chile, Ireland, Luxembourg, Mexico and New Zealand, 2021; International Committee of the Red Cross (ICRC), 'ICRC position on autonomous weapon systems', 12 May 2021; and CCW Convention, GGE on Emerging Technologies in the Area of LAWS, Statement by the Holy See, 1st session of 2021, 1st meeting, Audio recording, 3 Aug. 2021.

may not only be lawful but also enhance compliance with IHL.[14] As a means to ensure compliance with IHL, the GGE also discussed the possibility of limiting AWS to target only objectives that are military in nature and only objects, not humans. The proposed limits, which were put forward by the ICRC in particular, divided the GGE and did not reach consensus.[15] In the light of the continuing lack of clarity around how to ensure compliance with IHL in relation to AWS, the GGE considered the value of creating a compendium that would map and clarify relevant rules of IHL applicable to AWS.[16] Some delegations, however, raised concerns that a compendium could give the wrong impression that IHL was sufficient to address the challenges posed by AWS.[17]

As part of the GGE's discussions around IHL, the risk of bias was the subject of increased debate in 2021. Several delegations—such as the Group of 13 as well as Austria, and jointly Brazil, Chile and Mexico—expressed concern that targeting based on algorithms risks amplifying social bias, posing challenges to compliance with IHL, most notably the principle of distinction (between civilians and combatants).[18] Others, such as Russia and the USA, argued that it was premature to include the risk of bias in the GGE's

---

[14] See e.g. CCW Convention, GGE on Emerging Technologies in the Area of LAWS, 'US proposals', Commentary by the United States, 11 June 2021; CCW Convention, GGE on Emerging Technologies in the Area of LAWS, 'Considerations for the report of the Group of Governmental Experts of the High Contracting Parties to the Convention on Certain Conventional Weapons on Emerging Technologies in the Area of Lethal Autonomous Weapons Systems on the outcomes of the work undertaken in 2017–2021', Commentary by Russia, 2021 (unofficial translation); and CCW Convention, GGE on Emerging Technologies in the Area of LAWS, Statements by France and Japan, 1st session of 2021, 1st meeting, Audio recording, 3 Aug. 2021.

[15] The ICRC as well as Argentina, Palestine and the Philippines were among those in favour of imposing such limits. ICRC (note 13); CCW Convention, GGE on Emerging Technologies in the Area of LAWS, 'Commentary of the Republic of the Philippines on the normative and operational framework in emerging technologies in the area of lethal autonomous weapon systems', Commentary by the Philippines, 2021; and CCW Convention, GGE on Emerging Technologies in the Area of LAWS, Statements by Argentina and Palestine, 1st session of 2021, 2nd meeting, Audio recording, 3 Aug. 2021.
France, the Netherlands and Switzerland were among the delegations that argued against the legal feasibility of the proposals. CCW Convention, GGE on Emerging Technologies in the Area of LAWS, Statement by France, 2nd session of 2021, 6th meeting, Audio recording, 29 Sep. 2021; and CCW Convention, GGE on Emerging Technologies in the Area of LAWS, Statements by the Netherlands and Switzerland, 2nd session of 2021, 9th meeting, Audio recording, 30 Sep. 2021.

[16] See e.g. CCW Convention, GGE on Emerging Technologies in the Area of LAWS, Statements by Portugal and the United Kingdom, 3rd session of 2021, 4th meeting, Audio recording, 3 Dec. 2021.

[17] See e.g. CCW Convention, GGE on Emerging Technologies in the Area of LAWS, Statements by Palestine and the Philippines, 3rd session of 2021, 4th meeting, Audio recording, 3 Dec. 2021.

[18] See e.g. CCW Convention, GGE on Emerging Technologies in the Area of LAWS, 'Joint working paper', Commentary by Costa Rica, Panama, Peru, the Philippines, Sierra Leone and Uruguay, 2021; CCW Convention, GGE on Emerging Technologies in the Area of LAWS, Statement by Austria, 1st session of 2021, 10th meeting, Audio recording, 9 Aug. 2021; and CCW Convention, GGE on Emerging Technologies in the Area of LAWS, Joint statement by Brazil, Chile and Mexico, 2nd session of 2021, 3rd meeting, Audio recording, 27 Sep. 2021.

consensus recommendations, but that the issue could constitute an area of future work.[19]

Finally, the GGE considered the relevance of including other areas of international law, such as international human rights law (IHRL) and international criminal law (ICL), in its consensus recommendations. While several states and civil society groups argued in favour of doing so, no consensus was reached and IHL remained the primary focus of the GGE.[20]

Human–machine interaction

The GGE has established that certain types and degrees of HMI are needed across the life cycle of AWS to ensure compliance with IHL.[21] However, the challenge facing the GGE in 2021 was to identify concrete recommendations on what type and degree of HMI would be needed in all or some circumstances.

The GGE focused, in particular, on what measures would be needed for IHL compliance in the use phase of an AWS, but did not reach further consensus despite the concrete proposals submitted by the Chair.[22] However, the GGE did agree on the importance, going forward, of identifying good practice for HMI to strengthen compliance with IHL. In their discussions on HMI, delegations returned to the question of whether IHL compliance requires humans to exercise 'control', 'judgement' or 'involvement' and what term the GGE's recommendations should use. Although the majority argued that 'human control' is the appropriate standard, the term was not adopted as consensus language due to opposition from, among others, Canada, Israel and the USA.[23]

---

[19] See e.g. CCW Convention, GGE on Emerging Technologies in the Area of LAWS, Statement by the USA, 1st session of 2021, 10th meeting, Audio recording, 9 Aug. 2021; and CCW Convention, Statement by Russia (note 10).

[20] See e.g. CCW Convention, GGE on Emerging Technologies in the Area of LAWS, Statements by Amnesty International, the Philippines, Sri Lanka and the UK, 2nd session of 2021, 7th meeting, Audio recording, 29 Sep. 2021; CCW Convention, GGE on Emerging Technologies in the Area of LAWS, Statements by Austria, Brazil, Chile, Cuba and Mexico, 2nd session of 2021, 8th meeting, Audio recording, 29 Sep. 2021; and CCW Convention, GGE on Emerging Technologies in the Area of LAWS, 'Working paper to be submitted by the Bolivarian Republic of Venezuela on behalf of the Non-Aligned Movement (NAM) and other states parties to the Convention on Certain Conventional Weapons (CCW)', Working paper submitted by Venezuela, 2021.

[21] Guiding principle (c). CCW Convention, CCW/GGE.1/2019/3 (note 3), annex IV, para. (c).

[22] See e.g. CCW Convention, GGE on Emerging Technologies in the Area of LAWS, Statements by Israel, Japan and the UK, 2nd session of 2021, 9th meeting, Audio recording, 30 Sep. 2021; CCW Convention, GGE on Emerging Technologies in the Area of LAWS, Statement by Austria, 3rd session of 2021, 5th meeting, Audio recording, 6 Dec. 2021; and CCW Convention, GGE on Emerging Technologies in the Area of LAWS, Statement by Peru on behalf of the then Group of 11 (Argentina, Costa Rica, Ecuador, El Salvador, Nigeria, Palestine, Panama, Peru, the Philippines, Sierra Leone and Uruguay), 3rd session of 2021, 5th meeting, Audio recording, 6 Dec. 2021.

[23] See e.g. CCW Convention, Statement by Israel (note 10); and CCW Convention, GGE on Emerging Technologies in the Area of LAWS, Statement by Canada, 2nd session of 2021, 5th meeting, Audio recording, 28 Sep. 2021; and CCW Convention, GGE on Emerging Technologies in the Area of LAWS, Statement by the USA, 2nd session of 2021, 1st meeting, Audio recording, 24 Sep. 2021.

Human responsibility and accountability

In 2019 the GGE reached consensus that responsibility for decisions to use force involving AWS must be retained by humans as accountability cannot be transferred to machines.[24] Yet questions on how to ensure human responsibility and accountability in practice had remained largely unaddressed by the GGE. Deliberations reached a more granular level in 2021, however, as the GGE attempted to identify concrete recommendations to submit at the RevCon.[25] The GGE discussed different options and challenges related to holding, most notably, individuals and states accountable for potential violations of IHL in the development and use of AWS. Many delegations emphasized in particular the importance of ensuring a 'responsible human chain of command and control'.[26] The discussions, nevertheless, revealed conceptual confusion and a lack of clarity around the different responsibility frameworks.[27] Although the consensus was that ensuring human responsibility and accountability is of key significance, the shared view was that further work and clarification were needed in this area.

Weapon reviews

It is well established in the GGE that weapon reviews are essential means to ensure compliance with IHL.[28] The inclusion of this aspect in the GGE's consensus recommendations was therefore largely supported. The GGE agreed that AWS pose specific challenges for weapon reviews and that sharing of good practices related to the review process is beneficial.[29] The chair's paper, however, gave rise to discussions on the extent to which reviews should be

---

[24] Guiding principles (b) and (d). CCW Convention, CCW/GGE.1/2019/3 (note 3), annex IV, paras (b) and (d).

[25] See e.g. CCW Convention, Commentary by Austria, Brazil, Chile, Ireland, Luxembourg, Mexico and New Zealand (note 13); CCW Convention, Commentary by the USA (note 14); CCW Convention, GGE on Emerging Technologies in the Area of LAWS, 'Switzerland's food for thought as requested by the Chair of the Group of Governmental Experts (GGE) on Emerging Technologies in the Area of Lethal Autonomous Weapons Systems (LAWS) within the Convention on Certain Conventional Weapons (CCW)', Commentary by Switzerland, 2021; and CCW Convention, GGE on Emerging Technologies in the Area of LAWS, Statement by the UK, 1st session of 2021, 3rd meeting, Audio recording, 4 Aug. 2021.

[26] See e.g. CCW Convention, GGE on Emerging Technologies in the Area of LAWS, 'Discussion paper: Building on Chile's proposed four elements of further work for the Convention on Certain Conventional Weapons (CCW) Group of Governmental Experts (GGE) on Emerging Technologies in the Area of Lethal Autonomous Weapons Systems (LAWS)', Commentary by Australia, Canada, Japan, the UK and the USA, 2021; and CCW Convention, Commentary by Austria, Brazil, Chile, Ireland, Luxembourg, Mexico and New Zealand (note 13).

[27] Some delegations pointed out, for instance, that the term 'human responsibility' used in the chair's paper is not a legal term and suggested that more accurate terms would, among others, be 'individual criminal responsibility' or 'individual accountability'. See e.g. CCW Convention, GGE on Emerging Technologies in the Area of LAWS, Statements by Austria and Cuba, 3rd session of 2021, 5th meeting, Audio recording, 6 Dec. 2021.

[28] Guiding Principle (e). CCW Convention, CCW/GGE.1/2019/3 (note 3), annex IV, para. (e).

[29] CCW Convention, GGE on Emerging Technologies in the Area of LAWS, 'Commonalities in national commentaries on guiding principles', Working paper by the Chair, Sep. 2020, paras 13, 14 and 21(a); and CCW Convention, CCW/GGE.1/2019/3 (note 3), annex IV, para. 17(i).

subject to international standards or left to the discretion of states. India, for instance, stated that the chair's paper was overly prescriptive and stressed that weapon reviews are a national matter.[30]

Ethical considerations

The ethical considerations posed by AWS, and how these should be addressed in the consensus recommendations, were the subject of increased attention in 2021. The issue was raised at a number of sessions by civil society groups and several states, including the Campaign to Stop Killer Robots, the Group of 13 and Austria.[31] These delegations argued that targeting based on algorithms gives rise to fundamental ethical concerns, which should be reflected explicitly in the GGE's consensus recommendations. In contrast, the USA pointed out that, in some instances, AWS could improve rather than contravene ethical standards.[32] This viewpoint was based on, among other things, the perceived benefits of accuracy and combat protection associated with the use of AWS. The GGE did not reach an agreement but recognized that further deliberations on ethical considerations remained an area for future work.

Options for addressing the challenges posed by AWS

A central component of the GGE's mandate was to recommend options related to the governance of AWS. This issue was considered of particular importance in 2021 as it connected to recommendations around what a future mandate potentially should aim to achieve. While most states' views on the matter remained unchanged, dicussions in 2021 provided an opportunity for delegations to expand on their positions. Notably, arguments in favour of new, legally binding rules to address the challenges posed by AWS gained

---

[30] CCW Convention, GGE on Emerging Technologies in the Area of LAWS, Statement by India, 2nd session of 2021, 9th meeting, Audio recording, 30 Sep. 2021.

[31] See e.g. CCW Convention, GGE on Emerging Technologies in the Area of LAWS, Statement by Austria, 1st session of 2021, 2nd meeting, Audio recording, 3 Aug. 2021; CCW Convention, GGE on Emerging Technologies in the Area of LAWS, 'Elements for a future normative framework conducive to a legally binding instrument to address the ethical humanitarian and legal concerns posed by emerging technologies in the area of (lethal) autonomous weapons (LAWS)', Commentary by Brazil, Chile and Mexico, 2021; CCW Convention, GGE on Emerging Technologies in the Area of LAWS, Statement by Ireland, 2nd session of 2021, 1st meeting, Audio recording, 24 Sep. 2021; CCW Convention, Working paper submitted by Venezuela (note 20); CCW Convention, GGE on Emerging Technologies in the Area of LAWS, Statement by the Philippines on behalf of the then Group of 11 (Argentina, Costa Rica, Ecuador, El Salvador, Nigeria, Palestine, Panama, Peru, the Philippines, Sierra Leone and Uruguay), 3rd session of 2021, 3rd meeting, Audio recording, 3 Dec. 2021; ICRC (note 13); and CCW Convention, GGE on Emerging Technologies in the Area of LAWS, 'Recommendations on the normative and operational framework for autonomous weapon systems', Commentary by the Campaign to Stop Killer Robots, June 2021.

[32] CCW Convention, GGE on Emerging Technologies in the Area of LAWS, Statement by the USA, 2nd session of 2021, 11th meeting, Audio recording, 1 Oct. 2021.

further momentum in 2021. The ICRC, which has followed the debate since the beginning, joined a large number of delegations in recommending the adoption of legally binding rules on certain types and uses of AWS.[33] Despite the significance of the ICRC's announcement, several states (including many major military powers) repeated their warning against premature regulation, pointing to the potential humanitarian and military benefits associated with AWS.[34] According to this line of argument, positive obligations accompanied by clarification of existing law would be sufficient to address the challenges posed by AWS.[35] This view was endorsed by the USA, in particular, which in 2021 made great efforts to promote the idea of establishing a code of conduct.[36] Finally, a few delegations, most notably Russia, continued to oppose the creation of new norms or rules. Russia argued that existing IHL is sufficient to address the challenges posed by AWS.[37] The Russian delegation did, however, express support for the creation of non-binding instruments, such as a manual or a compendium.[38] While the various options outlined by the delegations are not necessarily mutually exclusive, the GGE remained divided in terms of what type and combination of measures would be adequate responses to the challenges posed by AWS.

Despite the continued divergence in this area among delegations, growing support emerged in 2021 for a so-called two-tier approach. Following a two-tier approach, a future normative framework would include both prohibitions and regulations. The pertaining challenge, however, would be to agree what

---

[33] ICRC (note 13). A large number of states and civil society groups have already recommended the need to adopt a legally binding instrument. These include: the 55 members of the African Union, Argentina, Austria, Brazil, the Campaign to Stop Killer Robots, Chile, China, Costa Rica, Cuba, Ecuador, El Salvador, Guatemala, The Holy See, Kazakhstan, Mexico, New Zealand, the Non-Aligned Movement, Pakistan, Palestine, Panama, Peru, the Philippines and Uruguay. In addition, UN Secretary-General António Guterres has expressed support for this view on several occasions.

[34] In varying degrees, these states include: Australia, France, India, Israel, Japan, the Republic of Korea, Russia, the UK, the USA and Turkey.

[35] See e.g. CCW Convention, GGE on Emerging Technologies in the Area of LAWS, 'Written contributions on possible consensus recommendations in relation to the clarification, consideration and development of aspects of the normative and operational framework on emerging technologies in the area of lethal autonomous weapons systems', Commentary by the UK, June 2021; CCW Convention, GGE on Emerging Technologies in the Area of LAWS, 'Proposals for consensus in relation to the clarification, consideration and development of aspects of the normative and operational framework', Commentary by Portugal, June 2021; CCW Convention, GGE on Emerging Technologies in the Area of LAWS, Statement by Israel, 3rd session of 2021, 4th meeting, Audio recording, 3 Dec. 2021; and CCW Convention, GGE on Emerging Technologies in the Area of LAWS, Statement by Australia, 3rd session of 2021, 7th meeting, Audio recording, 7 Dec. 2021.

[36] CCW Convention, GGE on Emerging Technologies in the Area of LAWS, Statement by the USA, 3rd session of 2021, 7th meeting, Audio recording, 7 Dec. 2021.

[37] CCW Convention, Commentary by Russia (note 14).

[38] CCW Convention, GGE on Emerging Technologies in the Area of LAWS, Statement by Russia, 2nd session of 2021, 7th meeting, Audio recording, 29 Sep. 2021.

types of AWS should be subject to either prohibition or regulation.[39] In this regard, consensus seemed to emerge around two aspects: first, to regulate based on *how* AWS are used, rather than the level of autonomy; and second, to prohibit AWS that cannot be used in compliance with IHL.[40] The GGE also considered proposals to prohibit 'inherently unpredictable' AWS and AWS that cannot be used without 'meaningful human control'.[41] Even though the GGE did not manage to agree on the details of a two-tier approach, the framework could provide part of the GGE's consensus recommendations.

Outlook

Failed attempts to agree on substantive consensus recommendations

After almost a decade of discussions within the forum of the CCW Convention, the GGE was expected to submit substantive consensus recommendations at the RevCon on the clarification and potential development of the normative and operational framework for AWS. This was also supposed to include recommendations for a future GGE mandate. In an attempt to make progress, the GGE Chair suggested taking a gradual approach at the RevCon. Under this approach, the GGE would (*a*) consolidate the progress made in a political declaration, and (*b*) adopt a new mandate that would work towards the adoption of an 'instrument on the regulation of weapons systems'.[42]

Most delegations engaged constructively with the Chair's proposal, although they expressed diverging preferences on the content and scope of the political declaration and the instrument. Regarding the political declaration, which was based on the substantive elements of the chair's paper, some delegations—including India, Turkey and the USA—argued that it was premature for the GGE to adopt a political declaration as currently

---

[39] E.g. as expressed in: CCW Convention, GGE on Emerging Technologies in the Area of LAWS, 'Elements for possible consensus recommendations', Commentary by Finland, June 2021; and CCW Convention, GGE on Emerging Technologies in the Area of LAWS, Statement by Switzerland, 2nd session of 2021, 5th meeting, Audio recording, 28 Sep. 2021.

[40] The USA, Austria, Ireland, Palestine and the Republic of Korea were among the majority of delegations in favour of regulating based on use. CCW Convention, Statement by the USA (note 23); CCW Convention, GGE on Emerging Technologies in the Area of LAWS, Statements by Austria and Ireland, 2nd session of 2021, 5th meeting, UN Web TV, 28 Sep. 2021; CCW Convention, GGE on Emerging Technologies in the Area of LAWS, Statement by Palestine, 2nd session of 2021, 6th meeting, Audio recording, 28 Sep. 2021; and CCW Convention, GGE on Emerging Technologies in the Area of LAWS, Statements by the Republic of Korea, 2nd session of 2021, 7th meeting, Audio recording, 29 Sep. 2021.

[41] See e.g. ICRC (note 13); CCW Convention, Commentary by Costa Rica, Panama, Peru, the Philippines, Sierra Leone and Uruguay (note 18); and CCW Convention, Commentary by the Campaign to Stop Killer Robots (note 31).

[42] CCW Convention, GGE on Emerging Technologies in the Area of LAWS, Draft report of the 2021 session, CCW/GGE.1/2021/CRP.xx, Nov. 2021, para. 55(b), (c).

drafted, as it was too far-reaching and did not reflect consensus language.[43] In their view, a political declaration should be based on past consensus, as reflected in, among other things, the GGE's guiding principles. Meanwhile, other delegations, such as Austria, Brazil, Chile, Ireland and Mexico, argued that a political declaration merely reflecting the guiding principles was not representative of the progress made over the past years and that it should be more ambitious.[44] The GGE also discussed the purpose of the political declaration. While some delegations were content with the adoption of a political declaration in itself, several others argued that it should serve only as an interim step to making more substantial progress—for example, as a step towards adopting a legally binding instrument.[45]

With regard to the new mandate, the GGE largely supported the adoption of a more expansive mandate as proposed by the Chair. Several delegations argued that a new mandate should enable the GGE to negotiate a legally binding instrument.[46] Others, meanwhile, stressed that the mandate should not prejudge the outcome, raising concerns that use of the term 'instrument' suggested a preference for the adoption of a legally binding instrument.[47] Finally, a few delegations, most notably Russia, opposed the Chair's suggestion entirely and argued for the adoption of a roll-over mandate, meaning that the GGE would simply renew its mandate from 2019.[48]

[43] See e.g. CCW Convention, GGE on Emerging Technologies in the Area of LAWS, Statements by India, Turkey and the USA, 3rd session of 2021, 1st meeting, Audio recording, 2 Dec. 2021; and CCW Convention, GGE on Emerging Technologies in the Area of LAWS, Statement by Russia, 3rd session of 2021, 3rd meeting, Audio recording, 3 Dec. 2021.

[44] See e.g. CCW Convention, GGE on Emerging Technologies in the Area of LAWS, Joint statements by Brazil, Mexico and Chile, and statements by Austria and Ireland, 3rd session of 2021, 1st meeting, Audio recording, 2 Dec. 2021.

[45] See e.g. CCW Convention, Joint statements by Brazil, Chile and Mexico, and statement by Ireland (note 44); and CCW Convention, GGE on Emerging Technologies in the Area of LAWS, Statement by Sierra Leone on behalf of the then Group of 11 (Argentina, Costa Rica, Ecuador, El Salvador, Nigeria, Palestine, Panama, Peru, the Philippines, Sierra Leone and Uruguay), 3rd session of 2021, 4th meeting, Audio recording, 3 Dec. 2021.
While not supporting a legally binding instrument, Switzerland and some other delegations argued that a political declaration should not be the final outcome. See e.g. CCW Convention, GGE on Emerging Technologies in the Area of LAWS, Statement by Switzerland, 3rd session of 2021, 1st meeting, Audio recording, 2 Dec. 2021.

[46] See e.g. CCW Convention, Joint statements by Brazil, Mexico and Chile (note 44), statement by Sierra Leone on behalf of the then Group of 11 (Argentina, Costa Rica, Ecuador, El Salvador, Nigeria, Palestine, Panama, Peru, the Philippines, Sierra Leone and Uruguay), and statement by the Campaign to Stop Killer Robots, 3rd session of 2021, 1st meeting, Audio recording, 2 Dec. 2021; and CCW Convention, GGE on Emerging Technologies in the Area of LAWS, Statement by Namibia on behalf of the African Group, 3rd session of 2021, 3rd meeting, Audio recording, 3 Dec. 2021.

[47] See e.g. CCW Convention, GGE on Emerging Technologies in the Area of LAWS, Statement by the USA, 3rd session of 2021, 10th meeting, Audio recording, 8 Dec. 2021.

[48] See e.g. CCW Convention, Commentary by Russia (note 14); CCW Convention, GGE on Emerging Technologies in the Area of LAWS, Statement by India, 3rd session of 2021, 1st meeting, Audio recording, 2 Dec. 2021; and CCW Convention, Statement by Russia (note 43).

As a way forward, the Chair encouraged delegations to embrace 'constructive ambiguity' in the consensus recommendations.[49] However, the inflexibility exercised by some delegations prevented the GGE from reaching substantive agreement at its final meeting in December. In particular, Russia's opposition was considered by many delegations to have been a significant obstacle to making substantial progress. By the end of the meeting, the GGE had managed to agree only on a few paragraphs, which reflected what was perceived as the absolute minimum and made no recommendations regarding a future mandate.[50] The substantial sections that were intended to form the basis of a political declaration were instead turned into a 'Chairperson's summary' and therefore did not carry the same weight.[51] Many delegations considered the lack of agreement on substantial recommendations as a significant failure that neither did justice to the progress made over the past years nor reflected the urgency of the issue.[52]

New mandate, new divisions

Because the GGE failed to make recommendations regarding a new mandate, the future of discussions on AWS within the framework of the CCW Convention was left to be decided at the RevCon. However, thanks to informal consultations and political will, the GGE managed to agree on a compromise text for a future mandate, which was then adopted at the RevCon. Going forward, the GGE is mandated to 'consider proposals and elaborate, by consensus, possible measures . . . related to the normative and operational framework on emerging technologies in the area of lethal autonomous weapon systems, building upon the recommendations and conclusions contained in the reports of the Group of Governmental Experts'.[53]

The new mandate allocated 10 days for the GGE to meet in 2022, although most delegations expressed a preference for 15 or 20 days.

While reaching an agreement could be considered something of an achievement, the new mandate was significantly less ambitious than what the majority of delegations wanted and several expressed their deep disappointment with the outcome of the GGE's work. It was a widely held view that a few states had misused their veto power and not practised the consensus-seeking

---

[49] See e.g. CCW Convention, GGE on Emerging Technologies in the Area of LAWS, Statement by the Chair, 3rd session of 2021, 10th meeting, Audio recording, 8 Dec. 2021.

[50] E.g. one of the paragraphs read as follows: 'The Group considered different proposals on how to reflect the deliberations including possible conclusions and recommendations of the Group, but no consensus was reached.' CCW Convention, GGE on Emerging Technologies in the Area of LAWS, Draft report of the 2021 session, CCW/GGE.1/2021/CRP.1, 8 Dec. 2021, para. 17.

[51] CCW Convention, CCW/GGE.1/2021/CRP.1 (note 50), annex III.

[52] See e.g. CCW Convention, GGE on Emerging Technologies in the Area of LAWS, Statement by the Campaign to Stop Killer Robots, 3rd session of 2021, 10th meeting, 8 Dec. 2021.

[53] CCW Convention, Sixth Review Conference, Draft Final Document of the Sixth Review Conference, CCW/CONF.VI/11, Geneva, 13–17 Dec. 2021, 10 Jan. 2022, part III.

behaviour needed in a forum like the CCW Convention. For instance, in a rare joint statement, Austria, Belgium, Brazil, Chile, Finland, Germany, Ireland, Italy, Luxembourg, Mexico, the Netherlands, New Zealand, Norway, South Africa, Sweden and Switzerland expressed their frustration with the process and noted that those who invoke a veto 'should do so responsibly and seldom, and only when all other avenues are exhausted'.[54]

While discussions on AWS will continue within the framework of the CCW Convention in 2022, the culmination of events in December 2021 may feed concerns as to whether the CCW Convention remains the appropriate forum to address the challenges posed by AWS. Time will tell whether the GGE will be able to make satisfactory progress or whether the large group of states advocating a legally binding instrument will seek alternative paths for doing so outside the CCW Convention.

---

[54] CCW Convention, GGE on Emerging Technologies in the Area of LAWS, Joint statement by Austria, Belgium, Brazil, Chile, Finland, Germany, Ireland, Italy, Luxembourg, Mexico, the Netherlands, New Zealand, Norway, South Africa, Sweden and Switzerland, 3rd session of 2021, 10th meeting, 8 Dec. 2021.

III. The withdrawal of Russia from the Treaty on Open Skies

ALEXANDER GRAEF

In January 2021 Russia announced that it would withdraw from the 1992 Treaty on Open Skies.[1] It took this decision following the withdrawal by the United States in November 2020. Russian President Vladimir Putin signed the withdrawal law in June 2021 and, in accordance with treaty regulations, the Russian withdrawal came into effect six months later, on 18 December 2021.[2]

The Open Skies Treaty has been in force since 1 January 2002 and, prior to the withdrawal of Russia and the USA, had 34 states parties across Europe, North America and northern Asia. It established a regime of unarmed aerial observation flights over the entire territory of participating states on a reciprocal basis. As neither Russia nor the USA is now party to the treaty, no other state party can conduct overflights over their territories. Without these two states, the future of the treaty is uncertain, even though the remaining 32 parties have pledged to continue to implement it.

This section first reviews the consequences of the US withdrawal and its relevance for Russia in 2021. It then discusses the Russian withdrawal procedure and international reactions to it.

The impact of the US withdrawal on the treaty and Russian reactions

The coming into force of the US withdrawal on 22 November 2020 acceler-ated Russian attempts to receive additional security guarantees from the treaty's other remaining states parties. On 12 November 2020 Russian Foreign Minister Sergey Lavrov indicated that Russia required the other parties 'to legally confirm in writing that . . . they will not prohibit flights over any part of their territory regardless of whether US bases are located there [and] strongly commit not to transmit data on flights over Russia to the United States'.[3] In parallel, Russia stopped conducting overflights and introduced strict Covid-19 quarantine rules for foreign inspection team members, which essentially ruled out timely treaty implementation.[4] Nevertheless, on 11 December 2020 Russia submitted a draft decision to the Open Skies

---

[1] For a summary and other details of the Treaty on Open Skies see annex A, section II, in this volume. On the US withdrawal see Davis, I., 'The withdrawal of the United States from the Treaty on Open Skies', *SIPRI Yearbook 2021*.

[2] Russian Ministry of Foreign Affairs, 'Foreign Ministry statement on the withdrawal of the Russian Federation from the Treaty on Open Skies', 20 Dec. 2021.

[3] Russian Ministry of Foreign Affairs, 'Foreign Minister Sergey Lavrov's interview with Russian and foreign media on current international issues', 12 Nov. 2020.

[4] Gavrilov, K., Head of the Russian Delegation, Statement, 4th plenary meeting, 83rd session, Open Skies Consultative Commission (OSCC), Vienna, 14 Dec. 2020.

Consultative Commission (OSCC) to amend the treaty rules concerning data security and to restate the right to access all national territory, which was originally to be discussed further at a regular OSCC meeting scheduled for 25 January 2021.

However, in his annual news conference on 17 December 2020, President Putin openly remarked that Russia could not allow North Atlantic Treaty Organization (NATO) members to conduct overflights, which would 'make everything available to our US partners'. In his view Russia was 'forced to respond' to such issues of concern.[5]

In an unexpected diplomatic note on 22 December 2020, the Russian Ministry of Foreign Affairs pushed ahead, bypassing the OSCC process, and requested that other states parties confirm their prior acceptance of the Russian draft decision before 1 January 2021, in a legally binding form; otherwise, Russia would initiate withdrawal procedures. On 30 December 2020, 16 European states parties rejected this ultimatum, although they remained open to further discussions within the OSCC.[6] As a result, the Russian Foreign Ministry announced on 15 January 2021 that it would begin domestic procedures for withdrawal from the treaty and would, on completion, send the notification to the treaty depositaries, Canada and Hungary.[7]

Nevertheless, even after this announcement, Russian officials continued to emphasize that Russia was willing to 'somehow adjust the decision to launch internal procedures' for withdrawal if the USA sent a 'clear and unambiguous message' that it was ready to return to the treaty.[8] In a plenary meeting of the OSCC on 22 February, the head of the Russian delegation, Konstantin Gavrilov, stated that the Russian withdrawal procedures would be 'completed by summer 2021'.[9] The US government would have to make a decision by then, otherwise Russia would submit its withdrawal notification to Canada and Hungary. In parallel, however, Russia pointed out that it would not accept any special procedures intended to ease the return of the USA.[10]

---

[5] President of Russia, 'Vladimir Putin's annual news conference', 17 Dec. 2020.

[6] Krüger, P.-A. and Mascolo, G., 'Der Himmel könnte sich schließen' [The sky could close], *Süddeutsche Zeitung*, 3 Jan. 2021.

[7] Russian Ministry of Foreign Affairs, 'Statement by the Ministry of Foreign Affairs of the Russian Federation on the beginning of domestic procedures for the withdrawal of the Russian Federation from the Treaty on Open Skies', 15 Jan. 2021.

[8] TASS, [Ryabkov: There is still time to rethink the situation around the Treaty on Open Skies], 11 Feb. 2021 (in Russian, author translation); and Gavrilov, K., Head of the Russian Delegation, Statement, 1st plenary meeting, 85th session, Open Skies Consultative Commission (OSCC), Vienna, 26 Apr. 2021.

[9] Gavrilov, K., Head of the Russian Delegation, Statement, 84th session, Open Skies Consultative Commission (OSCC), Vienna, 22 Feb. 2021 (in Russian, author translation).

[10] Yermakov, V., [Interview of the Director of the Department for Non-Proliferation and Arms Control of the Russian Foreign Ministry V. I. Yermakov to the international news agency 'Russia Today'], 25 Dec. 2020 (in Russian).

The position of the new US administration

As a presidential candidate, Joe Biden had condemned the decision of US President Donald J. Trump in May 2020 to withdraw from the treaty, stating that it would only 'exacerbate growing tensions between the West and Russia, and increase the risks of miscalculation and conflict'.[11] In addition, the National Defense Authorization Act for 2021, enacted by the US Congress on 1 January 2021 against Trump's presidential veto, stated that the Trump administration had not informed legislators of the US withdrawal prior to its announcement, despite a requirement to do so. The Congress also obliged the incoming Biden administration to provide a report before 1 March 2021, including a description of how the USA would replace intelligence, military-to-military contacts and diplomatic engagement lost as a result of leaving the treaty.[12] Moreover, on 26 January 2021 presidents Biden and Putin addressed the US withdrawal in their first telephone conversation.[13]

Parallel legal assessments and debate about the possibilities for the USA to rejoin the treaty, however, emphasized existing political difficulties. Without a two-thirds majority in the US Senate to approve renewed treaty membership, the Biden administration would be forced either to circumvent the Senate's prerogative for 'advice and consent', establishing a legal precedent, or to question the legality of the withdrawal decision by the Trump administration.[14] Nevertheless, the nomination by Biden of advocates for the Open Skies Treaty to central positions in the US Department of State raised expectations that the president might indeed be willing to consider renewing US treaty membership under certain circumstances. These nominations included, in particular, Bonnie D. Jenkins as Under Secretary of State for Arms Control and International Security and Alexandra Bell as Deputy Assistant Secretary in the Bureau of Arms Control, Verification and Compliance. At the beginning of February 2021, the State Department announced that the government was still 'studying the issues' and would 'take a decision in due course'.[15]

However, in a diplomatic memo released on 31 March 2021, the State Department told US allies and partners that rejoining the treaty 'that Russia continues to violate' would send the 'wrong message' and 'undermine the [US] position on the broader arms control agenda'.[16] A few days later,

---

[11] Biden, J., 'Statement by Vice President Joe Biden on President Trump's decision to withdraw from the Open Skies Treaty', Medium, 22 May 2020.

[12] National Defense Authorization Act for Fiscal Year 2021, US Public Law 116–283, signed into law 1 Jan. 2021, section 1232.

[13] President of Russia, 'Telephone conversation with US President Joseph Biden', 26 Jan. 2021.

[14] US Senate, 'Advice & consent', [n.d.]; and Rademaker, S., 'Are there shortcuts for the US to rejoin the Open Skies Treaty?', Lawfare, 15 Jan. 2021.

[15] US Department of State, 'Department press briefing', 2 Feb. 2021.

[16] Gould, J. and Mehta, A., 'Rejoining Open Skies would send "wrong message" to Russia, state tells partners', *Defense News*, 7 Apr. 2021.

on 3 April 2021, the US Air Force confirmed plans to retire its two Boeing OC-135B observation aircraft, previously used for overflight missions, and to fly them to Arizona in May and June for storage.[17] Nevertheless, the US State Department continued to claim publicly that no final decision had been made.[18] As Russia moved ahead with its domestic withdrawal procedures, however, the Biden administration officially informed Russia on 27 May 2021 that the USA would not rejoin the treaty.[19]

Russian withdrawal procedures and international reactions

Meanwhile, on 9 May 2021 President Putin introduced a draft law on withdrawal from the treaty to the lower house of the Russian Parliament, the State Duma, which the latter unanimously adopted on 19 May.[20] Two weeks later the upper house, the Federation Council, approved this decision, after which Putin signed the withdrawal law on 7 June 2021.[21]

On 16 June 2021 the Russian government also officially dissolved the group of states parties between Belarus and Russia, which had been declared upon signing the treaty in March 1992, and terminated the related implementation agreement from February 1995.[22] This arrangement had allowed Belarus to conduct joint flights with Russia and, thus, to make use of Russian equipment, based on a common active and passive quota of a maximum 42 overflights per year.[23]

Finally, on 18 June 2021 the Russian Ministry of Foreign Affairs officially submitted its withdrawal notification to the treaty depositaries.[24] In a statement following this notification, NATO urged Russia to 'use the remaining six months before its withdrawal takes effect to reconsider its decision and return to full compliance with the Treaty on Open Skies'.[25]

---

[17] Liewer, S., 'Offutt's Open Skies jets headed for desert scrapyard', *Omaha World Herald*, 3 Apr. 2021.

[18] Gould and Mehta (note 16).

[19] Heavey, S., 'US tells Russia it will not rejoin Open Skies arms control pact', 27 May 2021.

[20] [Draft federal law no. PR-767, 'On the withdrawal of the Russian Federation from the Treaty on Open Skies'], 9 May 2021 (in Russian).

[21] [Decree of the Federation Council of the Federal Assembly of the Russian Federation on the federal law 'On the withdrawal of the Russian Federation from the Treaty on Open Skies'], 2 June 2021 (in Russian); and [Federal law no. 158-FZ of 07.06.2019, 'On the withdrawal of the Russian Federation from the Treaty on Open Skies'], 7 June 2021 (in Russian).

[22] [Order of the Government of the Russian Federation, no. 1611-r of 16.06.2021], 16 June 2021 (in Russian).

[23] Under the treaty, states parties can form groups with varying rules as the allocation of overflight quotas. Russia and Belarus formed a group whereby they are effectively treated as a single entity: all observation flights conducted by either Russia or Belarus are conducted on behalf of the 'group' and charged against their total active group quota. An observing party may overfly Belarus or Russia (or both countries) and would count as one flight against the active quota of the observing party.

[24] Russian Ministry of Foreign Affairs, 'Foreign Ministry's statement following the Russian Federation's sending notifications to the states parties to the Treaty on Open Skies', 18 June 2021.

[25] NATO, 'Statement by the North Atlantic Council on the Treaty on Open Skies', Press release, 18 June 2021.

However, at the obligatory conference of states parties that convened on 20 July (after the minimum time period following notification), Russian Deputy Foreign Minister Sergey Ryabkov noted that Russia would not reverse its decision.[26]

Addressing the consequences of the Russian withdrawal

The Russian withdrawal requires the remaining 32 states parties to address several technical and political challenges. First, they will need to replace Russia as the chair of the OSCC informal working group on rules and procedures.[27]

Second, they will have to redistribute their annual active flight quotas. In the past almost one-third of all flights went over Russian (and Belarusian) territory. Since NATO members do not conduct flights over each other, Western interest in overflights is likely to shift to Belarus and Ukraine, and possibly Georgia and Bosnia and Herzegovina. In 2021, however, the states parties were unable to reach consensus about the distribution. At the annual quota conference in October 2021, some states applied for overflights of Russian territory in the following year, despite the Russian withdrawal decision, which Russia declined to accept.

Third, without access to Russian territory, missions in Europe may become too expensive for some states parties given the low cost–benefit ratio when overflying strategic partners. Canada, for example, used to conduct more than half of its flights over Belarus and Russia. Without the ability to conduct overflights of Russia, Open Skies missions in Europe might lose their purpose.

Finally, Sweden's decided to no longer offer its national aircraft for lease to other states parties in 2022. This will affect the ability of parties without aircraft to conduct overflights. Only 8 states currently possess certified aircraft equipped with sensors: Bulgaria, Canada, France, Hungary, Sweden, Romania, Turkey and Ukraine. Bulgaria, however, has stopped flying and is unlikely to resume. Canada and France share a single sensor pod, which can be mounted under the wing of their aircraft. The Swedish decision also increases the pressure on Germany and Romania to finalize ongoing certification processes of newly acquired aircraft for use under the treaty.

Outlook

The Russian and US withdrawals from the Treaty on Open Skies have put the treaty's long-term future at risk. In response, observers have suggested

---

[26] Russian Ministry of Foreign Affairs, 'Closing address by the Deputy Minister of Foreign Affairs of the Russian Federation SA Ryabkov at the Conference of States Parties to the Open Skies Treaty', 20 July 2021.
[27] Chernenko, Y., [Sky. Aircraft. Full stop], *Kommersant*, 18 Dec. 2021 (in Russian).

modernizing the treaty or using its framework for purposes other than military confidence building.[28] Proposals have envisioned establishing aerial observation regimes in other regions, including the Arctic, and introducing new sensor types for use in environmental monitoring and disaster relief.[29] The latter could include (near) infrared and radar sensors, which are, in principle, already allowed under the treaty, but also non-imaging sensors for air sampling and radiation measurement.[30] In July 2021 Germany illustrated these technical opportunities when taking digital-optical images of the devastating floods in western Germany with its new Open Skies Treaty aircraft (albeit outside the treaty framework).[31]

The treaty continued to face major challenges at the end of 2021. The states parties had still not reached consensus about the distribution of flight quotas for 2022 and Covid-19 quarantine regulations continued to affect implementation. The future membership of Belarus also looked uncertain as it did not possess its own aircraft and sensor kit, having earlier cooperated with Russia within the group of states parties. Moreover, in the past, points of entry for aircraft and airfields for use under the treaty and several other specifications were defined only for Russian territory, not Belarus.

Statements within the OSCC in late 2021 suggested that Belarus is, in principle, interested in continuing to implement the treaty although it had not yet made a final decision. Nevertheless, Belarus will not conduct or receive overflights in 2022.[32] However, Russian representatives have stated that, should Belarus decide to stay in the treaty, Russia is ready to offer technical support and provide aircraft and sensor equipment.[33] In addition, the new German and Romanian aircraft might become available for use under the treaty in late 2022.

---

[28] Gottemoeller, R. and Marvin, D., 'Reimagining the Open Skies Treaty: Cooperative aerial monitoring', *Bulletin of the Atomic Scientists*, 15 June 2021.

[29] Kertysova, K. and Graef, A., 'Open Skies in the Arctic: Challenges and opportunities', European Leadership Network, 20 May 2021; and Jones, P., 'Making a better Open Skies Treaty', James Martin Center for Nonproliferation Studies (CNS), Occasional Paper no. 50, Feb. 2021.

[30] The Open Skies Treaty permits 4 different sensor types: optical panoramic and framing cameras, video cameras, infrared line-scanning devices and sideways-looking synthetic aperture radar. Only the first 2 are currently in use. See Treaty on Open Skies (note 1), Article IV(1).

[31] German Federal Ministry of Defence (@BMVg_Bundeswehr), 'The aerial images show the extent of the #flood disaster: The #Federal Armed Forces are now supporting the local relief forces with high-resolution aerial images. Minister @akk has ordered reconnaissance flights with the Recce Tornado and the Open Skies Airbus A319 over the flooded area.', Twitter, 22 July 2021; and Kramp-Karrenbauer, A. (@akk), 'The A319, normally used for #OpenSkies, is now taking aerial photos of the flooded area. We make these available to the countries so that aid & reconstruction can be targeted. Our reconnaissance tornadoes are also in action. We will help as long as we are needed.', Twitter, 21 July 2021.

[32] Postnikova, E., [Silenced Treaty on Open Skies: What will happen with the Treaty on Open Skies after 18 December and under which conditions could Moscow and Washington return], *Izvestia*, 18 Dec. 2021 (in Russian).

[33] Postnikova (note 32).

IV. International transparency in arms procurement and military expenditure as confidence-building measures

PIETER D. WEZEMAN AND SIEMON T. WEZEMAN

Transparency in arms procurement and military spending remains an important element of conventional arms control and confidence building between states. States have created relevant instruments for this purpose within the United Nations and in several other multilateral organizations.

This section reviews the status in 2021 of the multilateral instruments to which states report—as a confidence-building measure (CBM)—on aspects of arms procurement and military spending.[1] It first looks at two instruments that have been created within the UN: the UN Register of Conventional Arms (UNROCA) and the UN Report on Military Expenditures (UNMILEX). It then provides an overview of developments in the transparency mechanisms of the Organization for Security and Co-operation in Europe (OSCE)— the only active CBM transparency instrument established by a regional organization. The activities under the instruments in 2021 mostly relate to states reporting on arms transfers, arms holdings and military spending in 2020. The section focuses on reports submitted by states in 2021, excluding any belated reports submitted in 2022.

The section does not discuss multilateral reporting on arms exports within the framework of arms trade regulations, such as the reporting obligations under the 2013 Arms Trade Treaty (ATT) or the European Union (EU) report on arms exports. Nor does it discuss public transparency, such as national arms export reports and military expenditure transparency at the national level.[2] While all these other transparency mechanisms may also help to build confidence between states and thus reduce the risk of conflict, that is not their primary function.

The United Nations Register of Conventional Arms

UNROCA was established in 1991 by the UN General Assembly. Its main aims are to enhance confidence between states, 'prevent the excessive and destabilizing accumulation of arms', 'encourage restraint' in the transfer and

---

[1] The section includes reporting by 31 Dec. 2021.

[2] On multilateral reporting on arms exports under the Arms Trade Treaty see chapter 14, section I; on the EU report see chapter 14, section IV; on national arms exports reports see chapter 9, section IV; and on military expenditure see chapter 8—all in this volume.

production of arms, and 'contribute to preventive diplomacy'.[3] However, while UNROCA's objectives relate to armament developments in general, its focus in terms of reporting is on arms transfers.

UN member states are requested to report annually, in a standardized format and on a voluntary basis, information on their exports and imports in the previous year of seven categories of major arms that are deemed to be 'indispensable for offensive operations'.[4] These categories are battle tanks, armoured combat vehicles, large-calibre artillery systems, combat aircraft, attack helicopters, warships, and missiles and missile launchers.

Since 2003, states have also been able to provide information on transfers of an eighth category: small arms and light weapons (SALW). The inclusion of SALW was largely related to efforts to prevent the illicit trade in these weapons, and not to UNROCA's function as a CBM between states.[5]

In addition, 'states in a position to do so' are invited—indicating a lower level of commitment—to provide information on their holdings of major arms and procurement of such arms through national production.[6]

Participation

The number of states submitting reports to UNROCA reached an all-time low in 2021 (for reporting year 2020).[7] In most years of the 1990s over 90 states reported to UNROCA and in the early 2000s over 110 states. However, from 2014 the number of UN member states submitting a report on exports or imports has never been higher than 48 per year. For reporting year 2019 only 40 submitted a report and for 2020 only 39.[8]

---

[3] UN General Assembly Resolution 46/36L, 'Transparency in armaments', 6 Dec. 1991, para. 2; and UN Office for Disarmament Affairs (UNODA), 'UN Register of Conventional Arms', [n.d.]. On the development of UNROCA see United Nations, General Assembly, 'Report on the continuing operation of the United Nations Register of Conventional Arms and its further development', A/74/211, 22 July 2019, paras 6–15.

[4] United Nations, General Assembly, 'Continuing operation of the United Nations Register of Conventional Arms and its further development', Note by the Secretary-General, A/71/259, 29 July 2016, para. 61(g).

[5] See e.g. United Nations, General Assembly, 'Continuing operation of the United Nations Register of Conventional Arms and its further development', Note by the Secretary-General, A/58/274, 13 July 2003, paras 92–108.

[6] UN General Assembly Resolution 74/53, 12 Dec. 2019.

[7] UNROCA submissions are made public in annual reports by the UN Secretary-General. The latest, covering most submissions in 2021 (for 2020), is available on the UN website (United Nations, General Assembly, 'United Nations Register of Conventional Arms', Report of the Secretary-General, A/76/130, 9 July 2021) while earlier annual reports are available on the UNODA website (<https://www.un.org/disarmament/convarms/register/>); most of those submissions as well as submissions that have been received after the compilation of the annual reports can also be found in the online UNROCA Database. All numbers mentioned here are based on the aggregation of reports in both sources as neither source by itself is complete.

[8] Figures are according to the public records available on 31 Dec. 2021. For more in-depth analysis of participation in the UNROCA reporting on arms transfers see Bromley, M. and Alvarado Cóbar, J. F., *Reporting on Conventional Arms Transfers and Transfer Controls: Improving Coordination and Increasing Engagement* (SIPRI: Stockholm, Aug. 2020).

Most of the states identified by SIPRI as large exporters of major arms in 2017–21 have been regular participants in UNROCA. In particular, the world's top 10 exporters have all submitted data for almost all of these five years. Of the 10 largest arms exporters in the period 2017–21, only the United States (by far the world's largest exporter of major arms) and China did not report in 2021, despite having done so every year in the previous decade.[9] Neither state has publicly explained the reason for not reporting in 2021. However, late reporting is not uncommon: for example, the USA belatedly submitted a report for 2019 in 2021.

Of the 10 largest arms importers in the period 2017–21, 7 (Saudi Arabia, Egypt, China, Algeria, Qatar, Pakistan and the United Arab Emirates) did not report to UNROCA for reporting year 2020.[10]

Annual reporting on arms exports and imports within the framework of the ATT involves use of reporting templates similar to those used for reporting on arms transfers within UNROCA, as well as the UNROCA definitions of major arms. However, out of 110 states parties to the ATT, 60 reported to the ATT for 2020. This was 21 more than to UNROCA.[11] Of the 52 that reported publicly to the ATT, and thus could have reported with little effort to UNROCA, only 34 did so. For example, Italy reported to the ATT but not to UNROCA.

The level of reporting on military holdings and arms procurement through national production was even lower than on arms transfers. Of the 39 reports for 2020, 19 included information on military holdings and only 8 included information on procurement from national production. India and Russia were among the states that submitted data for 2020 on arms transfers but did not provide data on holdings or arms procurement through national production.

Transparency versus data inaccuracies

Several submissions included significant information on arms transfers or details of such arms transfers that had not been available in the public domain before and therefore are likely to have contributed to increased transparency between states. For example, Belarus reported the export of 40 tanks to Uganda, France reported details on transfers of armoured vehicles to Saudi Arabia, and Turkey reported details about the number of armoured vehicles exports to several countries.

---

[9] On the largest exporters in 2017–21 see chapter 9, section II, in this volume.
[10] On the largest importers in 2017–21 see chapter 9, section III, in this volume.
[11] On ATT reporting see chapter 14, section I, in this volume.

However, there were again cases of significant omissions in some sub-missions.[12] For example in 2020 multiple sources identified deliveries from Russia of an estimated 2 combat aircraft to Algeria, an estimated 11 combat aircraft to Egypt and an estimated 6 combat aircraft to Syria. However, Russia did not include these transfers in its submission to UNROCA and the recipient states did not participate in UNROCA. In other cases, states provided the minimum requested data, but left out information essential for assessing the potential importance of the transfers.[13] For example, for 2020, France reported exports of missiles to Qatar and India, and the UK reported exports of missiles to Saudi Arabia, but neither provided descriptions or an indication of the types of the missiles involved. Other sources indicate that the French transfers included both short-range air-to-air missiles and air-to-surface cruise missiles with a range of about 300 kilometres.[14]

The United Nations Report on Military Expenditures

In 1980 the UN General Assembly agreed to establish an annual report in which all UN member states could voluntarily provide data on their military expenditure in the previous year.[15] The report, which has been known as the UN Report on Military Expenditures (UNMILEX) since 2012, aims to enhance transparency in military matters, increase predictability of military activities, reduce the risk of military conflict and raise public awareness of disarmament matters.[16]

The highest rate of participation in UNMILEX was reporting for 2001, when 81 states participated.[17] Of the 193 UN member states 44 have submitted information on their military spending for 2019, and on 31 December 2021

---

[12] See also: Wezeman, S. T., 'Reporting to the United Nations Register of Conventional Arms for 2017', SIPRI Background Paper, June 2019. The examples provided here are based on comparisons between the UNROCA submissions and the SIPRI Arms Transfers Database.

[13] States are requested to provide data on the identity of the UN member state to which they supply or from which they receive arms, and on the number of items in each category supplied. States are encouraged to add further details on the description of the arms and any comments on the transfers they want to share.

[14] Based on comparisons between the UNROCA submissions and the SIPRI Arms Transfers Database (note 12).

[15] UN General Assembly Resolution 35/142, 'Reduction of military budgets', 12 Dec. 1980, section B; and United Nations, General Assembly, 'Group of Governmental Experts to Review the Operation and Further Development of the United Nations Report on Military Expenditures', Note by the Secretary-General, A/72/293, 4 Aug. 2017, paras 2–5. For a detailed description of the history of the instrument see Spies, M., *United Nations Efforts to Reduce Military Expenditures: A Historical Overview*, UNODA Occasional Papers no. 33 (United Nations: New York, NY, Oct. 2019).

[16] United Nations, A/72/293 (note 15), para. 3.

[17] United Nations, 'Group of Governmental Experts on the Operation and Further Development of the United Nations Standardized Instrument for Reporting Military Expenditures', Note by the Secretary-General, A/66/89, 14 June 2011, p. 26.

only 43 had done so for 2020.[18] Of the 43 states that reported for 2020, 32 are in Europe, 4 in the Americas, 3 in Asia and Oceania, 3 in the Middle East and 1 in Africa. Of the 15 states that SIPRI identified as having the highest military spending levels in 2020, 7 did not report to UNMILEX, namely (in order of spending levels) the USA, China, the United Kingdom, Saudi Arabia, Australia, Canada and Brazil. The most significant omissions were the two states with the largest military expenditure: the USA, for which the most recent report is for 2015, and China, for which the most recent report is for 2017. While the UK, Canada and Brazil reported for 2019, they did not report in 2021 for 2020. In a positive development, South Korea submitted in 2021 a report for 2020 and a belated report for 2019.

In 2021 10 states participated in UNMILEX that had not done so in 2020, while 9 other states participated in 2020 but not in 2021. This might be explained by changes in personnel, poor institutional memory or underfunding.

Based on SIPRI military expenditure figures, the 43 states that reported for 2020 accounted for 25 per cent of total world spending in 2020.[19] In contrast to the low level of reporting to UNMILEX, almost all states provide information on their military spending at a national level. Of the 168 states for which SIPRI attempted to estimate military expenditure in 2020, 152 published their military budgets in official sources.[20]

Regional transparency mechanisms

In 2021 the only active regional efforts that aim at multilateral transparency in armaments were the information exchanges between the 57 participating states of the OSCE. The OSCE aims to 'contribute to reducing the dangers . . . of misunderstanding or miscalculation of military activities which could give rise to apprehension'.[21]

The Vienna Document 2011 on Confidence- and Security-Building Measures requires an annual exchange of information on part of the OSCE

[18] Tian, N., Lopes da Silva, D. and Wezeman, P. D., 'Transparency in military expenditure', *SIPRI Yearbook 2020*, pp. 264–66; United Nations, General Assembly, 'Objective information on military matters, including transparency of military expenditures', Report of the Secretary-General, A/74/155, 12 July 2019; United Nations, General Assembly, 'Objective information on military matters, including transparency of military expenditures', Report of the Secretary-General, A/75/140, 15 July 2020; and UNODA, 'Military expenditures', [n.d.].

[19] SIPRI Military Expenditure Database.

[20] SIPRI Military Expenditure Database. See also Wezeman, P. D. and Wezeman, S. T., 'Transparency in military expenditure', *SIPRI Yearbook 2020*, pp. 266–67.

[21] Conference on Security and Cooperation in Europe Final Act, Helsinki, 1 Aug. 1975, p. 10. For a brief description and list of states participating in the OSCE see annex B, section II, in this volume.

states' military holdings and procurement of major arms.[22] However, these reports are not made public. In addition, OSCE participating states have agreed to share information on imports and exports of major arms based on the categories and format of UNROCA.[23] Since 2017 these UNROCA-style submissions have been publicly available on the OSCE website.[24] In 2021, 45 of the 57 states reported on their arms transfers in 2020 to the OSCE. The main omission was the USA, which in 2021 submitted a belated report for 2019. Of the 45 states 16 did not submit equivalent reports to UNROCA in 2021.

Concerning military expenditure, the OSCE CBMs include a requirement for participating states to annually exchange information on military budgets.[25] Of the 57 OSCE participating states, 46 reported for 2020, 49 reported for 2019 and 49 for 2018.[26] However, these submissions are not publicly available.

In the Americas, the states parties of the Inter-American Convention on Transparency in Conventional Weapons Acquisition (Convención Interamericana sobre Transparencia en las Adquisiciones de Armas Convencionales, CITAAC) are required to submit annual reports on arms transfers. However, since 2015 there is only one public record of a state (Chile) having submitted information to CITAAC.[27] Chile included in its 2021 submission to UNROCA a copy of its 2020 submission to CITAAC.[28]

Conclusions

Fewer than one-quarter of UN member states participated in UNROCA or UNMILEX in 2021 and participation in both instruments declined slightly compared to the previous year. Only in Europe did most states participate in the reporting. Participation in the OSCE reporting on military expenditures also declined slightly. A noteworthy positive development was the USA

---

[22] Vienna Document 2011, para. 11 and annex III. For a summary and other details of the Vienna Document 2011 see annex A, section II, in this volume. See also OSCE, 'Ensuring military transparency—the Vienna Document', [n.d.].

[23] OSCE, Forum for Security Co-operation, 'Further transparency in arms transfers', Decision no. 13/97, 16 July 1997; OSCE, Forum for Security Co-operation, 'Changes in the deadline for the Exchange of Information on Conventional Arms and Equipment Transfers', Decision no. 8/98, 4 Nov. 1998; and OSCE, Forum for Security Co-operation, 'Updating the reporting categories of weapon and equipment systems subject to the Information Exchange on Conventional Arms Transfers', Decision no. 8/08, 16 July 2008.

[24] OSCE, 'Information Exchange on Conventional Arms Transfer', [n.d.].

[25] Vienna Document 2011 (note 22), paras 15.3–15.4.

[26] OSCE, Communications with author, 10 Jan. 2002.

[27] For a summary and other details of the convention see annex A, section II, in this volume. For the reports submitted up to 2015 see Organization of American States, Committee on Hemispheric Security, 'Inter-American Convention on Transparency in Conventional Weapon Acquisition (CITAAC)', [n.d.].

[28] United Nations, A/76/130 (note 7) pp. 19–20.

submitting reports in 2021 to UNROCA and OSCE, even if only belated reports for 2019. However, China not reporting to UNROCA in 2021 was a major setback.

Moreover, even where states participated in UNROCA and UNMILEX in 2021, only a few of them provided data that was comprehensive and detailed enough to use as an indicator of key trends in their arms procurements, arms transfers and military spending. At the regional level, only the information-sharing mechanisms within the OSCE framework appeared to have had a high level of participation.

The international transparency instruments described above continued to suffer from significant deficiencies, including a lack of participation, inaccuracies and a lack of relevant details in the reporting. These weaknesses limit their potential contribution to trust and confidence building in military matters in most parts of the world, at a time when distrust between states and groups of states is on the increase.

V. Cyberspace and the malicious use of information and communications technology

ALLISON PYTLAK

Cyber risks and the malicious use of information and communications technology (ICT) continued to intensify throughout 2021, in keeping with the broader growth in harmful cyber activity that has occurred over the past several years. This intensification also mirrored the heightened dependence on ICT during the Covid-19 pandemic, in which a growing number of industries and individuals increasingly used digital networks and devices to work, study and socialize. The number of malicious cyber operations targeting food, energy, information supply chains and critical infrastructure increased in 2021—and with diverse and significant offline impacts.[1]

In 2021 it is estimated that, each week, one in every 61 organizations was affected by ransomware, and the global annual cost of cybercrime is estimated to have been US$6 trillion.[2] Furthermore, an estimated 486 million people were affected by intentional internet shutdowns in 2021, which was 80 per cent more than during 2020.[3] Disinformation and propaganda campaigns, often state sponsored, affected domestic political processes as well as pandemic responses, and there is growing awareness of the extent to which spyware is being used by authorities to repress human rights.[4] Humanitarian actors can also be negatively affected by cyber operations, such as those that target critical infrastructure and impede relief work.[5]

As attack surfaces in cyberspace—that is, the number of points vulnerable to attack—expand and the threat landscape grows more complex, more effective cyber governance mechanisms are needed, as are efforts to increase cyber capacity and build confidence. Although all countries agree that international law is applicable to cyberspace and related actions, the novel characteristics of the cyber context generate ambiguity and uncertainty about how individual states interpret the law. This complicates the ability of the international community to meaningfully respond to violations and

---

[1] Center for Strategic and International Studies (CSIS), 'Significant Cyber Incidents' tracker, [n.d.].

[2] 'As battle against cybercrime continues during Cybersecurity Awareness Month, Check Point Research reports 40% increase in cyberattacks', Check Point blog, Oct. 2021; and Morgan, S., 'Cybercrime to cost the world $10.5 trillion annually by 2025', Cybercrime Magazine, 13 Nov. 2020.

[3] Apps, P., 'From Kazakhstan to Ethiopia, the growing internet shutdown', National Post, 12 Jan. 2022.

[4] On how elections and the pandemic response were affected by disinformation and propaganda see University of Oxford, 'Programme on Democracy and Technology'.

[5] International Committee of the Red Cross (ICRC), 'Eight digital dilemmas debate: Cyber operations against humanitarian organizations', Oct. 2021.

hold perpetrators to account.[6] This is further compounded by the political implications that accompany the technical attribution of operations as well as the ongoing role of proxy actors within such operations. In addition, more governments are outlining national cybersecurity strategies and doctrines aimed at offensive or intrusive cyber operations.[7]

While the Covid-19 pandemic brought digital security threats more sharply into focus, it initially slowed efforts to further develop governance mechanisms.[8] However, in 2021 progress was made in relevant forums. Indeed, the virtual nature of meetings of relevant norm-setting bodies sometimes helped to facilitate broader and more diverse participation, although in a few contexts, meaningful participation remained difficult for non-governmental stakeholders.

Efforts to develop governance structures for ICT use and to achieve cyber-stability have developed through a patchwork of initiatives. Some have been state driven and based in the United Nations. Others have focused more on engaging with the technical community and private sector exclusively. Yet others have included a wider range of diverse stakeholders, including academia and civil society (e.g. the Global Commission on Stability in Cyberspace, the Paris Call for Trust and Security in Cyberspace, and the Cybersecurity Tech Accord). In varied yet largely reinforcing ways, these efforts have sought to elaborate deeper understandings about the applicability of international law to cyberspace or to establish norms and principles that can guide the behaviour of states and other actors.

This section outlines recent cyber governance initiatives at the multilateral, regional and national levels in turn, with a particular focus on current UN processes. This is followed by a description of non-governmental and collaborative initiatives.

---

[6] The applicability of international law, in particular the United Nations Charter, was first recognized by the 3rd UN Group of Governmental Experts on Developments in the Field of Information and Communications in the Context of International Security, in its consensus report of 2013 and later endorsed by the UN General Assembly. United Nations, General Assembly, Report of the Group of Governmental Experts on Developments in the Field of Information and Telecommunications in the Context of International Security, A/68/98, 24 June 2013; and UN General Assembly Resolution 70/237, 23 Dec. 2015. Subsequent UN expert group reports and related General Assembly resolutions have reaffirmed this.

[7] Digital Watch, 'In context: The state of offensive cyber capabilities', Geneva Internet Platform, [n.d.].

[8] Richards, L., 'Cyberspace and the malicious use of information and communications technology', *SIPRI Yearbook 2021*, pp. 525–30.

Cyber governance structures within the United Nations

ICT in the context of international peace and security has been on the UN agenda since 1998, when Russia first tabled a resolution about 'information security' in the UN General Assembly's First Committee.[9]

Six UN Groups of Governmental Experts (GGEs) have been convened since 2004 to study the threats that come with the use of ICTs in the context of international security and to determine how these threats should be addressed.[10] Mandated by General Assembly resolutions adopted through the First Committee, the GGEs have reported their findings back to the UN membership. They have ranged in size from 15 to 25 states, and their meetings were always closed.

The report of the third group was welcomed for its breakthrough statement that international law is applicable to cyberspace.[11] The 2015 report of the fourth group set out 11 recommendations for state behaviour in cyberspace. The norms are concrete in setting out the positive actions that states should take—as well as actions to refrain from. Taken together, the norms variously do the following: highlight the applicability or recognition of existing law (i.e. to refrain from internationally wrong acts, and to respect human rights); indicate boundaries for items that should not be targeted or need protection (i.e. critical infrastructure and computer emergency response teams, supply chains); and encourage significant cooperation, information exchange and trust building (e.g. in response to incidents or for vulnerability disclosure).[12]

Amid intense politicization at the 2018 session of the First Committee, a sixth GGE was proposed, this time by the United States rather than Russia, the traditional sponsor.[13] The USA did so because Russia instead proposed creating the first ever open-ended working group (OEWG I) on cyber issues through a different resolution—'open' in the sense that all UN member states could participate.[14] Both the sixth GGE and OEWG I were established and commenced work in 2019.

---

[9] For more in-depth background on the UN cyber processes see Tiikk, E. and Kerttunen, M., 'Parabasis: Cyber-diplomacy in stalemate', Norwegian Institute of International Affairs (NUPI), 2018; Digitial Watch, 'UN GGE and OEWG', Geneva Internet Platform, [n.d.]; and UN Office for Disarmament Affairs (UNODA), 'Developments in the field of information and telecommunications in the context of international security', Fact sheet, July 2019.

[10] The timeframes of the six GGEs were as follows: first GGE (2004–2005), second GGE (2009–10), third GGE (2012–13), fourth GGE (2014–15), fifth GGE (2016–17), and sixth GGE (2019–21).

[11] United Nations, A/68/98 (note 6), para. 19.

[12] United Nations, General Assembly, Report of the Group of Governmental Experts on Developments in the Field of Information and Telecommunications in the Context of International Security, 22 July 2015, A/70/174, para. 13.

[13] UN General Assembly Resolution 73/266, 'Advancing responsible state behaviour in cyberspace in the context of international security', 22 Dec. 2018.

[14] UN General Assembly Resolution 73/27, 'Developments in the field of information and telecommunications in the context of international security', 5 Dec. 2018.

Like most international diplomatic processes, the Covid-19 pandemic made it hard for the GGE and OEWG I to meet as planned in 2020 and conclude their work within their mandated time frames. Extensions were granted, and both switched to virtual and informal meeting formats to maintain momentum and advance discussion.[15]

OEWG I

In March 2021, OEWG I held its final substantive session in a hybrid format, with some delegates participating live in New York and others attending virtually.[16] The aim was to adopt a substantive final report by consensus, which would include conclusions, recommendations and reflection of discussions held across the six thematic areas under the OEWG's consideration: threats; international law; rules, norms and principles; capacity building; confidence-building measures (CBMs); and regular institutional dialogue.

OEWG I adopted a final report, in what was widely described as a win for diplomacy and multilateralism because of the flexibility and compromise demonstrated by participating member states.[17] As in any consensus process, however, no one was completely satisfied. Some states, mainly those in the West, were uncomfortable with some of the compromises made during the final meeting of the session. Iran disassociated itself from 'parts of the report that do not match with its principles and positions', and Israel also disassociated itself from any reference to the need for a legally binding instrument.[18] Concerns included the removal of the reference to the applicability of international humanitarian law from the negotiated part of the report; references to the ordering of the subsections on law and norms; references to certain aspects of the UN Charter; and about binding instruments, among other points.[19]

---

[15] On developments in 2020 see Richards, L., 'Cyberspace and the malicious use of information and communications technology', *SIPRI Yearbook 2021*, pp. 525–30.

[16] Documents, working papers and other materials from all the OEWG substantive sessions can be found online at <https://www.un.org/disarmament/open-ended-working-group/> and <https://reachingcriticalwill.org/disarmament-fora/ict/oewg>.

[17] The final report of the 2019–21 OEWG consists of 2 main parts: a non-negotiated chair's summary (annex II), which includes those elements of the draft report that could not be agreed by consensus, with an annex of language or textual proposals made throughout the process; and the negotiated substantive report (annex I) outlining the negotiated conclusions and recommendations. These were issued along with a procedural report. United Nations, General Assembly, Report of the Open-ended Working Group on Developments in the Field of Information and Telecommunications in the Context of International Security, A/75/816, 18 Mar. 2021. An additional compendium of statements outlines positions on the final report. United Nations, General Assembly, Open-ended Working Group on Developments in the Field of Information and Telecommunications in the Context of International Security, 'Compendium of statements in explanation of position on the final report', A/AC.290/2021/INF/2, 25 Mar. 2021, Add.1, 14 Apr. 2021, and Add.2, 29 Nov. 2021.

[18] Pytlak, A., 'A win for diplomacy: Questions remain for cyber peace', *Cyber Peace & Security Monitor*, vol.1, no. 10 (17 Mar. 2021). Additional reporting and analysis of state positions can be found in other parts of the same edition of the *Monitor*.

[19] Pytlak (note 18).

Noteworthy aspects of the final OEWG I report include recognition of the potentially devastating humanitarian consequences of cyberattacks and acknowledging the impact of malicious ICT activity during the pandemic; progress on assessing the threat landscape (including attacks on health facilities and human rights implications); the reaffirmation of the applicability of international law, in particular the UN Charter, and of the normative framework; and agreement to implement several practical measures in the area of CBMs and capacity building.

Despite differences between states, the convening and conclusion of OEWG I was significant. It was the first time that a dialogue process on the subject of ICTs in the context of international peace and security had been convened by the UN, which made it possible for all states (regardless of size) to exchange views, begin to develop common understandings and identify gaps.[20] That the report, and by extension the wider UN membership, re-affirmed the outputs of the UN's five prior GGE's—which is referred to as the *acquis*—is important politically, even if it did not break new ground substantively.[21] Furthermore, over the course of OEWG I, multiple unique proposals were put forward by states and other stakeholders presenting suggestions about how to operationalize the UN cyber norms, for accountability mechanisms, and how to standardize information sharing, among others. While not all proposals were adopted or included in the final report, the process of developing and sharing these ideas helped to propel wider thinking and dialogue about cyber governance issues.

From OEWG I to OEWG II

One of the main points of contention among UN member states is about the future UN deliberations on international cyber governance and the form they will take. Cuba, Egypt, Russia and Venezuela, among others, have been calling for a legally binding instrument for many years. Some other states, including Costa Rica, Ecuador and Peru have indicated that they are open to developing a legal instrument, but not at this time. However, the majority of states—in particular, Australia, Canada, European Union (EU) members, Israel and the USA—believe that existing international law, coupled with the normative framework as developed within the UN, is sufficient to guide state behaviour in cyberspace. These differing views complicated how the

---

[20] It is not possible to include the full range of positions, proposals and dialogue that surfaced during the 2019–21 OEWG sessions. These can be accessed directly on the OEWG website, <https://www.un.org/disarmament/open-ended-working-group/>. Various civil society groups have also published reports and analysis. See e.g. Global Partners Digital, 'The OEWG's consensus report: Key takeaways', 18 Mar. 2021, DiploFoundation, 'What's new with cybersecurity negotiations? UN Cyber OEWG Final Report analysis', 19 Mar. 2021, and WILPF, *Cyber Peace & Security Monitor*, vol. 1, no. 10 (17 Mar. 2021).

[21] Gold, J., 'Unexpectedly, all UN countries agreed on a cybersecurity report. So what?', Council on Foreign Relations, 18 Mar. 2021; and ICT4Peace, 'The OEWG final report: Some progress, much remains unresolved', Mar. 2021.

section on 'regular institutional dialogue' was presented in the final report of OEWG I.[22] The politics around these different perspectives also underpin various other initiatives that are now the main vehicles for advancing cyber governance at the UN.

This is particularly relevant to the establishment of the UN's second OEWG on ICT (OEWG II), which was agreed during the 2020 session of the First Committee and before OEWG I had completed its work.[23] At the time, many states voted against or abstained from the Russia-led resolution, on the basis that the creation of a successor body was premature and would prejudge the outcomes of the OEWG in progress.[24] Nonetheless, the resolution secured sufficient votes to be adopted. OEWG II has a longer time frame (2021–25) than OEWG I, which is a source of concern to those who do not want to wait five years for the UN to adopt decisions or act on what is an increasingly pressing security matter.

In addition, a proposal introduced by Egypt and France in 2020 to develop a politically binding programme of action (POA) on state behaviour in cyber space has now been endorsed by more than 50 states.[25] Inspired somewhat by the UN Programme of Action to Prevent, Combat and Eradicate the Illicit Trade in Small Arms and Light Weapons in All Its Aspect (on which see section I), the initial proposal was articulated during 2021 through working papers submitted to the OEWG I by Egypt and France, and informal discussion among its supporters.[26] Generally, POA-supporting states suggest that the instrument could reflect the *acquis*, be action-oriented rather than deliberative, and become a mechanism to facilitate capacity building. OEWG II could be a space to further develop thinking around a POA, but there is also a concern that doing so might see the POA proposal being stunted by those who do not support it. It is not yet clear if a negotiation mandate for a POA will be sought at the 2022 session of the First Committee or if another avenue will be pursued.

OEWG II held its first substantive session in December 2021, chaired by Ambassador Burhan Gafoor of Singapore. It mainly focuses on the same six thematic topics as its predecessor. At the December 2021 session, many states

---

[22] United Nations, A/75/816 (note 17), annex I, paras 68–79.

[23] Note that the name of OEWG II is slightly different than that of OEWG I: 'Open-ended Working Group on *security of and in the use of* information and communications technologies 2021–2025'.

[24] United Nations, General Assembly, First Committee, 'Developments in the field of information and telecommunications in the context of international security', Draft resolution, A/C.1/75/L.8/Rev.1, 26 Oct. 2020.

[25] United Nations, Open-ended Working Group on Developments in the Field of Information and Telecommunications in the Context of International Security, 'The future of discussions on ICTs and cyberspace at the UN', Submission by France and others, 2 Dec. 2020.

[26] United Nations, 'Working paper for a Programme of Action (POA) to advance responsible state behaviour in the use of ICTs in the context of international security', Dec. 2021; and Pytlak, A., *Programming Action: Observations from Small Arms Control for Cyber Peace* (Women's International League for Peace and Freedom: New York, Feb. 2021).

emphasized two important points about the second OEWG: that it should be action oriented; and that they should not be required to wait until the end of its mandate to make decisions or produce results. Many also stressed the need for exchange about how international law is being applied in national cyber strategies and action.[27]

The sixth GGE on responsible state behaviour in cyberspace

In May 2021 the sixth GGE released its final report as well as a compendium containing national views about how international law applies to state use of ICT, which had been submitted on a voluntary basis.[28] The report is notable for providing additional layers of understanding and guidance for implementing the UN norms. This is done through the inclusion of explanatory or contextual information in relation to each norm, as well as recommended actions for their implementation.

By taking this approach, the report provides an updated assessment of ICT threats, including references to the Covid-19 pandemic and operations targeting health infrastructure; considers some of the complexities relating to technical and political attribution; describes what states might consider as critical infrastructure; gives significant consideration to protecting supply chain integrity; and provides specific actions to take as confidence- and transparency-building measures and in capacity building. The perennially thorny issue of the applicability of international humanitarian law was partially resolved, in that states 'took note' of its applicability only in situations of armed conflict; agreed to further study the applicability of the principles of international humanitarian law; and recalled that these principles do not legitimize or encourage conflict.

The sixth GGE was also more consultative than its predecessors, having held a series of regional consultations for non-group members, some of which were also open to non-governmental stakeholders.

Participation by non-governmental stakeholders

An issue that has dominated both OEWGs is the participation of non-governmental stakeholders in formal meetings. Ahead of the first OEWG session, in 2019, all organizations that lacked accreditation from the UN Economic and Social Council (ECOSOC) had their requests to participate anonymously vetoed; this pattern was repeated ahead of the second session,

---

[27] United Nations, Open-ended Working Group on security of and in the use of information and communications technologies, 1st substantive session, Statements, 13–17 Dec. 2021.

[28] United Nations, General Assembly, 'Report of the group of governmental experts on advancing responsible state behaviour in cyberspace in the context of international security', A/76/135, 14 July 2021; and 'Official compendium of voluntary national contributions on the subject of how international law applies to the use of information and communications technologies by states', submitted by participating governmental experts in the GGE, A/76/136, 13 July 2021.

in 2020. Such a blanket rejection is extremely rare in General Assembly-based forums and generated significant concern, particularly given the significant role that non-governmental stakeholders, including the private sector, play in the ICT environment. No official reason for the accreditation denials was provided; most assume it was either politically motivated or because objecting states prefer to limit the role of civil society, including the private sector, generally. Throughout the OEWG I process and especially in 2021, some governments worked with civil society and the private sector to organize informal opportunities for stakeholders to input their views, and its chair was also receptive to creating such opportunities.[29]

During the June 2021 organizing meeting for OEWG II, Canada and other states requested greater transparency in the accreditation process and, ultimately, improved stakeholder access to future formal OEWG meetings.[30] These requests were not taken on board by the incoming OEWG II chair when he outlined meeting modalities ahead of the December 2021 session. Dozens of states protested these modalities when the session was convened on 13 December, stalling the adoption of the session's agenda, and the topic became the focus of informal consultations throughout the week.[31] As of early 2022, a compromise had not been reached on this matter (in relation to the OEWG's second session, in March 2022), and the continued sidelining and exclusion of relevant civil society stakeholders risked damaging OEWG II's credibility and its practical impact in the world outside the UN.

Finally, it is worth noting how other parts of the UN system are addressing cyber-related topics. First, Estonia convened the first ever UN Security Council open debate on cybersecurity in June 2021.[32] Second, the International Telecommunication Union (ITU) is providing technical coordination and standards development. Third, a process is underway to negotiate a new treaty on cybercrime, initiated in the General Assembly's Third Committee (the Social, Humanitarian and Cultural Committee).[33] Fourth, human rights bodies have adopted resolutions or issued statements of concern regarding the human rights impact of digital technologies over recent years; notably, in 2021 the UN Working Group on Mercenaries

---

[29] One example is the Let's Talk Cyber Initiative, <https://letstalkcyber.org/>.

[30] Pytlak, A., 'Building on—and establishing—foundations', *Cyber Peace & Security Monitor*, vol. 2, no. 1 (3 June 2021), pp. 3–4.

[31] Pytlak, A., 'Summary: Civil society participation modalities', *Cyber Peace & Security Monitor*, vol. 2, no. 3 (21 Dec. 2021), pp. 3–6.

[32] Permanent Mission of Estonia to the United Nations, 'Maintaining international peace and security in cyberspace', Concept Note to the UN Security Council High-level Open Debate on Cyber Security, 29 June 2021.

[33] UN Office on Drugs and Crime, 'Ad-Hoc Committee to Elaborate a Comprehensive International Convention on Countering the Use of Information and Communications Technologies for Criminal Purposes', [n.d.].

published a report on cyber mercenaries and human rights.[34] Finally, the UN secretary-general gave priority to reducing cyber risks in 'Our Common Agenda', released in September 2021, where he also referenced the need for a ban on cyberattacks against civilian infrastructure.[35]

Regional cyber governance initiatives

Regional efforts at cyber governance have the potential to be somewhat less politically challenging than those that are global, and it is widely recognized that existing regional good practice should be built upon and accounted for within global initiatives. This point was made repeatedly by states and other actors during many of the multilateral forums described above. In some regions, collaboration has been more practical and technical (rather than political), particularly given the transboundary nature of ICT threats and infrastructure. Elsewhere, activities have focused on building common policies and understanding. The following examples of recent developments or events are meant to illustrate recent regional initiatives, but are by no means exhaustive.

The Association of Southeast Asian Nations (ASEAN) has long been active in coordinating around cyber issues, particularly in building resilience and protecting critical infrastructure.[36] The ASEAN Cybersecurity Coordinating Committee (ASEAN Cyber-CC) was established in late 2020 and is mandated to work across sectors on cybersecurity issues. ASEAN holds annual ministerial conferences on cybersecurity issues and has recently launched a regional action plan on the implementation of the norms of responsible state behaviour in cyberspace, in line with UN norms.[37] South East Asia is also home to two cybersecurity centres of excellence, in Bangkok and Singapore.

In June 2021 South Korea and the Organization for Security and Co-operation in Europe (OSCE) co-convened the third Inter-Regional Conference on Cyber/ICT Security.[38] In 2013 the OSCE began developing a

---

[34] United Nations, General Assembly, 'The human rights impacts of mercenaries, mercenary-related actors and private military and security companies engaging in cyberactivities', Report of the Working Group on the use of mercenaries as a means of violating human rights and impeding the exercise of the right of peoples to self-determination, A/76/151, 15 July 2021.

[35] United Nations, *Our Common Agenda*, Report of the secretary-general (United Nations: New York, 2021).

[36] Van Raemdonck, N., 'Cyber diplomacy in Southeast Asia', EU CyberDirect, May 2021.

[37] Yu, E., 'Asean champions regional efforts in cybersecurity, urges international participation', ZD Net, 6 Oct. 2021.

[38] Organization for Security and Co-operation in Europe (OSCE), 'Cyber/ICT security between OSCE and Asian regions focus of OSCE and Republic of Korea-hosted discussion', 24 June 2021.

set of cyber CBMs, of which there are now 16.[39] It launched a new training course on these measures in March 2021.[40]

In line with the above example, a growing number of cross-regional initiatives focus particularly on cyber capacity building. One example is the Latin America and the Caribbean Cyber Competence Centre (LAC4), which was established in 2021 in Santo Domingo as a collaboration with the EU's CyberNet to build ICT capacity in Latin America and the Caribbean. The EU published a cybersecurity strategy in late 2020 not only to focus on building resilience but also to lead dialogues on international norms and standards. In 2021 the EU joined the Paris Call.[41]

National cyber initiatives and policy

A growing number of states publish national policies and strategies on issues ranging from preventing and addressing cybercrime via data protection to building the resilience and capacity to respond to cyber threats. For most, this has necessitated creating new governmental entities to oversee or implement relevant initiatives; passing legislation; refining public–private partnerships; and developing bilateral cooperation agreements with other states.[42] In 2021 the ITU published the fourth edition of its Global Cybersecurity Index, which tracks a range of national efforts including governance and coordination mechanisms within countries that address cybersecurity.[43]

Throughout 2021 the UN Institute for Disarmament Affairs (UNIDIR) continued to update its Cyber Policy Portal, which provides the profiles of the national cyber policy documents of all UN member states, various intergovernmental organizations and multilateral frameworks.[44]

The evolution of national offensive cyber strategies and policies—often in connection with other military tactics or strategies—is also relevant to international cyber governance efforts. In general, it is difficult to determine the precise number of states with offensive cyber capabilities, in part because defining what that means is a matter of debate, and in part because of the intrinsically non-transparent nature of the subject. A few states have openly explained how they understand the term and their intentions around them,

---

[39] Organization for Security and Co-operation in Europe (OSCE), Permanent Council, 'OSCE confidence-building measures to reduce the risks of conflict stemming from the use of information and communication technologies', Decision no. 1202, PC.DEC/1202, 10 Mar. 2016.

[40] Organization for Security and Co-operation in Europe (OSCE) Secretariat, 'New e-learning course on OSCE cyber/ICT security confidence-building measures now available', 22 Mar. 2021.

[41] European Commission, 'New EU Cybersecurity Strategy and new rules to make physical and digital critical entities more resilient', 16 Dec. 2020.

[42] Calam, M. et al., 'Asking the right questions to define government's role in cybersecurity', McKinsey & Company, 19 Sep. 2018.

[43] International Telecommunication Union, 'Global Cybersecurity Index 2020', 2021.

[44] UNIDIR Cyber Policy Portal, <https://unidir.org/cpp/en/>.

including Australia, France, Germany and the USA.[45] While it could be argued that there is a benefit in states being transparent about their cyber abilities, the growing spread of offensive capabilities—if they can be neatly defined as such—raises other concerns about cyber-related militarism and the weaponization of technology. Moreover, two nuclear-armed states, the United Kingdom and the USA, have indicated in recent years that they would consider responding to a highly destructive cyber incident with nuclear weapons.[46] In 2021, UNIDIR launched a research paper series to consider the national doctrines and cyber capabilities of 15 countries across diverse global regions, which has aided in facilitating transparency among states.[47]

Towards the end of 2021 and in connection with the December 2021 session of the OEWG II, a few states (including China, Estonia, France and Italy) provided national views on how specific legal principles apply in cyberspace.[48] Others indicated during the session that they are engaging in domestic processes to outline these views. Clarifying how, at a national level, states understand and interpret international law as relevant to cyber actions was a recommendation from OEWG I and the sixth GGE and will therefore be important for ongoing cyber governance efforts.

Non-governmental and collaborative initiatives

A range of non-governmental actors are currently undertaking diverse initiatives to deepen understandings of cyber norms, governance and legal questions, which are sometimes carried out in partnership with states or international organizations.

---

[45] Relevant resources for comparative analysis include a 2021 survey from the International Institute for Security Studies that assesses how 15 states approach cyber capability in the context of power. International Institute of Security Studies (IISS), *Cyber Capabilities and National Power: A Net Assessment* (IISS: London, [2021]). The Belfer Center at Harvard University publishes an annual Cyber Power Index that measures 30 countries' cyber capabilities in the context of 7 national objectives. Voo, J. et al., *National Cyber Power Index 2020: Methodology and Analytical Considerations* (Belfer Center for Science and International Affairs: Cambridge, MA, Sep. 2020). On the countries mentioned in the text see Hansen, F. and Uren, T., 'Australia's offensive cyber capability', The Strategist, 10 Apr. 2018; Schultze, M. and Herpig, S., 'Germany develops offensive cyber capabilities without a coherent strategy of what to do with them', Council on Foreign Relations, 3 Dec. 2018; Stroebel, W. P., 'Bolton says US is expanding offensive cyber operations', *Wall Street Journal*, 11 June 2019; and Parly, F., French Minister of Armed Forces, 'Stratégie cyber des Armées' [Cyber strategy of the armed forces], Speech, Paris, 18 Jan. 2019.

[46] US Department of Defense (DOD), *Nuclear Posture Review 2018* (DOD: Arlington, VA, Feb. 2018); and British Parliament, House of Commons Library, 'Integrated Review 2021: Increasing the cap on the UK's nuclear stockpile', Briefing Paper no. 9175, 21 Mar. 2021.

[47] Kastelic, A., *International Cyber Operations: National Doctrines and Capabilities*, International Cyber Operations Research Paper Series no. 1 (UN Institute for Disarmament Research (UNIDIR): Geneva, 2021).

[48] United Nations, Open-ended Working Group on security of and in the use of information and communications technologies, 'Member State views and inputs', 2021.

The Global Commission on the Stability of Cyberspace is a multi-year, multi-stakeholder and non-UN process that produced a set of eight norms of responsible cyber behaviour. It launched a new paper series in 2021 that focuses on cyberstability and explores the expanding 'constellation' of related cyber initiatives and changing conditions in cyberspace.[49]

The Cybersecurity Tech Accords bring together more than 150 technology companies under a common commitment to protect cyberspace. In 2021 and in collaboration with the Paris Call, it advocated for improved stakeholder access to the UN cyber processes, as based on experiences with multistakeholder governance models.[50]

The Cooperative Cyber Defence Centre of Excellence (CCDCOE) of the North Atlantic Treaty Organization (NATO), the International Committee of the Red Cross (ICRC) and other partners provided a 2021–22 update to their collaborative Cyber Law Toolkit.[51] Based on 25 hypothetical scenarios, the toolkit is an interactive web-based resource for legal professionals who work at the intersection of international law and cyber operations.

Established in 2020, the Oxford Process on International Law Protections in Cyberspace is an initiative of the Oxford Institute for Ethics, Law and Armed Conflict (ELAC) and Microsoft. It has identified five statements on international law protections that consider how international law applies to specific sectors and objects.[52] The fourth and fifth of these statements, on the Regulation of Information Operations and Activities, and on Ransomware Activities, were developed in 2021.

Another ongoing initiative is the Tallinn 3.0 process. The process seeks to update the *Tallinn Manual 2.0 on International Law Applicable to Cyber Operations* and reflect on current state practice regarding cyber operations. The new manual will consider activities and statements delivered in international forums, such as the UN processes, alongside academic publications and multistakeholder initiatives.[53] The project is hosted by the CCDCOE, although the earlier manuals have not been endorsed as NATO documents. The *Tallinn Manual 3.0* is anticipated to be released in 2025–26.[54]

A prominent message from many civil society actors following the UN and other multilateral cyber governance processes in 2021 has been their

---

[49] Klimburg, A. (ed.), *New Conditions and Constellations in Cyber* (The Hague Centre for Strategic Studies. The Hague, Dec. 2021).

[50] 'The third anniversary of the Paris Call and results from Working Group 3: Advancing a multistakeholder approach', Cybersecurity Tech Accord, Nov. 2021.

[51] Cyber Law Toolkit, 2021/22 update.

[52] Oxford Institute for Ethics, Law and Armed Conflict (ELAC), 'The Oxford process on international law protections in cyberspace', University of Oxford, May 2020.

[53] NATO Cooperative Cyber Defence Centre of Excellence, 'CCDCOE to host the Tallinn Manual 3.0 process', 2020.

[54] Dunlap, C., 'International law and cyber ops: Q & A with Mike Schmitt about the status of Tallinn 3.0', 3 Oct. 2021, Lawfire blog.

call for human-centric approaches to cybersecurity and governance. A human-centric approach builds on earlier relevant concepts of 'human security' and 'humanitarian disarmament' by questioning whose security is at the core of policy and normative efforts and, within that, seeking to better highlight—and prevent—the human cost of cyber operations.[55] This approach also aligns with the protection of human rights and fundamental freedoms even when considering cyber operations within the framing of 'international peace and security', much in the way that conventional arms control instruments are increasingly motivated by humanitarian concerns (see section I). Subsequently, documenting and exploring the human cost of cyber operations is becoming more of a focus for some non-governmental actors and is likely to influence their inputs into cyber governance and norm-building processes.[56]

Within the push for human-centric approaches to cyber governance is a growing interest in addressing the gendered impact of cyber operations and the gender dimensions of cyber diplomacy more broadly. In 2021 a diverse range of publications and capacity-building activities sought to advance earlier research on this subject, and the final OEWG I report included recognition of women's participation in cybersecurity, with some governments having advocated for more specific recommendations in this area.[57] This is in line with increased support for addressing the gender dimensions of violence and conflict in other weapon-related forums.

Conclusions

While 2021 is generally considered to have been a productive year for cyber governance mechanisms, real-world events overtook the pace of diplomacy and multilateralism. The ability of existing frameworks to prevent cyber harm and maintain cyber peace and stability is being severely tested. There are ample normative frameworks, as well as guidelines within existing law, for state behaviour and the governance of ICTs.[58] This is not the ungoverned and unruly sphere it is sometimes portrayed as. However, further clarity

---

[55] E.g. Deibert, R. J., 'Toward a human-centric approach to cybersecurity', *Ethics and International Affairs*, Dec. 2018; and Kumar, S., 'The missing piece in human-centric approaches to cyber norms implementation: The role of civil society', *Journal of Cyber Policy*, vol. 6, no. 3 (2021).

[56] E.g. CyberPeace Institute, 'Cyber Incident Tracer #HEALTH',.

[57] United Nations, A/75/816 (note 17), annex I, para. 12 and annex II, para. 37. See also e.g. Millar, K., Shires, J. and Tropina, T., *Gender Approaches to Cybersecurity: Design, Defence and Response* (UN Institute for Disarmament Research: Geneva, 2021); and Sharland, L. et al., *System Update: Towards a Women, Peace and Cybersecurity Agenda* (UN Institute for Disarmament Research: Geneva, 2021).

[58] For an overview of the frameworks and how they overlap see Brown, D., Esterhuysen, A. and Kumar, S., *Unpacking the GGE's Framework on Responsible State Behaviour: Cyber Norms* (Association for Progressive Communications and Global Partners Digital: 2019); and the Carnegie Endowment for Peace, 'Cyber norms index and timeline', [n.d.].

on some core legal questions is required, as is improved transparency and capacity building.

Bringing the diverse patchwork of existing frameworks together under a single roof—perhaps via a UN programme of action—could help to create an environment with greater potential for accountability mechanisms and transparency. Calls for accountability mechanisms are growing stronger, particularly from the non-governmental community. Yet what will ultimately be most crucial for the effectiveness of any governance model are trust and political will.

VI. Developments in space security

NIVEDITA RAJU

Developments in space security in 2021 were defined by the proliferation of counterspace technologies, reported weapon tests and growing lunar ambitions. Space security also received dedicated focus at the national level, as evidenced by new space commands established by the German and British governments.[1] The need for stronger governance to curb threats to space activities further encouraged states to move towards concrete action in the United Nations General Assembly.

This section outlines three key issues in space security in 2021. First, overall stability continued to be unsettled by the development and demonstration of offensive counterspace capabilities.[2] Reported weapon tests in space by China and Russia were particularly controversial. Second, the year saw rising interest in lunar activities. Several states expressed lunar ambitions through the formation and development of two distinct international partnerships: one led by the United States and the other led by China and Russia. The absence of any dedicated cooperation mechanism between these two partnerships is potentially destabilizing. In addition, US military interests in lunar activities expanded. Third, and more positively, 2021 witnessed widespread support for new measures on space security in the General Assembly. States, international organizations and civil society representatives contributed to discussions on norms, rules and responsible behaviour, which were summarized in a report by the UN secretary-general. A consensus-based open-ended working group (OEWG) will be convened to move discussions forward.

Reports of weapon tests by China and Russia

'Counterspace' refers to capabilities or techniques used to gain an advantage over a rival in space. These can include offensive and defensive elements. In recent years there has been a surge in the development of different types of counterspace capability, principally by China, Russia and the USA.[3] In 2021 reported weapon tests in space by China and Russia drew international criticism, especially from the USA.

---

[1] Siebold, S., 'New German space command to tackle Russian, Chinese threat, overcrowding', Reuters, 13 July 2021; and British Ministry of Defence, 'UK Space Command officially launched', 30 July 2021.

[2] Weeden, B. and Samson, V. (eds), *Global Counterspace Capabilities: An Open Source Assessment* (Secure World Foundation: Washington, DC, Apr. 2019). On developments in 2019 and 2020 see Porras, D., 'Creeping towards an arms race in outer space', *SIPRI Yearbook 2020*, pp. 513–18; and Raju, N., 'Developments in space security, 2020', *SIPRI Yearbook 2021*, pp. 531–36.

[3] eds Weeden and Samson (note 2).

China's fractional orbital bombardment system test

A fractional orbital bombardment system (FOBS) is a weapon-delivery system that partially enters into orbit and then, rather than completing a full rotation, deorbits to reach its target. In October 2021 the *Financial Times* reported that in August China had conducted a test of a FOBS that deployed a hypersonic glide vehicle.[4] China maintained that the test only involved a reusable space launch vehicle.[5] Subsequent reports suggested that two tests had occurred, in July and August.[6] The reports were based on limited information released by US sources. In the absence of verified open-source information, these reports fuelled speculation and exaggerated claims, including those from US officials, that the test was close to a 'Sputnik moment'.[7]

FOBS are not new. The technology was developed and deployed by the Soviet Union in the 1960s and 1970s.[8] However, more recently, alarmist views have arisen about the new hybrid technology of FOBS paired with hypersonic glide vehicles. FOBS were designed by the Soviet Union to bypass the US network of radar systems in the north and instead attack targets through the South Pole undetected.[9] The principal advantages were overcoming anti-ballistic missile (ABM) systems and challenging the adversary's ability to predict the intended target.[10] However, some have questioned the military effectiveness of FOBS.[11] Others state that FOBS cannot be used to conduct a surprise nuclear attack on the USA due to the latter's sophisticated space situational awareness (SSA) capabilities.[12] Experts also note that US vulnerability to Chinese attacks existed prior to this FOBS test, given China's existing nuclear and conventional arsenal.[13]

There are different views on whether FOBS violate Article IV of the 1967 Outer Space Treaty, which prohibits the placement of weapons of mass

---

[4] Sevastapulo, D., 'China tests new space capability with hypersonic missile', *Financial Times*, 16 Oct. 2021.

[5] Tian, Y. L., 'China denies report of hypersonic missile test, says tested space vehicle', Reuters, 18 Oct. 2021.

[6] Sevastapulo, D., 'China conducted two hypersonic weapons tests this summer', *Financial Times*, 21 Oct. 2021.

[7] Martin, P., 'US general likens China's hypersonic test to a "Sputnik moment"', Bloomberg, 27 Oct. 2021.

[8] Jasani, B., 'Military satellites', *SIPRI Yearbook 1977*, table 5.17, p. 170.

[9] Siddiqi, A. A., 'The Soviet fractional orbiting bombardment system (FOBS): A short technical history', *Quest, The History of Spaceflight Quarterly*, vol. 7, no. 4 (2000); and Bowen, B. and Hunter, C., 'Chinese fractional orbital bombardment', Asia-Pacific Leadership Network, Policy Brief no. 78, 1 Nov. 2021.

[10] Siddiqi (note 9).

[11] Siddiqi (note 9).

[12] Bowen and Hunter (note 9).

[13] Grego, L., 'A nuclear arms race is unavoidable without serious intervention', *Financial Times*, 27 Oct. 2021; and Bowen and Hunter (note 9).

destruction (WMD) in orbit around the Earth.[14] It largely depends on the interpretation of 'orbiting' and whether FOBS can be considered to have been 'placed in orbit' even when they do not complete a full rotation in orbit. Nonetheless, China's test is expected to further widen mistrust between China and the USA, propel the cycle of weapon proliferation and accelerate the pace at which states are moving into an arms race. Statements from US officials support this bleak outlook.[15] These developments further highlight the complex relationship between nuclear weapons, missile defence and space security.

Russia's direct-ascent anti-satellite weapon test

In November 2021 Russia conducted a direct-ascent anti-satellite (ASAT) weapon test using the PL-19 Nudol ABM system to intercept one of its own defunct satellites in orbit, Cosmos-1408. Although Russia had tested the Nudol on several occasions, this was the first instance of a collision with a target.[16]

The intercept took place at an altitude of approximately 480 kilometres in low-Earth orbit, creating significant debris in what is the busiest environment for space activities. The debris created was initially estimated by US Space Command to comprise 1500 trackable fragments.[17] Based on these figures, 904 fragments have been publicly catalogued.[18] This count will fluctuate due to various actors' ability to track and observe the debris and due to fragments gradually re-entering the Earth's atmosphere.

The test was a stark reminder of how space debris endangers the space activities of all states. The hazards of space debris were evident soon after the test, when the US National Aeronautics and Space Administration (NASA) reported that the International Space Station (ISS) had to take emergency measures to avoid the risk of collision with the debris from Russia's test.[19] A study by commercial firm COMSPOC (based on estimates from US Space Command) suggests that the Russian test posed direct risks to spacecraft of other states as well as the ISS.[20] However, the official Russian statement denied that the test posed 'any obstacles or difficulties to the functioning of

---

[14] For a summary and other details on the Treaty on Principles Governing the Activities of States in the Exploration and Use of Outer Space, including the Moon and Other Celestial Bodies (Outer Space Treaty) see annex A, section I, in this volume.

[15] Erwin, S., 'Mike Griffin critical of US response to China's advances in hypersonic weapons', SpaceNews, 30 Nov. 2021.

[16] eds Weeden and Samson (note 2), pp. 2–16; and McDowell, J., 'Space activities in 2021', 3 Jan. 2022, p. 54.

[17] United States Space Command, 'Russian direct-ascent anti-satellite missile test creates significant, long-lasting space debris', SpaceRef, 15 Nov. 2021.

[18] Hitchens, T., 'Russian ASAT debris imperils DOD, NRO sats, while ISS risks increase: COMSPOC', Breaking Defense, 4 Jan. 2022.

[19] NASA, 'NASA administrator statement on Russian ASAT test', 15 Nov. 2021.

[20] COMSPOC, 'COMSPOC's latest analyses of the Russian ASAT event', 29 Dec. 2021.

orbital stations and spacecraft, or to other space activities'. The statement also claimed that the test was conducted 'in strict conformity with international law'.[21]

Arguments can be made that the intentional creation of large amounts of debris violates elements of the Outer Space Treaty. Article IX of the treaty provides a series of obligations for states to follow.[22] These include the duty to 'avoid . . . harmful contamination' of outer space and 'where necessary, . . . adopt appropriate measures' to carry out this duty; and a requirement that states conduct activities with 'due regard to the corresponding interests of all other States Parties to the Treaty'. Furthermore, Article IX states,

If a State Party to the Treaty has reason to believe that an activity or experiment planned by it or its nationals in outer space . . . would cause potentially harmful interference with activities of other States Parties in the peaceful exploration and use of outer space . . . it shall undertake appropriate international consultations before proceeding with any such activity or experiment.

Russia's failure to consult can arguably be an additional violation of the treaty.

Several actors, including states, companies and civil society, have condemned ASAT tests as irresponsible and called for them to be prohibited.[23] These public reactions reflect the nascent movements towards an instrument prohibiting debris-creating kinetic ASAT tests. Indeed, earlier in 2021 an international open letter had proposed a multilateral treaty to ban kinetic ASAT tests.[24] US officials also expressed support for such a ban.[25] Russia's test revived the urgency of agreeing new measures regarding these tests.[26]

Growing interest in lunar activities

The legal regime for lunar activities is distinct from activities elsewhere in outer space under international law. States are legally obligated by the Outer Space Treaty to use the Moon and other celestial bodies 'exclusively' for peaceful purposes.[27] There are also blanket prohibitions on certain activities: 'The establishment of military bases, installations and fortifications, the

---

[21] Russian Ministry of Foreign Affairs, 'Comment by Foreign Ministry Spokeswoman Maria Zakharova on aspects of the space activities of Russia and other states', 16 Nov. 2021.

[22] Outer Space Treaty (note 14), Article IX.

[23] Raju, N., 'Russia's anti-satellite test should lead to a multilateral ban', Commentary, SIPRI, 7 Dec. 2021.

[24] Raju (note 23); and Byers, M. et al., 'Kinetic ASAT test ban treaty', Open letter, Outer Space Institute, 2 Sep. 2021.

[25] Smith, M., 'Space Council condemns Russian ASAT test: DOD calls for end to debris-creating tests', Space Policy Online, 1 Dec. 2021; and Hitchens, T., 'Biden's space policy nominee backs ban on destructive ASAT testing, pushes norms', 13 Jan. 2022, Breaking Defense.

[26] Byers et al. (note 24).

[27] Outer Space Treaty (note 14), Article IV.

testing of any type of weapons and the conduct of military manoeuvres on celestial bodies'.[28] The Moon therefore has a special legal status, with a higher standard of non-militarization than the rest of outer space.[29] This legal standard requires emphasis in the light of renewed lunar exploration ambitions and growing military focus in 2021.

International partnerships

In 2021 two distinct international partnerships for lunar exploration and resource utilization developed. The first is the Artemis Accords, which is led by the USA and by the end of 2021 included 14 other states.[30] The second involves a memorandum of understanding (MOU) announced by China and Russia in May 2021 for a joint international lunar research station, which invites other states to collaborate on this venture.[31] China and Russia have reportedly approached the European Space Agency (ESA) to join.[32]

With similar timelines and purposes, it is unclear how these two initiatives can be conducted simultaneously without any dedicated coordination mechanisms between the states leading them. For example, lunar resource utilization is a key objective for both partnerships. Yet, the Moon does not have plentiful, evenly distributed resources, and states are therefore likely to direct activities to a few resource-rich regions, or to specific areas that offer observational advantages.[33] As a result, new protocols will be required between participating states to ensure that no conflict arises out of competition for these locations and resources. Such cooperation, even involving rival states, is not unimaginable: NASA and the China National Space Administration (CNSA) have previously cooperated to exchange data and even provide monitoring and observational support.[34] However, in the absence of these dedicated mechanisms, the potential for miscommunication and magnified tensions leading to conflict on the Moon is likely to grow.

---

[28] Outer Space Treaty (note 14), Article IV.

[29] See Porras (note 2). See also Raju, N., 'Trends in lunar exploration: Examining the governance challenges', eds T. Ray and R. P. Rajagopalan, *Digital Debates: Cyfy Journal 2021* (Observer Research Foundation and Global Policy Journal: New Delhi, 2021).

[30] The Artemis Accords: Principles for Cooperation in the Civil Exploration and Use of the Moon, Mars, Comets, and Asteroids for Peaceful Purposes, opened for signature 13 Oct. 2020.

[31] Joint statement between China National Space Administration and the State Space Corporation 'Roscosmos' regarding cooperation for the construction of the International Lunar Research Station, 9 Apr. 2021.

[32] TASS, 'ESA mulls joining Russian–Chinese lunar station project', 27 Oct. 2021.

[33] Elvis, M., Krolikowski, A. and Milligan T., 'Concentrated lunar resources: Imminent implications for governance and justice', *Philosophical Transactions of the Royal Society A: Mathematical, Physical and Engineering Sciences*, vol. 379, no. 2188 (2021), p. 7.

[34] Foust, J., 'NASA exchanged data with China on Mars orbiters', SpaceNews, 30 Mar. 2021. Also see Xinhua, 'NASA's lunar orbiter has its third, overhead look on China's Chang'e-4 probe', 15 Feb. 2019.

Military interest in lunar activities

In May 2021 the US Air Force Research Laboratory released a primer on cislunar security, which was 'targeted at military space professionals . . . to develop plans, capabilities, expertise, and operational concepts'.[35] The primer refers to the MOU signed in September 2020 between NASA and the US Space Force (USSF), in particular quoting,

As NASA's human presence extends beyond ISS to the lunar surface, cislunar, and interplanetary destinations, and as USSF organizes, trains, and equips to provide the resources necessary to protect and defend vital US interests in and beyond Earth-orbit, new collaborations will be key to operating safely and securely on these distant frontiers.[36]

It then addresses the scope for the detection and surveillance of activities in cislunar space.[37] The primer indicates an expansion of US military interest in lunar activities, in particular the USSF's drive for enhanced surveillance and monitoring in cislunar space.[38]

Growing military interest in lunar activities was again evidenced when the Defense Advanced Research Projects Agency (DARPA), the research and development arm of the US Department of Defense (DOD), announced the intent to commence manufacturing processes on the Moon.[39] As the Outer Space Treaty requires that the Moon be used 'exclusively for peaceful purposes', DARPA's announcement was immediately questioned by experts in the space sector as possibly violating international law.[40] As a result, some experts recommended the termination of these USSF and DARPA ventures in cislunar space, and alternatively suggest that these programmes be reassigned to NASA for civilian uses only.[41] This would ensure that the non-militarization standard for the Moon continues to be strictly maintained. Clarifications regarding intent in cislunar space, in addition to limitation of military interests, are therefore needed.

---

[35] Holzinger, M. J., Chow, C. C. and Garretson, P., *A Primer on Cislunar Security* (Air Force Research Laboratory: Kirtland AFB, NM, May 2021), p. 3.

[36] Holzinger et al. (note 35), p. 3.

[37] Holzinger et al. (note 35) pp. 13–18.

[38] Hitchens, T., 'AFRL jumpstarts early research on cislunar monitoring, satellite servicing', Breaking Defense, 17 Dec. 2021.

[39] Erwin, S., 'DARPA to survey private sector capabilities to build factories on the Moon', SpaceNews, 7 Feb. 2021.

[40] Hitchens, T., 'DARPA space manufacturing project sparks controversy', Breaking Defense, 12 Feb. 2021.

[41] Byers, M. and Boley, A., 'Cis-lunar space and the security dilemma', *Bulletin of the Atomic Scientists*, 17 Jan. 2022.

Other states have also expressed interest in cislunar space, such as China.[42] Amid unclear rhetoric and military interest, there is a need for clarity on permissible activities in the lunar environment.

Looking ahead: Discussions on responsible behaviour in space

The need to prevent an arms race in outer space was acknowledged at the Conference on Disarmament (CD) in 2021, although no further measures were adopted.[43] The UN Committee on the Peaceful Uses of Outer Space (COPUOS) also convened its 64th session, where delegations exchanged views on ways to maintain peaceful uses of space.[44] These included discussions on the continued implementation of the Guidelines for the Long-term Sustainability of Outer Space Activities, adopted by the committee in 2019.[45] However, at the multilateral level, it was developments through the United Kingdom-sponsored resolution at the UN General Assembly that made the most substantive progress. This approach may hold the key to overcoming the current impasse in space security governance.[46]

In December 2020 the General Assembly adopted a resolution on 'Reducing space threats through norms, rules and principles of responsible behaviours'. This resolution invited states to

study existing and potential threats and security risks to space systems . . . characterize actions and activities that could be considered responsible, irresponsible or threatening . . . and share their ideas on the further development and implementation of norms, rules and principles of responsible behaviours and on the reduction of the risks of misunderstanding and miscalculations with respect to outer space.[47]

The resolution aims to advance space security discussions on the prevention of an arms race in outer space (PAROS), which has been a priority for the CD for decades, but has made little progress due to political and technical hurdles.[48] It adopts a fresh approach that focuses on behaviour rather than capabilities and hardware. The resolution invited states to submit their views, which were then summarized in a report by the UN secretary-

---

[42] Chinese State Council, *China's Space Program: A 2021 Perspective*, White paper (State Council Information Office: Beijing, Jan. 2022).

[43] United Nations, General Assembly, Report of the Conference on Disarmament, 2021 session, A/76/27, 14 Sep. 2021.

[44] United Nations, General Assembly, Report of the Committee on the Peaceful Uses of Outer Space, 64th session, A/76/20, 21 Oct. 2021.

[45] United Nations, A/76/20 (note 46), annex II.

[46] Porras (note 2).

[47] UN General Assembly Resolution 75/36, 'Reducing space threats through norms, rules and principles of responsible behaviours', 7 Dec. 2020, para. 5.

[48] Porras (note 2).

general.[49] Thirty states, the European Union (EU) and several international and non-governmental organizations submitted responses. The submissions exhibit common concerns: the shared importance of space for all states and the risks posed by the proliferation of counterspace technologies, including both kinetic capabilities (which rely on motion-based destruction to destroy targets) and non-kinetic capabilities (such as lasers and electronic interference).

Most submissions referred to the hazards of space debris, with a few expressly proposing a ban on kinetic ASAT tests that generate debris. Some submissions also raised the need to specifically regulate non-cooperative rendezvous and proximity operations, which is when space objects come into contact with, or in close proximity to, each other. The submissions also contain recommendations for SSA data-sharing and increased transparency.

The secretary-general's report was followed by a resolution in the General Assembly in December 2021 to convene an open-ended working group to 'make recommendations on possible norms, rules and principles of responsible behaviours relating to threats by States to space systems, including . . . how they would contribute to the negotiation of legally binding instruments, including on the prevention of an arms race in outer space'.[50] The OEWG will convene in 2022 and 2023 over four sessions and, working by consensus, will submit a report to the General Assembly at its 78th session.[51]

Continuing to build the momentum to enhance the security of outer space through norms of behaviour, in July 2021 the US Secretary of Defense published a formal memorandum stating that the DOD would, unless otherwise directed, follow five 'Tenets of responsible behavior in space': (*a*) operating with due regard, (*b*) limiting 'long-lived debris', (*c*) avoiding creation of harmful interference, (*d*) maintaining safe separation and safe trajectory, and (*e*) communicating and notifying to enhance safety and stability.[52] While this declassified memorandum is a positive starting point for discussions on responsible behaviour in space, many of these concepts require legal and technical clarification as well as consensus-building among states as to their common understanding. The OEWG provides the ideal forum for these discussions.

With the potential to overcome the ongoing space security stalemate, this resolution and the OEWG could evolve space security governance at a time when transparency and cooperation are urgently needed.

---

[49] United Nations, Report of the Secretary-General, 'Reducing space threats through norms, rules and principles of responsible behaviours', A/76/77, 13 July 2021.

[50] UN General Assembly Resolution 76/231, 'Reducing space threats through norms, rules and principles of responsible behaviours', 30 Dec. 2021, para 5(c).

[51] UN General Assembly Resolution 76/231 (note 52), para. 5(d).

[52] US Secretary of Defense, 'Tenets of responsible behavior in space', Memorandum, 7 July 2021.

14. Dual-use and arms trade controls

Overview

During 2021 a range of global, multilateral and regional efforts took place that were aimed at strengthening controls on the trade in conventional arms and in dual-use items connected with conventional, chemical, biological and nuclear weapons and their delivery systems. Membership of the different international and multilateral instruments that seek to establish and promote agreed standards for the trade in arms and dual-use items remained unchanged. The global Covid-19 pandemic continued to limit in-person meetings for most of the year, although a growing willingness to replace these with online or hybrid meetings did allow some plenaries and intersessional processes to take place. The election of President Joe Biden in the United States saw a reversal of some of the policies adopted by the previous administration on the United Nations sanctions on Iran and the Arms Trade Treaty (ATT) and a return to greater engagement in international and multilateral export controls instruments and processes. However, the Biden administration continued to seek allies' support for the USA's use of national and multilateral export controls measures to restrict transfers of dual-use items to China. This has led China to seek international support for its opposition to what it views as the misuse of export control measures for national economic and security purposes. Divisions between the USA and China may weaken the increasingly fragile international consensus concerning the use of multilateral export controls as non-proliferation tools.

The seventh conference of states parties (CSP7) to the ATT was conducted under the presidency of Ambassador Lansana Gberie of Sierra Leone (see section I). The theme of the conference was 'Strengthening efforts to eradicate the illicit trade in small arms and light weapons (SALW) and ensure efficient stockpile management'. The meeting was held in a hybrid format with some delegates participating in person in Geneva and others joining online, making it more interactive than CSP6 which was held under a written procedure. However, Covid-19 restrictions meant that work in the newly established Diversion Information Exchange Forum (DIEF) could still not begin. Negative trends in the number of states submitting required initial reports on treaty implementation and annual reports on arms transfers, and in the number of states not making reports publicly available, persisted in 2021. Of the 105 annual reports on transfers in 2020 that were due by the end of 2021, 63 were either not submitted (45) or only made available to states parties (18).

During 2020, 13 UN embargoes, 21 European Union (EU) embargoes and 1 League of Arab States embargo were in force (see section II). No new multi-

lateral arms embargo was imposed. Ten of the EU arms embargoes matched the scope of those imposed by the UN; three were broader in terms of duration, geographical scope or the types of weapon covered; and eight had no UN counterpart. The single Arab League arms embargo, on Syria, had no UN counterpart. The level of international consensus around decisions about lifting and extending UN arms embargoes was greater in 2021 than in 2020. Examples include the Biden administration abandoning the Trump administration's unilateral attempt to reimpose UN sanctions on Iran; and China and Russia voting in favour of the arms embargo on South Sudan, after having abstained in previous years. However, as in previous years, investigations by UN-appointed panels and groups of experts revealed numerous reported cases of violations, particularly in connection with the embargoes on Libya and non-governmental forces in Yemen. Also of concern were reports of states—including China and Russia—seeking to block the release of the reports produced by panels and groups or to influence their work.

Covid-19 pandemic restrictions continued to affect the work of the four multilateral export control regimes—the Australia Group (on chemical and biological weapons), the Missile Technology Control Regime (MTCR), the Nuclear Suppliers Group (NSG), and the Wassenaar Arrangement on Export Controls for Conventional Arms and Dual-use Goods and Technologies (WA)—but the nature and extent of the disruption varied (see section III). The annual plenaries of the AG and the WA could not be held but the NSG and MTCR plenaries did go ahead, albeit with a smaller participation of state representatives. The pandemic continued to limit the regimes' ability to take major decisions and to discuss political and technical topics, such as amendments to their control lists. It also contributed to reduced levels of transparency and outreach activities. However, unlike in 2020, small amendments were made to the control lists of the MTCR and the WA.

To implement these four regimes in its single market, the EU has established a common legal basis for controls on the export, brokering, transit and transshipment of dual-use items, software and technology and, to a certain degree, military items (see section IV). The EU is the only regional organization to have developed such a framework. In 2021 the EU adopted a new version of the EU dual-use regulation and began work on clarifying how its new provisions will be implemented. The review and recast was dominated by debates about whether EU-level processes should play a more prominent role in decision-making concerning the content and implementation of member states' export controls. Developments in the European Parliament indicate these debates look set to continue. The EU and the USA deepened their cooperation on export control issues in 2021, but underlying differences within the EU and between the EU and the USA may limit their eventual impact.

MARK BROMLEY

I. The Arms Trade Treaty

GIOVANNA MALETTA AND ANDREA EDOARDO VARISCO

The 2013 Arms Trade Treaty (ATT) is the first legally binding international agreement to establish standards for regulating the international trade in conventional arms and preventing their illicit transfers.[1] As of 31 December 2021, 110 states were party to the ATT and 31 had signed but not yet ratified it. There were no new states parties in 2021.[2]

The Covid-19 pandemic continued to affect the proceedings and meetings of the ATT, which had been severely impacted over the course of 2020.[3] During 2021, the Working Group on Effective Treaty Implementation (WGETI), the Working Group on Transparency and Reporting (WGTR) and the Working Group on Treaty Universalization (WGTU) held only one set of preparatory meetings in a virtual format on 26–29 April.[4] The WGTR and the presidency of the seventh conference of states parties (CSP7) also held an additional round of informal virtual consultations on 28–30 June.[5] States parties continued to consult remotely in the run-up to CSP7, to finalize documentation for submission and consideration during the conference.[6]

CSP7 was held during 30 August to 3 September 2021 under the presidency of Ambassador Lansana Gberie of Sierra Leone, whose thematic focus was 'strengthening efforts to eradicate the illicit trade in small arms and light weapons (SALW) and ensure efficient stockpile management'.[7] Participating in CSP7 were 103 states and 40 delegations from regional and international organizations, non-governmental organizations (NGOs), research institutes, industry associations and national implementing agencies.[8] In an attempt

---

[1] For a summary and other details of the Arms Trade Treaty see annex A, section I, in this volume. The 2001 UN Firearms Protocol is also legally binding but only covers controls on the trade in firearms. UN General Assembly Resolution 55/255, Protocol against the Illicit Manufacturing of and Trafficking in Firearms, their Parts and Components and Ammunition, supplementing the UN Convention against Transnational Organized Crime (UN Firearms Protocol), adopted 31 May 2001, entered into force 3 July 2005.

[2] Arms Trade Treaty, 'Treaty status', accessed on 18 Dec. 2021; and Arms Trade Treaty, 'States Parties to the ATT (in order of deposit of instrument of ratification, approval, acceptance, or accession)', 7 Aug. 2020.

[3] See Varisco, A. E., Maletta, G. and Robin, L., 'The Arms Trade Treaty', *SIPRI Yearbook 2021*, pp. 555, 563.

[4] Arms Trade Treaty, CSP7 President, 'Announcement: Confirmation of the format of the preparatory meeting for the seventh Conference of States Parties', 22 Feb. 2021.

[5] Arms Trade Treaty, 'CSP7 informal consultations: 28–30 June 2021', [n.d.].

[6] Arms Trade Treaty, CSP7, 'Final report', ATT/CSP7/2021/SEC/681/Conf.FinRep.Rev1, 2 Sep. 2021, para. 5.

[7] Arms Trade Treaty, CSP7 President, 'Strengthening efforts to eradicate the illicit trade in small arms and light weapons and ensure efficient stockpile management', Draft working paper, ATT/CSP7/2021/PRES/659/Conf.SALWPSSM.Rev3, 14 July 2021, p. 1.

[8] CSP7 attendees comprised 86 states parties, 15 signatory states, 2 observer states, 7 observer organizations (including the European Union) and 33 civil society organizations. See Arms Trade Treaty, ATT/CSP7/2021/SEC/681/Conf.FinRep.Rev1 (note 6), paras 11–15.

to promote more interactive meetings and move away from the silence procedure format adopted for the sixth conference of states parties (CSP6), CSP7 took place in a hybrid format. This meant that a limited number of delegates were able to attend the conference in person in Geneva while others could participate virtually.[9] Side events were conducted in a virtual format. Because December 2020 marked the sixth anniversary of the entry into force of the treaty, in accordance with Article 20 of the ATT, CSP7 was the first conference where states parties could propose amendments to the treaty. However, none was proposed.

CSP7 concluded with the election of Ambassador Thomas Göbel of Germany as the president of the eighth conference of states parties (CSP8) to be held in August 2022. Ambassador Göbel announced that the main themes of the German presidency will be universalization, post-shipment controls and 'stocktaking with regard to achievements and shortcomings in implementation of the ATT'.[10]

This section summarizes key ATT-related developments during 2021 and at CSP7. First, it focuses on issues related to treaty implementation, including the thematic discussions on illicit SALW trade and stockpile management. Next, it looks at the status of ATT transparency and reporting, followed by the status of universalization and developments regarding the provision of international assistance. Finally, it analyses issues related to the financial health and functioning of the treaty, before concluding with a reflection on CSP7's major achievements and shortcomings, and the prospects for CSP8.

Treaty implementation

Tackling the illicit trade in small arms and light weapons

The decision of the Sierra Leonean presidency to make illicit trade in SALW and stockpile management the thematic focus of CSP7 aimed to link efforts to implement the ATT to the 'global framework' for arms control, disarmament and non-proliferation and, in particular, to instruments promoting effective SALW control and stockpile management. In a draft working paper circulated and reviewed during the CSP7 meetings cycle, the CSP7 president outlined the relevance of the ATT as a tool to prevent diversion and address the illicit trade in SALW. The working paper also described synergies between the treaty and the UN Programme of Action (UNPOA) on SALW as well as a number of other relevant international and regional instruments.[11] Issues related to diversion of SALW and stockpile management were also addressed during the seventh biennial meeting of states parties to the UNPOA (BMS7)

---

[9] Arms Trade Treaty, 'Participation in CSP7 and testing of platform', [n.d.].
[10] Arms Trade Treaty, 'President', [n.d.].
[11] Arms Trade Treaty, ATT/CSP7/2021/PRES/659/Conf.SALWPSSM.Rev3 (note 7), pp. 1–4.

that took place in July 2021.[12] The CSP7 president's paper suggested that states parties further strengthen the implementation of ATT provisions on diversion by increasing cooperation in the post-delivery phase, including through the promotion of effective security and management of national stockpiles.[13] CSP7 positively received both the working paper and the thematic discussion that it generated, and endorsed the proposed set of possible areas for further consideration by states parties.[14]

The proposals included encouraging ATT stakeholders to map and make better use of existing guidelines and tools in the field of SALW control and stockpile management as developed in the context of other relevant instruments. CSP7 also decided that the WGETI should address 'post-delivery cooperation experiences' in its discussions and consider compiling a list of existing assistance programmes that address illicit trade in SALW and stockpile management, and make it available to states in need of support in this field.[15]

Developments in the Working Group on Effective Treaty Implementation

States parties adopted the revised multi-year workplans for the WGETI and its sub-working groups via silence procedure in February 2021, after failing to do so as part of the CSP6 decision-making process.[16] The WGETI is divided into three sub-working groups covering specific areas of ATT implementation, namely Article 6 ('Prohibitions') and Article 7 ('Export and Export Assessment'), Article 9 ('Transit or Trans-shipment'), and Article 11 ('Diversion').

The sub-working group on Articles 6 and 7 continued to encourage states parties to share information on their interpretation of key treaty terms (such as 'serious', 'facilitate' and 'overriding' risk) and their national practices in relation to 'mitigating measures'.[17] As part of these efforts, in 2020 the facilitator of the group developed a template to seek relevant inputs from states parties. These inputs will also inform the drafting of a voluntary guide to implementing articles 6 and 7, which is also part of the group's multi-year work programme for 2020–23. The facilitator presented results of this

---

[12] Developments in the UNPOA on SALW and BMS7 are addressed in chapter 13, section I, in this volume.

[13] Arms Trade Treaty, ATT/CSP7/2021/PRES/659/Conf.SALWPSSM.Rev3 (note 7), p. 5.

[14] Pytlak, A., 'CSP7 report: Thematic discussion', *ATT Monitor*, vol. 14, no. 4 (8 Sep. 2021), p. 5; and Arms Trade Treaty, ATT/CSP7/2021/SEC/681/Conf.FinRep.Rev1 (note 6), para. 21.

[15] Arms Trade Treaty, ATT/CSP7/2021/SEC/681/Conf.FinRep.Rev1 (note 6), para. 21(b) and (e).

[16] Arms Trade Treaty, ATT/CSP7/2021/SEC/681/Conf.FinRep.Rev1 (note 6), para. 23. See also Varisco, Maletta and Robin (note 3), p. 556.

[17] Arms Trade Treaty, CSP7, Working Group on Effective Treaty Implementation (WGETI), Letter from the chair, ATT/CSP7.WGETI/2021/CHAIR/655/M.LetterWorkPlans, 31 Mar. 2021, pp. 4–5.

'unpacking' exercise during the CSP7 preparatory meetings in April 2021.[18] The report prompted some scepticism and raised concerns among both states parties and NGO representatives, who cautioned against setting prescriptive definitions going beyond the text of the ATT and flagged the risks of unnecessary clarifications of basic notions already enshrined in international humanitarian law or already analysed by legal scholars.[19] Taking into account the results of the exercise and the inputs shared in the discussion that followed, in the intersessional period leading up to CSP8 the facilitator of the sub-working group will continue leading this work by drafting and presenting the first chapter ('Key concepts') of the above-mentioned voluntary guide.[20]

In the sub-working group on Article 9, states shared details on their national practices for implementing and enforcing transit and trans-shipment controls with a view to achieving a common understanding of the key terms of this provision.[21] CSP7 confirmed that in the run-up to CSP8 the work of the group will focus on the measures to regulate the transit and trans-shipment of arms by land.[22]

Finally, the sub-working group on Article 11 continued to promote the effective implementation of treaty provisions addressing the risk of diversion. Specifically, the facilitator of the group prepared a draft voluntary paper that outlined elements of a process for assessing the risk of diversion.[23] It was first presented during the preparatory meetings in the spring and later endorsed by CSP7 'as a living document of a voluntary nature to be reviewed and updated regularly' by the group.[24] Based on its multi-year work plan, the work of the sub-working group during the CSP8 cycle is expected to focus on the role of transit and trans-shipment states in preventing diversion.[25] Also relevant to the work of the sub-working group on Article 11 was the endorse-

---

[18] Arms Trade Treaty, ATT/CSP7.WGETI/2021/CHAIR/655/M.LetterWorkPlans (note 17), annex A, pp. 8–10; and Arms Trade Treaty, CSP7, WGETI, Chair's draft report, ATT/CSP7.WGETI/2021/CHAIR/675/Conf.Rep, 22 July 2021, para. 7.

[19] See Varisco, A. E., Maletta, G. and Robin, L., *Taking Stock of the Arms Trade Treaty: Achievements, Challenges and Ways Forward*, SIPRI Policy Report, Dec. 2021, pp. 20–21; Arms Trade Treaty, ATT/CSP7.WGETI/2021/CHAIR/675/Conf.Rep (note 18), para. 10; Pytlak, A. and Geyer, K., 'A whole lot of unpacking going on', *ATT Monitor*, vol. 13, no. 2 (11 Feb. 2020), p. 1; Geyer, K., 'Summary: Sub-working group on Articles 6 and 7', *ATT Monitor*, vol. 13, no. 2 (11 Feb. 2020), pp. 3–4; Pytlak, A., 'One more time for the people in the back—transparency (still) matters!', *ATT Monitor*, vol. 13, no. 4 (27 Aug. 2020); Geyer, K. and Pytlak, A., 'News in brief', *ATT Monitor*, vol. 13, no. 4 (27 Aug. 2020), pp. 5–6; and Rafferty, J., 'Summary: Sub-working group on Articles 6 and 7', *ATT Monitor*, vol. 14, no. 2 (5 May 2021), pp. 8–11.

[20] Arms Trade Treaty, ATT/CSP7/2021/SEC/681/Conf.FinRep.Rev1 (note 6), para. 24.

[21] Arms Trade Treaty, ATT/CSP7.WGETI/2021/CHAIR/675/Conf.Rep (note 18), para. 12.

[22] Arms Trade Treaty, ATT/CSP7/2021/SEC/681/Conf.FinRep.Rev1 (note 6), para. 24.

[23] Arms Trade Treaty, ATT/CSP7.WGETI/2021/CHAIR/675/Conf.Rep (note 18), annex A.

[24] Arms Trade Treaty, ATT/CSP7.WGETI/2021/CHAIR/675/Conf.Rep (note 18), annex A, p. 6; and Arms Trade Treaty, ATT/CSP7/2021/SEC/681/Conf.FinRep.Rev1 (note 6), para. 25.

[25] Arms Trade Treaty, 'Multi-year work plan for the WGETI Sub-working Group on Article 11', Mar. 2021, p. 5.

ment of the working paper presented by the Argentinian president of CSP6 on the role of transparency and information exchange in preventing diversion.[26] The paper, which was among the decisions that CSP6 did not adopt, identified the Diversion Information Exchange Forum (DIEF) as one of the tools through which states are recommended to share information that could help detect and prevent cases of diversion.[27]

The Diversion Information Exchange Forum

The DIEF is a subsidiary body established by CSP6. In 2021 the DIEF was unable to convene as the Covid-19 pandemic prevented in-person meetings, something which states have identified as a necessary condition for discussing sensitive matters related to diversion. As recommended by the DIEF chair's report, CSP7 mandated the CSP8 president to arrange the first meeting of this body as soon as in-person meetings are possible. CSP7 also decided to postpone the review of the usefulness of the DIEF 'at the first CSP following two cycles of DIEF meetings'.[28]

Transparency and reporting

States parties to the ATT have two reporting obligations: under Article 13(1), within one year after entry into force at national level, to provide an initial report to the ATT Secretariat of 'measures undertaken in order to implement' the treaty and report when appropriate 'on any new measures undertaken in order to implement' the treaty; and under Article 13(3), to submit an annual report to the Secretariat on 'authorized or actual exports and imports of conventional arms'. As of 31 December 2021, 26 out of 110 (24 per cent) states parties that were due to submit an initial report had failed to do so.[29] Of the five states parties that were due to submit an initial report to the Secretariat in 2021—Afghanistan, China, Namibia, Niue, and Sao Tomé and Principe— only China fulfilled this requirement and it decided to restrict access to its initial report for states parties. Therefore, the total number of restricted access initial reports is 20 (24 per cent of total initial reports submitted).[30]

---

[26] Arms Trade Treaty, ATT/CSP7/2021/SEC/681/Conf.FinRep.Rev1 (note 6), para. 28; and Arms Trade Treaty, CSP6 President, 'Transparency and exchange of information: Its role in the prevention of diversion', Working paper, ATT/CSP6/2020/PRES/611/Conf.TranspInfExch.Rev4, 6 July 2021.

[27] Arms Trade Treaty, ATT/CSP6/2020/PRES/611/Conf.TranspInfExch.Rev4 (note 26), p. 2.

[28] Arms Trade Treaty, ATT/CSP7/2021/SEC/681/Conf.FinRep.Rev1 (note 6), para. 27; and Arms Trade Treaty, Diversion Information Exchange Forum, 'ATT Diversion Information Exchange Forum chair's report to CSP7', ATT/CSP7.DIEF/2021/CHAIR/673/Conf.Rep, 16 July 2021.

[29] ATT Secretariat, 'Initial reports', Status at 10 Feb. 2022.

[30] The countries that submitted restricted access initial reports are Benin, Botswana, Burkina Faso, Cameroon, Chile, China, Cyprus, Greece, Guatemala, Honduras, Kazakhstan, Madagascar, Maldives, Malta, Mauritius, Nigeria, Saint Vincent and the Grenadines, Senegal, Palestine and Tuvalu. ATT Secretariat, 'Initial reports' (note 29).

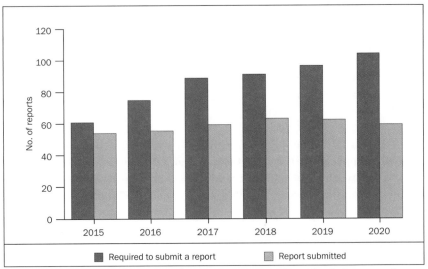

Figure 14.1. Number of Arms Trade Treaty states parties submitting annual reports, 2015–20

Source: ATT Secretariat, 'Annual reports', Status at 25 Oct. 2021.

Out of 105 states required to submit an annual report, 60 (57 per cent) submitted an annual report for 2020 and fulfilled their annual reporting obligations.[31] The percentage of annual reports submitted by states parties for 2020 is lower than in 2019 (the year that had the lowest percentage of submissions before 2020) and represents the lowest compliance rate of any year so far.[32] This downward trend in annual reporting means that a higher percentage of state parties failed to fulfil their annual reporting obligations and the number of annual reports due but not submitted has increased every year (figure 14.1).[33] Declining rates of report submissions are not unique to the ATT: the number of states submitting their reports to the UN Register of Conventional Arms (UNROCA) for the year 2020 also reached the lowest level in 2021.[34]

Of the annual reports submitted, more than 75 per cent were on time, which represents the highest rate of timely submissions ever. This was a positive development compared to a significant drop in the timeliness of submissions

---

[31] ATT Secretariat, 'Annual reports', Status at 25 Oct. 2021.

[32] The total number of annual reports submitted is not the lowest, but the percentage of reports submitted is the lowest due to a higher number of states parties. Barbados, Cameroon, Canada and Palau submitted an annual report for the first time. In previous years, they had either not submitted a report (Barbados and Cameroon) or no annual report was due (Canada and Palau).

[33] On compliance rate in 2019 see Varisco, Maletta and Robin (note 3), pp. 557–58.

[34] For UNROCA data see chapter 13, section IV, in this volume.

for 2019 reports, which was likely caused by the impact of Covid-19.[35] States parties can also submit reports belatedly and for several years' backlog: for example, in 2021 Antigua and Barbuda submitted annual reports covering six years from 2015 through 2020.[36]

The number of annual reports that are available only for states parties is also increasing, as 18 states parties submitted a restricted access annual report for 2020.[37] This means that, of a total of 105 annual reports due for 2020, 63 reports were either not submitted (45) or not made public (18). Interestingly, the list of states parties that have submitted a restricted-access annual report for 2020 also includes countries that made their submission public in the context of other reporting instruments such as the UNROCA (e.g. Bulgaria, Cyprus, Greece and Lithuania). In addition, nine ATT states parties indicated in their annual reports that they had withheld some information that was commercially sensitive or related to national security, as allowed under Article 13.3.[38] At CSP7, South Africa voiced some concerns about reporting fatigue and reiterated that withholding this kind of information 'is permitted under, and consistent with' Article 13 'without prejudice and need not be the subject of further discussion or the need for any self-justification'.[39] Although making reports public is not a treaty obligation, this growing tendency goes against one of the treaty's main purposes of promoting transparency in the international arms trade.[40]

CSP7 acknowledged the trends identified above in its final report by emphasizing 'the significance of transparency and reporting', recalling 'that transparency is a key purpose of the Treaty' and expressing 'its concern for the low rate of compliance with the reporting obligations'.[41]

Finally, during 2021 the WGTR completed its work on revisions of the initial and annual reporting templates. The changes introduced aim to provide clarifications to states parties and address issues of user friendliness,

---

[35] Parker, S., 'Arms Trade Treaty: Status of reporting', Presentation at the working group meetings and CSP8 informal preparatory meeting, 17 Feb. 2022. See also ATT Secretariat, 'ATT Working Groups' and 1st CSP8 informal preparatory meetings, day 3, as delivered', YouTube, 17 Feb. 22, 00:20:40–00:31:35.

[36] Stohl, R., Fletcher, R. and Dick, S., 'Taking stock of ATT annual reports', Stimson Center Arms Trade Treaty—Baseline Assessment Project report, Feb. 2022, p. 7.

[37] The 18 states are Albania, Antigua and Barbuda, Barbados, Benin, Bulgaria, Cameroon, Cyprus, El Salvador, Georgia, Greece, Kazakhstan, Lithuania, Maldives, Malta, Mauritius, North Macedonia, Panama and Palestine. Benin, Bulgaria, El Salvador and Panama had submitted public annual reports for 2019.

[38] The nine states are Argentina, Chile, Finland, Hungary, Republic of Korea, Mexico, Montenegro, Norway and Sweden.

[39] Arms Trade Treaty, ATT/CSP7/2021/SEC/681/Conf.FinRep.Rev1 (note 6), annex B: Statement by South Africa on the report of the Working Group on Transparency and Reporting (WGTR). See also Pytlak, A., 'The fuel that perpetuates conflict', ATT Monitor, vol. 14, no. 4 (8 Sep. 2021), p. 3.

[40] Arms Trade Treaty (note 1), article 1. See also Arms Trade Treaty, ATT Working Group on Transparency and Reporting (WGTR), Co-chairs' draft report to CSP7, ATT/CSP7.WGTR/2021/CHAIR/676/Conf.Rep, 22 July 2021, pp. 2, 6 and 7.

[41] Arms Trade Treaty, ATT/CSP7/2021/SEC/681/Conf.FinRep.Rev1 (note 6), para. 26.

Table 14.1. Arms Trade Treaty numbers of ratifications, accessions and signatories, by region

Region	States	States parties	Signatories	Non-signatories
Africa	53	28	12	13
Americas	35	27	3[a]	5
Asia	29	6	7	16
Europe	48[b]	41	2	5[b]
Middle East	16[c]	2[c]	4	10
Oceania	16[d]	6[e]	3	7[f]
Total	197	110	31	56

Notes: The treaty was open for signature until it entered into force in Dec. 2014. Existing signatories may accept, approve or ratify the treaty in order to become a state party. A non-signatory state must now directly accede to the treaty in order to become a state party.

[a] This figure includes the United States. On 18 July 2019, the USA announced its intention not to become a state party to the treaty.

[b] This figure includes the Holy See.

[c] This figure includes Palestine.

[d] This figure includes Niue and the Cook Islands.

[e] This figure includes Niue.

[f] This figure includes the Cook Islands.

Source: United Nations, UN Treaty Collection, Status of Treaties, ch. XXVI Disarmament: 8. Arms Trade Treaty.

inconsistencies and omissions identified in the previous templates.[42] The revisions received broad support from states and other delegates at CSP7, which endorsed the revised templates and recommended they be used by states parties in compiling their initial and annual reports.[43]

Treaty universalization and international assistance

Status of universalization

During 2021 no new state joined or ratified the ATT, leaving the number of states parties at 110 (table 14.1). In presenting the status of treaty participation, the ATT Secretariat noted that the overall picture remains positive, but also stressed continued regional disparities and the decreasing ratification rate since adoption of the ATT.[44] During the high-level opening panel of CSP7, Gambia announced its decision to join the treaty.[45] However, by the end of 2021 it had still not become a state party. During the CSP7 session on universalization, the United States announced that the Biden administration was 'determining the proper relationship' of the USA with the ATT as part of

[42] Arms Trade Treaty, ATT/CSP7.WGTR/2021/CHAIR/676/Conf.Rep (note 40), para. 26, annexes C and E. Annexes B and D of the document include all adjustments to the reports in track changes.

[43] Arms Trade Treaty, ATT/CSP7/2021/SEC/681/Conf.FinRep.Rev1 (note 6), para. 26(g)–(h).

[44] Rafferty, J., 'CSP7 report: Treaty universalization', *ATT Monitor*, vol. 14, no. 4 (8 Sep. 2021), p. 13.

[45] Faye, S. O., Gambian Minister of Defence, Statement at the opening session of CSP7, Geneva, 30 Aug. 2021.

a wider process of revising its conventional arms transfer policy.[46] Still, by the end of 2021 the USA had not finalized this revision process and therefore its official position—which is that the USA 'does not intend to become a party to the treaty' and therefore 'has no legal obligations arising from its signature'—remained unchanged.[47]

Despite the challenges created by pandemic-related restrictions on travel and meetings, the WGTU and the CSP7 president conducted limited outreach activities whenever possible.[48] The Sierra Leonean presidency adopted a universalization strategy which differentiated non-party states into countries that were close to joining the ATT and countries that indicated joining the treaty as a long-term prospect. Outreach activities were therefore tailored accordingly. These included the organization of two online outreach meetings targeting states that are not yet part of the ATT, of which one specifically addressed states that were considered likely to join the treaty. The president of Sierra Leone, Julius Maada Bio, also wrote to the heads of non-states parties to encourage them to join the treaty.

Further, the CSP7 presidency cooperated with the Inter-Parliamentary Union to engage parliamentarians around the world in the universalization of the ATT. The European Union (EU) also contributed to universalization efforts by sponsoring the printing of copies of the Universalization Toolkit in all United Nations languages. CSP7 adopted recommendations, formulated by the WGTU, to further strengthen universalization efforts.[49] These included continued outreach and coordination among relevant stakeholders and making use of the UN Human Rights Council's Universal Periodic Review mechanism to make the case for treaty accession.[50]

International assistance

The ATT Secretariat reported to the CSP7 on the activities implemented by the Voluntary Trust Fund (VTF) over the previous year.[51] The VTF continues to have a good financial basis for carrying out its work. Since its establishment in 2016, the VTF has received over $10 million in voluntary contributions from 28 states.[52] These contributions have supported, or are supporting, 65 projects aimed at helping states to strengthen or build capacity to comply

---

[46] US Department of State, Statement to CSP7, 30 Aug.–3 Sep. 2021.

[47] See United Nations, UN Treaty Collection, Status of Treaties, ch. XXVI Disarmament: 8. Arms Trade Treaty, endnote 3.

[48] Arms Trade Treaty, CSP7, Working Group on Treaty Universalization (WGTU), ATT/CSP7. WGTU/2021/CHAIR/677/Conf.Rep, 27 July 2021, paras 6–9.

[49] Arms Trade Treaty, ATT/CSP7/2021/SEC/681/Conf.FinRep.Rev1 (note 6), para. 22.

[50] United Nations Human Rights Council, 'Universal periodic review', [n.d.].

[51] ATT Secretariat, 'Report on the work of the ATT Voluntary Trust Fund (VTF) for the period August 2020 to August 2021', ATT/VTF/2021/CHAIR/678/Conf.Rep, 20 July 2021.

[52] ATT Secretariat, ATT/VTF/2021/CHAIR/678/Conf.Rep (note 51), para. 7.

with their ATT obligations. African states continue to be the largest group among beneficiaries of the VTF.[53]

Notwithstanding the limitations imposed by the pandemic, the Secretariat and the VTF continued to conduct limited outreach activities to promote the objectives of the fund and support the submission of good quality proposals. These activities included the production of two additional instructional videos on how to complete the grant application and budget forms.[54] In order to limit the pandemic-related disruptions to the implementation of assistance activities, the Secretariat also provided guidance to states, on the sidelines of CSP7, on how to apply for VTF funding in a way that makes provision for the impact of the pandemic on project implementation.[55]

Two other developments in 2021 could have a positive impact on the co-ordination of efforts in support of ATT implementation and support the Secretariat's task to 'facilitate the matching of offers of and requests for assistance' as defined in Article 18. In April, the Council of the EU approved funding for a project to provide support for various activities implemented by the Secretariat, including the creation of a database to match assistance needs and resources. The project also foresees a 'training the trainers' programme to support the creation of a pool of ATT experts at the regional and local level.[56] In addition, the amended template to submit the ATT initial report adopted at CSP7 (discussed earlier in this section) will now allow states parties to provide additional details on requests and offers of assistance.

The financial situation of the ATT

All ATT states parties and signatories, as well as states attending CSPs as observers, are required to make financial contributions to cover the costs of organizing the CSPs, subsidiary body meetings and the work of the ATT Secretariat.[57] However, the ATT is facing a difficult financial situation caused by partial or delayed payment of assessed contributions, which was noted with concern at CSP7.[58] As of 29 October 2021, 64 out of the 153 states that

---

[53] For a complete list of projects and beneficiaries see annexes B, C, D, E and H of ATT Secretariat, ATT/VTF/2021/CHAIR/678/Conf.Rep (note 51).

[54] ATT Secretariat, 'Arms Trade Treaty (ATT)—Voluntary Trust Fund (VTF) grant application form overview', YouTube, 6 Jan. 2022; ATT Secretariat, 'Arms Trade Treaty (ATT)—Voluntary Trust Fund (VTF) budget form', YouTube, 7 Jan. 2022.

[55] Remarks by the ATT Secretariat at the CSP7 side event 'The ATT Voluntary Trust Fund (VTF): VTF projects in the time of Covid', 31 Aug. 2021.

[56] Council Decision (CFSP) 2021/649 of 16 Apr. 2021 on Union support for activities of the ATT Secretariat in support of the implementation of the Arms Trade Treaty, *Official Journal of the European Union*, L133, 20 Apr. 2021, p. 60.

[57] Arms Trade Treaty, First Conference of States Parties (CSP1), 'Financial Rules for the Conferences of States Parties and the Secretariat', ATT/CSP1/CONF/2, 25 Aug. 2015, Rules 5.1, 5.2 and 6.

[58] Arms Trade Treaty, ATT/CSP7/2021/SEC/681/Conf.FinRep.Rev1 (note 6), para. 31. See also Varisco, Maletta and Robin, 'The Arms Trade Treaty' (note 3), pp. 562–63; and Varisco, Maletta and Robin (note 19), pp. 27, 29–30.

have been obliged to make contributions since 2015 were behind with their payments, creating an accumulated deficit of $473 432.[59] Solutions to the financial situation proposed in past years include the full application of Financial Rule 8.1(d) which—among other things—would potentially lead to limitations being placed on the voting rights of states in financial arrears for two or more years that have not entered into arrangements with the Secretariat in relation to the discharge of their financial obligations.[60]

To solve this problem the fifth conference of states parties (CSP5) mandated the ATT Management Committee to prepare guidelines on the implementation of Financial Rule 8.1(d).[61] CSP6 rejected the initial procedure proposed by the committee and deferred the matter to CSP7.[62] As mandated by states parties in February 2021, the committee prepared a revised draft procedure regarding Rule 8.1(d) which was considered and adopted at CSP7.[63] The procedure approved allows states in arrears to comply with their financial obligations through a single- or multi-year payment plan. It foresees a series of steps to follow when making such financial arrangements with the ATT Secretariat.[64]

Conclusions

The ATT continues to face long-standing challenges posed by downward trends in reporting, ratifications and financial contributions. In addition, the Covid-19 pandemic continued to have an impact on ATT meetings and processes. The hybrid format adopted for CSP7 represented an improvement compared to CSP6, enabling more interaction among participants and, more generally, allowing a larger attendance from capitals or from stakeholders

---

[59] ATT Secretariat, 'Status of contributions to ATT budgets', 29 Oct. 2021.

[60] Arms Trade Treaty, ATT/CSP1/CONF/2 (note 57), Rule 8.1; Varisco, Maletta and Robin (note 19), pp. 29–30; and Maletta, G. and Bromley, M., 'The Arms Trade Treaty', *SIPRI Yearbook 2019*, pp. 529–31.

[61] Arms Trade Treaty, Fifth Conference of States Parties (CSP5), 'Final report', ATT/CSP5/2019/SEC/536/Conf.FinRep.Rev1, 30 Aug. 2019, para. 35.

[62] Arms Trade Treaty, Sixth Conference of States Parties (CSP6), 'Final report', ATT/CSP6/2020/SEC/635/Conf.FinRep.Rev1, 21 Aug. 2020, para. 42; and Varisco, Maletta and Robin (note 3), p. 563. See also Arms Trade Treaty, CSP6 President-designate, 'Decision 15: Management Committee proposal on the draft elements for a Secretariat's procedure regarding Rule 8(1)D', ATT/CSP6.MC/2020/ MC/631/ Decision.FinArr8(1)d, 29 July 2020; Arms Trade Treaty, Management Committee, 'Draft elements for a Secretariat's procedure regarding Rule 8(1)d (reference paper)', ATT/CSP6.MC/2020/MC/609/ Conf.PropFinArr8(1)d, 17 July 2020; and Arms Trade Treaty, CSP6 President-designate, 'Decision 16: Application of Rule 8(1)d on the ATT Sponsorship Programme and Voluntary Trust Fund', ATT/CSP6. MC/2020/MC/632/Decision.ImpFR8(1)d, 29 July 2020.

[63] Arms Trade Treaty, Management Committee, 'Draft elements for a procedure regarding Rule 8(1) d (revised version based on comments received during the CSP6 cycle, the CSP7 informal preparatory meeting and intersessional consultations)', ATT/CSP7.MC/2021/MC/674/Conf.PropFinArr8(1)d, 16 July 2021; and Arms Trade Treaty, ATT/CSP7/2021/SEC/681/Conf.FinRep.Rev1 (note 6), para. 32.

[64] Arms Trade Treaty, Management Committee, 'Elements for a procedure regarding Rule 8(1)d', Sep. 2021; and Arms Trade Treaty, 'Procedure to follow when applying to make a financial arrangement with the ATT Secretariat in terms of Rule (1)d of the ATT Financial Rules', [n.d.].

with limited travel budgets. However, hybrid and virtual meetings present some limitations in terms of inclusivity and transparency. For example, some delegations have limited access to stable and secure internet connections or find it difficult to participate due to differences in time zones. While the ATT Sponsorship Programme will continue to provide financial support to delegates with limited means to attend ATT meetings in Geneva in person, current travel restrictions, disparities in Covid-19 vaccination roll-out around the world and differences in vaccine authorization policies are factors likely to limit in-person participation in the foreseeable future. This risks creating 'a hierarchy' that privileges delegates in the room (who, e.g., will be more able to engage in informal diplomatic interactions) over those attending online.[65] The reduced meeting times imposed by the virtual and hybrid formats also risk shrinking opportunities for meaningful discussion of issues related to treaty implementation. For instance, stricter time management at CSP7 led statements and interventions being cut short while the conference ended up concluding one day earlier than originally scheduled. This raises questions about the current format and length of CSPs and whether more time could instead be dedicated to intersessional work.

Finally, representatives of civil society organizations participating in the conference—although still stressing the existence of a discrepancy between states' commitments under the ATT and their practices—positively noted how discussions at CSP7, mostly as a result of the efforts made by Sierra Leone, appeared to be more substantial than in the past.[66] In addition, they also welcomed the 'stocktaking' initiative launched by the incoming German CSP8 presidency as the opportunity to assess, among other things, the outputs of previous meetings cycles.[67]

---

[65] Varisco, Maletta and Robin (note 19), pp. 27 and 33.

[66] See e.g. Pytlak (note 39), pp. 1–4.

[67] Women's International League for Peace and Freedom, 'Statement to the preparatory meeting of the seventh Conference of States Parties to the Arms Trade Treaty', 30 Apr. 2021.

II. Multilateral arms embargoes

MARK BROMLEY AND PIETER D. WEZEMAN

The United Nations Security Council uses its powers under Chapter VII of the UN Charter to impose arms embargoes—that is, restrictions on transfers of arms and related services and, in certain cases, dual-use items—that are binding for all UN member states and which form part of what the UN generally refers to as 'sanctions measures'.[1] During 2021, 13 UN arms embargoes were in force (table 14.2). The European Union (EU) also imposes arms embargoes under its Common Foreign and Security Policy (CFSP) that are binding for EU member states and which form part of what the EU generally refers to as 'restrictive measures'.[2] During 2021, 21 EU arms embargoes were in force. Of these EU embargoes, 10 matched the coverage of a UN arms embargo; 3 (Iran, South Sudan and Sudan) were broader in duration, geographical scope or the types of arms covered; while 8 had no UN counterpart. The Arab League had one arms embargo in place (on Syria) that also had no UN counterpart. In addition, one voluntary multilateral embargo imposed by the Conference on Security and Co-operation in Europe (CSCE, now renamed the Organization for Security and Co-operation in Europe, OSCE) was in force for arms deliveries to forces engaged in combat in the Nagorno-Karabakh area.[3] No new multilateral arms embargo was imposed in 2021.[4]

Multilateral arms embargoes varied in coverage of items (table 14.2). Most covered arms, military materiel and related services. Some UN and EU arms embargoes also covered certain exports or imports of dual-use items that can be used both for civilian purposes and to produce, maintain or operate conventional, biological, chemical or nuclear weapons.[5] Certain EU arms embargoes also covered equipment that might be used for internal repression or certain types of communication surveillance equipment. Multilateral arms embargoes also varied in the types of restrictions imposed and recipients targeted. Some placed a ban on all transfers to the state in question, while others banned transfers to a non-state actor or group of non-state actors. Certain

---

[1] United Nations, Security Council, 'Sanctions', [n.d.].

[2] These form part of what the EU generally refers to as 'restrictive measures'. European Council, 'Sanctions: How and when the EU adopts restrictive measures', [n.d.].

[3] Conference on Security and Co-operation in Europe, Committee of Senior Officials, Statement, annex 1 to Journal no. 2 of the Seventh Meeting of the Committee, Prague, 27–28 Feb. 1992.

[4] The last time a new multilateral arms embargo was imposed was in 2018, by the UN on South Sudan.

[5] The UN and EU embargoes on Iran and North Korea apply to dual-use items on the control lists of the Nuclear Suppliers Group (NSG) and the Missile Technology Control Regime (MTCR). The UN and EU embargoes on Somalia apply to certain dual-use items on the control lists of the Wassenaar Arrangement that can be used to produce, maintain and operate improvised explosive devices. The EU embargo on Russia applies to transfers to military end-users of all items on the EU's dual-use list. For details of the NSG, MTCR and the Wassenaar Arrangement see annex B, section III, in this volume.

Table 14.2. Multilateral arms embargoes in force during 2021

Target (entities or territory covered)[a]	Date embargo first imposed (duration type)	Materiel covered[a]	Key developments, 2021
United Nations arms embargoes			
Afghanistan (Taliban: NGF)	16 Jan. 2002 (OE)	Arms and related materiel and services	
Central African Republic (government: PT; NGF)	5 Dec. 2013 (TL)	Arms and military materiel (small arms exempted for government)	Extended until 31 July 2022
Democratic Republic of the Congo (government: PT; NGF)	28 July 2003 (TL)	Arms and military materiel	Extended until 1 July 2022
Iran (whole country: PT)	23 Dec. 2006 (TL)	Items related to nuclear weapon delivery systems; Items used in the nuclear fuel cycle	
Iraq (NGF)	6 Aug. 1990 (OE)	Arms and military materiel	
ISIL (Da'esh), al-Qaeda and associated individuals and entities (NGF)	16 Jan. 2002 (OE)	Arms and military materiel	
Korea, North (whole country)	15 July 2006 (OE)	Arms and military materiel; Items relevant to nuclear, ballistic missiles and other weapons of mass destruction related programmes	
Lebanon (NGF)	11 Aug. 2006 (OE)	Arms and military materiel	
Libya (government: PT; NGF)	26 Feb. 2011 (OE)	Arms and military materiel	
Somalia (government: PT; NGF)	23 Jan. 1992 (TL)	Arms and military materiel; Components for improvised explosive devices	Extended until 15 Nov. 2022
South Sudan (whole country)	13 July 2018 (TL)	Arms and military materiel	Extended until 31 May 2022
Sudan (Darfur: PT)	30 July 2004 (OE)	Arms and military materiel	
Yemen (NGF)	14 Apr. 2015 (OE)	Arms and military materiel	
European Union arms embargoes without UN counterpart or with broader scope than UN embargoes on the same target			
Belarus (whole country)	20 June 2011 (OE)	Arms and military materiel; Dual-use materiel for military use or military end-user; Communication surveillance equipment	Coverage expanded[c]; Extended until 28 Feb. 2022
China[b] (whole country)	27 June 1989 (OE)	Arms	
Egypt[b] (whole country)	21 Aug. 2013 (OE)	Equipment which might be used for internal repression	

Target (entities or territory covered)[a]	Date embargo first imposed (duration type)	Materiel covered[a]	Key developments, 2021
Iran (whole country)	27 Feb. 2007 (TL)	Equipment which might be used for internal repression; Communication surveillance equipment	Extended until 13 April 2022
Myanmar (whole country)	29 July 1991 (TL)	Arms and military materiel; Communication surveillance equipment	Extended until 30 April 2022
Russia (whole country)	31 July 2014 (TL)	Arms and military materiel; Dual-use materiel for military use or military end-user	Extended until 31 Jan. 2022
South Sudan (whole country)	18 July 2011 (OE)	Arms and military materiel	
Sudan (whole country)	15 Mar. 1994 (OE)	Arms and military materiel	
Syria (whole country)	9 May 2011 (OE)	Equipment which might be used for internal repression; Communication surveillance equipment	
Venezuela (whole country)	13 Nov. 2017 (OE)	Arms and equipment which might be used for internal repression; Communication surveillance equipment	Extended until 14 Nov. 2022
Zimbabwe (whole country)	18 Feb. 2002 (OE)	Arms and military materiel	Extended until 22 Feb. 2022

League of Arab States arms embargoes

Syria (whole country)	3 Dec. 2011 (OE)	Arms	

ISIL = Islamic State in Iraq and the Levant; NGF = non-governmental forces; OE = open-ended; PT = partial, i.e. embargo allows transfers to the state in question provided the supplier or recipient state has received permission from, or notified, the relevant United Nations sanctions committee or the UN Security Council; TL = time-limited.

[a] The target, entities and territory, and materiel covered may have changed since the first imposition of the embargo. The target, entities and material stated in this table are as at the end of 2021.

[b] The EU embargoes on China and Egypt are political declarations whereas the other embargoes are legal acts imposed by EU Council decisions and EU Council Regulations.

[c] Coverage in Belarus expanded to include dual-use materiel for military use or military end-user and communication surveillance.

Sources: United Nations, Security Council, 'Sanctions', [n.d.]; and Council of the EU, 'EU sanctions map', Updated 10 Feb. 2022. The SIPRI Arms Embargo Archive provides a detailed overview of most multilateral arms embargoes that have been in force since 1950 along with the principle instruments establishing or amending the embargoes.

UN arms embargoes were 'partial', in that they allowed transfers to the state in question provided the supplier or recipient state had received permission from, or notified, the relevant UN sanctions committee or the UN Security Council.

During 2021, as in previous years, the various UN investigations on the implementation of UN arms embargoes highlighted issues of varying types and substance. Unlike the UN, the EU, the Arab League and the OSCE do not have systematic mechanisms in place for monitoring compliance with their arms embargoes.

This section reviews significant developments and implementation issues in UN, EU and OSCE arms embargoes in 2021. In particular, the section highlights cases where new embargoes or amendments to embargoes were implemented, debated or demanded, and gives examples of actual or alleged violations.

United Nations arms embargoes: Developments and contraventions

During 2021 the UN introduced no new arms embargoes. Few significant amendments to existing embargoes were made.

This subsection provides a concise overview of the most notable developments in UN arms embargoes in 2021 in relation to Afghanistan, the Central African Republic (CAR), Iran, Democratic People's Republic of Korea (DPRK, North Korea), Libya, Myanmar, South Sudan, Sudan and Yemen. It discusses changes in embargoes, proposed embargoes and differences among UN Security Council members about UN arms embargoes. It also highlights notable violations of UN arms embargoes in 2021, or the lack thereof, primarily based on reports by UN panels and groups of experts that monitor UN arms embargoes. Such reports are the most detailed source of information on arms embargo violations. However, the ability of these groups and panels to provide a comprehensive picture of arms embargo implementation is constrained by the limited resources at their disposal, the fact that they must conduct their investigations under difficult and often dangerous circumstances, and—since 2020—the limitations on travel imposed due to the Covid-19 pandemic. Despite being established by the UN Security Council, groups and panels regularly report a lack of cooperation from states in their investigations. Also in 2021 there were allegations that China and Russia in particular again tried to limit the independence of certain groups and panels, and to block appointments of potential members in order to influence the outcome of their investigations.[6] In December 2021 the UN Security Council

---

[6] Lynch, C., 'Sunset for UN sanctions?', *Foreign Policy*, 14 Oct. 2021; Lynch, C. 'The worst bloody job in the world', *Foreign Policy*, 20 Oct. 2021; and Lynch, C., 'Russia's sanctions problem', *Foreign Policy*, 22 Oct. 2021.

adopted Resolution 2616 which outlined a range of steps aimed at improving compliance with UN arms embargoes. These included—where relevant and appropriate—giving peace operations a more direct role in assisting national authorities with detecting and combating embargo violations.[7] The resolution also requested 'the full cooperation' of member states with the corresponding panel of experts. It was adopted by a vote of 12 in favour, with China, India and Russia abstaining. China and Russia focused in their objections on the resolution's linking of peacekeeping missions to monitoring arms embargoes and did not mention the resolution's request for cooperation with the panels of experts.[8]

Afghanistan (the Taliban)

Since 2000 there have been several UN Security Council resolutions that imposed a full UN arms embargo on the Taliban and other groups that threaten the peace, stability and security in Afghanistan. Multiple sources have indicated that Taliban forces have over many years captured and stolen large amounts of weapons and ammunition from the Afghan armed forces.[9] It is likely that it was these weapons that the Taliban used to sustain its military operations, including the offensive that gave them control over the whole of Afghanistan in 2021.[10] In contrast, the reported violations of the UN embargoes have been limited in scope.[11] For example, the UN monitoring team reported in 2019 and 2020 that it had received information from the Afghan government indicating that new and refurbished small arms and light weapons (SALW) had reached the Taliban from abroad.[12] The monitoring team also reported that the Taliban had acquired dual-use items on the international commercial market and repurposed them for use in combat operations. This included civilian night-vision equipment, ammonium nitrate for making explosives, and small drones for adaption to reconnaissance and

---

[7] United Nations, 'Security Council resolves to consider during mandate renewals role of peace operations in curbing illicit weapons flow, adopting Resolution 2616 (2021) by recorded vote', Meeting coverage SC/14751, 22 Dec. 2021.

[8] United Nations, SC/14751 (note 7).

[9] Mitzer, S. and Oliemans, J., 'Disaster at hand: Documenting Afghan military equipment losses since June 2021 until August 14, 2021', *Oryx*, 23 June 2021; Broder, J. and Yousafzai, S., 'Arming the enemy in Afghanistan', *Newsweek*, 18 May 2015; Bodetti, A., 'How the US is indirectly arming the Taliban', The Diplomat, 13 June 2018; and Kuimova, A. and Wezeman, S. T., 'Transfers of major arms to Afghanistan between 2001 and 2020', SIPRI Topic Backgrounder, 3 Sep. 2021.

[10] On the conflict in Afghanistan see chapter 4, section III, in this volume.

[11] On the supply of arms to the Afghan armed forces see Kuimova and Wezeman (note 9).

[12] United Nations, Security Council, 'Tenth report of the analytical support and sanctions monitoring team pursuant to Resolution 2255 (2015) concerning the Taliban and other associated individuals and entities constituting a threat to the peace and stability and security of Afghanistan', S/2019/481, 13 June 2019, para. 83; and United Nations, Security Council, 'Eleventh report of the analytical support and sanctions monitoring team pursuant to resolution 2501 (2019) concerning the Taliban and other associated individuals and entities constituting a threat to the peace and stability and security of Afghanistan', S/2020/415, 27 May 2020, para. 97.

attack roles.[13] However, in 2021 the team did not mention anything about possible arms supplies from abroad to the Taliban. In addition, US allegations in 2017 that Russia had supplied SALW to the Taliban have never been independently confirmed.[14] The embargo continued to be in force after the Taliban seized Afghanistan in late 2021.

Central African Republic

The UN arms embargo on CAR bans any arms transfers to non-state armed groups while permitting deliveries to the government's security forces of most SALW if the government provides advance notification to the relevant UN sanctions committee, and other arms if they have received advance approval from the relevant committee. The embargo was first imposed in 2013 and has since been extended every year. Over the years numerous violations have been reported. In 2021 the panel of experts reported how, during fighting in early 2021, the state security forces lost weapons due to soldiers abandoning their posts, deserting or joining the ranks of the main armed group, the Coalition des patriotes pour le changement (CPC).[15]

With regard to arms supplies to the state security forces, the panel concluded that deliveries of equipment occurred 'at a pace unprecedented' since 2013, 'some of which were non-compliant and others in violation of the embargo'.[16] For example, the panel had obtained evidence that suggested that in early 2021 thousands of SALW and ammunition had been supplied from Sudan to CAR security forces without the proper advance notifications, or, in the case of larger calibre ammunition, without having received an exemption from the relevant UN sanctions committee.[17]

While the aim of preventing weapons reaching non-state groups in CAR has been widely supported, the restrictions on arms supplies to CAR security forces have been the subject of debate in the UN Security Council. In 2021 for the first time one of the five permanent members, China, abstained from the vote as it found that the draft resolution had not taken its concerns into account. China argued that as general elections had been held successfully and the security situation had improved in CAR, there was a 'growing disconnect between the Council's sanctions and the evolving situation on the

---

[13] United Nations, S/2019/481 (note 12), para. 84; United Nations, S/2020/415 (note 12), para. 97; and United Nations, Security Council, 'Twelfth report of the analytical support and sanctions monitoring team pursuant to resolution 2557 (2020) concerning the Taliban and other associated individuals and entities constituting a threat to the peace and stability and security of Afghanistan', S/2021/486, 1 June 2021, paras 87–89.

[14] Azami, D., 'Is Russia arming the Afghan Taliban?', BBC World Service, 2 Apr. 2018.

[15] United Nations, Security Council, 'Final report of the Panel of Experts on the Central African Republic extended pursuant to Security Council Resolution 2536 (2020)', S/2021/569, 25 June 2021, para. 63.

[16] United Nations, S/2021/569 (note 15), p. 3.

[17] United Nations, S/2021/569 (note 15), 25 June 2021, p. 2, para. 74 and p. 83.

ground' and that sanctions were increasingly threatening CAR's sovereignty.[18] Other Security Council members highlighted the need for CAR to have established adequate stockpile controls and to meet other benchmarks, including security sector reforms, set by the Security Council for lifting the restriction on arms supplies to CAR security forces.[19]

Iran

In accordance with the terms of the 2015 Joint Comprehensive Programme of Action (JCPOA), the UN embargo on transfers of arms to and from Iran were lifted in October 2020.[20] At that time the United States claimed that these restrictions, along with other UN sanctions that had been lifted under the terms of the JCPOA, were still in force due to the USA initiating the JCPOA's so-called 'snapback mechanism' in September 2020. This assertion was made despite the fact that the USA withdrew from the JCPOA in May 2018. The other signatories of the JCPOA saw no legal basis for the US claim. The US government also underlined that the USA would use its 'domestic authorities' to sanction any individual or entity involved in supplying arms to Iran.[21] In February 2021 President Joe Biden informed the UN Security Council that the USA had withdrawn these claims, made under the Trump administration, about the reimposition of UN sanctions on Tehran and that the Biden administration no longer contested the expiration of the arms embargo in October 2020.[22] In 2019 the US Defense Intelligence Agency claimed that Iran was 'evaluating and discussing' weapons acquisitions from Russia and China and that, if the UN arms embargo were lifted, Iran would potentially try to purchase—specifically—Su-30 combat aircraft, Yak-130 trainer aircraft, T-90 tanks and S-400 air defence systems from Russia.[23] These claims were later repeated by Trump administration officials during debates about the lifting of the Iran sanctions in 2020.[24] As of December 2021 there were no signs that these acquisitions had taken place.

The UN sanctions on the transfer to and from Iran of items that could contribute to the development of nuclear weapon delivery systems, unless these items have been approved in advance by the UN Security Council, will remain in force until 18 October 2023. Equivalent controls on transfers

---

[18] United Nations, 'Adopting Resolution 2588 (2021) by 14 votes in favour, 1 abstention, Security Council extends mandate of Expert Panel on Central African Republic, renews arms embargo', Meeting coverage SC/14590, 29 July 2021.

[19] United Nations, SC/14590 (note 18).

[20] On developments in the JCPOA see chapter 11, section II, in this volume.

[21] See Wezeman, P. D., 'Multilateral embargoes on arms and dual-use items', section II in 'Dual-use and arms trade controls', *SIPRI Yearbook 2021*, pp. 568–69.

[22] Lederer, E. M., 'Biden rescinds Trump's sanctions on Iran', AP News, 19 Feb. 2021.

[23] US Defence Intelligence Agency (DIA), *Iran Military Power: Ensuring Regime Survival and Securing Regional Dominance* (DIA: Washington, DC, Aug. 2019), p. 88.

[24] Brennan, D., 'Iran's foreign minister mocks "desperate" Pompeo over proposed arms embargo', *Newsweek*, 24 June 2020.

to Iran of items that could contribute to Iran's activities related to uranium enrichment, nuclear fuel reprocessing or heavy water, will remain in place until 18 October 2025. The JCPOA Procurement Channel, which was created to approve exemptions to these restrictions, continued its work during 2021 but without the involvement of the USA, due its withdrawal from the JCPOA. During 2021 one exemption request was submitted and one was approved.[25] The UN secretary-general's regular reports to the Security Council on the implementation of UN Security Resolution 2231 details investigations of transfers that may have taken place without the required prior approval of the procurement channel. The report of December 2021 stated that during 2021 the UN Secretariat was analysing evidence provided by Israel concerning Iran's transfer of 'UAV [uncrewed aerial vehicle] systems and capabilities to its proxies in Lebanon, Iraq, Syria and Yemen'.[26] It also noted that the Secretariat had sought information from Norway about an apparent attempt to transfer nuclear technology to Iran.[27] In September 2021 Norwegian authorities charged a German–Iranian national working at a technical university with violating Norway's export controls by hosting guest researchers from Iran and giving them access to technology covered by the scope of the UN sanctions.[28] The December report also noted that the Secretariat had sought information from Germany about an apparent attempt to transfer nuclear technology to Iran.[29] In September 2021 German police arrested a German–Iranian national suspected of exporting equipment to be used in Iran's nuclear and missile programmes.[30] In this case the items were not covered by the scope of the UN sanctions but were covered by the EU sanctions on Iran.[31]

North Korea

The UN arms embargo on North Korea prohibits transfers to and from North Korea of arms and items relevant to the development of nuclear weapons or

---

[25] United Nations, Security Council, 'Report of the Joint Commission to the Security Council on the status of the Procurement Working Group's decisions and on any implementation issues', S/2021/992, 8 Dec. 2021; and United Nations, Security Council, 'Report of the Joint Commission to the Security Council on the status of the Procurement Working Group's decisions and on any implementation issues', S/2021/578, 24 June 2021, para. 7.

[26] United Nations, Security Council, 'Implementation of Security Council Resolution 2231 (2015)', Secretary-General's report, S/2021/995, 8 Dec. 2021, para. 21.

[27] United Nations, S/2021/995 (note 26), 8 Dec. 2021, para. 12.

[28] 'Norway charges professor with violating sanctions on Iran', AP News, 29 Sep. 2021.

[29] United Nations, S/2021/995 (note 26), 8 Dec. 2021, para. 11.

[30] 'Germany arrests man for shipping equipment for Iran's nuclear programme', Reuters, 14 Sep. 2021.

[31] German Federal Court of Justice (GBA), Public Prosecutor, 'GBA: Festnahme wegen mutmaßlicher Verstöße gegen das Außenwirtschaftsgesetz' [GBA: Arrest for alleged violations of the Foreign Trade Act], Press release, 14 Sep. 2021.

ballistic missiles.[32] In 2021, the UN expert panel on North Korea reported that, despite a worsening economic situation and the imposition of border restrictions in response to the Covid-19 pandemic, Pyongyang 'maintained and improved its ballistic missile and nuclear infrastructure' and 'continued to seek material and technology for these programmes overseas'.[33] The panel repeated allegations made by states and reported in previous panel reports concerning cooperation between North Korea and both Syria and Iran on 'missile-related projects' and efforts by North Korean officials to 'sell weapons in Africa and South-East Asia', but did not provide any additional details.[34]

During 2021 the panel paid particular attention to the potential role of international collaboration between universities and research institutes in enabling access to knowledge and technology relevant to North Korea's nuclear weapons and missile programmes. The UN arms embargo requires states to prevent specialized teaching or training of DPRK nationals within their territories or by their nationals of disciplines which could contribute to the DPRK's proliferation sensitive nuclear activities or the development of nuclear weapon delivery systems.[35] In particular, the panel investigated cases of collaboration between North Korean and Chinese academics on 'composite structures and vibration analysis', noting that both processes 'have industrial applications but are essential in the design of both nuclear equipment and ballistic missile programmes'.[36] In response to questions from the panel about the nature of this joint work, China responded that there were 'no prohibited academic exchanges, scientific cooperation or joint studies between Chinese universities with the DPRK'.[37]

Libya

The UN arms embargo on Libya bans arms transfers and technical assistance related to military activities to non-state armed groups but permits deliveries to the internationally recognized Government of National Accord (GNA), provided that the transfers have been approved in advance by the UN sanctions committee for Libya. In March 2021 the GNA and the Libyan House of Representatives—which is supported by the Libyan National Army (LNA), also known as the Haftar Army—formed a Government of National Unity.[38] However, throughout 2021 there was no substantial progress on

---

[32] On developments in North Korea's nuclear weapons programme see chapter 10, section IX, in this volume.

[33] United Nations, Security Council, Midterm report of the 1718 Panel of Experts, S/2021/777, 8 Sep. 2021, Summary.

[34] United Nations, S/2021/777 (note 33), para. 21.

[35] UN Security Council Resolution 2270, 2 Mar. 2016, para. 5.

[36] United Nations, S/2021/777 (note 33), para. 11.

[37] United Nations, S/2021/777 (note 33), 8 Sep. 2021, para. 11.

[38] On developments in Libya see chapter 6, section IV, in this volume.

creating a unified military structure' and the LNA remained in existence as an independent force.[39]

Since the imposition of the embargo in 2011, the UN panel of experts on Libya has reported on many cases of violations and named the governments of Russia, Turkey and the United Arab Emirates, among others, as having delivered weapons in contravention of the embargo's terms.[40] In March 2021 the panel of experts reported that in 2020 and the first months of 2021, the arms embargo had remained 'totally ineffective' and that several states had extensively supported parties to the conflict in complete disregard for the UN sanctions measures.[41] The panel also noted that the states that supplied arms had control of the entire supply chain, which complicated the detection, disruption or interdiction of arms flows in contravention to the UN arms embargo.[42] Excerpts of a confidential report by the panel of experts, published by the press in December 2021, showed the panel's conclusion that while the intensity of arms supplies in violation of the embargo had diminished, the arms embargo remained totally ineffective throughout 2021. In particular, the panel noted that foreign fighters from Chad, Sudan and Russia remained active in Libya.[43]

Myanmar

In February 2021 Myanmar's elected government was overthrown in a violent military coup that was widely condemned and led to calls by states for the imposition of UN sanctions against Myanmar, including an arms embargo.[44] The UN General Assembly adopted in June 2021 a resolution which called upon all UN member states to prevent the flow of arms into Myanmar.[45] The call was the only element of actual pressure in a resolution that called on the armed forces of Myanmar to respect the 8 November 2020 general election in Myanmar, end the state of emergency and respect all human rights. The original draft resolution had included more forceful language, calling for an immediate suspension of the direct and indirect supply, sale or transfer of all weapons and munitions.[46] Of the 193 members of the General Assembly, 119 voted in favour of the resolution, 1 (Belarus) voted against and

---

[39] 'Libya holds talks about army unification', *Middle East Monitor*, 15 Dec, 2021.

[40] Wezeman (note 21), pp. 571–74. See also equivalent chapters in the *SIPRI Yearbook 2012* through *SIPRI Yearbook 2020*.

[41] United Nations, Security Council, Final report of the Panel of Experts on Libya established pursuant to Security Council Resolution 1973 (2011), S2021/229, 8 Mar. 2021, Summary, p. 2.

[42] United Nations, S2021/229 (note 41), Summary, p. 2.

[43] 'Fewer Libya arms embargo breaches but foreign fighters remain: UN panel', France 24, 1 Dec. 2021.

[44] Lederer, E. M., 'UN assembly condemns Myanmar coup, calls for arms embargo', PBS News Hour, 18 June 2021.

[45] UN General Assembly Resolution 75/287, 25 June 2021, para. 7.

[46] Nichols, M., 'UN vote on call to stop arms supply to Myanmar postponed', Reuters, 17 May 2021.

36 abstained.[47] Among the abstentions were China, Russia and India, which were the most important arms suppliers to Myanmar in 2017–2021.[48] During an informal Security Council meeting, the USA publicly suggested possible sanctions against the Myanmar military, including an arms embargo.[49] However, during 2021 there were no public indications of a draft resolution including an arms embargo having been circulated in the UN Security Council.

South Sudan

The UN arms embargo on South Sudan prohibits transfers of arms and military materiel to government forces and armed groups in South Sudan. Arms and related materiel, as well as technical training and assistance, that are provided solely in support of the implementation of the terms of the peace agreement in South Sudan are allowed if approved in advance by the UN sanctions committee for South Sudan. In April 2021 the embargo was extended with one significant amendment, the inclusion of 'benchmarks' which outlined specific areas where progress made on the part of the Revitalized Transitional Government of National Unity (RTGNU) and the South Sudanese defence and security forces could lead to the modification or lifting of the arms embargo.[50] These benchmarks included completing a Strategic Defense and Security Review process; forming a unified command structure for the Necessary Unified Forces; making progress on the disarmament, demobilization and reintegration process and on arms and ammunition stockpile management; and implementing a plan for addressing conflict-related sexual violence.

When the embargo was imposed in 2018 and when it was extended in 2019 and 2020, China and Russia abstained from the UN Security Council votes, arguing that the embargo's continuation in combination with targeted sanctions on South Sudanese individuals did not take into account progress in the peace process in South Sudan.[51] Despite both countries voting in favour of extending the sanctions on South Sudan in 2021, China stressed that it did not support the arms embargo and noted its hope that an assessment based on the new benchmarks would lead to the UN Security Council lifting the arms embargo as soon as possible.[52] India and Kenya voted against the extension, arguing that there had been significant developments towards peace and

---

[47] United Nations, General Assembly, 75th Session, Official record of the 83rd plenary meeting, A/75/PV.83, 18 June 2021, p. 5.

[48] See chapter 9, section III, in this volume.

[49] Lederer, E. M., 'US urges arms embargo and sanctions against Myanmar military', AP News, 9 Apr. 2021.

[50] UN Security Council Resolution 2577, 28 May 2021.

[51] Wezeman (note 21), pp. 570–71.

[52] United Nations, Security Council, 'United States of America: Draft resolution', S/2021/518, 1 June 2021, p. 23 (Annex 17, Chinese statement).

stability in South Sudan.[53] Kenya stressed that the African Union and the Intergovernmental Authority on Development had both called for lifting the arms embargo and other UN sanctions on South Sudan.[54]

During 2021 the UN panel of experts on South Sudan reported no cases of arms embargo violations. It did, however, note the widespread availability of ammunition in South Sudan.[55]

Sudan

The UN embargo on Sudan prohibits transfers to non-state actors in the region of Darfur. The UN panel of experts on Sudan reported that in 2021 one of the main armed groups in Darfur, the Sudan Liberation Army/Abdul Wahid, acquired weapons.[56] However, the panel did not provide the types or origins of the weapons. The panel also reported that SALW were brought into Darfur by cross-border dealers and offered at markets in Darfur.[57]

Yemen

The UN arms embargo on Yemen prohibits transfers to non-state actors in the country. However, the UN panel of experts on Yemen has reported continuous violations of the embargo since it was imposed in 2015. For 2021 the panel described how the evidence it had obtained showed that the Houthi rebels in Yemen had been able to produce UAVs and rockets using components sourced from the commercial market in Europe, the Middle East and Asia.[58] The panel also inspected SALW, including over 6000 assault rifles, seized by the USA on ships with Yemeni crews in the Arabian Sea.[59] Based on images of one of the seized cargoes and an inspection of the other, the panel concluded that many of the weapons had technical characteristics consistent with weapons made in China, including in 2016 and 2017. For other weapons the panel concluded that they had technical characteristics consistent with weapons made in Iran. Iran denied any involvement in the transport of the weapons whereas China had not yet responded to request from the panel. The panel drew no final conclusions about the intended final destination of the weapons nor about their immediate country of origin.

---

[53] United Nations, S/2021/518 (note 52), p. 24 (annex 18, Indian statement) and p. 25 (annex 19, Kenyan statement).

[54] United Nations, S/2021/518 (note 52), p. 25 (annex 19, Kenyan statement).

[55] United Nations, Security Council, 'Final report of the Panel of Experts on South Sudan submitted pursuant to Resolution 2521 (2020)', S/2021/365, 15 Apr. 2021, paras 84–86.

[56] United Nations, Security Council, 'Final report of the Panel of Experts on the Sudan', S/2022/48, 24 Jan. 2022, para. 53. On the armed conflict in Sudan see chapter 7, section IV, in this volume.

[57] United Nations, S/2022/48 (note 56), paras 77–89.

[58] United Nations, Security Council, 'Final report of the Panel of Experts on Yemen', S/2022/50, 26 Jan. 2022, pp. 23–25. On the armed conflict in Yemen see chapter 6, section V, in this volume.

[59] United Nations, S/2022/50 (note 58), pp. 26–32.

European Union arms embargoes: Developments and implementation challenges

During 2021 the EU introduced no new arms embargoes. However, it did expand the coverage of the embargo on Belarus. The European Parliament called for arms embargoes on Saudi Arabia and Ethiopia. Both within and among EU member states and in the European Parliament there have been continuous discussions since 2015 about the imposition of restrictions on arms supplies to Saudi Arabia in response to concerns about Saudi military operations in Yemen. In February 2016, October 2017, October 2018 and September 2020 the European Parliament adopted resolutions calling for an EU arms embargo on Saudi Arabia.[60] The European Parliament reiterated this call in a resolution adopted in February 2021.[61] In response to the violence in Ethiopia, which escalated further in 2021, the European Parliament called on EU member states to halt exports of arms and surveillance technology to Ethiopia that are being used to facilitate attacks on civilians and to perpetrate human rights violations.[62] The EU did not take any further steps to impose an actual EU arms embargo.

In June 2021 the EU expanded the coverage of its existing set of sanctions on Belarus. The decision was made following the unlawful forced landing of an intra-EU flight in Minsk in May 2021 in order to allow the authorities in Belarus to arrest opposition activist Roman Protasevich and his girlfriend Sofia Sapega. The expanded sanctions included flight restrictions, travel bans and asset freezes but also banned exports of dual-use items 'for military use in Belarus or for any military end-user in Belarus' and exports of 'equipment, technology or software intended primarily for use in the monitoring or interception' of telecommunications networks 'by, or on behalf of, the Belarusian authorities'.[63]

This is the second time the EU has included a ban on exports of dual-use items for a military use or for any military end-user in its sanctions measures. Equivalent restrictions have been part of the EU's sanctions on Russia since 2014. Ensuring full compliance with these restrictions has proved challenging given the wide range of items captured by the EU's dual-use list and efforts by Russian companies and the Russian government to mask the military purpose of acquisitions. In 2021 a report by Conflict Armament

---

[60] European Parliament resolution of 17 Sep. 2020 on Arms export: Implementation of Common Position 2008/944/CFSP, 2020/2003(INI), 17 Sep. 2020, para. 11. See also Wezeman (note 21), p. 575.

[61] European Parliament resolution of 11 Feb. 2021 on the humanitarian and political situation in Yemen, 2021/2539(RSP), 11 Feb. 2021, para. 13.

[62] European Parliament resolution of 7 Oct. 2021 on the humanitarian situation in Tigray, 2021/2902(RSP), 7 Oct. 2021, para. 25.

[63] Council Decision (CFSP) 2021/1031 of 24 June 2021 amending Council Decision 2012/642/CFSP concerning restrictive measures in view of the situation in Belarus, *Official Journal of the European Union*, L224, 24 June 2021.

Research documented several cases in which Russian military drones had been built using components produced in EU member states.[64] In 2021 media reports also alleged that attempts had been made by companies based in EU member states to supply small arms to Russia and Belarus.[65] Unlike in the case of UN arms embargoes there are no mechanisms in place to monitor the implementation of EU arms embargoes.[66]

This is the fourth time the EU has included a ban on exports of tele-communications monitoring systems in its sanctions measures. Similar restrictions are also part of the EU sanctions on Iran, Syria, Venezuela and Myanmar.[67] Controls on cybersurveillance items were also a key focus of the recent recast of the EU dual-use regulation which entered into force in 2021 and recent discussions between the EU and US on trade issues (see section IV in this chapter).

Conclusions

Several major differences in perceptions about UN arms embargoes that had been particularly pronounced in 2020 became less severe in 2021. For example, the new US administration did not pursue the previous administration's attempts to force other states to consider the UN arms embargo on Iran as being still in force. In addition, after the introduction of benchmarks for modifications of the embargo on South Sudan, China and Russia voted in favour of the arms embargo, after having abstained in previous years. However, in other cases views on the utility or desirability of multilateral arms embargoes were mixed, as could be witnessed when in the Security Council no draft was tabled for an embargo on Myanmar, despite a General Assembly resolution calling for member states to prevent arms flows to Myanmar. Similarly, the EU Council did not threaten or impose arms embargoes on Saudi Arabia or Ethiopia even when the European Parliament called for them.

Compliance with UN arms embargoes was mixed in 2021. There were reports of significant violations of the UN arms embargo on Libya, likely violations of the embargo on non-state actors in Yemen and contraventions of some of the restrictions on arms imports by the government of CAR. Cases of possible violations of the embargoes on Iran and North Korea involving research institutes and universities were also reported. As before, the UN Security Council did not take any actions against the countries reportedly

---

[64] Conflict Armament Research, *Weapons of the War in Ukraine: A Three-Year Investigation of Weapon Supplies into Donetsk and Luhansk* (Conflicts Armaments Research: London, Nov. 2021), p. 162.

[65] Rettman, A., 'EU arms firms trying to flout Belarus and Russia ban', *EU Observer*, 6 Oct. 2021.

[66] For a discussion of calls for the creation of mechanisms for monitoring EU arms embargoes see Bromley, M. and Wezeman, P. D., 'Multilateral arms embargoes', *SIPRI Yearbook 2020*, pp. 544–45.

[67] See European Commission, 'EU sanctions map', [n.d.].

linked to the embargo violations. In contrast there were no reports of, for example, major violations of the UN embargo on the Taliban in Afghanistan and the embargo on South Sudan. There were limited reports of violations of EU arms embargoes which again highlighted the potential need for more robust monitoring measures.

III. The multilateral export control regimes

KOLJA BROCKMANN

The Australia Group (AG), the Missile Technology Control Regime (MTCR), the Nuclear Suppliers Group (NSG) and the Wassenaar Arrangement on Export Controls for Conventional Arms and Dual-use Goods and Technologies (Wassenaar Arrangement, WA) are the four main multilateral export control regimes.[1] The regimes are informal groups of participating states which agree on guidelines for the implementation of export controls on goods and technologies in the areas of chemical and biological weapons, missiles and other weapon of mass destruction (WMD) delivery systems, nuclear fuel cycle technologies and nuclear weapons, and conventional arms and dual-use goods and technologies (table 14.3). Within each regime the participating states coordinate trade controls and related policies, share good practices on their implementation, and exchange information on proliferation cases, illicit acquisition attempts and licence denials, and in some cases licences granted. The participating states discuss technological developments and emerging technologies to continuously update the control lists defining relevant items that should be subject to controls. Through these functions, the regimes create important forums for exchanges among national policy and licensing officials, technical experts, and enforcement and intelligence officers—including across geopolitical divides. The participating states take all decisions in the regimes by consensus, and the resulting guidelines, control lists and good practice documents are politically rather than legally binding. Each participating state implements regime-prescribed trade controls and policies through national laws and their respective national export control systems. Despite the exclusive and non-binding nature of the regimes, their guidelines and control lists have been adopted by or adapted into the national export control systems of a large and increasing number of non-participating states—effectively creating international standards.[2]

In 2021 the Covid-19 pandemic continued to significantly affect the work of the regimes. Differences in the public health situation and related restrictions in the participating states, and the timing and severity of infection waves, meant that some of the regimes were more affected than others at the scheduled times of their annual plenary meetings and during their intersessional work. Restrictions on international travel and in-person meetings prevented the annual plenaries of the AG and the WA from taking

---

[1] For brief descriptions and lists of the participating states in each of these regimes see annex B, section III, in this volume.

[2] Bauer, S., 'Main developments and discussions in the export control regimes', *Literature Review for the Policy and Operations Evaluations Department of the Dutch Ministry of Foreign Affairs: Final Report* (SIPRI: Stockholm, Aug. 2017), p. 62.

place, while the NSG and MTCR plenaries did go ahead, albeit often with smaller delegations and, in the case of the MTCR, fewer states attending. The pandemic largely prevented the regimes from making progress on possible reform efforts and addressing structural and operational challenges.

In addition to these internal challenges, the effectiveness and legitimacy of the regimes were called into question by a range of external developments and initiatives. The United States and the European Union (EU) continued to identify emerging technologies and specific items that may warrant additional controls, including, so far mainly by the USA, expanded national controls. They also deepened their bilateral engagement on possible export controls outside of the regimes, particularly concerning controls based on national security and human rights reasons (see section IV in this chapter).[3] Nevertheless, the EU and the USA also continued to stress the importance of the regimes and their ongoing commitment to complying with their guidelines and principles. The EU in particular emphasized the primary role of the regimes in agreeing and harmonizing export controls. In the context of rising geopolitical tensions, much of the motivation of the USA behind these initiatives is building support for tighter restrictions on transfers of dual-use items to China. While China continues to comply with NSG principles and claims to adhere to the MTCR guidelines, it has been vocal in opposing EU and US initiatives outside of the regimes.[4] In November 2021 China secured the narrow adoption of a resolution in the United Nations General Assembly First Committee that took aim at the use of national and multilateral export control measures for national security purposes. The resolution noted 'with concern that undue restrictions on exports to developing countries of materials, equipment and technology, for peaceful purposes persist'.[5] In contrast, as part of the reform of its export control law, China also introduced controls based on national security rationales and reciprocal measures.[6]

The Australia Group

The AG provides a forum for participating states to coordinate and harmonize export controls on chemical and biological weapons and related dual-

---

[3] US Department of Commerce, Bureau of Industry and Security, 'Advance notice of proposed rulemaking: Review of controls for certain emerging technologies', *Federal Register*, vol. 83, no. 223 (19 Nov. 2018); Regulation (EU) 2021/821 of the European Parliament and of the Council of 20 May 2021 setting up a Union regime for the control of exports, brokering, technical assistance, transit and transfer of dual-use items (recast), *Official Journal of the European Union*, L206, 11 June 2021; and European Commission, 'EU–US launch Trade and Technology Council to lead values-based global digital transformation', Press release, 15 June 2021.

[4] Xinhua, 'White paper: China's export controls', *Global Times*, 29 Dec. 2021.

[5] UN General Assembly Resolution 76/234, 24 Oct. 2021, Preamble.

[6] Congressional Research Service, 'China issues new export control law and related policies', Insight paper no. 11524, 26 Oct. 2020.

Table 14.3. The four multilateral export control regimes

Regime (year established)	Scope	No. of participants[a]	2021 plenary chair	2021 plenary status
Australia Group (1985)	Equipment, materials, technology and software that could contribute to chemical and biological weapons activities	43	Australia	Cancelled
Missile Technology Control Regime (1987)	Unmanned aerial vehicles capable of delivering weapons of mass destruction	35	Russia	Sochi, 4–8 October 2021
Nuclear Suppliers Group (1974)	Nuclear and nuclear-related materials, software and technology	48[b]	Belgium[c]	Brussels, 22–25 June 2021
Wassenaar Arrangement (1996)	Conventional arms and dual-use items and technologies	42	Hungary	Cancelled

[a] Participant numbers are as of 31 December 2021.

[b] In addition, the European Union and the chair of the Zangger Committee are permanent observers of the Nuclear Suppliers Group.

[c] The Nuclear Suppliers Group changed its procedures so that participating states host a plenary at the end of their period as chair. At the 2021 NSG plenary Belgium handed the chair over to Poland for the 2021–22 period.

Sources: Australia Group; Missile Technology Control Regime; Nuclear Suppliers Group; and Wassenaar Arrangement on Export Controls for Conventional Arms and Dual-use Goods and Technologies.

use goods and technologies. In doing so, the AG seeks to reduce the risk of contributing to the proliferation of chemical and biological weapons.[7] The AG was created in 1985 upon an initiative by Australia. At the time there was significant momentum for strengthening trade control measures for the non-proliferation of chemical weapons after a UN investigation found that chemical weapons used in the 1980–88 Iran–Iraq war had been produced using precursor chemicals, equipment and materials procured from several Western states.[8] While the initial focus of the AG was consequently on chemical weapons and precursors, its coverage has since significantly expanded to include biological weapons and a wider range of equipment, materials and technology relevant to the development, production and use of chemical and biological weapons.[9] The AG is permanently chaired by Australia which also runs an informal secretariat situated within the Australian Department of Foreign Affairs and Trade.

The AG has 43 participants, including the EU which is a member with full voting rights. While the number of participants has increased considerably

[7] Australia Group, 'The Australia Group: An introduction', [n.d.]; and Australia Group, 'Objectives of the Group', [n.d.].

[8] Australia Group, 'The origins of the Australia Group', [n.d.].

[9] Australia Group (note 8).

from the original 18 in 1985, membership growth has largely stagnated, with the AG only admitting 2 new participating states in the last 10 years—Mexico (2013) and India (2018).[10] The AG encourages states not participating in the regime to become AG adherents by notifying the chair of their 'political commitment to adhere' to the guidelines and common control lists. The AG offers adherents access to additional information and assistance from AG participating states. Kazakhstan is the only state which has submitted the required notification.[11]

During 2021, the AG did not hold its regular annual plenary meeting in Paris, marking the second year in a row during which the regime did not convene its main decision-making body. In contrast to the other multilateral export control regimes, the AG did not issue any public statements or updates in any form on the continued implementation of its work in 2021. Despite consensus reached among the AG participating states in 2020 on resuming some of its official meetings in a virtual format, there was no reporting on any such meetings in 2021. The AG adopted one minor change to the Control List of Dual-use Biological Equipment and Related Technology and Software by adding a control on 'software designed for' already controlled nucleic acid assemblers and synthesizers.[12]

The Missile Technology Control Regime

The MTCR seeks to prevent the proliferation of missiles and other uncrewed delivery systems capable of delivering chemical, biological or nuclear (CBN) weapons. It was created in 1987 with the objective of contributing to preventing the proliferation of nuclear weapons by creating harmonized export controls on goods and technologies related to missiles capable of carrying such weapons.[13] Since then, the scope of the MTCR has expanded to include ballistic and cruise missiles, and all uncrewed aerial vehicles (UAVs) capable of delivering CBN weapons.[14] The MTCR's restrictive Category I covers missiles and UAVs 'capable of delivering a payload of at least 500 kg to a range of at least 300 km', or destined to be used to deliver CBN weapons. The MTCR participating states—referred to as 'the partners'—should exercise an 'unconditional strong presumption of denial' for transfers of items covered by Category I and should only diverge from this on 'rare occasions'.[15] Category II covers missiles and UAVs with a maximum range

[10] Australia Group, 'Australia Group participants', [n.d.].

[11] Australia Group, 'Australia Group adherents', [n.d.].

[12] Australia Group, 'Control list of dual-use biological equipment and related technology and software', 16 Aug. 2021.

[13] Missile Technology Control Regime, 'Frequently asked questions (FAQs)', [n.d.]. The G7 states are Canada, France, Germany, Italy, Japan, the United Kingdom and the United States.

[14] Missile Technology Control Regime (note 13).

[15] Missile Technology Control Regime (note 13).

of at least 300 km and a wide range of less-sensitive and dual-use goods, materials and technologies for missile, UAV and space-launch applications.[16] Partner governments should make transfers of such items subject to case-by-case licensing decisions and to a strong presumption of denial if they are 'intended for use in WMD delivery'.[17]

The membership of the MTCR has grown from the Group of Seven (G7) largest industrialized states to 35 participating states. Although several pending applications have been acknowledged in MTCR public statements—albeit without identifying the applying states—the regime's membership has not increased since the 2016 admission of India.[18]

Since 2014 the MTCR has had a formalized system for non-partner states to be recognized as 'adherents' to the MTCR guidelines and control lists. The MTCR invites all states to submit declarations of adherence and incentivizes becoming an adherent with invitations to technical outreach meetings, briefings on control list changes, meetings with the MTCR chair and access to some presentations from the MTCR Licencing and Enforcement Experts Meeting (LEEM).[19] However, since the creation of the adherent status, only three states have unilaterally declared their adherence: Estonia, Kazakhstan and Latvia. In 2021 no additional states declared their adherence.

The 2020 MTCR plenary meeting was set to take place in Innsbruck and had originally been postponed to March 2021, but the continued impact of the Covid-19 pandemic meant it had to be cancelled again. The partners did not find consensus on further postponing the 2020 plenary, with concerns including those from the incoming Russian chair that it would mean moving two plenaries too close together. As a result, Austria was unable to host a plenary during its chairship although informal consultations among some of the partners continued. The 2021 MTCR plenary took place according to the regular plenary schedule, from 4–8 October in Sochi, Russia, where Austria handed over the chair to Russia. However, officially due to national travel restrictions affecting many partners and concerns over the public health situation in Russia, several partners were unable or chose not to send a delegation, while many others only sent smaller delegations.[20] This also meant that discussions of a US proposal to change the parameters based on which UAVs are covered by Category I—and the USA's unilateral adoption of this change at the national level in 2020—were postponed again.[21]

---

[16] Missile Technology Control Regime, 'MTCR Guidelines and the Equipment, Software and Technology annex', [n.d.].

[17] Missile Technology Control Regime (note 13).

[18] Missile Technology Control Regime, 'Partners', [n.d.]; and Missile Technology Control Regime, 'Public statement from the plenary meeting of the Missile Technology Control Regime, Sochi, 8 October 2021', 26 Oct. 2021.

[19] Missile Technology Control Regime, 'Adherence policy', [n.d.].

[20] Regime delegate, Interview with the author, 27 Aug. 2021.

[21] Kimball, D. G., 'US reinterprets MTCR Rules', Arms Control Association, Sep. 2020.

As in the previous year, the Information Exchange Meeting (IEM) and the LEEM discussed 'ballistic missile developments and tests', 'proliferation trends and procurement activities', acquisition strategies, 'risks and challenges posed by intangible technology transfers', 'catch-all controls', 'transit and trans-shipment issues', 'outreach to industry' and 'national experiences to strengthen export control enforcement'.[22]

The MTCR plenary in Sochi adopted only minimal changes to the MTCR's Equipment, Software and Technology Annex, adding 'algorithms' and 'tables' to the list of examples provided of what can constitute controlled 'technical data' according to the Annex, and implementing several editorial changes.[23]

In the final days of the Austrian chairship, in September 2021 the Austrian chair conducted the MTCR's first outreach visit to Mexico.[24] The visit included a customs demonstration at Mexico City's airport. Following the handover of the MTCR chair to Russia, the Russian chair carried out the MTCR's eighth outreach mission to Kazakhstan in November 2021.[25]

The Hague Code of Conduct against Ballistic Missile Proliferation

The Hague Code of Conduct against Ballistic Missile Proliferation (HCOC) is a multilateral transparency and confidence-building measure covering ballistic missile and space-launch vehicle policies and activities.[26] It originated from discussions within the framework of the MTCR in 2002 but was created as an independent politically binding instrument that complements the MTCR in its goal of missile non-proliferation.[27] The HCOC is open for subscription by all states and currently counts 143 subscribing states. In 2021, no additional states subscribed to the HCOC.[28]

The HCOC is a political commitment by subscribing states to implement a set of transparency and confidence-building measures. Subscribing states commit to providing annual declarations on their national ballistic missile and space-launch vehicle programmes and policies. They also exchange pre-launch notifications on launches and test flights of ballistic missiles and

---

[22] Missile Technology Control Regime, 'Public statement from the plenary meeting of the Missile Technology Control Regime, Sochi, 8 October 2021' (note 18).

[23] Missile Technology Control Regime, 'Equipment, Software and Technology annex' [Current version, showing changes from previous version], 8 Oct. 2021.

[24] MTCR, @MTCR Chair, 'My gratitude goes to our Mexican colleagues for warmly welcoming us to the first outreach Meeting with @Mexico. Their excellent presentations and engaging questions manifested Mexico's high commitment and capacity. Looking forward to remain in contact with #Mexico. #MTCR', Twitter, 29 Sep. 2021.

[25] MTCR, @MTCR Chair, 'The MTCR carried out its eighth "outreach" mission to Kazakhstan on November 24, 2021. The MTCR delegation received a warm welcome and held fruitful discussions with the country's government agencies, which displayed Nur-Sultan's strong commitment to non-proliferation.', Twitter, 22 Dec. 2021.

[26] Hague Code of Conduct, 'What is HCoC?', Feb. 2020.

[27] Brockmann, K., *Controlling Ballistic Missile Proliferation: Assessing Complementarity Between the HCoC, MTCR and UNSCR 1540*, HCOC Research Paper no. 7 (June 2020).

[28] Hague Code of Conduct, 'List of HCoC subscribing states', Feb. 2020.

space launch vehicles.[29] The HCOC does not have a verification mechanism for subscribing states' declarations and notifications.

The 20th annual regular meeting of the HCOC was held in Vienna on 7–8 July 2021 under the chairship of Argentina. Delegations from 77 of the 143 subscribing states registered to attend, the highest number of participating delegations since these numbers have been reported in the meeting press releases. On assuming the HCOC chair, Argentina outlined its key objectives for the period 2021–22 as continuing to work towards universalization and full implementation, and preparing activities to mark the occasion of the 20-year anniversary of the Code.[30]

As the previous HCOC chair, Switzerland had organized and participated in a range of outreach meetings in the 2020–21 period, notably a series of HCOC outreach activities funded by the EU and implemented by the Foundation for Strategic Research (FRS). In March 2021 the Swiss chair and the Geneva Centre for Security Policy conducted a regional outreach seminar for the Middle East and North Africa region.[31] The FRS organized an expert mission to South Sudan and a regional outreach seminar for francophone countries in March 2021, a regional outreach seminar for Latin America in April 2021, and a virtual outreach seminar for CARICOM countries in June 2021.[32] Since taking over as chair in July, Argentina also participated in outreach activities and public meetings on behalf of the HCOC, including a virtual outreach meeting with the Democratic Republic of Congo in November 2021.[33]

The Nuclear Suppliers Group

The NSG seeks to contribute to the non-proliferation of nuclear weapons by implementing guidelines for export controls on transfers of nuclear and nuclear-related material, equipment, software and technology. It was established in 1974 as a reaction to India's first nuclear test, the first explosion of a nuclear weapon by a state not recognized as a nuclear-weapon state by

---

[29] Hague Code of Conduct, 'How to join HCoC', Nov. 2018.

[30] Hague Code of Conduct, '20th regular meeting of the subscribing states to the Hague Code of Conduct against Ballistic Missile Proliferation (HCOC)', Press release, July 2021.

[31] Swiss Security Policy (Swiss Federal Department for Foreign Affairs International Security Division), @SecurityPolCH, 'Today, following up on [Swiss flag] efforts to increase universalisation of #HCoC, we held an event with @TheGCSP discussing the Code and ballistic missile activities with states from the MENA region. Thanks to @SIPRIorg, @FRS_org and @MFA_Austria for the valuable insights!', Twitter, 11 Mar. 2021.

[32] Foundation for Strategic Research (FRS), 'Virtual seminar dedicated to CARICOM countries', 8 June 2021; FRS, 'Expert missions', [n.d.]; FRS, 'Virtual seminar dedicated to French-speaking countries', 31 Mar. 2021; and FRS, 'Virtual seminar dedicated to Latin American countries', 27 Apr. 2021.

[33] FRS, @FRS_org, 'La FRS a organisé dans le cadre du projet européen qu'elle met en œuvre sur le #HCoC un atelier de travail hybride consacré au Code et à la #prolifération balistique avec la République démocratique du Congo – avec @MJvanDeelenEU @gustavoainchil @gwg2k @odaunrec', Twitter, 23 Nov. 2021.

the Treaty on the Non-proliferation of Nuclear Weapons (NPT).[34] The NSG currently has 48 participating governments. In addition, the European Commission and the chair of the Zangger Committee have permanent observer status. The membership of the NSG has grown from an initial seven participating governments, but no new states have been admitted to the group since 2013.[35] The possible admission of additional states into the NSG, including several pending requests from states, is an ongoing subject of discussion among participating governments, but in 2021 there was again no consensus for new admissions.[36] The long-standing question on the possible participation of states not party to the NPT continued to be discussed at the NSG plenary regarding its 'technical, legal and political aspects'.[37]

In 2021 the NSG convened for its annual plenary, after the 2020 plenary was postponed because of the Covid-19 pandemic.[38] The plenary was hosted in Brussels on 24–25 June 2021 by the outgoing Belgian chair, with consultative group meetings taking place on 22–23 June. This marks a change to the NSG's chairing system where from now on each NSG plenary chair will host a plenary at the end of their term in office rather than at its beginning, as was previously the case.[39] The participating governments also 'underscored their strong resolve to protect continuity and enhance the vitality of the NSG' despite the challenges arising from the 'restricted working conditions imposed by' the Covid-19 pandemic.[40] Poland assumed the NSG chair for the period 2021–22 and the chair of the Technical Experts Group was handed over from a Swedish expert to a US expert.[41]

The NSG plenary exchanged information on global proliferation challenges, reiterating its support for the NPT, and further discussed plans to promote the NSG guidelines at the rescheduled NPT review conference.[42] The participating governments also reaffirmed their commitment to and support for the relevant UN Security Council resolutions concerning the Democratic People's Republic of Korea, Iran and the Joint Comprehensive Plan of Action (JCPOA).[43] They also received a briefing on the work of the JCPOA Procurement Channel. The NSG continued its discussions of technical issues and proposals to update and clarify the NSG controls lists, and participating governments exchanged information and best practices on

---

[34] Nuclear Suppliers Group, 'About the NSG', [n.d.].

[35] Nuclear Suppliers Group, 'Participants', [n.d.].

[36] Nuclear Suppliers Group, 'Public statement: Plenary meeting of the Nuclear Suppliers Group', Brussels, 24–25 June 2021, p. 2.

[37] Nuclear Suppliers Group (note 36), p. 2.

[38] Brockmann, K., 'The multilateral export control regimes', *SIPRI Yearbook 2021*, pp. 584–85.

[39] Nuclear Suppliers Group (note 36), p. 1.

[40] Nuclear Suppliers Group (note 36), p. 1.

[41] Nuclear Suppliers Group (note 36), p. 3.

[42] Nuclear Suppliers Group (note 36), p. 1.

[43] For a discussion of developments related to the JCPOA see chapter 11, section II, in this volume.

licensing and enforcement, including concerning transit and trans-shipment issues.[44]

The NSG did not conduct any outreach missions to non-participating states during 2021 due to the pandemic situation. Participating states exchanged views at the plenary on national practices in awareness-raising and engagement with industry and with academic and research institutions.[45]

The Wassenaar Arrangement

The Wassenaar Arrangement was created in 1996 as the successor to the cold war–era Co-ordinating Committee for Multilateral Export Controls (COCOM). Moving away from the COCOM's approach of export controls targeting a specific group of adversarial states, the WA participating states—notably including Russia and the USA—seek to prevent transfers that contribute to 'destabilising accumulations' of conventional weapons and dual-use goods and technologies that could threaten international and regional security and stability, as well as transfers to terrorists. Through the WA the participating states also aim to promote 'transparency and greater responsibility' in the transfers of such weapons and technologies. The WA has 42 participating states. Despite some expansion beyond the original 33 participating states, the WA has not admitted any additional state since the admission of India in 2017.[46]

The WA was forced to cancel its annual plenary again in 2021 due to the global pandemic and the local public health situation in Vienna. The WA was able to resume 'some in-person meetings' throughout the year and 'cooperated intersessionally'. The participating states also continued 'the comprehensive and systematic review of the WA Control Lists' and managed to agree on changes to the control lists.[47] The changes include a new control list item covering 'computer-assisted-design software tools for high-end components' and expanded coverage of 'metallic and organic substrates used in highly sophisticated applications'. The participating states also agreed on several decontrols and adjustments relaxing controls on high-performance computers, multi-mode lasers and radars now commonly used in anti-collision systems in automobiles.[48]

At the end of 2021, Hungary handed over the plenary chair of the WA for 2022 to Ireland. South Africa assumed the chair of the general working

---

[44] Nuclear Suppliers Group (note 36), p. 2.

[45] Nuclear Suppliers Group (note 36), p. 3.

[46] Wassenaar Arrangement, 'About us', Updated 17 Dec. 2020.

[47] Wassenaar Arrangement, Statement issued by the plenary chair, Vienna, 23 Dec. 2021.

[48] Wassenaar Arrangement (note 47).

group, Malta continued to chair the experts group and Switzerland assumed the chair of the WA's licensing and enforcement officers meeting for 2022.[49]

To mark the occasion of its 25-year anniversary, the WA conducted a 'practical workshop' in a virtual format, bringing together 13 WA participating states and more than 100 officials from 24 non-participating states. The workshop included briefings from the WA head of secretariat and the chairs of the WA's experts group and licensing and enforcement officers meeting on recent updates, changes to the WA control lists and 'developments in licensing and enforcement'. Several WA participating states also shared perspectives on control list issues and 'licensing processes, internal compliance programmes, catch-all controls, and strategic risk assessment', and engaged in an informal dialogue with non-participating states. The WA chair and secretariat also hosted a visit by the 2021 UN disarmament fellows in September 2021.[50]

Conclusions

The global Covid-19 pandemic continued to test the resilience of the functions of the multilateral export control regimes and demonstrated the limitations resulting from their reliance on in-person annual plenaries as central decision-making bodies. The focus on continuing intersessional work highlighted the commitment of states to the regimes' work, but it was often less inclusive if conducted by smaller groups of participating states. The pandemic also highlighted the issue of transparency, as most of the regimes' limited communications and publications are usually connected to the plenaries or are statements made during public events and outreach activities, many of which were cancelled in 2021. Rising geopolitical tensions, a growing tendency towards creating mechanisms for adopting national controls outside of the regimes, and criticism towards the legitimacy of the regimes levelled through the UN General Assembly have challenged the unique position of the regimes. This highlights the continued need for the regimes to strengthen their implementation and functions and to explore complementary ways towards more openness.

---

[49] Wassenaar Arrangement (note 47).
[50] Wassenaar Arrangement, 'Outreach', Updated 23 Dec. 2021.

IV. Developments in the European Union's dual-use and arms trade controls

MARK BROMLEY, KOLJA BROCKMANN AND GIOVANNA MALETTA

The European Union (EU) is currently the only regional organization with a common legal framework for controls on the export, brokering, transit and trans-shipment of dual-use items and also, to a certain extent, military items. The key elements of this legal framework are the EU's arms embargoes, dual-use regulation, foreign and direct investment (FDI) screening regulation, common position on arms exports, directive on intra-Community transfers, and anti-torture regulation. Developments in EU arms embargoes are addressed in section II of this chapter. During 2021 the EU adopted a new version of the dual-use regulation and began clarifying how it will be implemented at the national level. The EU and its member states also reported on steps taken to implement the FDI screening regulation, which entered into force in 2020. The EU and the United States took steps to develop expanded processes of cooperation and consultation on export controls. No major developments took place in the common position on arms exports, the directive on intra-Community transfers or the anti-torture regulation. However, there were efforts in the European Parliament to create a new mechanism at the EU level to inform and harmonize implementation of aspects of the common position.

The EU dual-use regulation

The EU dual-use regulation covers controls on the export, re-export, brokering and transit of dual-use goods, software and technology. The regulation is directly applicable law in EU member states but is implemented and enforced via their national control systems. In 2011 the EU began a process of review of the 2009 version of the regulation, which led to a legislative process for a 'recast' that concluded with a final compromise text in November 2020 after a 'trilogue' between the European Commission, the European Parliament and the Council of the EU.[1] The regulation was recast as Regulation (EU) 2021/821, which was adopted by the European Parliament in May 2021 and entered into force on 9 September 2021.[2]

Regulation (EU) 2021/821 introduces several new elements and modifications to the dual-use regulation. These include new EU general export

---

[1] Council of the European Union, 'New rules on trade of dual-use items agreed', Press release, 9 Nov. 2020.

[2] Regulation (EU) 2021/821 of the European Parliament and of the Council of 20 May 2021 setting up a Union regime for the control of exports, brokering, technical assistance, transit and transfer of dual-use items (recast), *Official Journal of the European Union*, L206, 11 June 2021.

authorisations (EUGEAs) for goods that employ cryptography and intra-company transfers of 'technology', expanded mechanisms of intra-governmental information sharing and public reporting, and a new catch-all control for non-listed cybersurveillance items. It also expanded the scope for member states to create national control list items and a new system of 'transmissible' controls that allow one member state to apply catch-all controls to exports of non-listed items for which another member state has created such national controls.[3] For some of these issues the Commission and the European Parliament made proposals that were broader in scope than the changes eventually adopted but that were narrowed down during the negotiating phases due to opposition from EU member states. For the same reason, Regulation (EU) 2021/821 did not include other proposals made by the Commission and the European Parliament—including agreed standards on how to regulate the use of cloud computing to store and share controlled software and technology, new EUGEAs on low-value shipments and 'other dual-use items', and greater standardization in the amount of time states take to process licences and the penalties associated with non-compliance.

The views of the Commission and the European Parliament on the one hand and EU member states on the other regarding the merits of particular changes to the regulation largely reflected two underlying differences about its future development. The first concerned the extent to which aspects of the regulation's implementation should be made subject to EU-level decision-making processes or remain under the control of member states. The second concerned the extent to which the range of items it controls should remain exclusively tied to the lists adopted in the multilateral export control regimes or be supplemented by items controlled on the basis of autonomous EU decisions. Many of the proposals that were put forward by the Commission and the European Parliament and opposed by member states would have shifted some decision-making powers towards the EU and away from member states or the regimes.[4]

Perhaps the most significant change introduced by Regulation (EU) 2021/821 is a new catch-all control for non-listed cybersurveillance items. Both the Commission and the European Parliament had initially pro-posed more extensive measures, including a unilateral control list for cyber-surveillance items and a catch-all control linked to human rights concerns. The new catch-all control that was agreed through the trilogue requires exporters to apply for a licence for the export of unlisted cybersurveillance

---

[3] For a more detailed analysis of the changes introduced by Regulation (EU) 2021/821 see Bromley, M., Brockmann, K. and Maletta, G., 'Developments in the European Union's dual-use and arms trade controls', *SIPRI Yearbook 2021*; and Bromley, M. and Brockmann, K., 'Implementing the 2021 recast of the EU Dual-Use Regulation: Challenges and opportunities', EU Non-Proliferation and Disarmament Consortium, Non-Proliferation and Disarmament Paper no. 77 (Sep. 2021).

[4] Bromley and Brockmann (note 3).

items if they have 'been informed by the competent authority that [the items] may be intended, in their entirety or in part, for use in connection with internal repression and/or the commission of serious violations of human rights and international humanitarian law'.[5] Exporters are also required to inform their national authorities if they are 'aware according to [their] due diligence findings' of any such risks.[6] A key test for the dual-use regulation will be if and how the new catch-all is utilized, and which exports of non-listed cybersurveillance items are controlled and prevented. For example, members of the European Parliament have indicated that they would like to see the catch-all used to control exports of facial recognition systems and biometric systems, which are not currently captured by dual-use export controls.[7] Regulation (EU) 2021/821 commits the Commission and the Council to producing guidelines to help exporters apply the catch-all. During 2021 the Commission and EU member states began work in the Surveillance Technology Expert Group (STEG)—a subsidiary body of the EU Dual-Use Coordination Group—on producing these guidelines, which they aim to publish by September 2022.[8] Among other things, the guidelines will aim to clarify the regulation's definition of cybersurveillance items and what is required of exporters under the 'due diligence' procedures referred to in the catch-all control.[9]

Another key focus for the recast was creating a more harmonized application of the dual-use regulation, including by achieving a more uniform interpretation of some of the concepts it references, such as the exemptions for 'basic scientific research' and information that is 'in the public domain'. The need for more clarity and uniformity in the application of these exemptions has been highlighted in discussions about compliance with dual-use export controls by universities and research institutes.[10] Regulation (EU) 2021/821 does not provide more specific definitions of the exemptions for 'basic scientific research' and information that is 'in the public domain' but notes that more detailed guidelines are needed.[11] In September 2021 the EU published a new set of guidelines, specifically targeted at research and academia, on how to set up and implement internal compliance programmes

---

[5] Regulation (EU) 2021/821 (note 2), Article 5(1).

[6] Regulation (EU) 2021/821 (note 2), Article 5(1).

[7] See e.g. Gregorová, M., INTA Rapporteur, European Parliament, 'The European Parliament's expectations for more effective controls on cybersurveillance technologies', Presentation at the 2020 Export Control Forum (virtual meeting), 11 Dec. 2020.

[8] Farcas-Hutchinson, C., National Expert, DG TRADE, 'Export control of cyber-surveillance items in the EU', Presentation at the 2021 Export Control Forum, Brussels, 8 Dec. 2021.

[9] Farcas-Hutchinson (note 8).

[10] See e.g. Branislav, A. and de Bie, J. J. C., 'From a practical view: The proposed dual-use regulation and export control challenges for research and academia', Fraunhofer and TNO, Dec. 2017.

[11] Regulation (EU) 2021/821 (note 2), Preamble para. 13.

(ICPs).[12] The new guidelines outline frameworks for research organizations and researchers to use when establishing ICPs and for member states to use when developing outreach programmes targeted at research organizations and researchers.[13] The guidelines seek to provide clarity on the scope of the decontrols on 'basic scientific research' by introducing two criteria to assist in determining whether they are relevant: the technology readiness level (TRL) and the prevalence of industry funding.[14] TRLs were originally developed by the US National Aeronautics and Space Agency (NASA) to be 'a type of measurement system used to assess the maturity level of a particular technology'.[15] They have previously also been adopted within the framework of EU research funding mechanisms such as Horizon 2020.[16]

Another key focus of the recast was improving the ability of the EU and EU member states to respond to international and national security challenges posed by the development and proliferation of emerging technologies.[17] The efforts undertaken by the USA to introduce national controls on a range of emerging technologies, and growing concerns over China's foreign and domestic policies related to many areas of emerging technology, were key drivers for creating new mechanisms.[18] The recast seeks to address these challenges by increasing the scope for member states to adopt national controls on unlisted items and creating a mechanism to make these controls transmissible so that they can be applied as a catch-all control by other EU member states.[19]

The new measures introduced by the dual-use regulation also connect with wider efforts by the EU and EU member states to keep pace with developments in emerging technologies and, where deemed necessary, to take steps to restrict certain transfers through dual-use export controls or implement other regulatory measures. Drawing from a series of technical workshops that took place in 2019–20, the EU published a series of fact sheets on relevant emerging technologies in September 2021.[20] The fact sheets list

---

[12] Commission Recommendation (EU) 2021/1700 of 15 Sep. 2021 on internal compliance programmes for controls of research involving dual-use items under Regulation (EU) 2021/821 of the European Parliament and of the Council setting up a Union regime for the control of exports, brokering, technical assistance, transit and transfer of dual-use items, *Official Journal of the European Union*, L338, 15 Sep. 2021.

[13] Commission Recommendation (EU) 2021/1700 (note 12), p. 1.

[14] Commission Recommendation (EU) 2021/1700 (note 12), p. 19.

[15] Tzinis, I., 'Technology readiness level', NASA, 29 Oct. 2012 (updated 2 Apr. 2021).

[16] European Commission, 'Horizon 2020—Work programme 2016–2017: General annexes', [n.d.], p. 29.

[17] Bromley, Brockmann and Maletta (note 3); and Bromley and Brockmann (note 3).

[18] US Department of Commerce, Bureau of Industry and Security, 'Advance notice of proposed rulemaking: Review of controls for certain emerging technologies', *Federal Register*, vol. 83, no. 223 (19 Nov. 2018); and Bromley, Brockmann and Maletta (note 3).

[19] Bromley and Brockmann (note 3).

[20] See e.g. European Commission, 'Emerging technologies: Developments in the context of dual-use export controls', Fact sheet, Sep. 2021.

the industries developing and utilising each technology, their 'export control relevant' applications within the military and 'public security agencies', how they are currently captured by dual-use export controls, and the extent to which they are the subject of discussions within the export control regimes about creating new control list categories or modifying existing ones.[21] In 2021 the EU also established the Emerging Technology Expert Group (ETEG) as a subsidiary body of the EU Dual-Use Coordination Group. The ETEG will draw on expertise of member states 'to help develop an EU framework to address the risks associated with trade and technology transfers of such emerging technologies'.[22]

The EU foreign direct investment screening regulation

The FDI screening regulation is focused on enabling the EU and EU member states to identify and respond to cases where FDI might allow foreign companies and governments to own and control critical infrastructure such as transport hubs, energy grids and telecommunications networks, or to gain access to knowledge and technology which may or may not be subject to export controls but which could benefit their defence and security capabilities. The regulation does not require EU member states that do not have a screening mechanism to put one in place; it only establishes basic requirements that should be common to any such mechanism. Nevertheless, the regulation obliges member states to share information about FDI cases that are being screened, while creating a mechanism for other EU member states to provide comments and for the Commission to issue non-binding opinions on certain cases.[23]

The EU has not framed the FDI screening regulation as being focused on any particular foreign state. However, negotiation and adoption of the regulation took place against a background of heightened concern about Chinese investments.[24] While the levels of Chinese FDI in Europe have declined since 2016—particularly sharply during the Covid-19 pandemic—concerns about their origin and purpose have persisted. For example, in September 2021 the Italian authorities announced that they were charging six individuals in connection with the sale of a 75 per cent stake

---

[21] European Commission (note 20).

[22] European Commission, Directorate-General for Trade, 'Commission's actions to implement new EU Export Control Regulation', Memo, 9 Sep. 2021.

[23] Regulation (EU) 2019/452 of the European Parliament and of the Council of 19 Mar. 2019 establishing a framework for the screening of foreign direct investments into the Union, *Official Journal of the European Union*, L79 I, 21 Mar. 2019, Preamble para. 19.

[24] Hanemann, T. and Huotari, M., *EU–China FDI: Working Towards Reciprocity in Investment Relations*, Mercator Institute for China Studies (MERICS) Papers on China, Update no. 3 (MERICS: Berlin, May 2018); and Nienaber, M., 'German minister ups rhetoric against takeovers ahead of China trip', Reuters, 29 Oct. 2016.

in Alpi Aviation—a manufacturer of military drones—to a Hong Kong–based company in 2018.[25] The authorities alleged that the sale inflated the true value of the company, sought to mask the true actors behind the Hong Kong–based company—discovered to be two government-owned companies in China—and took place without the prior consent of the Italian authorities.[26]

In November 2021 the Commission published the first annual report on the implementation of the FDI screening regulation.[27] The report was published together with the 2021 edition of the Commission's annual report on the implementation of the dual-use regulation, emphasizing the extent to which the two instruments have a shared focus on regulating transfers of sensitive goods and technologies.[28] The report noted that more than 400 transactions had been notified by member states since the FDI screening regulation's entry into force. Until 30 June 2021, the Commission had received 265 notifications for screening and issued an opinion in around 3 per cent of these cases.[29] Over 90 per cent of the cases submitted came from only five member states: Austria, France, Germany, Italy and Spain.[30] Among the countries of origin of investors in the notified FDI cases, the largest share came, in decreasing order, from the USA, the United Kingdom, China, Canada and the United Arab Emirates.[31] The report also noted that as of 1 July 2021, 18 EU member states had FDI screening mechanisms in place, compared with 11 in 2017.[32] The report identified six additional member states as having initiated consultative or legislative processes that are expected to lead to the introduction of such mechanisms.

Member states have welcomed the regulation and its cooperation mechanism. However, several member states also noted the need for clarity of key concepts; resource constraints; and implementation challenges, including 'tight deadlines' and the amount of requests for information related to multi-jurisdictional transfers.[33] Proposals for addressing these challenges included the production of guidelines on notification requirements 'to sharpen the focus and avoid "overloading" the system'.[34]

---

[25] Italian Finance Police, 'Violazione alla legge sui materiali d'armamento—Denunciate 6 persone' [Violation of the law on military goods—6 people reported], Press release, 6 Sep. 2021.

[26] Italian Finance Police (note 25).

[27] European Commission, 'Trade and security: Commission highlights work to defend EU interests and values', Press release, 23 Nov. 2021.

[28] European Commission, 'First annual report on the screening of foreign direct investments into the Union', Report to the European Parliament and the Council, COM(2021) 714, 23 Nov. 2021, p. 1.

[29] European Commission (note 27).

[30] European Commission (note 28), p. 11.

[31] European Commission (note 28), p. 14.

[32] European Commission (note 27).

[33] European Commission (note 28), pp. 15–17.

[34] European Commission (note 28), pp. 17–18.

European and United States cooperation on export controls

Cooperation between the EU and European states and the USA on export controls and trade policy more generally deepened in 2021. These efforts included a particular focus on export controls on emerging technologies and cybersurveillance items and FDI screening mechanisms. The USA has taken a range of steps in recent years to expand its controls in all these areas.[35] In contrast to the EU policy instruments that have been developed, those in the USA are very clearly motivated, in large part, by an attempt to tighten controls on transfers of dual-use items to China to both influence its domestic and foreign policy choices and limit its ability to gain access to technology that could benefit its defence industrial capabilities.

The EU–US Trade and Technology Council

In June 2021 the EU and the USA launched the EU–US Trade and Technology Council (TTC). The TTC will have ten working groups on a wide range of trade and technology topics, two of which are on the 'misuse of technology threatening security and human rights' and export controls.[36] The USA and the EU held the inaugural meeting of the TTC in September 2021 in Pittsburgh.[37] The outcome document outlines a number of steps that both parties commit to taking for improved coordination in identifying challenges and policy responses in the fields of emerging technology, FDI, export controls and artificial intelligence. The document also contains thinly veiled references to China and the need to focus efforts in all of these areas on controlling transfers to China, referring to shared concerns about the 'civil-military fusion policies of certain actors' which 'undermine security interests, and challenge the objective assessment of risks by the competent authorities and the effective implementation of rules-based controls in line with internationally-agreed standards'.[38] On export controls, there is also an emphasis on working through the regimes and avoiding autonomous measures: 'The USA and the European Union recognize the importance, where appropriate and feasible, of consultations prior to the introduction of controls outside the multilateral regimes.'[39]

---

[35] See e.g. US Department of Commerce, Bureau of Industry and Security, 'Information security controls: Cybersecurity items; delay of effective date', *Federal Register*, vol. 87, no. 8 (12 Jan. 2022), pp. 1670–71; and Jackson, J. K., 'The Committee on Foreign Investment in the United States (CFIUS)', Congressional Research Service (CRS), 26 Feb. 2020.

[36] European Commission, 'EU–US launch Trade and Technology Council to lead values-based global digital transformation', Press release, 15 June 2021.

[37] White House, 'US–EU Trade and Technology Council inaugural joint statement', Briefing Room statement, 29 Sep. 2021.

[38] White House (note 37).

[39] White House (note 37).

Although the EU and the USA are taking steps to coordinate their export control policies, there is continued tension around the extraterritorial application of US export control and sanctions instruments. In 2021 the EU moved ahead with its attempts to update the blocking statute 'to further deter and counteract the unlawful extra-territorial application of sanctions to EU operators by countries outside the EU'.[40] The original EU blocking statute was adopted in 1996 and seeks to protect EU operators against the extra-territorial application of the US sanctions on Cuba and Iran.[41]

Bilateral cooperation on controls on exports of cybersurveillance items

Separately, the USA is also seeking to build a broader coalition of states that would agree to apply common standards on exports of surveillance technologies. On the final day of the 'summit for democracy', which was held in December 2021 and organized by the USA, four states—Australia, Denmark, Norway and the USA—formally launched the Export Controls and Human Rights Initiative. In a joint statement the group of states noted that 'authoritarian governments increasingly are using surveillance tools and other related technologies in connection with serious human rights abuses'.[42] Substantively, the group has committed to developing 'a voluntary written code of conduct intended to guide the application of human rights criteria to export licensing policy and practice' and to engaging in 'further coordination with other governments, as well as consult[ing] with industry and academia'.[43]

Although the Export Controls and Human Rights Initiative pursues similar goals on exports of cybersurveillance items to those being pursued under the TTC, the USA did not channel this former initiative via the EU. This was reportedly due to the fact that EU-wide cooperation with the USA's summit for democracy was blocked by Hungary, which had not been invited to participate.[44]

The EU common position on arms exports

The EU common position on arms exports (EU common position) covers controls on the export, transit, trans-shipment and brokering of military equipment and technology. As an instrument of the EU's common foreign and

---

[40] European Commission, 'Blocking statute: Protecting EU operators, reinforcing European strategic autonomy', [n.d.].

[41] European Commission (note 40).

[42] White House, 'Joint statement on the Export Controls and Human Rights Initiative', Briefing Room statement, 10 Dec. 2021.

[43] White House, 'Export Controls and Human Rights Initiative launched at the Summit for Democracy', Briefing Room fact sheet, 10 Dec. 2021.

[44] Vela, J. H., 'Brussels Playbook: Putin–Biden talks—Belgium's new COVID measures—NFI to the democracy summit', *POLITICO Brussels Playbook*, 3 Dec. 2021.

Table 14.4. Submissions of information to the European Union annual report on arms exports, 2011–20

Annual report	Year covered	No. of states obliged to make submissions	No. of states making submissions	No. of states making full submissions[a]	Proportion of states making full submissions (%)
23rd	2020	27[b]	27	23	85
22nd	2019	28	28	21	75
21st	2018	28	28	21	75
20th	2017	28	27[c]	19	68
19th	2016	28	27[c]	19	68
18th	2015	28	27[c]	19	68
17th	2014	28	28	21	75
16th	2013	28	27[c]	21	75
15th	2012	27[d]	27	20	74
14th	2011	27	27	18	67

[a] A 'full submission' is taken to be data on the financial value of both arms export licences issued and actual exports, broken down by both destination and European Union (EU) military list category.

[b] The United Kingdom officially left the EU on 31 January 2020 and was not obliged to submit data for 2020.

[c] Greece did not submit data to the 16th, 18th, 19th and 20th reports.

[d] Croatia joined the EU in 2013 and was not obliged to submit data for 2012. It submitted data for the first time to the 16th report.

Sources: European External Action Service (EEAS), 'Arms Export Control—Arms Trade Treaty'; and Council of the European Union, 'Twenty-third annual report according to Article 8(2) of Council Common Position 2008/944/CFSP defining common rules governing the control of exports of military technology and equipment', ST/12189/2021/INIT, Official Journal of the European Union, C515, 21 Dec. 2021.

security policy (CFSP), EU member states are legally obliged to implement its provisions, but the European Court of Justice (ECJ) and other EU bodies have no powers of sanction in cases of non-compliance. In 2021 the Council Working Party on Conventional Arms Exports (COARM) continued work on implementing the Council conclusions on arms exports that were agreed in 2019.[45] The 2019 conclusions were adopted following the last review of the EU common position and outlined a series of tasks for COARM to undertake to further improve transparency and convergence in arms export controls.[46] The tasks included harmonizing end-user certificates (EUCs) 'for the export of small arms and light weapons and their ammunition' at the EU level. In January 2021, EU member states agreed a Council decision establishing

[45] Council of the European Union, 'Council conclusions on the review of Council Common Position 2008/944/CFSP of 8 December 2008 on the control of arms exports', 12195/19, 16 Sep. 2019. COARM brings together EU member state officials working on arms export controls and is chaired by the European External Action Service (EEAS).

[46] See Bromley, M. and Maletta, G., 'Developments in the European Union's dual-use and arms trade controls', *SIPRI Yearbook 2020*, pp. 562–64.

common elements that should be included in such EUCs.[47] In 2021 COARM also started working on the development of a closed database for EU licensing officers, to provide them with access to reports and sources on the potential recipients of their arms exports.[48]

September 2021 saw the adoption of the 23rd EU annual report on arms exports, which includes details on the financial value and number of member states' export licences, the value of their actual exports, and the aggregated data on licence denials in 2020. This publication date continues the trend in improved timeliness of the report's release and indicates that the reporting deadlines agreed after the 2019 review have had a positive impact.[49] The annual report shows that 85 per cent of EU member states submitted complete data for 2020 on licences granted and actual exports, broken down by the categories of the EU military list (table 14.4). However, not all EU member states currently provide disaggregated data on actual exports, which limits the comparability of the information included in the report.[50] Following the review of the common position, COARM has started a discussion on how to improve reporting on the value of actual exports, although this did not produce any tangible outcome in 2021.[51]

Draft proposal for an EU regulation on arms export controls

In October 2021 Hannah Neumann, a German member of the European Parliament and rapporteur for the parliament's report on arms exports, presented a proposal on behalf of the Greens/European Free Alliance (EFA) parliamentary group for an EU regulation that would establish an EU regime for arms export control.[52] The aim of the proposed regulation is to reduce discrepancies among EU member states' policies on arms export control and prevent their weapons exports from being misused or diverted,

[47] Council Decision (CFSP) 2021/38 of 15 Jan. 2021 establishing a common approach on the elements of end-user certificates in the context of the export of small arms and light weapons and their ammunition, *Official Journal of the European Union*, L14, 18 Jan. 2021.

[48] European Union, Statement on treaty implementation at Arms Trade Treaty, Seventh Conference of States Parties, Geneva, 30 Aug.–3 Sep. 2021; and Council of the European Union, 'Twenty-third annual report according to Article 8(2) of Council Common Position 2008/944/CFSP defining common rules governing the control of exports of military technology and equipment', ST/12189/2021/INIT, *Official Journal of the European Union*, C515, 21 Dec. 2021, p. 4.

[49] European External Action Service (EEAS), '23rd annual report on arms exports launched today (28/9): EU is a transparent and responsible trader in arms', 28 Sep. 2021; and Council of the European Union, 'User's guide to Council Common Position 2008/944/CFSP (as amended by Council decision (CFSP) 2019/1560) defining common rules governing the control of exports of military technology and equipment', 12189/19, 16 Sep. 2019, p. 154.

[50] Belgium, Cyprus, Germany, Greece and Latvia do not provide details on value of actual exports. Council of the European Union, ST/12189/2021/INIT (note 48), p. 8.

[51] Council of the European Union, ST/12189/2021/INIT (note 48), p. 4.

[52] German Green Party and European Free Alliance (Greens/EFA), 'How to prevent EU produced weapons from fuelling conflict', Webinar, YouTube, 12 Oct. 2021; and Neumann, H., Draft proposal for a 'Regulation of the European Parliament and of the Council setting up a Union regime for the control of arms exports', 12 Oct. 2021.

by strengthening the role of the EU in this area. The proposal assumes that greater involvement of EU institutions in arms export control is both necessary to guarantee a stricter application of export control standards, and legitimate because the EU's budget is increasingly being used to support the development of the European defence industrial base.[53]

The proposal suggests several amendments to the language of the EU common position's export licensing criteria, adding explicit references to the risk of corruption and gender-based violence. One of the measures foreseen in the proposal is the creation of an EU Common Risk Assessment Body comprising independent experts nominated by the European Commission. Although EU member states would keep their prerogative on arms export control decisions, the body would be tasked with creating and periodically updating a list of countries where—based on an assessment of their internal situation, end-users and the items exported—there is a risk of the criteria being violated.[54] As an EU regulation, the proposed regime would also give the Commission the ability to oversee implementation and allow the ECJ to sanction cases of violations.[55]

The German Green Party (of which Neumann is a representative) is part of the new German government that took office after the September 2021 elections. The coalition agreement that will guide the work of the new government includes specific provisions regarding arms export controls, including the adoption of a more restrictive arms export policy at the national level and cooperation for corresponding efforts at the EU level.[56] Despite Germany's likely support for the proposal, it is expected that the draft regulation in its current form will encounter opposition from other EU member states, particularly France, that prefer maintaining national control over export licensing decision-making.[57]

Conclusions

The recast EU dual-use regulation and the FDI screening regulation have provided the EU and EU member states with a broader set of tools to control transfers and acquisitions of dual-use items and sensitive technologies and to coordinate their efforts in these areas. Despite a strong push from the Commission and the European Parliament during the review of the EU

---

[53] Neumann, H., 'A European arms export control: My draft regulation', 4 Nov. 2021; Greens/EFA, 'FAQs on EU arms exports', [n.d.]; and Neumann (note 52).

[54] Neumann (note 52), paras 22–25

[55] European Union, 'Types of legislation', [n.d.]; and Greens/EFA (note 53).

[56] Social Democratic Party of Germany, Free Democratic Party and Alliance 90/The Greens, 'Mehr Fortschritt wagen: Bünd. für Freiheit, Gerechtigkeit und Nachhaltigkeit' [Daring more progress: Alliance for freedom, justice and sustainability], Nov. 2011, p. 146.

[57] Sprenger, S., 'German proposal for an EU arms-export regime faces uphill battle', *Defence News*, 17 Dec. 2021.

dual-use regulation to devolve certain aspects of decision-making to the EU level, ultimate control over which items are subject to licensing requirements and which exports are approved remains in the hands of the member states. However, the proposal put forward in the European Parliament by the Greens/ EFA parliamentary group on embedding the provisions of the EU common position into an EU regulation indicates that debates about the extent to which issues concerning export controls are determined at the EU or member state level are likely to continue. Deeper EU–US cooperation and coordination on export controls and trade policy more generally appears to be high on the agenda for both the US Biden administration and the EU and its member states. However, substantive progress on these issues may prove challenging due to underlying differences both within the EU and between the EU and the USA about the eventual goal of these efforts.

Annexes

Annex A. Arms control and disarmament agreements

Annex B. International security cooperation bodies

Annex C. Chronology 2021

Annex A. Arms control and disarmament agreements

This annex lists multi- and bilateral treaties, conventions, protocols and agreements relating to arms control and disarmament. Unless otherwise stated, the status of agreements and of their parties and signatories is as of 1 January 2022. On the International security cooperation bodies mentioned here, see annex B.

Notes

1. The agreements are divided into universal treaties (i.e. multilateral treaties open to all states, in section I), regional treaties (i.e. multilateral treaties open to states of a particular region, in section II) and bilateral treaties (in section III). Within each section, the agreements are listed in the order of the date on which they were adopted, signed or opened for signature (multilateral agreements) or signed (bilateral agreements). The date on which they entered into force and the depositary for multilateral treaties are also given.

2. The main source of information is the lists of signatories and parties provided by the depositaries of the treaties. In lists of parties and signatories, states whose name appears in italics ratified, acceded or succeeded to, or signed the agreement during 2021.

3. States and organizations listed as parties had ratified, acceded to or succeeded to the agreements by 1 January 2022. Since many agreements delay the entry into force for a state for a certain period after ratification or accession, when that occurred late in 2021 the agreement may not have fully entered into force for that state by 1 January 2022.

4. Former non-self-governing territories, upon attaining statehood, sometimes make general statements of continuity to all agreements concluded by the former governing power. This annex lists as parties only those new states that have made an uncontested declaration on continuity or have notified the depositary of their succession. The Russian Federation continues the international obligations of the Soviet Union.

5. Unless stated otherwise, the multilateral agreements listed in this annex are open to all states, to all states in the respective zone or region, or to all members of a certain international organization for signature, ratification, accession or succession. Not all the signatories and parties are United Nations members. Taiwan, while not recognized as a sovereign state by many countries, is listed as a party to the agreements that it has ratified.

6. Where possible, the location (in a printed publication or online) of an accurate copy of the treaty text is given. This may be provided by a treaty depositary, an agency or secretariat connected with the treaty, or in the *United Nations Treaty Series* (available online at <https://treaties.un.org/>).

I. Universal treaties

Protocol for the Prohibition of the Use in War of Asphyxiating, Poisonous or Other Gases, and of Bacteriological Methods of Warfare (1925 Geneva Protocol)

Signed at Geneva on 17 June 1925; entered into force on 8 February 1928; depositary French Government

The protocol prohibits the use in war of asphyxiating, poisonous or other gases and of bacteriological methods of warfare. The protocol remains a fundamental basis of the international prohibition against chemical and biological warfare, and its principles, objectives and obligations are explicitly supported by the 1972 Biological and Toxin Weapons Convention and the 1993 Chemical Weapons Convention.

Parties (147): Afghanistan, Albania, Algeria, Angola, Antigua and Barbuda, Argentina, Armenia, Australia, Austria, Bahrain, Bangladesh, Barbados, Belgium, Benin, Bhutan, Bolivia, Brazil, Bulgaria, Burkina Faso, Cabo Verde, Cambodia, Cameroon, Canada, Central African Republic, Chile, China, Colombia, Costa Rica, Côte d'Ivoire, Croatia, Cuba, Cyprus, Czechia, Denmark, Dominican Republic, Ecuador, Egypt, El Salvador, Equatorial Guinea, Estonia, Eswatini, Ethiopia, Fiji, Finland, France, Gambia, Germany, Ghana, Greece, Grenada, Guatemala, Guinea-Bissau, Holy See, Hungary, Iceland, India, Indonesia, Iran, Iraq, Ireland, Israel, Italy, Jamaica, Japan, Jordan, Kazakhstan, Kenya, Korea (North), Korea (South), Kuwait, Kyrgyzstan, Laos, Latvia, Lebanon, Lesotho, Liberia, Libya, Liechtenstein, Lithuania, Luxembourg, Madagascar, Malawi, Malaysia, Maldives, Malta, Mauritius, Mexico, Moldova, Monaco, Mongolia, Morocco, Nepal, Netherlands, New Zealand, Nicaragua, Niger, Nigeria, North Macedonia, Norway, Pakistan, Palestine, Panama, Papua New Guinea, Paraguay, Peru, Philippines, Poland, Portugal, Qatar, Romania, Russia, Rwanda, Saint Kitts and Nevis, Saint Lucia, Saint Vincent and the Grenadines, Saudi Arabia, Senegal, Serbia, Sierra Leone, Slovakia, Slovenia, Solomon Islands, South Africa, Spain, Sri Lanka, Sudan, Sweden, Switzerland, Syria, Taiwan, Tajikistan, Tanzania, Thailand, Togo, Tonga, Trinidad and Tobago, Tunisia, Turkey, Uganda, UK, Ukraine, Uruguay, Uzbekistan, USA, Venezuela, Viet Nam, Yemen

Notes: On joining the protocol, some states entered reservations which upheld their right to employ chemical or biological weapons against non-parties to the protocol, against coalitions which included non-parties or in response to the use of these weapons by a violating party. Many of these states have withdrawn these reservations, particularly after the conclusion of the 1972 Biological and Toxin Weapons Convention and the 1993 Chemical Weapons Convention since the reservations are incompatible with their obligation under the conventions.

In addition to these, 'explicit', reservations, a number of states that made a declaration of succession to the protocol on gaining independence inherited 'implicit' reservations from their respective predecessor states. For example, these implicit reservations apply to the states that gained independence from France and the UK before the latter states withdrew or amended their reservations. States that acceded (rather than succeeded) to the protocol did not inherit reservations in this way.

Protocol text: League of Nations, *Treaty Series*, vol. 94 (1929), <https://treaties.un.org/doc/Publication/UNTS/LON/Volume 94/v94.pdf>

Convention on the Prevention and Punishment of the Crime of Genocide (Genocide Convention)

Opened for signature at Paris on 9 December 1948; entered into force on 12 January 1951; depositary UN Secretary-General

Under the convention any commission of acts intended to destroy, in whole or in part, a national, ethnic, racial or religious group as such is declared to be a crime punishable under international law.

Parties (152): Afghanistan, Albania*, Algeria*, Andorra, Antigua and Barbuda, Argentina*, Armenia, Australia, Austria, Azerbaijan, Bahamas, Bahrain*, Bangladesh*, Barbados, Belarus*, Belgium, Belize, Benin, Bolivia, Bosnia and Herzegovina, Brazil, Bulgaria*, Burkina Faso, Burundi, Cabo Verde, Cambodia, Canada, Chile, China*, Colombia, Comoros, Congo (Democratic Republic of the), Costa Rica, Côte d'Ivoire, Croatia, Cuba, Cyprus, Czechia, Denmark, Dominica, Ecuador, Egypt, El Salvador, Estonia, Ethiopia, Fiji, Finland, France, Gabon, Gambia, Georgia, Germany, Ghana, Greece, Guatemala, Guinea, Guinea-Bissau, Haiti, Honduras, Hungary*, Iceland, India*, Iran, Iraq, Ireland, Israel, Italy, Jamaica, Jordan, Kazakhstan, Korea (North), Korea (South), Kuwait, Kyrgyzstan, Laos, Latvia, Lebanon, Lesotho, Liberia, Libya, Liechtenstein, Lithuania, Luxembourg, Malawi, Malaysia*, Maldives, Mali, Malta, Mauritius, Mexico, Moldova, Monaco, Mongolia*, Montenegro*, Morocco*, Mozambique, Myanmar*, Namibia, Nepal, Netherlands, New Zealand, Nicaragua, Nigeria, North Macedonia, Norway, Pakistan, Palestine, Panama, Papua New Guinea, Paraguay, Peru, Philippines*, Poland*, Portugal, Romania*, Russia*, Rwanda, Saint Vincent and the Grenadines, San Marino, Saudi Arabia, Senegal, Serbia*, Seychelles, Singapore*, Slovakia, Slovenia, South Africa, Spain, Sri Lanka, Sudan, Sweden, Switzerland, Syria, Tajikistan, Tanzania, Togo, Tonga, Trinidad and Tobago, Tunisia, Turkey, Turkmenistan, Uganda, UK, Ukraine*, United Arab Emirates*, Uruguay, USA*, Uzbekistan, Venezuela*, Viet Nam*, Yemen*, Zimbabwe

* With reservation and/or declaration.

Signed but not ratified (1): Dominican Republic

Convention text: United Nations Treaty Collection, <https://treaties.un.org/doc/Treaties/1951/01/19510112 08-12 PM/Ch_IV_1p.pdf>

Geneva Convention (IV) Relative to the Protection of Civilian Persons in Time of War

Opened for signature at Geneva on 12 August 1949; entered into force on 21 October 1950; depositary Swiss Federal Council

The Geneva Convention (IV) establishes rules for the protection of civilians in areas covered by war and in occupied territories. Three other conventions were formulated at the same time, at a diplomatic conference held from 21 April to 12 August 1949: Convention (I) for the Amelioration of the Condition of the Wounded and Sick in Armed Forces in the Field; Convention (II) for the Amelioration of the Condition of the Wounded, Sick and Shipwrecked Members of Armed Forces at Sea; and Convention (III) Relative to the Treatment of Prisoners of War.

A party may withdraw from the convention, having given one year's notice. But if the party is involved in an armed conflict at that time, the withdrawal will not take effect until peace has been concluded and that party's obligations under the convention fulfilled.

Parties (196): Afghanistan, Albania*, Algeria, Andorra, Angola*, Antigua and Barbuda, Argentina, Armenia, Australia*, Austria, Azerbaijan, Bahamas, Bahrain, Bangladesh*, Barbados*, Belarus, Belgium, Belize, Benin, Bhutan, Bolivia, Bosnia and Herzegovina, Botswana, Brazil, Brunei Darussalam, Bulgaria, Burkina Faso, Burundi, Cabo Verde, Cambodia, Cameroon, Canada, Central African Republic, Chad, Chile, China*, Colombia, Comoros, Congo (Democratic Republic of the), Congo (Republic of the), Cook Islands, Costa Rica, Côte d'Ivoire, Croatia, Cuba, Cyprus, Czechia*, Denmark, Djibouti, Dominica, Dominican Republic, Ecuador, Egypt, El Salvador, Equatorial Guinea, Estonia, Eritrea, Eswatini, Ethiopia, Fiji, Finland, France, Gabon, Gambia, Georgia, Germany*, Ghana, Greece, Grenada, Guatemala, Guinea, Guinea-Bissau*, Guyana, Haiti, Holy See, Honduras, Hungary, Iceland, India, Indonesia, Iran*, Iraq, Ireland, Israel*, Italy, Jamaica, Japan, Jordan, Kazakhstan, Kenya, Kiribati, Korea (North)*, Korea (South)*, Kuwait*, Kyrgyzstan, Laos, Latvia, Lebanon, Lesotho, Liberia, Libya, Liechtenstein, Lithuania, Luxembourg, Madagascar, Malawi, Malaysia, Maldives, Mali, Malta, Marshall Islands, Mauritania, Mauritius, Mexico, Micronesia, Moldova, Monaco, Mongolia, Montenegro, Morocco, Mozambique, Myanmar, Namibia, Nauru, Nepal, Netherlands, New Zealand*, Nicaragua, Niger, Nigeria, North Macedonia*, Norway, Oman, Pakistan*, Palau, Palestine, Panama, Papua New Guinea, Paraguay, Peru, Philippines, Poland, Portugal*, Qatar, Romania, Russia*, Rwanda, Saint Kitts and Nevis, Saint Lucia, Saint Vincent and the Grenadines, Samoa, San Marino, Sao Tome and Principe, Saudi Arabia, Senegal, Serbia, Seychelles, Sierra Leone, Singapore, Slovakia, Slovenia, Solomon Islands, Somalia, South Africa, South Sudan, Spain, Sri Lanka, Sudan, Suriname*, Sweden, Switzerland, Syria, Tajikistan, Tanzania, Thailand, Timor-Leste, Togo, Tonga, Trinidad and Tobago, Tunisia, Turkey, Turkmenistan, Tuvalu, Uganda, UK*, Ukraine*, United Arab Emirates, Uruguay*, USA*, Uzbekistan, Vanuatu, Venezuela, Viet Nam*, Yemen*, Zambia, Zimbabwe

 * With reservation and/or declaration.

Convention text: Swiss Federal Department of Foreign Affairs, <https://www.fdfa.admin.ch/dam/eda/fr/documents/aussenpolitik/voelkerrecht/geneve/070116-conv4_e.pdf>

Protocol I Additional to the 1949 Geneva Conventions, and Relating to the Protection of Victims of International Armed Conflicts

Protocol II Additional to the 1949 Geneva Conventions, and Relating to the Protection of Victims of Non-International Armed Conflicts

Opened for signature at Bern on 12 December 1977; entered into force on 7 December 1978; depositary Swiss Federal Council

The protocols confirm that the right of parties that are engaged in international or non-international armed conflicts to choose methods or means of warfare is not unlimited and that the use of weapons or means of warfare that cause superfluous injury or unnecessary suffering is prohibited.

Article 36 of Protocol I requires a state party, when developing or acquiring a new weapon, to determine whether its use could be prohibited by international law.

Parties to Protocol I (174) and Protocol II (169): Afghanistan, Albania, Algeria*, Angola*, Antigua and Barbuda, Argentina*, Armenia, Australia*, Austria*, Bahamas,

Bahrain, Bangladesh, Barbados, Belarus*, Belgium*, Belize, Benin, Bolivia*, Bosnia and Herzegovina*, Botswana, Brazil*, Brunei Darussalam, Bulgaria*, Burkina Faso*, Burundi, Cabo Verde*, Cambodia, Cameroon, Canada*, Central African Republic, Chad, Chile*, China*, Colombia*, Comoros, Congo (Democratic Republic of the)*, Congo (Republic of the), Cook Islands*, Costa Rica*, Côte d'Ivoire, Croatia*, Cuba, Cyprus*, Czechia*, Denmark*, Djibouti, Dominica, Dominican Republic, Ecuador, Egypt*, El Salvador, Equatorial Guinea, Estonia*, Eswatini, Ethiopia, Fiji, Finland*, France*, Gabon, Gambia, Georgia, Germany*, Ghana, Greece*, Grenada, Guatemala, Guinea*, Guinea-Bissau, Guyana, Haiti, Holy See*, Honduras, Hungary*, Iceland*, Iraq[1], Ireland*, Italy*, Jamaica, Japan*, Jordan, Kazakhstan, Kenya, Korea (North)[1], Korea (South)*, Kuwait*, Kyrgyzstan, Laos*, Latvia, Lebanon, Lesotho*, Liberia, Libya, Liechtenstein*, Lithuania*, Luxembourg*, Madagascar*, Malawi*, Maldives, Mali*, Malta*, Mauritania, Mauritius*, Mexico[1], Micronesia, Moldova, Monaco*, Mongolia*, Montenegro*, Morocco, Mozambique, Namibia*, Nauru, Netherlands*, New Zealand*, Nicaragua, Niger, Nigeria, North Macedonia*, Norway*, Oman*, Palau, Palestine, Panama*, Paraguay*, Peru, Philippines*, Poland*, Portugal*, Qatar*, Romania*, Russia*, Rwanda*, Saint Kitts and Nevis*, Saint Lucia, Saint Vincent and the Grenadines*, Samoa, San Marino, Sao Tome and Principe, Saudi Arabia*, Senegal, Serbia*, Seychelles*, Sierra Leone, Slovakia*, Slovenia*, Solomon Islands, South Africa, South Sudan, Spain*, Sudan, Suriname, Sweden*, Switzerland*, Syria*[1], Tajikistan*, Tanzania, Timor-Leste, Togo*, Tonga*, Trinidad and Tobago*, Tunisia, Turkmenistan, Uganda, UK*, Ukraine*, United Arab Emirates*, Uruguay*, Uzbekistan, Vanuatu, Venezuela, Viet Nam[1], Yemen, Zambia, Zimbabwe

* With reservation and/or declaration.
[1] Party only to Protocol I.

Signed but not ratified Protocols I and II (3): Iran, Pakistan, USA

Protocol I text: Swiss Federal Department of Foreign Affairs, <https://www.fdfa. admin.ch/dam/eda/fr/documents/aussenpolitik/voelkerrecht/geneve/77prot1_ en.pdf>

Protocol II text: Swiss Federal Department of Foreign Affairs, <https://www.fdfa. admin.ch/dam/eda/fr/documents/aussenpolitik/voelkerrecht/geneve77/prot2_ en.pdf>

Antarctic Treaty

Signed by the 12 original parties at Washington, DC, on 1 December 1959; entered into force on 23 June 1961; depositary US Government

The treaty declares the Antarctic an area to be used exclusively for peaceful purposes. It prohibits any measure of a military nature in the Antarctic, such as the establishment of military bases and fortifications, and the carrying out of military manoeuvres or the testing of any type of weapon. The treaty bans any nuclear explosion as well as the disposal of radioactive waste material in Antarctica.

States that demonstrate their interest in Antarctica by conducting substantial scientific research activity there, such as the establishment of a scientific station or the dispatch of a scientific expedition, are entitled to become consultative parties. Consultative parties meet at regular intervals to exchange information and hold consultations on matters pertaining to Antarctica, as well as to recommend to their governments measures in furtherance of the principles and objectives of the treaty. Consultative parties have a right to inspect any station or installation in Antarctica to ensure compliance with the treaty's provisions.

Parties (54): Argentina*, Australia*, Austria, Belarus, Belgium*, Brazil*, Bulgaria*, Canada, Chile*, China*, Colombia, Cuba, Czechia*, Denmark, Ecuador*, Estonia, Finland*, France*, Germany*, Greece, Guatemala, Hungary, Iceland, India*, Italy*, Japan*, Kazakhstan, Korea (North), Korea (South)*, Malaysia, Monaco, Mongolia, Netherlands*, New Zealand*, Norway*, Pakistan, Papua New Guinea, Peru*, Poland*, Portugal, Romania, Russia*, Slovakia, Slovenia, South Africa*, Spain*, Sweden*, Switzerland, Turkey, UK*, Ukraine*, Uruguay*, USA*, Venezuela

* Consultative party (29) under Article IX of the treaty.

Treaty text: Secretariat of the Antarctic Treaty, <https://www.ats.aq/documents/ats/treaty_original.pdf>

The Protocol on Environmental Protection (**1991 Madrid Protocol**) was opened for signature on 4 October 1991 and entered into force on 14 January 1998. It designated Antarctica as a natural reserve, devoted to peace and science.

Protocol text: Secretariat of the Antarctic Treaty, <https://www.ats.aq/documents/recatt/Att006_e.pdf>

Treaty Banning Nuclear Weapon Tests in the Atmosphere, in Outer Space and Under Water (Partial Test-Ban Treaty, PTBT)

Signed by three original parties at Moscow on 5 August 1963 and opened for signature by other states at London, Moscow and Washington, DC, on 8 August 1963; entered into force on 10 October 1963; depositaries British, Russian and US governments

The treaty prohibits the carrying out of any nuclear weapon test explosion or any other nuclear explosion (*a*) in the atmosphere, beyond its limits, including outer space, or under water, including territorial waters or high seas; and (*b*) in any other environment if such explosion causes radioactive debris to be present outside the territorial limits of the state under whose jurisdiction or control the explosion is conducted.

A party may withdraw from the treaty, having given three months' notice, if it decides that its supreme interests have been jeopardized by extraordinary events related to the treaty's subject matter.

Parties (126): Afghanistan, Antigua and Barbuda, Argentina, Armenia, Australia, Austria, Bahamas, Bangladesh, Belarus, Belgium, Benin, Bhutan, Bolivia, Bosnia and Herzegovina, Botswana, Brazil, Bulgaria, Cabo Verde, Canada, Central African Republic, Chad, Chile, Colombia, Congo (Democratic Republic of the), Costa Rica, Côte d'Ivoire, Croatia, Cyprus, Czechia, Denmark, Dominican Republic, Ecuador, Egypt, El Salvador, Equatorial Guinea, Eswatini, Fiji, Finland, Gabon, Gambia, Germany, Ghana, Greece, Guatemala, Guinea-Bissau, Honduras, Hungary, Iceland, India, Indonesia, Iran, Iraq, Ireland, Israel, Italy, Jamaica, Japan, Jordan, Kenya, Korea (South), Kuwait, Laos, Lebanon, Liberia, Libya, Luxembourg, Madagascar, Malawi, Malaysia, Malta, Mauritania, Mauritius, Mexico, Mongolia, Montenegro, Morocco, Myanmar, Nepal, Netherlands, New Zealand, Nicaragua, Niger, Nigeria, Norway, Pakistan, Panama, Papua New Guinea, Peru, Philippines, Poland, Romania, Russia, Rwanda, Samoa, San Marino, Senegal, Serbia, Seychelles, Sierra Leone, Singapore,

Slovakia, Slovenia, South Africa, Spain, Sri Lanka, Sudan, Suriname, Sweden, Switzerland, Syria, Taiwan, Tanzania, Thailand, Togo, Tonga, Trinidad and Tobago, Tunisia, Turkey, Uganda, UK, Ukraine, Uruguay, USA, Venezuela, Yemen, Zambia

Signed but not ratified (10): Algeria, Burkina Faso, Burundi, Cameroon, Ethiopia, Haiti, Mali, Paraguay, Portugal, Somalia

Treaty text: Russian Ministry of Foreign Affairs, <https://mddoc.mid.ru/api/ia/download/ ?uuid=561590f5-ed1a-4e2a-a04e-f715bccb16ad>

Treaty on Principles Governing the Activities of States in the Exploration and Use of Outer Space, Including the Moon and Other Celestial Bodies (Outer Space Treaty)

Opened for signature at London, Moscow and Washington, DC, on 27 January 1967; entered into force on 10 October 1967; depositaries British, Russian and US governments

The treaty prohibits the placing into orbit around the earth of any object carrying nuclear weapons or any other kind of weapon of mass destruction, the installation of such weapons on celestial bodies, or the stationing of them in outer space in any other manner. The establishment of military bases, installations and fortifications, the testing of any type of weapon and the conducting of military manoeuvres on celestial bodies are also forbidden.

A party may withdraw from the treaty having given one year's notice.

Parties (112): Afghanistan, Algeria, Antigua and Barbuda, Argentina, Armenia, Australia, Austria, Azerbaijan, Bahamas, Bahrain, Bangladesh, Barbados, Belarus, Belgium, Benin, Bosnia and Herzegovina, Brazil, Bulgaria, Burkina Faso, Canada, Chile, China, Cuba, Cyprus, Czechia, Denmark, Dominican Republic, Ecuador, Egypt, El Salvador, Equatorial Guinea, Estonia, Fiji, Finland, France, Germany, Greece, Guinea-Bissau, Hungary, Iceland, India, Indonesia, Iraq, Ireland, Israel, Italy, Jamaica, Japan, Kazakhstan, Kenya, Korea (North), Korea (South), Kuwait, Laos, Lebanon, Libya, Lithuania, Luxembourg, Madagascar, Mali, Malta, Mauritius, Mexico, Mongolia, Morocco, Myanmar, Nepal, Netherlands, New Zealand, Nicaragua, Niger, Nigeria, Norway, Pakistan, Papua New Guinea, Paraguay, Peru, Poland, Portugal, Qatar, Romania, Russia, Saint Vincent and the Grenadines, San Marino, Saudi Arabia, Seychelles, Sierra Leone, Singapore, Slovakia, Slovenia, South Africa, Spain, Sri Lanka, Sweden, Switzerland, Syria, Taiwan, Thailand, Togo, Tonga, Tunisia, Turkey, Uganda, UK, Ukraine, United Arab Emirates, Uruguay, USA, Venezuela, Viet Nam, Yemen, Zambia

Signed but not ratified (23): Bolivia, Botswana, Burundi, Cameroon, Central African Republic, Colombia, Congo (Democratic Republic of the), Ethiopia, Gambia, Ghana, Guyana, Haiti, Holy See, Honduras, Iran, Jordan, Lesotho, Malaysia, Panama, Philippines, Rwanda, Somalia, Trinidad and Tobago

Treaty text: British Foreign and Commonwealth Office, Treaty Series no. 10 (1968), <https:// assets.publishing.service.gov.uk/government/uploads/system/uploads/attachment_data/ file/270006/Treaty_Principles_Activities_Outer_Space.pdf>

Treaty on the Non-Proliferation of Nuclear Weapons (Non-Proliferation Treaty, NPT)

Opened for signature at London, Moscow and Washington, DC, on 1 July 1968; entered into force on 5 March 1970; depositaries British, Russian and US governments

The treaty defines a nuclear weapon state to be a state that manufactured and exploded a nuclear weapon or other nuclear explosive device prior to 1 January 1967. According to this definition, there are five nuclear weapon states: China, France, Russia, the United Kingdom and the United States. All other states are defined as non-nuclear weapon states.

The treaty prohibits the nuclear weapon states from transferring nuclear weapons or other nuclear explosive devices or control over them to any recipient and prohibits them from assisting, encouraging or inducing any non-nuclear weapon state to manufacture or otherwise acquire such a weapon or device. It also prohibits non-nuclear weapon states parties from receiving nuclear weapons or other nuclear explosive devices from any source, from manufacturing them, or from acquiring them in any other way.

The parties undertake to facilitate the exchange of equipment, materials, and scientific and technological information for the peaceful uses of nuclear energy and to ensure that potential benefits from peaceful applications of nuclear explosions will be made available to non-nuclear weapon states party to the treaty. They also undertake to pursue negotiations in good faith on effective measures relating to cessation of the nuclear arms race at an early date and to nuclear disarmament, and on a treaty on general and complete disarmament.

Non-nuclear weapon states parties undertake to conclude safeguard agreements with the International Atomic Energy Agency (IAEA) with a view to preventing diversion of nuclear energy from peaceful uses to nuclear weapons or other nuclear explosive devices. A Model Protocol Additional to the Safeguards Agreements, strengthening the measures, was approved in 1997; additional safeguards protocols are signed by states individually with the IAEA.

A review and extension conference, convened in 1995 in accordance with the treaty, decided that the treaty should remain in force indefinitely. A party may withdraw from the treaty, having given three months' notice, if it decides that its supreme interests have been jeopardized by extraordinary events related to the treaty's subject matter.

Parties (192): Afghanistan*, Albania*, Algeria*, Andorra*, Angola*, Antigua and Barbuda*, Argentina*, Armenia*, Australia*, Austria*, Azerbaijan*, Bahamas*, Bahrain*, Bangladesh*, Barbados*, Belarus*, Belgium*, Belize*, Benin*, Bhutan*, Bolivia*, Bosnia and Herzegovina*, Botswana*, Brazil*, Brunei Darussalam*, Bulgaria*, Burkina Faso*, Burundi*, Cabo Verde, Cambodia*, Cameroon*, Canada*, Central African Republic*, Chad*, Chile*, China*†, Colombia*, Comoros*, Congo (Democratic Republic of the)*, Congo (Republic of the)*, Costa Rica*, Côte d'Ivoire*, Croatia*, Cuba*, Cyprus*, Czechia*, Denmark*, Djibouti*, Dominica*, Dominican Republic*, Ecuador*, Egypt*, El Salvador*, Equatorial Guinea, Eritrea*, Estonia*, Eswatini*, Ethiopia*, Fiji*, Finland*, France*†, Gabon*, Gambia*, Georgia*, Germany*, Ghana*, Greece*, Grenada*, Guatemala*, Guinea, Guinea-Bissau*, Guyana*, Haiti*, Holy See*, Honduras*, Hungary*, Iceland*, Indonesia*, Iran*, Iraq*, Ireland*, Italy*, Jamaica*, Japan*, Jordan*, Kazakhstan*, Kenya*, Kiribati*, Korea (South)*, Korea (North)‡, Kuwait*, Kyrgyzstan*, Laos*, Latvia*, Lebanon*, Lesotho*, Liberia*, Libya*, Liechtenstein*, Lithuania*,

Luxembourg*, Madagascar*, Malawi*, Malaysia*, Maldives*, Mali*, Malta*, Marshall Islands*, Mauritania*, Mauritius*, Mexico*, Micronesia*, Moldova*, Monaco*, Mongolia*, Montenegro*, Morocco*, Mozambique*, Myanmar*, Namibia*, Nauru*, Nepal*, Netherlands*, New Zealand*, Nicaragua*, Niger*, Nigeria*, North Macedonia*, Norway*, Oman*, Palau*, Palestine, Panama*, Papua New Guinea*, Paraguay*, Peru*, Philippines*, Poland*, Portugal*, Qatar*, Romania*, Russia*[†], Rwanda*, Saint Kitts and Nevis*, Saint Lucia*, Saint Vincent and the Grenadines*, Samoa*, San Marino*, Sao Tome and Principe, Saudi Arabia*, Senegal*, Serbia*, Seychelles*, Sierra Leone*, Singapore*, Slovakia*, Slovenia*, Solomon Islands*, Somalia, South Africa*, Spain*, Sri Lanka*, Sudan*, Suriname*, Sweden*, Switzerland*, Syria*, Taiwan*, Tajikistan*, Tanzania*, Thailand*, Timor-Leste, Togo*, Tonga*, Trinidad and Tobago*, Tunisia*, Turkey*, Turkmenistan*, Tuvalu*, Uganda*, UK*[†], Ukraine*, United Arab Emirates*, Uruguay*, USA*[†], Uzbekistan*, Vanuatu*, Venezuela*, Viet Nam*, Yemen*, Zambia*, Zimbabwe*

* Party (183) with safeguards agreements in force with the IAEA, as required by the treaty, or concluded by a nuclear weapon state on a voluntary basis. In addition to these 183 states, as of 1 Jan. 2022 Cabo Verde, Guinea, Guinea-Bissau, Palestine and Timor-Leste had each signed a safeguards agreement that had not yet entered into force.

[†] Nuclear weapon state as defined by the treaty.

[‡] On 12 Mar. 1993 North Korea announced its withdrawal from the NPT with effect from 12 June 1993. It decided to 'suspend' the withdrawal on 11 June. On 10 Jan. 2003 North Korea announced its 'immediate' withdrawal from the NPT. A safeguards agreement was in force at that time. The current status of North Korea is disputed by the other parties.

Treaty text: International Atomic Energy Agency, INFCIRC/140, 22 Apr. 1970, <https://www.iaea.org/sites/default/files/publications/documents/infcircs/1970/infcirc140.pdf>

Additional safeguards protocols in force (139): Afghanistan, Albania, Andorra, Angola, Antigua and Barbuda, Armenia, Australia, Austria, Azerbaijan, Bahrain, Bangladesh, Belgium, Benin, Bosnia and Herzegovina, Botswana, Bulgaria, Burkina Faso, Burundi, Cambodia, Cameroon, Canada, Central African Republic, Chad, Chile, China, Colombia, Comoros, Congo (Democratic Republic of the), Congo (Republic of), Costa Rica, Côte d'Ivoire, Croatia, Cuba, Cyprus, Czechia, Denmark[1], Djibouti, Dominican Republic, Ecuador, El Salvador, *Eritrea*, Estonia, Eswatini, Ethiopia, Euratom, Fiji, Finland, France, Gabon, Gambia, Georgia, Germany, Ghana, Greece, Guatemala, Haiti, Holy See, Honduras, Hungary, Iceland, India, Indonesia, Iraq, Ireland, Italy, Jamaica, Japan, Jordan, Kazakhstan, Kenya, Korea (South), Kuwait, Kyrgyzstan, Latvia, Lesotho, Liberia, Libya, Liechtenstein, Lithuania, Luxembourg, Madagascar, Malawi, Mali, Malta, Marshall Islands, Mauritania, Mauritius, Mexico, Moldova, Monaco, Mongolia, Montenegro, Morocco, Mozambique, Namibia, Netherlands, New Zealand, Nicaragua, Niger, Nigeria, North Macedonia, Norway, Palau, Panama, Paraguay, Peru, Philippines, Poland, Portugal, Romania, Russia, Rwanda, Saint Kitts and Nevis, Senegal, Serbia, Seychelles, Singapore, Slovakia, Slovenia, South Africa, Spain, Sweden, Switzerland, Tajikistan, Tanzania, Thailand, Togo, Turkey, Turkmenistan, Uganda, UK, Ukraine, United Arab Emirates, Uruguay, USA, Uzbekistan, Vanuatu, Viet Nam, *Zimbabwe*

[1] A separate additional protocol is also in force for the Danish territory of Greenland.

Note: Taiwan has agreed to apply the measures contained in the Model Additional Protocol.

Additional safeguards protocols signed but not yet in force (14): Algeria, Belarus, Bolivia, Cabo Verde, Guinea, Guinea-Bissau, Iran*, Kiribati, Laos, Malaysia, Myanmar, Timor-Leste, Tunisia, Zambia

* Iran notified the IAEA that as of 16 Jan. 2016 it would provisionally apply the Additional Protocol that it signed in 2003 but has not yet ratified. It has not been applied since 23 Feb. 2021.

Model Additional Safeguards Protocol text: International Atomic Energy Agency, INFCIRC/540 (corrected), Sep. 1997, <https://www.iaea.org/sites/default/files/infcirc540c.pdf>

Treaty on the Prohibition of the Emplacement of Nuclear Weapons and other Weapons of Mass Destruction on the Seabed and the Ocean Floor and in the Subsoil thereof (Seabed Treaty)

Opened for signature at London, Moscow and Washington, DC, on 11 February 1971; entered into force on 18 May 1972; depositaries British, Russian and US governments

The treaty prohibits implanting or emplacing on the seabed and the ocean floor and in the subsoil thereof beyond the outer limit of a 12-nautical mile (22-kilometre) seabed zone any nuclear weapon or any other type of weapon of mass destruction as well as structures, launching installations or any other facilities specifically designed for storing, testing or using such weapons.

A party may withdraw from the treaty, having given three months' notice, if it decides that its supreme interests have been jeopardized by extraordinary events related to the treaty's subject matter.

Parties (95): Afghanistan, Algeria, Antigua and Barbuda, Argentina, Australia, Austria, Bahamas, Belarus, Belgium, Benin, Bosnia and Herzegovina, Botswana, Brazil*, Bulgaria, Canada*, Cabo Verde, Central African Republic, China, Congo (Republic of the), Côte d'Ivoire, Cuba, Cyprus, Czechia, Denmark, Dominican Republic, Eswatini, Ethiopia, Finland, Germany, Ghana, Greece, Guatemala, Guinea-Bissau, Hungary, Iceland, India*, Iran, Iraq, Ireland, Italy*, Jamaica, Japan, Jordan, Korea (South), Laos, Latvia, Lesotho, Libya, Liechtenstein, Luxembourg, Malaysia, Malta, Mauritius, Mexico*, Mongolia, Montenegro, Morocco, Nepal, Netherlands, New Zealand, Nicaragua, Niger, Norway, Panama, Philippines, Poland, Portugal, Qatar, Romania, Russia, Rwanda, Saint Kitts and Nevis, Saint Vincent and the Grenadines, Sao Tome and Principe, Saudi Arabia, Serbia*, Seychelles, Singapore, Slovakia, Slovenia, Solomon Islands, South Africa, Spain, Sweden, Switzerland, Taiwan, Togo, Tunisia, Turkey*, UK, Ukraine, USA, Viet Nam*, Yemen, Zambia

* With reservation and/or declaration.

Signed but not ratified (21): Bolivia, Burundi, Cambodia, Cameroon, Colombia, Costa Rica, Equatorial Guinea, Gambia, Guinea, Honduras, Lebanon, Liberia, Madagascar, Mali, Myanmar, Paraguay, Senegal, Sierra Leone, Sudan, Tanzania, Uruguay

Treaty text: British Foreign and Commonwealth Office, Treaty Series no. 13 (1973), <https://assets.publishing.service.gov.uk/government/uploads/system/uploads/attachment_data/file/269694/Treaty_Prohib_Nuclear_Sea-Bed.pdf>

Convention on the Prohibition of the Development, Production and Stockpiling of Bacteriological (Biological) and Toxin Weapons and on their Destruction (Biological and Toxin Weapons Convention, BWC)

Opened for signature at London, Moscow and Washington, DC, on 10 April 1972; entered into force on 26 March 1975; depositaries British, Russian and US governments

The convention prohibits the development, production, stockpiling or acquisition by other means or retention of microbial or other biological agents or toxins (whatever their origin or method of production) of types and in quantities that have no justification of prophylactic, protective or other peaceful purposes. It also prohibits weapons, equipment or means of delivery designed to use such agents or toxins for hostile purposes or in armed conflict. The destruction of the agents, toxins, weapons, equipment and means of delivery in the possession of the parties, or their diversion to peaceful purposes, should be completed not later than nine months after the entry into force of the convention for each country.

The parties hold annual political and technical meetings to strengthen implementation of the convention. A three-person Implementation Support Unit (ISU), based in Geneva, was established in 2007 to support the parties in implementing the treaty, including facilitating the collection and distribution of annual confidence-building measures and supporting their efforts to achieve universal membership.

A party may withdraw from the convention, having given three months' notice, if it decides that its supreme interests have been jeopardized by extraordinary events related to the treaty's subject matter.

Parties (184): Afghanistan, Albania, Algeria, Andorra, Angola, Antigua and Barbuda, Argentina, Armenia, Australia, Austria*, Azerbaijan, Bahamas, Bahrain*, Bangladesh, Barbados, Belarus, Belgium, Belize, Benin, Bhutan, Bolivia, Bosnia and Herzegovina, Botswana, Brazil, Brunei Darussalam, Bulgaria, Burkina Faso, Burundi, Cabo Verde, Cambodia, Cameroon, Canada, Central African Republic, Chile, China*, Colombia, Congo (Democratic Republic of the), Congo (Republic of the), Cook Islands, Costa Rica, Côte d'Ivoire, Croatia, Cuba, Cyprus, Czechia*, Denmark, Dominica, Dominican Republic, Ecuador, El Salvador, Equatorial Guinea, Estonia, Eswatini, Ethiopia, Fiji, Finland, France, Gabon, Gambia, Georgia, Germany, Ghana, Greece, Grenada, Guatemala, Guinea, Guinea-Bissau, Guyana, Holy See, Honduras, Hungary, Iceland, India*, Indonesia, Iran, Iraq, Ireland*, Italy, Jamaica, Japan, Jordan, Kazakhstan, Kenya, Korea (North), Korea (South)*, Kuwait*, Kyrgyzstan, Laos, Latvia, Lebanon, Lesotho, Liberia, Libya, Liechtenstein, Lithuania, Luxembourg, Madagascar, Malawi, Malaysia*, Maldives, Mali, Malta, Marshall Islands, Mauritania, Mauritius, Mexico*, Moldova, Monaco, Mongolia, Montenegro, Morocco, Mozambique, Myanmar, Nauru, Nepal, Netherlands, New Zealand, Nicaragua, Niger, Nigeria, Niue, North Macedonia, Norway, Oman, Pakistan, Palau, Palestine, Panama, Papua New Guinea, Paraguay, Peru, Philippines, Poland, Portugal, Qatar, Romania, Russia, Rwanda, Saint Kitts and Nevis, Saint Lucia, Saint Vincent and the Grenadines, Samoa, San Marino, Sao Tome and Principe, Saudi Arabia, Senegal, Serbia, Seychelles, Sierra Leone, Singapore, Slovakia*, Slovenia, Solomon Islands, South Africa, Spain, Sri Lanka, Sudan, Suriname, Sweden, Switzerland*, Taiwan, Tajikistan, Tanzania, Thailand, Timor-Leste, Togo, Tonga, Trinidad and Tobago, Tunisia, Turkey, Turkmenistan, Uganda, UK*, Ukraine, United Arab Emirates, Uruguay, USA, Uzbekistan, Vanuatu, Venezuela, Viet Nam, Yemen, Zambia, Zimbabwe

* With reservation and/or declaration.

Signed but not ratified (4): Egypt, Haiti, Somalia, Syria

Treaty text: British Foreign and Commonwealth Office, Treaty Series no. 11 (1976), <https://assets.publishing.service.gov.uk/government/uploads/system/uploads/attachment_data/file/269698/Convention_Prohibition_Stock_Bacterio.pdf>

Convention on the Prohibition of Military or Any Other Hostile Use of Environmental Modification Techniques (Enmod Convention)

Opened for signature at Geneva on 18 May 1977; entered into force on 5 October 1978; depositary UN Secretary-General

The convention prohibits military or any other hostile use of environmental modification techniques that have widespread, long-lasting or severe effects as the means of destruction, damage or injury to states parties. The term 'environmental modification techniques' refers to any technique for changing—through the deliberate manipulation of natural processes—the dynamics, composition or structure of the earth, including its biota, lithosphere, hydrosphere and atmosphere, or of outer space. Understandings reached during the negotiations, but not written into the convention, define the terms 'widespread', 'long-lasting' and 'severe'.

Parties (78): Afghanistan, Algeria, Antigua and Barbuda, Argentina*, Armenia, Australia, Austria*, Bangladesh, Belarus, Belgium, Benin, Brazil, Bulgaria, Cabo Verde, Cameroon, Canada, Chile, China, Costa Rica, Cuba, Cyprus, Czechia, Denmark, Dominica, Egypt, Estonia, Finland, Germany, Ghana, Greece, Guatemala*, Honduras, Hungary, India, Ireland, Italy, Japan, Kazakhstan, Korea (North), Korea (South)*, Kuwait*, Kyrgyzstan, Lithuania, Laos, Malawi, Mauritius, Mongolia, Netherlands*, New Zealand*, Nicaragua, Niger, Norway, Pakistan, Palestine, Panama, Papua New Guinea, Poland, Romania, Russia, Saint Lucia, Saint Vincent and the Grenadines, Sao Tome and Principe, Slovakia, Slovenia, Solomon Islands, Spain, Sri Lanka, Sweden, Switzerland*, Tajikistan, Tunisia, UK, Ukraine, Uruguay, USA, Uzbekistan, Viet Nam, Yemen

   * With reservation and/or declaration.

Signed but not ratified (16): Bolivia, Congo (Democratic Republic of the), Ethiopia, Holy See, Iceland, Iran, Iraq, Lebanon, Liberia, Luxembourg, Morocco, Portugal, Sierra Leone, Syria, Turkey, Uganda

Convention text: United Nations Treaty Collection, <https://treaties.un.org/doc/Treaties/1978/10/19781005 00-39 AM/Ch_XXVI_01p.pdf>

Convention on the Physical Protection of Nuclear Material and Nuclear Facilities

Original convention opened for signature at New York and Vienna on 3 March 1980; entered into force on 8 February 1987; amendments adopted on 8 July 2005; amended convention entered into force for its ratifying states on 8 May 2016; depositary IAEA Director General

The original convention—named the **Convention on the Physical Protection of Nuclear Material**—obligates its parties to protect nuclear material for peaceful purposes while in international transport.

The convention as amended and renamed also obligates its parties to protect nuclear facilities and material used for peaceful purposes while in storage.

A party may withdraw from the convention, having given 180 days' notice.

Parties to the original convention (164): Afghanistan, Albania, Algeria*, Andorra, Angola, Antigua and Barbuda, Argentina*, Armenia, Australia*, Austria*, Azerbaijan*, Bahamas*, Bahrain*, Bangladesh, Belarus*, Belgium*, Benin, Bolivia, Bosnia and Herzegovina, Botswana,

Brazil, Bulgaria, Burkina Faso, Cabo Verde, Cambodia, Cameroon, Canada*, Central African Republic, Chad, Chile, China*, Colombia, Comoros, Congo (Democratic Republic of the), *Congo (Republic of the)*, Costa Rica, Côte d'Ivoire, Croatia, Cuba*, Cyprus*, Czechia, Denmark, Djibouti, Dominica, Dominican Republic, Ecuador, El Salvador*, Equatorial Guinea, Eritrea*, Estonia, Eswatini, Euratom*, Fiji, Finland*, France*, Gabon, Georgia, Germany*, Ghana, Greece*, Grenada, Guatemala*, Guinea, Guinea-Bissau, Guyana, Honduras, Hungary, Iceland, India*, Indonesia*, Iraq, Ireland*, Israel*, Italy*, Jamaica, Japan, Jordan*, Kazakhstan, Kenya, Korea (South)*, Kuwait*, Kyrgyzstan, Laos*, Latvia, Lebanon, Lesotho, Libya, Liechtenstein, Lithuania, Luxembourg*, Madagascar, Malawi, Mali, Malta, Marshall Islands, Mauritania, Mexico, Moldova, Monaco, Mongolia, Montenegro, Morocco, Mozambique*, Myanmar*, Namibia, Nauru, Netherlands*, New Zealand, Nicaragua, Niger, Nigeria, Niue, North Macedonia, Norway*, Oman*, Pakistan*, Palau, Palestine, Panama, Paraguay, Peru*, Philippines, Poland, Portugal*, Qatar*, Romania*, Russia, Rwanda, Saint Kitts and Nevis, Saint Lucia*, San Marino, Saudi Arabia*, Senegal, Serbia, Seychelles, Singapore*, Slovakia, Slovenia, South Africa*, Spain*, Sudan, Sweden*, Switzerland*, Syria*, Tajikistan, Tanzania, Thailand, Togo, Tonga, Trinidad and Tobago, Tunisia, Turkey*, Turkmenistan, Uganda, UK*, Ukraine, United Arab Emirates, Uruguay, USA*, Uzbekistan, Viet Nam*, Yemen, Zambia, *Zimbabwe*

* With reservation and/or declaration.

Signed but not ratified (1): Haiti

Convention text: International Atomic Energy Agency, INFCIRC/274, Nov. 1979, <https://www.iaea.org/sites/default/files/infcirc274.pdf>

Parties to the amended convention (127): Albania, Algeria, Angola, Antigua and Barbuda, Argentina, Armenia*, Australia, Austria, Azerbaijan*, Bahrain, Bangladesh, Belgium*, Benin, Bolivia, Bosnia and Herzegovina, Botswana, Bulgaria, Burkina Faso, Cameroon, Canada*, Chad, Chile, China*, Colombia, Comoros, Costa Rica, Côte d'Ivoire, Croatia, Cuba, Cyprus, Czechia, Denmark, Djibouti, Dominican Republic, Ecuador, El Salvador, Eritrea, Estonia, Eswatini, Euratom*, Fiji, Finland, France, Gabon, Georgia, Germany, Ghana, Greece, Hungary, Iceland, India, Indonesia, Ireland, Israel*, Italy, Jamaica, Japan, Jordan, Kazakhstan, Kenya, Korea (South), Kuwait, Kyrgyzstan, Latvia, Lesotho, Libya, Liechtenstein, Lithuania, Luxembourg, Madagascar, Mali, Malta, Marshall Islands, Mauritania, Mexico, Moldova, Monaco, Montenegro, Morocco, Myanmar*, Namibia, Nauru, Netherlands, New Zealand, Nicaragua, Niger, Nigeria, North Macedonia, Norway, Pakistan*, Palestine, Panama, Paraguay, Peru, *Philippines*, Poland, Portugal, Qatar, Romania, Russia, *Rwanda*, Saint Kitts and Nevis, Saint Lucia, San Marino, Saudi Arabia, Senegal, Serbia, Seychelles, Singapore*, Slovakia, Slovenia, Spain, Sweden, Switzerland, Syria*, Tajikistan, Thailand, Tunisia, Turkey*, Turkmenistan, UK, Ukraine, United Arab Emirates, Uruguay, USA*, Uzbekistan, Viet Nam

* With reservation and/or declaration.

Note: In addition to the 127 states that had ratified the amended convention as of 1 Jan. 2022, Malawi ratified it on 11 Feb. 2022 and Brazil on 18 Mar.

Amendment text and consolidated text of amended convention: International Atomic Energy Agency, INFCIRC/274/Rev.1/Mod.1 (Corrected), 18 Oct. 2021, <https://www.iaea.org/sites/default/files/publications/documents/infcircs/1979/infcirc274r1m1c.pdf>

Convention on Prohibitions or Restrictions on the Use of Certain Conventional Weapons which may be Deemed to be Excessively Injurious or to have Indiscriminate Effects (CCW Convention, or 'Inhumane Weapons' Convention)

Opened for signature with protocols I, II and III at New York on 10 April 1981; entered into force on 2 December 1983; depositary UN Secretary-General

The convention is an umbrella treaty, under which specific agreements can be concluded in the form of protocols. In order to become a party to the convention a state must ratify at least two of the protocols.

The amendment to Article I of the original convention was opened for signature at Geneva on 21 November 2001. It expands the scope of application to non-international armed conflicts. The amended convention entered into force on 18 May 2004.

Protocol I prohibits the use of weapons intended to injure using fragments that are not detectable in the human body by X-rays.

Protocol II prohibits or restricts the use of mines, booby-traps and other devices. *Amended Protocol II*, which entered into force on 3 December 1998, reinforces the constraints regarding anti-personnel mines.

Protocol III restricts the use of incendiary weapons.

Protocol IV, which entered into force on 30 July 1998, prohibits the employment of laser weapons specifically designed to cause permanent blindness to unenhanced vision.

Protocol V, which entered into force on 12 November 2006, recognizes the need for measures of a generic nature to minimize the risks and effects of explosive remnants of war.

A party may withdraw from the convention and its protocols, having given one year's notice. But if the party is involved in an armed conflict or occupation at that time, the withdrawal will not take effect until the conflict or occupation has ended and that party's obligations fulfilled.

Parties to the original convention (125) and protocols I (118), II (95) and III (115): Afghanistan[2], Albania, Algeria[2], Antigua and Barbuda[2], Argentina*, Australia, Austria, Bahrain[5], Bangladesh, Belarus, Belgium, Benin[2], Bolivia, Bosnia and Herzegovina, Brazil, Bulgaria, Burkina Faso, Burundi[4], Cabo Verde, Cambodia, Cameroon[6], Canada*, Chile[2], China*, Colombia, Costa Rica, Côte d'Ivoire[4], Croatia, Cuba, Cyprus*, Czechia, Denmark, Djibouti, Dominican Republic[6], Ecuador, El Salvador, Estonia[2], Finland, France*, Gabon[2], Georgia, Germany, Greece, Grenada[2], Guatemala, Guinea-Bissau, Holy See*, Honduras, Hungary, Iceland, India, Iraq, Ireland, Israel*[1], Italy*, Jamaica[2], Japan, Jordan[2], Kazakhstan[2], Korea (South)[3], Kuwait[2], Laos, Latvia, Lebanon[2], Lesotho, Liberia, Liechtenstein, Lithuania[2], Luxembourg, Madagascar, Maldives[2], Mali, Malta, Mauritius, Mexico, Moldova, Monaco[3], Mongolia, Montenegro, Morocco[4], Nauru, Netherlands*, New Zealand, Nicaragua[2], Niger, North Macedonia, Norway, Pakistan, Palestine[2], Panama, Paraguay, Peru[2], Philippines, Poland, Portugal, Qatar[2], Romania[2], Russia, Saint Vincent and the Grenadines[2], Saudi Arabia[2], Senegal[5], Serbia, Seychelles, Sierra Leone[2], Slovakia, Slovenia, South Africa, Spain, Sri Lanka, Sweden, Switzerland, Tajikistan, Togo, Tunisia, Turkey*[3], Turkmenistan[1], Uganda, UK*, Ukraine, United Arab Emirates[2], Uruguay, USA*, Uzbekistan, Venezuela, Zambia

* With reservation and/or declaration.
[1] Party only to 1981 protocols I and II.
[2] Party only to 1981 protocols I and III.

[3] Party only to 1981 Protocol I.
[4] Party only to 1981 Protocol II.
[5] Party only to 1981 Protocol III.
[6] Party to none of the original protocols.

Signed but not ratified the original convention and protocols (4): Egypt, Nigeria, Sudan, Viet Nam

Parties to the amended convention (86): Afghanistan, Algeria, Albania, Argentina, Australia, Austria, Bangladesh, Belarus, Belgium, Benin, Bosnia and Herzegovina, Brazil, Bulgaria, Burkina Faso, Canada, Chile, China, Colombia, Costa Rica, Croatia, Cuba, Czechia, Denmark, Dominican Republic, Ecuador, El Salvador, Estonia, Finland, France, Georgia, Germany, Greece, Grenada, Guatemala, Guinea-Bissau, Holy See*, Hungary, Iceland, India, Iraq, Ireland, Italy, Jamaica, Japan, Korea (South), Kuwait, Latvia, Lebanon, Lesotho, Liberia, Liechtenstein, Lithuania, Luxembourg, Malta, Mexico*, Moldova, Montenegro, Netherlands, New Zealand, Nicaragua, Niger, North Macedonia, Norway, Panama, Paraguay, Peru, Poland, Portugal, Romania, Russia, Serbia, Sierra Leone, Slovakia, Slovenia, South Africa, Spain, Sri Lanka, Sweden, Switzerland, Tunisia, Turkey, UK, Ukraine, Uruguay, USA, Zambia

* With reservation and/or declaration.

Parties to Amended Protocol II (106): Afghanistan, Albania, Argentina, Australia, Austria*, Bangladesh, Belarus*, Belgium*, Benin, Bolivia, Bosnia and Herzegovina, Brazil, Bulgaria, Burkina Faso, Cabo Verde, Cambodia, Cameroon, Canada*, Chile, China*, Colombia, Costa Rica, Croatia, Cyprus, Czechia, Denmark*, Dominican Republic, Ecuador, El Salvador, Estonia, Finland*, France*, Gabon, Georgia, Germany*, Greece*, Grenada, Guatemala, Guinea-Bissau, Holy See, Honduras, Hungary*, Iceland, India, Iraq, Ireland*, Israel*, Italy*, Jamaica, Japan, Jordan, Korea (South)*, Kuwait, Latvia, Lebanon, Liberia, Liechtenstein*, Lithuania, Luxembourg, Madagascar, Maldives, Mali, Malta, Mauritius, Moldova, Monaco, Montenegro, Morocco, Nauru, Netherlands*, New Zealand, Nicaragua, Niger, North Macedonia, Norway, Pakistan*, Panama, Paraguay, Peru, Philippines, Poland, Portugal, Romania, Russia*, Saint Vincent and the Grenadines, Senegal, Serbia, Seychelles, Sierra Leone, Slovakia, Slovenia, South Africa*, Spain, Sri Lanka, Sweden*, Switzerland*, Tajikistan, Tunisia, Turkey, Turkmenistan, UK*, Ukraine*, Uruguay, USA*, Venezuela, Zambia

* With reservation and/or declaration

Parties to Protocol IV (109): Afghanistan, Algeria, Albania, Antigua and Barbuda, Argentina, Australia*, Austria*, Bahrain, Bangladesh, Belarus, Belgium*, Benin, Bolivia, Bosnia and Herzegovina, Brazil, Bulgaria, Burkina Faso, Cabo Verde, Cambodia, Cameroon, Canada*, Chile, China, Colombia, Costa Rica, Croatia, Cuba, Cyprus, Czechia, Denmark, Dominican Republic, Ecuador, El Salvador, Estonia, Finland, France, Gabon, Georgia, Germany*, Greece*, Grenada, Guatemala, Guinea-Bissau, Holy See, Honduras, Hungary, Iceland, India, Iraq, Ireland*, Israel*, Italy*, Jamaica, Japan, Kazakhstan, Kuwait, Latvia, Lesotho, Liberia, Liechtenstein*, Lithuania, Luxembourg, Madagascar, Maldives, Mali, Malta, Mauritius, Mexico, Moldova, Mongolia, Montenegro, Morocco, Nauru, Netherlands*, New Zealand, Nicaragua, Niger, North Macedonia, Norway, Pakistan, Panama, Paraguay, Peru, Philippines, Poland*, Portugal, Qatar, Romania, Russia, Saint Vincent and the Grenadines, Saudi Arabia, Serbia, Seychelles, Sierra Leone, Slovakia, Slovenia, South Africa*, Spain, Sri Lanka, Sweden*, Switzerland*, Tajikistan, Tunisia, Turkey, UK*, Ukraine, Uruguay, USA*, Uzbekistan

* With reservation and/or declaration.

Parties to Protocol V (96): Afghanistan, Albania, Argentina*, Australia, Austria, Bahrain, Bangladesh, Belarus, Belgium, Benin, Bosnia and Herzegovina, Brazil, Bulgaria, Burkina Faso, Burundi, Cameroon, Canada, Chile, China, Costa Rica, Côte d'Ivoire, Croatia, Cuba, Cyprus, Czechia, Denmark, Dominican Republic, Ecuador, El Salvador, Estonia, Finland, France, Gabon, Georgia, Germany, Greece, Grenada, Guatemala, Guinea-Bissau, Holy See*, Honduras, Hungary, Iceland, India, Iraq, Ireland, Italy, Jamaica, Korea (South), Kuwait, Laos,

Latvia, Lesotho, Liberia, Liechtenstein, Lithuania, Luxembourg, Madagascar, Mali, Malta, Mauritius, Moldova, Montenegro, Netherlands, New Zealand, Nicaragua, North Macedonia, Norway, Pakistan, Palestine, Panama, Paraguay, Peru, Poland, Portugal, Qatar, Romania, Russia, Saint Vincent and the Grenadines, Saudi Arabia, Senegal, Sierra Leone, Slovakia, Slovenia, South Africa, Spain, Sweden, Switzerland, Tajikistan, Tunisia, Turkmenistan, Ukraine, United Arab Emirates, Uruguay, USA*, Zambia

  * With reservation and/or declaration.

Original convention and protocol text: United Nations Treaty Collection, <https://treaties.un.org/doc/Treaties/1983/12/19831202 01-19 AM/XXVI-2-revised.pdf>

Convention amendment text: United Nations Treaty Collection, <https://treaties.un.org/doc/Treaties/2001/12/20011221 01-23 AM/Ch_XXVI_02_cp.pdf>

Amended Protocol II text: United Nations Treaty Collection, <https://treaties.un.org/doc/Treaties/1996/05/19960503 01-38 AM/Ch_XXVI_02_bp.pdf>

Protocol IV text: United Nations Treaty Collection, <https://treaties.un.org/doc/Treaties/1995/10/19951013 01-30 AM/Ch_XXVI_02_ap.pdf>

Protocol V text: United Nations Treaty Collection, <https://treaties.un.org/doc/Treaties/2003/11/20031128 01-19 AM/Ch_XXVI_02_dp.pdf>

Convention on the Prohibition of the Development, Production, Stockpiling and Use of Chemical Weapons and on their Destruction (Chemical Weapons Convention, CWC)

Opened for signature at Paris on 13 January 1993; entered into force on 29 April 1997; depositary UN Secretary-General

The convention prohibits the development, production, acquisition, transfer, stockpiling and use of chemical weapons. The CWC regime consists of four pillars: disarmament, non-proliferation, assistance and protection against chemical weapons, and international cooperation on the peaceful uses of chemistry. The convention established the Organisation for the Prohibition of Chemical Weapons (OPCW) as its implementing body.

Each party undertook to destroy its chemical weapon stockpiles by 29 April 2012. Of the seven parties that had declared stocks of chemical weapons by that date, three had destroyed them (Albania, India and South Korea). Libya and Russia completed the destruction of their stockpiles in 2017 and Iraq did so in 2018, while the USA continues to destroy its stocks. The stockpile of chemical weapons that Syria declared when it acceded to the CWC in 2013 was destroyed in 2016, although gaps, inconsistencies and discrepancies in the 2013 declaration continue to be investigated. Old and abandoned chemical weapons will continue to be destroyed as they are uncovered from, for example, former battlefields.

A party may withdraw from the convention, having given 90 days' notice, if it decides that its supreme interests have been jeopardized by extraordinary events related to the treaty's subject matter.

Parties (193): Afghanistan, Albania, Algeria, Andorra, Angola, Antigua and Barbuda, Argentina, Armenia, Australia*, Austria*, Azerbaijan, Bahamas, Bahrain, Bangladesh, Barbados, Belarus, Belgium*, Belize, Benin, Bhutan, Bolivia, Bosnia and Herzegovina, Botswana, Brazil, Brunei Darussalam, Bulgaria, Burkina Faso, Burundi, Cabo Verde, Cambodia, Cameroon, Canada,

Central African Republic, Chad, Chile, China*, Colombia, Comoros, Congo (Democratic Republic of the), Congo (Republic of the), Cook Islands, Costa Rica, Côte d'Ivoire, Croatia, Cuba*, Cyprus, Czechia, Denmark*, Djibouti, Dominica, Dominican Republic, Ecuador, El Salvador, Equatorial Guinea, Eritrea, Estonia, Eswatini, Ethiopia, Fiji, Finland, France*, Gabon, Gambia, Georgia, Germany*, Ghana, Greece*, Grenada, Guatemala, Guinea, Guinea-Bissau, Guyana, Haiti, Holy See*, Honduras, Hungary, Iceland, India, Indonesia, Iran*, Iraq, Ireland*, Italy*, Jamaica, Japan, Jordan, Kazakhstan, Kenya, Kiribati, Korea (South), Kuwait, Kyrgyzstan, Laos, Latvia, Lebanon, Lesotho, Liberia, Libya, Liechtenstein, Lithuania, Luxembourg*, Madagascar, Malawi, Malaysia, Maldives, Mali, Malta, Marshall Islands, Mauritania, Mauritius, Mexico, Micronesia, Moldova, Monaco, Mongolia, Montenegro, Morocco, Mozambique, Myanmar, Namibia, Nauru, Nepal, Netherlands*, New Zealand, Nicaragua, Niger, Nigeria, Niue, North Macedonia, Norway, Oman, Pakistan*, Palau, Palestine, Panama, Papua New Guinea, Paraguay, Peru, Philippines, Poland, Portugal*, Qatar, Romania, Russia, Rwanda, Saint Kitts and Nevis, Saint Lucia, Saint Vincent and the Grenadines, Samoa, San Marino, Sao Tome and Principe, Saudi Arabia, Senegal, Serbia, Seychelles, Sierra Leone, Singapore, Slovakia, Slovenia, Solomon Islands, Somalia, South Africa, Spain*, Sri Lanka, Sudan*, Suriname, Sweden, Switzerland, Syria*, Tajikistan, Tanzania, Thailand, Timor-Leste, Togo, Tonga, Trinidad and Tobago, Tunisia, Turkey, Turkmenistan, Tuvalu, Uganda, UK*, Ukraine, United Arab Emirates, Uruguay, USA*, Uzbekistan, Vanuatu, Venezuela, Viet Nam, Yemen, Zambia, Zimbabwe

* With reservation and/or declaration.

Signed but not ratified (1): Israel

Convention text: United Nations Treaty Collection, <https://treaties.un.org/doc/Treaties/1997/ 04/19970429 07-52 PM/CTC-XXVI_03_ocred.pdf>

Comprehensive Nuclear-Test-Ban Treaty (CTBT)

Opened for signature at New York on 24 September 1996; not in force; depositary UN Secretary-General

The treaty would prohibit the carrying out of any nuclear weapon test explosion or any other nuclear explosion and urges each party to prevent any such nuclear explosion at any place under its jurisdiction or control and refrain from causing, encouraging or in any way participating in the carrying out of any nuclear weapon test explosion or any other nuclear explosion.

The verification regime established by the treaty will consist of an International Monitoring System (IMS) to detect signs of nuclear explosions, an International Data Centre to collect and distribute data from the IMS, and the right to on-site inspection to determine whether an explosion has taken place. Work under the treaty will be implemented by the Comprehensive Nuclear-Test-Ban Treaty Organization (CTBTO).

The treaty will enter into force 180 days after the date that all of the 44 states listed in an annex to the treaty have deposited their instruments of ratification. All 44 states possess nuclear power reactors or nuclear research reactors. Pending entry into force, a Preparatory Commission is preparing for the treaty's implementation and the establishment of the CTBTO and the IMS.

After entry into force, a party will be able to withdraw from the treaty, having given six months' notice, if it decides that its supreme interests have been jeopardized by extraordinary events related to the treaty's subject matter.

States whose ratification is required for entry into force (44): Algeria, Argentina, Australia, Austria, Bangladesh, Belgium, Brazil, Bulgaria, Canada, Chile, China*, Colombia, Congo (Democratic Republic of the), Egypt*, Finland, France, Germany, Hungary, India*, Indonesia, Iran*, Israel*, Italy, Japan, Korea (North)*, Korea (South), Mexico, Netherlands, Norway, Pakistan*, Peru, Poland, Romania, Russia, Slovakia, South Africa, Spain, Sweden, Switzerland, Turkey, UK, Ukraine, USA*, Viet Nam

* Has not ratified the treaty.

Ratifications deposited (170): Afghanistan, Albania, Algeria, Andorra, Angola, Antigua and Barbuda, Argentina, Armenia, Australia, Austria, Azerbaijan, Bahamas, Bahrain, Bangladesh, Barbados, Belarus, Belgium, Belize, Benin, Bolivia, Bosnia and Herzegovina, Botswana, Brazil, Brunei Darussalam, Bulgaria, Burkina Faso, Burundi, Cabo Verde, Cambodia, Cameroon, Canada, Central African Republic, Chad, Chile, Colombia, *Comoros*, Congo (Democratic Republic of the), Cook Islands, Costa Rica, Côte d'Ivoire, Congo (Republic of the), Croatia, *Cuba*, Cyprus, Czechia, Denmark, Djibouti, Dominican Republic, Ecuador, El Salvador, Eritrea, Estonia, Eswatini, Ethiopia, Fiji, Finland, France, Gabon, Georgia, Germany, Ghana, Greece, Grenada, Guatemala, Guinea, Guinea-Bissau, Guyana, Haiti, Holy See, Honduras, Hungary, Iceland, Indonesia, Iraq, Ireland, Italy, Jamaica, Japan, Jordan, Kazakhstan, Kenya, Kiribati, Korea (South), Kuwait, Kyrgyzstan, Laos, Latvia, Lebanon, Lesotho, Liberia, Libya, Liechtenstein, Lithuania, Luxembourg, Madagascar, Malawi, Malaysia, Maldives, Mali, Malta, Marshall Islands, Mauritania, Mexico, Micronesia, Moldova, Monaco, Mongolia, Montenegro, Morocco, Mozambique, Myanmar, Namibia, Nauru, Netherlands, New Zealand, Nicaragua, Niger, Nigeria, Niue, North Macedonia, Norway, Oman, Palau, Panama, Paraguay, Peru, Philippines, Poland, Portugal, Qatar, Romania, Russia, Rwanda, Saint Kitts and Nevis, Saint Lucia, Saint Vincent and the Grenadines, Samoa, San Marino, Senegal, Serbia, Seychelles, Sierra Leone, Singapore, Slovakia, Slovenia, South Africa, Spain, Sudan, Suriname, Sweden, Switzerland, Tajikistan, Tanzania, Thailand, Togo, Trinidad and Tobago, Tunisia, Turkey, Turkmenistan, Uganda, UK, Ukraine, United Arab Emirates, Uruguay, Uzbekistan, Vanuatu, Venezuela, Viet Nam, Zambia, Zimbabwe

Signed but not ratified (15): China, Egypt, Equatorial Guinea, Gambia, Iran, Israel, Nepal, Papua New Guinea, Sao Tome and Principe, Solomon Islands, Sri Lanka, Timor-Leste, Tuvalu, USA, Yemen

Note: In addition to the 170 states that had ratified the treaty as of 1 Jan. 2022, Gambia ratified it on 24 Mar. 2022 and Tuvalu on 31 Mar.

Treaty text: United Nations Treaty Collection, <https://treaties.un.org/doc/Treaties/1997/09/19970910 07-37 AM/Ch_XXVI_04p.pdf>

Convention on the Prohibition of the Use, Stockpiling, Production and Transfer of Anti-Personnel Mines and on their Destruction (APM Convention)

Opened for signature at Ottawa on 3–4 December 1997 and at New York on 5 December 1997; entered into force on 1 March 1999; depositary UN Secretary-General

The convention prohibits anti-personnel mines (APMs), which are defined as mines designed to be exploded by the presence, proximity or contact of a person and which will incapacitate, injure or kill one or more persons.

Each party undertakes to destroy all of its stockpiled APMs as soon as possible but not later than four years after the entry into force of the convention for that state party. Each party also undertakes to destroy all APMs in mined areas under its jurisdiction or control not later than 10 years after the entry into force of the convention for that state party. Of the 164 parties, 162 no longer had stockpiles of APMs and 30 of the 63 parties that reported areas containing APMs had cleared them by 1 January 2022. A three-person ISU, based in Geneva, provides advice and technical support on implementing the convention to the states parties.

A party may withdraw from the convention, having given six months' notice. But if the party is involved in an armed conflict at that time, the withdrawal will not take effect until that conflict has ended.

Parties (164): Afghanistan‡, Albania, Algeria, Andorra, Angola‡, Antigua and Barbuda, Argentina*‡, Australia*, Austria, Bahamas, Bangladesh, Barbados, Belarus, Belgium, Belize, Benin, Bhutan, Bolivia, Bosnia and Herzegovina‡, Botswana, Brazil, Brunei Darussalam, Bulgaria, Burkina Faso, Burundi, Cabo Verde, Cambodia‡, Cameroon, Canada*, Central African Republic, Chad‡, Chile*, Colombia‡, Comoros, Congo (Democratic Republic of the)‡, Congo (Republic of the), Cook Islands, Costa Rica, Côte d'Ivoire, Croatia‡, Cyprus‡, Czechia*, Denmark, Djibouti, Dominica, Dominican Republic, Ecuador‡, El Salvador, Equatorial Guinea, Eritrea‡, Estonia, Eswatini, Ethiopia‡, Fiji, Finland, France, Gabon, Gambia, Germany, Ghana, Greece*†, Grenada, Guatemala, Guinea, Guinea-Bissau, Guyana, Haiti, Holy See, Honduras, Hungary, Iceland, Indonesia, Iraq‡, Ireland, Italy, Jamaica, Japan, Jordan, Kenya, Kiribati, Kuwait, Latvia, Lesotho, Liberia, Liechtenstein, Lithuania*, Luxembourg, Madagascar, Malawi, Malaysia, Maldives, Mali, Malta, Mauritania‡, Mauritius, Mexico, Moldova, Monaco, Montenegro*, Mozambique, Namibia, Nauru, Netherlands, New Zealand, Nicaragua, Niger‡, Nigeria‡, Niue, North Macedonia, Norway, Oman‡, Palau, Palestine‡, Panama, Papua New Guinea, Paraguay, Peru‡, Philippines, Poland*, Portugal, Qatar, Romania, Rwanda, Saint Kitts and Nevis, Saint Lucia, Saint Vincent and the Grenadines, Samoa, San Marino, Sao Tome and Principe, Senegal‡, Serbia*‡, Seychelles, Sierra Leone, Slovakia, Slovenia, Solomon Islands, Somalia‡, South Africa, South Sudan‡, Spain, Sri Lanka†‡, Sudan‡, Suriname, Sweden, Switzerland, Tajikistan‡, Tanzania, Thailand‡, Timor-Leste, Togo, Trinidad and Tobago, Tunisia, Turkey‡, Turkmenistan, Tuvalu, Uganda, UK*, Ukraine†‡, Uruguay, Vanuatu, Venezuela, Yemen‡, Zambia, Zimbabwe‡

* With reservation and/or declaration.
† Party with remaining APM stockpile.
‡ Party with areas containing uncleared APMs.

Signed but not ratified (1): Marshall Islands

Convention text: United Nations Treaty Collection, <https://treaties.un.org/doc/Treaties/1997/09/19970918 07-53 AM/Ch_XXVI_05p.pdf>

Rome Statute of the International Criminal Court

Opened for signature at Rome on 17 July 1998 and at New York on 18 October 1998; entered into force on 1 July 2002; depositary UN Secretary-General

The Rome Statute established the International Criminal Court (ICC), a permanent international court dealing with accusations of genocide, crimes against humanity, war crimes and the crime of aggression. The ICC can investigate and prosecute an alleged crime that takes place on the territory of a state party, is committed by a state party or is referred to it by the UN Security Council. The ICC may only prosecute a crime if the domestic courts are unwilling or unable to do so.

The *Amendment to Article 8 adopted on 10 June 2010* makes it a war crime to use chemical weapons and expanding bullets in non-international conflicts. A series of *Amendments to Article 8 adopted on 14 December 2017* make it a war crime to use weapons which use microbial or other biological agents, or toxins; weapons the primary effect of which is to injure by fragments undetectable by x-rays in the human body; and blinding laser weapons. The *Amendment to Article 8 adopted on 6 December 2019* makes intentional use of starvation of civilians a war crime. Amendments to Article 8 enter into force for the parties that have accepted them one year after that acceptance.

Amendments adopted on 11 June 2010 define the crime of aggression. The ICC's jurisdiction over the crime of aggression was activated on 17 July 2018. From that date, the ICC may investigate an apparent act of aggression committed by a state that is party to the statute (and that has not opted out of jurisdiction over the crime of aggression) on the territory of another party; such acts on or by any state (regardless of whether it is a party to the statute) may also be referred to the ICC by the UN Security Council.

A state may withdraw from the statute and the ICC by giving 12 months' notice. Burundi withdrew from the statute and the ICC on 27 October 2017 and the Philippines on 17 March 2019.

Parties to the Rome Statute (123): Afghanistan, Albania, Andorra, Antigua and Barbuda, Argentina*, Australia*, Austria, Bangladesh, Barbados, Belgium, Belize, Benin, Bolivia, Bosnia and Herzegovina, Botswana, Brazil, Bulgaria, Burkina Faso, Cabo Verde, Cambodia, Canada, Central African Republic, Chad, Chile, Colombia*, Comoros, Congo (Democratic Republic of the), Congo (Republic of the), Cook Islands, Costa Rica, Côte d'Ivoire, Croatia, Cyprus, Czechia, Denmark, Djibouti, Dominica, Dominican Republic, Ecuador, El Salvador, Estonia, Fiji, Finland, France*, Gabon, Gambia, Georgia, Germany, Ghana, Greece, Grenada, Guatemala, Guinea, Guyana, Honduras, Hungary, Iceland, Ireland, Italy, Japan, Jordan*, Kenya, Kiribati, Korea (South), Latvia, Lesotho, Liberia, Liechtenstein, Lithuania, Luxembourg, Madagascar, Malawi, Maldives, Mali, Malta*, Marshall Islands, Mauritius, Mexico, Moldova, Mongolia, Montenegro, Namibia, Nauru, Netherlands, New Zealand*, Niger, Nigeria, North Macedonia, Norway, Palestine, Panama, Paraguay, Peru, Poland, Portugal*, Romania, Saint Kitts and Nevis, Saint Lucia, Saint Vincent and the Grenadines, Samoa, San Marino, Senegal, Serbia, Seychelles, Sierra Leone, Slovakia, Slovenia, South Africa, Spain, Suriname, Sweden*, Switzerland, Tajikistan, Tanzania, Timor-Leste, Trinidad and Tobago, Tunisia, Uganda, UK*, Uruguay, Vanuatu, Venezuela, Zambia

* With reservation and/or declaration.

Signed but not ratified (31): Algeria, Angola, Armenia, Bahamas, Bahrain, Cameroon, Egypt, Eritrea, Guinea-Bissau, Haiti, Iran, Israel*, Jamaica, Kuwait, Kyrgyzstan, Monaco, Morocco, Mozambique, Oman, Russia*, Sao Tome and Principe, Solomon Islands, Sudan*, Syria, Thailand, Ukraine†, United Arab Emirates, USA*, Uzbekistan, Yemen, Zimbabwe

* These states have declared that they no longer intend to become parties to the statute.
† Although Ukraine is not a party to the statute, it has accepted the jurisdiction of the ICC with respect to alleged crimes committed on its territory since 21 Nov. 2013. This jurisdiction extends to action committed by citizens of non-parties to the statute on Ukrainian territory but, since Ukraine itself is not a party, not the crime of aggression without a referral from the UN Security Council.

Parties to the Amendment to Article 8 of 10 June 2010 (40): Andorra, Argentina, Austria, Belgium, Botswana, Chile, Costa Rica, Croatia, Cyprus, Czechia, El Salvador, Estonia, Finland, Georgia, Germany, Guyana, Latvia, Liechtenstein, Lithuania, Luxembourg, Malta, Mauritius, *Mongolia*, Netherlands, New Zealand, North Macedonia, Norway, Palestine, Panama, Paraguay, Poland, Portugal, Samoa, San Marino, Slovakia, Slovenia, Spain, Switzerland, Trinidad and Tobago, Uruguay

Note: In addition to the 40 states that had ratified the amendment as of 1 Jan. 2022, Italy and Sweden ratified it on 26 Jan. 2022 and Romania on 14 Feb.

Parties to the Amendments of 11 June 2010 defining the crime of aggression (41): Andorra, Argentina, Austria, Belgium, Bolivia, Botswana, Chile, Costa Rica, Croatia, Cyprus, Czechia, Ecuador, El Salvador, Estonia, Finland, Georgia, Germany, Guyana, Iceland, Ireland, Latvia, Liechtenstein, Lithuania, Luxembourg, Malta, *Mongolia*, Netherlands, North Macedonia, Palestine, Panama, Paraguay, Poland, Portugal, Samoa, San Marino, Slovakia, Slovenia, Spain, Switzerland, Trinidad and Tobago, Uruguay

Note: In addition to the 41 states that had ratified the amendment as of 1 Jan. 2022, Italy and Sweden ratified it on 26 Jan. 2022.

Parties to the Amendment to Article 8 of 14 December 2017 on weapons which use microbial or other biological agents, or toxins (9): Croatia, Czechia, Latvia, Luxembourg, Netherlands, New Zealand, *Norway*, Slovakia, Switzerland

Note: In addition to the 9 states that had ratified the amendment as of 1 Jan. 2022, Liechtenstein ratified it on 21 Jan. 2022, Sweden on 26 Jan. and Romania on 14 Feb.

Parties to the Amendment to Article 8 of 14 December 2017 on weapons the primary effect of which is to injure by fragments undetectable by x-rays in the human body (9): Croatia, Czechia, Latvia, Luxembourg, Netherlands, New Zealand, *Norway*, Slovakia, Switzerland

Parties to the Amendment to Article 8 of 14 December 2017 on blinding laser weapons (9): Croatia, Czechia, Latvia, Luxembourg, Netherlands, New Zealand, *Norway*, Slovakia, Switzerland

Note: In addition to the 9 states that had ratified the amendment as of 1 Jan. 2022, Romania ratified it on 14 Feb. 2022.

Parties to the Amendment to Article 8 of 6 December 2019 on intentional starvation of civilians (6): Andorra, *Croatia*, Netherlands, New Zealand, *Norway*, *Portugal*

Note: In addition to the 6 states that had ratified the amendment as of 1 Jan. 2022, Liechtenstein ratified it on 21 Jan. 2022 and Romania on 14 Feb.

Statute text: United Nations Treaty Collection, <https://treaties.un.org/doc/Treaties/1998/07/19980717 06-33 PM/Ch_XVIII_10p.pdf>

Text of the Amendment to Article 8 of 10 June 2010: United Nations Treaty Collection, <https://treaties.un.org/doc/Treaties/2010/10/20101011 05-46 PM/CN.533.2010.pdf>

Text of the Amendments of 11 June 2010 defining the crime of aggression: United Nations Treaty Collection, <https://treaties.un.org/doc/Treaties/2010/06/20100611 05-56 PM/CN.651.2010.pdf>

Text of the Amendment to Article 8 of 14 December 2017 on weapons which use microbial or other biological agents or toxins: United Nations Treaty Collection, <https://treaties.un.org/doc/Publication/CN/2018/CN.116.2018-Eng.pdf>

Text of the Amendment to Article 8 of 14 December 2017 on weapons the primary effect of which is to injure by fragments undetectable by x-rays in the human body: United Nations Treaty Collection, <https://treaties.un.org/doc/Publication/CN/2018/CN.125.2018-Eng.pdf>

Text of the Amendment to Article 8 of 14 December 2017 on blinding laser weapons: United Nations Treaty Collection, <https://treaties.un.org/doc/Publication/CN/2018/CN.126.2018-Eng.pdf>

Text of the Amendment to Article 8 of 6 December 2019 on intentional starvation of civilians: United Nations Treaty Collection, <https://treaties.un.org/doc/Publication/CN/2020/CN.394.2020-Eng.pdf>

Convention on Cluster Munitions

Opened for signature at Oslo on 3 December 2008; entered into force on 1 August 2010; depositary UN Secretary-General

The convention's objectives are to prohibit the use, production, transfer and stockpiling of cluster munitions that cause unacceptable harm to civilians. It also establishes a framework for cooperation and assistance to ensure adequate provision of care and rehabilitation for victims, clearance of contaminated areas, risk-reduction education and destruction of stockpiles. The convention does not apply to mines.

Each party undertakes to destroy all of its stockpiled cluster munitions as soon as possible but not later than eight years after the entry into force of the convention for that state party. The first deadlines for stockpile destruction were in 2018. Each party also undertakes to clear and destroy all cluster munitions in contaminated areas under its jurisdiction or control not later than 10 years after the entry into force of the convention for that state party. The first deadlines for clearance were in 2020.

A three-person ISU, based in Geneva, was established in 2015 to, among other things, provide advice and technical support to the parties.

A party may withdraw from the convention, having given six months' notice. But if the party is involved in an armed conflict at that time, the withdrawal will not take effect until that conflict has ended.

Parties (110): Afghanistan, Albania, Andorra, Antigua and Barbuda, Australia, Austria, Belgium, Belize, Benin, Bolivia, Bosnia and Herzegovina, Botswana, Bulgaria, Burkina Faso, Burundi, Cabo Verde, Cameroon, Canada, Chad, Chile, Colombia*, Comoros, Congo (Republic of the), Cook Islands, Costa Rica, Côte d'Ivoire, Croatia, Cuba, Czechia, Denmark, Dominican Republic, Ecuador, El Salvador*, Eswatini, Fiji, France, Gambia, Germany, Ghana, Grenada, Guatemala, Guinea, Guinea-Bissau, Guyana, Holy See*, Honduras, Hungary, Iceland, Iraq, Ireland, Italy, Japan, Laos, Lebanon, Lesotho, Liechtenstein, Lithuania, Luxembourg, Madagascar, Malawi, Maldives, Mali, Malta, Mauritania, Mauritius, Mexico, Moldova, Monaco, Montenegro, Mozambique, Namibia, Nauru, Netherlands, New Zealand, Nicaragua, Niger, Niue, North Macedonia, Norway, Palestine, Palau, Panama, Paraguay, Peru, Philippines, Portugal, Rwanda, Saint Kitts and Nevis, Saint Lucia, Saint Vincent and the Grenadines, Samoa, San Marino, Sao Tome and Principe, Senegal, Seychelles, Sierra Leone, Slovakia, Slovenia, Somalia, South Africa, Spain, Sri Lanka, Sweden, Switzerland, Togo, Trinidad and Tobago, Tunisia, UK, Uruguay, Zambia

    * With reservation and/or declaration.

Signed but not ratified (13): Angola, Central African Republic, Congo (Democratic Republic of the), Cyprus, Djibouti, Haiti, Indonesia, Jamaica, Kenya, Liberia, Nigeria, Tanzania, Uganda

Convention text: United Nations Treaty Collection, <https://treaties.un.org/doc/Publication/CTC/26-6.pdf>

Arms Trade Treaty (ATT)

Opened for signature at New York on 3 June 2013; entered into force on 24 December 2014; depositary UN Secretary-General

The object of the treaty is to establish the highest possible common international standards for regulating the international trade in conventional arms; and to prevent and eradicate the illicit trade in conventional arms and prevent their diversion.

Among other things, the treaty prohibits a state party from authorizing a transfer of arms if they are to be used in the commission of genocide, crimes against humanity or war crimes. The treaty also requires the exporting state to assess the potential for any arms proposed for export to undermine peace and security or be used to commit serious violations of international humanitarian law or international human rights law. This assessment must take into account the risk of the arms being used to commit or facilitate serious acts of gender-based violence or serious acts of violence against women and children.

Each party must submit an annual report on its authorized or actual exports and imports of conventional arms.

The treaty established the ATT Secretariat, based in Geneva, to support the parties in its implementation. Among other tasks, it collects the annual reports submitted by each party on imports and exports of conventional arms.

A party may withdraw from the treaty, having given 90 days' notice.

Parties (110): Afghanistan, Albania, Antigua and Barbuda, Argentina, Australia, Austria, Bahamas, Barbados, Belgium, Belize, Benin, Bosnia and Herzegovina, Botswana, Brazil, Bulgaria, Burkina Faso, Cabo Verde, Cameroon, Canada, Central African Republic, Chad, Chile, China, Costa Rica, Côte d'Ivoire, Croatia, Cyprus, Czechia, Denmark, Dominica, Dominican Republic, El Salvador, Estonia, Finland, France, Georgia, Germany, Ghana, Greece, Grenada, Guatemala, Guinea, Guinea-Bissau, Guyana, Honduras, Hungary, Iceland, Ireland, Italy, Jamaica, Japan, Kazakhstan*, Korea (South), Latvia, Lebanon, Lesotho, Liberia, Liechtenstein*, Lithuania, Luxembourg, Madagascar, Maldives, Mali, Malta, Mauritania, Mauritius, Mexico, Moldova, Monaco, Montenegro, Mozambique, Namibia, Netherlands, New Zealand*, Niger, Nigeria, Niue, North Macedonia, Norway, Palau, Palestine, Panama, Paraguay, Peru, Poland, Portugal, Romania, Saint Kitts and Nevis, Saint Lucia, Saint Vincent and the Grenadines, Samoa, San Marino, Sao Tome and Principe, Senegal, Serbia, Seychelles, Sierra Leone, Slovakia, Slovenia, South Africa, Spain, Suriname, Sweden, Switzerland*, Togo, Trinidad and Tobago, Tuvalu, UK, Uruguay, Zambia

* With reservation and/or declaration.

Signed but not ratified (31): Andorra, Angola, Bahrain, Bangladesh, Burundi, Cambodia, Colombia, Comoros, Congo (Republic of the), Djibouti, Eswatini, Gabon, Haiti, Israel, Kiribati, Libya, Malawi, Malaysia, Mongolia, Nauru, Philippines, Rwanda, Singapore, Tanzania, Thailand, Turkey, Ukraine, United Arab Emirates, USA*, Vanuatu, Zimbabwe

* This state has declared that it no longer intends to become a party to the treaty.

Note: In addition to the 110 states that had ratified the treaty as of 1 Jan. 2022, the Philippines ratified it on 24 Mar. 2022.

Treaty text: United Nations Treaty Collection, <https://treaties.un.org/doc/Treaties/2013/04/20130410 12-01 PM/Ch_XXVI_08.pdf>

Treaty on the Prohibition of Nuclear Weapons (TPNW)

Opened for signature at New York on 20 September 2017; entered in force on 22 January 2021; depositary UN Secretary-General

In its preamble, the treaty cites the catastrophic humanitarian and environmental consequences of the use of nuclear weapons and invokes the principles of international humanitarian law and the rules of international law applicable in armed conflict. The treaty prohibits parties from developing, testing, producing, manufacturing, acquiring, possessing or stockpiling nuclear weapons or other nuclear explosive devices. Parties are prohibited from using or threatening to use nuclear weapons and other nuclear explosive devices. Finally, parties cannot allow the stationing, installation or deployment of nuclear weapons and other nuclear explosive devices in their territory.

The treaty outlines procedures for eliminating the nuclear weapons of any party that owned, possessed or controlled them after 7 July 2017, to be supervised by a 'competent international authority or authorities' to be designated by the states parties. Each party is required to maintain its existing safeguards agreements with the IAEA and must, at a minimum, conclude and bring into force a comprehensive safeguards agreement with the agency. The treaty also contains provisions on assisting the victims of the testing or use of nuclear weapons and taking necessary and appropriate measures for the environmental remediation of contaminated areas.

Membership of the treaty does not prejudice a party's other, compatible international obligations (such as the NPT and the CTBT). A party may withdraw from the treaty, having given 12 months' notice, if it decides that its supreme interests have been jeopardized by extraordinary events related to the treaty's subject matter. But if the party is involved in an armed conflict at that time, the withdrawal will not take effect until it is no longer party to an armed conflict.

Ratifications deposited (59): Antigua and Barbuda, Austria, Bangladesh, Belize, Benin, Bolivia, Botswana, *Cambodia*, *Chile*, *Comoros*, Cook Islands*, Costa Rica, Cuba*, Dominica, Ecuador, El Salvador, Fiji, Gambia, *Guinea-Bissau*, Guyana, Holy See, Honduras, Ireland, Jamaica, Kazakhstan, Kiribati, Laos, Lesotho, Malaysia, Maldives, Malta, Mexico, *Mongolia*, Namibia, Nauru, New Zealand, Nicaragua, Nigeria, Niue, Palau, Palestine, Panama, Paraguay, *Peru*, *Philippines*, Saint Kitts and Nevis, Saint Lucia, Saint Vincent and the Grenadines, Samoa, San Marino, *Seychelles*, South Africa, Thailand, Trinidad and Tobago, Tuvalu, Uruguay, Vanuatu, Venezuela, Viet Nam

* With reservation and/or declaration.

Signed but not ratified (30): Algeria, Angola, Brazil, Brunei Darussalam, Cabo Verde, Central African Republic, Colombia, Congo (Democratic Republic of the), Congo (Republic of the), Côte d'Ivoire, Dominican Republic, Ghana, Grenada, Guatemala, Indonesia, Libya, Liechtenstein, Madagascar, Malawi, Mozambique, Myanmar, Nepal, Niger, Sao Tome and Principe, Sudan, Tanzania, Timor-Leste, Togo, Zambia, Zimbabwe

Note: In addition to the 59 states that had ratified the treaty as of 1 Jan. 2022, Côte d'Ivoire ratified it on 23 Mar. 2022.

Treaty text: United Nations Treaty Collection, <https://treaties.un.org/doc/Treaties/2017/07/20170707 03-42 PM/Ch_XXVI_9.pdf>

II. Regional treaties

Treaty for the Prohibition of Nuclear Weapons in Latin America and the Caribbean (Treaty of Tlatelolco)

Original treaty opened for signature at Mexico City on 14 February 1967; entered into force on 22 April 1968; treaty amended in 1990, 1991 and 1992; depositary Mexican Government

The treaty prohibits the testing, use, manufacture, production or acquisition by any means, as well as the receipt, storage, installation, deployment and any form of possession of any nuclear weapons by any country of Latin America and the Caribbean and in the surrounding seas.

The parties should conclude agreements individually with the IAEA for the application of safeguards to their nuclear activities. The IAEA has the exclusive power to carry out special inspections. The treaty also established the Agency for the Prohibition of Nuclear Weapons in Latin America and the Caribbean (Organismo para la Proscripción de las Armas Nucleares en la América Latina y el Caribe, OPANAL) to ensure compliance with the treaty.

The treaty is open for signature by all the independent states of Latin America and the Caribbean. A party may withdraw from the treaty, having given three months' notice, if it decides that its supreme interests or the peace and security of another party or parties have been jeopardized by new circumstances related to the treaty's content.

Under *Additional Protocol I* the states with territories within the zone—France, the Netherlands, the UK and the USA—undertake to apply the statute of military denuclearization to these territories.

Under *Additional Protocol II* the recognized nuclear weapon states—China, France, Russia, the UK and the USA—undertake to respect the military denuclearization of Latin America and the Caribbean and not to contribute to acts involving a violation of the treaty, nor to use or threaten to use nuclear weapons against the parties to the treaty.

Parties to the original treaty (33): Antigua and Barbuda[1], Argentina[1], Bahamas, Barbados[1], Belize[2], Bolivia[1], Brazil[1], Chile[1], Colombia[1], Costa Rica[1], Cuba, Dominica, Dominican Republic[3], Ecuador[1], El Salvador[1], Grenada[1], Guatemala[1], Guyana[3], Haiti, Honduras[1], Jamaica[1], Mexico[1], Nicaragua[1], Panama[1], Paraguay[1], Peru[1], Saint Kitts and Nevis[1], Saint Lucia[1], Saint Vincent and the Grenadines[4], Suriname[1], Trinidad and Tobago[1], Uruguay[1], Venezuela[1]

[1] Has ratified the amendments of 1990, 1991 and 1992.
[2] Has ratified the amendments of 1990 and 1992 only.
[3] Has ratified the amendment of 1992 only.
[4] Has ratified the amendments of 1991 and 1992 only.

Parties to Additional Protocol I (4): France*, Netherlands*, UK*, USA*

Parties to Additional Protocol II (5): China*, France*, Russia*, UK*, USA*

* With reservation and/or declaration.

Original treaty text: *United Nations Treaty Series*, vol. 634 (1968), <https://treaties.un.org/doc/Publication/UNTS/Volume 634/v634.pdf>

Amended treaty text: Agency for the Prohibition of Nuclear Weapons in Latin America and the Caribbean, Inf.11/2018, 5 June 2018, <https://www.opanal.org/wp-content/uploads/2019/10/Inf_11_2018_Treaty_Tlatelolco.pdf>

South Pacific Nuclear Free Zone Treaty (Treaty of Rarotonga)

Opened for signature at Rarotonga on 6 August 1985; entered into force on 11 December 1986; depositary Secretary General of the Pacific Islands Forum Secretariat

The South Pacific Nuclear Free Zone is defined as the area between the zone of application of the Treaty of Tlatelolco in the east and the west coast of Australia and the western border of Papua New Guinea and between the zone of application of the Antarctic Treaty in the south and, approximately, the equator in the north.

The treaty prohibits the manufacture or acquisition of any nuclear explosive device, as well as possession or control over any such device by the parties anywhere inside or outside the zone. The parties also undertake not to supply nuclear material or equipment, unless subject to IAEA safeguards, and to prevent the stationing or testing of any nuclear explosive device in their territories and undertake not to dump, and to prevent the dumping of, radioactive waste and other radioactive matter at sea anywhere within the zone. Each party remains free to allow visits, as well as transit, by foreign ships and aircraft.

The treaty is open for signature by the members of the Pacific Islands Forum. If any party violates an essential provision or the spirit of the treaty, every other party may withdraw from the treaty, having given 12 months' notice.

Under *Protocol 1* France, the UK and the USA undertake to apply the treaty prohibitions relating to the manufacture, stationing and testing of nuclear explosive devices in the territories situated within the zone for which they are internationally responsible.

Under *Protocol 2* China, France, Russia, the UK and the USA undertake not to use or threaten to use a nuclear explosive device against the parties to the treaty or against any territory within the zone for which a party to Protocol 1 is internationally responsible.

Under *Protocol 3* China, France, Russia, the UK and the USA undertake not to test any nuclear explosive device anywhere within the zone.

Parties (13): Australia, Cook Islands, Fiji, Kiribati, Nauru, New Zealand, Niue, Papua New Guinea, Samoa, Solomon Islands, Tonga, Tuvalu, Vanuatu

Parties to Protocol 1 (2): France*, UK*; *signed but not ratified (1)*: USA

Parties to Protocol 2 (4): China*, France*, Russia*, UK*; *signed but not ratified (1)*: USA

Parties to Protocol 3 (4): China*, France*, Russia*, UK*; *signed but not ratified (1)*: USA

* With reservation and/or declaration.

Treaty text: Pacific Islands Forum Secretariat, <https://www.forumsec.org/wp-content/uploads/2018/02/South-Pacific-Nuclear-Zone-Treaty-Rarotonga-Treaty-1.pdf>

Protocol texts: Pacific Islands Forum Secretariat, <https://www.forumsec.org/wp-content/uploads/2018/02/South-Pacific-Nuclear-Zone-Treaty-Protocols-1.pdf>

Treaty on Conventional Armed Forces in Europe (CFE Treaty)

Original treaty signed by the 16 member states of the North Atlantic Treaty Organization (NATO) and the 6 member states of the Warsaw Treaty Organization (WTO) at Paris on 19 November 1990; entered into force on 9 November 1992; depositary Dutch Government

The treaty sets ceilings on five categories of treaty-limited equipment (TLE)—battle tanks, armoured combat vehicles, artillery of at least 100-mm calibre, combat aircraft and attack helicopters—in an area stretching from the Atlantic Ocean to the Ural Mountains (the Atlantic-to-the-Urals, ATTU). The treaty established the Joint Consultative Group (JCG) to promote its objectives and implementation.

The treaty was negotiated by the member states of the WTO and NATO within the framework of the Conference on Security and Co-operation in Europe (from 1995 the Organization for Security and Co-operation in Europe, OSCE).

The **1992 Tashkent Agreement**, adopted by the former Soviet republics with territories within the ATTU area of application (with the exception of Estonia, Latvia and Lithuania) and the **1992 Oslo Document** (Final Document of the Extraordinary Conference of the States Parties to the CFE Treaty) introduced modifications to the treaty required because of the emergence of new states after the break-up of the USSR.

A party may withdraw from the treaty, having given 150 days' notice, if it decides that its supreme interests have been jeopardized by extraordinary events related to the treaty's subject matter.

Parties (30): Armenia, Azerbaijan, Belarus, Belgium[2], Bulgaria[2], Canada[2], Czechia[2], Denmark[2], France, Georgia, Germany[2], Greece, Hungary[2], Iceland[2], Italy[2], Kazakhstan, Luxembourg[2], Moldova[2], Netherlands[2], Norway, Poland, Portugal[2], Romania, Russia[1], Slovakia[2], Spain, Turkey[2], UK[2], Ukraine, USA[2]

[1] On 14 July 2007 Russia declared its intention to suspend its participation in the CFE Treaty and associated documents and agreements, which took effect on 12 Dec. 2007. In Mar. 2015 Russia announced that it had decided to completely halt its participation in the treaty, including the JCG.

[2] In Nov.–Dec. 2011 these countries notified the depositary or the JCG that they would cease to perform their obligations under the treaty with regard to Russia.

The first review conference of the CFE Treaty adopted the **1996 Flank Document**, which reorganized the flank areas geographically and numerically, allowing Russia and Ukraine to deploy TLE in a less constraining manner.

Original (1990) treaty text: Dutch Ministry of Foreign Affairs, <https://repository.overheid.nl/frbr/vd/004285/1/pdf/004285_Gewaarmerkt_0.pdf>

Consolidated (1993) treaty text: Dutch Ministry of Foreign Affairs, <https://wetten.overheid.nl/BWBV0002009/>

Flank Document text: Organization for Security and Co-operation in Europe, <https://www.osce.org/library/14099?download=true>, annex A

Concluding Act of the Negotiation on Personnel Strength of Conventional Armed Forces in Europe (CFE-1A Agreement)

Signed by the parties to the CFE Treaty at Helsinki on 10 July 1992; entered into force simultaneously with the CFE Treaty; depositary Dutch Government

This politically binding agreement sets ceilings on the number of personnel of the conventional land-based armed forces of the parties within the ATTU area.

Agreement text: Organization for Security and Co-operation in Europe, <https://www.osce.org/library/14093?download=true>

Agreement on Adaptation of the Treaty on Conventional Armed Forces in Europe

Signed by the parties to the CFE Treaty at Istanbul on 19 November 1999; not in force; depositary Dutch Government

With the dissolution of the WTO and the accession of some former members to NATO, this agreement would have replaced the CFE Treaty's bloc-to-bloc military balance with a regional balance, established individual state limits on TLE holdings, and provided for a new structure of limitations and new military flexibility mechanisms, flank sub-limits and enhanced transparency. It would have opened the CFE regime to all other European states. It would have entered into force when ratified by all of the signatories.

The **1999 Final Act of the Conference of the CFE States Parties**, with annexes, contains politically binding arrangements with regard to Georgia, Moldova and Central Europe and to withdrawals of armed forces from foreign territories (known as the Istanbul commitments). Many signatories of the Agreement on Adaptation made their ratification contingent on the implementation of these political commitments.

Ratifications deposited (3): Belarus, Kazakhstan, Russia*[1]

   * With reservation and/or declaration.

Signed but not ratified (27): Armenia, Azerbaijan, Belgium, Bulgaria, Canada, Czechia, Denmark, France, Germany, Georgia, Greece, Hungary, Iceland, Italy, Luxembourg, Moldova, Netherlands, Norway, Poland, Portugal, Romania, Slovakia, Spain, Turkey, Ukraine[2], UK, USA

[1] On 14 July 2007 Russia declared its intention to suspend its participation in the CFE Treaty and associated documents and agreements, which took effect on 12 Dec. 2007. In Mar. 2015 Russia announced that it had decided to completely halt its participation in the treaty, including the JCG.

[2] Ukraine ratified the Agreement on Adaptation on 21 Sep. 2000 but did not deposit its instrument with the depositary.

Agreement text: Dutch Ministry of Foreign Affairs, <https://repository.overheid.nl/frbr/vd/009241/1/pdf/009241_Gewaarmerkt_0.pdf>

Treaty text as amended by 1999 agreement: SIPRI Yearbook 2000, <https://www.sipri.org/sites/default/files/SIPRI Yearbook 2000.pdf>, appendix 10B

Final Act text: Organization for Security and Co-operation in Europe, <https://www. osce.org/library/14114?download=true>

Treaty on Open Skies

Opened for signature at Helsinki on 24 March 1992; entered into force on 1 January 2002; depositaries Canadian and Hungarian governments

The treaty obligates the parties to submit their territories to short-notice unarmed surveillance flights. The area of application initially stretched from Vancouver, Canada, eastward to Vladivostok, Russia.

The treaty was negotiated between the member states of the WTO and NATO. Since 1 July 2002 any state can apply to accede to the treaty. A party may withdraw from the treaty, having given six months' notice. The USA withdrew from the treaty on 22 November 2020 and Russia withdrew on 18 December 2021.

Parties (32): Belarus, Belgium, Bosnia and Herzegovina, Bulgaria, Canada*, Croatia, Czechia, Denmark, Estonia, Finland, France, Georgia, Germany, Greece, Hungary, Iceland, Italy, Latvia, Lithuania, Luxembourg, Netherlands, Norway, Poland, Portugal, Romania, Slovakia, Slovenia, Spain*, Sweden*, Turkey, UK, Ukraine

  * With reservation and/or declaration.

Signed but not ratified (1): Kyrgyzstan

Treaty text: Canada Treaty Information, <https://www.treaty-accord.gc.ca/text-texte.aspx?id =102747>

Treaty on the Southeast Asia Nuclear Weapon-Free Zone (Treaty of Bangkok)

Signed by the 10 member states of the Association of Southeast Asian Nations (ASEAN) at Bangkok on 15 December 1995; entered into force on 27 March 1997; depositary Thai Government

The South East Asia Nuclear Weapon-Free Zone includes the territories, the continental shelves and the exclusive economic zones of the states parties. The treaty prohibits the development, manufacture, acquisition or testing of nuclear weapons inside or outside the zone as well as the stationing and transport of nuclear weapons in or through the zone. Each state party may decide for itself whether to allow visits and transit by foreign ships and aircraft. The parties undertake not to dump at sea or discharge into the atmosphere anywhere within the zone any radioactive material or waste or dispose of radioactive material on land. The parties should conclude an agreement with the IAEA for the application of full-scope safeguards to their peaceful nuclear activities.

The treaty is open for accession by all states of South East Asia. If any party breaches an essential provision of the treaty, every other party may withdraw from the treaty.

Under a *Protocol* to the treaty, China, France, Russia, the UK and the USA are to undertake not to use or threaten to use nuclear weapons against any state party to the treaty. They should further undertake not to use nuclear weapons within the zone. The protocol will enter into force for each state party on the date of its deposit of the instrument of ratification.

Parties (10): Brunei Darussalam, Cambodia, Indonesia, Laos, Malaysia, Myanmar, Philippines, Singapore, Thailand, Viet Nam

Protocol (0): no signatures, no parties

Treaty text: ASEAN Secretariat, <https://asean.org/treaty-on-the-southeast-asia-nuclear-weapon-free-zone/>

Protocol text: ASEAN Secretariat, <https://asean.org/protocol-to-the-treaty-on-the-southeast-asia-nuclear-weapon-free-zone/>

African Nuclear-Weapon-Free Zone Treaty (Treaty of Pelindaba)

Opened for signature at Cairo on 11 April 1996; entered into force on 15 July 2009; depositary Secretary-General of the African Union

The African Nuclear Weapon-Free Zone includes the territory of the continent of Africa, island states members of the African Union (AU) and all islands considered by the AU to be part of Africa.

The treaty prohibits the research, development, manufacture and acquisition of nuclear explosive devices and the testing or stationing of any nuclear explosive device in the zone. Each party remains free to allow visits and transit by foreign ships and aircraft. The treaty also prohibits any attack against nuclear installations. The parties undertake not to dump or permit the dumping of radio-active waste and other radioactive matter anywhere within the zone. Each party should individually conclude an agreement with the IAEA for the application of comprehensive safeguards to their peaceful nuclear activities. The treaty also established the African Commission on Nuclear Energy (AFCONE) to ensure compliance with the treaty.

The treaty is open for accession by all the states of Africa. A party may withdraw from the treaty, having given 12 months' notice, if it decides that its supreme interests have been jeopardized by extraordinary events related to the treaty's subject matter.

Under *Protocol I* China, France, Russia, the UK and the USA undertake not to use or threaten to use a nuclear explosive device against the parties to the treaty.

Under *Protocol II* China, France, Russia, the UK and the USA undertake not to test nuclear explosive devices within the zone.

Under *Protocol III* France and Spain are to undertake to observe certain provisions of the treaty with respect to the territories within the zone for which they are internationally responsible.

Parties (42): Algeria, Angola, Benin, Botswana, Burkina Faso, Burundi, Cabo Verde, Cameroon, Chad, Comoros, Congo (Republic of the), Côte d'Ivoire, Equatorial Guinea, Eswatini, Ethiopia, Gabon, Gambia, Ghana, Guinea, Guinea-Bissau, Kenya, Lesotho, Libya, Madagascar, Malawi, Mali, Mauritania, Mauritius, Mozambique, Namibia, Niger, Nigeria, Rwanda, Sahrawi Arab Democratic Republic (Western Sahara), Seychelles, Senegal, South Africa, Tanzania, Togo, Tunisia, Zambia, Zimbabwe

Signed but not ratified (12): Central African Republic, Congo (Democratic Republic of the), Djibouti, Egypt, Eritrea, Liberia, Morocco, Sao Tome and Principe, Sierra Leone, Somalia, Sudan, Uganda

Parties to Protocol I (4): China, France*, Russia*, UK*; *signed but not ratified (1)*: USA*

Parties to Protocol II (4): China, France*, Russia*, UK*; *signed but not ratified (1)*: USA*

Parties to Protocol III (1): France*

   * With reservation and/or declaration.

Treaty text: African Union, <https://au.int/sites/default/files/treaties/37288-treaty-0018_-_the_african_nuclear-weapon-free_zone_treaty_the_treaty_of_pelindaba_e.pdf>

Agreement on Sub-Regional Arms Control (Florence Agreement)

Adopted by the 5 original parties at Florence and entered into force on 14 June 1996

The agreement was negotiated under the auspices of the OSCE in accordance with the mandate in Article IV of Annex 1-B of the 1995 General Framework Agreement for Peace in Bosnia and Herzegovina (Dayton Agreement). It sets numerical ceilings on armaments of the former warring parties. Five categories of heavy conventional weapons are included: battle tanks, armoured combat vehicles, heavy artillery (75 mm and above), combat aircraft and attack helicopters. The limits were reached by 31 October 1997; by that date 6580 weapon items, or 46 per cent of pre-June 1996 holdings, had been destroyed. By 2014 a further 3489 items had been destroyed voluntarily.

   The implementation of the agreement was monitored and assisted by the OSCE's Personal Representative of the Chairman-in-Office and the Contact Group (France, Germany, Italy, Russia, the UK and the USA) and supported by other OSCE states. Under a two-phase action plan agreed in November 2009, responsibility for the implementation of the agreement and mutual inspection was transferred to the parties on 5 December 2014, following the signing of a new set of amendments to the agreement. The Sub-Regional Consultative Commission (SRCC) monitors implementation.

Parties (4): Bosnia and Herzegovina, Croatia, Montenegro, Serbia

Agreement text: RACVIAC–Centre for Security Cooperation, <https://web.archive.org/web/20170405151539/www.racviac.org/downloads/treaties_agreements/aIV.pdf>

Inter-American Convention Against the Illicit Manufacturing of and Trafficking in Firearms, Ammunition, Explosives, and Other Related Materials (CIFTA)

Opened for signature by the member states of the Organization of American States (OAS) at Washington, DC, on 14 November 1997; entered into force on 1 July 1998; depositary General Secretariat of the OAS

The purpose of the convention is to prevent, combat and eradicate the illicit manufacturing of and the trafficking in firearms, ammunition, explosives and other related materials; and to promote and facilitate cooperation and the exchange of information and experience among the parties. A party may withdraw from the convention, having given six months' notice.

Parties (31): Antigua and Barbuda, Argentina*, Bahamas, Barbados, Belize, Bolivia, Brazil, Chile, Colombia, Costa Rica, Dominica, Dominican Republic, Ecuador, El Salvador, Grenada, Guatemala, Guyana, Haiti, Honduras, Mexico, Nicaragua, Panama, Paraguay, Peru, Saint

Kitts and Nevis, Saint Lucia, Saint Vincent and the Grenadines, Suriname, Trinidad and Tobago, Uruguay, Venezuela

* With reservation.

Signed but not ratified (3): Canada, Jamaica, USA

Convention text: OAS, <https://www.oas.org/en/sla/dil/inter_american_treaties_A-63_illicit_manufacturing_trafficking_firearms_ammunition_explosives.asp>

Inter-American Convention on Transparency in Conventional Weapons Acquisitions

Opened for signature by the member states of the OAS at Guatemala City on 7 June 1999; entered into force on 21 November 2002; depositary General Secretariat of the OAS

The objective of the convention is to contribute more fully to regional openness and transparency in the acquisition of conventional weapons by exchanging information regarding such acquisitions, for the purpose of promoting confidence among states in the Americas. A party may withdraw from the convention, having given 12 months' notice.

Parties (17): Argentina, Barbados, Brazil, Canada, Chile, Costa Rica, Dominican Republic, Ecuador, El Salvador, Guatemala, Mexico, Nicaragua, Panama, Paraguay, Peru, Uruguay, Venezuela

Signed but not ratified (6): Bolivia, Colombia, Dominica, Haiti, Honduras, USA

Convention text: OAS, <https://www.oas.org/en/sla/dil/inter_american_treaties_A-64_transparency_conventional_weapons_adquisitions.asp>

Protocol on the Control of Firearms, Ammunition and other related Materials in the Southern African Development Community (SADC) Region

Opened for signature by the members states of SADC at Blantyre on 14 August 2001; entered into force on 8 November 2004; depositary SADC Executive Secretary

The objectives of the protocol include the prevention, combating and eradication of the illicit manufacturing of firearms, ammunition and other related materials, and the prevention of their excessive and destabilizing accumulation, trafficking, possession and use in the region. A party may withdraw from the protocol, having given 12 months' notice.

An agreement amending the protocol was approved by the 40th ordinary SADC summit on 17 August 2020. The agreement broadens the scope of the protocol to include other conventional weapons, aligns it with the ATT and other international and regional conventions, and incorporates contemporary best practices and standards on corruption, tracing and cooperation. It is subject to ratification.

Parties (11): Botswana, Eswatini, Lesotho, Malawi, Mauritius, Mozambique, Namibia, South Africa, Tanzania, Zambia, Zimbabwe

Signed but not ratified (2*): Congo (Democratic Republic of the), Seychelles[†]

* Three member states of SADC—Angola, the Comoros and Madagascar—have neither signed nor ratified the protocol.

† Seychelles signed the protocol in 2001 but did not ratify it before withdrawing from SADC in 2004. It rejoined SADC in 2008.

Protocol text: SADC, <https://www.sadc.int/files/8613/5292/8361/Protocol_on_the_Control_of_Firearms_Ammunition2001.pdf>

Nairobi Protocol for the Prevention, Control and Reduction of Small Arms and Light Weapons in the Great Lakes Region and the Horn of Africa

Signed by the 10 member states of the Nairobi Secretariat on Small Arms and Light Weapons and the Seychelles at Nairobi on 21 April 2004; entered into force on 5 May 2006; depositary Regional Centre on Small Arms in the Great Lakes Region, the Horn of Africa and Bordering States (RECSA)

The objectives of the protocol include the prevention, combating and eradication of the illicit manufacture of, trafficking in, possession and use of small arms and light weapons (SALW) in the subregion. Its implementation is overseen by RECSA.

Parties (12): Burundi, Central African Republic, Congo (Democratic Republic of the), Congo (Republic of the), Djibouti, Eritrea, Ethiopia, Kenya, Rwanda, South Sudan, Sudan, Uganda

Signed but not ratified (3*): Seychelles, Somalia, Tanzania

* The accuracy of this list is uncertain. Some or all of these 3 states may have ratified the treaty. They all participate in the implementation activities of RECSA.

Protocol text: RECSA, <https://web.archive.org/web/20210702090958/www.recsasec.org/wp-content/uploads/2018/08/Nairobi-Protocol.pdf>

ECOWAS Convention on Small Arms and Light Weapons, their Ammunition and Other Related Materials

Adopted by the 15 member states of the Economic Community of West African States (ECOWAS) at Abuja, on 14 June 2006; entered into force on 29 September 2009; depositary President of the ECOWAS Commission

The convention obligates the parties to prevent and combat the excessive and destabilizing accumulation of SALW in the ECOWAS member states. The convention bans the transfer of SALW into, through or from the territories of the parties. The ECOWAS member states may, by consensus, grant a party an exemption for national defence and security needs or for use in multilateral peace operations. Possession of light weapons by civilians is banned and their possession of small arms must be regulated. Each party must also control the manufacture of SALW, establish registers of SALW and establish a national commission to implement the convention.

A party may withdraw from the treaty, having given 12 months' notice, if it decides that its supreme interests have been jeopardized by extraordinary events related to the treaty's subject matter.

Parties (14): Benin, Burkina Faso, Cabo Verde, Côte d'Ivoire, Ghana, Guinea, Guinea-Bissau, Liberia, Mali, Niger, Nigeria, Senegal, Sierra Leone, Togo

Signed but not ratified (1): Gambia

Convention text: ECOWAS Commission, <https://web.archive.org/web/20180127191610/documentation.ecowas.int/download/en/legal_documents/protocols/Convention on Small Arms and Light Weapons, their Ammunitions and other Related Matters.pdf>

Treaty on a Nuclear-Weapon-Free Zone in Central Asia (Treaty of Semipalatinsk)

Signed by the 5 Central Asian states at Semipalatinsk on 8 September 2006; entered into force on 21 March 2009; depositary Kyrgyz Government

The Central Asian Nuclear Weapon-Free Zone is defined as the territories of Kazakhstan, Kyrgyzstan, Tajikistan, Turkmenistan, Uzbekistan. The treaty obligates the parties not to conduct research on, develop, manufacture, stockpile or otherwise acquire, possess or have control over nuclear weapons or any other nuclear explosive device by any means anywhere. A party may withdraw from the treaty, having given 12 months' notice, if it decides that its supreme interests have been jeopardized by extraordinary events related to the treaty's subject matter.

Under a *Protocol* China, France, Russia, the UK and the USA undertake not to use or threaten to use a nuclear explosive device against the parties to the treaty.

Parties (5): Kazakhstan, Kyrgyzstan, Tajikistan, Turkmenistan, Uzbekistan

Parties to the protocol (4): China, France*, Russia, UK*; *signed but not ratified (1)*: USA

  * With reservations and/or declaration.

Treaty and protocol text: United Nations Treaty Series, vol. 2970 (2014), <https://treaties.un.org/doc/Publication/UNTS/Volume 2970/Part/volume-2970-I-51633.pdf>

Central African Convention for the Control of Small Arms and Light Weapons, Their Ammunition and All Parts and Components That Can Be Used for Their Manufacture, Repair and Assembly (Kinshasa Convention)

Opened for signature by the 10 member states of the Communauté économique d'États de l'Afrique Centrale (CEEAC, Economic Community of Central African States) and Rwanda at Brazzaville on 19 November 2010; entered into force on 8 March 2017; depositary UN Secretary-General

The objectives of the convention are to prevent, combat and eradicate illicit trade and trafficking in SALW in Central Africa (defined to be the territory of the members of CEEAC and Rwanda); to strengthen the control in the region of the manufacture, trade, transfer and use of SALW; to combat armed violence and ease the human suffering in the region caused by SALW; and to foster cooperation and confidence among the states parties.

A party may withdraw from the treaty, having given 12 months' notice.

Parties (8): Angola, Cameroon, Central African Republic, Chad, Congo (Republic of the), Equatorial Guinea, Gabon, Sao Tome and Principe

Signed but not ratified (3): Burundi, Congo (Democratic Republic of the), Rwanda

Treaty text: United Nations Treaty Collection, <https://treaties.un.org/doc/Treaties/2010/04/20100430 01-12 PM/Ch_xxvi-7.pdf>

Vienna Document 2011 on Confidence- and Security-Building Measures

Adopted by the participating states of the Organization for Security and Co-operation in Europe at Vienna on 30 November 2011; entered into force on 1 December 2011

The Vienna Document 2011 builds on the 1986 Stockholm Document on Confidence- and Security-Building Measures (CSBMs) and Disarmament in Europe and previous Vienna Documents (1990, 1992, 1994 and 1999). The Vienna Document 1990 provided for annual exchange of military information, military budget exchange, risk reduction procedures, a communication network and an annual CSBM implementation assessment. The Vienna Document 1992 and the Vienna Document 1994 extended the area of application and introduced new mechanisms and parameters for military activities, defence planning and military contacts. The Vienna Document 1999 introduced regional measures aimed at increasing transparency and confidence in a bilateral, multilateral and regional context and some improvements, in particular regarding the constraining measures.

The Vienna Document 2011 incorporates revisions on such matters as the timing of verification activities and demonstrations of new types of weapon and equipment system. It also establishes a procedure for updating the Vienna Document every five years. However, no updates were agreed in 2016 and 2021, and the process of modernizing or adapting the document remains frozen.

Participating states of the OSCE (57): See annex B

Document text: Organization for Security and Co-operation in Europe, <https://www.osce.org/files/f/documents/a/4/86597.pdf>

III. Bilateral treaties

Treaty on the Limitation of Anti-Ballistic Missile Systems (ABM Treaty)

Signed by the USA and the USSR at Moscow on 26 May 1972; entered into force on 3 October 1972; not in force from 13 June 2002

The parties—Russia and the USA—undertook not to build nationwide defences against ballistic missile attack and to limit the development and deployment of permitted strategic missile defences. The treaty prohibited the parties from giving air defence missiles, radars or launchers the technical ability to counter strategic ballistic missiles and from testing them in a strategic ABM mode. It also established a standing consultative commission to promote its objectives and implementation. The **1974 Protocol** to the ABM Treaty introduced further numerical restrictions on permitted ballistic missile defences.

In 1997 Belarus, Kazakhstan, Russia, Ukraine and the USA signed a memorandum of understanding that would have made Belarus, Kazakhstan and Ukraine parties to the treaty along with Russia as successor states of the USSR and a set of agreed statements that would specify the demarcation line between strategic missile defences (which are not permitted under the treaty) and non-strategic or theatre missile defences (which are permitted under the treaty). The

1997 agreements were ratified by Russia in April 2000, but the USA did not ratify them and they did not enter into force.

On 13 December 2001 the USA notified Russia that it had decided to withdraw from the treaty, citing the ballistic missile threat to its territory from other states; the withdrawal came into effect six months later, on 13 June 2002.

Treaty text: *United Nations Treaty Series*, vol. 944 (1974), <https://treaties.un.org/doc/Publication/UNTS/Volume 944/v944.pdf>

Protocol text: US Department of State, <https://2009-2017.state.gov/t/avc/trty/101888.htm #protocolabm>

Treaty on the Limitation of Underground Nuclear Weapon Tests (Threshold Test-Ban Treaty, TTBT)

Signed by the USA and the USSR at Moscow on 3 July 1974; entered into force on 11 December 1990

The parties—Russia and the USA—undertake not to carry out any underground nuclear weapon test having a yield exceeding 150 kilotons. The 1974 verification protocol was replaced in 1990 with a new protocol.

Either party may withdraw from the treaty, having given the other 12 months' notice, if it decides that its supreme interests have been jeopardized by extraordinary events related to the treaty's subject matter.

Treaty and protocol texts: *United Nations Treaty Series*, vol. 1714 (1993), <https://treaties.un.org/doc/Publication/UNTS/Volume 1714/v1714.pdf>

Treaty on Underground Nuclear Explosions for Peaceful Purposes (Peaceful Nuclear Explosions Treaty, PNET)

Signed by the USA and the USSR at Moscow and Washington, DC, on 28 May 1976; entered into force simultaneously with the TTBT, on 11 December 1990

The parties—Russia and the USA—undertake not to carry out any individual underground nuclear explosion for peaceful purposes having a yield exceeding 15 kilotons or any group explosion having an aggregate yield exceeding 150 kilotons; and not to carry out any group explosion having an aggregate yield exceeding 1500 kilotons unless the individual explosions in the group could be identified and measured by agreed verification procedures. The treaty established a joint consultative commission to promote its objectives and implementation. The 1976 verification protocol was replaced in 1990 with a new protocol.

The treaty cannot be terminated while the TTBT is in force. If the TTBT is terminated, then either party may withdraw from this treaty at any time.

Treaty and protocol texts: *United Nations Treaty Series*, vol. 1714 (1993), <https://treaties.un.org/doc/Publication/UNTS/Volume 1714/v1714.pdf>

Treaty on the Elimination of Intermediate-range and Shorter-range Missiles (INF Treaty)

Signed by the USA and the USSR at Washington, DC, on 8 December 1987; entered into force on 1 June 1988; not in force from 2 August 2019

The treaty obligated the original parties—the USA and the USSR—to destroy all ground-launched ballistic and cruise missiles with a range of 500–5500 kilometres (intermediate-range, 1000–5500 km; and shorter-range, 500–1000 km) and their launchers by 1 June 1991. The treaty established a special verification commission (SVC) to promote its objectives and implementation.

A total of 2692 missiles were eliminated by May 1991. For 10 years after 1 June 1991 on-site inspections were conducted to verify compliance. The use of surveillance satellites for data collection continued after the end of on-site inspections on 31 May 2001.

In 1994 treaty membership was expanded to include Belarus, Kazakhstan and Ukraine in addition to Russia and the USA.

On 2 February 2019 the USA notified the other parties that it would withdraw from the treaty in six months, citing the alleged deployment by Russia of a missile in breach of the treaty's limits. The USA and then Russia also suspended their obligations under the treaty. The withdrawal came into effect on 2 August 2019.

Treaty text: United Nations Treaty Series, vol. 1657 (1991), <https://treaties.un.org/doc/Publication/UNTS/Volume 1657/v1657.pdf>

Treaty on the Reduction and Limitation of Strategic Offensive Arms (START I)

Signed by the USA and the USSR at Moscow on 31 July 1991; entered into force on 5 December 1994; expired on 5 December 2009

The treaty obligated the original parties—the USA and the USSR—to make phased reductions in their offensive strategic nuclear forces over a seven-year period. It set numerical limits on deployed strategic nuclear delivery vehicles—intercontinental ballistic missiles (ICBMs), submarine-launched ballistic missiles (SLBMs) and heavy bombers—and the nuclear warheads they carry.

In the Protocol to Facilitate the Implementation of START (**1992 Lisbon Protocol**), which entered into force on 5 December 1994, Belarus, Kazakhstan and Ukraine also assumed the obligations of the former USSR under the treaty alongside Russia.

Treaty and protocol texts: US Department of State, <https://2009-2017.state.gov/t/avc/trty/146007.htm>

Treaty on Further Reduction and Limitation of Strategic Offensive Arms (START II)

Signed by Russia and the USA at Moscow on 3 January 1993; not in force

The treaty would have obligated the parties to eliminate their ICBMs with multiple independently targeted re-entry vehicles (MIRVs) and reduce the number of their deployed strategic nuclear warheads to no more than 3000–3500 each (of which no more than 1750 were to be deployed on SLBMs) by 1 January 2003. On 26 September 1997 the two parties signed a *Protocol* to the treaty providing for the extension until the end of 2007 of the period of implementation of the treaty.

The two signatories ratified the treaty but never exchanged the instruments of ratification. The treaty thus never entered into force. On 14 June 2002, as a response to the taking effect on 13 June of the USA's withdrawal from the ABM Treaty, Russia declared that it would no longer be bound by START II.

Treaty and protocol texts: US Department of State, <https://2009-2017.state.gov/t/avc/trty/102887.htm>

Treaty on Strategic Offensive Reductions (SORT, Moscow Treaty)

Signed by Russia and the USA at Moscow on 24 May 2002; entered into force on 1 June 2003; not in force from 5 February 2011

The treaty obligated the parties to reduce the number of their operationally deployed strategic nuclear warheads so that the aggregate numbers did not exceed 1700–2200 for each party by 31 December 2012. The treaty was superseded by New START on 5 February 2011.

Treaty text: United Nations Treaty Series, vol. 2350 (2005), <https://treaties.un.org/doc/Publication/UNTS/Volume 2350/v2350.pdf>

Treaty on Measures for the Further Reduction and Limitation of Strategic Offensive Arms (New START, Prague Treaty)

Signed by Russia and the USA at Prague on 8 April 2010; entered into force on 5 February 2011

The treaty obligates the parties—Russia and the USA—to each reduce their number of (*a*) deployed ICBMs, SLBMs and heavy bombers to 700; (*b*) warheads on deployed ICBMs and SLBMs and warheads counted for deployed heavy bombers to 1550; and (*c*) deployed and non-deployed ICBM launchers, SLBM launchers and heavy bombers to 800. The reductions were achieved by 5 February 2018, as required by the treaty.

The treaty established a bilateral consultative commission (BCC) to resolve questions about compliance and other implementation issues. A protocol to the treaty contains verifications mechanisms.

The treaty followed on from START I and superseded SORT. After being in force for an initial period of 10 years, the treaty was extended on 3 February 2021 for a further period of 5 years, until 5 February 2026. It cannot be extended further but may be superseded by a subsequent agreement. Either party may also withdraw from the treaty, having given the other three months' notice, if it decides that its supreme interests have been jeopardized by extraordinary events related to the treaty's subject matter.

Treaty and protocol texts: US Department of State, <https://2009-2017.state.gov/t/avc/newstart/c44126.htm>

Annex B. International security cooperation bodies

This annex describes the main international organizations, intergovernmental bodies, treaty-implementing bodies and transfer control regimes whose aims include the promotion of security, stability, peace or arms control and lists their members or participants as of 1 January 2022. The bodies are divided into three categories: those with a global focus or membership (section I), those with a regional focus or membership (section II) and those that aim to control strategic trade (section III).

The member states of the United Nations and organs within the UN system are listed first, followed by all other bodies in alphabetical order. Not all members or participants of these bodies are UN member states. States that joined or first participated in the body during 2021 are shown in italics. The address of an internet site with information about each organization is provided where available. On the arms control and disarmament agreements mentioned here, see annex A.

I. Bodies with a global focus or membership

United Nations (UN)

The UN, the world intergovernmental organization, was founded in 1945 through the adoption of its Charter. Its headquarters are in New York, United States. The six principal UN organs are the General Assembly, the Security Council, the Economic and Social Council (ECOSOC), the Trusteeship Council (which suspended operation in 1994), the International Court of Justice (ICJ) and the Secretariat.

The General Assembly has six main committees. The First Committee (Disarmament and International Security Committee) deals with disarmament and related international security questions. The Fourth Committee (Special Political and Decolonization Committee) deals with a variety of subjects including decolonization, Palestinian refugees and human rights, peacekeeping, mine action, outer space, public information, atomic radiation and the University for Peace.

The UN Office for Disarmament Affairs (UNODA), an office of the UN Secretariat, promotes disarmament of nuclear, biological, chemical and conventional weapons. The UN also has a large number of specialized agencies and other autonomous bodies.

UN member states (193) and year of membership

Afghanistan, 1946
Albania, 1955
Algeria, 1962
Andorra, 1993
Angola, 1976
Antigua and Barbuda, 1981
Argentina, 1945
Armenia, 1992
Australia, 1945
Austria, 1955
Azerbaijan, 1992
Bahamas, 1973
Bahrain, 1971
Bangladesh, 1974
Barbados, 1966
Belarus, 1945
Belgium, 1945
Belize, 1981
Benin, 1960
Bhutan, 1971
Bolivia, 1945
Bosnia and Herzegovina, 1992
Botswana, 1966
Brazil, 1945
Brunei Darussalam, 1984
Bulgaria, 1955
Burkina Faso, 1960
Burundi, 1962
Cabo Verde, 1975
Cambodia, 1955
Cameroon, 1960
Canada, 1945
Central African Republic, 1960
Chad, 1960
Chile, 1945
China, 1945
Colombia, 1945
Comoros, 1975
Congo, Democratic Republic of the, 1960
Congo, Republic of the, 1960
Costa Rica, 1945
Côte d'Ivoire, 1960
Croatia, 1992
Cuba, 1945
Cyprus, 1960
Czechia, 1993
Denmark, 1945
Djibouti, 1977
Dominica, 1978
Dominican Republic, 1945

Ecuador, 1945
Egypt, 1945
El Salvador, 1945
Equatorial Guinea, 1968
Eritrea, 1993
Estonia, 1991
Eswatini, 1968
Ethiopia, 1945
Fiji, 1970
Finland, 1955
France, 1945
Gabon, 1960
Gambia, 1965
Georgia, 1992
Germany, 1973
Ghana, 1957
Greece, 1945
Grenada, 1974
Guatemala, 1945
Guinea, 1958
Guinea-Bissau, 1974
Guyana, 1966
Haiti, 1945
Honduras, 1945
Hungary, 1955
Iceland, 1946
India, 1945
Indonesia, 1950
Iran, 1945
Iraq, 1945
Ireland, 1955
Israel, 1949
Italy, 1955
Jamaica, 1962
Japan, 1956
Jordan, 1955
Kazakhstan, 1992
Kenya, 1963
Kiribati, 1999
Korea, Democratic People's Republic of (North Korea), 1991
Korea, Republic of (South Korea), 1991
Kuwait, 1963
Kyrgyzstan, 1992
Laos, 1955
Latvia, 1991
Lebanon, 1945
Lesotho, 1966
Liberia, 1945
Libya, 1955

Liechtenstein, 1990
Lithuania, 1991
Luxembourg, 1945
Madagascar, 1960
Malawi, 1964
Malaysia, 1957
Maldives, 1965
Mali, 1960
Malta, 1964
Marshall Islands, 1991
Mauritania, 1961
Mauritius, 1968
Mexico, 1945
Micronesia, 1991
Moldova, 1992
Monaco, 1993
Mongolia, 1961
Montenegro, 2006
Morocco, 1956
Mozambique, 1975
Myanmar, 1948
Namibia, 1990
Nauru, 1999
Nepal, 1955
Netherlands, 1945
New Zealand, 1945
Nicaragua, 1945
Niger, 1960
Nigeria, 1960
North Macedonia, 1993
Norway, 1945
Oman, 1971
Pakistan, 1947
Palau, 1994
Panama, 1945
Papua New Guinea, 1975
Paraguay, 1945
Peru, 1945
Philippines, 1945
Poland, 1945
Portugal, 1955
Qatar, 1971
Romania, 1955
Russia, 1945
Rwanda, 1962
Saint Kitts and Nevis, 1983
Saint Lucia, 1979
Saint Vincent and the Grenadines, 1980
Samoa, 1976
San Marino, 1992
Sao Tome and Principe, 1975

Saudi Arabia, 1945
Senegal, 1960
Serbia, 2000
Seychelles, 1976
Sierra Leone, 1961
Singapore, 1965
Slovakia, 1993
Slovenia, 1992
Solomon Islands, 1978
Somalia, 1960
South Africa, 1945
South Sudan, 2011
Spain, 1955
Sri Lanka, 1955
Sudan, 1956

Suriname, 1975
Sweden, 1946
Switzerland, 2002
Syria, 1945
Tajikistan, 1992
Tanzania, 1961
Thailand, 1946
Timor-Leste, 2002
Togo, 1960
Tonga, 1999
Trinidad and Tobago, 1962
Tunisia, 1956
Turkey, 1945
Turkmenistan, 1992
Tuvalu, 2000

Uganda, 1962
UK, 1945
Ukraine, 1945
United Arab Emirates, 1971
Uruguay, 1945
USA, 1945
Uzbekistan, 1992
Vanuatu, 1981
Venezuela, 1945
Viet Nam, 1977
Yemen, 1947
Zambia, 1964
Zimbabwe, 1980

Non-member observer states (2): Holy See, Palestine

Website: <https://www.un.org/>

UN Security Council

The Security Council has responsibility for the maintenance of international peace and security. All UN members states must comply with its decisions. It has 5 permanent members, which can each exercise a veto on the Council's decisions, and 10 non-permanent members elected by the UN General Assembly for two-year terms.

Permanent members (the P5): China, France, Russia, UK, USA

Non-permanent members (10): Albania[†], Brazil[†], Gabon[†], Ghana[†], India[*], Ireland[*], Kenya[*], Mexico[*], Norway[*], United Arab Emirates[†]

   [*] Member in 2021–22.
   [†] Member in 2022–23.

Website: <https://www.un.org/securitycouncil/>

Conference on Disarmament (CD)

The CD is intended to be the single multilateral arms control and disarmament negotiating forum of the international community. It has been enlarged and renamed several times since 1960. It is not a UN body but reports to the UN General Assembly. It is based in Geneva, Switzerland.

Members (65): Algeria, Argentina, Australia, Austria, Bangladesh, Belarus, Belgium, Brazil, Bulgaria, Cameroon, Canada, Chile, China, Colombia, Congo (Democratic Republic of the), Cuba, Ecuador, Egypt, Ethiopia, Finland, France, Germany, Hungary, India, Indonesia, Iran, Iraq, Ireland, Israel, Italy, Japan, Kazakhstan, Kenya, Korea (North), Korea (South), Malaysia, Mexico, Mongolia, Morocco, Myanmar, Netherlands, New Zealand, Nigeria, Norway, Pakistan, Peru, Poland, Romania, Russia, Senegal, Slovakia, South Africa, Spain, Sri Lanka, Sweden, Switzerland, Syria, Tunisia, Turkey, UK, Ukraine, USA, Venezuela, Viet Nam, Zimbabwe

Website: <https://www.un.org/disarmament/conference-on-disarmament/>

UN Disarmament Commission (UNDC)

The UNDC in its original form was established in 1952. After changes of name and format, it became the Conference on Disarmament in 1978. In that year, the UN General Assembly re-established the UNDC in its current form. It meets for three weeks each year in New York to consider a small number of disarmament issues—currently two substantive items per session—and formulate consensus principles, guidelines and recommendations. It was unable to reach agreement on any such outcome in 2000–16 or 2018–21, but in 2017 adopted consensus recommendations on 'Practical confidence-building measures in the field of conventional weapons'.

Members (193): The UN member states

Website: <https://www.un.org/disarmament/institutions/disarmament-commission/>

UN Peacebuilding Commission (PBC)

The PBC was established in 2005 by the General Assembly and the Security Council to advise them on post-conflict peacebuilding and recovery, to marshal resources and to propose integrated strategies.

The General Assembly, the Security Council and ECOSOC each elect seven members of the PBC for two-year terms; the remaining members are the top five providers of military personnel and civilian police to UN missions and the top five contributors of funds to the UN. Additional states and organizations participate in country-specific meetings on countries on the PBC agenda.

Members (31): Bangladesh*‖, Brazil*†, Bulgaria**†, Canada*#, China*‡, Colombia*§, Costa Rica*†, Dominican Republic**†, Egypt*†, Ethiopia*‖, France*‡, Germany*#, India*‖, Japan*#, Kenya*‡, Korea (South)*§, Latvia*§, Lebanon*†, Mexico*‡, Netherlands*#, New Zealand*§, Nigeria*§, Pakistan*‖, Portugal*§, Thailand*§, Russia*‡, Rwanda*‖, South Africa*†, Sweden*#, UK*‡, USA*‡

  * Member until 31 Dec. 2022.
  ** Member until 31 Dec. 2023.
  † Elected by the General Assembly.
  ‡ Elected by the Security Council.
  § Elected by ECOSOC.
  ‖ Top 5 contributor of personnel.
  # Top 5 contributor of funds.

Website: <https://www.un.org/peacebuilding/commission/>

International Atomic Energy Agency (IAEA)

The IAEA is an intergovernmental organization within the UN system. It is mandated by its Statute, which entered into force in 1957, to promote the peaceful uses of atomic energy and ensure that nuclear activities are not used to further any military purpose. Under the 1968 Non-Proliferation

Treaty and the nuclear weapon-free zone treaties, non-nuclear weapon states must accept IAEA nuclear safeguards to demonstrate the fulfilment of their obligation not to manufacture nuclear weapons. Its headquarters are in Vienna, Austria.

Members (173): Afghanistan, Albania, Algeria, Angola, Antigua and Barbuda, Argentina, Armenia, Australia, Austria, Azerbaijan, Bahamas, Bahrain, Bangladesh, Barbados, Belarus, Belgium, Belize, Benin, Bolivia, Bosnia and Herzegovina, Botswana, Brazil, Brunei Darussalam, Bulgaria, Burkina Faso, Burundi, Cambodia, Cameroon, Canada, Central African Republic, Chad, Chile, China, Colombia, Comoros, Congo (Democratic Republic of the), Congo (Republic of the), Costa Rica, Côte d'Ivoire, Croatia, Cuba, Cyprus, Czechia, Denmark, Djibouti, Dominica, Dominican Republic, Ecuador, Egypt, El Salvador, Eritrea, Estonia, Eswatini, Ethiopia, Fiji, Finland, France, Gabon, Georgia, Germany, Ghana, Greece, Grenada, Guatemala, Guyana, Haiti, Holy See, Honduras, Hungary, Iceland, India, Indonesia, Iran, Iraq, Ireland, Israel, Italy, Jamaica, Japan, Jordan, Kazakhstan, Kenya, Korea (South), Kuwait, Kyrgyzstan, Laos, Latvia, Lebanon, Lesotho, Liberia, Libya, Liechtenstein, Lithuania, Luxembourg, Madagascar, Malawi, Malaysia, Mali, Malta, Marshall Islands, Mauritania, Mauritius, Mexico, Moldova, Monaco, Mongolia, Montenegro, Morocco, Mozambique, Myanmar, Namibia, Nepal, Netherlands, New Zealand, Nicaragua, Niger, Nigeria, North Macedonia, Norway, Oman, Pakistan, Palau, Panama, Papua New Guinea, Paraguay, Peru, Philippines, Poland, Portugal, Qatar, Rwanda, Romania, Russia, Saint Lucia, Saint Vincent and the Grenadines, *Samoa*, San Marino, Saudi Arabia, Senegal, Serbia, Seychelles, Sierra Leone, Singapore, Slovakia, Slovenia, South Africa, Spain, Sri Lanka, Sudan, Sweden, Switzerland, Syria, Tajikistan, Tanzania, Thailand, Togo, Trinidad and Tobago, Tunisia, Turkey, Turkmenistan, Uganda, UK, Ukraine, United Arab Emirates, Uruguay, USA, Uzbekistan, Vanuatu, Venezuela, Viet Nam, Yemen, Zambia, Zimbabwe

Notes: North Korea was a member of the IAEA until June 1994. In addition to the 173 members as of 1 Jan. 2022, the IAEA General Conference had also approved the membership of Cabo Verde, the Gambia, Guinea, Saint Kitts and Nevis, and Tonga; each will take effect once the state deposits the necessary legal instruments with the IAEA.

Website: <https://www.iaea.org/>

International Court of Justice (ICJ)

The ICJ was established in 1945 by the UN Charter and is the principal judicial organ of the UN. The court's role is to settle legal disputes submitted to it by states and to give advisory opinions on legal questions referred to it by authorized UN organs and specialized agencies. The court is composed of 15 judges, who are elected for terms of office of nine years by the UN General Assembly and the Security Council. Its seat is at The Hague, the Netherlands.

Website: <https://www.icj-cij.org/>

Bilateral Consultative Commission (BCC)

The BCC is a forum established under the 2010 Russian–US Treaty on Measures for the Further Reduction and Limitation of Strategic Offensive Arms (New

START, Prague Treaty) to discuss issues related to the treaty's implementation. It replaced the joint compliance and inspection commission (JCIC) of the 1991 START treaty. The BCC is required to meet at least twice each year in Geneva, Switzerland, unless the parties agree otherwise. Its work is confidential.

Website: US Department of Defense, Office of the Assistant Secretary of Defense for Acquisition, <https://www.acq.osd.mil/asda/ssipm/sdc/tc/nst/index.html>

Commonwealth of Nations

Established in its current form in 1949, the Commonwealth is an organization of developed and developing countries whose aim is to advance democracy, human rights, and sustainable economic and social development within its member states and beyond. It adopted a charter reaffirming its core values and principles in 2012. The members' leaders meet in the biennial Commonwealth Heads of Government Meetings (CHOGMs). Its secretariat is in London, UK.

Members (54): Antigua and Barbuda, Australia, Bahamas, Bangladesh, Barbados, Belize, Botswana, Brunei Darussalam, Cameroon, Canada, Cyprus, Dominica, Eswatini, Fiji, Gambia, Ghana, Grenada, Guyana, India, Jamaica, Kenya, Kiribati, Lesotho, Malawi, Malaysia, Maldives, Malta, Mauritius, Mozambique, Namibia, Nauru, New Zealand, Nigeria, Pakistan, Papua New Guinea, Rwanda[†], Saint Kitts and Nevis, Saint Lucia, Saint Vincent and the Grenadines, Samoa, Seychelles, Sierra Leone, Singapore, Solomon Islands, South Africa, Sri Lanka, Tanzania, Tonga, Trinidad and Tobago, Tuvalu, Uganda, UK[*], Vanuatu, Zambia

[*] CHOGM host in 2018 and Chair-in-Office in 2018–22.
[†] CHOGM host in 2022 and Chair-in-Office from 2022.

Note: Zimbabwe (which withdrew in 2013) applied to rejoin the Commonwealth in May 2018.

Website: <https://www.thecommonwealth.org/>

Comprehensive Nuclear-Test-Ban Treaty Organization (CTBTO)

The CTBTO will become operational when the 1996 Comprehensive Nuclear-Test-Ban Treaty (CTBT) has entered into force. It will resolve questions of compliance with the treaty and act as a forum for consultation and cooperation among the states parties. A Preparatory Commission and provisional Technical Secretariat are preparing for the work of the CTBTO, in particular by establishing the International Monitoring System, consisting of seismic, hydro-acoustic, infrasound and radionuclide stations from which data is transmitted to the CTBTO International Data Centre. Their headquarters are in Vienna, Austria.

Signatories to the CTBT (185): See annex A

Website: <https://www.ctbto.org/>

Financial Action Task Force (FATF)

The FATF is an intergovernmental policymaking body whose purpose is to establish international standards and develop and promote policies, at both national and international levels. It was established in 1989 by the Group of Seven (G7), initially to examine and develop measures to combat money laundering; its mandate was expanded in 2001 to incorporate efforts to combat terrorist financing and again in 2008 to include the financing of weapon of mass destruction (WMD) proliferation efforts. It published revised recommendations in 2012, which are updated regularly. Its secretariat is in Paris, France.

Members (39): Argentina, Australia, Austria, Belgium, Brazil, Canada, China, Denmark, European Commission, Finland, France, Germany, Greece, Gulf Cooperation Council, Hong Kong (China), Iceland, India, Ireland, Israel, Italy, Japan, Korea (South), Luxembourg, Malaysia, Mexico, Netherlands, New Zealand, Norway, Portugal, Russia, Saudi Arabia, Singapore, South Africa, Spain, Sweden, Switzerland, Turkey, UK, USA

Website: <https://www.fatf-gafi.org/>

Global Initiative to Combat Nuclear Terrorism (GICNT)

The GICNT was established in 2006 as a voluntary international partnership of states and international organizations that are committed to strengthening global capacity to prevent, detect and respond to nuclear terrorism. The GICNT works towards this goal by conducting multilateral activities that strengthen the plans, policies, procedures and interoperability of its partner. The partners meet at biennial plenaries. Russia and the USA act as co-chairs and Morocco leads the implementation and assessment group.

Partners (89): Afghanistan, Albania, Algeria, Argentina, Armenia, Australia, Austria, Azerbaijan, Bahrain, Belarus, Belgium, Bosnia and Herzegovina, Bulgaria, Cabo Verde, Cambodia, Canada, Chile, China, Côte d'Ivoire, Croatia, Cyprus, Czechia, Denmark, Estonia, Finland, France, Georgia, Germany, Greece, Hungary, Iceland, India, Iraq, Ireland, Israel, Italy, Japan, Jordan, Kazakhstan, Korea (South), Kyrgyzstan, Latvia, Libya, Lithuania, Luxembourg, Madagascar, Malaysia, Malta, Mauritius, Mexico, Moldova, Montenegro, Morocco, Nepal, Netherlands, New Zealand, Nigeria, North Macedonia, Norway, Pakistan, Palau, Panama, Paraguay, Philippines, Poland, Portugal, Romania, Russia, Saudi Arabia, Serbia, Seychelles, Singapore, Slovakia, Slovenia, Spain, Sri Lanka, Sweden, Switzerland, Tajikistan, Thailand, Turkey, Turkmenistan, UK, Ukraine, United Arab Emirates, USA, Uzbekistan, Viet Nam, Zambia

Official observers (6): European Union, International Atomic Energy Agency, International Criminal Police Organization (INTERPOL), UN Interregional Crime and Justice Research Institute, UN Office of Counter-Terrorism, UN Office on Drugs and Crime

Website: <https://gicnt.org/>

Group of Seven (G7)

The G7 is a group of leading industrialized countries that have met informally, at the level of head of state or government, since the 1970s. The presidents of the European Council and the European Commission represent the European Union at summits.

Between 1997 and 2013 the G7 members and Russia met together as the Group of Eight (G8). Following Russia's annexation of Crimea, the G7 states decided in March 2014 to meet without Russia until further notice.

Members (7): Canada, France, Germany[†], Italy, Japan[‡], UK[*], USA

  [*] G7 presidency and summit host in 2021.

† G7 presidency and summit host in 2022.
‡ G7 presidency and summit host in 2023.

Website: <https://www.international.gc.ca/world-monde/international_relations-relations_internationales/g7/index.aspx>

Global Partnership against the Spread of Weapons and Materials of Mass Destruction

The Global Partnership was launched in 2002 by the G8 to address non-proliferation, disarmament, counterterrorism and nuclear safety issues. The members meet twice each year, hosted by the state holding the G7 presidency, with the main goal of launching specific projects to tackle the abuse of weapons and materials of mass destruction and reduce chemical, biological, radioactive and nuclear risks. The Global Partnership was extended for an unspecified period in May 2011.

Members (31): Australia, Belgium, Canada, Chile, Czechia, Denmark, European Union, Finland, France, Georgia, Germany, Hungary, Ireland, Italy, Japan, Jordan, Kazakhstan, Korea (South), Mexico, Netherlands, New Zealand, Norway, Philippines, Poland, Portugal, Spain, Sweden, Switzerland, UK, Ukraine, USA

Note: Russia was a founding partner of the Global Partnership, but it ceased to be a partner following its exclusion from the G8.

Website: <https://www.gpwmd.com/>

International Criminal Court (ICC)

The ICC is a permanent international court dealing with the crime of genocide, crimes against humanity, war crimes and the crime of aggression. Its seat is at The Hague, the Netherlands, and it has field offices in the Central African Republic, Côte d'Ivoire, the Democratic Republic of the Congo, Georgia, Kenya, Mali and Uganda. The court has 18 judges and an independent prosecutor, elected by the assembly of states parties for nine-year terms.

The court's powers and jurisdiction are defined by the 1998 Rome Statute and its amendments. While the ICC is independent of the UN, the Rome Statute grants the UN Security Council certain powers of referral and deferral.

Parties to the Rome Statute (123) and its amendments: See annex A

Website: <https://www.icc-cpi.int/>

Non-Aligned Movement (NAM)

NAM was established in 1961 as a forum for non-aligned states to consult on political, economic and arms control issues and coordinate their positions in the UN.

Members (120): Afghanistan, Algeria, Angola, Antigua and Barbuda, Azerbaijan*, Bahamas, Bahrain, Bangladesh, Barbados, Belarus, Belize, Benin, Bhutan, Bolivia, Botswana, Brunei Darussalam, Burkina Faso, Burundi, Cabo Verde, Cambodia, Cameroon, Central African Republic, Chad, Chile, Colombia, Comoros, Congo (Democratic Republic of the), Congo

(Republic of the), Côte d'Ivoire, Cuba, Djibouti, Dominica, Dominican Republic, Ecuador, Egypt, Equatorial Guinea, Eritrea, Eswatini, Ethiopia, Fiji, Gabon, Gambia, Ghana, Grenada, Guatemala, Guinea, Guinea-Bissau, Guyana, Haiti, Honduras, India, Indonesia, Iran, Iraq, Jamaica, Jordan, Kenya, Korea (North), Kuwait, Laos, Lebanon, Lesotho, Liberia, Libya, Madagascar, Malawi, Malaysia, Maldives, Mali, Mauritania, Mauritius, Mongolia, Morocco, Mozambique, Myanmar, Namibia, Nepal, Nicaragua, Niger, Nigeria, Oman, Pakistan, Palestine Liberation Organization, Panama, Papua New Guinea, Peru, Philippines, Qatar, Rwanda, Saint Kitts and Nevis, Saint Lucia, Saint Vincent and the Grenadines, Sao Tome and Principe, Saudi Arabia, Senegal, Seychelles, Sierra Leone, Singapore, Somalia, South Africa, Sri Lanka, Sudan, Suriname, Syria, Tanzania, Thailand, Timor-Leste, Togo, Trinidad and Tobago, Tunisia, Turkmenistan, Uganda[†], United Arab Emirates, Uzbekistan, Vanuatu, Venezuela, Viet Nam, Yemen, Zambia, Zimbabwe

* NAM chair in 2019–23 and summit host in 2019.
[†] NAM chair from 2023 and summit host in 2023.

Note: A 60th anniversary commemorative summit was held in Serbia in 2021.

Website: <https://www.namazerbaijan.org/>

Organisation for Economic Co-operation and Development (OECD)

Established in 1961, the OECD's objectives are to promote economic and social welfare by coordinating policies among the member states. Its headquarters are in Paris, France.

Members (38): Australia, Austria, Belgium, Canada, Chile, Colombia, *Costa Rica*, Czechia, Denmark, Estonia, Finland, France, Germany, Greece, Hungary, Iceland, Ireland, Israel, Italy, Japan, Korea (South), Latvia, Lithuania, Luxembourg, Mexico, Netherlands, New Zealand, Norway, Poland, Portugal, Slovakia, Slovenia, Spain, Sweden, Switzerland, Turkey, UK, USA

Website: <https://www.oecd.org/>

Organisation for the Prohibition of Chemical Weapons (OPCW)

The OPCW implements the 1993 Chemical Weapons Convention (CWC). Among other things, it oversees the destruction of chemical weapon stockpiles and associated infrastructure, implements a verification regime to ensure that such weapons do not re-emerge, provides assistance and protection to states parties threatened by such weapons, and facilitates and engages in international cooperation to strengthen treaty compliance and to promote the peaceful uses of chemistry. In addition to the responsibility to investigate alleged use of chemical weapons, in 2018 the OPCW gained the power to attribute responsibility for any chemical weapon use on the territory of a member state if requested to do so by that state.

The work of the OPCW and its Technical Secretariat is overseen by the Executive Council, whose 41 members are elected for two-year terms by the Conference of States Parties. It is based in The Hague, the Netherlands.

Parties to the Chemical Weapons Convention (193): See annex A

Website: <https://www.opcw.org/>

Organisation of Islamic Cooperation (OIC)

The OIC (formerly the Organization of the Islamic Conference) was established in 1969 by Islamic states to promote cooperation among the members and to support peace, security, and the struggle of the people of Palestine and all Muslim people. Among its organs are the Independent Permanent Human Rights Commission (IPHRC) and the Islamic Development Bank (IDB). Its secretariat is in Jeddah, Saudi Arabia.

Members (57): Afghanistan, Albania, Algeria, Azerbaijan, Bahrain, Bangladesh, Benin, Brunei Darussalam, Burkina Faso, Cameroon, Chad, Comoros, Côte d'Ivoire, Djibouti, Egypt, Gabon, Gambia, Guinea, Guinea-Bissau, Guyana, Indonesia, Iran, Iraq, Jordan, Kazakhstan, Kuwait, Kyrgyzstan, Lebanon, Libya, Malaysia, Maldives, Mali, Mauritania, Morocco, Mozambique, Niger, Nigeria, Oman, Pakistan, Palestine, Qatar, Saudi Arabia, Senegal, Sierra Leone, Somalia, Sudan, Suriname, Syria, Tajikistan, Togo, Tunisia, Turkey, Turkmenistan, Uganda, United Arab Emirates, Uzbekistan, Yemen

Website: <https://www.oic-oci.org/>

II. Bodies with a regional focus or membership

African Commission on Nuclear Energy (AFCONE)

AFCONE was established by the 1996 African Nuclear-Weapon-Free Zone Treaty (Treaty of Pelindaba) to ensure compliance with the treaty and to advance the peaceful application of nuclear science and technology in Africa. Its seat is in Pretoria, South Africa.

Parties to the Treaty of Pelindaba (42): See annex A

Website: <https://www.afcone.org/>

African Union (AU)

The AU was formally established in 2001 and launched in 2002. It replaced the Organization for African Unity (OAU), which had been established in 1963. Membership is open to all African states. The AU promotes unity, security and conflict resolution, democracy, human rights, and political, social and economic integration in Africa. Its main organs include the Assembly of Heads of State and Government (the supreme body), the Executive Council (made up of designated national ministers), the AU Commission (the secretariat), the Pan-African Parliament, and the Peace and Security Council. The AU's headquarters are in Addis Ababa, Ethiopia.

Members (55): Algeria, Angola, Benin, Botswana, Burkina Faso, Burundi, Cabo Verde, Cameroon, Central African Republic, Chad, Comoros, Congo (Democratic Republic of the), Congo (Republic of the), Côte d'Ivoire, Djibouti, Egypt, Equatorial Guinea, Eritrea, Eswatini, Ethiopia, Gabon, Gambia, Ghana, Guinea*, Guinea-Bissau, Kenya, Lesotho, Liberia, Libya, Madagascar, Malawi, Mali†, Mauritania, Mauritius, Morocco, Mozambique, Namibia, Niger, Nigeria, Rwanda, Sahrawi Arab Democratic Republic (Western Sahara), Sao Tome and Principe, Senegal, Seychelles, Sierra Leone, Somalia, South Africa, South Sudan, Sudan‡, Tanzania, Togo, Tunisia, Uganda, Zambia, Zimbabwe

* Guinea was suspended from the AU on 10 Sep. 2021 following the military coup of 5 Sep.

† Mali was suspended from the AU on 1 June 2021 following the military coup of 24 May. It had previously been suspended on 19 Aug. 2020 following the military coup of 18 Aug. That suspension was lifted on 9 Oct. 2020 after agreement on an 18-month transition to a civilian-led government.

‡ Sudan was suspended from the AU on 26 Oct. 2021 following the military coup on the previous day. It had previously been suspended between 6 June and 6 Sep. 2019.

Note: In addition to the 3 member states of the AU suspended as of 1 Jan. 2022, Burkina Faso was suspended on 31 Jan. 2022 following the military coup of 24 Jan.

Website: <https://www.au.int/>

Peace and Security Council (PSC)

The PSC is the AU's standing decision-making organ for the prevention, management and resolution of conflicts. Its 15 members are elected by the Executive Council subject to endorsement by the Assembly. It is the main pillar of the African Peace and Security Architecture (APSA).

Members for a 3-year term 1 Apr. 2019–31 Mar. 2022 (5): Algeria, Burundi, Kenya, Lesotho, Nigeria

Members for a 2-year term 1 Apr. 2020–31 Mar. 2022 (10): Benin, Ghana, Cameroon, Chad, Djibouti, Egypt, Ethiopia, Malawi, Mozambique, Senegal

Members for a 3-year term 1 Apr. 2022–31 Mar. 2025 (5): Cameroon, Djibouti, Morocco, Namibia, Nigeria

Members for a 2-year term 1 Apr. 2022–31 Mar. 2024 (10): Burundi, Congo (Republic of the), Gambia, Ghana, Senegal, South Africa, Uganda, Tanzania, Tunisia, Zimbabwe

Website: <https://www.peaceau.org/>

Asia–Pacific Economic Cooperation (APEC)

APEC was established in 1989 as a regional economic forum to enhance open trade and economic prosperity in the Asia–Pacific region. Since 2001 the forum has been engaged in helping to protect the economies in the region from terrorism. A task force established in 2003 became the Counter-Terrorism Working Group in 2013. The APEC Secretariat is based in Singapore.

Member economies (21): Australia, Brunei Darussalam, Canada, Chile, China, Hong Kong, Indonesia, Japan, Korea (South), Malaysia, Mexico, New Zealand*, Papua New Guinea, Peru, Philippines, Russia, Singapore, Taiwan, Thailand†, USA‡, Viet Nam

* Host of APEC Economic Leaders' Meeting in 2021.
† Host of APEC Economic Leaders' Meeting in 2022.
‡ Host of APEC Economic Leaders' Meeting in 2023.

Website: <https://www.apec.org/>

Association of Southeast Asian Nations (ASEAN)

ASEAN was established in 1967 to promote economic, social and cultural development as well as regional peace and security in South East Asia. Development of the ASEAN Political–Security Community is one of the three pillars (along with the Economic and Sociocultural communities) of the ASEAN

Community, which was launched in 2015 as a framework for further integration. The ASEAN Secretariat is in Jakarta, Indonesia.

Members (10): Brunei Darussalam*, Cambodia†, Indonesia, Laos, Malaysia, Myanmar, Philippines, Singapore, Thailand, Viet Nam

* ASEAN chair and summit host in 2021.
† ASEAN chair and summit host in 2022.

Website: <https://www.asean.org/>

ASEAN Regional Forum (ARF)

The ARF was established in 1994 to foster constructive dialogue and consultation on political and security issues and to contribute to confidence-building and preventive diplomacy in the Asia-Pacific region.

Participants (27): The ASEAN member states and Australia, Bangladesh, Canada, China, European Union, India, Japan, Korea (North), Korea (South), Mongolia, New Zealand, Pakistan, Papua New Guinea, Russia, Sri Lanka, Timor-Leste, USA

Website: <https://aseanregionalforum.asean.org/>

ASEAN Plus Three (APT)

The APT cooperation began in 1997, in the wake of the Asian financial crisis, and was institutionalized in 1999. It aims to foster economic, political and security cooperation and financial stability among its participants.

Participants (13): The ASEAN member states and China, Japan, Korea (South)

Website: <https://aseanplusthree.asean.org/>

East Asia Summit (EAS)

The East Asia Summit started in 2005 as a regional forum for dialogue on strategic, political and economic issues with the aim of promoting peace, stability and economic prosperity in East Asia. The annual meetings are held in connection with the ASEAN summits.

Participants (18): The ASEAN member states and Australia, China, India, Japan, Korea (South), New Zealand, Russia, USA

Website: <https://eastasiasummit.asean.org/>

Collective Security Treaty Organization (CSTO)

The CSTO was formally established in 2002–2003 by six signatories of the 1992 Collective Security Treaty. It aims to promote military and political cooperation among its members. Under Article 4 of the 1992 treaty, aggression against one member state is considered to be aggression against them all. An objective of the CSTO is to provide a more efficient response to strategic problems such as terrorism and narcotics trafficking. Its seat is in Moscow, Russia.

Members (6): Armenia, Belarus, Kazakhstan, Kyrgyzstan, Russia, Tajikistan

Website: <https://odkb-csto.org/>

Commonwealth of Independent States (CIS)

The CIS was established in 1991 as a framework for multilateral cooperation among former republics of the Soviet Union. The institutions of the CIS, including the Council of Defence Ministers, were established by the 1993 Charter. Their headquarters are in Minsk, Belarus.

Members (10): Armenia, Azerbaijan, Belarus, Kazakhstan, Kyrgyzstan, Moldova, Russia, Tajikistan, Turkmenistan*, Uzbekistan

* Turkmenistan has not ratified the 1993 CIS Charter but since 26 Aug. 2005 has participated in CIS activities as an associate member.

Note: Although Ukraine did not ratify the CIS Charter, it was an unofficial associate member from 1993. Ukraine decided to end its participation in CIS institutions in May 2018; it completed the process of withdrawing from the CIS coordination bodies in Feb. 2019. It continues to withdraw from CIS agreements.

Website: <https://www.cis.minsk.by/>

Communauté économique des États de l'Afrique Centrale (CEEAC, Economic Community of Central African States, ECCAS)

CEEAC was established in 1983 to promote political dialogue, create a customs union and establish common policies in Central Africa. It also coordinates activities under the 2010 Central African Convention for the Control of Small Arms and Light Weapons, Their Ammunition and All Parts and Components That Can Be Used for Their Manufacture, Repair and Assembly (Kinshasa Convention). Its secretariat is in Libreville, Gabon.

The **Council for Peace and Security in Central Africa (Conseil de paix et de sécurité de l'Afrique Centrale, COPAX)** is a mechanism for promoting joint political and military strategies for conflict prevention, management and resolution in Central Africa.

Members (11): Angola, Burundi, Cameroon, Central African Republic, Chad, Congo (Democratic Republic of the), Congo (Republic of the), Equatorial Guinea, Gabon, Rwanda, Sao Tome and Principe

Website: <https://ceeac-eccas.org/>

Conference on Interaction and Confidence-building Measures in Asia (CICA)

Initiated in 1992, CICA was formally established in 1999 as a forum to enhance security cooperation and confidence-building measures among the member states. It also promotes economic, social and cultural cooperation. Its secretariat is in Astana, Kazakhstan.

Members (27): Afghanistan, Azerbaijan, Bahrain, Bangladesh, Cambodia, China, Egypt, India, Iran, Iraq, Israel, Jordan, Kazakhstan*, Korea (South), Kyrgyzstan, Mongolia, Pakistan, Palestine, Qatar, Russia, Sri Lanka, Tajikistan, Thailand, Turkey, United Arab Emirates, Uzbekistan, Viet Nam

* Chair from 2020.

Website: <https://www.s-cica.org/>

Council of Europe (COE)

The Council was established in 1949. Membership is open to all European states that accept the principle of the rule of law and guarantee their citizens' human rights and fundamental freedoms. Its seat is in Strasbourg, France. Among its organs are the Council of Ministers, the Parliamentary Assembly, the European Court of Human Rights and the Council of Europe Development Bank.

Members (47): Albania, Andorra, Armenia, Austria, Azerbaijan, Belgium, Bosnia and Herzegovina, Bulgaria, Croatia, Cyprus, Czechia, Denmark, Estonia, Finland, France, Georgia, Germany, Greece, Hungary, Iceland, Ireland, Italy, Latvia, Liechtenstein, Lithuania, Luxembourg, Malta, Moldova, Monaco, Montenegro, Netherlands, North Macedonia, Norway, Poland, Portugal, Romania, Russia, San Marino, Serbia, Slovakia, Slovenia, Spain, Sweden, Switzerland, Turkey, UK, Ukraine

Note: Following Russia's invasion of Ukraine on 24 Feb. 2022, the Committee of Ministers suspended Russia from its rights of representation in the Committee of Ministers and the Parliamentary Assembly on 25 Feb. On 15 Mar. Russia formally notified the COE that it would withdraw, with effect from 31 Dec. 2022. On 16 Mar. the Committee of Ministers expelled Russia with immediate effect.

Website: <https://www.coe.int/>

Council of the Baltic Sea States (CBSS)

The CBSS was established in 1992 as a regional intergovernmental organization for cooperation among the states of the Baltic Sea region. Its secretariat is in Stockholm, Sweden.

Members (12): Denmark, Estonia, European Union, Finland, Germany, Iceland, Latvia, Lithuania, Norway, Poland, Russia, Sweden

Note: Following Russia's invasion of Ukraine on 24 Feb. 2022, Russia was suspended from the CBSS on 3 Mar.

Website: <https://www.cbss.org/>

Economic Community of West African States (ECOWAS)

ECOWAS was established in 1975 to promote trade and cooperation and contribute to development in West Africa. In 1981 it adopted the Protocol on Mutual Assistance in Defence Matters. Its Commission, Court of Justice and Parliament are based in Abuja, Nigeria.

Members (15): Benin, Burkina Faso, Cabo Verde, Côte d'Ivoire, Gambia, Ghana, Guinea*, Guinea-Bissau, Liberia, Mali[†], Niger, Nigeria, Senegal, Sierra Leone, Togo

* Guinea was suspended from the AU on 8 Sep. 2021 following the military coup of 5 Sep.

† Mali was suspended from ECOWAS on 30 May 2021 following the military coup of 24 May. It had previously been suspended on 20 Aug. 2020 following the military coup of 18 Aug. That suspension was lifted on 6 Oct. 2020 after agreement on an 18-month transition to a civilian-led government.

Notes: In June 2017 ECOWAS agreed in principle to admit Morocco as its 16th member. In addition to the 2 member states of ECOWAS suspended as of 1 Jan. 2022, Burkina Faso was suspended on 28 Jan. 2022 following the military coup of 24 Jan.

Website: <https://www.ecowas.int/>

European Union (EU)

The EU is an organization of European states that cooperate in a wide field, including a single market with free movement of people, goods, services and capital, a common currency (the euro) for some members, and a Common Foreign and Security Policy (CFSP), including a Common Security and Defence Policy (CSDP). The EU's main bodies are the European Council, the Council of the European Union (also known as the Council of Ministers or the Council), the European Commission (the secretariat), the European Parliament and the European Court of Justice.

The CFSP and CSDP are coordinated by the High Representative of the Union for Foreign Affairs and Security Policy, assisted by the European External Action Service (EEAS) and the EU Military Staff.

The principal seat of the EU is in Brussels, Belgium.

Members (27): Austria, Belgium, Bulgaria, Croatia, Cyprus, Czechia, Denmark, Estonia, Finland, France, Germany, Greece, Hungary, Ireland, Italy, Latvia, Lithuania, Luxembourg, Malta, Netherlands, Poland, Portugal, Romania, Slovakia, Slovenia, Spain, Sweden

Website: <https://europa.eu/>

European Atomic Energy Community (Euratom, or EAEC)

Euratom was created by the 1957 Treaty Establishing the European Atomic Energy Community (Euratom Treaty) to promote the development of nuclear energy for peaceful purposes and to administer (in cooperation with the IAEA) the multinational regional safeguards system covering the EU member states. The Euratom Supply Agency, located in Luxembourg, has the task of ensuring a regular and equitable supply of ores, source materials and special fissile materials to EU member states.

Members (27): The EU member states

Website: <https://euratom-supply.ec.europa.eu/>

European Defence Agency (EDA)

The EDA is an agency of the EU, under the direction of the Council. It was established in 2004 to help develop European defence capabilities, to promote European armaments cooperation and to work for a strong

European defence technological and industrial base. The EDA's decision-making body is the Steering Board, composed of the defence ministers of the participating member states and the EU's High Representative for Foreign Affairs and Security Policy (as head of the agency). The EDA is located in Brussels, Belgium.

Participating member states (26): The EU member states other than Denmark

Note: The EDA has signed administrative arrangements with Norway (2006), Switzerland (2012), Serbia (2013) and Ukraine (2015) that enable these states to participate in its projects and programmes.

Website: <https://eda.europa.eu/>

Permanent Structured Cooperation (PESCO)

The Council of the EU established PESCO in 2017 as a framework to deepen security and defence cooperation between EU member states. Through joint projects, it aims to increase the military capabilities available to EU member states. The EDA and the EEAS jointly act as the PESCO secretariat.

Participating member states (25): The EU member states other than Denmark and Malta

Website: <https://pesco.europa.eu/>

Gulf Cooperation Council (GCC)

Formally called the Cooperation Council for the Arab States of the Gulf, the GCC was created in 1981 to promote regional integration in such areas as economy, finance, trade, administration and legislation and to foster scientific and technical progress. The members also cooperate in areas of foreign policy and military and security matters. The Supreme Council (consisting of the head of each member state) is the highest GCC authority. Its headquarters are in Riyadh, Saudi Arabia.

Members (6): Bahrain, Kuwait, Oman, Qatar, Saudi Arabia, United Arab Emirates

Website: <https://www.gcc-sg.org/>

Intergovernmental Authority on Development (IGAD)

IGAD was established in 1996 to expand regional cooperation and promote peace and stability in the Horn of Africa. It superseded the Intergovernmental Authority on Drought and Development (IGADD), which was established in 1986. Its secretariat is in Djibouti.

Members (8): Djibouti, Eritrea, Ethiopia, Kenya, Somalia, South Sudan, Sudan, Uganda

Website: <https://www.igad.int/>

International Conference on the Great Lakes Region (ICGLR)

The ICGLR, which was initiated in 2004, works to promote peace and security, political and social stability, and growth and development in the Great Lakes region. In 2006 the member states adopted the Pact on Security, Stability and Development in the Great Lakes Region, which entered into force in 2008. Its executive secretariat is in Bujumbura, Burundi.

The ICGLR Joint Intelligence Fusion Centre (JIFC) and the Expanded Joint Verification Mechanism (EJVM) were launched in 2012 in Goma, Democratic Republic of the Congo. The JIFC collects, analyses and disseminates information on armed groups in the region and recommends action to member states. The EJVM monitors and investigates security incidents.

Members (12): Angola, Burundi, Central African Republic, Congo (Republic of the), Congo (Democratic Republic of the), Kenya, Rwanda, South Sudan, Sudan, Tanzania, Uganda, Zambia

Website: <https://www.icglr.org/>

League of Arab States

The Arab League was established in 1945 to form closer union among Arab states and foster political and economic cooperation. An agreement for collective defence and economic cooperation among the members was signed in 1950. In 2015 the Arab League agreed to create a joint Arab military force for regional peacekeeping, but no progress in its establishment has been subsequently made. The general secretariat of the Arab League is in Cairo, Egypt

Members (22): Algeria, Bahrain, Comoros, Djibouti, Egypt, Iraq, Jordan, Kuwait, Lebanon, Libya, Mauritania, Morocco, Oman, Palestine, Qatar, Saudi Arabia, Somalia, Sudan, Syria*, Tunisia, United Arab Emirates, Yemen

* Syria was suspended from the organization on 16 Nov. 2011.

Website: <http://www.leagueofarabstates.net/>

North Atlantic Treaty Organization (NATO)

NATO was established in 1949 by the North Atlantic Treaty (Washington Treaty) as a Western military alliance. Article 5 of the treaty defines the members' commitment to respond to an armed attack against any party to the treaty. Its headquarters are in Brussels, Belgium.

Members (30): Albania, Belgium, Bulgaria, Canada, Croatia, Czechia, Denmark, Estonia, France, Germany, Greece, Hungary, Iceland, Italy, Latvia, Lithuania, Luxembourg, Montenegro, Netherlands, Norway, North Macedonia, Poland, Portugal, Romania, Slovakia, Slovenia, Spain, Turkey, UK, USA

Website: <https://www.nato.int/>

Euro-Atlantic Partnership Council (EAPC)

The EAPC brings together NATO and its Partnership for Peace (PFP) partners for dialogue and consultation. It is the overall political framework for the bilateral PFP programme.

Members (50): The NATO member states and Armenia, Austria, Azerbaijan, Belarus, Bosnia and Herzegovina, Finland, Georgia, Ireland, Kazakhstan, Kyrgyzstan, Malta, Moldova, Russia, Serbia, Sweden, Switzerland, Tajikistan, Turkmenistan, Ukraine, Uzbekistan

Website: <https://www.nato.int/cps/en/natohq/topics_49276.htm>

Istanbul Cooperation Initiative (ICI)

The ICI was established in 2004 to contribute to long-term global and regional security by offering practical bilateral security cooperation with NATO to countries of the broader Middle East region.

Participants (34): The NATO member states and Bahrain, Kuwait, Qatar, United Arab Emirates
   Note: In addition to the 34 participating states, Oman and Saudi Arabia participate in selected activities within the ICI framework.

Website: <https://www.nato.int/cps/en/natohq/topics_52956.htm>

Mediterranean Dialogue

NATO's Mediterranean Dialogue was established in 1994 as a forum for political dialogue and practical cooperation between NATO and countries of the Mediterranean and North Africa. It reflects NATO's view that security in Europe is closely linked to security and stability in the Mediterranean.

Participants (37): The NATO member states and Algeria, Egypt, Israel, Jordan, Mauritania, Morocco, Tunisia

Website: <https://www.nato.int/cps/en/natohq/topics_52927.htm>

NATO–Georgia Commission (NGC)

The NGC was established in September 2008 to serve as a forum for political consultations and practical cooperation to help Georgia achieve its goal of joining NATO.

Participants (31): The NATO member states and Georgia

Website: <https://www.nato.int/cps/en/natohq/topics_52131.htm>

NATO–Russia Council (NRC)

The NRC was established in 2002 as a mechanism for consultation, consensus building, cooperation, and joint decisions and action on security issues. It focuses on areas of mutual interest identified in the 1997 NATO–Russia Founding Act on Mutual Relations, Cooperation and Security and new areas, such as terrorism, crisis management and non-proliferation.

Participants (31): The NATO member states and Russia

Note: In Apr. 2014, following Russian military intervention in Ukraine, NATO suspended all practical cooperation with Russia, although political dialogue in the NRC continues at the ambassadorial level or above.

Website: <https://www.nato.int/nrc-website/>

NATO–Ukraine Commission (NUC)

The NUC was established in 1997 for consultations on political and security issues, conflict prevention and resolution, non-proliferation, transfers of arms and technology, and other subjects of common concern.

Participants (31): The NATO member states and Ukraine

Website: <https://www.nato.int/cps/en/natohq/topics_50319.htm>

Organisation Conjointe de Coopération en matière d'Armement (OCCAR, Organisation for Joint Armament Cooperation)

OCCAR was established in 1996, with legal status since 2001, to provide more effective and efficient arrangements for the management of specific collaborative armament programmes. Its headquarters are in Bonn, Germany.

Members (6): Belgium, France, Germany, Italy, Spain, UK

Participants (7): Finland, Lithuania, Luxembourg, Netherlands, Poland, Sweden, Turkey

Website: <https://www.occar.int/>

Organismo para la Proscripción de las Armas Nucleares en la América Latina y el Caribe (OPANAL, Agency for the Prohibition of Nuclear Weapons in Latin America and the Caribbean)

OPANAL was established by the 1967 Treaty of Tlatelolco to resolve, together with the IAEA, questions of compliance with the treaty. Its seat is in Mexico City, Mexico.

Parties to the Treaty of Tlatelolco (33): See annex A

Website: <https://www.opanal.org/>

Organization for Democracy and Economic Development–GUAM

GUAM is a group of four states, established to promote stability and strengthen security, whose history goes back to 1997. The organization was established in 2006. The members cooperate to promote social and economic development and trade in eight working groups. Its secretariat is in Kyiv, Ukraine.

Members (4): Azerbaijan, Georgia, Moldova, Ukraine

Website: <https://guam-organization.org/>

Organization for Security and Co-operation in Europe (OSCE)

The Conference on Security and Co-operation in Europe (CSCE), which had been initiated in 1973, was renamed the OSCE in 1995. It is intended to be the primary instrument of comprehensive and cooperative security for early warning, conflict prevention, crisis management and post-conflict rehabilitation in its area. Its headquarters are in Vienna, Austria, and its other institutions are based elsewhere in Europe.

The OSCE Troika consists of representatives of the states holding the chair in the current year, the previous year and the succeeding year. The Forum for Security Cooperation (FSC) deals with arms control and confidence- and security-building measures.

Participants (57): Albania, Andorra, Armenia, Austria, Azerbaijan, Belarus, Belgium, Bosnia and Herzegovina, Bulgaria, Canada, Croatia, Cyprus, Czechia, Denmark, Estonia, Finland, France, Georgia, Germany, Greece, Holy See, Hungary, Iceland, Ireland, Italy, Kazakhstan, Kyrgyzstan, Latvia, Liechtenstein, Lithuania, Luxembourg, Malta, Moldova, Monaco, Mongolia, Montenegro, Netherlands, North Macedonia[‡], Norway, Poland[†], Portugal, Romania, Russia, San Marino, Serbia, Slovakia, Slovenia, Spain, Sweden[*], Switzerland, Tajikistan, Turkey, Turkmenistan, UK, Ukraine, USA, Uzbekistan

[*] Chair in 2021.
[†] Chair in 2022.
[‡] Chair in 2023.

Website: <https://www.osce.org/>

Joint Consultative Group (JCG)

The JCG is an OSCE-related body established by the 1990 Treaty on Conventional Armed Forces in Europe (CFE Treaty) to promote the objectives and implementation of the treaty by reconciling ambiguities of interpretation and implementation. Its seat is in Vienna, Austria.

Parties to the CFE Treaty (30): See annex A

Note: In 2007 Russia suspended its participation in the CFE Treaty, and in Mar. 2015 it announced that it had decided to completely halt its participation in the treaty, including the JCG.

Website: <https://www.osce.org/jcg/>

Minsk Group

The Minsk Group supports the Minsk Process, an ongoing forum for negotiations on a peaceful settlement of the conflict in Nagorno-Karabakh.

Members (13): Armenia, Azerbaijan, Belarus, Finland, France*, Germany, Italy, Russia*, Sweden, Turkey, USA*, OSCE Troika (North Macedonia, Poland and Sweden)

  * The representatives of these 3 states co-chair the group.

Website: <https://www.osce.org/mg/>

Open Skies Consultative Commission (OSCC)

The OSCC was established by the 1992 Treaty on Open Skies to resolve questions of compliance with the treaty.

Parties to the Open Skies Treaty (32): See annex A

  Note: The USA withdrew from the treaty and the OSCC on 22 Nov. 2020 and Russia withdrew on 18 Dec. 2021.

Website: <https://www.osce.org/oscc/>

Organization of American States (OAS)

The OAS, which adopted its charter in 1948, has the objective of strengthening peace and security in the western hemisphere. Its activities are based on the four pillars of democracy, human rights, security and development. Its general secretariat is in Washington, DC, USA.

Members (35): Antigua and Barbuda, Argentina, Bahamas, Barbados, Belize, Bolivia, Brazil, Canada, Chile, Colombia, Costa Rica, Cuba*, Dominica, Dominican Republic, Ecuador, El Salvador, Grenada, Guatemala, Guyana, Haiti, Honduras, Jamaica, Mexico, Nicaragua, Panama, Paraguay, Peru, Saint Kitts and Nevis, Saint Lucia, Saint Vincent and the Grenadines, Suriname, Trinidad and Tobago, Uruguay, USA, Venezuela

  * By a resolution of 3 June 2009, the 1962 resolution that excluded Cuba from the OAS ceased to have effect; according to the 2009 resolution, Cuba's participation in the organization 'will be the result of a process of dialogue'. Cuba has declined to participate in OAS activities.

Website: <https://www.oas.org/>

Organization of the Black Sea Economic Cooperation (BSEC)

The BSEC initiative was established in 1992 and became a full regional economic organization when its charter entered into force in 1999. Its aims are to ensure peace, stability and prosperity and to promote and develop economic co-operation and progress in the Black Sea region. Its permanent secretariat is in Istanbul, Turkey.

Members (13): Albania, Armenia, Azerbaijan, Bulgaria, Georgia, Greece, Moldova, North Macedonia, Romania, Russia, Serbia, Turkey, Ukraine

Website: <https://www.bsec-organization.org/>

Pacific Islands Forum

The forum, which was founded in 1971 as the South Pacific Forum, aims to enhance cooperation in sustainable development, economic growth, governance and security. It also monitors implementation of the 1985 South Pacific Nuclear Free Zone Treaty (Treaty of Rarotonga). Its secretariat is in Suva, Fiji.

Members (18): Australia, Cook Islands, Fiji, French Polynesia, Kiribati, Marshall Islands, Micronesia, Nauru, New Caledonia, New Zealand, Niue, Palau, Papua New Guinea, Samoa, Solomon Islands, Tonga, Tuvalu, Vanuatu

Note: Following a dispute over the appointment of a new secretary-general, in Feb. 2021 Kiribati, Marshall Islands, Micronesia, Nauru and Palau agreed to initiate the formal process of leaving the forum. In Feb. 2022 the 5 states 'temporarily rescinded' their withdrawal after the new secretary-general agreed to resign early, in June 2022.

Website: <https://www.forumsec.org/>

Regional Centre on Small Arms in the Great Lakes Region, the Horn of Africa and Bordering States (RECSA)

The Nairobi Secretariat on Small Arms and Light Weapons was established to coordinate implementation of the 2000 Nairobi Declaration on the Problem of Illicit Small Arms and Light Weapons in the Great Lakes Region and the Horn of Africa. It was transformed into RECSA in 2005 to oversee the implementation of the 2004 Nairobi Protocol for the Prevention, Control and Reduction of Small Arms and Light Weapons. It is based in Nairobi, Kenya.

Members (15): Burundi, Djibouti, Central African Republic, Congo (Democratic Republic of the), Congo (Republic of the), Eritrea, Ethiopia, Kenya, Rwanda, Seychelles, Somalia, South Sudan, Sudan, Tanzania, Uganda

Website: <https://www.recsasec.org/>

Regional Cooperation Council

The RCC was launched in 2008 as the successor of the Stability Pact for South Eastern Europe that was initiated by the EU at the 1999 Conference on South Eastern Europe. It promotes mutual cooperation and European and Euro-Atlantic integration of states in South Eastern Europe in order to inspire development in the region for the benefit of its people. It focuses on six areas: economic and social development, energy and infrastructure, justice and home affairs, security cooperation, building human capital, and parliamentary cooperation. Its secretariat is in Sarajevo, Bosnia and Herzegovina, and it has a liaison office in Brussels, Belgium.

Participants (46): Albania, Austria, Bosnia and Herzegovina, Bulgaria, Canada, Council of Europe, Council of Europe Development Bank, Croatia, Czechia, Denmark, European Bank for Reconstruction and Development, European Investment Bank, European Union, Germany, Finland, France, Greece, Hungary, International Organization for Migration, Ireland, Italy, Kosovo, Latvia, Moldova, Montenegro, North Atlantic Treaty Organization, North Macedonia, Norway, Organisation for Economic Co-operation and Development, Organization for Security and Cooperation in Europe, Poland, Romania, Serbia, Slovakia, Slovenia, South East European Cooperative Initiative, Spain, Sweden, Switzerland, Turkey,

UK, United Nations, UN Economic Commission for Europe, UN Development Programme, USA, World Bank

Website: <https://www.rcc.int/>

Shanghai Cooperation Organisation (SCO)

The SCO's predecessor group, the Shanghai Five, was founded in 1996; it was renamed the SCO in 2001 and opened for membership of all states that support its aims. The member states cooperate on confidence-building measures and regional security and in the economic sphere. Its secretariat is in Beijing, China. The SCO Regional Anti-Terrorist Structure (RATS) is based in Tashkent, Uzbekistan.

Members (8): China, India, Kazakhstan, Kyrgyzstan, Pakistan, Russia, Tajikistan, Uzbekistan

Website: <http://eng.sectsco.org/>

Sistema de la Integración Centroamericana (SICA, Central American Integration System)

SICA was launched in 1993 on the basis of the 1991 Tegucigalpa Protocol. Its objective is the integration of Central America to constitute a region of peace, freedom, democracy and development, based on respect for and protection and promotion of human rights. The SICA headquarters are in San Salvador, El Salvador.

The **Comisión de Seguridad de Centroamérica (CSC, Central American Security Commission)** was established by the 1995 Framework Treaty on Democratic Security in Central America. Its objectives include following up on proposals on regional security, based on a reasonable balance of forces, strengthening civilian power, and eradicating violence, corruption, terrorism, drug trafficking and arms trafficking.

Members (8): Belize, Costa Rica, Dominican Republic, El Salvador, Guatemala, Honduras, Nicaragua, Panama

Website: <https://www.sica.int/>

Southern African Development Community (SADC)

SADC was established in 1992 to promote regional economic development and the fundamental principles of sovereignty, peace and security, human rights and democracy. It superseded the Southern African Development Coordination Conference (SADCC), established in 1980. Its secretariat is in Gaborone, Botswana.

The **SADC Organ on Politics, Defence and Security Cooperation (OPDS)** is mandated to promote peace and security in the region.

Members (16): Angola, Botswana, Comoros, Congo (Democratic Republic of the), Eswatini, Lesotho, Madagascar, Malawi, Mauritius, Mozambique, Namibia, Seychelles, South Africa, Tanzania, Zambia, Zimbabwe

Website: <https://www.sadc.int/>

Sub-Regional Consultative Commission (SRCC)

The SRCC meets regularly to monitor implementation of the 1996 Agreement on Sub-Regional Arms Control (Florence Agreement) in the former Yugoslavia. Representatives of the Contact Group consisting of France, Italy, Germany, Russia, the UK and the USA also take part in these sessions.

Parties to the Agreement on Sub-Regional Arms Control (4): See annex A

Unión de Naciones Suramericanas (UNASUR, Union of South American Nations)

UNASUR is an intergovernmental organization with the aim of strengthening regional integration, political dialogue, economic development and coordination in defence matters among its member states. Its 2008 Constitutive Treaty entered into force on 11 March 2011 and it was intended to gradually replace the Andean Community and the Mercado Común del Sur (MERCOSUR, Southern Common Market). Its headquarters were in Quito, Ecuador.

The **Consejo de Defensa Suramericano (CDS, South American Defence Council)** met for the first time in March 2009. Its objectives are to consolidate South America as a zone of peace and to create a regional identity and strengthen regional cooperation in defence issues.

Members (5): Bolivia, Guyana, Peru, Suriname, Venezuela

Notes: Argentina, Brazil, Chile, Colombia, Ecuador, Paraguay and Uruguay withdrew from UNASUR during 2019–20. Peru suspended its participation in Apr. 2018. Bolivia suspended its participation in Nov. 2019 but resumed again in Nov. 2020.

At a summit in Santiago, Chile, on 22 Mar. 2019, Argentina, Brazil, Chile, Colombia, Ecuador, Guyana, Paraguay and Peru launched a process to form a new regional group, known as the Forum for the Progress of South America (Foro para el Progreso de América del Sur, PROSUR).

Website: <http://www.unasursg.org/>

III. Strategic trade control regimes

Australia Group (AG)

The AG is an informal group of states and the European Commission formed in 1985. The AG meets annually to exchange views and best practices on strategic trade controls in order to ensure that dual-use material, technology and equipment are not used to support chemical and biological warfare activity or weapon programmes.

Participants (43): Argentina, Australia*, Austria, Belgium, Bulgaria, Canada, Croatia, Cyprus, Czechia, Denmark, Estonia, European Commission, Finland, France, Germany, Greece, Hungary, Iceland, India, Ireland, Italy, Japan, Korea (South), Latvia, Lithuania, Luxembourg, Malta, Mexico, Netherlands, New Zealand, Norway, Poland, Portugal, Romania, Slovakia, Slovenia, Spain, Sweden, Switzerland, Turkey, UK, Ukraine, USA

* Permanent chair.

Website: <https://www.australiagroup.net/>

Hague Code of Conduct against Ballistic Missile Proliferation (HCOC)

The principle of the 2002 HCOC is the need to curb the proliferation of ballistic missile systems capable of delivering WMD. Subscribing states commit to exercise restraint in the development, testing and deployment of such missiles, to issue pre-launch notifications and to provide annual declarations on their policies concerning ballistic missiles and space-launch vehicles. The Ministry for Foreign Affairs of Austria acts as the HCOC Secretariat.

Subscribing states (143): Afghanistan, Albania, Andorra, Antigua and Barbuda, Argentina[†], Armenia, Australia, Austria, Azerbaijan, Belarus, Belgium, Benin, Bosnia and Herzegovina, Bulgaria, Burkina Faso, Burundi, Cabo Verde, Cambodia, Cameroon, Canada, Central African Republic, Chad, Chile, Colombia, Comoros, Congo (Republic of the), Cook Islands, Costa Rica, Croatia, Cyprus, Czechia, Denmark, Dominica, Dominican Republic, Ecuador, El Salvador, Equatorial Guinea, Eritrea, Estonia, Ethiopia, Fiji, Finland, France, Gabon, Gambia, Georgia, Germany, Ghana, Greece, Guatemala, Guinea, Guinea-Bissau, Guyana, Haiti, Holy See, Honduras, Hungary, Iceland, India, Iraq, Ireland, Italy, Japan, Jordan, Kazakhstan, Kenya, Kiribati, Korea (South), Latvia, Lesotho, Liberia, Libya, Liechtenstein, Lithuania, Luxembourg, Madagascar, Malawi, Maldives, Mali, Malta, Marshall Islands, Mauritania, Micronesia, Moldova, Monaco, Mongolia, Montenegro, Morocco, Mozambique, Netherlands, New Zealand, Nicaragua, Niger, Nigeria, North Macedonia, Norway, Palau, Panama, Papua New Guinea, Paraguay, Peru, Philippines, Poland, Portugal, Romania, Russia, Rwanda, Saint Kitts and Nevis, Saint Vincent and the Grenadines, Samoa, San Marino, Senegal, Serbia, Seychelles, Sierra Leone, Singapore, Slovakia, Slovenia, Somalia, South Africa, Spain, Sudan, Suriname, Sweden, Switzerland*, Tajikistan, Tanzania, Timor-Leste, Togo, Tonga, Tunisia, Turkey, Turkmenistan, Tuvalu, Uganda, UK, Ukraine, Uruguay, USA, Uzbekistan, Vanuatu, Venezuela, Zambia

　* Chair in 2020/21.
　[†] Chair in 2021/22.

Website: <https://www.hcoc.at/>

Missile Technology Control Regime (MTCR)

The MTCR, established in 1987, is an informal group of countries that seeks to coordinate national export licensing efforts aimed at preventing the proliferation of missiles and other delivery systems capable of delivering WMD. The partner countries apply the Guidelines for Sensitive Missile-Relevant Transfers. The MTCR has no secretariat. A point of contact based in the Ministry for Foreign Affairs of France distributes the regime's working papers and hosts regular policy and information-exchange meetings.

Partners (35): Argentina, Australia, Austria*, Belgium, Brazil, Bulgaria, Canada, Czechia, Denmark, Finland, France, Germany, Greece, Hungary, Iceland, India, Ireland, Italy, Japan, Korea (South), Luxembourg, Netherlands, New Zealand, Norway, Poland, Portugal, Russia[†], South Africa, Spain, Sweden, Switzerland[‡], Turkey, UK, Ukraine, USA

　* Chair in 2020/21.
　[†] Chair in 2021/22.
　[‡] Chair in 2022/23.

Website: <https://www.mtcr.info/>

Nuclear Suppliers Group (NSG)

The NSG, formerly also known as the London Club, was established in 1975. It coordinates national transfer controls on nuclear materials according to its Guidelines for Nuclear Transfers (London Guidelines, first agreed in 1978), which contain a 'trigger list' of materials that should trigger IAEA safeguards when they are to be exported for peaceful purposes to any non-nuclear weapon state, and the Guidelines for Transfers of Nuclear-Related Dual-Use Equipment, Materials, Software and Related Technology (Warsaw Guidelines). The NSG Guidelines are implemented by each participating state in accordance with its national laws and practices. The NSG has no secretariat. The Permanent Mission of Japan to the IAEA in Vienna acts as a point of contact and carries out practical support functions.

Participants (48): Argentina, Australia, Austria, Belarus, Belgium*, Brazil, Bulgaria, Canada, China, Croatia, Cyprus, Czechia, Denmark, Estonia, Finland, France, Germany, Greece, Hungary, Iceland, Ireland, Italy, Japan, Kazakhstan, Korea (South), Latvia, Lithuania, Luxembourg, Malta, Mexico, Netherlands, New Zealand, Norway, Poland[†], Portugal, Romania, Russia, Serbia, Slovakia, Slovenia, South Africa, Spain, Sweden, Switzerland, Turkey, UK, Ukraine, USA

* Chair in 2020/21.
[†] Chair in 2021/22.

Note: In addition, the European Union and the chair of the Zangger Committee are permanent observers.

Website: <https://www.nuclearsuppliersgroup.org/>

Proliferation Security Initiative (PSI)

Based on a US initiative announced in 2003, the PSI is a multilateral forum focusing on law enforcement cooperation for the interdiction and seizure of illegal WMD, missile technologies and related materials when in transit on land, in the air or at sea. The PSI Statement of Interdiction Principles was issued in 2003. The PSI has no secretariat, but its activities are coordinated by a 21-member Operational Experts Group.

Participants (107): Afghanistan, Albania, Andorra, Angola, Antigua and Barbuda, Argentina*, Armenia, Australia*[†], Austria, Azerbaijan, Bahamas, Bahrain, Belarus, Belgium, Belize, Bosnia and Herzegovina, Brunei Darussalam, Bulgaria, Cambodia, Canada*, Chile, Colombia, Croatia[†], Cyprus, Czechia[†], Denmark*, Djibouti[†], Dominica, Dominican Republic, El Salvador, Estonia, Fiji, Finland, France*[†], Georgia, Germany*[†], Greece*, Holy See, Honduras, Hungary, Iceland, Iraq, Ireland, Israel, Italy*[†], Japan*[†], Jordan, Kazakhstan, Korea (South)*[†], Kyrgyzstan, Kuwait, Latvia, Liberia, Libya, Liechtenstein, Lithuania[†], Luxembourg, Malaysia, Malta, Marshall Islands, Micronesia, Moldova, Mongolia, Montenegro, Morocco, Netherlands*[†], New Zealand*[†], North Macedonia, Norway*[†], Oman, Palau, Panama, Papua New Guinea, Paraguay, Philippines, Poland*[†], Portugal*[†], Qatar[†], Romania, Russia*, Saint Lucia, Saint Vincent and the Grenadines, Samoa, San Marino, Saudi Arabia, Serbia, Singapore*[†], Slovakia, Slovenia[†], Spain*[†], Sri Lanka, Sweden, Switzerland, Tajikistan, Thailand, Trinidad and Tobago, Tunisia, Turkey*[†], Turkmenistan, UK*[†], Ukraine[†], United Arab Emirates[†], USA*[†], Uzbekistan, Vanuatu, Viet Nam, Yemen

* Member of the Operational Experts Group.
[†] PSI exercise host, 2003–21.

Website: <https://www.psi-online.info>

Wassenaar Arrangement on Export Controls for Conventional Arms and Dual-Use Goods and Technologies (Wassenaar Arrangement, WA)

The Wassenaar Arrangement was formally established in 1996 as the successor to the cold war-era Co-ordinating Committee for Multilateral Export Controls (COCOM). It aims to promote transparency and responsibility in the transfers of conventional weapons and dual-use goods and technologies. Participating states seek to prevent transfers of armaments and sensitive dual-use goods and technologies that contribute to destabilizing accumulations of weapons, as well as transfers to terrorists. The WA Secretariat is located in Vienna, Austria.

Participants (42): Argentina, Australia, Austria, Belgium, Bulgaria, Canada, Croatia, Czechia, Denmark, Estonia, Finland, France, Germany, Greece, Hungary*, India, Ireland[†], Italy, Japan, Korea (South), Latvia, Lithuania, Luxembourg, Malta, Mexico, Netherlands, New Zealand, Norway, Poland, Portugal, Romania, Russia, Slovakia, Slovenia, South Africa, Spain, Sweden, Switzerland, Turkey, UK, Ukraine, USA

  * Chair in 2021.
  [†] Chair in 2022.

Website: <https://www.wassenaar.org/>

Zangger Committee

Established in 1971–74, the Nuclear Exporters Committee, called the Zangger Committee, is a group of nuclear supplier countries that meets informally twice a year to coordinate transfer controls on nuclear materials according to its regularly updated trigger list of items which, when exported, must be subject to IAEA safeguards. It complements the work of the Nuclear Suppliers Group.

Members (39): Argentina, Australia, Austria, Belarus, Belgium, Bulgaria, Canada, China, Croatia, Czechia, Denmark, Finland, France, Germany, Greece, Hungary, Ireland, Italy, Japan, Kazakhstan, Korea (South), Luxembourg, Netherlands, New Zealand, Norway, Poland, Portugal, Romania, Russia, Slovakia, Slovenia, South Africa, Spain, Sweden, Switzerland, Turkey, UK, Ukraine, USA

Website: <http://www.zanggercommittee.org/>

Annex C. Chronology 2021

This chronology lists the significant events in 2021 related to armaments, disarmament and international security. Keywords are indicated in the right-hand column.

January

5 Jan.	Six Gulf states, including Saudi Arabia, sign an agreement to ease the blockade with Qatar, in place since 2017.	Gulf States; Qatar; Saudi Arabia
6 Jan.	Supporters of outgoing United States President Donald J. Trump storm the US Capitol, disrupting certification of the 2020 presidential election and forcing Congress to evacuate. Five people die in the rioting.	USA
15 Jan.	European Union (EU) member states establish a common approach on end-user certificates in the context of the export of small arms and light weapons (SALW) and their ammunition.	EU; export controls; SALW
15 Jan.	Russia announces that it will begin domestic procedures for withdrawal from the 1992 Treaty on Open Skies.	Russia; Treaty on Open Skies
17 Jan.	Russian opposition leader Alexei Navalny is arrested immediately on his return to Russia, after recovering from nerve-agent poisoning.	Russia
20 Jan.	Joe Biden is inaugurated as the 46th president of the USA.	USA
22 Jan.	The 2017 Treaty on the Prohibition of Nuclear Weapons (TPNW), the first legally binding international agreement to comprehensively prohibit nuclear weapons, comes into effect.	TPNW
26 Jan.	The number of confirmed Covid-19 cases exceeds 100 million worldwide.	Covid-19
30 Jan.	The Russian–Turkish Joint Monitoring Centre (RTJMC) in Azerbaijan becomes operational. It will monitor implementation of the Nov. 2020 ceasefire agreement between Armenia and Azerbaijan.	Armenia; Azerbaijan; RTJMC; Russia; Turkey

February

1 Feb.	A coup in Myanmar removes Aung San Suu Kyi from power and restores military rule, leading to widespread demonstrations across the country.	Myanmar
1 Feb.	The number of Covid-19 vaccinations administered worldwide exceeds 100 million.	Covid-19
2 Feb.	Russian opposition leader Alexei Navalny is jailed for three and a half years over alleged parole violations in Moscow.	Russia
3 Feb.	The USA and Russia extend their New START nuclear arms control agreement for five years. It is the last remaining nuclear arms deal between the two countries.	New START; Russia; USA

4 Feb.	US President Biden announces changes in US policy towards Yemen, including ending the designation of the Houthis as a foreign terrorist organization and terminating support for the Saudi Arabian-led coalition's 'offensive operations' in the conflict.	Saudi Arabia; UAE; USA; Yemen
4 Feb.	The International Criminal Court (ICC) convicts Ugandan Lord's Resistance Army Commander Dominic Ongwen of war crimes and crimes against humanity.	ICC; Uganda
9 Feb.	A joint World Health Organization (WHO)–China investigation into the source of the Covid-19 outbreak concludes that a Wuhan laboratory leak is 'extremely unlikely', with a 'natural reservoir' of bats being a more likely origin.	China; Covid-19; WHO
13 Feb.	Former US President Trump is acquitted in a second Senate impeachment trial on the charge of incitement of insurrection, after senators vote 57 to 43 in favour of conviction, less than the two thirds majority required for impeachment.	USA
15 Feb.	Nigerian Ngozi Okonjo-Iweala becomes the first woman and the first African to lead the World Trade Organization (WTO).	WTO
18 Feb.	In Yemen, the United Nation's emergency relief coordinator warns of the 'worst famine the world has seen in decades'.	Yemen
19 Feb.	The USA officially rejoins the 2015 Paris Agreement on climate change, 107 days after leaving it.	Paris Agreement; USA
22 Feb.	Luca Attanasio, the Italian ambassador to the Democratic Republic of the Congo (DRC), is murdered near Goma.	DRC; Italy
24 Feb.	The UN-backed COVAX vaccine-sharing initiative for middle- and low-income countries delivers its first Covid-19 vaccines, delivering 600 000 doses for healthcare workers in Ghana.	COVAX; Covid-19; Ghana
25 Feb.	India and Pakistan announce a ceasefire agreeing to the 'strict observance of the truce along the Line of Control' between the Indian and Pakistani controlled parts of Kashmir.	India; Kashmir; Pakistan
25 Feb.	The Armenian military calls for Prime Minister Nikol Pashinyan to resign. Pashinyan accuses the military of attempting a coup.	Armenia
28 Feb.	Myanmar security forces open fire on protests around the country, killing at least 18 people.	Myanmar
March		
2 Mar.	The USA applies sanctions on seven senior Russian government officials and 14 entities associated with Russian biological and chemical agent production, in response to allegations of Russian cyberespionage and the poisoning of Russian opposition leader Alexei Navalny.	Russia; sanctions; USA
3 Mar.	During anti-coup protests in Myanmar, 38 people are killed by security forces.	Myanmar
3 Mar.	The ICC announces an investigation into the 'Situation in the State of Palestine', focusing on events beginning in 2014.	ICC; Israel; Palestine
7 Mar.	Explosions at a military base in Bata, Equatorial Guinea, likely from faulty storage of dynamite, kill at least 98 people and injure over 400.	Equatorial Guinea

9 Mar.	China and Russia agree to build an international lunar research station and collaborate on lunar missions.	China; Russia; space security
10 Mar.	A unified government is formed in Libya for the first time since 2014. The Government of National Unity, headed by Prime Minister Abdelhamid Dabaiba and a three-person Presidency Council, was accepted by both the Tripoli-based Government of National Accord and the rival Tobruk-based House of Representatives.	Libya
15 Mar.	Armed attackers kill at least 58 people in the Tillabery region in the south-west of Niger.	Niger
16 Mar.	The British government announces an increase to the upper limit of its nuclear stockpile, up to no more than 260 warheads from the previously announced 180 in 2015.	Nuclear weapons; UK
22 Mar.	The EU, the United Kingdom, the USA and Canada impose sanctions on Chinese officials over alleged human rights abuses against Uighurs in China.	China; sanctions
25 Mar.	The number of Covid-19 vaccinations administered worldwide exceeds 500 million.	Covid-19
20 Mar.	The number of confirmed cases of Covid-19 worldwide reaches a quarter of a million and the death toll surpasses 10 000.	Covid-19
26 Mar.	Kyrgyzstan and Uzbekistan reach agreement on their long-standing border disputes.	Kyrgyzstan; Uzbekistan
27 Mar.	In protests against the military coup in Myanmar, 114 people are killed by the armed forces.	Myanmar
27 Mar.	Iran and China sign a 25-year cooperation agreement in Tehran, guaranteeing Chinese investment of $400 billion and Iranian oil supply in return.	China; Iran
27 Mar.	Militants attack the town of Palma, northern Mozambique, killing dozens in an escalation of violence in the area.	Mozambique
30 Mar.	Twenty-five heads of government and international agencies call on the international community to work together towards a new international treaty for pandemic preparedness and response.	Pandemic treaty
April		
2 Apr.	Russia warns the North Atlantic Treaty Organization (NATO) against sending any troops to aid Ukraine, amid reports of a large Russian military build-up on its borders.	NATO; Russia; Ukraine
6 Apr.	The USA and the remaining parties to the 2015 Joint Comprehensive Plan of Action (JCPOA)—Iran, China, Russia, the EU and the E3 (France, Germany and the UK)—begin talks in Vienna, Austria, to restore the agreement. Six rounds of negotiations are held until 20 June, but the diplomatic process ends without positive results.	Iran; JCPOA; USA
11 Apr.	Iran accuses Israel of 'nuclear terrorism' and vows revenge after a large explosion destroys the internal power system of the Natanz uranium enrichment plant.	Iran; Israel
14 Apr.	US President Biden says 'It's time to end America's longest war', confirming his decision to withdraw all US troops from Afghanistan by 11 Sep. 2021.	Afghanistan; USA

15 Apr.	The USA announces extensive new sanctions on 32 Russian entities and individuals, and formally attributes the 2019–20 SolarWinds hacking attack to Russia's foreign intelligence agency. In response, Russia expels 10 US diplomats and blacklists 8 US officials.	Russia; sanctions; USA
17 Apr.	The global death toll from Covid-19 surpasses 3 million.	Covid-19
20 Apr.	Chadian President Idriss Déby is killed in clashes with rebel forces after 30 years in office. The constitution is suspended and a Transitional Military Council is established to govern the country for 18 months.	Chad
21 Apr.	Russian President Vladimir Putin warns the West not to cross a 'red line' in his state of the union address, while massing 100 000 Russian troops on the border with Ukraine.	Russia
22 Apr.	World leaders mark Earth Day by hosting a virtual summit on climate change. At the summit, more ambitious targets for greenhouse gas emission reductions are proposed, including a 40 per cent cut by 2030 for the USA.	Climate change; USA
24 Apr.	The number of Covid-19 vaccinations administered worldwide exceeds 1 billion. Half of these doses have been administered in just three countries: China, India and the USA.	Covid-19
28 Apr.	The EU approves the EU–UK Trade and Cooperation Agreement, governing the relationship between the EU and the UK after Brexit.	Brexit; EU; UK
28 Apr.	At least 55 people are killed and nearly 50 000 more are displaced in one of the most serious clashes in Central Asia following border disputes between Kyrgyzstan and Tajikistan. A ceasefire is agreed on 1 May.	Kyrgyzstan; Tajikistan
29 Apr.	China and Russia sign a memorandum of understanding for a joint international lunar research station.	China; Russia
29 Apr.	The number of confirmed Covid-19 cases exceeds 150 million worldwide.	Covid-19
May		
3 May	A temporary 'state of siege' in the North Kivu and Ituri provinces of the DRC is declared by President Felix Tshisekedi. Special measures introduced include the replacement of all civil authorities with military authorities granted the power to arrest and prosecute civilians. The state of siege was still extant at the end of Dec. 2021.	DRC
10 May	Violence breaks out in the ongoing Israeli–Palestinian conflict and continues until a ceasefire comes into effect on 21 May. It is marked by protests and police riot control, rocket attacks on Israel by Hamas and Palestinian Islamic Jihad, and Israeli airstrikes targeting the Gaza Strip.	Israel; Palestine
12 May	The International Committee of the Red Cross (ICRC) recommends that states adopt new legally binding rules on the development and use of autonomous weapon systems (AWS).	AWS; ICRC
15 May	Fighting between Israeli forces and Palestinians continues to escalate, as the death toll exceeds 150. An Israeli airstrike destroys a high-rise office building in Gaza occupied by AP News, Al Jazeera and other media outlets.	Israel; Palestine
18 May	India reports over 4500 deaths from Covid-19 within 24 hours, the highest single-day toll recorded in any country.	Covid-19; India

23 May	Belarus is accused of 'state-sponsored hijacking', after diverting Ryanair Flight 4978 to detain journalist Roman Protasevich.	Belarus
24 May	A military coup in Mali removes interim President Bah Ndaw and acting Prime Minister Moctar Ouane from power. This leads to the country being suspended from the Economic Community of West African States (ECOWAS) and the African Union (AU), as well as France suspending its military operations in Mali.	AU; ECOWAS; France; Mali
27 May	The USA notifies Russia that it will not be rejoining the Treaty on Open Skies.	Russia; Treaty on Open Skies; USA
31 May	The AU Peace and Security Council decides to end the Human Rights Observers and Military Experts Mission in Burundi.	AU; Burundi; peace operations
June		
1 June–30 Sep.	During its monsoon season, India experiences a series of deadly floods that claim 1282 lives.	Climate change; India
5 June	At least 160 people are killed by suspected Islamist extremists in Solhan, Burkina Faso, amid a deepening security crisis in the region.	Burkina Faso
8 June	France suspends aid and military cooperation in the Central African Republic (CAR) because of what it says is the government's failure to stop 'massive disinformation campaigns' against France.	CAR; France
10 June	Amid a rapid escalation of tensions between Mali and France, French President Emmanuel Macron announces a drawdown of the 5000 Operation Barkhane troops in Mali.	France; Mali
14 June	NATO leaders commit to updating the alliance's strategic concept, with the aim of considering new threats and clarifying that the principle of collective defence also applies to threats in space and cyberattacks.	NATO
15 June	The EU–US Trade and Technology Council (TTC) is launched, with 10 working groups on a wide range of trade and technology topics.	EU–US Trade and Technology Council
16 June	At a summit meeting, US President Biden and Russian President Putin agree to begin dialogues about nuclear arms control and cybersecurity.	Russia; USA
18 June	Russia submits its notification of withdrawal from the Treaty on Open Skies to the treaty depositaries.	Russia; Treaty on Open Skies
23 June	A summit of the Southern Africa Development Community (SADC) establishes the SADC Mission in Mozambique (SAMIM), in response to escalating violent extremism in the northern Mozambican province of Cabo Delgado.	Mozambique; SADC; SAMIM
23 June	Representatives of Libya's new interim Government of National Unity take part in an international conference co-sponsored by the UN and Germany in Berlin, aimed at renewing foreign commitment to supporting Libya's peace process.	Libya
25 June–mid July	An extreme heat wave affecting much of western North America results in over 1000 deaths.	Climate change; North America
29 June	Estonia convenes the first ever UN Security Council open debate on cybersecurity.	Cybersecurity; Estonia

29 June	The number of Covid-19 vaccinations administered worldwide exceeds 3 billion.	Covid-19
30 June	Reports indicate that China is building more than 100 silos for intercontinental ballistic missiles (ICBMs) in a desert near the north-western city of Yumen.	China; ICBMs
July		
1 July	President Xi Jinping gives an address at celebrations in Tiananmen Square, Beijing, to mark the 100-year centenary of the Chinese Communist Party.	China
2 July	US troops hand over Bagram airbase, the hub of the US war effort inside Afghanistan, to the Afghan government.	Afghanistan; USA
7 July	The USA publishes a memorandum stating that it will follow five 'Tenets of Responsible Behavior in Space'.	Space security; USA
7 July	Haitian President Jovenel Moïse is assassinated and a state of emergency is declared across the country.	Haiti
8 July	US President Biden specifies a new completion date of 31 Aug. 2021 for the US withdrawal from Afghanistan.	Afghanistan; USA
8 July	The number of deaths from Covid-19 surpasses 4 million.	Covid-19
12 July	The Council of the EU establishes the EU Training Mission in Mozambique (EUTM Mozambique). The mission's aim is to build the capacity of Mozambican armed forces to combat armed groups in Cabo Delgado province.	EUTM; Mozambique
12–18 July	Europe's deadliest flooding since 1985 strikes western Germany and eastern Belgium, killing 240 people and causing $43 billion in damage.	Climate change; Europe
17–19 July	Flooding kills more than 300 people in central China's Henan province, as a year's worth of rain falls in just three days.	China; climate change
18 July	An international investigation (Pegasus Project) reveals that spyware sold by Israel's NSO Group to different governments is being used to target heads of state, along with thousands of activists, journalists and dissidents around the world.	Israel; Pegasus Project
26 July	Tunisian President Kais Saïed sacks the country's prime minister and senior ministers, and suspends parliament for 30 days—a move political opponents call 'unconstitutional' or a coup. The suspension is later extended to Dec. 2022.	Tunisia
26 July	Iraq and the USA hold another round of strategic dialogue and agree to end the presence of US combat troops in Iraq by the end of 2021, at which point the US security relationship will transition to an advisory role.	Iraq; USA
26–27 July	The biennial meeting of states on the implementation of the UN Programme of Action to Prevent, Combat, and Eradicate the Illicit Trade in Small Arms and Light Weapons in All Its Aspects (UNPOA) agreed several gender-related provisions to mainstream gender perspectives into SALW control policies.	UNPOA
27 July	China tests a missile with a hypersonic weapon system, later called 'very close' to a Sputnik moment by a US general.	China; USA
August		
4 Aug.	The number of confirmed Covid-19 cases surpasses 200 million worldwide.	Covid-19

8 Aug.	More than 51 people are killed in northern Mali after attacks on three villages by armed jihadists.	Mali
9 Aug.	The Intergovernmental Panel on Climate Change (IPCC) releases the first part of its Sixth Assessment Report, which concludes that the effects of human-caused climate change are now 'widespread, rapid, and intensifying'. The report is described as a 'Code Red for humanity'.	Climate change; IPCC
14 Aug.	A 7.2-magnitude earthquake strikes Haiti, killing more than 2100 people.	Haiti
15 Aug.	Afghanistan's capital, Kabul, is captured by the Taliban; and the Afghan government surrenders to the Taliban.	Afghanistan; Taliban
24 Aug.	The US intelligence community delivers a classified report on the Covid-19 pandemic origins to President Biden, and releases a short, two-page unclassified summary three days later. The several agencies making up the intelligence community remain divided on the question.	Covid-19; USA
26 Aug.	As many as 200 people are killed, including 13 US military personnel, in attacks on Kabul airport by the Islamic State–Khorasan Province.	Afghanistan; USA
29 Aug.	A US drone strike in Afghanistan kills 10 civilians, including 7 children, and not an Islamic State extremist as first claimed.	Afghanistan; USA
29 Aug.	A missile and drone attack on al-Anad airbase in the south of Yemen kills at least 30 soldiers. It is one of the deadliest attacks in recent years.	Yemen
30 Aug.	The USA withdraws its last remaining troops from Kabul airport, ending 20 years of operations in Afghanistan.	Afghanistan; USA

September

5 Sep.	Guinea's President Alpha Condé is detained in a military coup.	Guinea
7 Sep.	A National Unity Government—a parallel administration in exile—declares a 'people's defensive war' against the military junta in Myanmar.	Myanmar
9 Sep.	A revised EU dual-use regulation covering controls on the export, re-export, brokering and transit of dual-use goods, software and technology enters into force. Regulation (EU) 2021/821 introduces several new elements and modifications to the dual-use regulation.	EU dual-use regulation
10 Sep.	UN Secretary-General António Guterres launches his 'Our Common Agenda' report, reflecting on the solutions needed to move away from divisiveness and fragmentation in the world and to build on lessons learned from recent crises, including Covid-19 and the climate crisis.	Our Common Agenda; UN Secretary-General
13 Sep.	Israeli Prime Minister Naftali Bennett makes his first official visit to Egypt in a decade for talks with Egyptian President Abdel Fattah al-Sisi in Sharm el-Sheikh.	Egypt; Israel
14 Sep.	North Korea demonstrates two short-range ballistic missiles that land just outside Japan's territorial waters. Only hours later, South Korea demonstrates its first submarine-launched ballistic missile (SLBM), making it the first non-nuclear weapon state to develop a SLBM capability.	Missile proliferation; North Korea; South Korea

16 Sep.	Australia, the UK and the USA jointly announce a new trilateral security partnership named AUKUS, which includes a pledge to provide Australia with the technology to build eight nuclear-powered submarines.	AUKUS; Australia; UK; USA
16 Sep.	At a mini summit of the International Conference on the Great Lakes Region, a joint road map to revitalize the peace process in CAR is adopted, notably calling for the declaration of a ceasefire by the CAR government.	CAR
16 Sep.	France announces that it has killed the leader of the Islamic State in the Greater Sahara, Adnan Abu Walid al-Sahrawi.	France; Islamic State in the Greater Sahara
20–21 Sep.	The second review conference of the Convention on Cluster Munitions (CCM) adopts the Lausanne Action Plan to support implementation of the CCM in 2021–26, including 50 concrete actions.	CCM; cluster munitions
21 Sep.	In his address to the 76th session of the UN General Assembly, UN Secretary-General Guterres voices concern that 'military coups are back', blaming a lack of international unity in response to military interventions.	Military coups; UN General Assembly; UN Secretary-General
21 Sep.	World leaders address climate change at the UN General Assembly. US President Biden pledges to double financial aid to developing countries, while Chinese President Xi says China will stop coal-fired projects abroad.	China; climate change; UN General Assembly; USA
28 Sep.	France and Greece make a defence cooperation agreement that will allow them to come to each other's aid in the event of an external threat.	France; Greece
29 Sep.	Tunisian President Kais Saied appoints Najla Bouden Romdhan as Tunisia's, and the Arab world's, first woman prime minister.	Tunisia
30 Sep.	At the second meeting of the USA–Russia bilateral Strategic Stability Dialogue, two expert working groups are established: Principles and Objectives for Future Arms Control; and Capabilities and Actions with Strategic Effects.	Russia; strategic stability; USA
30 Sep.	The Organization for Security and Co-operation in Europe (OSCE) Observer Mission at the Russian Checkpoints Gukovo and Donetsk is discontinued, following Russia's objection to a further mandate extension.	OSCE; Russia; Ukraine
October		
3 Oct.	The International Consortium of Investigative Journalists and assorted media partners publish a set of 11.9 million documents leaked from 14 financial services companies (Pandora Papers), revealing offshore financial activities that involve multiple current and former world leaders.	Pandora Papers
6 Oct.	The WHO endorses the first malaria vaccine.	Malaria; WHO
7 Oct.	During the 76th session of the First Committee of the UN General Assembly, Russia and China release a joint statement for the first time on strengthening the Biological and Toxin Weapons Convention (BWC).	BWC; China; Russia
8 Oct.	The Nobel Peace Prize is awarded to journalists Maria Ressa of the Philippines and Dmitry Muratov of Russia 'for their efforts to safeguard freedom of expression'.	Nobel Peace Prize

18 Oct.	Russia announces that it will cease diplomatic engagement with NATO, in the latest sign of unravelling relations between Russia and the West.	NATO; Russia
25 Oct.	After several rumoured coup attempts and one failed coup attempt on 21 Sep. 2021 in Sudan, the Sudanese military launches a coup against the government. Prime Minister Abdalla Hamdok, senior officials and political activists are arrested, triggering widespread protests and condemnation.	Sudan
31 Oct.– *13 Nov.*	The 2021 United Nations Climate Change Conference (COP26) is held in Glasgow, after being postponed in 2020 due to Covid-19. Agreements reached include a phase-down of coal power, a 30 per cent cut in methane emissions by 2030, plans for a halt to deforestation by 2030 and increased financial support for developing countries.	Climate change; COP26

November

1 Nov.	The number of recorded deaths from Covid-19 surpasses 5 million.	Covid-19
2 Nov.	An attack by a jihadist group in south-western Niger kills 69 people, including a local mayor.	Niger
9 Nov.	The EU accuses Belarusian President Alexander Lukashenko of an 'inhuman, gangster-style approach' to thousands of migrants massing on the border with Poland in freezing conditions.	Belarus; EU; migration
14 Nov.	An attack on a military police outpost near a gold mine in Inata, northern Burkina Faso, kills at least 53 people.	Burkina Faso
15 Nov.	During a meeting, Chinese President Xi and US President Biden agree to begin discussions on strategic stability, although the precise format remains unclear.	China; strategic dialogue; USA
15 Nov.	Russia draws international condemnation following an anti-satellite (ASAT) test that creates a cloud of space debris.	ASAT; Russia
26 Nov.	The WHO convenes an emergency meeting amid concerns over Omicron, a highly mutated variant of Covid-19 first identified in South Africa that appears more infectious than Delta.	Covid-19
29 Nov.	The parties to the JCPOA—Iran, China, Russia, USA, the EU and the E3—resume talks in Vienna (the 7th round), leading to an 8th round of talks on 27 Dec. but with no agreement in sight.	Iran; JCPOA; USA;
29 Nov.– *3 Dec.*	The second session of the Conference on the Establishment of a Middle East Zone Free of Nuclear Weapons and Other Weapons of Mass Destruction takes place at UN Headquarters in New York, USA. Among other issues, the conference report reaffirms the importance of Israel's accession to the Non-Proliferation Treaty (NPT).	Israel; WMD-Free Zone in the Middle East

December

1 Dec.	Meeting in a special session, the second ever since the WHO's founding in 1948, the World Health Assembly agrees to start a global process on a treaty to strengthen pandemic prevention, preparedness and response.	Pandemic treaty
3 Dec.	Reflecting the continuation of a process begun in 2007, the five permanent members of the UN Security Council (China, France, Russia, the UK and the USA—the P5) release a 'Joint Communique of the Non-Proliferation Treaty P5 Nations' on their joint obligations and aims under the NPT.	Nuclear non-proliferation; P5

4 Dec.	The killing of 14 civilians by the Indian Army in Nagaland increases tensions and leads to calls for the repeal of the 1958 Armed Forces (Special Powers) Act.	India; Nagaland
6 Dec.	Former Myanmar leader Aung San Suu Kyi is sentenced to four years (later reduced to two) for inciting public unrest and breaching Covid-19 protocols.	Myanmar
7 Dec.	During a video call, US President Biden warns Russian President Putin that the USA and its allies would meet a military invasion of Ukraine with strong economic penalties, moves to bolster Ukrainian defences and the fortifying of support for NATO member states in Eastern Europe.	Russia; Ukraine; USA
9–10 Dec.	A virtual Summit for Democracy, is hosted by the USA 'to renew democracy at home and confront autocracies abroad'.	Summit for Democracy; USA
12 Dec.	The Group of Seven (G7) calls on Russia to de-escalate and pursue diplomatic channels as Russia–Ukraine tensions grow.	G7; Russia; Ukraine
15 Dec.	The EU Training Mission in the Central African Republic (EUTM RCA) suspends its training activities in CAR due to the growing influence of Russian private military companies (PMCs).	CAR; EU; PMCs; Russia
16 Dec.	Typhoon Rai strikes the Philippines, resulting in at least 457 deaths and affecting 10.6 million people.	Climate change; Philippines
17 Dec.	Russia releases two draft security agreements, one with NATO and the other with the USA, which set out a number of proposals to change the European security framework. Most of the proposals are not new and are at odds with the views of many Western countries.	NATO; Russia; USA
18 Dec.	Russia withdraws from the Treaty on Open Skies.	Russia; Treaty on Open Skies
19–21 Dec.	At the sixth review conference of the Certain Conventional Weapons Convention (CCW Convention), a few countries prevent progress on the main agenda item—a possible new protocol on AWS—as well as efforts to strengthen controls on incendiary weapons and mines other than anti-personnel mines.	CCW Convention
22 Dec.	The UN Security Council adopts Resolution 2616, which outlines a range of steps aimed at improving compliance with UN arms embargoes. These include giving peace operations a more direct role in assisting national authorities with detecting and combating embargo violations.	UN arms embargoes
24 Dec.	A resolution in the UN General Assembly establishes an open-ended working group (OEWG) to reduce space threats and 'make recommendations on possible norms, rules and principles of responsible behaviours relating to threats by States to space system'.	OEWG; space security

About the authors

Dr Lucie Béraud-Sudreau (France) is the Director of the SIPRI Military Expenditure and Arms Production Programme, where her work focuses on the dynamics and implications of global military spending, arms production and transfers. Previously, she was a Research Fellow for Defence Economics and Procurements at the International Institute for Strategic Studies (IISS).

Kolja Brockmann (Germany) is a Researcher in the SIPRI Dual-use and Arms Trade Control Programme. He joined SIPRI in 2017 and conducts research in the fields of export control, non-proliferation and technology governance. He focuses on the multilateral export control regimes, controls on emerging technologies, particularly additive manufacturing, and missile technology.

Mark Bromley (United Kingdom/Sweden) is the Director of the SIPRI Dual-use and Arms Trade Control Programme, where his work focuses on national, regional and international efforts to regulate the international trade in conventional arms and dual-use items. Previously, he was a Policy Analyst for the British American Security Information Council (BASIC).

Laura Bruun (Denmark) is a Research Assistant at SIPRI, working on emerging military and security technologies. Her focus is on how emerging military technologies, notably autonomous weapon systems (AWS), affect compliance with and interpretation of international humanitarian law.

Dr Marina Caparini (Canada) is the Director of the SIPRI Governance and Society Programme. Her research focuses on inclusive peacebuilding and the nexus between security and development. She works on security sector governance, policing and peace operations.

Dr Ian Davis (United Kingdom) is the Executive Editor of the SIPRI Yearbook and an Associate Senior Fellow within Conflict and Peace at SIPRI. From 2014–16 he was the Director of SIPRI's Editorial, Publications and Library Department.

Dr Tytti Erästö (Finland) is a Senior Researcher in the SIPRI Nuclear Disarmament, Arms Control and Non-proliferation Programme. Her research interests include the Iran nuclear deal, the Treaty on the Prohibition of Nuclear Weapons (TPNW), efforts to establish a weapons of mass destruction-free zone in the Middle East, United States–Russian arms control, missile defence, and the global disarmament and non-proliferation regime more generally.

Shivan Fazil (Iraq) is a Researcher in the SIPRI Middle East and North Africa Programme. His work mainly focuses on drivers of conflict, peacebuilding and governance in Iraq, where he has worked for over six years with various organizations, most recently with the United States Institute of Peace.

Vitaly Fedchenko (Russia) is a Senior Researcher in the SIPRI Weapons of Mass Destruction Programme, responsible for nuclear security issues and the political, technological and educational dimensions of nuclear arms control and non-proliferation.

Dr Alexander Graef (Germany) is a Researcher working within the Arms Control and Emerging Technologies research area at the Institute for Peace Research and Security Policy (IFSH) at the University of Hamburg.

Annelies Hickendorff (Netherlands) is a Research Assistant in the SIPRI Sahel/West Africa Programme. She has been involved in multiple studies contributing to a better understanding of local security perceptions in the region.

Dr Una Jakob (Germany) is a Senior Researcher in the International Security research department at the Peace Research Institute Frankfurt (PRIF). Her research interests include the disarmament and non-proliferation of chemical and biological weapons (CBW), with a particular focus on CBW norm dynamics, regime evolution and investigations of alleged CBW use.

Matt Korda (Canada) is an Associate Researcher with the SIPRI Nuclear Disarmament, Arms Control and Non-proliferation Programme, and a Senior Research Associate and Project Manager with the Nuclear Information Project at the Federation of American Scientists (FAS).

Hans M. Kristensen (Denmark) is the Director of the Nuclear Information Project at the Federation of American Scientists (FAS) in Washington, DC, and a SIPRI Associate Senior Fellow.

Alexandra Kuimova (Russia) is a Researcher in the SIPRI Arms Transfers Programme. Her areas of research include the monitoring of arms transfers, military spending and the arms industry, as well as foreign and defence policies.

Dr Moritz Kütt (Germany) is a Senior Researcher at the Institute for Peace Research and Security Policy at the University of Hamburg, working within the Arms Control and Emerging Technologies research area.

Dr Filippa Lentzos (Norway) is a Senior Lecturer in Science & International Security at King's College London, where she is jointly appointed in the Department of War Studies and the Department of Global Health & Social Medicine.

Xiao Liang (China) is a Research Assistant in the SIPRI Military Expenditure and Arms Production Programme. He collects and analyses data on military spending and the arms industry. His research areas cover the opportunity costs and reduction of military spending, the relationship between military aid and development assistance, and regional trends in the Asia-Pacific.

Dr Jaïr van der Lijn (Netherlands) is the Director of the SIPRI Peace Operations and Conflict Management Programme. He is also an Associate Fellow at the Radboud University Nijmegen.

Dr Diego Lopes da Silva (Brazil) is a Senior Researcher in the SIPRI Military Expenditure and Arms Production Programme. He holds a PhD in Peace, Defence and International Security Studies from São Paulo State University.

Giovanna Maletta (Italy) is a Researcher in the SIPRI Dual-use and Arms Trade Control Programme. Her research covers issues related to the implementation of international and regional instruments in the field of arms export controls, with a particular focus on the Arms Trade Treaty (ATT) and the European Union (EU) and its member states.

Alexandra Marksteiner (Austria/Germany) is a Researcher in the SIPRI Military Expenditure and Arms Production Programme.

Dr Zia Mian (United States) is the Co-Director of the Program on Science and Global Security at Princeton University's School of Public and International Affairs. A physicist, his work focuses on nuclear weapon non-proliferation, arms control and disarmament, and nuclear energy issues.

Dr Claudia Pfeifer Cruz (Brazil) is a Researcher in the SIPRI Peace Operations and Conflict Management Programme. Her research focuses on global developments in peace operations, peace operations and human rights, and women's participation in peace operations; and she maintains SIPRI's database on multilateral peace operations.

Dr Pavel Podvig (Russia) is a Researcher in the Program on Science and Global Security at Princeton University and a Senior Researcher at the United Nations Institute for Disarmament Research (UNIDIR).

Allison Pytlak (Canada) is the Disarmament Programme Manager for the Women's International League for Peace and Freedom (WILPF). In this role, she contributes to the organization's monitoring and analysis of United Nations disarmament processes, including those on cybersecurity.

Nivedita Raju (India) is a Researcher in the SIPRI Weapons of Mass Destruction Programme. She conducts research on space security and gender issues. Her subject expertise is space law and policy, space security, international law and feminist legal theory; and her regional expertise is India, South Asia and the Middle East.

Dr Lora Saalman (United States) is a Senior Researcher within SIPRI's Armament and Disarmament, and Conflict, Peace and Security research areas. She also serves as a Member of the Committee on International Security and Arms Control (CISAC) and as an Adjunct Senior Fellow at the East–West Center.

Timo Smit (Netherlands/Sweden) is a Senior Researcher in the SIPRI Peace Operations and Conflict Management Programme. He is in charge of SIPRI's database on multilateral peace operations and conducts research on trends in peace operations and various related thematic issues.

Dan Smith (Sweden/United Kingdom) is the Director of SIPRI. He has a long record of research and publication on a wide range of conflict and peace issues. His current work focuses on the relationship between climate change and insecurity, on peace and security issues in the Middle East and North East Asia, and on global conflict trends.

Dr Issaka K. Souaré (Guinea) is an Associate Senior Researcher working with the SIPRI Sahel/West Africa Programme. With about 20 years of work experience on peace and security issues, his current work focuses on conflict and peace, as well as governance dynamics in Africa.

Fei Su (China) is a Researcher in the SIPRI China and Asia Security Programme. Her research interests focus on regional security issues in East Asia, with a special interest in North Korea, China's foreign and security policy, and maritime affairs.

Dr Nan Tian (South Africa) is a Senior Researcher in the SIPRI Military Expenditure and Arms Production Programme, where he leads the Military Expenditure Project. His research interests focus on the causes and impact of military expenditure and civil conflict, and the issues relating to transparency and accountability in military budgeting, spending and procurement.

Dr Andrea Edoardo Varisco (Italy/United Kingdom) is the Director of the SIPRI Arms Transfers Programme. He has worked as Acting Director of the SIPRI Dual-use and Arms Trade Control Programme and as Head of Analytics for Conflict Armament Research.

Pieter D. Wezeman (Netherlands/Sweden) is a Senior Researcher in the SIPRI Arms Transfers Programme. He has contributed to many SIPRI publications since 1994, including SIPRI's annual reviews of global trends in arms transfers, arms industry, military expenditure and multilateral arms embargoes.

Siemon T. Wezeman (Netherlands) is a Senior Researcher in the SIPRI Arms Transfers Programme. His areas of research include the monitoring of arms transfers and the use of weapons in conflicts, transparency in arms transfers, and the development of conventional military technologies and doctrines.

Dr Jingdong Yuan (United States/Canada) is an Associate Professor at the Centre for International Security Studies, University of Sydney, and an Associate Senior Fellow at SIPRI. His research focuses on Indo–Pacific security, Chinese foreign policy, Sino–Indian relations, China–European Union relations, and nuclear arms control and non-proliferation.

Errata

SIPRI Yearbook 2021: Armaments, Disarmament and International Security

Page 560, Table 14.1   Under number of signatories for Asia, *for* '6' *read* '7'

Under number of non-signatories for Asia, *for* '17' *read* '16'

Under total number of signatories, *for* '30' *read* '31'

Under total number of non-signatories, *for* '57' *read* '56'

Errata for this printed version of *SIPRI Yearbook 2022* will appear at <http://www.sipri.org/yearbook/> and in *SIPRI Yearbook 2023*.

Index

Abiy Ahmed 226, 228
Abkhazia 146
ABM Treaty (Anti-Ballistic Missiles Treaty, 1972) 669–70
  1974 Protocol 669
Aerojet Rocketdyne 291
Afghanistan:
  1979–2021 timeline 116–17
  armed conflict 13, 103, 105
    2021 developments 113–20
    consequences 119
    fatalities 27, 29, 35, 105, 114
    internationalization 29
  arms embargo 596, 599–600, 609
  arms imports 323–24
  ATT reporting 587
  children 39
  climate change and 107
  cluster munitions 522, 523
  corruption 64–65
  Covid-19 pandemic 119
  displacement 37
  EUPOL Afghanistan 63–64
  failure of interventions in 69, 70
  food insecurity 38
  human rights 119, 120
  ISAF 50, 52, 59, 63–64, 67, 68, 116
  Islamic State 106, 117–18, 119–20, 707
  landmines 524, 525
  military expenditure 277
  Pakistan and 126
  RSM 28, 45, 49–50, 52, 56, 58, 59, 63–64, 68–69, 70, 73, 107
  SALWs 599–600
  Taliban victory 103–104, 107, 113, 114–18, 277, 324, 707
  terrorism 36
  UNAMA 64, 72, 113
  US–Taliban agreement 52, 107, 114
  US withdrawal 20, 21–22, 50, 61
    announcement 703
    Bagram airbase 706
    geopolitics 68, 69
    military expenditure and 244, 255, 268
    policy 64, 66
    post-withdrawal policy 164
    Taliban return 114–18
    timetable 706, 707
  Western withdrawal 3, 21–22, 103, 107
    consequences and outlook 119–20
    consolidating trends 67–9
    inspiration for armed groups 66–67
    peace operations after withdrawal 63–69
    statebuilding and 64–66
Africa:
  armed conflicts 13, 193–239
    Central Africa 194, 215–23
    Covid-19 pandemic and 197
    dynamics 195
    East Africa 194, 224–29
    election violence 200–201, 204–205
    external factors 199–200
    fatalities 193, 195, 196
    internal conflicts 210–14
    internalization 193, 195
    key general developments 195–201
    North Africa 156, 158, 179–84
    overview 193–94
    water disputes 201
    West Africa 193–94, 202–14
  armed groups 197–98
    transnational 203–204
  arms exports 304
  arms imports 297, 299, 303
    2017–21 period 317–22
  criminal networks 198, 210
  identity militias 198
  Kinshasa Convention (2010) 668–69
  military coups 193, 200–201, 205–206
  military expenditure 243, 248, 251, 256, 257, 262–65
  peace operations 196–97, 200
    West Africa 207–10
  Pelindaba Treaty (1996) 664–65
  water insecurity 201
  see also individual countries
African Commission on Nuclear Energy (AFCONE) 683
African Union (AU) 683–84
  arms imports and 317
  climate change and 40–41
  Guinea and 206
  Human Rights Observers (HROs) 49–50
  Mali and 206, 705
  Peace and Security Council (PSC) 40–41, 50–51, 232, 683, 684, 705
  peace operations 56–58, 72

AMISOM 28, 45, 54, 56–58, 61, 66,
  70, 72, 231–32
MISAC 72
MISAHEL 72
Mission in Libya 56, 72
MOUACA 56, 72
Observer Mission in Burundi 28,
  49–50, 72, 705
UNAMID 28, 52, 53–54, 61, 238
Agenda 2030 243, 253, 531
aggression:
  ICC and 653, 654, 681
  Ukraine war 4, 11–12, 487
Airbus 292, 293
Aïvo, Frédéric Joel 204–205
al-Kadhimi, Mustafa 165
al-Qaeda 22, 66, 198
al-Qaeda in the Arabian Peninsula 162,
  187
al-Sadr, Muquada 168
al-Shabab 57, 67, 70, 194, 229–32, 264
Algeria:
  arms imports 317–18
    Germany 318
    Russia 311, 312, 318, 554
    transparency 554
    UNROCA and 553
  military expenditure 262–63
  Morocco and 156, 184
Aliyev, President Ilham 140–41
Almaz-Antey 294
Alpi Aviation 625
Americas:
  armed conflicts
    Central America 88–91
    fatalities 78
    key developments 77–81
    North America and Caribbean 82–87
    overview 75–76
    South America 92–102
    survey 75–102
  arms exports 304
  arms imports 297, 299, 322–23
    2017–21 period 317
  authoritarianism 79–80
  CIFTA (1997) 665–66
  CITAAC 556, 666
  Covid-19 pandemic 80–81
  food insecurity 81
  gang violence 33, 76, 77–79, 82, 86, 87,
    88, 89, 91, 92, 100
  heat waves 705
  military expenditure 244, 248, 256,
    257, 265–71

OPANAL 692
peace operations 76, 77
Tlatelolco Treaty (1967) 659–60
see also individual countries
AMISOM (AU Mission to Somalia) 28,
  49, 54, 56–58, 61, 66, 70, 72, 231–32
Angola:
  armed conflict 195
  arms imports 318–19
  cluster munitions 522
  contribution to peace operations 48
  landmines 525
  military expenditure 256, 264
Antarctic Treaty (1959) 639–40
Antohi, Florian 491
Antonov. Anatoly 441
apartheid 177
APM Convention (1997) 652–53
  2021 developments 513, 516
  MSP19 526
  prohibitions 524
  states parties 524, 525
  see also landmines
Arab League 173, 582, 595, 597, 690
Arab Spring 157–58, 161, 179
Argentina:
  ATT and 587
  authoritarianism 79
  BWC and 490
  HCOC and 616
  HEU facilities 430
Arias, Fernando 508, 511
armed conflicts:
  2021 developments
    conflict management 22–23
    consequences 35–41
    overview 27–28
    significant features 33–35
    survey 29–44
  Africa 13, 193–239
    armed groups 197–98
    Central Africa 194, 215–23
    East Africa 194, 224–29
    election violence 200–201, 204–205
    external factors 199–200
    fatalities 193, 195, 196
    internationalization 193
    key general developments 195–201
    North Africa 156, 158, 179–84
    overview 193–94
    water disputes 201, 224, 228
    West Africa 193–94, 202–14
  Americas
    Central America 88–91

North America and Caribbean 82–87
overview 75–76
South America 92–102
survey 75–102
armed groups 33–34
arms transfers and 297–98, 302–303
Asia–Oceania
East Asia 109–12
key developments 105–108
overview 103–104
South Asia 113–26
South East Asia 127–35
survey 103–35
categories of violence 37
child soldiers 34, 39
classification 30–32
civil wars 32
extrastate 32
interstate (international) 32
intrastate (non-international) 32
subnational 32
Covid-19 and 28, 44, 197
definitions 30–33
displacement 35, 36–37, 40
economic costs 39
environmental costs 39–41
Europe 137, 139–63
key developments 139–41
Russia–Western relations 141–46
Ukraine see **Ukraine**
unresolved conflicts 146–48
fatalities 35–36
methodology 32
regional breakdown 36
food insecurity see **food insecurity**
global casualties 27
global developments 27–28
humanitarian violations 34–35
Middle East 155–91
key developments 157–63
overview 155–56
sexual violence see **sexual violence**
Ukraine see **Ukraine war**
way forward 23–24
see also individual countries
armed uncrewed aerial vehicles see
UAVs
Armenia:
arms imports: Russia 313
attempted coup 702
Azerbaijan and see **Nagorno-
Karabakh conflict**
cluster munitions 521, 522
military expenditure 283

OSC and 59
UAVs and 528
arms control:
conventional arms see **conventional
arms control**
nuclear weapons see **nuclear arms
control**
trade see **arms trade control**
treaties 635–73
regional treaties 659–60
universal treaties 636–58
see also specific weapons
arms embargoes:
2021 table 596–97
Arab League 582, 595, 597
European Union 582, 595, 598, 608,
609
OSCE 595, 598
scope 595–98
survey 595–609
United Nations
2021 developments 582, 595–606
assessment 608–609
UNSC Resolution 2616 599, 710
see also individual countries
arms industry:
2002–20 total sales 288
2011–20 sales trends 289
2019–20 regional and national shares
290
2020 developments 287–96
Covid-19 pandemic and 244, 287–89,
293
top 100 companies 289–96
see also individual companies;
individual countries
arms trade control:
Covid-19 and 581, 582
multilateral export control regimes
582, 610–19
overview 581–82
transparency: ATT 587–90
see also specific treaties
Arms Trade Treaty (ATT, 2013) 657
2021 developments 583–94
assessment 593–94
Covid-19 and 581, 583
CSP5 593
CSP6 585, 587, 593
CSP7 581, 583–94
CSP8 587
Diversion Information Exchange
Forum (DIEF) 581, 587
entry into force 584

funding 592–93
implementation 584–87
international assistance 591–92
ratification statistics 590
reporting requirements 553, 587–90
SALWs and 530, 581, 583–84, 584–85
states parties 583, 590
UAVs and 516, 527
USA and 581, 582, 590–91
universalization 590–91
Voluntary Trust Fund 591–92
working groups 585–87
arms transfers:
1950–2021 trends 300
2017–21 developments 299–303
exporters 304–16
importers 317–33
2021 key developments 300–302
armed conflicts and 297–98, 302–303
control *see* **arms trade control**
Covid-19 and 244, 300–301
definitions 302
exporters 297
40 largest exporters 306–307
2017–21 developments 304–16
regional breakdown 310
types of arms 308, 309
financial value 298, 334–39
2011–20 table 336–39
methodology and transparency 334–35
importers 297–98
2012–16 regional breakdown 322
2017–21 developments 317–33
2017–21 regional breakdown 322
2017–21 top importers 320–21
Africa 317–22
Americas 322–23
Asia–Oceania 323–28
Europe 328–30
Middle East 330–33
methodology 302
overview 297–98
survey 297–339
transparency 334–35, 551–57
ATT and 553, 587–90
inaccuracies 553–54
regional mechanisms 555–56
UNMILEX 551, 554–55
UNROCA 551–54, 588
Vienna Document 144, 555–56
Artemis Accords 576
ASAT tests 574–75, 579, 709
ASEAN (Association of Southeast

Asian Nations) 684–85
ASEAN Plus Three (APT) 685
Bangkok Treaty (1995) 663–64
BWC and 486
China and 110
cybersecurity 566
East Asia Summit (EAS) 685
Myanmar and 104, 107, 131
non-interference approach 131
Regional Forum (ARF) 685
Aselsan 296
Asia–Oceania:
armed conflicts
Central Asia 107–108
East Asia 109–12
fatalities 105, 106
Kashmir disputes 120–24
key developments 105–108
overview 103–104
South Asia 113–26
South East Asia 127–35
survey 103–35
arms exports 304
arms imports 297, 299, 323–28
2017–21 period 317
China 314
France 313, 323
Germany 314
Russia 311
South Korea 316
United States 305
CICA 686–87
climate change and 106–107
counterterrorism 103
Covid-19 pandemic 103, 106, 108, 277–78
military expenditure 243–44, 245–48, 251, 256, 257, 262, 271–78
peace operations 107
Rarotonga Treaty 660
Semipalatinsk Treaty (2006) 668
see also individual countries
Asia-Pacific Economic Cooperation (APEC) 684
Assad, Bashar al- 168, 169, 172–73
Assistance Association for Political Prisoners 129
Astana Group 172
AstraZeneca 473
Attanasia, Luca 702
AUKUS 21, 109, 111, 275–76, 301, 325–26, 708
Aung San Suu Kyi 127, 128, 130, 701, 710

Australia:
arms imports 297, 299, 323, 325–26
France 301, 325–26
Spain 325
top importer 317
United Kingdom 301, 315, 325–26
United States 305–308, 325–26
AUKUS 21, 109, 111, 275–76, 301,
325–26, 708
chemical/biological weapons and
CNS-acting chemicals 509
China and 275–76
contribution to peace operations 63
cybersecurity and 562, 568, 627
EWIPA and 519
France and 276, 301, 325–26
HEU and 301
military expenditure 258, 259, 275,
275–76, 555
Australia Group 697
2021 developments 611–13
Control List 613
Covid-19 and 610–11
participants 612–13
scope 582, 610, 611–12
Austria:
AWS and 535, 536, 539, 542, 544
EU and PESCO 8
EWIPA and 520
FDI screening 625
authoritarianism: Americas 79–80
autonomous weapons systems (AWS):
2021 developments 513, 532–44
CCW and 516, 532–44, 710
11 Guiding Principles 533–34, 542
characterization 534–35
consensus failure 541–43
ethics 539
fully vs partially autonomous 534–35
human accountability 538
human–machine interaction 537
ICRC and 535, 536, 540, 704
IHL and 535–37, 538, 540, 541
IHRL and 537
new mandate 543–44
options 539–41
Protocol 516
way forward 541–44
weapon reviews 538–39
AVIC 292
AWS *see* **autonomous weapons systems**
Azerbaijan:
Armenian conflict *see* **Nagorno-
Karabakh conflict**

arms imports: Russia 313, 329
BWC and 491
cluster munitions 521, 522
EWIPA and 520
military expenditure 283

Babcock International 292
Bahrain:
normalization agreement with Israel
175
Qatar and 159
Syria and 173
Yemen war and 185
Baissuanov, Arman 484
Bajwa, General 123–24
Bako, Malam 204
**Bangkok Treaty (Treaty on the
Southeast Asia Nuclear-Free Zone,
1995)** 663–64
Bangladesh:
contribution to peace operations 28,
61, 62
Covid vaccination 474
Islamic State 106
refugees from Myanmar 132
Barkhane, Operation 66, 193, 199, 204,
207–208, 209, 705
Barnawi, Abu Musab al- 204
Barrow. President Adama 205
Bazoum, Mohamed 204
Beavogui, Mohamed 206
Belarus:
arms embargo 596, 607
arms exports 319, 553
arms imports from Russia 312–13, 329
Canada and 549
migrants 709
Myanmar and 605
NATO and 549
nuclear weapons: relinquishment 11
Open Skies Treaty and 548, 549, 550
political crisis 137
Protasevitch affair 142, 607, 705
Russia and 137
arms transfers 312–13, 329
military exercises 145
Open Skies Treaty 548
Western relations 142–43
Belgium:
arms imports 329
AWS and 544
EWIPA and 519
floods 706

US nuclear weapons in 352
Bell, Alexandra 547
Ben Embarek, Peter 477, 478
Benin:
    armed conflict 193, 195, 202
    presidential elections 202, 204–205
Bennett, Naftali 405, 707
Bharat Electronics 295
Biden, President Joe:
    1st year in office 19–21
    Afghan policy 21–22, 64, 114, 115, 117,
        120, 703, 706
    arms exports and 308–310, 311
    arms trade control 581, 582, 590–91
    Chinese relations 441–42, 581
    climate change policy 708
    counterterrorism 80
    Covid-19 pandemic and 479, 481
    EU relations 631
    Haiti and 87
    Iran and 16, 450, 457, 581, 582, 601
    Israeli policy 177, 405
    Middle East relations 10
    military expenditure 268
    nuclear arms control 435, 437, 440, 467
    nuclear policy 343, 346, 354, 373
    Open Skies Treaty and 547–48
    Putin meeting 20, 144, 435, 440, 705,
        710
    Taiwan policy 112
    Ukraine war and 154
    Xi Jinping meeting 435, 443, 709
    Yemen war and 189, 702
Biketawa Declaration 63
**Bilateral Consultative Commission
    (BCC)** 437, 438, 672, 678–79
bin Laden, Osama 116
BINUH (UN Integrated Office in Haiti)
    72
Bio, President Julius Maada 591
**Biological and Toxin Weapons
    Convention (BWC, 1972)** 644–45
    9th review conference 472, 483, 484,
        486, 489, 491, 495
    2021 MSP 471–72, 483, 490–91
    meetings of experts 483–85
    states parties 483
    UNGA 1st Committee and 485–89, 708
    working capital fund 489, 490
biological weapons:
    2021 disarmament developments
        483–95
    BWC *see* **Biological and Toxin
        Weapons Convention**

geopolitics and 483, 492–95
    Tianjin Biosecurity Guidelines 484
    Ukraine: Russian allegations 4
    UNSGM and 484–85, 487–88
    see also **Australia Group**
Blinken, Anthony 441, 442
Boeing 289
Boko Haram 194, 203, 204, 208, 213,
    215, 216, 221, 319
Bolivia: authoritarianism 79
Bolsonaro, President Jair 80, 99, 100
Bosnia and Herzegovina:
    cluster munitions 522, 523
    Dayton Peace Agreement 60
    EUFOR Althea 60, 72
    landmines 525
    OHR 59–60, 69, 73
    Open Skies Treaty 549
    OSCE Mission 73
    unresolved conflict 147
Botswana:
    arms imports 318, 319
    contribution to peace operations 48
Bouba, Hassan 220
Bouden Romdhan, Naija 708
Bozizé, President François 218
Brazil:
    armed conflict 75, 77, 92, 99–102
        armed groups 99, 100
        blurred nature 100
        fatalities 27, 29, 35–36, 98, 99
        political violence 79
    arms exports 319
    arms imports 323
    authoritarianism 79
    AWS and 535, 536, 542, 544
    BWC and 490
    cluster munition production 522
    Covid-19 and 80, 99–100, 474, 475
    displacement 81
    gang violence 92, 100
    HEU facilities 430
    military expenditure 270, 555
Brexit 704
Budapest Memorandum 11
Buhari. President Muhammadu 67–68
Bukele, President Nayib 75, 89, 270
Bulgaria:
    cluster munitions 523
    Covid-19 deaths 475
    Open Skies Treaty and 549
    UNROCA and 589
Burkina Faso:
    armed conflict 193, 195, 202

fatalities 27, 29, 210, 211, 705, 709
internal conflict 210–11
transnational armed groups 203
climate change and 203
contribution to peace operations 62
Covid-19 pandemic 202
displacement 37, 211
human insecurity 206–207
Operation Barkhane 207–208
Burundi:
2020 elections 50–51
armed conflict 193
AU Observer Mission 28, 49–51, 72, 705
contributions to peace operations 61
HROs and MEs Mission 49–51, 56
Bush, President George W. 22, 116
BWC *see* **Biological and Toxin Weapons Convention**

Cabo Verde:
Covid-19 203
elections 202, 204
CAE 296
Cambodia:
cluster munitions 522
landmines 525
Cameroon:
armed conflict 193, 194, 215–17
anglophone region 216–17
fatalities 27, 29, 216
Lake Chad region 215–16
transnational armed groups 203, 213, 215
Boko Haram 215, 216
contribution to peace operations 62
displacement 37
food insecurity 216
landmines 524
Campaign to Stop Killer Robots 539
Canada:
arms imports 305, 315, 322
arms industry 290, 295, 296
AWS and 537
Belarus and 549
China and sanctions 703
cybersecurity and 562, 565
EWIPA and 519
FDI 625
military expenditure 258, 265, 266, 555
Open Skies Treaty and 549
Russia and 549

Ukraine and 153
Yemen and 185
CARICOM 529, 616
Castro, President Xiomara 76, 90–91
CCW (Inhumane Weapons Convention, 1981) 648–50
5th review conference (2016) 517–18
6th review conference 513–14, 515–516, 520, 525–26, 528, 532–33, 710
2021 developments 513
2021 meetings 516
autonomous weapons systems and 513, 532–44, 710
Covid-19 and 515–516
EWIPA and 520
incendiary weapons 517–18
landmines 515, 525–26
Protocols 515–516, 524, 648–50
scope 515
states parties 515
UAVs and 528
CEEAC (Economic Community of Central Africa, ECCAS) 686
Kinshasa Convention (2010) 668–69
Centauri 291
Central African Republic (CAR):
armed conflict 193, 194, 195
2021 developments 217–20
fatalities 27, 29, 218
internalization 218–19
armed groups 33, 600
arms embargo 596, 600–601
China and 600–601
conflict management 45
displacement 37
elections 200, 218, 219–20
failed coup 193, 200
food insecurity 38
France and 219, 705
peace operations 46, 65
EUAM RCA 73
EUTM RCA 58, 69, 73, 194, 219, 710
MINUSCA 49, 51, 53, 54, 55, 61, 72, 217, 218, 220
MOUACA 56, 72
peace process 708
Political Agreement 217, 219–20
Russia and 194, 199, 218–19
SALWs 600
sexual violence 217
Special Criminal Court 220
Wagner Group in 58, 69
Centre for Chemistry and Technology 472, 511

CFE Treaty (Treaty on Conventional Armed Forces in Europe, 1990) 661–63
  Agreement on Adaptation (1999) 662
  CFE-1A Agreement (1992) 662
  Concluding Act on Personnel Strength (1992) 662
  Final Act (1999) 662–63
  Flank Document (1996) 661
  Tashkent Agreement (1992) 661
Chad:
  armed conflict 193, 221–22
  Boko Haram 203, 213, 221
  cluster munitions 522
  displacement 221
  food insecurity 221
  landmines 525
  military coup 193, 200, 264
  military expenditure 265
  Operation Barkhane 207–208
Chávez, President Hugo 101
chemical weapons:
  2021 developments 472
  CNS-acting chemicals 509–10
  CWC see **Chemical Weapons Convention**
  destruction: United States 511
  novichok 472, 504–506
  outlook 512
  Syrian use allegations 472, 496–503
    2nd Report 500–502
      compliance procedure 502–503
      investigations 496–500
  Ukraine: Russian allegations 4
  see also **Australia Group**
Chemical Weapons Convention (CWC, 1993) 650–51
  5th review conference 511
  2021 developments 472
  Article IX: novichok and 506
  Article XI 510
  Article XII (compliance procedure) and Syria 502–503
  CNS-acting chemicals and 509–10
  CSP25 472, 500–503, 507
  CSP26 507, 508, 508–509
  OPCW see **OPCW**
  states parties 504
  see also **chemical weapons**
child soldiers 34, 39, 191, 213
children: armed conflicts and 39
Chile:
  arms imports 323, 556
  AWS and 536, 542, 544

  cluster munitions 522, 523
  military expenditure 270
China:
  1969 clash with Soviet Union 12
  Afghan policy 22, 65
  African policy 199
  arms embargoes and 582, 596
    CAR 600–601
    Libya 605
    North Korea 603
    South Sudan 605
    United Nations 599
    Yemen 606
  arms exports 297, 299, 304
    Africa 317, 318, 319
    developments 314
    geopolitics 311
    lack of transparency 334
    Myanmar 328
    Pakistan 314, 324–25, 403
    Thailand 301
    UNROCA and 553
  arms imports 297, 299, 326–27
    conflicts and 302
    Russia 311, 312
    top importer 317, 323, 326
  arms industry 244, 287, 290, 291–92
  arms trade control and 581, 611
    ATT reporting 587
  ASEAN and 110
  Australia and 275–76
  biological weapons and
    BWC 486, 495, 708
    geopolitics 492–95
    United States 492–93
  Bosnia and 60
  British relations 111, 703
  Canadian relations 703
  Central African Republic and 600–601
  climate change policy 21, 41, 708
  cluster munition production 522
  Communist Party centenary 706
  Covid-19 pandemic
    origins 471, 477–82, 702
    vaccination 474
  cybersecurity and 568
  East Africa and 224
  economic growth 20
  Ethiopia and 227
  EU relations 624–25, 703
  FDI: EU control 624–25
  floods 706
  French relations 111
  GDP 272–73

geopolitics 19–21, 28, 69, 311, 471
  biological weapons control and
    492–95
Indian relations
  clashes 104, 277, 391
  Kashmir 107, 120–22
  nuclear weapons 387, 391
Iran and 18–19, 449, 457, 703
Japanese relations 110–11, 274, 302
landmines 525
maritime disputes 110, 302
Middle East policy 10, 159
  nuclear free zone 464
military expenditure 255
  2017–21 components 272
  2021 changes 272–74
  increase 243–44, 255–56, 259, 271
  military burden 273
  top spender 257, 272
  transparency 555
model Xiaolang villages 122
Myanmar and 131–32, 328, 605
NATO and 10
Nigeria and 199
nuclear arms control 435
  CTBT and 466, 467
  NPT 447, 460
  USA and 435, 437, 446–47, 709
nuclear weapons see **nuclear weapons**
OPCW and 508
outer space and
  Moon 514, 578, 703
  Russian partnership 576, 704
  tests 514, 572–75
Pakistani relations 314
Philippines and 110, 111
Russian relations 45
  bilateral cooperation 137, 141
  BWC and 493
  moon partnership 576, 704
  nuclear arms control 435
  Ukraine war and 10
Syria and chemical weapons 501
Taiwan and 3, 12, 105, 111–12, 327
threat perceptions 323, 324
UAVs 527
Uighurs 703
Ukraine war and 10
US relations 16–17, 50
  2021 developments 20–21
  arms transfers and 310, 581
  biological weapons 492–93
  dual use technologies 623
  geopolitics 311

military expenditure and 269
nuclear arms control 435, 437,
  446–47, 709
post-Afghanistan 68
sanctions 703
space developments 574
strategic stability dialogue 441–45,
  448
Taiwan and 3, 12, 105, 111–12, 327
trade war 21
trend 103, 105, 109–12
Western relations 109
China Aerospace Science and Industry
  Corporation (CASIC) 292
China Electronics Technology Group
  Corporation (CETC) 292
China South Industries Group
  Companies (CSGC) 292
CICA (Conference on Interaction and
  Confidence-Building Measures in
  Asia) 686–87
CIFTA (Inter-American Convention
  Against the Illicit Manufacturing
  and Trafficking in Firearms,
  Ammunition, Explosives and Other
  Related Materials, 1997) 665–66
CITAAC (Inter-American Convention
  on Transparency in Conventional
  Weapons Acquisitions) 556, 666
civil wars: definition 32
climate change:
  2021 developments 13–15
  armed conflicts and 40–41
  Asia–Oceania 106–107
  Central Africa 215
  Chinese policy 21, 708
  COP26 14–15, 21, 253, 709
  Earth Day 704
  East Africa 224–25
  floods 706
  food insecurity: West Africa 203
  heat waves 705
  IPCC 13–14, 707
  Middle East 162
  military expenditure and 243, 253
  Paris Agreement 14, 243, 253, 702
  US policy 704, 708
  water insecurity: Africa 201
Clinton, Bill 405
Cluster Munition Coalition 521–22
cluster munitions:
  2021 developments 521–23
  clearance 522
  destruction 522–23

use and production 521–22
Cluster Munitions Convention (2008)
656
2nd review conference 523, 708
2021 developments 513, 516
Lausanne Action Plan 523
unconditional prohibition 521
Coalition for Economic Preparedness
Innovations (CEPI) 473
Collective Security Treaty
Organization (CSTO) 685–86
Colombia:
armed conflict 75, 77, 92–98
assassinations 79, 98
fatalities 27, 29, 94
outlook 98
armed groups 94–97, 101
arms imports 323
authoritarianism 79
Covid-19 97
displacement 37
EWIPA and 519
landmines 524
MAPP/OEA 73
military expenditure 270, 271
peace agreement (2016) 93, 101
protests 97–98
UNVMC 72, 93–94
Commonwealth of Independent States
(CIS) 686
Commonwealth of Nations 679
Comoros: CTBT and 465–66
Comprehensive Nuclear-Test-Ban
Treaty (CTBT, 1996) 651–52
25th anniversary 436, 465–69
CTBTO 466, 469, 679
executive secretary 466–67
impact 468–69
objectives 466, 468
operation 466
P5 declaration 447, 468
ratifications 465–66
COMSPOC 574
Condé, President Alpha 205–206, 707
Conference on Disarmament (CD) 443,
460, 578, 676
confidence-building measures:
arms procurement transparency 551,
557
ASEAN 685
biological weapons 490, 645
CICA 686–87
conventional arms control 514
cyberpace 561, 562, 567, 570

Europe 144
HCOC 615
nuclear non-proliferation 469
Open Skies Treaty 514, 550
SCO 696
UNDC 677
Congo (DRC):
armed conflicts 193, 194, 195
2021 developments 222–23
children 39
eastern DRC 223
fatalities 27, 29, 223, 702
arms embargo 596
cluster munitions 522, 523
contribution to peace operations 48
displacement 37, 223
food insecurity 38
HCOC and 616
landmines 526
MONUSCO 45, 54–55, 61, 70, 72, 222
peace operations 65
sexual violence 223
state of siege 704
Convention on the Physical Protection
of Nuclear Material and Nuclear
Facilities (1980) 646–47
conventional arms control:
categories of weapons 513
cluster munitions 521–23
EWIPA *see* **EWIPA**
humanitarian disarmament 513, 515
incendiary weapons 515, 516, 517–18
landmines *see* **landmines**
Open Skies *see* **Open Skies Treaty**
overview 513–514
SALWs *see* **SALWs**
transparency 514, 551–57
ATT and 553
inaccuracies 553–54
regional mechanisms 555–56
UNMILEX 551, 554–55
UNROCA 551–54, 588
treaties 513, 515–31
UAVs *see* **UAVs**
Wassenaar Arrangement 582
see also specific weapons
Cooperative Cyber Defence Centre for
Excellence (CCDCOE) 569
COPUOS (UN Committee on the
Peaceful Uses of Outer Space) 578
Costa Rica:
cybersecurity and 562
EWIPA and 520
UAVs and 528

Council of Europe 687
Council of the Baltic Sea States (CBSS)
687
counterterrorism:
  Afghanistan and 118
  Africa 67–68, 198
  Asia 103, 105, 106
  East Africa 224
  GICNT 680
  Operation Barkhane 66, 193, 199,
    207–208, 209, 705
  UAVs and 527
  United States 80
counterspace 572
coups *see* **military coups**
Covax 473–74, 702
Covid-19 pandemic:
  2021 developments 15–16, 471–72,
    473–82
  Afghanistan 119
  Africa 197, 202–203
  Americas 80–81
  armed conflicts and 28, 44, 197
  arms industry and 244, 287–89, 293
  arms trade control and 581, 582, 583
  arms transfers and 244, 300–301
  Asia–Oceania 103, 106, 108, 277–78
  authoritarianism and 79–80
  Bangladesh 474
  Brazil 80, 99–100, 474, 475
  Bulgaria 475
  CCW and 515–516
  China *see* **China**
  Colombia 97
  cyberspace and 558, 559
  El Salvador 89
  Europe 278–79
  France 281, 293
  gender–race divides 476–77
  Guatemala 90
  health and mortality impacts 474–76
  India 108, 276, 295, 474, 475, 704
  Indonesia 474
  Iraq 165, 167
  Japan 274
  Lithuania 475
  Mali 202
  Mexico 475
  Middle East 155, 157
  milestones 473–77
  military expenditure and 243, 245,
    248–55, 257
  multilateral export control regimes and
    582, 610–11

Niger 202
Nigeria 202–203
North Macedonia 475
Omicron variant 474, 482, 709
OPCW and 472, 507
origins 471, 477–82, 702, 707
Pakistan 277, 474
pandemic treaty 482
peace agreements and 41
peace operations and 55
Peru 475
Philippines 474
preparedness 471, 703, 709
quarantine regulations 550
research studies 477–82
Russia 144, 294, 475, 545
school closures 477
security and 16
Singapore 278
socio-economic impact 13, 38, 471,
  476–77
South Africa 474
statistics 15, 474–76, 701, 703, 704,
  706, 709
Thailand 135
Tunisia 183
United Kingdom 279, 474, 476–77
United States 81, 144, 301, 471, 474,
  475, 477, 479, 481, 701
vaccination 15–16
  Africa 197
  Americas 81
  equity issues 253, 473–74, 594
  low-income countries 702
  milestones 473
  statistics 701, 703, 704, 706
  West Africa 202–203
Croatia:
  arms imports: France 314
  cluster munitions 523
  landmines 525
  military expenditure 280
CTBT *see* **Comprehensive Nuclear-
  Test-Ban Treaty**
**CTSAMVM (Ceasefire and
  Transitional Security Arrangements
  Monitoring and Verification
  Mechanism)** 58, 73
Cuba:
  authoritarianism 79
  BWC and 486
  CTBT and 466
  cybersecurity and 562
  displacement 81

EWIPA and 520
UAVs and 528
UN sanctions and 627
CWC *see* **Chemical Weapons Convention**
Cybersecurity Tech Accord 559, 569
cyberspace:
  mercenaries 565–66
  national initiatives 567–68
  NGOs 568–70
  regional initiatives 566–67
  regulation 514, 558–71
  UN framework 514, 560–66, 568
cybersurveillance 621–22, 627
Cyprus:
  landmines 526
  peacekeeping 147
  Turkey and 147
  UNFICYP 72
  unresolved conflict 146, 147
  UNROCA and 589
Czechia: arms exports 330

Dabaiba, Abdelhamid 181
Darboe, Ousainou 205
Dassault Aviation Group 293
Déby, Mahamat 221
Déby, President Idris 221
Denmark:
  cybersecurity and 627
  Joint Expeditionary Force 9
developing countries:
  BWC and 486
  China and 611
  climate change and 253
Diab, Hassan 163
displacement:
  Americas 81
  armed conflicts and 35, 36–37, 40
  Brazil 81
  Burkina Faso 37, 211
  Chad 221
  Congo (DRC) 37, 223
  Cuba 81
  East Africa 224
  Ethiopia 37, 225, 226
  Guatemala 37, 81
  Haiti 37, 76
  Honduras 37, 81
  Iraq 167
  Libya 37, 182
  Myanmar 37, 132
  Niger 212

Nigeria 37, 213
Sahel 40, 211
Somalia 37, 231
South Sudan 37, 234, 238
Sudan 37, 238
Syria 37, 171
Ukraine war and 5
West Africa 206
Doumbouya, Mamadi 205–206
drones *see* **UAVs**
droughts 103, 104, 106, 113, 119, 166, 201, 206, 215, 224, 225, 231
drug trafficking 75, 82–83, 89, 90, 91, 95, 100, 101
dual-use trade control:
  arms embargoes 595
    Belarus 607
  European Union 582
    2021 developments 620–33
    assessment 630–31
    common position 627–30
    cybersurveillance items 621–22
    FDI 624–25
    guidelines 622–23
    Regulation 620–24, 707
    Russian acquisitions 607–608
    Wassenaar Arrangement 582
Duque Márquez, President Ivan 94, 98
Duterte, President Rodrigo 134

ECOMIG (ECOWAS Mission in Gambia) 58, 72
Economic Community of West African States *see* **ECOWAS**
ECOSOC (UN Economic and Social Council) 564–65, 674, 677
ECOWAS (Economic Community of West African States) 687–88
  Guinea and 206
  Mali and 205, 206, 705
  peace operations 56
    ECOMIG 58, 72
  SALW Convention (2006) 667–68
Ecuador: cybersecurity and 562
Edge 296
Egypt:
  armed conflict 155, 156, 157, 179, 302
  arms embargo 596
  arms imports 297, 299, 332–33
    armed conflict and 302
    France 313, 314, 322
    Germany 315, 332
    Italy 315, 332

Russia 301, 311, 312, 332, 333
South Korea 316
top importer 317, 330
United States 305, 314, 332
UNROCA and 553
cluster munitions 522
contribution to peace operations 62
CTBT and 466
CWC and 504
cybersecurity and 562, 563
East Africa and 224
Israeli relations 707
landmines 524
Mediterranean conflicts and 147
MFO in the Sinai Peninsula 59, 61, 73
Middle East diplomacy 160
military coup 314, 332
Qatar and 159
Syria and 173
Turkey and 159
UAVs 527
USA and
    arms imports 305, 314, 332
    military aid 332
    military coup 332
water dispute 201, 224
Yemen war and 185
El Salvador:
armed conflict 75, 77, 88–89
authoritarianism 79
Covid-19 89
displacement 37
food insecurity 81
gang violence 88
military expenditure 270
organized crime 270
Elbit Systems 295
Enmod Convention (1977) 646
environment:
armed conflicts and 39–41
see also **climate change**
Equatorial Guinea: explosions 702
Eritrea:
landmines 526
Tigray conflict 226–27
Estonia:
arms exports: Ukraine 329–30
arms imports 328–29
CTBT and 467
cybersecurity and 565, 568, 705
Joint Expeditionary Force 9
Ethiopia:
armed conflict 3, 22, 193, 194, 195
    2021 developments 225–29

fatalities 27, 29, 226
outlook 229
sexual violence 34
Tigray 226–28
arms embargo and EU 607, 608
arms imports 318, 319
cluster munitions 522
contributions to peace operations 28,
   61
displacement 37, 225, 226
elections 200, 228
food insecurity 38
humanitarian crisis 225–26
landmines 525
Russia and 199
Sudan and 228, 238
UAVs 34, 227, 319
water dispute 201, 224, 228
**EUAM Iraq (EU Advisory Mission in
Iraq)** 73
**EUAM RCA (EU Advisory Mission in
the CAR)** 73
**EUAM Ukraine (EU Advisory Mission
in Ukraine)** 73
**EUBAM Libya (EU Integrated Border
Management Assistance Mission in
Libya)** 73
**EUBAM Rafah (EU Border Asistance
Mission for the Rafah Crossing
Point)** 72
**EUCAP Sahel Mali (EU CSDP Mission
in Mali)** 73, 209
**EUCAP Sahel Niger (EU CSDP Mission
in Niger)** 73, 209
**EUFOR Althea (EU Military Operation
in Bosnia Herzegovina)** 60, 72
**EULEX Kosovo (EU Rule of Law
Mission in Kosovo)** 72
**EUMM Georgia (EU Monitoring
Mission in Georgia)** 72
EUNAVFOR (Naval Force) Atalanta
62–63
EUNAVFOR (Naval Force) Med Irini
63
**EUPOL Afghanistan (EU Police
Mission in Afghanistan)** 63–64
**EUPOL COPPS (EU Police Mission for
the Palestinian Territories)** 72
Euratom 688
**Euro-Atlantic Partnership Council
(EAPC)** 691
Eurocorps 9
Europe:
armed conflicts 137

key developments 139–41
Russia–Western tensions 141–46
see also **Nagorno-Karabakh
conflict; Ukraine**
arms exports 304
arms imports 297, 299, 328–30
2017–21 period 317
Germany 314
South Korea 316
United States 305
arms industry 290
Covid-19 pandemic 278–79
floods 706
military expenditure 244, 248, 251,
256–57, 262, 278, 278–83
Regional Cooperation Council 695–96
see also individual countries
**European Convention on Mutual
Assistance in Criminal Matters** 506
**European Court of Human Rights:
Turkish Kurds and** 174
European Defence Agency (EDA) 689
European Peace Facility (EPF) 279
European Union (EU) 688
arms embargoes 582, 595, 607–608,
609
table 596–97
ATT and 591, 592
Belarus and sanctions 142
China and 624–25, 703
Common Foreign and Security Policy
627–28
Covid-19 pandemic: origins 479
cybersecurity and 562, 567
dual-use trade control 582, 620–31,
707
European Defence Fund 279
incendiary weapons and 517
Iraq and 167–68
JCPOA and 457–59
Mediterranean conflicts and 147
multilateral export control and 611
Myanmar and 131
NSG and 617
OPCW and 508
outer space and 579
peace operations 58, 62–63
Africa 196–97
EUAM Iraq 73
EUAM RCA 73
EUAM Ukraine 73
EUBAM Libya 73
EUCAP Sahel Mali 73, 209
EUCAP Sahel Niger 73, 209

EUFOR Althea 60, 72
EULEX Kosovo 72
EUMM Georgia 72
EUNAVFOR Atalanta 62–63
EUNAVFOR Med Irini 63
EUPOL Afghanistan 63–64
EUPOL COPPS 72
EUTM Mali 54, 58–59, 73, 208–209
EUTM Mozambique 28, 46, 49, 56,
58, 73, 197, 706
EUTM RCA 58, 69, 73, 194, 219, 710
EUTM Somalia 58, 72
table 72–73
PESCO 8–9, 689
Russian relations 137, 141, 144–45,
607–608
SALWs and 701
Turkey and 147
Ukraine war and 6–9, 70
USA and 631
cybersurveillance 627
dual use trade control 620
EU–US Trade and Technology
Council 626–27, 705
export control cooperation 582, 608,
626–27
**EUTM Mali (EU Training Mission
Mali)** 54, 58–59, 73, 208–209
**EUTM Mozambique (EU Military
Training Mission in Mozambique)** 28,
46, 49, 56, 58, 73, 197, 706
**EUTM RCA (EU Training Mission in
the CAR)** 58, 69, 73, 194, 219, 710
**EUTM Somalia (EU Training Mission
Somalia)** 58, 72
EWIPA:
2021 developments 513, 516, 518–20
move to regulate 518–19
political declaration 513, 519
UNSC and 520
explosive remnants of war (ERWs) 515,
517, 524

**Fiji Islands: contribution to peace
operations** 63
Financial Action Task Force (FATF)
679–80
Fincantieri 293, 315
Finland:
arms imports 329
AWS and 544
EU and PESCO 8
Eurocorps 9

Joint Expeditionary Force 9
military expenditure 280
NATO membership issue 7
fissile material:
  2021 global stocks 424–32
    HEU 426–27
    plutonium 428–29
  Argentina 430
  categories 341, 424–25
  China 426, 428, 430, 432
  France 426, 428, 430, 432
  Germany 430
  HEU
    2021 global stocks 426–27
    Australian submarines 301
    production method 424
    worldwide enrichment facilities
      430–31
  India 426, 428, 430, 432
  Iran 426, 435–36, 450–56
    centrifuges 454–55
    HEU 450, 452–54, 455
    Israel and 703
    plutonium 455–56
    see also **JCPOA**
  Israel 405–407, 426, 428, 432
  Japan 428, 432
  North Korea 410
    HEU 416–17, 426, 430
    plutonium 415–16, 428, 432
  Pakistan 426, 428, 430, 432
  plutonium
    2021 global stocks 428–29
    2021 reprocessing facilities 432
    production method 424–25
  Russia 426, 428, 430, 432
  United Kingdom 426, 428, 430, 432
  United States 426, 428, 430, 432
fissile material cut-off treaty (FMCT)
  447
Flank Document (1996) 661
FLIR Systems 291
floods 40, 103, 106, 113, 190, 201, 215,
  224, 231, 234, 238, 550, 706
Florence Agreement (1996) 665, 697
Floyd, Robert 467
food insecurity:
  Americas 81
  armed conflicts and 5–6, 37–38, 40
  Cameroon 216
  Chad 221
  El Salvador 81
  Guatemala 81
  Honduras 81

Myanmar 38, 104
Somalia 38, 231
South Sudan 38, 207, 234
Ukraine war and 5–6
Venezuela 102
West Africa 203, 206–207
Yemen 38, 207
foreign direct investment: EU control
  624–25
**fractional orbital bombardment
  systems (FOBS)** 573–74
France:
  African conflicts and 199
  arms exports 280, 297, 299, 304, 305
    Africa 317
    Asia–Oceania 313, 323
    Australia 301, 325–26
    Botswana 319
    Brazil 323
    developments 313–14
    Egypt 313, 314, 322
    India 313, 324, 325, 394, 554
    Morocco 318
    Nigeria 319
    Qatar 313, 331, 554
    Romania 329
    Saudi Arabia 553
    transparency 553, 554
    UAE 314, 331
    Ukraine 330
  arms industry 290, 292, 293
  Australia and 276, 301, 325–26
  AWS and 535–36
  Cameroon and 216
  Central African Republic and 219, 705
  Chinese relations 111
  Covid-19 281, 293
  cybersecurity and 563, 568
  EWIPA and 519
  FDI screening 625
  Greek defence agreement 9, 148, 708
  Iran and 18–19, 449
  Iraq and 165
  Mali and 65, 67, 68, 193, 705
  Middle East and 160, 464
  military expenditure 257, 281
  Minsk Group 141, 153
  NPT recognized nuclear state 460
  nuclear arms control 17, 441, 447, 448
  nuclear weapons *see* **nuclear weapons**
  Open Skies Treaty and 549
  Operation Barkhane 66, 193, 199, 204,
    207–208, 209, 705
  peace operations 65–66

Russia and 144, 504, 505, 506
Sahel and 65, 67
Syrian peace process and 172
Yemen and 185
Francese, Tancredi 491
Freedom House 79
Fujitsu 295

G5 Sahel 203, 208, 319
G5 Sahel Joint Force 62, 208, 210, 212
G7 (Group of Seven) 154, 480, 680–81, 710
G20 (Group of Twenty) 120
Gaddafi, Muammar 179, 286
Gafoor, Burhan 563
Gambia:
    ATT and 590
    ECOMIG 58, 72
    presidential elections 202, 205
Gavi 473
Gavrilov, Konstantin 546
Gberie, Lansana 581, 583
General Dynamics 289–90
Geneva Conventions 637–39
Geneva Protocol (1925) 636
Georgia:
    cluster munitions 522
    EUMM Georgia 72
    NATO–Georgia Commission 691
    Open Skies Treaty 549
    Russian invasion (2008) 4
Germany:
    arms exports 297, 299, 304
        Algeria 318
        Brazil 323
        developments 314–15
        Egypt 315, 332
        Europe 328
        Israel 333, 408–409
        Saudi Arabia 331
        South Korea 313–15, 327
        Ukraine 330
    arms imports 329
    arms industry 290, 292, 293–94
    AWS and 544
    BWC and 486
    cluster munitions 522
    cybersecurity and 568
    East Africa and 224
    EU defence and 8–9
    FDI screening 625
    floods 706
    HEU facilities 430

Iran and 449, 602
Libyan peace process and 181
military expenditure 256, 281
Minsk Group 153
Morocco and 184
new government 281
Open Skies Treaty and 549, 550
outer space security 572
peace operations and 65
Russian novichoks and 504, 505, 506
Syrian peace process and 172
TPNW and 463–64
Ukraine war and 7
US nuclear weapons in 352, 353
Ghali, Brahim 184
Ghani, President Ashraf 64–65, 277
Global Commission on Stability in Cyberspace 559, 569
Global Cybersecurity Index 567
Global Initiative to Combat Nuclear Terrorism (GICNT) 680
Global Partnership against the Spread of Weapons and Materials of Mass Destruction 681
Göbel, Thomas 584
Goïta, Assimi 205
Gorbachev, Mikhail 18–19., 435, 440
Greece:
    arms imports: France 314
    cluster munition production 522
    French defence agreement 9, 148, 708.
    landmines 525
    military expenditure 280
    Turkey and 147, 148
    UNROCA and 589
Grenada: cluster munitions 523
Griffiths, Martin 132
Group of 13 539
Groupf Seven (G7) 154, 480, 680–81, 710
Grundberg, Hans 189
GUAM (Organization for Democracy and Economic Development) 693
Guatemala:
    armed conflict 75, 77, 89–90
    authoritarianism 79
    Covid-19 90
    displacement 37, 81
    food insecurity 81
    gang violence 88, 89
Guinea:
    armed conflict 195
    military coup 193, 200, 202, 205, 205–206, 264, 707

military expenditure 265
Guinea-Bissau: landmines 526
Gulf Cooperation Council 159, 286, 689
Guterres, Antonio 15, 22–23, 44,
  200–201, 462, 540n33, 707, 708
Guzmán, Joaquin 'El Chapo' 82–83.

Hadi, President Abdrabbuh Mansur
  185
Hague Code of Conduct against
  Ballistic Missile Proliferation 615–16,
  698
Haiti:
  armed conflict 75, 77, 82, 86–87
  assassination of president 76, 86, 706
  authoritarianism 79
  BINUH 72
  displacement 37, 76
  earthquake 87, 707
  food insecurity 38
  gang violence 82, 86, 87
  mass protests 86
  UN Integrated Office 87
Hamas 156, 175, 176, 704
Hamdok, Abdalla 237, 709
Hanwha Aerospace 295
Harris 291, 295
Hecker, Siegfried 416
Henry, Ariel 87
Hensoldt 293
Hernández, President Juan Orlando
  76, 91
Hexcel 288
Hezbollah 159, 163
highly enriched uranium (HEU) *see*
  fissile material
Hindustan Aeronautics 295
HIV 476
Hoffmann, Wolfgang 467
Honduras:
  armed conflict 75, 76, 77, 90–91
  assassinations 79
  authoritarianism 79, 90–91
  displacement 37, 81
  food insecurity 81
  gang violence 88, 90, 91
  homicide rate 90
  migration from 91
  poverty 91
Houti, Hussein Badredi al- 185
Hu Jintao, President 443
Human Rights Watch 177, 517
human trafficking 182

humanitarian disarmament: concept
  513, 515
Hungary:
  Open Skies Treaty and 549
  Wassenaar Arrangement and 618
hurricanes 81, 91

Iceland:
  EWIPA and 520
  Joint Expeditionary Force 9
ICRC (International Committee of the
  Red Cross):
  on armed groups 33
  AWS and 535, 536, 540, 704
  CNS-acting chemicals and 509, 510
  on Colombia 92, 95
  cybersecurity and 569
  EWIPA and 519–20
  incendiary weapons and 517
identity militias 36, 198
identity politics 105, 125, 221
IGAD (Intergovernmental Authority
  on Development) 689–90
  CTSAMVM 58, 73
  peace operations 56, 73
IHI Corporation 295
improvised explosive devices (IEDs)
  517, 524, 526
IMT (International Monitoring Team)
  in Mindanao 59, 73
incendiary weapons 515, 516, 517–18
India:
  armed conflicts 103, 105
    arms imports and 302
    fatalities 124
    internal conflicts 124–26
    Kashmir 107, 120–24, 277, 325
  arms embargoes and 599
  arms exports to Myanmar 328
  arms imports 299, 323, 324–25
    France 313, 324, 325, 394, 554
    Russia 311, 313, 324
    top importer 317
    transparency 554
    United States 311
  arms industry 290, 295–96
  Australia Group and 613
  AWS and 541–42
  BWC and 486, 489, 491
  Chinese relations
    clashes 104, 277, 391
    geopolitics 311
    Kashmir 107, 120–22

nuclear weapons 387, 391
  threat perception 324
climate change and 107
cluster munitions 522
Covid-19 pandemic 108, 276, 295
  deaths 474, 475, 704
East Africa and 224
farmers' protests 125
floods 705
Hindu–Muslim tensions 125
Islamic State 106
landmines 524, 525
military expenditure 276–77
  increase 244, 255–56, 271, 276
  military burden 259
Myanmar and 328, 605
Nagaland killings 125, 710
nuclear arms control 17, 448
  CTBT and 466, 469
nuclear weapons *see* **nuclear weapons**
Pakistani conflict 27, 29, 104
  arms imports and 324–25
  border clashes 391
  ceasefire 107, 122–23, 702
  Kashmir 122–24, 277, 325
  nuclear posture 398
  UNMOGIP 72
peace agreement 42
peace operation contributions 61
Syrian chemical weapons and 501
Vibrant Villages Programme 122
Wassenaar Arrangement and 618
Indian Ordnance Factories 295
indigenous people 79–80, 96, 98, 214
Indonesia:
  armed conflict 103, 105, 132–33
  arms imports 301, 305, 314, 315
  contribution to peace operations 61, 62
  Islamic State 106
  military expenditure 277, 278
  South Korea and 278
Indus Water Treaty (1960) 123
INF Treaty (Intermediate Range Nuclear Forces, 1987) 144, 368, 671
Inhumane Weapons Convention *see* **CCW**
Inter-American Convention on Transparency in Conventional Weapons Acquisitions (CITAAC, 1999) 556, 666
Intergovernmental Panel on Climate change (IPCC) 13–14, 707
International Agency for Biological Safety 485

International Atomic Energy Authority (IAEA) 677–78
  fissile material declarations 424, 425
  Iran and 18, 436, 449, 450–57
  Israeli fissile material and 405
  Middle East nuclear free zone and 465
  North Korea and 415–16, 417
International Campaign to Ban Landmines (ICBL) 524
International Conference on the Great Lakes (IGGLR) 690
International Court of Justice (ICJ) 678
International Criminal Court (ICC) 681
  Israel–Palestinian conflict and 176–77, 702
  Ongwen trial 702
  Philippines investigation 134
  Rome Statute 653–55
International Crisis Group 174
International Labour Organization 476
International Monetary Fund (IMF) 165, 248, 249, 260
International Network on Explosive Weapons (INEW) 518–19, 520
International Panel on Fissile Material (IPFM) 405, 424
International Telecommunication Union (ITU) 565, 567
International Union of Pure and Applied Sciences (IUPAC) 511
Iran:
  allies 155, 158
  armed conflict 37
  arms embargoes 332, 595
    EU 597, 608
    UN 596, 601–602
  arms exports to Yemen 602, 606
  arms imports 332, 601
  Astana Group 172
  biological/chemical weapons and 486, 488, 510, 612
  China and 18–19, 703
  cluster munitions 522
  CTBT and 466
  cybersecurity and 561
  displacement 37
  East Africa and 224
  Ethiopia and 227
  fissile material 426, 435–36, 703
    JCPOA and 450–56
  interstate revalries 155, 158

Iran–Iraq war: chemical weapons 612
Iraq and 155, 158, 164, 165, 602
Israel and 158–59, 285, 286
  arms embargo 602
  arms imports and 333
  cyberattacks 453–54
  drones 452
  nuclear issues 409, 456, 703
Kurds 166–67
landmines 524
Lebanon and 155, 158, 602
military expenditure 257–58, 259,
  284–85
nuclear deal 10
nuclear technology
  2021 developments 18–19
  JCPOA *see* **JCPOA**
OPCW and 508
SALWs and 529, 530
Saudi Arabia and 159–60
Syria and 155, 158, 169, 285
  arms transfers 602
  chemical weapons 501
UAVs 527
UN arms embargo 332
USA and 10, 16, 18, 160, 164
  sanctions 284–85, 449, 458, 459,
   581, 582, 627
Yemen and 155, 158, 185, 189, 602, 606
Iraq:
2003 war 147
armed conflict 155, 164–68
  fatalities 27, 29, 166, 167
  forever war 68
armed groups 33
arms embargo 596
cluster munitions 522
Covid-19 165, 167
displacement 167
economy 165
failures of interventions in 68, 69
Iran and 155, 158, 164, 165, 602
Iran–Iraq war: chemical weapons 612
Islamic State 161–62, 164
Kurds 165, 166–67, 173–74
landmines 525
Middle East diplomacy 159–60
NMI 59, 73
parliamentary elections 167–68
peace operations 65
  EUAM Iraq 73
Turkey and 166, 167, 173–74
UAVs 527
US-led war 116

US withdrawal 255, 706
USA and 161, 165–66
Ireland:
AWS and 542, 544
CTBT and 467
EU and PESCO 8
EWIPA and 513, 516, 519
MOTAPM and 526
Wassenaar Arrangement and 618
**ISAF (International Security
  Assistance Force)** 50, 52, 59, 63–64,
  67, 68, 116
Islamic State:
Afghanistan 117–18, 119–20, 707
Asia 106
Iraq 161–62, 164
Libya 181
Syria 161–62, 168, 169
Islamic State Central Africa Province
229
Islamic State Khorasan Province 707
**Islamic-State-Sinai Province (Wilayat
Sinai)** 179
**Islamic State West Africa Province
(ISWAP)** 203, 204, 215, 216
Israel:
arms exports 304
arms imports 333, 408–409
arms industry 290, 295
AWS and 537
cluster munition production 522
CWC and 504
cybersecurity and 561, 562
defence agreements 148
Egyptian relations 707
fissile material 405–407
government changes 285
international crimes 177
Iran and 158–59, 285, 286
  arms imports 333, 602
  cyberattacks 453–54
  nuclear issues 409, 456, 703
landmines 525
Lebanon and 333
military expenditure 258, 259, 284,
  285–86
normalization agreements (Abraham
  Accords) 175
nuclear non-proliferation and 17
  Middle East nuclear free zone 464
  NPT 405, 465
nuclear weapons *see* **nuclear weapons**
Palestinian conflict *see* **Israel–
  Palestine conflict**

Pegasus Project 706
Syria and 333
UAE and 160–61
UAVs 527
USA and 155, 156, 158, 175, 178, 285, 333, 405
Israel Aerospace Industries 295
Israel–Palestine conflict:
2021 developments 27, 156–57, 175–78
arms imports and 333
EUBAM Rafah 73
EUPOL COPPS 72
fatalities 155, 176, 177
Gaza escalation 175–77, 704
humanitarian crisis 175
ICC investigation 176–77, 702
nature of conflict 29
outlook 178
USA and 156, 175, 178
Issoufou, Mahamadou 204
Istanbul Cooperation Initiative (ICI) 691
Italy:
arms exports 304, 315
Brazil 323
Egypt 315, 332
Kuwait 315, 332
Pakistan 325
Qatar 315, 331
transparency 553
UAE 331
arms imports 329
arms industry 290, 293
AWS and 544
China and: FDI 624–25
cybersecurity and 568
East Africa and 224
FDI screening 625
Ivory Coast: armed conflict 195

Japan:
arms imports 302, 323, 326, 327
arms industry 290, 294–95
AWS and 535–36
Chinese relations 110–11, 274, 302
Covid-19 and 274
East Africa and 224
fissile material 428, 430, 432
military expenditure 259, 272, 274
Myanmar and 132
North Korea and 274
Russian relations 274
Ukraine war and 9–10

US relations 109, 112
JCPOA:
2021 developments 435–36, 449–59
arms embargo and 601–602
Comprehensive Safeguards Agreement Additional Protocol 451–52
outstanding issues 456–57
diplomatic efforts to restore 457–59
Iranian diplomacy 285
Iran's nuclear programme development 450–56
NPT and 461
NSG and 617
Procurement Channel 602
resuming negotiations 703, 709
UNSC Resolution 2231 449
uranium enrichment 435–36
USA and 16, 18, 160, 436, 449–50
arms embargo 601, 608
change 581
diplomacy 457–59
withdrawal 160, 449
Jenkins, Bonnie 440, 442, 445, 494, 547
Johnson & Johnson 473
Joint Control Commission (JCC) Peacekeeping Force 59, 73
Jordan:
contribution to peace operations 62
Middle East diplomacy 160
military expenditure 284
Syria and 173
Yemen war and 185

Kanu, Nnamdi 214
Karakaev, Sergey 361, 362, 363
Kashmir disputes 107, 120–24, 277, 325
Kawasaki Heavy Industries 295
Kazakhstan:
arms imports from Russia 312–13
International Agency for Biological Safety and 485
military expenditure 271
nuclear weapons: relinquishment 11
KBR 291
Keita, President Ibrahim Boubacar 205
Kenya:
armed conflict 193, 195, 264
climate change 225
contributions to peace operations 61
military expenditure 264
Ukraine war and 11
Kerry, John 443

KFOR (Kosovo Force) 54, 61, 73
Khan, Imran 123, 126
Kiir, President Salva 233
Kim Jong Un 410, 411, 419, 422
Kimani, Martin 529
Kinshasa Convention (Central African SALW Convention, 2010) 668–69
Kmentt, Alexander 463–64
Kongsberg Gruppen 294
Korea, Democratic People's Republic of (DPRK, North Korea):
    arms embargo 596, 602–603
    China and 603
    climate change and 107
    cluster munitions 522
    CTBT and 466
    CWC and 504
    ending Korean War 103, 107, 109
    Japanese relations 274
    nuclear non-proliferation and 17
    nuclear weapons *see* **nuclear weapons**
    South Korea and 275, 315, 411, 422, 423
    US relations 109–10, 411, 435
Korea, Republic of (ROK, South Korea):
    arms exports 304, 316
    arms imports 302, 314–15, 323, 326, 327
    arms industry 290, 295
    cluster munitions 522
    cybersecurity and 566–67
    ending Korean War 103, 107, 109
    military expenditure 244, 258, 259, 272, 274–75, 275
    NNSC 59, 73
    North Korea and 275, 315, 411, 422, 423
    SLBMs 707
    USA and 12, 109, 327
Kosovo:
    cluster munitions 522
    EULEX Kosovo 72
    KFOR 54, 61, 73
    OMIK 73
    Serbian border 146–47
    UNMIK 72
Krauss-Maffei Wegmann 294
KRET 294
Kubiš, Ján 181–82
Kurds:
    Iran 166–67
    Iraq 165, 166–67, 173–74
    Syria 170, 171, 172, 173–74
    Turkish conflict 27, 29, 173–74
Kuwait:
    arms imports 315, 332
    military expenditure 284
    Syria and 173
    Yemen war and 185
Kuzmanovska Biondic, Elena 484
Kyrgyzstan:
    military expenditure 271
    Tajik conflict 27, 29, 103, 105, 108, 704
    Uzbek agreement 107–108, 703

L3 technologies 291
L3Harris Technologies 291, 295
Lake Chad Basin Commission 208
landmines:
    2021 developments 523–26
    CCW Convention 515
    clearance and destruction 525
    use and production 524–25
    see also **APM Convention**
Laos: cluster munitions 522
Latin America and the Caribbean Cyber Competence Centre (LAC4) 567
Latvia:
    arms imports 328–29
    Joint Expeditionary Force 9
Laukkanen, Kimmo 483
Lavrov, Sergey 545
LAWS (lethal autonomous weapons systems) *see* **autonomous weapons systems (AWS)**
Lebanon:
    2020 Beirut explosion 163
    armed conflict 155, 157, 162–63
    arms embargo 596
    cluster munitions 522, 523
    Hezbollah 159, 163
    Iran and 155, 158, 602
    Israel and 333
    UNIFIL 54, 55, 61, 72
Lenderking, Tim 189
Leonardo 293
Lesotho: contribution to peace operations 48
Liang Wannian 477
Libya:
    armed conflict 155, 156
    2021 developments 179–83
    fatalities 182
    nature of conflict 157
    outlook 183

proxy war 180
armed groups 33
arms embargo 582, 596, 603–604
arms imports 317, 604
cluster munitions 522
displacement 37, 182
elections 181–82
foreign fighters 604
Government of National Unity 703
humanitarian situation 182–83
Islamic State 181
Mediterranean conflicts and 147
peace agreement (2020) 28, 43, 159
peace operations
  AU Mission 56, 72
  EUBAM Libya 73
  EUNAVFOR Irini 63
  UNSMIL 72
peace process 180–82, 705
Qatar and 286
Russian arms to 604
Turkey and 147, 604
UAE and 331, 604
United Nations and 65, 182–83, 183
LIG Nex1 295
Lithuania:
arms exports to Ukraine 330
arms imports 328–29
Covid-19 pandemic 475
EWIPA and 519
Joint Expeditionary Force 9
UNROCA and 589
Lockhead Martin 289, 291
López Obrador, President Manuel Andrés 84–85, 86
Lukashenko, President Alexander 142–43, 709
Luxembourg: AWS and 544

Machar, Riek 233
Macron, President Emmanuel 8, 65, 67, 209, 375, 705
Madagascar: armed conflict 193
Madougou, Reckya 204–205
Maduro, President Nicolás 101, 102
Mailu, Cleopa 490
malaria 238, 476, 708
Malawi: contribution to peace operations 48
Malaysia:
Islamic State 106
military expenditure 277
Thai conflict and 135

Mali:
armed conflict 193, 202
  conflict management 45
  external interventions 199
  fatalities 27, 29, 210, 212, 707
  internal conflict 211–12
  transnational armed groups 203
armed groups 67
arms imports 318, 319
climate change and 201, 203
Covid-19 pandemic 202
displacement 37
France and 65, 67, 68, 193, 705
human insecurity 206
landmines 212
military coup 193, 200, 202, 205–206, 264, 705
military expenditure 265
peace operations 46, 65
  EUCAP Sahel Mali 73, 209
  European Union 62
  EUTM Mali 54, 58–59, 73, 208–209
  French withdrawal 67
  MINUSMA 28, 49, 54, 55–56, 57, 61, 65, 68, 72, 207, 208, 210, 212
  Operation Barkhane 66, 193, 199, 204, 207–208, 209, 705
peace process 42, 211
Russia and 199, 209–10, 319
statebuilding 65
Wagner Group in 66
Malta: Wassenaar Arrangement and 619
MAPP/OEA (OAS Mission to Support the Peace Process in Colombia) 73
Mauritania:
cluster munitions 522, 523
contribution to peace operations 62
landmines 526
Operation Barkhane 207–208
Regional Advisory and Coordination Cell (RACC) 209
MBDA 292, 293
Mediterranean Dialogue 691
Melrose Industries 292–93
Mercosur 529
Mexico:
Australia Group and 613
authoritarianism 79
AWS and 536, 542, 544
Covid-19 deaths 475
MCTR and 615
migration from 81
military expenditure 269–70

USA and 81, 82–3
violence 75, 77
  against journalists 79, 84
  assassinations 79, 84
  cartels 82–84, 100
  disappearances 84
  fatalities 27, 29, 35, 83
  gangs 82, 100
  homicide rate 82
  military law enforcement 84–85
  organized crime 82–86
  outlook 85–86
**MFO (Multinational Force and
  Observers) in the Sinai Peninsula** 59,
  61, 73
Microsoft 569
Middle East:
  armed conflicts 155–91
    alliances and diplomacy 158–61
    fatalities 157, 158
    key developments 157–63
    overview 155–56
  arms exports 304
  arms imports 297, 299, 330–33
    2017–21 period 317
    France 313
    Germany 314
    Italy 315
    Russia 311
    South Korea 316
    United States 305
  Covid-19 pandemic 155, 157
  military expenditure 244, 248, 251,
    256–57, 257, 262, 284–86
  nuclear free zone 436, 464–65, 709
  UNTSO 72
  see also individual countries
Mikati, Najib 163
military coups:
  Africa 193, 200–201, 205–206
  Armenia 702
  CAR 193, 200
  Chad 193, 200, 264
  Egypt 314, 332
  epidemic 23
  Guinea 193, 200, 202, 205–206, 264,
    707
  Myanmar 3, 127–30, 701, 707, 710
  Niger 193, 200, 202, 204, 205
  Sudan 193, 196, 200, 237, 264, 709
  United Nations and 23, 708
military expenditure:
  2012–21 trends 255–57
  2021 global developments 245–61

economic data variations 248
  GDP and 248–50
  largest spenders 257–59
  opportunity costs 252–55
  priorities 250–52
  Africa 243, 248, 251, 256, 257, 262–65
  Americas 244, 248, 256, 257, 265–71
  Asia–Oceania 243–44, 245–48, 251,
    256, 257, 262, 271–78
  climate change and 243
  Covid-19 pandemic and 243, 245,
    248–55, 257
  definitions 260
  Europe 244, 248, 251, 262, 278–83
  increase 39, 243
  Middle East 244, 248, 251, 256, 257,
    262, 284–86
  military burden 245–47, 256, 257, 259
  overview 243–44
  regional data 249, 254, 256
    2021 developments 262–86
  sources of information 260–61
  transparency: UNMILEX 551, 554–55
Miller, Austin 115
Min Aung Hlaing 130, 131
Minsk Group 141, 694
Minsk process 140–41
Minsk Protocol 51
**MINURSO (UN MIssion for the
  Referendum in Western Sahara)** 72,
  184
**MINUSCA (UN Multidimentional
  Integrated Stabilization Mission in
  the CAR)** 49, 51, 53, 54, 55, 61, 65, 72,
  217, 218, 220
**MINUSMA (UN Multidimentional
  Integrated Stabilization Mission in
  Mali)** 28, 49, 54, 55–56, 57, 61, 65, 68,
  72, 207, 208, 210, 212
**MISAC (AU Mission for the CAR and
  Central Africa)** 72
**MISAHEL (AU Mission for Mali and
  the Sahel)** 72
**Missile Technology Control Regime
  (MCTR)** 698
  2021 developments 613–16
  Covid-19 and 582, 611, 614
  Hague Code of Conduct 615–16, 698
  Information Exchange Meeting 615
  LEEM 614, 615
  scope 582, 610, 612, 613
  UAVs and 516, 527, 528, 613–14
Mistura, Staffan de 184
Mitsubishi Electric 295

Mitsubishi Heavy Industries 295
MNJTF (Multinational Joint Task Force) 62, 208
Moderna 473
Modi, Narendra 122
Moïse, President Jovenel 86, 706
Moldova:
  JCC 59, 73
  OSCE Mission 73
  Trans-Dniester 59, 73, 146
Montenegro: cluster munitions 523
MONUSCO (UN Oganization Stabilization Mission in the DRC) 45, 54–55, 61, 70, 72, 222
Moon:
  2021 developments 514, 572
  growing interest in 575–78, 703, 704
  international partnerships 576
  military interest in 577–78
  Outer Space Treaty and 575–76, 577
Moon Jae-in, President 109–10
Morocco:
  Algeria and 156, 184
  armed conflict 157, 184
  arms imports 317–18
  Germany and 184
  military expenditure 262–63
  MINURSO 72, 184
  normalization agreement with Israel 175
  Spain and 184
  US relations 318
  Western Sahara 72, 156, 184, 522
  Yemen war and 185
MOTAPMs (mines other than anti-personnel mines) 516, 524, 526
MOUACA (AU Military Observer Mission in the CAR) 56, 72
Mozambique:
  armed conflict 193, 194
    2021 developments 229–31
    Cabo Delgado 229–31
    fatalities 27, 29, 228, 229, 703
    internationaization 229
    outlook 231
  cluster munitions 523
  displacement 37
  Jihadists 198
  peace operations 45
    EUTM Mozambique 28, 46, 49, 56, 58, 73, 197, 706
    SAMIM 28, 46, 47–48, 49, 56, 58, 73, 197, 230, 705
Muratov, Dmitry 708

Myanmar:
  2020 elections 127–28
  armed conflicts 13, 103, 104, 105
    2021 developments 127–32
    armed groups 105–106
    arms imports and 328
    fatalities 27, 29, 35–36, 128, 702
    impact of coup on 130–31
  arms embargo 597, 604–605, 608
  arms imports 327–28
  ASEAN and 104, 107, 131
  Belarus and 605
  Chinese relations 131–32, 328, 605
  crimes against humanity 128–29
  displacement 37, 132
  European Union and 131
  food insecurity 38, 104
  humanitarian crisis 132
  India and 328, 605
  Japanese relations 132
  landmines 524
  military coup 3, 127–30, 701, 707, 710
    impact on existing armed conflicts 130–31
    international response 131–32
  peace process 43
  political protests 129, 702, 703
  Rohingya 128, 130, 132, 328
  Russian relations 131–32, 328, 605
  sanctions on 131
  terrorism 36
  Thai relations 132
  USA and 131, 605

Nagorno-Karabakh conflict:
  2021 developments 137, 139–41
  arms embargo 595
  cluster munitions 521–22
  continuation 4, 22
  drone use 34, 528
  fatalities 43, 140
  interstate conflict 27, 29
  landmines 524
  military expenditure and 283
  Minsk process 140–41
  OSCE role 59, 73
  peace agreement (2020) 28, 43, 137
  peace operations 63, 137, 140, 313
    OSCE PRCIO 73
    RTJMC 28, 46, 47, 59–60, 73, 701
  renewed clashes 140–41
  Russia and 46, 47, 63, 137, 140, 313, 701

Nairobi Protocol on SALW (2004) 667
Nakai, Kazahiro 483–84
Nakamitsu, Izumi 461–62, 486
Namibia: ATT reporting 587
NATO (North Atlantic Treaty
  Organization) 690–92
  Afghanistan: withdrawal 3, 103, 107,
    114–18, 268
  arms imports and 317
  Belarus and 549
  China and 10
  collective defence 143
  EAPC 691
  expansion 7, 10, 145
  Mediterranean issues 147
  military expenditure and 257, 280
  NATO–Georgia Commission 691
  NATO–Ukraine Commission 692
  peace operations 58
    fatigue 68
    geopolitics 70
    ISAF 50, 52, 59, 63–64, 67, 68, 116
    KFOR 54, 61, 73
    NMI 59, 73
    RSM 28, 45, 49–50, 52, 56, 58, 59,
      63–64, 68–69, 70, 73, 107
  Russia and 137
    militarization 143–44
    NATO–Russia Council (NRC) 143,
      146, 692
    Open Skies Treaty 546, 548–49
    security demands 145–46, 710
    Ukraine conflict 143–44, 703
    unravelling 709
  Sahel and 62
  strategic posture 705
  TPNW and 463–64
  Turkey and 148
  Ukraine conflicts and
    arms supplies 150
    Open Skies Treaty 549
    responses to 2022 war 8–9
    warnings 153, 710
  US nuclear forces in Europe and
    352–53
  Western Balkans 146–47
Naval Group 293
Navalny, Alexei 137, 141, 142, 472,
  504–506, 701, 702
Navantia 294
Ndaw, President Bah 205, 705
Nepal: contribution to peace
  operations 61, 62
Netherlands:

arms imports 328, 329
AWS and 544
HEU facilities 430
Joint Expeditionary Force 9
Neumann, Hannah 629–30
New START (Strategic Arms
  Reduction Treaty, Prague Treaty,
  2010) 672–73
  aircraft and air-delivered weapons 347,
    360
  Bilateral Consultative Commission 437,
    438, 672, 678–79
  compliance concerns 438–39
  data exchanges 438
  extension 16–17, 144, 435, 437–38, 701
    China and 442, 443
    NPT and 461
  inspections 437
  replacement issue 439, 440, 441
  Russian compliance 355, 361
  US compliance 343–46
New Zealand:
  AWS and 544
  contribution to peace operations 63
  EWIPA and 520
  Islamic State 106
Ngute, Joseph Dion 217
Nicaragua:
  authoritarianism 79
  elections 88
  political unrest 79, 88
Niger:
  armed conflict 193, 195, 202
    armed groups 203, 213
    fatalities 27, 29, 210, 212, 703, 709
  climate change and 203
  Covid-19 202
  displacement 212
  elections 200, 202, 204
  failed coup 193, 200, 202, 204, 205
  human insecurity 206
  landmines 524
  military expenditure 265
  Operation Barkhane 207–208
Nigeria:
  armed conflict 193–94, 195, 202
    fatalities 27, 29, 36, 213
  armed groups 33, 203, 204
  arms imports 318, 319
  Boko Haram 194, 213, 319
  child soldiers 213
  China and 199
  climate change and 203
  Covid-19 202–203

displacement 37, 213
human insecurity 38, 206, 207
Indigenous People of Biafra 214
landmines 524, 526
military expenditure 243, 263–64
Russia and 199
UAVs 527
USA and 199
Nkurunziza, President Pierre 50
NMI (NATO Mission in Iraq) 59, 73
NNSC (Neutral Nations Supervisory
  Commission) 59, 73
Nobel Peace Prize 708
Non-Aligned Movement (NAM) 484,
  486, 491, 681–82
Non-Proliferation and Disarmament
  Initiative (NPDI) 461
Non-Proliferation Treaty (NPT, 1968)
  642–43
  10th review conference 16, 17, 19, 436,
    460–62
  Article VI 461, 462
  India and 617
  Iranian membership 18
  Israel and 405, 465
  Middle East nuclear free zone and
    464–65
  NSG and 617
  P5 declaration 447, 460, 709
  recognized nuclear states 460
  TPNW and 436, 462, 463
NORINCO 292
Nort, Daan 512
North Korea see Korea, Democratic
  People's Republic of
North Macedonia:
  Covid-19 deaths 475
Northern Ireland: unresolved conflict
  146
Northrop Grumman 289, 291
Norway:
  arms embargoes and Iran 602
  arms imports 328, 329
  arms industry 290, 292, 294
  AWS and 544
  cluster munitions 523
  cybersecurity and 627
  Joint Expeditionary Force 9
  TPNW and 463–64
novichoks 472, 504–506
NPT see Non-Proliferation Treaty
nuclear arms control:
  bilateral developments 437–45
    Russia–US strategic stability

dialogue 440–41
  see also specific bilateral treaties
  JCPOA see JCPOA
  Middle East 463, 464–65
  multilateralism
    prospects 445–48
    treaties 436, 460–69
  overview 16–19, 435–36
  see also specific treaties
Nuclear Suppliers Group (NSG) 699
  2021 developments 616–18
  Covid-19 and 582, 611, 617
  origins 616–17
  participants 617
  scope 582, 610, 612, 616
nuclear weapons:
  China 341, 342
    2022 table 382–83
    aircraft and air-delivered weapons
      384–85
    competition 387
    data sources 380
    fissile material 426, 428, 430, 432
    hypersonic weapon system 387–88,
      706
    ICBMs 385–88, 706
    increased stockpiles 372
    India and 387, 391
    intermediate and medium range
      ballistic missiles 388–89
    land-based missiles 385–89
    no-first use policy 19, 381
    nuclear posture 380–84
    sea-based missiles 389–90
    survey 380–90
    tests 387–88
    US weapons and 387
  control see nuclear arms control;
    specific treaties
  cybersecurity and 568
  fissile material see fissile material
  France 341, 342
    2022 table 376
    aircraft and air-delivered weapons
      377–78
    fissile material 426, 428, 430, 432
    modernization 375–77
    nuclear posture 375
    sea-based missiles 378–79
    survey 375–79
    tests 379, 468
    transparency 375
  general rejection 12
  India 341, 342

2022 table 392
aircraft and air-delivered weapons
    393–94
China and 387, 391
cruise missiles 397
fissile material 426, 428, 430, 432
land-based missiles 394–96
non-transparency 391
NSG and 616–17
nuclear posture 391–93
sea-based missiles 396–97
survey 391–97
tests 469
Israel 341, 342
    2022 table 406
    aircraft and air-delivered weapons
        407
    fissile material 405–407, 426, 428,
        430, 432
    Iran and 159
    land-based missiles 407–408
    military posture 404–405
    non-transparency 404
    sea-based missiles 408–409
    survey 404–409
North Korea 341, 342
    2022 table 412–14
    cruise missiles 421–22
    data sources 410
    fissile material 410, 415–17, 426,
        428, 430, 432
    ICBMs 420–21
    justification 12
    land-based missiles 412–13, 418–22
    medium and intermediate range
        ballistic missiles 419–20
    nuclear doctrine 411–15, 418
    opacity 410
    sea-based missiles 413–14, 422–23
    short-range ballistic missiles 419,
        707
    South Korea and 275, 411
    survey 410–23
    targets 411–14
    tests 410, 417–18, 420, 421–22, 423,
        435
    warheads 417–18
overview 341
Pakistan 341, 342
    2022 table 400
    aircraft and air-delivered weapons
        399–401
    data sources 398
    fissile material 426, 428, 430, 432

India and 398
land-based missiles 401–403
non-transparency 398
role 398–99
sea-based missiles 403
survey 398–403
tactical weapons 398–99
tests 403, 469
relinquishment: former USSR states 11
Russia 341, 342
    2022 table 356–59
    aircraft and air-delivered weapons
        360–61, 367–68
    army weapons 368
    data sources 355
    fissile material 426, 428, 430, 432
    increased stockpiles 372
    land-based missiles 361–63
    military posture 359, 366, 370
    New START compliance 355, 361
    sea-based missiles 363–65, 366–67
    spending 283
    strategic forces 359–65
    survey 355–68
    tactical forces 365–68
    UK and 372
Soviet Union 11
transparency issue 341
United Kingdom 341, 342
    2022 table 370
    fissile material 426, 428, 430, 432
    increased stockpiles 372, 461, 703
    military posture 369–71
    modernization 372–74
    revised policy 371–72
    Russia and 372
    sea-based missiles 374
    survey 369–74
    transparency 369, 461
    USA and 373, 374
United States 341, 342
    2022 table 344–46
    aircraft and air-delivered weapons
        347–49, 352–53
    China and 387
    deployment in Europe 352–53
    deployment in South Korea 12
    fissile material 426, 428, 430, 432
    land-based missiles 349–50
    military posture 346–47, 370
    New START compliance 344–46
    Nuclear Posture Review (2018) 267,
        346–47, 365
    sea-based missiles 350–51, 353–54

sources of information 343
strategic forces 347–52
survey 343–54
tactical forces 352–54
tests 467
UK and 373, 374
warheads 351–52
world forces: 2021 table 342
Nukewatch 373
Nyusi, President Filipe 48

Obama, President Barack 10, 116, 346, 444
OCCAR (Organisation for Joint Armament Cooperation) 692
OECD (Organisation for Economic Co-operation and Development) 682
OHCHR (UN High Commissioner for Human Rights) 84, 95, 96, 97–98
OHR (Office of the High Representative in Bosnia Herzegovina) 59–60, 69, 73
Okonio-Iweala, Ngosi 702
Oman:
  arms imports from the UK 315
  military expenditure 284
  Syria and 173
OMIK (OSCE Mission in Kosovo) 73
Ongwen, Dominic 702
OPANAL (Agency for the Prohibition of Nuclear Weapons in Latin America and the Caribbean) 692
OPCW (Organisation for the Prohibition of Chemical Weapons) 682
  Advisory Board on Education and Outreach 512
  Africa Programme 510
  authority 472
  budget 2022–23 508–509
  capital fund 489
  Centre for Chemistry and Technology 472, 511
  CNS-acting chemicals and 509–10
  Covid-19 pandemic and 472, 507
  destruction of chemical weapons 511
  director-general 508
  international cooperation 510
  outlook 512
  Russian use of novichoks and 505–506
  Scientific Advisory Board 511–12
  Syrian chemical weapons and 496–502
    2nd Report 500–502

ad hoc mechanisms 498
investigations 496–500
verification regime 465
Open Skies Consultative Commission (OSCC) 694
Open Skies Treaty 663
  entry into force 544
  Russian withdrawal 514, 545, 546, 547
    consequences 549
  procedures 548–49, 701, 705, 710
  states parties 544
  US withdrawal 514, 544
    Biden administration and 547–48
    impact 544–45
  outlook 550, 705
  withering regime 144
Orbital ATK 291
Organization of American States (OAS) 694
  CIFTA (1997) 665–66
  CITAAC 556, 666
  Colombian peace process 94
  MAPP/OEA 73
  on Nicaragua 88
Organization of Islamic Cooperation (OIC) 683
Organization of the Black Sea Economic Cooperation (BSEC) 694
organized crime:
  Africa 198, 210
  Americas 78
  armed conflict and 31, 33
  Brazil 100
  Colombia 82
  El Salvador 270
  Guatemala 89
  Mexico 82–85
  Venezuela 102
Ortega, President Daniel 88
OSCE (Organisation for Security and Cooperation if Europe) 693–94
  arms embargo 595, 598
  arms transparency 514, 555–56. 557
  cybersecurity and 566–67
  Florence Agreement (1996) 665, 697
  Joint Consultative Group (JCG) 661, 693
  Minsk Group 141, 694
  Minsk process 140–41
  Minsk Protocol 51
  peace operations 58
    Mission to Bosnia and Herzegovina 73
    Mission to Moldova 73

Mission to Serbia 73
Mission to Skopje 73
Observer Mission at the Russian
    checkpoints Gukovo and Donetsk
    49–50, 51, 58, 69, 73, 151, 708
OMIK 73
PRCIO 73
Presence in Albania 73
SMM to Ukraine 59, 73, 151
Ukraine war and 28
Sub-Regional Consultative
    Commission (SRCC) 697
Ukraine war and 7–8
Vienna Document 144, 555–56, 669
**Oseguera Cervantes, Nemesio 'El
    Mencho'** 83
Otaibi, Mansour al- 464
Ouane, Moctar 205, 705
Ousmane, President Mahame 204
outer space:
2021 developments 514, 572–79, 703
ASAT tests 574–75, 579, 709
Chinese tests 572–74
counterspace 572
debris 575, 579, 709
fractional orbital bombardment
    systems (FOBS) 573–74
Moon *see* **Moon**
responsible behaviour 578–79, 706
Russian tests 572, 574–75
United Nations and 578–79, 710
Outer Space Treaty (1967) 641
Article IX 575
FOBS and 573–74
lunar prohibitions 575–76
Moon and 575–76, 577
Oxfam 476–77
**Oxford Institute for Ethics, Law and
    Armed Conflict (ELAC)** 569
**Oxford Process on International Law
    Protections in Cyberspace** 569

Pacific Islands Forum 63, 660, 695
Pakistan:
Afghanistan and 126
armed conflicts 103, 105
    arms imports and 302
    fatalities 27, 29, 126
    internal conflicts 125–26
    Taliban violence 104
arms exports 319
arms imports 314, 323, 324–25, 403,
    553

BWC and 491
climate change and 107
cluster munitions 522
contribution to peace operations 61
Covid-19 277, 474
Indian conflict 27, 29, 104, 277
    arms imports and 324–25
    border clashes 391
    ceasefire 107, 122–23, 702
    Kashmir 122–24, 277, 325
    nuclear posture 398
    UNMOGIP 72
Islamic State 106
landmines 524, 525
military expenditure 277
Nigeria and 319
nuclear arms control and 17, 448
    CTBT 466, 469
nuclear weapons *see* **nuclear weapons**
peace agreement 42
UAVs 527
USA and 124, 324, 324–25, 402–403
Palestinian Islamic Jihad 704
Panama:
BWC and 485
UAVs and 528
Pandora Papers 708
**Papua New Guinea: contribution to
    peace operations** 63
Paraguay: authoritarianism 79
Paris Agreement (2015) 14, 243, 253,
702
**Paris Call for Trust and Security in
    Cyberspace** 559, 569
Parolin, Pietro 217
Partial Test-Ban Treaty (PTBT, 1963)
640–41
Pashinyan, Nikol 702
peace operations:
2021 multilateral operations 45–51
    after Afghanistan 63–69
    closed operations 49–51
    largest operations 54
    new operations 46–49
    numbers 46, 47
    table 71–74
2021 trends 28, 45–74
ad hoc coalitions 59–60, 73
Afghanistan withdrawal and 63–69
    consolidating trends 67–9, 69–70
    inspiring armed groups 66–67
    state-building 64–66
African Union *see* **African Union**
Americas 76, 77

Asia–Oceania 107
conducting organizations 53–60
    regional organizations 56–59
personnel
    contributing countries 60, 61–62
    Covid-19 and 55
    deployments 51–53
    fatalities 28, 55–56, 57
    numbers 48, 52, 53
    trends 28
state-building and 64–66
United Nations 53–56, 65
    2021 operations 45–51
    Africa 65
    African contributors 200
    fatalities 55–56, 57
    numbers 28
West Africa 207–10
see also individual operations and
    countries
peace processes:
2012–21 numbers of agreements 40
2021 processes 41–44
see also **peace operations;** individual
    countries
**Peaceful Nuclear Explosions Treaty
(PNET, 1976)** 670
Pecsteen de Buytswerve, Marc 534
Pegasus Project 706
**Pelindaba Treaty (African Nuclear-
Weapon-Free Zone Treaty, 1996)**
664–65
Peraton 291
Perspecta 291
Peru:
    arms imports 323
    authoritarianism 79
    cluster munitions 523
    cybersecurity and 562
Pfizer/BioNTech 473
PGZ 294
Philippines:
    armed conflict 103, 104, 105
        2021 developments 133–34
        fatalities 27, 29, 134
    BWC and 489, 491
    Chinese relations 110, 111
    ICC investigation 134
    IMT in Mindanao 59, 73
    Islamic State 106
    landmines 524
    Typhoon Rai 710
    war on drugs 134
piracy 63, 224

plutonium *see* **fissile material**
**PNET (Peaceful Nuclear Explosions
Treaty, 1976)** 670
Poland:
    arms exports to Ukraine 330
    arms imports 328
    arms industry 290, 292, 294
    cluster munitions 522
    defence agreements 9
    NSG and 617
    Russia and 145
Proliferation Security Initiative (PSI)
699
Protasevich, Roman 142, 607, 705
Putin, President Vladimir:
    2021 Ukraine conflict 137
    Belarus and 143
    Biden meeting 20, 144, 435, 440, 705,
        710
    EU bans on 141
    Nagorno-Karabakh conflict and 140
    nuclear arms control 435, 440
    nuclear policy 360, 368
    Open Skies Treaty and 545–48
    Ukraine war and 10, 150 154, 704

Qatar:
    arms imports 331
        France 313, 331, 554
        Italy 315, 331
        top importer 330
        transparency 554
        United Kingdom 315
        United States 331
        UNROCA and 553
    East Africa and 224
    health spending 286
    Libya and 286
    Middle East relations 159, 701
    military expenditure 284, 286
    Syria and 286
    Yemen war and 185

Rafael 295
Raisi, President Ebrahim 436, 450, 458
**RAMSI (Regional Assistance Mission
to Solomon Islands)** 28, 63
**Rarotonga Treaty (South Pacific
Nuclear Free Zone Treaty, 1985)** 660
Raytheon Technologies 289, 291
Reagan, President Ronald 18–19, 435,
440

RECSA (Regional Centre on Small Arms in the Great Lakes Region, the Horn of Africa and Bordering States) 695
Red Cross *see* **ICRC**
refugees *see* **displacement**
Regional Cooperation Council 695–96
Ressa, Maria 708
Revete, Carlos Luis 'El Koki' 102
Rheinstall 293
Rodriguez Ramirez, Carmen 484
Romania:
  arms imports 329
  cluster munitions 522
  EWIPA and 520
  Open Skies Treaty and 549
Rome Statute of the International Criminal Court 653–55
Rouhani, President Hassan 454
RSM (Resolute Support Mission in Afghanistan) 28, 45, 49–50, 52, 56, 58, 59, 63–64, 68–69, 70, 73, 107
Russia:
  2014 invasion of Ukraine 4, 11–12
    NATO and 143–44, 703
  2021 Ukraine conflict 137
  2022 Ukraine war *see* **Ukraine war (2022)**
  Afghan policy 22, 65
  African policy 199
  armed forces: modernization 294
  arms embargoes and 582, 597
    Myanmar 605
    South Sudan 605
    United Nations 599
  arms exports 297, 299, 304–305
    Africa 317, 318
    Algeria 311, 312, 318, 554
    Angola 318
    Azerbaijan 313, 329
    Belarus 312–13, 329
    Egypt 301, 311, 312, 332, 333
    Ethiopia 319
    Europe 328
    India 311, 324, 325
    Indonesia 301
    Iran 601
    key developments 311–13
    Libya 604
    Mali 319
    Myanmar 328
    Nigeria 319
  arms industry 290, 294
  Astana Group 172

  AWS and 536–37, 540, 542
  Belarus and 137
    arms transfers 312–13, 329
    military exercises 145
    Open Skies Treaty 548
    Western relations 142–43
  biological/chemical weapons and 142
    BWC 484–85, 486–87, 495, 708
    CNS-acting chemicals 510
    geopolitics 492–95, 702
    novichoks 504–506
    OPCW 508
  Bosnia and 60
  Budapest Memorandum (1994) 11
  Canada and 549
  Central African Republic and 194, 199, 218–19
  Chechnya conflict 4, 142
  Chinese relations 45
    bilateral cooperation 137, 141
    BWC and 493
    Moon partnership 576, 704
    nuclear arms control 435
    Ukraine war and 10
  cluster munitions and 521, 522
  Covid-19 pandemic 144, 294, 475, 545
  cybersecurity and 142, 562
  EU and 137, 141, 144–45, 607–608
  EWIPA and 520
  France and 144, 504, 505, 506
  geopolitics 19–21, 28, 69, 70, 471
    biological weapons control and 492–95
  Georgia: 2008 invasion 4
  Germany and 504, 505, 506
  Iran and 18–19, 449, 457–59, 601
  Japan and 274
  landmines 524, 525
  Mali and 199, 209–10, 319
  MCTR and 614, 615
  Middle East policy 159, 464
  military expenditure 244, 255–56, 259, 282, 282–83
  military threats 256–57
  Minsk Group 141, 153
  Myanmar and 131–32, 328, 605
  Nagorno-Karabakh conflict and 46, 47, 59–60, 63, 73, 137, 140, 313, 701
  NATO and
    2014 invasion of Ukraine 143–44, 703
    NATO–Russia Council (NRC) 143, 146, 692
    security demands 145–46, 710

Ukraine conflict 143–44, 703
Navalny poisoning 141, 142, 472,
    504–506, 701, 702
New START *see* **New START**
nuclear arms control
    bilateral treaties 669–73
    CTBT and 467
    NPT 447, 460
    see also specific bilateral treaties
nuclear weapons *see* **nuclear weapons**
oil exports 282
Open Skies Treaty and 514, 545–50,
    701, 705, 710
OSCE and 7–8
outer space and
    ASAT tests 574–75, 709
    Chinese partnership 576, 704
    Moon 514, 576, 703, 704
    tests 514, 572, 574–75
Poland and 145
SALWs and 531
sanctions against 504–505
Sudan and 199
Sweden and 504
Syria and 148, 169, 170
    chemical weapons 496, 501, 503
    peace process 172
Turkish relations 148
UAVs 608
UK and 144, 504
Ukraine and *see* **Ukraine**
Ukraine war (2022) *see* **Ukraine war**
UNSC and climate change 41
US relations 137
    arms control 144
    arms transfers and 310
    Biden–Putin meeting 20, 144, 435,
        440, 705, 710
    biological weapons 492–93, 495
    Covid-19 pandemic and 144
    diplomacy 145
    military expenditure and 269
    multilateral arms control 445–46,
        447–48
    novichoks and 505
    nuclear arms control 435
    Open Skies Treaty and 545–46
    post-Afghanistan 68
    sanctions 141–42, 504–505, 702,
        704
    strategic stability dialogue 440–41,
        442, 448, 708
    Ukraine war and 3, 6–9, 710
    US–Russia Economic Dialogue 444

Wassenaar Arrangement and 618
Western relations 109
    Belarus and 142–43
    diplomacy 143–45
    militarization 143–44
    security demands 145–46
    tensions 141–46
Russian Electronics 294
Russian Helicopters 294
**Russian–Turkish Joint Monitoring
    Centre (RTJMC)** 46, 47, 59–60, 73, 701
Rwanda:
    Central African Republic and 218
    contribution to peace operations
        48–49, 61, 62, 230–31
Ryabkov, Sergey 438, 440, 441, 549

Saab 270, 294
SADC *see* **Southern African
    Development Community**
Safran 293
Sahrawi, Adnam Abu Walid al- 204
Saïed, President Kais 183, 706, 708
Salafis 161–62, 198
Sall, President Macky 202, 203
SALWs:
    2021 developments 514
    Afghanistan 599–600
    ATT 530, 581, 583–84, 584–85
    Central African Republic 600
    ECOWAS Convention (2006) 667–68
    EU exports 701
    ITI 514, 516, 529, 530
    Kinshasa Convention (2010) 668–69
    Nairobi Protocol (2004) 667
    RECSA 695
    regulation 516
    Sudan 606
    UN Programme of Action 514, 516,
        528–31, 563, 584, 706
    UNROCA and 553
    Yemen 606
**SAMIM (SADC Mission in
    Mozambique)** 28, 46, 47–48, 49, 56, 58,
    73, 197, 230, 705
San Marino: EWIPA and 520
Sapega, Sofia 142
Saudi Arabia:
    arms embargo and EU 607, 608
    arms imports 297, 299, 330–31
        armed conflicts and 302
        France 553
        Germany and 331

top importer 317, 330
United Kingdom 315
UNROCA and 553
USA 305–308, 310, 331
East Africa and 224
Iran and 159–60
military expenditure 244, 255, 257,
258, 259, 284, 555
Qatar and 159, 701
UAVs 527
Ukraine war and 10
USA and 155, 158, 305–308, 310, 331
Yemen war and 156, 185–91, 284,
308–309, 310, 607
Schmidt, Christian 60
Seabed Treaty (1971) 644
**Semipalatinsk Treaty (Treaty on
a Nuclear-Weapon-Free Zone in
Central Asia, 2006)** 668
Senegal:
armed groups 203
contribution to peace operations 62
landmines 525
peace agreement 42
Serbia:
cluster munitions 522
Kosovo border 146–47
landmines 525
OSCE Mission 73
sexual violence:
armed conflicts 34
Central African Republic 217
children and conflicts 39
Colombia 97
Congo (DRC) 223
East Africa 224
Ethiopia 227
Nigeria 213
South Sudan 234, 235, 605
Sudan 238
West Africa 206
**Shanghai Cooperation Organization
(SCO)** 121, 696
Sharma, Alok 15
Shekau, Abubakar 204, 213
Sherman, Wendy 440
**SICA (Central American Integration
System)** 696
Sierra Leone:
ATT and 594
SALWs and 584
Singapore:
arms industry 290, 295, 296
cluster munitions 522

Covid-19 278
military expenditure 277–78
Sinopharm 473
Sisi, President Abdel Fattah al- 707
Skopje, OSCE Mission to 73
Solomon Islands: RAMSI 28, 63
Somalia:
al-Shabab 67, 194, 232
armed conflict 193, 194, 195
2021 developments 231–33
fatalities 27, 29, 230, 231
children 34, 39
climate change 201, 225
cluster munitions 522
displacement 37, 231
food insecurity 38, 231
humanitarian crisis 231
landmines 526
peace operations 46
AMISOM 28, 45, 49, 54, 56–58, 66,
70, 72, 231–32
EUNAVFOR Atalanta 62–63
EUTM Somalia 58, 72
impact 66
UNSOM 72
political fragmentation 232–33
USA and 232
water insecurity 201
**SORT (Strategic Offensive Reductions
Treaty, Moscow Treaty, 2002)** 672
South Africa:
arms exports to Mali 319
ATT reporting 589
AWS and 544
contribution to peace operations 48
Covid-19 474
military expenditure 256, 264
Wassenaar Arrangement and 618–19
South Ossetia 146
South Sudan:
armed conflict 193, 194
2021 developments 233–36
fatalities 27, 29, 234, 235–36
armed groups 33, 233
arms embargoes 582, 595
European Union 597
United Nations 596, 605–606, 609
cluster munitions 522
CWC and 504
displacement 37, 234, 238
economic crimes 234
flooding 40, 234
food insecurity 38, 207, 234
HCOC and 616

human rights violations 234
humanitarian crisis 234
landmines 525
military expenditure 256, 264
peace agreement (2018) 42, 233, 235
peace operations 46
    CTSAMVM 58, 73
    UNMISS 54, 61, 72, 233, 235
sexual violence 234
Southern African Development Community (SADC) 696
peace operations 45, 56, 197
Protocol on the Control of Firearms (2001) 666–67
SAMIM 28, 46, 47–48, 49, 56, 58, 73, 197, 230, 705
Soviet Union:
1969 Chinese clash 12
invasion of Afghanistan 116
post-breakup conflicts 146–47
post-breakup nuclear weapons 11
space security *see* **outer space**
Spain:
arms exports 304, 325
arms industry 290, 292, 294
East Africa and 224
FDI screening 625
Morocco and 184
spyware 558, 706
Sri Lanka:
armed groups 105–106
Islamic State 106
landmines 525
ST Engineering 296
START I (Strategic Arms Reduction Treaty, 1991) 671
START II (Strategic Arms Reduction Treaty, 1993) 672
see also **New START**
Stockholm Initiative for Nuclear Disarmament 461
Stoltenberg, Jens 146
Sudan:
African Union and 237
armed conflict 193, 194, 195
    2021 developments 236–39
    fatalities 27, 29, 43, 238
    outlook 239
armed groups 197, 236
arms embargoes 595
    European Union 597
    United Nations 596, 606
arms imports 317, 606
cluster munitions 522

displacement 37, 238
Ethiopia and 228, 238
floods 238
food insecurity 38
humanitarian crisis 237–39
military coups 193, 196, 200, 237, 264, 709
military expenditure 256, 264
normalization agreement with Israel 175
peace agreements 42, 236
peace process 43, 196, 236–37
Russia and 199
sexual violence 238
UNAMID 28, 52, 53–54, 61, 238
UNITAMS 28, 46–47, 53–54, 72, 238–39
water dispute 201, 224, 228
Suga, Yoshihide 112
Sullivan, Jake 440–41, 442, 494
Sustainable Development Goals (SDGs) 243, 253–54, 531
Sweden:
arms exports 323, 325
arms industry 290, 292, 294
AWS and 544
EU and PESCO 8
Eurocorps 9
Joint Expeditionary Force 9
military expenditure 280
NATO membership issue 7
Open Skies Treaty and 549
Russian novichoks and 504, 505, 506
Switzerland:
arms imports 329
AWS and 544
CNS-acting chemicals and 509
EWIPA and 520
HCOC and 616
Syria:
armed conflict 155, 157, 158, 164
    2021 developments 168–73
    Arab world and 173
    ceasefire 43, 168, 169–70
    children 39
    drone use 34
    duration 171
    fatalities 27, 29, 36, 171–72
    international participants 169
    Mediterranean impact 147
    north-east 170–71
    north-west 169–70
armed groups 33
arms embargoes

Arab League 582, 595, 597
European Union 597, 608
arms imports 317
Bahrain and 173
chemical weapons *see* **chemical
weapons**
cluster munitions 521, 522
displacement 37, 171
Egypt and 173
elections 172–73
humanitarian crisis 38, 171–72
Iran and 155, 158, 169, 285, 501, 602
Islamic State 161–62, 168, 169
Israel and 333
Jordan and 173
Kurds 170, 171, 172, 173–74
Kuwait and 173
landmines 525
Middle East diplomacy 159
Oman and 173
peace processes 172–73
Qatar and 286
Russia and 148, 169, 170, 172, 496, 501,
503
Turkey and 148, 169, 170–71, 173–74
UAE and 173
UNDOF 54, 72
United Nations and 65, 488
USA and 169, 173

Taiwan:
arms imports 308, 327
China and 12, 327
China–US relations 3, 12, 105,
111–12
Tajikistan:
cluster munitions 522
Kyrgyz conflict 27, 29, 103, 105, 108,
704
military expenditure 271
Takuba Task Force 62, 193, 199, 208,
209, 210
Taliban 21–22, 52, 57, 63–65, 69, 70,
103–104, 107, 113–20, 126, 277, 324,
599–600, 609, 707
Tallinn 3.0 process 569
Tanzania:
contribution to peace operations 48
Mozambique conflict and 231
Tashkent Agreement (1992) 661
Tedros Adhanom Ghebreyesus 478,
480
Teledyne Technologies 291

Thailand:
armed conflict 103, 105, 135
arms imports from China 301
Covid-19 pandemic 135
landmines 524
military expenditure 278
Myanmar and 132
Thales 293
**Threshold Test-Ban Treaty (TTBT,
1974)** 670
ThyssenKrupp 293–94
Tlatelolco Treaty (1967) 659–60
Total 230
Tóth, Tibor 467
**Touadéra, President Faaustin-
Archange** 220
**TPNW (Treaty on the Prohibition of
Nuclear Weapons, 2017)** 658
MSP1 463–64
2021 developments 17–18, 462–64
entry into force 436, 462, 463, 701
NPT and 436, 462, 463
objectives 462–63
states parties 462
Trans-Dniester 59, 73, 146
Trump, President Donald:
Afghan policy 21–22
APM Convention and 526
arms transfers 309, 311
authoritarianism 80
Chinese relations 16–17
Covid-19 and 80, 477
geopolitics 19–20, 441
impeachment 702
Iran and 18, 449, 458
military expenditure 267
nuclear posture 346, 467
Open Skies Treaty and 547
Somali policy 232
Ukraine war and 8
Tshisekedi, President Felix 223
**TTBT (Threshold Test-Ban Treaty,
1974)** 670
tuberculosis 476
Tunisia:
Arab Spring 161
Covid-19 pandemic 183
emergency powers 161, 706
landmines 524
Prime Minister 708
protests 183–84
Turkey:
African policy 200
armed conflict 155, 157, 164, 174

arms exports 304, 324–25, 329, 330, 553
arms imports 308, 310–11, 315
arms industry 286, 290, 295, 296
Astana Group 172
AWS and 541–42
cluster munitions 522
Cyprus and 147
East Africa and 224
Egypt and 159
Ethiopia and 227
EU and 147
Greece and 147, 148
Iraq and 166, 167
Kurdish conflict 27, 29, 166, 173–74
landmines 525, 526
Libya and 147, 604
Middle East policy 159
military expenditure 286
NATO and 148
Open Skies Treaty and 549
RTJMC 28, 46, 47, 59–60, 73, 701
Russian relations 148
Syria and 148, 169, 170–71, 172
UAE and 159
UAVs 170, 527
US relations 308, 310–11
Western relations 147
typhoons 710

UAVs (armed uncrewed aerial vehicles):
2021 developments 516, 526–28
Afghanistan 117–18, 599–600, 707
arms transfers 319, 329, 602
counterterrorism 70
Ethiopia 34, 227, 319
EU control 625
humanitarian impact 513, 527
Iraq 165
Israel Iran relations 452, 602
MCTR and 516, 527, 528, 613–14
Mexican cartels and 83–84
Nagorno-Karabakh ceasefire and 47, 140
regulation 516, 527–28
Russia 608
Turkisn use 170, 527
Ukraine 329
use 34, 526–27
Yemen 185, 187, 606
Uganda:
armed conflict 193, 195, 264

arms imports from Belarus 553
contribution to peace operations 28, 61
electoral violence 200
military expenditure 264
war crimes 702
Ukraine:
2022 war see **Ukraine war (2022)**
armed groups 33
arms exports to Ethiopia 319
arms imports 150, 329–30
arms industry 290, 292, 294, 330
Budapest Memorandum (1994) 11
chemical/biological weapons and BWC 487
Russian allegations 4
cluster munitions 522
defence agreements 9
EUAM Ukraine 73
identity 150
independence (1991) 153
landmines 151, 525
military expenditure 283
Minsk Protocol 51, 152–53
NATO and Open Skies Treaty 549
NATO–Ukraine Commission 692
nuclear weapons: relinquishment 11
Open Skies Treaty and 549
OSCE Observer Mission at the Russian checkpoints Gukovo and Donetsk 28, 49–50, 51, 58, 69, 73, 151, 708
OSCE SMM 59, 73, 151
Russian occupation (2014-) 4, 11–12
2021 developments 149–54
biosecurity and 487
Crimea 148
Donbas 146, 148
humanitarian impact 150–51
internationalization of conflict 148–49
military expenditure and 283
military mobilization 151–52
NATO and 143–44, 703
nature of conflict 137
Russian war see **Ukraine war (2022)**
US military aid 283, 329
Ukraine war (2022):
aggression 11–12
collateral impact 23
consequences 5–12
displacement 5
escalation risk 5
food security and 5–6
international responses 9–12
see also individual countries

milestone 3
OSCE and 7–8
rule of law and 11
Russian military mobilization (2021)
    153–54, 283, 704
shock 3–12
USA and
    intelligence 145, 153
    Russian relations 3, 4
    warnings 710
war crimes 5
Western responses 6–9, 710
    military aid 6–7
    NATO 8–9
    NATO membership extension 7
    Russian relations 3, 4, 5
UkrOboronProm 294
**UN Disarmament Commission
    (UNDC)** 677
**UN OCHA (UN Office for the
    Coordination of Humanitarian
    Affairs)** 81
UN Peacebuilding Commission (PBC)
    677
**UNAMA (UN Assistance Mission in
    Afghanistan)** 64, 72, 113
**UNAMID (UN–AU Hybrid Operation
    in Darfur)** 28, 52, 53–54, 61, 238
**UNASUR (Union of South American
    Nations)** 697
**UNDC (UN Disarmament
    Commission)** 677
**UNDOF (UN Disengagement
    Oberserver Force)** 54, 72
UNDP (UN Development Programme)
    190
UNESCO 253–54
**UNFICYP (UN Peacekeeping Force in
    Cyprus)** 72
**UNIDIR (UN Institute for
    Disarmament Affairs)** 567, 568
**UNIFIL (UN Interim Force in
    Lebanon)** 54, 55, 61, 72
**UNISFA (UN Interim Security Force
    for Abyei)** 54, 61, 72
**UNITAMS (UN Integrated Transition
    Assistance Mission in Sudan)** 28,
    46–47, 53–54, 72, 238–39
United Aircraft Corporation 294
United Arab Emirates (UAE):
    arms exports to Mali 319
    arms imports 331
        conflicts and 302
        France 314, 331

Italy 331
South Korea 316
top importer 330
UNROCA and 553
USA and 301, 308, 309, 311
arms industry 290, 295, 296
BWC and 490
East Africa and 224
Ethiopia and 227
FDI 625
India–Pakistan conflict and 107,
    122–23
Israel and 160–61, 175
Libya and 331, 604
military expenditure 284
Qatar and 159
Syria and 173
Turkey and 159
UAVs 527
Ukraine war and 10
USA and 155, 158, 301, 308, 309, 311
Yemen war and 185, 187, 331
United Kingdom:
    arms exports 301, 304, 315, 325–26,
        331
    arms imports 328, 329
    arms industry 290, 292–93
    AUKUS 21, 109, 111, 275–76, 301,
        325–26, 461, 708
    Brexit agreement 704
    Budapest Memorandum (1994) 11
    BWC and 485, 486
    Cameroon and 216
    China and 111, 703
    Covid-19 pandemic 279, 474, 476–77
    cybersecurity 568
    Cyprus and 147
    defence agreements 9
    East Africa and 224
    Eurocorps 9
    EWIPA and 519
    FDI 625
    Iran and 18–19, 449
    Joint Expeditionary Force 9
    Middle East nuclear free zone and 464
    military expenditure 257, 258, 259,
        280–81, 555
    nuclear arms control 17, 441, 448
        NPT 447, 460
    nuclear weapons *see* **nuclear weapons**
    outer space security 572
    Russia and 144, 504–505, 506
    UAVs 527
    Ukraine and 51, 153

Yemen and 185
United Nations 674–76
  75th anniversary 23
  2030 Agenda for Sustainable
    Development 531
  chemical/biological weapons and
    Iran–Iraq war 612
    UNSGM 484–85, 487–88
  cluster munitions and 521
  Colombia and 93
  conventional arms control and 514
  Covid-19 and 44
  cyberspace and 514, 560–66, 568
  Ethiopia and 227
  Firearms Protocol 530
  food insecurity and 37–38
  Haiti and 87
  Honduras and 90
  Iraq and 167–68
  Libya and 180, 181–82, 183
  Middle East nuclear free zone and 464
  military coups and 23, 708
  military expenditure and 243, 254–55
  Morocco and 184
  Myanmar and 132
  'Our Common Agenda' 23–24, 67, 566,
    707
  outer space and 578–79
  peace operations see **peace operations**
  SALWs and 514, 516, 528–31, 563, 584,
    706
  Security Council see **United Nations
    Security Council**
  space security and 514, 572, 710
  Syria and 172
  TPNW and 463
  UAVs and 516, 527
  Ukraine war and 6, 9, 10, 11
  UNGA 1st Committee 674
    BWC and 485–89, 708
    cyberspace 560–65, 568
    EWIPA and 520
    IEDs 524
    SALWs 514, 516, 528–31, 584
    UAVs and 528
  UNGA 3rd Committee 565
  Women and Peace Agenda (WPS) 255,
    531
  Yemen and 188, 189, 190, 191
United Nations Human Rights Council:
  Israel–Palestinian conflict and 176
  on South Sudan 234
  Yemen and 191
United Nations Security Council 676

  Afghanistan and 65
  armed conflicts and
    climate change 41
    sexual violence 34
  arms embargoes 332, 595–606
  biological weapons and 488
  Bosnia and 60
  CTBT and 467–68, 469
  cybersecurity 705
  Cyprus and 147
  EWIPA and 520
  Iran and 18, 332
  Iraqi elections and 168
  Myanmar and 131
  peace agreements and 41
  Resolution 2231 (JCPOA) 449
  Resolution 2366 (Colombia) 93
  Resolution 2377 (Colombia) 93
  Resolution 2476 (Haiti) 87
  Resolution 2524 (Sudan) 46
  Resolution 2536 (CAR) 600
  Resolution 2559 (Sudan) 52
  Resolution 2574 (Colombia) 93
  Resolution 2577 (South Sudan) 605
  Resolution 2586 (Yemen) 188
  Resolution 2587 (Cyprus) 147
  Resolution 2588 (CAR) 601
  Resolution 2600 (Haiti) 87
  Resolution 2612 (Congo) 222
  Resolution 2616 (arms embargoes) 599,
    710
  scope of action 23
  Syrian chemical weapons and 501–502
  Ukraine war and 4, 11
United Shipbuilding Corporation 294
United States (USA):
  2020 presidential election 80
  Afghanistan see **Afghanistan**
  African policy 199
  APM convention and 526
  arms exports 297, 299, 304–11
    2021 developments 308–11
    Afghanistan 324
    Africa 317, 318
    Asia–Oceania 323
    Australia 301, 305–308, 325–26
    Egypt 305, 314, 332
    Europe 328, 329
    India 311
    Israel 333
    Kuwait 332
    Middle East 330
    Morocco 318
    Pakistan 324–25

Qatar 331
sanctions 310–11, 312, 314
Saudi Arabia 305–308, 310, 331
South Korea 327
Taiwan 308, 327
Ukraine 330
United Arab Emirates 301, 309, 311
arms imports 322
arms industry 244, 290
Covid-19 pandemic and 301
mergers 288, 291
space sector 291
top companies 289–91
arms trade control and
ATT 581, 582, 590–91
dual use items 623
multilateral control 611
transparency 553, 556–57
AUKUS 21, 109, 111, 275–76, 301,
325–26, 461, 708
AWS and 535–36, 536–37, 539, 540,
541–42
Belarus and 142
Budapest Memorandum (1994) 11
Capitol storming (Jan 2021) 3, 80, 701
chemical/biological weapons and
BWC 484, 486, 493–95
CNS-acting chemicals 509
destruction 472, 511
geopolitics 492–95
UNSGM 487–88
China and 16–17, 50
2021 developments 20–21
arms transfers and 310, 581
biological weapons 492–93
dual use technologies 623
geopolitics 311
hypersonic weapon system 706
military expenditure and 269
nuclear arms control 435, 437,
446–47, 709
nuclear estimates 380–90
space developments 573, 574
strategic stability dialogue 441–45,
448
Taiwan 3, 12, 105, 111–12, 112, 308,
327
trade war 21
trends 103, 105, 109–12
climate change and 21, 702, 704, 705,
708
cluster munitions 522
Colombia and 96
counterterrorism 22, 80, 187

Covid-19 and
arms transfers 301
deaths 81, 474, 475
origins 471, 477, 479, 481, 707
Russian relations 144
Cuba and 627
cybersecurity and 560, 562, 568
defence agreements 9, 148
East Africa and 224
East Asian politics 109–12
Egypt and 305, 314, 332
EU relations 631
cybersurveillance 627
dual use trade control 620
EU–US Trade and Technology
Council 626–27, 705
export control cooperation 582, 608,
626–27
EWIPA and 519
geopolitics 19–21, 311, 471, 492–95
Haiti and 86, 87
Indian nuclear estimates 395
Iran and 10, 160, 164, 284–85, 435,
449, 458, 459, 601, 608, 627
Iraq and 161, 164, 165–66, 706
Israel and 155, 156, 158, 175, 178, 285,
333, 405–406
Japanese relations 109, 112
JCPOA and see **JCPOA**
Korean War end 103
landmines 525, 526
Mexico and 81, 82–83
Middle East policy
allies 10, 155, 158
nuclear free zone 464
shrinking role 161, 164
migration from Latin America 81, 91
military expenditure 244, 256
2017–21 components 266
2021 overview 267–60
fall 255, 258, 265
military burden 259
top spender 257
transparency 555
Minsk Group 141, 153
Moroccan relations 318
Mozambique and 229–30
Myanmar and 131, 605
New START see **New START**
Nigeria and 199
North Korea and 109–10
ending Korean War 107
nuclear arms control 435
nuclear data 410, 417–18, 421–23

nuclear target 411
nuclear arms control
  bilateral treaties 669–73
  China and 435, 437, 446–47, 709
  CTBT and 466, 467
  INF Treaty withdrawal 368
  NPT 447, 460
  see also specific bilateral treaties
nuclear umbrella 461
nuclear weapons see **nuclear weapons**
Open Skies Treaty and 514, 545–50,
  705
outer space and 572
  Artemis Accords 576
  military interest 577
  Moon 572
  responsible behaviour 706
  Russian tests 574–75
Pakistan and 124, 324–25, 402–403
peace operation contributions 61, 68
Russian relations 137
  arms control 144
  arms transfers and 310
  Biden–Putin meeting 20, 144, 435,
    440, 705, 710
  biological weapons 492–93, 495
  Covid-19 pandemic and 144
  diplomacy 145
  military expenditure and 269
  multilateral arms control 445–46,
    447–48
  novichoks 505
  nuclear arms control 435
  Open Skies Treaty and 545–46
  post-Afghanistan 68
  sanctions 141–42, 504–505, 702,
    704
  security demands 145–46
  space developments 574–75
  strategic stability dialogue 440–41,
    442, 448, 708
  Ukraine war and 3, 4, 5, 6–9, 710
  US–Russia Economic Dialogue 444
SALWs and 529, 530
Saudi relations 155, 158, 308–309, 310,
  331
Somalia and 232
South Korea and 12, 109
Summit for Democracy 710
Syria and 169, 173
Turkey and 308, 310–11
UAE and 155, 158, 301, 308, 309
UAVs and 527–28, 707
Ukraine and

arms supplies 150, 330
intelligence 145, 153
military aid 283, 329
OSCE mission 51
war 3, 6–9, 710
warnings 154
watch level 151
Vietnam War 117
Wassenaar Arrangement and 618
Yemen and 185, 187, 189, 606, 702
**United Technologies Corporation
(UTC)** 289, 291
**UNMHA (UN Mission to Support the
Hodeidah Agreement)** 72, 188
**UNMIK (UN Interim Administration
Mission in Kosovo)** 72
**UNMILEX (UN Report on Military
Expenditures)** 551, 554–55
UNMISS (UN Mission in South Sudan)
54, 61, 72, 233, 235
**UNMOGIP (UN MIlitary Observer
Group in India and Pakistan)** 72
**UNODA (UN Office for Disarmament
Affairs)** 491, 528–29, 674
**UNROCA (UN Register of
Conventional Arms):**
  objectives 552–53
  OSCE and 556
  participation 552–53, 556–57, 588, 589
  progress 556–57
  transparency 551–54
**UNSMIL (UN Support Mission in
Libya)** 72
**UNSOM (UN Assistance Mission in
Somalia)** 72
**UNTSO (UN Truce Supervision
Organization)** 72
**UNVMC (UN Verification Mission in
Colombia)** 72, 93–94
Uzbekistan:
  Kyrgyz agreement 107–108, 703
  military expenditure 271

Vaccine Alliance 473
Vatican: UAVs and 528
Venezuela:
  armed conflict 37, 75, 77, 100–101,
    100–102
  arms embargo 597, 608
  arms imports 322–23
  authoritarianism 79, 102
  BWC and 490
  cybersecurity and 562

economic crisis 102, 323
food insecurity 102
landmines 524
UAVs and 528
Vienna Document (2011) 144, 555–56, 669
Viet Nam:
arms imports from Russia 311, 312
cluster munitions 522
US war 117

Wagner Group 58, 66, 69, 199, 210, 219
Wallace, Ben 372
Wang Yi 446–47
war crimes:
Afghanistan 115
CAR 220
Ethiopia 227
ICC jurisdiction 653–54, 681
Israel–Palestine conflict 176–77
Libya 183
Syria 169
Ukraine war 5
Yemen 191
Wassenaar Arrangement 700
25th anniversary 619
2021 developments 618–19
Control Lists 618
Covid-19 and 582, 610–11, 618
participants 618
scope 582, 610, 612
water disputes 41, 201, 224, 228
Western Sahara 72, 156, 184, 522
Win Myint, President 128
Woodward 288
World Health Organization (WHO):
Covid-19 and 15, 253, 471, 473–82, 709
malaria vaccine and 708
pandemic treaty 482
SAGO 471, 480–81

Xi Jinping, President 273, 435, 442, 443, 706, 709

Yang Jiechi 443
Yemen:
al-Qaeda in the Arabian Peninsula 162

arms embargo 185, 582, 596, 606, 607
arms imports 317, 330–31, 602
SALWs 606
UAVs 185, 187, 606
cluster munitions 522
food insecurity 38, 207
international crimes 191
Iran and 155, 158, 185, 189, 602, 606
landmines 525
Middle East diplomacy 160
Saudi Arabia and 156, 185–91, 284, 308–309, 310, 607
UAVs and 528
UNMHA 72, 188
USA and 185, 187, 189, 606, 702
Yemen war:
2021 developments 155, 156, 185–91
armed groups 33
arms imports and 330–31
conflict zones 187–88
displacement 37
drone use 34
fatalities 27, 29, 190, 191, 707
food insecurity 38, 207
humanitarian crisis 38, 190, 702
internalization 29
map: areas of control 186
outlook 191
peace process 43–44, 188–90
Riyadh Agreement (2019) 185–86, 187, 188
Saudi Arabia and 156, 185–87, 607
Stockholm Agreement (2018) 185, 188
United Nations and 65
USA and 189, 702

Zambada Garcia, Ismael 82–83
Zambia: electoral violence 200
Zangger Committee 612, 617, 700
Zelaya, President Manuel 91
Zelensky, President Volodymyr 151, 153
Zerbo, Lassina 466, 467
Zimbabwe:
arms embargo 597
contribution to peace operations 48
landmines 525
UNSGM and 487
Zlauvinen, Gustavo 462